THE OXFORD HANDBOOK OF

DANIEL DEFOE

THE OXFORD HANDBOOK OF
DANIEL DEFOE

Edited by
NICHOLAS SEAGER
and
J. A. DOWNIE

OXFORD
UNIVERSITY PRESS

Great Clarendon Street, Oxford, OX2 6DP,
United Kingdom

Oxford University Press is a department of the University of Oxford.
It furthers the University's objective of excellence in research, scholarship,
and education by publishing worldwide. Oxford is a registered trade mark of
Oxford University Press in the UK and in certain other countries

© the several contributors 2023

The moral rights of the authors have been asserted

First Edition published in 2023

All rights reserved. No part of this publication may be reproduced, stored in
a retrieval system, or transmitted, in any form or by any means, without the
prior permission in writing of Oxford University Press, or as expressly permitted
by law, by licence or under terms agreed with the appropriate reprographics
rights organization. Enquiries concerning reproduction outside the scope of the
above should be sent to the Rights Department, Oxford University Press, at the
address above

You must not circulate this work in any other form
and you must impose this same condition on any acquirer

Published in the United States of America by Oxford University Press
198 Madison Avenue, New York, NY 10016, United States of America

British Library Cataloguing in Publication Data
Data available

Library of Congress Control Number: 2023945032

ISBN 978-0-19-882717-7

DOI: 10.1093/oxfordhb/9780198827177.001.0001

Printed and bound by
CPI Group (UK) Ltd, Croydon, CR0 4YY

Links to third party websites are provided by Oxford in good faith and
for information only. Oxford disclaims any responsibility for the materials
contained in any third party website referenced in this work.

Preface

Daniel Defoe's enormous oeuvre, produced over four decades, is nothing less than a meeting house for all the major trends and debates of his era. His writings have a capacity, perhaps unmatched, to unlock multiple aspects of his age. To engage fully with Defoe is to access early eighteenth-century British culture, society, and thought in something approaching its entirety, because there are very few areas of human activity that Defoe did not write about. And he wrote in multiple genres, some of which were well established with a rich tradition, like satirical verse and conduct literature, but a number of which were newer or in flux and which his contributions helped to shape, including the travel book, periodical journalism, and not least extended prose fictions that would come to be called novels. He is a pivotal figure in literary history as well as the history of ideas.

What is more, Defoe's writings respond well to fresh investigation from evolving methods in humanities research, from new directions in the history of the book and of the cultural contexts of science to ecocriticism and global literary studies. Defoe, then, is a touchstone for humanities scholars. He is also one of the few eighteenth-century British authors with a worldwide reputation, and few undergraduate students of English will complete their programmes without studying him at some point. His fiction is of great interest to scholars and students beyond as well as within eighteenth-century studies. Postcolonial and eco-critics, for example, see *Robinson Crusoe* (1719) as a foundational work of imperial ideology; feminist critics wrestle with the constructions of gender in *Moll Flanders* (1722) and *Roxana* (1724); and historians of medicine, the emotions, and religion turn back to *A Journal of the Plague Year* (1722), such as during the COVID-19 pandemic, for its lessons on knowledge, feeling, and faith during a public health emergency.

But there is much more to Defoe than the burst of narratives, published in a fertile five-year rush, that have made him a household name. The fact that he was famous—or notorious—in his own day as a major journalist and controversialist, rather than as a 'literary' author, deserves to be acknowledged, as does the fact that even if he would have preferred a reputation as a *litterateur* rather than a *provocateur* it would have been as a poet rather than a novelist. More generally, Defoe was an important writer on politics and religion, science and nature, economics and trade, and much else. His writings, certainly his best works, usually stem from *experience* (as well as study). He was a failed merchant, semi-successful political agent, and divinity school dropout, and we feel confident asserting a close relationship between the life and the writings even though our biographical knowledge of Defoe is frustratingly limited in many respects.

For these reasons—the richness and diversity of his output, his impact on numerous genres of writing, the ongoing currency of his ideas to modern society and scholarship—Defoe is an ideal subject for an *Oxford Handbook*. He wrote so much, and in fields that have since his time been separated out as discrete disciplines, that few professional scholars would dare claim mastery of Defoe's oeuvre. The risk for the author of a book such as *Robinson Crusoe* that transcends its author is that the remainder of her or his writings go unnoticed, and when those writings are so voluminous the risk of neglect is only increased. This *Handbook* therefore tries to give a thorough picture of Defoe's ideas and writings, their contexts, and their endurance. There is no singular sense of Defoe that guides the volume, but there is a running debate: between Defoe as a defender of tradition and as a prophet of modernity.

Early on in his classic, three-volume history, *England Under Queen Anne*, G. M. Trevelyan turned to Defoe. 'When a survey is demanded of Queen Anne's island, of its everyday life far distant from the Mall and yet farther from the sound of war, our thoughts turn to Daniel Defoe', he explained. 'For Defoe was one of the first who saw the old world through a pair of sharp modern eyes'.[1] In this way, Trevelyan succeeded in capturing the twin aspects of Defoe's paramount importance as a writer: while he remains an unrivalled source for the realities of life in Britain at the turn of the eighteenth century, certain features of his prolific published output seem to bear the stamp of modernity. It was for this latter reason, presumably, that John Robert Moore entitled his influential biography *Daniel Defoe, Citizen of the Modern World* (1958), while more recently Pat Rogers has reasserted that *A Tour thro' the Whole Island of Great Britain* (1724–6) 'is a truly central work for our understanding of Britain at a crucial stage of its transition into modernity'.[2]

There is, however, a danger in privileging the portrait of Defoe as a 'progressive' author who held what we might consider to be 'liberal' opinions, for his manifest social conservatism precludes any simple depiction of him as some sort of democrat writing before his time. Thus in his eagerness to find ways in which Defoe's 'plebeian vitality' is expressed in his works, Christopher Hill, writing about *Robinson Crusoe*, concluded that 'the democratic revolution, defeated in politics, triumphed in the novel'.[3] It is now over fifty years since John Richetti drew attention to the 'teleological bias' evident in Ian Watt's classic account, *The Rise of the Novel: Studies in Defoe, Richardson and Fielding* (1957).[4] While Defoe's narratives almost certainly widened contemporary readers' horizons of expectation, the prefaces of *Robinson Crusoe*, *Moll Flanders*, *Colonel Jack* (1722), and *Roxana* each strenuously sought in their various ways to distinguish them from the novel as defined in Johnson's *Dictionary*—'A small tale, generally of love'.

---

[1] G. M. Trevelyan, *England under Queen Anne: Blenheim* (1930; repr. London: Collins, 1965), 13–14.
[2] Pat Rogers, *Defoe's Tour and Early Modern Britain: Panorama of the Nation* (Cambridge: Cambridge University Press, 2022), 129.
[3] Christopher Hill, 'Robinson Crusoe', *History Workshop Journal*, 10 (1980), 6–24 (22).
[4] John J. Richetti, *Popular Fiction Before Richardson: Narrative Patterns 1700–1739* (Oxford: Clarendon Press, 1969), 2.

Although he is still occasionally described as the first novelist, and *Robinson Crusoe* as the first novel, Defoe's reputation among his contemporaries was not that of a novelist, nor even a writer of fiction. 'A few days ago died Mr. Daniel Defoe, Sen. a person well known for his numerous and various writings', *The Grub-street Journal* reported on 29 April 1731: 'He had a great natural genius; and understood very well the trade and interest of this Kingdom. His knowledge of men, especially those in high life, (with whom he was formerly very conversant) had weaken'd his attachment to any Party; but in the main, he was in the interest of civil and religious liberty, in behalf of which he appear'd on several remarkable occasions'.[5] The obituary went on to mention *The Shortest-Way with the Dissenters* (1702) as one such occasion, but earlier contemporary references to Defoe's religious practices were often less than complimentary. 'He is a profest Dissenter', one account of the character of the 'author' of *The Review* conceded, 'tho' Reckoned of no morals'—therefore 'His Reputation amongst the fair Dealers of the City is very Foule'.[6] The anonymous author of *The Review Review'd. In a Letter to the Prophet Daniel in Scotland* found it hard to credit Defoe's own (entirely fictitious) account 'That some Merchants have employ'd you to contract for ten thousand Pounds of Salt yearly':

> He buy ten thousand Pounds of Salt! He buy ten thousand T—s. And, old Friend, it seems somewhat strange that you, who, when you were here [in London], could not be trusted for ten Pence, should when you are abroad, be trusted for ten thousand Pounds, when the People may easily be inform'd of your Character![7]

Defoe was disparaged as 'a Man of great Rashness and Impudence, a mean Mercenarie Prostitute, a State Mountebank, an Hackney Tool, a Scandalous Pen, a Foul-Mouthed Mongrel, an Author who writes for Bread, and Lives by Defamation, &c.'.[8] Contemporary assessments of Defoe's character appear far removed from the encomiums bestowed upon him by posterity for his numerous accomplishments, whether as brilliant polemicist, pioneer journalist, projector, social observer, creator of Robinson Crusoe, or even as the inventor of the novel.

Yet while the author of works as diverse as *The Review* (1704–13), *The Family Instructor* (1715), *A Tour thro' the Whole Island of Great Britain*, and *A Plan of the English Commerce* (1728) seems uniquely qualified as a commentator on his own age, it is equally important not to neglect or discount the manifold visionary features of his writings. Even if they were largely derided or ignored by his contemporaries, the innovative ideas he propounded on a wide variety of subjects—from his first full-length book *An Essay*

---

[5] *The Grub-street Journal*, no. 69 (29 April 1731).
[6] British Library, Add. MS 28094, ff. 165–6.
[7] Quoted in Maximillian E. Novak, 'A Whiff of Scandal in the Life of Daniel Defoe', *HLQ*, 34:1 (1970), 35–42 (37).
[8] Quoted in *A Just Reprimand to Daniel De Foe. In a Letter to a Gentleman in South Britain* (Edinburgh, [1707]), 7.

upon Projects (1697) through to late works like *Augusta Triumphans; or, The Way to Make London the Most Flourishing City in the Universe* (1728)—caught the attention of subsequent generations, so that the epithet 'Ingenious DANIEL DE FOE' seems entirely merited.[9]

The Oxford Handbook of Daniel Defoe is divided into four parts. Following Brian Cowan's chapter surveying Defoe's life and times, the first part contains ten chapters that address the genres and modes in which Defoe wrote. Here will be seen Defoe's adherence to certain literary traditions and ideas, as well as his experimental and innovative qualities. The second part features fourteen chapters that relate Defoe's writings to their social and historical contexts, again capturing the admixture of his conservative and progressive outlooks. The third part situates Defoe's writings with reference to various locations, working outwards from London to Britain, then Europe, and the world. The final part contains five chapters that tackle Defoe's posthumous critical and creative reception.

---

[9] He was styled thus on the title-page of the sale catalogue of his library in November 1731. *The Libraries of Daniel Defoe and Phillips Farewell: Olive Payne's Sales Catalogue*, ed. Helmut Heidenreich (Berlin: W. Hildebrand, 1970).

Contents

List of Figures — xiii
Abbreviations — xv
Notes on Contributors — xix

1. Defoe's Life and Times — 1
   BRIAN COWAN

PART I: GENRES

2. Defoe's Poetry — 29
   MAXIMILLIAN E. NOVAK

3. Defoe, Prose Fiction, and the Novel — 49
   GEOFFREY SILL

4. Defoe and Drama — 69
   CYNTHIA WALL

5. Dialogue and Didacticism: Defoe's Conduct and Advice Literature — 91
   PENNY PRITCHARD

6. The Great Polemicist: Defoe's Pamphlets and Tracts — 108
   JEFFREY HOPES

7. Defoe's Periodical Journalism — 125
   ASHLEY MARSHALL

8. Defoe and the Idea of Travel — 144
   PAUL BAINES

9. Defoe as Historian — 161
   REBECCA BULLARD

10. The Style of Defoe's Correspondence — 177
    MARC MIEROWSKY

11. Defoe and Satire 195
    JOSEPH HONE

PART II: CONTEXTS

12. Defoe and the Book Trade 215
    PAT ROGERS

13. Daniel Defoe and the Social Structure of Pre-Industrial England 232
    J. A. DOWNIE

14. Defoe and Economics: Industry, Trade, and Finance 249
    NICHOLAS SEAGER

15. Gender, Sexuality, and the Status of Women in Defoe's Writings 272
    PAULA R. BACKSCHEIDER

16. Family and Domesticity in Defoe's Writings 294
    LIZ BELLAMY

17. Defoe and Christianity 311
    DAVID WALKER

18. Defoe, Philosophy, and Religion 330
    JOHN RICHETTI

19. Defoe, Science, and Technology 345
    CHRISTOPHER F. LOAR

20. Defoe and Government: Propaganda and Principle 364
    D. W. HAYTON

21. Intelligence, Espionage, and the Ethics of Surveillance in Defoe's Writings 382
    KATHERINE ELLISON

22. Defoe and War 400
    SHARON ALKER AND HOLLY FAITH NELSON

23. Crime and the Law in Defoe's Works 417
    KATE LOVEMAN

24. Racial and National Identities in Defoe's Writings 436
    SRIVIDHYA SWAMINATHAN

25. Defoe and Ecology 451
    LUCINDA COLE

PART III: PLACES

26. Defoe and London 471
    BREAN S. HAMMOND

27. Defoe and Britain 488
    ADAM SILLS

28. Defoe's Europe: Allies and Enemies 505
    ANDREAS K. E. MUELLER

29. Defoe and Colonialism 524
    MARKMAN ELLIS

30. Defoe and the Pacific 544
    ROBERT MARKLEY

31. Africa and the Levant in Defoe's Writings 562
    REBEKAH MITSEIN AND MANUSHAG N. POWELL

PART IV: AFTERLIVES

32. The Celebrated Daniel De Foe: Publication History, 1731–1945 583
    NICHOLAS SEAGER

33. Defoe's Critical Reception, 1731–1945 610
    KIT KINCADE

34. Attribution and the Defoe Canon 629
    BENJAMIN F. PAULEY

35. Habits of Gender and Genre in Three Female Robinsonades, 1767–1985 645
    RIVKA SWENSON

36. Defoe on Screen: *Robinson Crusoe*, *The Red Turtle*, and Animal Rights 660
    ROBERT MAYER

Index 677

List of Figures

1.1 Frontispiece, Daniel Defoe, *A True Collection of the Writings of the Author of the True Born English-man* (1703). Courtesy of McGill University Library, Rare Books and Special Collections, shelf mark PR3401 1703. — 13

1.2 Frontispiece, Daniel Defoe, *Jure Divino: A Satyr. In Twelve Books. By the Author of The True-Born Englishman*. Courtesy of Lilly Library, University of Indiana, Bloomington, shelf mark PR3404 .J89. — 14

1.3 Portrait of Daniel Defoe, oil painting. © National Maritime Museum, Greenwich, London, Caird Collection BHC2648. https://collections.rmg.co.uk/collections/objects/14122.html. — 17

1.4 Frontispiece, P. Hills's pirated edition of *Jure Divino* (1706). Courtesy of Lilly Library, University of Indiana, Bloomington, shelf mark PR3404 .J89 1706. — 18

1.5 Frontispiece, Benjamin Bragg's piracy of *Jure Divino* (1706). Courtesy of Beinecke Rare Book and Manuscript Library, Yale University, shelf mark Ik D362 706Je. — 19

1.6 George Bickham, *The Whig's Medly* (1711). Courtesy of The Lewis Walpole Library, Yale University, shelf mark 711.00.00.01+. http://hdl.handle.net/10079/digcoll/549567. — 21

3.1 Frontispiece by [John] Clark and [John] Pine to Daniel Defoe, *Robinson Crusoe* (1719). Personal copy of Geoffrey Sill. — 54

4.1 Daniel Defoe, *The Family Instructor*, Volume II (1718), 180–3. Boston Public Library, Defoe 27.77 v.2. — 80

32.1 Frontispiece, *Satan's Devices; or, the Political History of the Devil: Ancient and Modern* (1819). © British Library Board. — 593

32.2 Frontispiece, *The History of the Plague Year in London, in the Year 1665* (1819). Personal copy of Nicholas Seager. — 598

32.3 Frontispiece, *The Fortunate Mistress* (1724). Boston Public Library, Defoe 27.26. — 603

32.4 Frontispiece, *Romances and Narratives by Daniel Defoe*, ed. G. A. Aitken, 16 vols (1895), vol. 13. Keele University Library. — 604

36.1 *The Red Turtle* (2016), dir. Michaël Dudok de Wit. — 670

Abbreviations

The place of publication for pre-1900 works is London, unless stated. Biblical references are to the Authorized Version. References to Defoe's writings use the 44-volume *Works* wherever possible (the series and individual volumes are listed below), except for the novels, which are widely available. Full references are given within chapters, except for the following abbreviations.

Defoe's Works

Appeal	Daniel Defoe, *An Appeal to Honour and Justice* (1715)
Correspondence	*The Cambridge Edition of the Correspondence of Daniel Defoe*, ed. Nicholas Seager (Cambridge: Cambridge University Press, 2022)
Letters	*The Letters of Daniel Defoe*, ed. G. H. Healey (Oxford: Clarendon Press, 1955)
Novels	Daniel Defoe, *Novels*, 10 vols, gen. eds P. N. Furbank and W. R. Owens (London: Pickering and Chatto, 2007–8)
	i. *Robinson Crusoe*, ed. W. R. Owens
	ii. *The Farther Adventures of Robinson Crusoe*, ed. W. R. Owens
	iii. *Serious Reflections … of Robinson Crusoe*, ed. G. A. Starr
	iv. *Memoirs of a Cavalier*, ed. N. H. Keeble
	v. *Captain Singleton*, ed. P. N. Furbank
	vi. *Moll Flanders*, ed. Liz Bellamy
	vii. *A Journal of the Plague Year*, ed. John Mullan
	viii. *Colonel Jack*, ed. Maurice Hindle
	ix. *The Fortunate Mistress*, ed. P. N. Furbank
	x. *A New Voyage Round the World*, ed. John McVeagh
PEW	Daniel Defoe, *Political and Economic Writings*, 8 vols, gen. eds P. N. Furbank and W. R. Owens (London: Pickering and Chatto, 2000)
	i. *Constitutional Theory*, ed. P. N. Furbank
	ii. *Party Politics*, ed. J. A. Downie
	iii. *Dissent*, ed. W. R. Owens
	iv. *Union with Scotland*, ed. D. W. Hayton
	v. *International Relations*, ed. P. N. Furbank

	vi. *Finance*, ed. John McVeagh
	vii. *Trade*, ed. John McVeagh
	viii. *Social Reform*, ed. W. R. Owens
RDW	Daniel Defoe, *Religious and Didactic Writings*, 10 vols, gen. eds P. N. Furbank and W. R. Owens (London: Pickering and Chatto, 2005–6)
	i. *The Family Instructor, Volume I*, ed. P. N. Furbank
	ii. *The Family Instructor, Volume II*, ed. P. N. Furbank
	iii. *A New Family Instructor*, ed. W. R. Owens
	iv. *Religious Courtship*, ed. G. A. Starr
	v. *Conjugal Lewdness*, ed. Liz Bellamy
	vi. *The Poor Man's Plea*, etc., ed. J. A. Downie
	vii. *The Complete English Tradesman, Volume I*, ed. John McVeagh
	viii. *The Complete English Tradesman, Volume II*, ed. John McVeagh
	ix. *The Commentator*, ed. P. N. Furbank
	x. *The Compleat English Gentleman*, ed. W. R. Owens
Review	*Defoe's Review* (1704–13), 9 vols, ed. John McVeagh (London: Pickering and Chatto, 2004–11)
SFS	Daniel Defoe, *Satire, Fantasy and Writings on the Supernatural*, 10 vols, gen. eds P. N. Furbank and W. R. Owens (London: Pickering and Chatto, 2003–4)
	i. *The True-Born Englishman and Other Poems*, ed. W. R. Owens
	ii. *Jure Divino*, ed. P. N. Furbank
	iii. *The Consolidator*, etc., ed. Geoffrey Sill
	iv. *Minutes of the Negotiations of Monsr. Mesnager*, etc., ed. P. N. Furbank
	v. *The Conduct of Christians made the Sport of Infidels*, etc., ed. David Blewett
	vi. *The Political History of the Devil*, ed. John Mullan
	vii. *A System of Magick*, ed. Peter Elmer
	viii. *An Essay on the History and Reality of Apparitions*, ed. G. A. Starr
TDH	Daniel Defoe, *Writings on Travel, Discovery and History*, 10 vols, gen. eds P. N. Furbank and W. R. Owens (London: Pickering and Chatto, 2001–2)
	i–iii. *A Tour thro' the Whole Island of Great Britain, Volumes I–III*, ed. John McVeagh
	iv. *A General History of Discoveries and Improvements*, etc., ed. P. N. Furbank
	v. *Due Preparations for the Plague*, ed. Andrew Wear
	vi. *Memoirs of the Church of Scotland*, ed. N. H. Keeble
	vii–viii. *The History of the Union of Great Britain*, ed. D. W. Hayton

OTHERS

Backscheider, *Daniel Defoe*	Paula R. Backscheider, *Daniel Defoe: His Life* (Baltimore, MD: Johns Hopkins University Press, 1989)
BJECS	*British Journal for Eighteenth-Century Studies*
Downie, *Robert Harley and the Press*	J. A. Downie, *Robert Harley and the Press: Propaganda and Public Opinion in the Age of Swift and Defoe* (Cambridge: Cambridge University Press, 1979)
ECF	*Eighteenth-Century Fiction*
ECS	*Eighteenth-Century Studies*
EHR	*English Historical Review*
Furbank and Owens, *Critical Bibliography*	P. N. Furbank and W. R. Owens, *A Critical Bibliography of Daniel Defoe* (London: Pickering and Chatto, 1998)
Furbank and Owens, *Political Biography*	P. N. Furbank and W. R. Owens, *A Political Biography of Daniel Defoe* (London: Pickering and Chatto, 2006)
HLQ	*Huntington Library Quarterly*
JECS	*Journal for Eighteenth-Century Studies*
MLR	*Modern Language Review*
Novak, *Daniel Defoe*	Maximillian E. Novak, *Daniel Defoe, Master of Fictions: His Life and Ideas* (Oxford: Oxford University Press, 2001)
N&Q	*Notes and Queries*
ODNB	*Oxford Dictionary of National Biography*
OED	*Oxford English Dictionary*
PBSA	*Papers of the Bibliographical Society of America*
PMLA	*Publications of the Modern Language Association of America*
PQ	*Philological Quarterly*
RES	*Review of English Studies*
Richetti, *Life of Daniel Defoe*	John Richetti, *The Life of Daniel Defoe: A Critical Biography* (Oxford: Wiley-Blackwell, 2005)
SEL	*Studies in English Literature, 1500–1900*
SP	*Studies in Philology*

Notes on Contributors

Sharon Alker is Mary A. Denny Professor of English and General Studies at Whitman College. With Holly Faith Nelson, she is coauthor of *Besieged: The Post War Siege Trope, 1660–1730* (2021) and coeditor of *James Hogg and the Literary Marketplace: Scottish Romanticism and the Working-Class Author* (2009) and *Robert Burns and Transatlantic Culture* (2012).

Paula R. Backscheider is the Philpott-Stevens Eminent Scholar at Auburn University. She is the author of *Daniel Defoe: Ambition and Innovation* (1986), *Daniel Defoe: His Life* (1989), *Reflections on Biography* (1999), *Eighteenth-Century Women Poets and Their Poetry: Inventing Agency, Inventing Genre* (2005), *Elizabeth Singer Rowe and the Development of the English Novel* (2013), and *Women in Wartime: Theatrical Representations in the Long Eighteenth Century* (2021).

Paul Baines is Professor of English at the University of Liverpool. He is the author of *The House of Forgery in Eighteenth-Century Britain* (1999), *The Long 18th Century* (2004), *Edmund Curll, Bookseller* (2007, with Pat Rogers), and *Daniel Defoe, Robinson Crusoe/Moll Flanders: A Reader's Guide to Essential Criticism* (2007). He is the coeditor of *The Poems of Alexander Pope* (2019).

Liz Bellamy teaches English at City College Norwich and the Open University. She is the author of *Commerce, Morality and the Eighteenth-Century Novel* (1998), *Samuel Johnson* (2005), and *The Language of Fruit: Literature and Horticulture in the Long Eighteenth Century* (2019), as well as editor of Defoe's *Moll Flanders* (2008) and *British It-Narratives, 1750–1830: Money* (2012).

Rebecca Bullard is Senior Tutor at Trinity College, University of Oxford. She is the author of *The Politics of Disclosure, 1674–1725: Secret History Narratives* (2009), editor of a special issue of *Etudes anglaises* entitled 'Daniel Defoe's *Robinson Crusoe*: A Gazetteer' (2019), and coeditor of *The Plays and Poems of Nicholas Rowe, Vol. I: The Early Plays* (2016) and of *The Secret History in Literature, 1660–1820* (2017).

Lucinda Cole is Associate Professor of English at the University of Illinois Urbana-Champaign. She is the author of *Imperfect Creatures: Vermin, Literature, and the Sciences of Life, 1600–1740* (2016) and articles in *English Literary History, Journal for Early Modern Cultural Studies, Journal for Critical Animal Studies*, and *Eighteenth-Century Fiction*. She edited a special issue of *Eighteenth-Century: Theory and Interpretation* entitled 'Animal, All Too Animal' (2011).

Brian Cowan is Associate Professor and Canada Research Chair in Early Modern British History at McGill University. He is the author of *The Social Life of Coffee: The Emergence of the British Coffeehouse* (2005), editor of *The State Trial of Doctor Henry Sacheverell* (2012), and coeditor of *The State Trials and the Politics of Justice in Later Stuart England* (2021).

J. A. Downie is Emeritus Professor of English at Goldsmith, University of London. He is the author of *Robert Harley and the Press* (1979), *Jonathan Swift: Political Writer* (1984), *To Settle the Succession of the State: Literature and Politics, 1678–1750* (1994), and *A Political Biography of Henry Fielding* (2009), as well as editor of *The Oxford Handbook of the Eighteenth-Century Novel* (2016).

Markman Ellis is Professor of Eighteenth-Century Studies at Queen Mary's, University of London. He is the author of *The Politics of Sensibility: Race, Gender and Commerce in the Sentimental Novel* (1996), *The History of Gothic Fiction* (2000), and *The Coffee House: A Cultural History* (2004). He is the coauthor of *Empire of Tea: The Asian Leaf that Conquered the World* (2019), and editor of *Eighteenth-Century Coffee House Culture*, 4 vols (2006) and *Tea and the Tea-Table in Eighteenth-Century England*, 4 vols (2010).

Katherine Ellison is Professor of English at Illinois State University. She is the author of *Fatal News: Reading and Information Overload in Early Eighteenth-Century Literature* (2006) and *A Cultural History of Early Modern English Cryptography Manuals* (2016), and coeditor of *Topographies of the Imagination: New Approaches to Daniel Defoe* (2014) and *A Material History of Medieval and Modern Ciphers: Cryptography and the History of Literacy* (2017).

Brean S. Hammond is Emeritus Professor of English Literature at the University of Nottingham. He is the author of *Pope and Bolingbroke: A Study of Friendship and Influence* (1984), *Professional Imaginative Writing in England, 1670–1740* (1997), *Making the Novel: Fiction and Society in Britain, 1660–1789* (2006, with Shaun Regan), *Jonathan Swift* (2010), and *Tragicomedy* (2021), as well as editor of John Vanbrugh's *The Relapse and Other Plays* (2004) and *The Double Falsehood* (2010) in the Arden Shakespeare.

D. W. Hayton is Emeritus Professor of History at Queen's University Belfast. He is the author of *Ruling Ireland, 1685–1742: Politics, Politicians and Parties* (2004), *The Anglo-Irish Experience, 1680–1730: Religion, Identity and Patriotism* (2012), and *Conservative Revolutionary: The Lives of Lewis Namier* (2019). He is the coeditor of *The History of Parliament: The House of Commons, 1690–1715* (2002), Jonathan Swift's *Irish Political Writings after 1725: A Modest Proposal and Other Works* (2018), and *The Correspondence of the Brodrick Family of Surrey and County Cork, Volume One: 1680–1714* (2019).

Joseph Hone is Academic Track Fellow in English Literature at the University of Newcastle. He is the author of *Literature and Party Politics at the Accession of Queen Anne* (2017), *The Paper Chase: The Printer, the Spymaster, and the Hunt for the Rebel Pamphleteers* (2020), and *Alexander Pope in the Making* (2021), as well as the coeditor of the forthcoming *Jonathan Swift in Context*.

Jeffrey Hopes is retired Professor of English Studies at l'Université d'Orléans. He is the author of *Gulliver's Travels* (2001) and of articles in journals including *Literature and History*, *Etudes anglaises*, and *Eighteenth-Century Fiction*. He is the coeditor of *Discours critique sur le roman, 1650–1850* (2010) and *Théâtre et nation* (2011).

Kit Kincade is Professor of English at Louisiana State University. She is the editor of Daniel Defoe's *An Essay on the History and Reality of Apparitions* (2007) and Clara Reeve's *The Old English Baron* (2010), and coeditor of *Topographies of the Imagination: New Approaches to Daniel Defoe* (2014).

Christopher F. Loar is Associate Professor of English at Western Washington University. He is the author of *Political Magic: Technology and Sovereign Violence in British Fiction, 1650–1750* (2014) and of articles in *Studies in English Literature*, *Eighteenth-Century Fiction*, *Eighteenth-Century Studies*, *Restoration*, *Genders*, and *Philological Quarterly*.

Kate Loveman is Associate Professor in English Literature at the University of Leicester. She is the author of *Reading Fictions 1660–1740: Deception in English Literary and Political Culture* (2008), *Samuel Pepys and his Books: Reading, Newsgathering, and Sociability, 1660–1703* (2015), and articles in *Journal of Social History*, *English Historical Review*, and *Review of English Studies*. She is the coeditor of *The Diary of Samuel Pepys* (2018).

Robert Markley is W. D. and Sara E. Trowbridge Professor of English at the University of Illinois, Urbana-Champaign. He is the author of *Two-Edg'd Weapons: Style and Ideology in the Comedies of Etherege, Wycherley, and Congreve* (1988), *Fallen Languages: Crises of Representation in Newtonian England, 1660–1740* (1993), *Dying Planet: Mars in Science and the Imagination* (2005), *The Far East and the English Imagination, 1600–1730* (2006), and *Kim Stanley Robinson* (2019).

Ashley Marshall is Professor of English at the University of Nevada, Reno. She is the author of *The Practice of Satire in England, 1658–1770* (2013), *Swift and History: Politics and the English Past* (2015), and *Political Journalism in London, 1695–1720: Defoe, Swift, Steele and their Contemporaries* (2020), and the editor of *Representation, Heterodoxy, and Aesthetics: Essays in Honor of Ronald Paulson* (2015).

Robert Mayer is Professor of English at Oklahoma State University. He is the author of *History and the Early English Novel: Matters of Fact from Bacon to Defoe* (1997) and *Walter Scott and Fame: Authors and Readers in the Romantic Age* (2017), the editor of *Eighteenth-Century Fiction on Screen* (2002), and coeditor of *Historical Boundaries, Narrative Forms: Essays on British Literature in the Long Eighteenth Century in Honor of Everett Zimmerman* (2007).

Marc Mierowsky is Lecturer in English and McKenzie Postdoctoral Fellow at the University of Melbourne. He is the author of articles in *The European Journal of Humour Research*, *Comedy Studies*, and *The Seventeenth Century*. He is coeditor of a forthcoming edition of Defoe's *The Fortunate Mistress* (2024, with Nicholas Seager).

Rebekah Mitsein is Associate Professor of English at Boston College. She is the author of *African Impressions: How African Worldviews Shaped the British Geographical Imagination across the Early Enlightenment* (2022), as well as articles in *Studies in Travel Writing*, *Journal for Early Modern Cultural Studies*, *Romanticism*, *Eighteenth-Century Fiction*, *Digital Defoe*, and *Studies in Eighteenth-Century Culture*.

Andreas K. E. Mueller is Professor of English at Metropolitan State University of Denver. He is the author of *A Critical Study of Daniel Defoe's Verse* (2010) and of articles in *Eighteenth-Century Life*, *Philological Quarterly*, and *The Eighteenth Century: Theory & Interpretation*. He is the coeditor of *Positioning Daniel Defoe's Non-Fiction: Form, Function, Genre* (2011) and *Robinson Crusoe After 300 Years* (2021).

Holly Faith Nelson is Professor of English at Trinity Western University. With Sharon Alker, she is coauthor of *Besieged: The Post War Siege Trope, 1660–1730* (2021) and coeditor of *James Hogg and the Literary Marketplace: Scottish Romanticism and the Working-Class Author* (2009) and *Robert Burns and Transatlantic Culture* (2012). She is also coeditor of *Topographies of the Imagination: New Approaches to Daniel Defoe* (2014), *Games of War in Early Modern English Literature: From Shakespeare to Swift* (2019), and *Borderlands: The Art and Scholarship of Louise Imogen Guiney* (2021).

Maximillian E. Novak is Distinguished Research Professor (Emeritus) at the University of California, Los Angeles. He is the author of *Economics and the Fiction of Daniel Defoe* (1962), *Defoe and the Nature of Man* (1963), *Realism, Myth and History in Defoe's Fiction* (1983), *Daniel Defoe: Master of Fictions* (2001), and *Transformations in Robinson Crusoe and Defoe's Other Narratives* (2014). He is the coeditor of Defoe's *An Essay upon Projects* (1999), *The Consolidator* (2001), *Robinson Crusoe* (2021), and *Farther Adventures* (2021).

Benjamin F. Pauley is Professor and Department Chair of English at Eastern Connecticut State University. He is the author of essays in *Reactions to Revolutions: The 1790s and their Aftermath* (2007), *Positioning Daniel Defoe's Non-Fiction: Form, Function, Genre* (2011), *Robinson Crusoe after 300 Years* (2021), and *The Oxford Handbook of Samuel Johnson* (2022).

Manushag N. Powell is Professor of English at Purdue University. She is the author of *Performing Authorship in Eighteenth-Century English Periodicals* (2012) and coauthor of *British Pirates in Print and Performance* (2015). She is coeditor of *Women's Periodicals and Print Culture in Britain, 1690–1820* (2018) and editor of Defoe's *Captain Singleton* (2019).

Penny Pritchard is Senior Lecturer in English at the University of Hertfordshire. She is the author of *The Long Eighteenth Century: Literature from 1660 to 1790* (2010) and *Before Crusoe: Defoe, Voice, and the Ministry* (2018), as well as articles in *Journal of Eighteenth-Century Studies*, *Journal of Religious History, Literature, and Culture*, and *Literature Compass*.

John Richetti is A. M. Rosenthal Professor of English (Emeritus) at the University of Pennsylvania. He is the author of *Popular Fiction Before Richardson: Narrative Patterns 1700–1739* (1969), *Defoe's Narratives: Situations and Structures* (1975), *Daniel Defoe* (1987), *The English Novel in History, 1700–1780* (1999), *The Life of Daniel Defoe: A Critical Bibliography* (2005), and *A History of Eighteenth-Century British Literature* (2017). He is editor of *The Cambridge Companion to the Eighteenth-Century Novel* (1996), *The Cambridge Companion to Daniel Defoe* (2008), and *The Cambridge Companion to Robinson Crusoe* (2018).

Pat Rogers is Distinguished University Professor Emeritus at the University of South Florida. His books include *Edmund Curll, Bookseller* (2007, with Paul Baines), *A Political Biography of Alexander Pope* (2010), *Documenting Eighteenth-Century Satire: Pope, Swift, Gay, and Arbuthnot in Historical Context* (2011), *The Poet and the Publisher: The Case of Alexander Pope, Esq., of Twickenham versus Edmund Curll, Bookseller in Grub Street* (2021), and *Defoe's Tour and Early Modern Britain: Panorama of the Nation* (2022).

Nicholas Seager is Professor of English Literature at Keele University. He is author of *The Rise of the Novel: A Reader's Guide to Essential Criticism* (2012), editor of *The Cambridge Edition of the Correspondence of Daniel Defoe* (2022), and coeditor of *The Afterlives of Eighteenth-Century Fiction* (2015), Samuel Johnson's *The Life of Richard Savage* (2016), and *The Cambridge Companion to Gulliver's Travels* (2023).

Geoffrey Sill is Emeritus Professor of English at Rutgers University. He is the author of *Defoe and the Idea of Fiction, 1713–1719* (1983) and *The Cure of the Passions and the Origins of the English Novel* (2001). He is the editor of *Walt Whitman of Mickle Street: A Centennial Collection* (1994) and Defoe's *The Consolidator* (2005), and the coeditor of *The Complete Plays of Frances Burney* (1995).

Adam Sills is Associate Professor of English at Hofstra University. He is the author of *Against the Map: The Politics of Geography in Eighteenth Century Britain* (2021) and of articles in *English Literary History*, *Journal of Narrative Theory*, and *Literature Compass*.

Srividhya Swaminathan is Associate Dean and Professor of English at St John's University. She is the author of *Debating the Slave Trade: Rhetoric of British National Identity, 1759–1815* (2009) and coeditor of *Invoking Slavery in the Eighteenth-Century British Imagination* (2013) and *The Cinematic Eighteenth Century History, Culture, and Adaptation* (2018).

Rivka Swenson is Associate Professor of English at Virginia Commonwealth University. She is the author of *Essential Scots and the Idea of Unionism in Anglo-Scottish Literature, 1603–1832* (2016) and coeditor of *Imagining Selves: Essays in Honor of Patricia Meyer Spacks* (2009).

David Walker is Professor of English at Northumbria University. He is the author of *The Discourse of Sovereignty, Hobbes to Fielding: The State of Nature and the Nature* *of the State* (2003, with Stuart Sim) and the coeditor of *Bunyan Studies: A Journal of Reformation and Nonconformist Culture*.

Cynthia Wall is William R. Kenan Jr Professor at the University of Virginia. She is the author of *The Literary and Cultural Spaces of Restoration London* (1998), *The Prose of Things: Transformations of Description in the Eighteenth Century* (2006), and *Grammars of Approach: Landscape, Narrative, and the Linguistic Picturesque* (2018). She is the editor of Pope's *The Rape of the Lock* (1998), Defoe's *A Journal of the Plague Year* (2003), and Bunyan's *The Pilgrim's Progress* (2008). She also coedited *Eighteenth-Century Genre and Culture: Serious Reflections on Occasional Forms* (2001) and *The Eighteenth Centuries: Global Networks of Enlightenment* (2017).

CHAPTER 1

DEFOE'S LIFE AND TIMES

BRIAN COWAN

Zealous Revolutioner

DANIEL DEFOE was born in the wake of one revolution, and he lived to help build the legacy of yet another one which he lived through. Defoe's life and times were thus shaped by two great revolutions of the Stuart age: the regicidal revolution of 1649 and the 'glorious' revolution of 1688–9. Defoe's birth coincided with the restoration of the Stuart monarchy in 1660—a moment that attempted, unsuccessfully, to efface the memory of two decades of civil wars and regime changes that preceded it. As a young man, Defoe joined the fight against the prospect of a popish successor to the throne by supporting the Duke of Monmouth's ill-fated rebellion (*Appeal*, 28).[1] Although Monmouth's attempted coup d'état failed in 1685, William of Orange's Glorious Revolution in 1688 succeeded beyond expectations. Henceforth, Defoe would defend the rectitude and greatness of 'the Revolution' as it would thereafter be known to him and his contemporaries. The revolutionary King William III became Defoe's hero, and throughout his life Defoe would insist that he had been a close confidant and advisor to the revolutionary king. Much of Defoe's political activities in the succeeding decades would be devoted to defending William's Glorious Revolution and to securing its enduring legacy. By the time of Defoe's death in 1731, the Jacobite menace that had threatened to undo the Glorious Revolution had receded, and the Protestant succession to a now united British throne appeared to be secure as a second Hanoverian king, George II, had succeeded to his throne without contest after the death of his father in 1727.

Defoe wrote ceaselessly about the Glorious Revolution and almost always with great praise and reverence for the nation's deliverance from the double threat of popery and arbitrary government that it heralded, but the regicidal revolution was never far

---

[1] Warrant to the Justices of Assize and Gaol Delivery for the Western Circuit (31 May 1687), TNA, SP 44/337, f. 281; Peter Earle, *Monmouth's Rebels: The Road to Sedgemoor 1685* (London: Weidenfeld and Nicolson, 1977), 180, 223 n. 39.

from his mind either. He drew upon the later Stuart debates about the English civil wars when he crafted his fictional *Memoirs of a Cavalier* (1720), a work which Nicholas Seager has argued was an attempt to moderate between the more partisan views of the war promoted by the posthumous publication of works such as John Toland's edition of Edmund Ludlow's *Memoirs* (1698–9) or the Earl of Clarendon's *History of the Rebellion* (1702–4). Pat Rogers notes that Defoe's *Tour thro' the Whole Island of Great Britain* (1724–6) 'never openly takes sides on the issues of the English Civil War, when (as often happens) the narrator comes on remnants of that great and divisive struggle'.[2] The challenge for Defoe, as for many of his contemporaries, was to acknowledge the divisive legacy of the civil wars without obviously aligning himself with either the regicidal or absolutist extremes of either side.

For most of his contemporaries, however, Defoe's views on the civil war era were far from moderate. Unlike the majority of his contemporaries, Defoe saw the revolution that ended Charles I's reign as an event akin to the more respectable glorious revolution that ended James VII and II's rule. In a pamphlet published early in Anne's reign, Defoe shocked many of his readers by declaring that the only difference between the two revolutions 'lyes here, the Whigs in 41. to 48. took up Arms against their King; and having conquer'd him, and taken him Prisoner, cut off his Head, *because they had him*: The Church of *England* took Arms against their King in 88. and did not cut off his Head, *because they had him not*. King *Charles* lost his Life, *because he did not run away*; and his Son, King *James*, sav'd his Life, *because he did run away*' (*PEW*, iii. 65). A few years later, in the *Review* (1704–13), Defoe would return to the topic where he would declare that there was little difference between 'the dry Martyrdom of King *James*, by his *Passive Obedience*, Church Subjects; and the wet Martyrdom of King *Charles* I, by People that never made any such Pretence'.[3]

Resistance was the common denominator between the two revolutions for Defoe; unlike most of his contemporaries, Defoe did not shy away from comparing the regicidal revolution with the Glorious Revolution. He made the analogy explicit in the preface to his longest poem, *Jure Divino* (1706), where he declared, despite acknowledging that 'some People will not bear the Comparison ... That the Parallel between the *Civil* War, or *Parliament* War, or *Rebellion*, call it which you will; and the Inviting over, Joyning with, and Taking up Arms under the Prince of *Orange*, against King *James*, seems to me to be very exact, the drawing such a Parallel very just, and the Foundation proceeding, and Issue just the same' (*SFS*, ii. 42, 43–4). Defoe could not understand 'How any People can then *Defend the inviting over the Prince of Orange*, to check the Invasions of King *James* II. and at the same time condemn the taking Arms against the Invasions of King *Charles* I' (*SFS*, ii. 44). Defoe even went so far as to claim that King James suffered *more* than his

---

[2] Nicholas Seager, '"A Romance the likest to Truth that I ever read": History, Fiction, and Politics in Defoe's *Memoirs of a Cavalier*', *ECF*, 20:4 (2008), 479–505; Blair Worden, *Roundhead Reputations: The English Civil Wars and the Passions of Posterity* (London: Penguin, 2001); Pat Rogers, *The Text of Great Britain: Theme and Design in Defoe's Tour* (Newark, DE: University of Delaware Press, 1998), 28–9.

[3] *Review*, ii. 804 (18 December 1705).

father Charles, whose execution was '*Une coup de Grace*', whereas for James his rebellious subjects 'were 11 years a Murthering of him, and he languish'd all that while under their Treachery' (*SFS*, ii. 49). Defoe's point was not to denigrate the Glorious Revolution, it was quite the opposite: he insisted that it had been achieved through resistance to the king's sovereign power and that resistance had been legitimate.

This was a highly controversial claim to make at the time. Queen Anne's reign saw the resurgence of a Tory ideology that abhorred all forms of resistance theory, even when applied to the Glorious Revolution. This Tory revanche put establishment Whigs on the defensive, and all but the most radical of them sought to temper their avowal of resistance theory, or even better to avoid the question altogether. Defoe's refusal to do either horrified many, and his equation of the revolution of 1649 with that of 1688 was explicitly condemned during the trial of Dr Henry Sacheverell.[4] After this official repudiation of his vigorous defence of resistance theory, very few other writers would dare to take it up again later in the eighteenth century.

Defoe was mainly known in his lifetime as a seditious writer with dangerously unorthodox views about resistance and revolution, but this is not how Defoe saw himself. Defoe consistently presented himself as a political moderate, a pragmatist, and a skilful politician who had access to and the esteem of the good and the great, above all his two heroes, King William III and the wily Robert Harley, whom Defoe did not hesitate to call 'Prime Minister' (*Letters*, 31). As important as they are for understanding Defoe's own self-regard and his public self-fashioning, these characteristics were guises adopted by a mercurial figure who delighted in presenting himself as a key player in the frenzied politics of post-revolutionary Britain. Defoe was not entirely wrong about this: through his varied and prolific writings, he managed to find himself embroiled in some of the major debates of his day. He wrote on politics, religion, economics, education, social policy, travel, and geography; he documented current events as well as writing histories.

Defoe's reputation in his own day was indelibly associated with his politics, and particularly his enthusiasm for the Revolution. When John Oldmixon identified Defoe as 'a Zealous Revolutioner and Dissenter' for the readers of his *History of England* (1735), he was merely repeating a standard opinion of the writer's significance.[5] Defoe's emergence in literary public opinion as a writer of genius emerged only posthumously, and even then the process was a slow one [SEE CHAPTER 33]. Robert Shiells was an early defender when he wrote the first substantive (albeit brief) biography of Defoe in *The Lives of the Poets* (1753), in which he argued against the derisive views of Pope and other arbiters of literary taste: 'De Foe can never with any propriety, be ranked amongst the dunces, for whoever reads his works with candour and impartiality, must be convinced that he was a man of the strongest natural powers, a lively imagination, and solid judgment,

---

[4] Brian Cowan (ed.), *The State Trial of Doctor Henry Sacheverell* (Malden, MA and Oxford: Wiley-Blackwell, 2012), 228; T. B. Howell (ed.), *A Complete Collection of State Trials*, 34 vols (London: Hansard, 1809–28), xv. 213, 324, 341.

[5] John Oldmixon, *The History of England, During the Reigns of King William and Queen Mary, Queen Anne, King George I* (1735), 235.

which ... ought not only to screen him from the petulant attacks of satire, but transmit his name with some degree of applause to posterity'. Even so, Shiells noted that Defoe's 'considerable name' was earned by 'his early attachment to the revolution interest, and the extraordinary zeal and ability with which he defended it'. Defoe was 'best known for the True-Born Englishman', Sheills added.[6]

It was only in the later eighteenth century, and particularly after the enterprising bookseller Francis Noble began to attribute fictional narratives such as *Moll Flanders* (1722) and *Roxana* (1724) to Defoe, that Defoe's reputation as an author of literary distinction, rather than a political writer who defended the Revolution interest, began to take shape.[7] In the nineteenth and twentieth centuries, Defoe's reputation as a 'master of fictions', grounded largely on the growing esteem for the novels he wrote between 1719 and 1724, dominated critical interest in him as a canonical author. Defoe is now probably best known as a fiction writer, and thanks largely to the prominence of his fictional writings in Ian Watt's influential *The Rise of the Novel* (1957), he is a key figure in debates about the 'rise of the novel' in the eighteenth century. Taken as a whole, Defoe's oeuvre (insofar as it can be known) illustrates the changing fortunes of literary production from the age of revolutions into which he was born to the subsequent century of politeness and sensibility in which his writings proved to become increasingly admired, reprinted, and in due course canonized.

He did not set out to be a writer, let alone a great one. Daniel Defoe was born as Daniel Foe, the son of James Foe (d. 1706), a successful London tallow chandler whose Puritanism would become known in his son's lifetime as 'Dissent' due to the ecclesiastical schism created by the 'Clarendon Code' of penal laws enacted in the early years of the Restoration.[8] Young Daniel grew up in the religious culture of late Puritanism and the political culture of what Mark Goldie has identified as 'Puritan Whiggery' [SEE CHAPTER 17]. His family's minister was the renowned Presbyterian Samuel Annesley, and he was educated at the Reverend Charles Morton's dissenting academy in Newington Green. It was in this nascent culture of Dissent that the young Defoe was raised. He was encouraged to begin training as a minister; had he done so, he would have been one of the first generation of Dissenting ministers wholly educated and ordained entirely outside the Church of England, but this was not to be.[9] It is possible that Defoe practised as a Dissenting preacher for a while when he was a young man in

---

[6] Robert Shiells, *The Lives of the Poets of Great Britain and Ireland*, 5 vols (1753), iv. 325, 313; Pat Rogers, *Grub Street: Studies in a Subculture* (London: Routledge, 1972), 311–27.

[7] P. N. Furbank, and W. R. Owens, 'Defoe and Francis Noble', *ECF*, 4:4 (1992), 301–15; P. N. Furbank and W. R. Owens, *The Canonisation of Daniel Defoe* (New Haven, CT: Yale University Press, 1988).

[8] George Southcombe, 'Dissent and the Restoration Church of England', in *The Later Stuart Church, 1660–1714*, ed. Grant Tapsell (Manchester: Manchester University Press, 2012), 195–216.

[9] Mark Goldie, *Roger Morrice and the Puritan Whigs* (London: Boydell, 2016), 194–5; Paula R. Backscheider, *Daniel Defoe: His Life* (Baltimore, MD: Johns Hopkins University Press, 1989), 7–21; Michael Watts, *The Dissenters: From the Reformation to the French Revolution* (Oxford: Oxford University Press, 1978), 315–16.

his twenties, and he would later pen a few lay sermons that were published, but he publicly acknowledged that 'the Pulpit is none of my Office—It was my disaster first to be set a-part for, and then to be set a-part from the Honour of that Sacred Employ'.[10]

Daniel chose instead to follow a secular life of trade and, ultimately, of professional writing. His life and his writings reflect the final phase of Puritanism in the age of revolutions. Certain Puritan themes remained central to Defoe's worldview: the importance of divine providence; the primacy of Biblical scripture as a guide to the divine plan; the centrality of faith to one's spiritual life; his orthodox trinitarianism; his plain style of prose expression; his respect for and even practice of lay preaching; and a rigorous sense of personal and social morality that found expression in his support for (and even participation in) the 'reformation of manners' movement.[11] Defoe's hostility to the theatre, which he described in distinctly Puritan terms as 'Nurseries of Crime, Colleges, or rather Universities of the Devil—Satan's Workhouse, where all the Manufactures of Hell are propagated', is exemplary of a worldview in which sin was omnipresent and a source of fear and social concern [SEE CHAPTER 4].[12] Indeed, Defoe's self-proclaimed conception of his position as a writer depended upon his notion that a satirist aims to provoke and chasten the consciences of his readers [SEE CHAPTER 11]. As he put it in the preface to *The True-Born Englishman* (1700/1), 'The End of Satyr is Reformation' (SFS, i. 83).[13] Defoe's vocation as a public satirist reflected the evolution of trends within Dissenting culture, particularly as Dissent came to reconcile itself with the emergence of a post-revolutionary public sphere.[14]

Over the course of Defoe's lifetime, the social and cultural worlds of Dissent became more securely urban and mercantile, just like Defoe himself. Without ever abandoning his piety, Defoe turned his talents towards the world around him. He sought to understand and describe that world for his contemporaries, and as it happens his works have become an invaluable guide to his world for later historians of his age.[15]

---

[10] *Review*, vi. 427 (22 October 1709); for speculation on Defoe's preaching, see Rogers, *Grub Street*, 316; Furbank and Owens, *Critical Bibliography*, 49, 246, 247 (nos 53(P), 250c, 250i).

[11] Katherine Clark, *Daniel Defoe: The Whole Frame of Nature, Time and Providence* (Houndmills: Palgrave Macmillan, 2007); G. A. Starr, *Defoe and Spiritual Autobiography* (Princeton, NJ: Princeton University Press, 1965); J. Paul Hunter, *The Reluctant Pilgrim: Defoe's Emblematic Method and Quest for Form in Robinson Crusoe* (Baltimore, MD: Johns Hopkins University Press, 1966); Charles Eaton Burch, 'Defoe and the Edinburgh Society for the Reformation of Manners', *RES*, 16:63 (1940), 306–12.

[12] *Review*, vi. 328 (1 September 1709).

[13] Ashley Marshall, 'Daniel Defoe as Satirist', *HLQ*, 70:4 (2007), 553–76; Ashley Marshall, *The Practice of Satire in England 1658–1770* (Baltimore, MD: Johns Hopkins University Press, 2013), 52–3, 153–68.

[14] Brian Cowan, 'The Public Sphere', in *The Cambridge History of Britain, vol. 3, Early Modern Britain, 1500–1750*, ed. Susan Amussen and Paul Monod (Cambridge: Cambridge University Press, forthcoming, c.2025); Mark Knights, *Representation and Misrepresentation in Later Stuart Britain: Partisanship and Political Culture* (Oxford: Oxford University Press, 2005).

[15] Peter Earle, *The World of Defoe* (London: Weidenfeld and Nicolson, 1976).

The Scribbler

Defoe's life as a writer mirrored substantial changes in English literary culture over his lifetime. Defoe claimed that his first publication was a 1683 tract in which he argued against supporting the Ottoman Turks in their war against the Catholic Habsburgs—a point 'which was taken very unkindly indeed' by his Whig friends—but no copy of this work survives, and it is unclear whether it ever existed (*Appeal*, 51). The first work of Defoe's which survives and can be definitively attributed to him is *A Letter to a Dissenter from a Friend at the Hague* (1688), in which he warned his Dissenting friends against the dangers of allying with King James II (*Appeal*, 51–2). He published at least ten more tracts in the 1690s.[16] Defoe is most often categorized as a characteristically eighteenth-century author, partly because the bulk of his publications were produced after 1700, but also because the concept of a 'long eighteenth century' beginning with the Restoration (and coincidentally the putative year of Defoe's birth) has long operated as a category of periodization in English literary and historical studies. The fact that Defoe's literary reputation, and particularly his reputation as a novelist, only grew in esteem over the course of the rest of the eighteenth century has helped to reinforce this notion of him as an eighteenth-century author.[17] Yet it is worth remembering that Defoe lived more than half of his life in the chronological seventeenth century, and his mental world was in many ways ensconced within the concerns of that revolutionary age. Like so many of his contemporaries, Defoe knew that the revolutions of the Stuart era had not been fully settled. They had simply created possibilities for seeing the world anew, and no one of his generation did more to exploit those new mental horizons in print than Defoe.

Print is the key for understanding Defoe's significance in his own day, but the print culture of his lifetime differed from the late Hanoverian and Victorian world that would canonize him as a great author. Defoe wrote in a time when authorship was considered to be an act rather than a profession, and quite often writing was a suspect act that was liable to get one in trouble.[18] Defoe learned this the hard way when he was prosecuted for seditious libel in 1703 for his authorship of *The Shortest-Way with the Dissenters* (1702). Defoe's experience of imprisonment—a large fine and three days of spectacular punishment in the pillory on 29, 30, and 31 July 1703—was a key turning point in his life: it signalled his moment of transition from a controversial scribbler to a writer with

---

[16] Furbank and Owens, *Critical Bibliography*, 8–17 (nos 4–13(P)).

[17] Lawrence Lipking, 'Inventing the Eighteenth Centuries: A Long View', in *The Profession of Eighteenth-Century Literature: Reflections on an Institution*, ed. Leo Damrosch (Madison, WI: University of Wisconsin Press, 1992), 7–25; Furbank and Owens, *Canonisation*; Brian Cowan, '"Restoration" England and the History of Sociability', in *British Sociability in the Long Eighteenth Century: Challenging the Anglo-French Connection*, ed. Valérie Capdeville and Alain Kerhervé (London: Boydell, 2019), 7–24.

[18] Mark Rose, *Authors in Court: Scenes from the Theater of Copyright* (Cambridge, MA: Harvard University Press, 2016), 1–10; Jody Greene, *The Trouble with Ownership: Literary Property and Authorial Liability in England, 1660–1730* (Philadelphia, PA: University of Pennsylvania Press, 2005).

privileged contacts at the highest levels of government.[19] Robert Harley, then Speaker of the House of Commons and soon to be made secretary of state for the Northern Department, contacted Defoe while he was imprisoned in Newgate with an offer of patronage and relief from his suffering.

In his personal apologia published after the Hanoverian accession, *An Appeal to Honour and Justice* (1715), Defoe drew a parallel between this offer from Harley and the Biblical encounter between Christ and the faithful blind man, who when asked '*What wilt thou that I should do unto thee?*' replied 'My Answer is plain in my Misery, Lord, that I may receive my Sight' (*Appeal*, 12).[20] To see, for Defoe, was to write. Harley's reprieve gave Defoe a chance to write again. Not long thereafter, Defoe would publish his *Essay on the Regulation of the Press* (1704), which argued against the restoration of pre-publication licensing, but also that authorial accountability should be established by a requirement that every published work should include the name of the author. Furthermore, he thought that authors should own 'an undoubted exclusive Right to the Property' of their works (*PEW*, viii. 158). Defoe was possibly the earliest advocate for an author's property rights in their writings; he argued for something closer to a common law right of property in an author's works: 'A Book is the Author's Property, 'tis the Child of his Inventions, the Brat of his Brain'.[21] This argument did not prevail in law, however. When a change in copyright came with the coming into effect of the Statute of Anne (8 Ann. c. 19) in 1710, property rights were granted not to authors but to booksellers, and only for a term of fourteen years for 'new books', with the possibility of extension for a second fourteen-year term. Copyright for 'existing books' was granted to their present owners for twenty-one years. The terms of the act would remain controversial, and Defoe's arguments for a common right of intellectual property in written works would be taken up most enthusiastically by the booksellers rather than authors until the matter was definitively settled in favour of fixed statutory limits by the Lords' decision in *Donaldson v. Becket* (1774).[22]

Defoe's writing career, despite his prodigious efforts and his relative success as a professional scribbler, relied upon a remarkably diverse stream of income from various sources, amongst which payment for copy was one of the least important. To be sure, he prospered more than most of his Grub Street contemporaries. Robert Harley's patronage was crucial in allowing Defoe to travel extensively whilst also maintaining his prodigious periodical and pamphlet writing in Anne's reign. Estimates regarding the amount of patronage Defoe received from the government vary considerably. An anonymous pamphlet, *The Republican Bullies* (1705), claimed that he received 'a handsome

---

[19] J. R. Moore, *Defoe in the Pillory and Other Studies* (Bloomington, IN: Indiana University Press, 1939); Thomas Keymer, *Poetics of the Pillory: English Literature and Seditious Libel, 1660–1820* (Oxford: Oxford University Press, 2019), 89–155.

[20] Defoe paraphrases Mark 10:51 and Luke 18:41.

[21] *Review*, vi. 649 (2 February 1710); Mark Rose, *Authors and Owners: The Invention of Copyright* (Cambridge, MA: Harvard University Press, 1993), 35, 39.

[22] Rose, *Authors and Owners*; Trevor Ross, *Writing in Public: Literature and the Liberty of the Press in Eighteenth-Century Britain* (Baltimore, MD: Johns Hopkins University Press, 2018).

Allowance, (viz.) 100 *l.* for the first Volume' of the *Review*. Novak estimates that he received £200 per annum from government secret service funds whilst writing the *Review* and other works; Downie's 'meanest estimate' is an annual income of £250 that may have been as high as £400; Backscheider contends that Defoe earned somewhere between £400 and £500 per year from at least 1707 until the death of the queen, thanks to his connections to Harley, Sunderland, and Godolphin.[23] Contemporaries certainly thought Defoe was well paid. Oldmixon claimed that Harley 'paid *Foe* better than he did *Swift*, looking on him as the shrewder Head of the Two for Business'.[24]

After Harley's fall from power and the Hanoverian accession in 1714, Defoe became more reliant upon commercial income from his relationships with the publishing industry; here too he was relatively well paid for his efforts. For pamphleteering, John Baker paid Defoe two guineas for every 500 copies of a sixpence pamphlet during the latter years of Anne's reign. Richard Janeway was more generous: on at least one occasion, he paid four guineas plus some free copies for every 1,000 pamphlets sold. Defoe had a similar arrangement with William Taylor, the publisher for the first edition of *Robinson Crusoe*. He was paid £10 for the original print run of 1,000 copies of the first volume, and £10 10s. more upon the printing of the second volume in 1,000 copies, along with provision for a supplementary payment of £5 if 500 copies of that printing were sold. For the third volume of *Crusoe*, Defoe was to be paid 15 guineas for every 1,000 copies printed.[25]

But it was through his ownership of several periodicals that Defoe may have made serious profits from his writing; Backscheider estimates that he earned perhaps as much as £1,200 per year by the 1720s.[26] As chief proprietor for the *Review*, Defoe had supplemented his small income from sales of the periodical, which was barely profitable, by selling advertisement space in its pages, and by collecting payments from readers for additional services rendered, such as offering advice on casuistic matters, problem solving, or in gratitude for having written something desirable in its pages. McVeagh estimates that he may have earned as much as £50 per year from advertisement revenues, but he garnered the rather more substantial sum of £1,300 annually from his 'Scandal Club business', although he only kept the latter running for less than two years from 1704 to 1705. The Scandal Club offered a section devoted to questions

---

[23] *The Republican Bullies: Or a Sham Battel Between Two of a Side* (1705), 4; Novak, *Daniel Defoe*, 211; J. A. Downie, 'Secret Service Payments to Daniel Defoe, 1710–1714', *RES*, 30:120 (1979), 437–41 (439); Paula R. Backscheider, 'Defoe, Daniel (1660?–1731)', *ODNB*, https://doi.org/10.1093/ref:odnb/7421.

[24] John Oldmixon, *The Life and Posthumous Works of Arthur Maynwaring* (1715), 276.

[25] Brean S. Hammond, *Professional Imaginative Writing in England, 1670–1740* (Oxford: Clarendon Press, 1997), 74, citing Backscheider, *Daniel Defoe*, 371, 434, 465; Henry Clinton Hutchins, *Robinson Crusoe and Its Printing 1719–1731: A Bibliographical Study* (New York: Columbia University Press, 1925), 40–1. For more on the printing of *Crusoe*, see Keith Maslen, *An Early London Printing House at Work: Studies in the Bowyer Ledgers* (New York: Bibliographical Society of America, 1993), 17–25, 57–61.

[26] Backscheider, *Daniel Defoe*, 465. Michael Harris, *London Newspapers in the Age of Walpole: A Study of the Origins of the Modern English Press* (Cranbury, NJ: Associated University Presses, 1987), 49–64, offers a less sanguine view of the profit potential of early eighteenth-century periodicals.

from readers, often of a personal or moral nature, that would be answered in the journal. Or, as Defoe put it, 'Here are Questions in Divinity, Morality, Love, State, War, Trade, Language, Poetry, Marriage, Drunkenness, Whoring, Gaming, Vowing, and the like'.[27] The business of answering questions and publishing puff pieces for readers was apparently a lucrative one. Defoe's erstwhile friend and Grub Street competitor John Dunton complained that the *Review*'s 'interloping' on Dunton's idea of answering readers' cases of conscience cost Dunton £200 in lost income; he also accused Defoe of 're-printing a Copy' of one of Defoe's earliest published poems, *The Character of the Late Dr. Samuel Annesley* (1697), which had allegedly been given to Dunton for publication but was in fact printed and sold by the bookseller Elizabeth Whitlock instead.[28] After the *Review*, Defoe would also manage periodicals such as *Mercator* (26 May 1713–20 July 1714), the *Monitor* (22 April–7 August 1714), the *Manufacturer* (30 October 1719–9 March 1721), the *Commentator* (1 January–6 September 1720), and the *Director* (5 October 1720–16 January 1721), and it was from these publications that he may have profited handsomely.

These earnings were considerable for a writer of his day, and Defoe may be considered one of the few Grub Street scribblers who managed to earn a respectable living from his pen. Samuel Johnson's annual income was under £100 for the first twenty years of his London career, which roughly coincided with the two decades succeeding Defoe's death in 1731.[29] Nevertheless, Defoe did not rely upon income from his writing alone, and he maintained a diversified income stream throughout his life.

Along with his work as a writer, Defoe remained active as a businessman and a high-risk investor in various projects [SEE CHAPTER 14]. His first major investment was his marriage on 1 January 1684 to a cooper's daughter, Mary Tuffley (1665–1732), who brought him a dowry of £3,700. This considerable sum allowed Defoe the capital and business networks he required to set up his trade as a wholesale hosier, and it did not take long before he had expanded his ventures to include overseas imports and exports in other wholesale goods such as tobacco, logwood, wine, spirits, and cloth. Some of his more speculative investments turned out to be unfortunate, such as his purchase of seventy civet cats for about £850 in April 1692. Two months later, he made an investment of £200 in a diving bell scheme designed to recover sunken treasure. Both cases resulted in lawsuits and recriminations with his business partners, including with his own mother-in-law, Joan Tuffley. In addition to these cases, Defoe's liabilities extended well beyond his ability to pay, and he found himself with £17,000 of debt claimed by his creditors. By the end of the year, Defoe was bankrupt and committed to the Fleet Prison on 29 October 1692; he was released upon recognizances but returned again on 12 February 1693.[30]

---

[27] John McVeagh, 'Introduction' to *Review*, i. xxiii, xxv, xxvii; *Review*, i. 391 (Supplement for September 1704).

[28] John Dunton, *The Life and Errors of John Dunton*, 2 vols (1818), ii. 423, 424.

[29] Robert D. Hume, 'The Economics of Culture in London, 1660–1740', *HLQ*, 69:4 (2006), 487–533 (526); J. A. Downie, 'Periodicals, the Book Trade and the "Bourgeois Public Sphere"', *Media History*, 14:3 (2008), 261–74.

[30] Backscheider, *Daniel Defoe*, 55–8.

This was a first-hand experience with what he would call 'the Poverty of Disaster' which 'falls chiefly on the middling Sorts of People, who have been Trading-Men, but by Misfortune or Mismanagement, or both, fall from flourishing Fortunes into Debt, Bankruptcy, Jails, Distress and all Sorts of Misery'.[31] In several works, Defoe defended the practice of declaring bankruptcy. He saw it as an honest and honourable recourse for a trader who had run into unforeseen financial difficulties: 'Certainly honesty obliges every man, when he sees that his stock is gone, that he is below the level, and eating into the estates of other men, to put a stop to it; and to do it in time, while something is left' (*RDW*, vii. 83). Bankruptcy and, even more so, imprisonment for debt were not uncommon experiences for middle-class traders in eighteenth-century England. Thirty-three thousand businesses went bankrupt in the eighteenth century, and over 300,000 people were imprisoned for debt. It has recently been estimated that perhaps 7% of all London men would experience incarceration for debt during their lifetime.[32] In 1709, Defoe estimated that there were 80,000 men imprisoned for debt in England, 'most of whom have Families, Wives, and Children innumerable, whose Miseries and Disasters are deriv'd from' such incarceration. Defoe's passion for this matter derived from his personal experiences with imprisonment.[33]

Somewhat miraculously, Defoe managed to settle his terms with his creditors, and he negotiated a relatively quick release from prison in 1693. It is not clear how he accomplished this. Defoe credited 'the late kings Bounty' (*Letters*, 17) with his financial salvation. Soon thereafter he 'was invited by some Merchants … to settle at *Cadiz* in *Spain*', but he demurred and instead was able to secure a new position from the crown 'without the least application' (*Appeal*, 5–6) as an accountant to the commissioners of the glass duty after his release.

Defoe managed around the same time to open a brick and pantile factory in Tilbury that promised to become very profitable given the growing market for building trades in the London area. He claimed to have employed 'a hundred Poor Familys at work and … Generally Made Six hundred pound profit per Annum' (*Letters*, 17). He was forced to sell the factory as a result of his prosecution for *The Shortest-Way*.[34] The timing of the sale was truly unfortunate, as it occurred just before the great storm of 26–7 November 1703, an event that immediately created substantial new demand for the factory's products. Rather than profiting from brick and pantile sales from the great rebuilding after the storm, Defoe turned to the book trade and rapidly published a series of tracts relating to the natural disaster: *The Lay-Man's Sermon*; a poem, *An Essay on the Late Storm*; and a journalistic account titled simply *The Storm* (1704).[35] Although

---

[31] *Review*, iv. 117 (3 April 1707).

[32] Tawny Paul, *The Poverty of Disaster: Debt and Insecurity in Eighteenth-Century Britain* (Cambridge: Cambridge University Press, 2019), 5, 45–6.

[33] *Review*, v. 676 (1 March 1709).

[34] Backscheider, *Daniel Defoe*, 63–6, 139–40.

[35] Defoe, *The Storm* (1704), ed. Richard Hamblyn (London: Penguin, 2003); Backscheider, *Daniel Defoe*, 141–5.

Defoe's business interests along with their accompanying debts would persist through his life, his two moments of imprisonment and prosecution for bankruptcy in 1692–3 and later for seditious libel in 1703 proved to be decisive in focusing his attention towards writing as both a source of income and a vocation [SEE CHAPTER 12].

Defoe's literary production was shaped by his experience of a series of personal misfortunes and twists of fate that were also key moments in his life. The bankruptcy proceedings prompted Defoe's emergence as a well-known writer, mainly of poems and satires, in the 1690s. Harley's reprieve granted after Defoe's second imprisonment and his pillorying a decade later initiated a new phase of work as propagandist for the government, in which he devoted himself primarily to journalism and pamphleteering [SEE CHAPTERS 6, 7, AND 20]. After the Hanoverian accession resulted in the fall from power of his primary patron, Robert Harley, Defoe would once again reshape his literary career as he began to concentrate on crafting and marketing narratives (both fictional and non-fictional or an amalgam of both) and guidebooks and didactic manuals such as *The Family Instructor* (1715, 1718), *The Compleat English Tradesman* (1725–7), and *A Tour thro' the Whole Island of Great Britain* (1724–6) [SEE CHAPTERS 3, 5, AND 8].

SELF-FASHIONING IN PRINT

Although Defoe is best known today as a novelist and a political commentator or propagandist, for much of his career as a writer he conceived of and presented himself to his publics primarily as a satirist. Throughout his lifetime and well afterwards, Defoe was best known as 'the author of the True-Born Englishman', a work that he significantly subtitled 'a satyr'. The first authorized collection of Defoe's writings was titled *A True Collection of the Writings of the Author of the True Born English-man* (1703); this was followed soon thereafter by *A Second Volume of the Writings of the Author of the True-Born Englishman* (1705).[36] Both volumes were reissued in 1710 as a two-volume collection. In 1721, Defoe published yet another collection of his writings with the title *The Genuine Works of Mr. Daniel D'Foe, Author of The True-Born English-Man, a Satyr*, which was largely a reprint of the earlier anthologies. These collections of Defoe's works sold well throughout his lifetime, and they were priced high enough to suggest that the works must have attracted a relatively wealthy readership.[37]

These various editions of Defoe's collected works, curated and edited by their author, offer some significant clues as to how Defoe conceived of his own authorial persona. The prominence of *The True-Born Englishman* as his most noteworthy work is clear. Perhaps because of the patriotic connotations evoked by the title, Defoe consistently wished to be known as the author of this 'satiric' poem. *The True-Born Englishman* was the first work

---

[36] For the unauthorized *Collection* of 1703, see Furbank and Owens, *Critical Bibliography*, 4.
[37] Marshall, 'Defoe as Satirist', x.

of his that sold well. Although he claimed that the work brought him no personal profit, Defoe proudly announced (with no doubt a substantial amount of hyperbole) that it had earned the booksellers over £1,000 profit through sales of nine authorized and twelve pirated editions, including 80,000 copies sold for '2d. or at a Penny'.[38] The size of these print runs is likely exaggerated: more reliable evidence for the authorized printing of Henry Sacheverell's best-selling sermon, *The Perils of False Brethren* (1709), indicates that the work sold just under 54,000 copies, and it is highly unlikely that Defoe's poem outsold Sacheverell's sermon.[39]

As a defence of King William and the Glorious Revolution, *The True-Born Englishman* suited Defoe's public self-fashioning as a vociferous defender of the Revolution cause and an intimate friend of the king. The scandal and spectacular punishment associated with *The Shortest-Way* may have brought Defoe more notoriety, his continuous writing for the *Review* for almost a decade may have secured him the nickname 'Mr. Review', and his authorship of *Robinson Crusoe* would seal his posthumous reputation as a novelist of great genius, but it was *The True-Born Englishman* that Defoe would continually refer back to as his most noteworthy work.

The frontispiece to Defoe's *True Collection* is an engraved portrait of the author (Figure 1.1). This portrait, drawn by Jeremiah Tavernier and engraved by Michael Van der Gucht, presented Defoe as he wished to be seen by his readers. He appeared handsome, well dressed, and spectacularly bewigged with a large perruque. Below his portrait appeared the words 'Daniel DeFoe, author of the Trueborn Englishman', along with a coat of arms. This rather august self-presentation was advertised for sale in the *Daily Courant* for 22 July 1703, just one week before Defoe's first day of punishment in the pillory. It was clearly designed to counter the now common image of Defoe as a rogue writer and a convicted criminal, and perhaps to capitalize upon his new-found notoriety. It also made the bourgeois tradesman appear as a gentleman worthy of respect. The portrait may have been printed and sold independently from the work. Although there is no evidence that such individualized sales were advertised, a copy of Defoe's pamphlet *Advice to All Parties* (1705) has the portrait inserted as a frontispiece. It also appears as the frontispiece to a copy of Defoe's *Second Volume of the Writings* (1705) and was tipped in to serve as the frontispiece for some editions of his *Jure Divino* as well. There are minor differences in the engravings for these works: some appear with attribution of the artists Tavernier and Van der Gucht, others do not; Defoe's eyes are reworked in later prints.[40] The image was obviously popular enough to demand a new execution of the original drawing for later printings.

Aside from the frontispiece to the *True Collection*, the only other work of Defoe's to include an authorial portrait was his major poem *Jure Divino* (1706) (Figure 1.2). Unlike his other works, most of which were composed and published with astounding

---

[38] Defoe, *A Second Volume of the Writings of the Author of The True-born Englishman* (1705), sig. A3r.
[39] Cowan (ed.), *The State Trial of Doctor Henry Sacheverell*, 209.
[40] Houghton Library, Harvard University, shelfmark *EC7 D3623 705a; McGill University Rare Books & Special Collections, shelfmarks PR3401 1703, PR3401 1705, and PR3404 J8 1706.

FIGURE 1.1 Frontispiece, Daniel Defoe, *A True Collection of the Writings of the Author of the True Born English-man* (1703). Courtesy of McGill University Library, Rare Books and Special Collections, shelf mark PR3401 1703.

FIGURE 1.2 Frontispiece, Daniel Defoe, *Jure Divino: A Satyr. In Twelve Books. By the Author of The True-Born Englishman*. Courtesy of Lilly Library, University of Indiana, Bloomington, shelf mark PR3404 .J89.

speed (often in less than a year), Defoe spent five years working on this poem. He also experimented with a subscription model for marketing and selling the folio edition for the substantial price of fifteen shillings. The experiment did not go as planned, however: the list of subscribers was not as substantial as he had hoped, and Defoe ultimately had to apologize for delays in publication. By the time it appeared, pirate editions were already in the works and would soon appear.[41] Defoe must have hoped that this publication would secure his reputation as a poet of major importance, and therefore he commissioned a more detailed and impressive version of the *True Collection* portrait from Van der Gucht, claiming that it had been 'prepar'd at the request of some of my Friends who are pleas'd to value it more than it deserves' (*Letters*, 124). It was printed as the frontispiece for the folio edition of *Jure Divino*. Here, Defoe's genteel dress and long wig appear even more elaborately detailed. The coat of arms is reproduced below, along with the Latin epigraph '*laudatur et alget*', identified as from Juvenal's first satire. The quote from Juvenal (*Satires* 1.74) reads '*probitas laudatur et alget*', or 'honesty is praised and is left to shiver'. Defoe significantly omits *probitas* from his epigraph, thus suggesting that it was the honest author himself who had once been praised for his work and then cruelly abandoned afterwards, which may be a reference to his prosecution for seditious libel in 1703.

This portrait may also have been sold independently. Defoe noted in a letter to his friend John Fransham that it cost one shilling (*Letters*, 124), a price that was close to the market rate for folio sized portraits. A few years later, unframed mezzotint print portraits of Henry Sacheverell would sell for one shilling and six pence. The British Museum and the Wellcome Library both hold a singular copy of the print in which the epigraph from Juvenal is printed around the oval coat of arms and the subject is identified below as 'Daniel De Foe, author of the True Born Englishman'.[42] These separates may have been sold for a shilling each at print shops or from booksellers, although no contemporary advertisements for them seem to have been placed in the newspaper press. Ads for such portraits tended to be reserved for clergymen or other figures of a higher social status than the struggling writer and bankrupted trader Defoe.

Defoe's investment in commissioning portraits for his *True Collection* and *Jure Divino* offers useful clues as to how he wished to be seen, and how he wished to have his authorized works recognized by his readers. The authorial portraits are testaments to his attempt to establish himself as a genteel author worthy of respect, rather than as a Grub Street scribbler. This was a cause that he took up in the *Review* at the same time. He admitted that he could not speak Latin with fluency: 'Latin, *Non ita Latinus sum ut Latine Loqui*—I easily acknowledge my self Blockhead enough, to have lost the Fluency of Expression in the

---

[41] Paula R. Backscheider, 'The Verse Essay, John Locke, and Defoe's *Jure Divino*', *ELH*, 55:1 (1988), 99–124; Margaret J. M. Ezell, *The Oxford English Literary History: Volume 5: 1645–1714, The Later Seventeenth Century* (Oxford: Oxford University Press, 2017), 482; John Robert Moore, *Daniel Defoe: Citizen of the Modern World* (Chicago, IL: University of Chicago Press, 1958), 236–9.

[42] *Post Boy*, no. 2301 (9–11 February 1710); British Museum [BM], registration no. 1872,0713.166; Wellcome Library Image Collection, no. 2425i (accessed 10 November 2020), https://wellcomecollection.org/works/u95mgb6n.

Latin'. This did not deter him however from challenging the Whig journalist John Tutchin (who had provoked the ire that had inspired *The True Born Englishman*) to a translation contest. He dared his adversary to translate one Latin, one French, and one Italian author into English and then to retranslate each, 'the English into French, the French into Italian, and the Italian into Latin'. Whoever managed to do this best and quickest would owe the other £20, a considerable sum. 'And by this', Defoe declared, 'he shall have an Opportunity to show the World, how much De Foe the Hosier, is Inferior in Learning, to Mr. Tutchin the Gentleman'.[43] Tutchin did not take him up on the challenge.[44] Defoe was aware that his bourgeois and Dissenting origins disadvantaged his authorial status as a polite writer, but he never renounced them. Instead, he struggled to convince his contemporaries that even a Dissenter from the middling sorts could outperform his gentleman rivals.

Further evidence that Defoe continued to seek genteel status throughout his life exists in the survival of a portrait of the author in oil on canvas (Figure 1.3). The 762 x 635 mm painting survives in the Caird collection of the National Maritime Museum in Greenwich, but the date of composition is unknown. If it was painted from the life, it must have been commissioned well after Defoe's earlier engraved portraits for his printed works, as the painted portrait represents a man considerably older in appearance than the pictures published in the 1700s when Defoe would have been in his forties. The Greenwich portrait was therefore probably painted in the 1710s or 1720s, or perhaps even later.[45] This is possibly the only surviving contemporary painting of Defoe, and it was not reproduced in print for popular consumption. Defoe presented himself in his writings as an expert on painting, and it is possible that he found some inspiration for his prose fictions in the works of contemporary Dutch realist painters.[46] It is plausible that he would have commissioned a formal portrait of himself later in life as a means of asserting his reputation as an accomplished man of means.

Defoe's efforts to establish himself as an author of recognized genius and politeness evidently did not pay off. The authorized portraits of Defoe as Juvenalian satirist and esteemed 'author of the True Born Englishman' were more than matched by less flattering images of him as a Grub Street hack who had stood in the pillory. Hills's pirate edition of *Jure Divino* included its own crude portrait of the author that was much less flattering and lacked the genteel coat of arms and Latin epigram (Figure 1.4). Another piracy by Benjamin Bragg included an even more damning image of Defoe standing in the pillory (Figure 1.5).[47] These critical effigies served to reinforce the general impression of Defoe as a writer who was not to be taken seriously, and they undermined his efforts to rehabilitate his public reputation

---

[43] *Review*, ii. 221–2 (31 May 1705).

[44] Brian Cowan, 'Daniel Defoe's *Review* and the Transformations of the English Periodical', *HLQ*, 77:1 (2014), 79–110 (95–8).

[45] National Maritime Museum, Caird Collection BHC2648, https://collections.rmg.co.uk/collections/objects/14122.html, (accessed 10 November 2020).

[46] Maximillian E. Novak, *Transformations, Ideology, and the Real in Defoe's Robinson Crusoe and Other Narratives* (Newark, DE: University of Delaware Press, 2015), 43–60.

[47] D. F. Foxon (ed.), *English Verse 1701-1750*, 2 vols (Cambridge: Cambridge University Press, 1975), D130 (Bragg), D131 (Hills); Janine Barchas, *Graphic Design, Print Culture and the Eighteenth-Century Novel* (Cambridge: Cambridge University Press, 2003), 42.

FIGURE 1.3 Portrait of Daniel Defoe, oil painting. © National Maritime Museum, Greenwich, London, Caird Collection BHC2648. https://collections.rmg.co.uk/collections/objects/14122.html.

in the wake of his spectacular punishment for *The Shortest-Way*. Other contemporary representations of Defoe made little effort to depict him realistically. His journalistic guise as Mr Review allowed him to be represented as a generic Whig writer, just one of 'the British Libellers' in *The Three Champions* (c.1710), who 'have *the Pillory* disgraced and may *the Gallows*', or one amongst several monstrous heads on a hydra-like beast in *Faction Display'd* (1709). In *A Character of a Turn-coat: Or, The True Picture of an English Monster* (1707), an effigy of Defoe is paired with one of Tutchin, in which both are depicted as two-faced, gender-bending, position-shifting, untrustworthy scribblers.[48] The overall effect of these caricatures was to present Defoe as an entirely untrustworthy writer.

---

[48] BM 1868,0808.3415 (Satires 1512); BM 1868,0808.3419 (Satires 1508); Houghton Library, Harvard University, Bute Broadsides C56.

FIGURE 1.4 Frontispiece, P. Hills's pirated edition of *Jure Divino* (1706). Courtesy of Lilly Library, University of Indiana, Bloomington, shelf mark PR3404 .J89 1706.

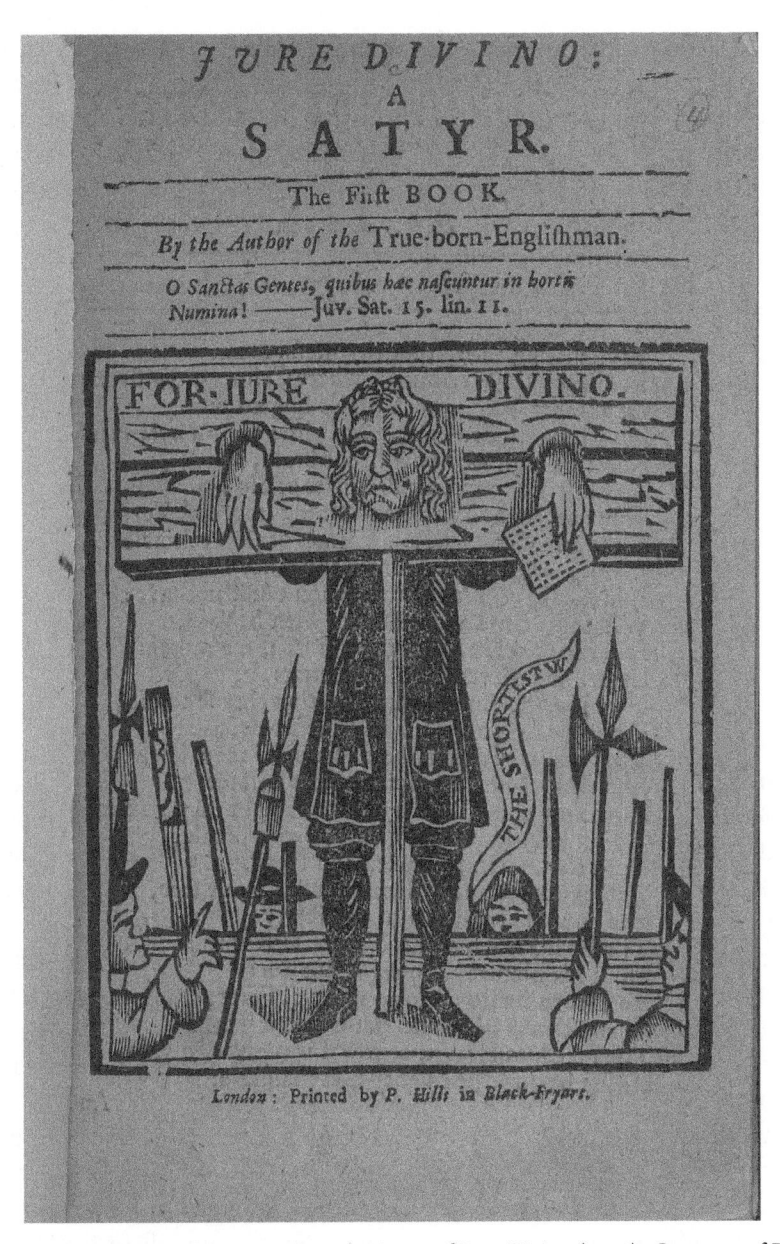

FIGURE 1.5 Frontispiece, Benjamin Bragg's piracy of *Jure Divino* (1706). Courtesy of Beinecke Rare Book and Manuscript Library, Yale University, shelf mark Ik D362 706Je.

The most sophisticated critical graphic satire of Defoe was George Bickham's *The Whig's Medly* (1711) (Figure 1.6). In this print, Defoe appears twice: first at the top as 'A Deformed head in the Pillory'. He also figures prominently in the centre of the image, depicted as a writer receiving advice from both the Pope and the Devil as he composes a text titled 'Resistance Lawful', a reference to Defoe's controversial advocacy of resistance theory in *Jure Divino* and the *Review*. The text below Defoe's head in the pillory reads:

> What awkward ill-look'd fellow's this?
> He has an ugly frightful phys;
> And sure as black his conscience is?
> Cadaverous, black, blue, and green.
> Not fit in publick to be seen.
> With dirt besmear'd, & goggle-ey'd
> With a long nose, & mouth as wide;
> With blobber lips, & lockram jaws,
> Warts, wrinkles, wens, & other flaws:
> With nitty beard, & neck that's scabby,
> And in a dress, that's very shabby.
> Who this should be I do not know,
> Unless a Whig? I guess he's so.
> If I am right, pray take a throw.

The recurrent rhyming of the last three lines with the name 'Defoe' must have been obvious to most contemporary readers of the print. Despite the fact that the print was produced in 1711, when Defoe was writing primarily in support of Harley's Tory ministry, Bickham has no reservations about associating him with the Whig cause. Surely the main reason for this was Defoe's strident defence of resistance theory and his consistent attacks on the resurgent high church cause epitomized by Dr Henry Sacheverell, whose sermons denigrated all justifications for resistance as sinful heresy. Defoe here is associated with the disgraced Oliver Cromwell, who 'is gone I fear to Hell, to be Protector', and the Calves Head Club, an imaginary club devoted to commemorating the regicide of Charles I by holding a feast on 30 January every year.[49]

Bickham's print confirms Defoe's contemporary reputation as a dangerous revolutionary subversive figure. It also invokes a graphic trope that had become common in the Sacheverell controversies, wherein a controversial writer is portrayed receiving counsel from nefarious figures such as the Pope, Oliver Cromwell, or the Devil. Both Sacheverell and his Whig nemesis Benjamin Hoadly were depicted in this manner, including in Bickham's own earlier print *The High Church Champion and His Two Seconds* (1709–10).[50] In *The Whig's Medly*, Bickham pays Defoe an ironic compliment by

---

[49] Edward Ward, *The Secret History of the Calves-Head Club* (1703).
[50] BM 1868,0808.3427 (Satires 1498); Brian Cowan, 'Hoadly the High and Sacheverell the Low: Religious and Political Celebrity in Post-Revolutionary England', in *Political and Religious*

FIGURE 1.6 George Bickham, *The Whig's Medly* (1711). Courtesy of The Lewis Walpole Library, Yale University, shelf mark 711.00.00.01+. http://hdl.handle.net/10079/digcoll/549567.

Practice in the Early Modern British World: Essays in Honour of Peter Lake, ed. Bill Bulman and Freddy Dominguez (Manchester: Manchester University Press, 2022), 158–78.

placing such a common scribbler in the company of clergymen, even if the intention is to satirize him.⁵¹

Defoe was unable to control the public reception of his authorial persona. Given the promiscuity of his writing practices, and his penchant for publishing anonymously or pseudonymously, it is hard to see how he could ever have succeeded in doing so. The first reason Defoe gave for publishing his self-justifying *Appeal to Honour and Justice* was, he said, because 'I think I have long enough been made *Fabula Vulgi* [the talk of the town], and born the Weight of general Slander' (*Appeal*, 2). Despite the fact that the vast majority of Defoe's publications appeared anonymously or pseudonymously, his authorial persona figured prominently, albeit rather unfavourably, in early eighteenth-century print culture. His conviction and punishment for seditious libel in 1703 proved to be difficult to surmount. While he would eventually emerge in the nineteenth century as a liberal culture hero who would be lionized as a martyr for the cause of freedom of speech, in his own day Defoe could never escape the stigma of his conviction for seditious libel.

The memory of his time in the pillory never left Defoe. Swift dismissively referred to Defoe in a pamphlet of 1709 as 'the Fellow that was *Pillor'd*, I have forgot his Name', who 'is indeed so grave, sententious, dogmatical a Rogue, that there is no enduring him'. A few years later, during Harley's administration, Joseph Addison noted that 'the Court found him [i.e., Defoe] such a False, Shuffling, Prevaricating Rascal, that they set him aside as a Person unqualify'd to give his Testimony in a Court of Justice; advising him at the same time, as he tender'd [i.e. valued] his Ears, to forbear uttering such notorious Falshoods as he had then Publish'd'.⁵² It was derisory comments such as these that encouraged Pope to include Defoe amongst his literary dunces in *The Dunciad* (1728), first as 'ear-less on high, stood pillory'd D—' and later in the *Dunciad Variorum* (1729) as 'Earless on high, stood un-abash'd Defoe', even when he would admit privately that 'there's something good in all he [Defoe] has writ'.⁵³

---

⁵¹ Mark Knights, 'Possessing the Visual: The Materiality of Visual Print Culture in Later Stuart Britain', in *Material Readings of Early Modern Culture: Texts and Social Practices, 1580–1730*, ed. James Daybell and Peter Hinds (Houndmills: Palgrave Macmillan, 2010), 85–122; Mark Hallett, *The Spectacle of Difference: Graphic Satire in the Age of Hogarth* (New Haven, CT: Yale University Press, 1999), 46–55. Bickham's graphic oeuvre was not obviously partisan. He produced works both critical and laudatory of Whigs and Tories alike. See https://www.britishmuseum.org/collection/term/BIOG19578 (accessed 27 September 2020).

⁵² Swift, *A Letter from a Member of the House of Commons in Ireland to a Member of the House of Commons in England, Concerning the Sacramental Test* (1709), 6, and Joseph Addison, *The Late Tryal and Conviction of Count Tariff* (1713), 12; both quoted in Thomas Keymer, 'Defoe's Ears: The Dunciad, the Pillory, and Seditious Libel', *Eighteenth-Century Novel*, 6–7 (2009), 159–96; Keymer, *Poetics of the Pillory*, 121–48.

⁵³ Keymer, *Poetics of the Pillory*, 100–1; Rogers, *Grub Street*, 311.

Allegorical and Historical Stories

Defoe tried to defend himself and his actions in *An Appeal to Honour and Justice*, a tract which served as a sort of personal memoir and defence of his public life and actions in support of the post-revolutionary governments. But the work also signalled a new interest in writing memoirs themselves, in both non-fictional and fictional forms. It is arguable that Defoe stumbled upon the fictional novel form through his experiments with memoir writing in the years following the Hanoverian accession, even if he had demonstrated an interest in fictional narratives throughout his life.[54] The manuscript of his 'Historicall collections, or, Memoires of passages & stories collected from severall authours', which he composed for his fiancée Mary Tuffley as a young man in 1682, contains a series of short stories and anecdotes of heroic tales drawn from a variety of sources ancient and modern.[55] It certainly demonstrates an early interest in fiction writing—and he incorporated fictional aspects to much of his published work, such as the satiric fantasy about a voyage to the moon in *The Consolidator* (1705)—but Defoe would not take to writing fiction *qua* fiction until much later in life. Even as he began to compose secret histories and novels in the early Georgian era, Defoe constructed and presented these fictional narratives under the guise of truth, much as he had done when writing his satires, histories, and political commentary. The much heralded 'realism' of Defoe's fiction emerged out of his skill in crafting stories replete with such detail that they seemed to be true to all but the most sceptical of readers.[56]

Before he wrote *Robinson Crusoe*, Defoe wrote several secret histories or otherwise contrived memoirs based upon claims to truth-telling that made the texts plausible if not entirely believable [SEE CHAPTER 9]. Despite denying his authorship (*Appeal*, 47), Defoe's *The Secret History of the White-Staff* in three parts (1714–15), along with *The Secret History of the Secret History of the White-Staff* (1715), was widely believed to be his work as it offered a strident defence of his patron Harley's conduct in office as Lord Treasurer. This work heralded the publication of similar works, such as *Minutes of the Negotiations of Monsr. Mesnager* (1717), before he produced the famous *Life and Strange Surprizing Adventures of Robinson Crusoe* (1719). Despite being marketed as the memoirs of a most remarkable life, *Crusoe*'s truth claims were flimsy, and the work was quickly criticized as an imposition upon the public. Charles Gildon's *Life and Strange*

---

[54] Paula R. Backscheider, *Daniel Defoe: Ambition and Innovation* (Lexington, KY: University Press of Kentucky, 1986), 125–35; Maximillian E. Novak, '*Robinson Crusoe* and Defoe's Career as a Writer', in *The Cambridge Companion to Robinson Crusoe*, ed. John Richetti (Cambridge: Cambridge University Press, 2018), 32–48.

[55] William Andrews Clark Library, UCLA, MS 1951.009.

[56] Maximillian E. Novak, 'Defoe's Theory of Fiction', *Studies in Philology*, 61:4 (1964), 650–68; Maximillian E. Novak, *Realism, Myth, and History in Defoe's Fiction* (Lincoln, NE: University of Nebraska Press, 1983); Novak, *Transformations, Ideology and the Real*; Geoffrey Sill, *Defoe and the Idea of Fiction, 1713–1719* (Newark, DE: University of Delaware Press, 1983).

Surprizing Adventures of Mr. D---- de F--, of London (1719) seized upon the narrative inconsistencies and absurdities in Defoe's *Crusoe* as a means of ridiculing the novel and denigrating Defoe's skills as an author. Gildon accuses Defoe of constructing a 'Fable' or a fiction without even a 'useful Moral, either express'd or understood' to justify its impostures; instead, he claims somewhat improbably that *Crusoe* was 'design'd against a publick Good' by scaring its readers from 'going to Sea', and thus will have the effect of impoverishing and endangering the British nation by discouraging maritime ventures. The novel's protagonist is no hero, but rather an incoherent and impious fool, much like its author. Later, Gildon argues that 'the Design of the Publication of this Book was not sufficient to justify and make Truth of what you allow to be Fiction and Fable; what you mean by Legitimating, Invention and Parable, I know not; unless you would have us think, that the Manner of your telling a Lie will make it a Truth'.[57]

Gildon's criticisms, while amusing at times, hardly affected the reception of the novel, aside from publicly outing Defoe as its author, but they bothered Defoe enough to provoke a response of sorts when he wrote the third book in his Crusoe trilogy, his *Serious Reflections During the Life and Surprising Adventures of Robinson Crusoe* (1720). Unlike the first two books, this work sought to justify his fictional tales of Crusoe by demonstrating—contra Gildon—that there were indeed wholesome morals to be derived from them. Furthermore, he embraced Gildon's satiric equation of Crusoe with Defoe himself. Here, Crusoe declares 'that the Story [in the first two novels], though Allegorical, is also Historical, and that it is the beautiful Representation of a Life of unexampled Misfortunes, and of a Variety not to be met with in the World'. He insists that 'the Adventures of Robinson Crusoe, are one whole Scheme of a real Life of eight and twenty Years, spent in the most wandring desolate and afflicting Circumstances that ever Man went through ... In a Word, there's not a Circumstance in the imaginary Story, but has its just Allusion to a real Story, and chimes Part for Part, and Step for Step with the inimitable Life of Robinson Crusoe' (*Novels*, iii. 51, 52–3).

Some critics have taken Defoe at his word and have attempted to read *Crusoe* as an autobiographical allegory, despite obvious difficulties in drawing the parallels too closely.[58] Certainly, Defoe's invocation of Crusoe's life of 'unexampled Misfortunes, and of a Variety not to be met with in the World' (*Novels*, iii. 51) fits well with the way in which he told his own life story as one of constant persecution intermittently interrupted by miraculous reprieves in *An Appeal to Honour and Justice*. It is on this very abstract level that the analogy between Crusoe's story and Defoe's life remains convincing. Any attempt to fix Defoe's authorial persona to a precise identity or meaning is bound to fail, not least because the writer himself was committed to using the affordances of early modern print culture to develop multiple personalities, different voices, and a radically

---

[57] Charles Gildon, *The Life and Strange Surprizing Adventures of Mr. D---- de F--, of London* (1719), 2–3, 33.

[58] George Parker, 'The Allegory of Robinson Crusoe', *History* 10:37 (1925), 11–25; and most recently in Michael Prince, *The Shortest Way with Defoe: Robinson Crusoe, Deism, and the Novel* (Charlottesville, VA: University of Virginia Press, 2019); *Novels*, iii. 11.

unfixed, perpetually labile identity.[59] In the published version of his 1976 Ford Lectures, J. P. Kenyon observed that 'despite the vast amount of work that has been done on Daniel Defoe, there is much in his life and work which is still mysterious'.[60] Kenyon's remark continues to ring true.

FURTHER READING

Paula R. Backscheider, *Daniel Defoe: His Life* (Baltimore, MD: Johns Hopkins University Press, 1989).

Paula R. Backscheider, 'Defoe, Daniel (1660?–1731)', *ODNB*, https://doi.org/10.1093/ref:odnb/7421.

Brian Cowan, 'Daniel Defoe's *Review* and the Transformations of the English Periodical', *HLQ*, 77:1 (2014), 79–110.

Laura A. Curtis, *The Elusive Daniel Defoe* (London: Vision, 1984).

Peter Earle, *Monmouth's Rebels: The Road to Sedgemoor 1685* (London: Weidenfeld and Nicolson, 1977).

Peter Earle, *The World of Defoe* (London: Weidenfeld and Nicolson, 1976).

P. N. Furbank and W. R. Owens, *The Canonisation of Daniel Defoe* (New Haven, CT: Yale University Press, 1988).

J. P. Kenyon, *Revolution Principles: The Politics of Party 1689–1720* (Cambridge: Cambridge University Press, 1977).

Thomas Keymer, *Poetics of the Pillory: English Literature and Seditious Libel, 1660–1820* (Oxford: Oxford University Press, 2019).

John Robert Moore, *Daniel Defoe: Citizen of the Modern World* (Chicago, IL: University of Chicago Press, 1958).

Maximillian E. Novak, *Daniel Defoe, Master of Fictions: His Life and Ideas* (Oxford: Oxford University Press, 2001).

Michael Watts, *The Dissenters: From the Reformation to the French Revolution* (Oxford: Oxford University Press, 1978).

---

[59] Laura A. Curtis, *The Elusive Daniel Defoe* (London: Vision, 1984).
[60] J. P. Kenyon, *Revolution Principles: The Politics of Party 1689–1720* (Cambridge: Cambridge University Press, 1977), 57.

PART I
GENRES

CHAPTER 2

DEFOE'S POETRY

MAXIMILLIAN E. NOVAK

When William Peterfield Trent (1862–1939), professor at Columbia University and admirer of Defoe, was trying to identify Defoe's writings among a wide amount of anonymous contemporary pamphlet literature, he hesitated over a poem that he thought likely to have been by Defoe. The problem, to his mind, was whether it was worth claiming a poetic effort for Defoe.[1] Trent was a poet himself—one who wrote in a late Victorian, semi-romantic style. For Trent, what Defoe wrote was hardly poetry. Keats had advised the poet 'to load every rift ... [of a poem] with ore'—with feeling-charged artistry, and for many of the poets Trent admired, this was the only acceptable kind of poetry.[2] But Defoe's *True-Born Englishman* was one of the more reprinted poems of the eighteenth century. And there is no question that Defoe always had an imaginative streak that may have found its best outlet in prose, but which he sometimes thought was best expressed in poetry.[3] Since that moment of Trent's hesitation, there has been some recognition of Defoe's talent as a poet. Andreas Mueller has devoted a critical volume to Defoe's poetry, and J. Paul Hunter has defended Defoe's occasional (if not entirely

---

[1] This occurs in one of the many manuscript listings that Trent made in which he debated with himself about ascribing works to Defoe. Trent disparaged Defoe's poetry throughout his unfinished manuscript bibliography, remarking of Defoe's *Jure Divino* (1706) that although Defoe had successfully worshipped the goddess of liberty, he had entirely failed to worship the goddess of poetry. The closest he came to putting this opinion in print came in a series of essays in *The Nation*. At one point he devoted a paragraph to various works in poetry and prose which, since they were 'worthless performances', might just as well be eliminated from any bibliography of Defoe. He remarked that as a poet 'Defoe was capable of execrable doggerel', and that various 'worthless performances' were of such 'slight consequence' that they might well be omitted. See the 'Trent Collection', The Beinecke Library, Yale University; and W. P. Trent, 'Bibliographical Notes on Defoe—I', *The Nation*, 84 (1907), 515–18 (516).

[2] John Keats, *Letters*, ed. Maurice Buxton Forman, 4th ed. (Oxford: Oxford University Press, 1952), 507–8. Keats was alluding to the vividly allegorical scene involving the temptation of Sir Guyon in Spenser's *The Faerie Queene*, II, vii, 28.

[3] The pattern of important writers of fiction beginning their careers as poets is hardly unusual; William Faulkner and Ernest Hemingway experimented with poetry in their early years. Some, such as George Eliot, Herman Melville, and D. H. Lawrence, continued to write poetry throughout their careers.

consistent) artistry and pointed to his standing as an important poet in the first decade of the eighteenth century.[4]

Early Poems and Influences

It is significant that the earliest work we have from Defoe is poetry—the very confessional 'Meditations' that he composed around 1682, when he was 22. He never published these poems, and they remained in manuscript until George Healey published an edition in 1946.[5] They reveal Defoe thinking of himself as a poet at this early point in his life. He was not a businessman who somehow fell into literature as the result of a series of bankruptcies. Poetry and a series of short fictions that he presented to his future wife, Mary Tuffley, around 1683, show that he was thinking imaginatively and creatively as a young man. He spoke of abandoning poetry around 1709, and so far as we know he did not publish many poems during the following decade. But he took the occasion of publishing *Serious Reflections ... of Robinson Crusoe* in 1720 to include a number of poems, and towards the end of his life he included a long poem in defence of the Christian concept of the Trinity in *A New Family Instructor* (1727).

When Defoe came to speak of the poets he most admired, they make up a pantheon of the great classical poets and of the most esteemed poets of the late seventeenth century. I will comment on these poets shortly, but before I do so I should note that, if we can tell from some of his quotations of various poets, Defoe also seems to have had a certain admiration for what might be called 'popular' poetry—poetry that, for the most part, avoided learned allusions and appealed to readers who enjoyed the heightened emotion of rhymed verse without too much complexity. These included Thomas Taylor 'the Water Poet' (1578–1653), George Wither (1588–1677), Thomas Jordan (1612–85), Charles Cotton (1630–87), and Robert Wild (1615–79). They were probably poets he encountered in his youth.[6] Taylor and Jordan were strongly connected with London. Jordan composed for London pageants. Wither was something of a rebellious spirit, who spent some time in prison. Defoe quoted a poem by him in *Serious Reflections* (1720):

---

[4] Andreas K. E. Mueller, *A Critical Study of Defoe's Verse: Recovering the Neglected Corpus of His Poetic Work* (Lewiston: Edwin Mellen Press, 2010); J. Paul Hunter, 'Poetic Footprints: Some Formal Issues in Defoe's Verse', in *Defoe's Footprints: Essays in Honour of Maximillian E. Novak*, ed. Robert Maniquis and Carl Fisher (Toronto: University of Toronto Press, 2009), 53–70. D. N. DeLuna argues that the methods used by Frank Ellis and those of the 'Yale School' of criticism did not use adequate critical tools in treating Defoe's poetry. 'Yale's Poetasting Defoe', *1650–1850*, 4 (1998), 345–62.

[5] *The Meditations of Daniel Defoe*, ed. George Harris Healey (Cummington, MA: Cummington Press, 1946).

[6] Defoe frequently quoted lines from the poet Samuel Butler (1612/13–80), whose burlesque poem *Hudibras* (1662, 1663, 1680) had a wide readership. Although he never appears to have imitated Butler's tetrameter couplets, Defoe probably admired Butler's wit and clever rhyming.

> The World and I may well agree,
>   as most that are offended;
> For I slight her, and she slights me,
>   and there's our Quarrel ended...[7]

He also found Wither's 'motto' attractive: nec habeo, nec careo, nec curo (I have not, I lack not, I care not). Like Wither, Defoe, in his later years, felt somewhat slighted by the world. He quoted Wild in *Robinson Crusoe* (1719) on the question of emotions.[8] This was not surprising, since Wild tended to maintain a heightened emotional tone in his poetry.

In treating these poets, John Dryden's Crites, one of the disputants in his *Essay of Dramatic Poesie* (1668), remarked of Wild that he was 'a very Leveller in Poetry, he creeps along with ten little words in every line, and helps out his Numbers with *For to* and *Unto*, and all the pretty Expletives he can find'.[9] Another Dryden spokesperson, Eugenius, however, remarks on Wild's popularity:

> Yet, assure your selves, there are multitudes who would think you malicious and them injur'd: especially him whom you first described; he is the very *Withers* of the City: they have bought more Editions of his Works then would serve to lay under all their Pies at the Lord Mayor's *Christmass*. When his famous Poem first came out in the year 1660, I have seen them reading it in the midst of Change-time; nay so vehement they were at it, that they lost their bargain by the Candles ends: but what will you say, if he has been received amongst great Persons?[10]

Dryden was attempting to distinguish between what he considered high and low poetry. In addition to an aesthetic distinction, the division included class separations. Although poems by the Presbyterian Wild appealed to a wide readership, such readers lacked a sense of what was required in true poetry—the poetry that should be read by the upper classes, all members of the Church of England, all supporters of the monarchy. Dryden was a better poet than any of those popular poets mentioned above, his verse tighter, his allusions and images often brilliant. On the other hand, these popular poets often had an energy which Defoe admired and imitated.

The first published poem by Defoe, *A New Discovery of an Old Intreague* (1691), had a Latin quotation from Ennius beginning '*Unus Nobis Cunctando Restituit*', alluding to the longer quotation: 'One man, by delay, saved the state; for he cared less for what was said than for the public welfare' (*SFS*, i. 35). Defoe may not have been responsible for every title page, but the ironic allusion certainly sounds like him. What is important

---

[7] Defoe, *Serious Reflections during the Life and Surprising Adventures of Robinson Crusoe* (1720), 260.
[8] Defoe, *The Life and Strange Surprizing Adventures of Robinson Crusoe*, ed. Maximillian E. Novak, Irving N. Rothman, and Manuel Schonhorn (Lewisburg, PA: Bucknell University Press, 2020), 45.
[9] John Dryden, *Works*, ed. Samuel Holt Monk et al., 20 vols (Berkeley, CA: University of California Press, 1956–2000), xvii. 11.
[10] Dryden, *Works*, xvii. 11–12.

here, however, is the Latin allusion—announcing that this was not a popular ballad, but rather a serious poem for upper-class readers. He placed it as the first work in *A Second Volume of the Writings of the Author of the True-Born Englishman* (1705), an indication that he took pride in its composition. He modelled his poem on the two great satiric poets of the Restoration, Dryden and Andrew Marvell, the first for his wit, the second for his ability to maintain a consistent tone of anger and indignation, somewhat in imitation of the Roman poet Juvenal.[11]

A New Discovery attacks the supporters of the exiled James II and their continued assaults upon William III (Nassau) and Mary II, in this case the 117 petitioners, hiding their demands behind a claim of restored rights. Defoe imagines the enemies of William assembling for their attacks. William seems at first unwilling to punish them:

> His Conquering Mercy did his Justice stay,
> And at his Peril let them disobey:
> Restraints to his own injur'd Passions gave,
> Their Folly pityed, and their Guilt forgave. (lines 639–42; *SFS*, i. 56)

But eventually William did punish these enemies of the state. Although at one point Defoe states that he will avoid the parallels with ancient Israel that Dryden used so masterfully in *Absalom and Achitophel* (1681), he uses some parallels immediately after this announcement. Some of his allusions are deliberately obscure, providing readers with a kind of older form of crossword puzzle as they were able (or not) to identify these references. Perhaps the most interesting thing about the poem is its commitment to satire ('Satyr') as a reforming mechanism. Defoe was to do better when he reached out to a larger, more general theme.

From the poets previously mentioned, all of whom were involved in political poetry, Defoe took the material and attitude for a series of poems attacking the enemies of King William. They were written in a lilting tone, stanzas of five lines of tetrameter and trimeter usually rhyming abaab with the improvisatory feel of a ballad. The rhymes are sometimes surprisingly witty, sometimes non-existent. They were aimed at mocking the Parliaments that had attacked the King. Defoe painted these legislators as feckless and incompetent. In *An Encomium upon a Parliament* (1699), he began by addressing them as 'Patriots', who had promised much but achieved little:

> Ye worthy Patriots go on
>   To heal the Nation's Sores,
> Find all Mens Faults out but your own,
> Begin good Laws, but finish none,
>   And then shut up your Doors. (lines 1–5; *SFS*, i. 59)

---

[11] Lines such as 'And did King *Jesus* Reign they'd murmur too' are taken directly from Dryden's *Absalom and Achitophel* (line 184; *SFS*, i. 43).

He ends with a '*Chorus*', suggestive of the musical quality of the work:

> *For shame leave this wicked Employment,*
> *Reform both your Manners and Lives;*
> > *You were never sent out*
> > *To make such a Rout,*
> *Go home and look after your W[ive]s.* (lines 101–5; *SFS*, i. 62)

Defoe was good at this kind of political balladry with its easy, popular wit and cheekiness. But the form had its limitations.

At this point in his career, Defoe appears to have had some aspirations to being accepted by a critical audience as an important poet. As has been mentioned, he had already published anonymously in 1691 a poem in pentameter couplets, *A New Discovery of an Old Intreague*, a satire on a petition that he considered part of a plot by the enemies of King William to undermine his reign—a poem reflecting the strong influence of Dryden and Marvell, who were acknowledged as the two most important satirists of the Restoration [SEE CHAPTER 11]. In his next important poem, *The Pacificator* (1700), he attempted to mediate between the quarrel involving the well-known poets Samuel Garth and Richard Blackmore. He produced a somewhat typical battle of the books poem of the time: in this case, a battle between the wits and the moralists.[12]

Defoe included himself in the list of poets at the end—poets who were to stick to their particular talents, with Defoe as the master of the 'Lampoon'. One wonders how many contemporaries would have filled in the name of the letters after 'F-e' (line 421; *SFS*, i. 76). I have never discovered a copy with 'Foe' filled out, but he may have been known to a small circle of poets surrounding the Earl of Dorset, poets writing in defence of King William. As W. R. Owens suggests, the lampoon had been designated as a somewhat doubtful category by John Dryden (*SFS*, i. 25). Whereas satire involved a more generous kind of attack, Dryden argued, the lampoon singled out the faults of individuals within society; whereas Dryden could point to his attack upon the Duke of Buckingham in *Absalom and Achitophel* as the kind of critique at which the victim might be amused, Defoe, in poems such as *Reformation of Manners*, presented a gallery of contemporaries upon whom the poet heaped as much scorn as possible. The effect was associated with the Roman satirist Juvenal and with Marvell, who used the 'advice to a painter' type of poem to attack Charles II and his government. Whatever the reason Defoe designated himself the master of the lampoon, it was a proper poetic positioning for his most successful poem—a poem in which he more or less berated the entire English nation for its racist pride, its xenophobia, and its ingratitude toward William III.

---

[12] Although mainly associated with Jonathan Swift, this form was part of the 'Quarrel between the Ancients and the Moderns' in France during the latter half of the seventeenth century. *The Pacificator* represented Defoe's attempt to enter the world of contemporary literary debate.

The True-Born Englishman (1700)

The True-Born Englishman had important, universal subjects. It also had a very specific theme. William had been almost ready to abdicate after the Parliament of 1698. He had written out a speech in which he stated that he had come over the Channel from Holland to rescue England from the tyranny of James II. Instead of gratitude for leading the nation in successful wars against James II and Louis XIV, he had had his Dutch guards dismissed, his grants of land to his favourites taken away, and the Dutch vilified, particularly in John Tutchin's poem, *The Foreigners* (1700). Defoe, who regarded William as a true hero, was able to summon up his indignation and rise above the anger he almost certainly felt, to reveal that the Englishman's pride in race was completely absurd [SEE CHAPTER 28]. History demonstrated that England was a hodgepodge of various invaders, many of doubtful pedigree. The name of one of the attacks upon Defoe's poem, *English Men No Bastards*, suggests the reaction of many of his readers. How dare anyone mock the purity of the English race? But that is just what Defoe did. And he did it in a way that left his enemies spluttering with indignation, yet it had to be an indignation that recognized that English claims to racial purity were illusory.

More than this, Defoe injected into *The True-Born Englishman* a political philosophy that rejected the concepts of hereditary virtue and race:

> Cou'd but our Ancestors retrieve their Fate,
> And see their Offspring thus degenerate;
> How we contend for Birth and names unknown,
> And build on their past Actions, not our own;
> They'd cancel Records, and their Tombs deface,
> And openly disown the vile degenerate Race:
> For Fame of Families is all a Cheat,
> 'Tis personal Virtue only makes us great. (lines 1209–16; SFS, i. 118)

This comes at the end of his contentious poem.[13] It embodies notions of equality that were part of the ideology associated with the Whig party—the party of the Revolution of 1688. It was an ideology that Defoe was to lay out a year later in his prose tract, *The Original Power of the Collective Body of the People of England*, or, as he referred to it, '*The Original Right* ... '.[14] This was a forceful statement of Defoe's political position, and Defoe, of course, was a writer of powerful prose. Owens seems to suggest that some of Defoe's prose footnotes in *Jure Divino* were superior to his poetry. This was certainly not true of his *True-Born Englishman*, which was among the most popular poems of the eighteenth century.

---

[13] This is probably a translation from Juvenal, *Satire* 8, verse 20: '*nobilitas sola est atque unica virtus*'.
[14] See John Robert Moore, *A Checklist of the Writings of Daniel Defoe* (Bloomington, IN: Indiana University Press, 1960), 17–18.

The opening lines of the poem present a witty image of a world governed by a seemingly generous Devil:

> Whereever God erects a House of Prayer,
> The Devil always builds a Chapel there:
> And 'twill be found upon Examination,
> The latter has the largest Congregation. (lines 56–9; *SFS*, i. 86)

As a subtext this Devil and his helpers are seen very much in terms of the opponents of William III. But most important is the way this Devil suited himself to the sins of the various nations of the world. Some of these sections are very witty:

> Ungovern'd Passion settled first in *France*,
> Where Mankind lives in haste, and thrives by Chance.
> A *Dancing Nation*, Fickle and Untrue:
> Have oft undone themselves, and others too:
> Prompt the Infernal Dictates to obey,
> And in Hell's Favour none more great than they. (lines 117–22; *SFS*, i. 88)

But it is when he comes to the English that the satire takes off. 'Ingratitude' is the great sin of the English. The supposed 'Antient Pedigree' of the English aristocracy dates no further back than some trooper in the army of William the Conqueror. 'A *Turkish* Horse can show more History', the poet remarks. Worse yet, they were French! England, he argues, has always been *'The Eternal Refuge of the Vagabond'* (lines 212, 227, 254; *SFS*, i. 91–2). But once arrived they foolishly pride themselves on their English heritage:

> Proudly they learn all Mankind to contemn,
> And all their Race are *True-Born Englishmen*. (lines 257–8; *SFS*, i. 92)

From the standpoint of poetry, the best passage is dedicated to the England of Charles II:

> The Civil Wars, the common Purgative,
> Which always use to make the Nation thrive,
> Made way for all that strolling Congregation,
> Which throng'd in Pious *Ch----s*'s Restoration,
> The *Royal Refugeé* our Breed restores,
> With *Foreign Courtiers*, and with *Foreign Whores*:
> And carefully repeopled us again,
> Throughout his Lazy, Long, Lascivious Reign,
> With such a blest and True-born *English* Fry,
> As much Illustrates our Nobility.
> . . . .
> Six Bastard Dukes survive his Luscious Reign,

> The Labours of *Italian Castlemain*,
> *French Portsmouth*, *Tabby Scot*, and *Cambrian*.
> Besides the Num'rous Bright and Virgin Throng,
> Whose Female Glories shade them from my Song. (lines 285–94, 303–7; *SFS*, i. 93)

The irony of the passage extends beyond the literal meaning that depicts a king who specialized in bringing back to England with him dozens of foreign courtiers and having children with a variety of mistresses. There was nothing 'careful' about his choice of such women. Nell Gwyn, for example, could not boast of any pedigree and had been the mistress of several men before Charles II took her from the stage. Having lived much of his life on the Continent, Charles himself was a 'Refugee', like so many who had poured into England to make up the race of mongrels that was the nation. Defoe reduces his status as a monarch to a single word. A monarch is no different in kind from any other refugee.

The entire group that came with Charles was anything but 'pious'. They were not a congregation, with the word's religious connotation; indeed, they were more like a collection of strolling players. But the passage is irreverent from the start. Charles I had become the equivalent of a saint in the Anglican Church, and the narrative surrounding him was central to the way the Church presented itself after 1660, the year of the Restoration. But the rebellion that started in 1642, and that resulted in his execution in 1649, is here treated as a kind of excretory moment in history, nothing unusual, just the slightly unusual event by which older forms are removed and replaced by newer ones. The reign of Charles II is described as 'Lazy, Long, … Lascivious', echoing in its final word the notion of luxurious or 'Luscious' as Defoe leads into the national variety of Charles's mistresses. Defoe's ironic evocation of pastoral imagery to cover the 'Virgin Throng', Charles's other mistresses, such as Moll Davis, has him seemingly reluctant to express his appreciation of this monarch, lest he seem too biased in his favour. The complex use of language, the ironic (over)use of alliteration, and the poetic allusions reveal Defoe's very conscious artistry as a satiric poet. Satire (especially the satire of the Restoration) aspired to a rough style, perhaps best exemplified in the work of John Oldham. But passages such as these show Defoe working smoothly as a skilled poet.

From this height, he falls into a rollicking satiric style as he imagines what the effect of Charles's love affairs will be on the nation:

> *French* Cooks, *Scotch* Pedlars, and *Italian* Whores,
> Were all made Lords, or Lords Progenitors,
> Beggars and Bastards by his new Creation,
> Much multipli'd the Peerage of the Nation;
> Who will be all, e're one short Age runs o're,
> As *True-Born* Lords as those we had before. (lines 312–17; *SFS*, i. 93)

Then, at line 334, he returns to his historical and political theme. There is no hereditary English nobility. England is a 'Modern' country, for better or for worse. Defoe attacks the various vices of the English, particularly their drunkenness, their self-importance, their admiration for wealth, their litigiousness. And from line 802, he begins his exposition of politics: English government has its origin in the mob. Government is a contract, and the people obey only as long as the leaders fulfil their role.

In the section labelled 'Britannia', Defoe expresses his admiration for William III:

> *My Hero, with the Sails of Honour furl'd,*
> *Rises like the Great Genius of the World.*
> *By Fate and Fame wisely prepared to be*
> The Soul of War, and Life of Victory.
> *He spreads the Wings of Virtue on the Throne,*
> *And ev'ry* Wind of Glory *fans them on.*
> *Immortal Trophies dwell upon his Brow,*
> *Fresh as the Garlands he has won but now.* (lines 905–12; SFS, i. 109–10)

There is nothing insincere in these lines. Defoe saw William as the heroic soldier and statesman who saved England and much of Europe from the depredations of Louis XIV. If these encomiastic verses seem to fall flat, it is partly because they lack the specificity of the satiric sections of the poem, partly because they attempt to create the kind of idealized figure that little comports with the notion we have of real personalities. Defoe was a hero worshipper. It made for poems such as his praise of Marlborough, *The Double Welcome* (1705)—idealizations that lack the critical judgements of poems such as Dryden's elegy on John Oldham or W. H. Auden's on Yeats.

At the beginning of *The True-Born Englishman*, Defoe called upon a personified concept of 'Satyr', using this device in a manner little different from Andrew Marvell's instructions to a painter to depict the ills of Restoration society. Now, towards the end of the poem, Defoe asks Satyr to continue his critique of the 'Unthankful Isle' and their ingratitude toward William, focusing on the character of Sir Charles Duncombe, whose speech displays a career of dishonest, immoral self-seeking. The 'Conclusion' sets out the main theme. The pride in nation and ancestry has no basis in reality. Only individual, '*Personal Virtue*' gives value to life. This powerful egalitarian message echoed through the centuries not merely in Defoe's popular poem, but as a subtext in all of Defoe's writings. During an age which produced hundreds of odes and descriptive poems of little value, Defoe's poem remained a brilliant combination of poetry and Whiggish politics.

SATIRES AND PANEGYRICS, 1702–5

Defoe continued to update *The True-Born Englishman*, including some additions in 1716. In the ninth edition (1701), he added a preface treating his concept of satire. Following Dryden, he argued that the purpose of satire was 'Reformation'. He wanted to reform the English out of their absurd anti-Williamite, anti-Dutch attitudes. In his *The*

Mock Mourners (1702), on those who hypocritically pretended to be mourning the death of King William, he followed the techniques that he used in *The True-Born Englishman*, with Britannia and Satyr carrying the burden of the criticism of a nation that had failed to appreciate the king.[15] But in *Reformation of Manners* (1702) and *More Reformation. A Satyr upon Himself* (1703), Defoe attempted a somewhat different tack. Frank Ellis compared *Reformation of Manners* to the end of Swift's *Gulliver's Travels* in its ironic stance.[16] The Societies for the Reformation of Manners had been formed in the early 1690s to improve the moral behaviour of the English. The problem, as Defoe saw it in 1702, was that the results of more than a decade of 'Black-Lists' of offenders had been the complete avoidance of any attacks upon the wealthy and the upper orders and a kind of war upon the poor. Defoe's poem was supposed to change that situation by a kind of grotesque series of pictures which revealed the moral failings of the wealthy and powerful. It was much the lesson of Defoe's earlier prose tract, *The Poor Man's Plea* (1698), but this time in an often pointed verse. Under the guise of criticizing the Roman port of Ostia, Defoe attacks London as a place that falsely claims to have reformed itself:

> How against Vice she has been so severe,
> That none *but Men of Quality* may swear:
> How Publick Lewdness is expell'd the Nation,
> That *Private Whoring* may be more in fashion. (lines 85–9; *SFS*, i. 159)

In the second part, the satirist, with the help of the personified Satyr, turns his eyes to another group, among whom there is another ample gallery of immoralists, with Defoe presenting a lengthy attack upon drunkards or 'Sots and the Church' and including a lengthy delineation upon virtue and vice. Somewhat in the manner of his *Pacificator*, he turned against a number of the 'Wits', including Dryden and D'Urfey:

> Let this describe the Nation's Character,
> One Man reads *Milton*, forty *Rochester*.
> This lost his Taste, *they say*, when h'lost his Sight,
> *Milton* had Thought, but *Rochester* had Wit.
> The Case is plain, the Temper of the Time,
> One wrote *the Lewd*, and t'other *the Sublime*.[17]

There is a degree of hypocrisy in this verse. Defoe admired Milton, but the sublime was not Defoe's best mode. Rochester's wit, on the other hand, was very much to Defoe's taste, and as shall be seen, Rochester's vision of human beings as political animals was

---

[15] Defoe identified the poem as both a satire and an elegy, seeming to confuse two forms. But Defoe used the notion of 'satire' for any poem with an argument. And it was an elegy for King William. See Mueller, *Defoe's Verse*, 68–9.

[16] Frank H. Ellis (ed.), *Poems on Affairs of State: Augustan Satirical Verse, 1660–1714*, 7 vols (New Haven, CT: Yale University Press, 1963–75), vi. 398–9.

[17] Defoe, *A True Collection of the Writings of The True-Born Englishman* (1703), 105.

to be shaped into a Defovian point of view.[18] The poem was apparently in its seventh edition within the year—most likely a success based on its scandalous list of sinners.

Between this poem and *More Reformation* (1703), Defoe published *The Spanish Descent* (1702), Defoe's most successful experiment in the sombre, often anguished satire that had been practised by Andrew Marvell in the early years of the Restoration. Just as Marvell had concentrated on the dubious successes of the war at sea against the Dutch, Defoe here takes on the failure of an expedition against the Spaniards at Cadiz, followed by the surprising success at Vigo. Defoe was to praise Marvell in *More Reformation* as a satirist who knew how to maintain a proper tone. Although Defoe never quite abandons the scepticism he displays at the beginning of the poem about war and blood spilled, particularly naval actions, he does end with fairly optimistic praise of Queen Anne. But at this time in his life, Defoe was captured by the state for what was considered a libellous prose tract: *The Shortest-Way with the Dissenters* (1702). He was forced to stand in the pillory and supposedly enjoined from writing for a period of years. As a result, Defoe became a celebrity of a kind. 'The Author of the *True-Born Englishman*' became the way in which Daniel De Foe became known to the reading public. His defiance of the ban against writing as well as his defiance of those who sentenced him became central to a series of poems between 1703 and 1704, which included *More Reformation* (1703), *A Hymn to the Pillory* (1703), and *An Elegy on the Author of the True-Born Englishman* (1704).

The first of these, *More Reformation*, is mainly interesting for its preface defending his practice of satire, including the ironic creation of the half-insane High Churchman in *The Shortest-Way with the Dissenters*. But in this poem, he is essentially apologetic. Satire, he states, should be general; he confesses that his satire was sometimes too specific. He repents of his crimes, but shares his guilt with the rest of humanity:

> For Innocence in Men, can not be meant.
> Of such as ne're offend, but as repent. (lines 103–4; SFS, i. 217)

Despite his seeming repentance, however, there is a degree of defiance. He asks what exactly his crime was and complains against an unfair punishment. It is as if Defoe was arguing with himself about what his reaction ought to be. He found his answer in *A Hymn to the Pillory*—defiance against an unfair system of justice. Although never as popular as *The True-Born Englishman*, this is, in many ways, Defoe's most powerful poem, directed against an unjust system of justice, the government, and a society which

---

[18] Defoe attacked Rochester again in *More Reformation*, but noted his repentance and his regret for certain poems and attacked women who enjoy what Defoe considered lewd plays:

> Like him they boldly venture on the Crime,
> But think not of Repenting too like him.
> Pleas'd with the Lines, he wish'd he had not Writ,
> They Court his Folly, and pass by his Wit. (lines 208–11; SFS, i. 175–6)

has moved in the direction of economic individualism and greed. He addresses the pillory as a symbol of all this corruption:

> Then Clap *thy Wooden Wings* for Joy,
>   And greet the Men of Great Employ;
> The Authors of the Nations discontent,
> And Scandal of a Christian Government.
> *Jobbers*, and *Brokers* of the City Stocks,
> With forty Thousand Tallies at their backs;
> Who make our Banks and Companies obey,
>   Or sink 'em all *the shortest way*. (lines 160–7; SFS, i. 245)

The pillory becomes the vehicle for Satyr to attack corrupt judges, lawyers, and the wealthy who revel in luxury on their country estates. This condition inverts the very concept of government:

> The first Intent of Laws
> Was to Correct th' Effect, and check the Cause;
>   And all the Ends of Punishment,
> Were only Future Mischiefs to prevent.
>   But Justice is Inverted when
>   Those Engines of the Law,
>   Instead of pinching Vicious Men,
>   Keep Honest ones in awe. (lines 397–404; SFS, i. 251)

Defoe then turns to his own situation: an innocent person punished by the government for no legitimate reason:

> Tell them it was because he was too bold,
> And told those Truths, which shou'd not ha' been told.
> Extoll the Justice of the Land,
> Who Punish what they will not understand.
>   Tell them he stands Exalted there,
>   For speaking what we wou'd not hear.
>   … … … … …
>   Tell 'em the M[en] that plac'd him here,
>   Are Sc[andal]s to the Times,
>   Are at a loss to find his Guilt,
>   And can't commit his Crimes. (lines 433–8, 449–52; SFS, i. 252–3)

Defoe abandoned iambic pentameter couplets for the version of the Pindaric ode that Cowley had explored in the middle of the seventeenth century.[19] He wanted to make a powerful statement of personal anger and succeeded brilliantly.

---

[19] Defoe had quoted Cowley's version of the second Olympic Ode of Pindar at the end of his preface to *The True Born Englishman*. He must have admired another of Cowley's imitations of Pindar, his 'Ode to Liberty', with its message involving freedom of poetic expression as well as political liberty.

An Elegy on the Author of the True-Born-English-Man was a more formal defence of himself as a poet. A Latin poem prefaced to the work celebrates the way in which the seven-year silence that was supposed to have been imposed upon Defoe by the law could not silence him. And, indeed, the frame of the poem—the supposition that he could no longer write to criticize those members of society who needed to be exposed—was clever. He writes the poem on the brink of a great silence that was supposed to descend upon him. But he seems to separate the voice of the poet from the writer—the voice from the hand of the writer:

> In vain they spend their Time and Breath
> To make me Starve, and die a Poet's Death:
> In *Butler's Garret* I shall ne'er appear,
> Neither his Merit nor his Fate I fear.
> ... ...
> I'm satisfy'd it never shall be said,
> But he that gave me Brains, will give me Bread. (lines 570–3, 576–7; SFS, i. 280)

The poem, then, goes from the paradox of the poet silenced, but apparently still writing, to the seeming possibility that he will 'come to Life again', to the seeming certainty that he will continue to write. Like what Mark Twain remarked of himself, it might have been said that rumours of Defoe's death were highly exaggerated. If the *Elegy* lacks the intense feeling of indignation that informed *A Hymn to the Pillory*, it is forceful enough.

In some ways this poem does represent the end of the stringent poetic satires. It was published with another poem, *The Storm. An Essay*. Once again Defoe writes as one under the sentence of poetic death. But the great storm of 1703, which caused so much damage to England, has awakened the poet in him:

> Tho' I have lost Poetick Breath,
> I'm not in perfect State of Death. (lines 11–12; SFS, i. 283)

He describes his condition as a poet as being in a state of limbo, but with this he moves on to a consideration of the storm as a sign of God's anger. As for many of these descriptive poems by Defoe, it may be said, what Swift said of Thomson's *Seasons*, later in the century—that it lacked method. Defoe was not sublime poet enough—not enough of a John Milton—to carry off such poems successfully:

> Plague, Famine, Pestilence, and War,
>   Are in their Causes seen,
> The true Originals appear
> Before the Effects begin:
> But Storms and Tempests are above our Rules,
>   Here our Philosophers are Fools.
> The *Stagyrite* himself could never show,
>   From whence, nor how they blow.
> Tis all Sublime, 'tis all a Mystery,
> They see no Manner how, nor Reason why. (lines 209–18; SFS, i. 288)

Defoe was doing a prose book on this storm, collecting reports of the damage. There is a certain pleasure in the rhyme, but beyond that there is little real poetic power. The great wind is supposed to have awakened him from his 'Satyr', from his 'sleep of legal Death', but he would never regain the satiric indignation that governed both *The True Born Englishman* and *A Hymn to the Pillory*.

Some of this loss of energy may be due to his adherence to a more formal kind of verse. The rollicking satire of the poems against King William's Parliaments is replaced by somewhat abstract accounts of the Battle of Blenheim in his panegyric, *A Hymn to Victory* (1704). Abstract figures like Victory and Fame drive the narrative. Prince Eugene, the brilliant Austrian general, is made into '*Eugenius*'; 'Marlbro' keeps his name but nothing more concrete. Defoe now speaks of his '*Muse*', which is incapable of describing the scene of battle. Defoe wrote a brilliant prose description of the battle of Blenheim in one of his periodicals.[20] He did not need to lose himself in abstract encomiastic verse. In fact, in his *The Double Welcome*, Defoe mostly avoided all the abstractions of his *Hymn to Victory* and presented a realistic picture of the grim ways in which soldiers often die:

> How has this wise pretending Age till now
> Talkt big of Fighting, never yet knew how;
> Our Soldiers tyr'd with strange Fateaguing Die,
> And in the *Ditch*, not *Bed* of Honour Lie;
> Starv'd with the Cold and Terror of the Night,
> But never show'd the *how* or *where* to fight. (lines 225–30; SFS, i. 333)

This poem welcomes Marlborough's return to help in the political battles at home, giving Defoe one more effort at satire—a form that kept his poetry closer to the realities of existence. Defoe claims this element of realist poetry as his talent:

> *Satyr has been her Talent*, Truth her Song,
> Truth *who can bear it!* sung too loud, too long.
> *Bright Truth!* that the Stranger to the Jingling Train,
> Makes all their Praises Satyrs, all their Satyrs vain,
> While Truth can neither this nor that explain. (lines 15–19; SFS, i. 327)

The weakness of his *Hymn to Victory* (1704) and his *Hymn to Peace* (1706) is his failure to do well in dealing with ideas and descriptions lacking concrete form.

Defoe had a tendency to make obscure allusions, a quality he showed from his first poem. As previously remarked it gave to some of these poems the quality of a crossword puzzle. Readers would fill in names identified by simply a first initial or by some obscure allusion. The most obscure poem along these lines was *The Dyet of Poland* (1705). The preface warns against '*Innuendo-Men*' who might think that he was actually writing

---

[20] Defoe, *The Master Mercury*, intro. Frank H. Ellis and Henry L. Snyder, Augustan Reprint Society No. 184 (Los Angeles, CA: William Andrew Clark Memorial Library, 1977), no. 4 (17 August 1704), 13–15.

about England rather than Poland (*SFS*, i. 343). At the end of this prose introduction, he plays with the reader about the author. Some might think it was by 'Daniel de Foe', some might think it was by the Man in the Moon, an allusion to Defoe's prose moon voyage, *The Consolidator* (1705).

What follows is a satire on the enemies of Augustus (Queen Anne) as she tries to get control of a nation filled with a strange gallery of political figures. In the end, Casimir (Godolphin) is appointed, Anne dismisses the Parliament, and all is well. Some of the characters are well drawn. Defoe is particularly amusing about Bromley (Bromsky), whom he satirizes for writing a travel book with vague bits of information which tell the reader nothing at all:

> Some Lands lye high, some lower still and lower
> And where the People are not *Rich*, THEY'RE POOR. (lines 852–3; *SFS*, i. 368)

Defoe's wit could sometimes sustain him when all else failed.

Politics and Poetry in 1706: *Jure Divino* and *Caledonia*

In 1706, Defoe produced his longest poem, a kind of epic 'satire' in twelve books intended to deal with the history of the errors that led to the belief in the divine right of kings and the resistance with which such ideas must be met. This is poetry as encapsulating ideas in pithy phrases:

> *Prayers* and *Tears* no Revolutions make,
> Pull down no Tyrants, will *no Bondage Break*. (Book II, lines 443–4; *SFS*, ii. 115–16)

Politics is about power. All would be 'Tyrants *if they durst*' (Book IV, line 78; *SFS*, ii. 148), so the people have to assert their rights continually and forcefully. The laws of Nature dictate self-defence and self-interest. As in his shorter poems, Defoe sends 'Satyr' to explore the history of the world and analyse human nature as governed by 'the Sense of Power Supream' (Book V, line 40; *SFS*, ii. 173) and pride. Much as in his *True-Born Englishman*, Defoe uses a large part of Book X to mock the concept of descent as not having any value, and in Book XI he extols what he considers to be the rule of the nation by the 'people', led by men of property. Book XII ends with praise of Godolphin, the keeper of the nation's credit, and of Queen Anne.[21]

---

[21] P. N. Furbank provides an excellent summary in his edition of *Jure Divino*. *SFS*, ii. 1–29.

The first six books involve some lively political poetry. It is a private taste, not the personal poetry, that most readers tend to like. He did not blend his own emotional experience with politics in the manner of W. H. Auden. And the relatively undramatic, often preachy tone precluded him from gaining some of the dramatic effects of two of the poets he imitated: Rochester and Milton.[22] But Defoe had a lively mind, and if one likes his ideas the poetry is occasionally stirring. It is difficult not to like poetry attacking tyranny and exalting human rights. How much better this is than, say, the praise of Godolphin, one of the leaders of the government under Queen Anne, for protecting the credit of the nation, should be obvious. Defoe advertised his work on the title page as 'A Satyr. In Twelve Books'. There is no question that the satiric power of the work fails badly in his historic survey of tyranny and the encomiums of the last two books. Satire works best in short bursts and with specific targets. Much of *Jure Divino* suffers from the same shortcomings as those of his poems devoted to abstract concepts. In *Jure Divino*, Defoe often drones on interminably.

It is worth mentioning two poems that he wrote before abandoning poetry for a time.[23] The first, *The Vision* (1706), was a short parody of the visionary speech of Lord Belhaven foreseeing the disasters that would be consequent upon the Union of England and Scotland [SEE CHAPTERS 20 AND 27]. Defoe satirized Belhaven's seeming adherence to the supposed Scottish ability of second sight, ending:

> And now the Exorcist in turn
> Like a Ghost in a Circle arises,
> Without any Tears he can Mourn,
> He is Extasie all and Surprises. (lines 100–3; *PEW*, iv. 204)

But the gist of *The Vision* was that no one understood him, that Belhaven was lost in a trance. It was an amusing poem—a return to the pure lampoons of his earlier poems. The second poem, also about Scotland and the Union, was *Caledonia*, published in December 1706 along with a list of subscribers that, in social status and number, as Pat Rogers observed, matched the kinds of lists that Alexander Pope was sometimes able to collect.[24] Although much of the poem was devoted to encomiums of the kind that produced some of Defoe's dullest poetry, the beginning involved a great deal of natural

---

[22] He took much of his view of human nature and some of the language at the beginning of *Jure Divino* from Rochester's *Satire against Reason and Mankind* (1674); he praises Milton for the depiction of the Fall in *Paradise Lost* in Book VII, *SFS*, ii. 232.

[23] In the *Review*, v. 264 (29 July 1708), in response to the request for a poem in praise of the victory against the French at Oudenarde, Defoe refused, saying that his '*Harps are long since hung on the Willows*'. The allusion was to Psalm 137:2: when exiled in Babylonia, the psalmist refuses to sing a song requested by his conqueror. Defoe was writing his *Reviews* from Scotland at the time, and he went on in this issue to complain of his 'banish'd Condition' and his 'distracted unsettled Circumstance'. His letters to Sunderland at this time complain of the failure to reward his efforts for the government (*Letters*, 259–64). The comment in the *Review* should be taken as a statement about writing poetry during this difficult period—a form of exile—not as an abandonment of poetry entirely.

[24] Pat Rogers, *Robinson Crusoe* (London: George Allen & Unwin, 1979), 102–3.

description of the kind that James Thomson was to popularize twenty years later with *Winter*.[25] In addition, Defoe commented extensively on economic subjects. He repeated several times in the poem a passage that seems awful to the modern ear, but which echoes the cry for economic development of the Enlightenment:

> 'Tis Blasphemy to say the Climate's curst,
> Nature will ne'er be fruitful *till she's forc't.*
> ... ...
> *To Court her's nonsense*, if ye will enjoy,
> *She must be ravish't*, When she's forc't she's free,
> *A perfect Prostitute to Industry.* (lines 1192–3, 1251–3; *PEW*, iv. 264, 266)

We who might groan at the sexism and have seen how industry is capable of ravishing nature to the point of destroying large parts of the planet might well wince at these lines, but they are clever for all that.[26]

LATER POEMS

W. R. Owens concludes his edition of Defoe's poetry with *A Hymn to the Mob* (1715), Defoe's ironic poem against the mob violence in England that was concurrent with the Jacobite rebellion in Scotland. Defoe had previously written against similar protests against the Union with Scotland, and there is nothing very new about Defoe's political attitude here. The preface fiercely attacks recent mob violence as part of the Jacobite plot against the reign of George I. But he allows a slight amount of paradox when he admits that 'in *England* the People govern' (*SFS*, i. 416).[27] While he admits that this only applies to the people as represented in Parliament, the argument allows for a radical streak that

---

[25] Defoe was probably trying to work in a poetic mode associated with descriptive Scottish poetry. Thus he describes himself in the Dedication as a painter attempting to present a true picture of Scotland to the world (*PEW*, iv. 211). See also James Sambrook, *James Thomson, 1700–1748* (Oxford: Oxford University Press, 1991), 34–5.

[26] In contrast, Defoe's *A Scot's Poem* (1707), which has much the same subject material as *Caledonia*, has only a few passages that might be considered more than an economic and political treatise in rhyme. The following is not untypical:

> *Coal, Cattle, Linen,* and all sorts of *Grain,*
> Shall to our Nation daily Riches gain,
> For then our *Linen,* from *Duty's* be exempt;
> And may be straight to their *Plantations* sent.
>
> Ellis (ed.) *Poems on Affairs of State*, vii. 263–4

[27] It should be remembered that during the last years of the reign of William III, Defoe was to argue that Parliament could fail to represent the will of the people.

is more present in the poem than in the preface. In Defoe's view, mob violence was a necessary part of what might be a righteous rebellion:

> Nor is thy Judgment *often wrong*,
> Thou seldom are mistaken, *never long*,
> However *wrong* in Means thou may'st appear,
> Thou gener'ly art in *thy Designe* sincere. (lines 189–92; SFS, i. 423)[28]

But in some instances, such as the riots against the Union and the Sacheverell riots of 1710, or these against George I, the mob's energy could be misplaced. This viewpoint—refusing to condemn the mob entirely—was radical enough in a Britain that, with a few exceptions, was to look disapprovingly at popular demonstrations for the next 300 years.

With the exception of a short break after 1709, Defoe continued to write poetry and indeed experiment with poetic techniques throughout his life. Indeed, after including a number of religious poems in *Serious Reflections during the Life … of Robinson Crusoe*, he added poems to a number of works, especially those on subjects bordering on the occult. One of these, 'On the Deaf and Dumb Being Taught to Speak', in *Mere Nature Delineated* (1726), involves meditations on silence, language, and sensation, subjects of particular importance for any reader of *The Life and Strange Surprizing Adventures of Robinson Crusoe* (1719). His poem on the deaf treated problems in epistemology. Much the same is true of his poem on the Trinity despite its religious subject matter:

> 'Tis not in Nature: Words are wanting here:
> Letters are scanty Sounds, and barren Speech
> Expresses nothing: High Conceptions fail;
> Image, Idea, Thought, tho' deep as Hell,
> Or rais'd to Heaven, can never enter there,
> Or guide us how to judge of what's beyond
> The *Adamantine Gates*, The Bounds of Time.[29]

Perhaps it is the lack of personal involvement with his subject that makes this less effective than our vivid understanding of Milton's comments on his blindness. At any rate, without questioning the sincerity of Defoe's beliefs, any reader would have to feel that

---

[28] Defoe gave a more negative picture of the mob in *A Scots Poem*:

> *A Mob's a Creature, never thinks, but raves,*
> *Hodge Podge of Women, Children, Fools, and Knaves.*
> *A Malecontent, deluded Animal.*
> *Without Grimace, within all Spleen and Gall.*
>
> Ellis (ed.) *Poems on Affairs of State*, vii. 253

Of course this was the description of a mob that had, to his mind, threatened to hang him.

[29] *A New Family Instructor*, RDW, iii. 281.

his treatment of the ineffable seems to operate better in a dramatic context—*A Journal of the Plague Year* (1722), for example—than it does here.

Probably more to his taste was the often satiric tone of the poems in *The Political History of the Devil* (1726). After describing the activities of the Devil in society, he summarizes his activities in a quatrain:

> Thus he walks up and down in compleat Masquerade,
>   And with every Company mixes,
> Sells in every Shop, works at every Trade,
>   And ev'ry Thing doubtful perplexes. (*RDW*, vi. 187)

If this is doggerel, it is interesting to note that one of his verses may have influenced William Blake's poem 'The Tyger'.[30] Defoe questions the origin of sin somewhat in the manner of Rochester's poem 'Upon Nothing' (1679):

> Tell us, sly penetrating Crime,
> How cams't thou there, thou fault sublime?
> How didst thou pass the Adamantine Gate,
>   And into Spirit thyself insinuate?
>   From what dark state? from what deep place?
>   From what strange uncreated race?
> Where was thy ancient habitation found,
> Before void Chaos heard the forming sound?
>   . . . .
> And how at first didst thou come there?
>   Sure there was a Time when thou wert not,
>   By whom wast thou created? and for what? (76–7)

Blake's concrete, powerful, ambiguous image of the tiger would have been beyond Defoe's gifts as a poet. Like Blake, Defoe is ambiguous about the origin of evil, but when he put the problem into a poem, the argument alone must have seemed paradoxical enough. Imagery would have been beside the point.

He also added a lengthy poem in blank verse on the Trinity to his *New Family Instructor* (1727). Whether this was more influenced by John Milton, whose 'manner' is announced as the inspiration for the kind of poetry that Defoe was imitating, or by the success of James Thomson's blank verse *Winter*, published in April 1726, just a few months before Defoe's work, is difficult to say.[31] He was certainly attempting to write a poem on what he considered a sublime subject. But one problem that Defoe has in conveying the depth of his belief in this difficult Christian doctrine is his tendency to

---

[30] For Blake's possible borrowing from Defoe, see Rodney M. Baine, 'Blake and Defoe', *Blake*, 6:2 (1972), 51–3.

[31] Thomson had called for an exalted type of poetry dealing with 'great and serious Subjects'. Sambrook, *James Thomson*, 43–4.

argue at length against the Deists and various opponents of belief in the Trinity, rather than presenting his private feelings.

* * *

Defoe was mainly a satirist whose excellence in poetry depended on witty turns of thought. Where he was able to place his poetry in a larger human construct, as he did with his *True-Born Englishman* and *A Hymn to the Pillory*—the evils of a racist nationalism, the evil power of the state in crushing the individual citizen—he was able to achieve a degree of greatness. He was also a confessional religious poet, as well as a didactic poet. Although he did not lack occasional verbal felicities that one associates with high art, for the most part he felt that he was combining the pleasure to be had in reading poetry with a way of thinking that was frequently unusual for his time.

Further Reading

D. N. DeLuna, 'Yale's Poetasting Defoe', *1650–1850*, 4 (1998), 345–62.

Frank H. Ellis (ed.), *Poems on Affairs of State: Augustan Satirical Verse, 1660–1714*, 7 vols (New Haven, CT: Yale University Press, 1963–75).

D. F. Foxon (ed.), *English Verse 1701–1750*, 2 vols (Cambridge: Cambridge University Press, 1975).

J. Paul Hunter, 'Poetic Footprints: Some Formal Issues in Defoe's Verse', in *Defoe's Footprints: Essays in Honour of Maximillian E. Novak*, ed. Robert Maniquis and Carl Fisher (Toronto: University of Toronto Press, 2009), 53–70.

Andreas K. E. Mueller, *A Critical Study of Defoe's Verse: Recovering the Neglected Corpus of His Poetic Work* (Lewiston: Edwin Mellen Press, 2010).

Maximillian E. Novak, *Daniel Defoe, Master of Fictions: His Life and Ideas* (Oxford: Oxford University Press, 2001).

CHAPTER 3

DEFOE, PROSE FICTION, AND THE NOVEL

GEOFFREY SILL

IN his *History of English Thought in the Eighteenth Century* (1876), Leslie Stephen, the editor of *Cornhill Magazine* and one of the most influential critics of the Victorian era, credited Defoe with being present at the birth of the novel, if not quite being the father of it: 'The English novel, as the word is now understood, begins with De Foe'. According to Stephen, Defoe drew on 'very crude rudiments' of fiction to fashion an original literary form that was taken up by writers of greater genius, notably Richardson, Fielding, and Smollett, who presented life in a more or less realistic manner. His success resulted from 'the rise of a class of comparatively educated and polished persons' that provided him with an audience.[1] Stephen's genealogy of the novel dominated criticism for some eighty years, until Ian Watt expanded upon it in *The Rise of the Novel* (1957) by adding 'formal realism' (particularity of representation, not mere naturalism), 'individualism' (particularity of character, place, and action, not mere types), and 'a more largely referential use of language' as the defining elements of the novel.[2]

Watt's *The Rise of the Novel* remains the starting point for many studies of the novel, though objections have been raised, in the six decades since it was written, to several components of its thesis: its teleological and 'evolutionary' notion of the novel's 'rise'; its assumption of a steady 'rise' in a literate middle class; its implication that the literary qualities of Defoe's novels were due to accident rather than artistic control and judgement; the exclusion of female and non-British writers from its coverage; and its

---

[1] Leslie Stephen, *The History of English Thought in the Eighteenth Century*, 2 vols (New York, 1876), ii. 379, 376. Stephen had previously published an important critical essay, 'Daniel Defoe', in *Cornhill Magazine*, vol. 23, no. 135 (March 1871), 310–20, which was reprinted as 'De Foe's Novels' in Leslie Stephen, *Hours in a Library*, 3 vols (London, 1874), i. 1–58.

[2] Ian Watt, *The Rise of the Novel: Studies in Defoe, Richardson and Fielding* (London: Chatto & Windus, 1957), 32.

general neglect of the religious and historical contexts of Defoe's fiction.[3] But perhaps the most problematic feature of the 'rise' thesis was the insistence of critics from Stephen to Watt that Defoe should be read as 'our first novelist'—that is, as the practitioner of a fully realized form of literary art, called the 'novel'.[4] Defoe, however, was quite clear on this point: he knew what novels were, and that was not what he was writing.[5] 'The World is so taken up of late with Novels and Romances', the fictitious 'editor' of *Moll Flanders* (1722) declares in the Preface, 'that it will be hard for a private History to be taken for Genuine, where the Names and other Circumstances of the Person are concealed, and on this Account we must be content to leave the Reader to pass his own Opinion upon the ensuing Sheets, and take it just as he pleases' (*Novels*, vi. 23). Some critics regard this disclaimer as disingenuous, but it provides an important clue to Defoe's intentions as a writer of prose fictions. The 'editor' asks us to read his text as a 'private History', rather than a novel or a romance, because the effect of the story depends on its being taken as a record based on fact, rather than fancy. Moll's 'private History', like that of Defoe's other fictional narrators, mixes private and public events and characters into a new hybrid form that prevents readers from associating them with the works of such writers as Aphra Behn, Delariviere Manley, and Eliza Haywood, whose works of 'amatory fiction' were collected and republished between 1696 and 1725 under the rubric of 'Novels',[6] while none of Defoe's fictions were called by that name on their title pages until the 'wildly garbled' edition of *Moll Flanders* published by Francis Noble in 1776.[7]

Typically for Defoe, a 'prose fiction' is a narrative in prose told by an imaginary narrator who speaks, generally in the first person, about either an event (or an entire life) that never happened, or a 'real' event that has been reimagined by the narrator.[8] The narrative draws on secret, private, and public materials unified by a single imaginary consciousness for the purpose of configuring a truth that is conveyed through the

---

[3] On the critical reception of Watt's thesis and its legacy, see Nicholas Seager, *The Rise of the Novel: A Reader's Guide to Essential Criticism* (Basingstoke: Palgrave Macmillan, 2012), 35–45. For an alternative theory to Watt's, see J. A. Downie, 'The Making of the English Novel', *ECF*, 9:3 (1997), 249–66.

[4] Watt, *Rise of the Novel*, 80.

[5] On the question of 'what novels were' prior to Defoe, see J. A. Downie, 'Mary Davys's "Probable Feign'd Stories" and Critical Shibboleths about "The Rise of the Novel"', *ECF*, 12:2–3 (2000), 309–26. Cf. J. Paul Hunter, *Before Novels: The Cultural Contexts of Eighteenth-Century English Fiction* (New York: Norton, 1990), 66–8.

[6] For the definition of 'amatory fiction', see Ros Ballaster, *Seductive Forms: Women's Amatory Fiction from 1684 to 1740* (Oxford: Clarendon Press, 1992); Toni O'Shaughnessy Bowers, 'Sex, Lies, and Invisibility: Amatory Fiction from the Restoration to Mid-Century', in *The Columbia History of the British Novel*, ed. John Richetti (New York: Columbia University Press, 1994), 50–72. Leah Orr uses 'amorous fiction' in preference to 'amatory fiction', and classifies amorous fiction as 'romance'. *Novel Ventures: Fiction and Print Culture in England, 1690–1730* (Charlottesville, VA: University of Virginia Press, 2017), 187–8.

[7] Furbank and Owens, *Critical Bibliography*, 200. Cf. P. N. Furbank and W. R. Owens, 'Defoe and Francis Noble', *ECF*, 4:4 (1992), 301–13.

[8] This necessarily reductive definition of 'prose fiction' in Defoe's canon draws in part on Lennard J. Davis, *Factual Fictions: The Origins of the English Novel* (Philadelphia, PA: University of Pennsylvania Press, 1983), 154–73.

fiction.[9] Of the 265 titles attributed to Daniel Defoe by P. N. Furbank and W. R. Owens in their *Critical Bibliography of Daniel Defoe*, some twenty may be called prose fictions under this definition.[10] These twenty prose fictions comprise about 7% of all of Defoe's writings (considering periodicals such as the *Review* as single titles). Of these twenty prose fictions, ten are secret histories or memoirs of supposedly historical events told by fictional persons—that is, narratives whose premise is that the events narrated are not imaginary [SEE CHAPTER 9].[11] The remaining ten fictions, discussed below, are works that, in the nineteenth and twentieth centuries, were commonly sold by booksellers and considered by critics as Defoe's 'novels'. These latter fictions, published between 1719 and 1724, enter much more deeply into the lives of the imaginary persons who claim to have written them, making their stories more credible, informative, and entertaining than the 'secret histories', each written to propagate support for a political figure or programme in the years 1711–18.[12]

A recent study of the history of the book trade in the early eighteenth century helps to place Defoe's writings amidst those of his contemporaries. In *Novel Ventures*, Leah Orr tabulates nearly 500 works of fiction published between 1690 and 1730, roughly the span of Defoe's career as a writer. She finds that 136 of these fictional works, or 29%, were labelled as 'Novels' on their title pages, while almost as many (130) claimed to be 'Histories', thirty-eight more were called 'Secret Histories', and eighty were 'Memoirs' or 'Letters'.[13] Orr's taxonomy of fiction supports what critics have long suspected: that 'novels' were a substantial part of the book market long before Defoe wrote fiction; that 'history' was used as often as 'novel' to describe a work of fiction; and that 'novel' usually meant amatory fiction, from which Defoe sought to differentiate his fictions by calling them 'histories'.

Orr divides fiction into two categories: 'fiction with purpose' and 'fiction for entertainment'. Though these categories seem arbitrary and clearly overlap, the distinction is useful because it avoids other, less useful binaries, such as the division between 'factual' and 'non-factual' fictions, or between 'realism' and 'romance' (9–10). 'Fiction with purpose' includes political and topical fiction, moral and social satire, and religious fiction; it is 'a means to an end rather than an end in itself' (183). Conversely, 'fiction for entertainment' is written to satisfy a reader's interest in crime and prostitution, adventure

---

[9] On the 'configuration' of truth in a historical or fictional narrative, see Hayden White, *The Content of the Form: Narrative Discourse and Historical Representation* (Baltimore, MD: Johns Hopkins University Press, 1987), 50–7.

[10] This list of 'prose fictions' includes the ten secret histories and the ten novels discussed below. Satires and parodies such as *The Consolidator* (1705), *A True Relation of the Apparition of One Mrs. Veal* (1706), *Atalantis Major* (1711), *Memoirs of Count Tariff* (1713), *The Quarrel of the School Boys at Athens* (1717), and *A Continuation of Letters Written by a Turkish Spy* (1718) are excluded.

[11] The differences between history and fiction are discussed by Hunter, *Before Novels*, 338–42.

[12] J. A. Downie, *Robert Harley and the Press: Propaganda and Public Opinion in the Age of Swift and Defoe* (Cambridge: Cambridge University Press, 1979), 186–95; Geoffrey Sill, *Defoe and the Idea of Fiction, 1713–1719* (Newark, DE: University of Delaware Press, 1983), 87–93.

[13] Orr, *Novel Ventures*, 17. Another 208 works of fiction did not specify a genre on their title pages.

and travel, or sentiment and romance and engages the reader with sympathetic (if unreliable) narrators, surprising adventures, and repentance after prosperity (227–36). In the case of Defoe, a purpose-driven book like *Robinson Crusoe* (1719) may derive its principal interest from Crusoe's extended, agonistic process of conversion, or from his struggle to distinguish the whisperings of Providence from his own desires and fears, while a book like *Moll Flanders* amuses the reader with a series of narrow escapes from the hellish fate that awaits Moll in Newgate prison, though her constant efforts (never quite effectual) to find a moral sentiment in her misadventures give her narrative the appearance of an ethical purpose and earn her the sympathy of readers disposed to hear her. As Orr concedes, the binary distinction between 'purpose' and 'entertainment' has its own problems, the chief of which is that most of Defoe's fictions claim to (and generally do) fit both categories (186). 'Modern readers', according to John Mullan, are 'thoroughly sceptical of the claims made in the prefaces of works like *Moll Flanders* and *The Fortunate Mistress* that those fictional autobiographies were published in order to teach virtue', but we cannot dispense with the claim entirely, because the narrator's horror of Newgate or of a misspent life is part of the story.[14] And because we are sceptical of the moral purpose, we find the fictions more entertaining, not less.

Rebecca Bullard has described the history and aims of the several dozen secret histories published in England during the same period studied by Orr.[15] Secret histories, beginning with *The Secret History of the Court of the Emperor Justinian*, written by Procopius in the sixth century but unpublished until 1623, typically were written to expose truths about public events or persons that had been concealed by official narratives. Bullard defines the 'secret history' as 'a revisionist form of historiography' that is 'bent on destroying the delusive stories which, it claims, are fabricated by those in positions of power' (139). Defoe commenced his string of secret histories with the two parts of *The Secret History of the October Club* (1711), which described the duplicitous efforts of a club of Jacobites, High-flyers, and Tory politicians to undermine the moderate policies of Robert Harley in the last years of the reign of Queen Anne.[16] After Harley's fall from power in 1714, Defoe defended the minister's conduct in *The Secret History of the White-Staff, Parts I and II* (1714), *A Secret History of One Year* (1714), *Memoirs of the Conduct of Her Late Majesty and Her Last Ministry* (1715), *The Secret History of the Secret History of the White Staff, Purse and Mitre* (1715), and *The Secret History of the White Staff, Part III* (1715).[17] As Harley's trial for treason approached, Defoe completed the conversion of the secret history genre into the 'private History' with his *Secret Memoirs of a Treasonable Conference at S..... House* (1716) and *Minutes of the Negotiations of Monsr. Mesnager*

---

[14] John Mullan, 'Introduction', *Novels*, vii. 9.

[15] Rebecca Bullard, 'Secret History, Politics, and the Early Novel', in *The Oxford Handbook of the Eighteenth-Century Novel*, ed. J. A. Downie (Oxford: Oxford University Press, 2016), 137–52.

[16] Novak, *Daniel Defoe*, 390–1.

[17] All of these secret histories are listed in Furbank and Owens's *Critical Bibliography*, except for *A Secret History of One Year* and *Memoirs of the Conduct of Her Late Majesty and Her Last Ministry*, which were recently reattributed to Defoe by Nicholas Seager in 'Literary Evaluation and Authorship Attribution, or Defoe's Politics at the Hanoverian Succession', *HLQ*, 80:1 (2017), 47–69.

(1717), a fictionalized account of the peace negotiations conducted in 1711 between the Harley ministry and the French envoy Nicolas Mesnager (1658–1714). Bullard calls Defoe 'the most sophisticated secret historian of the early eighteenth century', noting that his interest in exposing secrets, even of his own narrators, led to his 'highlighting the instability of any narrative grounded on secrets' (143). Defoe may not have been the father of the novel, but he was the progenitor in Britain of the fictional history of a private person with a secret to tell.

FICTIONS OF ADVENTURE: *THE LIFE AND STRANGE SURPRIZING ADVENTURES*, *THE FARTHER ADVENTURES*, AND THE *SERIOUS REFLECTIONS OF ROBINSON CRUSOE*

The first of Defoe's prose fictions that came in time to be read as 'novels' is *The Life and Strange Surprizing Adventures of Robinson Crusoe*, printed for William Taylor and published on 25 April 1719. The title page declares that the book was 'Written by Himself', as if it were the private history of a genuine person, similar to the *Minutes of the Negotiations of Mons. Mesnager* or the *Memoirs ... of the Duke of Shrewsbury* (1718).[18] The 'Editor' reinforces this claim to truth in the Preface when he declares that it is '*a just History of Fact; neither is there any Appearance of Fiction in it*', but that may be only the opinion of the unnamed editor, who is himself fictitious. The description of the book's contents on the title page focuses the reader's attention on Robinson's twenty-eight-year confinement on an island in the mouth of the Orinoco river, a location that seems plausible but cannot be positively identified. The fiction is made credible by opening and closing episodes that frame the story with apparently historical dates and details about Robinson's departure from home, his enslavement in Sallee, his rescue at sea by a Portuguese captain, his return to England on the anniversary of the Duke of Monmouth's rebellion, and the restoration of his wealth at approximately the time of the Glorious Revolution in England. Furthering the appearance of authenticity is an engraved frontispiece that depicts Robinson in a balletic pose, clothed in a well-tailored suit and cap of goatskins, his eyes cast down and away, his hands lightly grasping the stocks of two muskets, a fencing sword and pistol in his belt. Above his head are clouds, one dark and stormy, the other fair; at his feet are specimens of exotic tropical plants; to his right, a ship sails before a strong wind; and to his left, his fortifications surmount a patch of

---

[18] The *Memoirs of Publick Transactions in the Life and Ministry of His Grace the D. of Shrewsbury* was attributed to Defoe by Lee, Trent, Hutchins, Moore, and Novak, but has been disputed by Furbank and Owens in *Defoe De-Attributions: A Critique of J. R. Moore's Checklist* (London: Hambledon Press, 1994), 114–15.

cultivated ground. The frontispiece is not an illustration of any moment in the text, but rather an emblematic portrait of the supposed author with the themes of his book on display: the life of a mariner turned agriculturalist; his solitary struggle to survive and live with grace; his discovery of the delicate balance of power between humanity and nature; his conversion and deliverance by the Providence of God, assisted by his own passion and action; and his material deliverance a second time by the same Portuguese captain. The title page and frontispiece (Figure 3.1) together present *Robinson Crusoe* as a non-fictional history, while at the same time slyly admitting that the story is an allegorical and mythical tale with elements of romance.

Is there in *Robinson Crusoe* an allegorical or mythical realm of meaning that is accessible through the mundane world of Crusoe's ordinary experiences? Defenders of the 'realist' school of reading *Crusoe*, such as Leslie Stephen's daughter Virginia Woolf,

FIGURE 3.1 Frontispiece by [John] Clark and [John] Pine to Daniel Defoe, *Robinson Crusoe* (1719). Personal copy of Geoffrey Sill.

doubt that Defoe has anything but cheerless facts in mind: 'There are no sunsets and no sunrises; there is no solitude and no soul. There is, on the contrary, staring us fully in the face nothing but a large earthenware pot'. Yet Woolf, like her father, finds *Crusoe* to be a 'masterpiece', because Defoe, 'by reiterating that nothing but a plain earthenware pot stands in the foreground, persuades us to see remote islands and the solitudes of the human soul'.[19]

As Paul Baines has shown at length, criticism of *Robinson Crusoe* since Woolf has taught us much about what lies beyond the earthenware pot.[20] On the island, Crusoe virtually reinvents the progress of humankind from its Original Sin forwards. His own sin is his wilful passion to wander into places he has been warned against, by both his father and mother, and by a Bible-quoting captain who knows Crusoe was not meant for the sea. Crusoe's lust for adventure is, according to Christian orthodoxy, an illness of the spirit that must be cured if he is to live a peaceful and happy life.[21] His first shipwreck, his two years' captivity by the pirates of Sallee, and his limited success as a planter in Brazil all fail to warn him against the path he is on. To gratify his urge, Crusoe turns slave-trader and, on his first voyage to Africa, is cast away on a deserted island in the Caribbean. Here he remains for twenty-eight years, experiencing a range of passions— joy, grief, fear, anger, jealousy, even love (in his limited way) for his companion Friday— that were the stuff of seventeenth-century psychology. His spiritual growth (parallel to, but not the same as his religious awakening) finally reaches completion in his gratitude to the Samaritan-like Portuguese captain, the same who had saved him at sea years ago and who now redeems Crusoe's suffering by restoring his wealth. His story *is* a realistic tale about earthenware pots and so forth, but it is also a spiritual allegory about sins of passion, moments of introspection and revelation, and myths of redemption.[22]

On 20 August 1719, only four months after the *Strange Surprizing Adventures*, Taylor published *The Farther Adventures of Robinson Crusoe; Being the Second and Last Part of His Life*.[23] In the *Farther Adventures*, though Crusoe has achieved his goal of living an idyllic life as a gentleman farmer, he joins his nephew on a voyage to revisit his island, accompanied by Friday. He finds that a civil war between the Spaniards and the English settlers has divided the colony, whose unity Crusoe endeavours to restore. When after

---

[19] Virginia Woolf, 'Robinson Crusoe', in *The Second Common Reader*, ed. Woolf (1932; New York: Harcourt, Brace, & World, 1960), 45, 48.

[20] Paul Baines, *Daniel Defoe: Robinson Crusoe, Moll Flanders: A Reader's Guide to Essential Criticism* (Basingstoke: Palgrave Macmillan, 2007), esp. 58–67.

[21] For an account of the 'cure' of Crusoe's ill passions, see Geoffrey Sill, *The Cure of the Passions and the Origins of the English Novel* (Cambridge: Cambridge University Press, 2001), 93–106.

[22] For the original studies in a long-running debate about Christian themes in *Robinson Crusoe*, see G. A. Starr, *Defoe and Spiritual Autobiography* (Princeton, NJ: Princeton University Press, 1965), and J. Paul Hunter, *The Reluctant Pilgrim: Defoe's Emblematic Method and Quest for Form in Robinson Crusoe* (Baltimore, MD: Johns Hopkins University Press, 1966). For the allegorical significance of the Portuguese captain, see Geoffrey Sill, 'Robinson Crusoe, "Sudden Joy", and the Portuguese Captain', *Digital Defoe*, 10:1 (2018), www.digitaldefoe.org.

[23] The *Strange Surprising Adventures* is commonly referred to as 'Part I' of *Robinson Crusoe*, the *Farther Adventures* as 'Part II', and the *Serious Reflections* as 'Part III', and they will be so referenced here.

twenty-five days he leaves the island, more chaos ensues: Friday is killed when their ship is attacked off Brazil; his sailors commit a massacre on Madagascar and abandon him when he reproaches them; he joins an English merchant in a trading voyage to China, only to find that the ship they had bought was stolen, and he is pursued for a pirate; and at last, in Muscovy, he angrily attacks and burns a pagan idol, narrowly escaping the resentment of the Tartars. These cycles of fall and recovery recall his spiritual struggles in Part I, but in Part II the history is a public rather than a private one. Crusoe is now fighting a rear-guard action against sins not of his own making: murder, massacre, mutiny, deceit, paganism, and heathenism. Crusoe's war is indeed holy, especially as it models a plan to unite Roman Catholics and Protestants in the struggle to save and extend Christianity, but this holy war requires a narrator who 'takes a very bloody-minded view of Christian duty', unlike the penitent and tolerant narrator of Part I.[24] Whatever self-mastery and satisfaction Crusoe had acquired in Part I have been lost in Part II, and he is fortunate to regain his retirement in England after a journey of ten years and nine months.

After a pause of nearly a year, during which Defoe wrote several other fictions (discussed below), in August 1720 he published a third volume of Crusoe's life history, the *Serious Reflections during the Life and Surprising Adventures of Robinson Crusoe*. The three volumes were often printed together through the eighteenth century, but after 1790 Part III was generally abridged or dropped entirely. The more Defoe came to be read as a novelist, the more questions were raised about whether *Serious Reflections* was sufficiently novelistic to be part of the trilogy. The solitary narrator, Robinson Crusoe, comments on the discoveries made in his former travels, but also records new discoveries made during a voyage through the solar system. The voyage, he admits, may have been fictional: 'I really cannot tell; but I certainly made a Journey to all those supposed habitable Bodies in my Imagination' (235). This equivocal statement is Defoe's first suggestion that an imaginary voyage may be as 'real' as one taken by an ordinary traveller, and that fiction is therefore a valid form of knowledge. It is difficult to think of the *Serious Reflections* as a novel because of its lack of extension in time, its lack of continuous dramatic action, and its emphasis on abstract themes rather than particular persons or events; it is, nevertheless, an early and important instance of 'meta-fiction', a fictional commentary upon other works of fiction.

Leah Orr argues in her essay 'Providence and Religion in the Crusoe Trilogy' that the three parts of *Robinson Crusoe* were conceived as a single fiction, in which Crusoe progresses 'from conversion, to rethinking, to doubt'.[25] G. A. Starr, however, sees Part III not as the sequel to Parts I and II, but as the first of a sequence of books—*The Political History of the Devil* (1726), *A System of Magick* (1726), *An Essay on the History and Reality of Apparitions* (1727), and *A New Family Instructor* (1727)—in which Defoe explores the supernatural and man's relation to it.[26] Starr reads the *Serious Reflections* as 'a fascinating

---

[24] Leah Orr, 'Providence and Religion in the Crusoe Trilogy', *Eighteenth-Century Life*, 38:2 (2014), 1–27 (13–14).
[25] Orr, 'Providence and Religion', 4.
[26] G. A. Starr, 'Introduction', *Novels*, iii. 1.

early draft of a significant body of writing' on two dangerous threats to Christianity: at one extreme, scepticism, freethinking, deism, and atheism; and at the other, superstition, enthusiasm, and fanaticism, of which Roman Catholicism is the 'chief modern exemplar' (40). The medium between these extremes is not mere Protestant orthodoxy, but a meditation upon the practical, non-doctrinal form of religion that he developed on the island, and upon the spiritual truths which his voyages have revealed to him.

FICTIONS OF PURPOSE: *MEMOIRS OF A CAVALIER*, *A JOURNAL OF THE PLAGUE YEAR*, AND *A NEW VOYAGE ROUND THE WORLD*

If we grant that at least some of Defoe's prose fictions were written primarily to accomplish moral, political, or social purposes, we begin to see similarities among those works that focus on public and historical concerns such as war, epidemics, and exploration. These semi-fictional works are hybrids in that they draw on historical events that were still fresh in the English imagination, such as the First Civil War of 1642–6, the plague of 1665, and the voyages of explorers and buccaneers such as Sir John Narborough and William Dampier, whose non-fictional accounts were both published in the 1690s. J. A. Downie, following Maximillian Novak, has called these fictions 'propagandistic' because their purpose was to manipulate public opinion on behalf of certain political, economic, and legal initiatives that Defoe sought to encourage.[27] Yet they retain their capacity to entertain because the propagandistic purpose is moderated by the engaging voice of the imaginary narrator, who is caught up in the mundane details of the story as he or she lives it. There is little 'plot' in these stories because battles, mortality lists, and transcontinental treks shape the timeline, rather than human agency.

The first of these historical fictions, published in May 1720, was *Memoirs of a Cavalier*, the story of a 22-year-old English gentleman who travels to Italy, Austria, and Germany 'to satisfie my Curiosity, which was the chief End of my coming abroad' (68). After an affair with a courtesan in Italy that 'quite took away all the Gust to Vice that the Devil had furnished me with' (51–2), the Cavalier travels to Saxony, where he witnesses the sack of Magdeburg in 1631. His description of the sounds and sights of that day—'on a sudden I heard the dreadfullest Cry raised in the City that can be imagined, 'tis not possible to express the Manner of it, and I could see the Women and Children running about the Streets in a most lamentable Condition' (61)—anticipates the distress of the Saddler in Defoe's *A Journal of the Plague Year* (1722), who describes in similar terms the visitation of the plague in London in 1665. Such personal observations enliven the story of

---

[27] J. A. Downie, 'Defoe, Imperialism, and the Travel Books Reconsidered', *Yearbook of English Studies* 13 (1983), 66–83; Maximillian E. Novak, *Economics and the Fiction of Daniel Defoe* (Berkeley, CA: University of California Press, 1962), 142–3.

the Cavalier's service first in the Imperial army of Ferdinand II, then with the opposing forces of the Swedish king Gustavus Adolphus, and finally with the Royalist army of Charles I, fighting the Scots and Parliamentarians. The author of the Preface claims that the manuscript was written 'many Years ago', and was found 'by great Accident, among other valuable Papers in the Closet of an eminent publick Minister', but scholarship by A. W. Secord and others has shown that it was compiled from such printed sources as *The Swedish Intelligencer* (1632–3), Jean Le Clerc's *Life of the Famous Cardinal Duke de Richlieu* (1695), and the Earl of Clarendon's *History of the Rebellion* (1702–4).[28]

The information in the *Memoirs* was sufficiently accurate to make many early readers believe that the account was genuine, but the narrative is fictional in that it is recalled and configured as the object of a consciousness that is itself imaginary. Defoe's narrator, the Cavalier, improves on the raw data of history by recounting some of the most important military engagements of the 1630s and '40s as his own life story and by endowing that story with a private, polemical meaning. The brutal vitality of the Imperial soldiers under Count Tilly, the well-ordered, well-armed Swedish troops of Gustavus Adolphus, and the 'generaly tall swinging Fellows', the Scots, give way at the end of the book to the pitiful 'Rabble' and the incompetent officers of the Royalist army. Read as a novel, the *Memoirs* offers access to the exhilaration, followed by the disillusion, despair, and resignation of a young warrior in a failed cause; read as history, the book provides a generally truthful but 'sceptical and non-partisan' view of the English Civil War that was subsequently adopted by such historical novelists as William Godwin and Walter Scott.[29]

A Journal of the Plague Year was published in March 1722, a month after an equally long tract called *Due Preparations for the Plague*, which is a 'probable' attribution to Defoe.[30] The two books offer an interesting comparison in narrative method. *Due Preparations* uses fictional techniques to tell the story of a family that shut itself up in its own house to avoid the plague in 1665, and a second story of a sister who teaches her brothers how to prepare themselves spiritually for the plague in the same year. The stories do not share a first-person narrator and ultimately do not engage the reader deeply in the lives of either family. The *Journal*, however, is the testimony of an imaginary narrator—a Saddler in London whose full name is never disclosed, though he signs his journal at the end with the initials 'H. F.'—who remains in the city for the duration of the plague. The Saddler scrupulously observes the progress of the disease through the city and its effect on the citizenry in order, as he claims, to instruct future urban populations not only on how best to prepare for the plague, but also on how to return the city to some measure of civil behaviour when the disease finally regresses. He remains in the city despite the clear signs of Providence that he should leave, justifying his decision to stay by expressing the

---

[28] This scholarship is summarized in N. H. Keeble, 'Introduction', *Novels*, vi. 8–11. Cf. A. W. Secord, *Robert Drury's Journal and Other Studies* (Urbana, IL: University of Illinois Press, 1961), 72–133. Secord's account is reconsidered by Nicholas Seager, '"A Romance the Likest to Truth That I Ever Read": History, Fiction, and Politics in Defoe's *Memoirs of a Cavalier*', *ECF*, 20:4 (2008), 479–505.

[29] Seager, '"A Romance"', 504.

[30] Furbank and Owens, *Critical Bibliography*, 202–3, 204–5.

hope that his observations 'may be of some Moment to those who come after me, if they come to be brought to the same Distress' (*Novels*, vii. 30). His sense of public duty, which calls for a rational and objective response, is matched by his 'unsatisfy'd Curiosity' to see and hear the 'Groans and Exclamations' of the dying and their grieving survivors, with which he hopes to 'alarm the very Soul of the Reader' (103). The *Journal* is thus a hybrid in the way that it progressively reveals the inextricable confusion of public and private personalities. H. F. the Saddler's public purpose is to help his fellow citizens prepare for the next plague, but the only way he can do that is by passing through a personal hell similar to that of a Robinson Crusoe, a Moll Flanders, or a Roxana.

A New Voyage Round the World, by a Course never Sailed Before was published in November 1724, making it chronologically the last of the ten fictions by Defoe that are commonly read as novels. It is grouped here with the *Memoirs of a Cavalier* and *A Journal of the Plague Year* because like them it draws on historical materials—including Defoe's own proposal to William III for a colony in South America—to support the fiction of an anonymous narrator who advocates for the planting of a British colony in present-day Chile or Argentina, where the Spanish presence in South America is weakest.[31] The narrator, a Crusoe-like 'Captain' whose predominant passion is a 'Thirst of New Discoveries' (178), is employed by a company of merchants to determine the feasibility of such a project. Seeking to avoid detection by the Spanish, he sails 'by a Course never Sailed before' around the Cape of Good Hope, through Indonesia, and eastwards across the South Pacific, outside of the usual trade routes and against the trade winds, to Chile. Having saved a Spanish gentleman from being murdered, he is invited to reside in that gentleman's country house while he explores the countryside. Like Colonel Jack, the narrator and the Spanish gentleman vie in the richness of the gifts they can give each other, a code of gentility and free trade that surpasses nationality. The gentleman's desk drawers are crammed with gold dust and nuggets, so much gold that (as Crusoe also found) it becomes a 'Drug' that conflicts with the more profitable activities of exploration and improvement (184). Similarly, the rivers and mountains are littered with gold dust and nuggets which the Spanish, being 'so indolent, so slothful, and so satisfied' (209–10) with their present state, seldom bother even to pick up. Their indifference to any measures to improve or colonize their land is proof, in the Captain's view, that they do not 'possess' it by law, which gives the English the right to seize it. Though the novel's emphasis on material wealth is at times fatiguing, the *New Voyage* features some of Defoe's most powerful descriptive writing, particularly in the golden mountains of Chile where the Captain's party spends a night illuminated by volcanoes. Had the Whig political establishment not already turned its back on Defoe by this time, and had the merchant-adventurer audience to whom Defoe addressed the book given it any serious attention, it is possible that this 'fiction with purpose' might have resulted in a 'course never sailed before' for British trade in South America.

---

[31] John McVeagh, 'Introduction', *Novels*, x. 4–6. Cf. Pat Rogers, *Robinson Crusoe* (London: George Allen and Unwin, 1979), 26–7.

Fictions of Entertainment: *Captain Singleton*, *Moll Flanders*, and *Colonel Jack*

Less than two weeks after the publication of the *Memoirs of a Cavalier*, *The Life, Adventures, and Pyracies of the Famous Captain Singleton* was published in June 1720. Like the *Memoirs*, which mentions Gustavus Adolphus in its extended title, *Captain Singleton* authenticates itself by referring on its title page to a well-known pirate, Captain John Avery (also known as Henry Every), who had been the subject of numerous news reports, several books, ballads, and a play.[32] If *Captain Singleton* was conceived as an opportunity for Defoe to comment on the threat to trade posed by pirates, the story soon digresses into a transcontinental trek through uncharted jungles and deserts to the west coast of Africa.[33] Along the way Singleton and his Portuguese crew meet a naked Englishman who, expelled from the Royal African Company, has become a separate trader in the heart of Africa. He has amassed a fortune in gold, but with no way to transport it to the coast, it has no value to him, and he has reverted to a wild state of nature. Singleton rescues the man, who repays him by showing the crew his gold mines. In the course of things, both men acquire and then lose their golden fortunes, the Englishman to a French ship and Singleton to 'Spoilers' who waste his money (*Novels*, v. 121). Singleton 'rage[s] in my own thoughts' at their 'Ingratitude', but the loss of his money frees him to renew his piratical career, first with a mutineer named Captain Wilmot, then with the famous Captain Avery himself. He recruits a casuistical Quaker surgeon named William Walters, who becomes Singleton's spiritual advisor, as well as his tactician. When circumstances force a choice between Wilmot and William, Singleton chooses the Christian (though still covertly piratical) ethos represented by William, and after some further adventures William and Singleton return to England, where they now live, passing as Armenian merchants in order to conceal their past. Singleton is, like Crusoe, a bold adventurer, but a sequel titled *Serious Reflections of Bob Singleton* is unthinkable.

The central and most intriguing part of *Captain Singleton* is the journey across Africa, a continent about which Defoe had only the most rudimentary information [SEE CHAPTER 31]. Even such maps as those in John Ogilby's *Africa* (1670) and that of Herman Moll in the first volume of William Dampier's *A New Voyage Round the World* (1697) were based on 'indisputably wild and fabulous' guesses about the location of

---

[32] *The Life and Adventures of Captain John Avery* (1709), *The Successful Pyrate* by Charles Johnson (1712), and *The King of Pyrates* (1719). *The King of Pyrates*, published only a few months before *Captain Singleton*, was for some years thought to be Defoe's, but is disputed in Furbank and Owens, *Defoe De-Attributions*, 122.

[33] On Defoe's probable sources for the journey across Africa, see Arthur Wellesley Secord, *Studies in the Narrative Method of Defoe* (Urbana, IL: University of Illinois Press, 1924), 127–39.

lakes, waterfalls, and rivers, leaving Defoe with 'no recourse except his imagination'.[34] Singleton too has no facts at hand, other than the faulty memories of his Portuguese guide and crew, for whom he initially has great contempt. In the year that it takes to cross the continent, Singleton undergoes an enlightenment of sorts about the reliability and experience of the Portuguese, much as Crusoe had come to rely on the Portuguese captain for advice and assistance in his *Adventures*. If *Captain Singleton* is a novel in the 'secret history' tradition, the unknown territory that is explored and laid open is not merely the uncharted continent of Africa, but also Singleton's Anglocentric prejudice against the Portuguese, whom he comes to see as necessary partners in the British trade for gold, slaves, and ivory that Defoe had advocated in several pamphlets and in the *Review*.[35] In this way, *Captain Singleton* makes a strong case for the values of free trade and international commerce, even if Defoe himself was no defender of piracy.

Captain Singleton was followed by *The Fortunes and Misfortunes of the Famous Moll Flanders* (January 1722) and by *The History and Remarkable Life of the Truly Honourable Col. Jacque, commonly call'd Col. Jack* (December 1722). *Moll Flanders* appeared in a 'second' and a 'third edition' in 1722, and also in a 'second edition, corrected' by a new consortium of publishers, which went to a 'third edition, corrected' in that year. If each of these editions numbered 1,000 copies, then *Moll Flanders* may have sold some 5,000 copies in its first year. Perhaps because of the success of *Moll Flanders*, *Colonel Jack* bore a title-page price of 6s., a substantial sum in the 1720s. Three 'editions' of *Colonel Jack* were issued in 1723, but close inspection of the text shows that all three were identical except for the title pages, suggesting that the second and third 'editions' may have been only unsold copies of the first.[36] The price was reduced to 5s. for the third edition, but it may still have been too high; by 1734, *Colonel Jack* was advertised in the classifieds for 4s.[37] A fourth edition in 1738 and a fifth in 1739, said on the title pages to be 'Written by the Author of Robinson Crusoe', led to a brief revival for the novel, but it essentially lay dormant until it was praised by Charles Lamb as 'the most affecting natural picture of a young thief that was ever drawn' in a letter (1822) to Walter Wilson, who was then writing the first full-length biography of Defoe. Wilson printed the letter in his *Memoirs of the Life and Times of Daniel de Foe* (1830), which brought *Colonel Jack* to the attention of editors and critics of the nineteenth century.[38]

---

[34] Secord, *Studies in the Narrative Method*, 137.

[35] Defoe, *An Essay upon the Trade to Africa* (1711); *A Brief Account of the Present State of the African Trade* (1713); *Review*, v. 739–45 (31 March 1709); vii. 642–5, 650–3, 669–73; viii. 13–18, 46–50, 61–5, 74–8 (1, 6, 15, and 27 March; 10, 17, and 24 April 1711); viii. 700–3, 757–61 (22 March and 24 April 1712); ix. 171–8 (10 and 13 January 1713). See also *Atlas Maritimus* (1728), 238 and 252–3, in which the encounter in *Singleton* with a naked white man in Africa is retold.

[36] James E. May, 'Scribleriana Transferred', *The Scriblerian*, 15:2 (2013), 290. Cf. 'A Note on the Text', in Defoe, *Colonel Jack*, ed. Gabriel Cervantes and Geoffrey Sill (Peterborough, ON: Broadview Press, 2016), 51–4.

[37] *Daily Courant*, 1 May 1734; *Weekly Miscellany*, 11 May 1734.

[38] In addition to the letter, Wilson printed Lamb's critical essay, an 'Estimate of [Defoe's] Secondary Novels', *Memoirs of the Life and Times of Daniel de Foe*, 3 vols (London, 1830), iii. 428–9, 636–9. Lamb's comments on Defoe's novels are reprinted in *Colonel Jack*, ed. Cervantes and Sill, 401–5.

Like *Captain Singleton*, *Moll Flanders* and *Colonel Jack* are the 'private Histories' of imaginary narrators who inhabit identifiable public spaces, but are themselves secretive and pseudonymous. Moll does not know her own name, much less the name of the woman who gave birth to her in Newgate prison before being transported to Virginia. As an infant, Moll lives among 'a Crew of those People they call *Gypsies*' (28) until she is about 3 years old, so it is impossible for Moll to know anything about her mother or her kin. Moll seeks throughout her life to fill this void in her past by making every older woman into her lost mother. She is placed by the parish into the care of a broken gentlewoman—'my good old Nurse, Mother I ought rather to call her' (34)—who teaches her to read and to work with her needle. Moll's aspirations to be a gentlewoman herself are laughed off by her nurse and the ladies of the town, but her clever answers to them are rewarded with money, which becomes for Moll a 'drug' that, like gold for Crusoe and Singleton, she must have but cannot spend.

Four years after entering service in a Colchester family at 14, Moll is seduced by the elder son, 'a gay Gentleman that knew the Town' (36). A secret romance is followed by illness when her lover ultimately casts her off, and she is forced to marry the younger brother in the family, which completes her fall from innocence and leaves her with a cynical perspective on men and marriage. All of the 'Gentlemen' in her life are defined as such not by their manners or class, but by their willingness to spend money on Moll. Her Colchester husband dying, she marries a draper who is a 'Rake, Gentleman, Shop keeper, and Beggar all together' (67). This husband breaking, Moll enters the Mint to seek protection from his creditors, where she assumes the alias 'Mrs. Flanders'. Many years later, after a long decline from wife, mistress, and streetwalker to shoplifter and pickpocket, Moll enters Newgate prison, where she is derisively called 'Mrs. *Mary*, Mrs. *Molly*, and after that plain *Moll Flanders*' (225) by the other inmates. 'Moll Flanders', however, is the name of another prisoner, an old offender, and on the basis of this mistaken identity, Moll is sentenced to death for the felony of which she has been convicted. Her name, like her character, is a composite of what other people think her to be, a closely held secret that nearly results in her destruction.

Moll's conversion to Christianity in the depths of Newgate prison is similarly ambivalent. It is initiated by her 'old Governess', who 'acted a true Mother to me' (231). The governess first tries to assume the burden of Moll's guilt ('no Mother, no, *said I*, don't speak of that' [232]), then arranges for a minister who brings her to the point of remorse, if not penitence. The minister, believing in her sincerity, arranges for Moll's reprieve, while the governess bribes a court officer to convert her sentence to transportation. When she arrives in Virginia with her Lancashire husband, whom she persuades to escape trial by petitioning for transportation, she buys their freedom from the Captain and a local planter. Moll's thorough suborning of the judicial and penitential bases of transportation is entertaining to readers who read it as a 'novel', but it also has a historical purpose in that it provides a rationale for the recent passage of the Transportation Act of 1718, which allowed judges to sentence criminals to transportation as a form of punishment, rather than grant it as a favour.[39] It is transportation to America, not religion, that finally brings Moll to penitence.

---

[39] Dennis Todd, *Defoe's America* (Cambridge: Cambridge University Press, 2010), 159.

Moll's habit of concealing her name and origins reaches the height of irony in the famous incident, advertised on the title page, in which she is married 'once to her own Brother'. This man, Moll's third husband, owns a plantation in Virginia, to which Moll, who has deceived her husband about her fortune, allows herself to be 'Transported' (82). Moll's new mother-in-law, who she says 'was too kind a Mother to be parted with' (85), quickly becomes 'My Mother', a 'mighty cheerful good humour'd old Woman ... for her son was above Thirty', approximately (and impossibly) the same age as Moll. The mother 'frequently [tells her] old Stories of her former Adventures' (88), which leads Moll to imagine (though 'it might be difficult to convince her of the Particulars, and I had no way to prove them' [88]) that this 'old Woman' was in fact her own mother. One of these 'Particulars' is the name her mother had gone by in London, which affects Moll so deeply that 'I thought I should have sunk down in the place' (87). Moll does not say she recognizes the name, nor would it be possible for her to have known it, since she was separated from her birth mother at six months. Yet her imagination convinces her of the truth of this history, which must be kept secret because to expose it would cause her to be cast out; yet, to say nothing would be to commit both a crime and a mortal sin. To escape the dilemma, Moll tells her mother that she 'dar'd trust her with a Secret of the greatest importance': 'I began and told her the whole Story [of her birth in Newgate]' (80). When the mother later retells the story to Moll, 'she began to tell [the facts of the story] with Alterations and Omissions; but I refresh'd her Memory, and set her to rights in many things which I supposed she had forgot, and then came in so opportunely with the whole History, that it was impossible for her to go from it' (81). With Moll's coaching, the mother 'recovers' her memories of Newgate, which Moll uses to convince her 'mother' that she is indeed her birth mother, and the mother becomes Moll's ally in Moll's extrication of herself from her possibly incestuous (or perhaps merely confining) Virginia marriage. Whether the memories that Moll helped her mother 'recover' are right or wrong is never established, nor is it ever proven that her Virginia husband is her own brother; all we know for certain is that Moll has learned, through an adept use of secrets and ambiguities, how to control the story of her own life.

Jack's origin story and the history of his name are as ambiguous as Moll's. Jack is told that he is the son of a 'Gentlewoman' and a 'Man of Quality', but that for a surname, he might call himself 'Anything ... as Fortune and better Circumstances should give Occasion' (34). 'Jack' is a generic name for 'a man of the common people; a lad, fellow, chap; *esp.* an ill-mannered fellow, a knave' (*OED*), a stigma that he tries all his life to erase through a quest for gentility. Jack spends his life trying to become an adult, but he finds that he must continually take refuge in passing himself off as 'only a Boy', the guise of innocence that helped David slay Goliath.[40] Like Moll, he is forced by circumstances to take refuge in an alias, which is given to him by Frenchmen who do not understand

---

[40] For the background of this reading, see G. A. Starr, '"Only a Boy": Notes on Sentimental Novels', *Genre*, 10 (1977), 501–27; Geoffrey Sill, '"Only a Boy": George Starr's "Notes on Sentimental Novels" Revisited', in *Reflections on Sentiment: Essays in Honor of George Starr*, ed. Alessa Johns (Newark, DE: University of Delaware Press, 2016), 153–63.

'Jack', and so call him 'Monsieur Jacque', then 'Colonel Jacques', and finally 'Colonel Jacque', a bastardized title which he proudly emblazons on the title page of his memoirs. Like Moll, whose adoption of the alias 'Moll Flanders' exposes her to a capital conviction as an old offender, Jack's alias as 'Colonel Jacque' draws attention to his service as a Jacobite and exposes him to severe penalties.[41] The story of 'Colonel Jacque', who resembles in many ways the hero of *Memoirs of a Cavalier*, thus becomes a secret history within the public history of 'Col. Jack', a fable for the new Hanoverian age.

Jack's life, like Moll's, is full of secrets, but he is less skilful at keeping them. His honorific title, 'Colonel', was given to him not in the English army (from which he deserts), but by his Nurse, who calls each of her 'Jacks' by their rank in the household, 'Captain', 'Colonel', and 'Major' (34–5). If Colonel Jack holds a military rank, it is in the Jacobite army of James Francis Edward Stuart, whom Jack calls the '*Chevalier*' (a loyal Briton would call James the 'Pretender'), another secret that would ruin him if it were known. In 1715 Jack rejoins the Jacobite army at Preston, despite the importunities of his fourth wife Moggy, and he fears, even after fleeing to Virginia, that he will be recognized and prosecuted as a traitor. Rather than remaining out of sight on his plantation, where he is already prosperous, Jack impulsively sets out on a trading voyage to the West Indies, where he is forced to take refuge from the Spanish navy. After spending nearly a year in hiding, Jack arranges to smuggle woven goods into the Spanish colonies that are specifically proscribed under the Treaty of Utrecht, except as licensed in an *asiento*.[42] In the absence of an international agreement allowing free trade, or at least a letter of marque licensing him as a privateer, Jack must be considered a pirate, an outlaw identity consistent with those of his former lives as a thief and a Jacobite. In his secret history, Jack is a reformed thief, a freed slave, a rake-hero lover (sometimes comically so) of beautiful women, a recalcitrant rebel, and a free trader, while in public life he appears to be a respectable Protestant landowner, a dutiful husband, almost a gentleman. Again like Moll, Jack studies how to fashion his narrative, and ends his days (prior to returning to England) sitting in a country bower in Mexico, writing his memoirs and reflecting on his life with perfect lucidity, 'the Benefit of a violent Fit of the Gout' (263). Swift's Gulliver was yet four years away.

Defoe's 'Indisputably Great' Novel: *The Fortunate Mistress*

Defoe's last fiction but one, *The Fortunate Mistress: or, a History of the Life and Vast Variety of Fortunes of Mademoiselle de Beleau, afterwards call'd The Countess of*

---

[41] The joke on Jack, probably intended by Defoe, is that 'Jacques' is French for 'James', not 'John', which is the Colonel's proper name. 'Jacques' is the root word of 'Jacobite', an identity that Jack assumes in his quest for gentility.

[42] See Maximillian E. Novak, 'Colonel Jack's "Thieving Roguing" Trade to Mexico and Defoe's Attack on Economic Individualism', *HLQ*, 24:4 (1961), 349–53.

Wintselsheim, in Germany. Being the Person known by the Name of the Lady Roxana, in the Time of King Charles II, was published in February 1724 by a conger of publishers who had printed and sold other books by Defoe. No second edition or reprint is known to have been published in Defoe's lifetime. The subject matter of this private history—the life, errors, terrors, and secrets of a courtesan—and the supposed author's failure to make even the slightest effort at repentance, or to repair the ambiguities and loose ends of her life, may have perplexed readers who were looking for another *Moll Flanders* or *Colonel Jack*. If *The Fortunate Mistress* was not a success in its original form, a series of publishers, including Elizabeth Applebee (1740), C. Whitefield (1745), J. Cooke (1765), and Francis Noble and Thomas Lowndes (1775), did their best to make a conventional novel of it.[43] Some seventeen editions appeared between 1735 and 1775, at least six of them with 'continuations' that carried the story beyond the obscure and ambiguous ending of Defoe's original edition.[44] A 'lost' edition of 1735, *The Life and Adventures of Roxana, the Fortunate Mistress, or most Unhappy Wife*, was the first to replace 'The Fortunate Mistress' with 'Roxana' as the principal name in the title, and the novel was generally known thereafter as *Roxana*.

Roxana is the story of a woman born into a family of wealth and position who declines (reversing the trajectory of *Moll Flanders* and *Colonel Jack*) into poverty, despair, secrecy, anxiety, and depression. When her first husband, a well-to-do but lazy brewer, fails and deserts her, Roxana's cunning maid Amy devises a scheme to relieve her of her five children. Amy also persuades Roxana to accept the advances of her landlord, whose mistress she becomes. Roxana and Amy each have a daughter by him, though Roxana's child dies. The landlord, who is also a jeweller, is murdered, leaving Roxana with a secret cache of jewels, many secrets of conduct, and much guilt besides. After several more affairs, one with a Prince, and after dancing in a Turkish dress for a group of gentlemen, one of whom may be the King of England, Roxana accepts as her husband a rich Dutch merchant whose European title enables Roxana to be called 'your Ladyship' (*Novels*, ix. 204). Roxana is 'surpriz'd [with] Joy' (212) at her good fortune, though to herself she admits to suffering from 'a secret Hell within' (215) that is worsened by the fact that, not being a '*Roman-Catholic*', she cannot obtain absolution from a '*Father-Confessor*' (218). The novel appears to conclude at this point, without having explained the cause of her 'melancholly' (218). Soon after, however, the narrative loops back and inserts an episode that precedes her marriage: 'I must now go back to another Scene, and join it to this End of my Story, which will compleat all my Concern with *England*' (219). In this first-ever 'continuation', Roxana discovers that her cook-maid Susan is in a position to embarrass her and destroy her prospects for marriage. The young woman claims to have been a

---

[43] See John Mullan, 'The Textual History of *Roxana*', in Defoe, *Roxana*, ed. Mullan (Oxford: Oxford University Press, 1996), 331–9; P. N. Furbank, 'Appendix A', *Novels*, ix. 269–73.

[44] P. N. Furbank and W. R. Owens, 'The "Lost" Continuation of Defoe's *Roxana*', *ECF* 9:3 (1997), 299–308, which includes a list of eighteenth-century editions of *Roxana* compiled by Spiro Peterson in 'Defoe's *Roxana* and its Eighteenth-Century Sequels' (unpublished doctoral thesis, Harvard University, 1953).

member of Roxana's family in London, and at first identifies Amy as her mother. Upon Amy's denial, Susan fastens upon Roxana and pursues her relentlessly. There are numerous ambiguities and contradictions in her story, such as her persistent references to the wife of a ship captain as her 'Sister', though the captain's wife is clearly not Roxana's child. Yet Roxana is driven by guilt and fear to believe that Susan's story is true, despite evidence to the contrary.[45] In this way *Roxana* reverses the lost-mother theme of *Moll Flanders*, in that the story is here told by the mother, Roxana (who prefers not to be found), instead of the young woman, Susan, who seeks to discover that either Amy or Roxana is her mother.

Another ambiguity that contributes to the novel's complexity is the social relationship between Roxana and her maid. Amy knows Roxana's desires better than Roxana does, and she acts on them when Roxana is immobilized by her anxieties. It is Amy who tracks down the Dutch merchant whom Roxana has spurned and brings him over to England to renew the courtship. It is Amy who remains behind in England to deal with 'the Girl' (as Roxana repeatedly calls her) while Roxana escapes to Holland with her new husband, who does not (and must not) know the girl's story. In a fit of anger, Roxana enjoins Amy from murdering 'my Child' (255), and forbids Amy to come into her presence again if she does. Many readers are puzzled when, in the penultimate paragraph but one, Amy rejoins Roxana in Holland without having given 'full Satisfaction to my Friend the Quaker, that she had not murther'd my Child' (267). The conundrum may be resolved (though made even more horrific) by the supposition that Amy has come to Holland because she knows that the child she has murdered is not Roxana's, but her own.

Like Defoe's other prose fictions that are now read as novels, *Roxana* flouts the conventions of the 'amatory fiction' that was the basis of many novels in Defoe's time. The 'fortunate' ending in which she is married to a European Count, with whom she has a son for whom she feels 'the natural affections of a Mother' (217), is disrupted by the interpolation of a fifty-page episode in which her hopes for a peaceful retirement are entirely blasted. Her triumphal charade as 'The Countess of Wintselsheim', as the title page calls her, is undercut by the secret history of her more modest origins, her abandonment of her children, her life as a courtesan, and her rejection of the girl who claims kinship with her. Her narrative, in which she tries to confess her secrets and find absolution, turns into a thicket of ambiguities about the fate of her children, her relationships with the men who fathered them, the identity of the girl who saw her in the Turkish dress, and Amy's threats to murder the girl. Postmodern readers have accepted, even applauded these ambiguities as reflections of the chaotic world in which Roxana (analogically, every woman) lives, though Defoe's original readers were probably puzzled by these loose ends. Time has finally caught up with *Roxana*, and made of it what Virginia

---

[45] For the argument that Susan is not Roxana's daughter, see Geoffrey Sill, '*Roxana*'s Susan: Whose Daughter Is She Anyway?', *Studies in Eighteenth-Century Culture*, 29 (2000), 261–72.

Woolf, the daughter of Leslie Stephen, conceived it to be: one of 'the few English novels which we can call indisputably great'.[46]

After *Roxana* and *A New Voyage Round the World*, Defoe wrote no more books that could now be considered 'novels', though he continued to employ the techniques of prose fiction in works such as *Religious Courtship* (1722), *An Essay on the History and Reality of Apparitions* (1727), and *A New Family Instructor* (1727). Paula Backscheider suggests that the burdens of illness and business failures after 1724 led to 'phantasms of disorder' in Defoe's mind, to which he responded with a series of books that laid out 'an astonishingly detailed, carefully ordered construct' for the reordering of Great Britain, but which may have precluded him from writing fiction.[47] Maximillian Novak thinks that the aging Defoe 'was recycling material, reissuing earlier tracts, and reviving old ideas' in his last years, in an effort 'to be sure that everyone understood what he meant', which might explain the turn away from fiction.[48] Perhaps slow sales of such books as *Colonel Jack*, *The Fortunate Mistress*, and *A New Voyage Round the World* made booksellers hesitant to pay Defoe what he wanted for the rights to new fiction. Or perhaps Defoe felt that he had penetrated the secret history of humanity to the bottom, and there was nothing more to be found there. For reasons only he knew, he passed on, leaving behind him the foundations of the modern novel.

Further Reading

Ros Ballaster, *Seductive Forms: Women's Amatory Fiction from 1684 to 1740* (Oxford: Clarendon Press, 1992).
Lennard J. Davis, *Factual Fictions: The Origins of the English Novel* (Philadelphia, PA: University of Pennsylvania Press, 1983).
P. N. Furbank and W. R. Owens, 'Defoe and Francis Noble', *ECF*, 4:4 (1992), 301–13.
J. Paul Hunter, *Before Novels: The Cultural Contexts of Eighteenth-Century English Fiction* (New York: Norton, 1990).
J. Paul Hunter, *The Reluctant Pilgrim: Defoe's Emblematic Method and Quest for Form in Robinson Crusoe* (Baltimore, MD: Johns Hopkins University Press, 1966).
Maximillian E. Novak, *Economics and the Fiction of Daniel Defoe* (Berkeley, CA: University of California Press, 1962).
Leah Orr, *Novel Ventures: Fiction and Print Culture in England, 1690–1730* (Charlottesville, VA: University of Virginia Press, 2017).
Nicholas Seager, *The Rise of the Novel: A Reader's Guide to Essential Criticism* (Basingstoke: Palgrave Macmillan, 2012).
Geoffrey Sill, *The Cure of the Passions and the Origins of the English Novel* (Cambridge: Cambridge University Press, 2001).

---

[46] Virginia Woolf, *The Common Reader, First Series* (1925; New York: Harcourt, Brace & World, 1953), 90. Woolf included *Roxana*, along with *Robinson Crusoe* and *Moll Flanders*, among the titles she would carve 'on any monument worthy of the name of monument' to the memory of Defoe.
[47] Backscheider, *Daniel Defoe*, 510.
[48] Novak, *Daniel Defoe*, 680.

Geoffrey Sill, *Defoe and the Idea of Fiction, 1713–1719* (Newark, DE: University of Delaware Press, 1983).

G. A. Starr, *Defoe and Spiritual Autobiography* (Princeton, N.J.: Princeton University Press, 1965).

Ian Watt, *The Rise of the Novel: Studies in Defoe, Richardson and Fielding* (London: Chatto & Windus, 1957).

CHAPTER 4

DEFOE AND DRAMA

CYNTHIA WALL

'THE Advocates for the Stage', Defoe argues in the Preface to *Moll Flanders* (1722),

> have in all Ages made this the great Argument to persuade People that their Plays are useful, and that they ought to be allow'd in the most civiliz'd, and in the most religious Government; Namely, That they are applyed to vertuous Purposes, and that by the most lively Representations, they fail not to recommend Vertue, and generous Principles, and to discourage and expose all sorts of Vice and Corruption of Manners.[1]

Indeed, *Moll Flanders* adheres to 'this Fundamental': 'there is not a superlative Villain brought upon the Stage, but either he is brought to an unhappy End, or brought to be a Penitent' (5). Defoe liberally employs theatrical vocabulary throughout his works, being especially fond of the 'Stage of Life'. From his contemporary Charles Gildon to a host of twentieth-century critics, it has become axiomatic that, as a writer, Defoe is a 'Fabulous *Proteus*'.[2] Defoe himself admitted that 'we live in a general Disguise, and like the Masquerades, every Man dresses himself up in a particular Habit'.[3] Every one of his fictional characters acts a part at one point or another. In the *Review* in 1705 he muses that if the play-going audience would simply hiss the naughty bits off the stage, 'a Noble Sublime Piece of Wit, and True Invention' would generate a delighted *new* group in the seats.[4] So why didn't Defoe—who wrote poems, satires, pamphlets, letters, conduct books, trade manuals, political treatises, economic theories, religious tracts, travel narratives, histories, and novels—try his hand at a Noble Sublime Piece of Wit and True Invention? *Why didn't Defoe write plays?*

---

[1] Defoe, *Moll Flanders*, ed. G. A. Starr and Linda Bree (Oxford: Oxford University Press, 2011), 4–5.
[2] Charles Gildon, *The Life and Strange Surprizing Adventures of Mr. D--- De F-- of London, Hosier*, 2nd ed. (1719), iii–iv.
[3] Defoe, *A System of Magick* (1727), *SFS*, vii. 242.
[4] *Review*, ii. 151 (3 May 1705).

This chapter will look at the well-known reasons why he didn't ('*Puritan!*') and also at why and how, in short, he did. His published views against contemporary drama will provide a sort of historical platform against which to measure the figures of speech, the theatrical familiarity, and the dramatic structures within Defoe's works. As David Marshall puts it: 'To read Defoe—his printed or personated characters—is to enter the theater'.[5]

The Dissenter and 'The Errors of the Stage'

On 2 September 1642, in the first year of the English Civil War (1642–51), the increasingly dominant Puritans succeeded in getting Parliament to close down all the theatres:[6] in order to 'appease and avert the Wrath of God' that was manifesting in 'a Cloud of Blood by a Civil War', the order declared that 'Public Stage-plays', which 'do not well agree … with the Seasons of Humiliation' because they 'too commonly expres[s] lascivious Mirth and Levity … shall cease, and be forborne', and instead everyone should just stay home and give themselves up to 'profitable and seasonable considerations of Repentance, Reconciliation, and Peace with God'.[7] Puritans had long and complicated arguments for banning stage plays; as J. Paul Hunter itemizes: 'The objections to acting, for example, included worries about the representation of immoral, inappropriate, or incendiary acts and about the falseness to self or integrity involved in an actor's pretending to be someone else; and objections to the public viewing of theater included both fears of sheeplike collective thinking and moblike collective action'.[8] In 1648 all the theatres and playhouses were ordered to be pulled down, the actors to be seized and whipped, and anyone caught attending a play to be fined five shillings. While the theatres were restored in 1660 (now with women as actors, *à la française*) upon the restoration of Charles II, the vein of Puritan mistrust was pulsing—and not very far under the skin. In 1698, towards the end of what we loosely call 'Restoration drama'—that exhilarating run of witty sex and sexy wit glamorized by Aphra Behn, William Congreve, John Dryden, Thomas D'Urfey, George Etherege, Thomas Otway, John Vanbrugh, and William Wycherley—Jeremy Collier, a Nonjuring clergyman, published his *Short View of the Immorality of the English Stage*. '[N]*othing has gone farther in Debauching the Age than*

---

[5] David Marshall, *The Figure of Theater: Shaftesbury, Defoe, Adam Smith, and George Eliot* (New York: Columbia University Press, 1986), 75.

[6] 'The Errors of the Stage' comes from the *Review*, ii. 152 (3 May 1705).

[7] *Acts and Ordinances of the Interregnum, 1612–60*, ed. C. H. Firth and R. S. Rait, 3 vols (London: H. M. Stationery Office, 1911), i. 26–7.

[8] J. Paul Hunter, 'Protesting Fiction, Constructing History', in *The Historical Imagination in Early Modern Britain*, ed. Donald R. Kelley and David Harris Sacks (Washington, D.C.: Woodrow Wilson Center Press; Cambridge: Cambridge University Press, 1997), 298–317 (303).

the Stage Poets', he argues; '*like* Foot-Pads, *they must not only* Rob, *but* Murther' with their lewdness and atheism.[9] All those playwrights came under fire for their profanity and blasphemy, not least Shakespeare. (About Ophelia, Collier says, since Shakespeare 'was resolv'd to drown the Lady like a Kitten, he should have set her a swimming a little sooner' to protect her reputation [6].) The work had great impact: Congreve and D'Urfey were prosecuted; the actors Thomas Betterton and Anne Bracegirdle were fined. Several writers replied in print—Congreve, Vanbrugh, D'Urfey, and others—but Collier trounced them. As Samuel Johnson noted: 'contest was his delight, he was not to be frighted from his purpose or his prey'.[10] Congreve, Vanbrugh, and George Farquhar continued to write this kind of play, but with decreasing appeal; the 'reformed' drama of Colley Cibber and his successors took its place.

Defoe was born into this anti-theatrical company. He received a robust Dissenting education and trained (abortively) for the Presbyterian ministry [SEE CHAPTER 17]. In his first major published work, *An Essay upon Projects* (1697), he *anticipated* Collier in proposing an academy or society for the improvement of language and literature, in which the theatre and its performances would be improved as well:

> All the Disputes about Precedency of Wit, with the Manners, Customs, and Usages of the Theatre wou'd be decided here; Plays shou'd pass here before they were Acted, and the Criticks might give their Censures, and damn at their pleasure; nothing wou'd ever dye which once receiv'd Life at this Original: The Two Theatres might end their Jangle, and dispute for Priority no more; Wit and Real Worth shou'd decide the Controversy, and here shou'd be the *Infallible* Judge. (*PEW*, viii. 114–15)

The *Review* is where Defoe published his first diatribes against the theatre. On 3 May 1705, Defoe was agitated by the opening of '*the* Queen's New Theatre *in the* Hay-Market':

> We have lately Erected at the Cost and Charges of several Pious Charitably Disposed Christians, a Noble and Magnificent Fabrick, near the *Hay-market*, in the Liberties of *Westminster*.
> The Name of this Thing (for by its Outside, it is not to be Distinguish'd from a *French Church* or a Hall, or a Meeting-House, or any such usual Publick Building) is a Theater, or in *English*, a Play-House.

This 'Thing' is an imposter, a deceiver, disguising itself as a church or hall in 'its Beauty, its Stupendious Height, [and] the Ornament and Magnificence of its Building' (ii. 150). In fact, as Defoe concludes in a few pungent couplets, after he has reprinted the prologue spoken at the opening of the new theatre, the Stupendious Magnificence is really

---

[9] Jeremy Collier, *A Short View of the Profaneness and Immorality of the English Stage*, 5th ed. (1730), A4r–v.

[10] Samuel Johnson, 'Congreve', in *The Lives of the Poets*, 4 vols, ed. Roger Lonsdale (Oxford: Clarendon Press, 2006), iii. 69.

> A *Lay-stall* this, *Apollo* spoke the Word,
> And straight arose a *Playhouse* from a T—.
> Here *Whores in Hogstyes*, Vilely blended lay,
> Just as *in Boxes*, at our *Lewder Play*. (ii. 153)

The language here is violent, vulgar, and completely unambiguous.

A year later, in the *Review* for 20 June 1706, the diatribe is taken up again. It turns out that, in order to '[Defray] the Charge of repairing and fiting up the Chappel in *Russel-Court*', a production of *Hamlet* ('with singing by Mrs *Hughes*, &c. and Entertainment of Dancing by Monsieur *Cherrier*, Miss *Samlow* his Scholar, and Mr. *Evans* Boxes 5*s*. Pitt 3*s*. first Gallery 2*s*. upper gallery 1*s*.') will be performed at the Theatre Royal in Drury Lane. Upon which, the Reviewer concludes: '*If the D—l be come over to us*, and assists *to support the Church*; The D—l must be in it, *if the Church be in Danger*'.[11] By 3 August 1706, the Reviewer is pushing harder against this unholy collaboration between Church and stage. Charles Leslie's *The Rehearsal*, responding to the *Review*'s criticisms, gets a knockout double punch: first, that 'Poor Gentleman! this Author has always the Misfortune to defend the *Church* to her Disadvantage' (*Review*, iii. 475), and second, in a little textual proto-Sternean mini-drama of its own:

> But says this *Church* Defender, has not the *Church* express'd her Dislike of these things, and have not thousands of Mr. *Colliers* Book against the Stage been dispers'd?—Yes Sir, they have—But by whom—Not by any of the Ministers of the *Russel-Court* Chapel; for they, in particular Mr. ----- rather chose to turn Sollicitors for the Play-house, and to disperse the Play-house Tickets, selling them for the Profit of the *Church*, and it will be prov'd, that Mr. ---- acknowledg'd, he had sold as many as came to 50*l*. (ii. 475–6)

Plays promote (or enact) profanity and lewdness; theatres pretend to look like churches; plays are staged to support chapels; not all of Mr Collier's thousands of dispersed books have dented the enthusiasm of Church-supporters selling tickets to the playhouse to support the Church.

In all, Defoe wrote over a dozen *Review* essays against the theatre between 1705 and 1709. On 25 June 1706, Defoe noted that his earlier observations about the playhouse funding the Church 'have made some noise in the World' (iii. 390)—they have even earned the soubriquet 'Defoe's Sermon' in the streets.[12] On 8 August, Defoe follows the theatre to Oxford, where certain actors from both companies (already 'Indicted for Blasphemy and Prophaneness') plan to 'assist in the accomplishing, *Anglicè*, *debauching* the Morals of the Sons of our chief Families, and the young Generation of the Nation's Instructors' (iii. 485). Later contributions (10 August and 26, 29, and 31 October 1706) offer various suggestions for theatrical reform, urging playwrights to enact

---

[11] *Review*, iii. 380 (20 June 1706).
[12] Edward G. Fletcher, 'Defoe and the Theatre', *PQ*, 13 (1934), 382–9 (383).

virtue, wit, learning, eloquence, and polite language; critics to praise those qualities; and audiences to appreciate them. In 1707 he compares the price of plays (six shillings a dozen, sixpence apiece) to sermons: at 1s. 6d. a dozen (1½ pence apiece), virtue is a steal. In August and September 1709, he comments on the suspension of the theatres by Queen Anne (which in September he seems to celebrate as permanent, but which lasted only until 23 November). Throughout his diatribes, as J. A. Downie has argued, runs a political vendetta: 'In Defoe's eyes the words vice and tory were virtually synonymous, so he professed to recognise a connection between High-Church toryism and the flourishing of the stage'. Unfortunately for Defoe's argument, however, '[t]he complexion of early eighteenth-century drama was', in fact, in Defoe's own camp: 'decidedly whiggish'.[13] The Haymarket Theatre was designed by Sir John Vanbrugh and supported by the 'ultra-whig' Kit-Cat Club. Defoe did acknowledge this, pointing to the rivalry between the Haymarket as the *'Low-Church Play-House'* and Drury Lane Theatre as the *'High-Church Play-House'* (iii. 392), but as Downie demonstrates, 'the political activities of both theatres, despite Defoe's classification, would appear to have been whig-orientated'.[14]

His own party, in fact, propped up the theatrical scene, a fact which Downie persuasively argues Defoe could not bring himself fully to admit. Instead he aimed his propaganda at the High Church Tories; his rhetorical efforts at reformation thus combined political with religious invective.

Downie concludes his analysis of Defoe's characterization of the theatre in *The Review* by quoting the pamphlet responding to 'Defoe's Sermon', *Remarks on the Review, Numb. 74. Concerning the New Chappel in Russel-Court, Covent-Garden.* 'Its concluding words are perhaps a fitting judgement on Defoe's writings on the theatre, at least when they involved anti-High-Church propaganda':

> I appeal to any Sober Unprejudiced Person, what Regard is to be given to such a Lying, False Tongue, who throws out his Invectives like poison'd Arrows, without regarding Truth, Manners, Decency, Religion, or any thing in Authority.[15]

And yet, even in the *Review*, Defoe's criticisms of the theatre are not one-sided, lying, vicious poisoned arrows. (Defoe never in his entire life had only one side to him. Even three-dimensionality is an understatement.) His *Review* criticisms, like Jeremy Collier's, attack the current practices of plays, not the genre itself. The Preface to Collier's *Short View* begins: '*BEING convinc'd that nothing has gone farther in Debauching the Age than the Stage Poets and Play-house, I thought I could not employ my Time better than in Writing against them*' (A4). But the Introduction opens with a definition: 'THE Business

---

[13] J. A. Downie, 'Defoe's *Review*, the Theatre, and Anti-High-Church Propaganda', *Restoration and 18th-Century Theatre Research*, 15:1 (1976), 24–32 (27).

[14] Downie, 'Defoe's *Review*', 29.

[15] Downie, 'Defoe's *Review*', 30; *Remarks on the Review, Numb. 74.* (1706), 8.

of *Plays* is to recommend Vertue, and discountenance Vice' (1). In the *Review* of 8 August 1706, Defoe concedes: 'I'll readily allow you in the Lawfulness of Representations, and that Plays abstracted from the Leudness and Vice of their Practice, may in themselves be innocent' (iii. 487). He then acknowledges that sober plays will not sell: 'In short, the Players know better than to act dull Sobriety on the Stage; abstract the leud and the prophane, there's not a Play now will bear acting' (iii. 488). Two months later he takes the actors' point of view:

> If you will have us reform our Plays, and give sober Turns to our Language; if you will have dull Vertue run thro' all our Plots, if every Hero must be a good Christian, if the Beau must not swear, the Bully swagger, the Fop talk Blasphemy, nor the Rake beastlily; Why then, Gentlemen, you must petition the QUEEN for an Allowance or Stipend to us, to maintain the Actors and Undertakers, with a Price to the Poets and Composers, that the Plays may be acted *Gratis*, and the Doors set open for the People to come in for nothing. (iii. 655 [26 October 1706])

Defoe comes up with a number of solutions, including having the government (or volunteers) fund the actors and playwrights so they would not suffer from the closing down of the theatres; alternatively, he would arrange that

> the Taste of the Town shall be chang'd—That the Ladies shall no more love to be made blush in the Boxes (for we know Blushing has long since been banish'd from the Gallaries). That Bawdy and Blasphemy shall no more please the Auditory—That they shall make right Judgments of Things, and never take Prophaneness for Wit, clap a nasty Jest, and like the Representations of Lewdness, under the Foppish Disguises of Love and Gallantry. I grant, this is a very hard Article, but the Difficulty has this Advantage in it, That while this last Article is un-reforrm'd—do but secure the Players to reform the first, and you effectually suppress the Stage, for no Body will give 6*d*. to see a Play. (vi. 325 [30 August 1709])

In short, he would like either to change the world, or else '[buy] Vice out of the Nation if I could, since I cannot get it pull'd down any other way' (vi. 331 [1 September 1709]).

Dramatic Techniques

Towards the close of his career as a hired party writer, Defoe turned to a genre he would approach in a way '*entirely New*' and perhaps 'something *Odd*' (*RDW*, i. 46)—a conduct manual, *The Family Instructor* (1715). The fifth and last dialogue of the first part, *Relating to Fathers and Children*, begins with Mother talking to the 'obstinate and refractory', 'hot and insolent' elder daughter about the rules changing now that Father is home, and there will be no more going to the park after church on the sabbath. Elder Daughter snarks back, and then:

> [*Here the Daughter turns away, and with a kind of a humming low Voice*, sings *the Tune of* a new *Play-house* Song. (113)

Mother, not surprisingly, is incensed, and the argument heats up rapidly, with jeering laughter, a box on the ear, more insolence, and then:

> *Dau.* You have done your worst.
> [*The Mother provok'd highly by her Tongue, follows her, and goes into her Chamber, but she had gone into another Room, and the Mother seeing the Closet-door open in her Chamber, goes in, and takes away* all her Books, PLAYS, SONGS, &c. *leaving only her* Bible, Prayer-books, *and two or three good Books in their Room.* (114)

Mother then soliloquizes: 'These are the cursed Roots from whence this blessed Fruit grows up! Here her Sabbath-Days Study! and the Bait to all her Pleasures. These shall be the first Sacrifice to the blessed Resolution I have taken *of reforming my Family*'. This is followed by another stage direction:

> [*The Mother brings them all down Stairs, and after looking over the Particulars, threw them all into the Fire.* (114)

But—but—*this looks like a play!* we murmur in surprise. It has speech-prefixes, stage directions, and everything! Most Defoe scholars, from his own day to the present, have remarked on his use of dialogue, an ancient and popular genre of its own [SEE CHAPTER 5]. Anna Lætitia Barbauld commented that among Defoe's most popular works 'were his Family Instructor and Religious Courtship. They both consist of dialogues on religious and moral subjects, relative to the conduct of life in its various situations and occurrencess [sic]'.[16] Walter Wilson condescends to approve: 'Historical dialogues, when written with spirit, are particularly acceptable to the inferior classes, and to young people in general, who make themselves parties to the conversation, and can fix the subject, with a slight effort, upon their memories'.[17] Paula Backscheider notes that the dialogue form was not in fact '*entirely New*', as Defoe claimed; earlier conduct books had used it. What was original, she argues, is the depth of detail and the 'leisurely

---

[16] Anna Lætitia Barbauld, *The British Novelists; with An Essay; and Prefaces, Biographical and Critical*, 50 vols (1810), xvi, iv.

[17] Walter Wilson, *Memoirs of the Life and Times of Daniel De Foe*, 3 vols (1830), iii. 521.

narration'.[18] Barbauld agrees: 'They have not the least pretensions to elegance, and an air of religious austerity pervades the whole of them; but their dramatic form of dialogues, supported with much nature and feeling, and the interest which his manner of writing has thrown into the familiar stories and incidents of domestic and common life, has made these publications, especially the former, exceedingly popular to this day among those whose religious opinions are similar to his own'.[19] Robert Shiells commented that in *Religious Courtship* and *The Family Instructor*, writings of 'a serious and religious turn' are written 'not in a dry dogmatic manner, but in a kind of dramatic way, which excites curiosity, keeps the attention awake, and is extremely interesting, and pathetic'.[20]

In fact, in the Preface to *The Family Instructor*, Defoe acknowledges: '*The whole Work being design'd both to divert and instruct, the Author has endeavoured to adapt it as much as possible to both those Uses, from whence some have call'd it* a Religious Play'. He really wanted to write a '*Drammatick Poem*', he confesses, but that would have put too much '*Restraint*' on his '*Excursions*'. So he concludes: '*As to its being called* a Play, be it called so if they please; *it must be confest, some Parts of it are too much acted in many Families among us*' (44). All the world's a stage, of course. There is, in that sense, a realism to the dramatic form.

Maximillian Novak's take on Defoe's dialogues in *The Family Instructor* and elsewhere is that, while he had certainly read his Congreve, and represents the quarrelling couple as a sort of Fainall and Marwood of *The Way of the World*, his dialogues are emphatically not dramatic in the strictly theatrical sense, but rather 'intended to show quarrels as they are heard in everyday life'.

Novak acknowledges the stage directions and makes a comparison to the fascination with soap operas 'on radio or television'. He thus grants the dramatic power to the 'novelistic' values of the dialogues while acknowledging the presence of the dramatic structures.[21] Another way of putting this is that Defoe was playing creatively with both forms, embedding drama in prose, and novels in plays.

What did Defoe actually know about drama? For all that critics have assumed his 'familiarity with the theatre',[22] the sales catalogue of Defoe's library, notwithstanding its limitations as a resource for ascertaining which books Defoe actually owned, contains a 'limited number of playwrights [which] seems to reflect his critical attitude towards the theatre'.[23] Of course, one does not have to read plays, or buy published plays, in order to know plays. One just has to attend them. But we have no record of Defoe attending

---

[18] Backscheider, *Daniel Defoe*, 363.

[19] Barbauld, *British Novelists*, xvi. iv.

[20] Quoted in Theophilus Cibber, *The Lives of the Poets of Great Britain and Ireland. By Mr. Cibber, and other Hands*, 5 vols (1753), iv. 322–3.

[21] Novak, *Daniel Defoe*, 526–7.

[22] Frank Bastian, *Defoe's Early Life* (Totowa, N.J.: Barnes & Noble Books, 1981), 49–50.

[23] *The Libraries of Daniel Defoe and Phillips Farewell: Olive Payne's Sale Catalogue (1731)*, ed. Helmut Heidenreich (Berlin: W. Hildebrand, 1970), xxvii, citing R. Stamm, 'Daniel Defoe: An Artist in the Puritan Tradition', *PQ*, 15 (1936), 225–46 (234), and *Der aufgeklärte Puritanismus Daniel Defoes* (Zürich, 1936), 244–84. See James Kelly, 'Defoe's Library', *The Library*, 3:3 (2002), 284–301.

the theatre either. Backscheider notices a certain 'softening' of Defoe's attitude towards the theatre in the 1720s, 'since he had castigated the Spectator for doing more evil by "recommending the Play-Houses... than all the Agents of Hell ever employed before"'.[24] She points to *A New Family Instructor* (1727), in which the Brother assents that in any genre (even Romances) 'where the Moral of the Tale is duly annex'd, and the End directed right, wherein it evidently accords; the enforcing sound Truths; making just and solid Impressions on the mind; recommending great and good Actions, raising Sentiments of Virtue in the Soul, and filling the Mind with just Resentments against wicked Actions of all Kinds' (*RDW*, iii. 66), such reading is fit for family reading. In the journal *The Commentator*, Defoe points to himself as a 'Well-Wisher of the *Drama*, ... having in a former Paper recommended Plays as the most innocent Diversions'.[25] Yet even in the 1720s, as Backscheider demonstrates, Defoe directed criticism, and more rarely praise, towards the theatre. One way or another, Defoe knew his drama. Defoe acted his drama. Defoe wrote his drama.

The Drama in the Works

Defoe's conduct books are often considered in relation to his later novels; as Backscheider describes them, '[w]hat was original about Defoe's conduct book[s] was his fully realized, even leisurely narration, the individualized characters, the realistic dialogue, and, above all, his analytical interest in relationships' (363)—that is to say, their proto-novelism.[26] I have argued elsewhere[27] that the format of *The Pilgrim's Progress* (a book Defoe quotes frequently) looks in many places something like a play in the middle of transforming itself into a novel:

> Now I saw in my Dream, that just as they had ended this talk, they drew near to a very *Miry Slough*, that was in the midst of the Plain, and they being heedless, did both fall suddenly into the bogg. The name of the Slow was *Dispond*. Here therefore they wallowed for a time, being grieviously bedaubed with the dirt; And *Christian*, because of the burden that was on his back, began to sink in the Mire.
>   Pli. *Then said* Pliable, *Ah, Neighbour* Christian, *where are you now?*
>   Ch. Truly, said *Christian*, I do not know.
>   Pli. At that, *Pliable* began to be offended; and angerly said to his Fellow, *Is this the happiness you have told me all this while of?*[28]

---

[24] Backscheider, *Daniel Defoe*, 519.
[25] Defoe, *The Commentator*, no. 14 (15 February 1720), *RDW*, ix. 69–70.
[26] Backscheider, *Daniel Defoe*, 363.
[27] Cynthia Wall, 'Bunyan and the Early Novel', in *The Oxford Handbook to John Bunyan*, ed. Michael Davies and W. R. Owens (Oxford: Oxford University Press, 2018), 521–36 (531–3).
[28] John Bunyan, *The Pilgrim's Progress*, ed. Cynthia Wall (New York: W. W. Norton, 2009), 15.

The stage directions are given; then the novelistic narrative, complete with recorded dialogue, fills the interior spaces. In tracing the form of dialogue in English literature from its origins in Plato, Cicero, and Lucian, to their influences on medieval through nineteenth-century literature, Elizabeth Merrill demonstrates that dialogue in fictionalized texts of the late seventeenth and early eighteenth centuries increasingly wobbled between dramatic and novelistic form (playing with the idea of quotation marks along the way) until it finally settled down around the mid-eighteenth century into a more consistently narrativized format.[29]

In the following sections, I want to turn attention to the dramatic qualities of Defoe's dialogues. First, I will spotlight the dialogic episodes in a number of works for their likenesses to *playbooks*, recreating the stage on the page. Second, I will argue that various memorable scenes in Defoe's novels are memorable precisely because they resemble (or in fact *are*) a staged scene, frontlit, tableauxed.

Textual Plays

In Defoe's *The Family Instructor*, the dialogue is straightforwardly in dialogue/drama format:

> I Was looking up there, *says the Child,* pointing up in the Air.
> Father. Well, and what did you point *thither* for, and then point *to the Ground*, and then to your self afterwards, what was that about?
> Child. I was *a wondring*, Father.
> Fath. At *what*, my Dear?
> Child. I was a wondring what Place *that* is.
> Fath. That is the *Air*, the *Sky*.
> Child. And what is beyond that, *Father*.
> Fath. Beyond! *my Dear,* why above it all *there is Heaven.* (48)

But a few years later, in Volume II of *The Family Instructor* (1718), Defoe embraces not only the format, but the lexicon of the theatre. The Preface spells it out:

> *If Novelty had only recommended the First Part, then indeed we might suggest, that the Thoughts of People being once entertain'd, could no more be pleas'd again with the same Scheme: But this can no way affect us here; for if Novelty, the modern Vice of the reading Palate, is to judge of our Performance, the whole Scene now presented, is so perfectly new, so entirely differing from all that went before, and so eminently directed to another Species of Readers, that it seems to be more new than it would have been, if no other Part had been publish'd before it; nay, to any considering People that reflect*

---

[29] Elizabeth Merrill, *The Dialogue in English Literature* (New York: Burt Franklin, 1911), 74 (see also 2–3, 7–8, 59).

upon the differing Scenes of Human Life, and the several Stations we are plac'd in, and Parts we act, while we are passing over this Stage; it cannot but be known, that there are Follies to be exposed, Dangers to be caution'd against, and Advices to be given, particularly adapted to the several Stages of Life. (RDW, ii. 3–4)

This conduct book is even *newer* than the last, with its emphasis on Performance, Scene, Parts acted, this Stage, and all the scenes acted and parts performed throughout the stages (and on the stage) of Life. And while Volume I had its bits of stage direction along with steady speech-prefixes, those stage directions tended to be minimal, and often as much Bunyanesque marginal commentary: '[*Here the Child cries, and the Father blusht, /or at least ought to have done so*' (50); '[*Here Conviction works in / the Child, the Child weeps*' (52); [* *Conviction of Sin thus working up to a love / to God, a fear of God, and a desire of / serving God, which is* Holiness; *may be / very well allowed here to be an Appearance / of converting Grace in the Heart of a little One. /* [The Father takes notice of it as such]' (54); '[* *Here the Child is silent, and / Tears fall from its Eyes*' (61).

Volume II of *The Family Instructor* blends a rich narrative with an even richer mixture of tenses, dialogue, and stage directions. Part II features a basically good but short-tempered man—a prosperous London merchant—whose kind first wife died and whose second wife is a good housewife but an indifferent stepmother; he has made his children so afraid of him that any attempt to instruct them backfires. Figure 4.1 depicts the beginning of one story, starting on page 180 with 'a good grave Christian' hearing domestic violence before knocking on his neighbour's door. We get novelistically detailed action-narrative, which continues through the next paragraph, as the Good Neighbour enters and pretends not to notice that the Father opens the door with a cane in his hand, making tactful noises about some other business that brought him there, before the Father proceeds to an explanation of his son's misdemeanours and punishment. The Neighbour pretends to be reassured because of course the Father was joking—no self-respecting man who wanted to be a good father could possibly say, much less do, such violent things to his child. Why not? says belligerent Father. Because in so doing, 'you make your self dreadful to the Child, and that's the way to drive him to Extremities; and that again is the Road to his Destruction'—not to mention the fact that a man in a temper cannot presume to correct a child's temper. After a page or so of more moral dialogue, the scene begins to shift with the Neighbour enjoining the Father to 'lay aside your Passion for the Present, and let us go take a Pint of Wine somewhere, for I have a Mind to talk a little with you'. We get more drama—dialogue and directions—before it concludes with prose narrative in which 'his Family Governess' tries to incite the Father to further violence. I would say this scene offers a bit more than Barbauld and Backscheider's 'leisurely narration'—it is a fully directed dramatic scene, with props, emotional cues, spatial direction, and even a sort of curtain up ('And thus the Dialogue came in'—even if the actors push through the curtain before it is *quite* up from the narrative) and a curtain down, back to narrative. The proto-novel frames the embedded play.

Thus the second volume of the *Family Instructor* extends and expands, quite self-reflexively, the deliberate use of dramatic structures in the creation of its scenes. The rest

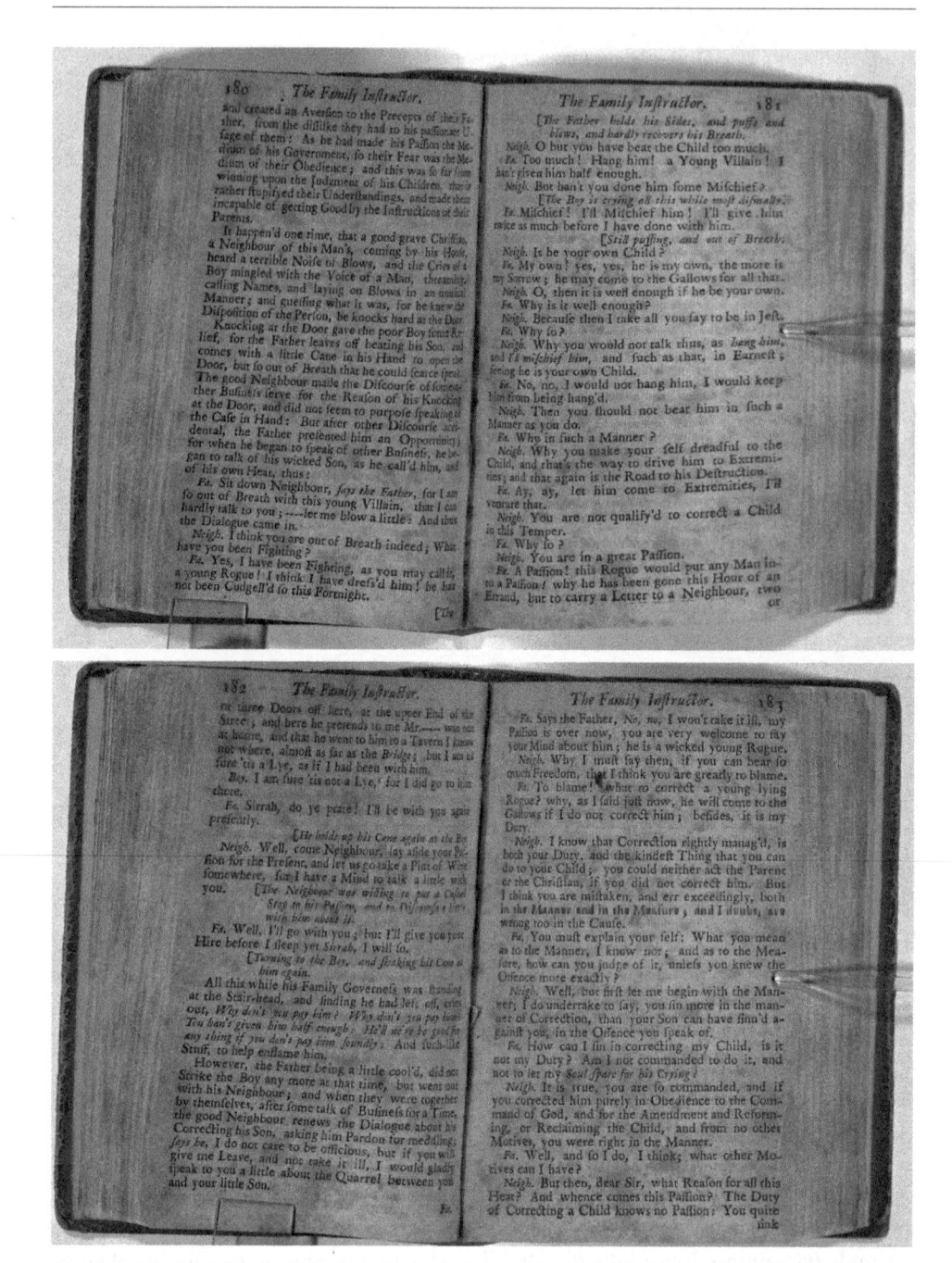

FIGURE 4.1 Daniel Defoe, *The Family Instructor*, Volume II (1718), 180–3. Boston Public Library, Defoe 27.77 v.2.

of this section will point more briefly at two additional pairs of texts and the ways they similarly embed the dramatic structure of plays into their texts: the didactic manual *Due Preparations for the Plague* (1722) and its novelistic counterpart, *A Journal of the Plague Year* (1722); and *The Complete English Tradesman* (1725–7) paired with *The Compleat English Gentleman* (written c.1729, published 1890).

Defoe had published six novels by the time of *Due Preparations*, so he was quite comfortable within the genre's roomy parameters. *Due Preparations*, while bookended with facts and advice, is largely a series of dialogues among different family configurations. Defoe divides the work into 'Preparations against the Plague' and 'Preparations for the Plague' (*TDH*, v. 33). 'Preparations against' comprises both the public (governmental) and private (familial) strategies of prevention. 'Preparations for' are addressed to the soul. 'Preparations against' include explaining the current threat of plague from Marseille, the leading theories of contagion, geographical vulnerabilities, the role of the military, the shutting up of houses (for and against), explicit recommendations for London and the other large cities, what best to do with children and the poor, lessons from the Great Plague of 1665, and copious quotations from the leading expert Dr Mead. All this occurs in straight first-person narrative, with inset lists and statistics. There is no dialogue, no scene-setting. But when he gets to the 'preparations against' that are 'personal and particular'—'Family Preparations against the PLAGUE' (57)—we move almost at once into the personal and particular, rendered immediate and present-tense in dialogue: 'I shall here describe a Family so shut up, with the Precautions they used, how they maintained an absolute Retreat from the World, and how far they provided for it; it being partly Historical and partly for Direction; by which Pattern, if any Family upon the like occasion, thinks fit to act, they may, I doubt not, with the Concurrence of Providence hope to be preserv'd' (59). The family 'liv'd in' (it is a real family, *of course*, this being 'partly Historical') '*St. Albans Wood-Street*': a middle-aged father (a wholesale grocer, well-to-do) and mother, pretty healthy, with five children (three daughters and two sons), two maids, two apprentices, a porter, and 'a Boy' (whom he let go home at the threat of the coming 'desolation' [59]). We get the narrative details of the wicket made in the door and a rope-pulley attached to a window to let things in or out with safe social distancing. Much narrative spotlights the master's cleverness in shutting up his family, arranging for provisions (they would eat well for a long time, in candlelight), killing rodents, building a special little hutch for the poor porter, and such like, so that by

> the 14th of *July* he shut the Wicket of his Door up, and Bolted, Barr'd and Lock'd himself in with all his House, taking the Keys into his own keeping, declaring to all his Family, that if any one of them, though it were his eldest Son or Daughter, should offer to stir out without the Door, though it was but a Yard off, they should not come in again upon any Terms whatsoever.
>
> At the same time he Nail'd up all the Casements of his Window, or fasten'd the Wooden-shutters on the inside. (64)

More detailed novelistic narrative follows for several pages, then more embedded dialogue: 'They were answer'd by a strange Voice, who spoke in a melancholly Tone that *Abraham* the Porter was dead. And who, then, are you, says the Master to the Person that spoke? I am his poor distress'd Widow, Sir, says the Answerer, come to tell you that your poor Servant is gone' (68). The narrativized dialogue follows through to the end of the section.

But something different emerges in 'Preparations for the Plague' (*for the soul*). Here appear the speech-prefixes and bracketed stage directions that signal an embedded play: the ultimate drama. In the first edition, the section is framed by nine pages of narrative before the dialogues begin, and twenty-six after, leaving roughly *over one hundred pages* of dramatic dialogue in between (with a few intermissions of narratorial intervention)—the 'inwardness' of 'theatre', to play on Katharine Maus's terms.[30] We in the twentieth and twenty-first centuries are accustomed to thinking of the Novel as introducing 'interiority', psychological depth, three-dimensional or 'rounded' characters. But Defoe, like Bunyan, was a writer who understood that what contemporary drama promised was an insight into *the soul*. Dialogue embedded in didacticism vivisected the subject, opened up his or her insides (in the hands of Defoe and Bunyan, deepening the dialogue's exposure of 'thoughts' in Merrill's sense [3]); drama exposed the inner person in ways that fictional prose narrative had not yet discovered; the stage directions of a playbook could flay open even more reactions, motivations, intentions (see how '*the Child cries, and the Father blusht, / or at least ought to have done so*' [50]).

David Marshall elegantly analyses the story of the Three Men in *A Journal of the Plague Year* as an embedded play. The Three Men are John the 'Biscuit-Baker', his brother Tom the 'Sail-Maker', and the not-further-named 'Joiner' who find a way out, escaping plague-ridden London to tramp the countryside, devising Crusoe-esque dwellings, negotiating with hostile villagers, and manage to beat the system.[31] Marshall notes how the episode textually assumes the format of a play, with dialogue in the present tense and 'prefaced and vocalized by the silent names that stand for the characters'. He discusses the presence of dialogues in Defoe's work and eighteenth-century literature more generally, then concludes: 'What is remarkable here, however, is the considerable effort displayed by the narrator (that is, Defoe playing the part of the narrator) to keep this theatrical form before our eyes. The demands of exposition force him to interrupt the dialogue repeatedly', he says, pointing to the four footnotes the narrator interjects to explain some aspect of action or event that he somehow couldn't work into the dialogue itself, or even the stage directions (anticipating Samuel Richardson's Editorial Explanatory Interruptions in *Pamela* [1740]?).[32] Those footnotes include backstory or sidestory:

---

[30] Katharine Eisaman Maus, *Inwardness and Theater in the English Renaissance* (Chicago: University of Chicago Press, 1995).
[31] Defoe, *A Journal of the Plague Year*, ed. Cynthia Wall (1722; London: Penguin, 2003), 57, 117–39.
[32] Marshall, *Figure of Theater*, 82–3.

*It seems *John* was in the Tent, but hearing them call he steps out, and taking the Gun upon his Shoulder, talk'd to them as if he had been the Centinel plac'd there upon the Guard by some Officer that was his Superior.

*This frighted the Constable and the People that were with him, that they immediately changed their Note.

†They had but one Horse among them.

*Here he call'd to one of his Men, and bade him order Capt. *Richard* and his People to March the Lower Way on the side of the Marshes, and meet them in the Forest, which was all a Sham, for they had no Captain *Richard*, or any such Company. (132–4)

Actually, as we will see in the next section, apart from the they-only-had-one-horse detail (which would, if we think about it, be difficult to render in a stage scene, except by one of the actors soliloquizing, '*We're pretending we have a LOT of Horses*'), this scene recalls that in *Robinson Crusoe* where Crusoe stage-manages his motley crew to create the impression of a much larger and more organized colony on the island. The footnotes fill in the narratorial details of intention and effect. So, Marshall (and perhaps the rest of us) wonders, why didn't he just go for the third-person narrative to begin with?

> Rather than interrupting the format of the page to remind us of the difference between what John says, how the scene looks to the constable, and what is really going on, the narrator resorts to footnotes for the effect of dramatic irony. Such technical and textual devices may remind us that we are reading a book, but they provide us with the point of view that an audience to a play would have; and they show the extent to which the narrator is trying to maintain the dialogue form. Dramatic narrative—a text which acts like a play—is clearly desired in these pages.[33]

These footnotes play the role of *asides*: the first one tells the audience how John appears (or intends to appear) when he speaks his first line:

> [T]owards Evening they [the suspicious Country People] call'd from the Barrier, as above, to the Centinel at the Tent.
> *What do ye want?* says John* (132)

The footnote basically turns towards us and explains in a loud whisper that John steps out of the tent with his gun on his shoulder and acts authoritatively like a Centinel. The second footnote is actually more directorial. The 'playtext' reveals:

> *John.* It is you that threaten, not we: And since you are for Mischief, you cannot blame us, if we do not give you time for it; we shall begin our March in a Few Minutes.*
> *Const.* What is it you demand of us?

---

[33] Marshall, *Figure of Theater*, 83.

The asterisk alerts us that the stage manager is stepping in to tell the 'Constable and the People' actors that they were to 'immediately chang[e] their Note' (133). And, of course, the last footnote is the Defovian/[Richardsonian] Novelist/Editor, explaining the conjuror's trick. That is, the footnotes here take the reader backstage. The dramatic dialogue here is not, as in *The Family Instructor* or *Due Preparations for the Plague*, revealing the souls of the characters, but staging a performance for the in-text villagers. The reader is privileged to be shown the other side of the curtain, the artificiality of the props, the intended sleight-of-hand. As with Defoe's apparently repetitive digressions in his novels, a closer look at his dramatic dialogues reveals that what seems repeated is actually a subtle change-ringing of the bells.

Choosing a representative dialogue from *The Complete English Tradesman* is difficult, because they are all so *good*. There's the one about the shopkeeper who demonstrates the long-lasting power of 'courtesy, civility and good manners' as he patiently continues to serve the Lady and the citizen's wife, the latter somewhat sceptical of the Lady's aspersions against the shopkeeper based on her visiting day at Mrs. Whymsy's, where Lady Tattle prattled without proof about his rudeness and sauciness, and the citizen's wife engineers a test that tests but rewards that patience (*RDW*, vii. 91–7). Almost the entire nine pages in the original are occupied by dramatic dialogue; they have relatively few editorial interruptions or stage directions. The next dialogue appears in Letter XI, *Of the tradesman's marrying too soon*, in which a tradesman and his wife are living above their means, but she doesn't know it; he will not blame her, and acknowledges he should have told her. It is an intimate, poignant family drama, husband and wife loving and tender, as she tries to get him to tell her what is troubling him, the dialogue punctuated with frequent kisses, the discourse ordinary and repetitive, but all the more moving for that (123–8). And there's the wonderful Billingsgate catfight between the Mercer and the Lady in Letter XVIII, *Of the customary Frauds of Trade, which honest Men allow themselves to practise, and pretend to justify*:

> Lady. I like that colour and that figure well enough, but I don't like the silk, there's no substance in it.
> Mercer. INDEED, Madam, your Ladiship *lies*, 'tis a very substantial silk.
> Lady. NO, No, you *lie* indeed, Sir, 'tis good for nothing, 'twill do no service.
> Mer. PRAY, Madam, feel how heavy 'tis; you will find 'tis *a lie*; the very weight of it may satisfy you that *you lie*, indeed, Madam. . . .
> Lady. NO, that won't do neither; 'tis not a good colour.
> Mer. INDEED, Madam, *you lie*; 'tis as fine a colour as can be died.
> Lady. O fie! *you lie*, indeed, Sir; why it is not in grain.
> Mer. YOUR Ladiship *lies*, upon my word, Madam; 'tis in grain, indeed, and as fine as can be dyed. (198)

This one might not audition for Serious Drama, but perhaps a Monty Python episode?

In the end I plump for the extended drama in Letter XV, *Of Tradesmen ruining one another by Rumour and Clamour, by Scandal and Reproach*, because its protagonist is another Moll Flanders in engineering revenge on behalf of women against fickle men—albeit in this case Defoe's sympathies ultimately side with the tradesman. The story begins with narrative: a certain Lady, who had been courted by a London tradesman, finds herself jilted in favour of a woman with a little more money. The tradesman implied it was actually because of something 'which reflected a little on the person of the Lady' (161), and so the Lady plots revenge.

First she has it whispered to the new lady in his life that 'he was not only rakish and wicked, but in short, that he had the Foul disease' (161); then she sets up an extensive gossip network to broadcast her own prudence in refusing him, and the slow seepage of malice is extraordinarily delicate:

> WHY, says a Lady to one of these emissaries, what was the matter? I thought she was like to be very well married.
> O! no, Madam, by no means, *says the Emissary*.
> WHY, Madam, *says another Lady*, we all know Mr. H-------, he is a very pretty sort of a man.
> AY, Madam, *says the Emissary again*, but you know a pretty man is not all that's requir'd.
> Nay, *says the Lady again*, I don't mean so; he's no beauty, no rarity that way but I mean a clever good sort of a man in his business, such as we call a pretty tradesman.
> AY, *says the Lady employ'd*, but that is not all neither.
> WHY, *says the other Lady*, he has a very good trade too, and lives in good credit.
> YES, *says malice*, he has some of the first, but not too much of the last, I suppose.
> NO! *says the Lady*, I thought his credit had been very good.
> IF it had, I suppose, *says the first*, the match had not been broke off.
> WHY, *says the Lady*, I understood it was broken off on his side.
> AND so did I, *says another*.
> AND so did I indeed, *says a third*.
> O! Madam, *says the Tool*, nothing like it, I assure you.
> INDEED, *says another*, I understood he had quitted Mrs. -------- because she had not fortune enough for him, and that he courted another certain Lady, whom we all know. (161–2)

After three or four more pages of gossip and rumour-mongering about how the tradesman was 'deep in the bubbles' and 'was very near making a bubble of her, and 3000*l*. into the bargain', not to mention '*they say* they have made another discovery of him, in a worse circumstance than t'other … the foul disease, &c. I need say no more' (163–4), his doom is sealed:

> 2. *La.* YOU astonish me! why I always thought him a very civil, honest, sober man.
> 1. *La.* THIS is a sad world, Madam; men are seldom known now, 'till 'tis too late; but sometimes murther comes out seasonably, and so I understand 'tis here; for the Lady had not gone so far with him, but that she could go off again.
> 2. *La.* NAY, 'twas time to go off again, if 'twas so.

1. *La.* NAY, Madam, I do not tell this part of my own knowledge; I only heard so, but I am afraid there is too much in it.

The episode closes with narrative moralizing on 'this piece of hellish wildfire, upon the character and credit of a tradesman' (164), effectively corroborating the tradesman's 'real' reason for leaving the first lady (he 'courted another of a superior fortune indeed, *tho' not for that reason*' [164]). But notwithstanding this final judgement against the lady, Defoe saw fit to open the scene with the wrongs of woman, and the exquisite detail of the plot to discredit and destroy the faithless suitor both personally and financially recalls Moll's ingenuity in helping the captain's widow to remarry in a London where 'Marriages were … the Consequences of politick Schemes, for forming Interests, and carrying on Business, and that LOVE had no Share, or but very little in the Matter' (*Moll Flanders*, 57).

The sheer length of the dialogues within *The Complete English Tradesman*, and their granular detail, their real-time unrolling of ordinary bickering, ordinary negotiating, ordinary slandering, ordinary confessing, overlaps them more with the novel than drama, and yet the immediacy brought by the speech-prefixes, the rat-a-tat of *Mercer / Lady / Mer. / Lady / Mer. / Lady / Mer. / Lady* peels back the narratorial filter and leaves the two alone together on the stage in front of us.

I will close this section with a short example from *The Compleat English Gentleman*. Here Defoe presents his final argument on the true nature of a 'gentleman'—one not based on 'birth' or a classical education, but on wealth (which could be accumulated by trade); on a wide and deep education in 'Physicks', 'Natural Phylosophy', 'Astronomy', 'Geography', 'History', and 'eloquence … in the English tongue' and on the qualities of 'Honour, Virtue, Sense, Integrity, Honesty, and Religion'.[34] In short, as Michael Shinagel has pointed out, this model gentleman is 'none other than a transparent disguise for Defoe himself'.[35] The work is not dominated by dialogues, but features one in the first chapter, with two brothers arguing about 'learning and wit' (43–58); one in the third chapter about gentlemen's libraries (123–41); one in the first chapter of Part II among some gentlemen overseeing the rebuilding of an estate (271–5); and two novelistic rather than dramatic dialogues in the fourth and fifth chapters (that is, with nineteenth-century quotation marks only, and no speech-prefixes) (154–72, 188–207). Given the lack of concrete evidence about the existence of Defoe's own library, I thought I would bring in a few of his views about private libraries, through the lens of a rustic country gentleman and his friend:

Gentleman: 'Yes, my library deserves a room on purpose. I think I'll show it you by and by. Why, I have no books. What should I do with them?'
Friend: 'But your father Sir Anthony had a library, I don't doubt.'

---

[34] Defoe, *The Compleat English Gentleman*, ed. Karl D. Bülbring (London: David Nutt, 1890), 218–19, 21.

[35] Michael Shinagel, *Daniel Defoe and Middle-Class Gentility* (Cambridge, MA: Harvard University Press, 1968), 243.

> *Gentleman:* 'Yes, I'll giv you a catalogue of them. [a Bible; family records; prayer books; ballads; musical instruments; Foxe's *Book of Martyrs*; but no plays]'
> *Friend:* 'But I hope you have added to the stock since.'
> *Gentleman:* 'Not I! What should I do with books? I never read any. There's a heap of old journals and news letters, a bushell or two, I believ; those we have every week for the parson and I to talk over a little, while the doctor smokes his pipe'. (135)

Eventually the Friend talks the Gentleman into investing in a library, and in a novelistic turn in the episode the Gentleman goes to a London bookshop, looks around awhile, and then 'calls to the master of the shop. "Pray, Sir," says he, "what shall I giv you for all the books upon that side of your shop." It seems the books look'd all fair and new, and were most of them or many of them guilded and letter'd on the back' (138). The bookseller is a little taken aback at this way of buying books, but eventually 'gravely answer'd him that they came to 346 pound' (140). After a little back-and-forth, the deal is concluded, '[t]he books were taken down, pack'd up in cases, and went down by sea to Southampton, and from thence by land to the gentleman's fine house; where a room haveing been appointed before hand for that purpose, they were all in a very few dayes set up in their order in presses made on purpose with glass doors before them, that they might appear in all the extraordinary forms of a library' (141). The dramatic discourse about books resolves into a novelistic placement of the props into their beautiful glass-doored shelves; the immediate settles into the permanent, the performance into production.

Stage Sets

Another distinctive drama-in-prose feature of Defoe's works is the way he can set up, in narrative, a scene that is vivid precisely as a *mise en scène*. Occasionally in Defoe a small spare scene is set like a little stage for an actor to enter upon—a small cross-section of space and time, description and narration. Consider this moment in *Moll Flanders*:

> WANDRING thus about I knew not whither, I pass'd by an Apothecary's Shop in *Leadenhall-street*, where I saw lye on a Stool just before the Counter a little Bundle wrapt in a white Cloth; beyond it, stood a Maid Servant with her Back to it, looking up towards the top of the Shop, where the Apothecary's Apprentice, as I suppose, was standing up on the Counter, with his Back also to the Door, and a Candle in his Hand, looking and reaching up to the upper Shelf for something he wanted, so that both were engag'd mighty earnestly, and no Body else in the Shop. (160)

This scene is unusually still and drawn out. The focal point is the white bundle ('white' makes it gleam a bit more) on a stool, surrounded by the very key details of an absorbed maid and apprentice, the counter, the door, and the candle. The scene, like the bundle and Moll, is about to take off. This is a scene revealed by a just-drawn curtain;

its frontlit stillness invites Moll to snatch the bundle. She even has a prompter in the wings: "'twas like a Voice spoken to me over my Shoulder, take the Bundle; be quick; do it this Moment; it was no sooner said but I step'd into the Shop, and with my Back to the Wench, as if I had stood up for a Cart that was going by, I put my hand behind me and took the Bundle, and went off with it, the Maid or the Fellow not perceiving me, or any one else' (160). In this case, the Devil (aka Moll's Inner Promptings), offstage, cues her to move onto the stage and perform her theft; she does; curtain drops. We never see that apothecary shop again.[36]

Two more novelistic stage-sets to point to: the scene in *Robinson Crusoe* where, as David Marshall exquisitely analyses, Crusoe and his new allies 'stage a dramatic fiction to convince their enemy that they have fifty men instead of eight'.[37] And in *Roxana*, the elaborately staged scene where 'Roxana' earns her soubriquet (and in the part of her life where, she says, she 'began to act in a new Sphere'[38]) has a particularly fraught but momentarily invisible actor/audience drama of its own. Roxana dances her Turkish (er, French) solo performance (the costume is actually that, a costume: its girdle 'was set with Diamonds for eight Inches either way, only they were not true Diamonds; but nobody knew that but myself' [174]); the stage-set is actually that ('I kept my Station in my Drawing-Room, but with the Folding-Doors wide open' [173]); the audience includes, she's led to believe, a king. But we learn later that in the wings, unbeknownst to the woman centre-stage, is her daughter Susan, a maid in the house. We do not find this out until Roxana finally reveals it; in her retrospective autobiography, she of course knows that Susan is present at the Dance, but as the playwright she withholds the information until the final act. When Roxana's maid Amy and Susan strike up an intimacy, Roxana reveals that her daughter had been 'a Servant in my particular Family' (205); towards the very end, when Susan has stalked her mother to the Quaker's house, she excitedly tells the story of the event: 'O Madam! *says she*, we that were Servants, stood by ourselves in a Corner, but so, as we cou'd see more than some Strangers ... No indeed, Madam, *says she, I assure you*, my Lady was no Actress; she was a fine modest Lady, fit to be a Princess' (289). Thus the story that Roxana tells at the centre of the novel has embedded within it a story she only tells at the end. The drama of *Roxana* is the drama of a first-person narrator pulling curtains before her reader in the way that she herself had been, shall we say, becurtained. If a third-person narrator were to conceal this until the end, even in Defoe's day readers would have cried foul play. Susan could have been—but is not—Chekhov's gun; she is Roxana's subconsciously buried-mineprop, about to explode in the last act without being seen in the third.

While Defoe consistently embeds dramatic dialogues in his didactic works, his novels rarely employ the speech-prefix tactic. They do, however, employ the *strategies* of the

---

[36] For more detail on this scene, see Cynthia Wall, *The Prose of Things: Transformations of Description in the Eighteenth Century* (Chicago, IL: University of Chicago Press, 2006), 112.

[37] Marshall, *Figure of Theater*, 79. See Defoe, *Robinson Crusoe*, ed. Thomas Keymer (1719; Oxford: Oxford University Press, 2008), 224–9.

[38] Defoe, *Roxana*, ed. John Mullan (1724; Oxford: Oxford University Press, 1996), 172.

stage. Larger-than-life props, costumes, manufactured dialogue, and curtained, frontlit scenes embed themselves into his novels. The *characters* create the *mises en scène*.

THE SECRET HISTORY OF DRAMA

J. Paul Hunter argues that the 'Protestant holding back of fiction—a kind of damming up of the imaginative impulse—may have helped develop England's own unique contribution [to fiction], producing ultimately a version of fictional narrative that was more directly influenced by contemporary historical events and new cultural developments, as well as by Puritan habits of self-scrutiny and attitudes toward work, solitude, subjectivity, community, social ethics, and zealous didacticism, than the Continental version'.[39] Many Defoe scholars, past and present, have noted Defoe's ambivalence to the theatre, his love behind the hate. Hazlitt registered the contradictions: '*The Family Instructor* [is] a sort of controversial narrative, in which an argument is held through three volumes, and a feverish interest is worked up to the most tragic height, on "the abomination" (as it was at that time thought by many people, and among others by Defoe) of letting young people go to the play. The implied horror of dramatic exhibitions, in connexion with the dramatic effect of the work itself, leaves a curious impression'.[40] John Richetti argues along similar lines:

> Given his manifest delight throughout his career as a secret agent in dramatic impersonation and in his writing life his frequent recourse to mimicry of a wide range of characters, this antipathy to theatrical representation is puzzling, although not inconsistent with his moral posture and his religious affiliations. His performances as spy and political writer required the protective cloak of anonymity and secrecy, but he nonetheless condemned more overt forms of dramatic representation in his (self-appointed) capacity as public moral censor, which in the context of his writing career seems to be his favorite role.[41]

As a devout Dissenter, Defoe could not approve of Drama. As a chameleon, a fabulous Proteus, he could not *but* love drama. Hunter has argued that 'the politics of history have provided slippage, in the Williamite era, within habitual distinctions between fact and fiction'; regarding Defoe and drama, we might argue here that the politics of cultural history have dramatized a slippage, in the Defovean oeuvre, between the habitual distinctions of prose and plays. Defoe, like Bunyan, played with the plasticity of emerging genres, incorporating a variety of rhetorical techniques to render the ordinary

---

[39] Hunter, 'Protesting Fiction', 315.
[40] William Hazlitt, review of Wilson's *Memoirs* (1830), in *Defoe: The Critical Heritage*, ed. Pat Rogers (London: Routledge and Kegan Paul, 1972), 107.
[41] Richetti, *Life of Daniel Defoe*, 143–4.

dramatically, to open characters in daily life, to capture readers, and to flay souls. Defoe's dramas are textually embedded, prosaically tamed; but there they are, speech-prefixes, stage directions, dramatic interiority. *Why didn't Defoe write plays?* The Puritan Defoe might have suppressed any urge towards writing a play; the Protean Defoe read, watched, noted, critiqued—and *wrote* plays.

Further Reading

Leopold Damrosch, Jr., 'Defoe as Ambiguous Impersonator', *Modern Philology*, 71:2 (1973), 153–9.

J. A. Downie, 'Defoe's *Review*, the Theatre, and Anti-High-Church Propaganda', *Restoration and 18th-Century Theatre Research*, 15:1 (1976), 24–32.

Edward G. Fletcher, 'Defoe and the Theatre', *PQ*, 13 (1934), 382–9.

James Kelly, 'Defoe's Library', *The Library*, 3:3 (2002), 284–301.

David Marshall, *The Figure of Theater: Shaftesbury, Defoe, Adam Smith, and George Eliot* (New York: Columbia University Press, 1986).

John McVeagh, 'Defoe: Satirist and Moralist', in *The Cambridge Companion to Daniel Defoe*, ed. John Richetti (Cambridge: Cambridge University Press, 2008), 200–15.

Cynthia Wall, *Grammars of Approach: Landscape, Narrative, and the Linguistic Picturesque* (Chicago, IL: University of Chicago Press, 2019).

CHAPTER 5

DIALOGUE AND DIDACTICISM
Defoe's Conduct and Advice Literature

PENNY PRITCHARD

In Dialogue Three of Part One of *Religious Courtship* (1722), the father/brother character initially encountered in the book's first dialogue converses with his recently widowed sister about the irreligious behaviour of her husband over the course of their twenty-five-year marriage:

> *Bro.* I know he serv'd you many a merry Prank about your religious doings, such as putting every now and then a Ballad in your Prayer Book, or your Psalm Book; and I think he put the Story of *Tom. Thumb* once in one of Dr. *Tillotson*'s Sermons.
> *Sist.* No; 'twas two Leaves out of *Don Quixot*: He did a great many such things as those to me ... and every now and then he would paste a single printed Word, that he cut out of some other Book, just over another Word in [our children's] Books, so cunningly, that they could not perceive it, and make them read Nonsense. (*RDW*, iv. 87)

Sir James's cutting and pasting antics amongst his wife's religious books reflect *Religious Courtship*'s central motif: the misery caused by religious incompatibility within marriage. Coming from an author whose extensive canon comprised so many forms of popular writing, expressly religious and not, this compelling portrayal of religion quite literally interleaved with 'entertainment' gives pause for thought.[1] Defoe undoubtedly would have distanced his entire oeuvre from certain more secular forms of popular writing, such as the type of scurrilous ballad invoked here, but he had few qualms in

---

[1] On the association of 'entertainment' with popular literature in the early modern period, see William B. Warner, *Licensing Entertainment: The Elevation of Novel Reading in Britain, 1684–1750* (Berkeley, CA: University of California Press, 1998).

mixing together different aspects of popular writing, including though by no means limited to conduct literature.

Defoe's fundamental belief that literature's purpose was to underpin the tenets of the most important book of all—God's holy word in the Scriptures—meant that much of what he espouses in his conduct and advice literature is taken up in myriad forms and genres across his writings. In essence, *every* work of Defoe's is didactic: the author's impermeable nonconformist convictions associated the value of literature with its useful and practical benefits to readers.[2] Categorizing certain works by Defoe as 'conduct and advice literature', this chapter focuses on those texts which articulate the most conscious investment in Defoe's endeavour to provide moral and religious guidance for readers. In order to show nuance within Defoe's wider didactic project, it considers works with a specific literary format: a structure of multiple, interconnected fictional narratives relayed in dialogue [SEE CHAPTER 4]. This chapter's focus on dialogue serves to foreground how certain conduct works operate as a proving ground, first preliminary to, and then in parallel with, Defoe's use of the form in his novels.

Key to this consideration of dialogue in Defoe's conduct works is his deployment of multiple 'speaking' characters to enable readers to progress along a seemingly 'natural' path towards greater moral knowledge. In his comprehensive study of dialogue, Tullio Maranhão observes that 'dialogical knowledge is a game of instances of understanding, conditioned not by the logic of the categories of knowledge, but by shifts along a spiral line traced through the subject-speakers'.[3] Often summarized and supplemented by morally authoritative editorial personae, Defoe's dialogues are eclectic and expository, and they provide 'the opportunity to pursue the investigation of a given issue *laterally*' rather than linearly, particularly through the combination of expository conversations and accompanying commentary. This essentially investigative quality is one they share more generally with Platonic dialogues, in evidence for centuries prior to Defoe.[4]

Defoe's Didactic Oeuvre

Defoe's best-known and most enduring conduct writings are the three volumes of *The Family Instructor* (1715, 1718, and 1727) and *Religious Courtship* (1722). The trilogy focuses on domestic education, whereas the last named is about obeying religious precepts while seeking a partner in marriage. This chapter will focus on these books,

---

[2] On nonconformist attitudes towards the spiritual 'usefulness' of literature, including imaginative writing, see N. H. Keeble, *The Literary Culture of Nonconformity in Later Seventeenth-Century England* (Leicester: Leicester University Press, 1987), 135, 153.

[3] Tullio Maranhão, 'Introduction', in *The Interpretation of Dialogue*, ed. Maranhão (Chicago, IL: University of Chicago Press, 1990), 1.

[4] Jon R. Snyder, *Writing the Scene of Speaking: Theories of Dialogue in the Late Italian Renaissance* (Stanford, CA: Stanford University Press, 1989), 8. Defoe adopts a model of philosophical dialogue that Snyder shows had been in popular currency since the late Renaissance.

particularly their use of fictional dialogue. Dialogue featured in popular conduct literature for more than a century before *The Family Instructor*'s publication in 1715. But as Paula Backscheider observes, reflecting on the book's widespread influence, 'conduct books written after it were more often cast as stories, and the characters and their language became more realistic'.[5] The genre had achieved substantial popular recognition with readers prior to Defoe's contributions, but this investigation will explore examples of Defoe's innovations within the form, including realism, narrative, the employment of 'ordinary' conversational language, and the dynamic interrelation of dialogue and annotation. Before that, however, a survey of Defoe's other conduct books is useful.

The Complete English Tradesman (1725–7) is aptly described by Furbank and Owens as a 'summation of Defoe's ideas about the trading life'.[6] The final part of the work's full title indicates that it is 'Calculated for the Instruction of our Inland Tradesmen, and especially of YOUNG BEGINNERS' (*RDW*, vii. 27). In this respect, it has a narrower focus on the interests of merchants and therefore lacks the universality of address adopted by *The Family Instructor* and *Religious Courtship*. *The Complete English Tradesman*, though it accommodates some dialogue, utilizes an epistolary format, being framed as familiar letters. Michael Shinagel explains that *The Complete English Tradesman* 'was not only a practical manual on how to succeed in business but also a conduct book designed to dignify the profession and polish the men who practice it'.[7] It thus fits with Defoe's tracts promoting commerce during the 1720s, such as *A Plan of the English Commerce* (1728). Defoe also wrote what could be considered a companion piece: at his death, he left unfinished a manuscript called *The Compleat English Gentleman* (c.1729), a book of advice for noblemen, particularly enjoining them not to neglect education.

Towards the end of his life, Defoe produced a succession of moralistic works that belong, to various degrees, to the conduct book tradition. *Conjugal Lewdness: or, Matrimonial Whoredom* (1727) is dedicated to the didactic project of guiding readers in godly marital relations, including sexual propriety. It is therefore a sequel of sorts to *Religious Courtship*, in which Defoe had focused on lovers' actions before marriage. However, *Conjugal Lewdness* is rather different to *Religious Courtship* from a formal point of view, as Defoe departs from fictional narrative and dialogue. As a didactic prose treatise, *Conjugal Lewdness* fits readily with another important sub-category of Defoe's works in the late 1720s which address certain moral failings of the present age. These include, though are not limited to, those Defoe produced under the Andrew Moreton pseudonym, such as *Every-Body's Business is No-Body's Business* (1725), *The Protestant Monestary* (1726), *Parochial Tyranny* (1727), and *Augusta Triumphans* (1728). Novak has suggested that differences exist between the tone of *Conjugal Lewdness* and the Moreton

---

[5] Paula R. Backscheider, 'Introduction', in Defoe, *The Family Instructor* (1715): *A Facsimile Reproduction*, ed. Backscheider (Delmar, N.Y.: Scholars' Facsimiles and Reprints, 1989), 7.

[6] Furbank and Owens, *Critical Bibliography*, 216.

[7] Michael Shinagel, *Daniel Defoe and Middle-Class Gentility* (Cambridge, MA: Harvard University Press, 1968), 211.

titles, but their shared format aligns all of these works more closely with each other than with *Religious Courtship*.[8]

Defoe's stylistic innovations within fictional conduct literature are contemporaneous with novels such as *Robinson Crusoe* (1719) and *Moll Flanders* (1722), which themselves contain significant episodes of dialogic discourse. Defoe's reputation as an innovator within fictional prose narrative in the first decades of the eighteenth century is well-established; this chapter demonstrates that this period of innovation and experimentation should encompass all of his didactic fiction, including those traditionally categorized as conduct books.

Models and Contexts

In *Before Novels*, J. Paul Hunter reflects on the prevalence and importance of didacticism in late seventeenth- and early eighteenth-century literature, taken as a whole, and the challenges for modern readers in conceiving of a popular and commercial appeal for texts so unapologetically dedicated to moralism. Quite simply, Hunter argues, the risk of ignoring or rejecting the early modern period's cultural investment in didacticism is to fundamentally misconceive how novels came about in the first place:

> However alien to moderns such tones and aims may be, the didacticism of the early novel is central to the conception of the species. Its origins are so tied up with the needs of contemporary readers and its early history is so dependent on the didactic assumptions in popular non-narrative forms that to miss—or excuse—its characteristic didacticism is to misappropriate its features and misdefine its nature.[9]

Defoe clearly felt that his readers needed to be educated about the primacy of didacticism. The preface to *Moll Flanders* (1722) asserts that those finding less 'taste and relish in the Reading' of the parts of Moll's narrative dedicated to her repentance than those giving her criminal exploits are themselves to blame for their failure to enjoy 'the real worth of the Subject' (*Novels*, vi. 24). The sanctimony of this assertion speaks directly, if not conclusively, to the higher moral purpose Defoe associated with all of his works of fiction.[10]

Defoe's didactic project extended to his adoption of other popular religious genres beyond conduct literature; he employed the word 'sermon' in titles, for example, invoking connotations associated with sermonic literature, but these works were never meant to be read 'as' sermons.[11] Furthermore, Defoe's engagement with casuistical debate informs

---

[8] Novak, *Daniel Defoe*, 647, 663ff.
[9] J. Paul Hunter, *Before Novels: The Cultural Contexts of Eighteenth-Century English Fiction* (New York: W. W. Norton, 1990), 226.
[10] Bellamy notes that Defoe makes a similar point in *Conjugal Lewdness*. *Novels*, vi. 277.
[11] Penny Pritchard, *Before Crusoe: Defoe, Voice, and the Ministry* (New York: Routledge, 2019), 74–83.

a substantial component of *The Review* (1704–13), as well as the novels, but it never takes on the extensive commitment to advising readers on moral quandaries for which John Dunton's *Athenian Mercury* (1690–7) provided a model. This observation qualifies Starr's argument that Dunton's periodical was 'the medium through which traditional casuistry found its way into Defoe's fiction', with the conduct works identified by Starr as 'the next significant stage' in the 'transmutation of traditional cases of conscience into the materials of prose fiction'.[12] As a London-based Presbyterian, Defoe encountered ample alternative examples of traditional casuistry in popular contemporary religious writing, not least the highly successful and copious *Morning Exercise* volumes collated (and in some instances part-authored) by his childhood family minister, Dr Samuel Annesley, Dunton's father-in-law.

That said, Starr's assessment of dialogue's enabling the conduct works to take traditional casuistry to another level, through the seemingly 'organic' process of human exchanges in conversation, still rings true:

> Through dialogue we are persuaded that the speakers are groping their way toward principles of behaviour, not serving as mere mouthpieces for the author's predetermined views ... It is the very gradualness of this process, punctuated by doubts, tentative judgements, and changes of mind along the way, which allows an inductive spirit to prevail, and gives the eventual attitudes of Defoe's characters such persuasiveness as they possess.[13]

To view Defoe's conduct literature as merely a stage of 'progression' towards *Robinson Crusoe* and onwards is strictly inaccurate because Defoe returned to conduct writing in 1722 and 1727. As Starr puts it, in the conduct works 'cases of conscience are investigated in a "purer" form than in the novels. Defoe is more detached from the people whom he puts in casuistical predicaments, and more intent on the moral principles which character and action alike are designed to illustrate'.[14] Defoe's returns to the more comprehensive use of dialogue in 1722 and 1727 indicate his awareness that this device conduced to the success of his conduct writing. Novak says as much, and with greater diplomacy than Starr, when observing of Defoe's return in 1727 to books entirely comprising multiple dialogues that 'he may have tried to call attention to his ideas and enlarge his reading audience by using the *Family Instructor* format'.[15] Though modern readers value the complexity of judgement created by narrative perspective in the novels, related retrospectively, Defoe's continued incorporation of set-piece dialogues indicates his recognition of the purer dialogic form's commercial and educational benefits.

Dialogue-based conduct works had a long and successful history before Defoe, and the form was adapted over a significant period of time to meet the needs and interests

---

[12] G. A. Starr, *Defoe and Casuistry* (Princeton, NJ: Princeton University Press, 1971), 33.
[13] Starr, *Defoe and Casuistry*, 36–7.
[14] Starr, *Defoe and Casuistry*, 33.
[15] Novak, *Daniel Defoe*, 488. Cf. W. R. Owens's 'Introduction' to *A New Family Instructor RDW*, iii. 1–8.

of new generations of readers. Hunter notes that Arthur Dent's *The Plain Man's Pathway to Heaven* (1601) reached a twentieth edition by 1629 and a forty-first by 1831.[16] Regarding dialogue-based conduct works more contemporaneous with Defoe's own, William Darrell's *The Gentleman Instructed in the Conduct of a Virtuous and Happy Life* (1704) reached its twelfth edition in 1755 and, although Richard Baxter's *The Poor Man's Family Book* (1674) had only reached a sixth edition by 1697, it was still being reissued in 1776 in an abridged edition by Benjamin Fawcett entitled *Dialogues on Personal and Family-Religion, between a Minister and one of his Parishioners*.

Compared with Defoe's, the dialogues within Dent's or Baxter's conduct works might strike readers now as disappointingly rudimentary in terms of imaginative plot or characterization, yet even they present a degree of narrative interest otherwise absent from earlier conduct literature. Hunter notes the waning of popular interest in didactic formats such as sermons during the eighteenth century:

> Sermons were sometimes revised into other forms of discourse, but as sermons they had lost their market share long before the novel became popular. ... [T]heir diminished importance derives from shifts within the didactic context rather than from a steep decline in religiosity or a swelling of a secular spirit.[17]

Precisely what those 'shifts within the didactic context' were can be difficult to pin down, but what does seem to have been retained in the wake of sermons' popular decline is the enduring appeal of fictional narrative and the use of dialogue, those features most prominently shared between Defoe's conduct works and his contemporary novels. Beyond the sustained popular appeal of dialogue and narrative, Paula Backscheider offers a further compelling reason for Defoe's adoption of the conduct book genre in 1715:

> [Defoe] had been writing political tracts in support of the Tory ministry and Harley ... As the terms of the unpopular Treaty of Utrecht became known, he shared the opprobrium directed at the ministry by a disappointed populace. Because the treaty seemed to favor Catholic France over England's Protestant allies and to sacrifice the interests of British merchants, a group Defoe had always insisted he championed, people, and especially rival journalists, accused Defoe of being an unprincipled mercenary hack ... In addition, Defoe was under indictment for seditious libel. Accused of calling one of the new king's regents a 'Jacobite' ... he could expect to be pilloried again and fined heavily if convicted.[18]

---

[16] Hunter, *Before Novels*, 235.
[17] Hunter, *Before Novels*, 250–1.
[18] Backscheider, 'Introduction', 8. This context for the first publication of *The Family Instructor* is also discussed in Dessagene C. Ewing, 'The First Printing of Defoe's *Family Instructor*', PBSA, 65:3 (1971), 269–72 (269).

Defoe's 1715 move into conduct works offered him the prospect of commercial income under the cloak of respectable and unremarkable anonymity. His return to the form in 1718, 1722, and 1727 indicates that writing conduct books was financially profitable.[19]

Notable in Hunter's investigation of the myriad forms of early modern didactic writing is his estimation of their shared 'hortatory spirit, intense zeal, and intrusive concern for regulated behavior', as well as 'a basic worry about contemporary tendencies to ignore higher principles', both of which feature heavily in Defoe's contribution to the genre.[20] Hunter goes on to suggest more generally that the 'Guide tradition'—didactic works of practical divinity offering instruction for readers in their spiritual progress through life or in a particular vocation or role—demonstrates the extent to which a burgeoning contemporary print culture took up much of the function of guiding new generations 'who felt themselves cut adrift from the traditional systems of advice that had treasured the passing on of family habits and secrets from generation to generation'.[21] As far as the Guide tradition, defined in these terms, encompasses writing both religious and secular in application, it is unsurprising that many such works targeted younger readers. Conduct books were frequently directed from fathers or mothers to sons or daughters, or more generally to 'Youth'. A special case, however, needs to be made for religious guidebooks. Notwithstanding the fact that a considerable number of texts within this sub-genre do indeed focus on the moral failings of youth, with accompanying emphases on the importance of attending to the moral precepts set down by the previous generation, this is not the whole picture. Many conduct works necessarily took a broader view of readers in need of spiritual guidance; the endurance of Thomas Brooks's *Apples of Gold for Young Men and Women and a Crown of Glory for Old Men and Women* (1657), for example, attests to its positive reception by a multi-generational reading public over more than three decades, and conversely. It belongs to a prolific genre of religious writing which takes for its subject saintly or spiritually enlightened children who convert their adult relatives.[22]

Likewise, many narratives within Defoe's conduct writings emphasize the spiritual capacity of certain younger family members—as well as other social subordinates including servants and apprentices—to serve as religious mentors to their elders or masters. So prevalent is this feature of Defoe's conduct literature that I have suggested

---

[19] For details of published editions of Defoe's conduct works, see Laura A. Curtis, 'A Case Study of Defoe's Domestic Conduct Manuals Suggested by *The Family, Sex and Marriage in England, 1500–1800*', *Studies in Eighteenth-Century Culture*, 10 (1981), 409–28 (411, 424).

[20] Hunter, *Before Novels*, 252.

[21] Hunter, *Before Novels*, 253. Cf. J. Paul Hunter, *The Reluctant Pilgrim: Defoe's Emblematic Method and Quest for Form in Robinson Crusoe* (Baltimore, MD: Johns Hopkins University Press, 1966), 23–50.

[22] *Apples of Gold* reached its eleventh English edition by 1693. On saintly children in early modern conduct literature, including Defoe's *Family Instructor*, see Penny Pritchard, 'Young Saints and the Knots of Satan: Moral Exemplarity, Ministry, and Youth in Early Modern Dissenters' Writing', *JECS*, 41:2 (2018), 225–40. The extent to which *The Family Instructor* serves specifically as a guide for children's religious education through the moral exemplars of pious children is considered in Yannick Deschamps, 'The Education of Children in *The Family Instructor* (1715–1718) by Daniel Defoe', *LISA e-journal*. https://doi.org/10.4000/lisa.8932.

elsewhere how it calls into question the place (or absence) of more conventionally authoritative spiritual mentors, such as ministers, in meeting the spiritual needs of the populace.[23] As suggested by its title, however, the focus of *The Family Instructor* is first and foremost the provision of religious instruction within the domestic sphere alone [SEE CHAPTER 16]. Several Defoe scholars have identified the contextual significance of the 1714 Schism Act as, at the very least, the impetus for Defoe to take up his pen in the interest of guiding Dissenters towards proper principles of domestic religious instruction.[24] Though the Whig victory in the 1715 general election meant that the act's strictures on Dissenting academies and schools were never enforced, its proposal alone signalled, to many Dissenters, a return to the civil and religious persecution of earlier decades. Defoe expressed that anxiety in *The Weakest Go to the Wall* (1714). Simultaneously, Defoe observed with horror the rise of forms of freethinking, including deism and atheism, that challenged orthodox Christian doctrines. As such, Novak's assessment of the extent to which Defoe's own religious sensibilities broadly inspired the *literary* innovations embodied in *The Family Instructor* seem plausible:

> Until the end of his life, Defoe thought that contemporary Britain with its heretics, deists, and atheists formed a kind of wilderness through which the true Christian was forced to wander, and the religious controversies of the coming years were to reinforce that belief in him. The three volumes of *The Family Instructor* were calculated to war against such dangers, and to do that, Defoe was to create a domestic scenery of convincing reality.[25]

More recently, Andreas Mueller has presented the case for an alternative, though equally politically charged, reading of *The Family Instructor* as a response to contemporary social instability extending beyond the Dissenters' plight. Suggesting that Jacobite insurgency and 'the danger that this posed to the nation's basic political system and Protestant religion' lie behind the troubled domestic patriarchies represented within the dialogues, Mueller reads in Defoe's depiction of children's, servants', and apprentices' rejection of authority anxieties concerning the stability of the state itself.[26] Mueller's and other historicist readings of *The Family Instructor* offer the kind of valuable insights which enable readers to situate the conduct works into Defoe's wider canon and the early modern political milieu which inspired them. They demonstrate how such works strove to contribute to public debate, an intention which at first glance might seem to belie their narrowly domestic focus. Yet it is precisely through his calls for moral, religious, and

---

[23] Pritchard, *Before Crusoe*, 111–19.

[24] Irving N. Rothman, 'Defoe's *The Family Instructor*: A Response to the Schism Act', *PBSA*, 74:3 (1980), 201–20; Novak, *Daniel Defoe*, 483–9.

[25] Novak, *Daniel Defoe*, 484.

[26] Andreas K. E. Mueller, 'Daniel Defoe's *The Family Instructor*, The Schism Act, and Jacobite Unrest: The Conduct Book as Political Act', in *Positioning Daniel Defoe's Non-Fiction: Form, Function, Genre*, ed. Aino Mäkikalli and Andreas K. E. Mueller (Newcastle upon Tyne: Cambridge Scholars Publishing, 2011), 125–47.

educational reformation within the domestic sphere that Defoe, along with other early modern writers of fiction, carves out new space for the novel's promulgation of 'truths' which are seemingly universal and apolitical.[27]

Defoe's Dialogues in Action

Domestic disputes which threaten patriarchal stability abound in each volume of *The Family Instructor*, but often contingent upon their resolution is the intervention or 'voice' of humbler family members being heard by their superiors (as children to parents, or tenant labourers to their landowning masters, for example). Dialogues possess an inbuilt democratic ethos harking back to their Socratic origins.[28] Put to work within Defoe's conduct writing, however, the 'democracy' of dialogic exchange is a key device whereby children, poor labourers, or servants articulate Defoe's precepts, thereby serving as moral examples for society at large.

Given the case I am making in this essay for dialogue's significance in Defoe's didactic fiction, readers may recall the many episodes in his novels where formal dialogue quickly gives way to, or is interwoven with, the more familiar rhythms of prose narrative which can broadly be termed 'novelistic discourse'. These include the scene between Crusoe and Friday concerning the war customs of Friday's original nation (*Novels*, i. 215), or the episode in which Roxana and her lover the Prince are holidaying at the Palace of Meudon when a verbal exchange takes place between Amy and Roxana's Brewer husband (*Novels*, ix. 85–6). Rather than indicating an author progressively relinquishing a more restrictive format for the nuanced possibilities of novelistic discourse, these episodes showcase Defoe's mastery of a range of techniques, often juxtaposed, to further his didactic intentions. *A Journal of the Plague Year* (1722) contains an extended episode concerning three kinsmen who escape the Plague-ridden city; this narrative alternates (over twenty pages of the Pickering and Chatto edition of the text) between dialogue and prose. The formal flexibility illustrates the three kinsmen's practical resourcefulness but also supports the narrator H. F.'s intention to 'give an Account [of] what became of the great Numbers of People which immediately appear'd in the City as soon as the Sickness abated' (*Novels*, vii. 116–37). *A Journal of the Plague Year*'s wider didactic project speaks

---

[27] This reading of early modern fiction's politicization of the domestic sphere echoes the critical framework offered in Nancy Armstrong, *Desire and Domestic Fiction: A Political History of the Novel* (Oxford: Oxford University Press, 1987) and Part II of Michael McKeon, *The Origins of the English Novel, 1600–1740* (Baltimore, MD: Johns Hopkins University Press, 1987).

[28] For discussion of the democratic orientation of Socratic dialogue, see Arlene W. Saxonhouse, 'The Socratic Narrative: A Democratic Reading of Plato's Dialogues', *Political Theory*, 37:6 (2009), 728–53; David Robertson, 'Plato on Conversation and Experience', *Philosophy*, 84:3 (2009), 355–69.

to the universal need for all readers' spiritual preparation in the face of an unknown future.[29]

In this sense, many of Defoe's works proffer practical and moral advice to readers in formats which accommodate some dialogue without necessarily falling under the category of conduct writing; these include not only the aforementioned *Complete English Tradesman*, but also his unfinished *The Compleat English Gentleman* and, bound with it, the even more fragmentary *Of Royal Education*.[30] Even at the level of their titles, these works indicate a level of specificity in intended readership absent from the more universally applicable domestic treatises which I consider at greater length here, in which dialogue serves as the primary vehicle of literary expression.

In the dialogues of Defoe's conduct works, there is tantalizing evidence—in the marginalia and footnotes liberally appended to the first two volumes of *The Family Instructor* and *Religious Courtship*—of multiple occasions when Defoe opted to supplement the dialogue format with multiple, editorial, annotations. We cannot know, now, the stage at which these annotations were inserted in relation to the main body of the text; suffice to say that these marginal notes are so plentiful and varied in nature that they tempt speculation about Defoe's process of writing and editing these texts.[31]

For example, in the first dialogue in *Religious Courtship* a brief exchange takes place between the father and his oldest daughter concerning her younger sister's prospects for a happy marriage with a man whose religious convictions remain mysterious. The dialogue is peppered with paratextual notes; in some cases these notes function as simple 'stage directions' complementing verbal utterances with non-verbal communication, such as when the daughter's exclamation, 'O Dear, Sir, My Sister can never be satisfy'd so, sure', is accompanied by a note: 'He observes his Daughter concern'd at it, and that Tears stood in her Eyes' (37). Other notes function to provide a different narrative register betokening greater psychological and emotional complexity. Shortly after this exchange, the father's changing emotions and even his memories of past events as provoked by his oldest daughter's comments are revealed to the reader through a footnote, when the daughter recalls her late mother's deathbed advice to all three daughters to marry wisely. Her father's immediate and slightly tetchy response is 'Very well: that was as much to say, she had found the Inconvenience of it herself', but to this remark is appended the note 'Here his Conscience touch'd him again, though but slightly, and he fetch'd a Sigh, and said softly, If she did, it was nothing, but what she had too much Reason to do; for she liv'd but an uncomfortable Life with me, on that very Account' (39). The note extends the

---

[29] Just months before the publication of *A Journal of the Plague Year*, Defoe produced *Due Preparations for the Plague* (1722), which is a kind of conduct book offering both practical instruction and spiritual counsel to readers in the event that the recent visitation of plague in Marseilles spread to Britain.

[30] Furbank and Owens, *Critical Bibliography*, 267–8.

[31] The printing of Defoe's conduct works, and the question of later authorial 'insertions' into the texts, is considered by Ewing, 'First Printing'. Her brief investigation of the first printing of *The Family Instructor* is confined to a case for identifying Defoe's later insertion of an entire Dialogue (Dialogue Five) prior to printing.

dialogue considerably in adding emotional nuance to the father's words and therefore his characterization, in the extent of his regret for and mitigation of his first response to his daughter.

A key difference between Defoe's conduct literature and his novels is the latter's increasing orientation towards the interests of the individual.[32] Dialogues, characteristically, focus on individuals within groups and take for their guiding principle the interests of a wider community (the family, the neighbourhood, society at large). Defoe's novels necessarily complicate older cultural maxims by focusing primarily on a single protagonist's experience. One way in which this fundamental difference between Defoe's two modes of fictional narrative after 1715—those now called novels and those called conduct books—can be illustrated is to consider an instance in which the conduct works' scripted dialogue format seems to 'fail', arguably because it has placed disproportionate narrative emphasis on a single protagonist (at the expense of the wider community of characters in which that protagonist is placed). The protagonist in question features within several dialogues ostensibly set over many years' duration which, cumulatively, fashion a personal narrative burgeoning both in timescale and an emotional complexity not readily apparent elsewhere in Defoe's conduct literature.

This 'failed' dialogue comes in the fifth dialogue of Part Three of Volume One of *The Family Instructor*. It provides the closing episode of a narrative which began in the first dialogue of Part One, which originated with the father's grieved realization of his having neglected to provide adequate religious instruction for his family of five children. While the youngest three children were spiritually 'reclaimed' by his efforts in Part One, the more difficult challenge of converting his two oldest children (already young adults when he begins the task) is considered at length in Part Three. Dialogues One to Four in Part Three recount in elaborate detail the experiences of the oldest daughter/sister, beginning with her marriage to a pious gentleman who—despite the misgivings of both families concerning the daughter's irreligious ways—is prepared to take her without a portion, as she remains unrepentant and estranged from her father. These four dialogues also detail, after her marriage, the increasing unhappiness of domestic arrangements, due to her refusal to participate in family worship. A protracted series of marital disputes follows, concluding with the daughter suffering a near-fatal illness which brings her eventually to a deathbed conversion and, with her husband's assistance, reconciliation with her father (*RDW*, i. 243–309). These four dialogues are supplemented with the kind of notes previously described, but an additional function of the notes here is the avoidance of repetitive passages of narrative; these are seen frequently when a speaker must acquaint someone else with the whole of a previous dialogue's narrative content, and are often provided in the form of a summative note such as '*Here she relates to him*

---

[32] On the changing status of the individual in relation to early modern fiction, see Ian Watt, *The Rise of the Novel: Studies in Defoe, Richardson and Fielding* (London: Chatto and Windus, 1957), 180–215; McKeon, *Origins of the English Novel*, 90–6; Christopher Flint, *Family Fictions: Narrative and Domestic Relations in Britain, 1688–1798* (Stanford, CA: Stanford University Press, 1998); Lawrence Stone, *The Family, Sex and Marriage in England, 1500–1800* (London: Penguin, 1977).

all her own Story, from her Marriage to her Reconciliation with her Father, as related in the Dialogues foregoing' (317).

In Dialogues One to Four of Part Three of the first volume of *The Family Instructor*, the narratives are increasingly dedicated to describing the point of view of the oldest daughter/sister, and in Dialogue Three in particular the proportional focus on her individual emotional state is yet greater. This dialogue is prefaced with four and a half pages of editorial context which serves to resituate the reader in the updated place, time, and emotional state of the oldest daughter, now a wife and mother (277–80). One extended description of her thought processes while alone, her husband having departed after a bitter argument, witnesses her engaged in a self-recriminating monologue which belies her inner turmoil far beyond what was evident in the dialogue with her husband: '*What a Brute have I been* said she, *to the best Husband that ever Woman had ... What barbarous Language have I given him! And how calmly and tenderly has he returned all along, without one unkind Word*' (288–9).[33] There are brief returns to the original dialogic format but, given the duration over which the reader has been invited to trace this particular protagonist's development from teenage rebel in Part One to a married mother making a protracted journey towards repentance in Part Three, the reader is inevitably more invested emotionally in this protagonist, with all her fallibility and stubbornness, than any other character portrayed in *The Family Instructor*. Recalling Starr's estimation of Defoe's conduct literature, towards this character of the oldest daughter/wife and mother at least, Defoe seems anything but 'detached from the people whom he puts in casuistical predicaments'.

This becomes more apparent in comparison with the 'failed' final dialogue which witnesses the return of her intransigent brother, who had departed for the Continent in Dialogue One and thus has not been afforded the internal monologues or emotional insights accorded to his sister. Now a poverty-stricken invalid, broken in mind and body, having suffered both amputation of a wounded arm and financial bankruptcy, the brother remains unable to reconcile himself with his father. Despite the emotional pathos of its content, there is something frustratingly monochromatic in the following scene in which the converted adult sister, whose repentance has been traced in such vivid emotional terms for readers, exhorts her brother to make amends with their father:

> *Sister.* You cannot but own my father has been provoked.
> *Bro.* You were of another Mind *once Sister.*
> *Sister. Dear Brother*, I acknowledge with the greatest Affliction imaginable, That I was doubly unhappy in being so; that I was too much the wicked Instrument to encourage you in that course, which has reduced you to this Misery; and it has cost me more Tears than you can imagine, to think that I that loved you so dearly, should have so much Hand in your Ruin.

---

[33] The wife's 'introspective episode' passage in question is also discussed in Penny Pritchard, *Before Crusoe*, 128–9.

> *Bro.* It has cost me more Blood, than it hast cost you Tears.
> *Sister.* That may be true too, but my Repentance has been severe enough ... I was your unhappy Pattern before, *I pray GOD extend the same Grace to you now*, that as we sinned together, we may be Witnesses together of our Repentance. (317)

Given readers' familiarity with the many vicissitudes suffered and caused by the sister on her journey to repentance, as depicted over the four previous dialogues, emotional depth is disappointingly absent in this scene. Though they abound elsewhere in previous dialogues, the lack of appended notes makes this exchange frustratingly difficult to assimilate with the previous four dialogues' representation of the oldest daughter. In essence, the wider narrative's didactic importance has been 'hijacked' by increased focus on the sister's narrative as an individual, and here she serves as little more than a pious mouthpiece for repentance.

This observation has something to do with how the cumulative impact of narrative as it pertains to an individual protagonist, and the literary representation of subjective experience, will come to be seen as an integral part of how readers perceive the protagonists of novels. If the footnotes and prefatory descriptions appended to the first four dialogues of Part Three of *The Family Instructor* began to convey a more fully realized subjective representation of character in their portrait of the oldest daughter, the concluding scene from Dialogue Five undermines this portrait with an abrupt return to the strictures of the unadorned dialogue format.

Countering Religious Indifference

There is a sort of poignancy in the fact that the wider narrative of the family which concludes with this dialogue—notwithstanding the problematic portrait of the oldest sister described above—found its beginnings in the contrastingly 'childlike' simplicity of the opening dialogue of Volume One of *The Family Instructor*, in which the innocent questions of a boy of 'five or six years old' come to awaken in his father a life-changing realization of his paternal failure to instil godliness in his family through religious instruction (48–66). In returning to this first narrative, I want to explore another aspect of Defoe's conduct works, which is their shared consideration of the dangers of ever-present sin in the world. Defoe's *Family Instructor* volumes and *Religious Courtship*, in parallel with contemporary conduct works and other 'more' didactically orientated forms of popular religious writing from this period (such as pamphlets, sermons, catechisms, and works of casuistry) abound with expository and sometimes elaborate schemes of advice for readers, often supplemented with helpful scriptural references to heighten the moral usefulness of the proffered advice. All of these works are concerned with sins of omission, such as the neglect of family spiritual instruction, failing to attend to Sunday sermons, or failing to ensure one's future spouse is both religious and of the correct religion.

The material evidence of sin is usually only fleetingly referenced; one example can be seen in the oldest siblings' cherished playbooks destroyed by the parents in Part One of *The Family Instructor*. Yet, even given the relative economy of the dialogue format, the attention furnished on the 'pleasures' of sin in Defoe's conduct literature as a whole is nominal. A case in point may be found in the narrative concerning the middle daughter's marriage in *Religious Courtship*. This story, detailed in Dialogue Two of Part Two, plays out the emotional complexity of seemingly the most incompatible of marital arrangements in the union of a Protestant wife with an extremely wealthy—but devout Roman Catholic—husband whom she (otherwise) loves dearly. This portrait of an earthly union abounding in every possible material and emotional advantage, save that of religious compatibility, is significant for the extent of the sumptuous wealth implied in the description of the new husband's estate, though it is not his material wealth which presents the greatest danger to his wife's spiritual welfare. The real danger is, again, the sin of omission presented by the daughter's and father's failure to ensure that the potential husband is a Protestant. I will return to this episode in *Religious Courtship* in a moment. First, however, I will consider how this particular sin of omission—passive indifference towards Protestant religious conviction—forms the narrative basis on which much of *A New Family Instructor* (1727) is constructed.[34]

Although the work begins with eighteen pages of prefatory context, ostensibly intended to establish the narrative's setting and family circumstances, in truth it lacks altogether the vivid rendering of character and incident which have previously been considered in relation to the earlier *Family Instructor* volumes and *Religious Courtship*. What this work *does* contribute to the wider discussion of Defoe's conduct literature, however, is its return to older and more rigid tenets of the didactic tradition. As described by Hunter, such works 'share a view that the times have become luxurious, indulgent, and precarious for anyone trying to lead a life of righteousness'.[35]

In this case, the precariousness of a righteous life—that is, a life guided by unshakeable Protestant conviction—is contingent on the insinuating and subtle ways in which ill-prepared young men can be converted to Roman Catholicism while travelling in Italy. Despite the extent and vehemence of his father's admonitions against just such a fate, this is the inevitable result for the oldest son whose narrative occupies the first dialogue of *A New Family Instructor*, precisely because he chooses to ignore his father's precepts.

Contrasting with the more heedless paternal figures in the 1715 and 1718 volumes of *The Family Instructor*, the unswerving rectitude of the father in *A New Family Instructor* provides a reliably consistent moral compass by which the myriad topics covered in this voluminous text may be negotiated. The topics range from the comparative merits of reading didactic fiction versus the shortcomings of Romance in Dialogue Two, to the aberrations of contemporary irreligious practice such as deism and atheism in the first

---

[34] For an excellent overview of anti-Catholicism and contemporary religious controversy more generally, as it applies to *A New Family Instructor*, see Owens, 'Introduction', *RDW*, iii. 15–23.

[35] Hunter, *Before Novels*, 252.

dialogue in Part Two. But the father's reliability comes at the not inconsiderable expense of a relative lack of narrative interest and variety. Periodically, certain authorial gestures are made towards maintaining the work's narrative momentum. In Dialogue Six, a series of younger children under the father's instruction are introduced. Ultimately, however, even these characters are deployed to preserve the narrative impetus first witnessed in Dialogue One's warnings against the spectre of Roman Catholic conversion as these younger siblings fall prey to the oldest son's 'frightening' missionary tactics.

Indeed, here, the representation of the father's younger children as innocently vulnerable to the converting efforts of their oldest brother is unconvincing, not least because of this dialogue's prefatory description of

> Two younger Daughters, one about 11, the other 8 Years old; so that all of them were capable of entertaining early Notions of the Idolatry and Absurdity of the Popish Religion, the Frauds of the Priests, the Pageantry of their Worship, the villainous Characters of their Popes, and the general horrid Enthusiasms, Forgeries, and Falshoods, practised by their Saints, Priests, and other Promoters of Popish Cheats in the World. (165)

The dialogue then depicts the father's elaborate (and progressively text-based) proof of 'the Idolatry and Absurdity of the Popish Religion' for his daughters' benefit, beginning with biblical exegesis and papal history before he invokes a series of Roman Catholic texts evidencing the corrupt practices of selling pardons and penances. Contrasted with the manner in which the first volume of *The Family Instructor* in 1715 had presented a young child's questioning of his place in creation (with responses from a father obliged to use language of a register suitable for a child's comprehension), there is every evidence that Defoe's didactic intentions in *A New Family Instructor* have superseded his earlier commitment to engaging readers with narrative content.

Despite these marked differences, what these works share are general moral precepts against the dangers of spiritual complacency or indifference, and in the cases of *A New Family Instructor* and *Religious Courtship*, how these dangers particularly manifest the insidious threat posed by Roman Catholicism. It is vital to stress how Defoe posed this threat as subtle and seductive in nature. In Dialogue One of *A New Family Instructor*, the oldest son confidently assures his father that Roman Catholicism poses little danger to him while abroad as his father has 'not brought me up in Ignorance', despite his father's recommended spiritual prophylactic: six months' preparatory religious study in order to guard the strength of—what can only then be—thoroughly understood Protestant conviction (52ff). Indeed, the father specifically asserts that the 'Pageantry of the Popish Religion' itself poses no threat to the well-educated Protestant mind:

> I have seen all the Legerdemain of the Priests, and of their Worship; and I must say, that if the Subtlety of the Priests, their Sophistry in Argument, and the Use they make of those pompous Things, does not insnare and captivate the Mind, I am persuaded, very few Protestants would ever be perverted by what they should see; for that, (I

mean in their publick Worship) especially, take it in the Gross, and particularly as practised abroad; 'tis such a Piece of Pageantry, such a Puppet Show of Religion, that nothing from a well instructed Mind can be in any Danger from the Sight of it. (54)

Without this preparation, the father concludes, 'an indifferent Protestant is half a Papist' (58). The father's awareness of his son's lack of fervent Protestant conviction aligns with one of Defoe's most prevalent biblical references; at its heart, Revelation 3:16 asserts the dangers inherent in the sin of religious indifference and in *A New Family Instructor*, as elsewhere in Defoe's writings, even as early as 1698, this sentiment intimates the author's concern that a lack of spiritual conviction is tantamount to a loss of faith altogether.[36]

The grave danger of religious indifference, so much greater than the moral threat of material wealth, is a theme we can further recognize from Defoe's novels, including *Moll Flanders*, *Captain Singleton* (1720), and *Roxana*. Returning to the episode in Dialogue Two of Part Two in *Religious Courtship*, in which the middle daughter conducts a family tour of her new husband's London apartments, there is a scene which captures this point with consummate clarity. Despite their discovery of all of the articles necessary for conducting a Roman Catholic Mass contained within her husband's private closet, both the newly married wife and her sisters remain entirely ignorant of the objects' true significance:

After they had gone through several Apartments, and had admired the fine Paintings, as indeed they well deserved, they came to his Closet … they were surprized with the most charming Pictures that their eyes had ever beheld, with abundance of Rarities … and in a little Room on one side of his Closet, upon a Table cover'd with a Carpet of the finest Work they had ever seen, stood a Pix or Repository of the Host, all of Gold, and above them an Altar-Piece of most exquisite Painting. (179–80)

Distracted by the artistic merits and cultural richness on display in this 'little Room on one side of his Closet', the three sisters miss the clear and present spiritual danger before them. It is tempting indeed to see in their mis-seeing a metaphor for the seductive charms of material realism, compelling narratives, and entertainment to be enjoyed in the reading of literature contemporary with *Religious Courtship*. In this sense, Defoe's capacity for representing lived experience through the tapestry of vivid material detail and compelling narratives within his novels (and some of his conduct works) continues to distract his readers from his other, less seductive, didactic objectives.

---

[36] Revelations 3:16 ('So then because thou art lukewarm, and neither cold nor hot, I will spue thee out of my mouth') is as relevant here as it is to Defoe's *An Enquiry into the Occasional Conformity of Dissenters in Cases of Preferment* (1698) in expressing Defoe's overriding concerns about the parlous state of contemporary religion. Defoe's position is further discussed in Defoe, *The True-Born Englishman and Other Writing*, ed. P. N. Furbank and W. R. Owens (London: Penguin, 1997), xvii–xix.

Further Reading

Laura A. Curtis, 'A Case Study of Defoe's Domestic Conduct Manuals Suggested by *The Family, Sex and Marriage in England, 1500–1800*', *Studies in Eighteenth-Century Culture*, 10 (1981), 409–28.

J. Paul Hunter, *Before Novels: The Cultural Contexts of Eighteenth-Century English Fiction* (New York: W. W. Norton, 1990).

N. H. Keeble, *The Literary Culture of Nonconformity in Later Seventeenth-Century England* (Leicester: Leicester University Press, 1987).

Andreas K. E. Mueller, 'Daniel Defoe's *The Family Instructor*, The Schism Act, and Jacobite Unrest: The Conduct Book as Political Act', in *Positioning Daniel Defoe's Non-Fiction: Form, Function, Genre*, ed. Aino Mäkikalli and Andreas K. E. Mueller (Newcastle upon Tyne: Cambridge Scholars Publishing, 2011), 125–47.

Maximillian E. Novak, *Daniel Defoe, Master of Fictions: His Life and Ideas* (Oxford: Oxford University Press, 2001).

Penny Pritchard, *Before Crusoe: Defoe, Voice, and the Ministry* (New York: Routledge, 2019).

Irving N. Rothman, 'Defoe's *The Family Instructor*: A Response to the Schism Act', *PBSA*, 74:3 (1980), 201–20.

G. A. Starr, *Defoe and Casuistry* (Princeton, N.J.: Princeton University Press, 1971).

William B. Warner, *Licensing Entertainment: The Elevation of Novel Reading in Britain, 1684–1750* (Berkeley, CA: University of California Press, 1998).

CHAPTER 6

THE GREAT POLEMICIST
Defoe's Pamphlets and Tracts

JEFFREY HOPES

The issues of generic definition and terminology which have so preoccupied critics of Defoe's fiction are no less pressing when it comes to his non-fictional works and in particular the mass of writing subsumed under the categories of pamphlets and tracts. Literary approaches to genre tend to privilege a work's formal characteristics, but when he published *A True Collection of the Writings of the Author of The True Born English-Man* in 1703, Defoe referred to the various pieces it contained as 'writings' and 'tracts'. In the table of contents, further generic definitions are provided for the first five items; of the four poems, three are listed as satires and the fourth (*The Mock Mourners*) as a poem. In the second edition published two years later, *The Shortest-Way with the Dissenters*, which had landed Defoe in the pillory, is referred to as a pamphlet, but the generic term for the contents of the volumes is 'tracts', a term which encompasses writings both in poetry and prose. Other words used by Defoe are 'pieces', 'loose pieces', 'writings', 'things', and 'books' (though the whole collection is also described as a book). The subtleties of generic distinctions were not Defoe's concern, and he clearly thought they would not bother his readers either.

The term 'tract' derived from the learned *tractatus*, whereas 'pamphlet' carried connotations of scurrility and libel. To be known as a pamphleteer was to be sneered at as a hack writer churning out short, polemical pieces for monetary gain. Despite the poor reputation of the genre, their brevity made them more widely read than many longer pieces. In the words of the seventeenth-century Puritan theologian William Ames, 'the worth of a writing doth not consist, in bulk and belly, but in synewes, veynes, and artereyes, which with good blood and spirits, may be couched into a little body'.[1] Ames's definition perfectly fits so many of Defoe's early pamphlets, a form that is best defined by its pithiness, its cheapness, and above all its immediacy. These pamphlets

---

[1] William Ames, *A Fresh Suit against Human Ceremonies in God's Worship* (1633), 2.

were written 'to the minute'; they participated in an ongoing controversy or debate and had to be written, printed, and sold as quickly as possible. What makes Defoe such a superior pamphleteer to so many of his contemporaries is precisely this agility and a clear conception as to not just what he wants to say, but to whom he wants to say it and for what specific purposes. Such focus and flexibility were bound to give rise to accusations of inconsistency, opportunism, and scurrility. Yet for all his ability to adapt to changing circumstances, Defoe created in his pamphlets and tracts a body of work in which he forged a coherent view of the subjects he addressed.

In later years Defoe began to take up questions raised in *The Review* (1704–13) to develop them more fully in tracts which sought to convey the image of a detached and impartial commentator. Yet even when he attempted to adopt a distanced and measured style, Defoe found it hard to resist the cut and thrust of polemics. A good instance of this is the series of six *Essays at Removing National Prejudices* (1706–7) that he wrote to expound the benefits of the Anglo-Scottish Union [SEE CHAPTER 20].[2] The first two, written in England, and the third which appeared after he arrived in Edinburgh, are doggedly didactic, taking his readers through the advantages to both countries of working together and putting historical rivalries behind them. But already at the end of the third essay, Defoe is taking notice of the anti-Union writings that were circulating in the Scottish capital, such as Andrew Fletcher's *State of the Controversy betwixt United and Separate Parliaments* (1706). By the fourth essay, Defoe had read a number of such tracts, in particular one by William Hodges to which he replies. The essay thus veers from a calm, detached assessment of the pros and cons of the Union, to a tit-for-tat polemic with his opponents. Despite the way this disorganizes the fourth *Essay*, one senses that Defoe is pleased to be back in his element, refuting, accusing, and cajoling his adversary. The fifth *Essay*, which Defoe claims he had not originally planned, intermixes the polemics with detailed considerations on the commercial dimension of the Union. Finally, the sixth *Essay* addresses the accusations of inconsistency that Hodges had directed at Defoe for his position on petitioning parliament. Again Defoe admits that he thought the previous one would have been the last, 'But every Day brings with it New Occasions of Debate, and 'tis in Vain for me to resolve upon silence, unless I will abandon Truth, and see it every Day insulted with Errors, both in Practice and Opinion' (*PEW*, iv. 177). His compulsive need not just to expound his views but to defend them against his critics leads him from one polemic to the next. When there was no reaction to his tracts Defoe was miffed and disappointed, as when he complains at the lack of replies to *A New Test of the Church of England's Loyalty* (1702), a pamphlet of which he

---

[2] *An Essay at removing National Prejudices against a Union with Scotland* (1706); *An Essay at removing National Prejudices against a Union with Scotland Part II* (1706); *An Essay at removing National Prejudices against a Union with Scotland Part III* (1706); *A Fourth Essay, at removing National Prejudices; with some Reply to Mr. H—dges and some other Authors, who have printed their Objections against an Union with England* (1706); *A Fifth Essay, at removing National Prejudices; with a Reply to some Authors, who have printed their Objections against an Union with England* (1707); *Two Great Questions considered ... being A Sixth Essay at removing National Prejudices against the Union* (1707).

was clearly particularly proud. Undeterred, Defoe brought out *A New Test of the Church of England's Honesty* two years later, referring to the earlier work as 'a yet Unanswer'd Pamphlet' (*PEW*, iii. 189).

Defoe often revelled in the disreputable nature of pamphleteering. He was never more at home than when engaged in close combat with an opponent, trading arguments but also insults. One crucial aspect of Defoe's polemical strategy is authorship. Anonymity was an important weapon, and one that has led to continuing debate about Defoe attributions in our own time. Before 1702, the great majority of Defoe's pamphlets were published anonymously, including *The True-Born Englishman* (1700) itself, though its author was quickly identified and Defoe signed several subsequent tracts as 'by the author of the *True-Born Englishman*'.[3] He continued publishing anonymous tracts partly because he often did not want his identity to be acknowledged, as for the sulphurous *Legion* pamphlets that were condemned as seditious by Parliament, and partly because, as in the occasional conformity debate, he sought to give the impression that his arguments were those of several authors, not just one. Yet one can sense even at this early stage in his career a clear tension between Defoe's consciousness of the advantages of anonymity and his desire to enhance his reputation as a genuine writer.

Two events led to him being obliged to give much greater acknowledgement of his authorship: the unauthorized edition of *A Collection of the Writings of the Author of the True-Born Englishman* (1703) and the reaction to the publication of *The Shortest-Way with the Dissenters* (1702), whose strategy of extreme exemplification and exaggeration of the High-Church rhetoric of writers such as Henry Sacheverell and Charles Leslie depended on its anonymity, leaving readers to choose to read it as a High-Church tract or as a Dissenting attempt to discredit their opponents.[4] The revelation of Defoe's authorship forced him into a strategy of acknowledgement, explanation, and, towards the government, contrition.[5] But once he had survived the ordeal of imprisonment and the pillory, Defoe was quick to capitalize on the notoriety of his pamphlet, issuing sequels and explanations and signing *The Shortest Way to Peace and Union* (1703), amongst other works, as being by the author of *The Shortest-Way with the Dissenters*. Similarly, various later pamphlets on trade and foreign affairs were flagged as being 'by the author of *The Review*'. In the final years of his career as a writer, Defoe adopted the pseudonym Andrew Moreton, in order to establish continuity between his various writings on social policy, moral reform, and trade. Both anonymity and acknowledged authorship were conscious tools in the diffusion of Defoe's pamphlets and tracts, corresponding to the tactical requirements of his political allegiances and his own personal preference for alternate recognition and self-effacement. Such a strategy led Defoe into almost intractable difficulties following the death of Anne and the accession of George I when he

---

[3] This is notably the case of the poems *The Mock Mourners* (1702), *The Spanish Descent* (1702), and *More Reformation* (1703).

[4] See Joseph Hone, *Literature and Party Politics at the Accession of Queen Anne* (Oxford: Oxford University Press, 2017), 155–66.

[5] Paula R. Backscheider, 'No Defense: Defoe in 1703', *PMLA*, 103:3 (1988), 274–84.

switched his allegiance to the Whigs whilst continuing to defend the previous ministry. The *White-Staff* tracts of 1714–15 and two works of 1717 arguing against the ennoblement of foreigners are the most spectacular examples of this. In both cases, Defoe explicitly denied his authorship, and in doing so pointed to its probability.[6]

When surveying the themes broached by Defoe in these works, it is convenient to divide them into five main areas: politics, religion, trade and finance, foreign affairs, and social and moral reform. These are broadly the categories adopted by the editors of the Pickering Masters edition of *Defoe's Political and Economic Writings*, and I shall use these categories in what follows. Yet no one was more aware than Defoe of the ways in which these themes were inextricably linked. The religious questions that Defoe wrote about before 1715 were the object of intense political controversy which divided the nation on both political and religious lines. Questions of trade and finance were bound up both with the political divide between landed and monied interests and with the impact of the War of the Spanish Succession. Social and moral reform was strongly linked both to religious debate and to a political divide that Defoe was often keen to trace back to the opposition of Puritan Dissenters to the corrupt and debauched morals of the courts of Charles I and Charles II. The balance of power in Europe, the maintaining of which Defoe considered the prime justification for England's involvement in the War, was both one between France and the rest of Europe and between Protestant and Catholic powers, this despite the complex pattern of alliances which saw, for instance, the Catholic Austrian Habsburgs opposed to Louis XIV. For Defoe, as for the great majority of his contemporaries, Catholicism, tyranny, and poverty went together, as did Protestantism, liberty, and prosperity.[7]

Politics and Religion

Defoe declared in 1713 that 'Writing upon Trade was the Whore I really doated upon,'[8] but surveying his output from the end of the seventeenth century through to the beginning of *The Review* in 1704, it is clear that he was wedded to politics and religion. Defoe made his name as a radical Whig and a Dissenter, and it is the articulation of these two identities which dictates the nature of his output during this period [SEE CHAPTERS 17 AND 20].[9] Defoe's politics were rooted in the principles of the 1688

---

[6] *The Secret History of the White-Staff* (1714); *The Secret History of the White Staff Part II* (1714); *The Secret History of the Secret History of the White Staff, Purse and Mitre* (1715); *An Argument Proving that the Design of Employing and Enobling Foreigners, Is a Treasonable Conspiracy* (1717); *A Farther Argument against Ennobling Foreigners* (1717).

[7] In what follows, pressure of space prevents me from referring systematically to Defoe's biographers in whose works fuller analysis of his pamphlets and tracts can be found. Backscheider, *Daniel Defoe*; Novak, *Daniel Defoe*; Richetti, *Life of Daniel Defoe*; Furbank and Owens, *Political Biography*. J. A. Downie, *Robert Harley and the Press* remains indispensable for Defoe's political writings.

[8] *Review*, ix. 425 (11 June 1713).

[9] K. P. R. Clark, 'Defoe, Dissent, and Early Whig Ideology', *Historical Journal*, 52:3 (2009), 595–614.

Revolution. He consistently maintained that James had vacated the throne under pressure not just from Parliament and the Church, but from the people, or to be more exact, from the freeholders whose property ownership gave them a stake in the country. 'The *Freeholders* are the proper Owners of the Country', he writes in *The Original Power of the of the Collective Body of the People of England* (1702): 'It is their own, and the other Inhabitants are but Sojourners, like Lodgers in a House, and ought to be subject to such Laws as the Freeholders impose upon them, or else they must remove' (*PEW*, i. 121). It was to property holders that the responsibility for rebuilding a political system based on a contractual conception of government was devolved. The pamphlets that Defoe wrote in the first years of the eighteenth century sought to demonstrate how monarchical and parliamentary authority is meaningless without a clear recognition of its basis in popular consent. Discussing the oaths of allegiance in 1702, Defoe remarked that 'Government and Allegiance are both Conditional, and Oaths of Subjects are always to be consider'd in a Constructive Sence, with Conditions of Protection, and the like'.[10] This conditionality legitimizes, indeed necessitates, political debate. Addressing the king directly in one of his most cogent statements of Revolution Principles, Defoe states boldly that 'Your Majesty knows too well the Nature of Government, to think it at all the less Honourable, or the more Precarious, for being Devolv'd from and Center'd in the Consent of your People'.[11]

The four principles that Defoe sets out in opposition to those put forwards by Sir Humphry Mackworth in his *Vindication of the Rights of the Commons of England* (1701) make this clear. They can be summarized thus: all government was originally designed to protect the property of the governed; if governors, including the monarch, abuse their authority, power returns to the people; no collective or representative body is infallible; and all laws must derive from reason to be valid. This last principle is particularly important as, according to Defoe, everyone is a judge of reason 'and therefore in his proper place ought *to be allowed to give his Reason in Case of Dissent*' (*PEW*, i. 108). The argument formulated in *The Original Power*, as well as being a powerful statement of his political theory, had a specific purpose, however. It was designed to justify the right to petition Parliament, a right exercised notably by the Kentish petitioners who in May 1701 presented a list of grievances to the Tory-dominated Commons, only for their petition to be declared seditious. The petitioners appealed to the king to counter the tyranny of the House of Commons, which they claimed had failed to protect the interests of its electors. Parliaments to Defoe were fickle assemblies whose positions would change according to electoral fortunes. They had no more right to immunity from criticism than a tyrannical monarch. Defoe developed this line of thinking in *Some Remarks on the First Chapter in Dr. Davenant's Essays* (1704). Charles Davenant had denied that the people could retain any rights independently of their elected representatives, but Defoe asserted the contrary and pointed to the way that 'the People' constituted a collective,

---

[10] *A New Test of the Church of England's Loyalty*, PEW, iii. 69.
[11] *Original Power*, PEW, i. 101.

public opinion which politicians could no longer ignore: 'And tho' the Collective Body of the People are not a fourth Estate, yet they are the Center of the other three Estates, from whom constitution is derived, and for whom 'tis form'd' (*PEW*, i. 138). This is the essential justification for Defoe's activity as a pamphleteer at this time.

The right to appeal to Parliament or the monarch on the basis of reason also lies at the heart of Defoe's mistrust of parties and his gradual accommodation to Robert Harley's doctrine of moderation. Defoe's early pamphlets are Whig and Williamite, but already in 1701 he was deploring that England had become 'the most Divided, Quarrelsome Nation under the Sun'.[12] When the great storm struck England in November 1703, he interpreted it not just as a judgement on irreligion and immorality, but on factions and unnecessary disputes. Moderation was called for, and ''tis very hard that a word expressive of the most Glorious Principle in the World, should become the Brand of reproach, and a Badge of Infamy to Parties'.[13] The doctrine of moderation enabled him to appeal alternately to his fellow Whigs and to moderate Tories. In pamphlets such as *A Challenge of Peace* (1703) or *Advice to All Parties* (1705), Defoe defined his own Whig politics as moderate and those of his opponents as extremist. It was a stance that he also cultivated during the negotiations towards the Union, notably in the six *Essays at Removing National Prejudices*. He adopted the phrase 'Peace and Union', used by Anne in her speech to Parliament on 9 November 1703, to sum up the objective of a country united at home in face of the threat from abroad. Like the cry of moderation, it was a rhetorical trick, but it was effective in branding his political opponents as fanatics.

Defoe's analysis of political parties, however, was more sophisticated than such an appeal to a notional middle way might suggest. He frequently went back over the history of England since the Restoration or even before, to point out the origins of party differences, but it was from the 1688 Revolution that he dated the divisions of his own day. The crucial development was the split between the Old and the Modern Whigs, the former clinging to the Country principles of opposition to the court and the latter prepared to hold the reins of power, engage in European war and, so he hoped, defend the Dissenters. The division was above all, Defoe said, between those who were

---

[12] *The Free-Holders Plea against Stock-Jobbing Elections of Parliament Men* (1701), 1–2.

[13] *The Lay-Man's Sermon upon the Late Storm* (1704), 11. The debate about moderation illustrates the way in which Defoe's publications participated in ongoing pamphlet controversies and the extent to which the subjects of these controversies were interrelated. The Presbyterian James Owen published *Moderation a Virtue: Or, The Occasional Conformist Justify'd from the Imputation of Hypocrisy* in 1703. Defoe replied in *The Sincerity of the Dissenters Vindicated, from the Scandal of Occasional Conformity, with Some Considerations on a Late Book, Entitul'd, Moderation a Vertue* (1703). Other replies were forthcoming, notably Mary Astell, *Moderation Truly Stated: Or, A Review of a Late Pamphlet, entitul'd, Moderation a Vertue. With a Prefatory Discourse to Dr. D'Aveanant* (1704), Samuel Grascombe, *Occasional Conformity a Most Unjustifiable Practice. In Answer to a Late Pamphlet, entituled, Moderation a Virtue* (1704), and Charles Leslie, *The Wolf Stript of His Shepherd's Cloathing, in Answer to a Late Celebrated Book intitul'd Moderation a Virtue* (1704). Owen was supported by the anonymous *Moderation Pursued, By a Paper Written for the Vindicating of Our Liturgy and Church from any Malevolence to Meetings* (1704), and Owen replied to his High-Church opponents, Grascombe and Leslie, in *Moderation Still a Virtue: In Answer to Several Bitter Pamphlets* (1704).

out of office and those who were in. Defoe, somewhat idiosyncratically, saw himself as a modern Whig, but he considered that it was the failure of the Whigs to unite that allowed those opposed to the Revolution settlement to return to power: 'Thus the whole Overthrow of the *Whig* Interest was owing to the Self-interested Management of some of the *Whigs* themselves; and the letting in a Flood of *High Flyers* and *Jacobites*, became the consequence of Acting for private Interest, and in Defiance of Principle'.[14] It was nonetheless easier for Defoe to demonize the high flyers than to try to unravel the complexities of Whig divisions. This is what he did in the brilliantly excoriating satire of the two parts of *The Secret History of the October Club* (1711), the topic of which was the group of Tory malcontents formed in opposition to Harley's moderate policies. The pose of the 'secret history'—an account purporting to convey inside knowledge—allowed Defoe to invent meetings, debates, and speeches that unmasked their participants as Jacobites committed to purely self-interested policies (they wanted to abolish all taxes and regarded credit as a Whig plot) and intent on whipping up mob violence, particularly against Dissenters.

The most challenging moments in Defoe's career as a political pamphleteer were the succession crises of 1702 and 1714. The death of the Dutch William III, to whom Defoe had been unswervingly loyal, and the accession of the very English Queen Anne, whose commitment to promote and protect the Church of England revitalized the High-Church Tories, led Defoe to write a series of pamphlets defending the memory of the deceased king. Defoe was particularly concerned to establish Anne's legitimacy on the basis of the Act of Settlement (1701), not on hereditary right which risked subsequently legitimizing the claims of the Pretender. In *The Succession to the Crown of England Considered* (1701), well before William died, Defoe had set out the options for the succession following the loss of Anne's only surviving son, the Duke of Gloucester, in July 1700. The next year, the High-Church *persona* of *The Shortest-Way with the Dissenters* gives thanks in the name of the country for the death of a foreign monarch: 'god has at last heard her Prayers, and deliver'd her from the Oppression of

---

[14] *The Old Whig and Modern Whig Revived* (1717), SFS, iv. 192. The distinction between Old and Modern Whigs was popularized by the Tory Charles Davenant in his two dialogues between Tom Double and his friend Whiglove, *The True Picture of a Modern Whig* (1701) and *Tom Double Return'd out of the Country* (1702). Davenant returned to the theme in 1710 with *Sir Thomas Double at Court*. Davenant's pejorative use of the term 'Modern Whig' to mean a Whig acting out of self-interest rather than principle was highly influential, not just among Tories, but among those who considered themselves as Old (and so principled) Whigs. Defoe frequently pointed to the disastrous effects of what in *An Appeal to Honour and Justice* (1715) he termed 'that unkind Distinction of Old Whig, and Modern Whig, which some of the former were with very little Justice pleased to run up afterwards to an Extreme very pernicious to both' (10–11). As this suggests, he thought that Old Whigs were the enemies of moderation, and it is in this sense that Defoe, at least after the events surrounding *The Shortest-Way with the Dissenters*, considered himself a Modern Whig. Whilst he could at times agree with the criticism directed at Whig opportunists, he also thought that politics without power was ultimately sterile and risked allying discontented Whigs with other ousted groups such as the Jacobites. For Defoe's views on the distinction between Old and Modern Whigs, see notably *Eleven Opinions about Mr. H[arle]y* (1711), *PEW*, ii. 192–8.

the Stranger'. Now the throne is possessed by 'a Royal, *English*, True, and ever Constant Member of, and Friend to the Church of *England*' (*PEW*, iii. 97).

The events surrounding the death of Queen Anne and the Whigs' return to power gave rise to similar alarms as Defoe anticipated not just a Jacobite rebellion, but a backlash against the government for which he had been writing. He continued to defend Harley's (now the Earl of Oxford) politics of moderation in his three *White-Staff* tracts in 1714 and 1715, being careful nonetheless to admit some of his failings, and in a series of provocative pamphlets he raised the spectre of the Jacobite threat only to dismiss it, a tactic designed to both alarm moderate Tories and reassure those who might be tempted to panic, notably by provoking a credit crisis. *An Answer to a Question that No Body Thinks of, viz. But What if the Queen Should Die?* (1713) is a good example of these apparently contradictory arguments. Defoe reassured his readers that 'we do not believe the Ministry are in any Kind, or with any Prospect near, or remote, Acting for, or with a Design or View to bring in the Pretender', only to warn that this does not mean there is no threat to the succession, as the Jacobites within and outside the ministry are just sitting quiet until the Queen dies (*PEW*, i. 211). The Pretender, he assures his readers, can no longer rely on French support, but the Queen must die sometime, and Papists and Tories 'take their Obligations to the Queen, to End with Her Majesty's Life' (225). Such wavering reflects the unease with which Defoe viewed the advent of a Hanoverian monarchy, which he correctly sensed would bring back the Whigs and render vulnerable all those associated with the previous ministry, himself included. The uncertainty of this period, the numerous self-reflexive passages in Defoe's tracts, the tortuous strategies used to chart his route from Harleyan propagandist to Hanoverian Whig in the service of Townshend nonetheless writing for Tory newspapers give rise to new techniques of writing which can be seen as prefiguring his fictional works. One example of this is his 'Quaker' tracts, in which he adopts the style of a blunt, moralistic Quaker admonishing the faults of the likes of Thomas Bradbury, Henry Sacheverell, the Duke of Ormond, and the Earl of Mar.[15]

Defoe's Revolution principles were rooted in the securing of the Protestant succession and the protection that the Act of Toleration (1689) brought to Dissenters. In his pamphlets and tracts, Defoe frequently defines political divisions and parties in religious terms, using 'the High Church party' to refer to the Tories, for instance. Most importantly, he defended what he called the Dissenting interest, a distinct group of people with a shared, though diverse, religious identity which found only partial political expression through the Whig party. Defoe never forgave Shaftesbury for not having

---

[15] *A Friendly Epistle by Way of Reproof from One of the People called Quakers, to Thomas Bradbury, a Dealer in Many Words* (1715); *A Seasonable Expostulation with, and Friendly Reproof unto James Butler, who, by the Men of the World, is Still'd Duke of O--------d, Relating to the Tumults of the People* (1715); *A Sharp Rebuke from One of the People called Quakers to Henry Sacheverell, the High-Priest of Andrew's Holbourn* (1715); *A Trumpet Blown in the North and Sounded in the Ears of John Erskine, call'd by the Men of the World, Duke of Mar* (1716). For a study of the multiplicity of Defoe's voices, see Robert James Merrett, *Daniel Defoe: Contrarian* (Toronto: University of Toronto Press, 2013).

opposed the application of the Test Acts to Dissenters. In *The Weakest go to the Wall, or the Dissenters Sacrific'd by all Parties* (1714), he recounts how Shaftesbury gained the Dissenters' acquiescence to the acts by promising to engineer their exemption from the penal clauses, only to go back on his word. Alderman Love, a prominent Dissenter who made his objections known, becomes Defoe's mouthpiece on this question when he says that 'It is very hard my Lord ... *That the Dissenters who are Protestants, should suffer under the same Predicament as Popish Recusants, and that the Protestant Religion cannot be secur'd without our Ruin*'. 'Thus the Dissenters were cheated by the — – *for the first Time*, how often they have been so serv'd since, time will discover' (*PEW*, iii. 342), remarks Defoe in a clear reference to the failure of the Whigs to oppose the 1711 Occasional Conformity Act. Once the Test Acts were passed, he claims, they were principally used against Dissenters: 'The *Low-Church* Men were the Men who brought it in, all the Promises they made to the Dissenters were forgot, and all the Attempts which have been made since that to exempt the Dissenters from the Penalties of it have been rendred vain, and been principally opposed by the *Low-Church* Men' (342–3). Defoe's defence of the Dissenters was, however, not uncritical. Whilst many of these pamphlets attacked the High Church, particularly over the question of occasional conformity, he also berated his fellow Dissenters, deploring the way he thought the Toleration Act, which he wholeheartedly defended, had weakened their religious fervour and collective identity.

Defoe's attitude to occasional conformity, the practice whereby Dissenters could assume public office if they annually took communion at church, is a matter of some debate.[16] His first two pamphlets on the subject constitute a strong and cogent critique of a practice which he saw as not just hypocritical, but profoundly damaging to the credibility of Dissenters. In *An Enquiry into the Occasional Conformity of Dissenters* (1698), Defoe attacked Sir Humphrey Edwin, who had famously conformed in order to take office as Lord Mayor of London before attending a Dissenting service in full regalia accompanied by his sword bearer. When John Howe, a Presbyterian like Defoe, sought to defend Edwin, Defoe replied that what was most shocking in such acts was that it was precisely disagreement with church communion which constituted one of the fundamental reasons for Dissent. Howe had claimed that differences between Dissenters and the Church were relatively minor, to which Defoe replied, 'If we differ from the Establish'd Church in small things only, we are to blame to make the Breach so wide',

---

[16] Two recent articles have stressed, from differing points of view, the importance of the occasional conformity controversy. Mark Knights, 'Occasional Conformity and the Representation of Dissent: Hypocrisy, Sincerity, Moderation and Zeal', *Parliamentary History*, 24:1 (2005), 41–57; Brent S. Sirota, 'The Occasional Conformity Controversy, Moderation, and the Anglican Critique of Modernity, 1700–1714', *Historical Journal*, 57:1 (2014), 81–105. Yannick Deschamps argues that Defoe changed his attitude to occasional conformity in the course of the debate. 'Daniel Defoe's Contribution to the Dispute over Occasional Conformity: An Insight into Dissent and "Moderation" in the Early Eighteenth Century', *ECS*, 46:3 (2013), 349–61. I am grateful to Nicholas Seager for allowing me to see his unpublished work on Defoe and occasional conformity, in which he challenges Deschamps's interpretation.

asking if they had suffered persecution for unimportant differences of opinion? His typically pithy conclusion is, "'Tis manifest, Force cou'd not *compel*, why shou'd Occasion *invite?*".[17]

Because he was opposed to the practice of occasional conformity, Defoe urged Dissenters to stay out of the dispute, assuring them that the bill posed no threat to them or to the Toleration.[18] He returned to the theme in *The Shortest-Way with the Dissenters*, in which the narrator quotes Howe's reply to the preface to Defoe's 1701 edition of the *Enquiry*. If the differences between them and the Church are so minor, he argues, then the Dissenters will see reason: 'The Contagion will be rooted out; the Disease being cur'd, there will be no need of the Operation, but if they should venture to transgress, and fall into the Pit, all the World must condemn their Obstinacy, as being without Ground from their own Principles' (*PEW*, iii. 107). Minus the irony, this is exactly what Defoe had said about occasional conformity. Defoe is thus in agreement, on this question, with his High-Church *persona* in opposition to his fellow Dissenter John Howe.

By 1703 the passing of a bill penalizing occasional conformity became a real possibility. 'Laws against *Occasional Conformity*, and Compelling People who bear Offices to a Total Conformity, and yet Force them to take and serve in those publick Employments, cannot contribute to Peace and Union', Defoe argues.[19] In *Peace without Union*, Defoe accepts that the bill undermines the Toleration Act and that the question is not just one of Dissenters' consciences, but of the law and Dissenters' civil rights. Toleration, for Defoe, was a right, not a concession: "'Twas an Act of Honesty, not an Act of Charity; 'twas paying a Debt, not making a Loan".[20] In *A Serious Inquiry into this Grand Question; Whether a Law to Prevent the Occasional Conformity of Dissenters, would not be Inconsistent with the Act of Toleration, and a Breach of the Queen's Promise* (1704), Defoe puts his faith in the queen to protect Toleration, whatever Parliament might say. In the event, it was the House of Lords which defeated the occasional conformity bill, until a much-diluted bill was finally passed in 1711. It is clear that Defoe's opposition to both the practice of occasional conformity and to the bills to make it illegal was constant and reflected his desire to preserve both the integrity of Dissenters and their civic rights. Changes in emphasis from one pamphlet to another reflect the audience he was addressing, rather than any fundamental shift in his stance on the question.

When the divisions between the High and Low Church groupings in Convocation burst into open controversy, first over Henry Sacheverell's sermon *The Perils of False Brethren* (1709) and later during the Bangorian controversy, Defoe returned to his denunciation of High-Church rhetoric and the threat it posed to the Toleration Act. His reaction to the voluminous controversy provoked by Benjamin Hoadly's sermon *The Nature of the Kingdom, or Church of Christ* (1717) was to shower ironic praise on the

---

[17] Defoe, *A Letter to Mr. How* (1701), 19.
[18] See *An Enquiry into Occasional Conformity. Shewing that the Dissenters Are no Way Concern'd in it* (1702).
[19] *A Challenge of Peace* (1703), 4.
[20] *A New Test of the Church of England's Honesty*, *PEW*, iii. 194.

bishop and his Erastian views, not wanting to be seen too close to the Low Church in their battle with the High Church, however much he shared their detestation of a common enemy.[21] Subsequently, Defoe's writings on religion moved in a direction which almost entirely divorced them from politics.

Trade and Finance

The debate on occasional conformity led Defoe to set out the precise issues which separated Dissenters from the Church. But he also argued that to these real differences of religious conscience were added others that prevented a true understanding between them. In 1704 Defoe defined the Dissenting interest in quite different terms from those used in the religious controversies:

> The Dissenters in *England*, generally speaking, are the Men of Trade and Industry; and what Estates they have, lye principally in Stock of Goods, Houses, and Credit. No Publick Disaster can befal the Nation, but what affects their Estates more than other Mens; Banks Stocks, Trade Foreign and Domestick, These are the first Things that suffer on any Publick Disorder; and none of those People who are thus Embark'd in Trade, can be properly thought to desire Disasters and Revolutions, because they are generally the first that feel it.[22]

The loyalty of the Dissenters to the Revolution and to the reigning monarchs is a common theme of his, but here he also sets out their stake in society. Independent from both the landed and the monied interests, they are the guardians of the dignity and the usefulness of trade, of the production and exchange of goods. To Defoe, Britain was fundamentally a trading nation [SEE CHAPTER 14]. The *Memoirs of Count Tariff* (1713) presents a history of commerce from the Restoration onwards in fictional guise. The work was one of several written at the time of the negotiation of the commercial treaties which formed a crucial part of the Treaty of Utrecht. In *An Essay on the Treaty of Commerce with France* (1713), Defoe sought to explain and defend the text of a treaty which he knew people would not read and which many considered he should be opposing. His defensive tone is even more apparent in *Some Thoughts upon the Subject of Commerce with France* which appeared the same year, wherein he refutes accusations that he had changed opinion on the desirability of continuing to trade with France, even in time of war. Defoe's defence of treaties which lowered import tariffs on foreign goods laid him open once again to the charge of inconsistency. Both before and after the Treaty of Utrecht, he was a fervent advocate of protectionist measures to protect home-produced textiles, in particular

---

[21] Defoe's most significant contributions to the Bangorian controversy are *A Declaration of Truth to Benjamin Hoadly* (1717) and *The Conduct of Christians Made the Sport of Infidels* (1717).
[22] *The Dissenters Answer to the High-Church Challenge* (1704), PEW, iii. 48–9.

the wool trade, which he saw as 'the Life and Blood of the whole Nation, the Soul of our Trade, the Top of all Manufactures'.[23] He argued in particular for a complete ban on the import of calicoes and silks from India, China, and Persia.[24] In 1719 he came to the defence of the weavers in Spitalfields who had rioted against the sale of cheap calicoes which undercut their own silk production, calling them the 'poor mistaken tumultuous Weavers' and demanding, not for the first time, that the wearing of imported calicoes be banned altogether. By criticizing the women who 'dress more like the Merry-Andrews of *Bartholomew* Fair, than like the Ladies and Wives of a Trading People', he implicitly condoned the attacks that took place against women who had their clothes ripped from them.[25] Defoe was no free-trader. His priority was the defence of British manufactures against cheap foreign imports, whether these be printed calicoes or Dutch gin.[26] None of this prevented him from arguing for treaties which made international trade easier.

Defoe also endorsed the activities of the trading companies which handled colonial trade. His support for such ventures was not uncritical; he pointed for instance to the responsibility of the East India Company in the importation of calicoes. He also warned of the excessive use of bullion to pay for imports from India and China, arguing that Britain should be exporting more of its own textiles, however little adapted British woollens might seem to hot climates. In 1711, however, he defended the Royal African Company's monopoly against interlopers, and the following year he examined the activities of the South Sea Company, including the way it was used to transform government securities into South Sea stock, so reducing the national debt [SEE CHAPTERS 29, 30, AND 31]. Defoe defended the scheme and was also optimistic about the trading activities of the company, even if these would involve seizing American ports from Spain, an objective that was hardly compatible with the attempts to secure a negotiated peace.[27]

It was in the area of finance that Defoe penned some of his most original and important tracts, drawing on essays in *The Review* and seeking to explain the complexities of credit, funds, debt, and speculation at a time when these new phenomena had developed on a hitherto unheard-of scale. Two important essays of 1710 dealt with public credit and loans, the first expounding Defoe's almost mystical view of credit as

> a Consequence, not a Cause; the Effect of a Substance, not a Substance; 'tis the *Sunshine*, not the Sun; the quickning SOMETHING, *Call it what you will*, that gives Life

---

[23] *An Humble Proposal to the People of England* (1729), 57.

[24] See *Reflections on the Prohibition Act* (1708), 4, in which Defoe praises a law prohibiting use of manufactured silks from India, China, and Persia as 'one of the happiest and best Laws we enjoy, relating to Trade'.

[25] *A Brief State of the Question between the Printed and Painted Callicoes, and the Woollen and Silk Manufacture* (1719), 4, 11. Cf. *The Just Complaint of the Poor Weavers Truly Represented* (1719). On the calico riots and the English textile manufacture in general, see Mark Cameron Harris, 'The Moral Economy of the 1719–20 Calico Riots', (unpublished doctoral thesis, University of Alberta, 2015).

[26] *A Brief Case of the Distillers, and of the Distilling Trade in England* (1726).

[27] *An Essay upon the Trade to Africa* (1711); *An Essay on the South-Sea Trade* (1712); *The Trade to India Critically and Calmly Consider'd* (1720).

to *Trade*, gives Being to the Branches, and Moisture to the Root; 'tis the *Oil* of the Wheel, the *Marrow* in the Bones, the *Blood* in the Veins, and the *Spirits* in the Heart of all the Negoce, Trade, Cash, and Commerce in the World. (*PEW*, vi. 53)[28]

Credit for Defoe was rooted in moral trustworthiness and probity, whether it be in individual transactions or on the level of the state. In this sense he sees it as rooted in Protestant and particularly Dissenting values. *An Essay on Loans* is an admirably clear explanation of the way the War of the Spanish Succession had been financed. Defoe's enthusiasm for these new means of raising money did not extend to speculation, however. His earliest tract on finance and trade, *The Villainy of Stock-Jobbers Detected* (1701), is a denunciation of stock-jobbing, the manipulation of the market by the buying and selling of stocks for short-term profit, often using inside knowledge obtained from politicians. It is a theme he returned to in *The Anatomy of Exchange-Alley* (1719), his most ferocious assault on speculation. This pamphlet was written shortly before the search for speculative profit engendered the spectacular crashes in Britain and France which resulted from the attempts to absorb national debts using the South Sea Company in Britain and John Law's Mississippi Company in France. For all his denunciation of stock-jobbing, Defoe's fascination with these pieces of legerdemain meant that he only saw their dangers very late. In *The Chimera: or, The French Way of Paying National Debts, Laid Open* (1720), Defoe lavishes praise on Law only to insert a belated warning in a final sentence that he seems to have added at the last minute. *The Case of Mr. Law, Truly Stated* (1721) is an exercise in being wise after the event and compares the events in the two countries, concluding that the two companies 'were overturn'd by their own Bulk, the unperforming Machines blew themselves up by the Force of their own Motion, and the Projectors are overwhelm'd with them' (*PEW*, vi. 193–4).[29] In addition to pamphlets on specific subjects of trade and finance, towards the end of his life Defoe wrote a number of more general works designed to educate public opinion on subjects of which he considered there was much ignorance.[30] All of these works need to be read in conjunction with his longer treatises, notably *The Complete English Tradesman* (1725–7), *A Plan of the English Commerce* (1728), and *A Tour thro' the Whole Island of Great-Britain* (1724–6), the last of which contains numerous first-hand descriptions of manufacturing and trading activities.

---

[28] For an enlightening and provocative discussion of Defoe's conception of credit, see Sandra Sherman, *Finance and Fictionality in the Early Eighteenth Century: Accounting for Defoe* (Cambridge: Cambridge University Press, 1996).

[29] This tract was written as a reply to Eustace Budgell's *A Letter to Mr. Law, upon his Arrival in Great Britain* (1721).

[30] *Brief Observations on Trade and Manufactures* (1720); *A Plan of the English Commerce* (1728); *An Humble Proposal to the People of England, for the Encrease of their Trade* (1729); *The Advantages of Peace and Commerce* (1729).

Foreign Affairs

Defoe's writings on trade and finance are inextricably bound up with Britain's involvement in the War of the Spanish Succession and its aftermath. On no other subject was Defoe so vulnerable to accusations of being a turncoat, as his early support for the war gave way to his later propaganda in favour of a negotiated peace after 1710. Yet while here, as elsewhere, his pamphlets and tracts responded to the flux of rapidly changing events and the requirements of his political masters, there is more consistency in Defoe's approach than he is often given credit for. There were several justifications for the country's involvement in the war, and their relative importance changed over time. In one of his earliest pamphlets on the subject, *Lex Talionis* (1698), written after the signing of the 1697 Treaty of Ryswick, Defoe regretted that the Nine Years' War had been a war of states, not of religion. In 1701 he addressed William as the defender of the Protestant Religion. Liberty, property, and trade were important issues, '*But these are all Antecedent to the Great Relative* Religion; *These are all but Circumstances to the Great Essential Circles drawn about the Great Center Religion*'.[31]

The principal reason for the resumption of hostilities in 1701 was the French recognition of Carlos II's designation of the Bourbon Philip Duke of Anjou as the future King of Spain, but Defoe always made it clear that dynastic issues were secondary to the religious and commercial consequences of the alliance between France and Spain. Writing in November 1700, just before Louis XIV recognized Carlos II's will, Defoe was confident that Louis would not risk a war over the succession. If he did, the chief threat to Britain would be from French access to the riches of Spain's trans-Atlantic trade: 'If the French get *Spain*, they get the greatest Trade in the World in their Hands; they that have the most Trade, will have the most Money, and they that have the most Money, will have the most Ships, the best Fleet, and the best Armies; and if once the French master us at Sea, where are we then?'.[32] Defoe did not think, however, that on its own Louis's support for Philip, any more than his recognition of the Pretender as the rightful King of England, was sufficient justification for war.[33] It was the balance of power in Europe that mattered most. In this he adhered to William's policy of partitioning the Spanish throne. In 1711 he published *The Felonious Treaty*, a strong defence of William's secret Partition treaties in which he argued that though there was now no prospect of wresting the throne of Spain from the French, the objectives of partition could still be pursued by obtaining commercial concessions from Spain and providing support for the Barrier Treaty protecting Holland from the threat of French invasion via the Spanish Netherlands.

Defoe's earlier scepticism as to the chances of defeating France, as laid out in the early numbers of *The Review*, only changed following Marlborough's spectacular victories at

---

[31] *The Danger of the Protestant Religion Consider'd* (1701), *PEW*, v. 59.
[32] *Two Great Questions Consider'd* (1700), *PEW*, v. 39.
[33] See *Reasons against a War with France* (1701).

Blenheim and Ramillies in 1704 and 1706. It was in the pages of *The Review* that Defoe subsequently commented on the conduct of the war, only returning to it in his pamphlets when he became one of the chief propagandists for the drive for peace initiated by the Harley government after 1710. Defoe initially argued that peace should be negotiated jointly by all the confederates, but in 1712 he joined Swift in denouncing the way Britain had been betrayed by its allies, in particular the Dutch, who were accused of profiting from Britain's financing of the war effort for their own ends, but also the Holy Roman Empire, accused of disloyalty and a lack of commitment to the war. He did not subscribe, however, to the call from some Tories for a war against the Dutch.[34] As the peace negotiations drew to a conclusion, Defoe was at pains to present them not as an opportunity but as a blow to the Jacobites, and he sought to reassure those who thought the country had sold out to France, by opposing the destruction of the fortifications at Dunkirk which had been returned to Britain. Throughout the whole process of the peace negotiations then, Defoe asserted the essential coherence and continuity of the objectives that he had always held that Britain should pursue, through the negotiation of the peace as previously by the conduct of the war. Defoe's subsequent tracts on European affairs are few in number, but include two written at the end of the 1720s when the conflict with Spain was rekindled. Defoe joined the clamour for war from London merchants, arguing that Britain had nothing to lose. Once again, he underlined the connections between the Revolution principles of liberty, property, and religion and Britain's vital trading interests:

> Our Interest is our Trade; and our Trade is, next to our Liberty and Religion, one of our most valuable Liberties; if our Neighbours pretend to shut the Door against our Commerce, we must open it; and that by Force, if no other Means will procure it. To invade our Commerce is to invade our Property, and we may, and must defend it; and therefore I say, to invade our Trade is to begin a War; and will any Man then ask me, whether we shall have *War* or *Peace*?[35]

Even at this late stage in his writing career, Defoe's priorities had not changed. For all his recognition that peace was the necessary condition for commerce to flourish, if it came to a choice between the two, trade was worth going to war for.

Social and Moral Reform

One final heterogeneous group of pamphlets and tracts concerns the various moral and social questions that interested Defoe throughout his career. At the start of the century the campaign for moral reform was led by the Societies for the Reformation of Manners,

---

[34] See *A Farther Search into the Conduct of the Allies, and the Late Ministry* (1712); *An Enquiry into the Danger and Consequences of a War with the Dutch* (1712); *Imperial Gratitude* (1712).

[35] *The Evident Approach of a War* (1727), 32.

in which Dissenters were particularly active. Defoe's poems *Reformation of Manners* (1702) and *More Reformation* (1703) are linked to this movement, though they are also satires on the vices and hypocrisy of the rich and powerful. The need for the nation to reform remains a constant in Defoe's writing, though he frequently examines the social and economic effects of vice and luxury. In his earlier tracts, notably *The Poor Man's Plea* (1698), Defoe denounces the unequal treatment of rich and poor:

> 'Tis hard, Gentlemen, to be punish'd for a Crime, by a man as guilty as our selves; and that the Figure a man makes in the World, must be the reason why he shall or shall not by liable to a Law: This is really punishing men for being poor, which is no Crime at all; as a Thief may be said to be hang'd, not for the Fact, but for being taken. (*RDW*, vi. 29)

In words that anticipate *Moll Flanders* (1722) and *Roxana* (1724), he concludes that 'To think then to effect a Reformation by Punishing the Poor, while the Rich seem to Enjoy a Charter for Wickedness, is like *taking away the Effect, that the Cause my cease*' (32).

This streak in Defoe's tracts continues later, but it is accompanied by a clear distinction between what in the nineteenth century would be called the deserving and the undeserving poor. The deserving poor were those who worked hard to earn a living in often straitened circumstances, as at the time of the severe depression of 1717–19. The undeserving poor were 'a crowd of clamouring, unimploy'd, unprovided for poor People, who make the Nation uneasie, burthen the Rich, clog our Parishes, and make themselves worthy of Laws, and peculiar Management to dispose of and direct them'.[36] It was they who sank into drink, prostitution, and crime. Defoe was sympathetic to the plight of particular groups of workers, in particular in the textile industries, as we have seen, though he rejected their combinations (early trade unions). To other groups however he was intensely hostile. The hackney-coach drivers and the watermen of London provoked his ire, as did barmen and shoe-shiners. But it was the behaviour of servants that he criticized most, just like Jonathan Swift, deploring their insolence and seeking ways to reduce what he saw as their excessive wages.

In his old age Defoe became something of a grumpy, or as he put it himself, '*an over officious* Old Man',[37] observing the growth of the London he loved yet increasingly despairing of the social problems that seemed to plague it. Beginning with *The Great Law of Subordination Consider'd* (1724), an extraordinary catalogue of the insubordination of servants and others, and continuing with his Andrew Moreton tracts, Defoe painted a picture of a London beset by street robberies, gambling, and prostitution. He was not short of ideas as to how to put things right: better street lighting would make robbers more visible, and more and better trained watchmen would be able to catch them; female servants would be prevented from leaving service on a whim and sliding into prostitution; Protestant monasteries would be set up to form close-knit, virtuous communities. Over the whole country, he called for a reform of local government so

---

[36] *Giving Alms no Charity* (1704), *PEW*, viii. 174.
[37] *The Protestant Monastery* (1727), *PEW*, viii. 239.

that the cost of looking after the poor could be brought down and the venality of parish officers brought to an end. All of these ideas and others were submitted to Parliament in the vain hope that statesmen would still be reading his tracts.[38]

* * *

Forty-two years separate the publication of Defoe's earliest-known and probable-latest tracts, *A Letter to a Dissenter from his Friend at the Hague* (1688) and *A Brief State of the Inland or Home Trade, of England* (1730), forty-two years of political turmoil and religious conflict, of the expansion of trade and the creation of the institutions and practices of financial capitalism, a period dominated by a war which bankrupted the countries of Europe and which saw the gradual emergence of a modern, urban society. But they were also years of an unprecedented increase in the output of printed material, much of it for immediate consumption. Defoe's pamphlets and tracts are a significant part of this output and give us a unique insight into the subjects that fascinated him. His polemical involvement in these subjects hardly slackened, and right to the end he continued to cross swords with his adversaries, to instruct his readers, and to defend the causes he held dear. His pamphlets and tracts also give us an insight into the man himself, his obsessions, his phobias, his almost perverse tendency never to take the easiest and most direct route, the extraordinary range of his interests, and above all the virtuosity, the verve, and the tirelessness of his pen.

Further Reading

Paula R. Backscheider, *Daniel Defoe: His Life* (Baltimore, MD: Johns Hopkins University Press, 1989).
Paula R. Backscheider, 'No Defense: Defoe in 1703', *PMLA*, 103:3 (1988), 274–84.
K. P. R. Clark, 'Defoe, Dissent, and Early Whig Ideology', *Historical Journal*, 52:3 (2009), 595–614.
J. A. Downie, *Robert Harley and the Press: Propaganda and Public Opinion in the Age of Swift and Defoe* (Cambridge: Cambridge University Press, 1979).
P. N. Furbank and W. R. Owens, *A Political Biography of Daniel Defoe* (London: Pickering and Chatto, 2006).
Joseph Hone, *Literature and Party Politics at the Accession of Queen Anne* (Oxford: Oxford University Press, 2017).
Robert James Merrett, *Daniel Defoe: Contrarian* (Toronto: University of Toronto Press, 2013).
Maximillian E. Novak, Daniel Defoe, *Master of Fictions: His Life and Ideas* (Oxford: Oxford University Press, 2001).
John Richetti, *The Life of Daniel Defoe: A Critical Biography* (Oxford: Wiley-Blackwell, 2005).
Sandra Sherman, *Finance and Fictionality in the Early Eighteenth Century: Accounting for Defoe* (Cambridge: Cambridge University Press, 1996).

---

[38] The Moreton tracts are *Every-Body's Business, Is No-Body's Business* (1725); *Parochial Tyranny* (1727); *The Protestant Monastery* (1727); *Augusta Triumphans* (1728), and *Second Thoughts are best* (1729).

CHAPTER 7

DEFOE'S PERIODICAL JOURNALISM

ASHLEY MARSHALL

DANIEL DEFOE was a prominent and prolific journalist in late Stuart and early Hanoverian Britain, though his periodical writings continue to receive little critical attention. Even Maximillian E. Novak's chapter on 'Defoe's Political and Religious Journalism' has as much to say about complementary pamphlets as it does about Defoe's periodicals.[1] John McVeagh's edition (2003–11) of *The Review* (1704–13) will with any luck inspire more work on that important journal; some of the best recent commentary on it is to be found in Brian Cowan's and Nicholas Seager's review essays on McVeagh's edition.[2] Defovians have mined *The Review* for particulars, but few engage with it in its entirety or with Defoe's larger corpus of journalistic writing. As Cowan aptly observes, 'his relatively limited work as a novelist' has 'overshadow[ed] his prodigious achievement as a periodical essayist'.[3] Only one monograph has been devoted to *The Review*, and none to his broader periodical canon.[4] What scholars have not sufficiently explored is what makes *The Review* distinctive among contemporaneous papers; the particular nature of Defoe's late Stuart journalistic objectives has not been fully understood. Cowan has rightly highlighted the radicalism of *The Review*'s ideology, and that point will be amplified in what follows: Defoe is a Whig writing against Tories, but I shall argue that he also has a decidedly and radically Whig understanding of the role of journalism in cultivating public participation in government. This is especially true of Mr Review. Defoe's journalistic production changes markedly in the reign of George

---

[1] Maximillian E. Novak, 'Defoe's Political and Religious Journalism', in *The Cambridge Companion to Daniel Defoe* ed. John Richetti (Cambridge: Cambridge University Press, 2008), 25–44.

[2] Brian Cowan, 'Daniel Defoe's *Review* and the Transformations of the English Periodical', *HLQ*, 77:1 (2014), 79–110; Nicholas Seager, '"He reviews without Fear, and acts without fainting": Defoe's *Review*', *ECS*, 46:1 (2012), 131–42.

[3] Cowan, 'Daniel Defoe's *Review*', 79.

[4] William Lytton Payne, *Mr. Review: Daniel Defoe as Author of The Review* (New York: King's Crown Press, 1947).

I, when he becomes more anonymous and adversarial, and his relationship to the Whig party more complex.

Defoe belonged to a new culture of periodical journalism, a culture that emerged after the 1695 lapsing of the Licensing Act. The scale of periodical production in the generation after 1695 was unprecedented. The first daily newspaper appeared in the spring of 1702, moreover, which meant that there was not only an abundance of competing voices, but also a new craving for more immediate information. Defoe was an active contributor to this new culture—in his capacity as Mr Review, he wrote more than four million words, and he was involved in numerous other papers—as well as a meta-commentator on it. He frequently expresses his anxiety about the implications of a sudden surge of news-related publications, about the 'Loads of Weekly Journals!'.[5] *The Commentator* (a probable attribution), concisely captures one advantage of the emerging news culture: the free press is 'a *natural Appendix* to a just Government, as it gives every Man a Right to speak to it'.[6] Whether or not these are Defoe's words, the sentiment is in keeping with his comments in more solid attributions. Throughout *The Review* (and elsewhere), Defoe offered assessments of other outlets. This is central to his mission in the Scandal Club feature of *The Review*, where his 'Society' enumerates the falsehoods and partisan misrepresentation of rival papers. Elsewhere Defoe praised Jean de Fonvive's anti-Catholic *The Post Man* (1695–1730) as written 'most to the Purpose, and most worth Reading of any Paper yet Extant'.[7] He scrapped with Jonathan Swift (writing as Mr Examiner), Charles Leslie (*The Rehearsal*), and even his fellow Whigs John Tutchin and George Ridpath (*The Observator*) and Richard Steele (whose treatment of the Dutch in *The Guardian* of 1713 offended him).

In the new culture of daily news that emerged after 1695, and especially after Anne's accession in 1702, Defoe played a prominent role. My contention is that he also played a role different from any other contemporary journalist. Unlike more conservative periodical writers such as Swift, he engaged systematically with other periodicals and their authors, and his most important paper, *The Review*, represents a significantly different kind of enterprise from anything else written at the time. What ideology informs his journalism, and what is the nature of his particular contribution to the periodical culture of the early eighteenth century?

Defoe's Periodical Canon

Determining the number and nature of Defoe's contributions with any confidence is well-nigh impossible given the enormous uncertainties about attribution [SEE CHAPTER 34]. In addition to *The Review*, P. N. Furbank and W. R. Owens list three

---

[5] *The Commentator*, no. 3 (8 January 1720), *RDW*, ix. 25.
[6] *The Commentator*, no. 2 (4 January 1720), *RDW*, ix. 22.
[7] *Review*, ii. 118 (19 April 1705).

periodicals as definitively (and exclusively) by Defoe: *The Master Mercury* (1704), *Mercator* (1713–14), and *The Manufacturer* (1719–21). Three other journals—*The Monitor* (1714), *The Commentator* (1720), and *The Director* (1720–1)—are deemed 'probable' attributions. His contributions to papers run by other editors represent tricky cases. He was likely responsible for minor pieces in *The St. James's Post*, in *Applebee's Original Weekly Journal*, and in *The Universal Spectator*, all separate entries in Furbank and Owens's *Critical Bibliography* of Defoe's works. As they point out, Defoe was likely—briefly—a 'proprietor of the *Edinburgh Courant*, the *Scots Post-Man* and probably also the *Daily Post*, but it does not necessarily follow that he ever wrote for them'. He was in some fashion involved in *The White-hall Evening Post*, but we do not know the nature of his participation or what numbers he wrote, if any. He contributed to *The Flying-Post*, but to what extent is indeterminate; he insisted that he supplied only a few paragraphs, but that was likely a strategic understatement (*Letters*, 446). Defoe claimed to have had an editorial role in both *Mercurius Politicus* and Nathaniel Mist's *Weekly Journal*, and he almost certainly wrote 'extensively' for both, but as Furbank and Owens rightly conclude, trying to identify his contributions is a fool's errand.[8] In what follows, I will treat only those periodicals about which we can have reasonable confidence.

Mr Review

The Review (February 1704–June 1713) was one of the foremost papers of Anne's reign, and both in terms of word count and ideological argumentation it represents a major part of Defoe's canon. Critics, however, have shown relatively little interest in engaging with its contents or in placing it alongside contemporaneous periodicals. In the introduction to his edition, McVeagh explains Defoe's contribution as Mr Review in these terms:

> Defoe lifted periodical journalism out of rabid politics or whimsy and offered a civil and intelligent public discussion of modern affairs, in the process developing the kind of relationship with his readers which suggested the shared values which Steele and Addison would deepen with their reading public a few years later. Though literature may not have been Defoe's primary object, he made the *Review* in some ways the most interesting example—as it was the first—of a new genre: the eighteenth-century periodical essay.[9]

'Where Defoe's *Review* chiefly differs from [his] predecessors' outlets', he continues, 'is in its literary excellence', its 'intellectual range and energy' (i. xv). McVeagh's précis is not entirely wrong, though it does underestimate and obscure Mr Review's radical politics

---

[8] Furbank and Owens, *Critical Bibliography*, 242–60; quotation 242.
[9] *Review*, i. xiv.

and, yes, often 'rabid' partisanship. What it does not help us understand is how *The Review* connects with the broader periodical culture of the moment. What is the nature of the contents of Defoe's most important journal, and how (beyond 'intellectual range and energy') does it compare with those of other outlets?

At the centre of *The Review* is Mr Review himself, a confident, outspoken moralizer whom Defoe clearly wanted to be read as the author himself. In other words, Defoe does not create a clearly fictional persona, a 'character' à la Isaac Bickerstaff, but tries to appear as a man speaking directly and honestly to his readers. He assertively, if sometimes disingenuously, reminds readers of his own lack of artifice: 'I pretend to speak as plain *English* as any-body, and too plain for some People'.[10] The persona he projects depends upon this pose of unpolished candour. Unlike Swift in *The Examiner*, Defoe eschews anonymity, collapsing the distance between author and persona. The persecuted Mr Review is real, one and the same with the persecuted Daniel Defoe.

This voice unifies a paper that is anything but single-minded in its coverage. Mr Review comments widely on the state of England (and Scotland) and on the balance of power in Europe.[11] Over the course of its nine years, his paper—which changed titles several times,[12] but was always known as *The Review*—advocates 'PARTY-PEACE',[13] toleration of religious Dissent, the Protestant succession at home, and the Protestant interest abroad. But it is bigger than those concerns, more multidimensional, addressing issues related to partisan politics, the War of the Spanish Succession, the Union with Scotland, and religious controversies at home and abroad, as well as (for example) moral reform, Presbyterian confession, African trade, the treatment of insolvents, and the lamentable shortage of engineers in England. In the 'Scandal Club' sections of the paper—present only in 1704–5—he adds a more gossipy dimension, criticizing not only other journalists, but also any misbehaving citizens: the 'Society' behind the Club passes judgement on recalcitrant children, fops and snobs, adulterous husbands and faithless wives. This is as inclusive a paper as we find in late Stuart Britain. Some scholars have remarked upon the way the tittle-tattling 'distract[s] … from power politics';[14] conceivably Defoe imagined that his moral judgements might lend credence to his party-political ones. In any case, after the early years of *The Review*, the latter—very broadly defined—tend to dominate.

The Review varies across its lifespan in both focus and tone, though some preoccupations are constant, especially the dissemination of Whig notions about power,

---

[10] *Review*, i. 105 (29 April 1704).

[11] What follows in this section is a précis of an argument I have made in *Political Journalism in London, 1695–1720: Defoe, Swift, Steele and their Contemporaries* (Woodbridge: Boydell and Brewer, 2020).

[12] The original name was *A Weekly Review of the Affairs of France: Purg'd from the Errors and Partiality of News-Writers and Petty Statesmen, of all Sides*; after seven numbers Defoe dropped 'Weekly'. In February 1705, it changed to *A Review of the Affairs of France, with Observations upon Transactions at Home*; in 1707, the title became *A Review of the State of the British Nation*.

[13] Defoe uses this phrase frequently (for example, *Review*, ii. 2).

[14] McVeagh, 'Introduction', *Review*, i. xxxix.

religious toleration, and trade. Initially, Mr Review focuses primarily on the emergence of France as a power. From 1705, because of the general election, the perspective becomes less historical, more present-centred and topical, and more domestic. In 1705, Mr Review zeroes in on High Church Tories, and a year later he is predominantly occupied with matters relating to trade, credit, and debt. From fall 1706 and through 1707, his attention is directed at the Union, his aim to advocate for England's official connection to its Protestant northern neighbour. By 1708–9, in the wake of the abortive Jacobite invasion, Mr Review has returned to his attack on the high-flying Tories, renewing his assault on traitorous Jacobites masquerading as mere high Anglicans. 1708 is an election year, and Defoe works to convince readers 'that our *High-Flying* Gentlemen would be fatal to the Nation'.[15] The other *idée fixe* of 1708–9 is the War of the Spanish Succession, of which Mr Review is (at this point) unequivocally supportive. The following year, writing from Scotland, Defoe raises concerns about the ongoing Jacobite threat, champions the naturalization of foreign Protestants, and rebukes those who believe that Scottish Episcopalians have been persecuted for their religion. In 1710–11, he follows the trial of Henry Sacheverell and weighs in on the ministerial change that brought the Tories back to power. *The Review* of 1711–13—its last years—broadens out, holding forth on the war and the problem of acceptable peace terms, trade and public credit, the threat posed by the high Tory October Club, England's alliance with the Dutch, the question of toleration for Episcopalians in Scotland (which he opposes), and the security (or not) of the Protestant succession.

The political outlook and tone of *The Review* also change with circumstances [SEE CHAPTER 20]. Defoe's paper is initially moderately Tory; between 1708 and 1710, Mr Review is militantly anti-Tory and anti-High Church; after 1710, according to the standard account, Defoe writes as an apologist for Robert Harley, which means supporting Tory positions and policies that are out of sync with his own Whig values. *The Review* was perhaps launched at Harley's bidding, and J. A. Downie suggests that at its outset it served as a 'a tory organ', designed 'to cajole the moderate tories into maintaining their support for the government's war-effort'.[16] But Mr Review's position vis-à-vis the ministry became complicated, and in fact the degree to which *The Review* was a government paper varies from year to year (indeed more frequently). This reflects Defoe's own conflicted position: he clearly wished to be loyal to Harley, but he was also manifestly uncomfortable with the government's agenda under Harley's leadership. I have traced the party-political evolution of Defoe's paper elsewhere,[17] so will here offer only a précis.

Defoe could initially support Harley in good conscience. The hot-button issue of the 1704–5 parliamentary session was the high-flyers' attempt to 'Tack' the occasional conformity bill onto a money bill to force its passage. Harley enlisted moderate Tories to join

---

[15] *Review*, v. 141 (29 May 1708).
[16] J. A. Downie, *Robert Harley and the Press*, 65.
[17] See Ashley Marshall, 'Robert Harley and the Politics of Daniel Defoe's *Review*, 1710–13', *1650–1850*, vol. 24 (2019), 54–97.

with Whigs against this scheme, and throughout the 1705 election campaign Defoe zealously supported Harley's cause, seeking to alienate moderate Tories from the high-Tory Tackers. In 1706–8, the situation was more complex. While Defoe was espousing (some of) Harley's ideas, he was also working in Scotland as an intelligence agent, increasingly frustrated and disillusioned by Harley's non-communication, and less inclined to do the minister's bidding. In 1708, Harley was dismissed, freeing up Mr Review to serve—again, in good conscience—a Whig government, to voice his own solidly Whig principles, and to savage everything Tory. That he believed his polarizing declarations seems difficult to doubt: 'to *Act Legally*', pronounces Mr Review, 'is to *Act Whiggishly*', and 'A Tory by Principle, herds with a Jacobite, and a Jacobite by the very Nature of the Thing, shakes Hands with a Papist'.[18]

In 1710, Anne made a controversial ministerial change—out with the Whigs, in with the Tories—and *The Review* had again to shift its position. Defoe once more found himself to be Harley's man: Furbank and Owens aptly describe him as 'a would-be Whig and praiser of the old ministry', awkwardly obliged to serve the ousters of that ministry. He was playing a role, that is, that was 'hopelessly false'.[19] Downie maintains that, in 1710–13 as earlier, 'Defoe defended and justified the conduct of the government at all times', but this is not the case. Mr Review's ambivalence about the ministerial change is manifest, and he insists—seemingly cautioning the new leaders—that they must 'all be *Whiggs* in … Management'.[20] Defoe describes the Tories in October 1710 thus: they 'stick at nothing; they Bribe, Feast, make Drunk, and Debauch the People', and 'they regard no Justice, no Truth of Fact'.[21] Harley is building a (perhaps moderate) Tory administration; Mr Review is doggedly asserting that the Whigs and only the Whigs are the defenders of 1688, and that all Tories are enemies to the Revolution settlement and thus to the English constitution.[22] Downie also overstates the degree to which *The Review* promotes Harley's bid for a speedy settlement of the War of the Spanish Succession (1701–14). Like most of his contemporaries, Defoe was eager for a good peace but he routinely cautions that sufficiently favourable terms cannot be had until France has been roundly beaten. Eventually, by late 1711, as Downie points out,[23] Mr Review does change his tune, shifting from 'no peace without Spain' to 'no peace without partition'—a move that brings him more in line with Harley's and the Tory government's position. Is this a matter of Defoe selling out to support his boss and benefactor? Not necessarily. The First Partition Treaty (1698), dividing the Spanish empire, was the (temporary) achievement of Defoe's hero-king, William III. Defoe, moreover, persistently voices his concern for a (Protestant-favouring) balance of power in Europe, and significantly altered circumstances naturally affected the political calculus. When the

---

[18] *Review*, vii. 388, 482 (3 October 1710, 25 November 1710).
[19] Furbank and Owens, *Political Biography*, 124.
[20] *Review*, vii. 305 (19 August 1710).
[21] *Review*, vii. 409 (14 October 1710).
[22] See, for example, *Review*, vii. 306 (19 August 1710), vii. 458 (11 November 1710).
[23] Downie, *Robert Harley and the Press*, 140.

Austrian emperor Joseph I died abruptly in April 1711, he was succeeded by his brother, Charles. Charles was also the Allies' designee for the Spanish throne—but to give him both Austria and Spain would (many thought) be every bit as destructive to the balance of power in Europe as a Franco-Spanish union. Earlier advocates of Charles's accession began instead to clamour for a partition, Defoe among them.

Mr Review's position vis-à-vis successive ministries shifts, but the ideological basis of his periodical is staunchly Protestant Whig. In March 1711, Mr Review scorns those who 'deny Parliamentary Limitation of the Crown', and throughout he emphasizes the limits of royal power.[24] That such a committed Whig would affirm that '*It is the Undoubted Right of the Parliament of Great Britain, to Limit the Succession of the Crown*' is not surprising, but I do want to stress just how often he feels the need to remind his readers of this truth.[25] His rejection of *jure divino* dogma is total: 'the Phantastick Doctrine of the Divine Right of Princes has been most industriously supported by the Devil in the World'.[26] Like most late Stuart Whig journalists, Mr Review disparages the Tories for their 'abject Slavish Principles', their 'Non-Resisting Banter', their 'Passive Subjecting the Laws to the Will and Lust of a Tyrant', and so on.[27] He declares 'it Criminal for any Man to assert, *The Illegality of Resistance on any Pretence whatever*';[28] as Cowan has noted, Defoe's notions about resistance are not moderate but radical Whig. Mr Review not only reasoned that resisting James II in 1688 was legitimate, for example, but thought that such resistance 'could be used again'. This distinguishes him from Whigs like Robert Walpole, who were reluctant to present 1688–9 as a precedent for later revolutions.[29] *The Review* also quotes frequently from Defoe's own *Jure Divino* (1706), a twelve-book poem satirizing divine right that also serves as a paean to resistance—and a quite radical one.[30] Mr Review alludes to that poem in order to highlight the high-flyers' preference for tyranny over liberty, and to argue for man's natural inclination to abuse his power.[31] On three occasions he quotes at length from the poem, always challenging high-flying notions of non-resistance.[32] These moments also radicalize *The Review*, though its extensiveness and the miscellaneous nature of its focus have prevented most scholars (Cowan is the exception) from recognizing that radicalism.

---

[24] *Review*, viii. 14 (27 March 1711).
[25] *Review*, ix. 55 (16 September 1712).
[26] *Review*, vi. 35 (9 April 1709).
[27] *Review*, vii. 618 (13 February 1711).
[28] *Review*, vi. 593 (3 January 1710).
[29] Cowan, 'Daniel Defoe's *Review*', 87.
[30] For this argument, see Ashley Marshall, '"Treason and Loyalty go Hand in Hand": Moral Politics and Radical Whiggery in Defoe's *Jure Divino* (1706)', *SP*, 118:1 (2021), 145–80.
[31] *Review*, iv. 110 (1 April 1707); vi. 35 (9 April 1709). Defoe alludes to *Jure Divino* again in this context—'*all Men will be Tyrants if they can*'—in *Review*, viii. 452 (10 November 1711).
[32] On 27 August 1709, he takes roughly a hundred lines from Book VI again, though out of context the lines are less explicitly radical: '*Sure some of the Seraphick Race, / Too curious to survey th' Expanse of Space*', and so on (*Review*, vi. 321).

No other late Stuart periodical is like *The Review*. Defoe's paper is often described as a ministerial outlet,[33] insofar as it supports (some of) the initiatives of the successive governments under which it is written. Not only is the Whig *Review* ideologically remote from that other celebrated ministerial paper, the conservative, Tory *Examiner* (1710–14), but the two function very differently *as periodicals*. Their authors have entirely disparate attitudes towards and rhetorical relationships with their readers. Defoe is more inclined to engage with readers as citizens, whereas Mr Examiner—Swift in 1710–11, but other authors earlier and later—talks to readers as subjects, preaching obedience to rather than scrutiny of the powers-that-be. In his incisive commentary on the 1710 ministerial change—which *The Examiner* was launched to defend—Defoe indirectly invites readers to be sceptical of Anne's motives. His critical analysis of competing papers offers readers a model of inquiry and critique, whereas Mr Examiner shows no interest in cultivating readers' discernment. His objective is generating wholehearted support for the queen, her ministry, and their decisions. And for Defoe, politics are inseparable from religion; his ideological convictions and his partisan commitments have everything to do with his defence of the Protestant interest at home and abroad, about which Mr Examiner has very little to say.

In terms of ideology and of mission vis-à-vis readers, *The Review* shares much with *The Observator* of Tutchin and Ridpath, and with the ephemeral partisan papers of Steele. Tutchin and Ridpath not only promulgate radical Whig notions of power, but also encourage—like Defoe and unlike the Tories—a politically engaged, participatory public of readers. *The Review* is much wider-ranging than *The Observator* in its contents, however, offering more than a discourse upon political authority. This difference reflects different notions of ethos and journalistic authority. Mr Review's authority is first moral and then political, the latter to some extent earned by the former.

Ideologically, the Steele of *The Guardian* (1713) and *The Englishman* (1713–14, 1715)[34] is an ally of Mr Review's, but Defoe and Steele envision different roles for themselves. They diverge rhetorically and tonally. Defoe cannot quite manage to avoid the language and manner of Mr Examiner and other partisan controversialists; his métier is provocation and preachment. Steele consistently opposes and seeks to subvert his Tory rivals, but he does so in a series of papers that (mostly indirectly) contest foundational values rather than battling over particular issues. Most partisan journalists are fighting over the interpretation of the ministerial change, over trade, over war and peace, over toleration. Steele does not ignore these controversies, but he seems always preoccupied with the broader question of Tory authority—in social, ethical, cultural, religious, and political realms. Mr Review delights in the topical, though the topicality is so extensive and so cumulative that his mission nevertheless feels broader in scope than that of (say) *The Examiner*.

---

[33] Downie, *Robert Harley and the Press*, 64; Novak, *Daniel Defoe*, 395.
[34] Steele's *The Reader* (spring 1714) also has ideological connections with *The Review*.

Defoe's topicality is clear, too, in the short-lived *Master Mercury*, which overlapped briefly with *The Review* in 1704 and represents a kind of supplement to that paper. Defoe's animus is chiefly directed at Sir George Rooke, the Admiral of the Grand Fleet, and *The Master Mercury* takes pains to insinuate Rooke's cowardice. Defoe hoped to persuade the government that popular sentiment supported the removal of the Tory Rooke from his post. The 21 September issue acknowledges a recent English victory, for example, but also 'interpolate[s] details that call into question Rooke's judgment, loyalty, and personal bravery'.[35] Furbank and Owens describe *The Master Mercury* as a 'vendetta' against Rooke,[36] a short-lived but passionate campaign to turn public opinion against Defoe's target.

THE *MERCATOR*

Defoe's *Mercator: Or, Commerce Retrieved* (a triweekly running from May 1713 to July 1714) was the most prominent ministerial mouthpiece on the issue of the controversial Treaty of Commerce with France [SEE CHAPTER 14]. *The Mercator*, which overlapped briefly with *The Review* at the latter's end, was launched in response to 'a veritable snowstorm of pamphlets which threatened the government's plans, as both Whig opponents and anxious traders questioned the commercial management of the administration'.[37] *The Mercator* was designed to support the Treaty and to reveal its attackers as partyblind anti-patriots. Abel Boyer and other contemporaries attributed it to Defoe, who claimed partial responsibility for it in his *Appeal to Honour and Justice* (1715); epistolary evidence seems to confirm his authorship.[38]

The Mercator advocates the domestic and global value of free trade, including with France; it takes for granted that commerce is the most important part of national improvement. *The Mercator*'s primary aim was to challenge the '*general Opinion, That* England *loses by the Trade with* France' (no. 1). Here as elsewhere, Defoe uses the language of chicanery: his paper is meant '*to open Peoples Eyes*', whereas his rivals wish '*to blind and delude them*' (no. 15). Sensitive to popular anti-French sentiment, he doggedly maintains that England stands to gain more than France by this Treaty: '*The* French *take off Duties, Ours remain; the* French *bound*, Britain *left free*', and so on (no. 45). Defoe emphasizes, not always compellingly, that 'the Opposers of the Treaty of Commerce have their Eyes not upon the Merits of the Trade, but upon the Projects of Parties' (no. 109). For these 'Opposers' and for the people they have managed to bamboozle,

---

[35] Defoe, *The Master Mercury*, intro. Frank H. Ellis and Henry L. Snyder, Augustan Reprint Society, No. 184 (Los Angeles, CA: Williams Andrew Clark Memorial Library, 1977), vi.

[36] Furbank and Owens, *Critical Bibliography*, 249.

[37] Perry Gauci, *The Politics of Trade: The Overseas Merchant in State and Society, 1660–1720* (Oxford: Oxford University Press, 2001), 243.

[38] Furbank and Owens, *Critical Bibliography*, 250–1.

Defoe has nothing but disdain: their convictions are 'meer Delusion' (no. 148). After the Treaty was defeated, perhaps protesting too much, he contends, '*It can be no Damage to the Ministry, whether we accept this Treaty or no. But the Loss is to Trade, and the* British *Manufactures*' (no. 45).

The Mercator lived for another year beyond the vote against the Treaty. During that year Defoe exposes mistakes in Steele's treatment of trade in *The Guardian*, ridicules the idea that the Protestant Succession is in danger, and reflects on the limits of England's friendship with the Dutch. The *Mercator* is in many ways a Whig outlet, assuming the importance of 'the Liberties of England, and Privileges of Parliament' (no. 118) and of an Anglo-Dutch partnership, but keen to defend the ministry on the issue of the Treaty even after that Treaty is dead. Defoe was answered by *The British Merchant* (edited by Henry Martin), a topical paper meant to counter Defoe's own relentlessly topical propaganda.

Defoe was involved in a later trade-related periodical, *The Manufacturer* (October 1719–March 1721), 'commissioned ... by the London Company of Weavers to publicize the unemployment and destitution brought upon weavers by the importing of printed calicoes from India'.[39] This was a cause he could support without prevarication. As is often the case, Defoe's audience includes those he hopes to call to action: he appeals to parliament to revive old legislation regulating the importation of calico. Much, though not all, of Defoe's periodical writing has this kind of policy-driven pamphleteering quality: he often writes in very specific goal-orientated ways, labouring to spread opinion rather than to convey news. In that way, his late Stuart and early Hanoverian journalistic contributions are connected—though in many respects the latter is quite different from what Defoe wrote under Anne.

Defoe's Early Hanoverian Journalism

Defoe's situation at the time of Anne's death on 1 August 1714 cannot have been comfortable. He could cheerfully welcome a Whig regime that would protect interests near and dear to his heart, but he remained publicly associated with Harley, who was under suspicion of treason in 1714–15. The nature of his journalistic production in this period is difficult to assess in light of considerable attribution questions. Another problem is that Defoe seems to have been operating on both sides of the party divide during these years, raising familiar questions about his loyalty and honesty.[40] Defoe's late Stuart journalism has received relatively little critical attention, but his early Hanoverian journalism has had even less. His 1714–1720 periodical writing is scrappier, consisting not of a long-running commitment to a single journalistic voice like Mr Review, but a

---

[39] Furbank and Owens, *Critical Bibliography*, 253.
[40] What follows is indebted to the detailed discussion of Defoe's life and work during this time in Furbank and Owens, *Political Biography*.

series of miscellaneous contributions. He writes sometimes for but mostly against the government, and unlike *The Review* numbers, these contributions are anonymous or pseudonymous; Defoe-the-Hanoverian-journalist is slipperier than Defoe-the-late-Stuart-journalist, his ideological commitments harder to pin down.

At the time of Anne's death and George's accession, Defoe had been to some extent working for the Harley ministry—but he had also gotten involved with the sham *Flying-Post and Medley*, a paper devoted to criticizing that ministry.[41] The first journalistic project for Defoe after the collapse of the Tory ministry, in other words, was a trenchantly Whig paper penned against Anne's last government, though it does not specifically attack Harley. On 19 August 1714, the sham *Flying-Post* insinuated the covert Jacobite leanings of the Earl of Anglesey, who saw to it that all involved in the journal, including Defoe, were arrested. Defoe came to trial in June 1715 and was lucky not to be severely punished.[42]

Defoe appealed to Harley, explaining his involvement in the *Flying-Post* as his attempt to undermine the original *Flying Post* ('an Occasion Offred me which I Thought might be Improv'd Effectually to Overthrow it' [*Letters*, 446]). He not uncharacteristically holds that he is an innocent contributor wrongfully accused, and pleads with Harley in desperate (and probably disingenuous) ways. As Furbank and Owens note, this is not an anomalous letter. It resembles all too much the ones Defoe sent to undersecretary of state Charles Delafaye in 1718, eager to account for his awkward involvement in Mist's *Weekly Journal* and *Mercurius Politicus*.

Defoe's position vis-à-vis the Whig government between 1715 and 1718 is far from straightforward. The Anglesey affair left him worried that he would be forced into exile. In Defoe's telling, he decided to seek help from Chief Justice Parker, who not only put a stop to the proceedings against Defoe, but also recommended him to the secretary of state, Lord Townshend. In his 26 April 1718 letter to Delafaye, he explains his and Townshend's strategy for making the best use of his services: 'It was proposed ... That I should still appear as if I were as before under the Displeasure of the Governmt; and Seperated From the Whiggs; and That I might be more Servicable in a kind of Disguise, Than If I appeard openly'. To that end, he started up 'a Monthly Book called Mercurius Politicus', and also took 'a share in' another Tory venture, *Dyer's Newsletter*. Both *Mercurius Politicus* and the *Newsletter*, he continues, had 'To Pass as Tory Papers, and yet be Dissabled and Ennervated, So as to do no Mischief or give any Offence to the Governmt' (*Letters*, 451–3). In December 1716, Townshend was dismissed, which of course ended Defoe's employment with him.

Defoe's affirmation that he wrote against the government only to prevent more caustic criticism is naturally suspect. Whatever his intentions, in 1716–17 he was penning what served as (low-church) Tory propaganda. *Mercurius Politicus*[43] first appeared in May

---

[41] P. N. Furbank and W. R. Owens, 'Defoe and the Sham *Flying-Post*', *Publishing History*, 43 (1998), 5–15.

[42] Furbank and Owens, *Political Biography*, 139.

[43] On Defoe's involvement, see Furbank and Owens, *Critical Bibliography*, xxii–xxiii.

1716 as a rival to Abel Boyer's long-running Whig monthly, *The Political State of Great Britain* (1703–29). In 1717, John Toland complained that *Mercurius Politicus* 'frequently reflects upon the proceedings of the Government ... to the makeing [*sic*] of malicious and sometimes very dangerous insinuations'.[44] Toland's characterization is accurate.

Mercurius Politicus relies on other authors and texts to convey its ideology. The strategy is to quote at length from pamphlets, memorials, and speeches, all critical of the government, while recurrently claiming impartiality. In the opening issue, the author assures us that 'It is not the Business of these Collections to enter into the Debate'—but this statement of neutrality is followed by a long memorial calling for royal clemency toward the Scottish rebels, effectively a serious critique of the government's policy.[45] Such criticism ended abruptly in late 1718, about the time Defoe returned to the Whig fold,[46] but *circa* 1716–17 he was involved in opposition propaganda. His opposition might have been for purely mercenary reasons, or it could reflect actual disapproval of specific policies (for example, towards Spain). That said, as an opposition paper *Mercurius Politicus* is relatively bland, which is no doubt why it survived.

By the summer of 1717, Defoe had started writing for Nathaniel Mist's high-flying (even Jacobite) *Weekly Journal, or, Saturday's Post*—not at all a tame opposition outlet.[47] The government was annoyed by the weekly, and while Mist was frequently punished, prosecuting him only increased the popularity of his paper. As Paul Chapman points out, 'A government memorandum of 1722 complained that "There never was a Mist or any other Person taken up or tryed but double the number of papers were sold upon it". ... In 1741 the *Daily Gazetteer* recollected that "Mist's treasonable Papers were sold sometimes for Half a Guinea a-piece", such was the demand for them'.[48]

Rival journalists were quick to expose Defoe for his involvement in Mist's incendiary paper, and indeed his contributions were provocatively anti-government. On 1 February 1718, he penned a letter, signed by 'Sir Andrew Politick', and encouraging the editor to look into the Whig government's desire to embroil England in a costly war.[49] On 25 October of that year appears a still more inflammatory missive from the same knight, raising biting questions about the imminent war with Spain. The authorities branded that letter treason, and Mist named Defoe as the author. Defoe's *Review* had promulgated radically Whig ideals, and his early Hanoverian periodical work is likewise

---

[44] Toland, *The Second Part of the State Anatomy, &c.* (1717), 29.

[45] *Mercurius Politicus*, May 1716, 68.

[46] Furbank and Owens, *Political Biography*, 173.

[47] The paper became *Mist's Weekly Journal* in spring 1725; Mist fled to France in 1728, and his successor Charles Molloy resumed publication under the title *Fog's Weekly Journal*.

[48] Paul Chapman, 'Mist, Nathaniel (d. 1737)', *ODNB*. If true, this is an astonishing sum: according to MeasuringWorth.com, the 1720 retail price index value of 10*s* 6*d* would be £77; the 'labour value' would be £1,058; the income value would be £1,234. Half a guinea would represent two-thirds of the annual average household income for a week.

[49] Furbank and Owens, *Political Biography*, 161. They print the entirety of the 25 October 1718 letter in Appendix B (194–8).

radical—not so much in its ideology, less necessary to promulgate under a Whig regime, but in the boldness and fervency of its opposition.

Defoe's next periodical was the tri-weekly *White-hall Evening Post*, which commenced in September 1718. This paper started more or less at the time *Mercurius Politicus* was shifting away from criticism of the government. Furbank and Owens hypothesize that Defoe was pressured to terminate his opposition in the precarious aftermath of 'Sir Andrew's' sedition. What matters most for my purposes is that *The White-hall Evening Post* represents a notable shift from *Mist's*: throughout, the author positions himself on the side of the authorities, highlighting various kinds of policy-related progress made under the Hanoverian regime.

Something must be said here about another paper with which Defoe was long assumed to have been associated: John Applebee's *Original Weekly Journal*. Along with *Mist's* and *Read's*, Applebee's paper represents a new kind of enterprise emergent in George's reign: the weekly, including *Tatler*-esque essays, domestic and foreign news, local gossip, poems, criminal biographies, and editorials. Applebee launched his paper in October 1714 as a rival to *Mist's* and *Read's*; in 1720 the title changed to *Applebee's Weekly Journal*, and it ran until 1737. The first person to connect Defoe with *Applebee's* was William Lee, whose *Daniel Defoe: His Life and Recently Discovered Writings* (1869) added 300,000 words worth of contributions to the canon. Lee suggests—*sans* meaningful evidence—that Defoe began to write for the weekly on 25 June 1720 and continued to do so until 12 March 1726. Furbank and Owens point out that this attribution is based exclusively on internal evidence; no contemporary allusion to Defoe in relation to the paper has been found. Such a lack is conspicuous, if he was indeed involved: Defoe was a popular target for Whigs and Tories alike, and his connection with *Mist's* and other outlets hardly went unnoticed. Furbank and Owens's de-attribution has been contested by Novak, who argues for the restoration of some of *Applebee's* to the canon, again largely based on internal evidence.[50] I agree with Furbank and Owens that caution is in order.

The Journalist and the Public Sphere

I want to shift now away from a survey of Defoe's periodical contributions and towards a discussion of his role in and attitude towards the kind of public politics facilitated by a burgeoning news culture.

The sheer scale of newspaper production in Anne's reign is remarkable, and contemporaries voiced concern about the sudden proliferation of print matter. In 1704, some 44,000 copies of papers were printed weekly; by 1712, that number was more like 70,000. In 1709, at least eighteen papers appeared weekly or more often—fifty-five

---

[50] Maximillian Novak, 'Daniel Defoe and *Applebee's Original Weekly Journal*: An Attempt at Re-Attribution', *ECS*, 45:4 (2012), 585–608.

issues, all told, per week.[51] Between 1712 and 1716, as many as forty-five (mostly short-lived) journals were launched. Mr Review's lamentation that there are 'above two Hundred Thousand single Papers publish'd every Week in this Nation' (vii. 4) is hyperbolic, but it reflects his recognition of a news deluge. *The Commentator* characterizes competing partisan outlets as so much '*Nonsense and Forgery!*'—though the author, perhaps Defoe, also offers a more neutral summation of the significance of the rise of a daily newspaper press: because of such developments, this historical moment represents 'the *Dawn* of *Politicks* among the Common People'.[52]

Defoe is conscious of the connection between the press and the politics of the 'Common People', and he does perhaps more than any other contemporary journalist to appeal to and create 'public opinion'. Especially in *The Review*—my focus here—his attitude towards his readers is nevertheless complicated. Scholars routinely characterize Mr Review as a homiletic speaker, relying upon biblical authority and keen to tell his readers what and how to think. To some extent that is a fair characterization, but Defoe also manifestly believes in readers' discernment and encourages them to apply their own reason. This is not to deny his desire to instruct, or his considerable faith in the rightness of his own judgements. In *The Review*'s inaugural issue, Defoe conveys his wish to 'Set … the Affairs of *Europe* in a Clearer Light'—but he also immediately empowers his audience. 'When Matters are thus laid open, and stript from the false Glosses of Parties, Men are easily capable to Judge, what, and why Things are done'. Risking his own credibility, he calls into question the veracity and objectivity of journalists, significantly using first-person plural: 'we raise Clouds before Men's Eyes, and then complain no Body sees but our selves', and we 'Dose our Readers with continued Fumes of our own Brain'.[53] Over the course of *The Review*'s life, he becomes increasingly uneasy about the rational capacities of his 'poor blinded' fellow subjects.[54] What is consistent is his attempt to construct and strengthen a specifically Protestant public sphere, a transnational Protestant community threatened by 'Anti-Union, Oath-forgetting, Church-betraying, Queen-insulting' high-flying Tories and their Catholic allies abroad.[55]

Mr Review repeatedly suggests, implicitly or explicitly, a gap between the interests of high Tories and those of the nation. His aim is to contribute to 'the Publick Peace of *Protestants*', which is imperilled by 'our *Nation Disturbers*, the *High-Flyers*'.[56] Addressing his enemies, Defoe contends that 'the Queen, the House of Lords, the Bishops, the Moderate Clergy, and all the Gentlemen of *England*, that are troubled with the Faculty of Thinking, are so Engag'd against your Design', and so on; he defines rational,

---

[51] These numbers are given, with slight variations, in a number of sources. See, for example, Andrew Pettegree, *The Invention of News: How the World Came to Know about Itself* (New Haven, CT: Yale University Press, 2014), 245.

[52] *The Commentator*, no. 3, *RDW*, ix. 25; no. 2, *RDW* ix. 24. Furbank and Owens list this work as a probable attribution in the *Critical Bibliography*.

[53] *Review*, i. 6, 7 (19 February 1704).

[54] *Review*, vii. 56 (20 April 1710).

[55] *Review*, v. 137 (27 May 1708).

[56] *Review*, ii. 245 (7 June 1705); iv. 525 (7 October 1707).

civic-minded citizens as part of a united public from which high Tories have separated themselves.[57] The 'Gentlemen of the High-Church', he gravely concludes, can expect 'the Nations Resentment', and 'have shown themselves the whole Nation's Enemies'.[58] Defoe's ideal public is an electorate of Protestant voters who believe in Protestant unity and tolerance for Protestant Dissenters, fear Catholicism and Jacobitism, and denounce the bigoted violence of Tory mobs such as emerged during the Sacheverell trial.

What is Defoe's attitude towards that Protestant citizenship to which he appeals? Especially early on in *The Review*, he is highly conscious of his readers, and he comments upon their habits of reading. No. 5 opens with a 'DIGRESSION to the READER'. The Scandal Club of 1704–5 broadens out, but it begins as a vehicle with which Defoe can critique his brethren of the quill: the club's function is initially 'the Correction of Newspapers', which turned out to be so big a job that it represented a 'constant and intolerable' burden.[59] The club not only allows Defoe to roast his rivals; it also invites readers to exercise their own critical powers, and to learn to identify and call out the 'Blunders and Errors' of the press. In fact, Defoe goes so far as to attribute the exposure of such errors to 'the Clamour of the People', who have written passionate letters to the Scandal Club pushing club members to guarantee vengeance 'if the News-writers do not' reform.[60] The message about the popular role in reporting is clear: readers have the right to hold writers accountable. Of Defoe's contemporaries, only Steele would go as far in the direction of empowering readers to exercise their judgement, not only privately but publicly.[61]

When Mr Review logically dissects arguments made and conclusions offered in Tory outlets like *The Post Boy* and *The Rehearsal*, he is effectively fostering a culture of debate. He also tends to make cases rather than delivering judgements; he seems to want to persuade his readers so that they follow his logic rather than merely accepting his conclusions. He may not be democratic in the modern sense of the term, but he scorns elitism: 'It is easie to tell you the Consequences of Popular Confusions, Private Quarrels, and Party Feuds, without Reading *Virgil*, *Horace*, or *Homer*'.[62] Novak describes Mr Review as keen 'to satirize the wrong view and to assure his readers that his interpretation of events was the proper one',[63] but especially early on he seems also to empower his readers to exercise their own judgements.

By 1707–8, however, Mr Review's manner has changed: he begins to emphasize not the rational powers of 'the people', but instead their alarming credulity. Man is 'a short-sighted Creature, and weak in his politick Opticks'.[64] Mr Review complains not only about alarmist Tory 'Forgeries', but also about the reception of such deceptions:

---

[57] *Review*, ii. 163 (8 May 1705).
[58] *Review*, ii. 482 (9 August 1705); ii. 810 (20 December 1705).
[59] *Review*, i. 160 (30 May 1704).
[60] *Review*, i. 69 (8 April 1704).
[61] On this point, see Marshall, *Political Journalism*, Ch. 5.
[62] *Review*, ii. 227 (2 June 1705).
[63] Novak, 'Defoe's Political and Religious Journalism', 26.
[64] *Review*, iv. 650 (29 November 1707).

Really the Infirmity of our People is remarkable; in that they seem pleased with melancholly Reports, and willing to have things made worse to them than they are, that they appear gratify'd with the Phlegmatick Part, and love to be poring upon their Misfortunes, with the magnifying Glass of their own Hypocondriack Vapours; of these People I shall speak ... hereafter, but at present my Observations are not so much upon the Deluded, as upon the Deluders.[65]

Discouraged by party warfare at home in the spring of 1710, he complains thus: 'The People are fighting and quarrelling ... and yet do but ask the poor blinded Creatures *who* they are FOR, or who *against*, they cannot tell you'.[66] That said, he tends to blame the high-flyers rather than their gullible victims: '*To the Deluded*, impos'd upon, honest People, I say as before, all Manner of Tenderness and Kindness should be shown'.[67] Credulity is a major theme of *The Review*, the necessary counterpart to Defoe's relentless emphasis on the high-flying desire to mislead and bamboozle subjects. In the summer of 1710, relying upon a metaphor he uses frequently, he insists that his mission is to help prevent 'this Nation' from being 'overwhelmed by these rising Mists to the Ruine of her ... *Eye sight*'.[68] Here at least he is confident that 'their Eyes WILL be open'd'.[69]

Defoe's seemingly adversarial role—his peevish addresses to 'ENGLISH FOOLS!'—should not be read as disapproval of the importance of popular politics.[70] On the contrary, even this move seems to be about baiting readers into using their own critical facilities: 'our People want nothing *but to see what they are doing*'.[71] Mr Review's job is to translate Tory language—à la *The Shortest-Way with the Dissenters*—so that the people can know the actual intentions of the high-flyers. That his allusions to that scandalous pamphlet multiply in the middle years of *The Review* is unsurprising.[72] Every reference to *The Shortest-Way* represents an affirmation that 'the Nation can hardly know her Friends from her Enemies'. Such language represents an attempt to persuade his readers that his words and verdicts are to be trusted. Defoe disparages both Whig and Tory papers, all of them contributors to the partisan cacophony, and stands alone, the sole source of elucidation. 'In this wild Field', he concludes, 'leaving your *Examiners, Tattlers, Observators,* and a MEDLY of Moderns to toss the State in a Blanket among them; I shall for a while, talk to you'.[73] Despite his frustration with 'a Nation willing to be deluded', he works hard to politicize the people: 'I never was of their Opinion, whose Faith in Omnipotent Power led them to put all the Work upon GOD, and make themselves only

---

[65] *Review*, iv. 694 (18 December 1707).
[66] *Review*, vii. 56 (20 April 1710).
[67] *Review*, iv. 124 (8 April 1707).
[68] *Review*, vii. 188 (20 June 1710).
[69] *Review*, vii. 244 (18 July 1710).
[70] *Review*, vii. 265 (29 July 1710).
[71] *Review*, vii. 401 (10 October 1710).
[72] See for example *Review*, v. 98 (11 May 1708).
[73] *Review*, vii. 632 (22 February 1711).

Spectators'.[74] Mr Review challenges Tory journalists' assumption that subjects are meant to obey.

* * *

The early eighteenth century was a critical moment in the history of the news, and in the history of the public sphere. Defoe functioned in this new culture as a writer and editor, a minor contributor and a major provocateur, as an ally to and critic of other journalists. He was also a combatant—not only in the topical controversies covered and interpreted by his fellow journalists, but in the novel debates about what the role of journalism should be.

Defoe is an intensely public-minded journalist. His relentless topicality does not necessarily set him apart from other periodical writers, and neither does his willingness to challenge the authorities and risk punishment. Ideologically, *The Review* represents something more radical than most Whig outlets of the time, and that radicalism is one part of Defoe's contribution to the early eighteenth-century news culture. He is also unusually engaged with the reading public. Most modern readers think of journalism as inherently public-facing, but in the early years of a daily news culture, writers were not necessarily in agreement about the wisdom of offering a political education to ordinary citizens. The proper or best public role of journalism, in other words, was an open question. Defoe, Steele, and other Whig writers make clear that journalists could and should help citizens make more discerning judgements, whereas conservative authors such as Swift and Leslie worry about the potential for over-empowering subjects, inciting anti-institutional thinking or disaffection. On all sides, journalists and other commentators voice anxiety about whether subjects could read skilfully enough and sceptically enough to identify the misrepresentation of talented liars. Tory-leaning authors often respond to the burgeoning news culture with a reminder that ordinary citizens lack the experience to make political judgements, informed or not: 'it requires … many years experience in Politicks … to project or to penetrate into any of the sacred Mysteries of the State'.[75]

Mr Review does not accept that position: his emphasis on observation, his desperate plea that patriotic writers help the people improve their 'politick Opticks', signals an entirely different idea about public politics.[76] His alarm about journalism's negative potential now seems startlingly prescient: 'I Believe I may venture to affirm, that the main Foundation and Support of most of the Evils we complain of, is *False News*: So that some attempt must be made to remove the Loads of Forgery, Infamy and Absurdity which pass daily under the Name of *News*'.[77] Despite this scepticism, Defoe did not, like his more conservative counterparts, deny the politicizing and empowering value

---

[74] *Review*, iv. 650 (29 November 1707).

[75] Anon., *Arguments Relating to a Restraint upon the Press, Fully and Fairly handled in a Letter to a Bencher, from a Young Gentleman of the Temple* (1712), 30.

[76] *Review*, iv. 650 (29 November 1707).

[77] *The Commentator* (P), no. 2, *RDW*, ix. 21.

of journalism. Among contemporaneous periodical writers, Steele comes the closest to Defoe in privileging the act of reading and in helping citizens see themselves as thoughtful, rational judges of the competing news narratives they encountered on a daily basis. Few late Stuart journalists would go as far as Mr Review, who as early as December 1704 assures his readers that the right to question is universal: 'We now live under a Government that will hear Truth, and the freedom of the Press intimates any Man may write it'.[78] He occasionally voices concern about the 'Universal Pen and Ink Strife'—but he also celebrates the journalistic medium for its ability to cultivate a public sphere of vigilance and judgement-rendering.[79] The '*Publick Faults*' of news-writers and the governments they serve should receive, proclaims Mr Review, '*as Publick Censures*'.[80] No other journalist of this period is as prolific or as systematic in trying not only to shape public opinion, but to justify readers' right to know political truths and to assess the veracity of those who pretend to tell such truths.

Defoe's copious contributions make manifest that he consistently saw the periodical as a powerful vehicle in the battle over public opinion and for public support of one's positions. Even if we limit ourselves to the most certain attributions, Defoe's periodical canon is substantial, and his commentary on his fellow journalists and on the implications for journalism more broadly conceived is likewise rich and abundant. Though students of the long eighteenth century routinely acknowledge that Defoe was prolific as Mr Review, his role in the sudden emergence of a transformative new culture of daily 'news' has been vastly underappreciated. He aggressively championed public participation in affairs of state, calling for public judgement rather than docile acceptance of decrees from those with socio-political power. Modern scholars have been more interested in Swift's journalism than Defoe's, but Defoe occupies a position vastly more modern and what we would now call progressive than his rival's. Relative critical indifference to Defoe's periodical writings has meant missing out on this significant part of his mission as a writer. Not only does he advocate a surprisingly modern notion of public politics, but he also offers a model of journalism that seriously engages with its readership, a kind of journalism that teaches subjects to see themselves as citizens.

Further Reading

Brian Cowan, 'Daniel Defoe's *Review* and the Transformations of the English Periodical', *HLQ*, 77:1 (2014), 79–110.

J. A. Downie, *Robert Harley and the Press: Propaganda and Public Opinion in the Age of Swift and Defoe* (Cambridge: Cambridge University Press, 1979).

P. N. Furbank and W. R. Owens, *A Political Biography of Daniel Defoe* (London: Pickering and Chatto, 2006).

---

[78] *Review*, i. 606 (16 December 1704).
[79] *Review*, ii. 711 (8 November 1705).
[80] *Review*, ii. 51 (22 March 1705).

Ashley Marshall, 'Robert Harley and the Politics of Daniel Defoe's *Review*, 1710–13', *1650–1850*, 24 (2019), 54–97.

Ashley Marshall, *Political Journalism in London, 1695–1720: Defoe, Swift, Steele and their Contemporaries* (Woodbridge: Boydell and Brewer, 2020).

Ashley Marshall, '"Treason and Loyalty go Hand in Hand": Moral Politics and Radical Whiggery in Defoe's *Jure Divino* (1706)', *SP*, 118:1 (2021), 145–80.

Maximillian E. Novak, *Daniel Defoe, Master of Fictions: His Life and Ideas* (Oxford: Oxford University Press, 2001).

Maximillian E. Novak, 'Defoe's Political and Religious Journalism', in *The Cambridge Companion to Daniel Defoe*, ed. John Richetti (Cambridge: Cambridge University Press, 2008), 25–44.

Andrew Pettegree, *The Invention of News: How the World Came to Know about Itself* (New Haven, CT: Yale University Press, 2014).

Nicholas Seager, '"He reviews without Fear, and acts without fainting": Defoe's *Review*', *ECS*, 46:1 (2012), 131–42.

CHAPTER 8

DEFOE AND THE IDEA OF TRAVEL

PAUL BAINES

The de-attribution process has affected the travel shelf of Defoe's bibliography more than most: he no longer voyages alongside so many buccaneers, nor projects so many colonies. The boom in travel-writing, coincident with British commercial expansion in the late seventeenth century, took many forms: voyages, maps, gazetteers, surveys, descriptions, colonial proposals, and 'instructions for travel'; much was once assumed to be Defoe's.[1] But despite canonical losses, Defoe clearly thrived in and contributed enormously to a culture of travel writing, both in economic outlook, as an unabashed expansionist seeking new worlds to trade in, and, more ambivalently, in fiction.

For a writer of such global reach, Defoe's foreign ventures, if he had any, have left little documentary trace: no grand tour (an aristocratic luxury he derided), no Swiftian shuttling across the Irish Sea. Unlike the bookseller John Dunton, whose auto-fictional *A Voyage Round the World* (1691) was based on actual travels, Defoe may never have left mainland Britain; his passing remark about having lived in Spain constitutes a rare, and uncorroborated, claim to overseas experience.[2] Generally, Defoe wrote about Poland or the South Sea as he wrote about the moon: using books and imagination. His personal movements in Britain were, however, at once routine (in mercantile capacity), extensive, and risky. On one hand, the clandestine excursion to support Monmouth; on the other, the claim to have visited 'every Nook and Corner of... *England*... upon Publick Affairs,

---

[1] See Miles Ogborn and Charles W. Withers, 'Travel, Trade and Empire: Knowing Other Places, 1660–1800', in *A Concise Companion to the Restoration and Eighteenth Century*, ed. Cynthia Wall (Oxford: Blackwell, 2005), 13–35; William H. Sherman, 'Stirrings and Searchings (1500–1720)', in *The Cambridge Companion to Travel Writing*, ed. Peter Hulme and Tim Youngs (Cambridge: Cambridge University Press, 2002), 17–36.

[2] *Review*, vii. 592 (27 January 1711); see Frank Bastian, *Defoe's Early Life* (London: Macmillan, 1981), 92–4. For Defoe's consuming interest in travel writing, see Helmut Heidenreich (ed.), *The Libraries of Daniel Defoe and Phillips Farewell* (Berlin: Hildebrand, 1970), xix–xxi.

when I had the Honour to serve ... King *William*'.[3] Covert missions after release from prison in 1703, amply recorded in letters to Robert Harley as sponsor, combined risk and service. Travel often features in Defoe's writing as secret or spasmodic following painful restriction (such as Newgate and the pillory); the tension between this mode and regular motion or stasis is the focus of this chapter.

Projects and Storms

Defoe's promotion of travel began with visionary enthusiasm in *An Essay upon Projects* (1697). In the 'Introduction', Defoe decries the effects of the war on trade: blockades and sieges interrupted orderly commercial movement. Normally, merchants constitute a magician, even prophetic class:

> Every new Voyage the Merchant contrives, is a project ... Ships are sent from Port to Port, as Markets and Merchandizes differ, by the help of strange and Universal Intelligence; ... some are so exquisite, so swift, and so exact, that a Merchant sitting at home in his Counting-house, at once converses with all Parts of the known World. This, and Travel, make a True-bred Merchant the most Intelligent Man in the World, and consequently the most capable, when urg'd by Necessity, to Contrive New Ways to live. (*PEW*, viii. 36)

Defoe's vision includes, for Britain, a set of highways (55–70) purged of 'Floods, unpassable Sloughs, deep Cart-routs, high Ridges, and all the Inconveniences they now are full of' (57). His 'universal Correspondence' will clear impediments to movement, but also require ceaseless ambulatory surveillance, with commissioners travelling the roads to assess fluency. A system for physical travel (imagined from the road surface upwards) will need meta-travel to guarantee it.

Such wide-eyed imaginings were chastened in 1703 by the Great Storm, an explosive disruption of navigability by an opposite kind of travel: unplanned, chaotic, irresistible. *The Storm* (1704) presents movement with no predictable ordering at all, though the effect on trade is (as in war) registered as havoc. Theologians and scientists were unable to explain how the wind had kinetic agency without being observable: the wind was (like Fate or Fortune) capricious, random. The storm inverted normal relations of matter and motion: anchors broke, bricks flew, land became sea, trees moved in mysterious ways. Steeples blew down and re-erected themselves furlongs away; boats took to the air. The wind eddied through all compass-points at once. Crops and commodities, the stuff of mercantile travel, shifted pointlessly. The Navy could not navigate the island nation;

---

[3] *Review*, vii. 630 (22 Feb 1711).

ships were driven out 'into the Road', their survival or loss randomly apportioned.[4] Strange impetus travestied the static relations of things:

> The Water in the River of *Thames*, and other Places, was in a very strange manner blown up into the Air: Yea, in the new Pond in *James's Park*, the Fish, to the Number of at least two Hundred, were blown out and lay by the Bank-side, whereof many were Eye-witnesses. (46)

There was some narrative fascination in this prank-like, cack-handed witchcraft; it was nonetheless a kind of motion sickness over which Defoe was re-establishing control, recording events, statistics, measurements of damage. He collected and collated reports of an event that destroyed communication, the book replacing the devastation of time and space with trajectories of damage and repair. A pan-national account was assembled from pan-national estrangement; a collectively witnessed truth painstakingly retrieved from the fragmentations of overpowering traction.

Rambling Thoughts

These images—frictionless, ever-expanding trade, complicated by obstacles, disasters, and error—permeate Defoe's economic writings, including the *Review*. Movement was one of Defoe's most urgent signifiers of enrichment: *homo economicus* was *homo peregrinus*, as (in his favourite home-grown adage) an estate was a pond, but trade a spring. Since Defoe's protagonists all succeed as commercial agents, it is easy to align travel-fictions with a mercantile agenda; the variations on the theme are complex, however. No novelist has made protagonists travel so far, so energetically; not for Defoe the study of a restricted locale, provincial town or seaside resort. His hyperkinetic heroes circumnavigate the world, walk across Africa, map unknown islands, construct labyrinthine gazetteers of the inner city; they sail, ride, walk, run, and swim, but they never stay still. Though Moll and Roxana sometimes take trips with their lovers, there is little 'tourism'.[5] The fiction presents stop-go animation rather than regular movement, the blockages faced before (and after) getting on the boat. Prisons (including islands and lodgings) resemble psychological quagmires, extrapolated from the sloughs of despond and doubting castles of Bunyan's on-the-road spiritual template. Storms, shipwreck, and enemies animal, cannibal, piratical, or political impede the hero; overmastering these is one of the tasks.

Another is coming to an accommodation with the pattern of the stable economic world itself. Defoe's *Complete English Tradesman* (1725–7) stresses the virtues of stasis: the shop, counter, or warehouse where the trader must 'keep the Road, not

---

[4] Defoe, *The Storm*, ed. Richard Hamblyn (London: Penguin 2005), 140–3.
[5] 'Tourism' and 'tourist' post-date Defoe, but he uses 'tour' in several fictions, and, rarely 'trip'.

straggling into unknown By-paths of Trade, which he has never travelled in before, and where he does not know the Way in, or the Way out, but may be lost'. Let the 'Coach and the Chariot gallop, and drive, and Posts whip and spur', because 'the Plowman and the Carrier go soft and fair, and yet the last come with the greatest Certainty to the End of their Journey'. (Immediately afterwards, Defoe discusses actual 'English' wagons.) A 'Touring Fancy' must be controlled, for that way *Robinson Crusoe* lies—indeed, had already lain (*RDW*, viii. 35, 37). The fiction which preceded this hymn to immobility had already effected a breach with conduct-book sobriety, as individuals ditched the shop for the road, or were cast off the map. Their memoirs are not business-class travelogues, but travel meta-literature, resisting the description of mercantile routes by showing what happens off them; they decline to give on-board logbooks for already-known voyages.[6] Networks remain magically efficient but are not themselves interesting; homecomings are perfunctory. Fixed positions, social and geographical, are occupied by helpers (landlords, bankers); heroes experience, by contrast, powerful movement—flight, buccaneering, free-fall, recoil at the uncanny. They absorb the energy of movement they cannot control, mapping as they go, equipping the trade routes with more coordinates; but the fictions emphasize the risk that it will end in chaos. *An Essay upon Projects* frames this world; *The Storm* is closer to what happens in it.

In *The Storm*, Defoe records 'deliverances': a ship blown from the Downs to Norway, where it resumed its commercial route; several shipwrecked sailors, including one lone survivor, almost destroyed by mystical force, yet somehow preserved. *Robinson Crusoe* (1719) presented a hero salvaging himself from the wrack of the known world, economic trackways obliterated only to extend their global reach. The spiritual journey of Bunyan's pilgrim, always en route but often side-tracked, is hybridized with the navigation-obsessed *New Voyage Round the World* (1697) of William Dampier and *A Cruising Voyage Round the World* (1712) of Woodes Rogers (the most obvious of Defoe's sources among the travel-books booksellers were industriously promoting).[7] Defoe's fiction starts this world of motion with paternal, conduct-book recommendations *against* it, in favour of stable mercantile-domestic life. This position has however itself been achieved by travel: the Crusoes are True-Born Englishmen only as metics, the merchant father migrating from Bremen to Hull, marrying Britishness at York. Reversing the process, Crusoe (a folktale third son), is seduced by travel wonder; his 'Head began to be fill'd very early with rambling Thoughts'.[8] Travel is rebellion, truancy, the first voyage an escape via Hull, the stormy sea a Bunyanesque psychodrama even while Defoe draws on mariner-narrators for shipboard details. The next outing is a mercantile venture to

---

[6] Defoe could have known John Woodward's *Brief Instructions for Making Observations in all Parts of the World* (1696), a how-to guide for combining knowledge with commercial ambition; see Ilse Vickers, *Defoe and the New Sciences* (Cambridge: Cambridge University Press, 1996), 152–4. Crusoe starts a diary, but runs emblematically out of ink; Singleton says 'I kept no journal' three times.

[7] See J. A. Downie, 'Defoe, Imperialism, and the Travel Books Reconsidered', *Yearbook of English Studies*, 13 (1983), 66–83; Michael Seidel, *Robinson Crusoe: Island Myths and the Novel* (Boston, MA: Twayne, 1991).

[8] Defoe, *Robinson Crusoe*, ed. Michael Shinagel (New York: Norton, 1994), 4.

Guiana, thwarted by the first of many pirate encounters in Defoe. Crusoe's desperate escape from subsequent enslavement, in a stolen boat, and his panicked efforts at do-it-yourself orientation without navigational instruments, running from ethnographic terrors (howling animals, hostile 'savages'), are incomparably more detailed and personal than the 'very good Voyage' to Brazil (26) he makes once rescued.

The 'foolish inclination of wandring abroad' (29) from the plantation, 'preposterous' as it is (31), presents a psycho-social destiny. The shipwreck that destroys (and saves) Crusoe is recounted in slow-motion, immersing him in Storm-like power, and gradually establishing self-possession and control, from sandbank to rock to shore and the first self-made 'home'. Crusoe is soon experimenting with ways of getting off the island, using rafts to make short trips and mapping its coast to high specification. Forays from the hub then form a *Tour through the Whole Island of Robinson Crusoe*. By steps, 'ranging' for food becomes 'walking out', 'going abroad', or making 'rounds' (49, 53, 57, 70). The island is a prison, but also a topography onto which he projects, psychically and by literal footsteps, autonomous travel: he takes pedestrian dominion over it. Though cognates of 'voyage' and 'journey' dominate his language of travel, Crusoe uses the word 'tour' four times in this settled section. The pose is even open to irony, as in Crusoe's reflection on his status as a goatskin grandee, sauntering round his country estate. We 'take a Sketch of my Figure' only after he has confessed 'I could not but smile at the Notion of my travelling through *Yorkshire* with such an Equipage, and in such a Dress' (108).

These movements, translating spiritual wreck into secular mastery, Crusoe can control; his boating disasters (one too heavy to move, one almost getting him swept out to sea) remind him that control is insecure [SEE CHAPTER 18]. If Crusoe seems perforce the most 'settled' of escapee-protagonists, self-islanding is not permanent: the need to reconnect to a network is never extinguished. Defoe reboots him with the lone footprint, signalling the incursion of travellers from an off-grid elsewhere, curtailing his inland 'excursions' (123–4); he starts to explore withdrawal spaces, particularly caves. But the external map comes to him, as if by psychological traction: cannibals visit 'his' side of the island, then another European ship is driven onshore, giving Crusoe the opportunity to map the currents as he loots it. Friday embodies Crusoe's dream of an indigenous pilot, itself a psychological wedding of local with international systems; his preternatural swiftness constitutes a talismanic mobility. Through Friday, Crusoe knows where he is in relation to the Orinoco; they plot their own voyage and design their own boat. This is pre-empted by a further manifestation of the psychically necessary: another European ship. None of this is straightforward imperial progress to land-grab: the 'Europe' that arrives is quasi-piratical, in mutiny, a perverse Dampier-relic or rogue embassy from the trade routes. Crusoe's authority over the island has to be performed in a near-pantomime display (180–5). But he leaves on a functioning ship with a geo-located colony to his name: 'rambling' is reclaimed by economic circuitry.

If the voyage out was a Storm-like rupturing of inherited positions, reconnecting the colony to the map is easy. Portugal is the centre of his network; his financial power travels along known lines as magically as in *An Essay upon Projects*, and the castaway rejoins the world as a merchant prince. The final sections offer us aftershock reminders that travel is perilous: he returns to England by land, facing danger in the Pyrenees, thanks to wolves, bears, and feckless guides. But the European journey is too well known to require guide-book narration: 'I have nothing uncommon to take Notice of, in my Passage through *France*; nothing but what other Travellers have given an Account of, with much more Advantage than I can' (218). The book concludes at 'the centre of my Travels', in England physically, spread across the globe financially, the temptation to 'wandring Life' (219) teasingly unextinguished.

Farther Adventures of Robinson Crusoe (1719) announces itself with a map of global travels. There is much self-berating discussion of the rambling mentality, Crusoe protesting that he has tried to settle by farming some land. But there is less psycho-dramatic tension here: adventure morphs easily into merchant venturing. He embarks with his nephew, laundering a seemingly fateful power to a rational purpose: gain. Returning to the island (hard to locate but finally recognizable by its coastline) we meet a new chaos to be ordered by the Odyssean strongman: Crusoe retrieves stragglers who have wandered from the mapped zones, continues the process of division, establishes supply routes to the mainland, and pushes back the savage menace. This takes half the book. The second half establishes narrative routes into new territory, irresist-ible to his 'wandering Genius' (*Novels*, ii. 125–6). 'Descriptions of Places, Journals of our Voyages, Variations of Compass, Latitudes, Meridian-Distances, Trade-Winds, Situation of Ports, and the like' are avoided as 'tiresome' (127); Crusoe mentions other travel-narrators to avoid commenting on Sumatra and Siam (144–5). We are swiftly at Madagascar, prompting a new sequence of ethnographic encounters, including a geno-cidal attack from which Crusoe, often culturally-relativist, dissents; he is marooned, to relaunch the Crusoe enterprise. The next destination is mapped enough for him to attempt some gentlemanly anthropology, encountering the peoples of the world with more than trade in mind. But such normative travelogue is excursive: 'I shall make no more Descriptions of Countriess and People, 'tis none of my Business, or any part of my Design; but giving an Account of my own Adventures, through a Life of inimitable Wandrings' (140). Crusoe's real interest is in the logistics of his personal adventure, and he resists with increasing confidence an understood pressure to write as traveller-ethnographer: 'I am no more to describe People than Countries, any farther than my own Story comes to be concerned in them' (202).[9] Beyond the Great Wall of China (nei-ther a convincing obstruction nor worth tourist curiosity), everywhere seems possible for the super-traveller: Japan, the Philippines, Europe via Mexico. Defoe diverts Crusoe via the Muscovy caravan, along an established route, protected from attack, across deso-late terrain, the land equivalent of the navigational threats of the sea, as human and cli-matic violence threatens everywhere. Released from the pointless stasis of the Siberian winter, the caravan brings Crusoe, former castaway, now merchant freighted with

---

[9] See Joan Pau Rubiés, 'Travel Writing and Ethnography', in *Cambridge Companion to Travel Writing*, ed. Hulme and Youngs, 242–60.

money and projects, through deserts and Tartar hordes to the trouble-free route along the Elbe and the quick flit from the Hague to London.

Despite Crusoe's sense that 'a longer Journey' awaits him in the shape of death (217), *Serious Reflections during the Life and Surprising Adventures of Robinson Crusoe* (1720) reversed the Bunyan-Dampier polarity again by purveying a religious anthropology derived from Crusoe's 'wandring Years'. The 'Reflections' end with a global map of faiths and a '*Cruisado*' in pursuit of world domination (secure trade routes will be an additional benefit). The new 'travel' element comes in the 'Vision', a journey into cosmic space:

> my Imagination, *always given to wander*, took a Flight of its own; ... I had an invincible Inclination to travel, so I think I travelled as sensibly ... over all the Mazes and Wastes of infinite Space ... as ever I did over the Desarts of *Karakathay*, and the uninhabited Wasts of *Tartary*, and perhaps may give as useful an Account of my Journey. (*Novels*, iii. 236)

These final 'imaginary Travels' (237) prompt reflections on 'what we *are* ... and 'tis an Advantage worth Travelling for too' (248). By then, Defoe had published two other fictions demonstrating travel's generation of self-knowledge, wholly untroubled by the conduct-book injunction against travel as errancy.

Memoirs of a Cavalier (1720) separates its protagonist from paternal acres smoothly, the narrator asking his father's permission to travel in Europe, as soldier or tourist. But: 'I shall not trouble the Reader with a Journal of my Travels, nor with the Description of Places; which every Geographer can do better than I'. The Cavalier is deaf to the comedy of his comment on Paris: 'excepting the City it self, there was not much to be seen there'. Any conventional tourism is soon derailed by missing guides, footpads, a chance-medley killing necessitating a moonlight flit.[10] Exile in Italy brings the Cavalier into war, to observe contrasting versions of manoeuvre: ordered (assembling, marching, charging) and chaotic (roving, fleeing, deserting). His own displacement is partly repurposed as freedom through orderly narration of the disorders of war. The underlying territory is premapped, routes plugged into an already-plausible geography. Yet after capture, the Cavalier spends two years 'rather in wandring up and down, than travelling' (113), as if seeking a new, purposeful outlet for an essential mobility.

Part Two (again, the fiction appears to require this midway restart) takes the restless Cavalier into the English Civil War, observing the motions of armies at first hand and (seamlessly) by report [SEE CHAPTER 22]. All movement is essentially military, whether strategic (expeditions, troop manoeuvres, positioning of regiments) or (in defeat) chaotic: routs, scuffles in narrow lanes, sallies, misdirections in the night, desperate river crossings. The king's policy failures register as erratic *motion*, while Cromwell appears

---

[10] Defoe, *Memoirs of a Cavalier*, ed. James T. Boulton (Oxford: Oxford University Press, 1978), 11, 14. See James Buzard, 'The Grand Tour and After (1660–1840)', in *Cambridge Companion to Travel Writing*, ed. Hulme and Youngs, 37–52.

as a super-mobile force, a storm-cloud which 'rose out of the East, and spread ... into the North, 'till it shed down a Flood that overwhelmed the three Kingdoms' (186); the Scots are likewise an irresistible 'Storm' (191). The book is rich in details of villages, cities, gates, and bridges, like a spy-satellite vision, a news-hub of the war, itself essentially a mobile entity, depending on which groups clash and how their movements vectorize. All commercial travel suspended, the Cavalier 'ranges' over the kingdom, mapping himself against troop movements. His absence from the battle of Newbury, on a visit to Bath, registers the new normality of constant military regrouping against the old routines of place-centred tourism.

An abortive sea-voyage leads nowhere but signals the return from observer-historian towards economic-maritime self-seeking. In *Captain Singleton* (1720), there is no family to abandon, guiltily or otherwise: the narrator is abducted from his nursemaid on a walk, sold to a beggar, passed to a gypsy, and 'dragged about ... from one Part of the Country to another'. Too young for 'the Strolling Trade', he is 'frequently removed from one Town to another', then shipped to Newfoundland. His boat is taken by an '*Algerine* Rover'; he is rescued by a warship (*Novels*, v. 19–20). Within a dozen pages he is marooned at Madagascar, starting his free narrative from an old Crusoe haunt, origins erased by erratic, unfree movement.

Singleton reprises several Crusoe motifs: canoes, coastal explorations, fortifications; gutting a Dutch wreck shows Defoe looting his own materials. But Singleton now has charts, and improving navigational skills. The geographical crux of *Singleton* is choice: which direction to take, since, having no home, Singleton can go anywhere. His band make for Africa. Again, Singleton 'kept no Journal of this Voyage' (48); we have instead the planning that gets them there despite misadventures (logistical rather than spiritually inflected). This is only the first step back towards the atlas: the East coast of Africa is uncolonized and unmapped [SEE CHAPTER 31]. Remarkably, they head straight across the continent using a pocket compass, and the waterways on their charts. Progress is about practicalities: footwear, baggage (they enslave some local buffalo-drivers), mileage per day. But at the centre lies a horrifying blank:

> a vast howling Wilderness, not a Tree, a River, or a Green thing to be seen, for as far as the Eye could look; nothing but a scalding Sand, which, as the Wind blew, drove about in Clouds, enough to overwhelm Man and Beast; nor could we see any End of it ... (77)

Proceeding north nonetheless, they are prone to error (in the literal sense, wandering off); their bearings are upset by a mystifyingly gigantic inland sea. Always there is choice: north or south, left or right, land or water. Eventually a marooned white man (himself a mini-novel) guides them to a route—and riches. As the troop near Guinea, the rivers are literally lined with gold. Persistence has paid off: the hole in the global map is discovered to be a goldmine. Arrival at the west coast is told with Defoe's flattest affect; having traversed Africa on foot, Singleton simply boards a ship and reaches London inside a subordinate clause.

Defoe then retreads the landsman as a pirate. Normally pirates constitute, like storms, an obstacle to efficient commerce; experimentally imagined the other way round, 'cruising' presents the canniest travel Defoe can imagine, with little violence, and preternaturally smooth passages: West Indies, Brazil, East Indies, Red Sea, Maldives, Bay of Bengal, Formosa, the Spice Islands (on a whim). The unpredictable force of tropical storms is registered, and routes must be debated, but the crew go where they choose, intercepting, ambushing, chasing, escaping, returning to base in Madagascar, a site of desperate abandonment no longer. This piracy is close to trade: the home passage sees them pass for merchants going about their business, the picaresque laundered to a 'project'.

On Business

Defoe's next variant was the idea of travel by women.[11] *Moll Flanders* (1722) seems obliged to accord its female protagonist more desire for domesticity [SEE CHAPTER 16]. Moll is born in Newgate, the definitive place of non-movement. Her mother's transportation opens a deracination process resembling Singleton's: trafficked by gypsies, she wanders away at Colchester, finding a secure house of nurses and ladies (against the masculine 'wide world'). As a female child she is 'never out of the Doors';[12] as a woman without secure status, in domestic purdah, her seduction is via a fake errand, one of many delusive journeys, at Mile End, outside the town. Passive travel thereafter plays a significant role in Moll's marital adventures. Her second husband courts her via a 'ramble' to Oxford, in which she is invited to 'Travel like a Dutchess' (51–2); her third takes her to Virginia. The voyage is, despite its storms and pirates, minimized: 'I kept no Journal, neither did my Husband' (70). The real point is that being a passenger is a trap: Moll's new start implodes into a horrifying return to the mother, previously consigned to geographic oblivion, who is also the mother of her husband; diaspora reveals a fateful incest. Moll escapes this grotesque inverted stability, returning alone to England, with a new sense of independent mercantile purpose, checking her 'cargo' and 'lading' (88). Her inland journeys create new networks, which in turn easily return her to Virginia on her own economic terms. She goes on 'rambles' with a fourth husband (102), but the travel motif is strongest with the fifth ('Lancashire') husband. They delude each other by the use of hired coaches and potential 'estate' itineraries as false signs of wealth, but the 'telepathic' communication which recalls 'Jemy' to her side at the inn is a sign of something which transcends distance (120–2). Separated, Moll has a 'ramble' back to London (126) and industriously covers her tracks with false travel narratives. Now a richly knowledgeable mistress of English coach routes, she takes a tour with another man, crossing paths

---

[11] The journals of Celia Fiennes's travels were then unpublished.
[12] Defoe, *Moll Flanders*, ed. Albert J. Rivero (New York: Norton, 2004), 40.

with the Lancashire husband (a highwayman, or pirate of the road) and diverting pursuit from him: she understands travel well enough to fake it. Her famous comment that a woman without a protector is like 'a Bag of Money, or a Jewel dropt on the Highway, which is a Prey to the next Comer' (102–3) is a metaphorical prompt to walk off with the bag herself, grounded in an extraordinary amount of actual topographic detail.

Moll's adventures in thieving invert this exterior geography into the maze-like interior of London in a different 'wandring', Moll as a mobile crime unit developing new navigational command [SEE CHAPTER 26]. The breathless escape from the first theft sends her running through random alleys ('I think it was a Street that went thro' into *Fenchurch-street*', 151), but the deliberate disorientation of the child whose necklace she steals, and elaborate escape route, shows mastery of the A–Z:

> I went thro' into *Bartholomew Close*, and then turn'd round to another Passage that goes into *Long-lane*, so away into *Charterhouse-Yard* and out into *St. John's-street*, then crossing into *Smithfield*, went down *Chick-lane* and into *Field-lane* to *Holbourn-bridge*... (153).

Interludes at Bartholomew Fair and Bury Fair constitute further 'rambles', richly detailed. Moll even returns to Colchester, on a visit to Essex and Suffolk, with 'no little Pleasure' (210) though all her acquaintances are gone.[13] But much of Moll's roving is urban: theft from fixed places, via streets, lanes, alleys, and coach stops. All roads lead spiritually back to Newgate, the gravitational reverse of mobility, where the 'Lancashire' husband also arrives on the conventional arc of criminal destiny. Their reprieve from this, and transportation back to Virginia, return them to an indentured state (prison) which becomes a free estate (thanks to astute management). The book ends with one more routine crossing, Moll's rambles converted into travelling on business, her own 'Bag of Money' safely stowed.

A Journal of the Plague Year (1722) sees London thoroughfares from the perspective of the kind of fixed-location shopkeeper Moll robs. But here the travelling enemy is more like the storm. The plague acts like a mystical wind, not just because airborne dispersal was one of the theories of distribution, but because the plague goes wherever it wants: 'visitation' is one mode of arrival, like some official 'progress'. It reaches places, returns, spreads, draws, 'gets in among' people, or 'comes upon' them, without predictable itinerary. Gradually the human agency of its transmission becomes evident: people fatally bear it with them in their attempts to escape it, every man his own 'walking destroyer'.[14] As in *The Storm*, navigation is at a stand, merchants are stuck, roads blocked, travel for pleasure unthinkable. Consequently, travel acquires immense psychological

---

[13] Defoe was finalizing a land deal at Colchester, an old haunt, as *Moll Flanders* was being published; Pat Rogers, 'Daniel Defoe's Knowledge of Essex: The Evidence of *A Tour thro' the Whole Island of Great Britain*', *Essex Society for Archaeology and History*, 4th ser., 9 (2018), 127–41.

[14] Defoe, *A Journal of the Plague Year*, ed. Christopher Bristow, intro. Anthony Burgess (London: Penguin, 1981), 213.

urgency, focused on the choice: stay or go. People flee, remove, break out, run abroad; there is wandering guided only by desperation (73). 'H. F.' (unusually for a Defoe hero) stays, the still centre of a London as route-mapped as that of *Moll Flanders*. From his shop, formerly centre of an economic web, he watches micro-movements about the streets, including running 'up and down', a demented need to keep moving when there is nowhere to go (91).[15] He cannot evacuate, but can leave his house, on carefully considered routes round the City, watching the 'dead carts' rumble along, observing makeshift local trading routes, considering river traffic and seaborne navigation. He is one of the 'visitors' policing plague houses in which people are fatally imprisoned and from which desperate escape attempts are made. Others run haywire; H. F. walks the thoroughfares and fields at an orderly pace. Cordoned himself, he achieves a novelistic *excursus* in the story of 'travellers' who have left the city but cannot go anywhere else, and are stuck in liminal woods near a roadblock before finally acquiring the magical 'passport'. Even towards the end, H. F. watches alarmed as people 'ran all together promiscuously, sick and well' (239); normality is signalled by people moving coherently.

If *Plague Year* presented London in lockdown, all movement but the observer's pathological, *Colonel Jack* (1722) reopens the urban-picaresque geography of *Moll Flanders*, from the perspective of a freebooting picaro. Jack emerges from a folktale trio of Jacks who 'rambl'd about all three together' round Rosemary Lane and Rag Fair, lacking other place of origin (*Novels*, viii. 37). Of no fixed abode, he runs errands and navigates the thieving grounds (in the City, at Bartholomew Fair) and places of safety (Bethnal Green, Mile End, Whitechapel, Billingsgate). If Moll's criminal geography seems like an interior maze, Jack's moves outwards, to the edges. He flees 'into *Fenchurch-street*, through *Lime-street*, into *Leaden-hall street*, down St. *Mary axe*, to *London-Wall*, then thro' *Bishop gate*, and down old *Bedlam* into *Moor-fields* ... through *Long-alley*, and Cross *Hog-lane*, and *Holloway lane*, into the middle of the great Field ... call'd the *Farthing-pye-house-field* ...' (64). Later he walks to Scotland, using back roads and answering queries with Moll-like misdirection. At Edinburgh, 'Sick indeed of the wandering Life' (109), he enlists, deserts, and retraces his steps towards Newcastle, another kind of erasure. Geographic elements accelerate: he is 'trepanned' to Virginia as an indentured servant. After a 'very good Voyage' in which '[n]othing material happen'd to me' (119), 'rambling' Jack finds a settled 'place' and sense of self, escaping (like Moll) the gallows trajectory, a pilgrim's regress ineluctably followed by his namesakes.

But stability disappoints. Jack returns to Europe, surviving the usual Atlantic obstacles (storms, accidents, pirates) and hits an established route out of Bordeaux, strolling like a gentleman-merchant to England. Jack lacks the domestic security necessary for travel to be tourism: his relationships founder and London is dangerous for an ex-thief. He goes with the French army into Italy and reports (*Cavalier*-style) military manoeuvres, a circuit to Paris and travels via Norway and the Baltic, with another return (via Lille and Cologne) to London, where his movements are again chafingly restricted. He

---

[15] Crusoe 'run[s] about like a Mad-man' in despair (36).

marries a woman he meets in a coach, 'rambles' around Lancaster for a year after a fight, and returns to Virginia. Still he must move: witnesses to his 'cavalier' past at Preston arrive, necessitating further elaborate circumventions. Trade takes him to Antigua and confines him in Cuba. He writes his memoirs in exile, then heads via Cadiz to London, where the networks reassure him that everything thrives in Virginia. The English rogue still becomes the international gentleman-merchant, but the process now seems frenetic, entropic, a trap in itself.[16]

Grand Touring

Things turn darker still with *Roxana* (1724), an exotic pseudonym for another migrant (a refugee from Poitiers).[17] Economically speaking, Roxana picks up Moll's 'Bag of Money' and lodges it in the mechanisms of European banking; but mobility is once again the key existential element. Stuck in a domestic trap after her tradesman husband rides permanently away in fine travel equipage, a bad example from the conduct book, she becomes mistress to the landlord, who is then murdered on a business trip in France, leaving her vulnerable—but economically free. She is haunted by random reappearances of the first husband, now a soldier, whose indolence is represented as absence of purposeful movement: 'saving the necessary Motion of the Troops ... he was a mere motionless Animal' who 'never ... did any thing' but merely 'saunter'd about' (95). Roxana, by contrast, is always moving on, through increasingly important lovers. Her 'several Perambulations' (104) as a prince's trophy mistress round Paris, the Alps, and the Veneto look like the passivity of a '*Grand Tour*, as it may be call'd' (102), but she explicitly swerves normative travelogue, having 'no-Mind to write the History of my Travels on this side of the World' (103).[18] Roxana returns to England, but her real 'location' is the web of financial networks: a tremendous storm in the North Sea terrifies the maid Amy, but Roxana gets back on the ship to cash some bills. She is drawn to a Dutch merchant she meets in Paris; aligning the fiction with economic theory, Defoe has Roxana agree with the banker Sir Robert Clayton that merchants are true princes, and that (once more) 'an Estate is a Pond; but ... Trade was a Spring' (170). Her sons both become international merchants.

Roxana occasionally appears driven into metaphorical travel: after marriage she is 'like a Passenger coming back from the *Indies*, who having ... gotten a good Estate, with innumerable Difficulties and Hazards, is arriv'd safe at *London* ... and has the Pleasure of saying, he shall never venture upon the Seas any-more' (243); the shift of gender there

---

[16] In *Augusta Triumphans* (1728), Defoe cleansed London thoroughfares of 'Impudent Strumpets' and street-robbers: exactly his Molls and Jacks before transportation to Virginia (*PEW*, viii. 268).
[17] Roxana learns Turkish, perhaps in echo of Lady Mary Wortley Montagu's famous travels to Constantinople in 1716–18; *Roxana*, ed. Jane Jack (Oxford: Oxford University Press, 1981), 102.
[18] The phrase 'History of my Travels' is, however, used in both *Moll Flanders* (211) and *Cavalier* (55).

suggests the incomplete nature of Roxana's identification with Defoe's loaded mercantile gentlemen. But metaphor is no safe haven. As with Moll, and only partly for reasons of gender (it also affects Jack), free movement requires perennial reinvention of identity and covering of tracks. Roxana controls her public identity by controlling her address. Choices of lodging (the Quaker friend, the Dutch merchant) offer at once protection and the trap of discovery. Amy is a roving surveillance agent, plotting the movements of Roxana's contacts; the last sections dramatize tense cat-and-mouse contests, the detective researches of the daughter Roxana wants guiltily to avoid countered by bafflingly complex manoeuvres. Roxana gets stuck in a port while the escape ship is painfully in sight, agonizes over routes, exits through back doors, and approaches houses via alleyways. Escape to Holland offers not safety but a kind of doom, ominously foreshadowed in ambiguous final sentences.

A New Voyage Round the World (1724) liberated itself from such psychological culs-de-sac, taking ship for travel where there should be, finally, no constraints at all; the narrator is unnamed, existing only to voyage. As the (old) title for the (new) journey suggests, this text is closer to the maritime discourse of Rogers and Dampier than any of the other fictions. But the opening critique of 'the several Navigators whose Voyages round the World have been publish'd', for lack of 'that Variety which a Circle of that Length must needs offer' on one hand, and 'long Journals, and tedious Accounts of their Log-work' on the other, suggests those circumnavigations have become routine, already mapped, in effect static. This voyage is proposed as exploratory, in the observation-led manner of the Royal Society, though the crew are straightforwardly mercantile in outlook.[19] This division is not binding, however, since the narrator seeks less the travel that broadens the mind than the imperially useful new route revealing more worlds to colonize, especially where 'natives' are 'tractable and courteous' (145). The book revisits old haunts, including Madagascar and the Islas Juan Fernandez, home of the marooned ur-Crusoe. But Defoe propels his mariners further than ever along the trade routes: Arabia, India, Malaya, Borneo, the South Seas, the South polar region. Unexpectedly, the colonial dream focuses on a land crossing: confronted by the Andes, a seemingly impassable obstacle, the crew will break through with local knowledge (a courteous Spanish merchant) and careful exploration. They propose to cross the South American continent, observing the 'Passages of the Mountains, and the Wonders that were to be discovered on the other Side' (192); 'the more terrible and frightful, the more difficult and impracticable it was, provided it could be master'd at last, the more it would please me to attempt and overcome it' (193). The route is 'horrid and irregular ... nothing but Blackness and Terror all the Way' (195). Erupting volcanoes have nothing of sublime tourism to them, giving 'no Traveller any other Idea than that of being at the very Entrance into Eternal Horror' (204). But when they surmount the barrier, the narrative sees an open, fertile space that can be filled with a British colony. The hard-won landscape oozes gold,

---

[19] On these distinctions see Douglas Chambers, *The Reinvention of the World: English Writing 1650–1750* (London: Arnold, 1996), Ch. 3.

mapped (as in *Singleton*) by an expedition which part-walks, part-rafts across it, land unblocked by water. Boats meet them on the other side, in a joined-up colonial loop [SEE CHAPTERS 29 AND 30]. The *Voyage* presents obstacles to purposive motion overcome by intelligence and craft, an expansionist *Odyssey* without nostalgia (the return to London is Defoe's flattest yet).

THE WHOLE ISLAND

In 1734, 'Captain Richard Falconer', lamenting the dominance of *Crusoe*, *Moll Flanders*, and *Colonel Jack*, feared his own empiricist voyage narrative '*must in a short period ... strike to Sir* John Mandeville's *lying Travels, and Mademoiselle* Beleau's *unheard-of Intrigues*'.[20] Falconer does not quite identify *Roxana* as travel literature, but the alignment of Defoe's five-year fiction spree with false 'travels' is striking, especially since 'Falconer' was actually W. R. Chetwood, one of the original publishers of both *Moll Flanders* and *Colonel Jack*, now clambering aboard the *Crusoe* bandwagon. In supplanting the conventional logbook with personal meta-travelogues, full of accident, error, and entrapment, as well as 'discovery' and high-risk mercantile advancement, Defoe had changed the relation between traveller and narrative. Perhaps Swift's *Travels into Several Remote Nations of the World* (1726), with its deadpan cod-empiricism and hostility to colonial self-seeking, curtailed Defoe's explorations.[21] But by then he had embarked on a new travel project, dramatizing his own experiences, in *A Tour through the Whole Island of Great Britain* (3 vols, 1724–6). Even while writing *A Tour*, however, Defoe often refused to write about tourist things already described in a literature the conventions of which he flouts.[22]

In the Preface, Defoe states: 'seventeen very large circuits, or journeys have been taken through divers parts separately, and three general tours over almost the whole English part of the island; in all which the author has not been wanting to treasure up just remarks upon particular places and things'.[23] It is, intermittently, admitted that *A Tour* is not the research-based journey, beginning and ending at London, notebook-in-hand, that it must resemble. The start of Letter 3 indicates some of the reshapings that are required for literary pleasure (180), and the Preface to the Second Volume (239) elaborates the illusion of a 'journey, in a private capacity'; phrases such as 'I must travel

---

[20] *The Voyages, Dangerous Adventures and Imminent Escapes of Capt. Rich. Falconer* (1734), iv–v.
[21] Anna Neill, *British Discovery Literature and the Rise of Global Commerce* (Houndmills: Palgrave, 2002), studies Defoe's marine narrators, and Gulliver, respectively (Chs 3 and 4). The publication of *Gulliver's Travels* seems to have depressed the market in new fiction generally for a decade or so.
[22] See Pat Rogers, *The Text of Great Britain: Theme and Design in Defoe's Tour* (Newark, DE: University of Delaware Press, 1998).
[23] Defoe, *A Tour through the Whole Island of Great Britain*, ed. and abr. Pat Rogers (Harmondsworth: Penguin, 1971), 45.

no farther this way' (344) mean 'I must not *write* further in that direction'. 'I write ... in the person of an itinerant', Defoe explains. The pose is novelistically vivid: the start of Letter 4 pictures Defoe setting one foot in the sea 'beyond the farthest inch of dry land west', one of several Crusoe-esque gestures of completeness.

Defoe becomes his own mobile protagonist, relocating the hardships of his travellers to mainland Britain, relishing vistas of movement beyond roadblocks. The Brecon Beacons represent a greater barrier than the Alps and the Andes (375–7); the Black Mountains present 'a ridge of horrid rocks' and only a guide gets them through a 'desert' country 'full of horror'. Snowdon is a 'monstrous height' among 'unpassable heights'; Hannibal could not have got through (384, 390). Yet in the valleys, as in the land beyond the Andes, there is fertility, plenty, trade. Chatsworth, a scene of accomplished prosperity, lies adjacent to 'a vast and howling wilderness' (476), reminiscent of Singleton's African horror. The crossing from Rochdale to Halifax (487–90) resembles the passage through the Pyrenees in *Robinson Crusoe*. In Scotland Defoe encounters the 'wildest and most hideous aspect' of landscape in the 'monstrous and terrible' Enterkin Pass (591–5); the Cheviots are a horrifying obstacle. Hills resist travel; Defoe complains of the steepness of passages in Lincoln (410) and Edinburgh (576); he finds the road from Guildford to Farnham alarmingly narrow (158), and Bagshot Heath a 'Black Desert' (187). Hampstead Heath is fit only for 'a race of mountaineers' (339). These hardships are less a tourist complaint than a way of pitting difficult experience against potential improvement. The Scottish isles are too hard to get to, but Defoe does not despair of having it all mapped, one day (663, 669). *A Tour* suggests that Britishness thrives on the will to connect, despite geographical obstacles [SEE CHAPTER 27].

Defoe sometimes pictures himself taking a stroll round resorts such as Epsom. But his pleasures tend to 'prospect' form: Chester's city walls make 'a very pleasant walk ... from whence you may see the country round' (393); the road from Honiton has 'a beautiful prospect almost all the way to Exeter' (218). Pond is to spring as location is to road, and movement is the true mode of *A Tour*; the twelve miles *between* Nottingham and Derby 'are as agreeable ... as any spot of ground' (457–8). He avoids tourist-trap 'wonders'. The Peak points the comparison between routine shows and freshly observed domestic miracles: they miss the Giant's Tomb but find a cave-dwelling family and unexpected mining activity (462–9). Liverpool's rise as an international port is the real wonder, and Defoe lauds maritime hubs and their magically far-flung connectivity: Deal, Exeter, Falmouth, Hull—even York and Cambridge are, here, kinds of port. Rivers, with supplementary canals, plot the nation's navigability; the Thames has nothing of myth but is rather 'the channel for conveying an infinite quantity of provisions from remote counties to London, and enriching all the counties again ... by the return of wealth and trade from the city' (182). At Windsor, Defoe undertakes to 'leave talking of trade, river, navigation, meal and malt, and describe the most beautiful, and most pleasantly situated castle and royal palace, in the whole isle of Britain' (277). But generally, a place is nothing without connection to somewhere else. The only antiquities of any real interest are outcrops of Roman roads (Fosse Way, Watling Street), reminders of state facilitation of productive travel, like his 1697 *Project*, now emerging in postal networks and turnpike systems.[24]

Rope Makers' Alley

All the post-fiction schemes were on a grand scale, surveying mankind from China to Peru. In *A General History of Discoveries and Improvements ... in the Great Branches of Commerce, Navigation, and Plantation, in all Parts of the Known World* (1725–6), Defoe remapped history as a sequence of geographical expansions, the world a blank slate to fill with the knowledge borne of travel. He partly echoes an earlier 'Introductory Discourse on the History of Navigation', by Edmond Halley, prefacing a major travel collection. Halley commended the efforts of 'so many mariner and travellers' in advancing 'geography and hydrography' to 'some perfection'; an additional boon is that 'Trade is now raised to the highest pitch'.[25] Defoe reverses the equation: the Phoenician and Carthaginian traders were the drivers of knowledge. Learning spreads as commerce discovers things and establishes routes to exchange them. It is not a uniform 'progress', as the ruins of empires show; stop-start movement is historical as well as fictional. But decay and obstruction present redemptive opportunities: Defoe proposes to clear the sea of pirates, stabilize the economy of Africa, and (Chapter XXII) establish the colony in South America imagined in the *New Voyage*.

Defoe died in hiding from creditors, less on the run than terminally marooned. His last surviving letter finds him 'About two miles from Greenwich, Kent'.[26] His family 'dare not come by Water, and by Land there is no Coach'. He imagines a 'retired Lodging' in Enfield where (like Roxana) 'I might not be known'. Hemmed in, he reached for the safely transcendent conclusion of the *Farther Adventures*: 'I am so near my Journey's end, and am hastening to the Place where the Weary are at Rest ... May you Sail the dangerous Voyage of Life with *a forcing Wind*, and make the Port of Heaven *without a Storm*'.

Travel always suggested metaphor, a movement between zones. In the unfinished *Compleat English Gentleman*, Defoe was still thinking of book-travel as gentlemanly adventure in itself, an inspirational home truth from abroad, safe from the travails he had so intensely contemplated, and which would claim him in the end:

---

[24] See the Appendix to Volume 2, 429–47; Pat Rogers, 'Road-Testing the First Turnpikes: The Enduring Value of Daniel Defoe's Account of English Highways', *Journal of Transport History*, 40 (2019), 211–31.

[25] *A Collection of Voyages and Travels*, 4 vols (1704), i. lxix. Halley also wrote a preface to *Atlas Maritimus* (1728), which echoes, or incorporates, much thematically relevant work by Defoe.

[26] Defoe to Henry Baker, 12 August 1730, *Letters*, 473–6. Defoe died in Rope Makers' Alley, in the City, six months later.

> If he ... has not made the grand tour of Italy and France, he may make the tour of the world in books, he may make himself master of the geography of the Universe in the maps, atlasses, and measurements of our mathematicians. He may travell by land with the historian, by sea with the navigators. He may go round the globe with Dampier and Rogers, and kno' a thousand times more in doing it than all those illiterate sailors. He may make all distant places near to him in his reviewing the voiages of those that saw them ... The studious geographer and the well read historian travells with not this or that navigator or traveller ... he keeps them all company ... he discovers America with Columbus, conquers it with the great Cortez, and replunders it with Sir Francis Drake. (*RDW*, x. 167–8)

Further Reading

Douglas Chambers, *The Reinvention of the World: English Writing 1650–1750* (London: Arnold, 1996).

J. A. Downie, 'Defoe, Imperialism, and the Travel Books Reconsidered', *Yearbook of English Studies*, 13 (1983), 66–83.

Anna Neill, *British Discovery Literature and the Rise of Global Commerce* (Houndmills: Palgrave, 2002).

Pat Rogers, 'Road-Testing the First Turnpikes: The Enduring Value of Daniel Defoe's Account of English Highways', *Journal of Transport History*, 40 (2019), 211–31.

Pat Rogers, *The Text of Great Britain: Theme and Design in Defoe's Tour* (Newark, DE: University of Delaware Press, 1998).

Michael Seidel, *Robinson Crusoe: Island Myths and the Novel* (Boston, MA: Twayne, 1991).

Ilse Vickers, *Defoe and the New Sciences* (Cambridge: Cambridge University Press, 1996).

CHAPTER 9

DEFOE AS HISTORIAN

REBECCA BULLARD

DANIEL DEFOE wrote history from the very beginning of his long writing career. A manuscript entitled 'Historical Collections or Memoires of Passages & Stories Collected from Severall Authors', sent as a courting gift to his future wife Mary Tuffley in 1683, is among his earliest extant works.[1] In *The True-Born Englishman* (1700) and *Jure Divino* (1706) he situates contemporary political debates in the context of historical narratives about British national and political identities. In the preface to *The Storm* (1704) he reflects at length on 'the Duty of an Historian' to recount 'Matters of Fact' rather than 'Fable'.[2] And in one of the earliest issues of *The Review* (1704–13) he describes his journalistic practice as 'Writing a History by Inches'.[3] These early works indicate the depth and breadth of Defoe's engagement with ideas about and the practice of history writing. History could be ancient ('Historical Collections', for instance, offers violent and bloody anecdotes about historical figures including Alexander the Great) or contemporary: though aspiring to give an account of the rise of French greatness during the seventeenth century, *The Review* is also a history written 'a half Sheet' at a time about current events—a pace Defoe remarks is too slow for 'the Impatient World'.[4] It could concern natural history, as in *The Storm*, or political theory, as in *Jure Divino*. It could consist of eyewitness accounts, series of facts and figures, myths and legends, and political analysis. It frequently hybridized with other genres, including poetic satire, natural philosophy, and journalism.[5]

---

[1] On this manuscript, held in the William Andrews Clark Memorial Library, see Novak, *Daniel Defoe*, 38–40.

[2] Daniel Defoe, *The Storm*, ed. Richard Hamblyn (Harmondsworth: Penguin, 2005), 4–5.

[3] *Review*, i. 220 (4 July 1704).

[4] *Review*, i. 220 (4 July 1704).

[5] In this respect, Defoe's output sorts well with the expansive idea of eighteenth-century history writing offered by Noelle Gallagher, *Historical Literature: Writing about the Past in England, 1660–1740* (Manchester: Manchester University Press, 2012).

Defoe's early output is shot through with history, but none of his published works from this period is a work of full-scale history first and foremost.[6] That changed in 1709, with the publication in two volumes of *The History of the Union of Great Britain*. This chapter explores Defoe's evolving practice as a writer of history from 1709 until the early 1720s. In order to understand Defoe's sense of himself as an historian, we need to consider him not just as a writer, but also as a political agent. Though it might seem strange to us at 300 years' remove, there was no expectation in the early eighteenth century that history should strive for political impartiality or detachment; rather, it was almost always written with a partisan purpose in mind.[7] Defoe's career as a historian is inextricable from his relationship with one politician in particular: his patron Robert Harley, who was secretary of state for the Northern Department from 1704 until 1708, Chancellor of the Exchequer from 1710 to 1711, and Lord Treasurer from 1711 (the year he became Earl of Oxford) to 1714. Before examining Defoe's histories in detail, then, we need briefly to consider his career as Harley's agent.

Defoe worked for Harley from 1704 until 1714, with a hiatus from 1708 to 1710, as an intelligence gatherer and a political influencer [SEE CHAPTERS 20 AND 21]. His fact-finding tours around England during 1704 and 1705 were followed by extended visits to Scotland in the months leading to the passage of the Act of Union in 1707, and in its aftermath—an experience that led, eventually, to the publication of *The History of the Union*. Defoe's sense of pride at his new-found proximity to power (all the more remarkable given that Harley had rescued him, bankrupt, from Newgate prison in 1703) radiates from his letters of this period. He frequently offers Harley self-serving and apparently unsolicited advice about how to gain and hold power—a process in which 'A Scheme of Generall Intelligence' based on secret agents like Defoe himself are indispensable.[8] Paula Backscheider finds Defoe's 'self-importance and assurance' and his 'willing[ness] to sacrifice dignity and integrity' during this period of his life deeply unattractive.[9] It is—but it is also important, I think, to understanding his conception of himself as a historian.

Defoe's sense of himself as Harley's eyes and ears, and of his proximity to power, allow him to become, in *The History of the Union*, the kind of participant-historian that was familiar both from neoclassical histories such as the Earl of Clarendon's monumental *History of the Rebellion* (1702–4) and its classical antecedents.[10] And yet Defoe is not a

---

[6] Defoe's *History of the Kentish Petition* (1701) interprets recent events to intervene in an ongoing topical matter.

[7] Ashley Marshall, *Swift and History: Politics and the English Past* (Cambridge: Cambridge University Press, 2015).

[8] Defoe to Harley (July–August 1704), *Letters*, 28.

[9] Backscheider, *Daniel Defoe*, 182, 181.

[10] Clarendon offers his qualifications for writing the history of his own times as follows: 'I may not be thought altogether an incompetent person for this communication, having been present as a member of Parliament in those councils before and till the breaking out of the Rebellion, and having since had the honour to be near two great kings in some trust, so I shall perform the same with all faithfulness and integrity'. *The History of the Rebellion and Civil Wars in England, Begun in the Year 1641*, ed. W. Dunn Macray, 6 vols (Oxford: Clarendon Press, 1888), i. 3.

statesman like Clarendon or even his patron Harley, but a spy. Though he speculates in more than one letter to Harley on what he might do '*If I were a Publick Minister*', he acknowledges the 'Vanity of the expression'.[11] Spies were routinely denigrated in this period: 'A Man who is capable of so infamous a Calling as that of a Spy is not very much to be relied upon', wrote Joseph Addison in 1712, while Jonathan Swift went further, describing spies as 'the most accursed, and prostitute, and abandoned race, that God ever permitted to plague mankind'.[12] Moreover, Defoe was always aware of the fact that Harley ran many different agents at the same time, 'allowing none to know the whole Event of what they are employed to do'.[13] As Harley's agent, Defoe appears to feel both the self-confidence of the privileged insider and also the uncertainty and inevitable alienation and scepticism of the spy. Both of these attitudes can be felt in the histories that he published from 1709 onwards.

This chapter focuses on three different stages in Defoe's career as a historian. The first two parts address Defoe's histories that book-end Harley's ministry of 1710–14: *The History of the Union*, which he began while Harley was in the political ascendant and published just before his return to office, and *The Secret History of the White-Staff* (1714–15), which was published immediately after Harley's final fall from power. These histories depict a political world that is complex and difficult to comprehend, full of labyrinthine plots and secret political influences. The historian's role, according to Defoe, is to expose these hidden forces to public view—to offer a kind of 'perfect' or explanatory history of the recent past.[14] Yet the nature of this political terrain makes it impossible for a historian like Defoe to ever be fully confident of the completeness and accuracy of the narrative he presents to his readers. In these histories, then, we experience both the confidence of the partisan historian explaining the past according to a particular ideological model, and also the scepticism of the historian unsure that he has told, or could ever tell, his reader the whole truth about past events.

The final part of this chapter turns to the histories that Defoe wrote in the aftermath of Robert Harley's fall from power. *Minutes of the Negotiations of Monsr. Mesnager* (1717) and *Memoirs of a Cavalier* (1720) grew out of the historiographical methods that Defoe had developed earlier in his career. Like Defoe's earlier narratives, they are political histories that recount tumultuous events in Britain's recent past. And, like *The History of the Union* and *Secret History of the White-Staff*, they explore the possibilities

---

[11] Daniel Defoe to Robert Harley, 2 November 1704, *Letters*, 67.

[12] Joseph Addison, *The Spectator*, ed. Donald F. Bond, 5 vols (Oxford: Clarendon Press, 1965), no. 439, 24 July 1712; iv. 43; Jonathan Swift to Alexander Pope, 10 January 1721, *The Correspondence of Jonathan Swift, D. D.* ed. David Woolley, 5 vols (Frankfurt am Main: Peter Lang, 1999–2014), ii. 124.

[13] Defoe, *Minutes of the Negotiations of Monsr. Mesnager* (1717), *SFS*, iv. 42. Indeed, Defoe himself advised that Secretaries of State should 'have a Sett of Able heads, Under a Secret Management ... from whom to Receive Such Needfull Informations, as by Other Agents Under Them may be Obtain'd ... & yet These Secret heads Need Not Correspond'. Defoe to Harley, July–August 1704, *Letters*, 43.

[14] On 'perfect' history, see Barbara Shapiro, *Probability and Certainty in Seventeenth-Century England: A Study of the Relationships Between Natural Science, Religion, Law, and Literature* (Princeton, N.J.: Princeton University Press), 130–8.

and the limits of eyewitness history. These narratives, however, represent a significant development in Defoe's historiographical practice. With their fictional or fictionalized narrators, they blend memoir, fiction, and reportage to create a new form of history writing—one that gives priority to imaginative and affective engagement with the past.

The History of the Union (1709)

On 13 September 1706, Defoe set out for Scotland on Harley's instructions. His task was to promote the English government's policy of union between Scotland and England, to acquire intelligence about opposition to the Union, and 'By writing or Discourse, to Answer any Objections, Libells or Reflections on the Union, the English or the Court, Relateing to the Union'.[15] During his time in Scotland, Defoe published a number of pamphlets to this effect, but he also used writing as a pretext for gathering intelligence. In March 1707 he informed Harley that 'I have spies in the Commission, in the parliament, and in the assembly, and Undr pretence of writeing my hystory I have Every Thing told me'.[16] Perhaps at this stage the plan of writing a history was just a pretence, or perhaps there was an element of double bluff involved in Defoe's intelligence-gathering mechanism. In fact, both the partisan pamphlets and the secret intelligence that Defoe gathered in Scotland contributed to his first major work of history, *The History of the Union of Great Britain*, published towards the end of 1709, almost three years after the passage of the Act of Union.

Defoe deploys a variety of historiographical strategies over the course of the two volumes of *The History of the Union*, but the one that was to prove most significant for the development of his career as a historian is his emphasis on the importance of eyewitnessing and observation. Defoe repeatedly calls attention to himself as an '*Eye-Witness*' to the events that he recounts in *The History of the Union* (*TDH*, vii. 44, 143, 258), and he often positions himself rhetorically as an observer of the scenes that he describes. In his account of anti-Union riots in Edinburgh, for instance, he tells us that 'the Rabble ... went Roving up and down the Town, Breaking the Windows of the Members of Parliament, and Insulting them in their Coaches in the Streets'. He then swiftly moves the action from the street scene to his own position indoors as he reports that 'the Author of this had one great Stone thrown at him, for but Looking out of a Window' and that he 'was watch'd and set by the Mob'—singled out for his work in support of the Union (vii. 285–6). In this domesticated rendition of something akin to the battle scenes of classical historiography, Defoe ensures that his readers view anti-Union mob violence from—literally—his own perspective as a beleaguered eyewitness

---

[15] Defoe to Harley, September 1706, *Letters*, 126
[16] Defoe to Harley, March 1707, *Letters*, 211.

observer. Defoe the spy watches the mob, and the mob watches him back in a form of mutually hostile observation.

Defoe's run-in with the Edinburgh mob reveals the importance of observation to the practice of history writing, but also the dangers involved in historical looking. One of these dangers, of course, is that a single individual, no matter how well placed and well connected, cannot see everything. Defoe alerts his readers to this fact in a strikingly reflective methodological passage:

> I am not Insensible, That, in the strange Variety of Circumstances, Changes of Prospects, the Turns of Management, the Accidents and Niceties, with which [the Union] has been carryed on, the Infinite Difficulties the Zealous Promoters of it met with, the Restless Attacks of a Strong Party to Disappoint it, who never gave over their Struggle, no not even after it was done: In this Labyrinth of Untrode Paths, I may easily misplace some things, and omit others; and I cannot but Introduce my Account of it with this Caution, that tho' I believe no Man can have Collected with more Care, nor has had the Opportunity to Remark things with more Advantage, having been Eye Witness to much of the General Transaction, and furnish'd by the best Hands with every most secret Affair in the Carrying it on; yet many Minute Things may have past my Pen, which it is impossible for me to Attone for, but by making this *Proviso*, That the Reader may be assured, nothing Material can have slipp'd me; and I have used all necessary Caution to furnish my self with the whole Truth of Fact, whatever Omission of Circumstances I may make an Apology for. (*TDH*, vii. 143)

Here, Defoe challenges his authority as an observer and a historian even as he asserts it. The complexity of the Union's passage—the 'Labyrinth of Untrode Paths' through which it had to progress to come to fruition—makes it impossible for even for the most observant and well-informed intelligencer to be sure he has access to all of the relevant historical information. The difficulties that Defoe experiences are directly connected to the involved nature of his subject matter and the limits of his position as an observer. He cannot see into every nook and cranny of the Union. When he offers his readers 'the whole Truth of Fact', he suggests that his interpretation of events is correct, even if incomplete.

What does Defoe mean by 'Fact' here? Other commentators have pointed out the difficulties in navigating Defoe's use of this term, which in his time could mean an action or deed rather than the now more common sense of a known truth.[17] Elsewhere in the *History of the Union* Defoe asserts that this account is 'an Impartial and Unbyast History of Fact' (*TDH*, vii. 148). In both cases, however, the 'Fact' on which Defoe insists is not what many twenty-first-century readers would regard as impartial or unbiased. Defoe's

---

[17] Robert Mayer, History and the Early English Novel: Matters of Fact from Bacon to Defoe (Cambridge: Cambridge University Press, 1997).

narrative is a sustained, strenuous argument that any opposition to the Union proceeded overtly or covertly from the Jacobite faction—that is, from political supporters of the heir of the exiled monarch, James II. He insists that the Presbyterians who resisted the Union had been hoodwinked by the Jacobites. And to add weight to his positive arguments in favour of the Union, he includes a pre-history of the events of 1706 and 1707 in the form of a longitudinal narrative on ideas for a Union from medieval times to Anne's reign—a teleological account in which the completion of the Union is over-determined and providentially approved. In writing a 'History of Fact' Defoe constructs a highly partisan narrative of the events that led to the Union. If his readers come away from his *History* with a pro-Union understanding of the recent past, he has done his job correctly.

In order to navigate the labyrinthine events of the Union, Defoe suggests, his readers need a guide. He repeatedly returns to the metaphor of the *History* as a 'Thread'—a clue (in its literal sense) or ball of yarn used to guide a person through a maze.[18] He uses the material form of the book to reinforce this idea. In some places in his *History* he relegates material to appendices in order not to disrupt 'the Thread of the Story' (*TDH*, vii. 246). Elsewhere he includes documentary evidence 'as being not long enough to interrupt the Thread of this Discourse' (*TDH*, vii. 332). This kind of guidance takes a different form in the second volume of the *History*. Here, Defoe gives readers a series of verbatim reports of speeches from the Scottish Parliament, followed in each case by a set of 'Observations' to guide their interpretation. Difficult and dangerous as his task may be, Defoe presents it as indispensable if his readers are to navigate the 'Facts' of the Union aright.

Defoe's practice in *History of the Union* is closely related to his work as Harley's agent, but it also demonstrates a self-consciousness in his practice as a historian that extends into much of his later writing. In *History of the Union* he takes the idea of 'observation' in two different, but related, directions: he is an eyewitness narrator who observes events hidden from public view, and he is a synthesizer of events who creates for his readers a particular, politically inflected narrative thread. He encourages his readers to see his history not as a transparent window onto recent events, but rather as a narrative constructed from a position of privileged, but limited, knowledge. What emerges from the *History of the Union*, then, is not just an account of the Union itself, but also a reflection on the practice of writing history. The characteristics that we observe in this text—especially Defoe's interest in secret intelligence and hidden events and his self-consciousness towards narrative form—emerge once more the following decade in another Harley-inspired historical text, *The Secret History of the White-Staff*.

---

[18] 'clue, n.', *OED Online*, Oxford University Press, December 2019, www.oed.com/view/Entry/34830. Accessed 18 December 2019.

THE *SECRET HISTORY OF THE WHITE-STAFF* (1714–15)

After a period out of office between 1708 and 1710, Robert Harley returned to power the year after the publication of Defoe's *History of the Union*. In 1711 he rose still further, becoming Lord Treasurer—a post referred to as the White Staff, after its symbol of office—Earl of Oxford and Mortimer and, in effect, Queen Anne's prime minister.[19] His administration, which lasted until the summer of 1714, was especially controversial for its foreign policy. In 1713, Britain signed a peace treaty with France, bringing to an end Britain's involvement in a war that had lasted for more than a decade. Oxford's opponents seized on the peace as evidence that he was a friend of both France and, by extension, of the Jacobites—that is, supporters of James Francis Edward Stuart, son of James II, who claimed to be Britain's king in exile. Oxford was eventually dismissed a few days before the death of Queen Anne in the summer of 1714. Following the accession of the Hanoverian George I, the new Whig administration impeached Oxford in June 1715 on charges of high crimes and misdemeanours. They committed him to the Tower and demanded, in the words of the Whig polemicist John Dunton, his 'neck or nothing'.[20] At Oxford's downfall, Defoe too lost his off-the-books position as Harley's main propagandist, and his income. His *Secret History of the White-Staff* represents an attempt to exonerate his former patron from the charges that his political enemies laid at his door.

The secret history was a popular genre of history writing in late seventeenth- and early eighteenth-century England. Its practitioners claimed to expose the secrets of those in power, especially monarchs and ministers, laying bare stories of political and (often) sexual corruption.[21] Defoe had experimented with the form in 1711 in the two-part *Secret History of the October Club*: an account (notionally 'by a member') of the high Tory grouping who challenged Oxford's more moderate administration. But it was Oxford's political opponents who really seized on this genre of historiography, both during his ministry and, especially, after its collapse in 1714. Writers like John Dunton and John Oldmixon were determined to expose Oxford's political secrets as a popular counterpart to the more official impeachment process, and they used secret history in

---

[19] See Brian Hill, *Robert Harley: Speaker, Secretary of State and Premier Minister* (New Haven, CT: Yale University Press, 1988).
[20] John Dunton, *Neck or Nothing: In a Letter to the Right Honourable the Lord —— (1713)*.
[21] On secret history, see Rebecca Bullard, 'Introduction', in *The Secret History in Literature, 1660–1820*, ed. Rebecca Bullard and Rachel Carnell (Cambridge: Cambridge University Press, 2017), 1–14; Brian Cowan, 'The History of Secret Histories', *HLQ*, 81:1 (2018), 121–51.

order to do so.²² When Defoe decided to write his own secret history of Oxford's ministry, then, he was defending Oxford by coopting his opponents' historiographical form of choice.

Defoe's argument in *The Secret History of the White-Staff* is that, in spite of appearances to the contrary, Oxford was not working with or for the Jacobites during his ministry. In order to neutralize the political threat that the Jacobites posed, Defoe maintains, Oxford *appeared* to court this dangerous faction, but he did so in order to gather intelligence about them that would prevent their treasonous plots from coming to fruition. By making them believe that he was on their side, Oxford duped the Jacobites into 'believing the *White-Staff* was in their Interest; and by being made to entertain that Dream, they hamstringed their Cause, and suffered themselves ... to be made the Instruments and Agents to make that impossible, which they fancied they were bringing to pass' (*PEW*, ii. 273). The secret in this secret history, then, is not that Oxford was actually a Jacobite (as his opponents argued), but, rather, that in spite of appearing to side with the Jacobites, he was in fact working to bring about their downfall.

Defoe's convoluted argument might, with reason, remind us of the 'Labyrinth of Untrode Paths' through which he offers to guide his readers in his *History of the Union*. As in that earlier account, he represents political culture as complex and difficult for the casual observer to comprehend and navigate. Indeed, he uses a metaphor related to the labyrinth when he describes Oxford as 'the Clue'—that is, the thread—'we are to trace in this *Secret History*' (*PEW*, ii. 269). But he also moves beyond the metaphor of the labyrinth when he claims that his secret history exposes 'the several Springs and Wheels, Engines and Arts, by which both the Parties wrought in the violent Opposing one another' during Oxford's ministry.²³ Rather than a static maze, politics here becomes a system of dynamic, interlocking parts. Only a historian with privileged access to state secrets can hope to guide the unwary reader through such a complex mechanism.

Rather than telling the story of Oxford's ministry in chronological order, the three parts of this secret history go over the same period again and again, revising and supplementing the accounts offered in previous instalments. The second part begins with 'a brief Recapitulation of a Circumstance or two, which is but hinted lightly at in the first part, in order to preserve the Connection of the historical Relation of things, and, with the greater Clearness, to introduce the Matters which are behind'.²⁴ And the third part 'proceeds to what is yet behind, of Moment equal, and, perhaps, of Advantage much more to be known, than any thing which has been yet discours'd of'.²⁵ In both of these instances, Defoe uses a spatial metaphor to reflect on his work as a historian—each part of the secret history reveals information *behind* the material offered in the previous

---

[22] On secret histories in dialogue with Defoe's, see Rebecca Bullard, *The Politics of Disclosure, 1674–1725: Secret History Narratives* (London: Pickering and Chatto, 2009), 63–8, 135–47, and Gallagher, *Historical Literature*, 74–93.

[23] Defoe, *Secret History of the White-Staff... Part III* (1715), 20.

[24] Defoe, *Secret History of the White-Staff... Part II* (1714), 4.

[25] Defoe, *Secret History of the White-Staff... Part III*, 4.

part. The events of history exist not as a linear narrative, but rather as a series of springs, wheels, and cogs, each of which is driven by yet more carefully hidden movements. The material form of Defoe's secret history—not a single, extended narrative, but, rather, three pamphlets published over a period of months, each of which offers new and supplementary information about Oxford's ministry—reflects this sense of history as a series of revisions of received narratives of the past.

Even as he offers his readers more and more secret intelligence, however, Defoe also exercises scepticism towards the idea that *The Secret History of the White-Staff* gives a full account of its subject. He ends the third and final part by declaring that 'there are yet several large Fields that are not mentioned, or entred into, and which have some *Arcana* of publick Matters to bring to light, before the *History of the White-Staff* can be said to be compleat'.[26] What these 'large Fields' might be, Defoe does not say. Indeed, it is tempting to conclude that, after three separate instalments of this secret history, and in the face of an increasingly hopeless set of political circumstances (as Oxford faced inevitable impeachment charges), Defoe was becoming more interested in the idea of publishing history by instalments than in the particulars of Oxford's ministry.[27] Secret history is attractive to an author down on his luck, because it always leaves open the possibility that more secrets might be discovered and, therefore, furnish copy for future publications.

This might seem a rather cynical interpretation of Defoe's defence of his former patron, but it is in fact one that Defoe himself encouraged. Between the publication of the second and third instalments of *The Secret History of the White-Staff*, Defoe wrote and published one of the strangest and most surprising interventions in the historiography of Oxford's ministry: *The Secret History of the Secret History of the White-Staff* (1715). Also published anonymously and resembling closely the pamphlets that Defoe's enemies had published in response to his *Secret History of the White-Staff*, *The Secret History of the Secret History* makes an extraordinary claim: that both Defoe's secret histories and his political opponents' attacks on them were, in fact, nothing but a ruse by the booksellers of London to increase their revenue. 'The Writers of the Books', insists the narrator, 'sitting still all this while, had their leisure to Laugh at Mankind, and to please themselves with thinking how either Side fell into their Snare, and bought up many Thousands of the Books, which as shall presently be shewn, was the *Summa Totalis* of the Design' (*PEW*, ii. 299). The real secret in *The Secret History of the White-Staff*, according to this view, is that it is not a political defence of Oxford at all, but a ploy to generate copy.

What was Defoe doing in *The Secret History of the Secret History*? Why would he undermine his defences of Oxford in this way? It is difficult to say for sure, but what is apparent is that in *The Secret History of the White-Staff* and in *The Secret History of the Secret History* Defoe was developing ideas that he had already explored in *The History of*

---

[26] Defoe, *Secret History of the White-Staff... Part III*, 80.

[27] The secret committee that investigated Oxford's conduct in office began to meet in April 1715, and he was impeached in June. Defoe's response to the impeachment was *An Account of the Conduct of Robert Earl of Oxford* (1715).

the Union. In that earlier history, Defoe reflected self-consciously on the relationship between himself as historian, his readers, and his subject, even as he told the history of the Union. He presents himself as someone who had inside intelligence into the complex events that surrounded the passage of the Union, but he also acknowledges that those events were so complex that he might not, in fact, be able to offer a complete history. In the *History of the Union* he makes up for this deficiency by asserting a single salient 'fact': that the Jacobites were the driving force behind any opposition to the Union. By the time he came to write *The Secret History of the Secret History of the White-Staff*, however, he seems to have been more interested in the historiographical than in the political implications of his claims to reveal secrets. The historian is no longer a guide through a labyrinth, but has, rather, become a conspirator against the reading public. By pursuing the claim to reveal historical secrets to its fullest logical extent, Defoe undermines history itself.

Minutes and Memoirs

It is, perhaps, surprising that Defoe should return to writing history at all after the apparent cynicism of *The Secret History of the Secret History of the White-Staff*. No wonder, then, that when he does return, his narratives take a rather different—and rather more experimental—form from those he wrote earlier in his career. *Minutes of the Negotiations of Monsr. Mesnager* (1717) and *Memoirs of a Cavalier* (1720) share some characteristics with Defoe's earlier histories. Both, for instance, explore a complex political period in European political history—*Minutes of the Negotiations* concerns the negotiations that brought to an end the War of Spanish Succession in 1713, during the Earl of Oxford's ministry, and *Memoirs of a Cavalier* is set during the conflicts that ravaged Europe during the first part of the seventeenth century, including the Thirty Years' War and the English Civil Wars. Where these texts differ from those that came before them is in the kinds of narrator that Defoe deploys. *Minutes of the Negotiations* is narrated by a fictionalized version of a real-life French diplomat, and *Memoirs of a Cavalier* by an entirely fictional, unnamed supporter of Charles I. In both narratives, then, Defoe filters the events of the recent past through the lens of fiction. And in both, readers are asked to consider what that past looks like from a point of view that may well differ quite substantially from their own. The result is an exercise in imagining the world from a different point of view, and an increasingly expansive sense of how history might be written and experienced by its readers.

Minutes of the Negotiations of Monsr. Mesnager is, among other things, Defoe's final attempt to defend the Earl of Oxford. Published the month before Oxford's trial, it presents a first-person account of his ministry from the point of view of Nicolas Mesnager, a diplomat who was sent to London in 1710 to negotiate, in secret, the preliminaries of a peace treaty. According to Mesnager's account, Oxford did not commit the high crimes and misdemeanours of which he stood accused by the Whig ministry—but he did act in such a secretive and confusing manner as to generate suspicion, however unjustified. 'In publick Business', Mesnager writes, Oxford's 'Discourse is always reserved, communicating nothing' (*SFS*, iv. 42). He goes on to suggest that 'his being so absolute in his own Measures, as to enter into no Freedoms with any, has been the Cause that [Oxford] has broke with every Body first or last' (42). Secretive, controlling, and paranoid, Oxford is shown in this narrative to be an imperfect political manager, but not a traitor to Queen and country.

In some ways, *Minutes of the Negotiations* bears a strong resemblance to aspects of both *History of the Union* and *The Secret History of the White-Staff*. Defoe uses a by-now-familiar set of metaphors to describe the secretive and complex political landscape of the Oxford ministry. Oxford turns his political agents into '*Wheels in a Watch, perfectly passive, except as wound up, or screwed down by the Engineer, who was to be himself*' (50). This account aims to describe 'the first moving Springs' of the peace negotiations; Louis XIV is 'the Spring, and very Movement' behind the peace negotiations and 'a King, whose Soul was equal to all the Labyrinths and Meanders in the Politicks of all the Nations round him' (44, 37, 53). The political terrain in which both the British prime minister and the French king operate is, like the one described by Defoe in his earlier histories, convoluted and maze-like, full of secrets, hidden motives. Indeed, Oxford and Louis XIV appear well matched in their ability to negotiate this territory—perhaps justifying, according to Defoe, his master's secretive methods of political management.

In spite of these similarities, however, *Minutes of the Negotiations* differs from Defoe's earlier histories in one important respect: the nature of its narrator. Defoe signs the dedication of *The History of the Union* with his own name, and in *The Secret History of the White-Staff* he adopts a neutral, not readily identifiable, narrative persona (albeit one broadly sympathetic towards Oxford). *Minutes of the Negotiations*, on the other hand, presents itself as a first-person narrative written by someone who takes pride in being part of a French intelligence network in Britain, and who celebrates the French king as sincere, supremely good, and '*inspired from Heaven*' (36). Mesnager is not only an enemy to Britain, but also a non-English speaker and someone whose intelligence is often gleaned at second hand (115). Moreover, he stresses at various points in his narrative the gullibility of the English reading public (115–16). How, then, are Defoe's readers to interpret his account of the peace negotiations, and Oxford's conduct in them? How far can we trust this narrative? This 'insider' account of a sensitive period of recent history is a complex test case for approaches towards history. It offers readers an opportunity to develop a set of skills, rather than reliable information. It trains them to consider what the past might look like from different ideological perspectives, and to exercise scepticism towards history, even when—especially when—it purports to be written by an eyewitness.

Minutes of the Negotiations is a first-person narrative, but not a biography. Mesnager insists it is not 'an History of my Life, which was led in a more private Capacity' (25). Yet the use of a fictionalized narrator in this work seems to have inspired Defoe to begin to experiment with narrative forms, such as the memoir, that blur the boundaries between history and life-writing.[28] While *Minutes of the Negotiations* presents a fictionalized version of a real historical character, *Memoirs of a Cavalier* (1720) uses a fully fictional narrator—an English gentleman who enlists in the service of Gustavus Adolphus, King of Sweden, and Charles I during the European conflicts of the early seventeenth century. With its fictional first-person narrator, *Memoirs of a Cavalier* resembles in some ways its near contemporaries, *Robinson Crusoe* (1719) and *Moll Flanders* (1722). More than the texts that we have come to know as Defoe's novels, however, *Memoirs* asks its readers to keep in view both its narrator's own experiences and the wider set of public events to which he gives us access. This late stage in Defoe's writing career, so important to the development of the form that we have come to know as the novel, also represents an expansion in early eighteenth-century approaches towards history [SEE CHAPTER 3].

Memoirs of a Cavalier is a first-person narrative in distinct parts—an unusual structure among Defoe's mature, novel-length narratives, but one familiar from both *The History of the Union* and the multipart *Secret History of the White-Staff*, as well as *Memoirs of the Church of Scotland* (1717), a thoroughly-researched history of the Reformation in Scotland, the Church's persecution, and its eventual deliverance by the 1688–9 Revolution. Part 1 of *Memoirs of a Cavalier* addresses the unnamed narrator's exploits in central Europe and, in particular, his admiration for Gustavus Adolphus, under whom he serves. Part 2 brings the story back to England, and offers an account of the Cavalier's service under Charles I. As in Defoe's earlier histories, the two parts of the narrative both perform different kinds of historical work and also reflect on one another. In particular, the Cavalier's personal experience of two monarchs allows him to contrast Gustavus Adolphus and Charles, to the latter's discredit. 'When I was in *Germany* with the King of *Sweden*', the Cavalier recounts, 'we used to see the King with the General Officers every Morning on Horseback, viewing his Men, his Artillery, his horses, and always something going forward: Here [in England] we saw nothing but Courtiers and Clergymen, Bishops and Parsons, as busy as if the Direction of the War had been in them; the King was seldome seen among us, and never without some of them always about him'.[29] Just as, in *Minutes of the Negotiations*, a French spy questions the power of France to influence the Earl of Oxford, so in *Memoirs of a Cavalier* it is a supporter of Charles I, rather than a political opponent, who acknowledges, with regret, the weaknesses of his own side. Defoe is fascinated, it seems, by the idea of history as told not by the winning side, but by narrators of dubious faith who tell their stories from the edges and margins of the events they recount.

But just as significant as the contrast between Gustavus Adolphus and Charles I are the stylistic differences between the first and second part of *Memoirs of a Cavalier*. In

---

[28] Philip Hicks notes that 'unlike the historian, the writer of memoirs wrote from a patently personal perspective, often in the first person, and was not held to such high standards of impartiality as the historian'. *Neoclassical History and English Culture: From Clarendon to Hume* (Basingstoke: Macmillan, 1996), 11.

[29] Daniel Defoe, *Memoirs of a Cavalier*, ed. James T. Boulton (Oxford: Oxford University Press, 1991), 125–6.

Part 1, the Cavalier travels through Europe as a kind of military tourist. His observations on the conflicts he witnesses are strikingly dispassionate. He reports, for instance, that 'on the 16th of *November*, the Armies met on the Plains of *Lutzen*; a long and bloody Battle was fought; the *Imperialists* were entirely routed and beaten, 12000 slain upon the Spot, their Cannon, Baggage and 2000 Prisoners taken, but the King of *Sweden* lost his life, being killed at the Head of his Troops in the beginning of the Fight' (110). The Cavalier is no more moved when his own side, rather than the opposing one, suffers mass casualties. He notes that soon after the Battle of Lutzen 'we lost near 8000 Men upon the Spot, and above 3000 Prisoners, all our Cannon and Baggage, and 120 Colours' (118). There is a sense here of the overwhelming scale of conflict, but the bare facts feel inadequate to convey a sense of the human cost of warfare, or the human emotions involved. Even the death of the Cavalier's hero, Gustavus Adolphus, is tacked on to a catalogue of horrors, none of which seem in any way to horrify the Cavalier.

At the beginning of Part 2, when the scene moves to England and the outbreak of Civil War, the Cavalier comes to regard the emotional stupor of Part 1 with some astonishment. He speculates as to whether or not his experience of warfare in Germany 'had hardened me against the natural Tenderness which I afterwards found return upon me ... but I reflected upon my self afterwards with a great deal of Trouble, for the Unconcernedness of my Temper at the approaching Ruin of my native Country' (125). He is self-consciously emotional in his account of civil war—reporting, for instance, that 'It grieved me to the Heart, even in the Rout of our Enemies, to see the Slaughter of them; and even in the Fight, to hear a Man cry for Quarter in *English*, moved me to a Compassion which I had never been used to' (165). Even when he asserts that he was 'an Eye-witness of the Action', as at the siege of Leicester, his account focuses on the moral as much as the technical aspects of war: in this section he vigorously defends Charles's troops against the accusation that they committed atrocities, asserting that 'I never saw any Inclination in his Majesty to Cruelty' (242). The result is an account that seeks to give its readers not just information about the conflict or its causes, but a sense of how it felt to be involved [SEE CHAPTER 22].

The stylistic differences between Parts 1 and 2 may in part be a product of the sources on which Defoe drew in composing *Memoirs of a Cavalier*. As Arthur Wellesley Secord has shown, the Gustavus Adolphus sections in Part 1 rely on newspaper reports in *The Swedish Intelligencer* (1632–3), while Part 2 is based on a number of first-hand accounts of the Civil Wars, including those by Clarendon, Edmund Ludlow, and Bulstrode Whitelocke.[30] Defoe's use of these sources, however, suggests two quite different approaches towards history in Parts 1 and 2. The observational, data-driven approach of Part 1 comes to be associated, in Part 2, with a kind of impoverished detachment, while the heartfelt engagement of Part 2 offers a new way of understanding history—not through numbers, observations, and empirical eyewitnessing, but through an appeal to

---

[30] Arthur Wellesley Secord, *Robert Drury's Journal and Other Studies* (Urbana, IL: University of Illinois Press, 1961), 72–133.

the moral and affective aspects of human experience.[31] It anticipates the extraordinary and deeply moving work of historical fiction that Defoe would publish in 1722 as *A Journal of the Plague Year*.

DEFOE AS HISTORIAN

Defoe's approach towards history is, in many respects, typical of the time in which it is written. It was not only concerned with politics, but also self-consciously directed towards particular political and ideological ends. *History of the Union* was designed to promote the recent union between Scotland and England; *The Secret History of the White-Staff* and *Minutes of the Negotiations* defend Robert Harley, Earl of Oxford, from his detractors under the new, Whig political regime of the early years of Hanoverian rule. Even *Memoirs of a Cavalier*, which, set in the early seventeenth century, is less overtly connected to contemporary politics, nonetheless resonates with Harley's (and Defoe's) political beliefs. As Nicholas Seager has shown, Defoe's text draws on earlier histories of the Civil Wars written from both royalist and parliamentarian perspectives to promote a form of political moderation that had been a hallmark of Harley's politics—and to which Defoe still held fast, years after Harley's fall from power.[32] Twenty-first-century readers may look askance at such naked partisanship in history writing. Ashley Marshall reminds us, however, that history during the early eighteenth century 'was practical and ideologically loaded, not philosophical and academic'.[33] Readers throughout the 1710s and even, to some extent, the 1720s were living with the consequences of the events that Defoe described—whether those were the European struggles of the 1630s and 1640s or of the 1700s and 1710s. Defoe writes history that had a direct bearing on his readers' lives, and aims to teach them to interpret the recent past correctly, according to a particular set of ideological positions.

Defoe's histories also reflect wider contemporary practice in at least some of their techniques and methods. They are, for the most part, eyewitness accounts written by, or from the perspective of, participants in the events they describe, and they frequently claim to be based on insider knowledge. But while, in some ways, this emphasis on eyewitnessing and privileged information aligns Defoe's histories with what Barbara

---

[31] We might compare the stark stylistic differences between the rather dry, heavily researched first two parts of *Memoirs of the Church of Scotland*, which recount the period from the Reformation to the Restoration of Charles II, and the emotionally charged third part, which testifies to persecution that took place within the living memory of many of Defoe's readers.

[32] Nicholas Seager, '"A Romance the Likest to Truth that I Ever Read": History, Fiction, and Politics in Defoe's *Memoirs of a Cavalier*', *ECF*, 20:4 (2008), 479–505.

[33] Marshall, *Swift and History*, 4. On the polemical nature of history writing during the late seventeenth and early eighteenth centuries, see also Daniel Woolf, 'Historical Writing in Britain from the Late Middle Ages to the Eve of Enlightenment', in *The Oxford History of Historical Writing: Volume 3: 1400–1800*, ed. José Rabasa et al. (Oxford: Oxford University Press, 2012), 474–96 (484–9).

Shapiro has termed the emerging 'culture of fact' in eighteenth-century England, on the other hand it calls into question the extent and the reliability of the historian's knowledge and understanding.[34] Defoe's histories of the early and mid-1710s, with their focus on the labyrinthine politics of the Oxford ministry, reveal the difficulty of ever giving a complete account of the past, and leave themselves open to revision through future discoveries. His use of the memoir form was likewise vulnerable to attack on grounds of method. As far back as the 1680s, the French neoclassical theorist René Rapin had actively sought to distinguish between memoirists and historians:

> To relate the Actions of men without speaking of their *Motives*, is not to be accounted writing of History. Who does so, demeans himself as a *Gazeteer*, who thinks it enough to deliver the Events of things, without advancing to their Source. As *Caesar*, who simply gives an account of his Marches and his Encampings, without acquainting us with the Motives thereof: all in his Narration is too simple and too superficial; and true it is, that he writes onely Memoirs.[35]

When Defoe used fictionalized narrators to offer readers histories of their own times—as when he used secret histories—he chose a form that he knew was held in low esteem by many of his contemporaries.

Why would he do so? In part, his decision reflects the growing market in the early eighteenth century in forms of history other than the models presented by the kind of neoclassical 'perfect' history praised by commentators such as René Rapin. Daniel Woolf reminds us that 'history had arguably become by the early eighteenth century the single most commercially popular and fashionable published form of writing', and, as Noelle Gallagher among others has pointed out, much of this commercial growth was in 'models of historical representation that lay outside the conventional boundaries of history proper', including memoirs, satires, and secret histories.[36] As Defoe's career developed from something approaching 'history proper' in *History of the Union*, to the related, explanatory mode of secret history, to memoirs that are narrated at first from the perspective of an identifiable historical figure (Mesnager) and then by a fictional character (the Cavalier, as well as H. F. in *A Journal of the Plague Year*) we might sense in some ways a gradual movement away from humanistic, neoclassical history to forms of writing that are more self-confidently and self-consciously fictional and novelistic.

There is, however, more continuity across Defoe's career as a historian than this neat, developmental narrative at first suggests. The most distinctive aspect of Defoe's practice as a historian is his investment in the idea of a narrator who is, paradoxically, both a political insider who has access to privileged information, and an outsider who exists

---

[34] Barbara Shapiro, *A Culture of Fact: England, 1550–1720* (Ithaca, N.Y.: Cornell University Press, 2003).
[35] René Rapin, *Instructions for History, with a Character of the Most Considerable Historians Ancient and Modern*, trans. J. Davies (1680), 58.
[36] Gallagher, *Historical Literatures*, xv.

on the edges of courts, parliaments, and ministries, never sure of the extent of his own understanding of the situations on which he reports. His narrators often have personal connections with the very highest echelons of political power: the Cavalier knows Gustavus Adolphus and Charles I personally; Mesnager treats with Harley, St John, and other ministers; as secret historian, Defoe claims to have hidden intelligence about the White Staff; as the historian of the Union, he reports that he has access to ministers of the Church of Scotland, Members of Parliament, and their agents. They are always, however, conscious of the limitations of their account—of the inability of anyone, even an eyewitness (*especially* an eyewitness), to offer a definitive account of the past. The duty of an historian, his career implies, is to offer strategies for handling these limitations, whether through insistence on a particular ideological narrative, a sceptical approach towards history itself, or an imaginative or affective engagement with the past.

In *Colonel Jack* (1722), one of the novels that he wrote in the years after *Memoirs of a Cavalier*, Defoe's eponymous narrator—a reformed thief—is guided by a tutor who instructs him not only in religion, but also history: 'He read History to me;' Colonel Jack reports, 'and, where Books were wanting, he gave me Ideas of those things which had not been Recorded by our modern Histories, or at least that our Number of books would not reach'.[37] Like Colonel Jack's tutor, Defoe holds fast to the humanist belief that that history is crucial to a proper education—but he also suggests that history books are often insufficient to that end. Colonel Jack's tutor becomes a historian as well as a reader, supplementing the printed text with his own ideas, knowledge, and, perhaps, experience. Defoe's practice as a historian seems to suggest that he wished his own readers might do likewise.

Further Reading

Rebecca Bullard, *The Politics of Disclosure, 1674–1725: Secret History Narratives* (London: Pickering and Chatto, 2009).
Rebecca Bullard and Rachel Carnell (ed.), *The Secret History in Literature, 1660–1820* (Cambridge: Cambridge University Press, 2017).
Noelle Gallagher, *Historical Literature: Writing about the Past in England, 1660–1740* (Manchester: Manchester University Press, 2012).
Philip Hicks, *Neoclassical History and English Culture: From Clarendon to Hume* (Basingstoke: Macmillan, 1996).
Ashley Marshall, *Swift and History: Politics and the English Past* (Cambridge: Cambridge University Press, 2015).
Nicholas Seager, '"A Romance the Likest to Truth that I Ever Read": History, Fiction, and Politics in Defoe's *Memoirs of a Cavalier*', *ECF*, 20:4 (2008), 479–505.
Barbara Shapiro, *A Culture of Fact: England, 1550–1720* (Ithaca, N.Y.: Cornell University Press, 2003).

---

[37] Daniel Defoe, *Colonel Jack*, ed. Samuel Holt Monk (Oxford: Oxford University Press, 1965), 171–2.

CHAPTER 10

THE STYLE OF DEFOE'S CORRESPONDENCE

MARC MIEROWSKY

In *The Complete English Tradesman* (1725–7), Daniel Defoe offers a guide to writing letters that stresses plainness above all else. This advice need not be restricted to tradesmen, for, as Defoe insists, 'easy, plain, and familiar language is the beauty of speech in general, and is the excellency of all writing, on whatever subject, or to whatever persons' (*RDW*, vii. 52). The reason Defoe is so concerned with promoting a prose style that is comprehensible to all but at the same time resists the accusations of social levelling that were more commonly directed at print in this period becomes apparent when he reiterates his stylistic ideal and, in doing so, shifts the attention from writer to reader:

> If any man was to ask me, which would be supposed to be a perfect stile, or language, I would answer, that in which a man speaking to five hundred people, of all common and various capacities, idiots or lunaticks excepted, should be understood by them all in the same manner with one another and in the same sense which the speaker intended to be understood, this would certainly be a most perfect stile. (52)

Forgoing the typical metaphor that depicts letters as a written form of conversation,[1] Defoe opts instead for a comparison to mass communication. A plain style is that which can speak to a broad audience; it can impart a message that cuts across that audience's differences, unifying them in the process. Defoe spent much of his writing life honing this approach, with letters providing him an important but largely overlooked medium in which to do so.

Clare Brant places *The Complete English Tradesman* at a transitional point in the history of letter writing: two decades into a century during which men and women from

---

[1] Bruce Redford, *The Converse of the Pen: Acts of Intimacy in the Eighteenth-Century Familiar Letter* (Chicago, IL: University of Chicago Press, 1986), 1–7.

all classes began to write and receive letters. And yet despite this broadening of letter writing in practice—or, indeed, because of it—correspondents throughout the eighteenth century remained largely 'defined by class and sex'; the reception of their letters was bound closely to the social markers of their identity.[2] Defoe's defence of plainness as the basis for a common style is clearer in this light. Unlike the letter-writing manuals of the seventeenth century, which were concerned with the conversational maxims of the gentry, Defoe aimed to develop a style that could incorporate a broad spectrum of writers and readers.[3] Though quick to concede that most tradesmen will speak 'chiefly to other tradesmen', Defoe leaves open the possibility that 'private gentlemen … ministers of state, privy-counsellors, members of parliament' might require the tradesman's expertise on questions of national importance (60). The complete tradesman can speak to all but remains defined by his occupation. Like the chains of correspondence that reached across Britain in the early eighteenth century, carried by the Royal Mail, penny post, and personal delivery, his letters move through, without necessarily breaking down, social barriers.[4]

Throughout his career Defoe repeated the call for an unadorned 'natural' prose. Each time he did so, the terms of his intervention echoed closely the stylistic agenda of the Royal Society as laid out by Thomas Sprat in his 1667 *History*.[5] According to Spratt, the Royal Society expected its members to employ

> A close, naked, natural way of speaking; positive expressions; clear senses; a native easiness: bringing all things as near the Mathematical plainness, as they can: and preferring the language of Artizans, Countrymen, and Merchants, before that, of Wits, or Scholars.[6]

The extent to which this 'constant resolution' (as Sprat termed it) marked a decisive break in the history of prose style is the subject of a long-standing critical dispute.[7] It

---

[2] Clare Brant, *Eighteenth-Century Letters and British Culture* (Basingstoke: Palgrave Macmillan, 2006), 24, 37.

[3] On the difference between seventeenth- and eighteenth-century letter-writing manuals, see Victoria Myers, 'Model Letters, Moral Living: Letter-Writing Manuals by Daniel Defoe and Samuel Richardson', *HLQ*, 66:3–4 (2003), 373–91 (378).

[4] For a history of the postal system, see Kenneth Ellis, *The Post Office in the Eighteenth Century: A Study in Administrative History* (Oxford: Oxford University Press, 1969).

[5] Defoe asserted 'Plainness to be the Perfection of Language' in *Review*, vii. 650 (6 March 1711). He remarked on the 'Easie, Free Plainness, which is the Glory of the English Tongue' in *The Present State of the Parties in Great Britain* (1712), 318. Defoe also advocated plainness in *An Essay on the History and Reality of Apparitions* (1727), *SFS*, viii. 53, and *A New Family Instructor* (1727), *RDW*, iii. 248.

[6] Thomas Sprat, *History of the Royal Society*, ed. Jackson I. Cope and Harold Whitmore Jones (London: Routledge & Kegan Paul, 1959), 113.

[7] For Richard Foster Jones, Sprat's polemic is one in a series to mark the advent of plain style. For Morris Croll, Jones's chief antagonist, the 'plain style' of the Royal Society represents the end point of an anti-Ciceronian tradition that can be traced to Bacon, amongst others. For an overview, see Morris W. Croll, *Style, Rhetoric, and Rhythm: Essays by Morris W. Croll*, ed. J. Max Patrick and Robert O. Evans (Princeton, N.J.: Princeton University Press, 2015); Richard Foster Jones, 'Science and English Prose

is only recently, though, that John Guillory has pointed out that the dispute might stem from a false premise. If the writing of the Society members is anything to go by, then the 'resolution' Sprat speaks of is merely a 'clever rhetorical ploy', for not one of this august group of scientists, thinkers, and poets spoke anything like an artisan or tradesman. By Guillory's reckoning, plain style is thus better thought of as a 'purely conceptual entity'. Like the physicists' 'frictionless surface', it cannot exist in fact but serves as a projection; it is 'not the natural state of prose but its condition after the hypothetical removal of all traces of style'. It is, Guillory concludes, a device for 'discovering prose, for getting at its nature by imaginarily removing everything that might disturb its featureless surface'.[8]

Unlike the Society's members Defoe was fluent in the language of trade [SEE CHAPTER 14]. In his account, plainness means evacuating language of its 'rumbling' and 'bombast', its 'long harangues' and its 'flourishes' (*RDW*, vii. 47). Defoe pursues clarity but offers only the most general syntactic and lexical prescriptions. The strictures he enumerates in *The Complete English Tradesman* and elsewhere are general because the effect on readers is the ultimate metric; his is a pragmatics of plain style more than it is a semantics. Because letters offered a clearer sense of audience than other kinds of writing, they provided members of the Royal Society an arena in which to establish the perlocutionary effects of a plain style. In the same way, personal letters became the first medium and published letters the second through which Defoe could gradually announce, model, and test out a style of writing he hoped would have wide reach and salutary moral effects.

This emphasis on moral efficacy is why Defoe, though deviating often from what we might think of as the marks of clear, direct, and unornamented prose, returned to this ideal each time he was given the opportunity to reflect on the obligations of the correspondent. In *The Compleat English Gentleman* (1728–9?), he presents a plain form of letter writing as part of his programme to educate the gentry.[9] In *A Continuation of Letters Written by a Turkish Spy* (1718), his sequel to Giovanni Paolo Marana's *L'Espion du Grand Seigneur* (1684–6), Defoe adopts the authorial persona of the 'translator' who, when faced with 'the sublime Flights of the incomparable *Mahmut*', the Turkish spy embedded in Paris, reverts to

> the best Rule in all Tongues (*viz.*) to make the Language plain, artless, and honest, suitable to the Story, and in a Stile easie and free, with as few exotick Phrases and obsolete Words as possible, that the meanest Reader may meet with no Difficulty in the Reading and may have no Obstruction to his searching the History of things by their being obscurely represented. (*SFS*, v. 46)

Style in the Third Quarter of the Seventeenth Century', in *Seventeenth-Century Prose: Essays in Modern Criticism*, ed. Stanley Fish (Oxford: Oxford University Press, 1971), 53–89.

[8] John Guillory, 'Mercury's Words: The End of Rhetoric and the Beginning of Prose', *Representations*, 138:1 (2017), 59–86, esp. 68–71, 80–3.

[9] Defoe, 'The Compleat English Gentleman', BL Add. MS. 32555.

Defoe maintained a correspondence both as a means for conducting business and as a vehicle for sociability—the two ends of letter writing are inseparable, being linked by Defoe's helping to popularize the association between a well-managed correspondence and moral self-government. Presumably, the principles of good letter writing demonstrated in *The Complete English Tradesman*, *The Compleat English Gentleman*, and *A Continuation of Letters Written by a Turkish Spy* were drawn at least in part from Defoe's own experience as a tradesman, aspirant gentleman, and government agent. Like the narrator-protagonists at the end of his novels, these works look back upon a life lived in letters. Like Moll or Crusoe, Defoe can draw unifying principles from what has already been laid down—with the caveat that conduct literature and fiction put these principles at one remove from his personal correspondence.

The goal of this chapter is not to hold the letters Defoe wrote throughout his life against the letter-writing manuals and exemplary letters he published in his final decade. Instead, my method here is to canvass his letters, both personal and published,[10] to show how 'the Plainness' Defoe professed in both 'Style and Method'[11] resulted from a concerted attempt to confront the moral and political questions attendant on addressing a wide audience. As critics have noted, Defoe's approach to language took its bearings from the new science and Dissenting preaching, acquiring from each a way to apprehend the world and to interpret events so as to shape the consciences of his readers as political subjects.[12] Plain style was associated with both discourses, and so it is only natural that Defoe had recourse to plainness when justifying the reach of his work. As a 'method', plainness became an umbrella term for his attempts to strengthen for his own ends the bonds that drew these subjects together.

Paula Backscheider notes that Defoe's letters 'exhibit the attention to detail and presentation, the economy, and the accumulative syntax that are the hallmarks of his prose'.[13] In comparison to the career of Samuel Richardson, the century's other great exponent of letter-writing manuals, letters do not hold a prominent position in Defoe's novels, and so their importance to the development and theorization of his prose style generally goes unremarked. Alan T. McKenzie's observation that Defoe's letters demand 'far more attention to local historical detail than to niceties of style' reflects the prevailing attitude. The term 'niceties' is a holdover from scholarship that regards a balanced elegance as the height of style and dismisses Defoe's prose as unstylish by minimizing the importance of its precision and variety.[14] Without neglecting the communicative rationality

---

[10] I use the term 'personal' to refer to letters Defoe wrote and sent and 'published' for those letters he printed and disseminated to the reading public.

[11] Defoe, *Serious Reflections ... of Robinson Crusoe* (1720), *Novels*, iii. 76.

[12] Ilse Vickers, *Defoe and the New Sciences* (Cambridge: Cambridge University Press, 1996), 1–55; G. A. Starr, *Defoe and Casuistry* (Princeton, N.J.: Princeton University Press, 1971), 1–50.

[13] Paula R. Backscheider, 'Accounts of an Eyewitness: Defoe's Dispatches from the Vale of Trade and the Edinburgh Parliament House', in *Sent as a Gift: Eight Correspondences from the Eighteenth Century*, ed. Alan T. McKenzie (Athens, GA: University of Georgia Press, 1993), 21–47 (24).

[14] Alan T. McKenzie, 'Introduction', in *Sent as a Gift*, ed. McKenzie, 1–20 (1). Stanley Fish reflects this prejudice when he voices his concern that his analytical method might be undermined by a writer such as Defoe, the effect of whose prose on the reader he suspects to be accidental. 'The Reader in

and historical circumstances of the letters, this chapter first examines how Defoe's commitment to plainness as a correspondent allowed him the means to define himself as a public writer. In the sections that follow I trace how the stylistic catch-all 'plain' gave Defoe the opportunity to set out a theory of writing that might unify populations and, somewhat ironically, to claim that plainness provided moral justification for the shifts in character and perspective of pamphleteering, journalism, and fiction. While my primary aim is to integrate the letters into literary-critical study, I also draw attention to the significance of Defoe's letters as a manuscript resource. The letters serve as a corrective to earlier scholarship on the basic elements of Defoe's style, which was fundamentally weakened by a reliance on texts adulterated by compositors and editors.[15] Laid bare in the letters themselves are the mutually implicated developments of Defoe's style and politico-ethical thought. Here we have the punctuation, syntax, additions, revisions and corrections, habits of trope and thought that make the style, as the style makes the man, the spy, the satirist, the pamphleteer, the journalist, and, finally, the novelist.

THE HUMBLE SERVANT AND GRATEFUL CORRESPONDENT

The earliest letters to have survived were written in 1703 when Defoe was on the run following the disastrous reception of *The Shortest-Way with the Dissenters* (1702). After it was revealed that the pamphlet—apparently a High-Church call for England to do away with Dissenters in the same manner that France had dispatched its Protestants—was in fact the deadpan irony of one of the most ardent defenders of Dissent, resentment began to mount. On 3 January 1703, a warrant was issued for Defoe's arrest. Defoe's most recent biographers have traced his 'preoccupation with the possibilities of public credulity'[16] to the *Shortest-Way* affair, crediting the widespread outcry and Defoe's subsequent realization that he had the capacity to manipulate readers with the fiction he started promoting at this time as a path to patronage and a pardon: that he had served as an agent to William III.[17]

Literature: Affective Stylistics', *New Literary History*, 2:1 (1970), 123–62 (147). Those who have tried to recuperate Defoe's style stress its multiplicity and Defoe's capacity to make his style suit its purpose, as in G. A. Starr, 'Defoe's Prose Style: 1. The Language of Interpretation', *Modern Philology*, 71:3 (1974), 277–94; P. N. Furbank and W. R. Owens, 'Defoe and the Improvisatory Sentence', *English Studies*, 67:2 (1986), 157–66.

[15] See Irving N. Rothman, 'Coleridge on the Semi-Colon in *Robinson Crusoe*: Problems in Editing Defoe', *Studies in the Novel*, 27:3 (1995): 320–40.

[16] Furbank and Owens, *Political Biography*, 31.

[17] See J. A. Downie, 'Daniel Defoe: King William's Pamphleteer?', *ECL*, 12:3 (1988), 105–17; P. N. Furbank and W. R. Owens, 'Defoe and King William: A Sceptical Enquiry', *RES*, 52:206 (2001), 227–32.

In promoting this apparent fiction, these letters contain some of Defoe's earliest reflections on the public function of his writing. In concert with his early verse and polemical pamphlets, they sketch his developing thoughts on the role writers might play in securing good will between the governed and their governors—a basic tenet of his system of government.[18] The letter form suited this kind of enquiry. Letters have an inherently 'mediatory' aspect, as Janet Gurkin Altman terms it; whether they act as bridge or barrier, they mediate social relations.[19] As Susan E. Whyman shows, eighteenth-century correspondents were keenly attuned to this aspect of letter writing, ever aware of the ways letters placed them in the social world. The act of corresponding gave writers moments of 'self-reflection' but it also demanded 'reciprocity'; the exchange of letters prompted correspondents to see themselves reflected in their interlocutors. The intersubjective bonds letter writing so entailed ended up forcing 'obedience to a social code', with correspondents developing and internalizing a spectatorial consciousness that in turn framed their actions in relation to what they owed the addressee—and how wider society might understand such obligations. Nowhere was the tension between the freedom for individual reflection and the constraints of social obligation more apparent, Whyman maintains, than 'in letters written to maintain patronage needs'.[20] Of the 278 surviving letters that were either written by or to Defoe, 186 were written to Robert Harley, and three were from Harley to Defoe. At least twenty-four more were written to men who can be thought of as potential patrons, amongst them Nottingham, Sunderland, Wharton, Godolphin, Halifax, Stanhope, and Delafaye. It is important to note that our perception of Defoe's correspondence is coloured by what survives. His letters give an important but partial account of how he negotiated service to members of the Triumvirate (Harley and Godolphin) and the Whig Junto (Halifax, Wharton, Sunderland). The battles between and shifting alliances amongst the two groups in pursuing ascendancy within the ministry characterized Anne's reign, repeatedly putting Defoe's politics and personal loyalties to the test [SEE CHAPTER 20].

The tension between the need for patronage and the desire to express his ideas freely is negotiated with typical guile in his first surviving letter, addressed to Daniel Finch, Earl of Nottingham, the secretary of state for the Southern Department, and responsible, as such, for prosecuting authors and publishers of seditious works. However proforma, Defoe is careful to address Nottingham as 'My Lord' and to refer to him throughout as 'yor Lordship'.[21] Defoe repeats the address and invocation to the point of cloyingness, willing, it seems, to perform the honorific gestures that communication between a fugitive and an earl required. Defoe was similarly genuflective towards Charles Spencer, Earl

---

[18] For this system, see *The Original Power of the Collective Body of the People of England* (1702), PEW, i. 99–128.

[19] Janet Gurkin Altman, *Epistolarity: Approaches to a Form* (Columbus, OH: The Ohio State University Press, 1982), 186.

[20] Susan E. Whyman, '"Paper Visits": The Post-Restoration Letter as Seen Through the Verney Family Archive', in *Epistolary Selves: Letters and Letter-Writers, 1600–1945*, ed. Rebecca Earle (Brookfield, VT: Ashgate, 1999), 15–36 (15, 19).

[21] Defoe to Nottingham, 9 January 1703, *Correspondence*, 1–5.

of Sunderland, in 1708—despite their political sympathies and the fact that Sunderland had earlier approached Defoe in an attempt to draw the writer from Harley's service into his own (*Correspondence*, 344–5). This is a representative sample of Defoe's surviving letters to Sunderland:

> But my L^d, According to ye Liberty I humbly Crav'd of yor L^{dpp}, and wch I had yor L^{dpps} p[er]missiona in, I Intreat yor L^{dpps} Pardon and Paćenće. (*Correspondence*, 450)

Furbank and Owens attribute Defoe's 'self-abasement' here to the haughty line Sunderland evidently took with the writer.[22] Comparing the tone in the letters to Nottingham and Sunderland with that Defoe adopts in letters to Harley—for the most part, far less sycophantic—reveals Defoe's capacity to modify his approach in accordance with the way his correspondents wielded their authority. Defoe had a preternatural ability to 'read Mankind' (132), as one correspondent put it. He realized that the social code that Whyman describes governed his potential patrons idiosyncratically. As a result, the politeness strategies he adopted are not simply conventional, but reveal much about how he licensed the often forthright counsel he offered statesmen.

In the letter to Nottingham Defoe's ultimate task is securing a pardon. In this pursuit Defoe shifts his position often. He acknowledges in one sentence that fleeing the law (as he had done) is in effect 'a kind of Raiseing Warr Against' Queen Anne, a standpoint at odds with his prostration of himself at 'her Majties feet' in the following paragraph (4–5). The shift in his position as writer is mirrored by the changing generic frame within which he classifies his request. At one point Defoe refers to himself as Queen Anne's 'Most Humble Petićoner' (5), invoking the form used by ordinary citizens to appeal to those in power. At another point he asks for a personal favour, a treatment befitting a gentleman and above what a petitioner might expect. The writer's request to be treated as a gentleman rests far more on what he could do than on who he was. When published, petitions demonstrated the support of signatories in order to extend that support amongst the reading public. Lurking behind Defoe's representation of himself as a 'Petićoner' is this generic fluidity and his own history of public petitioning.[23] He writes as if he is of the people, and yet in speaking for them (as he claims he did for William III and as he offers his potential patrons) he rises above them.

Defoe's approach to Nottingham establishes the role his letters would play in stabilizing his authorial persona to potential patrons as an intermediary between the people and their governors. Defoe was clearly aware that any letter he wrote would be interpreted through the prism of his reputation as both agitator and supposed agent to the late king. In a letter to Charles Montagu, Lord Halifax, in April 1705 he invokes his 'Dead Master' (135), William III, as the foundation of his political ideals. Defoe was aware too that any letter sent to a member of the ministry was likely to be seen by his

---

[22] Furbank and Owens, *Political Biography*, 91.
[23] On Defoe's public petitioning, see Mark Knights, *Representation and Misrepresentation in Later Stuart Britain* (Oxford: Oxford University Press, 2005), 124–5.

colleagues, because his letters served the function of intelligence reports, such as those sent from Scotland at the time of the passage of the Act of Union. With this knowledge of letter-writing culture, Defoe exploits the indeterminate position letters occupied as not quite in public, but not quite private either. Just as a petition has private and public manifestations and is able to accrue authority as it is passed between readers, so might this letter and, more generally, other letters Defoe wrote.

Defoe's confidence that he could gather support through a contiguous chain of readership underpins his letter to Nottingham. It is also the first instance of what would become one of the fundamental justifications for his later correspondence: that his capacity to move the reading public could serve a greater purpose. In the letter to Nottingham this justification emerges as Defoe disavows his 'Com̃on Fame' (4), one built on pamphlets like *Legion's Memorial* (1701), yet evokes his capacity to speak to all as a reason for the queen to grant a 'Remission' (6) of his offence. This double-edged argument culminates in his request to be reprieved as any criminal wishing to enter her majesty's military service would be, which Defoe qualifies in order to take into account his talents and status: 'At Least mÿ Lord This may Assure you, I am Ready wth my hand, my Pen, or mÿ head, to show her Maj^{tie} The Gratitude of a Pardoned Subject' (6). The idea that Defoe could serve the queen with his pen filters through to the subscription:

> May it Please yor Lordship
> yor Most Obedient, Distressed
> Humble Petic̈oner and Servt
> DeFoe (6)

Defoe made a point of signing letters to patrons as your 'Humble Servt', an ironic move in the case of those to Charles Delafaye, where such a signature masks the fact that he was probably duping its recipient with professions of political loyalty while actively writing against its recipient (831–2).[24] It did, however, convey genuine service to Godolphin, Harley, Halifax, and Sunderland. In the letter to Nottingham, the subscription—crucial to the epistolary mechanics of introspection and exchange—bridges speech and action, past and present. The individual letter wavers between what Altman terms closure and overture:[25] the signature closes the letter but holds out for more correspondence, performing the gratitude that would keep a 'Humble Servt' in his place if the proposal in this correspondence came to fruition.

Gratitude is a central theme in Defoe's correspondence. Circumstances certainly forced this emphasis. But to see the gratitude expressed in the early letters as merely reactionary would mean overlooking the importance of the concept to Defoe's ethical

---

[24] P. N. Furbank and W. R. Owens, 'Defoe, the De la Faye Letters, and *Mercurius Politicus*', *BJECS*, 23:1 (2000), 13–19.

[25] Altman, *Epistolarity*, 186.

thought.[26] Still a fugitive, Defoe opens a letter written in April 1703 to William Paterson, the Presbyterian banking projector, by thanking Paterson for his solicitude:

> I can Not Omitt That in ye Little Informaċon I have from my Very Few Friends I Meet wth from Every hand The Notiċes of yor Conċern for my Present Suffering, And as I am Assur'd my Gratitude for ye Kindness of my friends will be ye Last Vertue That will forsake me So my Senċe of yor Regard for me on whom I have Laid No Obligaċon Lays a Debt On Me I Can No Otherwise Pay Than by mÿ Thankfull Acknowledgements;[27]

The syntax is hypotactic and the punctuation characteristically erratic (a semi-colon and paragraph break serve as the endpoint to the sentence). Even so, there is an art to it, for the sentence performs in microcosm the actions of the letter. In bracketing out the syntactic constituents as he sees them, dividing the concern Paterson has shown from his own response with a comma and capitalizing 'And', Defoe dramatizes not simply the exchange of information letters facilitate, but the fellow-feeling they promote. As this exchange is recapitulated for the purpose of affirming its socially formative effects, Defoe's grammatical position shifts from subject to object, drawing the reader's attention from the back and forth of kindness, gratitude, and the acknowledgement of gratitude (as a means of repaying the kindness) to a system of virtue ethics in which gratitude is fundamental. It is the first virtue Defoe gives voice to and the last to forsake him when the ties that bind the commonwealth unravel around him. The economic metaphor, particularly pertinent given Paterson's expertise in finance, holds out that Defoe can repay the debts he owes the man in writing. As the letter progresses, Defoe leaves open the possibility that writing will be the means to pay his debts to society at large.

The way Defoe determines what he owes his correspondents and the mode of his repayment points to the moral economy in which his letter writing practice evolved. The letter to Paterson shows that Defoe worked from the Hobbesian notion that without gratitude civil society would cease to function. The ties gratitude binds find material acknowledgement in the obligations of correspondence, a medium built on the promise of future writing, and on the connections this writing can foster between political subjects.[28] Two instances illustrate this system and its limits. In 1705, Defoe wrote to Halifax, declaring himself 'a Plain and Unpolish'd Man ... Unqually'd to Make [the] formall Acknowledgements' (142) that would typically follow the generosity Halifax had shown him as intermediary for an anonymous benefactor (the Duchess of Marlborough). The same plainness of character that prevents an elaborate thanks allows for a kind of repayment that Defoe suggests will have wider utility: his

---

[26] See Maximillian E. Novak, *Defoe and the Nature of Man* (Oxford: Oxford University Press, 1963), 113–28.

[27] Defoe to William Paterson, April 1703, BL Add. MS. 70291, ff. 1–2 (1); cf. *Correspondence*, 11.

[28] Thomas Hobbes makes gratitude the third precept of natural law. *On the Citizen* (1642), ed. Richard Tuck (Cambridge: Cambridge University Press, 1998), 47.

service in 'promoteing the Generall Peace and Intrest of this Nacon' (86). Defoe thus posits a connection between plainness as humility, plainness as direct expression, and what he interprets as the national interest. And yet the evidence of the following year suggests that Defoe only wrote to Halifax with Harley's approval.[29] In 1708, Defoe offered a similar scheme of repayment to 'the Debt of Correspondence' (455) he owed Sunderland. His assertion is that 'plain, Naked and Unbyass't Acco[ts] both of Persons and of Things' (450) are a better form of repayment for Sunderland and the public than the rosy picture of Scotland that followed the failed Jacobite invasion. In this way, Defoe's gratitude authorizes his forthrightness; his debts compel him to speak plainly. In the case of Halifax, Defoe's gratitude-bound service 'keeps an Exact Unison with my Reason, my Principle, My Inclinacon, and The Duty Every Man Owes to his Country, and his Posterity' (142). He is similarly open and plain to Sunderland about the fact that he maintained his correspondence with Godolphin because he believed that the two were of 'One Intrest' in 'England', serving 'Truth, Liberty, & Peace' (456), ostensibly unaware of the mounting tension between them. The eye Defoe kept on the national interest allowed him to assert that he kept faith to his political principles. Because national interest is itself subjective, he had room enough to manoeuvre, favouring his personal obligations to Harley above the political affinity he felt for Halifax but turning towards Sunderland in the face of Godolphin's comparative coldness as a patron.

THE TWO KINDS OF COMPREHENSION

In August 1712, with Harley's increasingly High Tory approach to domestic and foreign policy weighing against him, Defoe sent his patron a letter that reassessed the terms of their relationship. In this 'singularly revealing letter', as James Sutherland classes it, one 'no biographer can afford to neglect',[30] Defoe makes the claim that he is 'Neither Employ'd, Dictated to, or Rewarded for, or in, what I write by any Person Und[r] Heaven' (698). Sutherland speculates that the writer's defensiveness in the face of accusations that he was Harley's tool prompted this effort to set down, for his patron, posterity, and himself that he 'never sold his pen'. Defoe was likely driven to make this claim by his failing health and the stretching of his political principles to the point of utter compromise. Even so, it does not mark a break from how he envisioned his service. When he reminds Harley, forcefully and on the face of it disingenuously, that he has always been allowed to 'Persue My Own Reason, and Principle' (698), Defoe uses the same words that in the letters to Halifax signified a natural consonance of ideals. As with all he served, or attempted to serve, Defoe measures what he owes as a man, correspondent, and writer against 'The good of my Country' (699). Setting his personal debts

---

[29] Paula R. Backscheider, 'Robert Harley to Daniel Defoe: A New Letter', *MLR*, 83:4 (1988), 817–19.
[30] James Sutherland, *Defoe* (London: Methuen, 1937), 190–2.

to Harley—'a Deep Senċe of Duty, and Gratitude for That Early goodness' (698) that Harley showed in securing Defoe's release from prison—against 'The Debt of justice to Truth, and Liberty' (699) allows him to argue that because he serves the nation, he does not write for a particular person. Defoe's assertion is far from unimpeachable. The kind of impartiality he projects here had been effective during Harley's tenure as secretary of state (1704–8) when Defoe's rhetoric echoed Harley's own efforts to reach above party. In August 1712, though, it seems to beg room for Defoe to disagree with the man to whom he considered himself indebted above all others. While there are enough instances of Defoe writing to direction to contradict his assertion of independence, there are also moments where Defoe wrote against Harley's wishes that might affirm it. That he felt the need to assert his independence here is evidence that he saw letters as a medium for crafting his historical reputation. The fact that this assertion rests on the notion of service he developed across his letters to Harley points to their utility as a medium for political theory as well as politics in practice.

In his first letter to Harley, written on 9 November 1703, shortly after the Speaker secured his release from Newgate, Defoe begins the process of outlining his theory of service as a public writer by elaborating upon the 'Vertue' of 'Gratitude' (27), extending it from his own ethical system towards the point at which it serves as the basis for public trust. It is gratitude that shapes the popular will, and it is through gratitude that the popular will can be incorporated into the organs of government. The process for incorporation is laid out in a series of letters written between July and September 1704, in which Defoe counsels Harley to undertake two discrete but overlapping ventures: the establishment of a system of secret intelligence and the tactical comprehension of Dissent. According to Manuel Schonhorn, these letters constitute a statement of principle that forms 'the bedrock' of Defoe's 'political imagination'.[31] Dig into this bedrock a little bit, and we find that the connection between the two schemes, and between Defoe's idea of political speech and action as a whole, is comprehension. The wide understanding of argument and the extension of Anglican settlement to encompass religious Dissenters served the same political function in broadening Harley's basis of support.

Some of the latitude Defoe takes in promoting this scheme to Harley—'yᵉ Plainess I have yor Leave to Use' (40)—can be traced to what he perceived as their shared confessional affiliation. Harley came from a family of Dissenters and, as Backscheider shows, would have understood Defoe's recourse to biblical types, such as the master-servant parable, as a kind of shorthand. In Backscheider's reading, Defoe's worry that he will become 'An Unprofitable Servant' (53), assuming the role of the "Tenth Leper" (744) from Luke 17:11–19, translates the obligation he feels into the unsolicited and unacknowledged 'advice and information' that would define his letters to Harley.[32] This higher

---

[31] Manuel Schonhorn, *Defoe's Politics: Parliament, Power, Kingship and Robinson Crusoe* (Cambridge: Cambridge University Press, 1991), 101. There is, however, no direct evidence that Harley read the memorandum.

[32] Paula R. Backscheider, 'Personality and Biblical Allusion in Defoe's Letters', *South Atlantic Review*, 47:1 (1982), 1–20 (1).

measure of service might have offered some solace in the face of Harley's long bouts of non-response. On a stylistic plane, the religious 'shorthand' Defoe adopts fits into a mode of argument by aphorism and exemplar that carries across all his letters and was to prove highly productive for him in other genres.

In the letter from July–August 1704, Defoe repays his debts to Harley, as the leper did to Jesus, with the same kind of plainness he would later offer Halifax and Sunderland. The counsel he offers is a path for installing the secretary as supreme minister, a position that would accommodate the managerial efficacy of French absolutism to the structures of British cabinet government. The need for a 'Supreme Ministry' is self-evident according to Defoe: 'Our Confusions in Council, Our Errors in Excecuting and Unwaryness in Directing from ye Multitude and bad Conduct of Ministers make it Too plain' (57). In this case, plainness is analogous to common sense; it is the means for expressing home truths and those truths themselves. In the form and content of this letter, Defoe accounts for this vital aspect of his plain style by outlining how common sense can be understood, expressed, and influenced in writing.

To this end, Defoe's argument proceeds by collecting common wisdom, accumulating aphorisms and historical exemplars, in a similar manner to his early manuscript 'Historical Collections',[33] albeit more tightly wound into a cohesive policy programme. These exemplars provide a precedent for the supreme ministry in the guise of the 'favourites' Defoe raises: men who have 'Serv'd the State Abstracted from his Own Intrest', and as a result were 'as Much ye Peoples favourite as ye kings' (58). Such favour would allow Harley to rise above the interest of 'Partyes' and avoid harassment by 'ye Mob', whose illegitimacy Defoe sets against the true and legitimate popularity of a leader who acts in the people's interest (58). What unites these 'favourites'—amongst them, Richelieu, Mazarin, Colbert, and Walsingham—is that they were all 'Master[s] of Intelligence' (58). The agents a supreme minister could disperse across England, Scotland, and at foreign courts would provide him a steady stream of intelligence. As an example of the form their correspondence might take, Defoe mentions 'a Book... Published in London about 7 or 8 yeares Ago Call'd Letters writ by a Turkish Spye' (66), a work that to his mind demonstrates how intelligence of his own people, of rival politicians at home, and of foreign courts would strengthen the political settlement.

The problem facing Defoe is that this kind of popular authority was likely to be thought radical, against which accusation he offers a set of aphorisms:

> Popular Fame Never Thinks a Man too high, Popular Hate Never Thinks him to Lowe.
> A Generous, free, Noble, Uncontracted Conduct, as Effectually Secures ye affeccons of ye People, as a Narrow, Covetous, Craving Spirit Effectually Engages Their Mortall Aversion....
> Nothing wins This Naćon like Generous, free Open handed Courtesye.[34]

---

[33] William Andrew Clark Memorial Library MS H6735M3.
[34] BL Lansdowne MSS 98, ff. 223–45 (224–5); cf. *Correspondence*, 59.

These remarks are set on their own lines and indented, functioning as headings that Defoe then substantiates with specific historical examples. They are at once gnomic and plain. They espouse a set of individual principles that can be abstracted—yet joined together they form a narrative that translates generosity into an aggregative concept of national interest. The upshot is that Harley should ensure that a diverse range of constituencies are 'Content'. Only then can there be 'Generall Union of Affeccon' (92). It follows that such contentment pivots on the same ethical maxim:

> We Say happyness Consists in being Content; but I Must Denye it, Unless ye Contentment be fixt on a Centre of Vertue, for a Vićous Man may So, be More happy Than a Vertuous ... A Man May be Popular without Merit, But That Popularity will Neither be usefull, nor Servićable. (41)

By stressing that popularity reflects the virtue of its possessor in neo-Harringtonian terms, Defoe aims to raise popular approval as an index for ethical political action.[35] And though the letter keeps the increasingly intractable Scots in sight, Defoe raises Dissenters as the case-in-point for how Harley's virtuous popularity might result in national unity.

Dissenters are in some ways an obvious choice, but in others a difficult one. Defoe's first published work, *A Letter to a Dissenter from his Friend at the Hague* (1688), established a pattern that alienated his coreligionists for most of his writing life. He was high-handed; he claimed to know more about their condition than they did and to speak for them better than they could speak for themselves. In short, he aimed to fashion the constituency according to his own principles for moral judgement. The published letter proved a useful medium for such engagement. Containing the intimacy of epistolary exchange but with the named correspondents betokening wider social types, this common polemical form both cultivated moral judgement through the perspective of the outsider and modelled correct interpretation of argument through the implied reader. In *A Letter to a Dissenter*, the 'Friend' writes from the 'Hague' because of its significance as the seat of the Protestant interest in Europe. The personal exchange between true Protestant friends is thus pitted against the false alliance that James II's offer to repeal the Test Acts presents. Defoe used public letters to varying degrees of success. In the second edition to his later *A Letter to the Dissenters* (1713), Defoe defends the pamphlet, which sought to woo nonconformists from the Whigs to the Tories, on the grounds that it '*could not fail to force its way into the Consciences and Understandings of all those, who were not prepossessed and prejudiced by Interest and Party*' (*PEW*, iii. 309). This constituency is strategically narrowed, but the point remains that published letters sought to shape the nature of the collective by their impact on the consciences of individual readers. This is why Defoe so often used the form when writing to allies, Dissenters, and Whigs, and

---

[35] For neo-Harringtonianism, see J. G. A. Pocock, *The Machiavellian Moment: Florentine Political Thought and the Atlantic Republican Tradition* (Princeton, N.J.: Princeton University Press, 1975).

especially so when he sought to fold these constituencies into a state with Harley as its premier minister.

The letters to Harley in mid-1704 and the letters, personal and published, through which Defoe promoted government through virtuous popularity draw an implicit parallel between comprehension as a socio-religious formation and the comprehension of argument. In the proposal, Harley's power would derive from his capacity to speak for Dissenters and to be seen as their 'friend'. As the Dissenters come to understand (or comprehend) that Harley is on their side, they will unite behind him and be comprehended into the broader polity he presides over. Plain style, so elaborated, becomes, then, a strategy to speak to and for the people—or to put it another way, to represent them. Defoe's role is to gather and communicate the knowledge required for Harley to be representative, to become, as St Paul advised, 'all Things to all men' (43).

All Things to All Men

Defoe's *A Continuation of Letters Written by a Turkish Spy* straddles the fluid divide between letter-writing manuals and epistolary fiction. The narrative unfolds through the correspondence of Mahmut, an Ottoman spy embedded in the court of Louis XIV, whose cover and social fluency reflect Defoe's ideal agent. Presented with Mahmut's outgoing correspondence only, the levels of masking and disclosure that Altman identified as one of the polarities of epistolarity are immediately apparent.[36] Mahmut is at his most guarded in the letters to 'Reis Effendi', a position he describes as 'Secretary of State' (*SFS*, v. 59) in a deliberate echo of that occupied by Harley for much of the time Defoe worked for him. His letters are most revealing when chastising his nephew (101–2), or discussing his hopes and disappointments, or jesting with his friend '*Mustapha Osman*' (123–6; 228–9). Likewise, Defoe's guard is at its lowest when he worries about how much money his son Benjamin is spending at university,[37] or when he reveals to his friend John Fransham the 'most difficult time' (*Correspondence*, 315) he is experiencing in Scotland, or when he banters with Edward Owen in mock formal tone (173–9). When arranging the financial conditions of his daughter Sophia's marriage to Henry Baker, Defoe gives voice to his concern, no doubt inflected by his guilt for a life lived on the cusp of financial ruin, that he can 'hardly hope to do Equally for all ye Rest [of his children], as I shall for my Dear Sophie' (858). We can only guess at how many of Defoe's letters to family and friends have been lost. From what survives, it is clear that familiar letters occasioned moments of reflection in a correspondence otherwise beholden to pressures to craft a certain image for his patrons and posterity. That such moments are then echoed in his *Continuation of Letters Written by a Turkish Spy* marks the work as transitional: a

---

[36] Altman, *Epistolarity*, 186.
[37] Paula R. Backscheider, 'John Russell to Daniel Defoe: Fifteen Unpublished Letters from Scotland', *PQ*, 61:2 (1982), 161–77.

midpoint between his polemical letters and his later novels, carrying much of the argumentative force of the former and moving towards the sense of interiority that was central to the emergence of the latter.

In depicting a Turkish spy in Paris, Defoe utilizes a similar framework to that which first structured the *Review*, the periodical he founded in 1704. In the early issues, before the paper became Defoe's personal vehicle for wide-ranging commentary on current affairs, the *Review* aimed to provide a 'Compleat History of *France*'.[38] Mr Review depicted French 'Greatness'[39] with the intention of urging English action. Like Defoe's 1704 memorandum addressed to Harley, the *Review* is preoccupied with deficiencies in the English administrative state. As in the memorandum and *A Continuation*, the *Review* identifies Mazarin and Richelieu as exemplary statesmen. The *Review* was designed to represent French victories without exaggeration, avoiding the '*French* Rhodomantades' that Defoe found in competitor periodicals.[40] At the same time it steers clear of the complacency that would take hold in readers should it exaggerate English triumphs. The stylistic corollary to this editorial agenda is detailed in the preface to the paper's first collected edition as a language '*explicit, easie, free, and very plain*'.[41] There is a sense that correspondence might guide this awakening, with the *Review* conducting extended discussion with its readers through letters, be they genuine or written by Defoe. Though Mahmut's letters are not as directly responsive, in providing a behind-the-scenes look at operations of two imperial powers, France and the Ottoman Empire, they work like Defoe's *Review* to raise the consciousness of English readers. As Mahmut chronicles the ascendance of both powers but particularly of France in the 1680s and 1690s, readers are not simply led to endorse Defoe's ideal for a centralized English state, but poised in readiness for a French incursion, a cause Defoe had fought since at least 1701.[42]

As Mahmut's letters move between topics, the spy is fleshed out, his professional opinions made comprehensible as his personal beliefs are brought to the fore. No longer one of the archetypes Defoe deployed in polemical letters, he becomes a narrator. This humanizing effect is most keenly felt when the spy defends his religion. According to Arthur Weitzman, Mahmut's defence of Islam against the barbarity of Christianity in Marana's *L'Espion* cuts both ways: 'On the one hand it boldly rips the fabric of Christian self-righteousness ... while on the other hand, it subtly cuts the inner lining of all dogmatic and absolute opinions'.[43] In Defoe's sequel Mahmut's critique of French Catholicism redounds upon an English Protestantism plagued with division. And so while humanizing the Turkish Spy as witty, thoughtful, and urbane in order to undermine Eurocentric notions of Turks as despotic barbarians is consistent across Marana's

---

[38] *Review*, i. 6 (19 February 1704).
[39] *Review*, i. 13 (26 February 1704).
[40] *Review*, i. 6 (19 February 1704).
[41] Preface to the *Review*, i. 3.
[42] Defoe's participation in what J. A. Downie terms 'the paper war of 1701' captures this concern. *Robert Harley and the Press*, 41–56.
[43] Giovanni P. Maraña, *Letters Writ by a Turkish Spy*, ed. Arthur J. Weitzman (New York: Columbia University Press, 1970), xiv.

and Defoe's works, Defoe's version presses the levels of comparison and analogy inherent to this characterization to argue for a more comprehensive Protestant Settlement. In a letter to the great Mufti, Mahmut lays waste the idea of papal infallibility before remarking upon the Reformation that the misrule of popes precipitated. Amidst his analysis he stops to discuss the case of the Huguenots:

> By far the honester and wiser Sect of the *Nazareens,* than those who are called *Catholicks,* and therefore have been persecuted and even extirpated out of the Kingdom of *France;* and they do not fail to expose it daily, when they are in Companies and Societies where they can do it freely, the Cheats and Impositions, and the Absurdities of the *Catholicks:* There are divers Sects of these People, who have broken off from the great Mufty [i.e. the Pope] ... *Lutherans* from *Luther, Calvinists* from *Calvin,* and the like; and though I look upon these to be, as above, the better Sort by far, as to their Morality, and as to their Principles; yet they differ again one from another, and separate even in Charity and Affection, as much as the *Ottomans* and *Persians* do, about the Successors to our Great Prophet *Mahomet;* Nay, they have likewise proceeded to Persecution, and even to Blood. (70)

The hypotactic syntax is characteristic of Defoe's letter-writing style, and in this case it allows him to direct attention from the persecution of the Huguenots (a focal point in English debates over the incorporation of foreign and Dissenting Protestants) to a history of the Reformation, a moral comparison of Catholics and Protestants, and finally to a broader comparison between divisions in Christianity and those in Islam. The superiority Mahmut finds amidst the Huguenots in particular and Protestantism in general is threatened by a failure to unify found not just in Christianity, but in Protestantism.

Throughout the letters Mahmut collects instances of Christian disunity. He is appalled to find the French allying themselves with the Ottomans against the Germans (100), as indeed was Defoe, though he relishes how it serves Ottoman interests, as do all wars where Nazareens cut 'one another in pieces' (174). Mahmut questions the lack of a pan-Christian alliance, a prospect few English readers would have relished. But with the stick comes the carrot, and just as he shows weaknesses in Christian Europe and failures of France even to aid its Jacobite allies, his more positive references to Protestant England establish a theological and political basis for greater unity. In a letter to 'Simeon Ben Habbakkuk, a Jew at Salomica', he makes the case for religious law free from rabbinic interference. Mahmut's case is based on the last books of the Pentateuch which

> contain a recapitulation by *Moses* to the People, of all that God commanded him to say to them; wherein he tells them, the whole substance of the Command, the plainness of it, and particularly that it needs no Oral Exposition, or Addition. (95)

The implicit sanction of a religion free from clerical legislation relies on the levels of refraction involved in the epistolary narrative, wherein a Muslim agent writes to a Jewish friend only to be read by English Protestants. What emerges is a monotheism pared back to textual revelation and the rational interpretations of individual laymen.

The letter exchange provides the layers of defence needed to put forth an argument for a Protestantism of high latitude, one that encompasses Defoe's Presbyterianism and renders plainness a Protestant virtue.

The same process of temporal as well as geopolitical and religious refraction is at play in a letter of 1691 sent to the Kaimicham, in which Mahmut praises William III. Like the letter to Ben Habbakkuk, this exchange is designed to cultivate in English readers an external moral perspective on their own affairs. The fictional frame is that the letter was written shortly after William's triumph over James II at the Battle of the Boyne. When Mahmut refers to William's triumph over a superior army 'by plain fighting', stressing that 'the Slaughter was not great, but the Victory plain, and confess'd by the Flight of that unfortunate Prince, the Deposed King' (145), he takes for granted a 'plain' interpretation of one of the most contentious questions in seventeenth-century political thought: the justification for the Revolution of 1688–9. The plainness contained in the content of this letter and conveyed by its style are aided by a form that mimics the acts of transmission and reception to involve English readers in a discussion on national values. As a rational outsider writes to his colleague, the English are presented with an image of themselves. This image is then made more 'plain' by the translator, so that in the end the religious settlement Defoe idealizes and the basis for a Protestant English state he believed was now in *de facto* operation are taken as givens.

This argument by plainness is hard to refute logically. By assuming as fact a set of values that all hold, Defoe aims to bring more readers to those values. But the question that has tugged at this chapter remains how a writer of such ingenuity and variety, whose career culminated in fiction, could make the case that his was a 'plain style'. In the final book of *Continuation of Letters Written by a Turkish Spy*, Defoe signals with sly awareness this paradox, when Mahmut complains to the Mufti that:

> These *Nazareens* are the most addicted to Fiction and Forgery of any People that ever I met with; it is a received Custom among them, that whenever they have to do with any Sect or Opinion of People, differing from their own, the first thing they go about is, to represent them as monstrous and unnatural; either in Person or in Principle, or perhaps in both; dressing them up in ridiculous Shapes, and imposing a Thousand Stories about them upon the Credulity and Ignorance of the Vulgar, that they may entertain immoveable Prejudices and Aversions against the Persons and the Principles they profess. (219)

Mahmut's depiction as humane, rational, and complete as a spy, correspondent, and man stands in contrast to the idea of fictionalization he voices. Though Defoe spilled plenty of ink attacking groups whose opinions differed from his own, he nonetheless found a measure of justification for his writing in his overarching quest for unity. Implicit to this justification is a defence of fiction by virtue of its reach, its ability to see through the perspective of another, and its capacity thereby to bring readers into relation with one another: elements that are consonant with Defoe's outward-looking letter-writing practice.

Further Reading

Janet Gurkin Altman, *Epistolarity: Approaches to a Form* (Columbus, OH: The Ohio State University Press, 1982).

Paula R. Backscheider, 'Accounts of an Eyewitness: Defoe's Dispatches from the Vale of Trade and the Edinburgh Parliament House', in *Sent as a Gift: Eight Correspondences from the Eighteenth Century*, ed. Alan T. McKenzie (Athens, GA: University of Georgia Press, 1993), 21–47.

Paula R. Backscheider, 'John Russell to Daniel Defoe: Fifteen Unpublished Letters from Scotland', *PQ*, 61:2 (1982), 161–77.

Paula R. Backscheider, 'Personality and Biblical Allusion in Defoe's Letters', *South Atlantic Review*, 47:1 (1982), 1–20.

Clare Brant, *Eighteenth-Century Letters and British Culture* (Basingstoke: Palgrave Macmillan, 2006).

J. A. Downie, *Robert Harley and the Press: Propaganda and Public Opinion in the Age of Swift and Defoe* (Cambridge: Cambridge University Press, 1979).

P. N. Furbank and W. R. Owens, 'Defoe, the De la Faye Letters, and *Mercurius Politicus*', *BJECS*, 23:1 (2000), 13–19.

P. N. Furbank and W. R. Owens, 'Defoe and the Improvisatory Sentence', *English Studies*, 67:2 (1986), 157–66.

Victoria Myers, 'Model Letters, Moral Living: Letter-Writing Manuals by Daniel Defoe and Samuel Richardson', *HLQ*, 66:3–4 (2003), 373–91.

Bruce Redford, *The Converse of the Pen: Acts of Intimacy in the Eighteenth-Century Familiar Letter* (Chicago, IL: University of Chicago Press, 1986).

G. A. Starr, *Defoe and Casuistry* (Princeton, N.J.: Princeton University Press, 1971), 1–50.

G. A. Starr, 'Defoe's Prose Style: 1. The Language of Interpretation', *Modern Philology*, 71:3 (1974), 277–94.

CHAPTER 11

DEFOE AND SATIRE

JOSEPH HONE

DANIEL DEFOE was the single most prolific satirist of the early eighteenth century. Over a period of thirty-six years beginning in 1691, he produced around fifty satirical or partially satirical works in verse and in prose.[1] Defoe began his career with satire and, at least until 1706, primarily thought of himself as an author of poetical satires [SEE CHAPTER 2]. For some time, he was best known as 'the Author of *The True-Born Englishman*', the sobriquet under which many of his individual satires were published after 1700 in addition to his two volumes of collected writings in 1703 and 1705.[2] He opened the first volume with a flurry of three verse satires: *The True-Born Englishman* (1700, but likely published in January 1701), *The Mock Mourners* (1702), and *Reformation of Manners* (1702). He opened the second volume with another pair: *A New Discovery of an Old Intreague* (1691) and *More Reformation* (1703). His crowning achievement in the mode was an ambitious and elaborately annotated twelve-book satire, *Jure Divino* (1706). Published in folio with a large frontispiece portrait of its author, *Jure Divino* emphatically announced Defoe as an eminent author of satire (**Figure 1.2**).

Despite his massive output, literary scholars have been reluctant to accept Defoe into the pantheon of great eighteenth-century satirists. Critics of 'Augustan' satire in the twentieth century dismissed him as an 'inept' and 'resolutely non-Augustan' oddity.[3] So he has remained. Notwithstanding important revisionist criticism by scholars such as Ashley Marshall, Defoe is rarely considered as a satirist.[4] My aim in this chapter is to

---

[1] Ashley Marshall, 'Daniel Defoe as Satirist', *HLQ*, 70:4 (2007), 553–76.

[2] Novak, *Daniel Defoe*, 148–57; Christopher Borsing, *Daniel Defoe and the Representation of Personal Identity* (London: Routledge, 2017), 13–36; Backscheider, *Daniel Defoe*, 126–7.

[3] Martin C. Battestin, *The Providence of Wit: Aspects of Form in Augustan Literature and the Arts* (Oxford: Oxford University Press, 1974), 224; David Nokes, *Raillery and Rage: A Study of Eighteenth-Century Satire* (Brighton: Harvester, 1987), 34. Defoe receives a single mention, though not for his satires, in Ian Jack, *Augustan Satire: Intention and Idiom in English Poetry 1660–1750* (Oxford: Clarendon Press, 1952); he is mentioned not at all in James Sutherland, *English Satire* (Cambridge: Cambridge University Press, 1958); cf. Pat Rogers, *The Augustan Vision* (London: Methuen, 1974).

[4] Marshall, 'Defoe as Satirist'; Joseph Hone, 'Daniel Defoe and the Whig Tradition in Satire', *ELH*, 84:4 (2017), 865–90; D. N. DeLuna, 'Yale's Poetasting Defoe', *1650–1850*, 4 (1998), 345–62; D. N. DeLuna,

convey the importance of satire in Defoe's literary career and to demonstrate that Defoe was often a less conventional—and more exciting—satirist than most scholars have assumed. Defoe had very clear ideas about the legitimate targets and methods of satire. He believed that satire could and ought to reform society. The battle between Protestant constitutional monarchy and popish absolutism was his central theme. Politics and theology were entirely intertwined with morality and society.

There was no fixed idea of satire in Defoe's lifetime.[5] Rather, there were many different traditions of satire with which he engaged, ranging from the classical tradition to contemporary manuscript libels and printed collections of *Poems on Affairs of State*. The purpose of this chapter is therefore not to disentangle Defoe's many and varied satirical texts into discrete categories. That would serve little purpose. Rather, I want to document the rhetorical strategies that underpin Defoe's satires, ranging from occasional squibs to *Jure Divino* and the ironical succession pamphlets of 1713. Tracing the development of Defoe as a satirist during the reigns of William and Anne can help suggest new ways of thinking not only about the trajectory of his literary career, but also about satire's moral status during a period of intense political unrest.

Theorist

Defoe was seldom a self-reflexive writer. He wrote no manifesto on prose fiction, periodical journalism, or political pamphleteering, despite those being the genres for which he is best known. Yet he did provide multiple theoretical frameworks for his satires. His very earliest attempt in the mode, *A New Discovery of an Old Intreague* (1691), opens with a preface explaining that '*The End of* Satyr *ought to be, exposing Falshood, in order to Reformation. As all Warrings are Unlawfull whose Aim is not Peace; so Satyrs not thus meant, are no more* Satyrs *but* Libells' (*SFS*, i. 37). A decade later, in his preface to *The True-Born Englishman*, Defoe repeated the same basic point: '*The End of Satyr is Reformation: And the Author, tho he doubts the Work of Conversion is at a general Stop, has put his Hand to the Plow*' (83). The common theme is moral reform.

Defoe's belief that the satirist could root out vice has its origins in the contemporary movement to reform English manners.[6] Before the accession of William and Mary in

---

'Discovering Defoe's Satire' (unpublished doctoral thesis, Johns Hopkins University, 1993). Cf. George Southcombe, 'The Satire of Dissent', in *The Oxford Handbook of Eighteenth-Century Satire*, ed. Paddy Bullard (Oxford: Oxford University Press, 2019), 56–73.

[5] Ashley Marshall, *The Practice of Satire in England, 1658–1770* (Baltimore, MD: Johns Hopkins University Press, 2013), 39–69.

[6] T. C. Curtis and W. A. Speck, 'The Societies for the Reformation of Manners: A Case Study in the Theory and Practice of Moral Reform', *Literature and History*, 3 (1976), 45–64; David Hayton, 'Moral Reform and Country Politics in the Late Seventeenth-Century House of Commons', *Past and Present*, 128:1 (1990), 48–91; Craig Rose, 'Providence, Protestant Union and Godly Reformation in the 1690s', *Transactions of the Royal Historical Society*, 3 (1993), 151–70; Shelley Burt, 'The Societies

1689, the Stuart court was seen to encourage licentious behaviour. Lewdness, vulgarity, and libertine impiety were all closely associated with Restoration decadence, whereas godliness was a product of the new revolution settlement.[7] It was therefore essential that Defoe, as a firm supporter of the new establishment, wrote his satires from a position of moral authority. He explained his position explicitly in the preface to *Reformation of Manners*: 'That no Man is qualified to reprove other Mens Crimes, who allows himself in the Practice of the same, is very readily granted, and is the very Substance and Foundation of the following Satyr' (155). The same point was more elaborately voiced in *More Reformation* (1703):

> Satyr is Nonsense, when it comes from those
> Who practise all the Errors they expose; . . .
> But let the Man that pens thy History
> Correct his own, and first repent like thee:
> He's welcome then his Satyr to advance,
> And gorge his rising Spleen with thy Mischance:
> 'Tis vain against thy Crimes to raise a Storm,
> Let those recriminate who first reform:
> Let them expose thy Errors to the Town,
> As freely as if they themselves had none:
> Thou shalt go unreprov'd 'till they repent,
> But first let them reform, and thou'rt content.
> (lines 111–38; *SFS*, i. 217)

Defoe was confident that he had '*as good a Title to Animadversion as another, since no Man can charge him with any of the Vices he has repov'd*' (155). Serious moral failings would be enough to disqualify him from the role of satirist. He needed to be beyond reproach, of unquestionable moral integrity. '*I recommend my Practice to all my Friends, if they would be Satyr free*' (212).

Success was crucial. The reference to the '*Plow*' in the preface to *The True-Born Englishman* alludes to a passage from Luke 9:62, where Christ explains 'No one who puts his hand to the plough and looks back is fit for the kingdom of God'. By putting his hand to the plough, Defoe had committed himself to eradicating vice. Thus, in *A New Discovery*, Defoe promised that '*If no Reformation follows, I must do as* Providence *does, let you alone to your Own Wills, and as I never drew Pen before, so expect no Second*

---

for the Reformation of Manners: Between John Locke and the Devil in Augustan England', in *The Margins of Orthodoxy: Heterodox Writing and Cultural Response, 1660–1750*, ed. Roger D. Lund (Cambridge: Cambridge University Press, 1995), 149–69.

[7] Tony Claydon, *William III and the Godly Revolution* (Cambridge: Cambridge University Press, 1996); Tony Claydon, 'Protestantism, Universal Monarchy and Christendom in William's War Propaganda, 1689–1697', in *Redefining William III: The Impact of the King-Stadholder in International Context*, ed. Esther Mijers and David Onnekink (Aldershot: Ashgate, 2007), 125–42; Kevin Sharpe, *Rebranding Rule: The Restoration and Revolution Monarchy, 1660–1714* (New Haven, CT: Yale University Press, 2013), 367–73.

Item' (37). His satires would be no more than mere *'Banters'*, claimed the preface to *The True-Born Englishman*, until *'our Magistrates and Gentry reform themselves by way of Example'* (83). In Defoe's hands, satire became a vehicle for his evangelical mission. His aim was not simply—or only—to preach to the choir, but rather to increase the overall stock of moral Englishmen.

Moral reformation often featured in contemporary dissertations on satire, though was rarely such a priority. Defoe's prefatory statements about the *'End of Satyr'* manifestly drew on John Dryden's preface to *Absalom and Achitophel* (1681), which closed with a similar point: *'The true end of Satyre, is the amendment of Vices by correction. And he who writes Honestly, is no more an Enemy to the Offendour, than the Physician to the Patient, when he prescribes harsh Remedies to an inveterate Disease'*.[8] Dryden elaborated on this theme in his *Discourse on the Original and Progress of Satire* (1692), explaining that the only two acceptable motives for writing lampoons were revenge and 'to make examples of vicious men'. For while satirists 'have no Moral right on the Reputation of other Men', it was 'an Action of Virtue' to expose 'Crimes and Follies: Both for their own amendment, if they are not yet incorrigible; and for the Terrour of others, to hinder them from falling into those Enormities, which they see are so severely punish'd, in the Persons of others'.[9] Doubtful that satire would have any effect on 'incorrigible' offenders, Dryden instead thought satire, by making 'examples of vicious men', would be more effective as a deterrent. Defoe understood this argument. In an issue of *The Review* (1704–13), he reflected on the 'Lampoons and Satyrs' of Dryden and his contemporaries, which 'Wounded, and at last went far in Ruining the Parties they were pointed at'.[10] But in Defoe's judgement that was ultimately bad practice and made the satirist no better than his victims, especially once they had reformed: 'All Satyr ceases when the Men repent, / 'Tis Cruelty to lash the Penitent' (*SFS*, i. 212). Dryden aimed to 'ruin' and 'lash' offenders; Defoe sought to persuade them to change their ways.

Defoe was very clear about what satire should *not* be. Any satires that did not aim to reform their targets 'are no more *Satyrs* but *Libells*' (37). Technically a legal term drawn from common law, 'libel' had come to denote a particular kind of scurrilous poetry, packed with personal invective and character assassination, and usually circulated in manuscript or printed surreptitiously.[11] This distinction between libel and 'true' satire

---

[8] *The Works of John Dryden*, ed. H. T. Swedenberg et al., 20 vols (Berkeley, CA: University of California Press, 1956–2000), ii. 5.

[9] Dryden, *Works*, iv. 59–60.

[10] *Review*, viii. 20 (29 March 1711).

[11] On seditious libel, see Philip Hamburger, 'The Development of the Law of Seditious Libel and the Control of the Press', *Stanford Law Review*, 37 (1985), 661–765; Ian Higgins, 'Censorship, Libel and Self-Censorship', in *Jonathan Swift and the Eighteenth-Century Book*, ed. Paddy Bullard and James McLaverty (Cambridge: Cambridge University Press, 2013), 179–98; Andrew Benjamin Bricker, *Libel and Lampoon: Satire in the Courts, 1670–1792* (Oxford: Oxford University Press, 2022); Joseph Hone, 'Legal Constraints, Libellous Evasions', in *The Oxford Handbook of Eighteenth-Century Satire*, ed. Bullard, 525–41; Thomas Keymer, *Poetics of the Pillory: English Literature and Seditious Libel, 1660–1820* (Oxford: Oxford University Press, 2019).

was a common one among satirists, although nobody quite agreed on a precise definition.[12] Writing in the *Tatler* in 1709, Richard Steele claimed that 'the Satyrist and Libeller differ as much as the Magistrate and the Murderer. In the Consideration of human Life, the Satyrist never falls upon Persons who are not glaringly faulty, and the Libeller on none but who are conspicuously commendable'.[13] The problem of defining satire in such relative terms was that Steele's idea of the 'glaringly faulty' and the 'conspicuously commendable' was very different to Defoe's. Often the disagreement boiled down to basic partisan differences. When the critic and poet John Dennis denounced the great satires of Dryden and Samuel Garth as 'Libels which have pass'd for Satires', he explained that 'they are every where full of Flattery or Slander, and a just Satire admits of neither'. *Absalom and Achitophel* and *The Medal* (1682) were singled out as particularly egregious examples: 'How many were abus'd only for being true to the Religion and Liberties of their Country? And on the other side, some were extoll'd only for being false to both'.[14] Writing from opposing political sides, Dennis and Dryden had fundamentally different views about who were the rightful targets of satire. For one, Shaftesbury and Monmouth were heroes of English Protestantism; for the other, they were irredeemable villains. So the difference between satire and libel was often nothing more than a matter of perspective.

Defoe addressed this conundrum in the preface to *More Reformation*, in which he outlined three basic rules that governed his own selection of satirical targets. Firstly, hypocrites who claim virtue but are truly wicked men are always fair game: *'If I have singled out any Men by Characters, it has either been such as pretending to reform others, and execute the Laws against Vice, have been the great Examples and Encouragers of it in their own Example and Practice'*. Secondly, men who suffer ill fortune should not be lampooned: *'I never Reproach'd any Man for having his House burnt, or his Ships cast away, or his Family ruin'd; I never Lampoon'd a Man because he could not pay his Debts, or for his being a Cuckold'*. Thirdly, religious difference alone is insufficient cause for satire: *'I never reproach'd any Man for his Opinion in Religion, or us'd him the worse for differing in Judgment from me'* (*SFS*, i. 211). There were, of course, major exceptions to that last rule. Religious ambodexters were a perennial favourite target; Catholics were often victims of Defoe's scorn; so too were Protestant Dissenters who occasionally conformed in order to hold public office. *'I do own that I shall never see a notorious scandalous Magistrate, a whoreing drunken Clergy-man, a leud debaunch'd Justice of the Peace, a publick blasphemeing Atheist'*, continued Defoe in the preface to *More Reformation*, *'but I shall be apt to have a fling at him my way'* (212).

By concentrating his energies on sinful behaviour and moralizing, Defoe ostensibly distanced himself from the parallel tradition of partisan libel. In the aftermath of his

---

[12] Marshall, *Practice of Satire*, 40–3.

[13] Joseph Addison and Richard Steele, *The Tatler*, ed. Donald F. Bond, 3 vols (Oxford: Clarendon Press, 1987), ii. 74.

[14] John Dennis, *The Critical Works of John Dennis*, ed. Edward Niles Hooker, 2 vols (Baltimore, MD: Johns Hopkins University Press, 1939–43), ii. 201.

prosecution for writing *The Shortest-Way with the Dissenters* (1702)—on which, more in due course—he conspicuously denounced political libel. '*Satyr* has no business with the Crown', he wrote in *More Reformation* (line 546). Addressing a personified 'Satyr', Defoe instructs:

> No more shalt thou old *Marvell*'s Ghost lament,
> Who always rally'd Kings and Government:
> Thy lines their awful Distance always knew,
> And thought that Debt to Dignities was Due.
> Crowns should be counted with the things Divine,
> On which Burlesque is rudeness and profane. (lines 534–9; *SFS*, i. 228)

Defoe excoriates the oppositional tradition of libellers such as Andrew Marvell, whose dissident satirical writings had been republished in recent years by the radical clique of 'commonwealth' Whigs who set themselves against the corruption and apostasy of those 'court' Whigs who took government posts under William III.[15] Utterly consistent with his earlier prefaces on the purpose of satire, the focus here is on the uncouth behaviour of radical Whig libellers such as John Tutchin, whose verse was strongly influenced by Marvell.[16] Instead of following that example, Defoe urged his fellow satirists to 'go about it like Poets' in a manner 'suitable to the Quality of the Persons, and the Dignity of Satire'.[17] He made a similar point in *The Pacificator* (1700), which closed by warning readers to 'No Banters, no Invective lines admit, / Where want of Manners, makes up want of Wit' (lines 429–30; *SFS*, i. 76). Truthfully, Defoe could not separate private conduct from public affairs. For all his posturing, Defoe's targets were no less partisan than those of Dryden or Dennis. By championing the reformation of English manners, Defoe implicitly—and often explicitly—aligned himself with the cause of Protestantism and constitutional monarchy.

Reformer

To what extent did Defoe practise what he preached? How did he go about 'exposing Falshood, in order to Reformation', persuading the wicked to change their ways? His principal rhetorical technique was antithesis. Defoe not only excoriated vice; he promoted corresponding virtues. Through this strategy Defoe differentiated his satires from mere libels and lampoons. Whereas poets such as Dryden and Rochester exposed moral failings simply with the intention of 'wounding' or even 'ruining' their peers,

---

[15] Joseph Hone, 'John Darby and the Whig Canon', *Historical Journal*, 64:5 (2021), 1257–80.
[16] Hone, 'Defoe and the Whig Tradition', 874–8.
[17] *Review*, ix. 304 (28 March 1713).

Defoe supplied practical examples of positive conduct to guide future behaviour.[18] His satires contain an equal dose of panegyric, the purpose of which is threefold: to provide a positive exemplar for moral reform; to distinguish sinful behaviour from virtue; and to expose the folly of poets who attack the same behaviours that Defoe praises as virtuous.

This strategy is ubiquitous in the earliest poems, most notably in *The True-Born Englishman*.[19] Having reeled off a litany of vices associated in the popular imagination with rival nations—pride for Spain, lust for Italy, drunkenness for Germany, passion for France, and so on—Defoe unmasks ingratitude as the governing sin of England. At the same moment, he commands:

> *Satyr* be kind, and draw a silent Veil
> Thy *Native England*'s Vices to conceal:
> Or if that Task's impossible to do,
> At least be just, and show her Virtues too;
> *Too Great the first, Alas! the last too Few.* (lines 145–9; *SFS*, i. 89)

Parts one and two of the poem outline the '*Breed*' and the '*Manners*' of the English, before leading to '*Britannia*'s Song', in which the heroic deeds of William III are rehearsed at length.[20] Unfortunately, Defoe writes, the English have vilified and plotted against this virtuous king at every turn. The effect of this contrast is designed to be instructive:

> The Fact might very well be answer'd thus;
> He has so often been betray'd by us;
> He must have been a Madman to rely
> On *English* Gentlemen's Fidelity.
> For laying other Arguments aside,
> This Thought might mortify our *English* Pride,
> That Foreigners have faithfully obey'd him,
> And none but *Englishmen* have e're betray'd him. (lines 1029–36; *SFS*, i. 113)

Structurally, the satire moves from diagnosis to cure. Following the example of the king and his most loyal counsellors, Englishmen could yet reform their manners, if they chose to do so: 'Examples are for Imitation set, / Yet all men follow Virtue with Regret' (lines 1207–8; *SFS*, i. 118). *The Mock Mourners*, 'A Satyr, By way of Elegy on King *William*', is likewise only satirical insofar as it provides a model for reformed English behaviour.

---

[18] On Defoe's complex relationship with Rochester's poetry, see John McVeagh, 'Rochester and Defoe: A Study in Influence', *SEL*, 14:3 (1974), 327–41; but cf. Hone, 'Defoe and the Whig Tradition', 870–4.

[19] For a parallel reading, see J. A. Downie, *To Settle the Succession of the State: Literature and Politics, 1678–1750* (Basingstoke: Macmillan, 1994), 53–4.

[20] On Defoe's praise of William III, see Manuel Schonhorn, *Defoe's Politics: Parliament, Power, Kingship and Robinson Crusoe* (Cambridge: Cambridge University Press, 1991), 43–88; P. N. Furbank and W. R. Owens, 'Defoe and King William: A Sceptical Enquiry', *RES*, 52:206 (2001), 227–32; Andrew McKendry, '"No Parallels from Hebrew Times": Troubled Typologies and the Glorious Revolution in Daniel Defoe's Williamite Poetry', *ECS*, 50:1 (2016), 81–99.

Confronted by gleeful Englishmen who only pretend to mourn their king, Defoe once again recommends they imitate William's conduct:

> Thou, Satyr, shalt the grateful Few rehearse,
> And solve the Nation's Credit in thy Verse;
> Embalm his Name with Characters of Praise,
> His Fame's beyond the Power of Time to rase
> From him let future Monarchs learn to Rule,
> And make his lasting Character their School,
> For he who wou'd in time to come be Great,
> *Has nothing now to do but imitate.*
> Let dying Parents when they come to bless,
> Wish to their Children only his Success,
> Here their Instructions very well may end,
> *William*'s Example only recommend,
> And leave the Youth his History t'attend. (lines 520–32; SFS, i. 151)

Defoe was addressing two audiences here: the diligent child who wishes to emulate William's 'Success', and 'future Monarchs', specifically the new Queen Anne: 'In *William*'s Steps sedately she proceeds, / *William's a Patern to immortal Deeds'* (lines 561–2; SFS, i. 152). By counterbalancing his satirical attack on English ingratitude with praise of the king as a pattern of virtue, Defoe aimed both to reform English manners and to counsel English rulers.[21]

Everyday morality was inseparable from statecraft. Defoe saw private vice as the foundation of misrule. Therefore, even a catalogue of private depravity such as *Reformation of Manners* necessarily addresses issues of poor governance. Having listed all manner of wickedness and misconduct across the city and country, Defoe turns his attention 'To States and Governments':

> *Vertue*'s their Life and Being, *Vice* their End:
> *Vertue* establishes, and *Vice* destroys,
> And all the Ends of Government unties:
> *Vertue*'s an *English* King and Parliament,
> *Vice* is *a Czar of* Muscow *Government*:
> *Vertue* sets bounds to Kings, and limits Crowns,
> *Vice* knows no Law, and all Restraint disowns:
> *Vertue* prescribes all Government by Rules,
> *Vice* makes Kings Tyrants and their Subjects Fools.
> (lines 898–906; SFS, i. 181)

---

[21] See Joseph Hone, *Literature and Party Politics at the Accession of Queen Anne* (Oxford: Oxford University Press, 2017), 43–7, 126–8.

English constitutional monarchy is established on the bedrock of a virtuous polity which 'sets bounds' for rulers and 'limits Crowns'. Vice leads the way to slavery and foreign despotism. Moral reform is portrayed simply as a means of securing the revolution settlement. Equally, though, Defoe's strategy of formal contrast between vice and virtue helps distinguish egregious from upstanding Englishmen. Petty villains and rogues are unmasked as insidious enemies of the state. The incursion of praise and positive exemplars serves to make these negative aspects of satire even more pointed. With their sharply opposing contraries, Defoe's satires occupy an absolute moral landscape.

No satire is more morally authoritative or ambitiously reforming than *Jure Divino*. When the poem first appeared in 1706, the title page labelled it 'A SATYR' in massive block capitals. And yet, as John Richetti has observed, 'the satire so prominent in the title tends to be ignored or given second place to the illustration of his notions about constitutional and contractual monarchy'.[22] In truth, the satire and the political theory are inseparable. In the poems on everyday English manners, Defoe explained how a virtuous polity was the foundation of constitutional rule. Now he turned his attention to the upper echelons of constitutional rule: how a virtuous monarchy can encourage a virtuous polity. The specific focus had changed, but *Jure Divino* firmly belongs to the same satirical project as *The True-Born Englishman*, *The Mock Mourners*, *Reformation of Manners*, and other poems. Only when a monarch rules by godly principles can they be said to have any sort of right to the throne. 'Kings are not Kings *Jure Divino*, that when they break the Laws, trample on Property, affront Religion, invade the Liberties of Nations, *and the like*, they may be opposed and resisted by Force' (*SFS*, ii. 38), explained Defoe in the preface. In a recent essay, Ashley Marshall has suggested that this strain of 'resistance theory' aligns the poem with the radical fringe of the Whig project.[23] But it is important to understand that the right to resist tyrants underpinned the entire spectrum of Whig political thought, including the moderate loyalism espoused by Defoe. Indeed, the central argument of *Jure Divino* is that the central tenets of Whig political theory, including resistance, are consistent with support for the revolution settlement and the rule of Queen Anne. No monarch who upholds godly, virtuous rule could be opposed by upstanding Whig citizens. Resistance might be legitimate under the right circumstances, he argued, but not during the reigns of William III or Anne. This message was surely aimed at the Whig dissidents who had earlier opposed the revolution settlement on the grounds that it did not go far enough. Defoe sought to illustrate that the 'radical' principles espoused by oppositional Whigs were in fact consistent with support for the present regime. *Jure Divino* is 'radical' only insofar as it coopts those ideas for defenders of the government.

---

[22] Richetti, *Life of Daniel Defoe*, 105. Cf. Paula R. Backscheider, 'The Verse Essay, John Locke, and Defoe's *Jure Divino*', *ELH*, 55:1 (1988), 99–124; D. N. DeLuna, '*Jure Divino*: Defoe's "whole Volume in Folio, by Way of Answer to, and Confutation of *Clarendon*'s History of the Rebellion"', *PQ*, 75:1 (1996), 43–66; Manuel Schonhorn, *Defoe's Politics*, 124–40; Hone, 'Defoe and the Whig Tradition', 879–84.

[23] Ashley Marshall, '"Treason and Loyalty Go Hand in Hand": Moral Politics and Radical Whiggery in Defoe's *Jure Divino* (1706)', *SP*, 118:1 (2021), 145–180.

Jure Divino ranges widely, from the origins of pagan society in the distant past to the present day. Defoe sought and deployed examples from history, scripture, and myth to disprove Tory theories of divine monarchy.[24] The first two books progress through the pagan gods and Hobbesian ideas about the origins of government all the way to the example of Saul and his descent into tyranny. In the mode of classical Whig resistance theorists such as Algernon Sidney, Defoe argues that God grants power to wicked men only because he also left mankind with the liberty to defend itself from evil.[25] Historical examples affirm that all nations in all ages have dethroned tyrants and defended their freedoms. Further examples are marshalled to illustrate the nonsense of hereditary succession:

> If Kings by *Jus Divinum* wear the Crown,
> By nat'ral Devolution handed down;
> Let them go back and trace the Sacred Claim,
> They'll find *the Genealogy so lame*;
> So full of Usurpations, such a Crowd,
> Of *false Successions, spurious Births*, and *Blood*;
> Such *Perjuries*, such *Frauds* to wear a Crown,
> *They'd blush* their *ill born Ancestors* to own.
> (Book IX, lines 29–36; *SFS*, ii. 273)

Defoe's treatment of the divine right theorists is unabashedly hostile. Eventually, in Book X, he addresses the English monarchy directly: the corruption of the original Saxon constitution by William the Conqueror, the bloody rebellions and murders by which early kings claimed their thrones, the 'vast Extent of *Royal Crime*' (Book X, lines 146; *SFS*, ii. 299).[26]

But these negative illustrations of royal absolutism are more than counterbalanced by the positive exemplars of monarchy which we have come to learn were an integral

---

[24] On that tradition, see Mark Goldie, 'Tory Political Thought, 1689–1714' (unpublished doctoral thesis, University of Cambridge, 1978); James Daly, *Sir Robert Filmer and English Political Thought* (Toronto: University of Toronto Press, 1979); Cesare Cuttica, *Sir Robert Filmer and the Patriot Monarch: Patriarchalism in Seventeenth-Century Political Thought* (Manchester: Manchester University Press, 2012).

[25] See Blair Worden, 'The Commonwealth Kidney of Algernon Sidney', *Journal of British Studies*, 24:1 (1985), 1–40; Jonathan Scott, *Algernon Sidney and the Restoration Crisis, 1677–1683* (Cambridge: Cambridge University Press, 1991).

[26] On the Saxon constitution in Whig political thought, see Mark Goldie, 'The Ancient Constitution and the Languages of Political Thought', *Historical Journal*, 62:1 (2019), 3–34. Cf. J. G. A. Pocock, *The Ancient Constitution and the Feudal Law* (Cambridge: Cambridge University Press, 1957); R. J. Smith, *The Gothic Bequest: Medieval Institutions in British Political Thought, 1688–1863* (Cambridge: Cambridge University Press, 1987); Janelle Greenberg, *The Radical Face of the Ancient Constitution: St Edward's 'Laws' in Early Modern Political Thought* (Cambridge: Cambridge University Press, 2006); Julia Randolph, *Common Law and Enlightenment in England, 1689–1750* (Woodbridge: Boydell and Brewer, 2013); Ashley Walsh, 'The Saxon Republic and Ancient Constitution in the Standing Army Controversy, 1697–1699', *Historical Journal*, 62:3 (2019), 663–84.

element of Defoe's satirical technique. Having debunked the hereditary principle and absolute monarchy, the final two books are given over entirely to eulogy of William III, Anne, and their counsellors:

> SATYR, from Fact, to Consequence descend,
> Just Princes and just Governments defend;
> Where Kings and People with a joint Assent,
> Move in the Grand Machine of Government:
> In proper Sphere, respective Parts perform,
> And General Good's to both the General Charm:
> There Peace and Property go Hand in Hand,
> These freely Bow, and gently those Command.
>   Princes and People join in publick Peace,
> Both seek and understand their Happiness:
> Those softly guide, these chearful Homage pay;
> Those Rule by Law, and these by Choice Obey:
> Commence the Parts of Rule in just Consent,
> And jointly drive the Wain of Government:
> In gentle Yoke of due Subservience draw,
> People to Monarchs, Monarchs to the Law;
> In spight of Blood, Possession, or of Line,
> These are the Governments that are Divine.
> (Book XI, lines 1–18; *SFS*, ii. 316)

The essential argument is summarized in the last few lines: divine government has nothing to do with lineage or patriarchal forms of monarchy; it simply observes the rule of law and governs by public consent. That is God's will. But there are also a few key phrases in this passage which underscore what Defoe saw as the duty of satire: 'just Governments defend', and a few lines later: 'Impartial SATYR, challenge all Mankind, / And leave the just Remark, for Ages yet behind' (Book XI, lines 22–3; *SFS*, ii. 317). Like his contemporaries, Defoe agreed that satire ought to excoriate malfeasance; yet he believed that it should also 'defend' the public good, be 'Impartial', and leave 'just Remark[s]'. Satire was a servant of justice, and justice required that virtue be rewarded no less than vice be punished. Nowhere is this contrast voiced with greater clarity than the final lines of *Jure Divino*, where Defoe anticipates a sequel devoted entirely to praise of Anne:

> SATYR when next our Muse *inspir'd with Rage*,
> Comands in just Defence of Truth t'engage;
> By Foils present, and make a new Essay;
> And try our Vice, by Vertue to display:
> Learn by the soft and milky Way to soar,
> A Path that SATYR never trod before;
> By just Antithesis illustrate Crime,
> And see how strangely Vice and Vertue Chime:

> Let gentler Scenes guild thy aspiring Verse,
> And Britain's Pride, in Britain's Queen rehearse;
> Let the Reverse of Tyranny be known,
> And *ANN*'s inlighten'd Character be shown:
> Her Panegyrick stabs a Tyrant's Praise,
> As Hell's long Night's described by Heav'n's long Days.
> (Book XII, lines 470–83; *SFS*, ii. 358)

The lines project a distinctive vision of a new British politics founded on Williamite principles of constitutional monarchy, liberty of conscience, and a morally virtuous body politic. In an ideal world there would be no more vice to expose, only virtue; no tyrants to reform, only godly monarchs. And yet, beyond its status as a paradigm for virtuous rule, Defoe's praise of constitutional monarchy also has a negative edge. Just as *Jure Divino* shows how 'radical' Whig ideas are consistent with the revolution settlement, and should not be used to oppose it, so too the poem illustrates the delusion of high-flying Tories who espouse the divine right of kings. Earnest, truthful praise of revolution principles unmasks the falsehood of Tory political thought. 'Every Panegyrick upon King *William*, was a Ballad upon King *James*, and a Lampoon upon Divine Right', wrote Defoe in the preface (*SFS*, ii. 40). The text of the poem follows this strategy. Next to Anne, tyrants would be seen in their true light: 'just Antithesis' will 'illustrate Crime'. There was no need to reform Anne as a ruler. Instead, Defoe would use Anne's example to persuade supporters of absolutism that constitutional monarchy was preferable to divine right. He could reform High Church misconceptions about the source of Anne's authority: not God, but popular consent.

Defoe's reforming energies had a limit, though. *Jure Divino* was written for an elite audience schooled in Whig political theory. His ideal readers would be sensitive to his moral lessons. But there would always be a minority of irredeemably wicked men who would never be receptive to his arguments, as he explained in *More Reformation*:

> For when to Beasts and Devils men descend,
> Reforming's past, and Satyr's at an end.
> No decent Language can their crimes rehearse,
> They lye below *the Dignity of Verse*.
> But if among thy Lines he would have place,
> Petition him to *Counterfeit some Grace*,
> Let him like something of a Christian sin,
> Then thou't ha' some pretence to bring him in. (lines 630–7; *SFS*, i. 231)

Once a target could not be reformed, it was no longer worthy of satire. In short, Defoe conceived of satire as a positive enterprise designed to help redeem Christians from their sins. He simply did not have satirical 'victims' in the manner of Dryden; rather he illustrated examples of virtuous and wicked behaviour, and expected properly attuned readers to follow the correct path. For a parallel example, look to *The Mock Mourners*, where Defoe refused to address the most egregious crimes of his countrymen: 'Blush,

Satyr, when such Crimes we must reveal, / And draw a silent Curtain to conceal' (lines 541–2; *SFS*, i. 151). Certain crimes were not worth exposing—not because they were small fry, but rather because they were beyond the pale. The only appropriate treatment was silence.

LIBELLER

Defoe's reforming satires are all emphatically public documents. He was a proud reformer of English manners and so acknowledged his reforming satires on their title pages. These were texts through which he sought to construct his public reputation. Yet there was another side to Defoe's career as a satirist. Despite his pretentions to moral guardianship, he was, on multiple occasions, convicted of seditious libel. Indeed, his contemporary reputation was that of a libeller.[27] When *Jure Divino* was pirated by Henry Hills, the title page was adorned with a woodcut of Defoe slumped gloomily in the pillory, the standard punishment for libellers (**Figure 1.5**).[28] In 1705 a new pack of playing cards likewise included an image of Defoe in the pillory, surrounded by guards and a braying crowd.[29] George Bickham's famous medley print of 1711 illustrating the most egregious crimes of the Whigs was crowned with an image of Defoe, goggle-eyed and warty, staring out from the pillory (**Figure 1.6**).[30] When Alexander Pope turned his attention to hack journalists in *The Dunciad* (1728), he portrayed Defoe in the pillory with sliced ears, another historic punishment for libel.[31]

Defoe's reputation for libel stemmed not from any of his verse satires, but rather from one of his anonymous pamphlets, *The Shortest-Way with the Dissenters* (1702). In response to a Tory resurgence in the early months of Queen Anne's reign, Defoe assumed the voice of an anonymous High Church zealot proposing to rid the nation of religious Dissenters, even at the cost of genocide. He segues from a proposal to exile nonconformists—'they are to be rooted out of this Nation'—to straightforward murder: 'Now *let us Crucifie the Thieves*' (*PEW*, iii. 109). At the heart of the book is a twisted reading of Queen Anne's first speech to parliament, in which she promised to support 'the Interests and Religion of the Church of England, and … those who have the truest Zeal to support it'.[32] Naturally, this speech was popular among churchmen;

---

[27] Thomas Keymer, 'Defoe's Ears: *The Dunciad*, the Pillory, and Seditious Libel', *Eighteenth-Century Novel*, 6–7 (2009), 159–96; Andreas K. E. Mueller, 'A "Body Unfitt": Daniel Defoe in the Pillory and the Resurrection of the Versifying Self', *The Eighteenth Century*, 54:3 (2013), 393–407.

[28] Keymer, *Poetics of the Pillory*, 132–5.

[29] Joseph Hone, 'A New Portrait of Defoe in the Pillory', *N&Q*, 63:1 (2016), 70–1.

[30] British Museum, item 1873,0712.795. See Mark Hallett, 'The Medley Print in Early Eighteenth-Century London', *Art History*, 20:2 (1997), 214–37.

[31] Alexander Pope, *The Dunciad (1728) and The Dunciad Variorum (1729)*, ed. Valerie Rumbold (Harlow: Longman, 2007), 55–6.

[32] *The History and Proceedings of the House of Commons*, 12 vols (1742), iii. 202–3.

pamphleteers quickly coopted and manipulated her statement to demonstrate her support for a resurgent Tory party. By stating bluntly some of the implicit assumptions and desires behind Tory polemic, Defoe's aim was to expose the violence behind High Church appropriations of Anne's rhetoric. He also unveiled the Jacobite biases which animated Tory propagandists in the wake of Anne's accession.[33]

Whether or not *The Shortest-Way* was originally and wholly conceived as a satire (my own stance is it was not), that is what Defoe sought to claim once he was exposed as the author.[34] Modern literary critics have discovered a few potential markers of irony in the pamphlet.[35] But Defoe's contemporary readers, taking the book at face value with an eye to the news, failed to get the joke. Whatever ironic markers Defoe may have embedded into the pamphlet, they were not obvious enough. Whereas Defoe *ex post facto* passed off *The Shortest-Way* as 'an Irony not Unusual' (*PEW*, iii. 114), contemporaries saw only 'Malicious Banters' and 'Spightful and Seditious *Sarcasm*'.[36] His attempt to save face by crying 'irony' did not work. He was charged with seditious libel and sent to Newgate. While awaiting punishment, in a last-ditch effort to counter his emerging reputation for libel, Defoe consciously sought to entrench his status as a reforming satirist, standing above the fray. He issued the first volume of his collected writings one week before his date in the pillory; he signed poems as 'the Author of *The True-Born Englishman*', reminding readers of his previous loyalist credentials before this debacle; he wrote *A Hymn to the Pillory*, a bitter protestation of innocence which combined a sophisticated satire against corruption with entreaties for the mob to look kindly on him.[37] Unlike his earlier bungled efforts, that last move *did* work. Tory journalists such as William Pittis were appalled by the sympathetic crowd who 'Hallow'd him down from his Wooden Punishment, as if he had been a *Cicero* that had made an Excellent Oration in it, rather than a *Cataline* that was Expos'd and Declaim'd against There'.[38]

Despite the manifest risks associated with ironic writing, this early incident did not stop Defoe from using the same basic technique in later pamphlets. During the succession crisis of 1713 he wrote a flurry of similar pamphlets exposing the logic of Jacobite polemic, starting with *Reasons Against the Succession of the House of Hanover* and followed by *And What if the Pretender Should Come?* and *An Answer to a Question that No Body thinks of, viz. But What if the Queen Should Die?* Despite the flagrant ironic

---

[33] Hone, *Literature and Party Politics*, 132–51.

[34] Hone, *Literature and Party Politics*, 155–65; Ashley Marshall, 'The Generic Context of Defoe's *The Shortest-Way with the Dissenters* and the Problem of Irony', *RES*, 61:249 (2010), 234–58; Kate Loveman, *Reading Fictions, 1660–1740: Deception in English Literary and Political Culture* (Aldershot: Ashgate, 2008), 134; but cf. J. A. Downie's critique in 'Review of Hone, *Literature and Party Politics*', *RES*, 69:292 (2018), 993–5.

[35] J. A. Downie, 'Defoe's *Shortest Way with the Dissenters*: Irony, Intention and Reader-Response', *Prose Studies*, 9:2 (1986), 120–39; Howard D. Weinbrot, *Literature, Religion, and the Evolution of Culture, 1660–1780* (Baltimore, MD: Johns Hopkins University Press, 2013), 66–89.

[36] *The Fox with His Fire-Brand Unkennell'd and Insnar'd* (1703), 20.

[37] Backscheider, *Daniel Defoe*, 126–7.

[38] *Heraclitus Ridens*, no. 2 (3–7 August 1703).

voice of the first two pamphlets, caricaturing the attitudes of Jacobite writers, Defoe once again faced prosecution, much to his horror:

> The Books I have written are as plain a Satyr upon the Pretender and his Friends, as can be written, if they are view'd Impartially; but being written Ironically, all the first Part, if taken asunder from the last Part, will read, *as in all Ironical speaking must be,* just contrary ... if what I have written be the strongest Irony, and consequently the greatest push that I could make against the Pretender's Interest, then this Prosecution must be Malicious and Abominable. Nor is this Irony concealed, *as has been suggested formerly*; but it is express'd plainly, and explicitly, in words at length.[39]

That Defoe returned to irony at this later moment of crisis suggests he considered it an important satirical technique. His indignation that he had not 'concealed' his irony likewise suggests he had learned something from the incident with *The Shortest-Way*, if not the wisdom to remain silent. Only Harley's intervention prevented a return to the pillory.[40]

Do these duplicitous ironic pamphlets fulfil the definition of satire as earlier delineated by Defoe? Ten years before *The Shortest-Way* he had written that 'The End of Satyr ought to be exposing Falshood, in order to Reformation' (*SFS*, i. 37). This had been the guiding principle behind all his verse satires. Had he forgotten the lesson? For while the ironic pamphlets certainly exposed the falsehoods peddled by Jacobite agitators, and may even have opened the eyes of 'those People who the *Jacobites* had deluded', they did little to reform the vices of their core targets (*Appeal*, 27).[41] Besides irritation, *The Shortest-Way* had no impact on the morale of the High Church brigade. Nor did the ironic pamphlets of 1713. So the only tenable conclusion is that Defoe did not judge these prose satires by the same standards as his verse satires. The same vices that he believed lay 'below *the Dignity of Verse*' were perfectly appropriate to be tackled in prose, an altogether more boisterous literary form. Equally, the ironic and dissembling aspects of these pamphlets were calculated to distance their anonymous author from the moral guardian responsible for *The True-Born Englishman*. Though their targets are the same, Defoe the covert ironist is very different to Defoe the verse satirist.

If not 'satires' in the sense previously elucidated by Defoe, are these pamphlets then 'libels', as the government claimed? The circumstances of publication suggest Defoe was alert to their potentially seditious content. Whereas Defoe openly claimed the vast majority of his poetic satires, he always published his ironic pamphlets anonymously and

---

[39] *Review*, ix. 334–5 (16 April 1713); cf. TNA, SP 34/37/205.
[40] Novak, *Daniel Defoe*, 424–31.
[41] See Nicholas Seager, '"She Will Not Be that Tyrant They Desire": Daniel Defoe and Queen Anne', in *Queen Anne and the Arts*, ed. Cedric D. Reverand II (Lewisburg, PA: Bucknell University Press, 2015), 41–55. In *Review*, vi. 84 (3 May 1709), Defoe explained that he was attempting to persuade 'Men of Reason among our *Jacobites*, that their Cause is near its End, and that it is Time for them to lay it down'. Most Jacobites were not so reasonable.

took precautions to ensure he would not be discovered.[42] In 1702 he had employed an experienced press agent, Edward Bellamy, to deliver the manuscript of *The Shortest-Way* anonymously to George Croome, a printer at Bridewell suspected of harbouring Jacobite views.[43] No bookseller or publisher was involved in the clandestine production process. Bellamy was supposed to be a safe pair of hands, but cracked under interrogation and admitted that he was working for Defoe. The 1713 pamphlets were all anonymously printed by Richard Janeway, a specialist in radical literature, and issued for sale by the trade publisher John Baker. When writing out the manuscripts, Defoe purportedly disguised his handwriting to avoid suspicion among the printers. Even if this is true, his efforts were sloppy. Once Janeway's men were seized and questioned, they admitted to recognizing Defoe's handwriting. Their evidence led to Defoe's arrest a few days later.[44]

The wild variance between the publication strategies of a poem such as *Jure Divino*—an expensive subscription publication, advertised in *The Review*, with Defoe's engraved portrait furnishing the frontispiece—and a pamphlet such as *Reasons Against the Succession of the House of Hanover* underscores the generic gap between Defoe's reformist verse satires and his controversial ironic pamphlets. The aim of the poems was to persuade villainous citizens to lead more virtuous lives, though in practice Defoe was suggesting that both Tories and radical Whigs ought to adhere to mainstream Whig principles. The aim of the ironic pamphlets was to unmask the seditious undertones of Tory polemic, helping readers understand the polemical contours of early eighteenth-century journalism and pamphleteering. These were stealthily educational primers, not blunt reforming satires. One after another, each dealt with the most touchy political topic of the day: royal succession. At its core, *The Shortest-Way* exposed the overlap between High Church ranters such as Sacheverell and more brazen exponents of a Jacobite succession. The 1713 pamphlets all made the same argument. It was not an argument Defoe dared to make in verse.

In this chapter I have attempted to chart Defoe's career in satire as Defoe himself would have seen it. Defoe was a verse satirist first and foremost. His aim was moral reform; his central technique was antithesis between vice and virtue. His prose writings are fundamentally different in both aim and technique. If the caution I have exhibited in separating Defoe's verse satires from his prose pamphlets appears contrived or unnecessary, that is because recent criticism has tended to emphasize the rhetorical affinities between satires across a variety of forms while overlooking the differences. What we mean by satire is very different to what Defoe meant by satire. To deny that Defoe used satirical techniques such as irony in his pamphlets would be wrong. But equally, to suggest

---

[42] Press spies and messengers were always on the hunt for the authors of libels: see Henry L. Snyder, 'The Reports of a Press Spy for Robert Harley: New Bibliographical Data for the Reign of Queen Anne', *The Library*, 5th ser., 22 (1967), 326–45.

[43] Paula R. Backscheider, 'No Defense: Defoe in 1703', *PMLA*, 103:3 (1988), 274–84 (276). According to John Dunton, 'Some would insinuate as though [Croome] favoured the Jacobites' (see John Nichols [ed.], *The Life and Errors of John Dunton*, 2 vols [London, 1818], i. 252). He was apprehended 'for treasonable Practices' in 1693 (TNA, SP 44/343/348).

[44] Novak, *Daniel Defoe*, 425–6.

that those pamphlets must therefore be labelled 'satires' is to misunderstand Defoe's very particular vision of satire, of what he believed satire could and ought to accomplish. Irony does not a satire make.

Further Reading

Paddy Bullard (ed.), *The Oxford Handbook of Eighteenth-Century Satire* (Oxford: Oxford University Press, 2019).
J. A. Downie, 'Defoe's *Shortest Way with the Dissenters*: Irony, Intention and Reader-Response', *Prose Studies*, 9:2 (1986), 120–39.
Ian Jack, *Augustan Satire: Intention and Idiom in English Poetry 1660–1750* (Oxford: Clarendon Press, 1952).
Joseph Hone, 'Daniel Defoe and the Whig Tradition in Satire', *ELH*, 84:4 (2017), 865–90.
Joseph Hone, *Literature and Party Politics at the Accession of Queen Anne* (Oxford: Oxford University Press, 2017).
Thomas Keymer, *Poetics of the Pillory: English Literature and Seditious Libel, 1660–1820* (Oxford: Oxford University Press, 2019).
Kate Loveman, *Reading Fictions, 1660–1740: Deception in English Literary and Political Culture* (Aldershot: Ashgate, 2008).
Ashley Marshall, 'Daniel Defoe as Satirist', *HLQ*, 70:4 (2007), 553–76.
Ashley Marshall, 'The Generic Context of Defoe's *The Shortest-Way with the Dissenters* and the Problem of Irony', *RES*, 61:249 (2010), 234–58.
Ashley Marshall, *The Practice of Satire in England, 1658–1770* (Baltimore, MD: Johns Hopkins University Press, 2013).
David Nokes, *Raillery and Rage: A Study of Eighteenth-Century Satire* (Brighton: Harvester, 1987).

PART II
CONTEXTS

CHAPTER 12

DEFOE AND THE BOOK TRADE

PAT ROGERS

Introduction

A paradox underlies the subject of this chapter. On the one hand we have seen a remarkable efflorescence in the study of book history over recent decades, which has yielded enormous new resources for the understanding of literature written in the past. Enumerative bibliography has benefitted from digital sources which enable us to locate and inspect thousands of titles which were once difficult to access. Physical bibliography has continued to push ahead, so that we can reconstruct with some exactitude the manner in which works were sent through the press. Publishers' records have been trawled for sales information, and authors' bank accounts ransacked for credits and debits. Yet we still know surprisingly little about the way that Daniel Defoe—one of the most prolific writers ever—interacted with editors, booksellers, and printers. The oddity of this situation amounts to a kind of cognitive dissonance in scholarly history. It needs a little more exploration and, where possible, explanation.

Central to our present grasp on the period of Defoe's lifetime are a few key events. They include the lapse of the Licensing Act in 1695, which saw an end to restrictions imposed in 1662 concentrating power in the government and in the reach of the Stationers' Company, a medieval guild that had enjoyed something close to a monopoly since Tudor times. The expiry of this measure opened up new avenues for expansion in both printing and bookselling, and it is not a mystery why the company should have tried hard to engineer its reintroduction.[1] A second measure of comparable importance was the Copyright Act of 1710, greeted with enthusiasm by members of the trade since

---

[1] A good outline of the issues discussed in this paragraph will be found in Peter Hinds, 'The Book Trade at the Turn of the Eighteenth Century', in *The Oxford Handbook of the Eighteenth-Century Novel*, ed. J. A. Downie (Oxford: Oxford University Press, 2016), 5–21.

it established clear rights to intellectual property, which they believed assured them of a perpetual claim to the titles they owned—a supposition which would not be successfully challenged in the English courts until 1774. The result was the appearance of a new and confident cadre of publishers, some not even members of the company, who were able to stretch the rules and augment their lists with items such as reprints of older works, translations, and books published in Ireland—none of which were covered by the 1710 legislation. This measure did much to institute modern copyright, and indeed intellectual property: we should be clear that the intended beneficiaries were mainly those who bought the property—booksellers—and not those who sold it—writers.

At the same time journalists had less to fear from official inquisitions, though they still might run into trouble with old laws imposing harsh penalties for offences such as seditious libel and scandalum magnatum (defaming peers). It is true that contemporaries such as Defoe himself experienced more liberty of the press than most of their predecessors, and far more than their colleagues under an absolutist regime across the Channel. Newspapers and other periodical organs (weekly, monthly, annual) flooded the capital and provincial towns [SEE CHAPTER 7]. In the view of some, it was this outburst of print that promoted the development of a relatively open society in Britain and supported the formation of a social and economic culture more hospitable to change than the advanced Enlightenment theorizing admired by the salonnières in Paris. This growth was not greatly slowed even by the imposition of a Stamp Tax (10 Anne, c.19) on newspapers in 1712, which actually survived until the nineteenth century. It had been designed to raise revenue, but also served as a backdoors way of reactivating censorship. This was something that the secretary of state, Lord Bolingbroke, may have wished to see, as Whigs such as Richard Steele proved formidable opponents to the government. The act divided supporters of the ministry: Jonathan Swift, an adherent of Robert Harley and Bolingbroke, had told his women friends in Dublin a year earlier, 'They are here intending to tax all little printed penny papers at a half-penny every half-sheet, which will utterly ruin Grubstreet'. The sentence ended in a way we might not expect: 'and I am endeavouring to prevent it'.[2] As it turned out, the press proved more resilient than Swift expected, and Grub Street had most of its finest hours yet to come. The measure did not yield everything that the government had hoped for, and the succeeding ministry felt obliged to introduce a new Stamp Act in 1725 (11 Geo. I, c.8) to close some loopholes that the trade had been able to exploit. But by that time Defoe's journalistic career was starting to wind down.

Another factor we need to consider is the intensely partisan nature of the age. In 1710 the trial of the high-flying clergyman Henry Sacheverell before the House of Lords inspired a cartload of pamphlets. The end of the Marlborough Wars in 1713 proved as contentious an issue in public opinion as the conflict itself had been. Then came the accession of the Hanoverians, almost immediately met by a Jacobite invasion of Scotland

---

[2] Jonathan Swift, *Journal to Stella*, ed. Abigail Williams (Cambridge: Cambridge University Press, 2013), 131. On the debates surrounding the Stamp Act, see J. A. Downie, *Robert Harley and the Press*, 149–61.

in 1715. The national wounds had hardly been repaired when the South Sea Bubble burst in 1720, a political as well as an economic crisis as its ramifications extended so deeply into the court, parliament, and the higher echelons of the business community. It was followed by the long ascendancy of Robert Walpole, the dominating figure in British life for a generation, who divided the chattering classes—among them members of the literary profession.

Defoe vs the Law

All these matters had their impact on writers. But what of Defoe? He ought to be among those most pervasively affected. His literary career as an author began almost at the moment that the Licensing Act lapsed, and this event to a degree enabled his career. From early on, however, he was in trouble with the authorities, and found that surveillance of the press had not gone away with the Act. It is enough here to instance only the more noteworthy cases.

The most famous by far concerns *The Shortest-Way with the Dissenters*, a parody of the alarmist rhetoric of High Church preachers such as Sacheverell. It was published at the end of 1702, and within weeks the machinery of government had started to clunk into action. On 3 January 1703, the secretary of state, the Earl of Nottingham, issued orders that Defoe was to be seized along with his papers, in order to face charges of 'high crimes and misdemeanours'. Defoe wrote to the Earl a few days later, claiming that he was 'Perfectly Free From any Seditious Designs', reflecting on a few incendiary clergymen, not the government (*Correspondence*, 5). He admitted that he had given great offence, but also explained his reluctance to surrender himself. The Whig publicity manager and the printer were soon arrested, and Defoe's involvement became publicly known. By 25 February Defoe had been indicted at the Old Bailey and a formal complaint lodged in parliament. Not for the first or last time, he had become a fugitive. When he could not be located by the messengers of the press, low-level commissars responsible for keeping tabs on the activities of the print trade, a proclamation was issued, offering £50 for information leading to his arrest. As is well known, he was caught in May hiding in the East End of London, and after being briefly bailed on a huge recognisance of £1,500, he was brought to court in July. What followed was almost a political show trial. Defoe was sentenced to stand in the pillory three times, fined about £135, and made to enter into an agreement for his good behaviour lasting no less than seven years. It is small wonder that historians have queried whether all this was strictly in accordance with the law. Defoe's biographer Paula Backscheider explains the reasons for this:

> Defoe's indictment and the summary of his trial have vestiges of the older language from other laws used to control the press. For example, he is accused of 'perniciously and diabolically' publishing 'without lawful Authority, with force and arms'. Since the Licensing Act had expired in 1695, there was no 'lawful Authority'. After the passage

of the Treason Trials Statute in 1696, it would have been inappropriate to prosecute Defoe for treason, the form from which the language 'with force and arms' came. His indictment and the court's ruling, however, conform to the use that the government would make of the law of seditious libel for the next fifty years.[3]

The impact of the trial was felt not just by authors, but also by members of the book trade, who needed to consider the implications of this judgement when publishing controversial items. Authors were sometimes more successful than Defoe in preserving their anonymity, but the law forbade booksellers from concealing their identity [SEE CHAPTER 34].

Defoe did not have to face the old sanctions against those judged to have calumniated their betters in print—though in *The Dunciad* (1728) Pope would refer with malicious inaccuracy to the episode: 'Earless on high, stood un-abash'd Defoe'.[4] Legend has it that he was protected as he stood on the rostrum, and pelted only by flowers. Still, with his natural flair for publicity, the condemned man was able to make a hearty meal of the occasion, arranging for his vigorous poem *A Hymn to the Pillory* (1703) to be handed out to the throng in attendance. Here he argued that justice was subservient to the whims of parties and governments, a claim as resonant as anything that John Milton had said in *Areopagitica* (1644), if less artistically couched. The actual sites of his public humiliation have their own symbolic meaning. The first took place close to the Royal Exchange, which Addison would hymn in the *Spectator* on 19 May 1711 as the nexus of British commerce (a central theme of Defoe's entire career as a writer), and which stood just yards from where he had set up as a young businessman [SEE CHAPTER 14]. The second was in Cheapside, another key artery of the City, down which Defoe had ridden in a torchlit procession to greet William III to the throne on Lord Mayor's Day in 1689. The third was alongside Temple Bar, the western limit of the City, close to the book trade milieu of Fleet Street, from which many of the author's publications would emerge and where his sometime enemy Edmund Curll (d. 1747) would later conduct his business. Defoe had attempted to speak truth to power, and the authorities had shown where power lay. They had ordered *The Shortest-Way* to be burnt by the common hangman, and they had exposed him to public disgrace across the city of which he was a liveryman and citizen. Somehow he had turned this ordeal into a triumph: the crowd 'Hallow'd him down from his Wooden Punishment, as if he had been a *Cicero* that had made an excellent Oration in it, rather than a *Cataline* that was Expos'd and Declaim'd against There'.[5]

The aftermath of the court proceedings holds equal significance. For one thing, once Defoe had been left to rot in prison for another four months, he was obliged prior to his release to pay fees for the time he had spent there. He only gained his freedom as a result of a deal cooked up by the Speaker of the Commons, Defoe's future patron Robert

---

[3] Backscheider, *Daniel Defoe*, 111.
[4] Alexander Pope, *The Dunciad*, ed. James Sutherland, 3rd ed. (London: Methuen, 1963), 117. The original reading was not 'un-abash'd' but 'pillory'd'.
[5] William Pittis, *Heraclitus Ridens*, no. 2 (3–7 August 1703).

Harley, which meant that the money owed could be paid surreptitiously out of secret service funds. It was not until July 1704 that a complete discharge was effected, when the queen issued a royal pardon. Defoe produced a collection of his writings, reprinting the flagitious pamphlet—in itself a brave gesture of defiant independence. Though his incarceration had cost him a great deal as far as his dreams of success in business went, it ultimately proved a boost to his literary career. He had been given the chance to open a long relationship with the man who would later become Lord Treasurer, Harley. The entire episode matters in literary history, but it also illuminates the development of the freedom of the press. Authors, publishers, and printers did not cease for a century or more to be harried and prosecuted. But from this time governments understood that they needed to be careful before they took on works by writers as talented as Defoe.

After this, Defoe could seldom feel entirely safe from legal constraints. Throughout his writing life, he found out the hard way that the press continued to face substantial harassment—even though it was no longer enough simply to have 'proffered or diffused heretical opinions' to be led to the stake, as Roger Chartier describes the fate risked by authors, printers, and booksellers in early modern history.[6] As late as 1720 he was in jeopardy because he was thought to have written an offensive piece in Nathaniel Mist's *Weekly Journal*, an organ in which he certainly was involved (see below). The printer was eventually convicted, and given a set of punishments, including the pillory, close to what Defoe had endured in 1703. As on that occasion, the offender was apparently protected by the mob, and his progress from the scaffold back to gaol was attended by a throng who made their support audible with loud huzzas. This time Defoe got away without sanctions, though he was required to give sureties of £400 in return for bail. He wrote to his contact in Whitehall, the under-secretary Charles Delafaye (d. 1762), that he 'had no Concern' in the most offensive paragraph in the newspaper article, and managed to convince his official minder that he had not repeated a misstep two years earlier, when he had 'by Inadvertence given Offence before'. This was a reference to a letter by 'Sir Andrew Politick' about the war with Spain that had appeared in Mist's paper. Both the printer himself and the bookseller Thomas Warner had confirmed Defoe as the author, just as had happened with *The Shortest-Way* (*Correspondence*, 847–8). In the grubby world of the popular press, one could not rely on colleagues to provide cover.

The most hazard that Defoe ever ran, apart from his troubles with *The Shortest-Way*, had faced him between 1713 and 1715. In the former year he was accused of having committed sedition amounting to treason in pamphlets relating to the succession, an intensely sensitive issue as the queen's health, never strong, began to decline further. A complaint was laid by three political writers, one of them Thomas Burnet (son of a latitudinarian bishop, and himself a regular thorn in the side of the Tories), as well as the editor of a Whig journal called *The Flying Post*. All three had recently found themselves

---

[6] Roger Chartier, *The Order of Books: Readers, Authors, and Libraries in Europe between the Fourteenth and Eighteenth Centuries*, trans. Lydia G. Cochrane (Stanford, CA: Stanford University Press, 1994), 50.

under prosecution by the government (*Correspondence*, 739–50). Events now moved swiftly, and a rapid summary must suffice:

> The printer, Richard Janeway, disclosed the author's name; a warrant was issued for Defoe's arrest and he was seized at Stoke Newington on 11 April. Through Harley's assistance he was released on bail on 13 April ... The informers had acted maliciously against Defoe; they were also determined to embarrass the Government. The Chief Justice [Thomas Parker] was a Whig; it would be claimed that the pamphlets were hostile to the Hanoverian Succession; and thus the Government could not openly protect Defoe. Defoe exacerbated the difficulties by vigorous protests in the *Review*, 16 and 18 April; on 22 April Parker committed him to prison for libel; and his release (on 2 May) came only when he apologized to the court (having printed his apologies in the *Review*, 28 April). Defoe petitioned the Queen for a general pardon to quash the original indictment; the pardon was signed by Bolingbroke for the Queen in November.[7]

One detail left out here is the fact that his bail was set at £1,600, a figure not far short of what a major state criminal might expect to face.

A year later, after the death of the queen, Defoe was in trouble again. He had published a letter in the *Flying Post* on 19 August 1714, which implied that the Earl of Anglesey—recently appointed a regent until George I should arrive to take up the throne—was actually a Jacobite. The printer of the paper, William Hurt, and its publisher (distributor), John Morphew, were arrested. Hurt was another to have been sentenced to a spell in the pillory, after he printed in 1713 what Swift called 'the cursedest Libel in Verse ... that ever was seen'.[8] He got his revenge after the Hanoverians came in, trapping a Jacobite bookbinder at work on a seditious pamphlet at 4 a.m. Such tit-for-tat exercises were common in the trade. Among the papers that the authorities seized was the compromising letter, inconveniently drafted in Defoe's own handwriting. He was promptly taken up and had to ask Robert Harley for help, claiming that he had been 'softening' the aggressive Whig rhetoric found in the original draft of the letter. It was not until the following summer that he came up for trial at the Guildhall, when he was found guilty. Sentence was deferred, and before a final decision could be taken the political climate had changed drastically—the former Tory leaders including Harley had been impeached, the Stuart rising had begun in Scotland, and Anglesey had compromised his own position. Defoe was able to plead his case with Lord Chief Justice Parker, so that he never came up for sentence. It was agreed that, in exchange for his freedom, he would infiltrate the Tory press and tone down attacks on the ministry (*Correspondence*, 821–7).

These instances show that for writers, journalists, printers, and publishers, the threat of prosecution was never very far away. The fact that Defoe wrote mostly in an anonymous or pseudonymous guise, as was then normal, did not grant him immunity.

---

[7] J. T. Boulton (ed.), *Daniel Defoe* (London: Batsford, 1965), 278.
[8] Swift, *Journal to Stella*, 517.

He was a particularly brave and sometimes reckless author, and yet his experiences do not distort reality, or exaggerate the sense of vulnerability many people in the book trade must have felt. But there are always contradictions surrounding his behaviour. In articles for the *Review*, some rehashed in *An Essay on the Regulation of the Press* (1704), he never tired of urging the government to take a stronger line against High Church 'libels', or calling for journals such as *The Flying Post* to be muzzled. Likewise, Edmund Curll volunteered to become government licenser of the press. It may be a good thing that he and Defoe never got together—they were sworn enemies, as this letter from 1718 indicates:

> Here has been a Very Barbarous attempt made by Curl ye Bookseller upon m^r Mist (Viz) to Trepann him into words Against ye Governm^t with a Design to Inform against him; I think Mist has Escaped him but if he brings it into yor Office I shall Lay a Clear state of the Matter before you. I kno' the Government is Sufficent to it Self for punishing Offendors, and is Above Employing Trepanns to Draw Men into Offences On Purpose to Resent them. (*Correspondence*, 845)

No warm feeling between brothers of the quill here, then.

Jure Divino, Piracy, and Publication by Subscription

With few exceptions, Defoe did not greatly avail himself of a form of publication which was becoming increasingly popular. This was the method of ensuring sales in advance by asking purchasers to put down a segment of the full price and then the remainder once the book came out. It was a way to reduce the risk—for one thing, if not enough subscribers had been found, the project could be abandoned before it reached the expenses of printing, paper, and binding, with money returned. Large and expensive editions were the most suitable vehicles. John Dryden had found it an effective way of issuing his translation of Virgil (1697), and Pope would make his fortune with his *Iliad* (1715–20): in each case the bookseller (respectively, Jacob Tonson and Bernard Lintot) had done well, but perhaps not quite so well as the author.

It is no surprise that Defoe steered clear of this method, because his first plan had backfired. He spent years on the composition of *Jure Divino* (1706), his most ambitious poem. When it was almost ready to come out in 1704, he had announced terms for purchasers in his journal, the *Review*. Subscriptions were to be taken in at sixteen places in London, as well as at most of the principal towns in England. The down payment would be 2*s*.6*d*., against a total cost of 10*s*., a good bargain for a folio volume of 100 sheets, that is 400 pages. In the end publication had to be delayed for a further two years, until the summer of 1706. In addition the list of subscribers, which would have been one of the best clues we have to Defoe's likely audience, was never printed. The obstacles have been summarized by Backscheider:

> *Jure Divino* may also have been delayed because of cost. Defoe complained in both the *Review* and the preface to the poem that subscribers failed to pay even the half crown. He says that 'not half' have paid the author, and that without the generous assistance of friends and other subscribers, he would not have been able to pay for paper and printing. One satiric attack … says that Matthews held back publication for a while for fear he would lose money on the poem. As further proof of his lowered status, some time before publication Defoe's subscribers refused to have their names listed on the pages usually reserved for this purpose.[9]

This passage supplies vital information that illustrates the relations of author, publisher, and readers in the period, and some of this needs to be explored in detail.

It shows that Defoe bore the expenses of the edition, and that *Jure Divino* was in a sense self-published, with John Matthews hired to perform the presswork for a fee (much as a jobbing printer might be asked to get out a business catalogue, say). This was a far more common procedure than we used to believe: J. A. Downie suggests that 'If authors really wanted to see their work in print, then the best way for them to achieve their objective, even after the passing of the Copyright Act, would have been to publish at his or her own risk' (one might even say, *especially* after passage of the act). The annual output of work labelled on their title-page 'printed for the author' actually went up steadily from 357 in the first decade of the eighteenth century to 2,522 in the last.[10] John Matthews, senior (d. c.1716) was 'an eminent printer', well established in the London trade. He was also the printer of Defoe's journal, the *Review*, and we must suspect that a similar arrangement was in place there.

There is a sad footnote: Matthews's son John succeeded to the business after his father died, but within two years he had run into desperate trouble. This was because he unwisely printed a number of seditious Jacobite items in the wake of the Rising of 1715–16. Once he was arrested and visited in gaol, prior to his release, by the high-flying printer and editor Nathaniel Mist (see below for Mist's connections with Defoe). In 1718 young Matthews goaded the ministry too far by issuing a short pamphlet entitled *Vox Populi, Vox Dei*. He ended up in Newgate prison, where he refused to divulge the identity of the author. In November 1719 he became the first and only printer to be accused of a treasonable libel and was duly hanged at Tyburn. He was 18 years of age. In response, the event became 'the occasion of riotous behaviour by apprentice and journeymen printers and resulted in the publication of at least five supposed dying declarations espousing the Jacobite cause'.[11] An elderly pressman who had assisted Matthews was expelled from the Society of Journeyman Printers for having sold him down the river in court. We

---

[9] Backscheider, *Daniel Defoe*, 189–90.

[10] J. A. Downie, 'Printing for the Author in the Long Eighteenth Century', in *British Literature and Print Culture*, ed. Sandro Jung (Cambridge: D.S. Brewer, 2013), 58–77 (61, 74).

[11] Paul Chapman, 'Matthews, John (1701?–1719)', *Oxford Dictionary of National Biography*, http://www.oxforddnb.com/view/10.1093/ref:odnb/9780198614128.001.0001/odnb-9780198614128-e-72387.

know that Defoe was prone to anxiety about his personal safety, but even he can hardly have feared such a drastic fate as the teenager received through his involvement in the printed word.

Jure Divino ought to have been Defoe's greatest coup as a professional author: the work deserved as much. In the event it was little short of a publishing disaster. A semi-respectable bookseller named Benjamin Bragg managed to produce a cheap version of the poem before Defoe had time to market his deluxe version with a portrait of the author at 13s. (65p). Bragg had naturally excluded his name from the imprint, but he had inserted an advertisement in the *Observator* on 20 July 1706, pointing out that the book had been available in town and country for some time 'for the Sole Benefit of the Author', but also that it required a further payment of one shilling from subscribers if they wanted the portrait. What Defoe must have found particularly galling was the fact that Bragg reprinted the preface to the work, containing as it did severe recrimination against some threatened piracies of which the author had evidently got wind. He fulminated with an understandable sense of injury in the *Review* on 3 August 1706: 'Whoever has a Mind to encourage such Robbery of other Mens Studies at their own Expence, may be furnished with the said Book at Mr. *Benjamin Bragg*'s, Publisher in ordinary to the Pyrates. As appears by setting his Name to their Advertisements'.[12] As well as stealing his material, the spurious edition was grossly incorrect: Defoe contemptuously adds, 'the Author undertakes at any time, to produce near one hundred Notorious Errors in one half of the Book—The Picture on the Book, which is but the Copy of a Copy, is about as much like the Author, as Sir *Roger L'Estrange*, was like the Dog *Towzer*'.[13] Here we see one side of piracy in the book trade, not always emphasized. A kind of Gresham's law has come into play, whereby superior works by major authors might be quickly replicated, or even driven out of circulation, in a bastard version by fringe operators. Adrian Johns aptly cites a later comment in the *Review* (3 December 1709), where Defoe compares the actions of offenders to those that footpads would take plundering on the highway, if there were no law to deter them, 'an Evil so fatal, and so just a Reproach to a well-govern'd Nation', that it is astonishing they are allowed to carry on with their thefts.[14] The Copyright Act, which was in the process of passing into law at this juncture, would do a little, but no more than that, to remedy the situation.

This was not the first time that Defoe suffered at the hands of pirates. He wrote bitterly of the way in which his earliest bestseller, *The True-Born Englishman* (1701), had been subjected to grievous breaches of what we should call intellectual property, citing it as a 'remarkable Example' of the frauds endemic in the book industry,

---

(Accessed 6 February 2019). A more detailed account will be found in James Sutherland, 'Young Matthews', in *Background for Queen Anne*, ed. James Sutherland (London: Methuen, 1939), 182–200.

[12] *Review*, iii. 479 (3 August 1706).
[13] *Review*, iii. 463 (27 July 1706).
[14] Adrian Johns, *Piracy: The Intellectual Property Wars from Gutenberg to Gates* (Chicago, IL: University of Chicago Press, 2009), 38.

by which the Author, tho' in it he eyed no Profit, had he been to enjoy the Profit of his own Labour, had gain'd above a 1000l. a Book that besides Nine Editions of the Author, has been Twelve Times printed by other Hands; some of which have been sold for 1d. others 2d. and others 6d. the Author's Edition being fairly printed, and on good Paper, and could not be sold under a Shilling. 80000 of the Small ones have been sold in the Streets for 2d. or at a Penny: And the Author thus abused and discourag'd had no Remedy but Patience.

Nor was this the only ground for complaint, as he had been able to observe 'monstrous Abuses' in the printing of these clandestine versions, with 'Twenty, Fifty, in some Places, Sixty Lines left out in a Place, others turn'd, spoil'd, and so intolerably mangled, that the Parent of the Brat could not know his own Child'.[15] This is a side of piracy that has been little discussed.

Returning to Defoe's subscription ventures, we need to take note of his poem *Caledonia* (1706), although it is a less instructive case in terms of the way campaigns were generally managed. The subscribers listed in the London edition had actually put down their names for the one that came out at Edinburgh in the previous year, as the work of Agnes Anderson, the royal printer. Defoe had petitioned the Privy Council for Scotland for the sole privilege of printing and selling the book, and they made a suitable grant. It is a highly unusual roster, containing only eighty-four names, far short of the average for a volume of such pretensions to gravitas: all are male, and all are Scottish. While the Edinburgh establishment and the ruling elite is well represented, especially the pro-Union faction, there is no depth of coverage. Two dukes (Queensberry and Argyll) stand out, along with two marquises; twenty-two earls (most notably the Unionist politician and future Jacobite leader Mar); six designated 'Lord', including some with a judicial title; and fifteen baronets and knights. Among the commoners there are also many prominent soldiers, lawyers, medical men, and landowners, but a singular absence of churchmen whose influence was so strong during negotiations over the Union. To say that the list was 'more prestigious than that of any other work in the century' is palpably exaggerating its standing.[16] Many subscription campaigns, in London especially, attracted a far larger clientele (sometimes by a factor of twenty or more), more members of the higher rungs of the peerage, more eminent figures in the professions, more of the upper gentry, more scientists and mathematicians, more artists and architects, more literary men, more subscribers from overseas, and self-evidently more royalty, women, and members of the clergy. Defoe must have been pleased with the results, after the debacle with *Jure Divino*, but apart from an effort with *The History of the Union* (1709), about which we know very little, he never went in for anything like this again.

One more case needs to be mentioned. This was *Atlas Maritimus & Commercialis* (1728), a vast compilation describing the coasts, ports, and harbours of the entire known

---

[15] *A Second Volume of the Writings of the Author of The True-Born Englishman* (1705), A3r. Italics reversed.

[16] Backscheider, *Daniel Defoe*, 223.

world. It took the form of a subscription volume running to more than 600 folio pages in two columns. The central aim of the volume was to promote a new globular projection for maps as an aid to navigation, for which a small group of entrepreneurial figures had obtained a royal warrant in 1721. The new system carried an endorsement by none other than Edmond Halley, a notable hydrographer among his other talents. It had been devised by a team including a mapmaker, an illustrator, a writer on navigation, and a bookseller—William Taylor (see below). Taylor had just made a killing with *Robinson Crusoe* (1719), and indeed the first hint of this project comes in an advertisement Taylor placed in *The Farther Adventures of Robinson Crusoe* (1719). It took several years before the work appeared, and then it can be seen to owe much to Defoe—the British sections are little more than a paraphrase of *A Tour thro' the Whole Island of Great Britain* (1724–6), and the entire work shows precise congruence in numerous details with what Defoe wrote elsewhere. However, it is highly unlikely that he had anything to do with an impressive subscription campaign, which yielded over 400 names with a galaxy of talent in areas such as the navy, mathematics, and navigation, as well as a good showing of aristocrats, politicians, and leading figures in overseas trade. There was a good showing of Scots, for what reason is not apparent.

Booksellers, Printers, and Editors

The term 'bookseller', as used in Defoe's time, is potentially misleading. It can refer in the modern way to someone who kept a shop and whose main business was to retail books. At other times it indicated a man or woman engaged in distributing stock, from a warehouse rather than a shop open to the public. However, it can also apply to someone who was responsible for issuing printed books, that is in effect the modern publisher. (That last named term generally signified the person we should call the editor of a book.) The categories may overlap, so that an individual operated in two or three of these capacities. Some booksellers had another line as printers, but most had not (see below for Defoe's contacts with printers). Certain booksellers also sold stationery, such as paper and ink, but that does not mean they would be called 'stationers', a word whose root sense at this time remained 'a bookseller; in wider sense, one engaged in one of the trades connected with book'.[17] We should note that membership of the Stationers' Company was no longer a requirement for setting up a successful business. Most of the leading booksellers had gone through an apprenticeship prior to achieving freedom of the guild, which gave them advantages including a recognized status in London municipal affairs. However, the company did not rule the roost as it once had done. Edmund Curll rejected an offer to qualify for admission, although he had begun by working under a master who belonged to the Stationers. Instead he chose to practise the trade by paying a fine and joining by

---

[17] *OED*, 'stationer', 1a.

'redemption' the ancient Company of Cordwainers, that is shoemakers and saddlers. (Defoe himself had joined the Company of Butchers, something he could do by patrimony since James Foe, his father, had been admitted.) Several members of the trade also moonlighted conducting book sales, a separate profession of auctioneers having only just started to emerge. Finally, it was common, too, for other goods to be sold as a sideline, most commonly patent medicines, pills, and potions. There were a few specialist branches: for example, publishers of atlases and topographical works would often sell globes as well. Printsellers for the most part confined themselves to graphic works such as engravings and etchings, eschewing letterpress.

Defoe worked with almost every conceivable segment of this broadly constituted trade. Most of the individuals concerned were based either in London or Edinburgh, but a few contacts are known with operators in the English provinces. It should be noted that Dublin functioned as a largely independent centre of the book trade. Since the British Copyright Act did not apply to Ireland until the union of 1801, and there was no recognized agreement, it was open to Irish publishers to reprint English books without acquiring the rights: they could be exported to the American colonies or marketed in England at a cheaper price than the homegrown product. As well as Cork, the subsidiary centre, a number of ports such as Waterford and Youghal regularly imported books from London, Amsterdam, and Paris for consumers in the Irish provinces. At least thirty works by Defoe were reprinted at Dublin in his lifetime, including some of his best-known items of fiction and non-fiction. In the imprint of these works are to be found the names of some of the most eminent members of the Dublin fraternity, including George Grierson (d. 1753), Thomas Hume (d. 1738), John Hyde (d. 1728), George Risk (d. 1762), Aaron Rhames (d. 1734), and Edward Waters (d. 1736, known for his association with Swift). Nevertheless, it is unlikely that Defoe had the slightest contact with these men, or even knew in some cases that the volumes had appeared.

For convenience, we can divide into two groups those among the London book trade with whom he intersected most often: trade publishers and general booksellers. There is a third category of mercuries, the people (often women) who actually hawked the stock around the streets of the capital—in the provinces their place might be taken by itinerant pedlars. Trade publishers generally did not buy the rights to works: rather, they made their living by providing a wholesaling service for retail booksellers, or by serving as distributors for authors who published at their own expense. Their names appear very frequently in imprints, but since they must often have operated at a distance from writers this fact can rarely be used to clinch an attribution of authorship in the case of anonymity. In the opening half of Defoe's career, up to 1714, the names most frequently found on his title-pages are those of John Morphew (d. 1720) and John Baker (d. after 1715). The first of these is named in all the important Tory pamphlets and newspapers of the later years of Queen Anne, including works by Swift, Delarivier Manley, and Matthew Prior, among many. Baker was his counterpart on the Whig side, issuing numerous tracts on behalf of the opposing party during the Harley administration of 1710–14. In sheer bulk they were outdone only by the durable James Roberts (d. 1754), who succeeded to the business of his mother-in-law Abigail Baldwin (d. 1713), and went on to produce many hundreds of items, mostly in line with Whig or government attitudes. The names of all these individuals are found repeatedly in the imprint of books by Defoe, but again we should not overemphasize the significance of this fact. It is, for instance, quite likely that some subsidy was made by the Whig hierarchy to both bookseller and author for some of the ten items in 1711 that bear Baker's name and are reliably attributed to Defoe (the count excludes second and later editions). In addition Baker took over the *Review* in 1710, while Morphew may have sold the journal at one stage. But we cannot infer a close relationship between Defoe and these two men on this evidence.

This caveat applies to the second category, booksellers who bought copyrights from an author. It would be altogether wrong to think that writers in this period would enjoy a cosy friendship with their publisher, as has sometimes happened in modern times. There was nothing corresponding with the mentoring role played by Maxwell Perkins in the case of major American writers of the twentieth century. Even a publisher as brash and self-confident as Curll knew his limitations when it came to fostering artistic creativity. Tim Severin has imagined that Defoe hobnobbed with William Taylor in Paternoster Row, to be given hints for the plot of *Crusoe*.[18] It is not at all likely.

The list of those who show up in the imprint of Defoe's productions is a long one: at least 150, even if we confine ourselves to solid attributions. In general, the individuals cannot be so readily identified with a particular camp in politics or religion. However, among those most often used in the 1720s, Arthur Bettesworth (d. 1739) commonly published items from a Low Church or Dissenting source. Others such as John Brotherton (d. 1756), William Rufus Chetwood (d. 1766), John Graves (d. 1726), William Meadows (d. 1760), and William Mears (d. c.1740) were involved in the great series of fictional works that Defoe produced in the first half of the decade. They also tended to toe the ministerial line. On the other hand, two important women figures in the trade, Anne Dodd (d. 1739) and Elizabeth Nutt (d. 1756), sometimes buck the trend. Nutt was the widow of the printer and publisher John Nutt (d. 1716), who issued many of Defoe's earlier works, and further expanded her husband's activities. She regularly employed Dodd, the most active of the mercuries or distributors, whose operations crisscrossed the entire network of outlets in the city. Nutt's daughters helped the business in local outlets at sites such as the Royal Exchange and the Savoy. More than once, the productions of these women fell foul of the authorities. Equally, there is the High-Church bookseller Charles Rivington (d. 1742), operating in St Paul's Churchyard, who consistently supported Tory or 'country' candidates in elections for the City of London. His name appears in the imprint of major works on commerce such as *The Complete English Tradesman* (1725–7).

Among those frequently encountered on title-pages is Thomas Warner, who succeeded Baker at the Black Boy in Paternoster Row in 1717, and worked from this address until 1734. In addition he may have taken over the role of trade publisher. We have already seen that Warner had testified against Defoe in 1718, stating that from what he had heard in conversation and for other mysteriously unspecified reasons, he

---

[18] Tim Severin, *In Search of Robinson Crusoe* (New York: Basic Books, 2002), 323–8.

believed Defoe to be the author of most of the article in question. Evidently there were no hard feelings, since Warner continues to appear in imprints right up to the time of Defoe's final publications. Other names recur, for example that of William Boreham, another resident of Paternoster Row, who figures only for a short period, 1718–20, and mostly in connection with the plight of the weavers at the time of the Calico Act. Boreham went bankrupt in 1721, a reminder that the book trade had its banal commercial risks as well as the perils of government displeasure.

It should be noted that Defoe's books do not make heavy use of the pseudonymous 'A. Moore' (sometimes J. Moor or other variants), who is generally located with studied vagueness 'near St. Paul's', as a device to evade the clutches of the law. It is found in works such as *The Case of Mr. Law, Truly Stated* (1721), which dipped into the still treacherous South Sea waters. Nor do we often encounter the formula 'sold by the booksellers of London and Westminster', an obvious give-away where surreptitious printings are in question. The pirate who caused the writer most grief was probably Henry Hills (d. 1711), always ready to pounce on items such as *The True-Born Englishman* and *A Hymn to the Pillory*. Edmund Curll does not seem to have got hold of any of Defoe's books, much as he would have liked to exploit his adversary.

The most important business in Paternoster Row, as far as Defoe's literary legacy goes, was undoubtedly that of William Taylor (d. 1724). It was he who published all three instalments of *Robinson Crusoe*, beginning with the first part that proved a runaway bestseller in 1719. Three more editions were called for in the same year, a fifth in 1720, a sixth in 1722. The second part was never quite as popular, but it did reach a fifth edition in 1726. For many years there was no call for a reprint of the religious musings that formed the third part. To a certain extent Taylor was responding to piratical reprints, notably one by T. Cox in London, one 'Printed for the Book-sellers of *London* and *Westminster*', and one by J. Hyde and others in Dublin. Abridgements soon began to appear, with a watered-down version of all three parts in 1722 printed by Edward Midwinter and sold by a team of booksellers including Bettesworth, Brotherton, and Meadows—all, it should be noted, purveyors of legitimate Defoe editions. Midwinter was often concerned with pamphlets and broadsides from his shop, which then stood in the unfashionable Pye Corner, Smithfield. This version reached a ninth edition by 1765, and stands at the beginning of all the derivative texts in various media—abridgements, chapbooks, serializations, Robinsonades, dramatizations, along with translations into scores of languages—which are discussed elsewhere in this volume [SEE CHAPTER 32].

Taylor died of a sudden fever, and his precious rights in *Crusoe* went soon after to John Osborn (d. 1734) and Thomas Longman (d. 1755), founder of the durable firm which lasted as an independent concern until recently, surviving even the loss of its premises in Paternoster Row to bomb damage in 1940. But by mid-century, the work had become 'more or less public property', a testimony to its place at the heart of the canon of modern literature. Taylor's family business had long used the sign of the ship, and his list contained a large number of works on travel and discovery, some of them included in the catalogue of his publications appended to editions of *Crusoe*. It may be that, before his death, he had recruited Defoe to work on *Atlas Maritimus*. As for the printing of the work, we know that it was carried out by the relatively obscure Henry Parker of Goswell Street, along with the great William Bowyer the elder (d. 1737), on a portion of the second and third editions, and Hugh Meere (d. 1723), the owner of a type foundry, known also for his work in printing reference works and some leading newspapers such as the *Daily Post*, in which Defoe is thought to have had a controlling interest.[19]

Not much has been discovered until now about those who printed Defoe's books, or the arrangements he may have made with them. Recent research by James E. May shows that most of the well-known printers of the day worked on items of his oeuvre.[20] One of these was John Barber (d. 1741), better known for his association with Swift and Pope, and for his activities as a Jacobite lord mayor of London. The list also includes John Darby, junior (d. 1733); Robert Tookey, to whom Defoe's ally Samuel Keimer (d. 1742) was apprenticed; and no less a figure than Samuel Richardson. We do not know how much contact went on between author and printer, but in the case of what may have been the last book that Defoe finished, *The Compleat English Gentleman* (unpublished until 1890), we have a letter to the eminent printer John Watts (d. 1763), dated 10 September 1729, in which he discusses revisions and proofs (*Correspondence*, 873–5). Among noted Scottish printers we find Agnes Anderson (d. 1716), who had inherited from her husband the patent as printer to the crown in Edinburgh, and who defended her monopoly with some vigour, turning her firm into the largest in the capital. From 1710 Defoe's books were sometimes printed in Edinburgh by John Moncur (d. 1729). Other items were reprinted in the city from the London editions by James Watson (d. 1722). The closest relation among all these may be with Keimer, who had worked for Watts. This eccentric Quaker issued up to five pamphlets by Defoe in 1715 (the estimate used to be higher), and he was the recipient of a sympathetic letter two years later when in prison as a result of his work on Mist's *Weekly Journal* (*Correspondence*, 828–30). He went on to set up a business in Philadelphia with the young Benjamin Franklin as foreman of the press.

In writing for the periodical press, Defoe, as far as we know, often acted as his own editor. His relations with Mist (d. 1737) were perhaps the most important he developed during the long course of his career as a newspaperman. The issues are too complex and too contested to be explored fully here. It is clear from correspondence with his controller, Delafaye, that he had been engaged by the ministry to tone down the violent Jacobite accents of Mist's *Journal*, but the exact degree to which he was able to perform this task remains uncertain. As for the *Review*, the journal that he ran from 1704 to 1713, the operative word must be 'singlehanded'. He had the backing of Harley, and some of the money he received from secret service funds, which ran to £400 per year, may have gone to subsidize production costs. But the printer John Matthews, senior, obviously had nothing to do with the content of the paper. Again, we should not postulate an

---

[19] On these matters, see Henry C. Hutchins, '*Robinson Crusoe*' and its Printing, 1719–1731: A Bibliographical Study (New York: Columbia University Press, 1925), quotation from 135; and K. I. D. Maslen, 'The Printers of *Robinson Crusoe*', *The Library*, 5th ser., 7 (1952), 124–31.

[20] I am greatly indebted to Professor May for sharing with me some results of his unpublished work.

intimate relationship in which a member of the book trade collaborates with the writer in a shared creative enterprise. That is not how things commonly worked.

Conclusion

We can hardly call Defoe a typical literary professional, as this category of writer has been explored by Brean Hammond.[21] A number of factors rule out this description, among them his exceptionally long and prolific career, the range of genres across which he worked, his heavy involvement in various forms of periodical, his close relations with the government, his willingness to write on both sides of an issue, his unusual background as a young man once aimed at the Dissenting ministry, his exposure to the world of business (right down to the first-hand observation of bankruptcy and a short spell in the debtors' gaol), the remarkable scope of his knowledge in many fields, and of course his immense talent as an author. Nevertheless, he probably had wider contacts with the book trade than anyone else in the entire century. His experience with regard to interventions by the law (on a more than average number of occasions), piracy (about average for a major writer), and subscription publishing (rather below average) falls into line with general norms. Defoe could not have practised his craft without the well-organized systems of production and distribution that had evolved in London especially; but the world of books would have been mightily impoverished if he had not seized the opportunities that presented themselves to him.

Further Reading

Paula R. Backscheider, *Daniel Defoe: His Life* (Baltimore, MD: Johns Hopkins University Press, 1989).

Roger Chartier, *The Order of Books: Readers, Authors, and Libraries in Europe between the Fourteenth and Eighteenth Centuries*, trans. Lydia G. Cochrane (Stanford, CA: Stanford University Press, 1994).

J. A. Downie, 'Printing for the Author in the Long Eighteenth Century', in *British Literature and Print Culture*, ed. Sandro Jung (Cambridge: D.S. Brewer, 2013), 58–77.

J. A. Downie, *Robert Harley and the Press: Propaganda and Public Opinion in the Age of Swift and Defoe* (Cambridge: Cambridge University Press, 1979).

Laurence Hanson, *Government and the Press 1695–1763* (Oxford: Clarendon Press, 1936).

Peter Hinds, 'The Book Trade at the Turn of the Eighteenth Century', in *The Oxford Handbook of the Eighteenth-Century Novel*, ed. J. A. Downie (Oxford: Oxford University Press, 2016), 5–21.

---

[21] Brean S. Hammond, *Professional Imaginative Writing in England 1670–1740: 'Hackney for Bread'*, (Oxford: Clarendon Press, 1997). See especially the discussion of Defoe's likely earnings for pamphlets and periodicals (74).

Henry C. Hutchins, *'Robinson Crusoe' and its Printing, 1719–1731: A Bibliographical Study* (New York: Columbia University Press, 1925).

Adrian Johns, *Piracy: The Intellectual Property Wars from Gutenberg to Gates* (Chicago, IL: University of Chicago Press, 2009).

K. I. D. Maslen, 'The Printers of *Robinson Crusoe*', *The Library*, 5th ser., 7 (1952), 124–31.

James Sutherland, *Defoe* (London: Methuen, 1937).

CHAPTER 13

DANIEL DEFOE AND THE SOCIAL STRUCTURE OF PRE-INDUSTRIAL ENGLAND

J. A. DOWNIE

From Dorothy George's *England in Transition* (1931) and G. M. Trevelyan's *English Social History* (1942) onwards, Gregory King's 'Scheme of the Income, and Expence, of the several Families of England; calculated for the Year 1688' has attracted widespread interest from historians. Until fairly recently, as Geoffrey Holmes first pointed out, it was taken 'as read that when Gregory King told posterity about the social structure of late seventeenth-century England, he knew what he was talking about'.[1] Thus in lauding King's 'political arithmetic', Peter Laslett referred to him as 'the first man to study the structure of a pre-industrial society'.[2] For all its superficial plausibility, however, what King's table actually presented was not an objective view of the state of the nation in 1688 based on hard evidence, but a polemical exercise undertaken by 'a thorough, divine right Tory'[3] with the explicit intention of demonstrating that the wealth of the nation had declined since the Revolution so that 'after the year 1695, the taxes actually raised will fall short, every year, more and more, to that degree, that the war cannot well be sustained beyond the year 1698 upon the foot it now stands'.[4] As an explanation of 'the veneration bestowed on King's table', Holmes suggested that it might have been because 'he speaks the language of our own generation. He speaks not with the tongues of men, but with the symbols of mathematicians'.[5] Hence, despite acknowledging that they were

---

[1] Geoffrey Holmes, *Politics, Religion, and Society in England 1679–1742* (London and Ronceverte: Hambledon Press, 1986), 283. See also Peter H. Lindert and Jeffrey G. Williamson, 'Revising England's Social Tables 1688–1812', *Explorations in Economic History*, 9:4 (1982), 385–408.

[2] *The Earliest Classics*, ed. Peter Laslett (no place: Gregg International Publishers Limited, 1973), 2.

[3] Holmes, *Politics, Religion, and Society*, 289.

[4] [Gregory King], *Natural and Political Observations and Conclusions upon the State and Condition of England, 1696*, in *The Earliest Classics*, ed. Laslett, 62.

[5] Holmes, *Politics, Religion, and Society*, 282–3.

in fact based on no more than 'informed guesswork', Laslett nonetheless praised King's 'national estimates' on the dubious grounds that 'no one else but he could have produced these figures'.[6]

No guesstimates were attached to the much more succinct list of classes published by Daniel Defoe in *The Review* for 25 June 1709:

> The People are divided into;
> 1. The Great, who live profusely.
> 2. The Rich, who live very plentifully.
> 3. The middle Sort, who live well.
> 4. The working Trades, who labour hard, but feel no Want.
> 5. The Country People, Farmers, &c. who fare indifferently.
> 6. The Poor, that fare hard.
> 7. The Miserable, that really pinch and suffer Want.[7]

Defoe, like King, had an ulterior motive for breaking down 'the ranks of People' in this way. He had just embarked on '*the long expected, and I confess, often promis'd Subject of Trade*'[8] in *The Review* in order to demonstrate 'the Advantages to *England* of the Encrease of People'[9] in the light of 'the great present Question now pretty much upon our Hands, what shall we do with a Matter of 10000 poor Refugee *Germans* come over hither from the *Palatinate*'.[10] As he was patently applying the language of his own day, however, Defoe's classification is of genuine interest as an indication of the way in which one contemporary understood the social structure of eighteenth-century England.

This is an important consideration. As Jonathan Barry has explained: 'Though literary critics, politicians and students have continued to see early modern England in terms of the rise of the middle class, few professional historians have dared to do so'.[11] Instead, for the past thirty years or so they have increasingly resorted to using the phrase 'the middling sort' to describe the various social divisions between the ruling elite—the nobility and gentry—and the labouring classes, whether in town or country. Thus Defoe's use of the term 'the middle Sort' assumes significance, particularly as he clarified what he meant in the course of the same essay in referring to 'the midling People of *England*, Citizens, Shopkeepers, Merchants, and Gentlemen; for the two first, I assure you, live as well as the last, and perhaps something better'.[12] As he was later to do in *The*

---

[6] *The Earliest Classics*, ed. Laslett, 4–5.
[7] *Review*, vi. 193 (25 June 1709).
[8] *Review*, vi. 184 (21 June 1709).
[9] *Review*, vi. 193 (25 June 1709).
[10] *Review*, vi. 187 (21 June 1709).
[11] Jonathan Barry, 'Introduction', in *The Middling Sort of People: Culture, Society, and Politics in England, 1550–1800*, ed. Jonathan Barry and Christopher Brookes (Basingstoke: Macmillan, 1994), 1–27 (1).
[12] *Review*, vi. 193 (25 June 1709). Defoe actually used the phrase 'the trading, middling sort of People in England' in *A Plan of the English Commerce* (1728), *PEW*, vii. 176.

Complete English Tradesman (1725–7) when explaining in some detail that 'a tradesman may on occasion keep company with gentlemen as well as other people', Defoe included gentlemen within the ranks of 'the middling People of *England*'. This passage offers significant insight into Defoe's thinking on the structure of society, even if there is perhaps a touch of special pleading on his part:

> Nor is a trading man, if he is a man of sense, unsuitable or unprofitable for a gentleman to converse with, as occasion requires; and you will often find, that not private gentleman only, but even ministers of state, privy-counsellors, members of parliament, and persons of all ranks in the government, find it for their purpose to converse with tradesmen, and are not asham'd to acknowledge, that a tradesman is sometimes qualified to inform them in the most difficult and intricate, as well as the most urgent affairs of government; and that has been the reason, why so many tradesmen have been advanc'd to honours and dignities above their ordinary rank. (*RDW*, vii. 60)

While it may be tempting to assume that here he was making an oblique reference to his own long association with Robert Harley, who from 1710 to 1714 was *de facto* prime minister of Great Britain, it appears that the 'tradesmen' Defoe had in mind were of much greater social standing than himself because he goes on to cite the examples of Sir Charles Duncombe, Sir Henry Furnese, Sir Charles Cook, Sir Josiah Child, and William Lowndes as 'men call'd out of their lower sphere for their eminent usefulness, and their known capacities' (61).

This is of considerable significance as far as our understanding of the fine gradations of rank in pre-industrial England is concerned. In the Preface to the first volume of *A Tour thro' the Whole Island of Great Britain* (1724), 'By a Gentleman', Defoe expressed his intention to offer 'an Account of the Encrease of Buildings, as well in Great Cities and Towns, as in the new Seats and Dwellings of the Nobility and Gentry; also the Encrease of Wealth, in many eminent Particulars'. Interestingly, however, when in the course of his second circuit he gets round to mentioning the proliferation of fine new buildings north of London, he observes that 'they are generally belonging to the middle sort of Mankind, grown Wealthy by Trade, and who still taste of *London*; some of them live both in the City, and in the Country at the same time: yet many of these are immensely Rich' (*TDH*, ii. 126). He returned to the subject in *The Complete English Tradesman* in citing the example of a tradesman who 'kept a country house about two miles from *London*, in the summer-time, for the air for his wife and children, and there he maintained them very comfortably' (135).

In providing these examples of tradesmen who had accumulated sufficient capital through trade to build desirable second residences outside London, the language Defoe uses once again draws attention to the growing number of men who, having made their fortunes through trade, aspired to be gentlemen. 'As there are several degrees of people employ'd in trade below these [i.e. tradesmen], such as *workmen, labourers,* and *servants*', he explained, 'so there is a degree of traders above them, which we call *merchants*' (36).

This corresponds to the social analysis offered thirty years later by James Nelson. 'Were we to subdivide the People, we might run it to an Infinity', Nelson suggested: 'to avoid Confusion therefore, I will select five Classes; *viz.* The Nobility, the Gentry, the genteel Trades, all those particularly which require large Capitals [sic], the common Trades, and the Peasantry'.[13] That this important distinction between the 'genteel' and the 'common' trades, with its interesting nod in the direction of the emergence of capitalism, accords with Defoe's earlier differentiation between merchants and lesser tradesmen is significant, and suggests that it had become more apparent in the intervening decades.

It is important to stress, however, that when Defoe referred to 'the middle Sort' in writing about 'the ranks of People' in England in *The Review* in 1709, it was in the course of his insisting on the vitality of 'the Numbers of the labouring and industrious People, whose Application to Trade and Manufactures are the Wealth and Strength of a Nation'.[14] He had no recourse to a vocabulary of upper, middle, and lower classes, let alone 'the middle class' as we mean it today, whether in the United States or the United Kingdom. This is a crucial consideration, given the continuing currency in Defoe scholarship of Michael Shinagel's fifty-year-old study, *Daniel Defoe and Middle-Class Gentility* (1968), the very title of which suggests some confusion about the English class system. In his Preface, Shinagel refers to 'Defoe's significant role as exemplar and exponent of middle-class gentility',[15] while Part I is entitled 'The Making of a Middle-Class Gentleman'.

It would not be stretching to argue that the concept of 'middle-class gentility' is actually a contradiction in terms. While Defoe, in common with his contemporaries, used terms like class, rank, and degree to describe the social structure of Great Britain, the categories into which he divided the inhabitants resembled Joseph Massie's *Calculations of Taxes for a Family of each Rank, Degree or Class: For One Year* (1756), which offered thirty examples of such calculations, beginning with 'N$^{o.}$ 1. A Nobleman, or Gentleman, who hath an Estate of Twenty Thousand Pounds a Year in Land', before concluding, by way of 'N$^{o.}$ 13. A Freeholder who hath an Estate of One Hundred Pounds a Year in Land', with 'N$^{o.}$ 30. A Husbandman, or Labourer, in the Country, whose Wages may be Five Shillings a Week, which amounts to Thirteen Pounds a Year'.[16]

Two passages in particular from Defoe's narratives spring to mind in relation to the concept of 'middle-class gentility', and, unsurprisingly, Shinagel devoted space to consideration of each: Crusoe's father's description of his own social status; and Moll's description of her second husband, the 'gentleman-tradesman'. Crusoe's father extols the advantages of what he calls

---

[13] James Nelson, *An Essay on the Government of Children, Under Three General Heads: Viz. Health, Manners, and Education* (1756), 273, cited in Penelope J. Corfield, *Language, History and Class* (Oxford and Cambridge, MA: Basil Blackwell, 1991), 101–2.

[14] *Review*, vi. 186 (21 June 1709).

[15] Michael Shinagel, *Daniel Defoe and Middle-Class Gentility* (Cambridge, MA: Harvard University Press, 1968), viii.

[16] Joseph Massie, *Calculations of Taxes for a Family of each Rank, Degree or Class: For One Year* (1756), n. p.

> the middle State, or what might be called the upper Station of *Low Life*, which he had found by long Experience was the best State in the World, the most suited to human Happiness, not exposed to the Miseries and Hardships, the Labour and Sufferings of the mechanick Part of Mankind, and not embarass'd with the Pride, Luxury, Ambition and Envy of the upper Part of Mankind. (*Novels*, i. 58)

Despite Defoe's use of the phrase 'the middle State', this is not the vocabulary of upper, middle, and lower or working classes into which, in socioeconomic terms, modern societies are usually divided. I have already drawn attention to the fact that Defoe included gentlemen within the ranks of 'the middling People of *England*' in *The Complete English Tradesman*. By explaining that Crusoe is located in 'the upper Station of *Low Life*', what Crusoe's father appears to be suggesting is that despite his getting 'a good Estate by Merchandise' before 'leaving off his Trade' (3), he is not really a member of the nobility and gentry who stood at the apex of the hierarchical social structure of England.

Moll's second husband is of even greater interest as far as the class terminology employed by Defoe is concerned. Left a widow 'with about 1200*l*. in [her] Pocket', she 'was Courted by several considerable Tradesmen'. 'I was not averse to a Tradesman', she acknowledges:

> but then I would have a Tradesman forsooth, that was something of a Gentleman too; that when my Husband had a mind to carry me to the Court, or to the Play, he might become a Sword, and look as like a Gentleman, as another Man; and not be one that had the mark of his Apron-strings upon his Coat, or the mark of his Hat upon his Perriwig; that should look as if he was set on to his Sword, when his Sword was put on to him, and that carried his Trade in his Countenance.
>
> WELL, at last I found this amphibious Creature, this *Land-water-thing*, call'd, *a Gentleman-Tradesman*; and as a just Plague upon my Folly, I was catch'd in the very Snare, which *as I might say*, I laid for myself; for I was not Trepan'd I confess, but I betray'd myself. (*Novels*, vi, 65, 66)

This is not straightforward. While it undoubtedly offers an additional interesting perspective on Defoe's idea of what constitutes a gentleman, as he employs one of his most striking figures in order to describe the ambiguous nature of 'this amphibious Creature',[17] it also insinuates that a gentleman-tradesman is neither one thing nor the other. In the sixteenth century, the right to wear a sword had been legally restricted by Elizabethan sumptuary laws (in theory at least) to 'Knights and Barons sonnes, and others of higher degree or place, and Gentlemen in ordinarie office attendant upon the Queenes Maiesties person'.[18] However, by the middle of the seventeenth century,

---

[17] Incidentally, the earliest instance of the word 'amphibious', cited by the *OED*, is from 1655. William Dampier also used it in *A New Voyage Round the World* (1697), 57.

[18] *A Booke containing all such Proclamations, as were published during the Raigne of the late Queene Elizabeth* (1618), f. 154.

according to *Judge Dodaridge, His Law of Nobility and Peerage* (1658), 'he is a Gentleman, who is so commonly taken, and reputed'.[19] Hence, perhaps, Moll's fancy to have a husband who 'might become a Sword, and look as like a Gentleman, as another Man', and two years later, in *The Great Law of Subordination Consider'd* (1724), Defoe appears to have been playing on the gradual disappearance of the clear-cut social distinction between those who were entitled to wear a sword and those who were not. 'Pray, where's your Sword, Esq; *William*? where's your Sword?', one insolent servant is sarcastically admonished. '*Liberty* has made you a Gentleman, I find that, and Gentlemen never go without a Sword' (*RDW*, vi. 59).

In *The Complete English Tradesman*, Defoe offered comments which might almost be regarded as a gloss on the pretensions and failings of the 'gentleman-tradesman'. 'I allow the tradesman to act the gentleman sometimes, and that even for conversation, at least if his understanding and capacity make him suitable company to them, but still his business is among those of his own rank' (63), he explained, before going on to describe the potentially disastrous consequences of a tradesman's neglecting his business: 'they are never at home, nor in their shop; one wears a long wig and a sword, I hear, and you see him often in the *Mall* and at court, but seldom in his shop, or waiting on his customers' (65). If this sounds remarkably similar to what happened to both Moll's second husband and Roxana's first, there are also sufficient grounds to think that in this instance, as so often in Defoe's writings, the subject matter is informed by autobiographical circumstances. 'One thing, Daniel, I want to know', the anonymous author of *The Review Review'd. In a Letter to the Prophet Daniel in Scotland* asked in 1706, 'is, whether you keep up your Beau Habit, your long Wig, with Tossels at the End of it, your Iron-bound Hat, and your blew Cloak? As also, whether you have left your old Wont, of holding out your little Finger to show your Diamond Ring? I would not for the World have your leave off your Beau Habit, to put on Scots Plad; that will turn your Squireship into a Highlander, and make thee a meer Ragamuffin'.[20]

A number of passages in *The Complete English Tradesman* might be deemed to have an autobiographical element, such as the anecdote about the tradesman 'who was such a sermon-hunter' that he 'us'd so assiduously to hunt out' the 'lectures and sermons preach'd in *London*, either in the churches, or meeting-houses, almost every day in the week', that he 'lost his trade, his shop was entirely neglected, the times which was proper for him to apply to his business was misapply'd, his trade fell off, and the man broke' (71). In the early 1680s, the young Daniel Foe attended the sermons of John Collins, transcribing them in his *Meditations*, by which time, as the earliest extant documentary record of the future author of *Robinson Crusoe* attests, he was already set up in business. Thus his marriage licence, dated 28 December 1683, refers to him as 'Daniel Foe, of St Michaell, Cornehill, Lond., Merch^t, Bach^r, ab^t 24'.[21] By the middle of the 1690s, however,

---

[19] *Judge Dodaridge, His Law of Nobility and Peerage* (1658), 147.
[20] Quoted in Maximillian E. Novak, 'A Whiff of Scandal in the Life of Daniel Defoe', *HLQ*, 34:1 (1970), 35–42 (39).
[21] *The Publications of the Harleian Society*, vol. 30 (1869), 155.

he was being named in legal documents as 'Daniel Defoe'.[22] Patently preoccupied with issues of status and entitlement, he described himself as 'a Gentleman' in his earliest extant letter, dated 9 January 1702 (i.e. 1703), and towards the end of his life he insisted, in *The Compleat English Gentleman*, that he had 'the honour to be rank'd, by the Direction of Providence, in the same Class' (*Correspondence*, 5; *RDW*, x. 37). Given all these circumstances, it is hardly surprising that Defoe's concern about his own social status should find its way into his fictional, as well as his non-fictional writings, but it is interesting that he appears to regard the pretensions of Moll and her second, gentleman-tradesman husband with a more jaundiced eye. The narrator explains how 'my new Husband coming to a lump of Money at once, fell into such a profusion of Expence, that all I had, and all he had before, if he had anything worth mentioning, would not have held it out above one Year' (61). As Moll's second husband ends up becoming bankrupt, one wonders whether, by 1722, Defoe, in his big house at Stoke Newington, viewed things rather differently at the end of a career in which he had gone from being a tradesman with pretensions of being a gentleman to finding himself on a number of occasions in a debtors' gaol.

The heroine's repeated aspirations to gentility are of course a recurring theme in *The Fortunes and Misfortunes of the Famous Moll Flanders*. At the outset, while she is living with her 'good old Nurse', she gains a reputation for being 'the little Lass that intends to be a Gentlewoman', despite the fact that the 'Gentlewoman' she admires turns out to be 'a Person of ill Fame, and has had two or three Bastards' (14). If one of the ironies of Defoe's narrative is that this is one ambition which Moll undoubtedly fulfils, there are a number of other occasions in the course of her varied career on which she is indeed taken for a gentlewoman, including the episode recounted by Kate Loveman in this volume in which, disguised in widow's weeds, she is mistakenly apprehended for stealing from a mercer's shop [SEE CHAPTER 23]. Moll explains how, having turned the tables on the put-upon mercer,

> at length we went all very quietly before the Justice, with a Mob of about 500 People at our Heels; and all the way I went I could hear the People ask what was the matter? and others reply and say, a Mercer had stop'd a Gentlewoman instead of a Thief, and had afterwards taken the Thief, and now the Gentlewoman had taken the Mercer, and was carrying him before the Justice; this pleas'd the People strangely ... (204)

In this instance, then, Moll's experiences which, according to the narrative chronology Defoe seems at pains to establish, take place sometime after the Restoration, would appear to bear out Sir John Dodderidge's contention that by that period 'he is a Gentleman'—or, in this case, a gentlewoman—'who is so commonly taken, and reputed' (147).

The theme of gentility also runs throughout *Colonel Jack* (1722), from the point at which his nurse bids the eponymous narrator to '*remember, that I was a Gentleman*'

---

[22] Spiro Peterson, 'Defoe and Westminster, 1696–1706', *ECS*, 12:3 (1979), 306–38 (332).

(*Novels*, viii. 10). Jack recounts how, on enlisting as a soldier, he 'Dream't of nothing but being a Gentleman Officer, as well as a Gentleman Soldier' (105)—an aim he is subsequently able to achieve on gaining command of a company in an Irish regiment in France. 'I was exceedingly pleas'd with my new Circumstances', he remarks, 'and now I us'd to say to my self, I was come to what I was Born to, and that I had never till now liv'd the Life of a Gentleman' (207). Innocent of any suspicion of ironic intent in Defoe's treatment of Jack's ambition, Shinagel regards it as a further example of the preoccupation with 'middle-class gentility' allegedly shared by the fictional character and his creator. But the gentility to which Jack aspires turns out to be a sham. He may believe himself to be a gentleman's son, but he only becomes a gentleman by deception. 'Much of the time, particularly in the central scenes set in London, Jack is not so much a gentleman, as someone dressed up to look like a gentleman', David Blewett sagely observes. 'Jack is almost as deluded about gentility as he is about Jacobitism'.[23]

In *The True-Born Englishman* (1700/1), Defoe satirized the English for boasting 'of Pedigree' even though England 'Borrows or makes her own Nobility':

> Wealth, howsoever got, in *England* makes
> Lords of Mechanicks, Gentlemen of Rakes.
> Antiquity and Birth are needless here;
> 'Tis Impudence and Money makes a P[ee]r. (lines 415–18; *SFS*, i. 96)

However, as *Judge Dodaridge, His Law of Nobility and Peerage* explained, 'our Law calleth none Noble, under the degree of a Baron, and not as forraign Countries do use to speak, with whom every man of Gentle Birth is counted Noble' (1). This is a most important observation because it emphasizes the crucial distinction between those who were gentlemen and those who were not. As well as offering additional interesting insights into how esquires and gentlemen were traditionally 'distinguished from the meaner sort of people' in medieval and early modern England, Dodderidge's treatise also included a section devoted to 'The Definition of Gentry, or civill Nobility' in which it was observed 'that Nobles are truly called Gentlemen, by the course and custome of *England*' (142). The stated intention was to distinguish between the nobility and gentry who together made up the landed aristocracy of England and the rest of the population. Thus when, in the Preface to *Jure Divino*, Defoe referred to 'All the Nobility, Gentry, Clergy, and Commons of *England*, who either invited over, or join'd with the Prince of *Orange*, and afterwards consented to his being made King', he was being thoroughly conventional in his description of the social orders of pre-industrial England (*SFS*, ii. 37). At the apex of the social hierarchy stood the hereditary peerage, the five ranks of the titled nobility—dukes, marquesses, earls, viscounts, and barons—who, along with the bishops, sat in the House of Lords.

---

[23] David Blewett, *Defoe's Art of Fiction: Robinson Crusoe, Moll Flanders, Colonel Jack and Roxana* (Toronto: University of Toronto Press, 1979), 99.

The Great, Who Live Profusely

In Defoe's lifetime, the wealthiest men in England were members of the peerage. King's 'Scheme of the Income, and Expence, of the several Families of England; calculated for the Year 1688' lists 160 'temporal lords' with an average yearly income per family of £2,800. However, the historian of the English aristocracy, J. V. Beckett, observes that the 'origin' of King's 'figures is obscure', and that 'the peerage figure looks suspiciously low', before going on to explain that:

> In 1683 rental receipts on the Earl of Rutland's estate totalled £14,482, while at about the same time the Earl of Devonshire's annual average income exceeded £17,000. The Duke of Newcastle's various estates netted about £25,000 annually in the 1690s. By the early years of the eighteenth century, King's figures were beginning to look even more unrealistic. The dukes of Newcastle, Bedford and Beaufort all had incomes in excess of £30,000, while four other magnates (the dukes of Ormonde, Somerset and Devonshire, and Lord Brooke) could boast between £20,000 and £30,000. Incomes in excess of £10,000 had become commonplace for peers above the rank of baron by 1710.[24]

Clearly, when he mentioned the 'Great, who live profusely', Defoe was referring to men such as these, who mostly derived their wealth from the rents they collected from their tenants. They were the ones who, when he embarked on his series of essays on trade in *The Review* at the beginning of 1706, he described as 'our *English* Quality'. However, he was far from impressed by their extravagant lifestyle. 'I grant, that the Luxury and Extravagancies of the *English* Nobility and Gentry, have been the Advantage of the Common People, and is a great support to some part of Trade', he conceded, before going on to ask: 'How many of these Great and Noble Families have been Impoverish'd by the Luxurious way of Living, which they have took up in these latter Ages of the World … How many of the best, and now the Wealthyest [sic] of our Families of *English* Gentry, have we seen deriv'd meerly from Trade, and top the Greatest and most Ancient Families, of our former Flourishing Quality?'[25]

It is noteworthy that in his consideration of the richest families in England, Defoe does not restrict his discussion to the nobility. As F. M. L. Thompson has pointed out: 'The landed aristocracy has always remained a body wider in membership than the nobility'.[26] The English aristocracy consisted of the nobility *and* the gentry, which is why Defoe elects to focus on 'the Luxury and Extravagancies of the *English* Nobility and Gentry', before going on to explain 'how have the Estates of these Great Families

---

[24] J. V. Beckett, *The Aristocracy in England 1660–1914* (Oxford: Basil Blackwell, 1986), 288.
[25] *Review*, iii. 58–9 (22 January 1706).
[26] F. M. L. Thompson, *English Landed Society in the Nineteenth Century* (London: Routledge and Kegan Paul, 1962), 14.

been swallow'd up, by the Commonalty and Tradesmen, who are now Richer all over the Nation, than the Men of Blood, Families and Inheritance, put them all together'.[27] Incomes of the landed gentry ranged widely. One Norfolk gentleman, Thomas Coke of Holkham, was worth £10,000 per annum—the income Jane Austen gave to her fictitious Fitzwilliam Darcy of Pemberley over a century later—while those who were able to exploit mineral resources on their land, such as Sir James Lowther of Whitehaven or George Bowes of Durham, 'were among the richest men in the kingdom, wealthier than most peers'.[28]

THE RICH, WHO LIVE VERY PLENTIFULLY

The dividing line between the great 'who live profusely' and the rich 'who live very plentifully' is perforce an imprecise one, but Massie offers some perspective in terms of the income of landed gentlemen. After considering noblemen or gentlemen owning estates of between £20,000 and £4,000 per year in land, Massie turned specifically to untitled landed gentlemen whose annual income ranged from £2,000 all the way down to £200. Evidently, gentlemen at the lower end of this scale should not be included amongst those who, in Defoe's terms, 'live very plentifully'. 'At a period when a labourer earned perhaps £20 a year in wages, the squire with a good rental income in the many hundreds or thousands of pounds was undoubtedly a gentleman', Douglas Hay and Nicholas Rogers observe. 'How much mattered: £500 yes, £300 probably, £150 doubtful'.[29] Hence the relevance of Defoe's rider that 'Citizens' and 'Shopkeepers' were able to 'live as well as' mere gentlemen, 'and perhaps something better'.[30] In 1709, however, anyone with an income of £1,000 or £2,000 a year would have been able to live sufficiently well to meet his description of 'the Rich, who live plentifully'. Taken together, Defoe's categories of 'The Great' and 'The Rich' would seem to comprise the 'group of 10,000–20,000 families who', according to Henry French, 'constituted the ruling elite throughout the early modern period'.[31]

Defoe seems to have been concerned about what he perceived as the decline of the gentry, and this fits in with the debate among historians about social and economic changes in England in the early modern period. Characteristically, Defoe linked the financial problems of the gentry after the Restoration with a decline in the nation's morals—a phenomenon which he blamed on the luxury of the Court of Charles II.

---

[27] *Review*, iii. 58 (22 January 1706).
[28] W. A. Speck, *Stability and Strife: England 1714–1760* (London: Edward Arnold, 1977), 37.
[29] Douglas Hay and Nicholas Rogers, *Eighteenth-Century English Society: Shuttles and Swords* (Oxford and New York: Oxford University Press, 1997), 23.
[30] *Review*, vi. 193 (25 June 1709). Interestingly, Massie's categories also overlap, as he considers the cases of London tradesmen who 'expend' between £100 and £300 a year.
[31] Henry French, '"Gentlemen": Remaking the English Ruling Class', in *A Social History of England 1500–1750*, ed. Keith Wrightson (Cambridge: Cambridge University Press, 2017), 270.

"Twas the Kings and the Gentry which first... degenerated from that strict Observation of Moral Virtues, and from thence carried Vice on to that degree it now appears in', he complained in *The Poor Man's Plea* (1698). 'From the Court Vice took its Progress into the Country; and in the Families of the Gentry and Nobility it harbour'd, till it took heart under their Protection, and made a general Sally into the Nation'. And Defoe suspected that there was a political motive behind this 'decaying Evil among the Gentry' which they were 'drawn into ... by the Luxury of the Court' (RDW, vi. 27–8). When he returned to the theme he had first expounded in *The Poor Man's Plea* a decade later in *The Review*, Defoe once again reminded the gentry and the clergy of their moral responsibilities. He was still harping on the same theme twenty years later when he came to write *The Compleat English Gentleman*, one of the purposes of which appears to have been to extend the argument of *The Great Law of Subordination Consider'd* that the nobility and gentry were failing in their duty to provide moral and spiritual leadership for the lower orders. He was at one with contemporaries such as Addison and Swift in attributing this abdication to the neglect of education across 'the untaught, unpolished, unimprov'd ... mass or bulk of the gentry [who] have the misfortune to be left behind, groveling in the dirt of ignorance' (80). Thus, according to Defoe, 'virtue, learning, a liberal education, and a degree of natural and acquir'd knowledge, are necessary to finish the born gentleman; and that without them the entitul'd heir will be but the shadow of a gentleman' (24).

The Middle Sort, Who Live Well

It is generally acknowledged, even by Marxisant historians, that the 'middling sort were not a middle class in any proto-Marxist sense of the term'. 'Although the term occasionally included the lesser gentry', Hay and Rogers explain, 'generally speaking, the term "middling sort" in the eighteenth century increasingly meant those in urban occupations: merchants, tradesmen, substantial shopkeepers, master manufacturers, as well as many in the emergent professions of medicine, teaching, the law, the civil and armed services'.[32] When Gregory King referred to 'traders' in 1696, however, he divided them into three categories with widely differing incomes: 'merchants and traders by sea' with £400 per annum; 'merchants and traders' with £200 p.a.; and 'shop-keepers and traders' with only £45 p.a.

When Defoe referred to the 'middle Sort, who live well' in 1709, therefore, he evidently meant those who had an income of several hundreds of pounds a year, whether from land or from other sources. This included substantial tradesmen as well as gentlemen and other freeholders.[33] (He considered farmers under a separate heading.) As so often in his writings, however, Defoe, in stating his case, had a polemical point

---

[32] Hay and Rogers, *Eighteenth-Century English Society*, 30.
[33] Nos 12 to 24 of Massie's *Calculations of Taxes for a Family of each Rank, Degree or Class* covered freeholders with estates of between £200 and £50 a year in land, farmers who expended between £150

to make. In attempting to allay the fears of those who thought that the nation was not in a position to accommodate 10,000 Palatine immigrants, Mr Review was 'upon examining the Advantages to *England* of the Encrease of People, and particularly as to the Consumption of the Produce of our Land'.[34] Defoe's insistence that 'Meer Want of People' was the reason why 'we have many Millions of Acres of Land in *England* untouch'd, that are to this day, just where the general Deluge left them', was designed to demonstrate how the influx of poor Palatines could be a blessing rather than a hindrance to the country.[35]

As a former 'middling tradesman' himself, Defoe was opinionated, if a little inconsistent, on the subject. Thus, while insisting in *The Complete English Tradesman* that 'the tradesman's proper business is in his shop or ware-house, and among his own class or rank of people' (61), he nonetheless 'allow[ed] the tradesman to act the gentleman sometimes, and that even for conversation' (63). As gentlemen 'put their younger sons apprentices to tradesmen', he maintained, 'it is no wonder that the tradesmen in *England* fill the lists of our nobility and gentry; no wonder that the gentlemen of the best families marry tradesmens daughters' (235). Defoe did not stop there. 'SOME of the greatest and best, and most flourishing families among not the gentry only, but even the nobility', he observed, 'have been rais'd from trade, owe their beginning their wealth, and their estates to trade' (232). While this might be regarded as another instance of Defoe's own preoccupation with what Shinagel called 'middle-class gentility', he seems more concerned with observing the growth in income of the average tradesman. Thus when he remarks that '400 *l.* ... is but an ordinary sum now for a tradesman to spend, whatever it has been esteemed formerly' (121), it leads on to his subsequent suggestion that 'as trade is now flourishing in *England*, and encreasing, and the wealth of our tradesman is already so great; 'tis very probable, a few years will shew us still a greater race of trade-bred Gentlemen, than ever *England* yet had' (237).

What is distinctive if not downright idiosyncratic about his social analysis is that, in his view, the political nation extended downwards beyond the nobility and gentry to include all freeholders. He was consistent on this score from one of the earliest pamphlets known to be his, *An Argument Shewing, That a Standing Army, With Consent of Parliament, Is not Inconsistent with a Free Government* (1697), directly addressed 'to the Honest well meaning English-Freeholder, who has a share in the *Terra firma*, and therefore is concern'd to preserve Freedom' (*PEW*, i. 65), through *The Original Power of the Collective Body of the People of England* (1702) where he insisted that 'the *Freeholders* are the proper Owners of the Country' (*PEW*, i. 121), to the couplet in *Jure Divino* in which he maintained that 'Reason makes it plain to understand, | They own the Government, that own the Land' (Book xi, lines 178–9; *SFS*, ii. 323). In taking up this position, Defoe suggests that he shared some opinions with radical Whigs such as John Trenchard and

---

and £40 a year, tradesmen in London who expended between £300 and £100, and tradesmen in the country who expended between £100 and £40 a year.

[34] *Review*, vi. 193 (25 June 1709).
[35] *Review*, vi. 194–5 (25 June 1709).

John Toland, whose ideas can be traced back to James Harrington. On this view, the people were divided into those who possessed property, real or personal, whether 'in Lands, Goods, or Moneys', and those who had to sell their labour who, in turn, were subdivided by Defoe into 'the labouring Poor' and 'the common People' (*RDW*, vi. 83).

THE WORKING TRADES, WHO LABOUR HARD, BUT FEEL NO WANT

Between the 'middle sort, who live well' and 'the labouring poor', however, were not only 'middling tradesmen', but manufacturers of various kinds. Gregory King estimated that in 1688 there had been 180,000 shopkeepers and tradesmen with an average yearly income of £45 in England, and 240,000 artisans and handicrafts with an average yearly income of £40. Sixty years later, in addition to tradesmen 'in the Country' expending between £100 and £40 pounds a year, Joseph Massie listed manufacturers 'of Wood, Iron ... Silk, &c. in *London*' with incomes of around £30 a year, and manufacturers 'of Wood, Iron ... Woollen Cloth, Stuffs, &c. in the Country' with incomes of around £20 a year.[36] In the essay in *The Review* in which Defoe divided the people into ranks, he suggested 'Tak[ing] the 4th Sort for the *Medium*'. In this category he included carpenters, smiths, weavers, 'what you will, that is industrious, works hard, and feels no Want, let him live in the Country or City, *North* or *South*, where you will'.[37] There can be no doubt, however, that wages were much higher in London, whether for craftsman or labourers. 'London workers continued to be the most highly paid, at least in terms of money wages, in England, and this may explain the continued immigration into the capital even when the population of the country itself grew only very slowly after the Restoration', Jeremy Boulton concludes. 'Labourers in the capital seem to have been paid usually at twice the rate of their counterparts in northern towns throughout the seventeenth century'.[38] Contemporaries understood that there were considerable variations in income not only between town and country, but also depending on where in England people resided. Hence, perhaps, Defoe's reference in *The Great Law of Subordination Consider'd* to 'the Poorer sort of People, Farmers, and Manufacturers of every kind, from *Lancashire* and *Westmoreland*, in the *North*; down to *Lincolnshire*, and *Leicestershire*, and thence into *Norfolk*, *Suffolk*, and *Essex*' (*RDW*, vi. 69).

---

[36] Massie, *Calculations*, nos 22–6, 28–9.

[37] *Review*, vi. 194 (25 June 1709).

[38] Jeremy Boulton, 'Wage Labour in Seventeenth-Century London', *Economic History Review*, 49:2 (1996), 268–90 (287). The tables for wages per day of craftsman and labourers in London presented by Boulton run from to 1574 to 1721, and indicate that in the early eighteenth century craftsman earned between 30*d*. and 36*d*. per day, while labourers earned between 22*d*. and 26*d*. per day (289).

The Country People, Farmers, &c. Who Fare Indifferently

Considerations such as these seem to have been behind Defoe's decision to subdivide the people into 'Country People, Farmers, &c.'. 'I believe I could make it out, that a poor labouring Man may live as cheap in *Kent* or *Sussex* as in the Bishoprick of *Durham*', he maintained in *Giving Alms no Charity* (1704), 'and yet in *Kent* a poor Man may earn 7s. 10s. 9s. a Week, and in the North 4s. or perhaps less' (*PEW*, viii. 176). Half a century later, Joseph Massie suggested that while the wages of 'A Husbandman, or Labourer, in the Country' might be five shillings a week, those of a labourer in London 'may be Nine Shillings a Week'.[39] In dividing the people into 'ranks' in *The Review*, Defoe was at pains to talk up the superior social conditions of the English; hence, presumably, his insistence that, as far as the consumption of provisions was concerned, 'the Farmers, my 5th Sort, *who by the way all over* England *live very well too*, can be suppos'd to under-do it', as much as 'the middle Sort of People ... over-do it'.[40] Gregory King estimated that there were 150,000 farmers in England and Wales in 1688 with an average yearly income per family of £44. Although Joseph Massie included 'N°. 18. A Farmer who expends Forty Pounds a Year', that was the lowest of the three headings under which farmers appeared. According to Massie, there were farmers who expended £150 and £100 a year, respectively—figures which seem more in line with Defoe's suggestion that 'the Farmers ... *by the way all over* England *live very well too*'.

The Poor, That Fare Hard

Gregory King estimated that there were 364,000 'Labouring People and Out Servants' with a yearly income per family of £15, and 400,000 'Cottagers and Paupers' with a yearly income per family of £6 5s. 'New evidence suggests that King's guesses on average family income are vindicated for lower-ranked occupations', according to Lindert and Williamson, but 'numerous 17th century documents strongly suggest that King grossly overestimated common laborers and paupers, while undercounting artisans'.[41] Wages at this level suggest that labourers and paupers did indeed 'fare hard', as Crusoe's father points out when trying to divert him from his 'meer wandring Inclination' by descanting on 'the Miseries and Hardships, the Labour and Sufferings of the mechanick Part of Mankind' (58). Nevertheless, in his various observations on the condition of 'the labouring Poor in *England*', Defoe maintained there was more than enough work

---

[39] Massie, *Calculations*, nos 27 and 30.
[40] *Review*, vi. 194 (25 June 1709).
[41] Lindert and Williamson, 'Revising England's Social Tables 1688–1812', 391, 387.

to keep 'the common People' in full employment, and therefore, as he put it in *Giving Alms no Charity*, 'the meanest Labours in this Nation afford the Work-men sufficient to provide for himself and his Family, and that could never be if there was a want of Work' (187). 'There is in England', he insisted, '*more Labour than Hands to perform it, and consequently a want of People, not of Employment*' (174). As his championing of the poor Palatines suggests, he was consistent on this score. Defoe was also confident that by the 1720s, strictly in terms of income, 'the Poor all over *England*, can now earn or gain nearly twice as much in a Day, and in some Places, more than twice as much as they could get for the same Work two or three Years ago'. He did not believe this made the labouring poor any better off, however, because they worked 'but two or three Days in the Week, or till they get Money enough to keep them the rest of the Week, and all the other part of their Time they lie in the Alehouse to spend it'.[42]

If he was consistent in maintaining that there was enough work for the labouring poor to be able to feed themselves, Defoe was also consistent in identifying 'a Dreadful Innundation of Vice and Immorality; infinitely more so than was the Case in former Days', as the principal reason that 'the Poor miserable People' of England were not in a happier condition.[43] He placed the blame for this state of affairs on a failure in leadership of 'the Nobility, Gentry, Justices of the Peace, and Clergy'. In attributing the decline in the manners of the common people fairly and squarely to the conduct of those in authority whose responsibility it was to provide moral leadership, so that, 'in a word, Order is inverted, Subordination ceases, and the World seems to stand with the Bottom upward' (51), he examined 'the general Behaviour of Workmen, and hir'd Labourers of both Sexes' (79), to conclude that 'the labouring Poor ... are indeed the Grievance of the Nation, and there seems an absolute Necessity to bring them, by severe regulations, to some State of immediate Subordination' (85).

THE MISERABLE, THAT REALLY PINCH AND SUFFER WANT

In drawing up his list of 'the ranks of People' in *The Review*, Defoe explicitly distinguished between 'the miserable Poor' and 'the working Poor'.[44] The latter, according to Defoe, were able to provide for their families through their labour. King's category of 'Labouring People and Out Servants' and their families added up to 1,275,000. Below these were cottagers and paupers, totalling a further 1,300,000, with an estimated yearly income per family of £6 10s. If King overestimated the number of common labourers,

---

[42] *Great Law of Subordination Consider'd*, RDW, vi. 85.
[43] *Great Law of Subordination Consider'd*, 51–2. Compare *Giving Alms no Charity*, 188, and *The Great Law of Subordination Consider'd*, 86.
[44] *Review*, vi. 193 (25 June 1709).

paupers, and vagrants, as Lindert and Williamson have suggested, it remains the case that we are speaking of a large body of people at the turn of the eighteenth century. In *Giving Alms no Charity*, Defoe was careful to scotch any suggestion 'that we are a poor Nation in general', but he nonetheless identified 'a crowd of clamouring, unimploy'd, unprovided for poor People, who make the Nation uneasie, burthen the Rich, clog our Parishes, and make themselves worthy of Laws, and peculiar Management to dispose of and direct them' (174). Economic conditions in England were generally favourable in the late seventeenth and early eighteenth centuries, yet poverty was recognized as a serious problem, and attempts were made through legislation to address it by such measures as the Workhouse Act of 1723, which was intended to deny the outdoor poor relief provided under the terms of the Elizabethan Poor Law. That a large proportion of the rural population nevertheless remained in receipt of outdoor relief during Defoe's lifetime offers an important perspective on his thinking on the subject of the 'Miserable, that really pinch and suffer Want'.

Conclusion

Perhaps as a consequence of John Robert Moore's representation of Defoe as a citizen of the modern world, there has been a tendency in recent scholarship to view him as some sort of liberal democrat writing before his time. What this fails to take into account is the manifest social conservatism of his ideas, perhaps best seen in *The Great Law of Subordination Consider'd*. Published in what proved to be the final decade of his life, this reveals a Defoe so concerned with the behaviour of the lower orders that he advocated 'severe regulations' to bring them 'to some State of immediate Subordination' (85). When taken in conjunction with his insistence that 'the *Freeholders* are the proper Owners of the Country: It is their own, and the other Inhabitants are but Sojourners, like Lodgers in a House, and ought to be subject to such Laws as the Freeholders impose upon them',[45] the strong suggestion is that he was an advocate of some sort of social hierarchy. The possession of landed property was key to Defoe's social and political thought, just as it was key to that of Addison and Steele, of Swift, Pope, and Gay, of Samuel Johnson, and any number of other contemporary and near-contemporary writers. It was a commonplace of the period that those who possessed a real and substantial stake in the nation—*real* estate—were the only true citizens, and therefore the notion that the poor should have a voice in how the country was governed was dangerous and absurd. On this view, Defoe's championing of trade should be considered as an indication of his life-long aspiration to become a true gentleman through the accumulation of wealth [SEE CHAPTER 14]. Hence his repeated insistence that tradesmen were becoming richer than gentry or, as he put it in *A Plan of the English Commerce* (1728):

---

[45] *Original Power of the Collective Body of the People of England, PEW*, i. 121.

THE rising Tradesman swells into the Gentry, and the declining Gentry sinks into Trade. A Merchant, or perhaps a Man of a meaner Employ thrives by his honest Industry, Frugality, and a long series of diligent Application to Business, and being grown immensely rich, he marries his Daughters to Gentlemen of the finest Quality, perhaps a Coronet; then he leaves the Bulk of his Estate to his Heir, and he gets into the Rank of the Peerage; does the next Age make any scruple of their Blood, being thus mix'd with the antient Race? Do we not just now see two Dukes descended by the Female Side, from the late *Josiah Child*, and the immediate Heir a Peer of *Ireland*? Many Examples of the like Kind might be given. (132)

On this view, Defoe aspired to authentic nobility, not to some kind of hybrid 'middle-class gentility'—an ambition which would have been perfectly in line with the wishes of the man who liked to be known as Daniel De Foe, Gentleman.

Further Reading

Jonathan Barry and Christopher Brookes (ed.), *The Middling Sort of People: Culture, Society, and Politics in England, 1550–1800* (Basingstoke: Macmillan, 1994).

J. V. Beckett, *The Aristocracy in England 1660–1914* (Oxford: Basil Blackwell, 1986).

Douglas Hay and Nicholas Rogers, *Eighteenth-Century English Society: Shuttles and Swords* (Oxford and New York: Oxford University Press, 1997).

Geoffrey Holmes, *Politics, Religion, and Society in England 1679–1742* (London and Ronceverte: Hambledon Press, 1986).

Peter H. Lindert and Jeffrey G. Williamson, 'Revising England's Social Tables 1688–1812', *Explorations in Economic History*, 9:4 (1982), 385–408.

Michael Shinagel, *Daniel Defoe and Middle-Class Gentility* (Cambridge, MA: Harvard University Press, 1968).

W. A. Speck, *Stability and Strife: England 1714–1760* (London: Edward Arnold, 1977).

Keith Wrightson (ed.), *A Social History of England 1500–1750* (Cambridge: Cambridge University Press, 2017).

CHAPTER 14

DEFOE AND ECONOMICS

Industry, Trade, and Finance

NICHOLAS SEAGER

'A Man Knowing in Universal Commerce'

CLOSING down his periodical the *Review* in 1713, Defoe acknowledged that 'writing upon Trade was the Whore I really doated upon'.[1] During the *Review*'s nine-year run, he often regretted having to set aside commerce while politics, religion, or war predominated.[2] He considered the subject abstruse and public understanding of it deficient; at one point he lamented, 'I Am very Unhappy, in that, while I am Entring this Dark Gulph of General Negoce, this hidden Mystery, this *half-known thing call'd Trade*, I speak to the Understandings but of a very few'.[3] Defoe feared that increasing specialization meant that few people could see the whole economic picture; he challenged readers, 'where shall you find a Man knowing in what we call Universal Commerce? Where are the Heads turn'd for the General Advantage of their Country, by seeing into the Scale of the World's Trade?'.[4] Across numerous publications—as economic theorist, historian, and journalist—Defoe presented himself as just such a patriotic polymath, qualified to treat comprehensively 'the Subject of Trade, *to me* a pleasant, and I hope *to you all*, a profitable Theme'.[5] The ambiguity of 'profitable' suggests that intellectual development and material gain remained compatible in Defoe's imagination, though he was no mere apologist for early capitalism.

---

[1] *Review*, ix. 425 (11 June 1713).
[2] E.g. *Review*, vii. 127 (25 May 1710).
[3] *Review*, i. 671 (6 January 1705).
[4] *A General History of Trade . . . June* (1713), 13.
[5] *Review*, viii. 13 (27 March 1711).

Defoe's writings echo the voices of ordinary people engaged in business, and we readily imagine him talking to tradesmen and manufacturers, observing operations and learning from first-hand experience across industries and regions of Britain.[6] He once described a succession of impersonations he adopted to coax Scottish merchants and manufacturers into supporting the Union:

> To ye Merchants I am about to Settle here in Trade, Building ships &c.; with ye Lawyers I want to purchase a House and Land to bring my family & live Upon it; ... to day I am Goeing into Partnership with a Memb^r of parliam^t in a Glass house, to morrow wth Another in a Salt work; wth ye Glasgow Mutineers I am to be a fish Merchant, wth ye Aberdeen Men a woollen, and with ye Perth and western men a Linen Manufacturer. (*Correspondence*, 275)

Defoe was playing up his credentials—as an undercover political operative and as a businessman—but several of these guises had a kernel of truth, and he may have been weighing his options when he wrote this in Edinburgh in 1706. He probably would have preferred to be a successful tradesman than a great writer. After a practical education that included casting accounts and learning about global geography and traffic, Defoe set out as a hosiery factor but also dealt in wine and textiles before establishing a brick and tile factory in Essex. Even after that failed, and while he supported himself mainly through writing, he continued to trade and invest. Notwithstanding his financial failures, Defoe was well-respected for his commercial knowledge even by opponents, albeit they superciliously told him to stick to what he knew: business, not politics.[7] Praise for his 'extensive knowledge in all the branches of the *British* Trade and Commerce' continued after his death.[8]

Defoe's writings on economics began with *An Essay upon Projects* (1697), which brimmed with civic-minded proposals on taxation, banking, insurance, stocks, transportation networks, and the like. He proclaimed that the ambitious ventures he calls 'Projects' were 'of publick Advantage, as they tend to Improvement of Trade, and Employment of the Poor, and the Circulation and Increase of the publick Stock of the Kingdom' (*PEW*, viii. 36). High employment, vigorous circulation, and maximized productivity to enable strong exports of manufactured goods: these are the pillars of Defoe's thinking on industry and trade. He distrusted economic activity that did not serve these aims. In *An Essay upon Projects* and then *The Villainy of Stock-Jobbers Detected* (1701), he criticized trading in exchequer notes and other paper securities, and his assault on this 'Trade founded in Fraud, born of Deceit, and nourished by Trick, Cheat, Wheedle, Forgeries, Falshoods, and all sorts of Delusions' intensified as he aged.[9]

---

[6] On Defoe's relish for local industrial parlance, see G. A. Starr, 'Defoe's Tour through the Dialects and Jargons of Great Britain', *MP*, 110:1 (2012), 74–95.

[7] E.g. Joseph Browne, *A Dialogue between Church and No-Church; or, A Rehearsal of the Review* (1706), 2.

[8] *Grub-street Journal*, 29 April 1731; *Read's Weekly Journal*, 1 May 1731; *The Complete English Tradesman*, 4th ed. (1738), x (quoted).

[9] *The Anatomy of Exchange-Alley* (1719), *PEW*, vi. 130.

Such trading, Defoe reasoned, even where there was a solid basis for the stocks, merely shifted wealth from one pocket to another, tying up money that could otherwise be productive.[10] Defoe embraced most aspects of the late seventeenth-century financial revolution.[11] He celebrated personal credit for facilitating trade and commended public credit for enabling large-scale warfare that allowed the state to defend commerce and increase national prosperity [SEE CHAPTER 22].[12] However, he regarded 'stock-jobbing' as a regrettable outgrowth of credit—it is 'among those Diseases which proceed from Plenty; for it sprung originally from Trade, and the Growth of Publick Credit'.[13] Defoe's outlook was dual, even Manichean: practised properly, commerce was essential to the divine plan, perhaps fallen humanity's best way to cooperate with Providence. But it was a slither away from being the devil's work.

In the *Review* Defoe took up causes stretching from the collectivist hospital established by Newcastle keelmen, who ferried coal down the Tyne, to the trading privileges of the Royal African Company (both the keelmen and the RAC paid him). Advising politicians, Defoe ranged from suitable tariffs on Scottish oats and herrings to the establishment of British colonies in Chile. Scholars rightly acknowledge Defoe's 'expansive global perspective on trade',[14] but he was as just as interested in small-time local industries as in international commerce—and he saw these as connected. He lived through financial developments which enabled Britain to become, in his own words, 'the most Flourishing and Opulent Country in the World' (*TDH*, i. 47). In *An Essay on Publick Credit* and *An Essay on Loans* (1710), Defoe evaluated the new mechanisms for funding state expenditure, especially war debt, showing his financial acumen and propagandist efficacy, as these tracts successfully supported the fiscal management of Robert Harley, Chancellor of the Exchequer. The 1710 essays' success resides in Defoe's presentation of Britain's evolving credit economy as Whiggish even under a Tory government. The modern financial system is thus a bulwark of liberty and Protestantism which makes self-interest (the desire for a secure return on investments) conducive to the national interest, public credit being a contract between the individual and the state.

Trade and patriotism, then, went hand in hand for Defoe. He produced periodicals to comment exclusively on national trade, including *Mercator* (1713–14), which advocated renewing trade with France following the War of the Spanish Succession,

---

[10] *Review*, ix. 150–1 (27 December 1712).

[11] P. G. M. Dickson, *The Financial Revolution in England: A Study in the Development of Public Credit, 1688–1756* (London: Macmillan, 1967).

[12] See, e.g., *Review*, vi. 174 (16 June 1709), which celebrates 'that wonderful Thing, we call CREDIT; the great Mystery of this Age, and the great Prop at this Time both of our Commerce and the War—A Thing, whether National or Personal, inestimable in Value'. See John Brewer, *Sinews of Power: War, Money, and the English State, 1688–1783* (Cambridge, MA: Harvard University Press, 1990).

[13] *Commentator*, *RDH*, ix. 82 (26 February 1720).

[14] Srinivas Aravamudan, 'Defoe, Commerce, and Empire', in *The Cambridge Companion to Daniel Defoe*, ed. John Richetti (Cambridge: Cambridge University Press, 2008), 45–63 (45).

and *The Manufacturer* (1719–21), which lobbied for legislation banning the use of imported Indian calicoes which, Defoe believed, damaged Britain's textile industries. Some of the most ambitious books of his later years—*A Tour thro' the Whole Island of Great Britain* (1724–6) and *A Plan of the English Commerce* (1728)—are proto-nationalistic projects, which give 'a View of the Country, its present State as to Fertility, Commerce, Manufacture, and Product' (*TDH*, iii. 11). Defoe holds out the hope that commercial relationships will unify Great Britain and promote the social harmony which religion and politics no longer could. These works exhibit his talents as an economic writer: a ready grasp of issues that befuddled others, lucid prose which brings abstract matters down to earth, and richly imaginative interweaving of ideas about trade into broader social, religious, philosophical, geographical, and political understanding.

His other major economic work of his late years, *The Complete English Tradesman* (1725–7), as Michael Shinagel explains, 'is not only a practical manual on how to succeed in business but also a conduct book designed to dignify the profession and polish the men who practice it'.[15] Defoe spent his career insisting that 'a True-Bred Merchant is a Universal Scholar', 'the most Intelligent Man in the World', and one whose 'learning excels the mere scholar in Greek and Latin'.[16] Yet *The Complete English Tradesman* is not just an exaltation of the merchant; it is also an investigation of his emotional and moral existence. For all that Defoe is considered the spokesman of the ascending mercantile class, more than any contemporary writer, especially those Augustans sniffy about commerce and finance,[17] he was fascinated by the psychology of the trading life and the potentially murky ethics of accumulation. Defoe is more the vigilant interrogator than 'the complacent apologist of nascent capitalism', as Ian Watt dubbed him.[18] Defoe explored the mental strains of money nowhere better than in his novels. In Robinson Crusoe's contemplation of value on a desert island, Captain Singleton's near-pathological antipathy to his pirate hoard, Moll Flanders's fateful confusion of love and money, Colonel Jack's measurement of self-worth by personal wealth, and Roxana's making a fortune but losing her soul, Defoe demonstrated insights into getting and keeping unmatched in British fiction until Dickens, Eliot, and Trollope. The next two sections of this essay analyse Defoe's ideas about the home trade and international commerce, respectively; the third addresses Defoe's ideas about commercial ethics; the fourth looks at money in the fiction.

---

[15] Michael Shinagel, *Defoe and Middle-Class Gentility* (Cambridge, MA: Harvard University Press, 1968), 211.
[16] *Review*, iii. 13 (3 January 1706); *An Essay upon Projects*, *PEW*, viii. 36.
[17] For the Augustan tradition, see Colin Nicholson, *Writing and the Rise of Finance: Capital Satires of the Early Eighteenth Century* (Cambridge: Cambridge University Press, 1994).
[18] Ian Watt, 'Robinson Crusoe as a Myth', *Essays in Criticism*, 1:2 (1951), 95–119 (106); cf. Isaac Kramnick, *Bolingbroke and His Circle: The Politics of Nostalgia in the Age of Walpole* (Oxford: Oxford University Press, 1968), 188–204.

'The Great Auxiliary': Trade and Industry at Home

Defoe embraced the early modern understanding that '*England* is a Trading Nation, that the Wealth and Oppulence of the Nation, is owing to Trade'. He painted a grim picture of how Britain would fare were trade to decline, using a favourite corporeal metaphor:

> Trade is the Life of the Nation, the Soul of its Felicity, the Spring of its Wealth, the Support of its Greatness, and the Staff on which both King and People lean, and which (if it should sink) the whole Fabrick must fall, the Body Politick would sicken and languish, its Power decline, and the Figure it makes in the World, grow by degrees, most Contemptibly Mean.[19]

As much as Protestantism and liberty—that is to say, religion and politics—the national character, and national interest, could be defined by trade, which is to say, economics. Defoe wrote:

> I divide the Care and Concern of the Nation among these Generals, Religion, Constitution, and Commerce; Trade, as it is the last of these three, is the first of all the subsequent Concerns of the Kingdom, and I rank it hand in hand with Religion and Constitution, not by Way of Equallity, but as it is the great Auxiliary, which enables us to protect, defend and preserve the other from all its Opposers.[20]

It made no sense to Defoe to separate the country's economic interests from its political and religious well-being.

The two main ideas about commerce which Defoe espoused were the vigorous circulation of goods domestically, and a favourable balance of exports to imports in international trade.[21] Fearing an interruption to healthful circulation, Defoe opposed proposals to erect municipal workhouses to spin wool, the industry he regarded as 'the Staple of our Trade, the Soul of our Commerce, the Original Foundation of our Wealth'.[22] He feared that these workhouses would make regions of England too self-sufficient and hence static:

---

[19] *Review*, ii. 18 (6 March 1705).
[20] *Review*, iv. 772 (20 January 1708).
[21] For Defoe and circulation in trade, see Peter Earle, *The World of Defoe* (London: Weidenfeld and Nicolson, 1976), 107–57; David Trotter, *Circulation: Defoe, Dickens, and the Economies of the Novel* (Basingstoke: Macmillan, 1988).
[22] *A Brief State of the Question between the Printed and Painted Callicoes* (1719), 29. Edgar Illingworth explains Defoe's adherence to the view that wool is the foundation of England's commercial greatness ('The Economic Ideas of Daniel Defoe' [doctoral thesis, University of Leeds, 1974], 182). Without denying the scale of the textile industry, Earle shows that Defoe's view is a bit out of date after 1700 (*World of Defoe*, 121–7).

> Manufactures and Trade are in this Nation like the Blood in the Body, they subsist by their Circulation; if once that Motion ceases, is inverted, or otherwise interrupted, it stagnates and corrupts or breaks out in Torrents beyond its ordinary Course, and these prove infallibly mortal, and incurably contagious to the Life of the Creature.[23]

Not only would labour assigned to unemployed paupers in one town take work from people already employed in some remote region, but, catastrophically, fewer people would be involved in distribution. Defoe believed that distribution employed more people than manufacture,[24] and so 'all Methods to bring our Trade to be manag'd by fewer hands than it was before, are in themselves pernicious ..., as it lessens the Employment of the Poor ... and tends to bring our Hands to be superior to our Employ'.[25] Defoe thus advocated the interdependence of separate regions of the nation, joined in a network in which London is the 'great Center of this Circulation, the Heart thro' which, by proper Pulsation, these Streams pass in their due Course' [SEE CHAPTER 26].[26] To illustrate the universal benefits of a genuinely national economy, Mr Review at one point runs through the 'Operations', spanning the length and breadth of England, that have gone into dressing him that day. 'From the first Principles of the Clothes to my wearing them, 100 Families have a Part of their Subsistence out of this one Suit of Clothes', he marvels.[27] Late in his career Defoe called for legislation against get-up-and-go pedlars who contracted circulation by cutting out middlemen such as factors and wholesalers. Due to this kind of activity, 'Trade is become vaguing and ambulatory', Defoe fretted, meandering motion antithetical to the regular, rhythmic pulsations of 'Circulation', 'the essential vital Part of the Prosperity of our Commerce'.[28]

Defoe followed the contemporaneous wisdom that 'the Multitude of People are the Strength of a Kingdom, and the Sinews of Trade' [SEE CHAPTER 27].[29] The populationist argument held that 'the more People, the more Trade; the more Trade, the more Money; the more Money, the more Strength; and the more Strength, the greater a Nation'.[30] He elaborated on the idea in *A Plan of the English Commerce*:

> Multitudes of People, if they can be put in a Condition to maintain themselves, must increase Trade, they must have Food, that employs Land; they must have Clothes, that employs the Manufacture; they must have Houses, that employs Handicrafts; they must have Household stuff, that employs a long Variety of Trades; so that in a Word Trade employs People, and People employ Trade. (*PEW*, vii. 136)

---

[23] *Review*, iv. 21 (18 February 1707).
[24] *Review*, ii. 59–61 (27 March 1705); iv. 21 (18 February 1707).
[25] *Giving Alms No Charity* (1704), *PEW*, viii. 183.
[26] *Review*, iv. 21 (18 February 1707).
[27] *Review*, vi. 221 (9 July 1709).
[28] *A Brief State of the Inland or Home Trade* (1730), 67.
[29] *Review*, i. 68 (8 April 1704).
[30] *Review*, vi. 186–7 (21 June 1709).

Greater population density reduced regional self-sufficiency. This conviction led Defoe to support schemes for settling Protestant immigrants in Britain.[31] It informed his support for England's union with Scotland: as a single polity, Britain would have a bigger population and a wider and easier circulation, hence 'their Riches shall not be our Poverty, nor their Encrease any way interrupt or interfere with Ours, but rather add to it'.[32] He was disappointed with post-Union developments which exposed English ignorance about Scottish circumstances, as England's elite continued to treat Scotland as a separate economy.[33]

Defoe contended that the circulation of trade within Britain enabled land to sustain more people than it naturally would, because multitudes could be employed by an extensive distribution network predicated on the mutual interdependence of regions: 'Trade is the Life of a Nations Wealth; Trade makes thousands live in a Country, more than the Lands can maintain; Trade makes the whole World live by, and depend upon one another'.[34] Defoe contributed to contemporaneous debates about the relative contributions of land and trade to national prosperity. The land-trade argument was occasioned by the fact that the financial revolution centred on the City of London and its bankers and merchants (predominantly Whigs, many of them Dissenters), and so raised their political influence to new heights, though the taxes which funded the national debt were mostly paid by landed men of Tory sympathies in an economy that was still predominantly agricultural despite the relative growth of industry and commerce. Defoe put commerce and manufacture on an equal footing with agriculture by contending that trade and industry sustained the value of estates. The equation seemed simple to him, such as when he anticipated a flourishing Scotland:

> If the Number of People Encreased, the Consumption of Provisions would Increase, and as the Value of Labour and rate of Labour shall rise the Price of Provissions would Rise and by Consequence land will be Improved and the Estates of Landed men will rise in Proportion. (*Correspondence*, 508)

On this basis, 'For the Landed Men to rail at Trade, is like the Members Mutinying against the Belly—'Tis from Trade as the Magazine, that Land receives its Value and Life'.[35] His attitude is captured in a metaphor repeated across his writings, 'That an Estate is a Pond; but that Trade was a Spring' (*Novels*, ix. 147). Defoe's writings, especially the *Tour*, portrayed an England comprising active manufacturing towns and regions more than an England made up of country estates as epicentres of regional economies.

---

[31] Daniel Statt, 'Daniel Defoe and Immigration', ECS, 24:3 (1991), 293–313.
[32] *An Essay at Removing National Prejudices against a Union with Scotland* (1706), PEW, iv. 58.
[33] *Correspondence*, 437–9; *Union and No Union* (1713) 9–24.
[34] *Review*, iv. 30 (22 February 1707).
[35] *Review*, iv. 768 (17 January 1708); viii. 89 (1 May 1711). On the land-trade debate in Defoe, see J. G. A Pocock, *The Machiavellian Moment: Florentine Political Thought and the Atlantic Republican Tradition* (Princeton, N.J.: Princeton University Press, 1975), 446–61. For a mature, detailed articulation of Defoe's idea on this, see *The Complete English Tradesman*, RDW, vii. 240.

Defoe argued that wages and prices should be kept high to sustain high levels of production, quality of goods, and consumption. Against the common judgement that high wages encouraged idleness, Defoe countered: 'If [workers'] Wages were low and despicable, so would be their Living; if they got little, they could spend but little, and Trade would presently feel it; as their Gain is more or less, the Wealth and Strength of the whole Kingdom would rise or fall' (*PEW*, vii. 178).[36] He was proud that English wages were higher than elsewhere in Europe, an obvious sign of prosperity and of course liberty, as well as a stimulus to trade.[37] Also against orthodox judgements about the need to minimize labour costs, Defoe approves a succession of middlemen handling goods, accreting value to them as the cycle proceeds, raising their ultimate price to the consumer.[38] 'The Circulation of Trade in *England* is the Life and Being of all our Home Trade', he wrote, 'And the Wealth that rolls from hand to hand, insensibly growing as it goes, is inexpressible'.[39] High prices, he maintained, ensured extensive employment, good wages, and high-quality goods. But he cautioned that high prices should be produced by extensive circulation, not by burdensome taxes.[40] In the *Tour*, 'Corporation-Tyranny', a residual medieval system of exclusive trading privileges, is among 'the greatest Inconveniencies of *Bristol*', whereas 'the rich Trading Towns in the *North*, such as *Manchester*, and *Rochdale*, *Sheffield*, *Wakefield*, *Gainsbro*', and the like, where they have no Corporation ... encrease, grow wealthy and populous and thrive.'[41]

For all his pragmatic plainness, Defoe also envisages economic growth as wondrous. Trade's operations are mysterious and magical because they make something from nothing, augmenting nature itself:

> Trade, like the Blood in the Veins, Circulates thro' the whole Body of Fraternities and Societies of Mankind, and Creates, ... a kind of Wealth which was never made before: For the Profits of Trade are an Encrease of Wealth, without an encrease of the Specie, and loading Men with Riches which were not found in the Creation.[42]

His celebrations of the beauty of commercial operations rise to lyricism, and he was rapturous when conveying his sense that the divine hand was discernible in the human organization of commerce as well as in the natural creation:

> Not the Variety of the Climates, not the Beauty of the Heavenly Bodies, not the Influences of the Elements in the Productions of Nature; not the Harmony of the

---

[36] See Richard C. Wiles, 'The Theory of Wages in Later English Mercantilism', *Economic History Review* 21:1 (1968), 113–26.

[37] *Review*, iv. 39–40 (27 February 1707).

[38] Thomas Keith Meier, *Defoe and the Defense of Commerce* (Victoria, B.C.: University of Victoria Press, 1987), 39.

[39] *Review*, vi. 221–2 (9 July 1709).

[40] *Review*, viii. 812, 822–4 (22 and 29 May 1712); *Fair Payment No Spunge* (1717), *PEW*, vii. 124.

[41] *TDH*, ii. 158; *Review*, v. 675 (1 March 1709).

[42] *A General History of Trade ... June*, 5–6.

Creation in general, or the wonderful Operations of the Parts in particular, afford more profitable, instructing, and diverting Observations, than the pleasing Diversity of Nature, from whence is derived the Foundations of Commerce, and the Chain of happy Causes and Consequences, which has now, more than ever, embark'd the whole World in a diligent Application to TRADE.[43]

He liked to shift between the cosmic and the prosaic, the global and the local. In *A Brief State of the Inland or Home Trade*, Defoe described the manufacture of a pin, not just the Crusoe style of this-then-this-then-this, but the complex social relations that ensue from its production to its use. Defoe marvels at the way in which 'even the least Pin contribute[s] its nameless Proportion to the Maintenance, Profit, the Support of every Hand, and every Family concerned in those Operations, from the Copper Mine in *Africa*, to the Retailer's-Shop in the Country Village, however Remote'.[44] He revelled in this mixture of the mundane and the mysterious, the intangible dynamic behind banal operations, the interconnectedness of disparate operations and their invisible cooperation to improve the human condition, notionally on a global scale.

'TRADE WITH EVERY NATION WE CAN BUBBLE': FOREIGN COMMERCE

In the wake of the Treaty of Utrecht (1713), Defoe boasted with justification that Britain conducted 'the greatest Trade of any Nation in the World'.[45] Across his lifetime Britain gained primacy in international trade thanks to state-led mercantilist policies directed to national prosperity: a large shipping industry, protectionist tariffs and prohibitions, import substitutions, export and re-export growth, and colonial expansion.[46] Defoe's association of the rise of British commerce with global improvement is ideological.

The orthodox view was that keeping wages at subsistence level was the way to convert labour into bullion through cheaper exports and hence favourable trade balances with competitors. By contrast, as we have seen, Defoe insisted that high wages improved productivity, whereas low wages diminished the quality of goods, compromised 'the Honour of the English Woolen Manufactures', and thereby damaged exports:

> To lower the Wages for our Poor's Work ... is of consequence to lessen the Value of their Goods, for this will be for ever true in Trade, that the less Wages you give the worse Work shall be done: It is the goodness of our Wages which we give above other

---

[43] *Review*, ix. 218 (5 February 1713).
[44] *A Brief State of the Inland or Home Trade*, 13.
[45] *Mercator*, no. 52 (19–22 September 1713).
[46] David Ormrod, *The Rise of Commercial Empires: England and the Netherlands in the Age of Mercantilism, 1650–1770* (Cambridge: Cambridge University Press, 2003).

Nations, which makes the Work our People do excel that of other Nations; ... in proportion to the Goodness of our Goods, they are made Cheaper by Englishmen than by any Nation in the World.[47]

Defoe wrote this defending the government's efforts to ratify a commercial treaty with France during 1713–14, an ultimately unsuccessful attempt to reverse fifty years of tariff-escalation and trade embargos between the two nations. Yet the principle is the same that Defoe touted in the preceding decade: so long as British wool is of the highest quality, it will hold its own despite higher prices caused by the high wages needed to sustain high employment at home. Trade with France, although it had been a losing game to England in the past, was viable in the early eighteenth century, even in wartime, Defoe insisted, because the balance favoured Britain. 'Our Trade to *France*, if open, would be to our Gain ... If it be to our Gain, it must be to their loss; ... We shall beggar them by it, and all Men will allow that's as quick a Way of Beating them, as to Fight them.'[48] He recognized that, for Britain, commerce was more vital than conquest in the pursuit of geopolitical dominance.

Defoe espoused classic mercantilist thought: support for foreign commerce where that produced a favourable balance of trade.[49] In this view, for all his emphasis on domestic circulation, Defoe says that inland trade only moves wealth around, whereas exporting manufactured goods in excess of imports, such that the difference of value had to be made up with bullion, increases national wealth. Yet Defoe's articulation of mercantilist principles is always qualified by his insistence that 'the Inland Trade of England ... is the foundation of all our wealth and greatness' (*RDW*, vii. 241):

> The Profit to a Nation is so much as any Thing is sold for Abroad more than it costs that Nation at Home; and indeed nothing else can be strictly call'd Gain to the publick Stock ... What comes from the Market Abroad to the Consumption at Home, is all so much sunk out of the publick Stock ... Our Consumption at home is, however, useful, as it circulates our Stock, separates it into small Parcels among the Poor, and causes the Return to enrich one Family by what another Family spends; and this, I say, is an inexpressible Benefit to the Nation, tho' not an actual Increase of its Wealth.[50]

For Defoe, international trade and domestic production and consumption needed to work in conjunction.

In the terms of Defoe's favourite haematological metaphor, the risk of importing more than one exports is bleeding out, which he expresses vividly with reference to imported Indian printed calicoes that, he feared, reduced the home demand for English-produced

---

[47] *Mercator*, no. 143 (22 April 1714); cf. *Some Thoughts on the Subject of Commerce with France* (1713), 45.
[48] *Review*, i. 672 (6 January 1705).
[49] On Defoe's mercantilism, see Maximillian E. Novak, *Economics and the Fiction of Daniel Defoe* (Los Angeles, CA: University of California Press, 1962).
[50] *Manufacturer*, nos 20 and 22 (6 and 13 January 1720).

woollens and drained the national treasure: '*Europe*, like a Body in a warm Bath, with its Veins open'd, lies bleeding to Death; and her Bullion, which is the Life and Blood of her Trade, flows all to *India*'.[51] In his outlook, laws such as the calicoes ban needed to channel private gain to public benefit, to encourage trade but also to make it beneficial to the nation as much as to the individual. Defoe defined the role of the state as 'to Enlarge, Encourage, Protect, and Support, the Commerce, by necessary Bounties, well-proportioned Customs, due Prohibitions, and avoiding all Clogs and Discouragements to the Merchants, such as foolish Prohibitions, discourageing Monopolies, and the like'.[52] Bans or restrictions on exporting wares made no sense: 'Manufacturing Nations ought never to Prohibit the Exportation of their own Manufactures to any Place whatsoever'.[53] One monopoly Defoe did support was that of the Royal African Company: he believed that only a state-approved corporation protected from private traders would sustain the necessary supply of slaves to the American colonies during downturns [SEE CHAPTER 31]. He called the African trade 'a Noble, Capital, and National Undertaking ... capable of being made perhaps, the Greatest and most Profitable this Nation is concern'd in; and a Trade, which without any Export *but of Trifles*, brings back the most solid, the richest, and the best Return in the World'.[54] Defoe minimizes the trade in people, and their forced labour, by focusing on the tip of the Triangle Trade: Britain's sending 'Baubles' to Africa and receiving goods from the Americas to re-export to Europe.

Defoe had a versatile programme for economic exploitation of distant lands and peoples. This included resource extraction under the guise of consensual exchange:

> We sufficiently possess a Nation when we have an open and free Trade to it; we know how to draw Wealth from all Nations, if we can but trade to them; the Value and Bulk of our own Manufactures have found the Way to make themselves necessary to all the World, and they force the Wealth from the best and richest Countries, be they never so remote.[55]

This was in 1707 when he was arguing *against* planting South Sea colonies, but when he argued *for* establishing them, just four years later, he did so because such colonies could send raw materials home and provide a market for British goods, especially woollen products [SEE CHAPTER 29]. Defoe explained that 'an Encrease of Colonies encreases People, People encrease the Consumption of Manufactures, Manufactures Trade, Trade Navigation, Navigation Seamen, and altogether encrease the Wealth, Strength and Prosperity of *England*' (*TDH*, vii. 319). In Defoe's view, trade was what distinguished ancient from modern colonialism: 'The Romans 'planted [colonies] for Conquest, we

---

[51] *Trade to India*, PEW, vii. 101.
[52] *Review*, vii. 632 (22 Feb 1711).
[53] *Mercator*, no. 23 (16 July 1713).
[54] *Review*, vii. 156 (8 June 1710).
[55] *Review*, iv. 521 (4 October 1707).

planted for Commerce; they planted to extend their Dominion, we to extend our Trade; and as the last is the best Foundation, so it is the surest Possession, and we will certainly continue longest; experience tells us so'.[56] As with trading with France during wartime, why fight when you can conquer with commerce and '*subdue whole Nations of Savages to a regular Life, and by that Means bring them to be subservient to Trade as well as to Government*' (PEW, vii. 121). Defoe recognized that '*Trading Nations*' outdid '*Fighting Nations*', that commerce was displacing conquest in the global system.[57] Trade fostered the peace that in turn nurtured trade, but it increased state power nonetheless.

Defoe was jealous of the relative self-sufficiency of Asian economies such as India, Japan, and China, which seemed wealthy because of advantageous trade balances with Europe.[58] 'They trade with *Europe* infinitely to its Loss, and to their own Gain', he wrote; and he proposed growing Asian staples like coffee and tea in Africa to redress this.[59] More generally, and in line with his theology of trade, Defoe argued that their relative autarky demonstrated that these nations were excluded from the divine purpose of global commerce. Versions of this idea are littered throughout Defoe's writings:

> There is a kind of Divinity in the Original of Trade ... God, in the Order of Nature, not only made Trade necessary to the making the Life of Man Easy, and towards accommodating one Part of the World with what they might want for their Conveniences, from another part; but also qualified, suited and adapted the Vegetative and Sensitive World, to be subservient to the Uses, Methods and Necessities which we find them now put to, by the ingenious Artists, for the Convenience of Trade? ... Providence has adapted Nature to Trade, and made it subservient in all its Parts, to the several necessary Operations of Commerce.[60]

The providential view of trade—predicated on the subservience of nature to human need and a fallen geography adapted from Thomas Burnet's *The Sacred Theory of the Earth* (1681)—finds expression in Defoe's writings at both national and international levels [SEE CHAPTER 19]. It explains why Britain is particularly blessed ('No Nation in the World has been equally furnished by Nature with the Principles of Manufacture, and the Advantages of Commerce'[61]), even though it gestures towards mutually beneficial international reciprocity:

> Every Nation has something to fetch from, and something to send to one another; every Nation something to spare, which another Country wants, and finds

---

[56] *A General History of Discoveries and Improvements* (1725-6), TDH, iv. 134. In this work, Defoe celebrates the commercial Phoenicians and Carthaginians rather than the bellicose Romans.
[57] *The Advantages of Peace and Commerce* (1729), 3.
[58] See G. A. Starr, 'Defoe and China', ECS 43:4 (2010), 435-54.
[59] *The Advantages of Peace and Commerce*, 17.
[60] *Review*, ix. 211 (3 February 1713).
[61] *A General History of Trade ... August* (1713), 7.

something wanting, another Country can spare; and this occasions Exchanging with those Countries, to the Advantage of both; and that we call TRADE.[62]

Defoe conceives the providential grant of 'exclusive Blessings to several parts of the World'—the divine dispersal of natural resources—as a spur to 'the Industry of Men, … Navigation, Plantation, Correspondence, and Commerce, to the Universal benefit of every part of the World'.[63] But Defoe decries the China and India trades because those nations export superfluities—luxury goods—that the English foolishly crave, and do not take English woollens.

For Defoe, commerce was beneficial at multiple levels: the human race, the nation, its citizenry, and the individual tradesman. It fostered peace and liberty and advanced human civilization; it made Britain powerful and protected its liberty and religion; it improved the standard of living for all classes of society; and it provided not only social and material benefits to the merchant, but intellectual and spiritual fulfilment too. But there is a murkier picture to all this, a concern that benignant commerce depended on personal selfishness.

'Lunacy in Trade': The Ethics of Commerce and Credit

In Defoe's economic thinking, merchants are 'the great Wheels of Trade, by which Commerce is carried round, and the Circulation of Trade in the World depends upon them'.[64] But he also fears for the merchant. The tradesman's vocation is inscrutable, unpredictable, and perilous. This calls up another facet of Defoe's economic writings—not the beautiful wonders and universal benefits of trade, but the anxiety of bewitchment and dementia:

> Trade is a Mystery, which will never be compleatly discover'd or understood; it has its Critical Junctures and Seasons, when acted by no visible Causes, it suffers Convulsion Fitts, hysterical Disorder, and most unaccountable Emotions—Sometimes it is acted by the evil Spirit of general Vogue, and like a meer Possession 'tis hurry'd out of all manner of common Measures; today it obeys the Course of things, and submits to Causes and Consequences; to morrow it suffers Violence from the Storms and Vapours of Human Fancy, operated by exotick Projects, and then all runs counter, the Motions are excentrick, unnatural and unaccountable—A Sort of Lunacy in Trade attends all its Circumstances, and no Man can give a rational Account of it.[65]

---

[62] *Review*, iii. 12 (3 January 1706).
[63] *Mercator*, no. 162 (5 June 1714).
[64] *Review*, viii. 336 (6 September 1711).
[65] *Review*, iii. 645 (22 October 1706).

Defoe found this temperamental quality, which leads him to metaphors of psychosomatic disorder, enticing rather than off-putting. It made him aware that the trading life was a hazardous one, materially, emotionally, and spiritually.

The tradesman had to weigh up competing demands on his time (prayer, leisure, and even family detract from tending the shop), tread an appropriate line between risk and caution, extend trust to others, attract and preserve trust in turn, live with the uncertainty of factors beyond his control, and make fine judgements about when to venture, play it safe, take on more debt, or call it a day and compound with creditors. A misstep could be fatal; calamity could be sudden and beyond prevention because 'the contingent nature of trade renders every man liable to disaster that is engag'd in it' (*RDW*, vii. 140).[66] Defoe's religious convictions led him to champion sedulity and probity in all walks of life, but most especially in commercial dealing, even if contemporaries doubted that he practised what he preached. 'FAIR DEALING is the Honour of Trade, and the Credit of the Tradesman', Defoe pronounced, but he knew from personal experience that messy reality could lead even the most conscientious man into other, deviant courses.[67] How could the pursuit of gain be squared with Christian ethics? At his most cynical, Defoe wrote that 'COMMERCE is turn'd into *Universal Pyracy*—Trade is little else, than the Extreme of Picking pockets—Juggle, Legerdemain, *Deceptio Visus* and most exquisite Fraud, seems to be the Essentials of general Negoce: To Circumvent one another, to Out-wit, *Anglicè* Deceive, to *Sharp*, Cozen and *Trick*—These are all become Vertues in Business.'[68] His extensive writings on bankruptcy tried to sort between honest men who go broke and admit it, and fraudulent ones who mislead their creditors.[69] As well as the legal consequences of bankruptcy, Defoe described the social stigma and emotional burden: the sense of helplessness, feeling of personal failure, and loss of manliness.

In *The Commentator*, in the wake of the South Sea Bubble (1720), when reckless speculation in a joint-stock company's shares crashed the market,[70] Defoe opined that 'he would be a Benefactor to the Age, who would stage any Project to restore the Morality of Commerce' (*RDH*, ix. 219). His *Complete English Tradesman* may be just such a project, though it too is riven by self-doubt and imponderable moral questions which are not only unanswered but are best left so:

> Custom indeed has driven us beyond the limits of our morals in many things, which trade makes necessary, and which we cannot now avoid; so that if we must pretend to go back to the literal sense of the command, if our yea must be yea, and our nay

---

[66] On the moral and social implications of 'credit' in this period—how new economic systems affected personal relations—see Craig Muldrew, *The Economy of Obligation: The Culture of Credit and Social Relations in Early Modern England* (Basingstoke: Palgrave, 1998).

[67] *A Brief State of the Inland or Home Trade*, 31.

[68] *Review*, vii. 147 (3 June 1710).

[69] See P. N. Furbank and W. R. Owens, 'Defoe and Imprisonment for Debt: Some Attributions Reviewed', *RES* 37:148 (1986), 495–502. On speculation and bankruptcy in the period, see Julian Hoppit, *Risk and Failure in English Business, 1700–1800* (Cambridge: Cambridge University Press, 1987).

[70] See John Carswell, *The South Sea Bubble*, rev. ed. (1960; London: Cresset Press, 1993).

nay; if no man must go beyond, or defraud his neighbour; if our conversation must be without covetousness, and the like, why then it is impossible for tradesmen to be Christians, and we must unhinge all business, act upon new principles in trade, and go on by new rules: in short, we must shut up shop, and leave off trade. (*RDW*, vii. 186).

The clash between worldly success and spiritual salvation is central to Defoe's fiction and non-fiction alike.

John McVeagh writes incisively on Defoe's moral quandaries: 'What strikes us is his sense that men have reached a stage at which they no longer have it in them to resist the economic imperative ... the expedient, that is the economically advantageous, has been raised as a principle of conduct above the just', so in Defoe we see 'the growing independence of the commercial rule of conduct from moral life'.[71] Although some still write about him as a naïve enthusiast for 'primitive accumulation',[72] Defoe moralizes against unscrupulous gain in many places and promotes moderation. He recognized that what he (being a good Puritan) called 'Avarice', and what we might call the profit motive, is self-perpetuating and has the ability to mask itself as a virtue: 'Avarice is rooted in Nature, and the Desire of getting increases as Gain increases ... Under the Disguise therefore of Industry, and Diligence in our Calling, all the Exorbitances of Crime are conceal'd; and the Devil maintains his Empire in the World';[73] and 'Avarice is often the Ruin of the greatest Tradesmen, when not satisfied with having gain'd a plentiful Fortune by their Diligence and Application, they are resolv'd to push at greater Things than they can grasp, launch out of their Depth in Trade, and blinded with the Vanity of their projected Hopes, do not see their Danger' (*RDW*, viii. 58). Almost every trading virtue is a potential vice.

Stock-jobbing is a flagrant example of unbridled acquisition as well as that vapourish, volatile quality that finance was assuming in this era. In the wake of the Bubble, Defoe decried 'those corrupt Projects of Stock-Jobbing and Bubbling, which ill designing Men draw People into, to the Ruin of their Fortunes'.[74] It typified for Defoe modern modes of 'getting Money by Trick and Craft, by Circumventing, Biting, and Sharping'.[75] Stock-jobbing is a regrettable outgrowth of personal credit, which Defoe celebrates for its ability to stimulate and facilitate trade.[76] But public joint stocks 'begot a New Trade ..., *Stock-Jobbing*, which was at first only the simple Occasional Transferring of Interest and Shares from one to another, as Persons alienated their Estates; but by the Industry of

---

[71] John McVeagh, *Tradefull Merchants: The Portrayal of the Capitalist in Literature* (London: Routledge and Kegan Paul, 1981), 54.
[72] Stephen Hymer, 'Robinson Crusoe and the Secret of Primitive Accumulation', *Monthly Review*, 23 (1971), 11–36; Michael Perelman, *The Invention of Capitalism: Classical Political Economy and the Secret History of Primitive Accumulation* (Durham, N.C.: Duke University Press, 2000), 139.
[73] *Commentator*, no. 46 (10 June 1720), *RDH*, ix. 198.
[74] *Brief Observations on Trade and Manufactures* (1721), *PEW*, vii. 113.
[75] *Manufacturer*, no. 55 (3 August 1720).
[76] *Review*, iv. 190 (8 May 1707).

the Exchange-Brokers, who got the business into their hands, it became a Trade; and one perhaps manag'd, with the greatest Intriegue, Artifice, and Trick, that ever any thing that appear'd with a face of Honesty could be handl'd with' (*PEW*, viii. 43). He fretted that all commerce exploited vanity and luxury: 'Since then our Vices are by Necessity, thus made Vertues in our Trade, we must allow those Things we call Superfluities, to be Necessaries in Trade'.[77] His conclusion that 'the Trade does not make the Vice, but the Vice makes the Trade' hardly solves the dilemma (*RDW*, viii. 211).

In writing about commercial behaviour, Defoe touted the Puritan emphasis on individual responsibility for decision-making, as well as virtues such as prudence, thrift, diligence, and perseverance. He had a strong concept of the calling, a sense of one's role in secular society appointed by Providence, and his own decision not to become a minister seems to have made him throw himself into trade as his calling, divinely approved but nonetheless fraught [SEE CHAPTER 17]. 'There are more People ruin'd in *England*, by over Trading, than for Want of Trade; and I would from my own unhappy Experience, advise all Men in Trade, to set a due Compass to their Ambition. Credit is a Gulph which it is easie to fall into, hard to get out of'.[78] Defoe's writings on credit have gained considerable recent attention. He was writing at a time when influential peers such as Jonathan Swift spoke to a widespread cultural anxiety about finance when he denounced credit as 'such a Complication of Knavery and Couzenage, such a Mystery of Iniquity, and such an unintelligible Jargon of Terms... as were never known in any other Age or Country of the World'. Swift saw a threat to social order because 'the Wealth of the Nation, that used to be reckoned by the Value of Land, is now computed by the Rise and Fall of Stocks', and 'that which was first a Corruption, is at last grown necessary, and what every good Subject must now fall in with'.[79]

Equally convinced the new finance was indispensable to a fiscal-military state, and also supporting the management of such a state by Tories after the governmental change in 1710, Defoe is less alarmist about credit than contemporaries. Natalie Roxburgh reads his interventions in debates over public credit as contributing to 'credible commitment', economic historians' term for citizens' faith in public institutions, in this case government fiscal management, as well as encouraging, as best he was able, financial rectitude in individual citizens.[80] For example, the much-discussed allegory of 'Lady Credit', imagined as a daughter of Money, which Defoe employed in the *Review*, combines an ideal of feminine punctiliousness and aristocratic uprightness to advocate 'honour' in financial dealing. Even if she can seem demure and yielding by turns, and thus typical of feminine changeability and subterfuge, Lady Credit is honest and chary of her reputation and virtue. She will avoid 'any place, where she has been ill Treated', and 'if you will entertain this Virgin, you must Act upon the nicest Principles of Honour, and

---

[77] *Review*, viii. 820 (27 May 1712).
[78] *Review*, iii. 41 (15 January 1706).
[79] Jonathan Swift, *Examiner*, no. 14 (2 November 1710).
[80] Natalie Roxburgh, *Representing Public Credit: Credible Commitment, Fiction, and the Rise of the Financial Subject* (London: Routledge, 2016).

Justice', Defoe warns.[81] In his historical account of finance leading up to the 1690s, Defoe describes Lady Credit being scared from Britain by such measures as Charles II's stop of the Exchequer (1672). In this account, she is like a sensible woman contemplating the terms of her marriage settlement, as Moll and Roxana must do. She accedes to England only when parliament secures loans, in William's reign in the 1690s. Thus, the new economic order must resemble a marriage (and a polity) based on fidelity and good usage. Defoe's masculinist metaphor renders an anxiety-inducing set of new and impersonal economic practices in domestic, personal terms that is comprehensible alike to Whiggish moneyed men and landed aristocrats.[82] The Lady Credit personification adapts traditional stigmatization of usury, also often expressed in the early modern period through sexist personifications about promiscuity and libidinous fecundity, to a new ethos of upstanding commercial conduct.[83] Defoe generally finds a way to square the circle of trading ethics, but the vividly described anxieties remain, nowhere more so than in his fiction.

FINANCE AND FICTIONALITY: MONEY AND THE NOVEL

Defoe's larger economic ideas—about circulation, wages, and mercantilism—inform and vitalize his fiction, but the treatment of money in his novels speaks more closely to the anguished moral philosophy of acquisition that comes through in his 1720s writings. Globetrotting Robinson Crusoe, long regarded as an embodiment of *homo economicus* but more recently reappraised for his religious and emotional as well as mercenary motives, memorably chances upon a small hoard when rummaging the wrecked ship for tools, and indulges in some grandiloquent moralism:

> I smil'd to my self at the Sight of this Money, O Drug! said I, aloud, what art thou good for, Thou art not worth to me, no not the taking off of the Ground, one of those Knives is worth all this Heap, I have no Manner of use for thee, e'en remain where thou art, and go to the Bottom as a Creature whose Life is not worth saving. However, upon Second Thoughts, I took it away.[84]

---

[81] *Review*, vii. 529 (21 December 1710).

[82] See Sandra Sherman, *Finance and Fictionality in the Early Eighteenth Century: Accounting for Defoe* (Cambridge: Cambridge University Press, 1996); Kimberley S. Latta, 'The Mistress of the Marriage Market: Gender and Economic Ideology in Defoe's *Review*', ELH 69:2 (2002), 359–83.

[83] On traditional ideas about usury, see Norman Jones, *God and the Moneylenders: Usury and Law in Early Modern England* (Oxford: Basil Blackwell, 1989). For the endurance of misogynistic anti-usury in Defoe, see Ann Louise Kibbie, 'Monstrous Generation: The Birth of Capital in Defoe's *Moll Flanders* and *Roxana*', PMLA 110:5 (1995), 1023–34.

[84] Defoe, *Robinson Crusoe*, ed. Thomas Keymer (Oxford: Oxford University Press, 2007), 50.

Marx used Defoe's castaway to illustrate an economic system based on the utilitarian theory of value—worth based on use, not barter—but exchange was always in Defoe's mind, even when his characters are isolated from commercial networks. When he finds money on the Spanish wreck, Crusoe reflects that "Twas to me as the Dirt under my Feet; and I would have given it all for three or four pair of *English* Shoes and Stockings' (163). In this, we hear Defoe's arguments that people across the world will gladly exchange their valuable raw materials for English woollens, the central idea of his last novel, *A New Voyage Round the World* (1724), in which indigenous Patagonians, surfeited with gold, yearn for British trade despite the Spanish claims to their territory. Crusoe's decision to take the money he finds on wrecks regardless of its uselessness in his predicament (indeed, on the second occasion he only regrets there is not more) is vindicated because although it grows 'rusty' and 'moulded' in a drawer (234), it is soon cleaned up and put to use when he is rescued. By that time, thanks to the improbably honest stewardship of his affairs by allies from Brazil to Britain, he is an extraordinarily wealthy man, as his survivalist labour on the island is rewarded with the fruits of the profit-directed labour of others on his real plantation, making *Crusoe* a fantasy of individual productivity divorced from social relations.[85]

Captain Singleton gets a comparable lesson in use value and exchange value when marooned 'entirely out of the way of all Commerce' in Africa, because 'our Money did us little Service, for the [indigenous] People neither knew the Value or the Use of it' and 'it was meer Trash to them'.[86] In theory, attitudes to money differentiate civilized Christians from heathen 'Savages', but the unregenerate Singleton's own outlook is scarcely more developed. When the group's time in Africa promises to become lucrative, he admits:

> I had no Notion of a great deal of Money, or what to do with my self, or what to do with it if I had it. I thought I had enough already, and all the Thoughts I had about disposing of it, if I came to *Europe*, was only how to spend it as fast as I could, buy me some Clothes, and go to Sea again to be a Drudge for more. (132)

The Britain to which he returns from Africa is still the world of economic predation Singleton left as a child who is literally bought and sold in the opening pages. It is as a pirate, a disruptor of the predictable circuits of international exchange, that Singleton develops from aimless profligacy to purposive prudence. His progress is abetted by Quaker William's reminders that the point of being a pirate is to make money rather than to fight, echoing Defoe's words on international trading: why fight the French or Spanish when you can out-trade them? Though he imbibes an acquisitive attitude, and seems to be developing into *homo economicus*, Bob's moral growth brings about an

---

[85] See David Wallace Spielman, 'The Value of Money in *Robinson Crusoe, Moll Flanders*, and *Roxana*', *MLR*, 107:1 (2012), 65–87 (70–6); Dennis Todd, *Defoe's America* (Cambridge: Cambridge University Press, 2010), 29.

[86] Defoe, *Captain Singleton*, ed. Shiv K. Kumar, intro. Penelope Wilson (Oxford: Oxford University Press, 1990), 45, 23.

internal conflict akin to Defoe's conduct-book tradesman, an echo of Crusoe's phrasing but now less practical and more anguished: 'As to the Wealth I had, which was immensely great, it was all like Dirt under my Feet; I had no Value for it, no Peace in the Possession of it, no great Concern about me for the leaving of it' (265). Back in Britain again, he contemplates giving it all to charity, an inversion of his gambling everything away earlier on, but alights on a kind of investment in William's necessitous sister and a commitment to live reclusively with William, ensuring the money will never circulate in Britain. Circulation, globally and domestically, is justified by the pirates' practice of it at sea and their exclusion from it once home.

After *Crusoe* and *Singleton*—individualistic adventure stories in distant locales—in *Moll Flanders*, *Colonel Jack*, and *The Fortunate Mistress* Defoe develops the social aspect of money's influence on the individual. These novels are concerned with the ways in which new sources of commercial wealth and institutions such as marriage, wage labour, the cash nexus, and a credit economy affect the behaviours of relatively ordinary people who occupy conditions ranging from abject penury to unimaginable prosperity. They represent the pursuit of personal wealth (through working, marriage, thieving, and whoring), but also imagine economic projects that will improve society: an orphans' hospital, transporting felons to grow colonies, and redressing certain laws, including marriage.

Defoe shows Moll's financial conditioning from a young age. As a poor infant, Moll associates her ability to please social superiors with monetary reward: the mayoress and her daughters 'lik'd my little Prattle to them ... and they gave me Money'; over time, 'they gave me Money oftner than formerly'. Avarice is not innate, as Moll reports, 'I gave it all to my Mistress Nurse', and she desires only economic independence through work, something she will eventually achieve illicitly.[87] Moll's class and gender are against her, of course, as one of the Colchester sisters says, because a young woman without capital is 'no Body' (20). The older brother in Colchester acts on this dehumanizing principle when he sexually assaults Moll and ends the attack with a gift of five guineas. 'I was more confounded with the Money than I was before with the Love', Moll says, and she is entranced by the wealth and the attention of a man 'already Rich to Excess', in a way that conflates the two: 'As for the Gold I spent whole Hours in looking upon it; I told the Guineas over and over a thousand times a Day' (26). When he promises marriage, it comes with 'a silk Purse, with an Hundred Guineas in it', which produces surely one of the most pathos-laden sexual transactions in modern fiction:

> So putting the Purse into my Bosom, I made no more Resistance to him, but let him do just what he pleas'd; and as often as he pleas'd; and thus I finish'd my own Destruction at once, for from this Day, being forsaken of my Vertue, and my Modesty, I had nothing of Value left to recommend me, either to God's Blessing, or Man's Assistance. (29)

---

[87] Defoe, *Moll Flanders*, ed. G. A. Starr (Oxford: Oxford University Press, 1971), 13.

The striking thing is not that Moll voices conventional morality about a fallen woman's status and prospects, but that Defoe refuses to uphold it. Moll lambasts herself for actions the socioeconomic causes of which she can neither control nor fully comprehend.

After her first husband dies, Moll acknowledges the reality of the marriage market, and of herself as both the negotiator and the object of her negotiations. She resolves that she will not be tricked again by *'that Cheat call'd Love'* (60), taking away from her Colchester experience not her first husband's willingness to marry her without a dowry, but rather her sister-in-law's advice, 'that Money only made a Woman agreeable' (67). The wealth that she possesses means that Moll is never close to the poverty that she pleads directs her into vice (120). She pursues marriage as the means to security. There are understandably many unsympathetic readings of Moll's actions that cite her reduction of relationships to monetary exchange,[88] but these do not always appreciate the challenge presented by her gender, the fact that she cannot readily convert the several hundred pounds she commands into a stable income, because 'when a Woman is thus left desolate and void of Counsel, she is just like a Bag of Money, or a Jewel dropt on the Highway, which is a Prey to the next Comer', whereas 'Men can be their own Advisers, and their own Directors, and know how to work themselves out of Difficulties and into Business better than Women' (128).[89] There is nothing mercenary in Moll's willingness to stick with her Lancashire husband 'till all my Money was spent' (157). When her final husband suffers a business loss and then dies, Moll is 'left in a dismal and disconsolate Case', watching her remaining wealth diminish, and apparently forgetting, whether or not we do, that her first nurse was a reduced gentlewoman who maintained herself honestly (189–90). The remaining parts of the novel, even if Moll becomes more callous, confirm the sense of the first half that morality, like survival, is easier for those with money.[90] Moll finds that a customer with cash on the hip will escape suspicion of theft, a transported felon who retains the proceeds of her crimes will find liberty in the New World, and a long-lost mother will ease her profitable reunion with her son with the gift of a stolen watch that carries an imagined sentimental value.

Colonel Jack in his infancy experiences a level of destitution that Moll never does, and, when he is first given some change by his brother, states: 'This was very welcome to me, who, as much as I was of a Gentleman, ... never had a Shilling of Money together before, in all my Life, not that I could call my own'.[91] He goes through the odd stage of feeling greater anxiety at having money than having none: 'Now as I was full of Wealth, behold!

---

[88] Spielman, 'Value of Money', 76–81.

[89] See Samuel L. Macey, *Money and the Novel: Mercenary Motivation in Defoe and His Immediate Successors* (Victoria, B.C.: Sono Nis Press, 1983), 42.

[90] 'The World has a very unhappy Notion of Honesty', Defoe wrote elsewhere: 'God's blessing may have made a rich Man—But why is he an honest Man, a fair Dealer, a punctual Merchant? The Answer is plain, Because he is a rich Man ... He has no Temptation, no wretched Necessity of Shifting and Tricking, which another Man flies to, to deliver himself from Ruin—The Man is not Rich, because he is Honest, but he is Honest because he is Rich' (*Review*, viii. 351 [15 September 1711]).

[91] Defoe, *Colonel Jack*, ed. Gabriel Cervantes and Geoffrey Sill (Peterborough, Ontario: Broadview, 2016), 72.

I was full of Care, for what to do to secure my Money I could not tell, and this held me so long, and was so Vexatious to me the next Day, that I truly sat down and cryed' (80). He becomes paranoid, cannot sleep, and wishes it away, though he despairs when he thinks he has lost it, wrapped in a linen rag, in a hollow tree, so when it is recovered Jack 'snatch'd it up, hug'd and kiss'd the dirty Ragg a hundred Times' (82). Jack's paltry money replaces loving relationships and intensifies his feelings of privation and vulnerability. He progresses to personal credit when given a bill of exchange as a reward, being the kind of criminal who does not love money for its own sake and is inclined to make restitution for his thefts, both to an indigent nurse (to whom he returns what he stole) and a well-to-do banker (who gets back what Jack cannot launder). When Jack is trepanned into indentured servitude in the Americas, his bill, the value of which has grown to £94 owing to his assiduous thievery, represents far more than the sum itself. It 'serves as the authenticating sign of his worth', its symbolic meaning more significant than its monetary value.[92] Just as being a street urchin with money would condemn him ('my Money would be my Crime' [80]), being the kind of man who has a bill of exchange, its value cleansed of its criminal origins, on a reputable citizen saves him. Though the 'bit of Paper' cannot instantly procure Jack's freedom in Virginia (163), it can go one better and pave a route to advancement from indentured servant to overseer and in time plantation owner. Even when financially secure, Jack is never quite able to rest content, as he fits in a 'Ramble of four and Twenty Years' (288), including touring Europe as a soldier, flirting with Jacobitism, a succession of marriages, and eventually engaging in an illegal trade with Spanish Americans that he acknowledges is 'contrary to all moderate Measures' (328). Nonetheless, a tidied-up finale sees him back in London with a steady income from his plantation, endowed by his wealth with 'Leisure to Repent' and 'to look back upon an ill-spent Life, bless'd with infinite Advantage' (340, 338). In *Moll* and *Jack*, Defoe produced comedies of the new economics of his era; in *The Fortunate Mistress*, he produced a tragedy.

Roxana progresses from financial victim to predator, from a woman starving alongside her five children to a woman who apparently connives in the killing of one of them to prevent the exposure of how her vast wealth was made. As a girl who 'wanted neither Wit, Beauty, or Money', Roxana is married off by her father with a generous dowry; her merchant brother then loses her independent wealth, her improvident husband mismanages the business such that 'the Money decreas'd apace', and she is incapacitated by her education from taking affairs in hand herself (*Novels*, ix. 24, 27). Left destitute, and incapable of supporting her family because hers is 'not a Town where much Work was to be had' (38), she benefits from models of selfless charity that never quite leave her, including a brother-in-law by marriage who views adopting his wife's nephews and nieces as lending to the Lord (36), and Roxana's maid Amy, who 'as long as she had any Money, when I had none, ... would help me out of her own' (32). After illicit

---

[92] See James Thompson, *Models of Value: Eighteenth-Century Political Economy and the Novel* (Durham, N.C.: Duke University Press, 1996), 109.

relationships with her landlord (a jeweller) and a German prince in France, she finds herself in possession of 'Money and Jewels, to a vast Value' (107), a remarkable transformation of her fortunes, but it is not until 'I had Paper ... for my Money' that Roxana is truly 'at Liberty to go to any Part of the World, and take Care of my Money myself' (111, 103). 'Now I was become, from a Lady of Pleasure, a Woman of Business, and of great Business too, I assure you', she says (117).

Roxana's treasure, her jewels and gold, is enticingly tactile and erotically charged, but it is also physically cumbersome and potentially incriminating. She must progress to the laundered and liquid assets of paper-based instruments of exchange, and that necessitates a new kind of financial literacy that adumbrates, or even allegorizes, the transformation of the English economy in Defoe's lifetime. With a stable money market and credit economy prevailing in Britain, wealth was self-reproducing to an unprecedented extent. Roxana seizes the opportunities therein, and Defoe grapples with the concomitant ethical problems. 'My Money being my great Concern at that time, I found it a Difficulty how to dispose of it, so as to bring me in an annual Interest', Roxana admits, so she enlists the aid of 'Sir *Robert* [Clayton], a Man thorowly vers'd in Arts of improving Money', who ensures that her wealth accrues from itself (142, 146). The entrepreneurial ideal clashes with traditional gender values, because Roxana would rather, in a sense, become a thriving trader than marry one. Marriage is anathema to Roxana, whose experience has been that a wife is 'upbraided with her very *Pin-Money*'—that is, denied for the most part any independent wealth—and even when an honourable offer comes her way, 'I construed it quite another Way, namely, that he aim'd at the Money' (118, 127). Despite knowing what she should do, and upbraiding herself for greed, Roxana cannot assuage her enterprising instincts: 'I aim'd at being a kept Mistress, and to have a handsome Maintenance; and that I was still for getting Money, *and laying it up too*' (147). She becomes so fantastically wealthy that 'the common Vice of all Whores, I mean Money, was out of the Question, nay, even Avarice itself seem'd to be glutted' (156), yet she promptly reveals her capacity for self-deceit on this last point: 'As Necessity first debauch'd me, and Poverty made me a Whore at the Beginning; so excess of Avarice for getting Money, and excess of Vanity, continued me in the Crime' (171). The sophistication of this novel is that Roxana's censure of her own industry and frugality (sex-work, thriftiness, and usury), which service her vanity and greed, could be the real meaning, making this a moral fable; or her moralism could be residual Puritan rhetoric that the novel invites us to disregard, recognizing in the heroine a model entrepreneur who, particularly as a woman denied much economic autonomy, capitalizes upon her only real asset, her enduring beauty, to succeed beyond her wildest dreams.[93] Defoe is an important figure in the economic history of the early eighteenth century not because he was the spokesman of a particular economic interest—the rising middle class—but

---

[93] See Bram Dijkstra, *Defoe and Economics: The Fortunes of 'Roxana' in the History of Interpretation* (Basingstoke: Macmillan Press, 1987); Helen Burke, '*Roxana*, Corruption, and the Progressive Myth', *Genre*, 23 (1990), 103–20.

because across his oeuvre he sought at once to understand, explicate, and interrogate the economic change through which he and his contemporaries lived.

Further Reading

John Brewer, *Sinews of Power: War, Money, and the English State, 1688-1783* (Cambridge, MA: Harvard University Press, 1990).
P. G. M. Dickson, *The Financial Revolution in England: A Study in the Development of Public Credit, 1688-1756* (London: Macmillan, 1967).
Bram Dijkstra, *Defoe and Economics: The Fortunes of 'Roxana' in the History of Interpretation* (Basingstoke: Macmillan Press, 1987).
Peter Earle, *The World of Defoe* (London: Weidenfeld and Nicolson, 1976).
Edgar Illingworth, 'The Economic Ideas of Daniel Defoe' (doctoral thesis, University of Leeds, 1974).
John McVeagh, *Tradefull Merchants: The Portrayal of the Capitalist in Literature* (London: Routledge and Kegan Paul, 1981).
Thomas Keith Meier, *Defoe and the Defense of Commerce* (Victoria, B.C.: University of Victoria Press, 1987).
Maximillian E. Novak, *Economics and the Fiction of Daniel Defoe* (Los Angeles, CA: University of California Press, 1962).
David Ormrod, *The Rise of Commercial Empires: England and the Netherlands in the Age of Mercantilism, 1650-1770* (Cambridge: Cambridge University Press, 2003).
J. G. A Pocock, *The Machiavellian Moment: Florentine Political Thought and the Atlantic Republican Tradition* (Princeton, N.J.: Princeton University Press, 1975).
Natalie Roxburgh, *Representing Public Credit: Credible Commitment, Fiction, and the Rise of the Financial Subject* (London: Routledge, 2016).
Sandra Sherman, *Finance and Fictionality in the Early Eighteenth Century: Accounting for Defoe* (Cambridge: Cambridge University Press, 1996).
James Thompson, *Models of Value: Eighteenth-Century Political Economy and the Novel* (Durham, N.C.: Duke University Press, 1996).
David Trotter, *Circulation: Defoe, Dickens, and the Economies of the Novel* (Basingstoke: Macmillan, 1988).

CHAPTER 15

GENDER, SEXUALITY, AND THE STATUS OF WOMEN IN DEFOE'S WRITINGS

PAULA R. BACKSCHEIDER

MOLL FLANDERS was uncomfortable disguised as a man and Roxana unself-consciously danced for a mimic Charles II-style gathering in a revealing harem outfit. These images from Defoe's two great novels about women tell us a lot about his attitudes towards women's gender and status. His other novels include one of the first portrayals of a woman addicted to alcohol and representations of women in dozens of countries in Asia, Europe, and Africa. Defoe had a lot of experience with women and a lot of opinions about them. He may have been apprenticed to a woman, and his first experience with the law was in making bail for Jane Foe and Mary Deering after their arrest at a conventicle. His first historical writing was for a woman, his wife-to-be Mary Tuffley.

He always thought he could give everyone in the world good advice, and in his first outpouring of such tracts, *An Essay upon Projects* (1697), he included two forward-looking ones for women's benefit. One was a detailed plan for insurance for widows, and the other was the better-known educational academy for women. He identified his late publications as 'a Testimony of my good Will to my Fellow Creatures'—not the more common 'fellowmen', but 'Fellow Creatures'.[1] Women are given multidimensional consideration in most of his writings throughout his life. The titles of his numerous late publications beginning in 1722 testify to the range and depth of his thinking about them.

Defoe was the subject of three publicly active queens. He made enough of a figure in a Lord Mayor's Day procession to honour Queen Mary and King William to be mentioned as one of the 'gallantly mounted and richly accoutred' members of a Royal Regiment of

---

[1] Defoe, *Augusta Triumphans* (1728), *PEW*, viii. 259. I am grateful to my Research Assistant, Katharine Brown, for her work on this essay.

Volunteer Horses, made up of 'chief Citizens'.[2] The regiment was commanded by one of the Council of Nine appointed to advise Queen Mary when William was abroad. Queen Anne was always on his mind. She interviewed him at Windsor about *The Shortest-Way with the Dissenters* (1702) before he was pilloried,[3] signed his pardon for it in July 1704, and pardoned him again in December 1713 for publishing pamphlets including *And What If the Pretender Should Come?*[4] In 1728 in *Augusta Triumphans*, he asked Queen Caroline to take up the cause of women sent to private madhouses, a cause he identified as for her sex: 'August Queen *Caroline!* ... Begin this Auspicious Reign with an Action worthy your illustrious Self, rescue your injur'd Sex' (*PEW*, viii. 275).

Increasing information about working women has been published in the last twenty-five years, and they were all around Defoe. His wife was significantly involved in his public and business life, and his writings frequently depict managerial women. A major collaborator in Scotland was a woman, the powerful printer to the crown, Agnes Campbell Anderson. One of his last major business investments included a mortgage financed by a woman, and he took his second daughter, Hannah, to Colchester to cosign a lease in 1722. He had invested well in the South Sea stock for her and his other daughters, and in that year her dividend had been an impressive £706.13.4.[5] The last disastrous legal action against him was initiated by two women, and one of them pursued him through Chancery and Exchequer beyond the grave.

Defoe lived a very long life, and the status of women was very different when he compiled *Historical Collections* (1682) to when he wrote the late works like *The Complete English Tradesman* (vol. I, 1725; Supplement, 1726; vol. II, 1727).[6] He wrote about women in novels, poetry, periodicals, histories, conduct and practical divinity books, and economic, crime, and social reform non-fiction. Each of these genres had conventions, histories, and somewhat discrete audiences, and Defoe knew that. The disciplines of literary history and criticism have changed substantially in the last thirty years. Decades of cultural studies and its saturation in the methodologies of anthropology render books like Shirlene Mason's *Daniel Defoe and the Status of Women* (1978) period pieces whose gaps and absences demand refinement and extension, and the decades of feminist criticism and women's studies have done the same with the topics of gender and sexuality, as one of my own first publications shows.[7]

---

[2] John Oldmixon, *History of England* (1735), 37. And for elaboration, see Backscheider, *Daniel Defoe*, 46–7. Unless otherwise noted, biographical information is from Backscheider, *Daniel Defoe*. I have added some information.

[3] The fullest account of this meeting is in Backscheider, 'No Defense: Defoe in 1703', *PMLA*, 103:3 (1988), 274–84, esp. 280–2, and see *Daniel Defoe*, 116–17.

[4] Defoe knew what a pardon should be like, and he checked Anne's carefully; he had been pardoned for his part in Monmouth's Rebellion on 31 May 1687. For some reason he seems not to have been covered by the King's General Pardon on 10 March 1686, or felt he was not safe.

[5] Backscheider, *Daniel Defoe*, 468.

[6] Stephen H. Gregg notes the debates and changing images of masculinity. *Defoe's Writings and Manliness: Contrary Men* (Aldershot: Ashgate, 2009), 12–13, 66, n. 19.

[7] Shirlene Mason, *Daniel Defoe and the Status of Women* (St. Alban's, VT: Eden Press, 1978); Paula Backscheider, 'Defoe's Women: Snares and Prey', *Studies in Eighteenth-Century Culture*, 5 (1976), 103–19.

My essay keeps Defoe's assignments of status firmly in mind, and I work with hierarchies, status markers, and status words [SEE CHAPTER 13]. The *OED* defines status as 'Position or standing in society, a profession, and the like'. 'And the like' adds a rather light-hearted phrase to the sober *OED*, but it captures the capacious nature of 'status'. More pertinent to Defoe is the definition for 'status' labelled 'Law': 'The legal standing or position of a person as determined by his membership of some class of persons legally enjoying certain rights or subject to certain limitations; condition in respect, e.g., of liberty or servitude, marriage or celibacy, infancy or majority'. This definition reminds us of the determining power of institutions—legal, religious, medical. Yet status is ordinarily conferred by a society that assigns material markers, such as location and dress, but it is also generated and assigned in relation to education, intelligence, temperament, problem-solving skills, wealth, gendered conduct, and behaviour (including lifestyle and sexual behaviour). As Thomas Hobbes wrote, 'For let a man (as most men do,) rate themselves at the highest Value they can; yet their true Value is no more than it is esteemed by others'. Defoe knew all of this, and his writing resonates to them and is corroborated by historians attempting to define status categories in this period with methods such as reconstructing 'the language of sorts'.[8]

In fact, one of his two earliest surviving compositions, *Historical Collections*, brings status into dramatic confluence and reveals Defoe's life-long conception of the sex. He begins one of the anecdotes about women by highlighting the importance of status: 'Canna wife to Synattus was Passionately loved by Synoris *of greater Quallity & Authority than Synattus*, who Attempted All ways and means to Attaine his desires, but in vaine' (emphasis mine). Frustrated, Synoris murders Synattus, and 'Renewed his suit to her'. Canna finally pretends to consent, and they go to the Temple of Diana to celebrate the marriage. She brings a secret potion, 'very Delightfull & pleasing to ye pallate; wch she Dranke to Synoris, and so poisoned him & her self too'.[9] Canna is a fascinating figure. Her faithfulness to her husband before and after his death is exemplary. But then, there is the dual-Defoe conception of the nature and capacity of women. She is the instrument of revenge, actualizes 'a life for a life', and is a murderer and a suicide, both acts of courage and neither virtuous nor feminine. Redolent, of course, with the stories of Bathsheba and Lucrece, Defoe's telling inscribes both women's vulnerability and women's frightening willingness to extract revenge and commit the most serious crimes. Volume I of *The Complete English Tradesman* has a long story of a woman's ruinous revenge on a tradesman who left her for a woman with a superior fortune (*RDW*, vii. 161–5), and Roxana's story is one of defying and then falling victim to the patriarchy.

I have divided this essay by topics that prioritize essential determinants of status in Defoe's work beginning with some of his most prominent status markers. Then I will explore sexuality and marriage, working women, and the imbrication of gender, status, and agency, another of Defoe's life-long preoccupations.

---

[8] Quoted in Alexandra Shepard, *Accounting for Oneself: Worth, Status, and the Social Order in Early Modern England* (Oxford: Oxford University Press, 2015), 1, 4–6.

[9] Defoe, *Historical Collections*, William Andrews Clark Memorial Library MS 1951.009, ff. 84–5.

Status Markers

Defoe's thinking about status and the attainment of it is of two kinds. One was status earned and maintained by hard work and some luck, but he also explored how it could be put on and then performed. His non-fiction spins out long stories of tradesmen who do everything right, patiently develop their businesses and their reputation, and become respected men in the community. In one example, all the status markers appear. 'If the Tradesman is risen from nothing to be an Alderman', Defoe begins. Then he mentions place, clothing, and signs of his elected office: 'the very Station of Life he fills up in the Place where he lives, declares it: His Fur-Gown and Gold Chain ... might be sufficient to tell the World he is rich' (*The Complete English Tradesman, Volume II, RDW*, viii. 116). Prosperity, sober dress, civic mindedness, and gender conformity confirm a comfortable, admirable status.

Moll becomes a rich, successful plantation owner in a happy marriage; Roxana becomes fabulously wealthy and even gains a title purchased by her Dutch husband. Here the fiction and the non-fiction diverge. Defoe's fictional characters have souls; their religion and the part religion plays both in identity and judgement are woven in.[10] Competence is another status marker for him. Criminal and sinful as it is, Defoe clearly relishes creating Jack's and Moll's extraordinary skill at petty thievery and the admiration of their peers. In the non-fiction, the reader's view is on the material and the external.

He understood that some held being in trade to be of lower status than other professions and wrote about women's pretentious efforts to obscure that position. Dressing and behaving like a gentlewoman (being a 'gay, delicate Lady') and stubbornly remaining ignorant of business details can turn ugly. In his tale, such a woman has to let an apprentice take over the business and then lets him 'creep to bed to her', even though she is 'old enough to be his mother'. She ends up marrying the apprentice and being abused by him. Defoe pursues this story relentlessly, as he emphasizes that this action cheats her children who should have inherited a thriving business (*The Complete English Tradesman, Volume I, RDW*, vii. 221–3). The consequences of her performance of femininity and ignorance of business are the loss of status for her sons and the total loss of it for herself.

Defoe's notices of status markers are highly visual and often performative. A couple in *The Family Instructor* (1715) goes to church to show and see fine clothes, and the child remarks on how his family 'take up the whole Night' afterwards talking about it (*RDW*, i. 32–3). In a catalogue of ways 'goods' counterfeit status he lists 'false gloss, a finer and

---

[10] After a hiatus in attention to religion, Defoe critics are again admitting its importance and publishing high-quality work. See Barbara M. Benedict's detailed paralleling of Roxana and Amy with attention to religious subtexts. 'The Sentimental Servant: The Danger of Dependence in Defoe's *Roxana*', in *Reflections on Sentiment: Essays in Honor of George Starr*, ed. Alessa Johns (Newark, DE: University of Delaware Press, 2016), 85–104, esp. 97–9.

smoother surface' and refers to whores who use make-up to turn 'tawny skin' pale (*The Complete English Tradesman, Volume I, RDW*, vii. 196). Moll Flanders is demoted to sleeping with one of the maids instead of with the oldest sister. These markers are everywhere, and some are likely forgotten. Entries totalling 5*s*. 6*d*. in a tradesman's 'Petty Cash-Book' include drink for the coachman and servants of the Duchess of --- while they waited and for a coach hire for a Lady's maid who 'came for Goods'. Not only are these necessary business, but they are signs of the tradesman's polish and classiness. Other such entries included pay for a woman that helped ladies out of coaches and escorted them into the shop and wine for women who were 'frighted' on the street. Fine holland shirts, white gloves, long perukes, and flashes of bright colours on coats and cloaks are purchased in many of his texts as individuals attempt to maintain or raise their status. Women bought them for men, as their appearance helped telegraph the woman's status. Moll Flanders takes 'especial care' to buy her last husband a 'handsome' scarlet cloak, silver hilted swords, fine fowling pieces, and even two long wigs, which must have attracted notice in their rural Maryland community. She declares that 'no Man in the World could deserve better of a Wife' and enjoys adorning him.[11]

Defoe had an eye for fashion. In *A General History of Discoveries and Improvements* (1725–6), part of his case for the achievements and importance of Carthage was that they 'dress'd well, and valued themselves upon it' (*TDH*, iv. 88). He took a special interest in what women wore on their heads, and his observations are as commercial as they are socially judgemental. He noted, for instance, the multiplication of shops specializing in commodes, the fashionable tall head pieces with a wire frame covered with silk or lace. In spite of frequent acknowledgement that spinning wool was the major opportunity for women and a secure and remunerative occupation, he gives more attention to head coverings. In a section of *The Complete English Tradesman, Volume II* that he styles as 'the Face of Trade in the City', he identifies 'two great Centers of the Women Merchants'. In the past, clustered in the Exchange Shops at the Royal Exchange and the New Exchange in the Strand were many millenary shops. Now, he says, the New Exchange has turned into 'a Looking-Glass Warehouse', and the millenary shops, head dressers, and commode shops are now scattered over the city (*RDW*, viii. 232–3). What women wore on their heads seemed particularly useful in signalling status. When Moll wants to find out about the health of a man with whom she had lived for six years, she puts on a round cap and straw hat as part of a disguise as a servant and gossips with one of his maids (97).

In fact, Defoe had considerable anxiety about the fluidity of dress and, therefore, status that women could assume. As evident as it is in the novels, especially *Roxana*, it became obsessive regarding servants. In *The Great Law of Subordination Consider'd* (1724), he complains that women servants dress with 'gaiety', spend their money on 'fine Cloaths, Laces, Hoops, &c.', and 'it is sometimes hard to know the Chamber-Maid from her Mistress', as they often have finer lace and silks than the mistresses (*RDW*, vi. 49; cf.

---

[11] Defoe, *Moll Flanders*, ed. Albert J. Rivero (New York: Norton, 2004), 265, 254.

81).¹² He asks repeatedly why women servants cannot be required to be 'distinguish'd by their Dress' (*Every-Body's Business, is No-Body's Business* [1725], *PEW*, viii. 220, 226). Kristina Booker identifies the fear of emulation as 'linked to anxieties about the social order and its signifiers', and this is certainly true of Defoe.¹³ Moll dresses carefully for her thefts, and just how dangerous that could make her hovers over an incident like the mirage of a skull. 'I was very well dress'd, and had my gold Watch', she says smugly as she aims at 'Sir *Thomas* ----'s eldest Daughter of *Essex*', whom she robs of a gold watch. Having learned what she needs to know from her footman, she says she put herself 'in a Rank with this young Lady', accompanies her to watch the king pass, and even lifts the child up to see him. This scene brings to mind the dreadful, arresting moment when Moll leads a child into a dark alley and has an impulse to kill her. She steals a necklace worth £12–14 from around the child's neck. The proximity to the child's throat and the location, the alley that leads into Bartholomew Close, one of the oldest parts of London with the narrowest, winding streets, add to the evil potential of the encounter.¹⁴ These necklaces, these material objects, raised the statuses of the children and the thief.

SEXUALITY AND MARRIAGE

Marriage was the most important determinant of a woman's status [SEE CHAPTER 16]. Although a wife could affect a husband's rank, it was she who moved into his social class. A wife's status was both public and private. Defoe frequently depicted the first and endlessly lectured about the second. Marriages were affective and business relationships, and a bad wife, especially a spendthrift, ruined a man and dropped his reputation. An unsatisfying companionate and sexual relationship could drive a man out of his home and even into the arms of a 'whore'. Again, the status of both husband and wife would plummet. Defoe's explanation of a husband's responsibilities extended to details. In spite of his muttering about how expensive maids were, he labelled them 'necessary as the bread he eats', especially if he multiplies apace, as Defoe had with his six living children (*The Complete English Tradesman, Volume I*, *RDW*, vii. 110, 120). He also insists that a man cannot expect a wife to 'be his bedfellow and his cook too'. He notes that wages have risen from £3–4 per year to as high as £8, because maids work less: where two sufficed, now five are often required, and he includes nurses and classifies kinds of maids. And he noted sex does take time, leisure, and good feeling. In addition to detailed descriptions and advice on managing a business, he wrote similarly about household management. In the first volume of *The Complete English Tradesman*, he tallied up the expenses of a

---

¹² See the embarrassing mistake of 'saluting' a chambermaid with the other ladies (185).
¹³ Kristina Booker, *Menials: Domestic Service and Cultural Transformation of British Society 1650–1850* (Lewisburg, PA: Bucknell University Press, 2018), 97–9, 105.
¹⁴ Defoe, *Moll Flanders*, 202–3, 153–4.

respectable tradesman and noted that most had two maid-servants, and they were an increasingly expensive 'tax' on them.

There is no doubt that Defoe carried an image of what a loving, respectful, supportive wife was, and his conception of a complete wife is multidimensional. One of his most succinct summaries is Crusoe's description of his dead wife in *The Farther Adventures of Robinson Crusoe* (1719):

> She was, in a few words, the stay of all my affairs, the centre of all my enterprises, the engine that, by her prudence, reduced me to that happy compass I was in, ... and did more to guide my rambling genius than a mother's tears, a father's instructions, a friend's counsel, or my own reasoning powers could do. I was happy in listening to her tears, and in being moved by her entreaties, and to the last degree desolate and dislocated in the world by the loss of her.

Like the exemplary wives throughout his work, she is a household manager and a partner in businesses and decisions. His final sentences extend to the affective aspects of marriage. She also gave him perspective on the larger world and life itself: 'I saw the world busy round me, one part labouring for bread, and the other part squandering in vile excesses ... as if daily bread were the only end of wearisome life, and a wearisome life the only occasion of daily bread'.[15] From the beginning, Defoe described his own wife as 'excellent' and virtuous, shared sophisticated political anecdotes with her, and wrote to and about her frequently with love and respect. He sent her, not one of his male friends or his lawyer, to discuss terms under which Defoe would surrender for publishing *The Shortest-Way with the Dissenters*. Later when he travelled for work, she was his 'faithful Steward' and managed the family well when he was irregularly paid.[16]

Religious Courtship (1722) establishes the importance of compatibility. As George Starr has written, 'much of the book chronicles the ways people can make one another miserable' (*RDW*, iv. 2). Bickering over servants, expenditures, and leisure time descends into dramatizations of discourses of abuse, ridicule, and torment. The most intense misery comes from different philosophies of child-rearing and especially religious differences. The youngest daughter, whom Starr describes as heroic, and one who discovers herself married to a 'Papist' are the most extreme examples. Alison Conway demonstrates that in *The Family Instructor* and *Religious Courtship* Defoe uses reflections on religious differences to explain some of the difficulties in family life.[17] Characters are worn down by harassment and insult, as is the wife who frequently finds an obscene ballad tucked in her Bible and the wife who is harangued about economy even as her husband keeps

---

[15] Defoe, *Farther Adventures of Robinson Crusoe*, in *The Works of Daniel Defoe*, ed. G. H. Maynadier, 16 vols (New York: Thomas Y. Crowell and Company, 1903), ii. 6–7.

[16] On Mary's management, see Backscheider, *Daniel Defoe*, 181, 201.

[17] These 'differences' are, of course, the most common in his time, Catholic-Protestant and Church of England-Nonconformist. Alison Conway, '"Unequally Yoked": Defoe and the Challenge of Mixed Marriage', in *Reflections on Sentiment*, ed. Johns, 11–28.

two horses and 'sits long at the *Fleece* every evening' (*The Complete English Tradesman, Volume I, RDW*, vii. 128).

The need is for a dual management of economic spaces and affective compatibility. In Volume I of *The Complete English Tradesman*, Defoe tells this story of a shopkeeper who needed to economize, and he argues that if his wife had 'any sense' she would assist him (*RDW*, vii. 121). Both husband and wife are responsible for the conduct and image that give desirable status. Defoe carefully dissects household expenses that he assigns to the wife's domain and recognizes their link to the family's status and also the error in the husband not communicating clearly their means. He admits that the husband is often the 'prompter' (112) of the wife's spending on dress and household expenses, and the correct amount of display and expense to be 'seen in good company' are mutual responsibilities (113). In an image reminiscent of Adam and Eve 'thus going hand in hand, she and he together' would bring their situation under control and their marriage into happy harmony (122).

Defoe believed wives should be useful, and one of his fullest illustrations of the arguments in his non-fiction is in *Colonel Jack*. It is sometimes said that Defoe invented the discourse of marital bickering, and the cross-examinations, harangues, and frustrations in the conduct book dialogues are of a piece with the miserable marriages in *Roxana* and especially *Colonel Jack*. The parade of wives in *Colonel Jack* begins with Jack's naïve attempts to marry as part of his climb to the status of 'gentleman'. Status is paramount. He classifies them coldly as two gentlewomen, a citizen, and a country wench.[18] His manhood is deeply interlocked with their status and behaviour. As Karen Downing notes, 'Marriage and family had long been integral to notions of successful male adulthood: heading a household and providing for its material needs "were the nub of independence"'.[19] After Jack's miserable failures in his marriage to an unfaithful spendthrift with whom he 'rallies' for hours, 'a clog', and a drunkard, he decides that his wisest choice would be to marry an upper Servant, 'a Nurse to my Children, and a House-keeper to my self', and he would not care whether she were a whore or not.[20] Moggy suits the job description in good and ironic ways. He finds out that she had 'slipped' and borne a child 'by a Gentleman of a great Estate ... who promised her Marriage', but she performs her job with Jack admirably, and they have children.

At this point, Jack seems to accept sexually active, disorderly women, and Defoe's rhetoric is thought-provoking in its strong similarity to what he often writes: 'Give me not poverty, lest I—'. Thus, he marries two such women, Moggy and, years later, his first wife, whom he divorced for adultery and profligate spending, when she turns up a transported criminal on his plantation. When he promotes her from a field hand to housekeeper, she proves to be an excellent manager who quickly gets everything in

---

[18] Defoe, *Colonel Jack*, ed. Gabriel Cervantes and Geoffrey Sill (Peterborough, ON: Broadview Press, 2016), 283.
[19] On Jack's masculinity, see Gregg's fine *Defoe's Writings and Manliness,* esp. Ch. 6; Karen Downing, *Restless Men: Masculinity and Robinson Crusoe, 1788–1840* (New York: Palgrave Macmillan, 2014), 151.
[20] Defoe, *Colonel Jack*, 234, 261, 278–9, 282.

order. She effects his disguised escape from being discovered as a Jacobite, helps him move cargo, and secures a pardon for him. She becomes his major agent when he is captured in Cuba; he writes to her, and she sends a shipload of easily traded, highly profitable goods for sale in Mexico and the Caribbean. She is Defoe's two-dimensional woman: bedfellow and partner. Jack says of the wife he has rediscovered on his plantation that after her 'fallen Flesh plump'd up', he 'sometimes' 'could not help having warm Desires towards her' and 'taking her into her first Station again' (295). Here and in his conduct and sociology writings, marriage is a 'station', a status for women, but one they must deserve and maintain. Jack learns that to be fully satisfied and happy, 'a settled family Life was the thing I Lov'd' (273), and that came only from intimate happiness and public sphere effectiveness.

What is especially interesting—and telling—at the time Defoe was at the peak of writing about women and sex acts, Eliza Haywood was finding ways to express that women enjoyed sex, some a lot and some too much. Defoe's women seem to lack anticipation and pleasure. Nowhere do we find Defoe's characters in fiction or non-fiction being described as Althea is in Haywood's *The Mercenary Lover* (1726). Althea recalls 'ruinous Delights' and her eyes telegraph 'ten thousand nameless Languishments, the Badges of Desire'.[21] The exception is Jemy, who comes back briefly after leaving Moll and 'almost stopped her breath with kisses'. She says they shared 'Extasies', but when he leaves her again, she quickly goes to London and begins to cultivate a new relationship (122–9). In one of her longest liaisons, Moll is described as yielding to 'mutual Inclinations' the first time she and the Bath gentleman have sex; quickly, however, she says, 'I resolv'd to let him lye with me, if he offer'd it; but it was because I wanted his help' (96).

With Jemy, sex finally becomes legitimate and one of Defoe's clear representations of sex as an essential, critical part of happiness in marriage. Moll believes the older brother in Colchester will marry her, but the relationship leads to 'whoredom' when she marries the younger, as she 'never was in Bed with my Husband, but I wish'd my self in the Arms of his Brother' (49). Sex becomes a commodity for Moll and her trade, as Defoe uses the word 'trade'. Defoe's world is full of women who have learned this trade, and seducing, carefully made-up women loaded with promises like Jack's first wife are found in almost every genre in his repertory. Desire and need for work continue to converge. He sometimes treats sexual behaviour and promiscuity as an addiction, and he endlessly warns men that women become 'the sex' and are dangerous snares for men and threats not only to their economic well-being, but even to financial structures.

Defoe's writings about marriage show strong evidence of his awareness of audience and his apprehension of societal change and the effect on status as well as happiness. In *Religious Courtship: Being Historical Discourses, on the Necessity of Marrying Religious Husbands and Wives Only*, he joined many people in the opinion that the nation was becoming increasingly and destructively secular, and his title accurately identifies his

---

[21] Eliza Haywood, *The Mercenary Lover: or, the Unfortunate Heiresses*, in *Selected Fiction and Drama of Eliza Haywood*, ed. Paula R. Backscheider (New York: Oxford University Press, 1999), 121–62 (152, 154).

opinion. In *The Family Instructor* and *A New Family Instructor* (1727), more emphasis is given to the negative results when sex and marriage are heavily contractual and in varying degrees mirror how trades are carried out. *Conjugal Lewdness* (1727) insists that loveless marriages are a form of prostitution and 'whoredom', and the now-initiated Moll sees that marriages are 'The Consequences of politick Schemes, for forming interests, ... And LOVE had no Share, or but very little in the Matter' (67).

As Liz Bellamy argues in her introduction, *Conjugal Lewdness* was published when there was 'increased awareness of, and anxiety about, erotic activity' as well as the 'propagation' of pornography ('Introduction', *RDW*, v. 1–21 [5], esp. 4–6). While Defoe's practical divinity books were largely about establishing good marriages and family relations and practices, *Conjugal Lewdness* was about sexual practices mostly within ongoing marriages. Detached from the blessing God made it at the creation and the religious emphasis on procreation, sex is also increasingly separated from companionate affection. 'Lasciviousness', an 'interest' motivating marriage, is the danger in this book. The word has an exaggerated phantasmagoric cast, as when he imagines 'our Lasciviousness, Sensuality, and ... all these our Distempers' as the cause of the rise in the number and wealth of doctors, surgeons, and even apothecaries (256). He is also aware of what Robert Merrett aptly identifies in Defoe's criticism of the current time, 'the secularization of sexuality'.[22]

In his fiction and this series of writings about marriage, Defoe seems to be writing for what he apprehends as his own socioeconomic-religious cohort. His worst examples of behaviour and disrespect for religion are landowning gentlemen and the prosperous London middle class. At its best, marriage is a symbiotic union between equals, between helpmeets who were friends, genuinely love each other, have sex, and want carefully nurtured children. He frequently calls husband and wife 'yoke-fellows' (*PEW*, viii. 271). 'Symbiotic' is a more precise term than 'equal', as gendered divisions of labour and location predominate, yet his exemplary couples are flexible and take on different tasks, as when the wife extends household management into partial or even full management of the business. *Conjugal Lewdness* is the fullest explication of compatibility, but the vision is consistent in his work. The younger daughter in *Religious Courtship* finally has a happy marriage with a husband who is 'suitable in Temper, Desires, Delights ... exemplar [sic] in Piety and Virtue' (*RDW*, iv. 149). He repeats this summary in nearly the same words in *Conjugal Lewdness*: 'The great Duty between the Man and his Wife, I take to consist in that of Love, in the Government of Affection, and the Obedience of a complaisant, kind, obliging Temper; the Obligation is reciprocal, 'tis drawing in an equal Yoke ... no imperious Command on one hand, no reluctant Subjection on the other'. He continues with references to mutual endeavours and, throughout, he describes the contrast between the peace of such a home and the 'bedlam' that comes of wrangling and contention of 'two *Devils* together in one House' (*RDW*, v. 43, 53, 94–5). To have such a marriage assures a well-governed family, and this achievement confers admirable status.

---

[22] Robert James Merrett, *Daniel Defoe: Contrarian* (Toronto: University of Toronto Press, 2013), 230.

Working Women

When asked how she will become a gentlewoman, Moll says she can earn three pence by spinning worsted, 'the chief Trade of that City'. A little later, she hears, 'if a young Woman have Beauty, Birth, Breeding, Wit, Sense, Manners, Modesty, and all these to an Extream; yet, if she have not Money, she's no Body' (12, 20). After marriage, money, the means to support oneself, garnered status. Not only does Defoe take this for granted, but some of his most detailed writing considers the imbrication of work and the status of a woman based on both society's opinions and personal attributes and accomplishments. A distinguished historian casually writes, 'In late seventeenth- and early eighteenth-century London, as we now know, most women, whether married, single or widowed, worked at least part of the time for wages or other remuneration, and they engaged in a wide range of types of work'. She reports that between 1680 and 1720, 84% of widows and spinsters performed paid work, and 60% of London married women also worked.[23] While poverty usually pushes Defoe's characters into crime or selling their bodies in marriages or back rooms, Defoe was living in what Peter Earle has called 'a city full of people'—working people. In other words, Defoe was surrounded by working women.

Spinning, the skill Moll was taught, was indeed a major occupation for women, perhaps employing over a million women and children by the mid-eighteenth century. It was a highly skilled occupation, and skilled women could earn as much as 3s. per week or even £11.4s. in a year. By the end of his life, the best could earn 9s. per week instead of the top amount of 12d. as maid-servants.[24] Economic historians have demonstrated that in Defoe's time, 35% of a family's income came from 'outwork' at home such as throwing silk (preparing raw silk for manufacture) and spinning wool, hemp, linen, silk, and other fabrics. As early as 1704 Defoe credited another queen, Elizabeth I, with bringing weaving and spinning wool to England, which provided new, profitable employments for women.[25] He saw queens as having a special interest in or at least duty to their women subjects. He wrote extensively about Queen Elizabeth I, and he gendered her actions and burnished their reception. In the first image of her in *Giving Alms No Charity* (1704), she is exercising 'goodness and forebearance' and wise, compassionate care for her people and for the Flemish citizens fleeing persecution. She 'cherish'd' and 'encourag'd' them, both actions often attributed to women's reactions to unfortunate people (*PEW*, viii.

---

[23] Margaret Hunt, 'Women and Money: Credit, Debt, and Status in the Eighteenth-Century London Court of Exchequer', in *Women and Credit in Pre-Industrial Europe*, ed. Elise M. Dermineur (Turnhout, Belgium: Brepols Publishers, 2018), 281–300 (282, 283 n.3). Cf. Jennine Hurl-Eamon, 'The Fiction of Female Dependence and the Makeshift Economy of Soldiers, Sailors, and their Wives in Eighteenth-Century London', *Labor History*, 49:4 (2008), 481–501.

[24] Defoe, *Great Law*, RDW, vi. 85–8.

[25] Craig Muldrew, '"Th' ancient Distaff" and "Whirling Spindle": Measuring the Contribution of Spinning to Household Earnings and the National Economy in England, 1550–1770', *Economic History Review*, 65:2 (2012), 498–526 (498, 521); largest industrial occupation, 523; on numbers in Defoe's time with percentages of work by women, 505–6, 509–10.

172).²⁶ She, like so many of Defoe's women figures, takes actions considered masculine. Once the Flemish people brought producing bayes, serges, stuff, and other fabrics to the country and taught English women to spin and fostered the trade, she passed laws obliging people to work and punishing 'vagrants', 'sturdy Beggars', and other able-bodied people who avoided work (178). *Giving Alms No Charity* is concerned with the growth of workhouses, begging, and criminalizing unemployment with, for instance, parish stocks, therefore linked to the benefits of creating work.

Recently published figures on women's earnings reveal the inadequacies that result from using the earnings of husbands alone. Estimates are that 70% of English households were poor enough to need the income of women and children.²⁷ Throughout Defoe's work are glimpses of randomly sighted working women. He describes women employed in 'the Prison' to clean the rooms, run errands, tend sick prisoners, and 'any such things as Occasion offer'd'.²⁸ In *A Journal of the Plague Year* (1722), which is based on actual policies and practices during the plague, Defoe included the 'full and nearly verbatim' official orders 'concerning the Infection of the Plague 1665' that included 'a detailed directive for the appointment of "Women-Searchers" in every Parish'. Women had been employed by the government for many years to 'search' bodies and determine causes of death. Paula McDowell includes broadsheet depictions of them. They are respectably dressed, carrying a long rod to indicate their occupation, and, when outdoors, wearing highly visible stovepipe hats.²⁹ Moll Flanders's governess is a pawn broker. Jennine Hurl-Eamon found evidence of an active, creative economy in 'liquefiable assets' such as pawned items from their homes or the homes and places they worked. If they owned the items, they could do this repeatedly, and pawning and selling clothes was the most common.³⁰ Obviously, many planned to redeem them.

Earle categorizes much women's work as 'casual, seasonal and makeshift' and Hurl-Eamon describes 'an economy of makeshift'.³¹ They have documented varied, numerous kinds of occupations available. Easton finds women passing as men working as labourers, butchers, cooks, porters, shipwrights, plasterers, stone-cutters, brick-layers, coachmen, and more.³² Many of the jobs women held were associated with gendered domestic roles, as they worked with food, drink, making and mending clothes, did housework, took in washing, cared for the elderly and sick, and undertook child care, including taking in and nursing bastard or parish children. Defoe devotes more time

---

[26] Interestingly, he foretold the effect of the development of frames on home hand spinning.
[27] See Muldrew, '"Th' Ancient Distaff"', 499, 501, 521.
[28] *Great Law, RDW*, vi. 159.
[29] Paula McDowell, 'Defoe and the Contagion of the Oral: Modeling Media Shift in *A Journal of the Plague Year*', *PMLA*, 121:1 (2006), 87–106, esp. 92–8. His *Due Preparations for the Plague* (1722) also includes women-searchers.
[30] Hurl-Eamon, 'Fiction of Female Dependence', 490–2.
[31] Hurl-Eamon, 'Fiction of Female Dependence', 483; Jennine Hurl-Eamon, *Marriage and the British Army in the Long Eighteenth Century* (Oxford: Oxford University Press, 2014), 133–5.
[32] Fraser Easton, 'Gender's Two Bodies: Women Warriors, Female Husbands and Plebeian Life', *Past and Present*, 180:1 (2003), 131–74, esp. 136–9.

to servant women than any other category of workers. He warns readers about them, counts them, lectures them, offers advice to them and employers, tells stories about them, and assigns various kinds of status. *The Great Law of Subordination* begins, 'The unsufferable Behaviour of Servants in this Nation is now (it may be hop'd) come to its Height'. He describes resistance to his insistence on the importance of the subject because men thought only 'a few Citizens Wives' and 'Gentlemens Footmen' were affected, but he has brought people to understand that 'Husbandmen are ruin'd, the Farmers disabled, Manufacturers and Artificers plung'd' and more (*RDW*, vi. 41). Booker points out how contemporary 'discourse frames servants as childlike ciphers, emptying them of adult reason and personal history'.[33] Although Defoe sometimes creates stories in which they have personal histories and explained motives, he most often treats them as a hoard of ciphers. Of all the groups of people about whom he writes, he shows them the least sympathy and differentiation and in most need of regulation. He describes women quitting a position and 'turning Whore' and '[flitting] from Bawdy-House to Service' back and forth and forming 'cabals' to set their own terms.[34]

London was teeming with single women, and Defoe often casts his subject of case studies as constantly on the market. We have taken a kind of sanguine look at the very large number of male characters depicted in Defoe's and other writers' novels who have to try new trades and fail or leave Great Britain to make a living. In contrast, Defoe represents employment for women as readily available. He insists that positions for servants are always available and even going unfilled. The balance of immigration into the city had shifted to women forming the majority, and estimates are that 'tens of thousands' of women followed the opportunities. Rising numbers of people seeking more and more servants created Defoe's sense of a horde of servants swarming through the city.[35] Women working in taverns, coffee houses, and inns seem in stable, happy situations, although they may be too busy flirting to serve him.[36] The problem for women is the status of the available jobs. Moll, Roxana, and Jack's first wife relentlessly struggle towards a means of climbing and remaining in a higher, more comfortable status. Moll bursts into tears and goes into hysterics at the prospect of going into service and doing housework, and, like Jack, develops an increasingly ambitious idea of remuneratively desirable work.

Defoe was writing at the time servants were becoming employees rather than members of households to be treated something like children. In *The Great Law of Subordination*, he specifies that the ones he is analysing have 'Bed and Board', yearly or monthly wages with food, lodging, and even washing (*RDW*, vi. 46).[37] He sees servants increasingly gouging employers and demanding independence, as the interviewee does

---

[33] Booker, *Menials*, 3.

[34] Defoe, *Augusta Triumphans*, *PEW*, viii. 269–70; *Every-Body's Business*, *PEW*, viii. 222, 224.

[35] Peter Earle, *A City Full of People: Men and Women of London, 1650–1750* (London: Methuen, 1998), 39–40.

[36] Defoe, *Every-Body's Business*, *PEW*, viii. 228–9.

[37] This treatise gives attention to male servants, among whom he includes apprentices, and clerks in the legal profession.

in *Every-Body's Business, is No-Body's Business* who expresses her right to work in her upscale clothes (*PEW*, viii. 227) and the servant does in *Religious Courtship* when she demands to spend her Sundays as she wishes and practise a religion different from her employer (*RDW*, iv. 222–31). For Defoe's servants, work is rarely something to do with pride and care; it is not a profession, but a struggle in changing times to set perimeters on what, how much, and how they will work. Margaret Hunt has established that about 20% of the plaintiffs in equity courts were women, and among the suits were marriage settlements, wage disputes, and debt and credit. She gives a good example of the murkiness over payment that emerged when women moved into households and, over time, experienced changing roles.[38]

Here and elsewhere Defoe is especially concerned with women servants' gossiping and revealing family secrets, a topic Haywood features in her *Present for a Servant-Maid* (1743). Interestingly, 'status contracts', one of the major kinds of legal contracts, 'almost always included ... the exchange of service, loyalty, etc., not primarily for money but for basic support'. As I do, Kristina Straub recognizes the 'opposition between financial motive and affective relationships' as part of a major social change, one that Defoe was trying to regulate. As might be expected, Defoe's fiction and non-fiction have many women who argue about their rights and sometimes appeal to legal institutions for relief. Many of these arguments are lengthy and even include the 'creative' movement and reference between status contracts (form and content heavily derived from the relative status of the parties) and money exchange contracts (based explicitly on monetary exchange) that Hunt says were typical of women in everyday life. She points out that women's litigating often included attempts to demonstrate that some sort of status contract, such as a promise of marriage, should be treated as a reinterpretation of a relationship that evolved into a monetary exchange.[39] Repeatedly Defoe's characters expect marriage, and then some circumstance, such as the man already being married, is revealed, and, as in the incident with Moll and the Bath gentleman, sex is bartered for support.

Straub also sees hopes and fears 'clustered around' servants, and disappointment or even surprise at what feels like betrayal is common in Defoe's conduct book texts.[40] Because of the difference in the 'relative status' of the two parties, there was 'an implied right of the superior party to discipline the inferior one',[41] and Defoe's texts often dramatize conflicts between masters or mistresses and a servant over this 'right'. He complains that it is common for servants now to exhibit 'daring Defiance of Correction' and to believe their 'due' perquisites include 'Tea, Sugar, Wine', or even linen.[42] These dialogues support Booker's argument that servants were supposed to 'practice the values of the

---

[38] Hunt, 'Women and Money', 282, 286–9.
[39] Hunt, 'Women and Money', 283–5, 291.
[40] Kristina Straub, *Domestic Affairs: Intimacy, Eroticism, and Violence Between Servants and Masters in Eighteenth-Century Britain* (Baltimore, MD: Johns Hopkins University Press, 2009), 5–12.
[41] Hunt, 'Women and Money', 283–4.
[42] Defoe, *Every-Body's Business*, *PEW*, viii. 225, 222.

master or mistress', as the Lady and the good servant Betty make clear.[43] But at the same time *Religious Courtship* was published, plays, periodicals, and other literature were satirizing or lamenting servants practising the profligate, pretentious, dishonest, and immoral behaviours of the upper classes.[44]

Defoe also writes extensively about a special kind of working woman, women who are business owners or partners, managers, and inheritors of businesses. Some of these talented women managers have natural skills, or learn them within marriage, or have to develop them out of necessity. As Christine Owen observes, Defoe departs from gendered roles in marriage and urges tradesmen to keep their wives informed about their business 'so that she may take over the business should anything happen to him'.[45] In his fiction, Defoe's most competent women managers are often widows and relatively minor characters like the Quaker woman in *Roxana* and Mother Midnight in *Moll Flanders*, whom Leon Guilhamet identifies with admiration as ethical and 'an honest broker'. He identified Moll herself as 'a living testimony to the transforming power of the ideals of trade and management' in harmony with the 'Whig assumption that industry and management can produce ... material and spiritual wealth'.[46] Notably, Defoe makes this possibility of success available to women and assumes the sex's capacity for industry and management.

Women's work conferred status as they moved through the city with money in their pockets, whether it be as seamstress, servant, sex worker, household manager, shop owner, or an upper-class wife doing what we would today call public relations and event planning. His books are full of women shopping, buying, selling, lending money, borrowing money, acquiring debts, cheating, and being cheated. A Supplement to *The Complete English Tradesman* lets us see women's mobility and immersion in the city by imagining 'Maid *Mary*' picking up ribbons and a silk handkerchief; 'Mrs. *Maukin* the Midwife' buying ready-made muslin aprons; Mrs. Carey's maid picking up 1,000 pins; 'Miss *Peggy*, at Cousin *Jacombs*' buying two yards of blue ribbon, fine garters and kid gloves, all on credit (*RDW*, vii. 342–3). Defoe was well aware of the development of women's advancements in commerce. Earle describes the clustering of industries in various parishes, and the rise of colonies, such as the women related to sailors in the silk trade in Rotherhithe.[47] Although Defoe refers to spinners, seamstresses, and other occupations for women that required long hours of sitting and working, he actually creates a picture of people in motion. Like Moll, they cruise the city looking for opportunities, secure or catch-as-catch-can, move from place to place as Jack's wives do, or even across the Channel as Roxana does.

---

[43] Booker, *Menials*, 5; *Religious Courtship*, *RDW*, iv. 222–31.

[44] An example in Defoe's time are Steele's essays in the *Spectator*, such as 11 June 1711.

[45] Christine Owen, 'Robinson Crusoe and the "Female Goddesses of Disorder"', in *Robinson Crusoe's Economic Man: A Construction and Deconstruction*, ed. Ulla Grapard and Gillian Hewitson (New York: Routledge, 2011), 163–83 (179).

[46] Leon Guilhamet, *Defoe and the Whig Novel: A Reading of the Major Fiction* (Newark, DE: University of Delaware Press, 2010), 126, 130–2.

[47] Earle, *City*, 13–16.

Gender, Status, and Agency

Moll tries to act like a woman, even a lady, and Roxana acts like a man. From the beginning of their stories, they are gendered contrasts. Moll is given the education of a gentlewoman by her nurse and then vicariously in the home where she is a companion and does sewing; she emerges gendered feminine. Her nurse is sober, pious, 'very Housewifly', and 'Mannerly', and Moll emerges grave and 'Mannerly'; even in old clothes, she would remain neat and clean. She has learned to sew and even spin worsted, the occupation that was recognized as woman's work while men sorted the wool, combed it because of the upper body strength required, and, after it was spun, performed the rest, including winding and pressing.[48] Moll goes on to use her lessons in social gendering to attract and keep men and also as a useful disguise when thieving.

In contrast, Roxana describes herself as 'sharp as a Hawk', and her discourse is quick, smart, satirical, and full of repartee. She is, as she says, 'a little too forward in Conversation' and bold.[49] All of these characteristics of speech are negatively reinforced in girls and women and associated with aggressive men. She declares that she sees that 'Liberty seem'd to be the Men's Property, I wou'd be a *Man-woman*; for as I was born free, I wou'd die so' (171). She refuses marriage repeatedly, sees marriage as 'a State of Inferiority, if not of Bondage' (171), and, when she finally marries the Dutch merchant, she insists on terms that keep her past and her finances secret and, she hopes, under her control. The conclusion to *Roxana* is so gothic because it raises the spectre of a revenge act, perhaps a murderous one, by Susan on Roxana or by Amy on Susan. Roxana's masculine gender characteristics generate the final paragraph of the novel, which alludes to a 'Course of Calamities' and also the masculine recognition of 'the Blast of Heaven' and the desperately needed but impossible repentance (329–30). In the gothic movement of the second half of the century, the consequences of evil are written on the bodies of women but on the souls of men—and on Roxana's soul. Roxana calls herself a She-Devil and like gothic men begins to question her sanity. She finds her imagination haunted with horrid visions—Susan with her brains knocked out and spilling or her head cut completely off (301, 325). Oliver Lindner points out that Roxana exercises power in a male role, 'the aggressor who employs sexual violence'. After forcing Amy's rape she continues to be portrayed in this role and as the unnatural 'murderous woman', a signifier of 'the apex of human atrocity'—'a startling disruption of the pattern of male agency which testifies to her aberrant womanhood'.[50]

Defoe was in the forefront of recognizing and representing the strains of change. His writings are filled with pictures of people struggling upwards, and, from statistical

---

[48] Defoe, *Moll Flanders*, 9, 12–13; Muldrew, '"Th'ancient Distaff"', 503–5.
[49] Defoe, *Roxana*, ed. Jane Jack (Oxford: Oxford University Press, 1964), 6.
[50] Oliver Lindner, '*Matters of Blood*': *Defoe and the Cultures of Violence* (Heidelberg: Universitätsverlag, 2010), 259, 265–6.

historians' work on explaining status in the period, one conclusion was that social judgement had become 'less about belonging to a "class" and more "a process of continual achievement"'; moreover, they have found the kind of frequent tallying up of monetary value that is often noted (or ridiculed) in *Moll Flanders* and *The Complete English Tradesman* as a rising status marker.[51] Moll defines 'Gentlewoman' in terms of agency, as she understands it as being 'able to Work for myself, and get enough to keep me without that terrible Bug-bear *going to Service*' and 'able to get my Bread by my own Work' (13–14). This achievement is a well-recognized test of status. As evidence, Alexandra Shepard contributes, 'Witnesses were regularly asked about how they maintained themselves ... Maintenance was in many ways a corollary of worth ... [the way] social/occupational status was asserted and understood'.[52] As Ellen Pollak notes, for Moll and Roxana 'their banishment *as women* from the privileges of economic independence puts their very lives in jeopardy' (emphasis mine).[53] In addition to widows who successfully assume their husbands' businesses or manage their inheritances carefully and live virtuous, respected lives, there are those who find themselves struggling to collect legitimate debts with inadequate documentation or lacking power to locate the debtor, or even ruined when an irresponsible husband dies and leaves his books incomplete and in disorder. His women characters are often widowed and cast into the world again as independent agents.[54] In his non-fiction work, Defoe frequently represents servants' desire and even coercive insistence on receiving wages, not just the older board wages (a contract for a combination of lodging, food, and clothing with irregular monetary payments that we would call tips or gifts).[55] Defoe both understood and feared the growing demand.

Modern editions of *Moll Flanders* provide maps that allow readers to see her circuitous flights through the City after thefts that scared her; maps and statistics in *A Journal of the Plague Year* starkly illuminate the progress of the plague, the clustering of masses of victims, and the parts of the city from which those who could departed for the country. In another attempt to render my topic manageable, my essay is strongly biased toward the city of London [SEE CHAPTER 26]. Space conferred status not only from its history, but what was immediately taking place there. Defoe knew the City deeply and

---

[51] Shepard, *Accounting*, 7, 82–113.

[52] Shepard, *Accounting*, 12, 149–50. A major method of hers is to analyse litigants' and witnesses' statements about themselves.

[53] Ellen Pollak, 'Gender and Fiction in *Moll Flanders* and *Roxana*', in *The Cambridge Companion to Daniel Defoe*, ed. John Richetti (Cambridge: Cambridge University Press, 2008), 139–57 (141). Kyung Eun Lo also connects Roxana, trade, and gender in 'The Pleasures and Perils of Female Consumption in Daniel Defoe's *Roxana*', *British and American Fiction*, 19:3 (2012), 259–82.

[54] See Karen Bloom Gevirtz, *Life After Death: Widows and the English Novel, Defoe to Austen* (Newark, DE: University of Delaware Press, 2005).

[55] See Roxann Wheeler, 'Powerful Affections: Slaves, Servants, and Labours of Love in Defoe's Writing', in *Defoe's Footprints: Essays in Honour of Maximillian E. Novak*, ed. Robert M. Maniquis and Carl Fisher (Toronto: University of Toronto Press, 2009), 126–52, esp. 132–6. She notes Defoe's consistent desire that the bond between master and servant (or slave) supersedes 'the cash nexus' (134).

intimately, and he learned about space and status young.[56] He was one of the earliest writers to identify occupations with locations and to convey our present theory of space as constituted by the people who use it and where gender, identity, and status are both revealed and created. Just as he wrote about colonies of spinners developing, so he often wrote about seamstresses and where they were located and migrated.[57] As Benjamin F. Pauley observes, 'If London had not existed, Daniel Defoe would have found it necessary to invent it'.[58] As a strategic act, William and Mary watched the procession from a specially prepared balcony at the Angel in Cheapside, a major commercial street in the heart of the Old City. Defoe was pilloried by the Royal Exchange on Cornhill almost within sight of his inner-city Freeman's Yard house.

His understanding of change extended into non-fiction texts in which he portrayed astute tradesmen's judgements about the commercial and status advantages of spaces, and he included women in these reports and, significantly, they are often examples of women's agency. In several publications, he discussed where women workers clustered, observing that they 'run to the Manufacturing-Towns' for higher wages. He noted that in counties near London such as Essex and Suffolk, and as far as Devon, they were paid as much as 15*d*. per day. The willingness to move for opportunities occurred in London as well. Defoe even presented going to America as a choice, an exercise of a woman's free decision to go 'away voluntarily to *Virginia*, and the neighbouring Colonies, meerly to seek their Fortunes'.[59] This passage was published two years after the publication of *Moll Flanders* and her transportation as a felon. She and the criminal women he saw passing in carts headed for ships to the colonies contrast with the agency exercised by free women like those whose names appear on the voluntary indenture slips in the London Metropolitan Archive.

In much of Defoe's writing there is a strong degree of equality between men and women. Here they can choose mobility to seek their fortunes, but they can also spend their money on drinks and become drunks. Defoe clearly believed that women should reserve sex for marriage, but he was aware of sex as 'a trade', an occupation requiring skill, and a commodity that could be part of a con job or bartered. Laura Rosenthal identifies the complexity of the gendered behaviour of sex workers; they are never, she says, 'simply masculine or feminine' because a woman 'claims the masculine position

---

[56] I am using space as Doreen Massey does in *Space, Place and Gender* (Cambridge: Polity Press, 1994). On London's space 'divided according to socioeconomic status' and Defoe's work, see Elizabeth Porter, 'A Metropolis in Motion: Defoe and Urban Identity in *A Journal of the Plague Year*', *Digital Defoe*, 7:1 (2015), 119–31.

[57] Earle, *City*, 140–2; *Complete English Tradesman, Volume II, RDW*, viii. 227–35.

[58] Benjamin F. Pauley, '"This Monstrous City": Imagining London in *A Tour Thro' the Whole Island of Great Britain*', in *Positioning Defoe's Non Fiction: Form, Function, Genre*, ed. Aino Makikalli and Andreas K. E. Mueller (Newcastle upon Tyne: Cambridge Scholars Publishing, 2011), 81–106 (81).

[59] Defoe, *Great Law, RDW*, vi. 85–86, 114. The London Metropolitan Archives holds over 6,000 of the 'plantation indenture' slips signed before a justice of the peace by those registering to go to America for three to seven years. CLA/047/LR/05/02/006; CLA/047/LR/05/01/001–003.

of self-ownership'.[60] In his economic treatises, he finds the same deceptive practices in dishonest tradesmen and prostitutes. Such shop keepers 'make a common whore of his tongue' (*Complete English Tradesman, Volume I, RDW*, vii. 197). Throughout, the status of sex workers is realistically represented, and the same factors—economics, polish, education, language—play crucial parts. Roxana can reach the heights of courtesanship, but there is always something a little déclassé about Moll. The eighteenth century tended to lump beauty with ambition as false and dangerous values, and Defoe sees the former as commodifiable and the latter as innate in most humans. Critics besides myself see Defoe imagining a certain androgyny necessary for success. Owen identifies early eighteenth-century values gendered feminine in *Robinson Crusoe* to argue that Defoe applies the feminine images, behaviours, and mores that the time associated with trade, credit, and luxury in positive ways that contribute to his successful trading mentality. She finds, for instance, that the widow who takes care of Crusoe's money 'signifies a public and feminine site of stability and trust'.[61]

His sharp recognition of change undoubtedly generated an important master strategy: building status ambiguity into his characters, especially the women. Women's status was more ambiguous than men's for various reasons, including recognition that dynastic bloodlines could trump sex.[62] It remained a question, however, whether rank could indeed elevate the status of a woman, as Jane Austen's problematic Lady Catherine demonstrates in *Pride and Prejudice* (1813). Defoe creates status ambiguity with concrete markers such as dress, living spaces, family connections, methods of transportation, friendships, locations of shopping, forms of recreation, and apparent education and accomplishments. An important part of his tactic is to include evidence that the woman is appropriately gendered and whether his characters know how to perform the sexed, classed body the situation demands. The contradictory fluidity that can be performed is illustrated in a short segment in *Moll Flanders*. When Moll is falsely accused of robbing the mercer and apprehended, she performs as a well-off gentlewoman and later receives generous damages when she and her attorney (part of her props) meet with him. She dresses in second mourning and wears a gold watch and pearl necklace that closes with a locket of diamonds. Only a few days later, she dresses like a beggar woman and a drawer asks her to hold a gentleman's horse with the assurance that the owner will give her something; she steals the horse (191–9).

In the readings of Moll's rank by the magistrate, mercer, and drawer, Defoe constructs a model example of status ambiguity [SEE CHAPTER 23]. Misty Anderson has described the eighteenth century as the time when people learned to 'read and perform class as it shifted from a marker of birth to a mobile amalgam of economic capital, gender scripts,

---

[60] Laura J. Rosenthal, *Infamous Commerce: Prostitution in Eighteenth-Century British Literature and Culture* (Ithaca, N.Y.: Cornell University Press, 2006), 10.

[61] Owen, 'Robinson Crusoe', 163–83; quotation, 179.

[62] See the summary of Thomas Smith's influential classification of 'sorts' of people and treatment of women from *De Republica Anglorum* in Shepard, *Accounting*, 3.

and social affect'.[63] Part of the 'creativity' in Defoe's women's stories was the result of the status ambiguity that he builds into his characters and examples. As Lindner points out, Moll's position within the gentlewoman's household is 'unstable, oscillating between that of a poor relative and that of a servant'.[64] Both Jemy and Moll perform stereotypically attractive genders, claim to be wealthy, and then discover that they both lied. What is revealed is that they were both negotiating a monetary contract under the guise of a traditional status contract and are left trapped in that contract because of status ambiguity. In his non-fiction, Defoe stages many debates, and status ambiguity marks a lot of the tactics in women's wrangling as they deploy gendered behaviour.

In fact, Defoe understood that the litigiousness of the times brings women into public life and marks their private discourses. Hunt writes, 'In the final analysis I do not think that the women who pleaded their cases in Exchequer, or Chancery ... were so very different from contemporaries who never made it to court',[65] and Defoe's countless examples of women in fiction and non-fiction pleading their cases reinforce her conclusion. Again, Defoe was in the forefront, as this example from *Historical Collections* shows a woman judging a king:

> An Old woman being wronged Lay Cryeing and Calling on [King Philip of Macedonia, father of Alexander the Great] to have ye hearing of her Cause, not Ceasing Dayly to Importune her King for justice. At last he Answered her he had no Leisure, she hearing him say so Cryed out, why then be no Longer King neither. Intimateing that when he ceased to Do Justice to his Subjects, he Ceased to be King (ff. 56).

Part of Defoe's recognition of the rising fluidity of status is expressed in creative efforts to expose and even regulate them. An example is a long anecdote about a coachman who had an affair with his employer's daughter and is finally fired. He comes back dressed 'very genteely' to fight his master. The weapons they individually have and choose are part of the class repartee. The coachman has acquired a sword, mark of the upper classes, and the master selects a pitchfork, a sign of his insulting identification of the coachman's class. As here, writing about women includes some hints of class warfare. He accuses women servants in particular of treachery towards 'Young-Ladies of Fortune'. Defoe's anxieties about servants, their duty to do their mistresses' will, the acceptance of that and its influence on them, their emulation and the evolution of roles and 'trust' in the household are nowhere more evident than in his depiction of Roxana and Amy. Somewhat ironically, *Roxana* was advertised at the back of *The Great Law of Subordination*. A vast literature going back for decades testifies to the importance of this text. Both Roxana

---

[63] Misty G. Anderson, 'Genealogies of Comedy', in *The Oxford Handbook of The Georgian Theatre, 1737–1832*, ed. Julia Swindells and David Francis Taylor (Oxford: Oxford University Press, 2014), 347–67 (355).
[64] Lindner, '*Matters of Blood*', 247.
[65] Hunt, 'Women and Money', 298.

and Amy increasingly advance by creating status ambiguity. Rather than a new interpretation, I want simply to acknowledge how much of Defoe's regulatory writing about servants and status are the very fabric of this novel.[66]

Stephen Gregg writes that Defoe's 'abiding interest was in *failures* of manliness'.[67] His abiding interest in women is not parallel. Rather it is in how women survive and what statuses they are assigned and can achieve. They dramatically live out the conclusion of Hunt and others that 'both married and unmarried women were more discursively entangled in the world of debt and credit, more conversant with monetary exchange contracts' and quite capable of leading the movement to reconceive status contracts into monetary exchanges'.[68] In the last analysis, Defoe realistically yields to his time's positioning of women, but his writing registers seismic changes. The highest status for women is good wife, and in this position, women have agency. They are managers, partners, and co-decision-makers. At the end, Moll has partnered with a husband and lives in secure prosperity.

Defoe recognizes servant maids as what working women will become—mobile, largely literate, forming information networks, and fighting to be paid, independent agents. As Earle proves, 'Few women engaged in the same occupation throughout their working lives',[69] and one of Defoe's chief complaints about servant women was their willingness to quit suddenly and move from household to household 'for every idle Disgust' (*Augusta Triumphans*, PEW, viii. 269). Another was their increasing demands for guaranteed perquisites, holidays, and salaries. Moreover, Defoe's servant women embody markers that were guides to status of occupation, such as the clothing they wore, their literacy, their recreational choices, and their shopping.

We have known for a long time how impressive was Defoe's foresight about economics and imperialism because of applications of these historical disciplines. Closely analysing status in his fiction and non-fiction together reveals how equally prescient he was regarding the progress of employment of women, the settling of London and its environs, and the imbrication of gender in every domain of life.

Further Reading

Paula R. Backscheider, *Daniel Defoe: His Life* (Baltimore, MD: Johns Hopkins University Press, 1989).

Barbara M. Benedict, 'The Sentimental Servant: The Danger of Dependence in Defoe's *Roxana*', in *Reflections on Sentiment: Essays in Honor of George Starr*, ed. Alessa Johns (Newark, DE: University of Delaware Press, 2016), 85–104.

---

[66] For recent studies, see Booker, *Menials*, 105–10; Dawn A. Nawrot, 'The Female Accomplice: Rape and Servant Problem in *Roxana*', ECF, 29:4 (2017), 563–82.

[67] Gregg, *Defoe's Writings and Manliness*, 1.

[68] Hunt, 'Women and Money', 297.

[69] Earle, *City*, 118; on examples of occupation changes and literacy, see 119–20.

Kristina Booker, *Menials: Domestic Service and Cultural Transformation of British Society 1650–1850* (Lewisburg, PA: Bucknell University Press, 2018).

Peter Earle, *A City Full of People: Men and Women of London, 1650–1750* (London: Methuen, 1998).

Karen Bloom Gevirtz, *Life After Death: Widows and the English Novel, Defoe to Austen* (Newark, DE: University of Delaware Press, 2005).

Stephen H. Gregg, *Defoe's Writings and Manliness: Contrary Men* (Aldershot: Ashgate, 2009).

Margaret Hunt, 'Women and Money: Credit, Debt, and Status in the Eighteenth-Century London Court of Exchequer', in *Women and Credit in Pre-Industrial Europe*, ed. Elise M. Dermineur (Turnhout, Belgium: Brepols Publishers, 2018), 281–300.

Shirlene Mason, *Daniel Defoe and the Status of Women* (St. Alban's, VT: Eden Press, 1978).

Robert James Merrett, *Daniel Defoe: Contrarian* (Toronto: University of Toronto Press, 2013).

Ellen Pollak, 'Gender and Fiction in *Moll Flanders* and *Roxana*', in *The Cambridge Companion to Daniel Defoe*, ed. John Richetti (Cambridge: Cambridge University Press, 2008), 139–57.

Laura J. Rosenthal, *Infamous Commerce: Prostitution in Eighteenth-Century British Literature and Culture* (Ithaca, N.Y.: Cornell University Press, 2006).

Alexandra Shepard, *Accounting for Oneself: Worth, Status, and the Social Order in Early Modern England* (Oxford: Oxford University Press, 2015).

CHAPTER 16

FAMILY AND DOMESTICITY IN DEFOE'S WRITINGS

LIZ BELLAMY

ALTHOUGH little read today, *The Family Instructor* (1715) was highly regarded throughout the eighteenth century, vying with *Robinson Crusoe* (1719) as Defoe's most popular work (*RDW*, i. 16, 331). Composed largely of dialogues, it opens with a conversation between a father and his youngest child, as they walk in the fields. The child, who is 'about five or six years old', exposes his utter ignorance of religion, causing the father to upbraid himself for neglecting his family's spiritual education (47, 48–66). After a similar exchange between the child and his mother, the parents agree to reform their household, compensating for former neglect by enforcing church attendance, prohibiting immoral occupations such as playing cards and reading romances, and introducing regular household prayers. Subsequent dialogues detail the progress and consequences of the reformation, as the couple's children respond to the new regime. P. N. Furbank argues that this work transformed the conventional conduct book, inventing 'a strange literary genre ... about religion but at the same time about power' (24). After the success of the first volume, Defoe produced *The Family Instructor II* (1718), *Religious Courtship* (1722), *A New Family Instructor* (1727), and *Conjugal Lewdness* (1727). These works contain warnings against miscellaneous modern evils, including excessive corporal punishment, foreign travel, and irreligious servants,[1] but their central concern is with domestic relationships. Families are put at the heart of moral debate, as Defoe dramatizes his moral strictures through case studies of inconsistent or tyrannical fathers, disobedient sons, saucy wives, and worldly daughters, as well as less memorable figures who model the devotion and moderation that the dialogues seek to promote.

---

[1] *RDW*, i. *passim*; *RDW*, ii. 125–47, 182–252; *RDW*, iii. 44; *RDW*, iv. 214–18, 221–65.

The Early Modern Family: Definitions and Debates

Raymond Williams traces the meaning of 'family' from the *OED* definition of 'A group of people living as a household' (2a) to a 'group of people consisting of one set of parents and their children, whether living together or not' (2b), arguing that the concept of 'the small kin-group, usually living in one house' became dominant between the seventeenth and nineteenth centuries.[2] This etymological perspective is part of a longstanding historical debate over whether, when, and how family structures changed in England. Lawrence Stone claims that the early modern period saw the emergence of the nuclear, individualistic 'affective family', which displaced traditional ideas of the household or extended kinship network under authoritarian patriarchal control.[3] Michael McKeon draws on histories of sexuality to describe a 'long-term and uneven shift' from 'patriarchalism', associated with Robert Filmer's location of monarchical authority in the role of the father, towards a concept of 'patriarchy', as the family became increasingly distinguished from the state, and family members from one another.[4] These approaches identify the long eighteenth century as a time when family structures were changing, focusing on the needs of individuals, and relationships between parents and children and husbands and wives, with a movement away from the extended family and unquestioning obedience to paternal authority.[5]

This view has been challenged by a counter tradition, drawing on demographic research questioning the assumption that English people lived in extended families before the late seventeenth century and emphasizing continuity rather than change in household structures.[6] Peter Laslett and Alan Macfarlane have traced the nuclear and

---

[2] Raymond Williams, *Keywords: A Vocabulary of Culture and Society* (London: Fontana, 1988), 132.

[3] Lawrence Stone, *The Family, Sex and Marriage in England 1500–1800* (London: Weidenfeld and Nicolson, 1977); quotations are from the revised and abridged edition (Harmondsworth: Penguin, 1990). Cf. Lawrence Stone, *Uncertain Unions and Broken Lives: Marriage and Divorce in England, 1660–1857* (Oxford: Oxford University Press, 1995). For revisions to this approach, see Ralph Houlbrooke, *Death, Religion, and the Family in England, 1480–1750* (Oxford: Oxford University Press, 1998); David Turner, *Fashioning Adultery: Gender, Sex and Civility in England, 1660–1740* (Cambridge: Cambridge University Press, 2002); Joanne Bailey, *Unquiet Lives: Marriage and Marriage Breakdown in England, 1600–1800* (Cambridge: Cambridge University Press, 2003).

[4] Michael McKeon, 'Historicizing Patriarchy: The Emergence of Gender Difference in England, 1660–1760', *ECS*, 28:3 (1995), 295–322 (300, 297, 298); Thomas Laqueur, *Making Sex: Body and Gender from the Greeks to Freud* (Cambridge, MA: Harvard University Press, 1992), 149. See also Tim Hitchcock, *English Sexualities, 1700–1800* (Basingstoke: Palgrave, 1997) and Randolph Trumbach, *Sex and the Gender Revolution: Volume One: Heterosexuality and the Third Gender in Enlightenment London* (Chicago, IL: University of Chicago Press, 1998).

[5] See, e.g., David Blewett, 'Changing Attitudes toward Marriage in the Time of Defoe: The Case of *Moll Flanders*', *HLQ*, 44:2 (1981), 77–88 (78).

[6] Peter Laslett, *The World We Have Lost* (New York: Scribner's, 1965); references are to the revised edition, *The World We Have Lost: Further Explored* (London: Routledge, 1983), 91.

affective family back to the sixteenth century and beyond, arguing that far from being a product of capitalism, the individualistic family was a crucial factor in its development.[7] Keith Wrightson has evaluated the debate, arguing that while advocates of change tend to suppress 'many of the complexities and variations of past realities' in the interests of constructing a determining master narrative, adherents of continuity 'over-modernize the distant past, by privileging ... similarities at the expense of differences of mentality, behaviour and context'. Wrightson suggests that historians should explore the complexity of concepts of the family as well as family structures, to show the 'interaction of forces of continuity and change in specific contexts'.[8] In this spirit, Naomi Tadmor analyses how words like 'family', 'kin', 'relations', 'connexions', and 'friends' are deployed in eighteenth-century texts, questioning the preoccupation with the nuclear family evident on all sides of the debate. Tadmor argues that while English people might have been living in families that could be retrospectively categorized as nuclear, their 'language usages' suggest the continuing importance of 'the household-family' and 'friendship-relationships' which 'included kinship ties, but also extended beyond them'.[9]

Defoe's writings have been invoked on all sides of the debate. While Christopher Flint argues that the moral treatises 'extoll the values of what Lawrence Stone calls the "closed domestic nuclear family"', Robert James Merrett believes 'Stone's thesis ... is not evident in Defoe's writings', highlighting instead the tension between secular and religious concepts of marriage.[10] Stone himself is equivocal. He cites *Conjugal Lewdness* as evidence that Defoe was 'a pioneering "liberal" on the marriage issue', revealing his 'revolutionary position' on children's rights, but sees the advocacy of 'strict self-control over sensual pleasure' as challenging the freedom of sexual expression associated with the new ideology, manifesting the 'counter-currents at work in eighteenth-century culture'.[11] This uncertainty over whether Defoe is revolutionary or reactionary exemplifies the 'textual elusiveness' and 'multiple and contrary stances' which have been identified as characteristic of his writing,[12] but it also highlights the complexity of ideas of the family, and the dangers of teleological approaches which project modern concepts of liberalism onto the past. In line with Wrightson's injunctions, this essay will suggest that Defoe's domestic ideology should be understood in the specific context of the class and gender

---

[7] Laslett, *World We Have Lost: Further Explored*, 81–105; Alan Macfarlane, *Marriage and Love in England: Modes of Reproduction, 1300–1840* (Oxford: Blackwell, 1986).

[8] Keith Wrightson, 'The Family in Early Modern England: Continuity and Change', in *Hanoverian Britain and Empire: Essays in Memory of Philip Lawson*, ed. Stephen Taylor, Richard Connors, and Clyve Jones (Woodbridge: Boydell, 1998), 1–22 (12–13, 21).

[9] Naomi Tadmor, *Family and Friends in Eighteenth-Century England: Household, Kinship and Patronage* (Cambridge: Cambridge University Press, 2001), 38–9, 21, 272.

[10] Christopher Flint, 'Orphaning the Family: The Role of Kinship in *Robinson Crusoe*', *ELH*, 55:2 (1988), 381–419 (381); Robert James Merrett, *Daniel Defoe: Contrarian* (Toronto: University of Toronto Press, 2013), 204.

[11] Stone, *Family, Sex and Marriage*, 188, 185, 328.

[12] Ellen Pollak, 'Gender and Fiction in *Moll Flanders* and *Roxana*', in *The Cambridge Companion to Daniel Defoe*, ed. John Richetti (Cambridge: Cambridge University Press, 2009), 139–57 (141); Merrett, *Daniel Defoe*, xiv.

tensions of the early eighteenth century, rather than as part of a grand narrative of historical progress.

There is further debate over how Defoe's didactic writings relate to his fiction. Some critics contrast the preoccupation with family life in the tracts with the apparent avoidance of domesticity in the novels.[13] It has been frequently noted that at the end of his *Life and Strange Surprizing Adventures*, Robinson Crusoe is married, fathers three children, is widowed and back on his travels within a single sentence (*Novels*, i. 284), while Moll Flanders notes of her marriage with Robin that it 'concerns the story in hand very little, to enter into the farther particulars of the Family, or of myself, for the five Years that I liv'd with this Husband' (*Novels*, vi, 65). Even if it is accepted that Defoe's fiction propounds a domestic ideology, there is little agreement over whether this is consonant with the non-fictional works. David Blewett argues that the novels can be read as exemplifications or 'negative illustrations' of ideas in the moral treatises, but Flint discerns a 'discursive gap' between Defoe's 'didactic narratives, which clearly unite story and family, and his novelistic treatments of character development, which study the disjunction between them'.[14] John Richetti proposes that the novels, and particularly those with female protagonists, liberate the subversion and 'wayward sexual individualism' that is 'contained' in the moral works.[15] This essay will address constructions of the family within some of Defoe's didactic and fictional writings to assess their ideological and historical significance and how they have shaped, and been shaped by, the genres which Defoe was developing.

FAMILY AND DOMESTICITY IN DEFOE'S DIDACTIC WORKS

After the revelations at the start of *Family Instructor I*, subsequent dialogues unfold the consequences of the parents' decision to run their household on strictly religious lines. While the tractable younger children sanctimoniously acquiesce, their older siblings, George and Mary, resent being deprived of entertainments that have previously received parental approval. The conversations are set out like philosophical dialogues, a technique Merrett relates to Defoe's 'contrarian ideology',[16] but the form also shapes how family life is portrayed. Participants are identified by relationships rather than names, so that Mary is *Sist.* when she is talking to her brother, but *Mist.* (for mistress) when she is addressing the *Maid*, Pru (*RDW*, i. 148). The universalizing function of this nomenclature, and the

---

[13] John Richetti, 'The Family, Sex, and Marriage in Defoe's *Moll Flanders* and *Roxana*', *Studies in the Literary Imagination*, 15:2 (1982), 19–35 (20).
[14] Blewett, 'Changing Attitudes', 85; Flint, 'Orphaning the Family', 411; cf. Merrett, *Daniel Defoe*, 216–17.
[15] Richetti, 'Family, Sex', 22–3.
[16] Merrett, *Daniel Defoe*, 216.

formality of the presentation of the interchanges, are in constant tension with lively dialogue which evokes individualized characters rather than types. Richetti refers to the 'controlled case histories' of the didactic writings,[17] yet many of the stories seem uncontrolled, as plots and characters assume autonomous life beyond their illustrative role. This is exemplified in the eighth dialogue of *Family Instructor I*, when Mary and George test their father's resolve by encouraging him to believe that they have gone to the park, against his express injunction. Modern readers may be torn between sympathy with the children's defiance and a sense that this goes against the grain of the moralistic narrative. The sympathetic response is validated, however, by the representation of the father's fury on discovering that his children have *not* disobeyed his commands (154–7). The irrational passion exhibited by the incarnation of patriarchal authority suggests that even in explicitly didactic works, Defoe cannot resist the temptation to present humanly fallible characters rather than exemplary stereotypes. The privileging of parental power associated with the conduct book is subverted by the dramatic potential of individuality, indicating that the balance of authority and individualism within the family remains unresolved, and the didactic tracts are negotiating the resultant tensions.

Each of the early dialogues ends with a 'Note' drawing moral conclusions, but these progressively dwindle, as the narrator increasingly assumes the role of telling the story rather than pointing to the moral. Defoe's subsequent didactic works incorporate extensive diegesis, developing complex domestic plots from the conflicts initiated in the conversations. The dialogue form is all but abandoned in *Conjugal Lewdness*, where the many practices that fall under the definition of 'matrimonial Whoredom' are illustrated through vignettes providing 'flagrant examples' (*RDW*, v. 34, 56). Nonetheless, the dialogic structure has an important function in enabling the externalization of moral dilemmas, as when the parents in *Family Instructor I* discuss the spiritual education of their family (*RDW*, i. 85–90), or when Mary and George consider their response to the new regime (143–5). It provides a format to expose the dramatic potential of the domestic, substantiating Furbank's emphasis on the genre's preoccupation with power. This is evident in the middle section of *Family Instructor I*, which expounds the master's paternal responsibility for his apprentices, apparently reinforcing Tadmor's arguments about the persistence of the household-family.[18] Yet the didactic tenor of the text indicates that the obligations outlined are not invariably recognized. Tom's master neglects domestic duties and does not provide family worship, so Tom attends prayers at a neighbouring house. When his father is summoned to discuss this apparent truancy, the dialogue between father and master concentrates on the role of the household head. To the master's question of whether he must be 'a Father and Master too?', the father replies that there is '*No question of it*; ... [the apprentice] is under your Family Care, *as to his Body, he is your Servant*; but as to his Soul, *I think*, he is as much your Son as any Child you have' (206). The father argues that a master is responsible for his household-family,

---

[17] Richetti, 'Family, Sex', 23.
[18] Tadmor, *Family and Friends*, 63.

but Tom's master is reluctant to accept the demands of this role. The tone of the debate and the use of persuasive language suggest that the father is advocating an emergent social model or a contested concept, rather than perpetuating an accepted residual form.

The household-family features in Defoe's fiction as well as the didactic works. In his first volume of adventures, Crusoe refers semi-ironically to his family of cats, dog, and parrot (*Novels*, i. 166), extending this in *The Farther Adventures* (1719) to include five English men, seventeen Spaniards, Friday's father, and the three men and five women rescued from the mainland. Crusoe describes himself as father to this diverse family, but paternalism is tempered with patriarchalism as he explains that 'they all voluntarily engag'd to me not to leave the Place without my Consent' (*Novels*, ii. 47, 75, 81). His self-construction combines roles of benevolent provider and imperialist legislator, for while the settlers 'voluntarily' subject themselves, they cannot depart without permission. Crusoe deploys domestic language to legitimize a social contract which reduces adult participants to dependants. In *Colonel Jack* (1722), Jack describes his plantations in Virginia as 'my several Families', encompassing not only his servants but also his slaves within the term (*Novels*, viii. 171; cf. 202, 220). Although some critics have associated Defoe with the traditional extended family,[19] his works cannot be easily accommodated into conventional paradigms based on a shift from a feudal to a capitalist structure, or from public to private ideology. Instead, both the fiction and non-fiction construct a domestic model which represents a radical mercantile appropriation of the extended family, framing economic and inherently exploitative relationships in the language of paternal duty and patriarchal authority.

Yet it is clear from the didactic works that Defoe sees parental power as limited and not absolute. In *Family Instructor II*, a neighbour interrupts a father who is violently beating his son, citing numerous instances where similar brutality has had terrible consequences. He warns the father that:

> Pity, not Passion, should influence you in the Conduct of your Child; and a sincere Zeal for his Soul's Good, should be the only Motive of Correction; all the Warmth that is not founded upon this Principle is sinful, ... 'tis a tyrannical Usurpation, not a Patriarchal or Paternal Exercise of legal Authority, and without doubt 'tis a great Sin. (*RDW*, ii. 133–4)

The legitimacy of an action derives from the intentions rather than the authority of the actor, and while the desire to prevent sin in the child legitimizes punishment, the need to avoid sin in the parent restrains its administration. 'Patriarchal' and 'Paternal' function as distinct yet cognate terms, but the juxtaposition of 'Patriarchal ... Authority' with 'tyrannical Usurpation' emphasizes the distinction between a father's power and

---

[19] Cynthia Wall, 'Domesticities and Novel Narratives', in *The Cambridge History of the English Novel*, ed. Robert L. Caserio and Clement Hawes (Cambridge: Cambridge University Press, 2012), 113–30 (116); Diana Brooke, 'Daniel Defoe: *The Family Instructor*' (unpublished doctoral thesis, Goldsmiths, University of London, 2016), 106.

absolutism. The neighbour again draws on political language to argue that fathers should not be 'Tyrants over our Children instead of Parents, and meer Magistrates in our Families instead of just Governours' (147). The *OED* defines a magistrate as an official 'charged with the administration of the law' (1a) whereas a governor is 'a person responsible for governing a society, institution' (1a), encompassing a variety of figures of temporal authority, such as guardians and private tutors (2a, 2b), as well as God (5c). Defoe represents the governor as responsible for the smooth and 'just' running of an establishment, whether a family, a household of servants and apprentices, or a plantation. While familial language legitimizes the power of the master or the plantation owner by locating it in a framework of affective relations, the language of governance operates as a counter movement, invoking a framework of legislative restraints to circumscribe parental power. The persistence of public and legal terminology reinforces the universalizing aspects of the individual narratives and their resistance to the relegation of discussions of domesticity to the realm of private discourse.

Defoe's didactic works are particularly preoccupied with the role of parents in selecting marriage partners. They endorse the view which Peter Earle identifies with the 'English middle class', that parents have the right to refuse consent, but not to force children to marry against their inclinations.[20] In *Religious Courtship*, the father recognizes the importance of affection and attraction between couples, but does not share his youngest daughter's scrupulousness over her suitor's religion (*RDW*, iv. 37–8). In a didactic version of what becomes the plot of the courtship novel, the daughter is torn between duty to her father and what she sees as her duty to God. The dilemma is exacerbated because she has promised to follow the 'Maxim' of her dying mother, not to marry '*any Man . . . that did not at least profess to be a* Religious Man' (32). The father's response to her refusal of the proposal—'from this time forward you are no Relation of mine, any more than my Cook-maid'—is clearly signalled as unjust when the narrative voice uses indirect speech to recount how:

> He made terrible Resolutions against her, that he would never give her a Farthing, that he would turn her out of doors; that she should go to Service, that he would make his Will, and whatever he left to the rest of his Children, it should be upon Condition, that they should never relieve her, nor own her, nor call her Sister, and that if they did, what they had should go to his eldest Son, and the like. (49–50).

The repetitions leading up to the final three words suggest a descent into vengeful and reiterative ramblings, distancing narrator and reader from the sentiments expressed and signalling the illegitimacy of this exercise of paternal power. *Conjugal Lewdness* is similarly unequivocal, with chapters on '*the absolute Necessity of a mutual Affection before* MATRIMONY' (*RDW*, v. 83–98) and the dangers of being '*Over-rul'd by Persuasion,*

---

[20] Peter Earle, *The Making of the English Middle Class: Business, Society and Family Life in London, 1660–1730* (London: Methuen, 1989), 185–91; cf. Defoe, *Family Instructor II*, *RDW*, ii. 153; *Religious Courtship*, *RDW*, iv. 32.

Interest, Influence of Friends, Force, and the like' (99–123). The narrator argues that 'As Matrimony should be the Effect of a free and previous Choice in the Persons marrying, so the breaking in by Violence upon the Choice and Affection of the Parties, I take to be the worst kind of *Rape*' (*RDW*, iv. 124).[21]

The juxtaposition of religious diction with discourses of natural jurisprudence and political economy emphasizes that the power of the father is limited by moral and spiritual rather than legal considerations. Filmerian concepts of patriarchal authority are replaced by paternal responsibilities that extend beyond immediate kin. While Defoe celebrates companionate marriage, he challenges the preoccupation with the nuclear family by constructing the mercantile household as an affective community fostering religious values that are of public significance. The child, servant, or apprentice has a duty to obey paternal authority, but only when it does not conflict with religious obligation. The power of the father is not absolute, since apprentices as well as daughters are justified in appealing to religion to legitimize acts of disobedience and can make autonomous judgements of where their duty lies. Tom the apprentice is vindicated in *Family Instructor I* because his truancy is motivated by religious devotion so that his master is finally induced to provide family worship and recognize his responsibilities to the family-household (*RDW*, i. 241). In *Religious Courtship*, the daughter's virtuous example leads to the conversion of her admirer and the father learns the importance of religious compatibility (*RDW*, iv. 67, 185–6).

Family Instructor II addresses issues of power and authority within marriage, as two husbands exchange notes on how their wives have mocked their conduct of family services. The men confide their feelings and expose the difficulties that husbands can face in exercising in practice the domestic authority they possess in theory, anticipating the evocations of male powerlessness in *Colonel Jack*.[22] For example, when one husband asks his wife to 'banter' on any subject except religion, she challenges him to 'exercise your Authority to stop my Mouth', warning that this may not be 'so easy as you imagine; for I will have my Liberty' (*RDW*, ii. 38). Political language is appropriated to justify blasphemous and disrespectful conduct, reinforcing the limitations of patriarchal power while signalling the illegitimacy of such usage. The trials of marital incompatibility are illustrated throughout *Conjugal Lewdness*, but the cautionary vignettes are interspersed with images of domestic harmony and advice on how to cultivate this. For Stone, the focus on sexual restraint runs contrary to an emergent ideology of individual fulfilment, while Merrett explores Defoe's negotiation of marriage as simultaneously a legal institution and a religious bond, showing how spiritual equality is elevated above the secular gender hierarchy.[23] But as the name suggests, there is extensive discussion within *Conjugal Lewdness* of the physical side of marital love. 'Repressive' readings tend to focus on chapters towards the end of the book in which the narrator condemns

---

[21] Merrett, *Daniel Defoe*, xvi identifies the metaphoric deployment of sexual terms with a 'semantic broadening' that challenges 'conventional mores'.

[22] Stephen H. Gregg, *Defoe's Writings and Manliness: Contrary Men* (Aldershot: Ashgate, 2009), 131.

[23] Merrett, *Daniel Defoe*, 201–10.

various forms of 'Matrimonial Whoredom', including 'Conjunctions' between 'two antient People' (*RDW*, v. 167), and '*a Husband knowing his Wife after Conception*' (198). Such practices are attacked on the grounds that sex is 'principally for the Procreation of Children' (62). Yet elsewhere the text contends that there is 'a Duty on both Sides, to yield, to please, and oblige one another, where no just Objections are to be made' (80). While the narrator condemns 'conjugal Violences' (76), for example recognizing and condemning marital rape, partners 'who decline one another criminally' are urged 'to consider the matrimonial Vow and Duty in all its Particulars' (80). Thus:

> The most modest and chast Virgin ... without the least Breach of Modesty, goes into what we call the naked Bed to [her Husband], and with him; lies in his Arms, and in his Bosom, and sleeps safely, *and with security to her Virtue*, all the Night. And this is her Place, her Property, her Privilege, exclusive of all others ... it is her Retreat, the Repository of her cares, as well as of her Delight, and of her Affection. (62)

Having largely abandoned the dialogue form of the earlier didactic works, conflicting views are incorporated within the omniscient narrative. But some of the apparent contradictions within the text can be resolved if a distinction is made between the love that is celebrated at the start of the book and the sensuality that is condemned at the end. True love is shown to have a physical dimension distinct from carnality. Husband and wife should be 'Lovers as well as Relatives' (73), but those who marry 'meerly to gratify the sensual Part', find, once they have satisfied their appetite 'in the Pleasures of the Marriage Bed', that 'all the rest ... is a Force, a Bondage; and they as heartily hate the State of Life as a Slave does his Lot in *Algier* or *Tunis*' (49). Defoe's emphasis on mutual respect and reciprocity within marriage can be related to emergent concepts of individualism, but this is not connected to sexual liberation.

The terms of the celebration of the 'Pleasure of a married State' in *Conjugal Lewdness* indicate why happy marriages might be regarded as antipathetic to the fictional form that Defoe is developing. This pleasure, we are told, 'consists wholly in the Beauty of the Union, the sharing Comforts, the doubling all Enjoyments; 'tis the Settlement of Life; the Ship is always in a Storm till it finds this safe Road, and here it comes to an Anchor' (84). Moll Flanders similarly remarks, on marrying her banker, that she 'seem'd landed in a safe Harbour, after the Stormy Voyage of Life past was at an end' (*Novels*, vi. 161). Pat Rogers and Cynthia Wall emphasize the significance of home-making activities in *Robinson Crusoe*,[24] yet these are confined to the island scenes and thus the 'Stormy Voyage of Life'. The minutiae of Crusoe's solitary existence may be suitable material for an adventure narrative, but the same is not true of the 'safe Harbour' of marriage. At the end of the first volume, Crusoe presents the domestic resolution in the laconic double negative that he married 'not either to my Disadvantage or Dissatisfaction' (*Novels*, i. 284). *The Farther Adventures* provides more information about this union and how his wife finally cures the 'Distemper' of a 'wandering Fancy', enabling Crusoe to embrace

---

[24] Pat Rogers, 'Crusoe's Home', *Essays in Criticism*, 24:4 (1974), 375–90; Wall, 'Domesticities', 114–15.

the lifestyle of 'a meer Country Gentleman' and achieve 'that middle State of Life' which his father 'so earnestly recommended' (*Novels*, ii. 6–9). Within a few pages, however, this 'Felicity' is interrupted by the wife's death, leaving Crusoe 'like a Ship, without a Pilot, that could only run afore the Wind' (9, 10). He tells the reader:

> It is not my Business here to write an Elegy upon my Wife, give a character of her particular Virtues, and make my Court to the Sex by the Flattery of a Funeral Sermon. She was, in a few Words, the Stay of all my Affairs, the Centre of all my Enterprizes, the Engine, that by her Prudence reduc'd me to that happy Compass I was in, from the most extravagant and ruinous Project that flutter'd in my Head ... and did more to guide my rambling Genius, than a Mother's Tears, a Father's Instructions, a Friend's Counsel, or all my own reasoning Powers could do. (9)

The portrayal of family life is ostensibly positive, but the metaphors are of confinement. The wife is a 'Stay' or brake. She is an 'Engine', but one that works to reduce the 'Compass' of her husband and counteract his projects. Marriage has terminated not only Crusoe's wandering, but also the 'rambling Genius' that is the essence of the picaresque novel. Thus, the suggestion that the evocation of domestic felicity is 'not [the] Business' of Crusoe implies that it is also not the business of fiction. It is only once the domestic moorings have been severed that Crusoe is free to embark on another narrative of miscellaneous adventures, having shed his remaining domestic impediments by leaving his children with the widow who had previously managed his fortune. He leaves his blood relations, to return to his island family.

While moral dialogue is increasingly replaced by narration in Defoe's didactic works, Crusoe's account of his return to the island incorporates dialogue in passages devoted to domestic themes. Conversations between Crusoe and reformed mutineer Will Atkins and between Atkins and his wife (101–8) celebrate marriage and paternal authority, as both men lament their filial disobedience (102). The dialogues are confined to the island episode, before Crusoe returns to a wandering life and the narrative to a picaresque structure. Robert Markley argues that by abandoning the island, Defoe rejects 'the discourses and practices of colonialism', and focuses for the rest of the novel on the opportunities of trade, replacing ideas of economic self-sufficiency with 'a discourse about the networks of communication and credit'.[25] He suggests that literary historians have underestimated the significance of the 'literary experimentation' of the trading narrative.[26] Yet the incorporation of domestic dialogues in the island scenes represents a different kind of experimentation, as Defoe draws on forms developed within the didactic works to explore the familial relationships that have been identified in the first *Crusoe* volume as outside the scope of the genre. The subsequent novels can be read

---

[25] Robert Markley, '"I have now done with my island, and all manner of discourse about it": Crusoe's *Farther Adventures* and the Unwritten History of the Novel', in *A Companion to the Eighteenth-Century English Novel and Culture*, ed. Paula R. Backscheider and Catherine Ingrassia (Oxford: Blackwell, 2005), 25–47 (32, 28).

[26] Markley, '"I have now done"', 45.

as responses to the challenge of fictionalizing the domestic, and the final section of this essay will explore aspects of these representations and their impact on the nascent novel form.

Fictionalizing the Domestic

Some critics have identified a clear distinction between the novels with male and those with female protagonists, arguing not only that domestic life is more central to *Moll Flanders* and *Roxana* (1724) than to *Robinson Crusoe*, *Captain Singleton* (1720), and *Colonel Jack*, but also that the female narratives manifest greater textual sophistication.[27] Yet while Defoe's novels are frequently categorized by gender, a different reading is achieved if they are viewed in terms of class [SEE CHAPTERS 13 AND 15]. From this perspective, Roxana is related to Crusoe rather than Moll. Roxana and Crusoe both open their narratives with the words 'I was born', introducing a brief family history, highlighting their foreign origins. Crusoe's father was 'a Foreigner of *Bremen*', while Roxana's parents are 'REFUGEES' from 'POICTIERS'. Crusoe describes himself as 'of a good Family', while Roxana's father 'was in very good Circumstances' (*Novels*, i. 57; ix. 23). It is only later that these characters fall into difficulties. Moll and Jack, by contrast, begin with references to the absence and unreliability of information about their origins, presenting themselves as outside the conventional familial structures and kinship networks that define social position (*Novels*, vi. 27–9; viii. 33–4). *Moll Flanders* and *Colonel Jack* can be viewed as companion pieces, sharing a narrative trajectory as well as a class basis, as their protagonists try to establish a position in the society from which they have been excluded. Moll strives to overcome her origins in Newgate to become a gentlewoman, and Jack has a similar ambition to acquire the status of a gentleman from being born a 'Son of Shame' (*Novels*, viii. 34). All Defoe's characters travel extensively [SEE CHAPTER 8],[28] but Moll and Jack also progress economically and socially. Patrick Parrinder distinguishes between centrifugal and centripetal narrative structures, suggesting that Defoe's 'fiction is centrifugal, his non-fiction centripetal, with London always at its centre'.[29] Yet if the novels are viewed as representing social rather than purely geographical movement, *Robinson Crusoe* and *Roxana* are centrifugal, showing the movement of the protagonists from the inside to the outside of society,

---

[27] Pollak, 'Gender and Fiction', 143, 149–51; Richetti, 'Family, Sex', 24. Cf. Gregg, *Defoe's Writings and Manliness*.

[28] Srinivas Aravamudan points out that *A Journal of the Plague Year* (1722) is the only 'novel' by Defoe that does not involve international travel. 'Defoe, Commerce, and Empire', in *Cambridge Companion to Daniel Defoe*, ed. Richetti, 45–63 (58).

[29] Patrick Parrinder, *Nation and Novel: The English Novel from its Origins to the Present Day* (Oxford: Oxford University Press, 2006), 66.

while *Moll Flanders* and *Colonel Jack* (and *Captain Singleton*) are centripetal, charting a journey from outside to inside.

The importance of marriage within this process is signalled on the title pages, with the account of how Moll Flanders 'was Twelve Year a *Whore*' and 'five times a *Wife* (whereof once to her own Brother)' (*Novels*, vi. 21), while the second edition of *Colonel Jack* explains that he 'was Five times married to Four *Whores*' (*Novels*, viii. 29), clarifying the first edition's claim that he 'married four Wives, and five of them prov'd *Whores*'.[30] Even if these title pages were the work of the printers rather than Defoe,[31] they acknowledge the structural significance of marriage. Unlike in the courtship novel, marriage is part of the problem rather than the solution. The unions are elements of an ongoing, if uneven, pursuit of social and financial stability, rather than the culmination of that pursuit. The absence of information on Moll's married life with Robin (*Novels*, vi. 65) does not necessarily denote absence of interest in marriage, and despite the 'refusal to domesticate the text' that Flint has identified,[32] *Moll Flanders* provides sustained consideration of issues arising from Robin's proposal. Moll's scruples over whether she should accept him after having been 'his Brother's Whore' (65) are rehearsed in long disputes with the elder brother, and there are protracted debates between Robin, his mother, and his siblings (45–65). The elder brother is anxious to promote the match for his own convenience, but the sisters express more mercenary views, encouraging domestic tensions. Like the deliberations over marriage on Crusoe's island, these conversations are presented as dialogue, invoking the form as well as the content of the didactic works (37, 60–2). Robin's proposal enables debate over the child's right to choose in a novel otherwise devoid of parental influence and demonstrates the potential of the family to furnish fictional drama.

Likewise, while Moll does not describe the 'uninterrupted course of Ease and Content' of her five years with the banker (162), the difficulty of ending his first marriage is extensively canvassed. Using the technique of paradox that Merrett identifies as characteristic of Defoe,[33] the banker is introduced as having '*a Wife, and no Wife*' (120), and his cuckolded condition is sketched in a vignette comparable to the monitory exempla of *Conjugal Lewdness*. The context is comic, as Moll tries to discuss her financial affairs, but the banker keeps returning to his marital woes (122). When the banker asks Moll '*what must a poor abus'd Fellow do with a* Whore?', Moll's advice is 'you must Divorce her' (122). Maximillian Novak and Lois Chaber argue that the novels are sympathetic to divorce, and Melissa Ganz suggests that *Moll Flanders* presents the case for reform of the marriage laws, but Merrett argues that divorce is presented as 'a form of unprincipled individualism'.[34] *Conjugal Lewdness* identifies marriage as unlawful without affection, but

---

[30] Defoe, *Colonel Jack*, ed. Samuel Holt Monk (Oxford: Oxford University Press, 1970), xxxi.
[31] Rodney M. Baine, 'The Evidence from Defoe's Title Pages', *Studies in Bibliography*, 25 (1972), 185–91 (186–8).
[32] Flint, 'Orphaning the Family', 410.
[33] Merrett, *Daniel Defoe*, 11.
[34] Maximillian E. Novak, *Defoe and the Nature of Man* (Oxford: Oxford University Press, 1963), 101–6; Lois A. Chaber, 'Matriarchal Mirror: Women and Capital in *Moll Flanders*', *PMLA*, 97:2 (1982), 212–26

the narrative voice explicitly disclaims the idea of 'Mr *Milton*' that this justifies divorce. Facilitating divorce 'would fill the World with Whoredom' (*RDW*, v. 96) and, developing the slavery image cited above, the narrator declares 'as you are once bound you must remain in Bonds; once in *Algier*, and ever a Slave' (96–7). Yet both *Moll Flanders* and *Colonel Jack* contain characters who escape their bonds by divorcing unsuitable partners, just as Crusoe escapes from slavery. For Moll's banker, divorce involves a protracted legal battle, giving Moll time to go to Lancashire, marry Jemy, separate, have a child, and put it out to nurse.

Social historians have traced the various mechanisms through which divorce could be obtained in the early eighteenth century.[35] Parliamentary divorce, which gave permission to remarry, was 'confined to men with great estates and titles', and Roderick Phillips estimates that on average there were one or two cases a year between 1670 and 1857.[36] For the banker, 'divorce' refers to a judgement in the ecclesiastical court, granting 'legal separation of bed and board'.[37] This did not convey the right to remarry, although in practice many people behaved as if it did.[38] The legal and moral ambivalence is acknowledged in the banker's letter to Moll, which conveys

> the surprizing News that he had obtain'd a final Sentence of Divorce against his Wife, and had serv'd her with it on such a Day, and that he had such an Answer to give to all my Scruples about his Marrying again, ... for that his Wife ... as soon as she had the account that he had gain'd his Point, had very unhappily destroy'd her self that same Evening. (*Novels*, vi. 148–9)

The banker assumes that Moll, as a respectable woman, will have 'scruples' about marriage to a divorced man, perhaps acknowledging the dubious legality of any subsequent nuptials. The reader recognizes the irony of this anxiety, since Moll receives the letter twenty-two days after giving birth to Jemy's child (148) and at a time when she has three husbands who are still very much alive. The references to 'a *Wife* and no *Wife*' (120, 121) recall Moll's description of herself after the desertion of the Gentleman Tradesman draper as having 'a Husband and no Husband' (69), reinforcing that in practice the early eighteenth century lacked the clear binarism of married and unmarried that informs didactic and legal writings. The variety of unions identified by social historians, combined with the absence of any effective system of recording, meant that although formal divorce was outside the scope of most couples, many relationships ended through desertion or separation, leading to bigamous or polygamous marriages like those of Moll and

---

(218); Melissa J. Ganz, '*Moll Flanders* and English Marriage Law', *ECF*, 17:2 (2005), 157–82 (165): Merrett, *Daniel Defoe*, 206.

[35] Stone, *Uncertain Unions*, 35–48; Roderick Phillips, *Untying the Knot: A Short History of Divorce* (Cambridge: Cambridge University Press, 1991), 64–119; Turner, *Fashioning Adultery*, 72–3, 145–53; Joanne Bailey, *Unquiet Lives*, 30–3.

[36] Stone, *Uncertain Unions*, 47; Phillips, *Untying the Knot*, 66.

[37] Stone, *Uncertain Unions*, 44–5; Bailey, *Unquiet Lives*, 51.

[38] Bailey, *Unquiet Lives*, 183–4.

Jack.[39] In this environment, Moll may have believed that she was effectively married to the elder brother (47–9), justifying her concerns about her incestuous relationship with Robin.[40]

Moll's most transitory unions, with the elder brother, the draper, and Jemy, are those in which she aspires to marry a Gentleman. In accepting the draper, Moll represents herself as having been 'hurried on (by my Fancy to a Gentlemen) to Ruin my self in the grossest Manner' (67), and in her marriage with Jemy she is blinded by 'the glittering show of a great Estate, and of fine Things' (128). In contrast, her more successful matches are those, with Robin, the banker, and her brother (up to the point where she discovers the incestuous connection), in which she marries for prudential reasons. She comments that she 'was not so much in Love with [the banker], as not to leave him for a Richer' (126), and like Crusoe, she describes her married life through negatives, telling the reader 'I kept no Company, made no Visits; minded my Family, and oblig'd my Husband' (162). These marriages are successful for the reasons that put them outside the 'business' of the novel: they are stable and uneventful, representing safe harbours in the voyage of life, and they fit with the strictures of *Conjugal Lewdness* in not being motivated by transitory passion. The characters from the 'middle State of Life' make the best husbands but are least suitable for fictional representation, and the centrality of money to domestic happiness is shown in the banker's inability to survive the loss of his credit (162). The problem with Moll's relationships with the elder brother, the draper, and Jemy is not that they are based on financial calculations, but rather that the calculations are inaccurate. The union with the elder brother is not a recognized marriage, and the draper and Jemy both manifest gentility through spending rather than accruing money. By the end of her story, Moll can be reunited with Jemy because she has the financial resources to acquire the luxury of a 'gentleman', particularly since this commodity can be maintained more cheaply in America than in England.

Moll uses mercantile language to describe a marriage market where 'The Men ... seem'd to Plie at every Door, and if the Man was by great Chance refus'd at one House, he was sure to be receiv'd at the next' (*Novels*, ii. 72). Men are figured as chapmen, vending their wares from door to door, but are themselves the goods, purchased with the woman's dowry. The objectification of men is paradoxically used by Moll to reinforce the powerlessness of women, but the situation is presented from a different perspective in *Colonel Jack*. Moll's marriages are detailed in the opening two-thirds of her novel, after a brief account of her childhood, and are only succeeded by her criminal 'adventures' when she is 'past the flourishing time' (*Novels*, vi. 162). The pattern is reversed in *Colonel Jack*. Jack starts with an account of his early life, criminal activities, desertion from the army, kidnapping, and experiences on the Virginia plantation, and it is in the final third of the novel that his adventures take marital form. Richetti dismisses Jack's marriages as 'merely entangling problems', which occur 'after he has established

---

[39] Bailey, *Unquiet Lives*, 168–92.
[40] Ganz argues that the exchange of vows means that Moll is married to the elder brother, although he denies making the vows. '*Moll Flanders* and English Marriage Law', 164–7.

himself as an individual' and are peripheral to Defoe's concern with 'individualism of a radical sort'.[41] Richetti's reading can be related to a critical tradition which, Maurice Hindle suggests, dismisses the second half of the novel as 'somewhat of a failure'. Hindle emphasizes the 'subtle *pattern*' of the last part of the narrative, and the importance of the 'Principle of Gratitude' within its moral scheme (*Novels*, viii. 26, 27–8), but it is also possible to see the marriages as having greater structural and ideological significance than Richetti and other critics have acknowledged, particularly when viewed as counterparts to Moll's unions.

Jack returns to London with the reputation of being 'vastly Rich' (171), yet he is 'a meer Boy in the Affair of Love, and knew the least of what belong'd to a Woman, of any Man in *Europe* of my Age' (172). The account of how he is courted by his first wife refers to 'Witch-Craft' and 'Magick', as 'like a Charm she had me always in her Circle' (172). While Moll describes the entrapment of her husbands from the female perspective, Jack constructs himself as the victim, drawing on the language of military conflict and hunting in recounting how 'She attack'd me without ceasing' and 'held me at Bay several Months' (172–3). Within a month of marriage, the relationship has failed as Jack is unable to make the transition from the passivity of courtship to the mastery of marriage. The wife proves to be 'a wild, untam'd Colt' (177), and Jack worries about the prospect of becoming 'a Beggar, and a Cuckold' (181). After his wife gives birth to an illegitimate child, he 'Sued her in the Ecclesiastical Court, in order to obtain a Divorce' (181). Like Moll's banker, having 'gain'd a legal Decree', Jack considers himself 'a Freeman once more', although he declares himself 'Sick of Wedlock' (181). He is, however, 'prevail'd with' to marry his Italian landlord's daughter, with whom he 'contracted a Kind of Familiarity' while a prisoner of war. He again presents his role as entirely passive, claiming he 'never intended' to marry, and the familiarity was 'perfectly undesign'd' (198).

After discovering his second wife's infidelity (204), Jack returns to England and, despite previous disappointments, aspires to 'a settled family Life' (208). He has some qualms about being 'a marry'd Man' but persuades himself that since his wife was 'a Whore', he would have obtained a divorce had he not been obliged to leave the country following a duel. He decides he is 'as much divorc'd, as if it had been actually done', so that his scruples 'vanish'd' (211–12). His third marriage founders when his wife turns to drink after an illness, losing 'her Beauty, her Shape, her Manners, and at last her Virtue' (213). When she dies, he takes a fourth wife 'as an upper Servant' to care for his children, but the union proves successful.[42] Like Mrs Crusoe, Moggy controls her husband's wandering, dissuading him from joining the 1715 Jacobite Rising, and provides the stability he has sought. The location of the marriages at the end rather than the start of *Colonel Jack* reinforces their significance as symbols of Jack's rejection of adventure in favour of the 'safe harbour' of family life, but it also suggests a recognition of the fictional potential

---

[41] Richetti, 'Family, Sex', 19.

[42] Jack's wives are all identified as 'Whores' on the title page, but Moggy only fits this description because she suffered a 'slip' in her youth.

of courtship and domesticity. While the didactic works present home as a locus for drama, the novels indicate that it can also provide resolution.

This is shown at the end of the novel when Jack returns to his plantation. As with *Moll Flanders*, the linear narrative eventually bends into a circle. Jack remarries his repentant first wife, and Moll is reunited with her Lancashire husband Jemy and the son from her incestuous marriage. These final unions anticipate the structural role of marriage in the mid-century novel, as the destination rather than the journey, although in both cases the significance of the domestic resolution is occluded by economic concerns. Jack explains that he has recorded his memoirs while confined in Cuba following some illicit trading, but his comments anticipate subsequent developments in the novel form:

> Perhaps, when I wrote these things down, I did not foresee that the Writings of our own Stories, would be so much the Fashion in *England*, or so agreeable to others to read, as I find the Custom, and the Humour of the Times has caus'd it to be ... 'tis evident by the long Series of Changes, and Turns, which have appear'd in the narrow Compass of one private mean Person's Life, that the History of Men's Lives may be many ways made Useful, and Instructing to those who read them, if moral and religious Improvement, and Reflections are made by those that write them. (263)

In identifying 'the Writings of our own Stories' as 'the Fashion' and in line with 'the Humour of the Times', Jack places the cultural importance of fiction in its location within 'the narrow Compass of one private mean Person's Life'. The adventures take place against a background of historical events, including European wars and the domestic upheavals of the Jacobite Rising, as well as changes in the systems of international trade, but the source of the drama and the 'Improvement' is private rather than public.

In the Preface to the *Serious Reflections during the Life and Surprising Adventures of Robinson Crusoe* (1720), Crusoe suggests that 'the Story, though Allegorical, is also Historical' and that 'there's not a Circumstance in the imaginary Story, but has its just Allusion to a real Story' (*Novels*, iii. 51, 52–3). The narratives of Moll and Jack show Defoe incorporating techniques deployed within the didactic works to present the 'real Story' of domestic life rather than the 'imaginary Story' of foreign adventure. Defoe's portrayal of family disputes within the didactic works is grounded in a mercantile model of the extended family, negotiating legal, customary, and religious concepts of domestic authority. The form of the moral dialogue provides a vehicle for representing internal debate and the tensions between the pursuit of selfhood and social obligation. As such, these writings anticipate the formalizing of generic conventions for fictionalizing the family in the emergent novel. *Roxana* has been identified as Defoe's most sophisticated text because it contains more interiority than its predecessors, but this psychological focus was facilitated by the development of methods for the exploration of marriage, internal debate, and domesticity in the earlier novels and didactic works. The didactic writings, and especially *Conjugal Lewdness*, challenge the patriarchal model to construct an image of marriage as the realization of individualism, rather than a threat to it, but also formulate strategies for the development of the domestic as a source of fictional drama rather than stability. While Markley has emphasized the fictional potential of the trading narrative of the *Farther Adventures*,[43] the endings of *Moll Flanders* and *Colonel Jack*, combined with the didactic works, demonstrate the narrative possibilities of the safe harbour of family life. These representations have shaped the expectations and affordances of the novel genre, but defy incorporation in a narrative of progress from a feudal to a modern social model.

Further Reading

Joanne Bailey, *Unquiet Lives: Marriage and Marriage Breakdown in England, 1600–1800* (Cambridge: Cambridge University Press, 2003).

David Blewett, 'Changing Attitudes toward Marriage in the Time of Defoe: The Case of *Moll Flanders*', *HLQ*, 44:2 (1981), 77–88.

Christopher Flint, 'Orphaning the Family: The Role of Kinship in *Robinson Crusoe*', *ELH*, 55:2 (1988), 381–419.

Melissa J. Ganz, '*Moll Flanders* and English Marriage Law', *ECF*, 17:2 (2005), 157–82.

Robert James Merrett, *Daniel Defoe: Contrarian* (Toronto: University of Toronto Press, 2013).

Ellen Pollak, 'Gender and Fiction in *Moll Flanders* and *Roxana*', in *The Cambridge Companion to Daniel Defoe*, ed. John Richetti (Cambridge: Cambridge University Press, 2009), 139–57.

John Richetti, 'The Family, Sex, and Marriage in Defoe's *Moll Flanders* and *Roxana*', *Studies in the Literary Imagination*, 15:2 (1982), 19–35.

Lawrence Stone, *The Family, Sex and Marriage in England 1500–1800* (1977; Harmondsworth: Penguin, 1990).

Lawrence Stone, *Uncertain Unions and Broken Lives: Marriage and Divorce in England, 1660–1857* (Oxford: Oxford University Press, 1995).

Naomi Tadmor, *Family and Friends in Eighteenth-Century England: Household, Kinship and Patronage* (Cambridge: Cambridge University Press, 2001).

David Turner, *Fashioning Adultery: Gender, Sex and Civility in England, 1660–1740* (Cambridge: Cambridge University Press, 2002).

---

[43] Markley, '"I have now done"', 45.

CHAPTER 17

DEFOE AND CHRISTIANITY

DAVID WALKER

> Wherever God erects a House of Prayer,
> The Devil always builds a Chappel there:
> And 'twill be found upon Examination,
> The latter has the larger Congregation.[1]

THE POLITICS OF RELIGION IN THE LATER SEVENTEENTH CENTURY

THE seventeenth century is arguably the wildest century in the political and religious history of Great Britain. It contained the peaks and troughs of civil war, regicide, republicanism, and restoration. The national church disestablished in the 1640s was revived in 1660, ushering in a period of persecution for Nonconformist Protestants. A century of turbulence culminated in the success (from Defoe's perspective) of the so-called Glorious Revolution of 1688, an event led by the Calvinist Dutchman William of Orange. The ensuing Toleration Act of 1689 still divides the opinion of historians concerning the extent to which the state had shifted from a policy of uniformity to one of pluralism: it guaranteed Dissenters freedom of worship though not full civic rights. These events changed forever the spiritual and temporal face of the British Isles. When the staunchly Anglican Queen Anne, the last Stuart eligible to sit on the British throne, died in 1714, an invasion of a different kind occurred when the new Hanoverian dynasty, headed by the Lutheran German George I, inherited a rich and modern country that could count itself as a significant power in Western Europe. It could have been very different: the Jacobite uprising of 1715 threatened a return to Roman Catholicism but did not ultimately destabilize the transition to a new dynasty. As Julian Hoppit has

---

[1] Defoe, *The True-Born Englishman* (1700/1), lines 56–9, *SFS*, i. 86.

remarked, 'one of the most remarkable features of the political landscape after 1715 was the success with which Jacobite threats were contained by George and the Whigs'. After the failure of the rebellion the Protestant succession was secure, and 'by 1720 the religious settlement of the 1690s was back in place'.[2] Even so, committed Christians like Defoe continued to see bogeymen in the form of heretics and atheists; Catholics, Anglicans, and Dissenters continued to disagree over finer points of Christianity, but now there were challenges to the very fundaments of the faith. Defoe lived through a period during which Christianity seemed fragmented, beleaguered, and precarious.

The political stability and relative religious freedom Defoe enjoyed in his final decade may have been inconceivable to him in his formative years. Throughout the 1660s a series of parliamentary acts subsequently—and erroneously—called the Clarendon Code severely limited Nonconformist worship.[3] The Code made illegal any form of conventicle designed for worship outside the Anglican Communion. As is often the case, persecution hardened resistance. The Church of England in its re-established form was extremely powerful and counted 'over 90 percent of the population' as members.[4] It was also vengeful in its persecution of Dissenters, aggressive and eager in its punishment of those who gathered in conventicles to express their faith. Manna for their vengeance were separatists such as Quakers and Baptists who filled the jails in the 1660s, '70s, and '80s. In the eyes of High Anglicans, sects such as these had demonstrated in the 1640s and '50s the potential of radical Puritanism for organization and agitation. Religion remained at the forefront of politics: 'Thus, the religious divisions which had been a key factor in the political life of England before the civil war and Interregnum continued to disrupt the nation after the Restoration'.[5] Those who chose not to conform lobbied aggressively against organized persecution. The religious landscape of English Protestant Dissent in the later seventeenth century demonstrated a growing antipathy towards the unified national Church inherited from the sixteenth-century Reformation. When it became clear that comprehension within the Church would not be available to them, Dissenters fought hard for toleration outside of it. Consequently, those who were persecuted were accused of clinging to the spirit of regicide and republicanism. *The Book of Common Prayer* (1662), revised and published in the same year that witnessed the passing of the Act of Uniformity, was vilified by Dissenters for its prescriptions on worship and was often lumped in with the persecutory legislation that unfolded in what was a very tense decade.[6]

---

[2] Julian Hoppit, *A Land of Liberty?: England 1689–1727* (Oxford: Oxford University Press, 2000), 383. For a detailed account of the Jacobite Rising of 1715, see Daniel Szechi, *1715: The Great Jacobite Rebellion* (New Haven, CT: Yale University Press, 2006).

[3] For the political and literary contexts, see Tim Harris, *Restoration: Charles II and his Kingdoms, 1660–1685* (London: Penguin, 2005), 53 (on the misnomer of the 'Clarendon Code'); and N. H. Keeble, *The Literary Culture of Nonconformity in Later Seventeenth-Century England* (Leicester: Leicester University Press, 1987), 45–55 (on the endurance of older, Elizabethan laws against nonconformity to the Church of England, as well the introduction of new ones at the Restoration).

[4] Hoppit, *Land of Liberty*, 208.

[5] Dewey Wallace, *Shapers of English Calvinism, 1660–1714: Variety, Persistence, and Transformation* (Oxford: Oxford University Press, 2011), 21.

[6] See John Bunyan's robust response to the new *Book of Common Prayer* in *I Will Pray with the Spirit* (1662), written from prison.

Daniel Defoe was born into a Presbyterian family in the year of the Restoration of the Church of England and monarchy, 1660. During his youth, the air was thick with prophecy and criticism of the openly wicked life lived by King Charles II and his courtiers and the women with whom they were acquainted. For those who worshipped outside conformity, events such as the 1665 plague and 1666 Great Fire of London could be attributed to an angry and jealous God punishing an unworthy people. The Foes, as upstanding and respected Nonconformists, made common cause with their preacher Samuel Annesley, deprived with many others of his living in 1662. The Foes settled in the parish of St Stephen Coleman Street: 'Not far away lived John Milton, and from the meeting place in Swan Alley there poured forth in vain the Fifth Monarchy Men in 1661 to rise against Charles II in the name of Jesus'.[7] Coleman Street area had 'a reputation for political and religious radicalism since the 1630s. Meetings were held there from which developed radical political and religious convictions held by two groups in particular, the Levellers and Fifth Monarchy men.'[8]

Defoe was brought up in this Nonconformist, Presbyterian environment. 1660 'abruptly cut across all the Interregnum religious experiments', says MacCulloch, as 'the leading episcopal clergy waiting in the wings made full use of this mood, completely outmanoeuvring the Presbyterians'.[9] Presbyterians, however, were resilient. They had spoken out in the 1590s under Elizabeth I, and again in the 1630s and '40s when they proved on occasion to be thorns in the side of Charles I's episcopal establishment. On the other hand, however, many opposed the regicide in 1649.[10] They often supported the monarchy and temperate forms of episcopacy and were as critical of the sects as were bishops. It was this tradition of Presbyterianism—reasonable and measured—to which Defoe was disposed, though Defoe defined himself generically as a Dissenter, rather than as a Presbyterian.[11] Richard Baxter's star 'as the voice of moderate Puritanism' was on the rise in the early to mid 1650s, and Baxter led the unsuccessful push for comprehension at the Restoration.[12] Keeble explains that 'their efforts toward comprehension (or "accommodation") in a more broadly based national church had been pursued in 1667 in a bill', but again 'these efforts came to nothing', resulting in a breakdown between Presbyterians and Baptists and Quakers.[13] Defoe lamented that comprehension failed, and he regretted that the Dissenters had not pressed for it again at the time of the Revolution.

---

[7] Novak, *Daniel Defoe*, 22.
[8] Stephen Porter, *Pepys's London: Everyday Life in London, 1650–1703* (Stroud: Amberley, 2012), 49–50
[9] Diarmaid MacCulloch, *Reformation: Europe's House Divided 1490–1700* (London: Allen Lane, 2003), 528–9.
[10] William Prynne and Richard Baxter were prominent in their opposition to the trial and execution of Charles in 1649. Both were dismissive of separatists.
[11] See further Katherine Clark, *Daniel Defoe: The Whole Frame of Nature, Time, and Providence* (Basingstoke: Palgrave Macmillan, 2007).
[12] Tim Cooper, *John Owen, Richard Baxter and the Formation of Nonconformity* (Farnham: Ashgate, 2011), 179.
[13] Keeble, *Literary Culture of Nonconformity*, 58.

By the time he reached adulthood Defoe had witnessed and participated in many of the twists and turns that characterize the persecutory history of religious Dissent in the second half of the seventeenth century. His father was particularly active in the closely fought municipal elections of the early 1680s that took place during and after the Exclusion Crisis (1678–81).[14] The crisis arose in the late 1670s, amidst the anti-Catholic backlash of the Popish Plot, when 'Reformed Protestants had come to agree with their onetime sectarian adversaries that the episcopal leadership of the church and the prospect of a Catholic successor endangered Protestantism and parliament'.[15] Dissenters joined Low Church Whigs in support of a parliamentary bill to exclude Charles II's brother James Duke of York from the succession. This is a further indication that politics and religion in this period were fellow travellers. All of this took place whilst Defoe was contemplating a radical change in his future: to withdraw from the training he was undergoing to become a Presbyterian preacher. His intention was to embrace the cut and thrust of a life in trade and commerce.

Defoe's *Meditations* (1681) in Context

Defoe in the 1680s was an eager Presbyterian, and it is natural therefore that his earliest known writings were about religion. The *Meditations*, composed in 1681, mark an auspicious event in the history of Nonconformist literature. They are what is thought to be his earliest literary work comprising a short sequence of seven highly emotive and inward-looking poems not published until the mid-twentieth century.[16] The immediate political context of Defoe's transition to a secular occupation in the early 1680s was the government's defeat of Exclusion in 1681. The personal context for the young Defoe was political as well as spiritual. The imminent move from his original ambition to be a minister in the Presbyterian Church to a career as a merchant in London's teeming metropolis may have been confirmed by the persecutory context. For Nonconformists, 1681 announced the beginning of a savage period of repression, as the victimization of religious Dissent was intensified and went unchecked for the remaining four years of Charles II's reign. Michael Watts informs us that, after the dissolution of the second and third Exclusion parliaments in 1681, '[f]or the rest of his reign Charles, now in receipt of French subsidies, could afford to do without Parliament and the Dissenters were

---

[14] For a brief but rigorous account of the London municipal elections in 1678 and James Foe's participation in them, see Backscheider, *Daniel Defoe*, 28. For more extensive coverage, see Gary De Krey, *London and the Restoration, 1659–1683* (Cambridge: Cambridge University Press, 2005), Chs 4–6; Mark Knights, *Politics and Opinion in Crisis, 1678–81* (Cambridge: Cambridge University Press, 1994).

[15] De Krey, *London and the Restoration*, 169.

[16] Strictly speaking there are only six fully worked out poems; the seventh is a fragment. George Harris Healey (ed.), *The Meditations of Daniel Defoe* (Cummington, MA: Cummington Press, 1946), v.

left to suffer the full force of royal vengeance'.[17] The Restoration in England and Wales from 1660 signalled the attempt to force the puritan and sectarian genie back into the bottle. This was resisted by a small but significant percentage of Nonconformists— as well as more dangerous separatists such as the Fifth Monarchy Men, who rebelled against the crown (disastrously, as it turned out) as we have seen in 1661, and paid a heavy price. Many others—Baptists, Quakers, Independents, Congregationalists, and Presbyterians—adopted a passive-aggressive stance: they would rather go to jail than conform to Anglicanism. To add insult to injury James II had a trouble-free accession to the throne, and from 1685 packed the universities and the army with Catholics. In doing so he confirmed in the minds of many Protestants that the country was on the high road to popery. Defoe urged his fellow Dissenters to resist James's Declarations of Indulgence, which he saw as an attempt to divide and conquer the Protestant interest and pave the way for Catholicism (*Appeal*, 51–2). Defoe's relationship to mainstream Dissent remained often fractious in later years.

Many Protestants believed that James's ultimate strategy was their eradication and the restoration of Roman Catholicism, a threat that hung over the nation like a black cloud alleviated by the successful invasion in 1688 by James's son-in-law, William of Orange, and the passing of the Toleration Act one year later. Although the Toleration Act was widely welcomed it did not extend liberty of conscience as far as it might: The Act 'did no more than exempt carefully defined classes of Dissenters ... The Toleration Act thus mitigated the religious, but not the political disabilities of the Dissenters'.[18] Groups not included in this dispensation were Quakers, Jews, and Catholics. England, Wales, Scotland, and Ireland were far from uniform. Dissenters caught in conventicles were still not protected by the law; on the contrary, 'with the doors locked, barred or bolted during any time of such meeting [... they] shall not receive any benefit from this law, but be liable to all the pains and penalties of all the foresaid laws'. Nor was it the case that exemptions from 'tithes or other parochial duties' would be countenanced.[19] Gordon J. Schochet is correct to remark that religious 'rights' and freedoms came late 'to the English speaking world ... Even then they were given grudgingly, and only partially'.[20]

From the early 1680s onwards, then, Defoe seems to have been in and around many of the controversial events and conspiracies of the day, be it with the pen or the sword. He narrowly escaped punishment for his participation in Monmouth's rebellion in 1685. The savagery of the state in the aftermath of James's victory and defeat of Monmouth

---

[17] Michael Watts, *The Dissenters: From the Reformation to the French Revolution* (Oxford: Oxford University Press, 1978), 253–4. See also Richard L. Greaves, *Secrets of the Kingdom: British Radicals from the Popish Plot to the Revolution of 1688-89* (Stanford, CA: Stanford University Press, 1992), 90–9.

[18] Andrew Browning (ed.), *English Historical Documents, Volume VIII, 1660-1714* (London: Eyre and Spottiswoode, 1953), 360, 401–2.

[19] See Browning, (ed.), *English Historical Documents*, 401–2.

[20] Gordon J. Schochet, 'The Act of Toleration and the Failure of Comprehension: Persecution, Nonconformity and Religious Indifference', in *The World of William and Mary: Anglo-Dutch Perspectives on the Revolution of 1688-89*, ed. Dale Hoak and Mordechai Feingold (Stanford, CA: Stanford University Press, 1996), 165–87 (165).

was extensive and ruthless. Judge Jeffreys's 'Bloody Assize' at Taunton passed death sentences resulting in over 200 men being hanged, drawn, and quartered, and a further 800 transported to the West Indies as slave labour, most of these Nonconformists. This was execution by other means. Working as a field hand on the sugar plantations was in effect a death sentence to those that were sent. Defoe was very fortunate to be given a special pardon on 31 May 1687.[21] That said, the narrow and seemingly unlikely escape from Jeffreys did not prevent him from writing prolifically on the major questions of the day in religion, politics, and economics. The last years of the seventeenth century and first decade of the eighteenth century would prove to be exciting on many fronts.

The *Meditations* demonstrates and contributes to an understanding of Defoe's mindset as he began a journey of discovery that led to a radical change of direction. These poems are considered here in relation to a crisis of vocation that Defoe experienced at this time, and his entry into the community of Dissenting networks, merchant guilds, and municipal politicians. Defoe was very close to completing his training for the Presbyterian priesthood when he decided to take a completely different path. He was acutely aware that he was living in times that were dangerous for Dissenters and yet very exciting. Many Nonconformist merchants and traders were intensely political animals, often working hand in glove with the emergent Whig faction in Parliament. The example was set very close to home. Defoe's father is a very good model of civic duty: James Foe was highly respected by many of his coreligionists and London citizens. He was a prominent and ambitious member of the Butchers' Guild and an active participant in city politics. The Dissenting community in London and their networks were at the forefront of guild management and municipal politics. For instance, the partisan shrieval elections fought in the early 1680s were intensely divisive. Whig candidates such as Slingsby Bethell and Henry Cornish revisited the language of arbitrary government and popish conspiracies, whilst Tories bemoaned what they saw as the return of the rebellious and republican discourse that they associated respectively with the freedom of political rhetoric in the 1640s and the nightmare of 'turning the world upside down'. Rehashing the rhetoric of 1641 was common to the understanding of both Whigs and Tories in the pamphlet literature of the day. It was sharply clear in the memories of the country. This was particularly evident in the tangled elections in London, and in the country more generally. 'Exclusion elections', says Richard Ashcraft, invoked a memorialization of the military, and he cites an example in Essex where 'the Whig candidate, Colonel Mildmay ... "appeared with about 1000 gentlemen and freeholders," and he was supported by Lord Grey with "about 2000 horse attending him"'. When they joined forces 'with other supporters they are reported to be 6000 strong'. Intimidation was clearly a valuable weapon in election politics. The militaristic elements in the Exclusion elections invoked the public memory of civil war and exercised considerable influence in what was still an unstable political and religious context. Many examples of this kind could be cited to force home the point.[22]

---

[21] Novak, *Daniel Defoe*, 83.

[22] Richard Ashcraft, *Revolutionary Politics and Locke's Two Treatises of Government* (Princeton, NJ: Princeton University Press, 1986), 166.

Gary De Krey, for instance, makes a very similar point when he asks the following question: 'Was the city, then, re-embarking on the courses of 1641?'. His answer is: 'That question was on the minds of many by 1679'.[23]

As is often the case, fraught political tensions in the country created a breeding ground for outstanding literature: Bunyan's allegorical fictions *The Pilgrim's Progress* (1678), *The Life and Death of Mr Badman* (1680), and *The Holy War* (1682), Dryden's *Absalom and Achitophel* (1681), Locke's *Two Treatises of Government* (written 1681, published 1689), alongside polemical writing such as Bunyan's *Israel's Hope Encouraged* (composed 1680–1, published posthumously 1692).[24] Bunyan's fiction and sermons strongly reflect the challenging socioeconomic and political context. Bunyan was sufficiently invested in the shrieval elections of the early 1680s to launch an attack. *Israel's Hope Encouraged* makes specific reference to topical events. Bunyan writes of 'days of trouble', citing the Popish Plot: 'For then we began to fear cutting of Throats, of being burned in our beds, and of seeing our Children dashed in pieces before our Faces'.[25] Vivid and horrific images presented in this work echo the rhetoric of anti-Catholicism found in Foxe's *Acts and Monuments* (1561), the pamphlet literature of the Irish rebellions from the 1590s and 1641, and, of course, the rabid anti-Catholicism of very many Protestants, be they Anglican or Nonconformist. Bunyan rarely comments negatively and directly on the immediate political context in which he writes. To do so on this occasion speaks perhaps to the seriousness of his concerns.

This context too was one with which Defoe was wrestling when he was reconsidering his vocation and facing hard choices. His true interests—he was now sure, says Backscheider—were in the realms of economics, trade, and politics: 'On the one hand he could embrace the obscure service of a Dissenting divine or the opportunities of trade and London's battle of wits with her monarchs; the probability of persecution or the hope of prosperity'.[26] In this tumultuous context, rendered here very briefly, Defoe relinquished the pursuit of a career in the ministry and became a wholesale hosier.

The *Meditations* apparently sprung from Defoe's attendance at a series of sermons delivered by the prominent Presbyterian/Congregationalist preacher John Collins in Pinner's Hall, a central venue for Nonconformist theology. 'The sermons', we are told, are 'discursive and dull (Mr Collins preached week after week from the same or almost the same text), and they tell us little enough about Defoe. The *Meditations* on the other hand are of the utmost interest and importance. They are Defoe's earliest work'.[27] 'At the time',

---

[23] Gary S. De Krey, *London and the Restoration 1659–1683* (Cambridge: Cambridge University Press, 2005), 164.

[24] Richard L. Greaves, *Glimpses of Glory: John Bunyan and English Dissent* (Stanford CA: Stanford University Press, 2002), 394–5.

[25] *Israel's Hope Encouraged*, ed. W. R. Owens, in *The Miscellaneous Works of John Bunyan*, gen. ed. Roger Sharrock, 13 vols (Oxford: Clarendon, 1975–94), xiii. 21.

[26] Backscheider, *Daniel Defoe*, 30.

[27] Andrew M. Wilkinson, 'The "Meditations" of Daniel Defoe', *MLR*, 46:3/4 (1951), 349–54 (350). On Collins see Francis Bremer and Tom Webster (eds.), *Puritans and Puritanism in Europe and America*, 2 vols (Santa Barbara, CA: ABC Clio, 2006), i. 58. Collins (c.1632–87) was born in England, educated in New England at Harvard College, and returned to England in 1653. In 1659 he was chaplain to

writes George Healey, Defoe 'was a well-educated youth of about 21, not yet married, ambitious, pious, and probably not wholly serene of mind'. Insofar as Defoe's withdrawal from his vocation is concerned, Healey refers us to *The Review* for 22 October 1709 (vi. 427) where Defoe '[y]ears later ... said that it had been his disaster first to be set aside for the ministry, ... but why his mind was changed, or exactly when, he never made clear'.[28] There are various views in this quotation from Healey's Introduction that are suggestive in their assumptions: 'not wholly *serene* of mind'—emphasis added—if true is a prompt, a trigger that is common when spiritual doubt leads to taking up the pen. Doubt often leads to enquiry, and also to uncertainty and scepticism. This is particular, but not exclusive, to those who follow a persecuted religion, entailing relentless introspection and forensic attention to one's spiritual welfare—concerns about election or salvation—and uncertainty of receiving God's grace. It is the uncertainty of election and salvation that lies at the heart of many despair-ridden narratives published in the sixteenth and seventeenth centuries. Calvinist theories of predestination were strict and forbidding, with little in the way of leeway, removed as they were from the Anglican or Arminian position of God's grace being potentially available to all.

The seventeenth century is particularly rich in the quality of its spiritual autobiographies in prose and poetry. Defoe's *Meditations* were perhaps the product of his state of mind in the early 1680s, and can be regarded as a spiritual autobiography by looking at the poems' form and content alongside the author's intention in relation to the context(s) in which they are written and the motivation that spurred him on. Unlike many people who wrote spiritual autobiographies, Defoe was young and filled with optimism. For John Richetti, 'Whatever his reasons in choosing a secular career, Defoe's youthful piety is probably not in question', and the poems 'are strongly expressive of genuine devotion'.[29] This does not, however, mean that Defoe did not wish to withdraw from entering the Presbyterian ministry. His links to the merchant world and his Presbyterian political networks were very strong. Nor is he being fickle. Business and religion in the Foe household is thought by all of Defoe's recent biographers to have been the bread and butter of conversation in the anxious world of municipal electoral politics and the oppressive arena of religious persecution. There is an element of conjecture in this assessment predicated on the later Defoe's amazingly diverse career. Maximillian Novak describes the tone and form of Defoe's *Meditations* as being to some extent indebted to Dryden, often cited as the most prominent living man of letters in the later seventeenth century. A more problematic influence in Novak's view, however, is the poetry of Rochester [SEE CHAPTER 2]. In 'Thou hast Made us & Not We', and in *Meditation* number 3, we read: 'If I my Self my Own First Being gave | And From that Primitive Nill | Into The Present Something Then Arose | Of Meer Power & Will | And

---

General Monck. 'He was one of the original six Pinner's Hall lecturers in 1672'. He was buried in the Nonconformist cemetery, Bunhill Fields. Collins is variously described as a Congregationalist and/or a Presbyterian.

[28] Healey, 'Introduction', in Defoe, *Meditations*, viii–ix.
[29] Richetti, *Life of Daniel Defoe*, 7.

Been my Self That Contradicction | Of Being, of its Self from Nothing Grown | Then I had been Indeed of Right My Owne.[30]

Novak has it that there are clear echoes of Rochester's 'Upon Nothing' and even some suggestion of the ideas presented in his 'Satire upon Mankind'.[31] The quotation above is part of the poem's first stanza. In the opening lines that precede it Defoe believes his reverence is intact. Accordingly, the subject matter in this poem is neither sycophantic towards God, nor apologetic. As with much poetry consisting of dialogues with God, the poet is polite and pious. Defoe's tone is far removed from the open anguish of John Donne in his religious verse, or George Herbert with his interest in speculative theology and the value of experience over abstraction. Defoe is, however, sceptical, and in this regard the stanza takes issue with the title and veers somewhat between the deity and the self. There is much in the devotional poetry of the seventeenth century upon which Defoe could draw. As Backscheider notes there are similarities here with Donne's *Holy Sonnets*, characterized by contradiction and argument, interrogation and self-aggrandizement. The poems 'have a restless frenetic quality ... a Donnian quality of fretting, of complexity, and of awareness of paradox'.[32] What makes Defoe different perhaps is the direction in which he is heading. Unlike Donne, Herbert, Baxter, and Bunyan, Defoe is not looking for spiritual certainty or evidence of election. Nor, at this time in his life, is he melancholic or suffering from a debilitating illness. Furthermore, he does not seek conflict or use the violent imagery we associate with many of Donne's religious poems. On the contrary, Defoe is happy enough to surrender to the greatness of God.[33] He is self-assured, and perhaps a little arrogant in the language that he uses, but he is nevertheless ever ready and happy to subordinate his own needs to a higher power. In short, perhaps, Defoe at this stage in his life is a young man in a hurry, and the energetic tone of the poems reflect enthusiasm and emotion, particularly joy.[34] Defoe's verse throughout the collection is written in the form of an irregular Pindaric ode, the traditional form used in the expression of literary emotion. In stanza 2 of 'Thou hast Made us', Defoe seems to shrug his shoulders in submission with the opening line: 'But Ah! How readily does My Wholl frame / Point to Thy Mighty hand'.[35] Here too Defoe is not crying out for confirmation of his salvation; nor does he beg or search for some

---

[30] For a brief but suggestive and interesting analysis, see Novak, *Daniel Defoe*, 59–60, where he sees in the *Meditations* the influence of Bunyan, Dryden, and Rochester.

[31] Novak, *Daniel Defoe*, 60.

[32] Backscheider, *Daniel Defoe*, 29.

[33] The theme of religious resignation is one that comes up in numerous examples of Defoe's personal writings. Examples in his correspondence include letters to Robert Harley, John Fransham, and Samuel Keimer, the last, as late as 1717, containing religious verse reminiscent of the *Meditations* (*Correspondence*, 139–40, 779–80, 828–30). On Defoe's religious poem 'Resignation', which survives in an autograph manuscript dated July 1708, see Frank H. Ellis, 'Defoe's "Resignaĉon" and the Limitations of "Mathematical Plainness"', *RES*, 36:143 (1985), 338–54.

[34] See S. Brynn Roberts, *Puritanism and the Pursuit of Happiness: The Ministry and Theology of Ralph Venning, c.1621–1674* (Woodbridge: Boydell Press, 2015). Roberts's title is clear in its attention to positive emotions under happiness rather than the restrictive stereotype of Puritans in the period.

[35] Defoe, 'Thou Hast made us & Not We', lines 12–13; Defoe, *Meditations*, 15.

defining sign of his election. Comparisons with Donne might therefore be overstated. In this quotation Defoe is plain in his speech. He is ready and willing to commit to his religion and to God. Kathleen Lynch persuasively argues that 'Donne's conflicted religious identity had been precisely tuned to King James's church and state. Pressured by the polemics of conversion, as he undoubtedly was, he refused to make any conversion from one confessional affiliation to another'.[36] Defoe's king and church is far different from the Jacobean Church, which was largely Calvinist. Charles II, on the other hand, was mostly thought in London at least to be a crypto-Catholic, and his Church was dominated by conflict from within—High and Low Church latitude men engaged in intellectual conflicts between reason and revelation.

The common understanding among his more recent biographers—Backscheider, Novak, Furbank and Owens, and Richetti—is that Defoe was on the verge of taking up a more secular career in commerce. The poems appear to confirm Defoe's spiritual contentment. The angst, where we find it, is specific to other matters. The evidence that Defoe questions his vocation is in the certain knowledge we have of his taking up a secular position soon after the writing of these poems, composed in the tightknit London merchant community and its links to Whig political networks. The emotionally wrought states demonstrated in the spiritual autobiographies of the early modern period, insofar as they affect Defoe's writing, is apparent in his fiction, particularly *Robinson Crusoe* (1719), where significant and influential critical work has elucidated that novel's religious commitments.[37] Providence in that novel is a word that carries a lot of theological freight and is summoned on a multitude of occasions as Crusoe undergoes a conversion experience based upon his reading of the Bible while marooned on his island.

DEFOE, THE REVOLUTION, AND DISSENT

Defoe was of course a confirmed and committed Williamite. He supported fully the Glorious Revolution of 1688 and the principle that parliament could limit the succession based on the nation's Protestant identity [SEE CHAPTER 20]. He also defended William's bellicose attitude towards the Catholic Sun King, Louis XIV, king of France, the

---

[36] Kathleen Lynch, *Protestant Autobiography in the Seventeenth-Century Anglophone World* (Oxford: Oxford University Press, 2012), 64. For Donne's supposed uncertainty about his religious affiliation, see John Carey, *John Donne: Life, Mind, and Art* (1981; London: Faber and Faber, 2008), Chs 1–2.

[37] G. A. Starr, *Defoe and Spiritual Autobiography* (Princeton, NJ: Princeton University Press, 1965); J. Paul Hunter, *The Reluctant Pilgrim: Defoe's Emblematic Method and Quest for Form in Robinson Crusoe* (Baltimore, MD: Johns Hopkins University Press, 1966); Stuart Sim, *Negotiations with Paradox: Narrative Practice and Narrative Form in Bunyan and Defoe* (London: Harvester Wheatsheaf, 1990), Chs 6–7. A new and persuasive argument on conversion narratives in all of their complexity can be found in Kathleen Lynch's *Protestant Autobiography*.

dominant power in late seventeenth-century Europe [SEE CHAPTER 28]. Defoe feared a religious war in Europe, and believed Protestant powers had to band together against threats from Versailles or the Vatican.[38] Throughout his life Defoe engaged rigorously in print with those aspects of religious change that eventually led to 'the comprehension proposals of 1689 and the Toleration Act, which were foreshadowed in the Petition of the Seven Bishops in June 1688'.[39] Defoe was at the forefront of religious controversy for all of his adult life, even when it seemed he was not. In *The Shortest-Way with the Dissenters* (1702), in which he uses irony to expose High-Church bigotry, Defoe's speaker scoffs at those Nonconformists who refused to take the Anglican Communion. Defoe himself was trenchantly opposed to occasional conformity, the means by which unscrupulous Nonconformists conformed, at the same time they were attending conventicles, in order to qualify for public office. He clashed with other Dissenters over his stance. However, he was equally opposed to legislation that would punish occasional conformists, and *The Shortest-Way* was occasioned by the first of three parliamentary bills introduced by Tories in the early years of Anne's reign. The anonymous publication of *The Shortest-Way* is a masterpiece of pamphlet literature, a brilliant demonstration of irony that apparently fooled many people into believing that its author was sincere in the belief that its negative representation of Dissenters should be taken at face value. The aftermath of outrage amongst the Dissenting community sees Defoe at the centre of his own controversy.

This notorious pamphlet is laced throughout with outrageous attacks upon those who maintained their religious position beyond the pale of the Established Church. Naturally enough, the pamphlet generated a storm of angry criticism from the Dissenting population, desperate to know who had written it. 'Even ye Dissenters Like Casha To Cæsar Lift up the first Dagger at me', Defoe complained while in hiding (*Correspondence*, 11). Defoe informs us tongue-in-cheek that 'it is now near Fourteen Years, that the Glory and Peace of the purest and most flourishing Church in the World has been Ecclips'd, Buffetted, and Disturb'd, by a sort of Men, who God in his Providence has suffer'd to insult over her, and bring her down' (*PEW*, iii. 97). In a pamphlet where every word seems quotable, Defoe writes in the borrowed voice of the Church of England in its attitude to Dissenters, applying the frequently levelled charges of regicide, revolution, and hatred towards the later Stuart monarchs:

> You have *Butcher'd* one King, *Depos'd* another King, and made a *mock King* of a Third; and yet you cou'd have the Face to expect to be employ'd and trusted by the Fourth;

---

[38] Defoe, *The Danger of the Protestant Religion Consider'd, from the Present Prospect of a Religious War in Europe* (1701).

[39] J. P. Kenyon, *The Stuart Constitution, Documents and Commentary* (Cambridge: Cambridge University Press, 1966), 365. See also Tony Claydon, *William III and the Godly Revolution* (Cambridge: Cambridge University Press, 1996); Scott Sowerby, *Making Toleration: The Repealers and the Glorious Revolution* (Cambridge, MA: Harvard University Press, 2013), and Harris, *Restoration*.

any body that did not know the Temper of your Party, wou'd stand amaz'd at the Impudence, as well as Folly, to think of it. (98)[40]

The reference to king-killing in 1649 evokes the Good Old Cause launched in 1641 and is the bread and butter of partisan rhetoric. Defoe's ventriloquizing of it heightens the irony. As Jonathan Scott writes: 'The loyalist rallying cry "41 again" had two meanings. It registered first the perception of the Dissenters' radical and intransigent opposition to the crown ... and the fact of political polarisation and a resulting belief in the proximity of civil war.'[41]

Defoe's public defence of William III in *The True Born Englishman* (1700/1) was widely known, and in *An Appeal to Honour and Justice* (1715) he makes his feelings especially clear. He supported fully the removal of James II. In Defoe's account, William himself was impressed with Defoe's loyalty and, according to Defoe, heaped gifts and regard upon him for writing the poem.[42] Defoe only mentions it to make clear his respect for King William: 'I take all Occasions to do for the expressing the Honour I ever preserv'd for the Immortal and Glorious Memory of that Greatest and Best of Princes, and who it was my Honour and Advantage to call Master as well as Sovereign' (*Appeal*, 6–7).

His antipathy in the *Appeal* towards serving a Catholic king, at this point, was firm and, in the wake of his writing for a Tory ministry accused of Jacobitism, timely. In his euphoric praise of William, Defoe reminds the country of

> The happy accession of His present majesty [George I] to the Throne, I cannot but advise them to look back, and call to mind who it was that first Guided them to the Family of *Hanover* ... the just authority of Parliament, in the undoubted Right of Limiting the Succession, and Establishing that Glorious Maxim of our Settlement, (viz.) *That it is inconsistent with the Constitution of this Protestant Kingdom to be Govern'd by a Popish Prince* ... and that it is to King *William*, next to Heaven it self, to whom we owe the Enjoying of a Protestant King at this time. (*Appeal*, 7–8)

Defoe's consistent defence of the Revolution settlement following William III's death was motivated by a conviction that Catholicism was tantamount to tyranny, a polity under which individuals would lose out not only temporally, but also in their religious freedom on which their salvation depended.

That Defoe was a proud Whig with Lockean views on patriarchy and property is evident in many of his works, the most famous of which is *Robinson Crusoe*. Another example is *Jure Divino* (1706), where Defoe's denunciation of the divine right theory of monarchy is trenchant:

---

[40] See Keeble, *Literary Culture of Nonconformity*, 70.

[41] Jonathan Scott, *England's Troubles: Seventeenth-Century English Political Instability in European Context* (Cambridge: Cambridge University Press, 2000), 435.

[42] For a sceptical take on Defoe's repeated claims about his work for William III, see Furbank and Owens, *Political Biography*, 26–32.

> *While* in the Infant-Ages of the Kind,
> Nature to first *Paternal Rule* confin'd;
> The Men untainted, and their Number few,
> The Patriarchal Government *might do*....
> There can be Pretence of Government,
> Till they that have the Property consent. (Book II, lines 70–3, 391–2; *SFS*, ii. 103, 114)

Defoe follows closely Locke's attack on Filmer's *Patriarcha*: Filmer has it, in Locke's paraphrase, that ' "Men are born in subjection to their parents", and therefore cannot be free. And this authority of parents, he calls "royal authority" '.[43] *Jure Divino* is a major satirical poem that celebrates the Williamite Revolution. It dismantles the idea that indefeasible hereditary right, passive obedience, and non-resistance is an ideal form of monarchical government and picks apart the notion of absolutist monarchy, whereby kings answer only to God. Christianity for Locke—and also for Defoe—has no truck with absolutist monarchy, a term they associate with tyranny.

It was at the start of Anne's reign that Defoe feared absolutism and persecution were being reasserted, and this led him to publish *The Shortest-Way with the Dissenters*. Novak has written that 'the narrative surrounding ... [the publication of *The Shortest-Way* and *A Hymn to the Pillory* (1703)] ... might be read as a triumph of journalistic integrity over the forces of government repression'. *The Shortest-Way* itself is much more than an exercise in irony, or an example of parody, says Novak. Instead it is a surgical satire on High-Church rhetoric 'and Defoe's High Churchman ... calls for outright violence and persecution of the Dissenters'.[44] D. N. DeLuna on the other hand, in her analysis of *The Shortest-Way*, concentrates on the pressing and controversial context of occasional conformity. For her *The Shortest-Way* participated aggressively in what was the hottest debate that 'came to monopolize the attention of Dissenters and then all politically aware Englishmen at the turn of the eighteenth century'. DeLuna reminds us that in 1702, 'the first year of Anne's reign, occasional conformity' was everywhere talked about. High-Church Tories sponsored the first Bill for Preventing Occasional Conformity in December 1702, the same month in which *The Shortest-Way* was published.[45] A Tory-packed reading of the bill in the Commons in November had already been passed.

Defoe's experience following his punishment for *The Shortest-Way* changed forever his relationship with the Dissenters. He felt that he had suffered for the cause but had been disowned. Soon after coming to an agreement to write for the ministry that had punished him—made possible by Queen Anne's removal from office of the High-Tory leaders—Defoe was writing Harley almost Machiavellian instructions on how to 'manage' the Dissenters, suggesting that they could be charmed with words

---

[43] John Locke, *Two Treatises on Government*, ed. Mark Goldie (London: Everyman, 1993), 7.

[44] Maximillian E. Novak, 'Defoe's Political and Religious Journalism', in *The Cambridge Companion to Daniel Defoe*, ed. John Richetti (Cambridge: Cambridge University Press, 2011), 25–44 (29); Novak, *Daniel Defoe*, 173.

[45] D. N. DeLuna, 'Ironic Monologue and "Scandalous *Ambo-dexter* Conformity" in Defoe's *The Shortest Way with the Dissenters*', *HLQ*, 57:4 (1994), 319–35.

that never need amount to concrete promises, let alone relief from civic disabilities (*Correspondence*, 88–92). Defoe's Dissenting credentials were clearly an asset to Queen Anne's ministers. Defoe built a network of mostly Nonconformist agents around the country to disseminate ministerial propaganda in 1705–6. His confessional identity as much as his head for commerce suited him to go to Scotland from autumn 1706 to early 1708, to persuade Church of Scotland ministers that the Anglo-Scottish Union would not spell the end for Presbyterianism there. And when, after 1710, Harley was unable to prevent the anti-Dissent legislation his Tory backbenchers demanded, it was again Defoe who defended the ministry, as best he was able. In *A Letter to the Dissenters* (1713) he produced a chilling series of warnings to his coreligionists, advising them against taking sides against the government lest more punitive laws followed. There was a tremendous backlash against the *Letter* in Nonconformist circles. By the end of Anne's reign, Defoe was as alienated from mainstream Dissent as he was from the Whig party. In *An Appeal to Honour and Justice* (1715), Defoe enumerated the occasions on which he had fallen out with the Dissenters in a manner that treads the line between apology and defiance. If Defoe was sometimes uncertain in aspects of his private faith, he was usually unequivocal in his convictions as a public voice on theological affairs. This self-assurance carries through to his late-career writings on Christianity. After writing conduct books like *The Family Instructor* and novels like *Robinson Crusoe*, in which characters struggle with correct religious conduct, Defoe wrote a string of works in the 1720s designed to bolster what he thought of as sound belief.

Defoe, Christianity, and the Occult

Unlikely as it may seem to some, Defoe had a strong interest since childhood in the occult. He was in good company, as Backscheider states: Raleigh, Boyle, Bacon, Dryden, and Newton especially took the study of the occult seriously, as scholars today have recognized.[46] Newton spent much of his time studying alchemy and wrote extensively on Christian theology, culminating in a *Treatise on Revelation*.[47] Newton, says Rob Iliffe, 'situated himself in a tradition of Protestant apocalyptic interpretation whose greatest exponent was the Christ's College fellow Joseph Mede'. Another friend, Henry More, was also the most prolific author of prophetic texts in late seventeenth-century England. At some point in the late 1670s, he began to devote himself to decoding the images in the prophetic books in the Bible, paying particular attention to Revelation. The enduring strength of belief in magic and supernatural practices is attested by the names mentioned above. Newton—perhaps the most intelligent man in the history

---

[46] Backscheider, *Daniel Defoe*, 520. See also Rob Iliffe, *Priest of Nature: The Religious Lives of Isaac Newton* (Oxford: Oxford University Press, 2017), 219; Jack M. Armistead, *Otherworldly John Dryden: Occult Rhetoric in his Poems and Plays* (London: Routledge, 2014).

[47] Iliffe, *Priest of Nature*, 171.

of the English Enlightenment—gave much of his time to working seriously on apocalyptic writings in the Bible and the workings of Satan's intentions. In *Priest of Nature: The Religious Worlds of Isaac Newton*, Iliffe reports Newton's opinion on miracles and the men who claimed them to be valid: 'Rather, the sheer number of false miracles were intended to ruin Christianity master-minded by a dark angel—Satan himself—who had fallen from heaven and who knew he had little time to play his tricks on Earth (Revelation 12:12).'[48]

Another prolific writer on supernatural matters was Richard Baxter, the moderate Presbyterian who wrote positively on the occult and published *The Certainty of the World of Spirits* (1691). Baxter applies a common-sense approach that satisfies his knowledge of God. In his preface, he suggests that the 'World of Spirits' is an extension of God's creation: 'It seemeth hard to unruly minds, that God should keep Intellectual souls, so strange to the unseen World of Spirits; that we know so little of them, and that our Knowledge of them, is no more by the way of sense: But there is in it, much of God's Arbitrary Sovereign Power, and much of his Wisdom, and much of his Justice, and also of his love.'[49] This is also the outlook that Defoe brought to his discussion of supernatural matters, particularly in his 1720s defences of Protestant orthodoxy. It marks him out not as a writer working against the grain of Enlightenment currents, but in tandem with them.

Eighteenth-century intellectuals took the supernatural seriously. The lure and magnetism of the subject was very strong. The writing of the day concerning magic and supernatural events in the early eighteenth century has been approached by some of the keenest historians of the Enlightenment. Modern historicism and new approaches by literary critics have uncovered significant evidence of belief and unbelief in the victory of science over religion, and others have argued strongly for the presence of alternative spiritual worlds. Jacob, for instance, starts with an emphatic point: 'The Enlightenment was an eighteenth-century movement of ideas and practices that made the secular world its point of departure. It did not necessarily deny the meaning or emotional hold of religion, but it gradually shifted attention away from religious questions toward secular ones'. This culminates, for instance, in '[a]reas of human behaviour once explained by concepts like miracles or original sin now received explanations inspired by physical science or the emerging studies of social and economic relations.'[50] Michael Hunter's *The Decline of Magic: Britain in the Enlightenment* opens with a similarly provocative Introduction entitled 'The Supernatural, Science and Atheism'. Here Hunter takes issue with 'Enlightenment commentators' who dismissed a variety of spiritual positions. Hunter instead uncovers changing attitudes to beliefs that were embraced by many, capturing folklore and superstition of such things as 'prophecies, ghosts, apparitions

---

[48] Iliffe, *Priest of Nature*, 171.
[49] Richard Baxter, *The Certainty of the Worlds of Spirits. And Consequently, Of the Immortality of Souls* (1691), Preface, 3.
[50] Margaret C. Jacob, *The Secular Enlightenment* (Princeton, NJ: Princeton University Press, 2019), 1–2.

and fairies'.⁵¹ Hunter is an eminent historian of science in the early modern period and a sceptic when it comes to the so-called decline of magic in the Enlightenment. Anthony Pagden too has recently pointed out that the old shibboleth of reason over passion maintained among Enlightenment intellectuals is 'simply false'. 'David Hume—who must rank, with Kant, as the greatest of the eighteenth-century philosophers—famously declared that "reason is and ought to be a slave of the passions and can never pretend to any other office but to serve and obey them" '.⁵²

Where though does this leave us with magic and Defoe? As a determined Presbyterian and a believer in supernatural events, Defoe, we can infer, would be more sympathetic to Hunter's position than that of Margaret Jacob. We know this too because freethinkers and the Deists—practically speaking—when they write do so by developing a 'cynical psychology'. Also, writes Hunter, 'Deists are a singular group of writers who were systematically sceptical about belief in the continuity of witchcraft and were even-handed in the relation of their phenomena in their publications'. Anthony Collins's *Discourse of Free-thinking* (1713) maintains that ' "the Devil's Dominion and Power" were "ever more or less extensive as Free-Thinking is discouraged or allow'd" '.⁵³

Defoe's antipathy to deism and associated heresies that promoted reason above faith make him seem reactionary. Defoe, as Roy Porter describes him, 'was a classic transitional figure, straddling the old world of distrustful Puritan asceticism and the new one of reason, desire, and abundance'. Effectively, Defoe was a polymath who could turn his hand to many fields of emergent discourses in science, journalism, political theory, and economics whilst similarly being fascinated by 'demonology and the supernatural— witness his *Political History of the Devil* and *System of Magick* (both published in 1726)', as well as being 'responsible for the century's most celebrated ghost story, *True Relation of the Apparition of One Mrs Veal* (1706) as well as a *History of Apparitions* (1727)'.⁵⁴ In his intellectual diversity Defoe fulfilled the criteria of the enlightened man, yet, as this catalogue of late-career publications indicates, Defoe remained committed to a world in which supernatural forces—the Devil, ghosts, and magicians—were in operation.

In the writings of his final decade, Defoe responded to what he saw as a rise in erroneous forms of belief, especially deism, which promoted human reason over salvation through faith.⁵⁵ Defoe fulminated against '*Deists*, *Atheists*, *Arminians*, and which is worse, *Arians*, *Socinians*, *Pelagians*, *Soul Sleepers*, and the like, who deny the most Fundamental Doctrines of the Christian Religion'.⁵⁶ G. A. Starr shows that his concerted

---

⁵¹ Michael Hunter, *The Decline of Magic: Britain in the Enlightenment* (New Haven, CT: Yale University Press, 2020), 1–2.

⁵² Anthony Pagden, *The Enlightenment and Why it Still Matters* (Oxford: Oxford University Press, 2013), xii.

⁵³ Hunter, *Decline of Magic*, 49.

⁵⁴ Roy Porter, *Enlightenment: Britain and the Creation of the Modern World* (London: Penguin, 2000), 383.

⁵⁵ Maximillian E. Novak, 'Defoe, the Occult, and the Deist Offensive during the Reign of George I', in *Deism, Masonry, and the Enlightenment: Essays Honoring Alfred Owen Aldridge*, ed. J. A. Leo Lemay (Newark, DE: University of Delaware Press, 1987), 93–108.

⁵⁶ *Review*, iv. 340 (17 July 1707).

campaign against heterodoxy began in earnest with the *Serious Reflections of Robinson Crusoe* (1720) and extends through to an anti-deist polemic, *Christianity Not as Old as the Creation* (1730), that might be his final published work.[57] The title of that tract bears explaining. It negates the title of Matthew Tindal's *Christianity as Old as the Creation* (also 1730), which had insisted that the Christian gospel merely republished reasonable ethical truths that nature planted in humanity. In this schema, Jesus was an important moral educator, but in no way divine or capable of miracles, and any parts of the scripture that contradict the evidence of our senses should be rejected. Defoe was committed to reasserting the orthodoxy of the Trinity, with Christ as a part of the godhead, and he ends *A New Family Instructor* (1727) with what may be his final poem, again a religious piece, this time in blank verse, 'Trinity: or, The Divinity of the Son', emphasizing the majesty and mystery of that doctrine (*RDW*, iii. 281–8). *A New Family Instructor*, though it continues the practical divinity of its two predecessors, is also committed to differentiating sound and erroneous versions of faith.

In the three supernatural treatises, all presented as histories, Defoe was steering between credulous superstition and sceptical freethinking.[58] For example, *The Political History of the Devil* mocks popular conceptions of Satan, such as insisting that features like the cloven hoof must be read as symbolic, but it also challenges Milton's representations of the fallen angels and heaven in *Paradise Lost*, objecting most stridently to what Defoe regarded as Milton's Arianism, a belief that again subordinates the Son to the Father. But Defoe's book explores the Devil's agency in the world—something felt vividly by Defoe's most famous fictional creations, including Crusoe, Moll, and Roxana—with a spirit of playfulness and satirical energy. He considers the Devil's role in perpetrating heinous political ideas such as absolutist monarchy, in enabling the rise of political schemers such as Cardinal Richelieu, and in egging men on to catastrophic actions such as the Crusades. Defoe realized that his use of satirical techniques could lead to accusations that the book is irreverent, even impious, but he considered the methods vital to cajole readers out of complacency on the question of sin. His willingness to explore and narrativize spiritual conflict, in evidence as early as the *Meditations* and as late as the novels, comes to the fore in *Political History*.

In *A System of Magick* Defoe explains that he writes satire to ridicule people into rational behaviour and belief [SEE CHAPTER 11]. The best thing he can do for people who believe that street conjurors are engaged in real necromancy is laugh at them: 'Satyr has reform'd the Age of many a Folly, which the Solid and the Solemn could never reach' (*SFS*, vii. 24). In *History of Apparitions*, he approaches reports of ghosts with a forensic, rationalist spirit, probing credibility to strike an appropriately moderate stance. The Christian supernaturalism that informs Defoe's worldview—Providence, spirits,

---

[57] Defoe, *Christianity Not as Old as the Creation: The Last of Defoe's Performances*, ed. G. A. Starr (London: Pickering and Chatto, 2012).

[58] Rodney M. Baine, *Defoe and the Supernatural* (Athens, GA: University of Georgia Press, 1968); Petra Schoenenberger, *Transformations of the Supernatural: Problems of Representation in the Work of Daniel Defoe* (Bielefield: Transcript, 2017).

and demonology—can easily be lumped together by modern readers. But in a climate in which attacks supposedly targeted at fallacious accretions to primitive Christianity seemed to Defoe to be striking at essential doctrines, it was vital that he sorted between, for example, faith in a system of angelic communication with humans through dreams and premonitions and disbelief at old wives' tales about chain-rattling spectres or witches.

Conclusion

It is remarkable that James Sutherland could write that 'Defoe was not a deeply religious man'.[59] From the time that he left off training for the ministry to embark on a secular career in trade, Defoe addressed the state of Christianity, and his own status as a Protestant Dissenter, in a fifty-year career that includes poetry, fiction, polemical writings, conduct literature, and long treatises, essays, and histories on religious subjects. This essay has shown that Defoe's Christianity was fundamental to his life and career. This began with the change in direction that saw him step away from a ministerial calling at a time when Dissenters faced intense persecution, and it produced his earliest literary works, poems in which he grappled with his spiritual condition. It proceeded through a phase in which Defoe defended the religious and political settlement of the 1688 Revolution, and in some ways culminated with his extensive, public defences of Christianity, which mark him out as at once an important figure in the English Enlightenment and the inheritor and transmitter of Puritan thought into the eighteenth century.

Further Reading

Paula R. Backscheider, *Daniel Defoe: His Life* (Baltimore, MD: Johns Hopkins University Press, 1989).
Rodney M. Baine, *Defoe and the Supernatural* (Athens, GA: University of Georgia Press, 1968).
Katherine Clark, *Daniel Defoe: The Whole Frame of Nature, Time, and Providence* (Basingstoke: Palgrave Macmillan, 2007).
Julian Hoppit, *A Land of Liberty?: England 1689–1727* (Oxford: Oxford University Press, 2000).
J. Paul Hunter, *The Reluctant Pilgrim: Defoe's Emblematic Method and Quest for Form in Robinson Crusoe* (Baltimore, MD: Johns Hopkins University Press, 1966).
Michael Hunter, *The Decline of Magic: Britain in the Enlightenment* (New Haven, CT: Yale University Press, 2020).
N. H. Keeble, *The Literary Culture of Nonconformity in Later Seventeenth-Century England* (Leicester: Leicester University Press, 1987).

---

[59] James Sutherland, *Defoe* (London: Methuen, 1937), 211.

Kathleen Lynch, *Protestant Autobiography in the Seventeenth-Century Anglophone World* (Oxford: Oxford University Press, 2012).

Maximillian E. Novak, *Daniel Defoe, Master of Fictions: His Life and Ideas* (Oxford: Oxford University Press, 2001).

Stuart Sim, *Negotiations with Paradox: Narrative Practice and Narrative Form in Bunyan and Defoe* (London: Harvester Wheatsheaf, 1990).

G. A. Starr, *Defoe and Spiritual Autobiography* (Princeton, NJ: Princeton University Press, 1965).

Michael Watts, *The Dissenters: From the Reformation to the French Revolution* (Oxford: Oxford University Press, 1978).

CHAPTER 18

DEFOE, PHILOSOPHY, AND RELIGION

JOHN RICHETTI

DANIEL DEFOE was not a philosopher in any formal or overt sense. That is to say, nowhere in his voluminous writings on a wide variety of subjects, in prose and verse, does he attempt to present a general and systematic theory about the nature of reality. He is not a metaphysician, although he is often enough an amateur but well-informed commentator on theological issues of the time, with particular views about the presence of spirits and angelic or providential participation in human events [SEE CHAPTER 17]. He was also an energetic and opinionated polemical moralist, as well as at his best a provocative thinker about moral and political topics, where he is philosophical to the extent that he understands morals and politics from a broad theoretical and historical perspective as well as from the outlook of a political operative and a writer of prose fictions and of political and historical tracts, two of his main employments. Very often he writes shrewdly as a psychologist and rationalist, something of what we might call an amateur epistemologist and thereby a consistent enemy of what he saw as vulgar superstition, which he attacks as the enemy of what he considered true or sound religious belief. He is always supremely, even obsessively, thoughtful, often enough to the point of deliberate paradox, a man whose long life of writing was defined by thorough engagement—in many formats and genres—with the realities and modalities of experience in the world of his times. Readers of his long prose fictions, what we now call novels by virtue of their realistic view of the world and the shrewdly observed human psychology that they present, will know that he deserves to be called an empiricist, an author whose characters as narrators of their lives dramatize with a never-failing exactness and steady gaze the things and phenomena, both natural and man-made, that constitute the world of human experience.

Consider in this regard a couple of key scenes from his first (and best) novel, *Robinson Crusoe* (1719). After the hero-narrator's escape in the early pages of his story from slavery in north Africa, Crusoe is eventually rescued by a Portuguese ship on its way to Brazil, and once there he decides to settle, prospering as a sugar planter. In due course, he and his fellow Brazilian planters decide to go on an (illegal) African expedition to buy more slaves for their plantations, but as fate would have it their ship is wrecked in a storm, with Crusoe the lone survivor on an island in the Caribbean. His vivid evocation of the waves that nearly drown him but at last carry him to the shore is radically exact, accurate and wholly precise in its rendering of the force of the water and his physical responses to its movements:

> The wave that came upon me again, buried me at once 20 or 30 foot deep in its own body; and I could feel my self carried with a mighty force and swiftness towards the shore a very great way; but I held my breath and assisted my self to swim still forward with all my might. I was ready to burst with holding my breath, when, as I felt my self rising up, so to my immediate relief, I found my head and hands shoot out above the surface of the water; and tho' it was not two seconds of time that I could keep my self so, yet it reliev'd me greatly, gave me breath and new courage. I was covered again with water a good while, but not so long but I held it out; and finding the water had spent it self and began to return, I strook forward against the return of the waves, and felt ground again with my feet.[1]

I know of no other description of an intense physical event in eighteenth-century prose fiction that matches this passage in its detailed (and to my mind accurate, as I remember from body-surfing as a boy, under less extreme conditions to be sure, on the ocean beaches off Long Island, east of New York City) rendering of an experience in which one's body is carried by waves towards a shore, and one has to by turns resist and co-operate with their back-and-forth motions. We can be reasonably sure that Defoe himself was never in this kind of desperate aquatic situation, but his imagining of it bespeaks a talent for convincingly and fully rendering physical phenomena. In moments like this, *Robinson Crusoe* is an experiment in exactly rendered empirical observation, as Defoe's narrator displays a sharp attentiveness to his environment that is philosophical in its notations and an evocation of phenomena that are of course essential here for his survival.[2]

In the early pages of his narrative, Crusoe wonders, of course, why he alone survived the wreck and gradually develops a religious outlook in which he thanks God's Providence for delivering him. But the immediate aftermath of his arrival on the island records his dazed confusion, a moment of inspired psychological and physical realism: 'I walk'd about on the shore, lifting up my hands, and my whole being, as I may say, wrapt up in the contemplation of my deliverance, making a thousand gestures and motions which I cannot describe, reflecting upon all my comrades that were were drown'd, and

---

[1] Daniel Defoe, *Robinson Crusoe*, ed. John Richetti (London: Penguin Books, 2001), 37–8.

[2] For the classic application to Defoe's fiction of the empiricist philosophy of John Locke (1632–1704), see Ian Watt, *The Rise of the Novel: Studies in Defoe, Richardson and Fielding* (London: Chatto and Windus, 1957). On Watt's influence, see John Richetti, 'The Legacy of Ian Watt's *The Rise of the Novel*', in *The Profession of Eighteenth-Century Literature: Reflections on an Institution*, ed. Leo Damrosch (Madison, WI: University of Wisconsin Press, 1987), 95–112.

that there should not be one soul sav'd but my self; for as for them, I never saw them afterwards, or any sign of them, except three of their hats, one cap, and two shoes that were not fellows' (38–9). Those frantic 'gestures and motions' that Crusoe cannot in any adequate way describe but simply evoke are eloquent in their deliberate vagueness and their elusive and erratic compulsions as they summon up his utterly confused mental state. But those hats, that cap, and the 'two shoes that were not fellows' signal a concrete and solid world of miscellaneous things that is touching in its bleakness as the only tokens of his drowned ship mates, but also both reassuring and threatening in its inexplicable if inevitable randomness. Here at the beginning of his isolation on the island, Crusoe's observations of himself and of the material world that surrounds him implicitly pose a philosophical problem that will recur in the rest of the narrative. The phenomenal world is in one sense crystal clear and readily available to ordinary if attentive observation, but in that clarity in this one exemplary moment of those pathetic material signs of his shipmates, that world resists final understanding in its threatening and miscellaneous quality and thereby may be said to dramatize the limits of empiricism as an explanatory approach to reality. Exact enumeration in this case and others provides no deep understanding; it merely renders a set of incidents and isolated phenomena.

Those limits and Crusoe's attempt to align them with his persistent yearning for evidence of a guiding Providence and meaningful order in his life come into sharp focus later in the narrative.[3] Crusoe is startled one day, surpris'd and perfectly astonish'd', when he notices 'something green, shooting out of the ground' and finds that it is 'perfect green barley of the same kind as our *European*, nay, as our *English* barley' (63). He quickly jumps to religious conclusions and providential explanations: 'I began to suggest that God had miraculously caus'd this grain to grow without any help of seed sown, and that it was so directed purely for my sustenance on that wild miserable place' (63). But after a thorough search of that part of the island that turns up no more of this barley, it occurs to Crusoe that he had 'shook a bag of chickens meat [left over from the ship] out in that place, and then the wonder began to cease; and I must confess, my religious thankfulness to God's Providence began to abate too upon the discovering that all this was nothing but what was common' (64). And yet in the same paragraph Crusoe develops another strategy as he comes to understand that it 'was really the work of Providence so to me, that should order or appoint, that 10 or 12 grains of corn should remain unspoil'd, (when the rats had destroy'd all the rest,) as if it had been dropt from Heaven; as also, that I should throw it out in that particular place, where it being in the shade of a high rock, it sprang up immediately; whereas, if I had thrown it any where else, at that time, it had been burnt up and destroy'd' (64).

---

[3] On Providence in Defoe's writings, see G. A. Starr, *Defoe and Spiritual Autobiography* (Princeton, NJ: Princeton University Press, 1965); J. Paul Hunter, *The Reluctant Pilgrim: Defoe's Emblematic Method and Quest for Form in Robinson Crusoe* (Baltimore, MD: Johns Hopkins University Press, 1966); and John Richetti, 'Secular Crusoe: The Reluctant Pilgrim Re-Visited', in *Eighteenth-Century Genre and Culture: Serious Essays on Occasional Forms: Essays in Honor of J. Paul Hunter*, ed. Dennis Todd and Cynthia Wall (Newark, DE: University of Delaware Press, 2001), 58–78.

Crusoe's logic is peculiar if striking, from a secular and materialistic view deeply flawed and facile, since he argues that all of the random acts and coincidences that led to the sprouting of the barley from a few seeds used to feed chickens on the ship that he had discarded are in fact not at all random, but arranged by a meticulous, overseeing Providence. Crusoe's empirical view of things, his remembering or reconstructing the chain of circumstances that somehow led to the sprouting of the barley, is transformed and redirected (indeed negated) by a religious ideology that employs exact empirical observation to understand the secret orderings of Providence, or, to take another more sympathetic view of Crusoe's understanding of the matter, transcends mere empirical observation, whereby what looks like the random and the accidental are actually the essential (if somewhat devious) method of providential arrangements. To be sure, the rest of Crusoe's story, on the island and throughout his subsequent travels and adventures, dramatizes him as a man of purposeful action, strategic planning, and decisive intervention, an effective force in his management of survival on the island, and of eventual deliverance from it rather than a passive observer of providential control. Indeed, in the second volume of Crusoe's life published a few months after part one, *The Farther Adventures of Robinson Crusoe* (1719), he is a powerful agent who returns to England with a fortune in profits from his mercantile dealings in the Far East, no thanks to Providence, which is simply not invoked in this part of his 'adventures'. In both of the first two volumes, Crusoe is far too busy planning and executing those plans to agonize more than this one time over the role Providence might be said to play in his life. In fact, in both parts of *Robinson Crusoe* this notion that Providence micro-manages everything may be said to disappear as no longer necessary to support or provoke Crusoe's religious consolations. Indeed, Crusoe makes the transition from shipwrecked, shocked, and nearly crazed loner to the calmly powerful 'ruler' of his island, domesticating its wilderness by cultivation, building a secure habitation, and eventually, as the conqueror of invading cannibals and later of English mutineers, founder of his island as a multiethnic colony, and then adventurous, world-travelling merchant in Southeast Asia and China [SEE CHAPTER 29].

Crusoe in his long sojourn on the island has some cultural shocks, notably when he discovers that cannibals come at times to slaughter their prisoners of war and eat them.[4] Naturally, Crusoe, when he stumbles upon the remains of a cannibal feast—'the shore spread with skulls, hands, feet and other bones of human bodies' (130)—is nauseated and vomits, and he thanks God that he is different from these savages. He makes furious plans to destroy them and prepares an elaborate ambush with his firearms. But eventually his lust to destroy the cannibals abates, and his thoughts take what might be called

---

[4] Maximillian E. Novak explores ways in which Defoe dramatizes the natural law theories of seventeenth-century philosophers including Samuel Pufendorf, Hugo Grotius, and Thomas Hobbes, in *Defoe and the Nature of Man* (Oxford: Clarendon Press, 1963). For a Hobbesian interpretation of Defoe's novels, see Virginia Ogden Birdsall, *Defoe's Perpetual Seekers: A Study of the Major Fiction* (Lewisburg, PA: Bucknell University Press, 1985).

a proto-anthropological turn, profoundly secular and rational, non-judgemental and relativistic, that is worth quoting at length:

> What authority or call I had, to pretend to be judge and executioner upon these men as criminals, whom Heaven had thought fit for so many ages to suffer unpunish'd, to go on, and to be, as it were, the executioners of his judgments one upon another. How far these people were offenders against me, and what right I had to engage in the quarrel of that blood, which they shed promiscuously one upon another. I debated this very often with my self thus; how do I know what God himself judges in this particular case; it is certain these people either do not commit this as a crime; it is not against their own consciences reproving, or their light reproving them, They do not know it to be an offence, and then commit it in defiance of divine justice, as we in almost all the sins we commit. They think it no more a crime to kill a captive taken in war, than we do to kill an ox; nor to eat human flesh, than we do to eat mutton. (135)

But in the discursive and oddly miscellaneous third volume of his story, *Serious Reflections During the Life and Surprising Adventure of Robinson Crusoe* (1720), Crusoe articulates at length a much more aggressively overt and complex theoretical view of human experience and providential management, presented in a series of moral and theological essays along with a set of distinctly unorthodox theological ruminations, including the most interesting and extravagant of Defoe's theological flights in three chapters of *Serious Reflections*: 'An ESSAY on the present State of RELIGION in the World', '*Of Listening to the Voice of* PROVIDENCE', and 'A VISION of the ANGELICK WORLD'. As G. A. Starr, the editor of the *Serious Reflections* volume in the Pickering & Chatto collected edition of Defoe's works, explains, the book represents an 'early draft' of a series of books that Defoe produced in the late 1720s, *The Political History of the Devil* (1726), *A System of Magick* (1726), *An Essay on the History and Reality of Apparitions* (1727), and *A New Family Instructor* (1727), all of which as Starr points out explore 'deviations from, and threats to, sound belief' as found in scepticism of various kinds such as Deism and atheism, that is to say the opponents of orthodox Christianity in the early eighteenth century as Defoe understood it in his fairly unorthodox way (*Novels*, iii. 1). These four books and the *Serious Reflections* constitute Defoe's most self-conscious polemical and theoretical discussions of what deserve to be called philosophical ruminations and explorations (moral and theological of course, rather than epistemological or metaphysical in purpose or in terminology). The shortest of these chapters in *Serious Reflections*, number 3, 'Of Atheistical and Prophane Discourse', sets the tone and outlines Defoe's perspective and intensely polemical stance, as well as his debater's wit: 'The Devil himself, who is allow'd to be full of Enmity against the supreme Being, has often set up himself to be worshipped as a God, but never prompted the most barbarous Nation to deny the Being of a God; and 'tis thought that even the Devil himself believ'd the Notion was too absurd to be imposed upon the World. But our Age is even with him for his Folly; for since they cannot get him to joyn in the Denial of a God, they will deny his Devilship too, and have neither one nor other' (115). Moreover, Crusoe/

Defoe laments that although political irreverence or dissent ('If a Man talk against the Government, or speak scurrilously of the King, he is had [sic] to the *Old Bayly*, and from thence to the Pillory, or Whipping-Post') is punished severely, nothing happens if a man 'speak Treason against the Majesty of Heaven, deny the Godhead of his Redeemer, and make a Jest of the Holy Ghost' (119).

But atheism and related denials or liberal modifications of religious orthodoxy such as Arianism and Socinianism are quickly dispatched in this short section. Equally brief sections deal with 'The Immorality of Conversation, AND The Vulgar Errors of Behaviour', 'Of reforming the Errors of Conversation', 'Of Lewd and Immodest Discourse', and finally 'Of Talking falsly'. Moral philosophy, in other words, and social reformation are less important for Defoe than proper and sound religion itself. What really seems to worry him is the decline of what he sees as true religious belief and action guided by that belief. Thus, the first of three substantial essays, on the present state of religion in the world, begins as a philosophical dialogue between Crusoe (in his thoughtful old age, as he informs us, 'arriv'd, after a long Course of infinite Variety, on the Stage of the World, to the Scene of Life, we call *Old Age*' [129]) and an 'old gentlewoman'. The essay soon becomes a cranky survey of the lack of actual or sincere (or for that matter 'true') religion around the world, including nominally Christian Europe, and, predictably, nobody in this survey comes off very well, although one is struck by Crusoe's moral condescension and high-minded superiority. As Crusoe observes at the outset of his dialogue: 'I found reason to think, that there was much more Devotion than Religion in the World; in a Word, much more Adoration than Supplication ... there is much more Hypocrisy than Sincerity' (133). To be sure and to be fair, Crusoe also worries at some length about the millions of individuals, more numerous than the inhabitants of Christendom, such as Muslims and pagans, who have never heard the Christian gospel. But he also observes that for these non-Christians 'as having not sin'd against saving Light, then their Ignorance and Pagan Darkness is not a Curse but a Felicity' (134). It follows, he goes on to say very shrewdly, that Christians are in more danger of damnation than uninstructed pagans, since they have sinned against that same 'saving Light' that others have not been exposed to.

Of course, Defoe as opposed to his alter ego had not as far as we know travelled anywhere near as much as Crusoe, although he was clearly very well read in travel writings [SEE CHAPTER 8]. This survey of religion in the world is made for the most part out of whole cloth and Defoe's fertile imagination, and it chiefly illustrates Defoe's characteristically pugnacious polemicizing rather than any extended or for that matter technical theological reasoning. However, this essay begins with Crusoe's summary of human psychology that he says has led him to turn away from his active, wandering life of adventure to the contemplative project of writing his *Serious Reflections*: 'There is an inconsiderate Temper which reigns in our Mind, that hurries us down the Stream of our Affections, by a kind of involuntary Agency, and makes us do a thousand things, *in the doing of which*, we propose nothing to our selves, but an immediate Subjection to our WILL, that is to say our Passion, even without the Concurrence of our Understandings, and of which we can give very little Account, *after 'tis done*' (129).[5] Such an interesting and sweeping theoretical statement about human psychology as fundamentally resistant to moral imperatives and concerned purely with personal fulfilment has little relevance to his search for authentic religious belief in the world, but can serve as the key to the next two essays in *Serious Reflections*, Chapter Five, 'Of Listening to the Voice of Providence', and the last and unnumbered section of the book, 'A Vision of the Angelick World', which forms a long coda or indeed a conclusion to Defoe's book, attempting to resolve in visionary fashion the problems and uncertainties that surround the notion of tracing and understanding providential control, which is a profound theological/philosophical issue that defies easy resolution, even for a fiercely committed Christian like Defoe.

'*Of Listening to the Voice of* PROVIDENCE' is more ambitiously theological than surrounding chapters, but almost recklessly anecdotal and particularized, as Crusoe seeks to pin down just how minutely thorough the workings of Providence are, and exactly how it operates in particular human lives, including of course his own. In his own terms and from the perspective of a devout Christian at the time, the following statement is completely logical: 'If Providence guides the World, and directs the Issues and Events of things, if it commands causes, and forms the Connection of Circumstances in the World … And above all, is the general Scope of Providence, and the Government of the World by the World by its Influence, be for our Advantage; then it follows necessarily, that it is our Business, and our Interest, *to listen to its Voice*' (184). But there are many cautions issued in what follows. Crusoe insists, of course, that there are 'Innumerable Instances' that present themselves 'every Day, in which the Providence of God speaks to us' (190). But note the qualification in the next paragraph, where Crusoe warns that we must not be 'utterly careless' and 'talk of trusting Providence', since we must 'use at the same Time, all Diligence in our Callings; so we are to trust Providence with our Safety, but with our Eyes open to all its necessary Cautions' (190).

But such caution is followed by several anecdotes of what a purely secular outlook might attribute to nothing more than coincidence and chance, even if they are remarkable nonetheless: Crusoe tells an elaborate story about some English soldiers in Flanders who are court-martialled for disobeying general orders (and not for plundering the local people, as we learn from a brutal story that Crusoe relates of revenge by the local people on the pillaging soldiers, two of whom escape). The general agrees to spare one of them, to be determined by throwing dice upon a drumhead. When the first throws two sixes, the other is distraught but overjoyed when he throws the same sixes. This symmetry continues as each of them throws identical dice, fives and then fours. When the general who ordered this is apprised, he pardons them both, '*I love*, says he, *in such*

---

[5] On Defoe's engagement with medical and philosophical ideas about 'the passions', see Geoffrey M. Sill, *The Cure of the Passions and the Origins of the English Novel* (Cambridge: Cambridge University Press, 2001).

extraordinary Cases to listen to the Voice of Providence' (192). Crusoe presents such an extraordinary case as a dramatic instance of providential arrangement, although he admits that it lacks the direct communication between God and man (at least to the Hebrew patriarchs and later to the Apostles) reported in Scripture. Nonetheless, he argues that there is still a clear if different connection between Heaven and earth: 'our Conduct in the inferior Life' wherein 'the Voice of God, even his immediate Voice from Heaven, is not entirely ceased from us, though it may have changed the Mediums of Communication' (193).

For evidence that is immediately available to the readers of *Serious Reflections*, Crusoe instances 'my own Story', the early details of which—ignoring the advice of friends and the entreaties of his parents, he went to sea and was shipwrecked, saved by another ship that sank soon after—constituted a clear providential warning; 'what Happiness might such a prudent Step have procured, what Miseries and Mischiefs would it have prevented in the rest of his unfortunate Life' (194). Crusoe piles up his evidence for clear providential guidance in his life and insists that with proper attention individuals (not Crusoe in his life, to be sure) may avoid calamities. For one instance, he cites 'an Acquaintance of mine' who took lodgings in a village near London and fell into bad company and was warned by various incidents—robbed on the highway, taken ill, terrified by 'a most dreadful Tempest of Thunder and Lightning'—so that 'he took it as a Warning from Heaven, and resolv'd not to go there again, and some Time after a Fire destroyed that House, very few escaping that were in it' (195). Crusoe also identifies those who ignore such signs: 'People that tye up all to Events and Causes, strip the Providence of God which guides the World of all it Superintendency, and leave it no room to act as a wise Disposer of Things' (195). With all these anecdotes, with his repetitive affirmation of providential control, Crusoe may be said to protest rather too much, but he is careful to posit a crucial exception, what he calls 'a much more rational System than that of tying up the Hands of the supreme Power to a Road of Things, so that none can be acted or permitted, but such as was so appointed before to be acted and permitted' (195). Thus Crusoe disavows a deterministic divine predestination; his view of Providence allows for individual agency and freedom of action. And yet, as he observes a bit later in this chapter, his belief in what he calls 'an invisible and powerful Hand' requires careful study to perceive 'the silent Actings of Providence, as well as those which are more loud, and which being declar'd, speak in publick' (196). Crusoe's arguments at moments like these in this chapter bespeak a sense of controversy and uncertainty surrounding his affirmations of providential activity, of a rival incredulity and secular or materialistic alternative to his position: 'These things may be jested with by the Men of Fashion; but I am supposing myself talking to Men that have a Sense of a future State, and of the Oeconomy of an invisible World upon them, and neither to Atheists, Sceptics, or Persons indifferent, who are indeed near of Kin to them both' (197).

These argumentative, polemical, and dialogical qualities of *Serious Reflections* are not central to the remarkable last chapter, 'A Vision of the Angelick World'. Crusoe here revisits some scenes in part one of *Robinson Crusoe* and reworks or retells them so that they record ghostly intimations of supernatural visitors and visions from the world of evil spirits on his island.[6] He remembers vivid nocturnal imaginings and physical symptoms that he fears were the result of a visit from the Devil. Noting that when Friday arrives, these visions and fears disappear (which implies that his visions are to a large extent functions of his radical solitude), Crusoe nonetheless affirms his belief 'that there is not only a World of Spirits, but that there is a certain knowledge of it' (228). And that knowledge does not come from actual 'Apparitions', but from the following ordinary itemized human events: 'Dreams, Voices, Noises, Impulses, Hints, Apprehensions, Involuntary Sadness, etc.' (229). On the one hand, Crusoe denies that spirits can be perceived; as immaterial substances they are not available to human sight. Such sightings are merely psychological illusions produced by the imagination in dark or murky environments, where people will 'see the Devil whether he be there or no; nay, they will be so perswaded, that they do see him, that their very Imagination will be a Devil to them where-ever they go' (227). But on the other hand, as Scripture in both Testaments makes clear (Crusoe cites numerous instances, Joseph and St Paul for his two chief examples) and his own dreams in these modern times have warned him of evils ahead: 'I never had any capital Mischief befel me in my Life, but I have had Notice of it by a Dream' (230). And yet not long after this, Crusoe modifies this confidence: 'The Maxim I have laid down to my self for my Conduct in this Affair is in few Words, that we should not lay too great Stress upon Dreams, and yet not wholly neglect them' (232).

In the pages that follow, Crusoe recalls a 'long Dispute' upon this subject between two of his acquaintances, one a clergyman, the other a layman, 'both very pious and religious Persons' (232), with the clergyman responding to the layman's scepticism about the significance of dreams. Shortly after this, the clergyman encourages Crusoe, and he recounts how after an extended discussion about whether the other planets are inhabited 'and of a Diversity of Worlds', he was 'like a Man transported into those Regions myself ... I certainly made a Journey to all those supposed habitable Bodies in my Imagination' (235). Even with this caveat that his journey takes place in his imagination, Crusoe's vision is comprehensive and vividly particular as he sees 'innumerable Armies of good and evil Spirits, who all seem'd busily employed, and continually upon the Wing ... pass'd between the Earth, which in this Part of my Travels I place below' (239). The sensational theological revelation from this vision is not simply that there is an invisible world of spirits, both good and evil, but that Satan has his kingdom in this realm, that he is '*the Prince of the Power of the Air*' (240). Furthermore, as Crusoe's vision expands, he explains how Satan sends his emissaries from this high eminence to various parts of the earth, although in Christendom ('the northern Parts of the temperate Zone') he cannot send squadrons of devils as he does to 'those blinded Parts of the World', but is 'obliged to carry on his Business among us by particular Agents upon particular Persons' (242). Nonetheless, Crusoe avers that despite the Devil commanding an 'infinitely great'

---

[6] On Defoe's relationship to contemporary attitudes to spirits, see Rodney M. Baine, *Daniel Defoe and the Supernatural* (Athens, GA: University of Georgia Press, 1968).

number of devils, 'the Numbers of good Angels or good Spirits' are 'equal at least in Number, but infinitely superior in Power' (242).

Crusoe/Defoe's insistence (and there are many more pages of such exposition) is compelling, if literally absurd and numbingly repetitive. 'A Vision' concludes with a conversion narrative that drops the visionary perspective as it tells the story of four university students who became atheists and were known as *'The Atheistical Club'* (261). One of their number, however, is terrified when a bolt of lightning comes frighteningly near him as he stands in a doorway to get out of the rain, and in his terror it flashes on him that there may well be a God. '*Where am I going! What am I going about! Who is it that has stopt me thus!* ... and with the rest came in this Thought, warm and swift as the Lightning, which had terrified him before, *What if there should be a God! What will become of me then!*' (262). At this point, 'a near Relation of his, a pious good Man' arrives and tries to comfort the terrified young man. But when one of the other atheistic students arrives and seeks to talk to his friend, this near relation denies him entrance and 'speaks aloud in the Person of his Friend thus: O SIR, Beseech them all to repent; for depend upon it, There is a GOD, tell them, I say so, and with that shut the Door upon him violently, giving him no Time to reply' (262–3). This moment, as remembered by one of the atheists and not remembered by the Gentleman who is the 'near Relation' who answered the door becomes a shocking revelation from the spirit world, from the deity as it were. Defoe's religious polemic is thus strangely contradictory, since readers know that the revelation is not from the spirit world and that the message of God's reality is a human opinion. But in his conclusion Defoe argues that it does not matter that the revelation is not directly from God, since the mistake shows 'how the Power of Imagination may be work'd up, by the secret Agency of an unknown Hand, how many Things concurr'd to make this Man believe he had seen an Apparition, and heard a Voice ... for many a Voice may be directed from Heaven, that is not immediately spoken from thence' (272). This is a remarkably secular modification of Crusoe's insistence on providential presence in human events.

Much of 'A Vision of the Angelick World' is in a format Defoe is fond of employing: an extended dialogue between the young atheist and a divinity student in the same college who has been reminded of the atheist by four lines of verse written on the back of the title page of a book he has been looking at in a bookseller's shop. As it happens, these are four lines from Defoe's poem 'The Storm. An Essay' (1704), which rehearse the Pascalian wager argument for the existence of God, and the student asks the atheist to read them aloud:

> But if it should *fall out*, as who can tell?
> That there MAY be a God, a Heaven and Hell:
> Had I not best consider well, for fear
> 'T should be *too late* when my Mistakes appear.

Overall, his mystical experience and vision of the angelic world that Crusoe evokes so vividly must speak to Defoe's deeply felt orthodox religious impulse and polemical fervour to promote that same orthodoxy. But in Defoe's writings such religious fervour shares the stage with the sharply focused empiricism and secular materialistic perspective of his narrative fictions (especially *A Journal of the Plague Year*, published just three years after the Crusoe trilogy) and of his later treatises: *The Political History of the Devil*, *A System of Magick*, and *An Essay on the History and Reality of Apparitions*. In their distinct ways, these books attack and ridicule superstition from the vantage point not just of Christian orthodoxy, but from Defoe's strict and often satirical rationalism that examines supernatural claims and finds them rooted in human psychological needs. The bubonic plague (The Black Death of the Middle Ages) that raged through parts of Europe in the late seventeenth and early eighteenth century came to England in 1665 (when Defoe was a child). Defoe's *A Journal of the Plague Year* (1722) is his terrifying evocation of its effects in London as written according to the title 'by a Citizen who continued all the while in London', self-identified in the text only by his initials and his profession, H. F., a saddler, all of whose friends and relatives have left the city to seek safety in the countryside. H. F. stays in the city and seeks to understand the causes of the plague as well as its possible cures. In that regard, H. F. expresses contempt for those who 'talk of its being an Immediate Stroke from Heaven, without the Agency of Means, having Commission to strike this and that particular Person, and none other; which I look upon with Contempt, as the Effect of manifest Ignorance and Enthusiasm'.[7] And yet, rather like Defoe himself, he values what he calls his 'strong Impressions', which convince him that God wants him to stay in London, 'the visible Call I seem'd to have from the particular Circumstance of my Calling ... also the Intimations which I thought I had from Heaven, that to me signify'd a kind of Direction' (12). To strengthen his resolve he resorts to bibliomancy and is confirmed in his views by the ninety-first psalm that his finger falls on: '*Thou shalt not be afraid for the terror by night, nor for the arrow that flieth by day: Nor the pestilence that walketh in darkness, nor for the destruction that wasteth at noon-day A thousand shall fall at thy side, and ten thousand as thy right hand: but it shall not come nigh thee*' (13). H. F.'s piety and confidence in divine guidance, along with his rational contempt for mere superstition, his interest in understanding the material causes of the plague, signal his intellectual affinity with the man who imagined his story. A bit later in H. F.'s narrative, he describes a group hallucination (one of many he observes) when a woman says she sees 'an Angel cloth'd in white, with a fiery Sword in his Hand, waving it, or brandishing it over his Head'. People around her agree and describe the same sight, but H. F. sees only a white cloud and reflects 'how the poor People were terrify'd by the Force of their own Imagination' (22–3).[8]

Years before he came in the 1720s to write the narrative fictions for which he is best known now, Defoe was a political journalist, notably in *The Review*, where his topics were history and politics for the most part, and where he is of course a resolutely secular

---

[7] Defoe, *A Journal of the Plague Year*, ed. Louis Landa (Oxford: Oxford University Press, 1969), 75.

[8] For a study of Defoe's relationship to scepticism, which also presents Locke as the main philosophical influence on Defoe, see Eve Tavor, *Scepticism, Society and the Eighteenth-Century Novel* (Basingstoke: Macmillan, 1987).

analyst and commentator. And yet even in this hard-hitting political periodical Defoe can be seen wondering if the direct hand of Providence can be observed in contemporary events. July 1706, for example, he labels 'a Month of wonders' in English victories in the war against France and her allies at Barcelona and at Ramillies (in modern Belgium). He insists that he has no special faith 'upon Days and Hours, Eclipses and Parallels; but I cannot believe, but they are sometimes directed' and there are coincidences that 'can never be human Direction' and 'must certainly come from God, or Devil'. He notes that natural phenomena such as eclipses of the sun and moon 'can portend nothing; but I cannot pretend to believe but that Providence often directs the Times and Connections of their otherwise natural Causes to concur in such a manner as may point out to us his Meaning' (9 July 1706).

How shall we explain Defoe's combination of polemical religious orthodoxy and vigorous secular rationalism, combined as here with hints of divine arrangements? What is the source, if any, of his complex and at times contradictory notions? As a Dissenter (a Protestant who did not conform to the tenets of the Church of England), the young Defoe could not attend either of the English universities, Oxford and Cambridge. Instead, he was a student for four years, 1674–9, at one of the schools that were founded by Dissenters to educate young men for the ministry. Defoe's teacher was Charles Morton (1627–98), who emigrated to New England in 1685 and became a professor and later vice-president at Harvard College, where he taught experimental science. Morton was an Oxford-trained (Wadham College) mathematician and a Baconian, a follower of the English philosopher, Francis Bacon (1561–1626), who was a proponent of modern scientific method in works such as *The Advancement of Learning* (1603).[9] In a manuscript (never printed in Defoe's lifetime but published in 1890), *The Compleat English Gentleman*, Defoe looked back with satisfaction and with superiority to the conventional university education of his day that emphasized the classical language: 'If then a man may be learned in all the wisdome and knowledge of God so as to be a complete Christian, and that without the knowledge of either Latin or Greek, I see not reason to scruple saying he may be a complete phylospher [sic] or a complete mathematician, tho' he has no skill in the learned languages'. Defoe describes with great enthusiasm his years in Morton's school, where the emphasis was on facts and science, with the master lecturing in English, and his instruction featuring lessons in English expression 'that taught his pupils to write a masculine and manly style'.

Of course, Defoe did not become a clergyman; he was for the rest of his very busy life a wholesale merchant as well as a voluminous author—a political journalist, miscellaneous writer on myriad subjects in prose and verse, as well as a government operative for the powerful politician Robert Harley, Earl of Oxford. Trade and commerce were subjects in much of his writing. To that extent, he was what we would now call a public intellectual. In one famous passage from his periodical, *The Review* (published

---

[9] For the influence on Defoe of Bacon and his followers in the early Royal Society, see Ilse Vickers, *Defoe and the New Sciences* (Cambridge: Cambridge University Press, 1996).

1704–13, twice a week and then three times a week and composed entirely by Defoe), he evokes 'A True-Bred Merchant', as a man who 'Understands Languages without Books, Geography without Maps, his Journals and Trading-Voyages delineate the World; his Foreign Exchanges, Protests and Procurations, speak all Tongues; he sits in his Counting-House, and Converses with all Nations, and keeps the most exquisite and extensive part of Human Society in a Universal Correspondence' (3 January 1706). Defoe's merchant is an absurdly glorified self-portrait, of course, and he defines himself in fantastically powerful intellectual terms [SEE CHAPTER 14]. His heroic merchant is nothing less than the most profound of scholars, and his commercial activities produce extensive and exact knowledge of the world (as well as profit, presumably). By virtue of his comprehensive understanding of the world in which he deals so powerfully and efficiently, the merchant acquires something like the contemplative and universalizing perspective that philosophy aspires to possess. In fact, Defoe's first major publication, when he was himself a young merchant (thirty-six or so), *An Essay upon Projects* (1697), is thoughtful as well as incredibly ambitious, something like a one-man think tank, but also shrewdly practical, proposing a new road system for England, pension and insurance arrangements for the poor, a new hospital for the insane, a new banking system for the nation, a military academy for training officers, a college for the education of women, and many other 'projects' equally innovative and progressive.

This same progressive and rational impulse is also on view in the three books on the supernatural that he published in rapid succession in the mid 1720s: *The Political History of the Devil*, *An Essay on the History and Reality of Apparitions*, and *A System of Magick; or, A History of the Black Art*, which a reader of this essay will recognize as recurring concerns for Defoe. All three books feature satirical condemnation of popular credulity and superstition. Without the fiction of the pious Crusoe that controls Defoe's approach to these matters in *Serious Reflections*, each of these tracts is intellectually sophisticated and theologically subtle. For one example among many, in the *Essay on the History and Reality of Apparitions*, Defoe dwells powerfully and eloquently on the way that imagination creates these spectres. Ghosts, he says, are projections that follow from human guilt, from a troubled conscience. 'My Purpose is to shew how Men's Guilt crowds their Imagination with sudden and surprizing Ideas of things; brings Spectres and Apparitions into their Eyes, when there are really no such things; forms Ghosts and Phantasms in their very View, when their Eyes are shut: They see sleeping, and dream waking; the Night is all Vision, and the Day all Apparition' (*SFS*, viii. 119). Defoe speaks in these books as essentially a sophisticated Enlightenment thinker, here as a close observer of human psychology. For example, here is his witty comment in *Political History of the Devil* about the reality of witchcraft: 'The strange Work which the Devil has made in the World by this Sort of his Agents call'd Witches, is such, and so extravagantly wild, that except our Hope that most of those Tales happen not to be true, I know not how any one could be easy to live near a Widow after she was five and fifty' (*SFS*, vi. 249).

Throughout the *Political History of the Devil*, Defoe ridicules conventional representations of Satan, with his cloven foot and brimstone, beginning the book with this observation: 'Children and old women have told themselves so many frightful things *of the Devil* ... that really it were enough to fright the Devil himself, to meet himself in the dark' (35). Defoe offers the sensible opinion 'that the *Devil* has no particular body; that he is a spirit, and that tho' he may, *Proteus* like, assume the appearance of either man or beast, yet it must be some borrow'd shape, some assum'd figure, *pro hac vice* [for that occasion], and that he has no visible body of his own' (65). In fact, Defoe at times goes even further and (almost) turns the Devil into a metaphor for human vice and folly. At one point he goes so far as to make demonic possession a misogynist joke: 'the walking Devils that we have generally among us, are of the female Sex; whether it be that the Devil finds less Difficulty to manage them, or that he lives quieter with them, or that they are fitter for his Business than the Men, I shall not enter into a Dispute about that; perhaps he goes better disguis'd in the fair Sex than otherwise' (229). This kind of jocularity recurs in the *Political History of the Devil*, underlining Defoe's rationalist contempt for folk beliefs about the devil, what John Mullan calls his history of human delusion (15). But at the same time Defoe takes the Devil very seriously and literally as a force and a person. He evokes him (here and elsewhere in his writing) as the 'Prince of the Air' and revises many aspects of Milton's Satan in the cosmology evoked in *Paradise Lost* by placing his version of the Devil in the infinite spaces of the new astronomy. Nevertheless, despite the numerous scriptural records of actual evil spirits conversing with humans (and with Christ for that matter), the Devil for Defoe is actually manifest in particular human behaviour. The Devil in human shape never in fact appears in Defoe's long narrative of devilish behaviour; he is a cause but a cause inferred rather than seen or in any sense perceived. For one example among many in this long book, Defoe recounts several stories of devilish temptation in dreams. But then he asks his readers if they think these dreams represent the Devil's work, and he concludes that they are the best proof of his existence:

> It is neither my Business or Inclination to turn Divine here, nor is the Age I write to sufficiently Grave to relish a Sermon, if I was disposed to preach, tho' they must allow the Subject would very well bear it; but I shall only ask them, if they think this is not the *Devil*, what they think it is? If they believe it is the *Devil*, they will act accordingly I hope, or let it alone, as Satan and they can agree about it.
> ... ...
> In short, I take Dreams to be the second Best of the Advantages the *Devil* has over Mankind; the first, I suppose, you all know (*viz.*) the Treachery of the Garrison within; by Dreams he may be said to get into the Inside of us without Opposition; here he opens and locks without a Key, and like an Enemy laying siege to a fortified City, Reason and Nature, the Governor of the City, keep him out by Day, and keep the Garrison true to their Duty; but in the Dark he gets in and parlees with the Garrison (the Affections and Passions) Debauches their Loyalty, stirring them up to Disloyalty and Rebellion, so they betray their Trust, Revolt, Mutiny, and go over to the Besieger. (259–60)

To be sure, this vivid allegory, with its tongue-in-cheek asides, proves nothing about the existence of the Devil, even if it cleverly imagines the Devil as an invader of the consciousness of a sleeper and the individual sleeper as a garrison seduced by his wiles. Of course, the garrison is manned by 'the Affections and Passions', which may be said to have a reality independent of Defoe's allegory and to that extent gives the game away. All Defoe can do is throw up his hands and say, if it is not the Devil what is it! Rhetorically, this is a clever move, but as a philosophical or theological statement it is meaningless. Defoe was honest enough to know that the Devil, in person and in plain view, could not really be found in contemporary life, despite his enduring presence in the Bible and in folklore; his existence could only be constructed from scriptural tradition and popular mythology and folk beliefs. It is to Defoe's credit that in this book he is honest about all this, that he insists on the plain and unremarkable truth and readily concedes that such truth does not lead to any revelation about the problem of evil. The Devil, such as he is, is in human nature.

Further Reading

Rodney M. Baine, *Daniel Defoe and the Supernatural* (Athens, GA: University of Georgia Press, 1968).

J. Paul Hunter, *The Reluctant Pilgrim: Defoe's Emblematic Method and Quest for Form in Robinson Crusoe* (Baltimore, MD: Johns Hopkins University Press, 1966).

Virginia Ogden Birdsall, *Defoe's Perpetual Seekers: A Study of the Major Fiction* (Lewisburg, PA: Bucknell University Press, 1985).

Maximillian E. Novak, *Defoe and the Nature of Man* (Oxford: Clarendon Press, 1963).

John Richetti, 'Secular Crusoe: The Reluctant Pilgrim Re-Visited', in *Eighteenth-Century Genre and Culture: Serious Essays on Occasional Forms: Essays in Honor of J. Paul Hunter*, ed. Dennis Todd and Cynthia Wall (Newark, DE: University of Delaware Press, 2001), 58–78.

Geoffrey M. Sill, *The Cure of the Passions and the Origins of the English Novel* (Cambridge: Cambridge University Press, 2001).

G. A. Starr, *Defoe and Spiritual Autobiography* (Princeton, NJ: Princeton University Press, 1965).

Eve Tavor, *Scepticism, Society and the Eighteenth-Century Novel* (Basingstoke: Macmillan, 1987).

Ian Watt, *The Rise of the Novel: Studies in Defoe, Richardson and Fielding* (London: Chatto and Windus, 1957).

CHAPTER 19

DEFOE, SCIENCE, AND TECHNOLOGY

CHRISTOPHER F. LOAR

> Infinite Experiments were made by the *Boyls* and *Newtons* of that Age; for all modern Knowledge seems to have built upon their first Experiments and to stand upon their Shoulders; Chymistry, Alchimy, Refining, Separating, Purging, Sublimating, and even to that yet unknown, tho' not unsought Mistery, call'd Transmutation, all had their rise and invention in these Ages, and much of it from these beginnings.[1]

IN this passage, Defoe makes a critical point about the forms of knowledge and practice we now typically call science and technology: in his reading, discovery proceeds from the experience of working and trading. The 'age' that Defoe refers to here is the age of Columbus, of geographic 'discovery', and of extractive imperial economies: the Boyles and Newtons of that earlier time were involved in the practical labour of mining and commerce. This assumption underlies many of Defoe's writings, in which scientific and technical knowledge is valuable inasmuch as it emerges from and is intertwined with work, trade, and the exploiting, disciplining, and improvement of the Earth [SEE CHAPTERS 14 AND 25]. Understanding this pragmatic streak in Defoe is crucial to grasping his attitudes towards secular science. He is attracted to knowledge production that emerges from necessity and that proceeds by observation and experiment; he is much less interested in speculation and cosmological theorizing. This is partly because his writings all evince his famous practicality and an interest in utility: what good is knowledge without application? But it also informs his understanding of how knowledge itself is generated: not simply or even primarily through reasoning, but first and

---

[1] Defoe, *A General History of Discoveries and Improvements*, TDH, iv. 196.

foremost through practice and experience. Science emerges from ad hoc practices—from labour, craft, and trade.

Understanding this pragmatism allows us better to situate Defoe's writings in the context of histories of science and technology. As scholars in those fields are at pains to point out, the aptness of these terms—*science* and *technology*—is open to serious question, since the term *science* in this period does not refer specifically to the natural philosophical and experimental practices that are the apparent antecedents of our own sense of that word.[2] Nor does *technology* carry anything very close to its present meaning until long after Defoe's death. Nevertheless, Defoe's writings do anticipate this distinction: his writings treat the rise of the 'new sciences' in the second half of the seventeenth century, the promulgation at an early stage of the corpuscular hypothesis, Newtonian science, experiment, and astronomy, while his writings on 'arts' and 'projects' often approach something like what we mean by *technology*. The latter practices are, in general, desirable, for they play an important role in reshaping and reforming nature. More abstract or speculative forms of knowledge are suspect; while inquiry into nature's workings is fine up to a point, it risks intruding on the role reserved for revelation and a providential understanding of the world.

To explore this tension, this chapter focuses on two concepts, roughly corresponding to our terms *science* and *technology*. In the first section, I consider Defoe's apparent views on how knowledge of non-human nature can and should be generated, and what relationship such knowledge has to spiritual truths. Some of Defoe's earliest writings examine the practices of the Royal Society; the role of observation in creating knowledge; and the relationship between knowledge, faith, and speculation. Like his contemporary Jonathan Swift, Defoe understands the knowledge produced by the New Sciences as sometimes too speculative and airy. But Defoe also engages obliquely and sometimes confusingly with problems of evidence and epistemology in many of his writings, borrowing somewhat eclectically from experimental methods in the service of establishing fundamental truths about the natural and supernatural worlds. His later writings on the natural and the supernatural offer a more clearly articulated approach to knowledge generation—one that has room for experiment and observation, but which consistently leaves space for faith as a critical component of human belief. I will then turn to discuss the related topics of applied sciences and technology. For Defoe, these applications are fundamentally progressive, orientated towards a future in which human thought, knowledge, and action improve the world and make it a better place through labour and commerce. Indeed, his writings often imagine that knowledge emerges originally from practice, rather than vice versa.

---

[2] For a brief and helpful discussion of this issue, see Gregory Lynall, *Swift and Science: The Satire, Politics and Theology of Natural Knowledge, 1690–1730* (Basingstoke: Palgrave Macmillan, 2012), 3–4. For a provocative and critical discussion of the term, see Tita Chico, *The Experimental Imagination: Literary Knowledge and Science in the British Enlightenment* (Stanford, CA: Stanford University Press, 2018), 5–10.

Practice and Improvement

Defoe's *General History of Discoveries and Improvements* (1725–6) offers a tour of an intermittently progressive human history, from the Great Deluge until the present moment. Noah's grape vines, first cultivated in the years following the Deluge, are perhaps the world's 'first *Improvement*'; the subsequent technological feat of the Tower of Babel, on the other hand, represents mere 'folly and madness' (*TDH*, iv. 29, 31). Following the confounding of languages, however, we see additional discoveries and improvements as Noah's descendants begin to spread out across the Earth. Defoe, following Walter Raleigh's *The History of the World* (1614), links these discoveries to their progressive adaptation to and manipulation of their environment. This progress takes the form of careful observation combined with hands-on practice. We can see this most clearly in the story of the Canaanites, later known as the Phoenicians, 'an Observing, Diligent, and Improving People' (*TDH*, iv. 38). And while Ham's descendants receive credit for their early discoveries in astronomy and chemistry, it is Shem's heirs the Phoenicians who first develop primitive boats, thus launching the human mastery of the sea that is crucial to the development of trade. Defoe presents the progressive development of boating as a fundamentally practical, technological process. The Phoenicians gradually came to learn their craft through casual observation of natural phenomena, such as bits of wood floating on the water. They soon turned to constructing rafts from oysters, leaves, and animal skins, used as early fishing vessels, staying very close to shore. Further progress is made primarily in response to challenges: when travelling into deeper waters, larger animals overset these primitive vessels, leading the Phoenicians to transform rafts into boats; later improvements lead to the invention of the sail. Defoe writes that 'From such small beginnings, was deriv'd that glorious piece of Knowledge, which is now so admirably improv'd, and is so deservedly rank'd among, and esteem'd the most useful part of the Mathematicks, I mean *Navigation*' (40). In this account of early human progress, we see certain persistent elements of Defoe's approach to knowledge production: practical activity to support the feeding of a growing population is transformed into a form of 'knowledge'—a *techne* that is a progressive emergence from that practical activity. Even mathematics is not primarily a high and abstruse art; it is, from the very beginning, intertwined with labour and, eventually, the development of the commercial systems in which Defoe placed his hope for a secular salvation of the globe.

Beginning with this emphasis helpfully allows us to supplement the dominant account of Defoe's approach to the sciences. The most influential and lucid treatment of Defoe's thinking on science as we now understand that term remains Ilse Vickers's *Defoe and the New Sciences*. For Vickers, the central fact of Defoe's thinking is the influence of Francis Bacon, which he would have absorbed while a student at Charles Morton's Newington Green Dissenting Academy. Morton had offered a natural philosophical curriculum that blended traditional science from the 'schools' with more contemporary experimental approaches.³ Yet Defoe's commitment to the ultimate power of Providence, and the risks of hubris in scientific inquiry, are clear and generally consistent throughout his career. It is in his more ambiguous and ambivalent treatments of these matters that we find revealing tensions and contradictions. Vickers convincingly traces a Baconian influence on Defoe's work throughout his career, seeing this influence in both Defoe's prose and his approach to education. Most subsequent research has taken Vickers as a guide or a starting point, though other scholars have provided additional contexts. For example, Al Coppola has persuasively interpreted Defoe's *A System of Magick* (1727) as a response to his perception of the excesses of public science in the 1720s.⁴ In this decade, lectures on Newtonianism were ragingly popular, even as they were caricatured in theatrical satires, most notably in the *Harlequin Doctor Faustus* craze. Defoe echoes the more indirect criticisms found on the London stage, suggesting that while there is nothing particularly wrong with the study of nature, especially for practical purposes, empirical study can combine with enthusiasm to promote deism and atheism. As Coppola writes, 'the "magick" that Defoe is most concerned with is being practiced by Newtonians like William Whiston who, emboldened by the Newtonian synthesis, were calling for a radical revision of Christian doctrine, if not outright atheism'. As he notes, Defoe's writings on magic 'trace the path by which specialist knowledge of nature was impressed into the service of power through cynical spectacles calculated to overawe credulous auditors— a characteristic stratagem of the Devil, according to Defoe, who taught men to apply just these skills of conjuration and craftsmanship, learned from natural philosophy, in political and religious discourse'.⁵

For Coppola, then, Defoe's approach to public science is a sceptical one: Newtonian lecturers tended towards speculative, impractical knowledge, and that knowledge in turn might seduce the unwitting to heretical views. But Defoe throughout his career remained admiring of the more practical and applied practices of 'art' and 'improvement', which align fairly closely with what we understand by the term *technology*. As Joseph Drury notes, Defoe's emphasis in his fiction, most notably *Robinson Crusoe* (1719), strongly links technological and moral progress. If the first part of Crusoe's time on his island is spent in the discovery of manufacturing processes and taming his surroundings—the work of the 'mechanic georgic', in Ann Van Sant's terms— the later portions are increasingly focused on Crusoe's disciplining of himself and of other men, most notably Friday.⁶ Drury identifies this as an important motif for later British novelists: the explicitly 'mechanic' aspects of discovery drop away, allowing for the growth of narratives emphasizing moral development and self-discipline.⁷ In two

---

³ Ilse Vickers, *Defoe and the New Sciences* (Cambridge: Cambridge University Press, 1996), 32–41; Novak, *Daniel Defoe*, 46–50; Backscheider, *Daniel Defoe*, 13–20.

⁴ Al Coppola, *The Theater of Experiment: Staging Natural Philosophy in Eighteenth-Century Britain* (Oxford: Oxford University Press, 2016), 136–9.

⁵ Coppola, *Theater of Experiment*, 138.

⁶ Ann Van Sant, 'Crusoe's Hands', *ECL*, 32:2 (2008), 120–37 (129).

⁷ Joseph Drury, *Novel Machines: Technology and Narrative Form in Enlightenment Britain* (Oxford: Oxford University Press, 2017), 27–8.

recent essays, Peter Walmsley has identified technology as a slippage point in Defoe's writings about 'savages'; while ostensibly less civilized peoples may display their inferiority through ignorance of craft and through poor workmanship, they may also display cleverness and skill, suggesting 'that skills are unevenly distributed culture by culture'.[8] Walmsley agrees that technology for Defoe is often an index of progress and civility, but that this progress is fragile and constantly subject to the hazards of degeneracy, paralleling the decline of human intellect and virtue following the Great Deluge.[9] And 'savage' technologies also serve as reminders of the link between knowledge and craft, between the work of the head and the work of the hand.[10] The work of hands as a source of knowledge—the idea that technology produces knowledge, rather than the other way around—is amply confirmed in Defoe's writings about the rise of science in the context of the rise of labour and commerce.

Speculation and Method

Two of Defoe's early works illustrate the tensions in his approach to science. In the early years of the eighteenth century, he published two volumes in close succession—*The Storm* (1704) and *The Consolidator* (1705)—that seem to register two different orientations towards the study of nature. The former imitates and borrows certain protocols and attitudes of the Royal Society, while the latter is partially imitative of Swift's satire of the excesses of experimental science in *A Tale of a Tub* (1704). These two works point towards a certain tension in Defoe's approach: a scepticism about the grander claims of science—particularly tendencies towards the idea that knowledge production could ever be separated from practical concerns and demonstration—that nevertheless continues to respect and make use of the protocols of empirical demonstration. His approach carves out an area of inquiry that is suitable for practitioners of science, but he is suspicious of theory-building and speculation. It is those areas, he seems to suggest, that are most subject to corruption, the most likely to encourage infidelity, and the least necessary, as the largest ontological questions of the universe are answered adequately by religious revelation.

This tension is well illustrated by *The Storm*. In this work, we find Defoe borrowing heavily from the observational protocols of the Royal Society; here, his Baconian influences chime nicely with their project of observation and synthesis of information

---

[8] Peter Walmsley, 'The African Artisan Meets the English Sailor: Technology and the Savage for Defoe', *Eighteenth Century: Theory and Interpretation*, 59:3 (2018), 347–68 (354).

[9] Walmsley, 'African Artisan', 350.

[10] Peter Walmsley, 'Robinson Crusoe's Canoes', *ECL*, 43:1 (2019), 1–23 (7–15). See also Van Sant, 'Crusoe's Hands', 129. Margaret Cohen has explored the relationship of craft and improvisation in *The Novel and the Sea* (Princeton, NJ: Princeton University Press, 2010), 60–87.

about a range of topics, including meteorology.[11] This book treats the hurricane that struck England in 1703; its readings of the storm blur lines between the material and the spiritual, as the storm has both physical and moral causes—an accident of the air, but also very likely a Divine judgement on the nation. In his treatment of the storm, Defoe reveals a familiarity with and investment in the methods and protocols of the Royal Society. The text's rhetoric is divided between this temptation to understand the storm in natural philosophical/scientific terms and an impulse to invest it with a providential meaning. Nevertheless, as Richard Hamblyn argues, *The Storm* is concerned with documentation and influenced by Royal Society procedures. Without rejecting providential explanations, it nevertheless seeks data and reliable witnesses. And while some aspects of God's non-human creation must not be probed too deeply, there is no harm in 'know[ing] all that the God of Nature has permitted'. He continues:

> To search after what God has in his Sovereignty thought fit to conceal, may be criminal, and doubtless is so; and the Fruitlessness of the Enquiry is generally Part of the Punishment to a vain Curiosity: but to search after what our Maker has not hid, only cover'd with a thin Veil of Natural Obscurity, and which upon our Search is plain to be read, seems to be justified by the very Nature of the thing, and the Possibility of the Demonstration is an Argument to prove the Lawfulness of the Enquiry.[12]

As Hamblyn points out, Defoe's journalistic writing exemplifies the growing emphasis on reliability and documentation in news media, a way of thinking that is also entangled with early scientific practice: 'Defoe's generation of journalists and reporters was the first to respond to the late-seventeenth-century rise of the empirical sciences, and they did so by emphasizing the need to gather first-hand evidence in support of a story'.[13] Robert Markley has also noted that *The Storm* refuses entirely to disentangle the empirical/material from the Providential. While Defoe understands the empirical requirements of witnessing as demanded by the protocols of the Royal Society, noting that many of his accounts come from 'worthy gentlemen', he never questions the higher, Providential nature of the non-human forces this book describes.[14] *The Storm* can be understood as an effort to work within the protocols of the Royal Society, now bleeding out into the world of journalism, while also explicitly retaining a commitment to the role of the Divine as the first cause.

Shortly after *The Storm* appeared, however, Defoe published *The Consolidator* (1705), which characterizes the Royal Society's procedures and proceedings quite differently. This peculiar and often obscure satiric work culminates with a voyage to the Moon,

---

[11] There is of course a massive literature on the Royal Society, its protocols, its self-representations, and its debts to Francis Bacon. These are conveniently summarized in Steven Shapin, *The Scientific Revolution* (Chicago, IL: University of Chicago Press, 1996), 80–109.

[12] Defoe, *The Storm*, ed. Richard Hamblyn (London: Penguin, 2005), 15.

[13] Hamblyn, 'Introduction', in *The Storm*, xxiv.

[14] Robert Markley, '"Casualties and Disasters": Defoe and the Interpretation of Climatic Instability', *Journal for Early Modern Cultural Studies*, 8:2 (2008), 102–24.

where is found a ludicrous society that satirically allegorizes contemporary English and European politics. Defoe's treatment of science, knowledge, and technological sophistication is not primarily to be found in his treatment of the lunar society, as one might expect, but rather on Earth, in the narrator's remarks on China.[15] The unnamed narrator travels first to China and then to the Moon on the feathered vessel that gives this work its title. The narrator's time in China is spent marvelling at that nation's technological and scientific accomplishments; the satiric voice in this text has little but praise for Chinese knowledge and cultivation. The '*Chineses*' (the narrator's term throughout the text) are masters of learning and 'useful Inventions' (*SFS*, iii. 30). The narrator promises to transmit more knowledge of the high state of Chinese science and engineering as a way of exposing 'the monstrous Ignorance and Deficiencies of European Science' and which will also transmit some of this great learning to European scholars and inventors. This will serve, he hopes, to 'abate the Pride and Arrogance of our Modern Undertakers of great Enterprizes, Authors of strange Foreign Accounts, Philosophical Transactions, and the like' (32). These discoveries all ultimately come from the lunar civilization, with which China has long been in contact; Chinese scientists, ahead of Europeans, are themselves merely heirs to this Moon-knowledge.

Defoe's satire has many targets, but among other things he suggests that the experimental practices of the Royal Society are potentially sacrilegious. The narrator, praising China, writes that:

> All our Philosophers are Fools, and their Transactions a parcel of empty Stuff, to the Experiments of the Royal Societies in this Country. Here I came to a Learned Tract of Winds, which outdoes even the Sacred Text, and would make us believe it was not wrote to those People; for they tell Folks whence it comes and whither it goes. There you have an Account how to make Glasses of Hogs Eyes, that can see the Wind; and they give strange Accounts both of its regular and irregular Motions, its Compositions and Quantities ... In these Calculations, some say, those Authors have been so exact, that they can, as our Philosophers say of Comets, state their Revolutions, and tell us how many Storms there shall happen to any Period of time, and when; and perhaps this may be with much about the same Truth. (34)

As the notes to the Stoke Newington edition underscore, this allusion is quite complicated; though this is a distorted image of the sacred text of John 3:8, it also perhaps casts an eye on Swift's Aeolus chapter in *A Tale of a Tub*, as well as Robert Boyle's and Edmond Halley's treatises on air and wind.[16] The passage may also glance back ironically at *The Storm*. While Defoe's earlier account had aimed at a more holistic

---

[15] Defoe's use of China in *The Consolidator* is part of a complex and rich debate in early eighteenth-century England about China and its relationship to modernity. For an illuminating discussion of this debate, see Eun Kyung Min, *China and the Writing of English Literary Modernity, 1690–1770* (Cambridge: Cambridge University Press, 2018), 1–88.

[16] Michael Seidel, 'Introduction', in *The Consolidator*, ed. Michael Seidel, Maximillian E. Novak, and Joyce D. Kennedy (New York: AMS Press 2001), xxi.

portrayal of an event that was simultaneously meteorological, spiritual, and social, the Royal Society here is targeted for its hubris in reducing this event to calculation and 'quantities'. *The Storm* seeks to reconcile the providential and the material, but Chinese natural philosophers prioritize the latter.

These misplaced priorities could even place one on the road to deism or atheism. Coppola has noted Defoe's later critique of this heresy in his discussion of magic, but his concern with deism and its links to the sciences is clear even earlier. The narrator notes that in modern England 'Phisicians are generally Atheists' and that 'Atheists are universally Fools, and generally live to know it themselves' (39). The accusation of atheism directed at experimental science might seem peculiar, since many of the most influential natural philosophers were famous for their piety (most notably Robert Boyle and Isaac Newton). Yet Defoe sees in their work a possible fetishizing or idolizing of 'Demonstrations', as opposed to 'Revelation'. In this section, the 'Great Eye' comes in as a figure for everything that is wrong with the world. The eye is what receives a demonstration; the eye does not need revelation. Defoe's traveller points to recent scientific researchers who

> to solve the Difficulties of Supernatural Systems, imagine a mighty vast Something, who has no Form but what represents him to them as one Great Eye: This infinite Optick they imagine to be *Natura Naturans*, or Power-forming; and that as we pretend the Soul of Man has a Similitude in quality to its Original, according to a Notion some People have, who read that so much ridicul'd Old Legend, call'd Bible, That Man was made in the Image of his Maker: The Soul of Man, therefore, in the Opinion of these Naturallists, is one vast Optick Power diffus'd through him into all his Parts, but seated principally in his Head. (50)

Defoe's narrator here reimagines the Christian deity as a perceiving, seeing power, and those who seek to see the hidden operations of the universe through experiment are imagined to be imitating that power. Really what this means is that these researchers can only imagine that power in the form of vision—their own fetishization, or idolization, of vision and perception is projected onto their deity. Anticipating Pope's seeker who wishes for insect-vision, as well as alluding to the rage for microscopes and telescopes, Defoe here suggests that there is a limit to Baconianism—prying into nature's hidden secrets threatens to lure seekers away from revelation.

Though *The Consolidator* criticizes airy speculating, it does not dismiss the observational protocols implicitly endorsed in *The Storm*. And indeed, Defoe's other writings often endorse these protocols, at least up to a point. They may even be used to explore phenomena not typically understood as scientific or material. Defoe is quite willing to borrow empirical methods from the natural sciences to examine questions that our own day typically considers matters of faith. His thinking seems to rest on a few assumptions. First, while Providence indeed governs all, he mocks those who emphasize it too much. In 1720's *Serious Reflections*, 'Crusoe' offers a sceptical reading of those who seek to see Divine power at work in even the most trivial occurrences:

> I am not answerable for any Extremes these Things may lead weak People into; I know some are apt to entitle the Hand of God, to the common and most ridiculous Trifles in Nature; as a religious Creature, I knew, seeing a Bottle of Beer being over ripe, burst out, the Cork fly up against the Ceiling, and the Froth follow it like an Engin, cried out, *O! the Wonders of Omnipotent Power*. (*Novels*, iii. 186)

As G. A. Starr notes, this passage pokes fun at what Defoe and his contemporaries might have considered 'enthusiasm', or an excess of religious zeal (*Novels*, iii. 12). A similar scepticism about enthusiasm is also visible in *A Journal of the Plague Year* (1722), where the search for an explanation leads to irrational beliefs and visions of non-existent apparitions; 'the Imagination of the People was really turn'd wayward and possess'd', the narrator H. F. laments.[17] For Crusoe and H. F., and perhaps for Defoe as well, scientific or naturalist explanations can provide an antidote to these extremes of enthusiastic or simple-minded religion.

Still, the enthusiast must not be confused with the cautious and receptive Christian who has 'an awful Regard to the Government of Providence in the World' and 'listens carefully to the Voice of Providence' (*Novels*, iii. 186–7). Nature can be allowed to follow its own course in trivial matters and ought not be overread for signs of 'omnipotent power', but the humble and careful Christian is attuned to subtler cues, which may come from the spirit world and invisible messengers [SEE CHAPTERS 18 AND 21]. Immaterial phenomena may be understood using methods akin to those in the experimental sciences. *Serious Reflections* offers comments on the 'invisible world' of spirits, which Defoe (or at least Crusoe) believes in. These spirits and their uncanny knowledge can be demonstrated empirically:

> How far they may or may not be concerned in the Influence of Providence, I also dare not say: But as the Verity of Astronomy is evidenced by the Calculation of Eclipses, so the Certainty of this Communication of Spirits is established by the Concurrence of Events with the Notices they sometimes give; and if it be true, as I must believe, that the Divine Providence takes Cognisance of all Things belonging to us, I dare not exclude it from having some Concern, *how much I do not say*, in these Things also. (187)

Crusoe does acknowledge that Divine Providence is difficult to understand; the 'Unchangeableness' of God's actions is hard to reconcile with the 'infinite Variation of his Providence' (196). But this difficulty, he concludes, is not so different from the difficulties faced by natural science. 'Why should we not as well say, nothing of God is to be understood, because we cannot understand it? Or that nothing in Nature is intelligible, but what we can understand?'. To fail to understand something does not imply that it does not exist: 'Who can understand the Reason, and much less the Manner of the needle tending to the Pole, by being touch'd with the Loadstone, and by what Operation

---

[17] Defoe, *A Journal of the Plague Year*, ed. Cynthia Wall (London: Penguin, 2003), 23.

the magnetic Vertue is conveyed with a Touch?' (196). It is striking that both the New Science and the practice of 'listening' that Crusoe advocates are in search of occult or hidden causes. And, in practice, both are in search of a fundamental Divine presence; natural philosophy reveals more about how the Divine works in the world, while listening to Providence provides evidence for how the Divine wishes one to act. As in so much of Defoe's writing on nature and philosophical inquiry, there is a distinction between mere knowledge and practical, applied action.

This distinction is quite prominent in his *A Journal of the Plague Year*, the work of Defoe's most commonly discussed in relation to problems of science and knowledge. Although the practical question of containing and suppressing the plague takes up a significant amount of attention in this text, scholars of science and literature have been especially drawn to Defoe's treatment of plague as a problem of knowledge. Plague is a natural mystery: an unknowable and invisible cause of profound and terrifying effects. For H. F. and other characters in this novel, plague hovers between the natural and the Providential, and the text famously walks a fine line between treating epidemic disease as an empirical and a spiritual problem. Defoe uses a range of techniques to make plague legible, some of which might be conceived of in terms of the New Science. While H. F. interpolates statistical data from the Bills of Mortality into his account, scholars such as Nicholas Seager have suggested that his treatment in the end suggests that plague as a social and spiritual phenomenon is not subject to definitive representation in cold statistics, and that an imaginative and probabilistic representation is the most appropriate mode for grasping plague's nature and significance.[18] Other scholars have noted that uncertain modes of representation—oral and sympathetic—can go too far; sympathetic energies can transform into contagious orality—or gossip—and interfere with the collection of useable data.[19] Data and observation might in turn produce practical, usable knowledge of how to respond to plague outbreaks, if not to its ultimate causes, which may remain forever unknowable.[20]

Indeed, Defoe seems to have had little patience for forms of natural inquiry that veered too far from the empirical. Unlike many practitioners of natural philosophy,

---

[18] Nicholas Seager, 'Lies, Damned Lies, and Statistics: Epistemology and Fiction in Defoe's *A Journal of the Plague Year*', *MLR*, 103:3 (2008), 639–53.

[19] Katherine E. Ellison, *Fatal News: Reading and Information Overload in Early Eighteenth-Century Literature* (London: Routledge, 2006), 89–107; Paula McDowell, 'Defoe and the Contagion of the Oral: Modeling Media Shift in *A Journal of the Plague Year*', *PMLA*, 121:1 (2006), 87–106.

[20] For other illuminating treatments of the *Journal* that consider questions related to natural philosophy, see Jayne Elizabeth Lewis, *Air's Appearance: Literary Atmosphere in British Fiction, 1660–1794* (Chicago, IL: University of Chicago Press, 2012), 111–29; Travis Chi Wing Lau, 'Defoe Before Immunity: A Prophylactic *Journal of the Plague Year*', *Digital Defoe*, 11 (2016), 23–39; Annika Mann, 'Isn't Contagion Just a Metaphor? Reading Contagion in Daniel Defoe's *A Journal of the Plague Year*', in *Transforming Contagion: Risky Contacts among Bodies, Disciplines, and Nations*, ed. Breanne Fahs, Annika Mann, Eric Swank, and Sarah Stage (New Brunswick, NJ: Rutgers University Press, 2018), 87–102; Geoffrey Payne, 'Distemper, Scourge, Invader: Discourse and Plague in Defoe's *A Journal of the Plague Year*', *English Studies*, 95:6 (2014), 620–36; and Helen Thompson, *Fictional Matter: Empiricism, Corpuscles, and the Novel* (Philadelphia, PA: University of Pennsylvania Press, 2016), 112–43.

Defoe was not attracted to imagination and speculation as sources of knowledge about the natural world. This tendency is particularly prominent in his comments on cosmology and the prospect of the geological history of the Earth and controversies over life on other worlds. In Defoe's supplement to his final book on Crusoe, *A Vision of the Angelick World*, Crusoe takes a quasi-imaginary voyage through the solar system. In a vision, our narrator soars above the Earth, reflecting on its small place in the vast range of creation; his sight also encompasses the greater order of the universe, with suns upon suns and their respective systems laid out neat and orderly 'without the least Confusion' (*Novels*, iii. 237). Among his other tasks is to dispel the popular idea that other planets might have inhabitants. He digresses briefly on what 'habitable' might mean:

> And first for the Word Habitable, I understand the meaning of it to be, that the Place it is spoken of, is qualify'd for the Subsistence and Existence of Man and Beast and to preserve the vegetative and sensitive Life; and you may depend upon it, that none of the Planets except the Moon, are in this Sense habitable; and the Moon, a poor little watery damp Thing, not above as big as *Yorkshire*, neither worth being called a World, nor capable of rendering Life comfortable to Mankind, if indeed supportable. (238)

Unlike some of his contemporaries, Defoe cannot imagine that living things might inhabit the environment of a place like Saturn, frozen from pole to pole, 'unless the Creator must be supposed to have created animal Creatures for the Climate, not the Climate for the Creatures' (238).

Expanding on this theme in *An Essay on the History and Reality of Apparitions* (1727), Defoe more explicitly compares his approach to that of natural philosophers of his time, who often speculated about the prospects for life of some sort on other planets. Defending his assertion that unembodied spirits may exist on earth and communicate with humanity, he pauses to introduce a digression on extraterrestrial life. Rather than the 'rational' belief in disembodied spirits and angels which he has been suggesting, here he identifies a theory that is 'as improbable' and 'much more inconsistent with the Christian Religion'—a theory which nevertheless 'Philosophy bids us call rational, and directs us to believe' (*SFS*, viii. 62). This 'improbable' idea is the possibility of life on other planets of the solar system, which some natural philosophers entertain even though

> both *Saturn* and *Jupiter* are uncomfortably dark, unsufferably cold, would congeal the very Soul (if that were possible) and so are not habitable on that Account; that *Mercury* and *Venus* are insufferably hot, that the very Water would always boyl, the Fire burn up the Vitals; and that, in short, no human Creatures could subsist in such Heat: But ... they will have God be obliged to create a Species of Bodies suitable to their several Climates. (62)

Defoe is at pains here to point out the counter-empirical reasoning embedded in these claims; astronomy and cosmology rely on speculation, just as much if not more than Defoe's own treatment of the invisible spirits which he senses but the existence of which cannot be empirically demonstrated. Likewise, he analogizes his theory of spirits to the New Sciences by explaining that both allow the formation of hypotheses that explain other phenomena. Referring indirectly to Christiaan Huygens's writings on astronomy, he writes that

> The great, and perhaps the strongest Argument which our learned Men produce for the Credit of their new Philosophy is, that by this they can the better solve the Difficulties of several other *Phænomena*, which before were hardly intelligible ...
>
> In like manner, tho' the Certainty of my Suggestion cannot be arrived to, or supposing it cannot, and that at best it is but a Speculation, scarcely can be called an *Hypothesis*, and that no Evidence can be given for it, yet this must be said of it, that by this Notion we may solve several other Difficulties which we cannot understand any other Way. (65)

As with many of Defoe's writings, it is difficult to pin down the precise tone of this claim, but one thing seems fairly clear: he sees the process of knowledge formation as one that is based on observation and generalization, at least when it comes to phenomena that are not specifically explicated by revelation. And this is true in the realm of spiritual as well as purely material phenomena.

THE PROGRESS OF SCIENCE

Despite Defoe's apparent scepticism about the airier aspects of early science, then, he nevertheless respects the truth claims of witnessing and experiment, seeing them as a guard against the excesses of enthusiasm, and, indeed, as broadly applicable to spiritual as well as physical matters. The principles of experimental science can lead to religious error, but they can also be adapted to spiritual purposes. In a related but different register, Defoe is also intrigued by science and technology as markers of progress—a progress that is, like the experimental method, linked with faith and Christianity, but through different pathways. The most important 'discoveries', as his later works suggest, are those that support 'improvement' and the transformation and exploitation of natural resources, and the flourishing of communication, commerce, and trade.

Defoe's later writings are full of discussions of early scientific and technological progress, most notably in his *A General History of Discoveries and Improvements* and *A System of Magick*. Both works borrow from a range of universal histories and scriptural scholarship to focus attention on humanity's development in the immediate wake of the Great Deluge. This is a crucial time for humanity, as in the interim between the Deluge and the revelation to Abraham, the world is largely bereft of prophecy, forced instead to rely on its own efforts to generate knowledge. In *General History* in particular, Defoe insists that scientific knowledge is driven by practical activity and engineering. Tracing a biblical chronology, he attributes some of the most significant early discoveries to Noah, as we have already seen, and to the descendants of his three sons. Their discoveries are not abstract or experimental, but rather grounded in practical agricultural and commercial activity. Noah himself appears as one of the Earth's first inventors and discoverers, and his Phoenician descendants, in particular, continue this tradition. There is, to be sure, a countervailing tendency, found most prominently in the offspring of Ham, whose civilizations make great progress in more abstract sciences such as astronomy and experimental science, as well as more 'wicked' pursuits such as magic. Prometheus is one such scientist: Defoe draws on ancient associations of this Titan with astronomy and feats of engineering, to euhemerize him as a Chaldean astronomer and inventor. Defoe offers an allegorical account of the myth of his punishment; the bird eating his liver is a figure for the desire for knowledge that consumed him. More literally, Defoe suggests, this astronomically inclined magus probably spent so much time lying on his back, watching the stars, that he contracted a liver disease (*TDH*, iv. 79).[21] The connection between this dubious figure of Prometheus and the study of the remote stars offers a sharp contrast to the practicality of the Phoenicians: practical problem-solving outdoes the speculations of idling stargazers.

Defoe's *System of Magick* also explores this period in the prehistory of science, during which a small number of extraordinary figures cultivate forms of knowledge that elevate them above the rest of humanity. These exceptional individuals may use their abilities to help humanity, as well as to increase their own influence and power. These figures are early magicians, which simply meant that they possessed knowledge not available to the common sort. Ancient magic was little more than what his own contemporaries would have called natural philosophy:

> In a Word, a *Magician* was no more or less in the ancient *Chaldean* Times, than a *Mathematician*, a Man of Science, who stor'd with Knowledge and Learning, as Learning went in those Days, was a kind of walking Dictionary to other People ... Men, *in a word*, who studied Nature, look'd up into, and made Observations from the Motions of the Stars and other heavenly Bodies, and who, *as 'tis said in the Scriptures*, understood the Signs of the Times, the Face of the Heavens, and the Influences of the Superior Luminaries there; who searched into the Arcana of Nature, and were Masters of *perhaps a little* experimental Philosophy. (*SFS*, vii. 29–30)

Through a slow process, the traditions of these magi became more widely distributed, which led them into the habit of pretending to ever-more secret affairs and knowledge, including occult knowledges such as astrology. The first true 'scientist' in Defoe's account was Abraham, from whom all the Chaldeans and Egyptians learned their astronomy and mathematics. He is also the first adherent of natural religion: his studies of the heavens would have led him to conclude that God exists, that order must have a creator, even before God's revelation to him: '*Abraham* learn'd to know the Creator, by the Contemplation of the Creature' (51). Later figures, however, sometimes pried

---

[21] Defoe repeats this interpretation in *An Essay upon Literature* (1726), *TDH*, iv. 303.

more deeply into hidden divine mysteries, opening the door to 'Diabolical things'. It is only at this point that *magic* becomes clearly distinguishable from practices that are the ancestors of the scientific method and observation. And, notably, these figures are those who have moved the farthest away from the demonstrable, the mechanical, and the practical, allowing their studies to encroach on theological topics best reserved for revelation.

Tracing the later progress of discovery, Defoe finds that knowledge passes through periods of stagnation as well as of growth. Often, predictably, there is a strong correlation between progress in knowledge and in other areas of human activity, such as commerce. In the earlier medieval world, for example, knowledge is in a state of stagnation:

> Every useful improving Thing was hid from them; they had neither look'd into Heaven or Earth, Sea or Land … they were confin'd and narrow'd in their Understandings, as they were in their Dwellings; they might be said not to know above a quarter part of the Globe, and not to understand a quarter part of that they knew. (*TDH*, iv. 175)

He goes on to describe them as having '*Philosophy* without Experiment' and 'ASTRONOMY without Demonstration', among their many limitations. In other words, to the extent that medieval Europeans created knowledge at all, it was of an impractical, abstract, or speculative form, akin to what we see in the more speculative forms of science that Defoe criticizes in the eighteenth century.

However, the fifteenth century sees an awakening of knowledge—knowledge driven by the pursuit of practical aims, commercial expansion, and empire. Spurred in large part by the discovery of the compass, which both derives from and fuels navigation and transoceanic commerce, the researchers of this era 'took the Alarm almost all together, preparing themselves as it were on a sudden, or by a general Possession or rather Inspiration to spread Knowledge through the Earth, and to search into every thing that it was possible to know' (*TDH*, iv. 177–8). The period from 1500 to 1700, Defoe points out, saw extraordinary technological, scientific, and geographical discoveries. Prior to that time, 'Nature being not enquir'd into, discover'd none of her Secrets to them, they neither knew, or sought to know, what now is the Fountain of all human Knowledge, and the great Mistery for the Wisest Men to search into, I mean *Nature*'. However, the discovery of the lodestone and the compass 'fir'd' the desire of Europeans to know more:

> Till then, *like* Solomon's *Fool*, they seem'd to have no delight in understanding that they seem'd to know but little but to be satisfied in their state of Ignorance, and not desire or at least not to search after an encrease of Knowledge, perhaps they believ'd, or at least fancy'd they could know no more than they did.
>
> But now having open'd a Door into the vast Ocean of Mathematical knowledge, it fir'd their Souls with a happy desire of knowing more; I say fir'd, because Mankind has ever since had an unquenchible Thirst after the compleat Discovery of Nature, and the highest degree of acquir'd Knowledge, and an indefatigable Application

to farther and farther Improvements in Arts and Science; in a word, in all possible Degrees of Learning and Knowledge. (*TDH*, iv. 174)

All this is to say: Defoe sees an acceleration in the desire to discover and to master the non-human things he calls 'Nature'. This acceleration is not surprisingly linked to the discovery of the compass, which seems to have awakened Europe to the practical possibilities afforded by this sort of inquiry.

This progressive account of human history is closely paralleled in Defoe's *An Essay upon Literature*, a little-discussed account of the origins of writing and printing. This history also traces a progressive narrative of the development and improvement of writing and, eventually, printing across centuries. However, this account is distinct in Defoe's work for locating the critical step in the propagation of knowledge—the quantum leap of oral into written language—as being a gift from God at the time of the handing down of the Ten Commandments. Defoe imagines this jump as too radical to have evolved from practical activity, which is why in this account no other cultural tradition developed writing independently. Even the wise ancient Egyptians were forced to rely on pictographic symbols, a 'poor Shift, compared to the present improvement of Letters' (*TDH*, iv. 231). Other peoples, in Defoe's reading, were even lower on the ladder, relying entirely upon 'meer Sound' and 'tradition' rather than writing. Defoe's account of an Algonquian messenger's first encounter with writing is illuminating:

> Nay, so ignorant were the *Americans* of the use or meaning of Letters, and writing Words upon Paper, which should be intelligible at a Distance, that they tell us the following Story, which happen'd at our first planting of *Virginia*: Viz. Captain *Smith*, one of the first Adventurers, happening to be taken Prisoner among the *Indians*, had leave granted him to send a Message to the Governor of the *English* Fort in *James Town*, about his Ransome; the Messenger being an *Indian*, was surpriz'd, when he came to the Governor, and was for kneeling down and Worshipping him as a GOD, for that the Governor could tell him all his Errand before he spoke one Word of it to him, and that he only had given him a piece of Paper: After which, when they let him know that the Paper which he had given the Governor had told him all the Business, then he fell in a Rapture the other Way, and then Capt. *Smith* was a Deity to be Worshipp'd, for that he had Power to make *the Paper speak*. (231)

This scene echoes many passages in the European colonial tradition in which white explorers or settlers, or their technology, are worshipped as gods by 'barbarous' peoples (not least in Defoe's own *Robinson Crusoe*). Writing, with its Divine origins, here becomes a mark of the superior knowledge and power of the European settler. And indeed, as Paula McDowell points out, the majority of the *Essay* is devoted not to the Divine origins of writing, but to its development and propagation by progressive European thinkers and traders.[22] Alphabetic writing and eventually print, for Defoe,

---

[22] Paula McDowell, 'Defoe's *Essay upon Literature* and Eighteenth-Century Histories of Mediation', *PMLA*, 130:3 (2015), 566–83.

come to elevate European knowledge above the oral traditions that predominate elsewhere in the world.

The history of European science, then, is intertwined with the development of exploration, commerce, and empire. Discovery is part of the drive towards economic growth and trade; idle speculation may not only be useless but actually dangerous, and impractical knowledge may lead to the circulation of the dangerous practices and ideas that go under the rubric of *magic*. Such technological progress, too, is interwoven with Defoe's religious beliefs, for economic progress is reflective of the Divine plan. We see this logic at work most clearly in his rejoinders to Thomas Burnet. Burnet's *Sacred Theory of the Earth* (1681, 1684, 1689) had attempted to reconcile spiritual and physical truths to explain the globe's apparent imperfections—its asymmetries and irregularities—as produced by the horrific action of the Great Deluge. For Defoe, such thinking was spurious. Defoe's comment on this work in a 1713 essay in *The Review* argues that not only is this a form of useless speculation; it fundamentally misrepresents the Divine plan for using geological irregularities as a spur to technological development and trade:

> But wise Providence having resolv'd Man to Eat his Bread with the Sweat of his Brow; that is, that he should obtain every thing he wanted, by the Labour of his Hand, the Application of his Head, and the Industrious Management of himself, and of the rest of the Creation; has, to this purpose, placed the several Blessings he has bestowed on the World for the Use and Convenience of Man, at the remotest Distance from one another, in the most Secret, Reserv'd and Inaccessible Parts, and shared to all Parts of the Earth, something essential to the other, so as to make a Universal Correspondence absolutely necessary.[23]

Defoe's generally positive image of a progressive history is somewhat tempered by his dim view of other spaces that have degenerated before fully exploiting their resources: '*Many parts of the World which have been peopled and planted, cultivated and improv'd have, by the fate of Nations been again laid wast, and have returned to their primitive, undiscovered State, and that before the native Wealth of those Countries had been fully improv'd, or their secret Treasure exhausted*' (*TDH*, iv. 21). Defoe perhaps predictably sees a responsibility for modern Europe to integrate these undepleted spaces into global networks of commerce [SEE CHAPTERS 29 AND 30]. The entirety of the *General History*, in fact, is closely linked with Defoe's narratives of progressive expansion of commerce and global economic productivity. Unsurprisingly, this narrative is linked to the disparaging attitude the narrative expresses towards Asian and African societies—particularly the Islamic world—for whom Defoe expresses little but contempt in this work: 'those nations,' he writes,

---

[23] *Review*, ix. 216 (5 February 1713). For a brief but useful discussion, see Marjorie Hope Nicolson, *Mountain Gloom and Mountain Glory: The Development of the Aesthetics of the Infinite* (New York: Norton, 1963), 258.

which being once at the Center of Commerce, as well as of Arts and Sciences, are since lay'd Desolate, and over run with a Barbarous People, who utterly neglecting those Improvements, have turn'd the most delicious Countries, formerly *flowing with Milk and Honey*, into a Desolate Howling Wilderness, and the most fruitful Provinces of *Asia*, *Greece*, and *Africa*, which formerly maintained Millions of Inhabitants, to be scarce able to feed the Wild Creatures that inhabit there. (25)

This progressive, if intermittent, mastery of nature is very much in line with much eighteenth-century thinking that goes under the banner of Enlightenment. So, too, is the use of this progress as a signifier for the value of European colonial projects, since these forms of knowledge and practice do appear as markers of progress vis-á-vis the cultural Others of the colonial world. In Defoe's later writing, technological progress is often associated with imperial projects of conversion and domination. That is to say, technology is often used to illustrate the difference between a civilized person and his or her barbarous or savage others. As Roxann Wheeler has observed, Defoe's scenes of the 'savage' worlds of central Africa and the Caribbean feature sequences in which Europeans assert their authority 'through the use of guns and through technological feats such as building ships, keeping meat from rotting, [and] removing salt from seawater', amounting at times to 'a glorification of European technology'.[24] *The Farther Adventures of Robinson Crusoe* (1719) also features an extended complaint that Europeans exaggerate the achievements of Chinese science and civilization, as Michael Adas has noted.[25] Defoe's use of technology as a foil for the cultural lack that characterizes savagery is most striking, perhaps, in *Robinson Crusoe*, with the title character's well-known demonstration of his firearm's power to cow Friday into a seemingly natural submission. Crusoe, at least, also associates his firearms with his religious civilizing mission. This technological superiority is perhaps more nakedly on display in the *Farther Adventures*, in which the title character disparages China's technological accomplishments and, later, uses his beloved gunpowder to destroy a monstrous Tatar idol. Defoe stages this sequence as a scene of potential enlightenment: Crusoe and his fellow travellers not only stuff the idol with gunpowder, they also force the idolatrous villagers to watch their deity's destruction. The sequence offers a picture of enlightened and technologically sophisticated Christians attempting to sway the superstitious and the idolatrous. Thus is technological prowess linked not only to power, but to the moral virtues of Christianity (*Novels*, ii. 196–7).

---

[24] Roxann Wheeler, *The Complexion of Race: Categories of Difference in Eighteenth-Century Culture* (Philadelphia, PA: University of Pennsylvania Press, 2000), 107–8.

[25] Michael Adas, *Machines as the Measure of Men: Science, Technology, and Ideologies of Western Dominance* (Cornell, N.Y.: Cornell University Press, 1989), 90.

Conclusion

Defoe's writings are dominated by this positive view of technological progress, but at times his writing does manifest other attitudes. As early as his *Essay upon Projects* (1697), Defoe had presented progress in the 'art of war' as a mixed blessing: 'Nor am I absolutely of the opinion that we are so happy as to be wiser in this age than our forefathers; though at the same time I must own some parts of knowledge in science as well as art have received improvements in this age altogether concealed from the former'. He continues:

> The Art of War, which I take to be the highest Perfection of Human Knowledge, is a sufficient Proof of what I say, especially in conducting Armies, and in offensive Engines; *witness* the new ways of Mines, Fougades, Entrenchments, Attacks, Lodgments, and a long *Et Cetera* of New Inventions which want Names, practised in Sieges and Encampments; *witness* the new sorts of Bombs and unheard-of Mortars, of Seven to Ten Ton Weight, with which our Fleets standing two or three Miles off at Sea, can imitate God Almighty himself, and rain *Fire and Brimstone* out of Heaven, as it were, upon Towns built on the firm Land; *witness also* our new-invented *Child of Hell*, the Machine, which carries Thunder, Lightning, and Earthquakes in its Bowels, and tears up the most impregnable Fortifications. (*PEW*, viii. 34)

In this, the introduction to his volume on the perils and profits of 'projecting' and improvement, Defoe gives voice to some of the ambivalence about technological improvement that we see in his later fiction [SEE CHAPTER 22].

All in all, however, this ambivalence is little more than an undercurrent of a generally positive attitude towards the empirical study of nature. Despite the dangers posed by airy speculations, the risks of excessive emphasis on materialist explanatory frameworks, and the sometimes alarming capabilities of contemporary technological developments, Defoe throughout his career retained his commitment to progressive technical development. And, in general, this commitment harmonizes with an approach to natural philosophy that appreciates its pragmatic power to explain and exploit nature, while steering away from speculation and excess. Contra the scientific role of literariness in British Enlightenment science outlined by Tita Chico, Defoe's science eschews the excesses of the non-literal, the speculative, and the imaginative. In her critique of recent critical studies into the field of literature and science, Chico notes that most such scholarship treats literature as necessarily 'belated'; in many of these studies, literature *follows* science, commenting on it after the fact.[26] Chico brilliantly explicates an alternative vision, of a 'literary knowledge' that evolves alongside and overlaps with the practices and ideas later identified with scientific disciplines. Defoe, however, might argue rather differently. With his suspicion of the speculative and the imaginative, his

---

[26] Chico, *Experimental Imagination*, 5–9.

writings suggest that the core element of the study of nature should be spontaneous engagement with reality as it confronts us, not the insubstantial realm of the imaginary.

Further Reading

Tita Chico, *The Experimental Imagination: Literary Knowledge and Science in the British Enlightenment* (Stanford, CA: Stanford University Press, 2018).

Al Coppola, *The Theater of Experiment: Staging Natural Philosophy in Eighteenth-Century Britain* (Oxford: Oxford University Press, 2016).

Helen Thompson, *Fictional Matter: Empiricism, Corpuscles, and the Novel* (Philadelphia, PA: University of Pennsylvania Press, 2016).

Jayne Elizabeth Lewis, *Air's Appearance: Literary Atmosphere in British Fiction, 1660–1794* (Chicago, IL: University of Chicago Press, 2012).

Steven Shapin, *The Scientific Revolution* (Chicago, IL: University of Chicago Press, 1996).

Ilse Vickers, *Defoe and the New Sciences* (Cambridge: Cambridge University Press, 1996).

Peter Walmsley, 'The African Artisan Meets the English Sailor: Technology and the Savage for Defoe', *Eighteenth Century: Theory and Interpretation*, 59:3 (2018), 347–68.

Peter Walmsley, 'Robinson Crusoe's Canoes', *ECL*, 43:1 (2019), 1–23.

Roxann Wheeler, *The Complexion of Race: Categories of Difference in Eighteenth-Century Culture* (Philadelphia, PA: University of Pennsylvania Press, 2000).

CHAPTER 20

DEFOE AND GOVERNMENT

Propaganda and Principle

D. W. HAYTON

DEFOE's friends in high places, especially Robert Harley, secretary of state 1704–8 and 'premier minister' 1710–14, were essential to him in providing a regular income and legal protection, but such connections tainted his reputation among contemporaries and to posterity. Writing for governments of different political complexions left him open to the accusation of being a 'mercenary scribbler'. Certainly, much of his journalism was propagandist; nor is the evidence of his private letters to the powerful particularly edifying. Nonetheless, while he frequently surrendered to the temptation of point-scoring to serve an employer, there were strong threads of consistency throughout his political writings: a revulsion from popery and absolute monarchy creating an overriding concern for the maintenance of the Revolution settlement; a veneration for the person and legacy of King William; a belief, shared with radical Whigs, that authority in the state rested on popular consent; and a commitment to toleration for Protestant Dissenters. He may thus be identified as a Whig by conviction. This did not mean, however, that he would always write on behalf of the Whig party, since its leaders did not themselves abide consistently by Whig principles.

REVOLUTION PRINCIPLES

King William was Defoe's hero, the man who had saved England from popish tyranny. Defoe's first published work after the Revolution, *A New Discovery of an Old Intreague* (1691), presented an idealized picture of the king, not merely as an instrument of Divine Providence, but almost as a *deus ex machina* in himself. 'Great Nassau' embodied the virtues of a martial hero and a wise and gentle ruler. This apotheosis did not mean that Defoe subscribed to the belief that the king ruled by divine right. William may have been God's instrument in saving his Protestant people, but his regnal authority derived ultimately from the people themselves.

William's reign opened in an atmosphere of uncertainty. Not only was he at war with Louis XIV; there was a strong Jacobite force in Ireland until 1691. William began therefore by seeking the broadest possible basis of support and appointed a 'mixed ministry' comprising men of different political complexions. He soon realized that cross-party coalitions were not only uneasy but inefficient in terms of parliamentary management; and so in 1693–4 he reconstructed his government on a more partisan basis, turning to a group of younger Whigs, among them the lawyer Sir John Somers, later Lord Somers, who became lord keeper (and subsequently lord chancellor), and Charles Montagu, later Lord Halifax, who took over at the treasury.

The leaders of William's Whig government, known collectively as the Junto, did not share the determination of their Exclusionist predecessors to restrict kingly power, especially at a time when war was making unprecedented demands on the treasury. Montagu organized a revolution in public finances, which strengthened the monarchy and furnished William with the troops and resources needed until the Treaty of Ryswick in 1697 brought the war to a conclusion. Successful as the Junto were in enabling the king to fight the French to a standstill, their policies nevertheless stirred up virulent opposition. The new financial system may have guaranteed parliament's place in the constitution, but this was not something back-bench MPs appreciated. Higher taxation and the wartime interruption to trade caused an economic depression. Moreover, landowners with unhappy experiences of borrowing money thought of the mounting public debt as 'the great mortgage' and were anxious to see it reduced. They were also alarmed by the king's insistence on retaining a standing army in peacetime, the consequence of his conviction that another war with the French was inevitable, and suspected William of having designs on their liberties. The Tory narrative, that William was bent on creating an absolute monarchy of his own, also attracted support from a minority of Whigs who retained a 'Country party' cast of mind.

In the House of Commons the onslaught on the ministry was led by Robert Harley, a flexible politician from an impeccably Whig background who was in the process of turning himself into a Tory.[1] From 1696–7 onwards, Harley harried the Junto on the issues of the standing army and instances of alleged corruption, especially the grants of Irish forfeited estates which William had made to his favourites. The king had always been the subject of scurrilous attacks from Jacobites on the subject of his nationality; economic stresses exacerbated English xenophobia, persuading William's critics that war was being waged for the benefit of the Dutch and to the detriment of England.

---

[1] For Harley's life and career, see Brian W. Hill, *Robert Harley: Speaker, Secretary of State and Premier Minister* (New Haven, CT: Yale University Press, 1988); the biography (by W. A. Speck) in *Oxford DNB*; and the entries in Eveline Cruickshanks et al. (ed.), *The History of Parliament: The House of Commons 1690–1715*, 5 vols (Cambridge: Cambridge University Press, 2002), iv. 244–80 and Ruth Paley (ed.), *The History of Parliament: The House of Lords 1660–1715*, 5 vols (Cambridge: Cambridge University Press, 2016), iii. 230–51.

Personal abuse of the king provoked Defoe to defend his hero in a lengthy poem which made his reputation. *The True-Born Englishman* (1700/1) was a direct reply to John Tutchin's *The Foreigners*, which had attacked the king himself. The conceit of Defoe's poem was that the Devil had found the means to rule all nations by their besetting sin; and that the besetting sin of the English was ingratitude. According to Defoe, the poem brought him to William's attention: Defoe wrote later that he was 'received … employed and … rewarded' by the king; indeed, that he was taken into the royal confidence (*Appeal*, 6). There is no supporting evidence for these claims, but there may have been a kernel of truth. Certainly, in *The True-Born Englishman* Defoe had vindicated William on a most tender point.

The parliamentary session of 1699–1700 was a catalogue of disasters, culminating in the passage of an act making void the grants of Irish forfeited estates. William began negotiations with the opposition, and entrusted management to those he considered 'moderate' men, the Court Tory Lord Godolphin and Robert Harley. The general election that followed, in January 1701, produced Tory gains but no outright majority in the Commons. The Junto remained ascendant in the Lords. The scene was thus set for a major confrontation that would obstruct business at a crucial time. The death of Carlos II of Spain in November 1700, bequeathing his kingdom to Louis XIV's grandson, made a resumption of war almost inevitable, and William needed a supportive parliament. The session began well enough; Harley was elected speaker, and there was no significant opposition to settling the succession to the crown in the Protestant house of Hanover. Soon, however, things took a turn for the worse. The Commons added a raft of additional clauses to the Bill of Settlement, to take place after the Hanoverian succession, which not only infringed on the royal prerogative, but constituted an indictment of many aspects of William's reign; and there was criticism in the Commons of the king's foreign policy, leading to the impeachment of several Junto ministers. By the prorogation it was clear that this parliament could not do the king's business. It was dissolved.

Before the election of January 1701, Defoe had written to justify in advance the king's likely response to the European crisis [SEE CHAPTER 28]. *The Two Great Questions Considered* emphasized that in the event of Louis XIV allowing his grandson to accept the Spanish crown the only course of action would be to act with European allies to contain the power of France. This chimed with arguments being put forwards by the Junto. While direct evidence of Defoe's connections with Junto ministers is elusive, he seems to have been a particular admirer of Somers. During the election campaign Defoe addressed voters directly, in *The Six Distinguishing Characters of a Parliament-Man*. While not explicitly partisan, this pamphlet served a party turn. Defoe focused on the European situation, and, looking beyond the security of the kingdom and the Protestant religion, dramatized the choice as between maintaining the Revolution settlement and restoring King James. The implications of Tory rhetoric were set out: anyone willing to countenance that 'the *French* and Popish Powers' should 'unite and possess *Flanders*', and who delighted in the prospect that the Dutch would be ruined, was, consciously or not, serving the interests of James II. 'Had the Nation seen with same Eyes as the late

Lord *Russel*, Earl of *Essex*, and the *Oxford Parliament*, did see, could they have been convinc'd by Argument that *It was inconsistent with the Constitution of this Protestant Kingdom to be govern'd by a Popish Prince*' (PEW, ii. 30). Defoe did not engage in a direct defence of the outgoing ministry, against those who depicted the 'new Whigs' as betrayers of their party's traditions. Instead, he focused on the danger of voting at this critical juncture for Tory candidates, who could not be trusted to support the Protestant interest at home and abroad. This was entirely appropriate to the thrust of the Whig election campaign.

Defoe made more impact with an intervention during the course of the 1701 parliament. The occasion was the so-called Kentish petition of April 1701, when a Whig-dominated grand jury petitioned the Commons to make good its promises to support the king's foreign policy, provoking Tory MPs to condemn the petition and order into custody those who presented it. The treatment of the petitioners became a *cause célèbre*. Defoe's was not the only voice raised on behalf of the petitioners. *Jura Populi Anglicani*, probably written by Somers, defended the subject's right to petition. In asserting that the Commons had overstepped its constitutional authority, the author in effect appealed to voters over the heads of their elected representatives. Defoe's response, the *Legion's Memorial*, went a step beyond and appealed directly to the people at large. It was written as a petition to Speaker Harley, in the name of 'many Thousands of the good People of *England*' (PEW, ii. 41). Rehearsing a range of grievances against the conduct of the Tory majority in the Commons, Defoe observed that 'it is the undoubted Right of the People of *England* to call them to an account' (45).

Although written explicitly against those who were obstructing William's intentions, the implications of the *Memorial* in terms of constitutional theory would not have been entirely welcome at court. Defoe ended with the remark that, should the Commons fail in their duty, 'you may expect to be treated according to the resentments of an injur'd Nation; for *Englishmen* are no more to be Slaves to Parliaments, than to a King' (45–6). The principle that authority in the state originated with the people was not in itself particularly radical. Many Whig backbenchers took the same view, but understood the will of the people as represented by the House of Commons. The version of popular sovereignty expounded by Defoe was more extreme, seemingly allowing for direct action. He developed his arguments in *The Original Power of the Collective Body of the People of England, Examined and Asserted* (1701), written in reply to the Tory MP Sir Humphry Mackworth's *A Vindication of the Rights of the Commons of England*, which had justified the impeachments as an essential element in England's mixed constitution, where sovereignty was held jointly by king, Lords, and Commons. For Defoe, sovereignty, however devolved, lay ultimately with 'the people'. He was careful to dedicate his pamphlet to the king, with extravagant praise of royal achievements, but he reminded William that even if the institution of monarchy was divinely instituted, it derived ultimately from the popular will. *Vox dei* and *vox populi* were identical.

Defoe's ideas of popular sovereignty belonged to the 'old Whig' tradition, exemplified in the republicanism of writers like Algernon Sydney. In another respect too, he seems to have situated himself at this point in his career at the radical end of the Whig spectrum, through comments on the possible reform of the electoral system. In *The Original Power of the Collective Body of the People of England*, Defoe equated 'the people' with freeholders.[2] Defoe presumably meant those entitled to vote in county elections, men with a freehold worth at least forty shillings a year. This was not in itself wholly at odds with mainstream contemporary thinking, Whig as well as Tory. Parliamentary proposals for electoral reform in this period did not extend the franchise, but focused on the imbalance between borough and county representation, and the corruption of borough elections. A failed bill in 1701 proposed increasing the electorates in smaller boroughs by admitting freeholders from the surrounding hundred.[3] Defoe, however, went further. He seems to have been in sympathy with the rather different remedy proposed by the 'commonwealth Whig' John Toland, whose *Art of Governing by Partys*, also published in 1701, argued for the disfranchisement of decayed boroughs, where there was no longer any genuine civic life, and their replacement by new corporations, 'where Towns are grown to considerable riches and extent', thereby enfranchising numbers of the urban 'middling sort'.[4] In *The Freeholder's Plea against Stock-Jobbing Elections of Parliament Men*, Defoe also protested against the debauching of electors by carpet-bagging London financiers. Once more he claimed to be speaking on behalf of 'the poor freeholders of England', but as his argument developed the emphasis fell on 'rotten boroughs', whose voters sold themselves to wealthy candidates or simply did the bidding of the local squire. This would not have been possible in populous constituencies, thriving centres of trade and industry which remained unrepresented.[5]

The fact that Toland was at this point in his career edging close to Robert Harley,[6] with whom Defoe would also in due course come to a working arrangement, is probably not significant. The burden of *The Art of Governing by Partys* was a denunciation of the 'new Whigs'—the Junto—who had become 'the most pliant gentlemen imaginable' in the service of the monarchy. It was of a piece with other attacks orchestrated by Harley. Defoe, on the other hand, remained at this point committed to the Whig cause, however much Somers and his colleagues had strayed from the path beaten by their Exclusionist predecessors. The European crisis required that the king be properly supported, and the behaviour of MPs in the 1701 parliament demonstrated that Tory MPs could not be trusted to do this. Defoe believed, or affected to believe, that Tories were at bottom Jacobites. And, as a Dissenter himself, he had other, powerful reasons to fear the influence of High Churchmen in politics.

---

[2] See Mark Knights, *Representation and Misrepresentation in Later Stuart Britain* (Oxford: Oxford University Press, 2005), 201.
[3] Cruickshanks et al. (ed.), *Commons 1690–1715*, i. 256.
[4] John Toland, *The Art of Governing by Partys* (1701), 76–7.
[5] Defoe, *The Free-Holders Plea against Stock-Jobbing Elections of Parliament Men* (1701), 16–20.
[6] Downie, *Robert Harley and the Press*, 42–5.

The Shortest-Way with the Dissenters

The passage of the Toleration Act in 1689 guaranteed Dissenters freedom of worship in registered meeting houses, which suited the largest groups of Nonconformists—Presbyterians, Independents (Congregationalists), and Baptists—if not the smaller sects. It did not provide full emancipation: Dissenters remained excluded from crown and municipal office, through the provisions of the Test and Corporation Acts. Paradoxically, the achievement of a statutory toleration highlighted the issue of political and civil rights through confirming the exclusion from the established church of those conservative Presbyterians, landed gentlemen and civic leaders, who expected to participate in public life and in order to do so carried out their legal obligations by attending their parish church once a year. Anglican outrage at 'occasional conformity' was one of the driving forces behind the re-emergence in the 1690s of a 'High Church' party among both clergy and laity. Unwilling to broach repeal of the Toleration Act, High Churchmen focused on the issue of occasional conformity, and in 1702, after the accession of the staunchly Anglican Queen Anne and the election of a Tory-dominated House of Commons, made their first attempt to outlaw the practice.

In *An Enquiry into the Occasional Conformity of Dissenters*, published in 1698, and addressed to a Dissenting audience, Defoe himself criticized 'occasional conformity', as a 'scandal': it was 'bantering with religion' (*PEW*, iii. 48). His outrage may well have been genuine: it is unnecessary to assume he was playing a part, since many Nonconformists, particularly those from an Independent or Baptist background, were disgusted by the notion of attending church in order to serve a turn. But it is worth noting that at this juncture it was in the interest of the Whig ministers that the issue of the defence of the ecclesiastical establishment should not come to the fore. The general election in 1698 was going to be difficult enough, given the unpopularity of the standing army, without enabling their opponents to raise another popular outcry. The Junto were grateful for support from Nonconformist voters, but were unwilling to do much to help if it meant gifting political opponents an opportunity to raise the cry of 'the church in danger'.

By 1702 the Junto were in opposition, and prepared to take a stronger line. Their control over the Lords enabled them to defeat the first Occasional Conformity Bill in 1702–3, and to thwart it in each of the following two sessions. For Defoe, the battle over the Occasional Conformity Bill was no longer simply about preventing Presbyterian mayors and aldermen from 'playing Bo-peep with God Almighty'; it had become a symbol of something more dangerous. High Church firebrands were using it as a means of attacking Dissent, with the underlying threat that some means might be found of undoing the Toleration Act. In the autumn of 1702 Defoe published two pamphlets on the issue. *An Enquiry into Occasional Conformity* once again took the view that occasional conformity was wrong, and thus that the true interests of the Dissenting community would not be harmed by the passage of the bill, an argument calculated to appeal to moderate Tories who were having second thoughts. His second contribution, *The*

Shortest-Way with the Dissenters, was a masterpiece of irony: written in the character of a red-hot Tory, it exposed the underlying intentions of the more violent High Churchmen by demanding that the only way of dealing with the cancer of Dissent within the body politic was surgical removal.

Unfortunately for Defoe, what the publication of *The Shortest-Way* exposed was that he lacked friends in government who could protect him. The ministry affected to take the text literally: a warrant was issued for his arrest. A feeble attempt to negotiate with the secretary of state, the High Tory Earl of Nottingham, failed, and Defoe was arrested and imprisoned. Instead of the favoured treatment he had received under King William, he now found himself subjected to hostile interrogations by Nottingham, who could not be persuaded into leniency by any promises of cooperation. After being sentenced to three spells in the pillory and imprisonment for seven years, Defoe approached the leaders of the ministry through the Quaker William Penn with a promise to make a full confession and name all his accomplices. When Nottingham came to Newgate to talk to him there was no offer, and in consequence no confession. It was enough to nurture in Defoe a life-long hatred of Nottingham. Having survived the pillory, he remained in Newgate until rescued by another, more sympathetic member of the administration, Robert Harley.

Defoe and Harley

Defoe seems to have made contact with Robert Harley for the first time in 1702. Then in prison for debt, Defoe approached Harley through an intermediary, in the hope of employment.[7] Although not holding office, Harley occupied a key role in the new ministry headed by Lord Treasurer Godolphin, being entrusted, as speaker, with management of the Commons. He was also known to patronize writers of varying stripes, including Toland. Defoe might seem guilty of a flagrant betrayal of his political hero, and a reversal of his previous party allegiance in thus turning to the man who had led opposition to King William's government in the turbulent sessions of 1697–9, and thus bore considerable responsibility for measures which William found personally insulting—the attempts to disband the army, and the resumption of Irish forfeitures. Yet there were mitigating factors: Harley's Nonconformist background and early espousal of Whig principles made him a relatively congenial employer; and his personal record in the 1701 parliament, as the architect of the Act of Settlement, was not exceptionable: he had not been responsible for the impeachments, nor for the condemnation of the Kentish petition. Moreover, he was identified with a 'moderate' stance on the issue of occasional conformity, and in the aftermath of the Tory triumph at the general election of 1702 seemed the Dissenters' best hope of restraining High-Church furies in

---

[7] Downie, *Robert Harley and the Press*, 60.

the new parliament. Throughout his political career, even when standing at the head of a Tory administration after 1710, Harley maintained connections with Nonconformist ministers.

Nothing came of these early solicitations, but following the publication of *The Shortest-Way with the Dissenters*, which served his own as well as the Whigs' purposes, Harley seems to have taken a greater interest. Once Defoe had been sentenced, Harley worked to secure his release, on security of good behaviour. This left Defoe dependent on Harley, not just for employment, but for his continued liberty.[8] In obtaining Godolphin's approval of Defoe's recruitment as a ministerial propagandist, Harley suggested that Defoe, as a Dissenter, might be particularly useful in Scotland. The ministry's management of Scottish politics was in chaos following the election of a new parliament in Edinburgh in 1703 and the failure of the Court party under the Duke of Queensberry to secure a working majority; moreover, the Scots were yet to settle the succession. In due course Defoe would be employed north of the border, but that was not the first service he undertook for Harley and Godolphin. A more pressing problem for the ministry was the insistence by hotter Tories in the Commons on legislating against occasional conformity. A second bill was threatened in the autumn of 1703, which was certain to be voted down in the Lords, creating an unnecessary political crisis. Defoe's pamphlet *A Challenge of Peace* (1703) followed other ministerial writers in urging both parties to come together behind the queen and her ministers, who were after all engaged in fighting a major war against the French on land and on sea: a peaceful settlement, rather than a fruitless political conflict, would be the 'shortest way with the Dissenters'.

Neither Defoe nor any other writer counselling moderation could prevail with the Tory leaders, and the sequence of events that Harley and Godolphin had feared came to pass, provoking a political crisis in February 1704 which saw High Churchmen, including Nottingham, ousted, and an influx of 'moderate' Tories into the administration, headed by Harley as secretary of state. The ministry now rested on a bloc of 'Court'-centred MPs, placemen, Harleyite Tories, and Whigs who preferred the careful stewardship of Godolphin to the strident partisanship of the Junto. But in a political world dominated by party allegiance, maintaining this kind of coalition was exceedingly difficult, and ministers required the case for 'moderation' to be made publicly and consistently. Defoe's periodical, the *Review*, the first issue of which appeared in February 1704, answered this need. The tone of the *Review* was carefully non-partisan—initially, the terms Whig and Tory seldom appeared in its columns—and the avowed purpose was to persuade readers that their duty was to support the administration in carrying on the war. This applied especially to Tories in parliament who, until the first of Marlborough's great victories, at Blenheim in the summer of 1704, were becoming critical of the expense of continental campaigns.[9] Such attitudes were reminiscent of

---

[8] Downie, *Robert Harley and the Press*, 60–4.
[9] Downie, *Robert Harley and the Press*, 65; Furbank and Owens, *Political Biography*, 34–6.

debates in William's reign, and fitted with Defoe's own overriding concern for the maintenance of the Revolution settlement and the defence of Protestantism at home and abroad.

Harley was closely involved with the production of the *Review* [SEE CHAPTER 7]. He also did whatever was necessary to protect his employee when indiscretions left Defoe open to prosecution. By the autumn of 1704 Defoe was not only writing propaganda for the secretary; he was also travelling the country gathering political intelligence. During these tours Defoe established a network of agents for the distribution of the *Review*, as a rival to the newsletters of John Dyer, which purveyed an intensely partisan message to Tories in the provinces.[10] The first test of Harley's propaganda machine came in the general election of 1705. The previous session had gone well, following the defeat in November 1704 of an attempt by Tory high-flyers to 'tack' a third Occasional Conformity Bill to the Land Tax Bill. A significant number of Tories either voted against the Tack, or abstained, marking a victory for Harleyite 'moderation'. Harley sought to follow this up at the general election of 1705, when the *Review* kept up a sustained onslaught on the 'Tackers', urging Tories who had refused to support the Tack to remain staunch. 'Moderation' was the *Review*'s catchword. Tories who had the public interest truly in view should 'Unite the Churches Safety and the Publick Interest together by promoting the Peace of all Parties'.[11]

Harley's strategy proved successful in the short term, but eventually the logic of party prevailed. The general election resulted in significant Tory losses and Whig gains, so that the two parties were more or less equal, with the Court group holding the balance. It became increasingly difficult to maintain Harley's 'moderating scheme' once the Junto acquired greater political leverage in the Commons. Harley and Godolphin began to diverge in their response to Whig assertiveness, Godolphin preferring to make limited concessions for short-term relief. In 1706 one of the Junto lords, Sunderland, was made secretary of state alongside Harley, but Whig demands did not stop there.

The *Review* continued to disseminate the Harleyite line, even to the extent of soft-pedalling enthusiasm for the war. Harley began to worry about the prolongation of the conflict, and the effect this was having on moderate Tory opinion. A second major victory in Europe, at Ramillies in 1706, gave the opportunity for a peace settlement before too much damage was done to the English economy. In this Defoe acted as Harley's mouthpiece, irrespective of what his true feelings might have been. It seemed a sharp reversal from the galloping martial enthusiasm of the *Review*'s first issues, and, taking a longer perspective, a very different message than the author had transmitted a decade earlier. 'All then we have to desire by this War, is a lasting, firm, solid and effectual Peace', Defoe wrote; England needed nothing more to make her 'the greatest Nation in the World' than 'Union at Home, and *Peace Abroad*'.[12]

---

[10] Downie, *Robert Harley and the Press*, 69–70.
[11] *Review*, ii. 318 (26 June 1705).
[12] *Review*, iii. 347 (4, 11 June 1706).

Union with Scotland

In the *Review* for 29 March 1707, Defoe celebrated the passage through the Westminster parliament of the Act of Union, a 'happy Conclusion' to which he had himself contributed.[13] His role had begun after the foundations had been laid. In the spring of 1706 the English and Scots appointed treaty commissioners; negotiations started in April 1706 and concluded in July; and during the following autumn and winter the two national parliaments considered bills to implement the treaty. The political narrative that led up to these discussions was serpentine: one detailed account has suggested that it was only in 1705–6 that Godolphin and Harley considered themselves likely to secure a political advantage from an incorporating union, which induced them to mobilize their adherents in England and their friends in Scotland, Queensberry's Court party, to support it.[14] But the project itself always appealed to Defoe, above all as a means of copper-fastening the Hanoverian succession. He commentated on the negotiations in the *Review*, and in May 1706 published two *Essays at Removing National Prejudices against a Union with Scotland*. The first appeared to be aimed primarily at an English audience, but the second was orientated towards Scottish readers, who were being bombarded with arguments that union represented a threat to Scotland's economy, with an imbalance in trade and higher levels of taxation (*PEW*, iv. 9–12).

Ministers considered the greatest danger to a union to come from Scotland. In England only the High Tories, who loathed the Scottish Presbyterian establishment and were openly contemptuous of Scots in general, would oppose it. The Junto, like Godolphin, expected to gain politically, believing that their own Scottish allies, the so-called Squadrone Volante, would prosper in elections to a united parliament.[15] In September 1706 Harley despatched Defoe to Scotland, to gather intelligence, and as far as possible to influence opinion, which he did by his pen, and through his personal contacts among merchants, lawyers, Presbyterian ministers, and members of the Scottish parliament. In this task Defoe was assisted by his agent, John Pierce, who was 'Very well known' among the radical—and highly agitated—Presbyterian ministers of the south-west (*Correspondence*, 283).[16] Defoe's reports to Harley, though a useful corrective to the optimistic accounts supplied by members of the Scottish Court party, were probably of less value than his conversations and writings in Edinburgh, which aimed at defusing popular reaction against the union. There were four more essays aimed 'at removing national prejudices', which targeted Scottish opponents of the union; *Caledonia* (1706), a verse tribute to the Scots nation, which embodied unionist views; and other minor contributions, including the satirical poem 'The Vision' (1706) directed

---

[13] *Review*, iv. 104 (29 March 1707).
[14] P. W. J. Riley, 'The Union of 1707 as an Episode in English Politics', *EHR*, 84:332 (1969), 498–527.
[15] Riley, 'Union'.
[16] W. R. Owens and P. N. Furbank, 'New Light on John Pierce, Defoe's Agent in Scotland', *Edinburgh Bibliographical Society Transactions*, 6 (1998), 134–43.

against the arch-patriot Lord Belhaven, who in the Scottish parliament had made an emotional appeal to Scottish patriotism by conjuring up a vision of national degradation (*PEW*, iv. 18–19, 21–2).

In a letter to Harley before his journey north, Defoe set out what he considered his principal objectives: to inform himself of 'Partys forming Against ye Union' and do what he could to 'prevent y^m'; to 'Dispose peoples minds to ye Union' by 'Conversation and ... all Reasonable Methods'; to answer objections in print; and lastly 'To Remove ye Jealousies and Uneasyness of people about Secret Designs ... against ye Kirk' (*Correspondence*, 215). The publication of the treaty had alarmed 'trading people' in Scotland, who had once looked forward to union but were now hostile.[17] An even stronger reaction was evident among churchmen. Even though the Scottish ecclesiastical establishment was guaranteed, ministers and laity became fearful for the continued existence of Presbyterianism in a united state and parliament in which the majority would be Episcopalian. Fears of economic oppression by the English, and simple Anglophobia, heightened the panic: there was a campaign of organized public protests and of local petitions. In Edinburgh Defoe felt himself threatened by the mob.[18]

Defoe's activities as a government agent in Scotland were denounced at the time, and have been condemned by modern-day Scottish nationalists, who depict him, somewhat melodramatically, as an English 'spy'. To one Scottish contemporary, the Jacobite George Lockhart, he was a 'wretch', one of a band of 'mercenary tools' working against the interests of Scotland, an accusation that Defoe felt obliged to refute in the *Review*.[19] There are of course some fragments of truth in these allegations, but only fragments. Defoe was employed by the English secretary of state; he supplied intelligence, albeit of a general, not confidential, nature; he concealed his true purposes in Scotland; he wrote to order, and usually anonymously; and he sought to persuade Scots that union was a good thing. However, his arguments in favour of union are not only internally consistent, but of a piece with his other writings in the political, religious, social, and economic objectives they pursued. The treaty promised to satisfy at a stroke several crucial objectives: it would establish an economic free-trade area which would create the conditions for massive economic improvement in both countries; and, even more importantly, it would guarantee the Revolution settlement.

Nonetheless, it would be naïve to think of Defoe's motives as wholly idealistic. Before taking the north road he tried to drive a hard bargain for his expenses, and referred to his family circumstances: the secretary should remember that 'you have a Widdo' and Seaven Children On yor hands' (*Correspondence*, 216). As Harley knew, Defoe was in

---

[17] Christopher A. Whatley (with Derek J. Patrick), *The Scots and the Union* (Edinburgh: Edinburgh University Press, 2006), 243–73.

[18] Whatley, *Scots and the Union*, 281–8; Karin Bowie, *Scottish Public Opinion and the Anglo-Scottish Union, 1699–1707* (Woodbridge: Boydell Press, 2007), 115–58; *Correspondence*, 227–8, 234–7, 244–7, 256–7, 278–88, 301.

[19] Daniel Szechi (ed.), *'Scotland's Ruine': Lockhart of Carnwath's Memoirs of the Union* (Aberdeen: Association for Scottish Literary Studies, 1995), 147; *Review*, iv. 441–6 (2 September 1707).

desperate straits financially, and had every incentive to escape across the border. Always alert for profitable opportunities, Defoe tried to put his time in Scotland to good use. His initial cover story, agreed with Harley, was that he was travelling on business. There was talk of various schemes in the commercial or manufacturing line (*Correspondence*, 275). The longer he stayed, however, and the more he published, the less plausible this pretext became, and he let it be known that the real reason was to further various literary schemes. There was even a degree of truth in this explanation, since some of Defoe's writings in the two years he spent in Scotland—*Caledonia*, and the massive *History of the Union* (1709)—were clearly written to make money, published as they were by subscription [SEE CHAPTER 12].

Once the Scottish parliament had passed the Union Bill, Defoe's work in Scotland was done, but he stayed on until November 1707, working on the *History*, and avoiding English creditors. Despite conflicts with Scottish patriots, he found living under a Presbyterian establishment relatively congenial; besides, he had made a number of useful contacts. He attempted several enterprises, including an abortive scheme to take over control of the *Edinburgh Courant*, and even enrolled his scapegrace son as a student at Edinburgh University.[20] After abandoning plans to reside permanently in Scotland, he still visited the country regularly. In his pamphlet writings his principal concern was now to defend the Church of Scotland from accusations, fanned by English High Churchmen, that it was persecuting the Episcopalian minority.[21] For all the airy dismissal in his pro-union writings of Presbyterian fears for their establishment, it had become apparent that there were those on both sides of the border with designs to subvert it.

Defoe had not been back in London for long when Harley fell from power. Junto pressure was remorseless, and in the winter of 1707–8 Harley made one last attempt to break free of the tightening vice by constructing a 'moderating scheme' which would build a coalition of Court Whigs and Court Tories to defeat 'the men of party'. In failing to carry this through he lost the trust of Godolphin, who came to believe that Harley was conspiring against him. Harley was dismissed.[22] Letters from Defoe condoled with the former secretary, promising to be 'The Servant of yor worst Dayes' and entreating Harley to 'Use me in Any Thing in wch I may Serve you' (*Correspondence*, 434). But it was not long before he had transferred his services to the new administration.

Godolphin did not immediately throw himself into the arms of the Junto, and, with the help of placemen, a group of Court Whigs, and the Queensberryites in Scotland, tried

---

[20] C. E. Burch, 'Defoe's Connections with the *Edinburgh Courant*', *RES*, 5:20 (1929), 437–40; Paula R. Backscheider, 'John Russell to Daniel Defoe: Fifteen Unpublished Letters from Scotland', *PQ*, 61:2 (1982), 161–77.

[21] In Defoe, *An Historical Account of the Bitter Sufferings and Melancholly Circumstances of the Episcopal Church in Scotland*... (Edinburgh, 1707); and Defoe, *The Scot's Narrative Examin'd; or, The Case of the Episcopal Ministers in Scotland Stated*... (1709), printed in *PEW*, iv. 267–360. See also *Review*, vi. 617–37, 678–81 (19, 21, 24, 26, 28 January, 16 February 1710).

[22] G. S. Holmes and W. A. Speck, 'The Fall of Harley in 1708 Reconsidered', *EHR*, 80:317 (1965), 673–98.

to retain some freedom of manoeuvre. Godolphin and the Junto each saw the general election in May 1708 as an opportunity. Scotland was a key battleground: Queensberry sought to maintain his position against the Junto's allies, the Squadrone. The conflict between the two factions was fought against a background of a failed invasion by the Pretender, which triggered the arrest of prominent Scottish Jacobite peers. Sunderland, as the responsible secretary of state, sought to take advantage of this situation through an agreement with the Duke of Hamilton, the man to whom Scottish Jacobites looked for political leadership, by which the arrested lords would be released in return for electoral assistance.[23]

In this complicated, and dangerous, situation Godolphin needed reliable information. He sent Defoe north again, to provide 'plain, naked and unbiassed accounts of persons and things', for which of course he was paid. At the same time Defoe was also approached by Sunderland. He reported to both, beseeching Sunderland not to let the treasurer know of their correspondence (*Correspondence*, 443–74).[24] Although Defoe denied that there was anything 'clandestine' in this arrangement, the reality was obvious (456). As far as Sunderland was concerned, there was little of political value in Defoe's letters. Godolphin, on the other hand, received valuable confirmation of the electoral alliance between the Squadrone and Scottish Jacobites. Despite Defoe's willingness to serve two masters, he may not have been quite as clever, or politically aware, as he thought he was, for in writing to Sunderland he artlessly expressed disapproval of the Squadrone's behaviour (*Correspondence*, 453). Comments in *The History of the Union* show that, for all his friendship with Queensberry's protégé, Sir John Clerk of Penicuik, Defoe had come to think better of the Squadrone, as representing the real Whig interest in Scotland.[25] That they should now be contemplating an electoral alliance with Jacobites he found shocking. Sunderland did not enlighten him.

Serving a Tory Ministry

Defoe's pen remained in the service of government while the Junto lords inexorably tightened their hold over Godolphin. The 1708 election proved to be a victory for the Whigs, which they exploited to the full. The *Review* became an organ of a Whig ministry. During the impeachment of the High Church preacher Dr Sacheverell in February 1710, a political gamble encouraged by the Junto which backfired spectacularly and paved the way for the Tory triumph at the general election in the following October, the *Review* damned both Sacheverell and his followers, especially Tory mobs rioting in

---

[23] P. W. J. Riley, *The English Ministers and Scotland 1707–1727* (London: Athlone Press, 1964), 103–10.

[24] W. R. Owens and P. N. Furbank, 'Defoe as Secret Agent: Three Unpublished Letters', *The Scriblerian*, 25:2 (1993), 145–53.

[25] Paula R. Backscheider, 'Defoe and the Clerks of Penicuik', *Modern Philology*, 84:4 (1987), 372–81 (372–5); *PEW*, vii. 177–8.

London.²⁶ This rhetoric came easily to Defoe, who despised Sacheverell and everything he stood for, and seems genuinely to have believed that Sacheverell's sermons were a denial of 'Revolution principles'.

Gradually, however, the Whigs' grip on power was prised away. During the summer the queen, advised by Harley, dismantled Godolphin's administration: Sunderland was removed in June, and Godolphin in August. Harley took Godolphin's place as chief minister, intending to construct another 'moderating scheme', retaining some Whigs in office and keeping out the more extreme Tories, such as Nottingham, who was left smouldering. Defoe had realized as soon as Sunderland was dismissed that Godolphin was doomed, and wrote to Harley suggesting a renewal of their previous relationship (*Correspondence*, 492–4). The *Review* began to play a different tune, regretting changes in the administration, and as hostile as ever to the High Tories, but emphasizing the necessity that the queen's business be carried on, and willing to argue that the new ministers were committed to the Revolution settlement, and in that respect were sufficiently 'Whig' to deserve popular support.²⁷ Defoe also attempted to assist in the most difficult task Harley faced: the maintenance of public credit during this period of seismic political change [SEE CHAPTER 14].²⁸

The general election in October 1710 changed the frame of reference. The Tory landslide, which many in the political nation had considered inevitable since the popular ferment over Sacheverell's impeachment, left Harley fighting a rearguard action against backbench Tory pressure for a thorough reformation of government. Harley's attempts to retain a few of the more amenable Junto ministers—Halifax, and even Somers— failed:²⁹ Whig party solidarity left Harley dependent on 'moderate' Tories. The story of his administration was one of a long campaign to resist demands for wholesale changes to men and measures. This was visible during the very first session of the 1710 parliament, with the establishment of a backbench Tory pressure-group, the so-called 'October Club'. Defoe naturally played his part, in the columns of *Review* and elsewhere, satirizing the October men as 'mad' and irresponsible, at best tools of the ministry's enemies, and at worst Jacobites.³⁰

Defoe continued to receive a steady income from government until the fall of Harley in 1714. He needed it, being pursued by creditors, one of whom had him arrested for debt in 1713, and worked hard for it (*Correspondence*, 733–5).³¹ The *Review* and other

---

²⁶ *Review*, vi. 564–6, 579–616, 705–13, 725–42 (3, 5, 7, 10, 12, 14, 17 January, 2, 4, 11, 16, 18 March 1710). I use the dates of the London printings, rather than Edinburgh. Defoe's condemnation of pro-Sacheverell addresses, denying that they represented 'the sense of the nation', was an apparent reversal of the position he had held over the Kentish petition in 1701 (Knights, *Representation and Misrepresentation*, 160).

²⁷ Furbank and Owens, *Political Biography*, 110–11.

²⁸ Downie, *Robert Harley and the Press*, 125.

²⁹ Paley (ed.), *Lords 1660–1715*, iii. 841–6; iv. 478: W. L. Sachse, *Lord Somers: A Political Portrait* (Manchester: Manchester University Press, 1975), 244.

³⁰ For example, *Review*, vii. 664–8 (13 March 1711); Defoe, *The Secret History of the October Club: From Its Original to This Time. By a Member* (1711).

³¹ Furbank and Owens, *Political Biography*, 113–15.

publications maintained a stream of Harleyite propaganda, designed to defend his employer from the denunciations of Whigs and malcontent Tories, and to present Harley as the only hope for stable government, the maintenance of public credit, and ultimately the security of the succession. Defoe was no longer the biggest cannon in Harley's arsenal, following the recruitment of Jonathan Swift, but the range and trajectory of his writings differed from Swift's. While Swift excoriated the Whigs and the Allies, Defoe's aim, as it had been during his previous employment by Harley, was to reassure moderates and wean Tories away from extremism. Once peace had been achieved, Defoe turned his attention to assisting Harley (now Earl of Oxford) in the most serious parliamentary crisis of his ministry: the defection in 1713 of a group of 'Hanoverian' Tories and Scots to join the Whig opposition to the commercial treaty concluded with France. Defoe began a new periodical, the *Mercator*, which set out the arguments in favour of the treaty.

Defoe's connections in Scotland were put to good use during Harley's ministry. In November 1710 he went to Edinburgh again to report on the elections. Not only was Harley concerned at the likely political complexion of the Scottish contingent in the Commons, and the representative peers, he was feeling his way towards a new strategy of managing Scotland, having recruited the former Court peer Lord Mar and a maverick Whig magnate, the Duke of Argyll, to replace Queensberry, and needed to understand how the fluid political situation was developing.[32] Defoe went north for a second time in the autumn of 1712, when Oxford's Scottish policy was on the point of disintegration. The assertiveness of Scottish Tory MPs in pushing for a toleration of Episcopalians, in alliance with the October Club; resentment among Scottish politicians at Oxford's failure to give them what they considered their due in terms of patronage; and discontent in Scotland over the imposition of the malt tax there in apparent contravention of the Treaty of Union: all combined to create a major political problem. Scottish involvement in the attack on the commercial treaty in 1713 was accompanied by a semi-serious attempt to repeal the Union.[33] Harley seems to have thought that Defoe could provide him with useful intelligence, although how useful he can have found Defoe's consistently optimistic reports is unclear. However, it is also possible that Defoe was at work trying to win over suspicious Scotsmen to the ministry's side. The involvement of one penurious Argyllite MP, Sir Alexander Cumming, in writing for Defoe's periodical the *Mercator* in support of the French commercial treaty, is suggestive.[34]

Working for Harley after 1710 severely tested Defoe's principles. He may still have believed that Harley's 'moderation' represented the best hope for the defence of the Revolution settlement and the Protestant succession, given the overwhelming Tory victory in the 1710 election, and the growing momentum behind the High Tory programme: a witch-hunt against members of the previous ministry, the strengthening of the confessional state, and peace at all costs. He was also given good reasons for

---

[32] Riley, *English Ministers and Scotland*, 150–8.

[33] Geoffrey Holmes and Clyve Jones, 'Trade, the Scots, and the Parliamentary Crisis of 1713', *Parliamentary History*, 1 (1982), 47–77.

[34] Cruickshanks et al. (ed.), *Commons 1690–1715*, iii. 807–8.

doubting the motives and integrity of the Junto, especially when the Whigs cynically joined Nottingham in the winter of 1711–12 to pass an Occasional Conformity Bill, in order to secure Nottingham's support in the Lords. In letters to Harley Defoe expressed his shock and distress at seeing the Dissenting interests 'Ruind', but at the same time was gratified that Dissenters would see that 'The Idols They adored have Appear'd capable of So Mean a Step, as to Sell The Party... into Perpetuall Tory bondage', reiterating what was a theme of Harley's correspondence with Nonconformist ministers (*Correspondence*, 669).[35] Nonetheless, Defoe's energetic defence of the peace of Utrecht does represent a *démarche*, particularly visible in the *Mercator*, where he admitted to changing his mind over the value of trade with France.[36] Swift's baiting of the Allies and the ministry's offhand treatment of the Dutch was not to Defoe's taste, and was certainly not consonant with the tenor of his writings in the 1690s. There are occasional indications that he found working for Harley after 1710 an uneasy experience. During his first visit to Scotland he had been scandalized by the behaviour of Argyll and Mar in backing electoral candidates who were, in his view. Jacobites. He published anonymously a pamphlet, *Atlantis Major*, full of 'bitter invective' against both magnates. Although he told Harley he had managed to get the work suppressed, it appeared in print six months later.[37]

THE HANOVERIAN SUCCESSION

Oxford's dismissal in July 1714 was soon followed by the death of Queen Anne, which ushered in a new political world. This was potentially disastrous as far as Defoe was concerned, but his own adroitness, and his usefulness to politicians, saved him. Even before Oxford's disgrace he was responsible for writing, again under cover, an ostensibly Whig newspaper, the *Flying Post and Medley*, which he explained to Oxford as a cunning move to disable the Whig propaganda machine by impersonating George Ridpath's *Flying Post* (*Correspondence*, 822). Its political slant was nonetheless strictly Whiggish. But he could not suddenly reinvent himself and undo the past. Publicly, he felt it necessary to defend himself from charges of having betrayed his principles by writing for a Tory ministry. In *An Appeal to Honour and Justice* (1715), he justified himself as a consistent advocate of 'moderation': 'the only Vertue by which the Peace and Tranquillity of this Nation can be preserv'd' (3–4). Privately, he still protested enduring loyalty to Oxford; and his *Secret History of the White-Staff*, written and published before George I's arrival in England, sought to exculpate his old master from the sins of the previous administration by showing the lord treasurer as striving to frustrate the intrigues of a cabal of colleagues, led by Lord Chancellor Harcourt. Oxford himself did not find the *Secret History* helpful, since it depicted him as the dupe of designing men: he assumed it

---

[35] Cruickshanks et al. (ed.), *Commons 1690–1715*, iv. 278.
[36] Downie, *Robert Harley and the Press*, 171; Furbank and Owens, *Political Biography*, 130.
[37] Furbank and Owens, *Political Biography*, 112–13.

was a ploy by the Whigs to discredit him.[38] Whether or not the pamphlet ultimately did Oxford any good is hard to judge: certainly it did not prevent his impeachment.

Within a year Defoe had become reconciled to the new Whig government and had briefly returned to the role of ministerial scribe. The process was remarkably similar to his recruitment by Harley in 1703–4. He was prosecuted for an unwise accusation made in his *Flying Post* against the Hanoverian Tory Lord Anglesey, that Anglesey had been actively involved in Tory schemes to remodel government before the queen died, in the interests of the Pretender, in his case purging the Irish military establishment. In Ireland Anglesey was accused of harbouring Jacobite sympathies, but in England his reputation was as a staunch Hanoverian, and Defoe faced trial for seditious libel.[39] He appealed to Lord Chief Justice Parker, who interceded for him with Lord Townshend, the Whig secretary of state. Legal proceedings were ended, and Defoe was engaged to produce a monthly periodical, *Mercurius Politicus*, in the service of government. Once more he wrote in masquerade, as a Tory, a stance which came easily to him. But six months later Townshend lost the secretaryship, and Defoe's secret service pension came to an end. This marked the end of his career as a government propagandist, though not the end of his involvement in writing about politics, which in the new world of Whig dominance, where divisions between competing Whig factions provided the dynamic of parliamentary conflict, presented a man of Defoe's background and principles with even more complex choices.[40]

Conclusion

Defoe's penchant for irony, and for writing in another character in order to put across a political message indirectly, can make it difficult to discover his intentions. For anyone seeking to identify a thread of consistency in his writings there are further complications; his perennial need for money, and addiction to subterfuge, in order to protect himself or simply for the love of fooling his readers. It was, after all, 'an age of plot and deceit; of contradiction and paradox'.[41] On occasion he wrote against himself, to cover his tracks. And of course he pursued vendettas, against other journalists and printers, and even, more dangerously, against individual politicians: men like Nottingham, Anglesey, and Harcourt.

To a few others he remained loyal: especially to the memory of King William, as a true Protestant hero; and to Robert Harley, with whom he seems to have established

---

[38] HMC, *Portland MSS*, v. 501.
[39] *Flying Post and Medley*, 19 August 1714; D. W. Hayton, *Ruling Ireland, 1685–1742: Politics, Politicians and Parties* (Woodbridge: Boydell Press, 2004), 180–4; Cruickshanks et al. (ed.), *Commons 1690–1715*, iii. 33.
[40] Furbank and Owens, *Political Biography*, 151–74.
[41] Knights, *Representation and Misrepresentation*, 356.

a genuinely close relationship. It is his association with Harley, above all else, which provides evidence for a hostile interpretation of his motives. In writing for government in 1704–8, and even more so in 1710–14, Defoe had to hold in check some of the radical Whig impulses found in his writings during the political crisis of 1700–2. But two clear threads remain visible: vehement opposition to popery and anything that smelt, however faintly, of Jacobitism; and a desire to maintain religious toleration for Dissenters. His strong support for the Anglo-Scottish Union was predicated on an understanding that the Union would guarantee the Revolution settlement and the Protestant succession. Harley's attractiveness as a patron was not merely in the sums of money he provided, but because he stood as a bulwark against the brand of High-Church Toryism that in Defoe's mind threatened to undo everything achieved in 1688 by King William and 'the good people of England'.

Further Reading

Paula R. Backscheider, *Daniel Defoe: His Life* (Baltimore, MD: Johns Hopkins University Press, 1989).
Karin Bowie, *Scottish Public Opinion and the Anglo-Scottish Union, 1699–1707* (Woodbridge: Boydell Press, 2007).
J. A. Downie, *Robert Harley and the Press: Propaganda and Public Opinion in the Age of Swift and Defoe* (Cambridge: Cambridge University Press, 1979).
P. N. Furbank and W. R. Owens, *A Political Biography of Daniel Defoe* (London: Pickering and Chatto, 2006).
Brian W. Hill, *Robert Harley: Speaker, Secretary of State and Premier Minister* (New Haven, CT: Yale University Press, 1988).
G. S. Holmes and W. A. Speck, 'The Fall of Harley in 1708 Reconsidered', *EHR*, 80:317 (1965), 673–98.
Mark Knights, *Representation and Misrepresentation in Later Stuart* Britain (Oxford: Oxford University Press, 2005).
Maximillian E. Novak, *Daniel Defoe, Master of Fictions: His Life and Ideas* (Oxford: Oxford University Press, 2001).
P. W. J. Riley, *The English Ministers and Scotland 1707–1727* (London: Athlone Press, 1964).
P. W. J. Riley, 'The Union of 1707 as an Episode in English Politics', *EHR*, 84:332 (1969), 498–527.
Christopher A. Whatley (with Derek J. Patrick), *The Scots and the Union* (Edinburgh: Edinburgh University Press, 2006).

CHAPTER 21

INTELLIGENCE, ESPIONAGE, AND THE ETHICS OF SURVEILLANCE IN DEFOE'S WRITINGS

KATHERINE ELLISON

In the late 1990s, computer programmers designed hypothetical organizational systems called the 'Defoe' and the 'Crusoe'. The 'Defoe' could handle information either sequentially or non-sequentially: errors in one step did not prevent the processor from moving to the next step. 'The Crusoe' worked through copies of itself made from underused information already in the processor.[1] Literary figures are often used to create memorable cultural references for designs, but the names Defoe and Crusoe, in this case, perpetuate a fascination with Defoe's depictions of information management in his fiction and during his career as secret agent for Robert Harley. In popular intelligence history, Defoe has earned the title 'father of the British Security Service (now MI5)'.[2] Defoe was not actually the 'father of British intelligence', or the first to envision a British intelligence system, but he did help build the cryptographic imaginary of the eighteenth century and argue for the necessary role of intelligence in governance and global trade.[3] He was one of the first writers to publicly consider the moral implications of intelligence. He consistently described how he saw his

---

[1] The 'Defoe' and the 'Crusoe' were VLIWs, or Very Large Instruction Word architectures. Anonymous, 'Crusoe Exposed: Transmeta TM5xxx Architecture 1' (2 January 2004), *real world technologies*, https://www.realworldtech.com/crusoe-intro. (Accessed 11 April 2018).

[2] John Laffin, *Brassey's Book of Espionage* (Ann Arbor, MI: University of Michigan Press, 1996), 30n.

[3] Sarah Myers West coins the term 'cryptographic imaginary' in 'Cryptographic Imaginaries and the Networked Public', *Internet Policy Review*, 7:2 (2018), https://policyreview.info/articles/analysis/cryptographic-imaginaries-and-networked-public. (Accessed 11 April 2018).

culture's information architecture working, and he aligns it with a theological vision of Divine surveillance and secret communication between invisible spirits and humanity. Manuel Schonhorn says of Defoe's information management skills that 'he was recognized correctly as a great political reporter and journalist, possessing heaps of information, but he was found unable to contain all that he knew within any conceptual framework'.[4] This essay attends to Defoe's ideas about a 'conceptual framework' for intelligence. Intelligence work, for Defoe, is not only about financial reward or political passion; he *does* consider carefully, and thoughtfully, the conceptual framework of the information he collects and reports because intelligence is central in his spiritual and imaginative worldview. In a 1693 publication that has been misattributed to Defoe but is often used in intelligence history to quote him, *A Dialogue Betwixt Whig and Tory*, the writer claims that intelligence 'is the Soul of Government'.[5] But in a letter to Harley in 1704, Defoe goes further: 'Intelligence is ye Soul of all Publick bussiness', he writes (*Correspondence*, 64).

In a range of writings and genres, from his letters to Harley to his *Review* essays (1704–13) and his novels, especially *Minutes of the Negotiations of Monsr. Mesnager* (1717) and *A Continuation of Letters written by a Turkish Spy in Paris* (1718), Defoe describes a surprisingly consistent intelligence system for information management that must have private as well as public functions. Agents report secret information at the same time that writers publish political essays that inform (or strategically misinform) readers, helping or hindering those readers as they try to interpret complex events. In a column of his *Review*, 'Mercure Scandale: or, Advice from the Scandalous Club' on 28 March 1704, Defoe refers to periodical essays like his own as 'Publick Intelligence'.[6] His later literary works are part of this vision, marking his shift from youthful optimism to experienced scepticism about the moral stakes of the intelligence professions. *The Political History of the Devil* (1726) describes secret agents and intelligence systems that are similar to the one he outlines in the 'Scheme of General Intelligence' for Harley in July or August 1704 but are used for tyranny. Intelligence in *Roxana* (1724), too, is depicted as a tool of moral depravity. Defoe is the first writer in British intelligence history to work as a secret agent and then describe, in such detail and across so many genres, the political, theological, and moral consequences of his culture of surveillance.

---

[4] Manuel Schonhorn, *Defoe's Politics: Parliament, Power, Kingship, and Robinson Crusoe* (Cambridge: Cambridge University Press, 1991), 2.

[5] Anonymous, *A Dialogue Betwixt Whig and Tory, alias Williamite and Jacobite* (1693), xi. Alan Marshall assumes *Dialogue* was written by Defoe, due to the attribution by John Robert Moore. Alan Marshall, *Intelligence and Espionage in the Reign of Charles II, 1660–1685* (Cambridge: Cambridge University Press, 1994). For evidence of the misattribution, see J. A. Downie, 'Daniel Defoe: King William's Pamphleteer?', *ECL*, 12:3 (1988), 105–17.

[6] *Review*, i. 52.

British Espionage and Intelligence Before Defoe

Early Renaissance intelligence was often rhetorically associated with the occult, but during the seventeenth century it became publicly recognized as a reputable profession with methods and practices that could be taught and mastered, thanks to the successes of Elizabeth I's network, the popularity of Francis Bacon's arguments for protected knowledge in *De Dignitate & Augmentis Scientiarum* (1623), and the later instructional manuals and literacy campaigns of Royal Society members, including John Wilkins, Samuel Morland, and John Falconer.[7] These works stress the need for secrecy in a culture of global competition for resources and knowledge, and they link political and military intelligence to a more personal, spiritual idea of intelligence as a means of interpreting the events in one's life. Bacon's *The Historie of the Raigne of King Henry the Seventh* (1622) offers an outline of how a centralized defensive political intelligence could work, which then becomes the basis for his depiction of espionage in *The New Atlantis* (1627). Wilkins's *Mercury; or the Secret and Swift Messenger* (1641) argues for intelligence as a legitimate discipline that should be studied as a liberal art and systematized as a national priority. Morland's undated 'A Brief Discourse Concerning the Nature and Reason of Intelligence', likely written under William III, argues that a permanent government intelligence service that oversees citizen surveillance is necessary for the healthy functioning of the nation.[8] Assumptions that intelligence was not professionalized until the nineteenth century have thus been debunked by early modern historians.[9] Peter Fraser, David Underdown, John Michael Archer, Alan Marshall, Julian Whitehead, Geoffrey Smith, and others have established that intelligence systems in use by a range of cultures during and before the seventeenth century were sophisticated, creative, and influential.[10]

One of the central assumptions in intelligence history of the seventeenth and early eighteenth centuries is that intelligence was existent but 'disorganized', in part because it was neither centralized nor well funded after the

---

[7] See Richard Kieckhefer, *Magic in the Middle Ages* (Cambridge: Cambridge University Press, 1989); John Henry, 'The Fragmentation of Renaissance Occultism and the Decline of Magic', *History of Science*, 46:1 (2008), 1–48.

[8] BL Add. MS. 47133, ff. 8–13.

[9] Michael Warner expresses this assumption in *The Rise and Fall of Intelligence: An International Security History* (Washington, D.C.: Georgetown University Press, 2014), 16.

[10] Peter Fraser, *The Intelligence of the Secretaries of State and their Monopoly of Licensed News, 1660–1688* (Cambridge: Cambridge University Press, 1956); David Underdown, *Royalist Conspiracy in England 1649–1660* (New Haven, CT: Yale University Press, 1960); John Michael Archer, *Sovereignty and Intelligence: Spying and Court Culture in the English Renaissance* (Stanford, CA: Stanford University Press, 1993); Julian Whitehead, *Cavalier and Roundhead Spies: Intelligence in the Civil War and Commonwealth* (Barnsley: Pen & Sword Military, 2009); Geoffrey Smith, *Royalist Agents, Conspirators and Spies: Their Role in the British Civil Wars, 1640–1660* (Farnham: Ashgate, 2010).

Restoration.[11] It is true that several diplomats, secretaries, and military personnel operated their own networks that, in many cases, did not communicate with one another. However, under Sir Joseph Williamson, for example, intelligence was closely managed, meticulously organized, and expertly streamlined. Centralization was his main goal.[12] Before Williamson had served in the same office as Harley, as secretary of state for the Northern Department, John Thurloe had also managed an effective spy network that, though massive, was tightly run. Much is also made of funding as a measure of sophistication. Samuel Pepys notes in his diary for 14 February 1668 that secretary Morris (Morice) complained of a low budget allotted him for intelligence that year, only £700 annually compared to Cromwell's previous allowance of £70,000. Fraser believes the allowance in 1668 would have been more along the lines of £2,000, the number that Paula Backscheider quotes.[13] What Morice does not mention is that this small allowance was supplemented by multiple grants and did not include funds not in the permanent budget, used for unforeseen situations. The likelihood is that secret intelligence was still a financial priority under Charles II just as it had been under Cromwell, but Pepys's colleagues, looking in hindsight, exaggerated the efficiency and grandeur of the Protectorate's security.

The role of intelligence in the persuasion of public opinion was also nothing new by Defoe's generation, and Harley was not the first to attempt to control the news. Charles II's administration strategically relayed carefully chosen private intelligence as public news, manipulating public opinion.[14] Even before Charles II, the office of the secretary of state not only received weekly reports from agents, but also intercepted private correspondence and collected 'open ordinary correspondence'—news from foreign and local gazettes, magazines, newsletters, and other publications.[15] Possibly written by John Wildman, an anonymous and undated 'A brief discourse concerning the business of intelligence and how it may be managed to the best advantage' advises Charles II on how to monitor the post office and also makes arguments that are similar to the scheme Defoe later proposed to Harley. Written after 1667 and early in his reign, 'A brief discourse' begins by suggesting Charles operate an extensive intelligence network, first by creating a small inner cabinet.[16] Next, Charles must interrupt and closely scrutinize all correspondence by mail, including letters sent through the central post office as well as letters sent by personal couriers. Finally, the discourse recommends Charles II spy on

---

[11] Gunther Rothenberg, 'Military Intelligence Gathering in the Second Half of the Eighteenth Century, 1740–1792', in *Go Spy the Land: Military Intelligence in History*, ed. Keith Neilson and B. J. C. McKercher (Westport, CT: Praeger, 1992), 99.

[12] Fraser, *Intelligence*, 47.

[13] Paula R. Backscheider, 'Daniel Defoe and Early Modern Intelligence', *Intelligence and National Security*, 11:1 (1996): 1–21 (17 n. 3).

[14] Fraser, *Intelligence*, 114.

[15] Fraser, *Intelligence*, 1.

[16] 'A brief discourse' is printed in C. H. Firth, 'Thurloe and the Post Office', *EHR*, 13:51 (1898), 527–33.

his own administration, ideally through a domestic servant. Lindsay O'Neill confirms that after 1670, the state closely monitored correspondence and news.[17]

The bureaucratic organization of intelligence that had already taken place before Defoe represented a significant theological shift and rethinking of the nature of truth. It signalled recognition that the monarch was not a deity. The monarch, Archer finds, 'became in effect an angel, not quite divine but endowed with intellectual powers unattainable by other mortals'.[18] In order for the 'angelic intelligence' of the monarch to function effectively, a network was needed to provide timely information by reliable labourers. Intelligence agents, as expert gatherers and distributors of information, were holders of *knowledge*, and the knowledge they accumulated, transferred to a political superior or monarch, secured that authority's image as divinely intelligent leader. Defoe would articulate a similar model, called the 'angelic ministry', in the last volume of the Crusoe trilogy.[19] In *Serious Reflections* (1720) and its addendum, *A Vision of the Angelick World*, Crusoe explains that space is crowded with angels who operate continuous surveillance, reporting to God and relaying God's intelligence to people, coded in signs that they must analyse and interpret.[20] Rodney M. Baine argues that Defoe's concept of the 'angelic ministry' is 'necessary not only for the full understanding of Defoe's heroes and heroines, but for the understanding of the writer's serious themes and purposes in his fiction'.[21] In this system, angels facilitate God's omniscience. Espionage also highlighted shifting notions of the nature of truth. Readers hungry for books on secrets operated under the idea that what is kept hidden must in some way be more authentic than what is transparent. Spies operated as witnesses to and messengers of truth. Rhetorically, this justified the increased surveillance that would characterize the period following the Wars of the Three Kingdoms and which Morland advocates in 'A brief discourse'. Jeremy Black confirms that the massive volume of intercepted dispatches from 1716 to 1766 proves the extent to which eighteenth-century intelligence shifted to a surveillance function.[22] During and after the Wars of the Three Kingdoms, then, intelligence and espionage became more publicly acknowledged and accepted as necessary political tools, used a set of methods that were promoted as legitimate professional pursuits, were already using the press to influence public opinion, and were theologically justified.

---

[17] Lindsay O'Neill, 'Dealing with Newsmongers: News, Trust, and Letters in the British World, ca. 1670–1730', *HLQ*, 76:2 (2013), 215–33 (216–17).

[18] Archer, *Intelligence*, 2.

[19] Katherine Ellison, 'Mediation and Intelligence in Defoe's *A Vision of the Angelic World*', in *Topographies of the Imagination: New Approaches to Defoe*, ed. Katherine Ellison, Kit Kincade, and Holly Faith Nelson (New York: AMS Press, 2014), 93–115.

[20] Defoe, *Serious Reflections During the Life and Surprising Adventures of Robinson Crusoe* (1720), 225; *A Vision of the Angelick World*, 14. The pagination restarts for *A Vision*.

[21] Rodney M. Baine, *Daniel Defoe and the Supernatural* (Athens, GA: University of Georgia Press, 1968), 35.

[22] Jeremy Black, 'Eighteenth Century Intercepted Dispatches', *Journal of the Society of Archivists*, 11:4 (1990), 138–43 (140). Cf. Jeremy Black, 'British Intelligence and the Mid-Eighteenth-Century Crisis', *Intelligence and National Security*, 2:2 (1987), 209–29.

Defoe's Education in Intelligence Before Harley

Defoe scholarship has provided much insight into espionage in the eighteenth century. J. A. Downie, P. N. Furbank and W. R. Owens, Backscheider, and others have provided invaluable information on Defoe's involvement in intelligence and, through their archival findings, have illuminated the complex networks that intensified and mediated the party divisions of the early eighteenth century [SEE CHAPTER 20]. Downie outlines Defoe's relationship with Harley and the ways in which that relationship created a 'propaganda machine'.[23] Furbank and Owens's account of Defoe's political career during the reigns of Queen Anne and George I emphasizes the alignment of his espionage activities, his public writings, and his private correspondence.[24] Backscheider argues that Defoe 'extended the possibilities of counter-insurgency, invented practices that survive to the present day, and earned the reputation of master spy'. Her focus on counter-insurgency is unique in eighteenth-century historical treatments of intelligence.[25] Insurgency and counter-insurgency are modern terms, ones that Defoe did not use to define his activities. Generally, an insurgency is an uprising, violent or non-violent, to overthrow a government or controlling party. It is organized, yet there is usually no coherent centre, and different undisciplined groups may be acting independently towards similar but not identical goals using uncoordinated, spontaneous combinations of surprise activities and attacks. Intelligence is thus crucial in preventing uprisings. Gathered information must be used to gain trust—trust is central in the management of both an insurgency and its counter. The goal in a counter-insurgency is not to subjugate the insurgents, but to persuade them to become loyal and peaceful. Counter-insurgency intelligence, then, is among the most difficult types of communication. Rhetorically skilled authors must understand their audience, appealing to hearts as well as minds. Backscheider isolates two of Defoe's strengths in this kind of intelligence: 'possessing a great deal of general knowledge and the ability to "accost" many kinds of people'.[26] I would specify that Defoe had a talent for contextualizing large quantities of disparate information, much like the processors that programmers named after him in the 1990s. He could analyse that information to know his audience, choosing genres that would move them.

It is rare to have a selection of letters documenting a spy's activities in addition to so many political publications that address the information in those letters and, furthermore, a selection of fictional works that dramatize intelligence networks in action.

---

[23] J. A. Downie, *Robert Harley and the Press*, 2. Cf. J. A. Downie, 'Secret Service Payments to Daniel Defoe, 1710–1714', *RES*, 30:120 (1979), 437–41.
[24] Furbank and Owens, *Political Biography*.
[25] Backscheider, 'Early Modern Intelligence', 1.
[26] Backscheider, 'Early Modern Intelligence', 18 n. 23.

The interrelations of these writings have helped scholars speculate about Defoe's early interest in intelligence and follow his career after his first letter to Harley on 9 November 1703, after a year of instability, financial ruin, and imprisonment for the publication of *The Shortest-Way with the Dissenters* (1702). Backscheider believes that even before that letter of gratitude in November 1703, Defoe was already a 'strong believer in intelligence' and had been exposed to intelligence early in his life, given he was born the year of Charles II's Restoration after the Wars of the Three Kingdoms and had read extensively about Sir Francis Walsingham's use of pamphleteering in Elizabeth I's intelligence system, as evidenced by his references to Walsingham in his 1704 memorandum.[27] Defoe had witnessed the effectiveness of information warfare in 1679 when Anthony Ashley Cooper, first Earl of Shaftesbury, introduced the Exclusion Bill attempting to keep James, Duke of York from inheriting the throne after Charles II. As elections to the new House of Commons were held in July and August, and as Shaftesbury circulated information to gain support and signatures in 1679 and 1680, networks were built across the countryside and in London, where coffee houses and other central meeting spaces were instrumental in swaying public opinion. Backscheider notes that Defoe copied the Whig strategy in his work for Harley to strengthen and report on support during elections and when he cultivated public opinion for the Anglo-Scottish Union in 1706 and 1707.

Defoe would have also learned about the importance of intelligence when he fought on the side of the Duke of Monmouth, the illegitimate son of Charles II vying for the throne after his father's death. Not only did James II's strategists receive intelligence about the locations of rebel arsenals and have them seized; they also anticipated Monmouth's plans and appeared to know where they would be before they arrived. Monmouth fell short in intelligence, and Defoe saw the consequences. As Backscheider points out, Monmouth did not adequately gather information about the geography of the battle site at Sedgemoor in July 1685, for example; his troops were uncertain of the depth of a stream and refused to cross, allowing them to be discovered, pursued, and killed.[28]

Beyond these experiences, there is little evidence that Defoe had played a more significant role in intelligence before 1704, though Defoe told Harley on 2 November 1704 that he served King William III 'in a kind like this' (*Correspondence*, 114). He reiterates this service under William several times in his correspondence; Downie notes that 'it is as if the record sticks whenever Defoe gets on to this favorite theme of his'.[29] John Robert Moore took Defoe at his word that he served William III, authoring forty-five documents as a propagandist, but Downie has convincingly rebutted the evidence for Defoe's authorship of those early publications and challenged Defoe's own proclamations that he worked in confidence for the former king.

---

[27] Backscheider, *Daniel Defoe*, 160; Backscheider, 'Early Modern Intelligence', 42.
[28] Backscheider, 'Early Modern Intelligence', 3.
[29] Downie, 'Daniel Defoe: King William's Pamphleteer?', 106.

Defoe's education about intelligence through reading is also difficult to trace, but it is certain that he read Jean Le Clerc's *The Life of the Famous Cardinal-Duke De Richlieu* (1695), translated by T. Brown, before his own intelligence service started. Geoffrey Sill believes that Defoe may have been reading Le Clerc's biography in May and June 1704, immediately before his first intelligence mission for Harley.[30] Le Clerc claims to have written a neutral biography of the famous cardinal and recounts that Richelieu conducted extensive research into his subjects and in preparation for policies. He emphasizes, too, that Richelieu had a talent for timing: he knew what information to provide or withhold, and when. He was also adept at handling (or leveraging) others' scandals. As Harley would as well, Richelieu oversaw the publication of pamphlets to further his causes, exercised control over the press, suppressed criticism, and employed many writers. Richelieu also actively engaged in revisionist history, editing past histories and accounts. Finally, Richelieu created the *Académie française* in 1635, which Defoe refers to several times as an admirable achievement. This educational institution, only for the French elite, promoted the proper use of the French language and arts. Politically, the *Académie* allowed Richelieu to control the teaching and learning of French citizens and provided an endless staff of creative minds. In *An Essay upon Projects* (1697), Defoe recommends the creation of an English language academy inspired by Richelieu's, but he emphasizes that the school would be primarily for merchants, not scholars: 'We want indeed a *Richlieu* to commence such a Work: For I am persuaded, were there such a *Genius* in our Kingdom to lead the way, there wou'd not want Capacities who cou'd carry on the Work to a Glory equal to all that has gone before them' (*PEW*, viii. 108).

Brown openly acknowledges Richelieu's faults in the first pages of his dedication to Erasmus Smith, a wealthy businessman, philanthropist, and educational theorist. Richelieu was brilliant, he notes, and he made France a global power by the late seventeenth century, but he also introduced unlimited monarchical power, destroyed the nobility, and was overly ambitious and vengeful. Le Clerc tries to focus not on whether Richelieu was good or evil, but on the *motive* behind his actions. Sill notes that it is this work that is 'Defoe's model for a history of the effect of the passions on human and state affairs'.[31] For Defoe, the biography provides a gauge for the ethical standards of intelligence work. In the scheme of general intelligence he describes to Harley in 1704, Defoe stresses that Richelieu's useful organizational strategies should be imitated, but not his corruption and immorality. The system Defoe proposes to Harley is undoubtedly akin to Richelieu's, but with modifications. Harley's moderation and patriotism, kept in check by an inner council, is the correction to Richelieu's despotism.

---

[30] Geoffrey Sill, *The Cure of the Passions and the Origins of the English Novel* (Cambridge: Cambridge University Press, 2001), 218 n. 21.

[31] Sill, *Cure*, 218, n. 21.

Defoe's Secret Service for Harley

The details of Defoe's decision to enter the world of intelligence as an agent and pamphleteer, and to serve Harley, have been well documented by Backscheider, Downie, Furbank and Owens, and others. Backscheider has even found accounts of Nottingham's interrogation of Defoe after his capture for the 1702 publication of *The Shortest-Way with the Dissenters*, which had serious consequences for Defoe's freedom and his finances. He stood for three days in the pillory in 1703, and later that year Harley paid £150 for his release from secret service funds, in exchange for Defoe's services.[32] On 9 November 1703, Defoe wrote to Harley to express his thanks and promises to 'Make Some Such Sort of Return as No Man Ever Made' (*Correspondence*, 27). In 1704, Defoe was pamphleteering, largely about the disunion of the Dissenters, and in August he accepted a commission to travel through the eastern counties of England to relay political opinions back to Harley. Defoe wrote in July or early August 1704 to Harley: 'I firmly believ This Journey may be the foundation of Such an Intelligence as Never was in England' (28). Earlier that year, Defoe had started the *Review* [SEE CHAPTER 7]. This paper, likely funded by Harley, allowed him to sway public opinion on issues he was privately observing in his travels, which Furbank and Owens detail in *A Political Biography of Daniel Defoe* (2006). Backscheider adds, though, that while the *Review* is sometimes a mouthpiece for Harley, there is evidence that Defoe started it independently.[33] He does sometimes critique administrative decisions too harshly for the Lord Treasurer, Sidney Godolphin, and Harley's taste, for example. Of these early tasks, Backscheider asserts that 'his first intelligence assignment broke no new ground', but his initial reports were 'specific, detailed and concise'.[34] His first letters to Harley demonstrate some trepidation about how the genres of intelligence writing function, specifically how to balance his personal views, imaginative style, attentive observations, and unsolicited advice with the directed reporting required of a spy, yet he was clearly committed to thorough information collection and sharpening his skills as a political agent.

In July or August 1704, Defoe sketched the central document for scholars interested in Defoe's clandestine work: his memorandum to Harley, which he referred to as 'a Scheme of Generall Intelligence' (*Letters*, 28). Defoe begins his scheme by arguing that England should create a Supreme Minister, acknowledging that the British constitution does not allow it and 'is Perticularly Jealous of Favourites' (29), and that not having this minister has in fact saved them from the despotism of singular figures like Richelieu. He acknowledges, too, that historically, chief ministers had served only for their own financial interests and ambitions, but he identifies two exceptions: Thomas Cromwell and Sir Francis Walsingham (30). 'Both These Dyed Poor', Defoe writes, 'They spent Their wholl

---

[32] Backscheider, 'Early Modern Intelligence', 4.
[33] Backscheider, *Daniel Defoe*, 152.
[34] Backscheider, 'Early Modern Intelligence', 4, 5.

Time in the Service of Their Country, and No Man would ha' Repin'd at Their Enjoying their Princes favour Longer' (31). He believes that Harley, too, works in the service only of the greater good of the government, that he is morally above corruption and could work from the position of Supreme Minister to unify Whigs and Tories. Defoe also suggests the creation of a small, trusted inner cabinet of experts to counsel the Supreme Minister, bypassing the traditional constitution of the privy council but ensuring that office does not abuse its power.

The key to success for Harley as the Supreme Minister is an intelligence network that extends to nearly every community in England and Scotland, so that the Supreme Minister can know, at all times, what citizens are thinking and feeling. Defoe cites one of his two intelligence influences, Gustavus Adolphus of Sweden, who would surprise citizens with 'Unlook'd for, Unask'd' 'Acts of Bounty' because his agents had informed him of what they needed (31). Though Schonhorn sees the suggestion of a Supreme Minister as the original—and dangerous—contribution of Defoe's scheme, it is this idealistic emphasis on governance through *knowing* one's citizens, in order to surprise them with courtesies and relief, that is different from previous intelligence schemes by Walsingham, Bacon, Wilkins, or Morland.[35] Like Wilkins and Morland, though, Defoe emphasizes the importance of instantaneous knowledge—the minister should react to public need *before* they have asked for help. This is the 'angelic ministry' that Archer describes as emerging during the seventeenth century.

The potential problem with gathering so much information is that the quantity can become overwhelming. Intelligence is meaningless without a way to categorize and analyse what has been collected, so Defoe emphasizes the importance of *organized* data collection. There should be complete lists of prominent families and their characters, detailed moral sketches of all clergy in all parts of England, and detailed descriptions of all politicians and leaders, in all cities and boroughs, with information about their party alliances (36). Indeed, he starts sending Harley lists in 1705, such as his 'An Abstract of My Journey with Casuall Observations on Publick Affairs' on 6 November (108). In numerous publications, Defoe describes how important it is, after one collects a volume of information, to keep it organized to facilitate analysis. In *The Consolidator* (1705), Defoe imagines a lunar community that creates maps of human politics, trade, and faith. Like Edmond Halley and William Dampier, Defoe was most interested in thematic mapping, or mapping of specific isolated phenomena to see trends across space. Thematic maps not only reveal how networks function, but they also provide persuasive evidence that can be shared with policy-makers. In *The Complete English Tradesman* (1725–7), an illiterate shop owner maintains an elaborate bookkeeping system that does not make sense to others but is a conceptual map of customer habits, allowing him to see his business from multiple data points (*RDW*, vii. 208–9). In *A Tour thro' the Whole Island of Great Britain* (1724–6), Defoe tries to map shifting trade routes. While collecting information for the *Tour*, Defoe even discovers what no one had noticed: the surge of deaths amongst

---

[35] Schonhorn, *Defoe's Politics*, 105–6.

the British peerage during the 1720s. Pat Rogers observes that Defoe was able 'to join the dots in a way no one else seems to have done'.[36]

Defoe's correspondence from his first contact with Harley until the latter's fall from power in 1708 indicates that he was endeavouring to ease the increasing friction in English-Scottish relations, writing prolifically in periodicals and pamphlets, and travelling frequently to gauge the political mood of the nation and, following the 1705 general election, give Harley information on the new members of parliament. Defoe's observations of the British navy led him to author a *Review* essay proposing a better way to man the fleet, and a committee of politicians took the plan seriously at the beginning of 1705. Defoe wrote a detailed plan, but it was rejected. His published writings saw more success. He finished and published *The Consolidator* and *The Dyet of Poland*—both of which were popular—and crafted political pamphlets like *The High-Church Legion* (17 July 1705), a response to *The Memorial of the Church of England* published only ten days earlier. In March 1705, Defoe increased the *Review* to three issues a week. In July, Defoe was eager to do more than write for Harley. He sent a brief memorandum asking for orders, a certificate for travel, and permission to leave his present location, which is undisclosed in the letter (*Correspondence*, 145). Defoe was then travelling in July to find out how elections had been conducted, what appeals of results were likely, and what kind of House of Commons the Godolphin ministry could expect in the autumn. He made an extensive tour of the south-west. In Dorset, he noted that there is 'Exceeding Harmony between the Dissenters and the Low Church', but in Salisbury ''tis quite Another Thing', and in Hoynton 'Here also Things are in Terrible Disordr' (94–5). He also discusses visits to Exeter, Totnes, Dartmoor, Plymouth, Crediton, Bideford, Bath, Bristol, and Gloucester, noting that 'I have Visited Every Town So Securely by being lodg'd among friends that I am Now under the Nose of the Justices Concern'd in the Enclos'd warrant and yet Out of their Danger' (99).[37] Defoe's 1705 information-gathering tour saw him move northward through the West Midlands, Lancashire, Yorkshire, East Midlands, and East Anglia. He rode during the day and then spent the late afternoons and evenings in public spaces, talking with community members about politics, or in private houses on appointment with individuals. Backscheider indicates that he must have moved quickly, staying only a night at each location, and his conversations were targeted: based on his knowledge of the towns from his own business dealings, he was able to identify influential and wealthy community members and even set up networks to relay information to him and to distribute publications. The extent of his network is reflected in a distribution list he sent Harley in 1706, by which means more than 2,000 copies of his *Remarks on the Letter to the Author of the State-Memorial*, a piece of ministerial counter-propaganda,

---

[36] Pat Rogers, 'Defoe and the Expiring Peerage', *Studies in Philology*, 102:4 (2005), 510–36 (519).

[37] The warrant here refers to an action taken by a justice of the peace when Defoe's letters concerning affairs of state, addressed to a probable pseudonym, 'Captain Turner', were opened by a real Captain Turner (*Correspondence*, 161–2).

were dispersed throughout England and Ireland.[38] Networks of this geographical reach are difficult to maintain, and they are built slowly.

Though Harley had already been doing much of what Defoe recommended in his scheme of 1704, Defoe's insistence that 'a Settl'd Intelligence in Scotland, a Thing Strangely Neglected There, is without a Doubt the Principall Occasion of the present Missunderstandings between the Two kingdomes' might have particularly resonated. In September 1706, Harley sent Defoe to Scotland to engage in the most significant intelligence assignment of his career: to promote the Union, which had been negotiated the previous spring and now required sanction from each nation's Parliament. Defoe recorded that he did not receive any explicit instructions from Harley about what he was supposed to do there. He wrote to Harley to clarify his sense of his task:

1   To Inform My Self of the Measures Takeing Or Partys forming Against the Union and Applye my Self to prevent them.
2   In Conversation and by all Reasonable Methods to Dispose peoples minds to the Union.
3   By writeing or Discourse, to Answer any Objections, Libells or Reflections on the Union, the English, or the Court, Relateing to the Union.
4   To Remove the Jealousies and Uneasyness of people about Secret Designs here against the Kirk, &c. (126)

Defoe had moved from data collection and commentary, through the *Review* and other publications, to direct intervention in conversations to sway opinion. Generally, this mission was conducted with more stealth than his earlier information-gathering trips. Defoe could convincingly explain that he was staying in Scotland to escape persecution for his publications and to rebuild his lost wealth through ventures that made sense in the region. After it had passed, he also claimed—initially as a ploy, though he did perform it—to be writing a history of the Union, for which he was given access to unpublished records. This project, in turn, helped him understand the complex family networks of Scottish communities, and with this knowledge he remained a valuable advisor on Scottish affairs to Godolphin and Harley for the rest of Queen Anne's reign.

The Scottish Parliament voted in favour of the Union on 4 November 1706, though the details of economic compensation, drawn out in the remaining articles of the Treaty, were still under negotiation. Defoe was in Scotland reporting to Harley on attitudes towards each article several times a week. On 19 November 1706, he reported that the Third Article, a highly controversial one that approved a single Parliament of Great Britain, had passed. He describes the threats to the Lord High Commissioner the Duke of Queensberry's personal security 'by the Rable in the street': he was 'Threatned with Daggers, pistols &c.' (151). Defoe saw his main task as helping to prevent those kinds of rabble. The negotiations required debate about excise taxes, and his accounting

---

[38] Pat Rogers, 'Defoe's Distribution Agents and Robert Harley', *EHR*, 121:490 (2006), 146–61.

experience was called on to help the committee calculate how two systems of taxation could be brought into line.[39] In his letter of 9 November, Defoe boasts that he is surprised by how influential he had managed to be: 'If Directed I might do more service to both Kingdomes than I Could have Expected' (144). His personal experience in trade was perhaps helpful, but it was his fast, sharp pen that was probably more useful. For example, Defoe wrote *The Vision, A Poem* (1706) as a response to the patriotic, anti-Union speech read for Parliament by John Hamilton, Lord Belhaven. Belhaven's speech did not sway the vote against the Union, but it did motivate passionate public reaction. Defoe quickly penned *The Vision* to neutralize the fervour; the poem is a satirical, insulting gesture of dismissal. It effectively trivializes Belhaven's serious, well-written rally of Scottish confidence and pride, a speech Novak notes was 'dignified oratory'.[40] After Defoe's *Vision* was published, anonymously, Belhaven responded with *A Scots Answer to a British Vision*, an attempt to match Defoe's teasing rhythm:

> Where Similes bite
> Thick Sculls do not know
> A Cat from a Kite,
> Their Pulse beats so low.
>   It is then no Wonder
>   That their pitiful Blunder
>   Pass for Lightning and Thunder.[41]

There is no evidence that Belhaven knew that Defoe was the author of *The Vision*. Defoe even brags to Harley, on 28 November, that Belhaven 'believs it my Ld Haddington', referring to Thomas Hamilton, sixth Earl of Haddington (*Correspondence*, 280). Regardless, Defoe does not let Belhaven have the last word. Proving his swiftness in meeting propaganda with his own, Defoe immediately circulated and then printed yet another response, *A Reply to the Scots Answer to the British Vision* (1706), a sarcastic encomium of Belhaven's genius for poetry and pathos. With this strategy, he can suppress counter-insurgency (with a playful smirk) before it even gains momentum. In a letter Backscheider recently discovered from Harley to Defoe on 21 November 1706, Harley says, 'The Ballad is the best answer to that stuff' (*Correspondence*, 265).[42]

Defoe's own reports of his effectiveness in Scotland are positive; he emphasized repeatedly that he had helped make the negotiations successful. He provided reports to Harley over the next year, remaining in Scotland until the last week of 1707 even though he wished to leave as soon as the articles he helped negotiate were ratified, on 16 January 1707. During this period, Defoe asked frequently for instructions and permission to return to England. Downie speculates that perhaps Defoe had not been as important as

---

[39] Novak, *Daniel Defoe*, 300.
[40] Novak, *Daniel Defoe*, 300.
[41] John Hamilton, Lord Belhaven, *A Scots Answer to a British Vision* (1706), lines 22–8; reproduced in *TDH*, iv. 379.
[42] Paula R. Backscheider, 'Robert Harley to Daniel Defoe: A New Letter', *MLR*, 83:4 (1988), 817–19.

he thought he was and that Harley was either keeping Defoe away or was not concerned enough about him to make him a priority.[43] On 12 June 1707, Harley wrote to Defoe to discharge him and turn his service over to Godolphin. Harley and Godolphin's relationship had been increasingly tense over differing opinions about the administration's membership as Godolphin became more dependent upon the Whig Junto, which among other factors would lead to Harley's resignation as secretary of state in February 1708.[44] Harley's tone in that letter, however, is not rudely dismissive. 'I hope I have not been an unprofitable Servant', Harley writes, 'I Am very sorry that you or your humble Servant should bear Reproach for doing what others could not' (*Correspondence*, 392). Defoe then considered Godolphin his employer, but still wrote to Harley throughout the rest of 1707, impatient about his lack of direction and remuneration from Godolphin. After he finally returned to London, Defoe tried to acclimate to the new political climate. On 10 February 1708, Defoe mentioned the rumours about Harley's resignation and vows his loyalty, though his sincerity has been questioned.[45] Godolphin sent Defoe back to Scotland that spring, but generally, he lacked the clear purpose he had previously.

Struggling with the complexity of the political relationships, from 1708 to 1710 Defoe was working increasingly in Whig interests in the *Review* as well as providing reports to the Whig Junto lord, Charles Spencer, third Earl of Sunderland, by May 1708, who Defoe had previously been warned was 'No Friend to me' (*Correspondence*, 373). Sunderland had been appointed secretary of state for the Southern Region, against Harley's wishes, culminating in the latter's fall. In Defoe's own account, given in *An Appeal to Honour and Justice* (1715), he had simply continued his work, reporting to Godolphin with Harley's blessing. In June 1710, however, Sunderland was dismissed, Godolphin followed in August, and Defoe returned to Harley's employment. Harley was adapting new strategies to regain Tory representation in the government that Defoe was only partially aware of, but he resumed sending reports to Harley, some of them coded. The coded letters indicate that he was increasingly concerned about anonymity and uncertain about who could be trusted. However, he was either not adept at cryptography or was forced to use an insecure system. 'In the late Election', Defoe writes, 'the Conduct of the D of 60, the E of 163, and the Earle of 194 is Very Perticular' (294). He mentions the prospect of impeachment of '140' and '193', Godolphin and Marlborough. The same numbers are used frequently throughout the letter, so if a reader did not deduce identities in one context, they surely would in another. On 6 December 1710, Defoe notes that in '212 you have Personally Spoken Against 214', which are easy to deduce by his syntax, and their closeness in number, as 'parliament' and the 'Pretender'. The key was unavailable to Healey, who deciphers the references in the footnotes of the *Letters*, but he was generally accurate. The key has since been discovered by Downie in Harley's voluminous

---

[43] J. A. Downie, 'Daniel Defoe and the General Election of 1708 in Scotland', *ECS*, 8:3 (1975), 315–28 (317–18).

[44] G. S. Holmes and W. A. Speck, 'The Fall of Harley in 1708 Reconsidered', *EHR*, 80:317 (1965), 673–98.

[45] Downie, 'General Election', 327.

papers, and it is printed in full in Nicholas Seager's edition of Defoe's correspondence.[46] The alphabetic order of this code system is quite basic relative to the more secure cipher systems in use at the time. Had Defoe desired an impenetrable algorithmic approach, instructional texts and knowledgeable cipherers were readily at hand. He must not have considered his information so sensitive that it needed complete protection, but again, it suggests intensified paranoia about the political situation and his part in it.

From 1710 to 1714, Defoe's public writing was in support of a Tory ministry, frequently urging government action against Whig journalists, and often needing Harley's assistance when rival journalists initiated prosecutions against him. There is speculation about Defoe's motives in the later years of his intelligence work when, after Harley's final dismissal, Anne's death, and the Hanoverian succession, he appears to have shifted his allegiance to serve the Whig ministry that was in power after the 1715 general election. Backscheider believes that Defoe worked in London in 'true counter-insurgency'.[47] In 1715, he was recruited by Whig secretary of state Charles Townshend, on the advice of Lord Chief Justice Parker, to infiltrate the Tory press, pretend to write for Tory causes, and secretly intercept and suppress their papers. On 26 April 1718, Defoe provided a brief history of his recruitment by the Whigs and affirmed his loyalty to the 'Present Governmt' to Charles Delafaye, undersecretary to the new secretary of state for the Northern Department, James, Earl Stanhope. He explained that his task is to 'appear as if I were as before under the Displeasure of the Governm^t; and Seperated From the Whiggs' (*Correspondence*, 834). He started the Tory periodical *Mercurius Politicus* in May 1716, and in June he ran the Tory *Dormer's News-Letter*. He also worked on *The White-hall Evening Post*, *The Manufacturer*, and *The Commentator*.[48] Defoe likely joined Nathaniel Mist's *Weekly Journal, or Saturday's Post* 'in ye Disguise of a Translator of the Forreign News', in August 1717 and began to write his own essays in January 1718, though it is difficult to confirm which essays those are (*Correspondence*, 835).[49] His goal, in these positions, was to take out the 'sting' of the papers, preserving the Tory style and content but reducing their potential damage to the government (*Correspondence*, 834). Defoe's remarks about his secret service in this capacity feign absolute loyalty to the new Whigs, but Furbank and Owens suspect Defoe may not have been fully honest to Delafaye, exaggerating his involvement and loyalty.[50] For his part, Defoe bemoaned that he must converse with 'Papists, Jacobites, and Enraged High Tories' who 'My Very Soul abhorrs', and he must frequently hear treasonous remarks 'and Smile at it all as if I Approv'd it'

---

[46] J.A. Downie, 'Defoe the Spy', *British Society for Eighteenth-Century Studies Newsletter*, 9 (1976), 17–18; *Correspondence*, 528–36.

[47] Backscheider, 'Early Modern Intelligence', 10.

[48] Backscheider, 'Early Modern Intelligence', 10.

[49] Two essays, which William Lee attributed to Defoe, are of note, though there is no concrete evidence that he wrote them: 'On Cypher-Writing' (22 June 1723) and 'On Cryptography' (17 August 1723). Both lament the popularity of cipher-writing as recreation. William Lee, *Daniel Defoe: His Life and Recently Discovered Writings*, 3 vols (1869), iii. 149–51, 172–5.

[50] P. N. Furbank and W. R. Owens, 'Defoe, the De la Faye Letters and *Mercurius Politicus*', *BJECS*, 23:1 (2000), 13–20.

(*Correspondence*, 836). Novak comments that, during this period, 'He appears to have considered himself an exile from his true political position and his true self'.[51]

INTELLIGENCE IN DEFOE'S FICTION

An Appeal to Honour and Justice and *Minutes of the Negotiations of Monsr. Mesnager* were both written during this period of propaganda work. Though it is ostensibly a transparently confessional account of his conduct, the *Appeal* spins events such that we might say it marks Defoe's transition from public, political pamphlet writing to fictional life writing. *Minutes of the Negotiations of Monsr. Mesnager* imitates Le Clerc's biography of Richelieu. Mesnager is a French agent whose employer resembles Harley in character. Defoe even mocks the instructions for his own spy mission in Scotland when Mesnager is sent to the Hague to conduct similar observation and receives a list like that which Defoe sent Harley in 1706. Through tongue-in-cheek parallels with his own experiences, Defoe is able to include information about England's inner-government workings from the perspective of a French spy. This looking inwards from an outsider perspective with insider knowledge also characterizes Mahmut's position in *A Continuation of Letters written by a Turkish Spy in Paris*. In both fictional representations, Defoe can compliment Harley's strengths and criticize his weaknesses. At one point, Defoe includes himself in the narrative of *Minutes*. Impressed by one of Defoe's writings, Mesnager attempts to bribe him with one hundred pistols to write for the French, but Defoe, incorruptible, informs the queen (*SFS*, iv. 64–5). John Richetti notes that with this move Defoe makes himself 'suddenly and effectively the political hero of the piece'.[52] Narratively, *Minutes* uses a plot structure that is reminiscent of Le Clerc's memoir of Richelieu, but Defoe is a more skilful writer and develops his characters more fully across space and time. He continued that experiment the next year in his continuation of Giovanni Paolo Marana's successful Turkish spy letters. In *Continuation*, Mahmut defines a spy: to be a spy is to be 'buried alive, among Infidels, and Strangers' (*SFS*, v. 59). Yet, his position grants him a privileged perspective on international politics.

Defoe's novels of 1720–2 depict occasional scenes of espionage, but *Roxana* is an extended moral meditation on intelligence. One of Roxana's lovers, the Prince, works in the secret service for the French government and is sent on a spy mission to Italy. Roxana also operates under paranoia about surveillance and enlists agents, like Amy and the Quaker gentlewoman, who provide intelligence and multiple perspectives on situations. Like Richelieu, though, Amy is a devilish figure, who apparently murders Roxana's daughter Susan.[53] Rebecca Bullard argues that Roxana mismanages Amy and

---

[51] Maximillian E. Novak, '"The Sum of Humane Misery"? Defoe's Ambiguity toward Exile', *SEL*, 50:3 (2010), 601–23 (603).

[52] Richetti, *Life of Daniel Defoe*, 180.

[53] Richetti, *Life of Daniel Defoe*, 37.

is naïve about the handling of secrets.[54] With Defoe's analysis of Richelieu in mind, the problem is not just poor handling: it is difficult, perhaps impossible, to be involved in intelligence without selling one's soul. The younger Defoe was hopeful that there could be moral balance. The older Defoe depicts characters who, time and again, fail to find it. The novel ends as Roxana leaves her affairs to her new 'faithful Spy', the Quaker gentlewoman, still invested in her secrecy and unable to give up her dependence on an intelligence agent.[55]

A main concern for Defoe, from his reading about and references to Richelieu to his later novels like *Roxana* and writings like *Every-Body's Business, is No-Body's Business* (1725) and *The Political History of the Devil*, is the balance between surveillance for necessary security and as the tool of tyranny. In *Every-Body's Business*, the domestic household government is analogous to the national government, and spying is out of hand. The servants are ruining the good families of London because they run surveillance on them and network with one another for higher pay. By the time he wrote *Political History*, Defoe understood the unavoidable necessity of espionage in modern politics, but he was clearly cynical about whether the government's soul can be saved once it engages and whether intelligence damages the morality of the people it serves. There, in response to the question of how he has gathered information about the devil, he notes that he cannot reveal his source, the cardinal rule of intelligence. He notes that this priority to protect one's source, and the public's acceptance of it, has allowed secret service agents and their handlers to commit many crimes and amass wealth. He implies that the informant he protects is Satan himself, who would punish him for disclosure (*SFS*, vi. 45–6).

The writings of Defoe's later career acknowledge that information can be collected and used by anyone with the ambition to leverage it, and the power that comes with managing that information is corruptive. *Every-Body's Business* confirms that Defoe's vision is also of a top-down information system; the labouring classes should not use surveillance to gather information on masters, better their finances, and destabilize the social hierarchy. Yet, he understood the importance of counter-insurgency intelligence to frustrate these kinds of uprisings. His own role in intelligence gathering and propaganda for Harley, suspected by many, contributed to a culture that at once valued the organized collection, management, and archiving of information and yet was wary of its potential to sway public opinion and influence government policy and structure. Defoe's novels further dramatize the personal and political advantages, as well as the moral sacrifices, of a life of espionage.

---

[54] Rebecca Bullard, *The Politics of Disclosure, 1674–1725: Secret History Narratives* (London: Pickering and Chatto, 2009), 152.

[55] Defoe, *Roxana*, ed. John Mullan (Oxford: Oxford University Press, 1996), 309.

Further Reading

Paula R. Backscheider, 'Daniel Defoe and Early Modern Intelligence', *Intelligence and National Security*, 11:1 (1996), 1–21.

Paula R. Backscheider, *Daniel Defoe: His Life* (Baltimore, MD: Johns Hopkins University Press, 1989).

J. A. Downie, 'Daniel Defoe and the General Election of 1708 in Scotland', *ECS*, 8:3 (1975), 315–28.

J. A. Downie, *Robert Harley and the Press: Propaganda and Public Opinion in the Age of Swift and Defoe* (Cambridge: Cambridge University Press, 1979).

Katherine Ellison, 'Mediation and Intelligence in Defoe's *A Vision of the Angelic World*', in *Topographies of the Imagination: New Approaches to Defoe*, ed. Katherine Ellison, Kit Kincade, and Holly Faith Nelson (New York: AMS Press, 2014), 93–115.

Peter Fraser, *The Intelligence of the Secretaries of State and their Monopoly of Licensed News, 1660–1688* (Cambridge: Cambridge University Press, 1956).

P. N. Furbank and W. R. Owens, 'Defoe, the De la Faye Letters and *Mercurius Politicus*', *BJECS*, 23:1 (2000), 13–20.

P. N. Furbank and W. R. Owens, *A Political Biography of Daniel Defoe* (London: Pickering and Chatto, 2006).

Alan Marshall, *Intelligence and Espionage in the Reign of Charles II, 1660–1685* (Cambridge: Cambridge University Press, 1994).

Maximillian E. Novak, *Daniel Defoe, Master of Fictions: His Life and Ideas* (Oxford: Oxford University Press, 2001).

Pat Rogers, 'Defoe's Distribution Agents and Robert Harley', *EHR*, 121:490 (2006), 146–61.

Manuel Schonhorn, *Defoe's Politics: Parliament, Power, Kingship, and Robinson Crusoe* (Cambridge: Cambridge University Press, 1991).

CHAPTER 22

DEFOE AND WAR

SHARON ALKER AND HOLLY FAITH NELSON

DURING much of Daniel Defoe's life, Britain was at war or threatening to go to war, from the second and third Anglo-Dutch Wars to the War of the Spanish Succession and beyond. Defoe had participated in combat himself, albeit briefly, when he joined Monmouth's rebels in 1685 and fought at Sedgemoor. At one point, under duress, he volunteered to serve again; in response to the threat of government discipline for publishing *The Shortest-Way with the Dissenters* (1702), Defoe wrote to the Earl of Nottingham, offering to become a volunteer officer in the War of the Spanish Succession for a year or more (*Correspondence*, 5–6). Defoe was also well aware, from personal experience, of the influence of war beyond the battlefield. A French naval battle with merchant ships in 1693, for instance, appears to have caused him financial losses.[1] This broad and persistent exposure to military matters made Defoe a keen student of war. He considers at great length in his writings both historical and contemporary warfare. However, his conception of warfare is not easily defined for two reasons: his writings on war are extensive and operate within a wide range of genres; and his work as a journalist and propagandist for several political leaders and parties [SEE CHAPTER 20] sometimes required him to vary positions on a given conflict.

In attempting to comprehend Defoe's overarching theory of war, we must negotiate, for example, his private letters to political correspondents in which he attempts to gain credit for offering advice on war measures; descriptions of soldierly experience in his fictional memoirs, such as *Memoirs of a Cavalier* (1720) and *Colonel Jack* (1722); and a wide variety of his historical, political, and journalistic works of prose non-fiction that document and evaluate actual military action. In the case of Defoe's prose non-fiction, this includes painstaking analysis of periodicals such as the *Review* (1704–13) and *The Master Mercury* (1704) that report on warfare (among other subjects) with as much immediacy as early modern methods of communication allow, as well as of works such as *A General History of Discoveries and Improvements in Useful Arts* (1725–6), which provides

---

[1] Novak, *Daniel Defoe*, 99.

a history of the art of war, focusing on technological developments in the instruments of combat. Paula Backscheider has pointed out that in relation to one war alone, Defoe could generate a multitude of works: 'He would produce thousands of pages on the Great Northern War ... in the shape of "lives", histories, periodical essays, news items, and a novel'.[2]

The various positions Defoe adopts on military matters have led to scholarly debate over his 'global' view of war, ranging from claims that, in the main, Defoe affirms military action, to assertions that, by in large, he critiques military undertakings and their consequences.[3] Others have turned to more 'local' aspects of Defoe's treatment of military issues, focusing, for instance, on his ideas about sufficient causes for a just or holy war, or his repeated defence of the provision of a standing army for William III [SEE CHAPTER 28].[4] Along the way, Defovians have worked to complicate local readings of war in specific texts, most recently in analyses of *Memoirs of a Cavalier*. This novel has been read over the last decade as an examination of how war rhetoric works to minimize, with limited success, the terrors of combat; as 'a study in evasion' that replaces affective accounts of catastrophic military injuries with statistical narratives; as a representation of past wars casting long shadows over modern political circumstances; and as a portrayal of the realities of urban warfare in which domestic and military space collide.[5] In the twenty-first century, therefore, research on war in Defovian texts increasingly drills down into the details of particular works.

If we wish, however, to balance this turn to the local with a global theory that synthesizes the treatment of war in Defoe's myriad works, we might consider his representation of warfare as a system.[6] In his prose non-fiction, Defoe shows a strong interest

---

[2] Backscheider, *Daniel Defoe*, 144.

[3] Sharon Alker explains, for example, that while Maximillian E. Novak's biography of Defoe 'foregrounds Defoe's long-term admiration of military matters', Paula R. Backscheider stresses 'that Defoe's work primarily critiques war' as a consequence of humanity's fallen nature. 'The Soldierly Imagination: Narrating Fear in Defoe's *Memoirs of a Cavalier*', *ECF*, 19:1 (2006), 42–68 (43).

[4] For Defoe's views on just or holy wars, see, for example, William James Roosen, *Daniel Defoe and Diplomacy* (Selinsgrove, PA: Susquehanna University Press, 1986), 50–5; and Robert James Merrett, *Daniel Defoe: Contrarian* (Toronto: University of Toronto Press, 2013), 93–4. For an introduction to Defoe's contribution to the standing army controversy, see Richetti, *Life of Daniel Defoe*, 72–6. Defoe's standing army pamphlets are *Some Reflections on a Pamphlet Lately Publish'd, Entituled, An Argument Shewing that a Standing Army is Inconsistent with a Free Government* (1697), *An Argument Shewing, That a Standing Army ... Is Not Inconsistent with a Free Government* (1698), and *A Brief Reply to the History of Standing Armies* (1698).

[5] Alker, 'The Soldierly Imagination'; Melinda Rabb, 'Parting Shots: Eighteenth-Century Displacements of the Male Body at War', *ELH*, 78:1 (2011), 103–35 (123); Nicholas Seager, '"A Romance the likest to Truth that I ever read": History, Fiction, and Politics in Defoe's *Memoirs of a Cavalier*', *ECF*, 20:4 (2008), 479–505; and Sharon Alker and Holly Faith Nelson, '(Re)Writing Spaces of War: Daniel Defoe and Early Modern Siege Narratives', in *Topographies of the Imagination: New Approaches to Daniel Defoe*, ed. Katherine Ellison, Kit Kincade, and Holly Faith Nelson (New York: AMS Press, 2014), 209–31.

[6] Maximillian E. Novak groups Defoe's 'presentation of warfare'—'aside from its political and economic dimensions'—into three categories: 'aesthetic, strategic, and pecuniary'. 'Defoe and the Art of War', *PQ*, 75:2 (1996), 197–213 (205). We are primarily concerned with the second of these.

in mapping out a system of war to reveal how it works on a large scale, across space and time. Even in his fiction, Defoe pays attention to how individuals move in and out of such a system, demonstrating how war presses upon those who encounter it. Defoe was, no doubt, fascinated by systems in general. In much of his writing he demonstrates an attraction to schemes, projects, and speculation. His prose non-fiction often thematizes the emergence and operation of systems, whether systems of magic, stock-jobbing, commerce, nation building (the Union), navigation, or warfare.

In *Invisible Hands: Self-Organization and the Eighteenth Century*, Jonathan Sheehan and Dror Wahrman foreground Defoe's fascination with the biblical metaphor of 'wheels within wheels' as he sought to understand increasingly complex sociopolitical operations. Defoe, they argue, is driven to make sense of the 'complexity that defied straightforward relationships of cause and effect', since he wished to describe 'situations in which unintended consequences, beneficial for the greater whole, emerged mysteriously from the unplanned, contradictory, self-propelled motions that were in the nature of the constituent parts'.[7] Warfare certainly comprises complex and layered situations—'wheels within wheels'—and Defoe delves deeply into its mechanics. In an age of ambitious military campaigns involving multiple nations and players, he sees a dynamic system of interrelated parts that is difficult to grasp. This chapter will identify intersecting elements of the system of war featured by Defoe in his war writings, taking into account that he is an early practitioner of deciphering and mediating what Mary Favret calls 'war at a distance'.[8] Defoe addresses the literal distance from military action and how he figuratively bridges it in the *Review* on 6 July 1708: 'We have been viewing things all the Winter in Perspective at a Distance and remote; and many a vain Hope, and many a true Fear we have suggested to our selves ... the Scene is now opened and every thing appears just as it really is'.[9] With the arrival and interpretation of new factual information, Defoe brings war into view, teaching his journal's readers not only what war is, but how it ought to be reported and consumed, just as he bridges this distance in his novels by imagining war up close through fictional military lives.

Writing the System of War: The 'Wheels within Wheels' of Military Conflict

Defoe's representation of war as a complex and multifaceted system is a response to shifts in the nature of warfare in his time. In *The Sociology of War and Violence*, Siniša

---

[7] Jonathan Sheehan and Dror Wahrman, *Invisible Hands: Self-Organization and the Eighteenth Century* (Chicago, IL: University of Chicago Press, 2015), 47, 50.

[8] Mary A. Favret, *War at a Distance: Romanticism and the Making of Modern Warfare* (Princeton, NJ: Princeton University Press, 2010), 10.

[9] *Review*, v. 214 (6 July 1708).

Malešević argues that the early modern period saw a profound change in the nature of warfare:

> Protestant military commanders planted the institutional seeds of military social organization that eventually gave birth to the modern bureaucratic nation-state ... The extensive development of social organization was also visible in the ever-increasing professionalization and bureaucratization of the military sphere.[10]

Defoe's work recognizes the increasing number of moving parts inherent in military action over a long period of time and a sprawling amount of space; and to comprehend it, he delves into the intricacy and dynamism at its heart. He also specifies that it is not a system that exists independently of other systems, economic, political, religious, or otherwise.

Writing for an emergent public sphere—in which he 'enthusiastically participated' to influence public opinion and policy—Defoe believed his readers required a thorough understanding of the nature and operation of war.[11] Such knowledge would not only make them cautious in drawing conclusions about military action; it would prevent them from succumbing to romanticized notions of war inherited from classical literature or to detached modern accounts of war in which actions and events are reduced to statistical facts and mathematical calculations. As a contributor to the emergence of war journalism in the *Review*, among other works, Defoe formulates a systemic account of war that requires readers to resist attributing to military men superhuman heroic qualities that are the province of literature rather than the actual sites of combat. Readers who hold inflated expectations are admonished not to let their imaginations run away with them: 'Nothing left will satisfie these hasty Gentlemen, than being at the Gates of *Paris*, plundering *Versailles*, overturning the whole Monarchy of *France* ... [D]o not make all your Footmen Horsemen, and your horses Eagles, and expect Armies, Generals, and Artillery can Fly'.[12]

In such passages, Defoe undoes the concept of war as a space of clear-cut victories and defeats, with larger-than-life generals at the helm who are worthy of excessive praise. Such hyperbole detracts from what the reader should focus on in a military leader, the virtue of prudence, which lies at the heart of the wise general. In fact, it is prudence that permits the general to synthesize the many types of knowledge needed for successful military strategy, which Defoe outlines in his account of a military academy in *An Essay upon Projects* (1697), and in his journalism. Defoe is thus inclined to praise the pragmatic ability of military leaders to navigate complex martial situations—for instance, winning battles amidst want and scarcity despite Parliament's refusal to give William III timely aid.[13] This is not to say that Defoe discounted military heroism. Far from it.

---

[10] Siniša Malešević, *The Sociology of War and Violence* (Cambridge: Cambridge University Press, 2010), 110.
[11] Richetti, *Life of Daniel Defoe*, 71.
[12] *Review*, vi. 161 (9 June 1709).
[13] *Review*, iii. 199–200 (30 March 1706).

He loudly and repeatedly praised William III, the Duke of Marlborough, Gustavus Adolphus, and Prince Eugene when the situation called for it. In his *Hymn to Victory* (1704), written after the battle at Blenheim in August 1704, Defoe '*rehearse*[*s*]' in his 'impartial Verse' the 'glorious Deeds' of Marlborough (lines 778–9), who, the poem suggests, had heightened 'English martial prowess ... on the battlefield' (*SFS*, i. 316).[14] Marlborough's valorous deeds render him the ultimate heroic warrior:

> 'Tis done! The Sound of Victory was heard
> As soon as *Marlbro*'s Conquering Troops appear'd.
>   Soon as he drew the *English* Sword,
> And gave *Queen ANN* for the *Victorious Word*,
>   *Victoria* let her Face be known,
> And gave him Earnest that she was his own.
> At *Schellemberg* the scatt'red Troops took Flight;
> *Valour* it self to VICT'RY must submit;
> And *English* Banners there, thro Seas of Blood,
> To *Danow*'s Stream the routed *French* pursu'd. (lines 504–13; *SFS*, i. 309)

The heroic Marlborough also looms large in 'On the Fight at Ramellies' (1706), in which he is shown scorching the 'bright Trophies' of the enemy and coercing with his sword 'insulting Tyrants' into suing for peace.[15] John McVeagh explains that the poem's 'poetic effusion was mocked' by at least one contemporary, so evidently Defoe was comfortable with the military heroic mode, even to the point of excess if it suited him.[16]

However, if Defoe, outside of such poetry, rejects the overly emotional heroic discourse of war that creates false expectations that winning one battle means the war is won, he also censures those who strip war of emotion entirely, viewing it as a measurable event readily solved by theoretical calculation. He sharply critiques

> a Sort of Arithmetical Gentlemen, who by Calculations, Calling up of Circumstances, deducting and allowing for Contingencies, dividing between Time and Strength, offensive and defensive, bring Causes and Consequences perfectly into Mathematical Demonstrations, and can tell you to so many Days, Hours, Minutes etc. how long a Town will hold out, how many Days open Trenches, how many Hours after the taking a Redout, and how many Minutes after a Counterscarp.[17]

If the former sort of gentlemen conceives of war as a matter of mythic grandeur, the latter views it in granular terms, but disconnected from a reality in which the messy disadvantages of poor location, weather, routes for provisions, health, and so on delay or halt progress. Such visions of warfare also tend to erase the suffering of combat. As we

---

[14] Stephen H. Gregg, *Defoe's Writing and Manliness: Contrary Men* (Aldershot: Ashgate, 2009), 32.
[15] 'On the Fight at Ramellies', *Review*, iii. 317–18 (21 May 1706).
[16] *Review*, iii. 319 n. 2 (21 May 1706).
[17] *Review*, iv. 474 (13 September 1707).

have argued elsewhere, Defoe disparages interpretations of war that privilege arrogant optimism and refuse to look more closely at the cost on the ground. At one point, during the War of the Spanish Succession, Defoe 'introduced a character named Mad Man to *The Review*' who enters into dialogue with Mr Review about military decisions. Mad Man 'spouts out excessive tactical discourse' in such a bombastic way that it serves to 'question its effectiveness and naive optimism', a posture that disregards the urban space that is destroyed during a siege.[18] To see warfare as purely mathematical or as reducible to a list of tactical terminology is to flatten the very complexities Defoe wants to bring to the fore.

Defoe represents the system of war in ways that privilege reality over both myth and mathematics in his account of a military academy in his *Essay upon Projects*. Given the complexity of modern warfare as Defoe conceives of it, it is unsurprising that the 'Academies for Military Studies' he imagines demand a substantial education for soldiers of various ranks who, in late seventeenth- and eighteenth-century England, must participate in a far more elaborate system of war than did soldiers of previous generations (*PEW*, viii. 115). The growing knowledge needed to excel in war supports his argument for a standing army, which can accrue more expertise over time than a militia, especially after a 'long Peace' that might lead England to 'a degree of Ignorance' that could be dangerous (*PEW*, viii. 116). Defoe notes that it is extraordinary that

> every thing shou'd be ready but the Soldier: Ships are ready, and our Trade keeps the Seamen always taught, and breeds up more; but Soldiers, Horsemen, Engineers, Gunners, and the like, must be bred and taught; men are not born with Muskets on their Shoulders, nor Fortifications in their Heads; 'tis not natural to shoot Bombs, and undermine Towns. (*PEW*, viii. 117–18)

At this academy composed of four colleges, each of which welcomes different types of students, Defoe asks that the following subjects be taught as part of the core curriculum: '*Geometry, Astronomy, History, Navigation, Decimal Arithmetick, Trigonometry, Dialing, Gauging, Mining, Fireworking, Bombarding, Gunnery, Fortification, Encamping, Entrenching, Approaching, Attacking, Delineation, Architecture, Surveying*' (*PEW*, viii. 123; two-column list without commas in original). These lessons should be supplemented by bodily exercises, including swimming, handling firearms, and horsemanship. The wide range of topics Defoe identifies as critical to training demonstrates just how intricate a system he believes warfare to be. The professional military man must combine in the decision-making process managerial abilities, engineering knowledge, technological expertise, and physical prowess. In other words, the dynamic, technologically advanced military system in which the soldier operates in Defoe's era cannot be navigated with limited or rapidly taught skills. The practitioner must synthesize multiple strands of knowledge, from a broad array of disciplines, when he confronts a precise military situation in a specific local context.

---

[18] Alker and Nelson, '(Re)Writing Spaces of War', 220–1.

Reading War at a Distance: Defoe's Prose Non-Fiction

While readers of Defoe's journalism and other historical works will not gain the level of specialized knowledge of warfare suitable for a soldier, they will acquire a comprehensive understanding of war as it evolved over time. Defoe makes five major claims in his 'military curriculum' for these lay readers. First, he claims that in order to comprehend modern warfare as a system, his readers, like soldiers, must employ military history with care, ideally placing distant and recent military events side by side to establish points of comparison that might help determine future action, which Defoe modelled in both the *Review* and *The Master Mercury*.[19] In, for example, the fourth issue of the latter, dated 17 August 1704, Defoe gives 'An Account of the Great Battle of Hochstetten', now known as Blenheim. After describing the 'terrible slaughter' that took place and Marlborough's tactical brilliance, he considers how to put the loss of the French troops into historical context. He first suggests that this may not be possible, claiming, 'As this is the greatest overthrow that ever the *French* met with for above 200 wars past, so we cannot find in any of our Histories an Action like it'.[20] Nevertheless, he then ploughs ahead with a historical example:

> The Great and Bloody Battel of *Leipsick*, between the brave *Gustavus Adolphus*, and old General *Tilly*, comes the nearest to it, in which the Imperial Army being 44000 Men, was Routed and entirely Beaten after a most Dreadful and Obstinate Fight. There was 8000 Foot at the end of the Battle retreated to a Village as the *French* did here, but with this difference, that as the *French* here laid down their Arms, the other fought to the last, would never accept of Quarter, though they knew their General was fled, but they were cut in pieces Rank and File as they were drawn up, and never turned their Backs.[21]

This passage is included in 'The Reflector', a commentary section in which Defoe expands on the factual descriptions shared earlier. The implication in this passage is that historically informed commentary serves an important function in making sense of current military events.

Comparative analysis, in Defoe's opinion, also guides readers in their consideration of future military directions. In a celebratory entry in the *Review* in July 1707, Defoe discusses the importance of momentum during warfare, affirming the importance of cumulative victories. In a discussion of a series of military shocks that France received in 1706, he turns to a classical analogy:

---

[19] Defoe published the short-lived *Master Mercury* anonymously.

[20] Defoe, *The Master Mercury*, intro. Frank H. Ellis and Henry L. Snyder, Augustan Reprint Society, No. 184 (Los Angeles, CA: Williams Andrew Clark Memorial Library, 1977), no. 4 (17 August 1704), 15.

[21] Defoe, *Master Mercury*, no. 4 (17 August 1704), 15.

> How near was the *Roman* Empire to an entire Overthrow and Dissolution, by the Loss of one general Battle at *Cannae*, and how to this Day do we reproach the Memory of that great General *Hannibal*, for that he did not march directly to the Gates of *Rome*, which if he had, he had put an End to the *Roman* Empire?—And how would such another Shock have torn it up by the Roots, and made them a meer Province of the *Carthaginian* Dominion.[22]

Defoe dedicated much space in early *Review* essays to praising the military might of the French, drawing some criticism as a result, but he insisted it was vital for the English to recognize the strengths and weaknesses of their opponents. He notes that whatever the French were in previous times when English armies frequently defeated them, they are now 'a Bold, Adventurous, Wise, Politick and Martial People'.[23] Therefore, in describing the defeats the French suffered at the hands of the British (and allies), Defoe affirms the latter's prowess while teaching the audience about the importance of military momentum. The reference to Hannibal, who ultimately did not 'put an end to the Roman Empire', serves as a warning that further action is needed to extend success beyond a single battle or siege to the entire campaign.

In addition to inviting readers to compare military events of the past and present, Defoe draws on history when he wants to discuss the virtues of military men or the character of the troops. For instance, he notes that in the Civil War, 'the King's Army and the Parliaments Army differ'd exceedingly in this; that the Kings army gave themselves a Loose to all Manner of Prophaneness, Vice, and ungoverned Debauchery, and the Parliament Soldiers were kept sober, strict and reform'd'.[24] And, of course, Parliament won the war. Defoe suggests thereby that a leader who promotes and enforces order and virtue in his soldiers remains vital to success in contemporary warfare, and he presents William III and Gustavus Adolphus as two such model leaders.

Recent military history was also a key part of Defoe's military lessons for readers, which he reveals not only in the *Review*, but also in a series of historically-based 'memoirs' with fictional narrators, such as *The History of the Wars, of his Present Majesty Charles XII* (1715), *An Impartial History of the Czar of Muscovy* (1723), and *The Impartial Account of the Late Famous Siege of Gibraltar* (1728).[25] The first two of these memoirs compile accounts of battles and sieges during the Great Northern War, which are obsessively relayed, as Novak notes, by 'two Scottish officers serving on opposite sides'. In these works, Novak finds that 'Defoe was merely taking advantage of the available sources from contemporary newsletters and doing little more than some occasional editing and rearranging of the texts … [T]hey are hardly more than an account of one

---

[22] *Review*, iv. 343 (19 July 1707).
[23] *Review*, i. 10 (19 February 1704).
[24] *Review*, iv. 623 (18 November 1707).
[25] While P. N. Furbank and W. R. Owens de-attributed these works from Defoe's canon, Paula Backscheider, Maximillian Novak, and Geoffrey Sill (among others) are wary of simply accepting such de-attributions. See Backscheider, *Daniel Defoe*, 592 n. 38.

battle after another'.[26] While this is true, making available this sequential account reveals the multidimensional nature of war, notably the interrelation of simultaneous events as the conflict unfolds and the varied elements, from engineering to diplomacy, that comprise the military system.

Second, while Defoe values using wars from the distant and recent past as interpretive lenses through which to clarify current conflict and future possibilities, he also recognizes that technological changes mean that knowledge of the history of conflict has its limitations. In his *Essay upon Projects*, written as a response to 'the present War with France' (*PEW*, viii. 29), Defoe writes,

> *witness* the new ways of Mines, Fougades, Entrenchments, Attacks, Lodgments, and a long *Et Cetera* of New Inventions which want Names, practised in Sieges and Encampments; *witness* the new sorts of Bombs and unheard-of Mortars, of Seven to Ten Ton Weight, with which our Fleets standing two or three Miles off at Sea, can imitate God Almighty himself and rain *Fire and Brimstone* out of Heaven, as it were, upon Towns built on the firm Land. (34)

In this passage, Defoe describes what we would now call 'shock and awe' techniques that increasingly render urban space the central site of combat. But, as Defoe explains, many of these new techniques lead to an oddly deflective method of engagement, or rather non-engagement, which differs from past military strategies. In the 'bloody Civil War', for example, 'fighting was the Business', as military personnel sought out direct combat, 'Battels, Surprizes, Storming of Towns, [or] Skirmishes'; but now, he concludes, it is not unusual to 'spend a whole Campaign in Dodging, or as 'tis genteely call'd, *Observing one another*, and then march off into Winter-Quarters' (116). Less blood might be spilled with the new military method in this and other cases, but it also 'spins Wars out to a greater length' (117). New developments in the art of war, therefore, do not necessarily lead to immediate success and can actually end up deferring conflict without any advantage gained.

Nevertheless, it is vital that soldiers and his readers understand new technologies, according to Defoe. In the early days of the *Review*, when Defoe details French military power, he lingers over the advanced fortifications of French towns because of the engineering expertise of Vauban, the French military engineer. Defoe explains that he will not 'Delineat the Fortifications of every Town, and tell ... [readers] how many Bastions, Gates, Guns, &c, Every Fortification contains; the Octogons, Pentagons, Hexagons, the Lines, Curtains, Tenails, Redouts, Horn Works, and all Monsieur *Vauban's* hard names'.[27] However, in this sentence alone he makes clear that British engineers and military leaders must take into account the technological prowess of their military opponents. John McVeagh explains that Defoe produces 'lesson[s]' for his readers on 'the anti-technological bias in English education', leaving Defoe wondering, 'where are

---

[26] Novak, *Daniel Defoe*, 482.
[27] *Review*, i. 158 (30 May 1704).

the Men that bend their mind to this [critical area of] Study?'.²⁸ Defoe intimates with this question that in critiquing military action, soldiers and readers must not only do so with knowledge of past conflicts, but also with a comprehensive understanding of new technologies and modern circumstances.

Third, in addition to addressing the tension between history and modernity in the art of war, Defoe enjoins his readers to withhold judgement and to stop assigning blame on reported military action until they have considered the logistics of setting in motion the apparatus of war when conflict sprawls across enormous swaths of territory with myriad moving parts (for example, people, arms, and supplies), each of which can influence the other. For instance, Defoe reprimands readers who are complaining, in late February 1708, that there is a deficiency of troops in Spain which caused the Battle of Almanza to go badly, explaining that the system of approving military action is complex and time consuming. He claims that far from involving a mismanagement of troops, a substantial amount of time was taken up by Parliament between providing

> for the Troops mentioned, and the Time of the Battle of *Almanza*, and … the Government could either send the Troops which were to be furnished thither, or recruit those which were there, and they will see, they had no Reason for the Reflections made, since the Parliament gave Money for the Troops but in *Feb* 1706/7; and the Battle of *Almanza* happen'd on *April* 14 the same Year; and to raise Troops or Recruits, ship them for *Spain,* and have them arrive there, and all in two Months, is an Expedition not known in these Ages of the World.²⁹

In this essay, Defoe addresses the difference between the perception of time and space by readers on English soil and the actual expenditure of time in international wars preparing soldiers and transporting them to the correct location. Defoe thus encourages readers studying war at a distance to keep in the forefront of their minds a realistic timeline of every aspect of military operations, as well as a sound knowledge of its sometimes immense geographic scale.³⁰

Defoe also directs his readers to consider the volatility and dynamism of campaigns, given the need of military forces to adapt continually to a wide variety of local, regional, national, and international circumstances. Since military success is contingent on numerous elements in the mutable system of war—from weather, disease, and transportation to political events and financial support—readers must recognize that adaptability is key, but that it is restricted by the nature of external conditions. It is not always

---

[28] John McVeagh, introduction to Defoe, *Review*, v. xix. The quotation from Defoe is taken from the 2 November 1708 issue.

[29] *Review*, iv. 859 (28 February 1708).

[30] Defoe also makes clear that the distant nature of war can cause issues within the military as well. The myriad decisions that take place in the planning of the war, for example, can actually disrupt success. In one instance, 'Conferences and Debates, [and] settling measures' take up the time of the Duke of Marlborough, who, in spring 1706, has 'not yet found it possible to put himself at the head of his Troops, or to open the scene of Action'. *Review*, iii. 296 (11 May 1706).

possible for military leaders to respond in the best possible way a reader might imagine because the resources simply are not always available. Their decisions may not be readily intelligible to those reading about them in a newspaper weeks or months after the fact. Writing about the Siege of Turin in 1706, Defoe tries to help readers decipher the true nature of a French loss that at first glance seems solely the result of mismanagement:

> The *French* had taken the right Measures, and calculated both the Time, as well as the Number of Troops for that Siege; and that nothing but the immediate Hand of invisible Providence sav'd it, by stopping Monsieur *Tholouse* and the *French* Fleet by Storms and contrary Winds, so that the Stores and Cannon could not be brought up.[31]

There is much, Defoe claims, that cannot be predicted either by military leaders or by war journalists. Failure in combat is not, therefore, always the result of military incompetence. Some circumstances cannot be anticipated by humankind.

Of course, for Defoe, that which is unforeseen by humans is not unknown by God. As Sheehan and Wahrman point out, the biblical 'wheels within wheels' trope so appealing to Defoe was often used to signify the invisible hand of Providence which 'fully determines the course of events' in the world.[32] Despite his emphasis on the materiality of war, Defoe periodically asserts, as he does in the *Review* on 23 September 1707, that Providence ultimately rules in military affairs, as in other worldly matters:

> GOD has, in his wonderful Providence, and by a long Series of differing Circumstances, exercised this Nation with a violent, a bloody, an expensive, and a ruinous War; the Necessity was Apparent, the Cause just and honourable; and tho' with infinite Hazards, Losses, Disasters, Ups and Downs, yet we have seen the proud Arm of our mighty Enemy stay'd, and his haughty Hand humbled to a great Degree.

Readers, therefore, should not panic at the thought of the volatility of war with France since, as Defoe later suggests, it has helped make the nation 'fit for [divine] Deliverance'.[33]

Fourth, to gain insight into the complexity and enormity of the system of warfare, the modern consumer of war reports must also be willing to master how it traverses other systems. We focus here on the financial system since, as Sheehan and Wahrman observe, Defoe was 'fascinated—spellbound—with this new presence [of credit] in economic life'.[34] Defoe recognizes that the financial revolution had a powerful impact on every aspect of human organization. Sheehan and Wahran theorize that

> Key to Defoe's mental image of this economic universe ... was 'the long Chain' of connections crisscrossing it from all sides. These largely invisible chains interlinking untold numbers of individuals accounted for the infinite generativeness or

---

[31] *Review*, iii. 435 (16 July 1706).
[32] Sheehan and Wahrman, *Invisible Hands*, 48.
[33] *Review*, iv. 492 (23 September 1707).
[34] Sheehan and Wahrman, *Invisible Hands*, 49.

destructiveness believed to characterize credit ... A battle in Turkey, Defoe once wrote, could reverse the fortunes of trade and credit throughout Europe without the people affected having any knowledge of the event that brought this about.[35]

In response to this reality, the economist Charles Davenant and others started to develop systems to aggregate information and to locate and interpret patterns.[36] As we have seen, throughout his war journalism Defoe participates in this education when he teaches his readers to collect information, weigh probabilities, and carry out comparative studies in comprehending the system of war. However, these activities become far more difficult when the reader must also account for the role played by the financial system in war—one wheel within many wheels. Still, this complicated interpretive practice is essential since money and war, for Defoe, are deeply interconnected. Not only does he believe that war disturbs and destabilizes economic systems; he also recognizes that 'Money is the Vitals of the War ... [since] the longest Purse is the Conquerer'.[37]

Defoe sets out to clarify how many aspects of combat are contingent on funding. Without money, Defoe writes,

> the Sinews are cut, and the Body becomes a Lump ... [T]heir Troops mutiny in Garrison, and are fain to fight all the Winter with Butchers and Bakers, their Officers have no Money, their Soldiers no Clothes, their Stores no Bread, their Dragoons and Troopers no Horses. In short, *France* is struck with a dead Palsie; as to their Cash, the Circulation stops, Credit suffers mortal Convulsions, and their Finances appear in the utmost disorder.[38]

Defoe breaks down for his readers the parts of the network of war that are dependent on systems of credit. What is an army travelling throughout the year in varied climates without clothes? How can their transportation work effectively without horses? If they have no bread, how can soldiers fight? It is not a surprise, then, that Defoe calls the Lord Treasurer (Godolphin) the 'General of Generals'.[39] If war is tied to financial systems, then military leaders need to have the wherewithal to navigate that system as well as to master strategic and tactical military planning. Likewise, consumers of war journalism must weave economic matters into their calculations and speculations.

Fifth, and finally, Defoe trains his readers to negotiate 'war at a distance' in all of its operational complexity. On the one hand, he gives them continual and orderly updates, encouraging them to feel as if they are participating in events as they occur, albeit from a place of 'privileged security'.[40] On the other hand, at times he intervenes to remind them that there is a lag time, to make visible mediation. In September 1706, he writes in

---

[35] Sheehan and Wahrman, *Invisible Hands*, 55.
[36] Sheehan and Wahrman, *Invisible Hands*, 59–62.
[37] *Review*, vi. 25 (7 April 1709).
[38] *Review*, vi. 25 (7 April 1709).
[39] *Review*, vi. 26 (7 April 1709).
[40] Favret, *War at a Distance*, 14, 39.

the *Review* of the effect of a post coming in between 'the Pen and the Press', or between 'the Press and the Publication', so that the author 'look[s] like a Conjurer, that prophesies after a thing has come to pass', making it clear to readers that the process of journalistic mediation adds another layer of complexity to making sense of the system of war.[41]

Given the distance of war and the fact that information relayed about it is always partial, Defoe also trains his readers to apply a hermeneutic of informed speculation when negotiating news from the front. For example, in August 1707 Defoe speculates in the *Review* about events that could compensate the French for the loss of Thoulon. While he waits for news in the mail, Defoe starts mapping out the state of things as they likely are, modelling a way of reading military news beyond the sheer mathematical by visualizing and assessing the condition of the fortifications of Thoulon, the number of soldiers in each army, the provisions, weapons, and supply line of the military leaders, and so on. He does something similar in the *Review* on 2 September 1708, in which he wonders what will happen now that Lille is besieged by the armies of the Duke of Marlborough and others and 'the Prosecution of the Siege so well secur'd, that there is no more question of its being taken'.[42] What, he asks, will the French do next? He again summarizes the state of affairs as they appear to stand and, in particular, the double duty the Duke of Marlborough faces since he must 'Cover the Siege, and protect the open Country of *Brabant* with the *Dutch-Flanders*'.[43] Defoe foregrounds his own uncertainty while playing this 'very difficult Game' in his mind.[44] He complicates the situation by speculating about how the Duke of Marlborough should respond if the French were to move their army. What should other players, such as the Duke of Berwick, do? Defoe reveals the complexity involved in guessing about potential moves in this specific game of war which leads him to his measured conclusion: Lille will be taken.

Reading War Nearby: Defoe's Prose Fiction

Thus far we have focused on Defoe's journalism, but it is in his novels that Defoe gives the reader the greatest sense of war nearby, through first-person narratives.[45] However, even in his novels Defoe situates the individual soldier's experience within the system of war. Defoe deals with military themes in several of his novels, but it is in *Colonel Jack* and *Memoirs of a Cavalier* that they feature most prominently, though there are violent conflicts in *Captain Singleton* and in the Crusoe novels, including a substantial reflection

---

[41] *Review*, iii. 560 (12 September 1706).
[42] *Review*, v. 331 (2 September 1708).
[43] *Review*, v. 331 (2 September 1708).
[44] *Review*, v. 331 (2 September 1708).
[45] In the case of Defoe's fiction, when we write of 'war nearby', we do not necessarily mean war in Britain, but war as directly experienced by a soldier.

on whether it is appropriate to use violent combat to convert people in 'foreign' nations in *Serious Reflections during the Life and Surprising Adventures of Robinson Crusoe* (1720) (*Novels*, iii. 207–19).[46] These first-person narratives focus on the experiences of male protagonists in a series of adventures, military and otherwise. In *Colonel Jack* and *Memoirs of a Cavalier*, military events are presented as (fictional) eyewitness testimony of an individual's enmeshment in the system of war. Though the protagonists recount an immersive experience in which they see various aspects of combat, they often make broader connections to the military campaigns of which they are a part and to warfare in general. Arthur Secord points out that in *Memoirs of a Cavalier* Defoe uses many historical sources to forge his broad descriptions of war, including the *Swedish Intelligencer* (1632–3), Bulstrode Whitelock's *Memorials of the English Affairs* (1682), and Clarendon's *History of the Rebellion* (1702–4).[47] To take one brief example of the intersection of soldier and system from *Memoirs of a Cavalier*, we might consider the moment in which the Cavalier travels with Sir John Hepburn to attack the fort of Oppenheim. After giving a detailed account of being 'set down within Musquet-shot of the Fort, under covert of a little Mount, on which stood a Wind-mill', the Cavalier moves to a more abstract discussion of the event that relates not only to the plan to storm the fort, but also to the king's grand design to cross the Rhine.[48] The narrating soldier appears compelled to explain his own role in the larger design, or system, of war.

In *Memoirs of a Cavalier* and *Colonel Jack*, Defoe recounts not one war, but multiple wars. He represents soldiers moving in and out of combat zones. The Cavalier initially fights on the Continent in various armies and ends up fighting on the royalist side of the Civil War. Colonel Jack becomes a military man three times. Initially, he joins a regiment in Scotland and finds it rather glamorous, particularly when he discovers his natural talent as a soldier: 'I took the Exercise so naturally, that the Serjeant that taught us to handle our Arms, seeing me so ready at it, ask'd me if I had never carryed Arms before'; but he quickly deserts when he realizes he will actually have to travel to Flanders to fight, something he would prefer not to do as an ordinary soldier.[49] In the second instance, after reading intently about war, and labouring as a servant on a plantation, he quarters with an English officer in Ghent right before a battle, and seems interested in witnessing events. Yet he misses much of the action and, at one point, while his friend's regiment is 'surrounded in a Village', he strolls away to see the countryside and the beauty of the fortifications of the towns (226). In the third instance, he actually joins a regiment and is involved in a series of martial actions.

---

[46] On this subject, see Nicholas Seager, 'Crusoe's Crusade: Defoe, Genocide, and Imperialism', *Etudes anglaises*, 72:2 (2019), 196–212.

[47] Arthur W. Secord, 'The Origins of Defoe's *Memoirs of a Cavalier*', in Arthur W. Secord, *Robert Drury's Journal and other Studies* (Urbana, IL: University of Illinois Press, 1961), 72–113.

[48] Defoe, *Memoirs of a Cavalier*, ed. James T. Boulton, intro. John Mullan (Oxford: Oxford University Press, 1991), 77.

[49] Defoe, *Colonel Jack*, ed. Gabriel Cervantes and Geoffrey Sill (Peterborough, ON: Broadview, 2016), 153.

We suspect that one of the reasons that Defoe weaves multiple wars into his novels is to produce the kind of comparative work undertaken in the *Review*. This quality of *Memoirs of a Cavalier* leads Backscheider to conclude that its 'first part ... make[s] the readers connoisseurs of armies and generals. The second strips away any illusions people may have about the glory of civil wars'.[50] The shift in these novels from micro-narratives of first-hand experience of military contexts and combat to macro-narratives of the war at large also allows Defoe to compare military leaders, measuring Tilly against Gustavus Adolphus, for example. In the case of *Colonel Jack*, it is the behaviour of the protagonist in battle that is compared to that of other military actors.

Representing war from the point of view of individual participants also enables Defoe to make visible the effects of soldierly action on the passions. Defoe has his first-person narrators write of both moments of horror and intense satisfaction. In *Memoirs of a Cavalier*, his representation of the sacking of Magdeburg is intended to generate in the character, and the reader, a sense of pure horror. The Cavalier declares:

> This Calamity sure was the dreadfullest Sight that ever I saw; the Rage of the *Imperial* Soldiers was most intolerable, and not to be expressed; of 25000, some said 30000 People, there was not a Soul to be seen alive, till the Flames drove those that were hid in Vaults and secret Places to seek Death in the Streets, rather than perish in the Fire.[51]

Such horror is amplified when the Cavalier fights in the Civil War and is shocked to hear his enemies cry out in English for mercy. He laments, 'It grieved me to the Heart, even in the Rout of our Enemies, to see the Slaughter of them; and even in the Fight, to hear a Man cry for Quarter in *English*, moved me to a Compassion which I had never been used to' (165). Descriptions of emotional suffering from an eyewitness to war permit Defoe to make visible the on-the-ground personal experience of barbarity that his journalistic accounts of war do not allow for. While war remains a system, it is still deeply personal.

Not all passions felt during war are negative, however. Despite his earlier desertion of the army, Colonel Jack remains fascinated by war. During his last military interlude, Jack experiences both hardship and glory as he spiritedly engages in several fights. On the one hand, he relates that 'I had the Misfortune to receive a Musquet shot, which broke my left Arm, and, that was not all, for I was knock'd down by a Gyant like a *German* Soldier' who was then shot and ended up falling on top of him, almost smothering him (259). On the other hand, Jack fervently celebrates his participation in the Cremona conflict, in which the Germans are secretly let into the town and Jack, in his Irish regiment, takes part in a rousing defence. The resulting victory is personally rewarding for him, allowing him to reaffirm his masculinity: 'I NOW had the satisfaction of knowing, and that for the first time too, that I was not that cowardly low spirited Wretch, that

---

[50] Backscheider, *Daniel Defoe*, 445.
[51] Defoe, *Memoirs of a Cavalier*, 44.

I was, when the Fellow Bullied me in my Lodgings' (248). For Defoe, military experience can result in profound self-insight and significantly transform character: 'Men never know themselves till they are tried, and Courage is acquir'd by time, and Experience of things' (248).

In conclusion, Defoe's mastery of the system of war and its mediation through journalism makes him an important figure in the emergence of war reporting. Bridging the pamphlets and emergent journalism of the Civil War and the more extensive reporting of the Napoleonic Wars (1803–15), he sought to ensure that readers were well informed of facts on the ground and well prepared to understand the complexity of modern warfare.[52] While he often promoted peace, and argued that war was most beneficial when it led to amity, he clearly recognized that his nation was increasingly in a permanent militarized state and that the citizenry therefore needed to comprehend war as a multifaceted system that was relevant to their everyday lives, despite its geographical distance. The novels, far more than the journalism, provide readers with knowledge and understanding of the local or microcosmic elements of war and also clarify, more so in *Colonel Jack* than in *Memoirs of a Cavalier*, that war is only one part of the military man's life.[53] The novels bridge the distance of war by staging scenes of war up close, revealing the passionate intensity of helping to bring about a victory or of grieving at the devastation of a fallen city.[54]

Therefore, Defoe's works encourage readers to approach news and narratives of war as cautiously and as comprehensively as possible. In a disorientating time when wars abroad were frequent, Defoe sets out strategies for reading and writing war at a distance that account for the entire military system with the goal of informing and training readers. The representation of the system and experience of war in his oeuvre accords with the goal of the *Review*: to set 'the Affairs of *Europe* in a Clearer Light'. Defoe thereby distinguished himself from the 'Street Scribblers' who published 'Unaccountable and Inconsistent Stories' of 'Great Victories when we are Beaten' and 'Miracles when we Conquer' that filled people's heads 'with wrong Notions of Things' and '[w]heedled' 'Nations … to believe in Nonsense and Contradiction'.[55] The path to epistemic clarity, accuracy, and wholeness offered by Defoe not only makes him a 'master of fictions', but indeed a master of the system of war.

Further Reading

Sharon Alker, 'The Soldierly Imagination: Narrating Fear in Defoe's *Memoirs of a Cavalier*', *ECF*, 19:1 (2006), 42–68.

---

[52] For information on journalism in the seventeenth century, see, for example, Jayne E. E. Boys, *London's News Press and the Thirty Years War* (Woodbridge: Boydell, 2011).

[53] At one point, Jack writes, 'But I hasten on to my own history, for I am not writing a journal of the wars, in which I had no long share' (255).

[54] Defoe, *Colonel Jack*, 248.

[55] *Review*, i. 6 (19 February 1704).

Sharon Alker and Holly Faith Nelson, '(Re)Writing Spaces of War: Daniel Defoe and Early Modern Siege Narratives', in *Topographies of the Imagination: New Approaches to Daniel Defoe*, ed. Katherine Ellison, Kit Kincade, and Holly Faith Nelson (New York: AMS Press, 2014), 209–31.

Paula R. Backscheider, *Daniel Defoe: His Life* (Baltimore, MD: Johns Hopkins University Press, 1989).

Mary A. Favret, *War at a Distance: Romanticism and the Making of Modern Warfare* (Princeton, NJ: Princeton University Press, 2010).

Maximillian E. Novak, Daniel Defoe, *Master of Fictions: His Life and Ideas* (Oxford: Oxford University Press, 2001).

Maximillian E. Novak, 'Defoe and the Art of War', *PQ*, 75:2 (1996), 197–213.

John Richetti, *The Life of Daniel Defoe: A Critical Biography* (Oxford: Wiley-Blackwell, 2005).

William James Roosen, *Daniel Defoe and Diplomacy* (Selinsgrove, PA: Susquehanna University Press, 1986).

Nicholas Seager, '"A Romance the likest to Truth that I ever read": History, Fiction, and Politics in Defoe's *Memoirs of a Cavalier*', *ECF*, 20:4 (2008), 479–505.

Jonathan Sheehan and Dror Wahrman, *Invisible Hands: Self-Organization and the Eighteenth Century* (Chicago, IL: University of Chicago Press, 2015).

CHAPTER 23

CRIME AND THE LAW IN DEFOE'S WORKS

KATE LOVEMAN

DEFOE's reputation as a prolific writer on crime is in certain respects undeserved. In the nineteenth century the unsubstantiated belief that Defoe had worked as a reporter with special access to Newgate prison led to many works on robberies and famous rogues being assigned to him. Nor was he quite so well versed in criminality on the high seas as was once thought, with the attribution of *A General History of the Pyrates* (1724–8) to him having proved suspect.[1] Defoe's knowledge of crimes did, however, include the committing of them. By 1720 he had been arrested and prosecuted multiple times for seditious libel. This included a conviction for *The Shortest-Way with the Dissenters* (1702), which led to him standing in the pillory and spending several months in Newgate. He obtained his release through political negotiation and the support of powerful officials.[2] When his canon is stripped of the most dubious attributions, the recurrent fascination with criminality remains impressive [SEE CHAPTER 34]. As significant, and less studied, is his interest in the law and its agents. In pamphlets and in prose fictions, Defoe's concern with the operation of justice led to strident polemic, scathing satire, and pointed appeals to readers' knowledge of the law and its representatives. In his novels, his protagonists' encounters with the legal system are also often intricately plotted moments when readers' perceptions of right and wrong, mercy and duty are put under pressure. Defoe's early satires offer evidence of his views on the legal system, its problems, and potential solutions [SEE CHAPTER 11]. These satires make for productive comparison with the representation of the law in *The Fortunes and Misfortunes of the Famous Moll Flanders* (1722) and *The History and Remarkable Life of the Truly Honourable Col. Jacque,*

---

[1] P. N. Furbank and W. R. Owens, *The Canonisation of Daniel Defoe* (New Haven, CT: Yale University Press, 1988), 72–4, 100–9; P. N. Furbank and W. R. Owens, *Defoe De-Attributions: A Critique of J. R. Moore's Checklist* (London: Hambledon Press, 1994), for example, 133–4, 136–41.

[2] Backscheider, *Daniel Defoe*, 106–25, 322–8, 378–80, 384, 433, 465. Defoe also had experience of arrest and gaol as result of civil prosecution for debts (58–60).

Commonly Call'd Col. Jack (1722). Little attention has been given to Jack's and Moll's early encounters with the law's representatives, despite the fact that these are moments on which the narrators themselves dwell. These episodes are also among the features that distinguish the two works from other criminal lives of the seventeenth and eighteenth centuries. More typically, pamphlets or a longer 'life' about a real criminal might describe the final trial in some detail, but otherwise limit or avoid mention of previous encounters with the law—although highwaymen were traditionally prone to robbing justices.[3] In contrast, Moll and Jack each have significant interactions with the legal system without coming before a judge, and indeed Jack evades trial altogether. The same verbal facility that makes them beguiling narrators is tested in their experiences with the law, in the process testing readers' notions of what constitutes justice.

THE LEGAL SYSTEM

Before considering the treatment of the law and crime in Defoe's works, it is helpful to understand certain principles of the eighteenth-century legal system and the demands these placed upon members of the public—especially in relation to Defoe's various target readerships. With frequent references to London's streets and officials, Defoe's works on crime primarily addressed London readers, and primarily those London readers with money to spend on non-essentials such as satirical poetry and scandalous prose. His pamphlets, especially when pirated, could sell for as little as a penny, but official editions cost considerably more: *The True-Born Englishman* (1700) retailed at one shilling.[4] This was at a time when the average daily wage for a London labourer, according to modern calculations, was two shillings.[5] The 'lives' in particular were costly: *Moll Flanders* was advertised at five shillings bound and *Colonel Jack* cost six.[6] Many of the individuals who could afford to purchase Defoe's works new or in official editions would be substantial householders within their parishes or citizens with voting rights in City institutions, and thus capable of exerting pressure for reform. Male readers might be called upon to act in particular cases as jurors or in other official capacities.

Early eighteenth-century justice has a reputation for harshness. This is largely on account of new legislation that expanded the range of property crimes for which men and women could be executed. Responding to concerns about the perceived growth in offences such as shoplifting and burglary, the government altered statutes to broaden

---

[3] For example, Alexander Smith, *The History of the Lives of the Most Noted Highway-men*, 2nd ed., 2 vols (1714), i. 5–6, 29–30.

[4] Defoe, *A Second Volume of the Writings of the Author of the True-Born Englishman* (1705), A3r.

[5] Jan Luiten van Zanden, 'Wages and the Cost of Living in Southern England (London) 1450–1700', International Institute of Social History, http://iisg.nl/hpw/dover.php. (Accessed 19 August 2019).

[6] *The Evening Post*, no. 1951, 27–30 January 1722; Defoe, *The History and Remarkable Life of the Truly Honourable Col. Jacque* (1723 [for 1722]), title-page.

the circumstances in which a criminal conviction could lead to death.[7] However, taking the passage of harsh statutes as proof of the rigour of the justice system is misleading. Evidence from court reports and other sources indicates widespread acceptance among legal officials and the public that the death penalty did not have to be strictly applied in order for it to be an effective deterrent. In practice, a range of steps were taken to prevent the accused from facing the gallows.[8] On the front line of the justice system were Justices of the Peace (JPs), who played a pivotal role in deciding whether or not a suspect would enter the system and which sanctions they would face. At a time when there was no police service, the local JP heard reports of crimes, issued warrants for arrest, determined the nature of the offence, decided whether the suspects brought before him should be committed for trial, and often imposed punishments for lesser crimes.[9] Norma Landau observes that a JP could take the role of 'arbiter and arbitrator of his community', while Dietrich Oberwittler argues that 'leniency rather than rigorous enforcement of the criminal law was characteristic of their judicial work'. When faced with crimes such as minor thefts, the measures open to JPs included encouraging an informal settlement between the accused and the victim or summarily dispatching the accused to a 'house of correction'. Being sent to a house of correction such as Bridewell meant the accused was not gaoled pending a trial, but instead was kept in detention for a short period. While there, they might be sentenced to undergo further punishment, such as labour or whipping, before being released.[10] As members of the gentry or well-to-do citizens, JPs had the power to affect perceptions of justice within their local area. The characters of London JPs were often well known in their jurisdictions and sometimes beyond; as a result they feature frequently in Defoe's writings on criminality.

JPs and judges had influence in shaping the charges and the types of conviction—but so too did juries and victims. Any one of these parties might act to keep the accused from execution. In cases of theft, the law was complex, with the nature of charges (and thus the penalties) determined by factors that included the amount stolen, the location and time of the theft, and whether violence or implied threat was present. If, for example, the goods were deemed to be worth over a shilling, this was 'grand larceny', a felony subject to the death penalty. A victim, a JP, or a jury (whose responsibilities included valuing stolen property), might therefore decide to undervalue goods if they did not feel the harshest penalties were warranted. Historians have detected a particular reluctance to carry out the death penalty for non-violent property crimes[11]—exactly the kinds of

---

[7] J. M. Beattie, *Policing and Punishment in London, 1660–1750: Urban Crime and the Limits of Terror* (Oxford: Oxford University Press, 2001), 19, 39, 316–17.

[8] Beattie, *Policing and Punishment*, 301; J. M. Beattie, *Crime and the Courts in England 1660–1800* (Princeton, NJ: Princeton University Press, 1986), 420–1.

[9] Beattie, *Crime and the Courts*, 36, 268–70; Norma Landau, *The Justices of the Peace, 1679–1760* (Berkeley, CA: University of California Press, 1984), 23–5.

[10] Landau, *Justices of the Peace*, 174; Dietrich Oberwittler, 'Crime and Authority in Eighteenth Century England: Law Enforcement on the Local Level', *Historical Social Research / Historische Sozialforschung*, 15:2 (1990), 3–34 (22, 17–20); Beattie, *Policing and Punishment*, 26–7.

[11] Beattie, *Crime and the Courts*, 38–9, 333, 406, 424; Oberwittler, 'Crime and Authority', 20.

offences in which Moll Flanders and Colonel Jack specialize. John Beattie argues that one of the major challenges for the eighteenth-century justice system was the limited range of punishments available for such crimes. Other than execution, the two main post-trial punishments for property crime were whipping (if the charge was petty larceny) or branding in the hand (if a defendant was convicted of a capital crime but able to plead clergy, thus reducing the punishment). Post-trial detention was not a standard sentencing option, so after corporal punishment the criminal would be released back into society—and perhaps return quickly to crime. Advocates of transportation saw it as a valuable middle way: it avoided the extremity of execution while nonetheless imposing a harsh punishment that removed the risk of the criminal reoffending within the local community. Transportation was not, however, a sentence formally available until 1718; prior to that it was only employed as a condition of a pardon, after a convict had been sentenced to death and reprieved.[12] Defoe's interest in transportation was partly that of a businessman: in 1688 he had traded in indentured labour and turned a profit from shipping people to Maryland.[13]

Early Satires

While historians have noted problems with the punishments available by statute, Defoe's consistent position in his early writings was that failures in the justice system stemmed not from problems with the laws themselves, but from the law's flawed agents. His anonymous pamphlet *The Poor Man's Plea* (1698) angrily accused the nation's elites of injustice. The authorial voice conceded that the laws passed as part of the recent move to reform manners and punish vice had sprung from noble motives. Yet these laws had proved not just futile, but vicious in their effects. Identifying himself as one of 'the *Plebeii*' he addressed the nation's 'Nobility, Gentry, Justices of the Peace, and Clergy':

> We do not find that all the Proclamations, Declarations, and Acts of Parliament yet made, have any *effective Power* to punish *you* for your Immoralities, as they do *us*. Now while *you* make Laws to punish *us*, and let *your selves* go free, though guilty of the same Vices and Immoralities, those Laws are unjust and unequal in themselves. (RDW, vi. 27–8)

Defoe attacked the inaction and hypocrisy of JPs. They seldom exercised their power, he argued, and when they did so they targeted 'the poor Commons' (28). In London, beggars and a few whores were punished, while rich drunkards and blaspheming merchants went free. Indeed, the Justices themselves were given to swearing and boozing, sentencing a drunkard with '*God damn him, set him in the Stocks*' (29). In

---

[12] Beattie, *Policing and Punishment*, 301–9, 442.
[13] Backscheider, *Daniel Defoe*, 485–6.

making the claim that the law's agents, not the law, were at fault Defoe was voicing a common complaint. However, he went further than most commentators in his willingness to point the finger at particular judges, JPs, and sheriffs. His most famous poem, *The True-Born Englishman*, echoed the arguments of *The Poor Man's Plea* for the magistrates and gentry to reform, before taking aim at 'A Modern Magistrate of Famous Note', who had made his fortune by stealing from the public revenue and from forgery: 'I hang poor Thieves for stealing of your Pelf / And suffer none to rob you, but my self', the magistrate announced. These lines had circulated in manuscript prior to their print publication.[14] Named as 'Sir C-----s D-----b' in some editions, the target was readily identifiable as Sir Charles Duncombe who, in 1699, had admitted involvement in a fraud concerning £10,000 of treasury funds. Soon after being tried and acquitted, Duncombe was chosen as a sheriff of London, a role that included overseeing two of the City's prisons and acting as a judge or JP in certain circumstances.[15]

In 1702, Defoe's poem *Reformation of Manners, A Satyr* expanded his allegations of corruption in general and in particular. The idea of a reformation of manners, he advised Londoners, had become so transparently ridiculous as to be a joke, with the crimes of legal officials among the most notable in a sink of vice. Among these villains was 'L--l, the *Pandor* of thy Judgement-Seat'. Sir Salathiel Lovell was the Recorder of London, the City's principal legal officer who sat as a judge at the Old Bailey court and also served as a JP. Lovell was alleged to be not just guilty of bribery, but of protecting thieves and profiting from crimes:

> He Trades in Justice, and the Souls of Men ...
> He has his Publick Book of Rates to show,
> Where every Rogue the Price of Life may know:
> And this one Maxim always goes before,
> He never hangs the Rich, nor saves the Poor....
> Fraternities of Villains he maintains,
> Protects their Robberies, and shares the Gains.
>
> (lines 131, 133–6, 141–2; *SFS*, i. 160–1)

A roster of other corrupt justices followed. 'F--e' (Sir Henry Furnese) was sarcastically named 'the City's New-reforming Magistrate', a man who would 'Take Money of the Rich, and hang the Poor' before sentencing to whipping the woman he had debauched (lines 178–9; *SFS*, i. 161). 'S--ple', 'C--le', and 'C--n' (Sir John Sweetapple, Sir William Cole, and Sir Robert Clayton) were all magistrates similarly given to whoring, filthy

---

[14] *The True-Born Englishman*, line 1045; *SFS*, i. 113; lines 1171–2; *SFS*, i. 117. Frank H. Ellis, 'Textual Notes', in *Poems on Affairs of State: Augustan Satirical Verse, 1660–1714, Volume 6: 1697–1704*, ed. Frank H. Ellis (New Haven, CT: Yale University Press, 1970), 762.

[15] E.g. *The True-Born Englishman* (1700, Wing D849), 62; Paula Watson and Perry Gauci, 'Duncombe, Charles (1648–1711), of Teddington, Mdx. Barford, Wilts', *The History of Parliament*, http://www.historyofparliamentonline.org/volume/1690-1715/member/duncombe-charles-1648-1711. (Accessed 26 February 2019); *The Compleat Sheriff* (1696), 196, 408.

speech, and irreligion.[16] Adding to the grim humour was that Defoe's attack on corrupt justices was itself bordering on the criminal, for it skirted the edges of the law on seditious libel. Conviction for seditious libel tended to require the naming of specific officials, so writers discouraged prosecution by supplying only certain letters of names. This technically turned the accusation into 'innuendo', which was subject to a jury's interpretation rather than presenting a clear-cut case.[17] Partially blanking out names also, of course, challenged readers to apply their local knowledge to solve the mystery—which might involve consulting others and so spread the scandal [SEE CHAPTER 2]. Defoe's favoured targets for satire and polemic meant that, as Paula Backscheider remarks, when he was prosecuted for *The Shortest-Way* he 'did not face friends' on the bench, having directly or indirectly attacked a number of his judges.[18] Shortly before standing in the pillory for seditious libel, he defiantly published the *True Collection* of his writings (1703), which included *Reformation of Manners*. While the professed intent of this selection was to show Defoe's enduring zeal for society's good, the fact that several of the pamphlets satirized men, such as Lovell, who had been involved in his prosecution must have been personally gratifying, and it pointedly demonstrated that he was uncowed.[19]

If, as *Reformation of Manners* argued, the 'useless Scare-Crows of neglected Laws' were no solution to stemming vice and crime, then what other ways were there to address the crisis? (line 292; *SFS*, i. 165). The answer, according to Defoe, was that *''tis Example must reform the Times'* (line 1231; *SFS*, i. 190). If magistrates were to abandon vice, they would be able to punish others without hypocrisy and set a fashion for virtue rather than for sinning.[20] Defoe thought what was needed was the replacement of current officeholders by 'another Set of Magistrates' entirely—'But God knows where the Men are to be found', he complained (lines 281, 283; *SFS*, i. 164). More practically, *The Poor Man's Plea* urged JPs to take a more active role: they need not be 'a *Passive Magistrate*', waiting for others to bring evidence, but should 'acquaint themselves with their Neighbourhood', take the initiative, and exercise justice impartially; if they made themselves available and trusted, informants would come to them (*RDW*, vi. 20–1). The explicit call in these early works was for positive examples whom the people would respect and emulate. In the absence of such paragons, Defoe's writing instead sought to change the 'fashion' for vice and mobilize the court of public opinion by shaming those who set poor examples. 1704 saw the inauguration of 'the Scandalous Club', a fictitious society, in Defoe's *Review*. Although it was set up with the declared purpose of critiquing false news, it soon began to resemble an alternative magistracy. It would not have escaped Defoe's contemporaries that the

---

[16] *The Genuine Works of Mr. Daniel D'Foe*, 2 vols ([1721]), ii. 2 (second pagination sequence) supplies a key. At the time of publication Furnese was sheriff of London; Clayton, a former Lord Mayor, was a JP for Surrey; Sweetapple and Cole had been sheriffs in 1695.

[17] Philip Hamburger, 'The Development of the Law of Seditious Libel and the Control of the Press', *Stanford Law Review*, 37:3 (1985), 661–765 (701, 749).

[18] Backscheider, *Daniel Defoe*, 109.

[19] *A True Collection of the Writings of the Author of The True-Born Englishman, Corrected by himself* (1703), A4r–A5v.

[20] Cf. *The Poor Man's Plea*, *RDW*, vi. 23–4, 35–6.

club sat in 'Sessions', as JPs did, to hear complaints brought before them and pronounce a verdict. The complainants included a whore cheated of payment by a rich citizen and a poor man who thought he had been unjustly put in the stocks for drunken fighting by a drunken magistrate. The editor gave the impression that he would very much like to name the most notorious cases, but was exercising restraint.[21] Faced with rampant vice and a broken judiciary, Defoe implied, the policing of behaviour and the work of reform fell to pamphleteers, journalists, and their readers.

THE LAW IN ACTION: *MOLL FLANDERS* AND *COLONEL JACK*

In *The Poor Man's Plea*, *The True-Born Englishman*, and *Reformation of Manners*, Defoe had launched caustic attacks on the corruption of London's magistracy. *Moll Flanders* and *Colonel Jack* took a different approach to the problems of the law while, like the pamphlets, inviting readers to apply their knowledge of gossip about London personalities to interpreting the text. The stories proposed various uses that readers might or should find for the criminal narrators' experiences. The preface to *Colonel Jack* anticipated that the work's readers would include 'wicked' ones, who might be brought to recognize their own misspent lives. *Moll Flanders* repeatedly urged readers to note how heedlessness or poverty might make them, like Moll, fall into crimes ranging from illicit sex to theft.[22] No reader could assume he or she would not become a criminal: all men and women being sinners, all needed to be alert to the prospect that they might slide from private vices to heinous crimes.[23] Great stress was also laid on the idea of the reader as a potential victim of crime. Both of Defoe's narrators, along with the prefatory material to *Moll Flanders*, presumed that readers would appreciate direct or tacit advice on avoiding becoming a victim of urban crimes and what to do if this happened: how to prevent your watch being stolen or your employer's parcel being snatched, how to seize upon a pickpocket, methods for recovering stolen goods, and so forth.[24] If the casting of readers as potential criminals and potential victims is manifest, what might be less apparent to modern readers is that in early modern England obtaining justice routinely meant victims acting as prosecutors. With most crimes the responsibility to prosecute fell to the victim. The victim arranged for the apprehension of the suspect, gave evidence

---

[21] *Review*, i. 17–18 (26 February 1704); i. 81–2 (15 April 1704); i. 88–9 (18 April 1704); i. 108–9 (29 April 1704).

[22] *Colonel Jack*, vi. Defoe, *The Fortunes and Misfortunes of the Famous Moll Flanders* (1721 [for 1722]), for example, vii, 233. On Moll's sexual 'crimes', see Kate Loveman, '"A Life of Continu'd Variety": Crime, Readers, and the Structure of Defoe's *Moll Flanders*', *ECF*, 26:1 (2013), 1–32 (16–17).

[23] On this belief see Andrea McKenzie, *Tyburn's Martyrs: Execution in England, 1675–1775* (London: Hambledon Continuum, 2007), 55–67.

[24] *Moll Flanders*, ix–x, 255, 260–1; *Colonel Jack*, 39–40, 56, 68.

to a grand jury (which determined if there was a case to answer), and then appeared at the trial to present the case, usually without legal representation. He or she organized other witnesses' appearances and bore the cost of prosecution.[25] In terms of time, money, and moral responsibility, this was not a burden lightly borne. Early in *Colonel Jack*, for example, an old woman whom Jack and his friend have robbed refuses to join in the prosecution of Jack's friend on religious principle: 'I would not Hang the poor Wretch for my Money, let him live and Repent' (107). Yet, as Defoe and others argued, if prosecution might mean causing another's death, inaction could be more culpable: it meant siding with the criminal against the law and failing to protect future victims.[26] In Defoe's writings, individuals—and individual readers—each bear a responsibility for the justice that their society doles out: it therefore behoved readers to be concerned about the state of the legal system and, it is implied, to take advantage of the opportunities Defoe's narratives offered to inform themselves about the processes of the law.

The laws defining offences and punishments were far from static, and this presents challenges when assessing the representation of crime and the law in Defoe's fictions. While *Moll Flanders* and *Colonel Jack* speak to eighteenth-century concerns, the protagonists' crime sprees take place in the seventeenth century. The final sentence of Moll's narrative states that it was 'Written in the Year 1683'—thirty-nine years before its publication in early 1722. Moll is almost seventy as the story ends, making her born around 1613 and putting her time as a thief in the 1660s and early 1670s.[27] On first reading, however, this chronology is not apparent: until the late reveal of '1683', Moll has given the impression that she is alive and writing contemporaneously with her first readers. There are allusions to legal processes that support the sense that her career as an infamous thief is after 1690.[28] In contrast, the time period of Jack's story is signalled to his readers early on by mention of a famous shipwreck, and it remains consistent during the first part of his story. Jack is born in late 1672 or early 1673, and his time as a thief in London ends around 1693.[29] In both works, the author manages to avoid significant mistakes in terms of projecting eighteenth-century laws or terms back into the seventeenth century and, with a few exceptions, is attentive to the specifics of processes and charges.[30]

---

[25] Beattie, *Crime and the Courts*, 35–6.
[26] See, for example, Defoe, *Religious Courtship* (1722), *RDW*, iv. 255–6; *Directions for Prosecuting Thieves* (1728), 1–2.
[27] *Moll Flanders*, 424. See also David Leon Higdon, 'The Chronology of *Moll Flanders*', *English Studies*, 56:4 (1975), 316–19.
[28] See note 49.
[29] *Colonel Jack*, 8, 22, 95, 97. As Samuel Holt Monk notes, in the latter part of the story Jack's counting of the years does not fit with the datable events. *Colonel Jack*, ed. Samuel Holt Monk (London: Oxford University Press, 1965), xxii.
[30] Exceptions include Moll's description of her indictment for 'Robbery and Housebreaking, that is for Felony and Burglary' (348). The second charge is then given as 'Burglary' (traditionally a nighttime offence), but the narrative continues to treat this charge as synonymous with 'Housebreaking'—a different, daytime, offence (352). Although Moll might be expected to know the difference, determining which of the two crimes had been committed could cause confusion, as the statute 12 Anne, c.7 (1713)

Colonel Jack and his foster brothers, Captain Jack and Major Jack, have their first serious encounter with the law in an episode set in the mid 1680s. At this point Colonel and Major Jack are begging, while Captain Jack has fallen in with a murderous gang of kidnappers. The gang are arrested and sent to Newgate for trial. Fortunately, as Captain Jack is 'not then much above 13 Year old', a senior magistrate intervenes to remove the risk of trial for a capital offence. Instead, the Captain is dispatched to Bridewell, the principal house of correction in London, for the court of governors there to determine a suitable punishment. Twelve-year-old Colonel Jack and the younger Major Jack are terrified by Captain Jack's sentence:

> The President of *Bridewell*, and who I think they call'd Sir *William Turner*, held preaching to him about how young he was, and what a pitty it was such a Youth should come to be hang'd, and a great deal more, and how he should take warning by it, ... and all this while the Man with a blue Badge on, lash'd him most unmercifully, for he was not to leave off till Sir *William* knock'd with a little Hammer on the Table. (13)

Combining corporal punishment with moral warning, what young Colonel Jack sees as 'unmerciful' whipping is in the legal context an act of mercy, saving the Captain's life while deterring him and others from crime and its fatal consequences. Jack at first suggests the measures were an effective deterrent: Captain Jack ceases his former habits for 'a great while'. Colonel and Major Jack do not feel the strokes of the whip as the Captain does, but nonetheless receive such 'sensible Impressions' that 'it might be very well said we were corrected as well as he' (14).

This episode appealed directly to Londoners' local knowledge, offering subtexts for early readers that tended to support concerns about whether justice was indeed being done. The magistrate William Turner (1615–93), whom Jack tentatively names, was President of Bridewell in the mid 1680s; he had also been Lord Mayor and later served as an MP for London. Turner was known for his conscientious actions in supporting the charities that aided orphans.[31] However, another strand of his reputation concerned the practice of using a hammer to end a whipping, his rigour in this ceremony, and the suspicion that this served his sexual appetites rather than justice. In 1683 (within a couple of years of Jack's supposed encounter), Turner was satirized in the dialogue *The Whores Rhetorick*. One woman remarked that if prostitutes used their wits they need 'not fear the Constables Staff, or the justices Warrant, a publick whipping, or a private one in *Bridewel*, where Sir *William* knocks, and keeps time with the Lash'.[32] Sir

---

noted, and this new law changed the specifics. A clearer inaccuracy concerns the claim that the law required two witnesses to convict Jemy of robbery (364): two witnesses was a legal requirement for treason cases only.

[31] Perry Gauci, 'Turner, Sir William (1615–93), of St. Paul's Churchyard, London', *History of Parliament*, http://www.historyofparliamentonline.org/volume/1690-1715/member/turner-sir-william-1615-93. (Accessed 26 February 2019).

[32] *The Whores Rhetorick* (1683), 37.

William's 'knocking' at the whipping of offenders was local legend, as well as being a source of lewd jokes. On his death in 1693, serious and satirical elegies noted his diligence in whipping. The mock-elegy *Good Sir W— Knock* relayed the prostitutes' lamentation: '*Knock Good Sir William*, was our *Tone*, / Now *Knock off Good Sir William's* all our *Moan*'.[33] After attacking Sir William's severity the whores concluded by observing the law's lack of justice: 'Oh *Bridewell*, what a Shame thy Walls Reproaches? / Poor *Whores* are Whip'd, whilst Rich Ones Ride in Coaches' (2). Nine years later, Defoe's *Reformation of Manners* would voice the same sentiment in reference to a 'Miss Morgan', mistress to Sir Charles Duncombe: 'And poor Street-Whores in *Bridewel* feel their Fate, / While Harlot M—n rides in Coach of State' (61). To the young Jack, Sir William was an unknown and terrifying figure; to readers well versed in London's recent history, however, the description recalled a famously active and harsh exponent of justice doling out exemplary punishment. It also, in recalling Turner's 'knocking', was likely to remind some readers of satires and gossip sceptical of the president's methods. Such doubts about the operation of justice prove well founded within Jack's narrative: what appears a brutal but effective punishment is quickly shown to be only the most short-term of solutions. Major Jack takes up pickpocketing 'within the Year', and Colonel Jack soon follows him into that profession; meanwhile Captain Jack returns to kidnapping, eventually ending on the gallows after a wicked career.[34]

Colonel Jack's poverty and lack of education mean his vicarious experience of justice is ineffectual in deterring him from crime. The lessons Moll takes from her encounters with JPs are also ineffectual, instead teaching her ways to exploit the law for profit. Critics have often noted that Moll's narrative is structured by patterns of repetition with variation.[35] Her three appearances before JPs can be numbered among these repetitions, and they model a decline. The first entails a wrongful arrest, which leads to Moll being brought before an unnamed JP. From this encounter, she emerges vindicated and considerably richer. The second sees Moll justly arrested but ingeniously extricate herself. Finally she is apprehended in a theft, and—her powers of persuasion failing—sent to Newgate. Only in the second of these episodes is the JP identifiable and, as with the early satires, this would require some detailed knowledge of local history on the part of readers. This second close shave with the law begins when Moll attempts to steal some silver plate from a goldsmith's workshop in Foster Lane, but is seized inside the shop by the goldsmith's vigilant neighbour. She improvises a cover story that she had come to buy silver spoons. The goldsmith is reluctant to have her arrested but wants to do 'Justice' to his neighbour who is 'violent' for prosecution (332–3). At stake here, although

---

[33] *Good Sir W— Knock. The Whores Lamentation for the Death of Sir W. T.* ([1693]), 2. 'Knock off' had been used in the sense of 'die' since at least 1672 (Thomas Shadwell, *The Miser* (1672), 76), while 'knock' had long had sexual connotations ('knock', sense 2e, *OED Online*, Oxford University Press, www.oed.com. [Accessed 20 August 2019]).

[34] *Colonel Jack*, 14, 150.

[35] For example, Maximillian E. Novak, 'Defoe's "Indifferent Monitor": The Complexity of *Moll Flanders*', *ECS*, 3:3 (1970), 351–65 (365); Lincoln B. Faller, *Crime and Defoe: A New Kind of Writing* (Cambridge: Cambridge University Press, 1993), 132–3.

it is not spelt out, is that Foster Lane was a neighbourhood of goldsmiths, and there was thus a strong public interest in pursuing prosecutions to deter thieves.

Moll tells the men she wants to go before a magistrate to clear herself and that she may seek 'reparation' (333): rather than just bluffing, she is apparently hoping to repeat her previous experience before a JP when she was able to turn a healthy profit from being falsely accused. At this point 'came by Sir T. B., an Alderman of the City, and Justice of the Peace, and the Goldsmith hearing of it goes out, and entreated his Worship to come in and decide the Case' (333). This, then, is an instance of a justice active and accessible to his community—just as *The Poor Man's Plea* had advocated. He hears the goldsmith who speaks with 'Moderation', then the neighbour whose 'Heat, and foollish passion' Moll judges helps her case, and finally Moll herself who, fortunately, has an old spoon which she offers up as evidence that she had come to match it to some new ones (333). The JP appears to believe her, but asks her to be generous and to not let the goldsmith lose his custom: will she still buy the spoons? This seems an admirable peace-making manoeuvre but is in fact a test: when Moll proves to have the money on her for the purchase, the JP is finally satisfied that she is a genuine customer. Moll buys the spoons and, as she puts it, 'came off with flying Colours' (335). Quick-thinking, rhetorical skill, and the forethought to go with money and props have allowed Moll to evade justice, despite what appear to be conscientious conduct and astute judgement by this JP.

Like the presence of Sir William Turner in Colonel Jack's narrative, there are allusions here that query juridical decisions. Foster Lane was in Aldersgate Ward, and the only 'Sir T. B' who was an alderman there in the late seventeenth or early eighteenth centuries was Sir Thomas Bludworth, alderman from 1663 to 1682.[36] Moll's oblique chronological references date the episode to Christmas Day 1673, confirming this identification.[37] What Bludworth was most famous for was not his years as alderman, but his stint as Lord Mayor of London in 1665-6 and, in particular, his response to the Great Fire. Samuel Pepys and other writers at the time recorded the Lord Mayor's inaction and failure to provide leadership.[38] In 1724 Defoe, in *A Tour thro' the Whole Island of Great Britain* (1724-6), summed up Bludworth's reputation with more sympathy than most. Bludworth was

> famous for the implacable Passion he put the People of *London* in, by one rash Expression, at the time of the Great Fire: (*viz.*) *That it was nothing, and they might Piss it out*; which was only spoken at the beginning of the Fire, when neither Sir *Thomas* or the Citizens themselves cou'd foresee the length it would go; and without

---

[36] Alfred P. Beaven, 'Aldermen of the City of London: Aldersgate Ward', *The Aldermen of the City of London Temp. Henry III–1912* (London, 1908), 1–8, British History Online, https://www.british-history.ac.uk/no-series/london-aldermen/hen3-1912/pp1-8. (Accessed 20 August 2019).

[37] See Higdon, 'Chronology of *Moll Flanders*', 319. To my knowledge, this identification has not been made by editors of *Moll Flanders*.

[38] See Carol Hartley, 'Bludworth, Sir Thomas (b. in or before 1623, d. 1682), Merchant and Mayor of London', *Oxford Dictionary of National Biography*, 24 May 2012, https://doi-org.ezproxy4.lib.le.ac.uk/10.1093/ref:odnb/73676. (Accessed 26 February 2019).

any design to lessen their endeavours to quench it: But this they never forgot, or forgave to him, or his Family after him; but fix'd the Expression on him, as a Mark of Indelible Reproach, even to this Day. (*TDH*, i. 182)

Even if Sir T. B. appears to behave without fault as a JP, he is deceived by Moll and releases her to steal again. For any reader (most likely to be a Londoner) who was capable of identifying Sir Thomas Bludworth, there was the reward of recognition and what looks very much like a sly bit of wit at the expense of a man famous for failure of judgement— the tendency of the allusion was to underscore the magistrate's error. Encouraging serious or facetious speculation among readers about whether Moll Flanders had indeed eluded capture by Thomas Bludworth would not have hurt sales of the book.[39] The portrayals of Bludworth and Turner are, nonetheless, very far from the corrupt magistrates depicted in earlier satires: reforming the magistracy would not solve the problems these two episodes present. These passages each show diligent officeholders pursuing different tactics, yet both, despite fulfilling their duties conscientiously, fail in detecting or deterring crime.

Negotiating Justice

Moll's and Jack's early interactions with the law have little to offer in terms of improvements that might be made to the justice system. Indeed, even the works' claims that better education and charitable support for abandoned children would reduce crime are undermined by the plots. As Aparna Gollapudi has noted, '*publick Schools, and Charities*', such as the preface to *Colonel Jack* recommends, might well have kept its narrator from crime given '*the generous Principles he had in him*', yet Captain Jack is presented as incorrigible by nature: education and support, it is implied, would not have kept him from criminality or the gallows.[40] Moll recommends a similar charitable institution when she observes that, as a baby born to a criminal mother in Newgate, she would have benefitted from a system in which such children are 'taken into the Care of the Government, and put into an Hospital call'd the *House of Orphans*' to be bred up to a trade or to service (2). Yet, from the time she can remember, she is brought up by a caring foster mother and watched over by the magistrates of Colchester, who have decided that, although she is not from their jurisdiction, she deserves charity. Her foster mother teaches her skills to support herself and—despite limited resources—raises all her charges 'as Mannerly and as Genteely, as if we had been at the Dancing School' (5).

---

[39] On the ways *Moll Flanders* encourages gossip, see Loveman, '"A Life of Continu'd Variety"', 19–26, and Kate Loveman, *Reading Fictions, 1660–1740: Deception in English Literary and Political Culture* (Aldershot: Ashgate, 2008), 146–7.

[40] *Colonel Jack*, iv, v; Aparna Gollapudi, 'Criminal Children in the Eighteenth Century and Defoe's *Colonel Jack*', *PQ*, 96:1 (2017), 27–53 (39, 42).

Moll's upbringing has all the benefits of a 'House of Orphans' and more, yet she still falls into crime. If these stories are cast as campaigning works, their arguments fall flat or—more charitably—the narratives tacitly concede that any crime-fighting projects will at best have a limited effect on complicated problems. What Defoe's narratives offer in place of wide-ranging solutions are, first, pragmatic examples for readers on how to manage encounters with legal officials and suspected criminals and, second, scenes that invite readers to test their judgements and appreciate the moral quandaries and risks involved in such encounters. All this comes in episodes replete with detail and dramatic twists, with two of Defoe's favourite motifs being the unjust accusation and turning the tables on accusers.

An excellent example of Defoe's method comes from Moll's first encounter with a JP from which, as already noted, she turns a substantial profit. This is one of the most sustained episodes in Moll's narrative—a sign that the author thought it of peculiar interest to readers. Moll, disguised as a widow and looking for opportunities to steal, is captured while walking in Covent Garden by a mob that has mistaken her for a woman in mourning dress who robbed a mercer. With the identification uncertain, Moll is forcibly detained in the mercer's shop, a constable called, and they await further witnesses. Moll's strategy is to play the outraged gentlewoman: she is indignant but initially polite to the constable, the mercer, and his journeyman. As her detention continues, she warns the mercer she will make herself 'amends upon him in a more legal way' and asks to send for 'Friends' to vindicate her character (a pretence) (297). When this request is denied, she calls for ink and paper—presumably she intends to be seen recording her treatment or to further her pretence of summoning help. This too is refused. The mercer mocks the constable when he suggests releasing Moll. Moll is then used 'barbarously' by the journeyman who roughly lays hands on her in order to search her. She spits in his face and demands 'that Villain's Name'; 'Dam her' he swears in response (298–9). From this point Moll's language to her readers casts the journeyman as the criminal—he is, she observes, an 'insolent Rogue' (299). When the long-awaited witnesses return, dragging with them the widow and the stolen goods found on her, the situation aligns with Moll's rhetoric: she now has the law on her side, and it is the victims of the theft who are in danger of prosecution for unlawful detention and assault. The mercer seeks to apologize, telling Moll 'that they had so many things of this nature put upon them every Day, that they cou'd not be blam'd for being very sharp in doing themselves Justice' (300). Moll demands reparation and to be taken before a magistrate. In Moll's words, the journeyman now 'look'd like a condemn'd Thief' (302)—rather than simply being cast as a criminal as before, he is now compared to one who has earned the harshest punishment. The scene ends in a fight as the mercer resorts to 'ill Language' to the constable and the journeyman resists arrest (302). In the confusion, the actual thief flees.

Moll relishes this reversal of fortune, and so does 'a Mob of about 500 People' that has gathered. It 'pleas'd the People strangely' to hear that 'the Gentlewoman' initially taken as a thief had arrested the mercer 'and was carrying him before the Justice' (303). The women in particular intimidate the mercer and throw mud. The JP hears the constable, the journeyman, and the mercer—who again attributes his severity to 'the great loss they have daily by Lifters and Thieves' (304). The JP implies that Moll should sue the mercer, binds him over to keep the peace, and sends the journeyman to Newgate for assaulting Moll and the constable. Moll and her Governess proceed to exploit the situation, negotiating with the mercer to avoid prosecution of him and his journeyman. A settlement is reached: Moll gets £150, a suit of silk, and a grovelling apology from the journeyman. The mercer loses his silk, his money, and only succeeds in dissuading Moll from her demand to publish 'the particulars in the common News Papers' (310). A published apology was one route by which disputes before JPs might be settled out of court.[41] In this case the merchant is apparently desperate to avoid further publicity; eighteenth-century readers would understand that such an apology would destroy his credit and his business.

What were readers to make of all this? On the one hand, sympathies are with Moll because she is unjustly accused and ill-treated—and because what happens to her might happen to any innocent party. This is the source of the mob's indignation: the women are enraged at the mercer because they have a stake in ensuring that women are not seized off the streets and their reputations threatened. Moll also earns readers' sympathies, or even admiration, through her dextrous management of the situation and by telling, as ever, a good tale. Yet any reader who cheers on Moll is in the position of the 'Mob' that has turned against the victim of the crime. As Moll pursues her advantage, the mercer's side of the story emerges. A man whose business is threatened by repeated shoplifting has to face a terrifying crowd, pays out substantial sums, and almost loses his business; his journeyman, a 'very poor' man with a family to support, has his health endangered by being sent to Newgate (310). Lincoln Faller argues that dialogue in this episode offers readers access to a range of perspectives, but that the rapid, complex action ultimately deters sympathy with or judgement of any party.[42] Such aloofness perhaps comes more easily to readers today, who are less likely than Moll's early readers to identify men or women equivalent to themselves in this scenario. Cumulatively the signals are to avoid unquestioning acceptance of Moll's account. With the criminal cast as a victim and the victims of theft becoming criminals, the episode prods readers to query what they hear and to be flexible in adapting their views to new information—qualities the narrative presents as valuable in life, not just in legal dealings. In practical terms, this episode is about how to conduct oneself in encounters with the law, and, in particular, what *not* to do. The journeymen and mercer court disaster not because they detain Moll, but because they disparage the constable, act out of passion, and diminish their authority through swearing and the use of force. Moll, in contrast, behaves proportionately. In acting the role of a virtuous woman she provides a model of how a respectable citizen should act if wrongly arrested. She only displays anger when openly insulted; she bolsters her authority by measured speech, by indications of her literacy, and by her

---

[41] Donna T. Andrew, 'The Press and Public Apologies in Eighteenth-Century London', in *Law, Crime and English Society, 1660–1830*, ed. Norma Landau (Cambridge: Cambridge University Press, 2002), 208–29 (210–12, 224).

[42] Faller, *Crime and Defoe*, 149–51, 158.

references to influential 'Friends'. She affects to respect the law's officials and due process in order to manipulate both.

The tactics that work for Moll here also work for Colonel Jack when, as a young man, he is finally brought before a magistrate on a warrant for 'a notorious Robbery, Burglary, and Murther' and threatened with the horrifying prospect of committal to Newgate (98). Although he is not guilty of these charges, he is in serious danger as he is guilty of related robberies. Jack possesses 'a natural Talent of Talking' (6). Aided by the JP's legal advice that he is not required to identify himself, he successfully argues against his accusers for over an hour—until it is discovered that the warrant is in fact for Captain Jack. At this point, as the JP remarks, Colonel Jack is entitled to sue the constable and the men who arrested him, but Jack settles for their returning to the place of his arrest to publicly declare his innocence: he is 'clear'd with Triumph' (101). Jack's reasoned, formal speech and his calm and respectful demeanour save him from committal to Newgate and raise him in the eyes of the magistrate and himself. He is a pickpocket who lacks both education and wealth, but the dubious implication here is that, with the help of a responsible JP and self-possession, even the poorest citizens can master the skills necessary to triumph against false allegations.

Jack's alarm at the prospect of committal stems from his belief that 'to go to *Newgate*, and to be hang'd were to me, as things which necessarily followed one another' (98). Moll shares this belief: committal to Newgate means 'an infamous Death' (337). She is finally arrested and committed when she is caught leaving a mercer's house with a bundle of silks. Unlike her previous two apprehensions, the circumstances mean she cannot come up with a plausible story: this is not a shop, so she cannot convincingly claim to have intended to pay for the silk. The mercer's wife is sympathetic to her plea that, as no goods had been lost, 'it would be cruel to pursue me to Death', but, with a constable already summoned, the mercer fears trouble for himself if he does not take the matter to a JP (336). Faced with a determined servant as a witness to Moll's intent to exit the house, the JP sends Moll to Newgate. It is this committal, not her arrest, that to Moll signals disaster. Her narrative from this point concerns the horrors of the prison and her progression towards repentance, and analyses of this part of the novel often focus upon these elements.[43] Less noted is that Moll's negotiations with justice are very far from over, and certainly not confined to a climatic trial appearance.[44]

---

[43] For example, G. A. Starr, *Defoe and Spiritual Autobiography* (Princeton, NJ: Princeton University Press, 1965), 155–60; Everett Zimmerman, *Defoe and the Novel* (Berkeley, CA: University of California Press, 1975), 88–96; Faller, *Crime and Defoe*, 122–8.

[44] Everett Zimmerman and Beth Swan both discuss Moll's final trial and her sense that justice can be manipulated. Swan's discussion usefully details the trial process, countering Zimmerman's argument that Moll's trial is legally flawed. Zimmerman, *Defoe and the Novel*, 102–3; Beth Swan, 'Moll Flanders: The Felon as Lawyer', *ECF*, 11:1 (1998), 33–48 (43–4). Gabriel Cervantes examines the legal contexts for transportation in 'Convict Transportation and Penitence in *Moll Flanders*', *ELH*, 78:2 (2011), 315–36. However, caution is needed with the mid eighteenth-century legal sources that these analyses cite to gloss Moll's situation, since her thieving takes place in the 1670s or, in the initially apparent timeline, the early 1700s.

Everyone Moll encounters is aware that, after being committed and even when convicted, those with money and 'Friends' can mitigate the effects of the law. She needs, as her gaoler remarks, 'very good Friends', meaning connections who are willing and able to exert their influence on officials to the point of bribery (349). 'Friends' also, as Moll's husband Jemy explains, means people you have won over through bribery. As Jemy, who is also in Newgate, puts it, 'the making of Friends, and soliciting his Case, had been very expensive' (384). In contrast with Defoe's early pamphlets, there is no inveighing against corruption. Moll is appalled by the depravity of Newgate and by the hypocrisy of the prison's chaplain, but the fact that justice can be bought is treated by all—Moll, Jemy, Moll's ally the Governess, and her gaoler—as an obvious and accepted fact: to them the system is not broken, this is how it functions. Moll fears for her fate as she lacks powerful friends, but she proves to have an astute agent in her Governess. What Moll calls the 'proper Methods' taken by the Governess on her behalf include: (1) attempting to 'tamper' with the two female witnesses; these servants prove, in Moll's words 'hard Hearted'—or honest—and refuse the bribe; (2) going to the mercer and his wife to plead for them to drop the case; this fails because the master has entered into recognisances to prosecute and does not want to lose his money; (3) offering to find 'Friends' to arrange to have the recognisance removed from the record, a step rejected by the master as unsafe (because it is illegal); and (4) attempting to persuade two members of the grand jury not to indict Moll as nothing was taken.[45] A number of these 'proper Methods' were crimes in themselves; others were on the borders of legitimate advocacy.

Moll's conviction and sentencing for felony is not a foregone conclusion since the circumstances offer scope for a sympathetic jury and judge to exercise discretion. She did not use force to enter the mercer's home and is thus not guilty of 'housebreaking' or 'burglary'.[46] She is indeed acquitted of this charge by the jury. The factors against Moll include the value of the goods and her reputation as an 'old Offender' (344). She is indicted for stealing silk worth £46 (350)—far too much for the jury to devalue down to less than one shilling, and so turn a capital felony to a petty larceny. Although sympathetic juries were occasionally known to produce spectacularly low valuations, this was also a theft difficult to value at below 10 shillings, the amount which (for most of the seventeenth century) allowed a convicted female felon to avoid a death sentence by pleading benefit of clergy.[47] The rumour that Moll is a career criminal crucially militates against the judge and jury exercising their influence in her favour, even if her prior crimes are not part of the legal record.[48] The jury convicts her of theft as a felony, making her acquittal for burglary 'small Comfort' since both are capital offences (352). The mercer desires

---

[45] *Moll Flanders*, 340–1, 347–8.

[46] Moll treats these charges as if they were synonymous; see note 30.

[47] Whether Moll was imagined by early readers as on trial in late seventeenth or the early eighteenth century, she did not have the option of pleading clergy. The statute 21 Jac I, c. 6 (1623) allowed women to plead benefit of clergy only for thefts that were below 10 shillings. In 1691, the statute 3 & 4 Wm & M c. 9 that allowed women benefit of clergy on the same terms as men also removed it for all thefts from dwelling houses of the type for which Moll was convicted.

[48] On the role of character, see Beattie, *Crime and the Courts*, 443–4.

mercy be shown in the sentencing (he is depicted all along as uneasy with being the prosecutor), but this request is ignored.

It is only once the death sentence is passed and her options apparently exhausted that Moll becomes penitent. For Moll, this is a process associated not with arguing and negotiation, but with silence. After becoming temporarily 'mute' when asked to speak in her mitigation, she then has 'no Tongue to speak, or Eyes to look up either to God or Man' on hearing the death sentence passed (352–3). Her actual conversion experience is unspeakable: she received 'Impressions ... not to be explain'd by words' upon her soul (355). Yet soon her ability to tell a plausible tale reasserts itself: she is able to recount to an 'honest friendly' minister 'all the Wickedness of my Life ... an Abridgement of this whole History' (355). The minister therefore hears *almost* what Moll's readers have been told—but not all of it. The minister has ostensibly been brought in by the Governess to support Moll in an emotional and religious capacity, yet the Governess has chosen a 'friendly' minister who proves a 'friend' in the sense that Moll has needed all along. He has the influence to get Moll a stay of execution, which she and the minister manage to convert into a pardon on condition of transportation.[49] When *Moll Flanders* was published transportation was newly available as a sentence, a measure of which Defoe evidently approved. Moll, however, is far from approving or accepting her situation. She alludes, in passing, to the fact that she hoped for an absolute pardon: she only offered her 'humble Petition for Transportation'—an appeal for a partial pardon with conditions—when she feared there was a serious risk of her appearing on the next 'dead Warrant' (361). The Governess, however (who was once transported herself but jumped ship in Ireland), is undefeated: 'Did you ever know one in your Life that was Transported, and had a Hundred Pound in his Pocket[?]' (363). This plan to bribe Moll's way out of transportation is abandoned only because she chooses to accompany Jemy, who has agreed to pay for the cost of his own transportation in order to avoid trial for highway robbery. On ship, they are able to use their ill-gotten gains to win over the crew and then to make arrangements to avoid being sold into bondage on arrival. Moll's continual efforts to evade the legal consequences of her actions, together with her readiness to continue to live from stolen money, and to continue to lie to Jemy, to her Virginian son, and to her Governess about her past and present, make her commitment to penitence at best tenuous. Aside from Moll's duplicity, what is striking about her ending is that each end proves to be another opportunity. For determined players such as Moll and the Governess, with verbal facility, money, and some connections, each stage of the legal process becomes the start of a negotiation, not a conclusion.

* * *

---

[49] The process Moll alludes to here is the one in place after 1689: she refers to keeping out of the 'dead Warrant' (a term from the 1690s) that listed those to be executed, and her petition is made via the Recorder of London, a post-Revolution arrangement (361). Cf. Beattie, *Policing and Punishment*, 347, 449.

Historians have argued that the legal system was not perceived as a remote, oppressive institution in this period; the courts were accessible to ordinary people, with the law seen as an arena for 'conflict and compromise'.[50] *Moll Flanders*, *Colonel Jack*, and Defoe's early satires support such an impression. In none of these works is the law portrayed as an unchallengeable or unknowable imposition from above. The satires call for the removal of specific London magistrates (Clayton, Furnese, Lovell) and protest directly to groups of readers ('the Nobility', 'the Gentry', 'the Clergy'), who are blamed for the failed system and deemed capable of altering it. These works convey that all readers, even the poorest, have a role in defining the public opinion that holds the legal system and its representatives to account. In the criminal narratives, significant power lies with officials and the wealthy evade justice, yet responsibility, and indeed power, is widely dispersed. The parties involved in determining arrests and prosecutions in *Moll Flanders* include a range of officials, householders, their relations, servants, and neighbours, along with the 'friends' (by affection and by bribery) of the accused. In convincingly detailing the social dynamics of imagined cases, *Moll Flanders* and *Colonel Jack* show how the problems of administering justice go beyond the laxness or corruption of officials. In certain of these episodes the author's tactics extended to including specific, sometimes cryptic, allusions to real-life magistrates—thereby appealing to a cohort among his readers who had detailed knowledge of London's geography, local legal history, and gossip or printed satire. These allusions ground the practice of justice in real personalities in ways that tend to underscore concerns about the fallibility of the system even when its agents are well intentioned. Surprisingly, given the corrupt London justice excoriated in the satires, Moll and Jack encounter conscientious and equitable magistrates. Yet the outcomes, if 'just' in terms of the circumstances, often remain unjust in the wider context: career criminals go unpunished, while victims go unrecompensed, see their livelihoods almost destroyed, or are labelled as criminals. In *Moll Flanders* and *Colonel Jack*, the qualities that the law is shown to reward—in a criminal, victim, prosecutor, or magistrate—include measured language, improvisation, self-command, and the tactical disclosure of only parts of one's knowledge. The narratives' repeated, if tacit, advice to readers is that the law favours not the innocent or truth-tellers, but skilful storytellers. Fittingly for an author who had found himself prosecuted more than once, Defoe's writings also caution readers against the presumption that they can easily remain on the right side of the law or aloof from its workings. Readers of his pamphlets, journals, and narratives are assumed to be deeply interested in the judicial system because they are at risk of becoming both victims and perpetrators of crime, and because—as prosecutors and as members of a public who hold local officials to account—they must serve as enforcers of the law.

---

[50] Oberwittler, 'Crime and Authority', 24; Beattie, *Crime and the Courts*, 197, 622.

Further Reading

Paula R. Backscheider, *Daniel Defoe: His Life* (Baltimore, MD: Johns Hopkins University Press, 1989).

J. M. Beattie, *Crime and the Courts in England 1660–1800* (Princeton, NJ: Princeton University Press, 1986).

J. M. Beattie, *Policing and Punishment in London, 1660–1750: Urban Crime and the Limits of Terror* (Oxford: Oxford University Press, 2001).

Lincoln B. Faller, *Crime and Defoe: A New Kind of Writing* (Cambridge: Cambridge University Press, 1993).

Aparna Gollapudi, 'Criminal Children in the Eighteenth Century and Defoe's *Colonel Jack*', *PQ*, 96:1 (2017), 27–53.

Norma Landau, *The Justices of the Peace, 1679–1760* (Berkeley, CA: University of California Press, 1984).

Norma Landau (ed.), *Law, Crime and English Society, 1660–1830* (Cambridge: Cambridge University Press, 2002).

Kate Loveman, '"A Life of Continu'd Variety": Crime, Readers, and the Structure of Defoe's *Moll Flanders*', *ECF*, 26:1 (2013), 1–32.

Dietrich Oberwittler, 'Crime and Authority in Eighteenth Century England: Law Enforcement on the Local Level', *Historical Social Research / Historische Sozialforschung*, 15:2 (1990), 3–34.

Beth Swan, 'Moll Flanders: The Felon as Lawyer', *ECF*, 11:1 (1998), 33–48.

CHAPTER 24

RACIAL AND NATIONAL IDENTITIES IN DEFOE'S WRITINGS

SRIVIDHYA SWAMINATHAN

To speak of race and nation in Daniel Defoe's writing is to speak of concepts in flux. For one, his sense of Englishness is situated in broader ideas about Britishness and Europeanness [SEE CHAPTERS 27 AND 28]. The traits associated with these various groups are often compared to 'Other' groups of 'foreign' or 'savage' or 'barbarous' origins.[1] However, none of his opinions about racial or national character appear fixed and often come into conflict within the same work. While Defoe offers many declaratives that categorize humans by race or nation, his ideas are not easily defined. He is better understood as creating mutable conceptual frameworks in response to developing ideas about hierarchies of civilization in which different ethnic, cultural, or national communities are situated. Indeed, his work is filled with more contradictions than truisms, so to attempt to find *a singular* sense of national or racial identity throughout his fiction and non-fiction would be a futile endeavour. Instead, a more fruitful enquiry might be had by following Roxann Wheeler's example in 'examining what constitute[es] human difference and how it [is] narrated' in Defoe's poetry and prose.[2] These works, regardless of genre, demonstrate the conflation of nation and race, the contradictions inherent in descriptions of specific peoples, and the burgeoning justifications for colonialism and imperialism that would form the backbone of English and British identity in the later part of the eighteenth century.

---

[1] An excellent study of the figure of the 'wild man', particularly relevant to Defoe's *Robinson Crusoe* (1719), is Richard Nash's *Wild Enlightenment: The Borders of Human Identity in the Eighteenth Century* (Charlottesville, VA: University of Virginia Press, 2003).

[2] Roxann Wheeler, *The Complexion of Race: Categories of Difference in Eighteenth-Century British Culture* (Philadelphia, PA: University of Pennsylvania Press, 2000), 6.

The complex sociopolitical context of Defoe's writing has been detailed in many excellent biographies.[3] Most relevant to the development of ideas of race and nation in Defoe are the accession to the throne of the Dutch William III in 1689, the Act of Union in 1707, and the strong commercial investment in colonial expansion in both the East and the West [SEE CHAPTERS 29 AND 30]. As *The True-Born Englishman* (1700/1) indicates, Defoe spoke with some approval of the mixing of peoples, specifically people of European origin. His notion of the English race and nation developed from a strong sense of pride in the enormous potential of the many 'peoples' of the British Isles to exert their control over the world stage. His enthusiastic support of the Act of Union binding England and Wales with Scotland stemmed from the new possibilities for commerce and the ability to combine resources for the benefit of the whole nation.[4] While Defoe's writing continued to address 'England' and the 'English', he used the terms as a shorthand for the whole island. For example, in the preface to *A Plan of the English Commerce* (1728), Defoe encompassed the 'British Dominions' in advocating for 'British commerce'. He also stated, 'Nothing is to me more evident, than that the civilizing the Nations where we and other Europeans *are already settled; bringing the naked Savages to Clothe, and instructing barbarous Nations how to live, has had a visible Effect already*.'[5] This statement reveals the mutability of race and nation as identities in a series of nested concepts. The British nested within a wider European context are marked as 'civilized' in contrast to wider global communities whom Europeans have an obligation to civilize.

The ideas concerning the conjunction of civilization and commerce outlined in his non-fiction form the backbone of Defoe's explorations of race, nation, and identity. Much of Defoe's fiction focuses on encounters with 'Others' and draws on national as well as racial stereotypes that are recognizable but not fixed. In *An Humble Proposal to the People of England* (1729), he comments admiringly on the ability of European countries to colonize and tame parts of the world. He mentions the Portuguese and their expansive empire stretching from Brazil to Africa to the East Indies. In the colonies of South America and Africa, 'the *Portuguese* have so civilized the Natives, and black Inhabitants of the Country, as to bring them, where they went even stark-naked as before, to clothe decently and modestly now, and to delight to do so'.[6] Defoe's comment demonstrates a hierarchical view of difference, but one that seems to intertwine the racial and the national. The distinction he makes between 'Native' and 'black' recognizes that different peoples occupy these varied geographic spaces, though both are able to change. Not only are they able to change, but they 'delight' in doing so. Accordingly, this essay explores the multifaceted representations of racial and national identity in Defoe's

---

[3] Backscheider, *Daniel Defoe*; Novak, *Daniel Defoe*; Richetti, *Life of Daniel Defoe*; Furbank and Owens, *Political Biography*.

[4] See Novak, *Daniel Defoe*, 319–23.

[5] Defoe, *A Plan of the English Commerce*, ed. John McVeagh, *PEW*, vii. 120.

[6] Defoe, *An Humble Proposal to the People of England for the Encrease of their Trade and the Encouragement of their Manufactures* (1729), 27. The context of the proposal was the ongoing trade war with Spain, which is why Defoe focused so much on colonial expansion. See Novak, *Daniel Defoe*, 688–9.

work to illustrate the interwoven frameworks or categories Defoe used to make sense of his world.

Englishmen: Nation and Race

For Defoe, the English represented the pinnacle of the civilizational order and had a God-given right to export their brand of civilization around the world. In *Maps of Englishness*, Simon Gikandi states: 'Questions of Englishness cannot be discussed except in relation to different forms of colonial alterity'.[7] Perhaps a better understanding of Defoe might be had by glossing his depictions of 'colonial alterity' with the concomitant discourses of civil society, servitude, and slavery. For however individualistic Defoe's characters may seem, their stories emphasize the manner in which they engage and navigate social networks in free and unfree conditions. For Defoe, race maps more clearly on to notions of civility and the advancement of civilization to which *all* nations are subject. How else could the Portuguese accustom people who were naked to enjoy being dressed? However, this hierarchy of civility does not exempt Europe from similar categorization and critique. Defoe does not define Englishness through alterity; rather, he measures all alterity, including European, by its degree of difference from Englishness.

In his political writings and adventure fiction, Defoe advocated for English commerce as necessary both to the prosperity of the nation and to the proper ordering of the civilized world. His works could be read as motivational in encouraging the English to take their rightful place in global enterprise. As Paula Backscheider states, Defoe 'virtually invented modern political propaganda' and that propaganda operated to influence behaviour both within and outside of the boundaries of nation.[8] As a 'spokesperson for the new world order of English Enlightenment', Defoe's writing adopted an authoritative voice on the peoples of the world.[9] In *An Humble Proposal to the People of England*, Defoe charges his countrymen with 'Indolence and Neglect' for falling behind the Portuguese, Dutch, French, and Spanish in their colonial acquisitions. He argues for further development of existing commercial ventures, such as factories on the West African coast [SEE CHAPTER 31]. He asks why the 'factories' have not been converted to 'populous and powerful Colonies, as they might be?'. Instead, England's factories are 'left to be ravag'd by the naked and contemptible Negroes'.[10] Defoe's statement performs

---

[7] Simon Gikandi, *Maps of Englishness: Writing Identity in the Culture of Colonialism* (New York: Columbia University Press, 1996), 50.

[8] Paula R. Backscheider, 'Defoe: The Man in the Works', in *The Cambridge Companion to Daniel Defoe*, ed. John Richetti (Cambridge: Cambridge University Press, 2008), 5–24 (5).

[9] Srinivas Aravamudan, 'Defoe, Commerce, and Empire', in *Cambridge Companion to Daniel Defoe*, ed. Richetti, 45–63 (46).

[10] Defoe, *Humble Proposal*, 45.

two kinds of dismissal of African sovereignty in their own lands. His characterization of the natives as 'naked and contemptible' strips them literally and figuratively of respect. On some level, this is a propagandistic move to stir English enterprise; however, it also reveals a bias against what he perceives as a less developed civilization. The 'ravaging' also negates claims that local communities have a native right to the property on which the 'factories' are built. This colonialist tactic of diminishing and dismissing indigenous Africans plays directly into developing discourses of national identity and the racial hierarchies of civilization.

However, even Defoe's sense of Englishness is not easily classified or always in touch with civilization.[11] In the 'Explanatory Preface' to *The True-Born Englishman*, Defoe states that an '*Unmix'd Nation*' is '*to Our Disadvantage*' because '*we have three Nations about us as clear from Mixtures of Blood, as any in the World, and I know not which of them I could wish our selves to be like*' (SFS, i. 79). His disparaging of the Scots, Welsh, and Irish on the grounds of 'racial purity' creates a curious slippage between notions of race and nation. The two terms appear synonymous, yet in contradiction, his view of the 'Other' separates race and nation (for example, Africans are a race, not a nation). For Defoe, there are decided limits to the valuing of a mixed nation. The many kinds of knowledge gained from European invaders creates a fluid, adaptive, and hybridized society. Yet, Defoe is aware that mixing with non-European groups is fraught with complications and failures.[12] So, to understand Defoe's concept of 'national identity', one needs to explore how he writes about 'nation' and 'character'.

Both *The True-Born Englishman* and *An Humble Proposal* lay out particular qualities of the Englishman that carry through Defoe's fictional work. *The True-Born Englishman* is a response to John Tutchin's attack on William III in *The Foreigners* (1700), and the poem outlines Defoe's particular worldview about the space and place of the English.[13] Defoe's mocking dismissal of the notion of pure descent negates the value of lineage in the idea of Englishness. Linda Colley characterizes his purpose as both 'deflating English conceit' and mounting 'a powerful demonstration of English confidence' over the Scots, Welsh, and Irish.[14] Defoe demonstrates and valorizes the mixed European ancestry of the English and their ability to absorb new forms of tradition. These new forms lead to a singular understanding of commerce and manufacturing that privileges the trader over the aristocrat. Srinivas Aravamudan's analysis of the poem in *Tropicopolitans* shows that 'the mongrel origins of "Englishness" get reworked into subtle dreams of imperialist mastery through transcultural subordination of Angles, Saxons, Normans,

---

[11] For example, Captain Singleton decidedly rejects his own 'English' identity when questioned by William the Quaker.

[12] Defoe does demonstrate an awareness of this mixing in Roxana's liaison with the foreign prince and the mention of Crusoe's friend who married an 'Indian wife' in the *Farther Adventures*. Crusoe's attempt to encourage mixing in his failed attempt to start a colony in *Farther Adventures* seems like a more positive representation, but I would argue these depictions are more for titillation than demonstration.

[13] See Novak, *Daniel Defoe*, 148–57 for the political occasion of this poem.

[14] Linda Colley, *Britons: Forging the Nation, 1707–1837* (New Haven, CT: Yale University Press, 1992), 15.

Scots, Picts, Welsh, and a host of others'.[15] In this poem, Defoe asks, 'why should not our neighbors be as good as we to derive from?', indicating that the English are not privileged over other Europeans by lineage. Defoe asserts that among '*all the Nations of* Europe ... *those Nations which are most mix'd, are the best, and have the least of Barbarism and Brutality about them*' (*SFS*, i. 79). In this surprising assertion, Defoe links ethnic mixing with greater sophistication and civility. However, he does not generally advocate ethnic mixing to civilize 'Native' and 'African'; those tasks can be accomplished through teaching alone.

What is more interesting is the turn Defoe makes to describe the qualities of unmixed European nations. His poem presents a litany of stereotypes about other European nations, carefully marking the negative qualities associated with their national characters.[16] The Devil presides over these misguided nations, deploying the seven deadly sins to infest each of their characters. The Spanish are plagued by 'Pride', the Italians by 'Lust', the Germans by 'Drunkeness', and so forth. England, by contrast, 'unpeopled lay' and became 'prey' to every invader. However, these invaders seeded the country with strengths through what Defoe characterizes as racial mixing:

> From whose mixt Relicks our compounded Breed,
> By Spurious Generation does succeed;
> Making a Race uncertain and unev'n,
> Deriv'd from all the Nations under heav'n. (lines 171–4; *SFS*, i. 89–90)

In these lines, Defoe demonstrates a slippage between racial, ethnic, and national identity. England is a nation of 'uncertain and uneven' peoples, but tracing true lines of descent is 'to value that which all wise men deride' (line 369; *SFS*, i. 95). While nations in Europe possess many negative traits, they are still unified by greater advancement over 'barbarous' or 'Savage' nations. Since England is a mix of all these groups, however 'uncertain and unev'n', they have the advantage of being less barbarous and brutal. Defoe consistently depicts civilizing as an aspirational quality to which all 'nations' must ascribe.

In *Captain Singleton* (1720), Defoe demonstrates the slippage of qualities associated with the interwoven concepts of race, nation, and civilization. At the opening of the novel, Bob Singleton recounts that he was kidnapped as a child and his only link to his lineage is his appearance: Singleton recounts that he was 'very well dress'd, [and] had a Nursery Maid to tend me'.[17] In this manner, Defoe erases any possibility of Singleton's tracing a pure lineage and presents his subsequent peripatetic childhood

---

[15] Srinivas Aravamudan, *Tropicopolitans: Colonialism and Agency, 1688–1804* (Durham, N.C.: Duke University Press, 1999), 91. Interestingly, Aravamudan links Defoe's negation of 'true-born' as opening the way for later eighteenth-century figures, specifically Olaudah Equiano, to claim Englishness.

[16] Defoe dismisses all the 'Pagan World' as under the Devil's sway. He does enumerate the sins of the Chinese, Persian, Moor, Tartar, and Jewish, perhaps as an inadvertent gesture towards cultural equality.

[17] Defoe, *The Life, Adventures, and Pyracies, of the Famous Captain Singleton*, ed. Shiv K. Kumar (Oxford: Oxford University Press, 1969), 1.

as a form of ethnic mixing. He is successively the son of a 'Beggar-Woman', a 'Gypsey', on the Parish accounts, and apprenticed to a 'Master of a Ship'. As Bob settles into life on board ship, his interactions with other nations resemble the prejudices of *The True-Born Englishman*. His ship is captured; his master is injured and 'very barbarously used by the *Turks*' until the ship is captured again by a Portuguese man of war (3). Though liberated from the 'barbarous' Turks, Singleton does not fare much better with the Portuguese. He is apprenticed to the ship's pilot from whom he learns to cheat. He describes the Portuguese as 'a Nation the most perfidious and the most debauch'd, the most insolent and cruel, of any that pretend to call themselves Christians, in the World' (6). Defoe's sense of competition with other imperial powers is the likely cause for this vilification of the Portuguese. Singleton is relentless in his discussion of their national character: 'Thieving, Lying, Swearing, Forswearing, joined to the most abominable Lewdness', he states, and later pronounces that 'they were generally speaking the most compleat Cowards that I ever met with' (6). At this early point in his narrative, Singleton views himself as English. He states, ''tis natural to an *Englishman* to hate a Coward, it all joined together to make the Devil and a *Portuguese* equally my Aversion' (7).

Captain Singleton provides numerous examples of the gradations of civility among the European 'races'. While Defoe begins with the premise that European nations are superior in commerce and trade to other parts of the world, he also acknowledges their flaws. During the incident with the slaving vessel, which will be discussed in greater detail later, Singleton is determined to discover what manner of 'whites' owned the vessel. The Africans do not speak any European language, but one makes clear that '[their enslavers] did not speak the same Language we spoke, nor the same our *Portuguese* spoke; so that in all Probability they must be *French* or *Dutch*' (161). When they decipher one man's story about a 'white man' who 'abused' (that is, raped) his wife and sixteen-year-old daughter, Singleton concludes the man was French, perhaps in keeping with the 'Ungoverned Passion' that is their national character.

Singleton is perhaps well positioned to critique other European powers because he has no claim to a home. He is constantly on the move during his narrative and relates to people essentially in terms of their use value. While he does create differing standards based on national and ethnic identifications, he is not keen to be associated with a particular identity. He calls himself an Englishman, but the identity is worn lightly. When he encounters the naked Englishman in the African interior, the Englishman is overjoyed at finding a fellow countryman; however, the enthusiasm is one-sided. Singleton feels no national affinity towards this man. This indifference to national identity carries through to the end of the novel when his companion, William, the Quaker, asks, 'art not thou an *Englishman?*'. Singleton's response is noteworthy: 'Yes, *says I*, I think so: you see I speak *English*; but I came out of *England* a Child, and never was in it but once since I was a Man, and then I was cheated and imposed upon, and used so ill, that I care not if I never see it more' (256–7).[18] In a sense, being born of a place does not guarantee

---

[18] William has a similar and rich dialogue with a Dutchman they encounter on their journey. For a full discussion of that incident and its implications for Defoe's understanding of slavery, see Srividhya

association with or loyalty towards it. Perhaps the place needs to earn the right to be identified with? As Ian Newman states: 'Singleton's rejection of geographical affiliation contains the possibility of a non-territorialized subjectivity that calls into question the naturalized discourse of the social contract, and assumptions of affiliation grounded in place and property'.[19] Singleton complicates both racial and national identification by this rejection of place.

This slippage between nation and race can be seen in Defoe's depiction of European characters. The sliding scale of civility to which Singleton refers maps onto the earlier commentary in *The True-Born Englishman*, without referring to fixed categories. As a contrast, in *Robinson Crusoe* the Portuguese are portrayed as kind and generous. The takeaway lesson might be that Defoe's sense of national identity ascribed almost exclusively to European nations the markers of higher degrees of civilization. The same distinction of nation does not seem to apply when Defoe writes characters of 'colonial alterity'. Perhaps to engage more fully with Defoe's nuanced construction of 'race' we need to consider his 'Other' characters in conjunction with emerging concepts of civilized society, servitude, and slavery. Defoe is a significant contributor to multiple discourses and is an 'influencer' of his time. In both non-fiction and fiction, his ideas about nation, identity, civility, and the innate capacities of man develop to serve a consistent ideology of commerce and empire.

Enslavement and Racial Identity

What complicates the notion of 'racial' identity in Defoe is that, as critics, we continue to look to his portrayal of 'Negro', 'African', 'Turk', and others only in terms of racial identity. However, George Boulukos comments in his reading of *Colonel Jack* (1722) that it is 'self-consciously set in a moment when racial categories are inchoate'.[20] The vague nature of the category is partly the result of a slippage of terminology. The *OED* provides a broad definition of 'race': 'An ethnic group, regarded as showing a common origin and descent; a tribe, nation, or people regarded as of common stock'.[21] The idea of common descent is integral to the construction of race and nation, so naming one set of identities as racial and one as national becomes thorny. Boulukos argues that 'race only becomes distinct from xenophobia when it is systematic, a primary category of identity, and

---

Swaminathan, 'Defoe's *Captain Singleton*: A Study of Enslavement', in *Invoking Slavery in the Eighteenth-Century British Imagination*, ed. Swaminathan and Adam R. Beach (Burlington, VT: Ashgate, 2013), 57–74.

[19] Ian Newman, 'Property, History, and Identity in Defoe's *Captain Singleton*', *SEL*, 51:3 (2011), 565–83 (570).

[20] George Boulukos, 'Daniel Defoe's *Colonel Jack*, Grateful Slaves, and Racial Difference', *ELH*, 68:3 (2001), 615–31 (615).

[21] 'race', n., *Oxford English Dictionary*. (Accessed 21 February 2019).

when it allows for systematic denigration of a given group or groups'.²² Defoe's writing demonstrates xenophobia with respect to his commentary on other European nations and the hierarchy among the 'civilized'. His depiction of non-European peoples lacks the nuances of distinction in civility; however, the question remains whether lack of civilization constitutes 'systematic denigration' so as to create a separate category called race. A clearer distinction might be drawn in looking at the relationship between servitude and enslavement. Roxann Wheeler maps out similarities in the obligations expected of the enslaved and servants, making qualities like 'gratitude' less convincing as a marker of enslavement. She points out that, 'historically, we are still in a world where power relations, while understood broadly as systemic, were thought about as interpersonal'.²³ The varied individual interactions described in Defoe's fiction demonstrate a fluidity in the construction of racial and national identities.

For both Boulukos and Wheeler, 'racial' is coded primarily in relation to enslavement, specifically New World enslavement. An examination of slavery in Defoe's fiction does support this conclusion as his characters encounter 'Others' either already enslaved or intended to be enslaved. However, what constitutes slavery and the association of that term with multiple states of being complicates any discussion of 'racial identity' in Defoe's fiction.²⁴ From the Hobbesian perspective, slavery is a consequence of war and the inability of the individual to accept sovereign authority. Hobbes elided the difference between voluntary and involuntary service by introducing the concept of 'Covenant' in response to conquest: 'It is not therefore the Victory, that giveth the right of Dominion over the Vanquished, but his own Covenant'.²⁵ Mary Nyquist, in her thorough examination of chattel slavery, states: 'While terminology was in comparative flux until the mid to latter seventeenth century, racialized distinctions between term-limited and permanent servitude had been established in the early stages of settlement, with irreversible status—a crucial attribute of chattel slavery—automatically assigned to enslaved Africans'.²⁶ For Nyquist, Hobbesian distinctions between slavery and servitude allow for the differing treatment of those coming under the dominion of the sovereign, and racial identity comes to take on a particular meaning in terms of length of service.

Both Hobbes and Locke in their theorizing about civil society, its relation to the monarchy, and its duty to the citizenry, ruminate on the concepts of servire (to serve) and

---

[22] George Boulukos, *The Grateful Slave: The Emergence of Race in Eighteenth-Century British and American Culture* (Cambridge: Cambridge University Press, 2008), 40.

[23] Roxann Wheeler, 'Powerful Affections: Slaves, Servants, and Labours of Love in Defoe's Writing', in *Defoe's Footprints: Essays in Honour of Maximillian E. Novak*, ed. Robert M. Maniquis and Carl Fisher (Toronto: University of Toronto Press, 2009), 126–52 (143).

[24] For a discussion of the varying usages of the term 'slavery' across the eighteenth century, see the introduction to *Invoking Slavery in the Eighteenth-Century British Imagination*, ed. Swaminathan and Beach, 1–19.

[25] Thomas Hobbes, *Leviathan* (1651), ed. Noel Malcolm, 3 vols (Oxford: Clarendon Press, 2012), ii. 312.

[26] Mary Nyquist, *Arbitrary Rule: Slavery, Tyranny, and the Power of Life and Death* (Chicago, IL: University of Chicago Press, 2013), 316. For a full discussion of Hobbes, see Ch. 9, 'Hobbes, Slavery, and Despotical Rule', 293–325.

servare (to save). These verbs form the crux of the distinction between those who voluntarily surrender their rights to the monarch and those whose rights are withheld, creating a distinction between servitude and slavery. In chapter 20 of *Leviathan*, Hobbes establishes two types of dominion, Paternal and by right of Conquest: 'Dominion acquired by Conquest, or Victory in war, … is the Dominion of the Master over his Servant'.[27] The distinction between servitude and slavery, therefore, lies in the willing acceptance or covenant with the Master; in a reversal, the servant is 'unbound' by his covenant while the slave is 'bound' by a lack. Nyquist argues that 'by reformulating the opposition between unbound and bound servant as one between servant and slave, Hobbes prepares the way for … the commodification of the enslaved'.[28] Conquest without covenant, for Hobbes, sets the stage for chattel slavery, which can only be maintained through a perpetual fear as the slave serves out of necessity, not desire. And, as the state of nature is predicated on perpetual war, the slave retains his right to resist and rebel. Locke takes up this Hobbesian formulation of the state of nature and associates slavery with war. Enslavement as a condition of war is antithetical to civil society, which eschews war as a means of self-preservation. However, Locke must also accommodate the burgeoning plantation society in the Americas. Though Hobbes's and Locke's theories are equally conflicted, both tacitly endorse war slavery and the absolute authority of the master over the life and death of the slave.[29] These ideas resonate in Defoe's fiction as fear of enslavement extends to all peoples, but only some people qualify for what Defoe regarded as legitimate enslavement.

For Defoe, 'war slavery' is a category to which all peoples are subject; however, he makes significant regional distinctions that begin to develop arguments for racialized identities in enslavement. Several of his novels demonstrate anxiety about being enslaved by the Barbary States or Turks. The awareness of British sailors being captured and enslaved likely came from the titillating narratives published in England.[30] The very real threat of enslavement for the English sailor is recognized immediately by Bob Singleton when he is marooned for mutiny off the East African coast. Similarly, Crusoe is taken as a 'slave' by a Turkish man-of-war on his second voyage as a 'Guinea trader'. For Crusoe, the condition of enslavement is anathema, but he is very comfortable with exercising mastery. Even as he escapes bondage, he takes on a Muslim 'servant' boy named Xury.[31] He escapes along the African coast, which he calls 'the truly *Barbarian* Coast, where whole Nations of Negroes were sure to surround us with their Canoes and destroy us' (22). Defoe uses an undifferentiated 'Nation' to characterize 'Negroes'

---

[27] Hobbes, *Leviathan*, ii. 312.

[28] Nyquist, *Arbitrary Rule*, 318.

[29] See Nyquist, *Arbitrary Rule*, 326–61 (Ch. 10, ' Locke's "Of Slavery", Despotical Power, and Tyranny'), and William Uzgalis, 'John Locke, Racism, Slavery, and Indian Lands', in *The Oxford Handbook of Philosophy and Race*, ed. Naomi Zack (Oxford: Oxford University Press, 2017), 21–30.

[30] See Adam R. Beach, 'The Good-Treatment Debate, Comparative Slave Studies, and the "Adventures" of T. S.', in *Invoking Slavery in the Eighteenth-Century British Imagination*, ed. Swaminathan and Beach, 21–36.

[31] Daniel Defoe, *Robinson Crusoe* (New York: The Modern Library, 2001), 21.

as a people, but they are to be feared. These are not a people with whom Crusoe feels he can negotiate or survive. Their state of (in)civility marks them as racialized and in later works, like *Colonel Jack* and its depiction of the American plantation economy, also marks them as more suitable for perpetual enslavement.

Another example shows more clearly how racial identity intersects with national identity in the state of slavery, which occurs with a very minor character in *Roxana* (1724). While she is the mistress of the '*Foreign Prince*', Roxana is presented with a 'little Female *Turkish* Slave'.[32] The history of the Turkish slave is given succinctly: 'the *Malthese* Man of War had, it seems, taken a *Turkish* Vessel ... in which were some Ladies bound for *Grand Cairo* in *Egypt*; and as the Ladies were made Slaves, so their fine Cloaths were thus expos'd' (193). One ship 'taken' by another provides the basis for the woman's loss of freedom as well as property in the form of her fine clothes. Roxana never questions the validity of this transaction, and this enslaved woman serves as a cultural interlocutor for Roxana, teaching her the speech and dress of her nation, which Roxana makes use of as a disguise in Paris. Roxana parasitizes the identity of her slave, literally and figuratively embodying the 'Turk', and then abandons her in Paris with no comment about what becomes of her. Just as with the term 'negro', this woman has no other name or identity than Turkish or Turk, yet her level of civility is more commensurate with the European. While 'Turk' clearly marks a national, or at least a religious, identity, does her enslavement also mark her as a racial 'Other'? Roxana's ability to assume her identity in disguise presents an answer, as does Singleton's experience being characterized as a Turk.

The conflict between service and slavery in the guise of racialized identity appears in *Captain Singleton* as well. The Portuguese pilot who takes him on as a servant refuses to compensate Singleton for any of the work, treating him as a slave rather than a servant. When Singleton complains to a priest, 'It was all one; neither the Priest or any one else could prevail with him, but that I was not his Servant but his Slave; that he took me in the *Algerine*; and that I was a *Turk*, only pretended to be an *English* Boy, to get my Liberty, and he would carry me to the Inquisition as a *Turk*' (8). The competing stories are interesting here, as the Pilot is technically telling the truth that Singleton was taken from Turkish ship. In that instance, Singleton is subject to war slavery through an act of conquest, but that conquest is mediated by national and ethnic affiliation. A Turk is enslaved, but an Englishman and fellow European is at liberty to serve. The mutability of both national and racial identity is clear if he can also accuse Singleton of merely playing English. Singleton is only entitled to wages as a European, but he has 'nobody to vouch for him' and prove his background. The complexity of enslavement as a racial marker also rests in the condition of slavery. Defoe makes no real distinction in the type of enslavement Singleton endures with the Pilot beyond his lack of wages. However, when Singleton is accused of treason by another ship's captain, which is punishable by death or exile, his 'master' intercedes on his behalf but has no control over Singleton's life. This

---

[32] Defoe, *Roxana*, ed. Melissa Mowry (Peterborough, ON: Broadview Press, 2009), 131.

incident can be read as challenging chattel slavery, as no masters appear to have actual control over life and death.

A similar moment of capture and enslavement is recounted in *Colonel Jack*. While transportation to the American colonies is a suitable punishment for criminals (as seen in *Moll Flanders*), the irony of Jack's position is that (though a criminal) he is kidnapped into transportation. After he and his companions realize they have been duped, they confront the captain who informs them they are 'Servants to be deliver'd at *Maryland*' to a specific man and were brought on board 'by the Owner's Agent'.[33] The implication of this statement points to a kind of slave trade operating in England that procured unwitting 'English' servants. Jack does not make a distinction between servitude and slavery when he informs the captain that 'we were not People to be sold for Slaves'; rather, they are 'Men of Substance' (162). In Jack's formulation, slavery is a condition to which Englishmen are susceptible through poverty. This comment shows awareness of debt slavery and indentured servitude in England. However, there is a visible lack of consent by these men that puts Jack in a liminal status when he does arrive in Maryland.

By contrast, Bob Singleton's narrative demonstrates a more profound association of race, inherent in the term 'Negro', and chattel slavery, albeit one mediated by his own lack of stability. In his trek across the continent, he demonstrates a belligerent attitude towards Africans and seeks to assert his mastery. He advises his crew 'to quarrel with some of the Negro Natives, take ten or twelve of them Prisoners, and binding them as Slaves, cause them to travel with us'. He proposes using the doctrine of war slavery for their convenience, which is rejected. But thankfully, 'we found some Knavery among them at last' (51). Perhaps to avoid any accusation of despotism, Singleton is required to find a premise, in this case 'Knavery', to justify the act of conquest and enslavement. There is no pretence for demanding servitude, of course, as the Europeans are also destitute and need to rely on forced labour. Defoe takes great pains to establish Singleton's poor upbringing as the possible reason behind some of his more mercenary tendencies. In this instance, Singleton operates from a point of self-preservation that sees the 'Negroes' in terms of use value. However, he can also concede that they possess kindness, generosity, and nobility of spirit, as in the case of the African Prince.[34] For Singleton, there is a civilizational divide that does not translate to a lack of humanity. In contrast to the later writing about 'African' peoples, he acknowledges that they are capable of the same range of personal attributes as Europeans.[35]

When he encounters the slave ship adrift in the ocean, Singleton displays the same confused association of Africans as the objects of chattel slavery who still manage to retain their humanity. Singleton and his crew respond first with fear when encountering

---

[33] Daniel Defoe, *Colonel Jack*, ed. Gabriel Cervantes and Geoffrey Sill (Peterborough, ON: Broadview Press, 2016), 160, 161.

[34] See Laura Brown, 'Defoe's "Black Prince": Elitism, Capitalism, and Cultural Difference', in *Defoe's Footprints*, ed. Maniquis and Fisher, 153–69 for an excellent reading of this incident in Singleton's story.

[35] See Peter Knox-Shaw, 'Defoe and the Politics of Representing the African Interior', *MLR*, 96:4 (2001), 937–51.

the 'Multitude of black Sailors' aboard the ship that looks adrift. When they board, he notices that there was 'not one Christian, or white Man, on board' (156). The category of 'white' is open to interpretation here, as 'Christian' seems to be a label broadly applicable across complexions. He later associates 'white' with European. In the following quotation, Singleton and William, the Quaker, each seek to influence the crew on what to do with people on the ship.

> I was struck with Horror at the Sight, for immediately I concluded, as was partly the Case, that these black Devils had got loose, had murthered all the white Men, and thrown them into the Sea; and I had no sooner told my Mind to the Men, but the Thought of it so enraged them, that I had much ado to keep my Men from cutting them all in Pieces. But *William*, with many Perswasions prevailed upon them, by telling of them, that it was nothing but what, if they were in the Negroes Condition, they would do if they could; and that the Negroes had really the highest Injustice done them, to be sold for Slaves without their Consent; and that the Law of Nature dictated it to them; that they ought not to kill them, and that it would be wilful Murder to do it. (156–7)

While Singleton's reaction seems in keeping with his perception of 'black Devils', William's comments stem partly from Quaker pacifism and partly from Hobbes (later, he also demonstrates a commercial savvy in proposing to sell the slaves when they get to the Caribbean). Describing the sailors' potential actions as 'wilful Murder' in retaliation for the obvious overthrow of the 'white' masters of the ship legitimizes the actions of the enslaved. Slaves have the right to rebel. To make his point, William presents the radical idea of empathizing with the 'Negroes Condition', one which they could share. The 'Injustice' done to them lies in the lack of 'Consent', tying the condition of enslavement to the radical notion of an illegitimate slavery. The idea that consent is needed to enslave 'Negroes' reframes Singleton's actions in Africa as legitimate conquest versus the sense that Africans on board the slave ship may have been kidnapped (therefore making them potentially like Colonel Jack).

Jack's experience on the plantation provides a clearer sense of how slavery becomes racialized through the contrast with servitude. When his 'master' learns how he came to the plantation, he acknowledges that Jack has been wronged. In his initial encounters on the plantation with the Master and the overseer, Jack sees himself as a 'poor half naked Slave'; he is performing the same labour and dressed in the same manner as the 'Negroes' on the plantation (172).[36] However, Jack is quickly promoted to 'overseer', which takes him out of the category of slave and places him in a new category of service. When Jack comments that he cannot be an overseer as he 'has no Cloaths to put on', he is provided with clothing and the injunction to dress in a room: 'go in there a Slave, and come out

---

[36] Dennis Todd provides an excellent reading of this 'conversion' of Jack from slave to master as predicated on taking Africans from 'savagery to civility'. *Defoe's America* (Cambridge: Cambridge University Press, 2010), 76–117.

a Gentleman' (172, 173). The sartorial distinction not only frees him from bondage, but also elevates his social status by connecting him to civility. Dress in the New World seems to be a marker of difference between enslaved and free. Clothing is a common marker of civilization throughout Defoe's novels. Thus, in removing from a condition of enslavement, Jack is marked not only by his dress, but also by his ability *to dress*.

As he develops his slave management style, Jack's perceptions of 'Negroes' also complicate received racial categories. Just as the African Prince in *Captain Singleton* is ennobled by his behaviour and Europeanized through his contact with 'whites',[37] the 'Negroes' on Jack's plantation benefit from his benign rule. When he is accused of being too lenient in refraining from whipping slaves, Jack asks, 'How cou'd I use this Terrible Weapon on the naked Flesh of my Fellow Servants, as well as Fellow Creatures?' (179). Jack's question comes from a feeling of camaraderie with those occupying the space of servant and slave. While Jack acknowledges different personality tendencies in the 'Negroes', he also takes 'whites' to task for their approach to management. Chattel slavery is founded on a principle of violence because there is no other impetus to work on behalf of the master. Yet, Jack's management style that alternates fear with 'Mercy' is intended to introduce a new form of governance to the plantation economy.[38] Though he never questions the legitimacy of African enslavement, he does offer this evaluation of their character:

> They had no Passion, no Affection to Act upon, but that of Fear, which necessarily brought Hatred with it; but that if they were used with Compassion, they would Serve with Affection, as well as other Servants: Nature is the same, and Reason Governs in just Proportions in all Creatures; But having never been let Taste what Mercy is, they know not how to act from a Principle of Love. (187–8)

Defoe does create racialized categories in drawing distinctions between 'white' and 'Negro' servants, but he also acknowledges a common humanity. In other words, his category is racialized only inasmuch as the practice of chattel slavery has created a difference between 'white' and 'black'.

When Colonel Jack is tricked into travelling to the American colonies as a bond servant, he is a complete stranger to plantation culture. After he is 'purchased', he asserts that 'The Master whose Service I was now gaged in, was a Man of Substance and Figure in the Country, and had Abundance of Servants, as well as *Negroes*, as *English*' (165). Not only does he include both himself and Africans in the category of 'Servant'; he designates each group as '*Negroes*' and '*English*'. He refers to himself alternately as 'Servant' and 'Slave', creating a slippage between the terms as markers of labour.[39] He also uses both

---

[37] See Brown, 'Defoe's "Black Prince"'.

[38] Dennis Todd reads this new style as a form of 'psychological and moral transformation' in 'material and social' conditions, in direct contrast to *Robinson Crusoe*. *Defoe's America*, 84.

[39] Gabriel Cervantes and Geoffrey Sill provide a detailed reading of how Jack uses race but also caution that Jack's 'racial progressiveness' is overstated. 'Introduction', in *Colonel Jack*, 23–9.

terms to describe the enslaved Africans brought to work on the plantation. While he eventually comes to describe the English as 'white', he always uses the marker of 'Negro' rather than 'black' to describe Africans. In this sense, the term slides between a racial and a national identity marker. As Roxann Wheeler has admirably demonstrated, in the eighteenth century skin colour was not as important a marker of racial difference as older concepts like civility.[40] Therefore, Colonel Jack's categories of 'Negro', 'English', or 'white' have differing cultural valences than later established phenotypic markers of race.

* * *

In surveying different forms of writing by Daniel Defoe, one can only conclude that he was a man of his time. He responded to the instability of cultural concepts like race, nation, slavery, and freedom by creating characters rife with contradictions. His opinions about national character or racial attributes were continuously tempered by the belief in change. Defoe viewed humankind as existing on a continuum from civility to savagery. While he privileged European and English culture above all others, he did not deny that those cultures had the ability to change. Similarly, he recognized the necessity of forced labour, servitude, and enslavement, but he was not wholly blind to the ethics of humane treatment. Thus, Defoe did not have a cohesive sense of racial or national identity, but he did have a pronounced one.

Further Reading

Srinivas Aravamudan, 'Defoe, Commerce, and Empire', in *The Cambridge Companion to Daniel Defoe*, ed. John Richetti (Cambridge: Cambridge University Press, 2008), 45–63.

Srinivas Aravamudan, *Tropicopolitans: Colonialism and Agency, 1688–1804* (Durham, N.C.: Duke University Press, 1999).

George Boulukos, *The Grateful Slave: The Emergence of Race in Eighteenth-Century British and American Culture* (Cambridge: Cambridge University Press, 2008).

Linda Colley, *Britons: Forging the Nation, 1707–1837* (New Haven, CT: Yale University Press, 1992).

Peter Knox-Shaw, 'Defoe and the Politics of Representing the African Interior', *Modern Language Review*, 96:4 (2001), 937–51.

Mary Nyquist, *Arbitrary Rule: Slavery, Tyranny, and the Power of Life and Death* (Chicago, IL: University of Chicago Press, 2013).

Srividhya Swaminathan 'Defoe's *Captain Singleton*: A Study of Enslavement', in *Invoking Slavery in the Eighteenth-Century British Imagination*, ed. Srividhya Swaminathan and Adam R. Beach (Burlington, VT: Ashgate, 2013), 57–74.

Dennis Todd, *Defoe's America* (Cambridge: Cambridge University Press, 2010).

---

[40] 'Throughout the eighteenth century older conceptions of Christianity, civility, and rank were *more explicitly* important to Britons' assessment of themselves and other people than physical attributes such as skin color, shape of the nose, or texture of the hair'. Wheeler, *Complexion of Race*, 7.

Roxann Wheeler, *The Complexion of Race: Categories of Difference in Eighteenth-Century British Culture* (Philadelphia, PA: University of Pennsylvania Press, 2000).

Roxann Wheeler, 'Powerful Affections: Slaves, Servants, and Labours of Love in Defoe's Writing', in *Defoe's Footprints: Essays in Honour of Maximillian E. Novak*, ed. Robert M. Maniquis and Carl Fisher (Toronto: University of Toronto Press, 2009), 126–52.

CHAPTER 25

DEFOE AND ECOLOGY

LUCINDA COLE

DANIEL DEFOE was born and died during The Little Ice Age, a 500-year period of short springs, long winters, truncated growing seasons, and frequently abrupt shifts in weather patterns. As a child, in 1664–5, he experienced one of the coldest English winters in recorded history, with the Thames turning into what Noah Webster calls 'a bridge of ice', followed by earthquakes in Coventry and Buckinghamshire, fairly close to his London home.[1] These years also brought plague, 'pestilential fevers', and mass death to London. The winter of 1683–4, about the time that Defoe first took up business, was described 'as the coldest that could be recollected by the oldest men living', during which 'Trees of large size split with frost'.[2] The last years of the seventeenth century, when Defoe began his career as a political writer, brought with them 'wet and cold summers, which prevented crops from arriving to maturity', and consequently Britain struggled with dearth and famine, especially in Scotland: 'Vast multitudes perished with hunger', writes Webster, '—the dead bodies lay scattered along the highways'.[3] Defoe also lived through the Great Storm of 1703, an extra-tropical cyclone, with winds reaching 110 mph, that devastated ships, trees, crops, and livestock across a wide swath of Wales and southern England and destroyed or damaged between 4 and 6% of England's housing stock.[4] In 1717 and 1718, right before Defoe published his first novels, much of the world struggled with cold and wet weather. America experienced snowstorms of over sixteen feet, the largest snowfall ever reported; plague took over 80,000 people in Aleppo; winter was cold in Europe; the 'greater number' of people who lived near slaughter-houses in Cork, died.[5] Before publishing *Robinson Crusoe* in his late 50s, then, Defoe had a lifetime of

---

[1] Noah Webster, *A Brief History of Epidemic and Pestilential Diseases, with the Principal Phenomena of the Physical World, which Precede and Accompany them, and Observations deduced from the Facts Stated*, 2 vols (Hartford, CT, 1799), i. 194.

[2] Webster, *Brief History*, i. 204.

[3] Webster, *Brief History*, i. 213.

[4] Robert Markley, '"Casualties and Disasters": Defoe and the Interpretation of Climatic Instability', *Journal of Early Modern Cultural Studies*, 8:2 (2008), 102–24 (106).

[5] Webster, *Brief History*, i. 225–6.

witnessing dramatic weather, occasional dearth, and periods of mass disease. These storms, fevers, freezes, plagues, and human and animal die-offs make their way into his writing, and, in complex ways, are related to concerns that we now identify under the rubric of ecology.

The exact *nature* of Defoe's understanding of these complex relationships, however, is not entirely equivalent to what we might call the 'ecological'. At a fundamental level, 'ecology' attributes to the non-human, natural world an independent or autonomous moral value; the interrelated health of land, oceans, and animal species is understood as a good in its own right. Defoe, however, follows a broadly Lockean paradigm in asserting that what is good is what can be put to human use. In his second *Treatise of Government* (1690), as Robert Markley argues, Locke counters the values and assumptions underlying a Hobbesian politics of scarcity by describing the Law of Nature in ways that invoke a Golden Age of unlimited resources; instead of individuals being pitted against each other in 'a continual struggle for limited resources', Locke's natural world 'suffers no consequences from human labor; no shortages of land or produce exist to provoke conflicts between the have and the have-nots'.[6] Locke's *Two Treatises*, in this respect, turns on the assumption that humans can use resources to improve or maintain living standards without ever exhausting them. Defoe extends this broad set of assumptions and values in texts otherwise as different as *The Storm* (1704), *Robinson Crusoe* (1719), *Captain Singleton* (1720), and *A Journal of the Plague Year* (1722). In his fiction and non-fictional work, he describes different ecologies—London's well-known suburbs or Africa's mysterious interior—in terms of an appropriative logic of goods that can be mined, harvested, traded for, transported, stored, prepared, and consumed, either now or in the future. In a post-Romantic understanding of ecology, then, Defoe's work, like Locke's, seems anti-ecological in its tendency to ignore environmental constraints and emphasize seemingly endless productivity. Nonetheless, recognizing how Defoe perceives the natural world and its resources allows us to read his work within the context of what we now think of as environmental economics. Whether he is writing about climate, foreign landscapes, or non-human animal populations, his emphasis on the infinite exploitability of God-given resources shapes his perception of humankind's duty to remake the natural world into a vast storehouse of useful goods.

Because it is driven by a market logic shaped by anthropocentric theologies, Defoe's view of nature is oddly abiotic; that is, in his writing we are less likely to encounter living landscapes and thriving species than we are warehouses of goods in the process—at least imaginatively—of being harvested. Even *The Storm*, arguably Defoe's most environmentally focused text, is less about the loss of life or the damage to species health than it is about the loss of property, the destruction (in his view) of valuable *things*: buildings, roof tiles, crops, livestock. In what follows, I trace Defoe's environmental economics through *The Storm*, *Robinson Crusoe*, *Captain Singleton*, and *A Journal of the Plague Year*, where

---

[6] Robert Markley, '"Land Enough in the World": Locke's Golden Age and the Infinite Extensions of "Use"', *South Atlantic Quarterly*, 98:4 (1999), 817–37 (828).

he projects onto landscapes real and imagined a view of a limitless Nature designed for human use, even as, like the businessman he was, his characters hedge their bets against an always threatening future [SEE CHAPTER 14]. Ultimately, I suggest that *A Journal of the Plague Year*, a text set squarely within urban London, is—however paradoxically—Defoe's most ecologically driven piece of writing because the novelist is forced to engage with contemporary theories of miasma—the environmentally determined beliefs about human and animal health—and consequently with what we would now call disease ecology.

'What is the Matter in the World?': *The Storm*

Like many of his predecessors and contemporaries, Defoe treats catastrophic weather events in theological as well as meteorological and climatological terms. *The Storm* is a syncretic text held together by accounts of the storm's violence and economic impact. Defoe begins by providing a historical and climatological overview of the reasons that he believes Britain is prone to 'very high Winds, and sometimes violent Tempests'.[7] Like Ralph Bohun and other seventeenth-century writers on meteorology, Defoe offers no fully scientific explanation for the windstorm of November 1703, arguing that 'the Winds are some of those Inscrutables of Nature, in which humane Search has not yet been able to arrive at any Demonstration' (32). Consequently, he refers any kind of teleological argument to his belief that 'where God has, as it were, laid his Hand upon any Place, and Nature presents us with an universal Blank, we are therein led as naturally to recognize the Infinite Wisdom and Power of the God of Nature' (32). The storm, then, offers a warning for the atheist. No atheist could have experienced 'the terrible Blasts of this Tempest', Defoe imagines, without trembling before a Divine Nature forcing him to confront some metaphysical questions: 'Am I not mistaken? ... What can all this be? What is the Matter in the World?' (15). *The Storm* looks back to a history of Biblical plague literature as well as to a tradition of physico-theology.[8]

If 'the Greatest and the Longest Storm that ever the World saw' lies beyond early eighteenth-century notions of physical causality, Defoe's theological presuppositions nonetheless allow him to sketch a proto-ecological and Lockean theory of improvement that makes it the duty and responsibility of pious Christians to transform the natural world. Sketching the history of the British Isles, Defoe argues against the idea

---

[7] Defoe, *The Storm*, ed. Richard Hamblyn (London: Penguin, 2005), 25.
[8] On phyisco-theology, see Robert Markley, *Fallen Languages: Crises of Representation in Newtonian England, 1660–1740* (Ithaca, N.Y.: Cornell University Press, 1993); and Courtney Weiss Smith, *Empiricist Devotions: Science, Religion, and Poetry in Early Eighteenth-Century England* (Charlottesville, VA: University of Virginia Press, 2016).

that England is more prone to storms than are other countries, but agrees that, prior to the draining of the fens, a project taken up under James I, England was susceptible to storms: in a primitive 'Nation ... full of standing Lakes', he writes, 'stagnated Waters, and moist Places, the multitude of Exhalations must furnish the Air with a quantity of Matter for Showers and Storms infinitely more than it can be now supply'd withal' (46). For Defoe, despite the known difficulties and ecological costs of widespread drainage—peat without water shrinks in ways that sometimes lower already lowlands—the transformation of marshes, fens, and moors into arable land for grazing and grains is a model of environmental economics.[9] The progress of the English, he writes, is measured by 'those vast Tracts of Land being now fenc'd off, laid dry, and turn'd into wholsome and profitable Provinces' (46). In the nineteenth century, the word 'province' denoted a biogeographical region, one characterized by particular flora and fauna; here, enclosed and planted, it means something akin to 'estate'. The 'standing Lakes, stagnated Waters, and moist Places' generate the matter or 'Exhalations' that Defoe, following Bohun, sees as furnishing the raw material for 'violent Tempests', but these habitats are described as though they did not harbour, in their own right, complex ecologies of plant, insect, and animal species. Both the creatures displaced by the drainage and the crops, livestock, and trees that supplant those creatures are subsumed within an abiotic balance sheet of profit and use rather than loss and waste. Land is defined in financial rather than ecological terms.

The Storm draws implicitly on the tradition of agricultural improvement literature promoted by English writers in the seventeenth century—among them, members of the Royal Society like Abraham Cowley and John Evelyn—to emphasize that profitability is akin to, or even evidence of, godliness. Financial devastation, accordingly, can be regarded as a sign of sinfulness. Especially along the coasts, destruction was catastrophic; over 100 vessels sank, many within sight of land, and about 8,000 sailors on both navy and merchant ships were lost.[10] The countryside was littered with thousands of dead sheep, cows, and horses. Defoe, like his contemporaries, treats these less as losses of life than as red ink on the sinful nation's collective balance sheet. The second and longer section of *The Storm* reprints accounts from reputable, gentlemanly eyewitnesses; Defoe uses these reports to highlight economic consequences in ways that erase differences between inanimate objects and living beings. Danial James, writing about the storm's effects on Bristol, describes both agricultural and commercial devastation. High winds 'blew down and scattered abundance of Hay and Corn Mows, besides almost Levelling many Orchards and Groves of stout Trees' (120). In the port of Bristol itself, 'the violent over-flowing of the Tide, occasion'd by the force of the Wind, ... did abundance of damage to the Merchants Cellers' (120). In 'the Marsh Country' along the River Severn, the storm destroyed 'Banks or Sea Walls, drowning abundance of Sheep, and other Cattle, washing some houses clear away, and breaking down part of others,

---

[9] See Eric H. Ash, *The Draining of the Fens: Projectors, Popular Politics, and State Building in Early Modern England* (Baltimore, MD: Johns Hopkins University Press, 2017).

[10] Markley, 'Casualties and Disasters', 106.

in which many Persons lost their Lives' (120). Like Defoe, James moves fluidly between damage to manmade structures—sea walls and commercial storehouses—and the destruction of trees, livestock, and crops.

The storm devastated an improved landscape that presumably set Britain apart from the absolutist politics, frequent food shortages, and rigid Catholic 'tyranny' of much of continental Europe.[11] The catalogues of disaster read like insurance adjustors' reports, lists of damages and material losses that, in turn, provoke grief for the fortunes lost and awe because, as bad as the devastation seems, it could have been so much worse. Although the rising Thames 'prov'd very prejudicial to abundance of People whose Cellars and Ware-houses were near the River', 'it was a special Providence that so directed the Waters' that they did not rise a foot higher, at which point 'all the Marshes and Levels on both sides the River [would have] been over-flowed, and a great part of the Cattle drowned' (35). The storm, then, represents both the mysterious workings of 'Divine Vengeance' (65) and a threat to a vision of agricultural and commercial productivity that was critical to England's self-definition as a bastion of agrarian, Protestant self-sufficiency. Defined in and through its productivity, the ravaged landscape appears less as a complex ecological system than as an overlay of theology, politics, and natural philosophy. The eyewitness accounts of potentially apocalyptic devastation that Defoe includes in *The Storm* move easily among accounts of uprooted trees, dead sheep, and ruined warehouses because all these signs of 'Divine Vengeance' throw into relief the limitations of a faith in Lockean productivity.

BIOINSECURITIES AND CRUSOE'S ISLAND

Defoe's first novel, set on an unpeopled island, seems to offer a good opportunity for the hero or novelist to take stock of and even analyse this pristine ecology. Yet his descriptions of the island's weather, in some ways, replicate what we saw in *The Storm*: threats to self and property, rather than to animal populations and indigenous species, drive the narrative. In an extended passage early in his twenty-eight years on the island, Crusoe describes an earthquake, followed by a hurricane, in considerable detail. 'The Motion of the Earth made [his] Stomach sick', filled him with 'Horror', and drove him first out of his cave, and then out of the flimsy shelter adjacent to it: 'I thought of nothing then', he says, 'but the Hill falling upon my Tent and all my houshold Goods, and burying all at once; and this sunk my very Soul within me a second Time'.[12] After the third shock passed, the wind rose into a 'most dreadful Hurricane' that struck the shore and tore up trees by the roots. The storm lasted for about three hours, then turned into a hard rain (70). Although Crusoe claims never to have experienced an earthquake—he

---

[11] Andrew McRae, *God Speed the Plough: The Representation of Agrarian England, 1500–1660* (Cambridge: Cambridge University Press, 1996), 3–18.

[12] Defoe, *Robinson Crusoe*, ed. Thomas Keymer (Oxford: World's Classics, 2007), 69.

is 'amazed' at 'the Thing it self, having never felt the like, or discours'd with any one that had'—he assumes a causal relationship between earthquakes and storms (69). Early writers on the nature of winds and the causes of storms, notably Ralph Bohun, cited by Defoe in *The Storm*, argue that violent tempests are the products of chemical reactions that occur in 'Subterraneall Kingdomes' and affect coal dust and other matter, producing earthquakes and volcanoes: 'Storms by Sea; *Winds*, and *Thunders*, in the *Air*; and *Earthquakes* under *Ground*' are all products of 'Subterraneall Storms'.[13] Crusoe calculates that because winds and rain were the 'consequences' of the earthquake, his tent and cave might be safe. The former, however, proves no match for the 'violent' rains, and the latter, he discovers, is in danger of flooding.

As in *The Storm*, this dramatic weather event functions primarily as a trigger for labour and improvement, about which Crusoe is explicit:

> This violent Rain forc'd me to a new Work, *viz*. To cut a Hole thro' my new Fortification like a Sink to let the Water go out, which would else have drown'd my Cave. ... It continu'd raining all that Night, and great Part of the next Day, so that I could not stir abroad, but my Mind being more compos'd, I began to think of what I had best do, concluding that if the Island was subject to these Earthquakes, there would be no living for me in a Cave, but I must consider of building me some little Hut in an open Place which I might surround with a Wall as I had done here, and so make my self secure from wild Beasts or Men; but concluded, if I staid where I was, I should certainly, one time or other, be bury'd alive. (70)

The storm triggers Crusoe's efforts to turn the island into what generations of critics have recognized as a refracted version of the English landscape, with crops (grapes, rice, and barley); domesticated animals (goats, cats, a dog); and enclosures (huts and walls). The ecology of the island, then, is quickly transformed from an environment prone to catastrophic destruction into Crusoe's property. Before his discovery of Friday, Crusoe's efforts to protect his crops and property ('houshold Goods') from natural disaster or potential competitors for his grain ('wild beasts or Men') signal an environment transformed (69–70).

In some sense, then, Crusoe interprets his island within a Lockean ideology of usefulness. He recognizes what we would call the biodiversity of the island, its flora and fauna, but frames it largely in terms of its use value. 'I had no Want of Food', he writes, 'and of that which was very good too ... especially Goats, Pidgeons, and Turtle or Tortoise; which, added to my Grapes, *Leaden-Hall* Market could not have furnish'd a Table better' (138). Nevertheless, his chief employment quickly becomes planting barley and rice—non-native crops—in order to have a 'good Quantity' of bread 'for Store, and to secure a constant Supply' (144). For much of the novel Crusoe devotes himself almost exclusively

---

[13] Ralph Bohun, *A Discourse Concerning the Origine and Properties of Wind* (Oxford, 1671), 27, 26. On tropical storms and the fears they provoked, see Matthew Mulcahy, *Hurricanes and Society in the British Greater Caribbean, 1624–1783* (Baltimore, MD: Johns Hopkins University Press, 2006).

to bread-making, employing all his 'Study' and 'Hours of Working' in creating the fences, instruments, and utensils required for seed and grain storage—Crusoe's insurance, as he sees it, against an always uncertain future.[14] Using a series of tools—traps, nets, guns, a dog, a scarecrow—to assert his dominance over the island's animal species, he transforms and increases his food supply, building up vast supplies despite the God-given sustenance that the island supplies. Having secured his grain against goats, hares, and birds, he eventually is able to produce 'forty Bushels of Barley and Rice at each harvest' (155), much more, he admits, than he can consume in a year.

For twenty-first-century readers, Crusoe's planting, provisioning, and hoarding may verge on a compulsive set of behaviours; J. M. Coetzee's *Foe* (1986) reinforces the sense of Crusoe as obsessive, if unproductive, building terrace after terrace on the island he occupies. But Crusoe's agricultural surpluses allow Defoe to solve—at least fictionally—the problem of food insecurity in the early eighteenth century. The provisioning of grain was, in the words of one agricultural historian, 'among the most serious of problems faced by local and state government in preindustrial England'.[15] Because a bad harvest or difficult winter could cause grain prices to double within a matter of months, grain storage was a hotly contested political issue that pitted grain merchants against the poor and those who did not grow their own food.[16] As Defoe's contemporary Charles Davenant wrote, 'in England, in a plentiful year, there is not above five months stock of grain at time of the succeeding harvest, and not above four months in an indifferent year, which is but a slender provision against any evil accident'.[17] 'Indifferent years' were common in Europe; 'evil accidents' includes storms like that of 1703, which destroyed both farmland and grain stores, and persistent periods of bad weather that were comparatively common during the Little Ice Age. On the island, Crusoe's corn crop is precious for two reasons. It allows him to replicate an emblematic English meal of bread and meat—an ideological marker of his control of the island. And the grain (unlike meat and fruit, which are subject to decay) allows Crusoe to safeguard some of his food

---

[14] See Thomas Kavanagh, 'Unraveling Robinson: The Divided Self in Defoe's *Robinson Crusoe*', *Texas Studies in Language and Literature*, 20:3 (1978), 416–32; Geoffrey Sill, *The Cure of the Passions and the Origins of the English Novel* (Cambridge: Cambridge University Press, 2001), 86–106; Maximillian E. Novak, *Transformations, Ideology, and the Real in Defoe's Robinson Crusoe and Other Narratives: Finding 'The Thing Itself*' (Newark, DE: University of Delaware Press, 2015); and Elizabeth R. Napier, *Defoe's Major Fiction: Accounting for the Self* (Newark, DE: University of Delaware Press, 2016).

[15] Randall Nielsen, 'Storage and English Government Intervention in Early Modern Grain Markets', *Journal of Economic History*, 57:1 (1997), 1–33 (1). Nielsen calls attention to the effects of climatic conditions on agriculture. See also H. H. Lamb, *Climate History and the Modern World*, 2nd ed. (New York: Routledge, 1995), 211–41; Brian Fagan, *The Little Ice Age: How Climate Made History 1300–1850* (New York: Basic Books, 2000); and Geoffrey Parker, *Global Crisis: War, Climate Change and Catastrophe in the Seventeenth Century* (New Haven, CT: Yale University Press, 2013).

[16] The Crown ordered the release of private stocks during times of dearth from the late sixteenth century on (Nielsen, 'Storage and English Government Intervention', 2), although the effectiveness of these proclamations is a matter of debate.

[17] Charles Davenant, *The Political and Commercial Works ... Relating to the Trade and Revenue of England, the Plantation Trade, the East-India Trade, and Africa Trade*, ed. Charles Whitworth, 5 vols (1771), ii. 224.

supply against contingencies and weather patterns because grain can be stored for long periods of time. The corn crop therefore becomes both a talismanic and practical safeguard against an uncertain future.

Robinson Crusoe's fantasy solution to contemporary grain problems reveals the novel's anti-ecological sleights-of-hand in another way as well. Vermin, as I have argued elsewhere, posed a persistent and dangerous threat to food supplies in England, on the continent, on board ships, and on island colonies.[18] Even in a good year, an estimated 20–30% of grain supplies would be lost to smutting (parasitic fungi) or insects, rats, and mice.[19] Rats in particular could eat shipboard provisions and then swim to islands, where they could destroy plantations. Such rodent populations generally arrived by ships, where rats were a constant source of trouble. William Dampier, leaving Cape Corrientes for the East Indies, describes the crew's fear at having their limited provisions ravaged by shipboard rats: 'We had not 60 days Provision ... and we had a great many rats aboard, which we could not hinder from eating part of our Maiz'.[20] Dampier's fellow buccaneer Woodes Rogers, a contemporary of Defoe, found that even when he stole grain from other ships, 'it was quickly much damag'd by the [shipboard] rats'.[21] When Rogers rescued the Scots sailor Alexander Selkirk, who was marooned on Juan Fernández off the Chilean coast, he describes in uncomfortable detail the rodent infestations brought to the islands by 'Ships that put in there to wood and water': 'The Rats gnaw'd his Feet and Clothes while asleep', Rogers writes, 'which oblig'd him to cherish the Cats with his Goats-flesh'.[22] Whether or not Selkirk was a model for Robinson Crusoe, Defoe was familiar with the problem of rats and their ability to decimate food supplies, on ships and on the islands they visited.

That Crusoe's island harbours no rats has far-reaching consequences for any ecological reading. Defoe mentions rats only three times in *Robinson Crusoe*, all of them in relation to his salvaged bag of grain, 'a little Remainder of *European* corn' that had been brought on board to feed some poultry that had been killed: 'there had been some Barly and Wheat together, but, to my great Disappointment, I found afterwards that the Rats had eaten or spoil'd it all' (94). He nevertheless shakes the bag out and one month later, miraculously, sees stalks of green, which lead him to a meditation on Providence: 'for it was really the Work of Providence as to me ... that 10 or 12 Grains of Corn should remain unspoil'd (when the Rats had destroy'd all the rest,) as if it had been dropt from Heaven' (115). In ecological terms, these 'unspoil'd' husks, free from rat urine, are not the real miracle; it is that the rats who helped themselves to the poultry feed disappear when the ship wrecked near the shore. The near-empty bag of grain reminds us that Crusoe represents

---

[18] Lucinda Cole, *Imperfect Creatures: Vermin, Literature, and the Sciences of Life, 1600–1740* (Ann Arbor, MI: University of Michigan Press, 2016), 143–71.

[19] During the seventeenth century, grain increasingly was moved from open-air ricks, where it was subject to rain and rodents, to barns, and then to raised platforms in barns.

[20] William Dampier, *A New Voyage around the World* (1703), 281.

[21] Woodes Rogers, *A Cruising Voyage Round the World* (1712), 220.

[22] Rogers, *Cruising Voyage*, 128.

a European food system—men grow grain, grain feeds fowl, grain and fowl feed men—extremely vulnerable to rodents. That rats are present only in their absence, in the traces of food they leave behind, suggests how Defoe's novel subordinates ecological reality to a larger theological and narrative perspective. The island's imagined environment is not an open, dynamic ecosystem, but a closed fantasy world in which Crusoe hunts, gathers, farms,stores and—eventually—sells under metaphysically secured conditions.

ELEPHANTS, IVORY, AND *CAPTAIN SINGLETON*

In his 1963 essay on realism in *The Life, Adventures, and Piracies of Captain Singleton*, Gary J. Scrimgeour comments that, while 'monstrous animals had been Africa's most famous product since classical times', Defoe's depiction of indigenous species is highly selective.[23] Unlike the contemporary descriptions of John Ogilby, William Bosman, and Denis di Carli, among others, Defoe's Africa includes no monkeys, no apes, no ostriches, and only a single serpent, of a 'hellish ugly deformed look and voice'.[24] Defoe also omits any mentions of Africa's seemingly omnipresent biting and stinging insects—'one of the great complaints of African travelers'—and instead uses encounters with dangerous animals as an occasion to emphasize how Englishmen 'use their own weapons in survival—palisades, gunpowder, and the great symbol of civilization, controlled fire'.[25] *Captain Singleton*, then, is in many ways as much of a fantasy as *Robinson Crusoe*; although employing the techniques of realism, the novel's descriptions of 'nature' must be understood as highly mediated and shaped by Defoe's conviction that the English should establish colonies in Africa to promote the nation's trade in ivory, gold, and slaves [SEE CHAPTER 31].[26] As he later argues in *Atlas Maritimus & Commercialis* (1728), Africa is a source of 'infinite riches' that are being grabbed by the Portuguese and the Dutch; but, with the right political, naval, and commercial initiatives, could just as easily be secured by the English.[27] In *Captain Singleton*, descriptions of elephants and

---

[23] Gary J. Scrimgeour, 'The Problem of Realism in Defoe's *Captain Singleton*', HLQ, 27:1 (1963), 21–37 (25).

[24] Scrimgeour, 'Problem of Realism', 25.

[25] Scrimgeour, 'Problem of Realism', 31.

[26] In addition to Scrimgeour, see Peter Knox-Shaw, 'Defoe and the Politics of Representing the African Interior', MLR, 96:4 (2001), 937–51; Lora E. Geriguis, '"A Vast Howling Wilderness": The Persistence of Space and Placelessness in Daniel Defoe's *Captain Singleton*', in *Topographies of the Imagination: New Approaches to Daniel Defoe*, ed. Katherine Ellison, Kit Kincade, and Holly Faith Nelson (New York: AMS Press, 2014), 185–207. The foundational account of Defoe and economics remains Maximillian E. Novak, *Economics and the Fiction of Daniel Defoe* (Berkeley, CA: University of California Press, 1962).

[27] On Defoe and the desire for inexhaustible resources, see Robert Markley, *The Far East and the English Imagination, 1600–1730* (Cambridge: Cambridge University Press, 2006), esp. Chs 5 and 6. Jeremy Wear extends this analysis in 'No Dishonour to Be a Pirate: The Problem of Infinite Advantage

elephant products help Defoe make that argument; at the same time though—perhaps unwittingly—they also demonstrate the devastating effects of European imperialism on the elephant population.

Halfway through the novel, on their 1,500-mile trek across Africa, Captain Singleton and his party of mutineers discover a vast elephants' graveyard. At this remote site, the usually understated Singleton reports that 'the Ground was scattered with Elephants Teeth, in such a Number, as is incredible'. Tusks in the graveyard, he asserts,

> may have lain there for some Hundreds of years, so seeing the Substance of them scarce ever decayes, they may lye there for ought I know to the End of Time. The Size of some of them is, it seems, to those to whom I have reported it, as incredible as the Number, and I can assure you, there were several so heavy, as the strongest Man among us could not lift. As to Number, I question not but there are enough to load a thousand Sail of the biggest Ships in the World, by which I may be understood to mean, that the Quantity is not to be conceived of; seeing that as they lasted in View for above eighty Miles Travelling, so they might continue as far to the right Hand, and to the left as far, and as many times as far, for ought we knew; for it seems the Number of Elephants hereabouts is prodigious great. (*Novels*, v. 83)

Singleton's insistence that the 'Quantity' of ivory is enough to load a 'thousand' of the 'Biggest ships in the World' reminds us of how crucial elephants and ivory were to international trade. Because ivory, Defoe argues in *Atlas Maritimus & Commercialis*, along with gold and jewels, can be obtained by trading 'mere Toys and Trifles scarce worth naming' to the Africans, it is incredible that the 'Marine and Trading Nations' of Europe are not pursuing these riches more fervently.[28] In this respect, Singleton's seemingly inexhaustible supply of tusks—a 'Quantity not to be conceived of'—functions metonymically for the 'prodigious great' supply of elephants. The dead elephants, in turn, stand in for the endless riches of Africa itself, a continent often signified on early modern maps by figures of the great beast. And where there is ivory, there must also be the manpower to transport it since, as Singleton says, some of the tusks are 'so heavy, as the strongest Man among us could not lift' them. Ivory, elephants, gold, and enslaved persons exist, then, as part of a complex chain of imperial desire.

Within this context, Defoe's enthusiastic description of this remote elephant graveyard raises questions not only about imperial practices, but about the ecological displacements that make such practices possible. Despite Singleton's jaunty reassurance that 'the Number of Elephants hereabouts is prodigious great', that the elephant graveyard is so far inland reminds us that by the late seventeenth century elephant populations in the West African coastal areas frequented by Europeans were already

---

in Defoe's *Captain Singleton*', *ECF*, 24:4 (2012), 569–96. On Defoe and the Royal African Company, see Tim Kiern, 'Daniel Defoe and the Royal African Company', *Bulletin of the Institute of Historical Research*, 61:145 (1988), 243–7.

[28] Defoe, *Atlas Maritimus & Commercialis: A General View of the World, So Far As It Relates to Trade and Navigation* (1728), 99.

depleted. According to the nineteenth-century historian Charles Frederick Holder, when the Portuguese first arrived on the African coast they found piles of ivory—'vast stores'—that were being used primarily for religious and ceremonial purposes, but these soon disappeared. 'The Portuguese collected all they could', he writes, 'and shipped the tusks to Europe, reaping a rich harvest, and so depleting the supply, that in the middle of the seventeenth century, it was almost exhausted again'.[29] In consequence, ivory hunters and traders pushed inland in search of elephant herds. John Frederick Walker finds 'abundant evidence' of increasingly international ivory trading and ivory-working 'deep in the interior'—and offers as a case study the situation of the Vili people in the coastal kingdom of Loango, who had been trading ivory with the Europeans since 1570. 'In 1608', he notes, 'they were selling twenty-three tons a year to the Dutch alone', but by the 1660s Vili hunters had to undertake 'journeys of three months' duration in the middle Congo before they could return with the ivory needed'.[30] In 1670, John Ogilby writes that while there are still 'many scurfed or hollow Teeth found in the Wilderness ... This Commodity, from the infinite abundance brought thence, within these fifty or sixty years, begins to abate much, because [hunters] are compell'd to fetch them further out of the Countrey'.[31] The idea that 'infinite abundance' can 'abate' suggests the limitations of the rhetoric that underlies Defoe's 'infinite Advantage'. In the sense that Ogilby implies, ecological limits—or in this case over-hunting—affects both the supply of elephants and ivory and the balance sheets of European traders.

William Bosman's late seventeenth-century expedition along the '*Tooth* and *Grain*' coast (that is, the present-day coasts of Ghana and Ivory Coast) found the peoples in village after village reporting '*that they had not at present any Elephant Teeth*'. The two villages that did have ivory forced Bosman to deal with them 'at the dearest rate', inflation that he attributes, in part, to the '*English* and *Dutch* interlopers', or non-company traders, who competed with the West Indies and Royal African Companies.[32] Such accounts demonstrate that ivory was hardly 'infinite'; by 1720, the year that *Captain Singleton* was published, Africa's elephants had long been in retreat away from encroaching human populations and destructive hunting practices.[33]

---

[29] Charles Frederick Holder, *The Ivory King: A Popular History of the Elephant and Its Allies* (New York: Charles Scribner's Sons, 1891), 218. In truth, elephant populations always had been subject to the demands of ivory. See John Frederick Walker, *Ivory's Ghosts: The White Gold of History and the Fate of Elephants* (New York: Grove Press, 2009). Walker reports that by the late sixth century 'not a single elephant could be found in Africa north of the Sahara' (47). Moreover, by the fifteenth century elephants had disappeared from the Indian Ocean coast 'and had to be sought hundreds of miles inland' (64).

[30] Walker, *Ivory's Ghosts*, 66.

[31] John Ogilby, *Africa, Being an Accurate Description of the Regions of Ægypt, Barbary, Lybia, and Billedulgerid, the Land of Negroes, Guinee, Æthiopia and the Abyssines* (1670), 530.

[32] Ogilby, *Africa*, 472, 487.

[33] Little information is available on the extent and movement of African elephant populations until the nineteenth century; even then, it remains largely anecdotal. See N. Thomas Håkansson, 'The Human Ecology of World Systems in East Africa: The Impact of the Ivory Trade', *Human Ecology*, 32:5 (2004), 561–91.

That once-plentiful elephants had by then to be hunted hundreds of miles inland therefore endows Singleton's elephant graveyard with a grimly ironic poignancy: he stumbles on this presumably inexhaustible source of treasure precisely at the time when great herds were on the wane, and ivory was becoming an even rarer and therefore more valuable commodity—so-called white gold. Indeed, Defoe's term 'Elephants teeth', more commonly used in this period than 'ivory', both recalls the living animal and casts it merely as an endlessly renewable delivery system for human exploitation and profit-taking.

Perhaps because Defoe casts the elephant primarily as an expendable resource, in marked contrast to the geographies and voyage narratives of the late seventeenth and early eighteenth centuries, *Singleton* contains no anthropomorphizing descriptions of individual elephants and no adventurous interludes devoted to elephant hunts. Singleton and his crew see elephants only from a distance, primarily in panoramic views of the African savannah. Singleton's first, indirect encounter with the animals comes via a second-hand description of how a scouting party negotiated their brush with a herd crossing the plains. His fellow sailors first saw a great 'Cloud of Sand'. Initially mistaking this cloud for an 'Army of Enemies', they conjectured it must be some 'vast Collection of wild Beasts' searching for food or water (83). Fearful that 'they should be all devoured or trampled under Foot by their Multitude', the group alters its course and sends out a native scout who, through sign language, comes back and conveys that it 'was a Great Herd or Drove, or whatever it might be called, of vast monstrous Elephants'.[34] This confusion about what to call the group of elephants may be significant; an elephant 'herd' is a family headed by a matriarch, whereas 'drove' commonly refers to a large mass of cattle, usually being driven to market. The African elephants both are and are not cattle, in part because, unlike cows, they were perceived as potentially dangerous to humans. Although Singleton's men are 'desirous' to see the live elephants—'it was a sight our Men had never seen', the hero tells us—they are also 'a little uneasy at the Danger too' (80). This danger is made more acute by the gunner in their party who wants to conduct a gruesome experiment about whether shot could penetrate an elephant; he wants to get close to an elephant, 'clapt his Piece to his Ear', and fire (83). The party fear that the herd, hearing the noise, 'should all turn upon, and pursue' them (83). This highly-mediated encounter reinforces an idea familiar in travellers' accounts—African elephants were capable of retribution when fired on—even as it introduces a new element that blurs the distinctions between human and animal intelligence and intentionality. Neither purveyors nor victims of violence, the herd functions in this scene as a kind of natural force, at once the object of a fascinated, European gaze and a group marked by a *collective* reciprocal intelligence, a *generalized* self-awareness: 'They were between 20 and 30 in Number, but prodigious great ones; and tho' they often shew'd our Men that they saw them, yet they did not turn out of their Way, or take any other Notice of them, than,

---

[34] Defoe, *Captain Singleton*, ed. Shiv K. Kumar, intro. Penelope Wilson (Oxford: World's Classics, 1990), 83.

as we might say, just to look at them' (84). That the elephants looked back, or 'shew'd our Men that they saw them', is as close as Defoe gets to endowing individual African elephants with the capacity for agency, intention, or sentience. His focus, however, remains on their species existence.

The next sighting, and citing, of live elephants occurs after Singleton and his men have passed the burial ground; through an extended figure, it again emphasizes the potential violence in the herd. Singleton sees an 'Abundance of Elephants at a Distance' and observes that they 'always go in very good Company', a military metaphor suggesting both danger and martial intentionality. Elephants, says Singleton, are

> always extended in a fair Line of Battle; and this, they say, is the way they defend themselves from their Enemies; for if Lions or Tygers, Wolves or any Creatures, attack them, they being drawn up in a Line, sometimes reaching five or six Miles in Length, whatever comes in their Way is sure to be trod under Foot, or Beaten in Pieces with their Trunks, or lifted up in the Air with their Trunks; so that if a hundred Lions or Tygers were coming along, if they meet a Line of Elephants, they will always fly back till they see Room to pass ... ; and if they did not, it would be impossible for one of them to escape; for the Elephant, tho' a heavy Creature, is yet so dextrous and nimble with his Trunk, that he will not fail to lift up the heaviest Lion, or any other wild Creature, and throw him up in the Air quite over his Back, and then trample him to Death with his Feet (89).

Singleton's elephants operate as a kind of automated war machine—literally, an 'invasive species'—moving across the desert in battle formation; these may be Hannibal's creatures, but they have no Hannibal, no human training, and no role in a human war. Instead, the elephants seem both to embody a refracted image of European aggressiveness and to constitute an elemental force that marks the limits of human control, force, and willpower. There are many such elephant armies, Singleton insists, their size rivalling that of their graveyard. 'We saw several Lines of Battle thus', he claims, one so long 'that indeed there was no End of it to be seen, and, I believe, their might be 2000 Elephants in a Row, or Line' (89). Defoe represents elephants in an aestheticized aggregate: as a 'vast Collection', moving across the savannah, markedly indifferent to the presence of others, mowing down threats, and eventually dropping ivory wherever they go to die.

By militarizing the elephants, Defoe splits the cultural reality of the international ivory and slave trades—in which Europeans, Africans, and elephants existed within complex, interdependent networks mediated by guns—into two mutually reinforcing caricatures: that of African humans as willing or cowed servants and that of African elephants as decontextualized landscape epiphenomena. At the beginning of his trek across the continent, the Africans whom Singleton encounters, awed by the Europeans' guns, allow themselves—and even their Prince—to be captured. Almost instantaneously, they become Friday-like caricatures of submission: they 'worshipped' us, Singleton reports, 'some kneeling, some throwing themselves flat on the Ground, made a Thousand antick Gestures, but all with Tokens of the most profound Submission' (53-4). He decides that by the 'Law of Arms' his party should take the natives 'Prisoners, and make them travel with us, and carry our Baggage' (54). Much like domesticated Asian elephants, the African humans henceforth serve as beasts of burden through the long trek across Africa, carrying 'very heavy' supplies, including 'Powder, and Shot, Lead', and 'Iron' (59). *Captain Singleton*'s elephants, in turn, removed from the populated coasts, shed their real species history, which includes domestication, and reappear as militarized 'lines' of biomass whose dominant features are their violence and their resistance to being numbered, counted, or even imagined. 'The Numbers of this kind of Creature that are in those Parts are inconceivable', says Singleton, 'as may be gather'd from the prodigious Quantity of Teeth, which I said we saw in this vast Desart' (90). Like the eighty miles of graveyard, the sublime elephant war machine stands as proof of the continent's inexhaustible resources. The novel's panoramic view of this 'vast' collection of elephants—both dead and alive—displaces the scenes of horrific violence recorded by Bosman and others. Through a series of occlusions, Defoe rewrites the African elephant, much in the same way as he rewrites African geography and ecology, obscuring the elephant's status as an intelligent agent trying to survive in an increasingly hostile environment, along with its membership in a family and genus that had lived and worked with humans throughout a long and interdependent history.

Disease Ecology, Cows, and *A Journal of the Plague Year*

Although one struggles to find in Defoe's early work and novels a relationship to nature and other species that resembles what we would identify as 'ecology', one not driven by human-centred, market-driven concerns, Christopher Loar argues convincingly that Defoe's plague writings offer 'an emergent form of ecological thinking' made possible and perhaps even necessary by contemporary disease theory.[35] Defoe shares with contemporary physicians and natural philosophers such as Thomas Sydenham, Richard Mead, and Richard Bradley, among many others, the understanding that plague is at some level an environmental problem 'produced by the weather (unfavorable winds or stagnant air), swarms of microscopic animals or particles, or some combination of the two'.[36] Although eighteenth-century writers disagreed about the nature and transmission of the plague, they acknowledged that the body is *in some sense* vulnerable to

---

[35] Christopher F. Loar, 'Plague's Ecologies: Daniel Defoe and the Epidemic Constitution', *ECF*, 32:1 (2019), 31–53 (31). On the relationship between ecology and plague more generally, see Cole, *Imperfect Creatures*, 1–80; Richard Barney and Helene Scheck, 'Early and Modern Biospheres, Politics, and Rhetorics of Plague', *Journal for Early Modern Cultural Studies*, 10:2 (2010), 1–22.

[36] Loar, 'Plague's Ecologies', 37.

both human and non-human environments: to the effluvia of human and animal others, to invisible *animacula*, to earthly exhalations, deadly putrefactions, *fomites* on traded goods. In eighteenth-century disease ecology, the human body is what Stacy Alaimo has identified as transcorporeal: far from being separated and cut off from the built environment and the natural world, it is embedded in it.[37] While characters and narrators in Defoe's *A Journal of the Plague Year* and *Due Preparations for the Plague* (1722) may sometimes exhibit hoarding and other prophylactic measures designed to ensure immunity, this 'Crusoe-esque isolation', Loar argues, is supplemented by a different ecology manifest in a new type of urban planning, one that deploys quantitative and qualitative information, to make a modern city.[38] 'The problem of the plague', he writes, 'is how to live as safely as possible in a perilous natural world—a "nature" that will not confine itself to the rural countryside or precolonial wilderness, but that fully inhabits society, the city, and the body'.[39] London in plague-ridden 1665, for Defoe, brings to the fore the qualifications and contexts that he could shunt aside in *Robinson Crusoe*.

If eighteenth-century theories of contagion allowed Defoe to imagine the human body as deeply entangled in the more-than-human world, his depiction of that world is surprisingly narrow and fiercely cosmopolitan and human-centred, especially compared to his well-known source texts.[40] The return of bubonic plague to France, as medical historians and Defoe scholars know, produced both general alarm and a rash of writings in England, including Nathanial Hodges's *Loimologia, or an Historical Account of the Plague in London in 1665*, which was translated into English and republished in 1720, along with John Quincy's remarks on the plague.[41] Defoe relied on both in crafting his *A Journal of the Plague Year*. But almost equally devastating and certainly more immediate for Defoe's eighteenth-century readers were the endemic cattle plagues which, between 1711 and 1714, killed over one and a half million cattle in England and, in 1720, ravaged north-east Germany, Italy, and parts of Switzerland and France.[42] One of the medical

---

[37] Stacy Alaimo first outlined this concept in *Bodily Natures: Science, Environment, and the Material Self* (Bloomington, IN: Indiana University Press, 2010).

[38] Loar, 'Plague's Ecologies', 43.

[39] Loar, 'Plague's Ecologies', 46.

[40] Scholars have argued that the concept of cosmopolitanism should be radically transformed in ways that are less nationalist and human-centred. See Rosi Braidotti, Patrick Hanifin, and Bolette B. Blaagarrd, *After Cosmpolitanism* (London: Routledge, 2013); Kaori Nagai, Karen Jones, Donna Landry, Monica Mattfield, Caroline Romney, and Charlotte Sleigh, *Cosmopolitan Animals* (Basingstoke: Palgrave Macmillan, 2015).

[41] Nathanial Hodges, *Loimologia, or an Historical Account of the Plague in London in 1665 ... To which is added, an Essay on the different Causes of Pestilential Diseases, and how they became Contagious*, 2nd ed. (1720). Hereafter cited parenthetically in the text.

[42] On the relationship among humoral theory, animal disease, and disease ecology, see Abigail Woods, Michael Bresalier, Angelo Cassidy, and Rachel Mason Dentiger (ed.), *Animals and the Shaping of Modern Medicine: One Health and Its Histories* (Basingstoke: Palgrave Macmillan, 2018), 11. On eighteenth-century cattle plagues, see Charles F. Mullet, 'The Cattle Distemper in Mid-Eighteenth-Century England', *Agricultural History*, 20:3 (1946), 144–65. On cattle plagues and theories of contagion, see Lise Wilkinson, 'Rinderpest and Mainstream Infectious Disease Concepts in the Eighteenth Century', *Medical History*, 28:2 (1984), 129–50. On eighteenth-century cattle plagues, contagion theory,

quandaries debated by Hodges, Quincy, and others was precisely the relationships between human and animal plagues. A cattle murrain preceded the human epidemic in Marseilles, a plague so severe that, according to reports, many people considered setting the whole town on fire. France eventually built a plague wall to separate the city from the rest of Provence.

Addressing cattle disease seven times in his short treatise, Hodges is concerned about the possible *proximity* of animal-to-human transmission. A Galenist, he regarded bubonic plague as arising from a 'poisonous Aura', from a 'Corruption of the nitrous Spirits in the Air' that affects many people at the same time; the 1665 infection, he believed, was imported from Holland in 'Packs of Merchandice'.[43] Although he rejects popular stories about direct transmission of cattle disease to humans, he agrees that humans and cattle can both be infected through a 'common cause', such as bad air, even if they respond differently.[44] Quincy similarly considers the possibility of what is now called zoonosis. Distinguishing between *epidemic* diseases that arise from a common cause, and *contagious* ones associated with 'subtle and active Particles' that, in his view, can 'penetrate the Pores of other Animals, and occasion a like Coagulation of their Blood', he holds open the possibility of cross-species infection: when the contagious particle is 'of that Nature' to 'Taint the Blood of other Animals', he writes, animals will be 'seized equally with Men'; if infection does not always occur, this is only because 'the Blood of Animals is different from humane Blood'. The contagion 'Particles', in other words, may not always find a suitable home, or host. Both of these texts, then, acknowledge that cattle suffer from diseases that are at least sometimes experienced by humans.[45] Epidemiologically, humans are *entangled* in a network of relations that includes cows, air, ships, packets of wool, pastures, cow keepers, government policies, animal spirits, blood—all evidence of a teeming and potentially infectious world.

Such questions invariably expand the networks of what we now call ecology by asking readers to rethink boundaries between animals and humans, health and environment. But one has to read carefully for signs of multispecies entanglements in Defoe's *Journal*. First, unlike Hodges's *Historical Account*, Defoe mentions cattle plague not at all, and cattle only twice, both in passing. He first refers to a group of people who, having fled London for the countryside near Henalt Forest, 'suffered' such 'great extremities' that they had turned outlaw: offering 'many violences to the county; they robbed and plundered, and killed cattle and the like'.[46] Second, he tells the story of a 'Citizen' who, having broken out of his house at Aldersgate, escapes to a garret room at an inn called 'the *Pyed Bull*'—a garret because the other rooms had been let to 'some Drovers being expected the next Day with Cattle' (85). The gentleman dies in the house, and within

and Defoe, see Lucinda Cole, 'What Is an Animal? Contagion and Being Human in a Multispecies World', *Lumen*, 40 (2021), 35–53.

[43] Hodges, *Loimologia*, 31–3.
[44] Hodges, *Loimologia*, 61.
[45] Hodges, *Loimologia*, 263.
[46] Defoe, *A Journal of the Plague Year* (1722), 171.

the week fourteen more people succumb to contagion. Although we see suggestions of an international cattle trade in the anticipated drovers, what these two stories have in common—and how they differ from Defoe's source literature—is that cattle are relegated to the background, removed to a shadowy landscape otherwise densely populated by humans alone.

And yet Defoe's *Journal* is markedly concerned with meat. Several passages in the novel focus on butchers and their 'tainted' or contaminated product: 'the Plague raged so violently among the Butchers, and Slaughter-Houses, on the other Side of our Street' that, rather than expose himself, the narrator prefers to go without eating meat (92); in the shambles near Newgate, two people fall dead, giving rise to the rumour that all the meat is 'infected' (279); the meat at Whitechapel was so 'dreadfully visited' that butchers began to slaughter cattle elsewhere, then bring the meat in on horses (92); people willing to venture to the shambles would not 'take [meat] of the Butcher's Hand, but take it off the Hooks themselves' (93). In Defoe's novel, then, living cattle are largely, although not completely, occluded by disembodied pieces of flesh that may, or may not, be a disease vector for humans. An international network of trade, mass animal die-offs, potentially cross-species pandemics, impassioned treatises on containment and cure, and coordinated systems of disease control are collapsed into scenes of human food insecurity and human fears of mortality in a city during England's last sustained experience of bubonic plague.

From a multispecies perspective, then, we can correctly describe Defoe's *A Journal of the Plague Year* as proto-ecological. By virtue of eighteenth-century theories of disease, some parts of the non-human world are endowed with agency in ways that elevate them to the position of what Bruno Latour would call an actant—that is, anything that modifies the behaviour of others through a series of actions.[47] In *A Journal of the Plague Year*, as Loar points out, actants include dung (human or otherwise); dead animals from the slaughter houses; 'Filthy unsufferable Smells' (45); and, I would add, potentially infected pieces of meat.[48] But there is no corresponding attention to lives other-than-the-human, no rethinking of 'life' itself as mortal and creaturely, no real sense of a shared world. Defoe's *Journal* resists being subsumed within the fantasy structures of 'infinite abundance', even as the cattle that populated both London and the English countryside disappear under the pressures of a disrupted and potentially infected human food supply. If the London plague, like the storm of 1703, signifies the eruption of God's vengeance on a sinful humankind, Defoe's belief that 'Nature plainly refers us beyond her Self, to the Mighty Hand of Infinite Power, the Author of Nature, and Original of all Causes' will always leave his depictions of the more-than-human world radically incomplete, without proximate causes, and in some sense beyond the parameters of epistemological inquiry.[49] Ready associations between virtue and abundance, or sin and scarcity,

---

[47] See, for example, Bruno Latour, *The Politics of Nature: How to Bring the Sciences into Democracy*, trans. Catherine Porter (Cambridge, MA: Harvard University Press, 2004), 75.
[48] Loar, 'Plague's Ecologies', 42.
[49] Defoe, *Storm*, 2.

ensure that Defoe's depictions of a devastated English countryside, Crusoe's unnamed island, the unknown interior of Africa, and the plague-stricken city of London are always embedded in other discourses, and mark trade-offs between prosperity and environmental constraints.

Further Reading

Lucinda Cole, *Imperfect Creatures: Vermin, Literature, and the Sciences of Life, 1600–1740* (Ann Arbor, MI: University of Michigan Press, 2016).

Brian Fagan, *The Little Ice Age: How Climate Made History 1300–1850* (New York: Basic Books, 2000).

Lora E. Geriguis, '"A Vast Howling Wilderness": The Persistence of Space and Placelessness in Daniel Defoe's *Captain Singleton*', in *Topographies of the Imagination: New Approaches to Daniel Defoe*, ed. Katherine Ellison, Kit Kincade, and Holly Faith Nelson (New York: AMS Press, 2014), 185–207.

Peter Knox-Shaw, 'Defoe and the Politics of Representing the African Interior', *MLR*, 96:4 (2001), 937–51.

Christopher F. Loar, 'Plague's Ecologies: Daniel Defoe and the Epidemic Constitution', *ECF*, 32:1 (2019), 31–53.

Robert Markley, '"Casualties and Disasters": Defoe and the Interpretation of Climactic Instability', *Journal of Early Modern Cultural Studies*, 8:2 (2008), 102–24.

Robert Markley, '"Land Enough in the World": Locke's Golden Age and the Infinite Extensions of "Use"', *South Atlantic Quarterly*, 98:4 (1999), 817–37.

Andrew McRae, *God Speed the Plough: The Representation of Agrarian England, 1500–1660* (Cambridge: Cambridge University Press, 1996).

Matthew Mulcahy, *Hurricanes and Society in the British Greater Caribbean, 1624–1783* (Baltimore, MD: Johns Hopkins University Press, 2006).

Geoffrey Parker, *Global Crisis: War, Climate Change and Catastrophe in the Seventeenth Century* (New Haven, CT: Yale University Press, 2013).

PART III
PLACES

CHAPTER 26

DEFOE AND LONDON

BREAN S. HAMMOND

ONE of Defoe's most recent biographers, John Richetti, wants us to know, before we know anything else about Defoe, that 'among the major eighteenth-century writers ... [Defoe] is almost unique as a Londoner born and bred'.[1] Defoe was in with the bricks—'literally', one is tempted to say. His Tilbury brickworks supplied some of the bricks for Greenwich Hospital, employing around a hundred workers at the end of the seventeenth century; and when, during the scandal provoked by *The Shortest-Way with the Dissenters* (1702), he wished to be perceived as a worthy burgher rather than a scurrilous libeller, he emphasized the utility of the brick manufactory and the opportunities it provided for ordinary Londoners to gain work and feed their families:

> Nor should the Author of this Paper boast in vain, if he tells the World, that he himself, before Violence, Injury, and Barbarous Treatment Demolish'd him and his Undertaking, Employ'd 100 Poor People in making *Pan-Tiles in England*, a Manufacture always bought in *Holland*, and thus he pursued this Principle with his utmost Zeal for the Good of *England*.[2]

Defoe's life triangulates around a group of London locations, none more evocative, perhaps, than the three sites where he stood in the pillory after the *Shortest-Way* jeu d'esprit went so shockingly awry: Cornhill near the Royal Exchange, Cheapside near the Conduit, and Fleet Street by Temple Bar.[3] Restless traveller though he was, Defoe's name conjures up the particular places of London with which he was associated—the Fleet, Newgate, Freeman's Yard, Stoke Newington.

In *The Fortunes and Misfortunes of the Famous Moll Flanders* (1722), Defoe's origins in the parish of St Giles Cripplegate and subsequent encyclopaedic knowledge of the London thoroughfares and alleys are very obviously put to work. A precursor of Dickens

---

[1] Richetti, *Life of Daniel Defoe*, 1.
[2] *Review*, ii. 55 (24 March 1705).
[3] Novak, *Daniel Defoe*, 186.

in this respect, Defoe deploys the streets of London almost as a supplementary character. When Moll steals a necklace from a child who had (perhaps) been at a dancing school in Aldersgate Street, her escape route is meticulously charted:

> I went thro' into *Bartholomew Close*, and then turn'd round to another Passage that goes into *Long-lane*, so away into *Charterhouse Yard* and out into *St. John's-street*, then crossing into *Smithfield*, went down *Chick-lane* and into *Field-lane*, to *Holbourn-bridge* ...[4]

Committing the crime in Aldersgate ward, the parish adjacent to that of Defoe's birth, Moll escapes through streets familiar to Defoe since childhood. Her route can be followed on John Strype's 1720 updating of Stow, *A Survey of the Cities of London and Westminster*, tempting us to suggest that such detail is lovingly supplied to secure the ends of an Ian Wattian 'realism'.[5] Even for the purposes of authenticity, however, there is more information here than a reader of fiction can require. Defoe is evincing his London pride, somewhat resembling modern Londoners whose initial conversation on arriving at a destination is to describe the streetwise and savvy route they took to get there. Cynthia Wall would argue that the very syntactical patterns of the prose are dictated by London topography in the above passage:

> Defoe's sentences are generally a series of clauses stitched together with colons and semi-colons ... The whole scene is related in one long paragraphical breath ... the event and the streetspaces are compressed, and in fact in their conceptual and topographical centre nestles Newgate Prison, the place Moll fears.[6]

Just three years after the publication of *Moll Flanders*, Defoe would give the following excited description of the same area in Letter II of the second volume of *A Tour thro' the Whole Island of Great Britain* (1724–6):

> From hence, let us view the Two great Parishes of St. *Giles's* and St. *Martin's in the Fields*, the last so increased, as to be above Thirty Years ago, formed into Three Parishes, and the other about now to be divided also.
> The Increase of the Buildings here, is really a kind of Prodigy; all the Buildings *North* of *Long Acre*, up to the *Seven Dials*, all the Streets from *Leicester Fields* and St. *Martin's Lane*, both *North* and *West*, to the *Hay-Market* and *Soho*, and from the *Hay-Market* to St. *James's street* inclusive, and to the Park Wall; then all the Buildings

---

[4] Defoe, *Moll Flanders*, ed. G. A. Starr (Oxford: Oxford University Press, 1981), 194.

[5] Ian Watt, *The Rise of the Novel: Studies in Defoe, Richardson and Fielding* (London: Chatto and Windus, 1957), esp. 1–34.

[6] Cynthia Wall, 'London and Narration in the Long Eighteenth Century', in *The Cambridge Companion to the Literature of London*, ed. Lawrence Manley (Cambridge: Cambridge University Press, 2011), 102–18 (114). Cf. Cynthia Wall, *The Literary and Cultural Spaces of Restoration London* (Cambridge: Cambridge University Press, 1998). On Defoe's punctuation and syntax, see also P. N. Furbank and W. R. Owens, 'Defoe and the "Improvisatory" Sentence', *English Studies*, 67:2 (1986), 157–66.

on the *North* Side of the Street, called *Picadilly*, and the Road to *Knight's Bridge*, and between that and the *South* Side of *Tyburn* Road, including *Soho-Square, Golden-Square*, and now *Hanover-Square*, and that new City on the *North* Side of *Tyburn* Road, called *Cavendish-Square*, and all the Streets about it.

This last Addition is, by Calculation, more in Bulk than the Cities of *Bristol, Exeter* and *York*, if they were all put together; all which Places were, within the Time mentioned, meer Fields of Grass, and employ'd only to feed Cattle as other Fields are. (*TDH*, ii. 78)

More obviously here, the street names are part of Defoe's great epic of transformation, of growth and progress—making the desert bloom—that is a predominant tonality in the description of London given in the *Tour*. It exemplifies the observation made by Pat Rogers that 'the materials of Defoe's fiction are often identical with the matter of his nonfictional works written at the same stage of his career', unsettling our contemporary conception, inapplicable to Defoe, that fiction and non-fiction are worlds apart.[7]

Defoe is, then, regarded as one of the chroniclers of London's irresistible development and growth after the Great Fire, an epicist of metropolitan progress. More precisely, his enthusiasm was harnessed by the emerging ascendancy of the City of London. Public credit and its palpable instruments, the Exchequer bills, enabled the financial system whose visible architectural manifestations were the Royal Exchange, Custom House, Excise Office, the Bank, and the headquarters of the great trading and insurance companies [SEE CHAPTER 14]. The *Tour* again:

The City ... has gained the Ascendant [over the Court], and is now made so necessary to the Court (as before it was thought rather a Grievance) that now we see the Court itself the Daily Instrument to encourage and increase the Opulence of the City, and the City again, by its real Grandeur, made not a Glory only, but an Assistance and Support to the Court. (*TDH*, ii. 87)

About those buildings that are great showpieces rather than palaces of utility, Defoe is less enthusiastic. Describing Wren's St Paul's Cathedral, he dwells uncomfortably on the constraints on situation and expense that the architect could not overcome; while on London's places of entertainment such as its theatres, he is completely silent. Nevertheless, the distance between Defoe's attitude to the city and its antithesis, the wild, undeveloped countryside, cannot be shown more dramatically than by citing his account of arrival in the county of Glamorgan:

Entring this *Shire*, from *Radnor* and *Brecknock*, we were saluted with *Monuchdenny-Hill* on our left, and the *Black-Mountain* on the right, and all a Ridge of horrid Rocks and Precipices between, over which, if we had not had trusty Guides, we should never have found our Way; and indeed, we began to repent our Curiosity, as not

---

[7] Pat Rogers, *The Text of Great Britain: Theme and Design in Defoe's Tour* (Newark, DE: University of Delaware Press, 1998), 25.

having met with any thing worth the trouble; and a Country looking so full of horror, that we thought to have given over the Enterprise, and have left *Wales* out of our Circuit. (*TDH*, ii. 173–4)

Alongside his satirical demythologizing of the so-called wonders of the Peak, this account of scenery later to be appreciated under the aspect of the 'sublime' makes clear by contrast Defoe's metropolitan affiliations.

Yet even in respect of cityspace, Defoe's thinking is not without nuance and complexity. Pat Rogers has argued convincingly that the *Tour* is permeated throughout by a threnodic, Virgilian sense of the 'tears of things', that its Whiggish 'onwards and upwards' paean to progress is at least tempered by an apprehension of decay and destruction, a tonality later to be given canonical expression in Shelley's *Ozymandias* (1818).[8] Defoe's London is conditioned also by proto-modernist intimations of the city as a terrifying site of anarchy and breakdown, and nowhere is that more powerfully expressed than in *A Journal of the Plague Year* (1722). Defoe had a longstanding interest in plague and how to control it. In an issue of his *Review* for 13 September 1711, he described a Danish outbreak, using letters from soldiers waiting to be stricken, to heartrending effect.[9] The occasion of the *Journal* is thought to be an outbreak of plague in Marseilles caused by the arrival from Syria of an infected ship in May 1720. Since there was some possibility of spread to England, Defoe was motivated to provide a fictionalized account of the horrors of 1665, focalizing the events of the plague year through the eyes of a saddler otherwise only designated H. F. The *Journal* is tendentious, its tendency being to oppose the practice of quarantining individual houses that, in 1665, resulted in the common incarceration of the sick and the healthy. First, this was impossible to enforce; second, those who would not, or could not, avoid observing the regulation were subjected to inhumane and appalling conditions: deprived of food and drink, closeted up with the dying and the dead, and highly likely to contract the disease. Some readers perceive, however, that the arguments put forwards in the *Journal* are not its thematic concern. There is a pressure amounting almost to allegory behind the text—not only the Biblical sense of a society being punished for sinfulness that is never far from contemporary thinking about epidemics and natural disasters, but also a conviction that the *Journal* cannot be referring to events that occurred sixty years previously. It must have some immediate significance for Defoe's readers in 1722.

Plague and the City

That significance, some have suggested, is the South Sea Bubble. Early in 1720, the South Sea Company, a company that had never made a trading profit—indeed, had

---

[8] Rogers, *Text of Great Britain*, esp. Chs 4 and 5.
[9] *Review*, viii. 347–50.

indulged in very little trade of any kind—was permitted to purchase the government's long-term funded or 'irredeemable' debt and convert it to South Seas stock. Parliament endorsed the scheme on 22 January 1720, resulting in the company outbidding the Bank of England by offering the Treasury £7.5 million for the right to assume its debt. The plan was to purchase the national debt at par (£100 share for every £100 of debt), and to offer government annuitants the opportunity to exchange their annuities for holdings of South Sea stock at whatever price the market then bore. Various forms of what would now be considered financial malpractice were used to prop up the value of the stock, ensuring that a company that had no business plan, no financial prospects whatsoever, and had never made a penny from any legitimate business, made itself the most powerful institution in Britain. Its capital value raised from shares topped £12 million, it owned half of the entire joint-stock capital of the nation, was indispensable to the country's economic security, and had as its governor King George I himself.[10] Provided the market kept rising, profits were unlimited. At its peak, the share price rose to £1,100. More than 450 MPs and 122 of the 200 peers were shareholders in the company at one time or another. But of course, the market did not keep rising.

Maximillian Novak argues that Defoe saw the bursting of the Bubble on an analogy with the spread of pestilence.[11] With hindsight, rising share prices could seem like the rising bills of mortality resulting from the plague. Similarities between the effects of avaricious greed—everyone wanting a piece of the South Sea action—and the contagiousness of plague could be perceived. Financial ruin, as also the plague, emptied the streets and turned usually busy thoroughfares into ghost streets. When the South Sea Company was first launched by Robert Harley in 1711, Defoe shared his patron's ambitions for it. *An Essay on the South Sea Trade* (1711) assured its readers that the company would establish British colonies in South America, bring home vast quantities of valuable commodities, provide new markets for English exports, and balance trade to the east (India) and to the west (South America). Fast forward to 1720, and Defoe is allegorizing the Bubble as a London fair, with the usual tricks and deceptions incident to such crowd-pleasing assemblies: '*Puppet-shows, Morrice-Dancers, Mimicks, Trumpeters, Tippling-Shops*, and other BUBBLES'.[12] In a letter published in *Applebee's Journal* on 20 October 1722, Defoe wrote in respect of the Bubble, and under the soubriquet T. Saddler: 'every Place is full of the Ruines of Exchange Alley, and the Desolations of the Bubble-Adventurers'.[13] H. F., the saddler whose memoirs of the plague year are recorded in *A Journal*, also calls attention to desertion and desolation:

> I cannot omit taking notice what a desolate Place the City was at that Time: the great Street I liv'd in, which is known to be one of the broadest of all the Streets of

---

[10] See John Carswell, *The South Sea Bubble* (London: Cresset Press, 1960); Helen Paul, *The South Sea Bubble: An Economic History of its Origins and Consequences* (London: Routledge, 2011).
[11] Maximillian E. Novak, 'Defoe and the Disordered City', *PMLA*, 92:2 (1977), 241–52.
[12] Defoe, *The Director*, no. 4 (14 October 1720), *PEW*, vi. 218.
[13] Quoted in Novak, 'Defoe and the Disordered City', 248.

> London ... the great Streets within the City, such as *Leaden-hall- Street, Bishopsgate-Street, Cornhill*, and even the *Exchange* it self, had Grass growing in them.[14]

City streets sprouting grass, the transformation of a thriving economic community into a country wasteland, represented for Defoe the destruction of an ideal. South Sea Company investment could have enabled individuals of the middling sort to aspire to wealth and position in the nation. The Royal Exchange was the thriving business centre of London, ensuring that the City would have at least parity with the Court in social importance; but it was the victim of its own avarice and so it was destroyed as if by plague. The extent of Defoe's disenchantment with the stock exchange can be measured by his 1719 essay *The Anatomy of Exchange-Alley*, subtitled 'Proving *that* Scandalous Trade, as it is now carry'd on, to be Knavish in its Private Practice, and Treason in its Publick'. The pamphlet begins by inventing a fictional story to show that stock-jobbing is one great confidence trick, ensnaring unsuspecting gulls in the same way as do the protagonists of his mature fiction. Later, Defoe takes us on one of his familiar tours round the purlieus of the London business world. One notes the coruscating, Swiftian irony of '*the Kingdom* of *Exchange-Alley* ... the Limits, are easily surrounded in about a Minute and a half':

> Stepping out of *Jonathan's* into the Alley, you turn your Face full *South,* moving on a few Paces, and then turning Due *East,* you advance to *Garraway's*; from thence going out at the other Door, you go on still *East* into *Birchin-Lane*, and then halting a little at the Sword-Blade Bank to do much Mischief in fewest Words, you immediately face to the *North*, enter *Cornhill*, visit two or three petty Provinces there in your way *West*: And thus having Box'd your Compass, and sail'd round the whole Stock-jobbing Globe, you turn into *Jonathan's* again; and so, as most of the great Follies of Life oblige us to do, you end just where you began. (*PEW*, vi. 143–4)

Having conducted us around the boundaries of this mock-heroic Lilliputian 'Kingdom' with its 'petty Provinces', Defoe takes his leave of us in Jonathan's coffee-house, a fittingly trivial palace for a discredited kingdom that requires ninety seconds to explore.

Disasters both natural and man-made have the potential to unleash anarchy upon a population concentrated in the narrow, winding alleyways and enclosed courtyards of a city such as London. *A Journal of the Plague Year*, despite its repeated assurances that the authorities coped well with plague and that charitable giving rose to the occasion, is one of the most powerful fictions of any era to present the possibility of urban breakdown under extreme circumstances. One of its disturbing leitmotifs is a repeated observation that despite the common adversity, there are people who try to profit out of it

---

[14] Defoe, *A Journal of the Plague Year*, ed. Louis A. Landa (1722; Oxford: Oxford University Press, 1972), 101.

through criminal activity: 'tho' it be something wonderful to tell, that any should have Hearts so hardned, in the midst of such a Calamity, as to rob and steal; yet certain it is, that all Sorts of Villanies, and even Levities and Debaucheries were practis'd in the Town, as openly as ever' (15). Defoe's readers had encountered one such hardened heart just two months earlier—Moll Flanders, who steals goods from people afflicted by fire. Later in the *Journal*, however, the narrator wishes to deny accounts of nurses murdering patients, and this leads him to discover the phenomenon of the urban myth. Defoe perceives very early that a feature of congested city communities is that they generate their own legends, stories repeated in awestruck verbatim by recounters who have no authority whatsoever for their truth:

> But these Stories had two Marks of Suspicion that always attended them, which caused me always to slight them, and to look on them as mere Stories, that People continually frighted one another with. (1.) That wherever it was that we heard it, they always placed the Scene at the farther End of the Town, opposite, or most remote from where you were to hear it: If you heard it in *White-Chapel*, it had happened at St. *Giles*'s, or at *Westminster*, or *Holborn*, or that End of the Town; if you heard of it at that end of the Town, then it was done in *White-Chapel*, or the *Minories*, or about *Cripplegate* Parish ... In the next Place, of what Part soever you heard the Story, the Particulars were always the same. (84–5)

But the inset narrative story of the three poor men of Wapping presents more realistic anxieties. They set out on a journey to avoid the plague on the principle that '*the whole Kingdom is my Native Country as well as this Town*' (124) and there is no legal right to prevent them from saving their lives, which puts them and the band of travellers they gather around them into conflict with local by-laws, watches, and constabularies. Represented on a quiet analogy with the exilic Jews, Defoe capitalizing on some of the success of *Robinson Crusoe* in the do-it-yourself aspects of the group's survival, this nomadic band fleeing from the spread of the infection poses the possibility that a committed mob might have violently faced down the London authorities determined to quarantine them. Even if the *Journal*'s official ideology is expressed in the statement that 'no Body perished for Want' (223), it is haunted by a subversive set of counter-claims showing that the poor had no alternative but to expose themselves repeatedly to mortal danger, to take on the worst jobs such as manning the 'dead carts', and to waste what meagre resources they had on absurd quack remedies. Standing as a fitting emblem of the exploited urban poor is the figure of '*Soloman Eagle*, an Enthusiast', who 'went about denouncing of Judgment upon the City in a frightful manner; sometimes quite naked, and with a Pan of burning Charcoal on his Head' (103). Reminiscent of Jonsonian figures such as Trouble-all from the play *Bartholomew Fair* (1614)—another of the great literary works to be created out of London topography—Soloman Eagle appears to be the deranged conscience of plague-stricken or Bubble-infected London. He is the dark underside of the progress narrative that Defoe is sometimes one-sidedly given the credit for having constructed.

Colonel Jack and London

On 20 December was published the last of Defoe's trilogy of masterpieces appearing in 1722, *Colonel Jack, or The History and Remarkable Life of the truly Honourable Col. Jacque.* Unmistakeably by the same hand as produced *Moll Flanders* and the *Journal*, *Colonel Jack* portrays a rogue with a conscience, whose story is told to illustrate how individuals born into unstable and poverty-stricken circumstances can rise above them and achieve a kind of gentility, provided they correctly identify what 'gentility' actually means. False forms of gentility, such as that implied by the code of honour that culminates in duelling, are set up to be rejected. Beyond that, and as in the other two major works of 1722, the story has particular theses to argue. In this case, Jack is used to show that kindness towards black slaves working the plantations is the most productive regime economically and that recipients of such benign treatment are naturally grateful. Taking its point of departure from the end of *Moll Flanders*, the story provides powerful propaganda for the American colonies as spaces where English criminals can start a new life with a clean sheet and can succeed in ways impossible to achieve in the old world.[15] At the novel's outset, however, that old world—the streets of London—is very powerfully evoked.

As in *Moll Flanders*, Jack lovingly describes the locations that gave him succour, identifying sites of manufacturing activity that doubled as hostels for the poor:

> As for Lodging, we lay in the Summer-time about the Watch-houses, and on Bulk-heads, and Shop-doors, where we were known; as for a Bed we knew nothing what belong'd to it for many Years after my Nurse died, and in Winter we got into the Ash-holes, and Nealing-Arches in the Glass-house, called *Dallows*'s Glass-house, near *Rosemary-Lane*, or at another Glass-house in *Ratcliff-high-way*.[16]

The annealing arches are those parts of the bottle factory where glass bottles were left to cool. They provide warmth for the sleeping urchins. Metropolitan readers can identify the location exactly from the naming of the specific bottle factory. This knowing readership is specifically addressed a little later in the narrative:

> Those who know the Position of the Glass-houses, and the Arches where they Neal the Bottles after they are made, know that those Places where the Ashes are Cast, and where the poor Boys lye, are Caveties in the Brick-work, perfectly close, except at the Entrance, and consequently warm as the Dressing-room of a *Bagnio*. (16)

---

[15] See Dennis Todd, *Defoe's America* (Cambridge: Cambridge University Press, 2010). Todd demonstrates that Defoe's fictional world is considerably at variance from the historical facts of indentured servitude in America.

[16] Daniel Defoe, *Colonel Jack*, ed. Samuel Holt Monk (Oxford: Oxford University Press, 1965), 9.

Accompanying the familiarity of location is a lexis that intensifies the sense the reader has of entering an urban subculture and learning its codes: terms such as 'Divers', glossed as 'Pick-pockets in the Town' (17); 'Coquets' (20), which are 'documents sealed by the officers of the custom-house, and delivered to merchants as a certificate that their merchandise has been duly entered and has paid duty';[17] 'Lug out' (20), meaning 'produce the spoils', the *OED* definition of which is illustrated with reference to *Colonel Jack*.[18] All of these are terms of art relating to the pickpocketing 'profession' and others, giving a sense of a technical vocabulary to which the reader is being given privileged access [SEE CHAPTER 23]. Exactly as in *Moll Flanders*, Jack describes the escape routes taken after his earliest pickpocketing expeditions: *Three-King-Court* to *Clements-Lane* to *Coleharbour* and over to St. *Mary Overs* Stairs (21); *Fenchurch-street* through *Lime-street* into *Leadenhall street*, down St. *Mary-axe*, to *London-Wall*, then through *Bishop gate*, and down old *Bedlam* into *Moorfields* (43). Such gazetteers as Jack repeatedly provides of his whereabouts and favourite haunts serve to distinguish *Colonel Jack* from the Spanish picaresque fictions to which it is sometimes compared. Defoe's London is much more solidly imagined than is the Seville of the picaresques.[19]

The combination of charismatic location and site-specific vocabulary is perfectly illustrated in Jack's account of his first highway robbery undertaken with his friend Will:

> We met at the lower part of *Gray's-Inn-Lane*, about an Hour before Sun-set, and went out into the Fields toward a place call'd *Pindar of Wakefield*, where are abundance of Brick-Kilns: Here it was agreed to spread from the Field Path to the Road way, all the way towards *Pancrass Church*, to observe any Chance Game, which as they call'd it, they might shoot Flying. (62)

In Pinder or Wakefield Fort, Defoe seems to have sought out a particularly resonant location, a place functioning not merely as a backdrop, but as a trigger for connotations that might invest his protagonist with some semblance of heroism. One of the chain of fortifications built around London as defences during the Civil War, the mound known as Pinder or Wakefield Fort, now the Mount Pleasant mail sorting office, had folkloric connotations. The story of George à Green, the Pinder (impounder of stray animals) of Wakefield, had been told most recently in 1706, in *The History of George a Green, Pindar of the Town of Wakefield*, signed by one N. W. His heroic resistance to factions rebelling against King Richard I, and in particular his forcing the rebels' messenger to swallow the three seals on their warrant document, is joyfully related there. Pindar of Wakefield is a site resonant, therefore, with London history and English folk myth. The metaphor of

---

[17] 'cocket, n. 2', *OED Online*, Oxford University Press, June 2018, www.oed.com/view/Entry/35400. (Accessed 13 July 2018).

[18] 'lug out, v. 5', *OED Online*, Oxford University Press, June 2018, www.oed.com/view/Entry/110978. (Accessed 13 July 2018).

[19] See further Brean Hammond, 'Defoe and the Picaresque', in *The Picaresque Novel in Western Literature: From the Sixteenth Century to the Neopicaresque*, ed. J. A. Garrido Ardila (Cambridge: Cambridge University Press, 2015), 140–56 (149–53).

wildfowl employed to describe the intended victims of highway robbery and the expression 'to shoot flying', meaning to shoot on the wing—that is, to ambush travellers—is recognized canting language of the period.

Unsurprisingly, Defoe's love-affair with London cooled as he aged. Its flipside is already embedded in *Colonel Jack*. When Colonel Jack returns to London in later life, it is a city in which he is elaborately double-bluffed by a seemingly genteel lady, is challenged to fight over a bill incurred by her, and is violently attacked by ruffians working for his wife's creditor. When in his late sixties Defoe came to publish the tract *Augusta Triumphans: or, The Way to Make London the Most Flourishing City in the Universe* (March 1728), he was decidedly jaded, seeing the city almost as a modern Sodom in urgent need of reform. As part of the suggestion for a foundling hospital, Defoe has occasion to consider bastardy, leading him to refer to an 'unhappy Gentleman toss'd from Father to Father', almost certainly Richard Savage, whose trial for murdering a man in a coffee-house brawl was the outstanding legal event of 1727 and whose final discharge was granted less than a fortnight before the publication of *Augusta Triumphans* (*PEW*, viii. 263).[20] Trading on such sensational topicalities, Defoe advances projects for preventing the murder of babies, suppressing phony madhouses that were being used to deprive married women of their liberty and provide their husbands with untrammelled access to their money and to other women, 'clearing the Streets of impudent Strumpets, Suppressing Gaming-Tables, and Sunday Debauches' (257), and limiting the sale of gin. London viewed through this set of projects anticipates that of Hogarth and recaps the career of his own Moll Flanders:

> A [servant] Girl quits a Place, and turns Whore; if there is not a Bastard to be murder'd, or left to the Parish, there is One or more unwary Youths drawn in to support her in Lewdness and Idleness; in order to which, they rob their Parents and Masters, nay, sometimes any Body else, to support their Strumpets; so that many Thieves owe their Ruin and shameful Deaths to Harlots. (269–70)

A little later, however, Defoe writes with uncommon sympathy for abused women:

> How hard is it for a poor industrious Woman to be up early and late, to sit in a cold Shop, Stall, or Market, all Weathers, to carry heavy Loads from one End of Town to the other, or to work from Morning till Night, and even then dread going Home for fear of being murder'd? (271)

One is struck by Defoe's divided ideological consciousness with respect to issues of gender [SEE CHAPTER 15]. Just as in the major fictions *Moll Flanders* and *Roxana* women are partly the victims of male exploitation deserving reader sympathy and partly experts in entrapment who engineer their own downfalls, the list of remediable social

---

[20] See Clarence Tracy, *The Artificial Bastard: A Biography of Richard Savage* (Cambridge, MA: Harvard University Press, 1953), esp. 82–92.

evils presented by *Augusta Triumphans* is ideologically both residual and emergent, positioned between older and gradually developing views of femininity. Some of the causes he espoused, such as the trenchant argument that domestic violence is criminal, are even today not fully resolved. But if Defoe had grown up in, say, Oakham in County Rutland, such a range of contradictory behaviours constituting femaleness would not have been thinkable.

In other social realms, *Augusta Triumphans* is surprisingly prophetic. Virtually all of the schemes Defoe advanced and institutional foundations he proposed, such as a University for London, would eventually be realized. Launching his proposal for the foundation of a music school for instrumentalists and singers, Defoe releases the likeable autobiographical information that he himself was 'accounted no despicable Performer on the Viol and Lute' in his youth (265). Sometimes branded a philistine on account of his Dissenting bias against the theatre—here, Defoe's attitudes did not deviate from those of his Puritan forefathers [SEE CHAPTER 4]—his enthusiasm for music is clear, though it takes the form, widely shared in the 1720s, of ideological dislike for Italian opera. Paying due credit to Corelli, Handel, Bononcini, and Geminiani, Defoe evinces the desire for a flourishing English musical tradition—perhaps even a native-language opera company. Such an emphasis on the cultural amenities of London prompts us to consider the broader implications of Defoe's metropolitanism.

DEFOE'S LONDON DISCOURSE

It remains to show that many of the matters Defoe took up, the causes he espoused, and the conversations in which he participated derived from his total immersion in the metropolitan public sphere. We begin with the issue of press freedom.

> The People of *England* do not believe the Parliament will make a Law to abridge them of that Liberty they should protect, for tho' it were more true than it is, that the Exorbitances of the Press ought to be restrain'd, yet I cannot see how the supervising, and passing all the Works of the Learned part of the World by one or a few Men, and giving them an absolute Negative on the Press, can possibly be reconcil'd to the liberty of the *English Nation*. (*PEW*, viii. 147)

Defoe published these words in 1704 in a tract entitled *An Essay on the Regulation of the Press*. In that pamphlet, Defoe spoke out against the reintroduction of press licensing, on the grounds that pre-publication censorship of print by government agents was a tool of party politics open to endless forms of corruption. His remedy for obscenity, scandal, and sedition was to make the law crystal clear and the punishments for breaking it equally so, in order that those who published offensive material would know they were doing so and would know exactly what to expect when they did. Towards the end, the argument shades into one about retention of authorial copyright: intellectual property is damaged by unauthorized abridgement of serious books and by publishers who undermine authorial labour by issuing cheap, inaccurate editions. Overall, Defoe makes a powerful, even if not strikingly original case for intellectual freedom and for the conditions in which it will flourish best. Appointing himself spokesman for 'the people of England', Defoe articulates very clearly here the role that he thinks public opinion should have in influencing parliamentary behaviour and shaping the law [SEE CHAPTER 12].

Daniel Defoe, this essay contends, could not have thought and written as he did had he grown up, say, in Salisbury in the 1730s rather than in London during the Restoration and 'Glorious Revolution' eras. Being a Dissenter, he could not attend university and the autodidactic aspects of his attitudes are omnipresent—his irrepressible enthusiasm, intellectual curiosity, love of schemes, projects, and arguments, his sometimes imperfect knowledge. Nevertheless, the education he received in the Dissenting academy run by Charles Morton in Newington Green was unique. It simply could not have been gained anywhere other than in (or just outside) London. As Ilse Vickers has shown, Morton based his curriculum upon the principles of Baconian science: 'Defoe's teacher was convinced that his reformed practical curriculum, his up-to-date information on experimental science, together with his defence of plain prose, would form his students' habit of mind and mode of expression'.[21] Defoe became a fierce defender both of practical education and of plainness of expression. In the *Review* for 16 December 1710, he hits out at a supposedly learned man, usually presumed to be his adversary Jonathan Swift:

> How often have I seen a Man boast of his Letters, and his Load of Learning, and be Ignorant in the common necessary Acquirements, that fit a Man either for the Service of himself or his Country ... I know [a man] that is an Orator in the Latin, a walking Index of Books, has all the Libraries in *Europe* in his Head ... but at the same time, he is a *Cynick* in Behaviour, a *Fury* in Temper, *Unpolite* in Conversation, *Abusive* and *Scurrilous* in Language, and *Ungovernable* in passion—Is this to be Learned? *Then may I be still Illiterate?*[22]

Swift clearly had need of one of his own 'flappers', the operatives who keep well-to-do Laputans on the straight and narrow in *Gulliver's Travels* (1726). When Defoe takes issue with the suave and gentlemanly *Spectator* (1711–12), it is because that publication prefers polite to plain speaking. Addison and Steele try to laugh us out of our follies, but Defoe prefers results: if, for instance, we wish to eradicate profanity, swearers 'must be spoke to in courser Language and plainer Words—And indeed, if I meddle with them, so they must'.[23]

Plain style became an issue for Defoe arising out of his first best-seller published at the end of 1700 or the start of 1701, the poem *The True-Born Englishman*. It provides

---

[21] Ilse Vickers, *Defoe and the New Sciences* (Cambridge: Cambridge University Press, 1996), 51.
[22] *Review*, vii. 521 (16 December 1710).
[23] *Review*, viii. 294 (14 August 1711).

a perfect example of the urban political conditions that produced Defoe's writing, of the unorthodoxy and boldness of his thought, and of the plainness of his style [SEE CHAPTER 10]. This is the poem's account of 'Englishness':

> Thus from a Mixture of all Kinds began,
> That Het'rogeneous thing, *An Englishman*:
> In eager Rapes, and furious Lust begot,
> Betwixt a Painted *Britton* and a *Scot*:
> Whose gend'ring Offspring quickly learnt to bow,
> And yoke their Heifers to the *Roman* Plough:
> From whence a Mongrel half-bred Race there came,
> With neither Name nor Nation, Speech or Fame.
> In whose hot Veins new Mixtures quickly ran,
> Infus'd between a *Saxon* and a *Dane*.
> While their Rank Daughters, to their Parents just,
> Receiv'd all Nations with Promiscuous Lust.
> This Nauseous Brood directly did contain
> The well-extracted Blood of *Englishmen*. (lines 334–47; *SFS*, i. 94)

The purpose of Defoe's poem is not to defend multiculturalism or immigration—though actually he was a proponent of immigration, campaigning in several issues of his *Review* for the settlement in England of Protestant refugees from the Palatinate in Germany.[24] In the above passage, he shows how the English are from their remote origins a bastard nation, whose ingratitude to the Dutch King William III, saviour of their bacon, can be explained on this basis. An outspoken critique of notions of family, pedigree, rank, and purity of blood just happens to be a by-product of the satirical invective. Though the poem scarcely *intends* to anticipate such sentiments as Burns's 'A Man's a Man for a' that' (1795), it nevertheless does have similar egalitarian implications. It is of a piece with the kinds of progressive thinking that we have encountered above in Defoe's views on such topics as women, freedom of thought, and even, in *Colonel Jack*, on slavery. Defoe did not oppose the institution of slavery—very few did in the 1720s—but he anticipated the arguments of the later-century ex-slave and campaigner Olaudah Equiano to the effect that only good treatment of slaves made economic, as well as moral sense. Of the poem's style, Defoe says in the Preface: '*without being taken for a Conjurer, I may venture to foretell, That I shall be Cavil'd at about my* Mean Stile, Rough Verse, *and* Incorrect Language' (83). His remark proved prophetic. William Pittis's *The True-Born Englishman: A Satire, Answered* (1701) is a paragraph-by-paragraph refutation of Defoe that castigates him, *inter alia*, for his prosaic poetry of statement—of a piece, as we have argued, with Defoe's Baconian precepts. Often ridiculed in his lifetime for the laboured nature of his writing—attacked by, for example, Swift for his lack of education and even

---

[24] Daniel Statt, 'Daniel Defoe and Immigration', *ECS*, 24:4 (1991), 293–313.

intelligence—Defoe was, as we have seen, a robust defender of the practical learning he did possess.[25]

These examples of Defoe's outspokenness underline the fact that metropolitanism was its constituting condition. London was a metropolis that grew vastly in population and in surface area during Defoe's lifetime. Milhous and Hume write that 'estimates vary disconcertingly, but in round figures ... between 1660 and 1700 the population of London jumped from a bit under 500,000 to upwards of 600,000. By 1750 it was pushing 700,000'.[26] Defoe was a creature of this growth and the rich opportunities for criminal activity that it furnished, treated in his great fictional works. Jonathan Pritchard has shown recently that London's expansion, too often believed to be uniformly genteel, brought in train an unprecedented degree of social intermingling: his argument is that even the most fashionable new addresses could not and did not exclude the urban poor and criminal strata.[27] Defoe did not need to look far, then, to do his research. Furthermore, his close-range observation both of the London poor and of London tradesmen, who could be criminalized for well-meaning business failure, afforded him a radical perspective on the relationship between poverty and crime. In the *Review* for 15 September 1711, he wrote:

> Let the honestest Man in this Town tell me[,] when he is sinking, when he sees his Family's Destruction in such an Arrest, or such a Seizure, and has his Friends Money by him, or his Employers Effects in his Hand; Can he refrain making use of it—? Can he forbear any more than a Starving Man will forbear his Neighbour's Loaf? Will the honestest Man of you all, if ye were drowning in the *Thames*, refuse to lay hold of your Neighbour who is in the same Condition, for fear he drown with you? Nay, will you not pull him down by the Hair of his Head. tread on him with your Feet, tho' you sink him to the Bottom, to get your self out?[28]

It is this distinctive metropolitan perception, summed up in the quotation from Proverbs 30:9 many times paraphrased by Defoe as '*Give me not Poverty, lest I Steal*', that frames the moral perspective of Defoe's major criminal fiction.

The political and financial revolutions of the Williamite period that created what is now termed the 'fiscal-military state', giving rise to the banking, stockbroking, and insurance industries centred on London that so engrossed Defoe, also produced an inexhaustible appetite for print controversy, of which he took supreme advantage. In February 1704, he commenced publication of the *Review*, which ran thrice weekly until

---

[25] See *Review*, vii. 514–18 (14 December 1710).
[26] Judith Milhous and Robert D. Hume, *The Publication of Plays in London 1660–1800: Playwrights, Publishers and the Market* (London: British Library, 2015), 91. Their figures draw on Roger Finlay, *Population and Metropolis: The Demography of London, 1580–1650* (Cambridge: Cambridge University Press, 1981), and E. A. Wrigley and R. S. Schofield, *The Population History of England, 1541–1871* (London: Edward Arnold, 1981).
[27] Jonathan Pritchard, 'Social Topography in *The Dunciad, Variorum*', *HLQ*, 75:4 (2012), 527–60.
[28] *Review*, viii. 352 (15 September 1711).

1713, becoming the most significant vehicle of rational public debate of its time, rivalled only post-1710 by the Addison-Steele periodicals *Tatler* and *Spectator* and by Jonathan Swift's *Examiner*. Jürgen Habermas's influential theory of the breakdown of absolute state control through the development of public opinion argues that in England after 1660, actual physical spaces developed to give new forms of polite conversation a local habitation and a name—London coffee-houses, clubs, and societies prominent among them—wherein the opinions of citizens could be expressed free from the trammels of the state and the church. Common people came to understand that they had a stake in their own governance, and in this new and unique realm of discursive sociability, they came together to discuss such matters.[29] Adrian Johns has argued that the combination of 'coffee, print and sociability' that constituted the public sphere required, as a sine qua non, *periodicity* of publication:

> Not just print, but cheap print, shared practices of reading, places in which to exercise that practice, and a routine of feedback by which readers' convictions could themselves be submitted to the commerce of print.[30]

Frequent periodical publication could alone achieve the to-and-fro and the speed of response that enabled claims and counter-claims, whether political, religious, ethical, or social, to be tested in the 'court' of public plausibility. Johns makes the further point that the 'plausibility of a broad realm of public reason depended, paradoxically, on the local integration of print into city culture'.[31]

In these terms, a strong case could be made for the *Review* as the single most important shaper of the 'public sphere' in the early eighteenth century [SEE CHAPTER 7]. We see in the range of Defoe's writing that this essay has covered precisely the combination of a transcendent order of books that nevertheless required, in Johns's words, 'neighbourhood knowledge, face-to-face relationships, chapel [guild] customs, and the proprieties of parish and ward'.[32] Defoe's range in the *Review* was much broader than that of specifically political rivals such as the *Examiner*, the sole rationale of which was to persuade the public to accept peace with France. Although he expressed deep respect for Addison's *Spectator*, his reservation was that its polite idiom was too often designed to head off at the pass intellectual combativeness and the coarseness of expression sometimes required by cut-and-thrust if truth was to be openly contested by reason. Some numbers of the *Review* are explicitly London-focused. That for 8 January 1713, for example, expresses the view that too many London shops are now trivial outlets for luxury goods and appetites:

---

[29] Richetti, *Life of Daniel Defoe*, 70.
[30] Adrian Johns, 'London and the Early Modern Book' in *Cambridge Companion to the Literature of London*, ed. Manley, 50–66 (63).
[31] Johns, 'London and the Early Modern Book', 64.
[32] Johns, 'London and the Early Modern Book', 64.

> Let any Man who thinks our Trade improved and encreased walk thro' the Principal Streets, where our Trade formerly flourished, such as *Cheapside, Corn-hill, Leadenhall-street, Newgate-street, Fleet-street, Snow-hill,* the *Strand, Pauls-Church-Yard, Paternoster-Row, Grace-Church-street, Cannon-street, Watling-street,* and such like Places. And, *First,* Let him reckon up all the Houses which are now to be Lett, and are actually Shut up, and then let him set aside all the Pastry-Cooks, Coffee-houses, Perriwig-makers, Cane Chair-Men, Looking-Glass Shops, Tinkers, *China,* or *Earthenware-Men*, Brandy-Shops, *and the like* ... and what a sad, tatter'd Condition will this *Improving City* look in?[33]

But even when London is not the explicit focus, the vast range of topics Defoe covers can only be furnished by a great metropolis. As for the 'bourgeois public sphere', the *Review* bears witness to the fault lines in the still-forming realm of public opinion, just as we saw earlier that Defoe's views on gender arise from both progressive and retrogressive structures of thought. Defoe's concept of what is open to rational discussion is fissured by crevices that come close to self-contradiction and even hypocrisy. Fiercely proclaiming his independence, disdainfully refuting the idea that his pen was ever for political hire—omitting to tell us that when he was in Scotland promoting the Union of the Scottish and English parliaments, he was being payrolled by Robert Harley—Defoe adopts the posture of a fearlessly outspoken defender of freedom who frequently has to use his cudgel to protect himself. Yet his plan in the *Review* of 1 September 1709 to suppress the stage through a government buy-out of the buildings and pensioning off of the entire London acting profession scarcely sits well with the freedoms of speech he proclaims with respect to the press. Defoe would gladly have suppressed the opinions of polemical adversaries such as John Tutchin, Jonathan Swift, and Charles Leslie.

One of Defoe's rhetorical triumphs is the preface he wrote for the eighth volume of the *Review* in July 1712, 'for the Support and Defence of TRUTH and LIBERTY', which speaks of the indignities and losses he has suffered (including the loss of his Tilbury brickworks during the *Shortest-Way* crisis). Defoe claims that he has expressed his 'Native, Free, Undirected Opinion' at all times, asserts his belief in Divine Providence, and predicts that one day he will be vindicated by those very Dissenters who once abused him [SEE CHAPTER 17] and understood by those readers now determined to misconstrue him. He rises to a rousing *apologia pro vita sua*:

> I have suffered deeply for cleaving to Principle; ... I was never so basely betrayed, *as by those* whose Families I had preserved from Starving; ... the People I have served, and love to serve, cut my Throat every Day because I will not cut the Throat of those that have served and assisted me—Ingratitude has always been my Aversion ... And now I live under universal Contempt, which Contempt I have learnt to Contemn, and have an uninterrupted Joy in my Soul, not at my being Contemn'd, but that no Crime can be lay'd to my Charge, to make that Contempt my Due.[34]

---

[33] *Review*, ix. 169 (8 January 1713).
[34] *Review*, viii. 2, 3, 7.

Self-aggrandizing heroism of this kind is easy to parody, and Defoe made himself a target by deploying it. Literary history has not been altogether kind to him, too frequently dismissing him as an effortful second-rater, whose work is laboured and clunky even at best. From the detached, classically inflected suburban perspective of such as Alexander Pope, so he seemed. But Defoe's strength and weakness is that he wrote from the dead centre of metropolitan life and events. He was immersed in those events, never detached, never less than fully committed to the arguments he made, the schemes and projects he devised, and the imaginative portraits that he conceived. London made him—and he remains—one of its greatest writers.

Further Reading

Judith Milhous and Robert D. Hume, *The Publication of Plays in London 1660–1800: Playwrights, Publishers and the Market* (London: British Library, 2015).
Maximillian E. Novak, *Daniel Defoe, Master of Fictions: His Life and Ideas* (Oxford: Oxford University Press, 2001).
Maximillian E. Novak, 'Defoe and the Disordered City', *PMLA*, 92:2 (1977), 241–52.
John Richetti, *The Life of Daniel Defoe: A Critical Biography* (Oxford: Wiley-Blackwell, 2005).
Pat Rogers, *The Text of Great Britain: Theme and Design in Defoe's Tour* (Newark, DE: University of Delaware Press, 1998).
Cynthia Wall, *The Literary and Cultural Spaces of Restoration London* (Cambridge: Cambridge University Press, 1998).
Cynthia Wall, 'London and Narration in the Long Eighteenth Century', in *The Cambridge Companion to the Literature of London*, ed. Lawrence Manley (Cambridge: Cambridge University Press, 2011), 102–18.
Ian Watt, *The Rise of the Novel: Studies in Defoe, Richardson and Fielding* (London: Chatto and Windus, 1957).

CHAPTER 27

DEFOE AND BRITAIN

ADAM SILLS

DANIEL DEFOE's conception of Britain, as a political, social, and cultural entity, is a fundamentally progressive one, especially when viewed in the context of more traditionally conservative evocations of Britain during the same period in which Defoe was active as an author, journalist, pamphleteer, and propagandist. For many writers and thinkers during the seventeenth and eighteenth centuries, Britain signified, more often than not, a deeply nostalgic and romantic ideal intended to conjure and establish its putative roots in classical antiquity as a territory within Rome's ever-expanding empire. Before the formation of modern-day England, Wales, and Scotland, Roman imperial forces conquered and ruled what they referred to as Britannia from roughly 43 to 410 AD, and it is this period that continues to inform Enlightenment conceptions of Britain from the Renaissance onwards, however misconstrued and erroneous those conceptions were. Hence, during Defoe's lifetime, the word Britain was often a kind of tacit shorthand for the myth of a unified Roman Britain, understood as a period of relative stability, peace, and prosperity in which the virtues of Roman civilization and culture were allowed to flourish and take hold in a profound and lasting manner. As Philip Ayres notes, 'At the same time that classical civic ideals were being adapted to current political purposes, the classical temperament was naturalised in a still profounder dimension by an intense focussing on Britain's own Roman past'.[1] We see this articulation of Roman Britain and its influence on the seventeenth and eighteenth centuries, for example, in many of the chorographies and atlases dedicated to mapping the vestiges of the Roman Empire, such as William Camden's *Britannia* (1586–1607), John Norden's *Speculum Britanniae* (1593), and John Speed's *The Theatre of the Empire of Great Britain* (1611–12), which continued to be published in successive editions throughout the following century. The interest in and engagement with Roman Britain continued to grow during the eighteenth century, with the publication of antiquarian works such as William Stukeley's *Itinerarium*

---

[1] Philip Ayres, *Classical Culture and the Idea of Rome in Eighteenth-Century England* (Cambridge: Cambridge University Press, 1997), 84.

Curiosum (1724), John Horsley's *Britannia Romana: or, the Roman Antiquities of Britain in Three Books* (1732), and William Roy's *The Military Antiquities of the Romans in Britain* (1793), among others. The bodying forth of the ruins and remains of Rome's occupation of Britain in the form of antiquarian topographies and maps helped to establish a direct and evidentiary connection between modern Britain and ancient Rome, or as Ayres puts it, 'the British had become genetically Roman'.[2]

To be sure, Defoe's understanding of Britain, while generally progressive in orientation, is no less imperial in its ambitions; however, rather than a vision of empire that looks to classical antiquity for its identity and sense of purpose, he eschews any mention of or reference to Roman Britain in the majority of his writings, instead choosing to focus on more present-day concerns, commerce and trade principally, as well as the impact of immigration and population growth on the economic health and well-being of Britain as a whole [SEE CHAPTER 14]. And on those occasions where he does turn to Britain's history, the picture he paints is quite different from those aforementioned admirers of Roman culture and civilization who wished to view themselves as their direct descendants and heirs. For example, in the 'Explanatory Preface' to *A True Collection of the Writings of Author of The True-Born Englishman* (1703), Defoe states that 'those nations which are most mixed are the best ... and have the least barbarism and brutality among them', an emphatic rejoinder to the xenophobic, anti-immigrant forces present in his own day, many of whom opposed the reign of William III due to his foreign birth and lineage.[3] *The True-Born Englishman* (1700/1) was written as a direct response to John Tutchin's *The Foreigners* (1700), a poem that depicts William as an illegitimate heir to the throne, one who levied exorbitant taxes on the gentry and nobility in order to maintain a standing army, and distributed wealth, land, and favours to his foreign-born allies rather than more deserving English subjects. Tutchin's argument, much like those we hear still today, is that an influx of immigrants and foreigners will only debase and corrupt the purity of the eponymous 'true-born' Englishman, and by extension the nation itself, bringing crime and poverty that can only diminish an otherwise prosperous economy and further undermine England's sovereignty at home and abroad. For Defoe, however, the case is just the opposite. As a proponent of mercantilism, he believed that an industrious and, just as importantly, growing population was the key to national wealth, regardless of one's nativity; more labouring bodies, immigrant or otherwise, would ultimately redound to the wealth and prosperity of the nation, hence Defoe's encouragement of immigration as a means of expanding England's population, which demographic historians argue contracted from roughly 1650 to 1720, including the catastrophic number of deaths due to the Great Plague and Fire in 1665 and 1666 respectively.[4] Pro-immigration policies, for Defoe, increased the ranks of potential Englishmen and, in turn, provided a much needed source of labour that would,

---

[2] Ayres, *Classical Culture*, 86.
[3] Defoe, *A True Collection of the Writings of Author of The True-Born Englishman* (1703), 1.
[4] Daniel Statt, 'Daniel Defoe and Immigration', *ECS*, 24:3 (1991), 293–313 (296).

counter to his detractors' assumptions, expand the national economy to the benefit of all.

This is a consistent line of argument in Defoe's early writings published both prior to and after *The True-Born Englishman*, including, among others, *An Essay upon Projects* (1697), *Some Sensible Queries on the Third Head, viz. a General Naturalization* (1697),[5] *Lex Talionis* (1698), and *Giving Alms No Charity* (1704).[6] Defoe's satirical poem, however, goes beyond making purely economic or political arguments in favour of the increased naturalization of foreign subjects and instead offers the moral justification that immigrants contribute to England's wealth precisely *because* they are not 'true-born'. As the above quotation suggests, there is something endemic to the English character that tends towards 'barbarism' and 'brutality' rather than the peace and prosperity that results from a 'mixed' nation. This moral quality to Defoe's arguments for increased immigration can be seen in the poem's introduction when he requests that Satyr:

> To Old *Britannia*'s Youthful Days retire,
> And there for *True-Born Englishmen* enquire.
> *Britannia* freely will disown the Name,
> And hardly knows her self from whence they came:
> Wonders that They of all Men should pretend
> To *Birth* and *Blood*, and for a Name contend. (lines 47–52; SFS, i. 86)

Ancient Britain, in this instance, would not recognize or understand the notion of a 'True-Born Englishman' and find it stranger still that such a person might claim '*Birth* and *Blood*' to a land that had been possessed by many peoples and many nations over its long and rather brutal history, well before the creation of modern-day England. This is, to be sure, no romantic or nostalgic evocation of England's past as some kind of pastoral idyll, a familiar and common trope during Defoe's own time, as I noted earlier, but rather a stark depiction of the whole of Britain as a land riven by violent conflict and perpetual conquest carried out by a succession of invaders, all of whom believed that they were somehow the first and best inhabitants of that land, including its most recent steward, the true-born Englishman himself. However, as Defoe's poem demonstrates, this is merely a fiction, an origin myth of pure, untainted ancestry: 'A *True-Born Englishman*'s a Contradiction, / In Speech an Irony, in Fact a Fiction'.[7] England, in fact, has many forebears, the blood of its citizens the product of their comingling over time: Romans, Gauls, Greeks, Lombards, Saxons, Danes, Scots, Picts, Celts, Normans, Angles, and Swedes, among other tribes and nations whose histories have intersected with the island

---

[5] On the attribution of this title, see J. R. Moore, 'Defoe's *Some Seasonable Queries*: A Chapter Concerning the Humanities', *Newberry Library Bulletin*, 6 (1965), 179–86; P. N. Furbank and W. R. Owens, *Defoe De-Attributions; A Critique of J. R. Moore's Checklist* (London: Hambledon Press, 1994), 7–8.

[6] Statt, 'Daniel Defoe and Immigration', 298.

[7] Defoe, *The True-Born Englishman*, lines 372–3; SFS, i. 95.

of Great Britain at some point in the past.[8] All have played their role in the formation of the true-born Englishman, even if that patrimony remains unrecognized and forgotten by those who would currently oppose the immigration of foreign subjects:

> Thus from a Mixture of all Kinds began,
> That Het'rogeneous Thing, *An Englishman*:
> In eager Rapes, and furious Lust begot,
> Betwixt a Painted *Britton* and a *Scot*:
> Whose gend'ring Offspring quickly learnt to bow,
> And yoke their Heifers to the *Roman* Plough:
> From whence a Mongrel half-bred Race there came,
> With neither Name nor Nation, Speech or Fame.
> In whose hot Veins new Mixtures quickly ran,
> Infus'd between a *Saxon* and a *Dane*.
> While their Rank Daughters, to their Parents just,
> Receiv'd all Nations with Promiscuous Lust.
> This Nauseous Brood directly did contain
> The well-extracted Blood of *Englishmen*. (lines 334–47; *SFS*, i. 86)

The true-born Englishman is thus mixed, the product of centuries and centuries of miscegenation, whether consensual or coerced; the nation too is the product of such mixing, understood here not as a monolithic, unified England, but more properly, as a heterogeneous and diverse Britain.

Defoe's understanding of the nation is, in this sense, a liberal and tolerant one, at least with respect to the question of immigration. Himself the descendent of Dutch Protestant immigrants, and, like William, an outsider of sorts, Defoe was a vocal supporter of the Foreign Protestants Naturalization Act of 1708, which, as its title suggests, allowed Protestant subjects from France, Holland, and Germany to emigrate to Britain and become naturalized citizens, provided that they took the sacrament in a Protestant church in Great Britain and swore an oath of allegiance and supremacy to the queen, as well as paid a fee of one shilling. Defoe wrote extensively in favour of the Act and the need for increased immigration in the *Review* and *A Brief History of the Poor Palatine Refugees Lately Arrived in England* (1709), again arguing that Britain could easily accommodate them and, more importantly, that they would provide a net economic benefit to the nation in the form of labour and an increase in the circulation of trade. However, despite the significant influx of roughly 14,000 Palatines, Suabians, and Lutherans, mostly fleeing war in their home countries, the Act was repealed only three years later in 1711 due to mounting Tory opposition, which viewed their presence as an undue burden on the nation and its resources, Defoe's arguments to the contrary notwithstanding.

---

[8] See Matthew Adams, 'Daniel Defoe and the Blooding of Britain', *BJECS*, 27:1 (2004), 1–15. Adams offers the important caveat that, while Defoe acknowledges that Britain is, in a word, a mongrel, the nation is not defined primarily by blood, but rather by laws and contracts that govern and protect the rights of property-holding citizens.

The demise of the Act did not signal the end of Defoe's support for a more diverse and heterogeneous Britain, however. His satirical 1717 essay, *An Argument Proving that the Design of Employing and Enobling Foreigners, is a Treasonable Conspiracy against the Constitution, Dangerous to the Kingdom, an Affront to the Nobility of Scotland in Particular, and Dishonourable to the Peerage of Britain in General*,[9] rehearses many of the same issues raised in *The True-Born Englishman*, albeit from the deeply ironic perspective of someone much closer to Tutchin's views on the subject than that of Defoe, hence the somewhat confusing and misleading title.[10] We understand the piece as satire not only because of Defoe's prior statements on the subject of population growth and immigration, but also his subsequent writings, *A Plan of the English Commerce* (1728) for example, which more or less conform to his belief that increased immigration is not only of economic benefit to the nation, but that labour and trade, regardless of one's origin or background, have a civilizing effect on the constitution and character of Britain itself. As with much of Defoe's corpus, economic and moral concerns are virtually indistinguishable and cannot be disentangled from one another. His thoughts on the subject of immigration, and its various impacts on Britain, are no exception in this regard. The nation is, for Defoe, defined less by blood or any specific ethnic or racial grouping, but rather by one's belief in and adherence to a system of laws intended to secure and guarantee the property rights of its citizens, the fruits of their labour as it were. Willing participation in such a system is as much a moral imperative for native and foreign-born alike as it is a political or economic one and thus essential to the character and identity of Great Britain.

For Defoe, one's national origin, ethnicity, and even religious affiliation are not necessarily defining qualities of the national character. He also rejects, by extension, the notion of a single, proper English language that should be spoken uniformly by Britain's varied subjects and citizens, although the eighteenth century would witness the beginnings of such a project to standardize English as a national language. Rather, Defoe appears to embrace the polyglot nature of English and the rich variety of languages, accents, and dialects that were spoken and written by the diverse peoples and cultures throughout Britain, none of which neatly conform to some putative national standard. This includes not only Welsh and Gaelic, found throughout Wales and Scotland, but also local and regional variants of English as spoken by so-called common people throughout Great Britain. Rather than stigmatize or deride such vernaculars and dialects, including the cant speech specific to a given area, profession, or class of people, Defoe instead champions a more pluralistic sense of the English language by taking the time to record in many of his writings its sheer diversity and heterogeneity, its various jargons and idioms, for the benefit of his reader, yet without really offering any judgement or correction to what he hears and transcribes. To his mind, the linguistic

---

[9] See Furbank and Owens, *Defoe De-Attributions*, 95–6.

[10] See Andreas K. E. Mueller, 'One of the Greatest Puzzles in Defoe Bibliography: John Toland, Daniel Defoe, and Ennobling Foreigners', in *Topographies of the Imagination: New Approaches to Daniel Defoe*, ed. Katherine Ellison, Kit Kincade, and Holly Faith Nelson (New York: AMS Press, 2014), 263–89.

diversity of Great Britain is, like the contributions of immigrants and foreigners to the economic prosperity of the nation, a strength and an asset, and certainly not a hindrance or barrier to national unity or a sense of collective identity:

> Defoe treats linguistic diversity not as an obstacle to communication, to be overcome by mandating standard English, but rather as an analogue to the diversity of natural resources that stimulates trade between one city or region and another ... [His] goal is not their erasure but fruitful reciprocity among them, on the model of profitable commercial relations between otherwise distant and dissimilar communities.[11]

Just as the diversity of Britain's natural resources encourages trade and commerce between its various localities and regions, so too does the plurality of vernacular Englishes found throughout Britain, precisely because it is the principal means by which trade and commerce are carried out by the merchant and labouring classes. It is the glue or tissue, as it were, that binds the nation together as the sum of its multifarious parts. This involves not only commercial activity between people and places marked by different local and regional languages and dialects, something which Defoe actively promoted throughout his career, especially in the case of Scotland, but also particular industries, professions, trades, crafts, and manufactures which are, for pragmatic and occupational reasons, steeped in their own varied iterations of the English language, their own vocabularies and idiomatic forms of speech. For Defoe, these modes of discourse are not deviations from or bastardizations of some primal, nativist sense of 'true' English, but rather the living and breathing embodiment of the language as it is actually spoken and written by diverse peoples across Britain, including Defoe himself, who frequently deployed in his writing the so-called plain, simple style with which he was raised as a Dissenter in London [SEE CHAPTER 10].

As many Defoe scholars have noted, the 'reality effect' he conjures in many of his novels is predicated, in part, on his familiarity and facility with Britain's colloquial forms of speech, no doubt the product of his journalistic methods and approach to fiction in general. Rather than the mannered, conventional style of many of his contemporaries, Defoe instead deploys the heterogeneity of vernacular speech in ways that reflect the nation in a more realistic fashion, attending to the discourse and rhythms of common, everyday life with which his readers would already be familiar. This includes the use of local and regional idioms and jargon whenever possible, especially as they relate to a particular profession or sub-culture, the world of criminals and criminality for example in *Moll Flanders* (1722), or the seafaring-life in *Robinson Crusoe* (1719) and *Captain Singleton* (1720). Defoe's narrators invite us into their world and, more importantly, their way of perceiving and communicating about that world, hence giving us a glimpse into the life of the nation that was perhaps previously unavailable or unknown to us. These various forms of cant, collectively, give us a richer, more complex, and perhaps

---

[11] G. A. Starr, 'Defoe's Tour through the Dialects and Jargons of Great Britain', *Modern Philology*, 110:1 (2012), 74–95 (80).

more authentic sense of Britain as a heterogeneous nation comprised of a multiplicity of languages, some familiar, others less so. As Janet Sorensen notes, 'In Defoe's novels, Britain is a Babel of regional, trade and craft, foreign, and cant languages … Yet there are no aspersions cast on the languages Defoe's narrators translate for their readers'.[12] Defoe offers no value judgements or criticisms about the rightness or wrongness of a given word, phrase, or expression, nor does he wring his hands about the deleterious effects of such 'linguistic confusion' on the nation, preferring only to represent and translate such vernacular speech for his reader, which is, in and of itself, a kind of value judgement given the general lack of such representation by other authors during the same period. Rather than a problem to be militated against or ignored altogether, Defoe sees the multiplicity of vernacular languages as an asset to be embraced and as a defining quality of British national identity.

However, as Sorensen rightly argues, that perspective is largely a privileged one, the product of the cosmopolitan traveller, such as Defoe, who not only has the freedom and mobility to experience and record Britain's linguistic diversity first-hand, in much the same fashion as a journalist would, but also the knowledge and ability to make sense of the polyglot and heterogeneous forms of speech he encounters and then to translate them for a broader readership. This is a far cry from advocating for or promoting a standardized English, but it is an attempt to unify the nation through the creation of a model British subject who, with respect to that heteroglossic confusion, is more liberal, tolerant, and—to return to my earlier point—civil towards the diverse peoples and cultures that make up the fabric of the nation. Defoe, in this sense, serves as our point of entry and guide to all things British, a model figure who will narrate its geography and its history for us so that we too may become fully participatory in the life of the nation. We see just such a construction of British national identity and subjectivity, not coincidentally, in Defoe's *A Tour thro' the Whole Island of Great Britain* (1724–6), whose very title makes clear his principal interest in serving as our guide to Britain, its various peoples, cultures, and languages and, more importantly, their relationship to one another [SEE CHAPTER 8]. Much like the touristic works that preceded it, such as Celia Fiennes's *Journeys* (published 1888) or John Macky's *Journey Through England in Familiar Letters* (1714–23), Defoe's *Tour* functions as a travel narrative that attempts to map Great Britain, including England, Scotland, and Wales, taking into account various places and people of historical or national significance, describing in great detail the features and contours of the land itself, and whenever possible recording local customs, habits, and traditions; however, unlike those previous accounts, Defoe's *Tour* remains committed to representing, first and foremost, the economic life of the nation in order to promote the view that intra-national trade and commerce are vital to the identity of Britain as a whole, if not its moral and spiritual well-being.

---

[12] Janet Sorensen, *Strange Vernaculars: How Eighteenth-Century Slang, Cant, Provincial Languages, and Nautical Jargon Became English* (Princeton, NJ: Princeton University Press, 2017), 63.

The *Tour* is, to be sure, an economic mapping of Great Britain, though a bit more speculative than actual on closer inspection, its treatment of Scotland in particular. Not that that lessens the value or importance of the work. As Christopher Parkes argues, 'Defoe saw in the discourse of thematic cartography the ability to transform physically and psychologically the landscape of Britain into a blueprint for economic development'.[13] Thomas Keith Meier reinforces this point, arguing that the *Tour* should be read as an extended defence of trade and commerce in keeping with, and in some ways, superior to Defoe's other economic writings. The *Tour*, he correctly insists, 'is as much a catalogue of Defoe's attitudes toward business as it is a collection of geographical facts about Britain'.[14] The result is an image of the nation that is, like the nature of trade and commerce itself, kinetic, dynamic, and constantly in flux. Defoe's mapping of the nation is the product of a narrator (ostensibly Defoe himself) who is able to comprehend these larger patterns of trade and commercial activity and, like his use of vernacular speech, translate them into the form of a travel narrative accessible to a general audience.[15] The *Tour* is an attempt to somehow capture that sense of ceaseless change and movement precipitated by economic activity, to submerge its reader into the ebb and flow of exchange, but on a national scale that allows one to see the interdependence of the various localities and regions which comprise the whole island of Great Britain. As G. A. Starr notes, 'Defoe finds beauty in the complex order of the system as a whole, in the distinctiveness and health of its constituent parts, and in the abundance that mercantile harmony produces: national unity, variety, and plenitude present a satisfying spectacle'.[16] The text thus allows the reader to experience the 'whole Island of Great Britain' as an integrated and knowable place, one whose identity is largely predicated on interconnected patterns of economic activity that touch upon and impact every corner of the nation.

Of course, to the untrained or inexperienced eye Britain appears to be anything but a harmonious and congruous whole, including to Defoe himself, who spends much of the *Tour* arguing for the need to reform and regulate intra-national trade and commerce in order to bring prosperity to those parts of Britain, Scotland most notably, where it is most wanting. Conversely, Defoe seeks to curtail the more pernicious effects of wealth and prosperity on those places, such as London, whose size, population, and appetites have grown 'monstrous' in his estimation, so much so that it threatens the economic and

---

[13] Christopher Parkes, '"A True Survey of the Ground": Defoe's *Tour* and the Rise of Thematic Cartography', *PQ*, 74:4 (1995), 395–415 (396).

[14] Thomas Keith Meier, *Defoe and the Defense of Commerce* (Victoria, B.C.: Victoria University Press, 1987), 57.

[15] Julian Fung argues that the *Tour*'s narrator is Anglican and so should not necessarily be identified with Defoe. 'Religion and the Anglican Narrator in Defoe's *Tour*', *SEL*, 53:3 (2013), 565–82.

[16] Starr, 'Defoe's *Tour*', 74–5. Cf. Terence N. Bowers, 'Great Britain Imagined: Nation, Citizen, and Class in Defoe's *Tour Thro' the Whole Island of Great Britain*', *Prose Studies*, 16:3 (1993), 148–78; Betty A. Schellenberg, 'Imagining the Nation in Defoe's *A Tour Thro' the Whole Island of Great Britain*', *ELH*, 62:2 (1995), 295–311; Pat Rogers, *The Text of Great Britain: Theme and Design in Defoe's Tour* (Newark, DE: University of Delaware Press, 1998).

moral fabric of the nation itself [SEE CHAPTER 26]. In the *Tour*, London is, to be sure, the centre from which all of Britain's commercial activity radiates and returns. As Defoe remarks in *A Brief State of the Inland or Home Trade, of England* (1730), 'Nature and the Course of Business has made *London* the Chief or Principal Market', which is largely due to its location with respect to the rest of the nation and the world.[17] It is also 'necessary there should be a Chief Market' according to Defoe, because it is, and will be, beneficial for all of England: 'Here the Main stream will run as to the Center, as the River to the Ocean, and as the Blood to the Heart; and it is certainly for the Health of the whole Body of Trade'.[18] However, as Defoe acknowledges in *A Plan of the English Commerce*, this analogy may easily run in the other direction: 'As the Veins may be too full of Blood, so a Nation be too full of Trade'. Likewise, 'the fine fresh Rivers, when they run with a full and gentle Stream, are the Beauty and Glory of a Country, ... but when swell'd by sudden and hasty Showers ... they turn frightful and dangerous, drown the Country, and sometimes the People' (*PEW*, vii. 259). Following Defoe's terrestrial and somatic metaphors, London has, in his estimation, overflowed its banks and glutted its circulatory system, endangering not only its own health and well-being, but that of the nation as well:

> It is the Disaster of *London*, as to the Beauty of its Figure, that it is thus stretched out in Buildings, just at the Pleasure of every Builder, or Undertaker of Buildings, and as the Convenience of the People directs, whether for Trade, or otherwise; and this has spread the Face of it in a most straggling, confus'd Manner, out of all Shape, uncompact, and unequal; neither long or broad, round or square; whereas the City of *Rome*, though a Monster for its Greatness, yet was, in a manner, round, with very few Irregularities in its Shape. (*TDH*, ii. 65)

Unrestrained and unregulated economic growth has affected London adversely according to Defoe, rendering it monstrous not only in terms of its 'straggling' and 'confused' geography, but also with respect to the impact such unbounded prosperity has on the rest of Great Britain, including other burgeoning centres of trade and commerce that must compete, directly or indirectly, with London. His comparison of London to ancient Rome is perhaps an apt one in this regard. For Defoe, the entire nation should ultimately benefit from the prodigious wealth and affluence of London, which in turn will reap the rewards from the sustained and reciprocal growth of markets throughout England, Scotland, and Wales; however, as with the imperial centre of the Roman Empire, that is not necessarily the case, as Defoe describes a London given over to avarice and gluttony at the expense of the overall health of the nation, Scotland in particular.

Defoe, in fact, devotes a considerable portion of the *Tour* to discussing the economic problems Scotland faces as it attempts to develop its trade and manufacturing such that it can compete with its counterparts to the south and so successfully contribute to the

---

[17] Defoe, *A Brief State of the Inland or Home Trade, of England* (1730), 15.
[18] Defoe, *Brief State*, 17.

general prosperity of Great Britain. However, in the course of his travels, including in parts of the Highlands, Defoe cannot help but note the enormous disparities that still exist between Scotland and England, despite his observations that the former possesses the necessary material and geographic conditions which might, at some point in the future, help close that gap. For example, upon entering Kirkcudbright, a coastal town, he says that the place 'is a surprise to a stranger'. The surprise results from his conflicting observations of, on the one hand, a 'People without Business' and a 'Port without Trade' and, on the other, all the materials and 'Opportunities' for trade, including a navigable river, a deep bay with an island to protect it from the sea, and a large salmon population as well as other varieties with which to build a sustainable fishing industry. Defoe, however, has difficulty reconciling the two realities:

> In a Word, it is to me the Wonder of all the Towns of *North-Britain*; especially, being so near *England*, that it has all the Invitations to Trade that Nature can give them, but they take no Notice of it. A Man might say of them, that they have the *Indies* at their Door, and will not Dip into the Wealth of them; a Gold Mine at their Door, and will not Dig it. (*TDH*, iii. 190)

To his credit, Defoe does not rationalize the problem by laying the blame for the current state of Kirkcudbright directly on the Scots themselves or insinuate that they are naturally predisposed to indolence, though he does acknowledge those detractors who explain the reasons for their poverty in just these terms. Instead, he reverses the formula to argue that indolence is an effect of poverty, not the other way around, and that the reasons for poverty are more complex in nature and thus harder to get at through mere topographical description. While he observes that the people not only *are* poor, but that they *look* poor as well, he goes on to suggest that the sober, grave mien of the townspeople, their general look of malaise and seriousness, may also be the surest sign that they could be a productive and diligent source of labour, if the conditions were right.[19] Defoe's survey of Scotland in the *Tour* is thus meant to underscore the sense of promise visible in the physical landscape, despite its current lack of use, and is clearly a plea for the further development and improvement of Scotland's natural resources and the increased integration of English and Scottish trade in order to substantiate and legitimate the 1707 Act of Union, of which Defoe was an ardent supporter and promoter.

In fact, Defoe was an instrumental figure in the ratification of the 1707 Act of Union that joined together the kingdoms of England and Scotland, having gone to Edinburgh in early October 1706 at the request of Robert Harley, Queen Anne's secretary of state, albeit as a spy whose real purpose there, while suspected by some, was never fully disclosed [SEE CHAPTERS 20 AND 21]. During his time in Edinburgh, which lasted

---

[19] Alistair M. Duckworth offers a similar reading of this passage. He argues that Defoe appropriates the classical *topos* of 'unbought provisions' found in many country house poems of the seventeenth century and simply applies it to the Scottish marketplace. '"Whig" Landscapes in Defoe's *Tour*', PQ, 61:4 (1982), 453–65 (459).

roughly until early January 1708, well after the Act of Union went into effect in May 1707, Defoe was tasked with promoting the virtues and benefits of the Union to Scottish parliamentarians, Presbyterian clergyman, and lay citizens, some of whom were resistant, if not outright hostile, to the idea of union in any form. As well, Defoe served as a conduit between the Scottish and English governments, regularly reporting his findings and impressions to Harley, who believed that Defoe's talents as a writer and journalist would serve his and England's interests well. He was not mistaken. In one early letter to Harley, dated 26 November 1706, Defoe champions his uncanny ability to tailor his character and his discourse to suit the diverse constituencies whom he would need to address and, ultimately, win over:

> I am Perfectly Unsuspectd as Corresponding with anybody in England. I Converse with Presbyterian, Espicopall-Dissenter, papist and Non Juror, and I hope with Equall Circumspection … I have faithfull Emissaries in Every Company And I Talk to Everybody in Their Own way. To the Merchants I am about to Settle here in Trade, Building ships &c. With the Lawyers I Want to purchase a House and Land to bring my family & live Upon it (God knows where the Money is to pay for it.) To day I am Goeing into Partnership with a Membr of parliamt in a Glass house, to morrow with Another in a Salt work. With the Glasgow Mutineers I am to be a fish Merchant, with the Aberdeen Men a woolen and with the Perth and western men a Linen Manufacturer, and still at the End of All Discourse the Union is the Essentiall and I am all to Every one that I may Gain some. (*Letters*, 158–9)

As noted previously, Defoe's understanding of the nation hinges on this idea of a heterogeneous, polyglot Britain that, rather than an unruly, cacophonous Babel of languages and cultures, can be made to cohere and coalesce into a unified national body, provided that one is open, willing, and able to accommodate oneself to those different voices and peoples. Defoe is, in this sense, both the master spy and the ideal British subject, mobile and flexible enough to speak to the Scots on their terms and in the idiom of whatever audience he is currently addressing, yet still able to do the bidding of his superiors at home in London by making political arguments for a unified Britain without rousing any suspicions. He can translate the cares and concerns of anti-Union Scots back to Harley in a fairly liberal and tolerant manner and, conversely, translate the pro-Union arguments of the Harley government to those in Scotland who still remain unconvinced, thus laying the groundwork for mutual understanding and agreement, which was Defoe's primary objective.

Of course, that act of translation is rendered somewhat easier when there already exists an underlying common discourse regarding the importance of trade and commerce to the Union's ultimate success, as we see in the *Tour* and elsewhere in Defoe's writings. He extols, for example, the economic benefits of a unified Great Britain to the Scottish people in the explicitly pro-Union poem *Caledonia* (1706):

> With Wealth and People, Happy, Rich and Free,
> You'd first *Improve the Land*, and then *the Sea*;

> Be Strong, be Great, be Rich, be *Europe's* Fear,
> Their War, their Wealth, their Trade, their Honours share.
> (lines 379–82; *PEW*, iv. 235)

In the poem, Defoe expresses great admiration for Scotland's 'Ancient Spirit', which he characterizes as a fierce, combative warrior culture that has protected them well from would-be invaders and outsiders, hence his spending considerable time recounting and praising the many brave and valorous acts committed in battle over the course of Scotland's history: 'Ages of Blood have brought them up to War / And their strong Legions breath in every Air' (lines 566–7; *PEW*, iv. 241). That said, Defoe believes that military strength and prowess are no longer the basis of true national power and wealth; rather, it is the expansion of trade and commerce and the improvement and development of the land that will form the foundation for a unified Great Britain and help guarantee its future success. As Laurence Dickey has argued, Defoe believed that 'a nation's "strength" lay more in its commercial wealth than in the martial valour of its people', dating back at least to his 1697 essay, *An Argument Shewing, That a Standing Army, With Consent of Parliament, is not Inconsistent with a Free Government*, in which he offers the following maxim: 'He who has the longest sword has yielded to them who had the longest purse'.[20] With this principle firmly in mind nearly a decade later, *Caledonia* sympathetically calls upon the Scottish people to embrace that so-called Ancient Spirit, not in the name of war or bloodshed, but rather in the service of new pursuits, new projects, new interests that will bring Scotland into a more prosperous and open relationship with Europe and the world as a source of economic wealth and power. The Union, Defoe concludes, will restore Scotland to its ancient glory and transform the Scottish national character ostensibly from barbaric warrior to civilized merchant, which would be to the benefit of Britain as a whole:

> Thus blest with Art, enricht with Heads and Hands,
> Producing Seas, and *more productive* Lands;
> The Climate sound, the People prompt and strong;
> *Why is her Happiness delay'd so long*? (lines 1175–8; *PEW*, iv. 264)

Scotland's 'happiness', as it were, Defoe suggests, will only be possible when '*Britain* be one, one End and Interest view, / And hand in hand *one Happiness* pursue' (lines 1006–7; *PEW*, iv. 259).

The only question that remained on this score, and one that was raised frequently during Defoe's time in Edinburgh, was who stood to gain and who stood to lose economically from the Act of Union, a subject with which Defoe was forced to contend in many of his writings given the widespread reservations regarding his otherwise sunny

---

[20] Laurence Dickey, 'Power, Commerce, and Natural Law in Daniel Defoe's Political Writings, 1698–1707', in *A Union for Empire: Political Thought and the Union of 1707*, ed. John Robertson (Cambridge: Cambridge University Press, 1995), 64, 68.

projections for Scotland's future. He wrote extensively in the *Review*, Defoe's London-based periodical, regarding the economic virtues of the Union to detractors and sceptics back home in England. As well, he crafted numerous essays, such as *Observations on the Fifth Article of the Treaty of Union* (1706), *An Enquiry into the Disposal for the Equivalent* (1706), and six parts of *An Essay at Removing National Prejudices Against a Union with Scotland* (1706–7), among others, which addressed the concerns and objections of those who opposed the Union on the grounds that it would ultimately redirect the wealth of Scotland towards England. For example, in *A Discourse Upon an Union of the Two Kingdoms of England and Scotland* (1707),[21] Defoe compares the future prosperity of Scotland to that of another part of Britain, Wales, arguing that the Union has not only been of immense benefit to the Welsh, but that given Scotland's geography, population, and abundance of natural resources, it far outstrips its neighbour to the south in terms of its potential contributions to the general wealth of the nation:

> The Interest of *England*, could not be less improved by Uniting *Scotland* to it, than by the Accession of *Wales*; the Strength of the former, is much beyond that of the other: Its Extent of Grounds and Number of Inhabitants, is much superiour. And besides, the Riches of *Scotland*, by joyning its Interest with our own, and by our giving it equal Encouragement for Trade, will prove more Considerable, than ever we have found the other to be.[22]

Later in the essay, Defoe acknowledges that the benefits of increased trade and commerce as a result of the Union may not be distributed equally across Scotland, that some markets and possibly whole towns and villages will likely shrink or even disappear over time; however, he insists that such losses are merely accidental and unintentional and that, in the long term, 'the whole will be enrich'd, and the *Publick* become a Gainer by it'.[23] Just as Defoe emphasizes the 'Whole Island of Great Britain' in the *Tour*, it is again the prosperity and integrity of the 'whole' that concerns him here, rather than the fortunes, or misfortunes as the case may be, of any one area or place within Britain.

While Wales perhaps provides an apt foil for Defoe in this instance, Ireland and its history with respect to England remained a sticking point for many Scots who objected to the Union, believing that the colonization of Ireland and its aftermath offered a more accurate picture of Scotland's likely future under a unified Great Britain, especially with respect to England's treatment of Irish Catholics and Dissenters there. Rather than equal citizens under a single crown and parliament, many Anglo-Irish subjects were instead treated like a conquered people, often deprived of basic rights and excluded from having any voice in their own governance.[24] Sympathetic to their plight, members of Scotland's

---

[21] See Furbank and Owens, *Defoe De-Attributions*, 31.
[22] Defoe, *A Discourse Upon an Union of the Two Kingdoms of England and Scotland* (1707), 18.
[23] Defoe, *Discourse Upon an Union*, 28.
[24] Defoe explicitly addressed the application of a religious test to Irish Dissenters in *The Experiment; or, the Shortest Way with Dissenters Exemplified* (1705).

Parliament and Presbyterian ministers saw in Ireland the seeds of their own demise as a sovereign nation and so resisted any arguments for the Union which promised otherwise. At issue was not simply the economic disparities between centre and margin, but rather religious difference, specifically, the authority and autonomy of the Presbyterian Church with respect to the Church of England, both of which had cause, however real or baseless, to fear the other within a unified Britain. Scottish clergymen feared the subversion and possible nullification of the Scottish Act of Security, which established the Presbyterian Church as an independent and autonomous ecclesiastical body apart from the Church of England, and during Defoe's time in Edinburgh, Presbyterian ministers frequently delivered sermons to the public on this very subject, stirring up fear and antipathy towards the Union. While Defoe found their accusations to be without grounds, and in some cases openly seditious, he, nevertheless, struck a sympathetic 'tone of impartiality and exculpation' in response to their concerns, often giving voice to their fears by acknowledging the tendentious and, at times, violent history between Scotland and England and, by extension, the Presbyterian and Anglican Churches.[25] As a Dissenter himself and so the victim of religious intolerance and persecution by the Church of England, Defoe innately understood the reasons and grounds for their objections to the Union; however, he used that sympathetic identification to, at once, draw Presbyterian clergy in but then show them that they have nothing to fear from the Union of Scotland and England, that the Presbyterian Church would remain an independent and autonomous ecclesiastical body whose religious authority and governance in Scotland would remain free from restriction and interference by the Anglican Church [SEE CHAPTER 17].

In Part III of his *An Essay at Removing National Prejudices Against a Union with England* (1706), Defoe makes this strategy explicit:

> Hitherto you have been jealous of *England*, putting upon you Episcopacy, Tyrany, &c. And I cannot say, 'tis without cause, and in case of Ruptures, War, diferent Soveraigns, and a Thousand Casualties and uncertainties, to which the Church as now Established is subject, both from *England* without, as distinctly and disunitedly consider'd, *Which after the Queen no Body can answer for*; and from a numerous and doubly Disaffected Party at Home: Who, I say, in case of those things, shall Answer, for what may or may not befal the present Establisht Church? I dare say, no man, that has a true Zeal for it can say, he is easy in the present condition of the Church, abstracted from this Union. (*PEW*, iv. 96)

Defoe also acknowledges that many of the long-held prejudices and animosities that have existed between the two churches are rooted in outright propaganda and groundless conspiracy theories that have been allowed to circulate unchecked and unexamined. In his essay *An Historical Account of the Bitter Sufferings, and Melancholly Circumstances of the Episcopal Church in Scotland* (1707), Defoe argues that accusations regarding scandals, misdeeds, and atrocities ascribed to the Presbyterian Church often

---

[25] Novak, *Daniel Defoe*, 344.

originated from within England itself to serve its own political purposes and are in no way rooted in fact or truth. Either way, Defoe openly agrees that the Scots have a legitimate reason to be apprehensive of the Union given the history he briefly outlines here, but he goes on to suggest that, rather than fear the possible diminution or destruction of the Presbyterian Church, the Scots should instead see the Act of Union as the instrument that will ultimately secure its authority and legitimacy well into the future:

> Upon an Union, all these fears vanish. 'Tis for ever rendered impossible to Overthrow the Settlement of the Presbyterian Church of *Scotland*; But by Subverting the constitution, by absolute Arbitrary Government, and the openest Bare-Fac'd Tyranny. The Church and the constitution, the Spiritual and Temporal Liberty, have the same Sanction, Subsist and Depend upon the same Security, are Defended by the same Power, Demanded by the same Right, Twisted and Connected together, cannot fall, but by the same Disaster, Nor stand, but by the Support of one another. (96)

It is an argument that Defoe fleshed out further in his *History of the Union between England and Scotland*, which he began writing in Edinburgh shortly after the Union passed but was not published until 1709, well after the Act of Union had been ratified by both English and Scottish parliaments.[26]

As Defoe notes in his dedicatory letter to Queen Anne, 'by the Union, they [Scotland] see themselves unalterably established, their *Church-Government* made a Fundamental of the Constitution, and the very *Church of England* engaged to preserve it intire' (*TDH*, vii. 38). The Scottish Parliament, wary of such promises, passed 'An Act for Securing the Protestant Religion and Presbyterian Church Government' on 12 November 1706, prior to the ratification of the Act of Union; however, that did not entirely resolve the issue, as there still remained considerable opposition from Jacobite forces in Scotland who, in their desire to see the Stuart monarchy restored, conspired with France in a failed invasion of north-east Scotland in 1708, the year following the Union, the events of which Defoe briefly details in the 'Preface' to the *History*. Recognizing that there remained many obstacles to the creation of a unified nation even after its legal establishment, Jacobitism perhaps most notably, *The History of the Union* represented Defoe's attempt to narrate and frame the Act of Union in 1707 in a way that made it appear as the logical and inevitable resolution to centuries of conflict and violence between the two kingdoms, beginning roughly with Edward I's attempts to unify England and Scotland through marriage in the thirteenth century. He then goes on to offer a detailed, journalistic accounting of present events that resulted in the Act of Union, including his own first-person narration of those events and an expansive appendix that includes various forms of documentary evidence, such as parliamentary debates and resolutions

---

[26] Defoe ultimately came to regret such arguments, as well as his participation in the Union, following the passage of the Church Patronage Act (1711) and the Scottish Episcopalians Act (1711), both of which directly contravened provisions in the Act of Union protecting the independence and sovereignty of the Church of Scotland. *Review*, viii. 533–6 (29 January 1712).

in England and Scotland at that time. In so doing, Defoe sought to justify and legitimate the Union to those who still opposed it, even after the Act of Union, and who perhaps would offer a history of the relationship between England and Scotland that differed greatly from Defoe's own political and ideological perspective. His *History of the Union* is thus a pre-emptive attempt to counteract such criticisms, by viewing the Union through the lens of a broader Providential history that, despite previous failed attempts and the present actions of its detractors, would ultimately see England and Scotland joined together once and for all [SEE CHAPTER 9]. The Union was, in this sense, more than simply an act of Parliament or a legal settlement for Defoe; rather, it was evidence of the hand of God working to effectuate the consolidation and integration of England and Scotland into a single nation, Britain, which was Defoe's true goal, above and beyond his duties to Harley and the Crown.

As Clare Jackson and others have argued, Defoe's interest in the Union went far beyond integrating the governments of Scotland and England; rather, the vision he offers is more akin to Benedict Anderson's notion of an 'imagined community' in which Scottish and English national identities are, over time, subsumed within a new and distinctly British national identity.[27] In Part III of his *An Essay at Removing National Prejudices* (1706), Defoe articulates this idea of uniting England and Scotland into one, indissoluble body:

> But if the Union be an Incorporation, a Union according to the extent of the Letter, it must then be a Union of the very SOUL OF THE NATION, all its Constitution, Customs, Trade and Manners, must be blended together, digested and concocted, for the mutual united, undistinguish't, good, growth and health of the one whole united Body. (*PEW*, iv. 94)

Jackson notes a similar evocation of the Union's true purpose in a later essay, *The Scots Nation and Union Vindicated* (1714), in which Defoe claims that 'there is not a *Scotsman* or an *Englishman* in the World, the Two Natures, nationally Speaking, being dissolved into One, *viz. Britain*'.[28] In many ways, the arguments Defoe offers here, as well as in *The History of the Union*, return us to many of the same ideas previously articulated in *The True-Born Englishman*, with which I began this essay. As Leith Davis observes, in the section titled 'A General History of Unions in Britain' Defoe does acknowledge that the 'blood' of the Scots is perhaps purer and less mixed than that of their fellow Englishmen, given their very different history and geography;[29] however, he suggests that their union would be a positive for Scotland for this very reason:

---

[27] Clare Jackson, 'Conceptions of Nationhood in the Anglo-Scottish Debates of 1707', *Scottish Historical Review*, 87 (Supplement 2008), 61–77; Katherine Clark, *Daniel Defoe: The Whole Frame of Nature, Time and Providence* (New York: Palgrave, 2007), 78–94; Leith Davis, *Acts of Union: Scotland and the Negotiation of the British Nation, 1707–1830* (Stanford, CA: Stanford University Press, 1999), 19–45.

[28] Defoe, *The Scots Nation and Union Vindicated* (1714), 14.

[29] Leith, *Acts of Union*, 41.

> 'Tis true, *England* is much more mixt in Blood, and the Reason of this is plain, in that, being a Nation powerful in Wealth, Fruitful in soil, and above all, increasing in Commerce, more Nations have sought to settle among them, numbers of People have flowed in upon them, from all Parts of the World, and blending their Blood with the most ancient Families, have destroyed all that can be called National, as to Antiquity among them, and they do not pretend to it. (*TDH*, vii. 82)

Scotland's homogeneity is, in short, part of the problem. It is a hindrance to its future economic health and prosperity, if not its moral and spiritual well-being. Mixed or mongrel nations, such as England, by contrast, face no such barriers and so have succeeded where Scotland and others have failed, at least in Defoe's estimation. The Union thus seeks to redress this imbalance through the further intermingling of the 'blood' of England and Scotland and, over time, the whole of Great Britain, which is both the product of that heterogeneity and the very process by which the national character is ultimately forged and secured.

Further Reading

Matthew Adams, 'Daniel Defoe and the Blooding of Britain', *BJECS*, 27:1 (2004), 1–15.
Terence N. Bowers, 'Great Britain Imagined: Nation, Citizen, and Class in Defoe's *Tour Thro' the Whole Island of Great Britain*', *Prose Studies*, 16:3 (1993), 148–78.
Katherine Clark, *Daniel Defoe: The Whole Frame of Nature, Time and Providence* (New York: Palgrave, 2007).
Leith Davis, *Acts of Union: Scotland and the Negotiation of the British Nation, 1707–1830* (Stanford, CA: Stanford University Press, 1999).
Christopher Parkes, '"A True Survey of the Ground": Defoe's *Tour* and the Rise of Thematic Cartography', *PQ*, 74:4 (1995), 395–415.
John Robertson (ed.), *A Union for Empire: Political Thought and the Union of 1707* (Cambridge: Cambridge University Press, 1995).
Pat Rogers, *The Text of Great Britain: Theme and Design in Defoe's Tour* (Newark, DE: University of Delaware Press, 1998).
Betty A. Schellenberg, 'Imagining the Nation in Defoe's *A Tour Thro' the Whole Island of Great Britain*', *ELH*, 62:2 (1995), 295–311.
Janet Sorensen, *Strange Vernaculars: How Eighteenth-Century Slang, Cant, Provincial Languages, and Nautical Jargon Became English* (Princeton, N.J.: Princeton University Press, 2017).
G. A. Starr, 'Defoe's Tour through the Dialects and Jargons of Great Britain', *Modern Philology*, 110:1 (2012), 74–95.
Daniel Statt, 'Daniel Defoe and Immigration', *ECS*, 24:3 (1991), 293–313.

CHAPTER 28

DEFOE'S EUROPE

Allies and Enemies

ANDREAS K. E. MUELLER

> 'I described to him the Country of *Europe*, particularly *England*, which I came from'.
>
> Daniel Defoe, *Robinson Crusoe* (1719)[1]

THE conceptualization of his place of origin offered by the Englishman Robinson Crusoe to his new companion and servant, the indigenous Carib Friday, echoes two key aspects of early eighteenth-century geographical, cultural, and political views of Europe. First, Crusoe views his native England as a constituent part of the larger geographical area.[2] England belongs to Europe: the twenty or so miles of North Sea water between the English and French coasts certainly offered something of a natural barrier, but, with the fastest Dover to Calais crossings taking around three hours, the Channel did not sever Britain from the continent. Second, while Europe was, to use Defoe's words, 'divided into a great Variety of separate Governments and Constitutions,'[3] with different languages and cultural customs, the historical interconnections between European nations and principalities—genetic, dynastic, constitutional, religious (a common Christian faith essentially distinguished Europeans from non-Europeans)—were perceived as coherent

---

[1] Defoe, *Robinson Crusoe*, ed. Thomas Keymer (Oxford: Oxford University Press, 2007), 187.

[2] William Roosen explains that Defoe's notion of Europe was characterized by a strong Western orientation: 'The most important part of Defoe's diplomatic world was made up of Britain, the Netherlands, France, and the Iberian peninsula. Italy, Scandinavia, Switzerland, and the territories of the Holy Roman Empire were important only insofar as their actions were related to, or were influential in, the affairs of the Maritime powers and France'. *Daniel Defoe and Diplomacy* (Selingsgrove, PA: Susquehanna University Press, 1986), 35–6.

[3] *Review*, iii. 342 (1 June 1706).

enough to reflect some of the unifying features of a 'country'. Crusoe's view of a specifically European England is hardly surprising: a York-born Englishman, he is the son of a German immigrant. But Crusoe's conceptualization of Europe as a broader, country-like entity reflects more than his own ancestry: in spite of an established tendency of England's inhabitants to regard their island nation as culturally and politically distinct from continental Europe, any sense of English—or British after the Union of 1707—exceptionalism sat alongside the recognition that the country's national heritage as well as her future were inextricably intertwined with those of other European nations.[4] Much like Defoe's Crusoe, the English considered themselves an 'elect nation',[5] but this did not make them isolationists: as Stephen Conway asserts, 'the eighteenth-century British showed themselves to be aware of their place *in* Europe'.[6] While the story is set in the seventeenth century, Defoe's famous adventurer appears to reflect this common eighteenth-century attitude: Crusoe is simultaneously and inextricably an Englishman *and* a European.

Defoe's deep interest in continental matters is evident across the entirety of his career as a journalist and novelist. Frequently referencing continued French military power and the threat of invasion, he was a vocal supporter of William III's pro-army policy during the Standing Army Controversy of 1697–9, publishing three pamphlets arguing for the necessity of a substantial professional military [SEE CHAPTER 22]. When the second Partition Treaty of March 1700 was jeopardized by Charles II's bestowal, shortly before his death on 1 November 1700, of the Spanish crown on Louis XIV's grandson, Defoe offered yet more detailed assessments of continental geopolitics in tracts such as *Two Great Questions Consider'd. I. What the French King will do, with Respect to the Spanish Monarchy. II. What Measures the English Ought to Take* (1700) and *The Danger of the Protestant Religion Consider'd, from the Present Prospect of a Religious War in Europe* (1701). The former pamphlet, produced before Louis recognized the transfer of the Spanish crown to the Duke of Anjou, stressed the ongoing territorial ambitions of the French king and anchored the safety of the all-important European balance of power in the alliance of the English and Dutch. The latter publication was produced after Louis's acceptance of Charles's will, and it framed, as its title suggests, all European wars as, in

---

[4] Patrick Collinson clarifies the relative interchangeability of 'English' and 'British', as well as the dominance of 'English' in these intertwined concepts: 'Out of the seventeenth century emerged and expanded something called Britain, its inhabitants sometimes called Britons, who proceeded to construct a British Empire (no one ever called it an English Empire), a joint enterprise which engaged Welsh, English and Scots as partners, and the Irish as, mainly, victims. England was in the driving seat of this new enterprise, and the English have always assumed, and still do, that for British you may read English, and vice versa'. *This England: Essays on the English Nation and Commonwealth in the Sixteenth Century* (Manchester: Manchester University Press, 2011), 2.

[5] Discussing the sixteenth-century roots of English exceptionalism, Collinson explains: 'That England, typologically Israel, was "an" elect nation was a commonplace, in the pulpit and elsewhere, but except as a rhetorical flourish—"God is English!"—the claim that England was the only elect nation, God's exclusive favorite, was rarer'. *This England*, 193.

[6] Stephen Conway, *Britain, Ireland, and Continental Europe in the Eighteenth Century: Similarities, Connections, Identities* (Oxford: Oxford University Press, 2011), 47. My emphasis.

essence, religious confrontations between Catholic and Protestant interests and nations, while reinforcing the need for an adequate army to counter the French adversary. At the same time Defoe made the point, in heroic couplets, that, due to England's long history of invasions and migratory waves from across the continent, an Englishman was a thoroughly European creature. The ironically titled verse satire *The True-Born Englishman* (1700/1) offered a piquant reflection on English national identity in relation to her European neighbours at a time of high international tensions and the threat of a new continental war. Defoe's most extensive commentary on European geopolitics came, however, in the most substantial project of his career as a political commentator and propagandist, the periodical *A REVIEW OF THE Affairs of FRANCE: AND OF ALL EUROPE, As Influenc'd by that NATION*. Employed by Robert Harley, Defoe began publication of the *Review* in February 1704, around two years after the start of the War of the Spanish Succession (1701–14), and he unwaveringly attempted to set 'the Affairs of *Europe* in a Clearer Light', usually in broad adherence to his employer's policies, until the final issue in June 1713 [SEE CHAPTERS 7 AND 20].[7] For almost two decades, then, Defoe's attention was thus directly focused on European matters, and even after the Treaty of Utrecht (1713) was followed by a relatively calm period in European geopolitics, Defoe did not lose sight of Britain's European neighbours: in 1717 the ostensible threat of a Swedish-supported Jacobite invasion drew public commentary from Defoe, as did British trade interests in relation to European competitors over the following years, in particular the textile and distilling trades [SEE CHAPTER 14].[8]

The present essay will chart some of the dominant attitudes towards Europe exhibited by Defoe in his propagandistic writings and in some of his later first-person fictions. A salient feature in Defoe's various analyses of European geopolitics and the crucial balance of power between Europe's most powerful nations is the centrality of national character as metonymically represented by the respective head of state. To Defoe and his contemporaries, the European balance of power was, as Jeremy Black has explained, 'an accurate model for the interpretation of international affairs when it was combined with the more random factor of the personal policies of rulers'.[9] The ways in which the different nation states and their rulers conducted themselves in political and trade negotiations, how their military leaders and soldiers behaved on the battlefield, and how temperamentally different, or not, the English were from their European neighbours featured strongly in Defoe's propagandistic writings concerning England's and Britain's relationship with its European neighbours and England's place in Europe. A second noteworthy aspect of Defoe's characterizations of continental Europeans is that a broadly sketched, potentially unflattering national character predicated on that

---

[7] On Defoe, Harley, and the *Review*, see Downie, *Robert Harley and the Press*, 57–79.
[8] Defoe, *What if the Swedes should Come?* (1717), *A Brief Sate of the Question, between the Printed and Painted Callicoes and the Woollen and Silk Manufacture* (1719), and *A Brief Case of the Distillers, and of the Distilling Trade in England* (1726).
[9] Jeremy Black, 'The Theory of the Balance of Power in the First Half of the Eighteenth Century: A Note on Sources', *Review of International Studies*, 9:1 (1983), 55–61 (57).

nation's ruler or an existing enmity between a given European nation and Britain did not automatically translate into a hostile depiction of an individual from that nation. In particular, in his fictions Defoe imagined mutually beneficial collaborations and trusting relationships between, for example, a Protestant Englishman and a Catholic Spaniard. The daily lived experience and conduct of the individual thus stood somewhat separated from European high politics.

Two major developments occurred during Defoe's lifetime with regards to England's role in and attitude towards Europe. First, the 1670s saw a reorientation of English propaganda from a demonization of the Dutch, who had humiliated Charles II in the second and third Anglo-Dutch Wars (1665–7, 1672–4) and who represented England's greatest global trade rival, to a condemnation after 1688 of the French as the most severe threat to the safety of the nation and, indeed, to the balance of power across Europe.[10] French territorial ambitions and political absolutism would remain a bogeyman in the English perception of European geopolitics until well after Defoe's death. Second, after 'a century of English military failure', the War of the Spanish Succession saw England emerge as a leading military force in Europe. In particular, the Duke of Marlborough's victory at Blenheim represented a 'real break' from England's century-long weakness in European warfare.[11] While Marlborough's continental victories dried up towards the end of this war, the Duke's military triumphs enhanced the self-image of the English as a bulwark of international Protestantism and as a counter-weight to the absolutist ambitions of Louis XIV. That is, the English assumed central importance in safeguarding the European balance of power that kept individual nations independent and French tyranny at bay.

WILLIAM III's EUROPEAN STRATEGY

Both of these contexts influenced Defoe's contributions to the Standing Army Controversy and *The True-Born Englishman*. The conclusion of the Nine Years' War with France in 1697 led to the question of whether a professional military force ought to be maintained during peace time. Wary of France's ongoing military might, William III believed it necessary to maintain a sizeable standing army to act as a deterrent and protect Britain from French invasion. However, resistance emerged in Parliament to the king's request for continued military funding: tired of high war taxation, the House of Commons voted to disband over 90% of the British army between 1697 and 1699. The two main justifications for this drastic reduction were that French military power had been sufficiently diminished in the war and an appeal to constitutional theory by

---

[10] Tony Claydon, *Europe and the Making of England, 1660–1760* (Cambridge: Cambridge University Press, 2007), 152.

[11] Claydon, *Europe*, 126–7.

claiming that a monarch with a large peacetime army stationed in Britain would destroy the nation's balanced constitution and inevitably lead to royal tyranny.[12]

Parliamentary attacks on William's request for a substantial peacetime army were anchored in older anti-Dutch sentiments and more general xenophobia. Echoing the mid-seventeenth-century English perception that Holland was 'on her way to universal dominance' due to the nation's aggressive global trade expansion, anti-army propagandists of the 1690s accused their Dutch king of wanting a standing army to establish his own absolute rule over Britain.[13] In addition, the contentious issue of Irish estates awarded to William's Dutch advisers, and the king's continued visits to his native Holland even after the arrival of peace, led many Englishmen to believe that the king 'loved no Englishman's face, nor his company'.[14] An illustrative example of Parliament's strong dislike of foreigners is Sir John Knights's well-known Commons speech against the naturalization bill, which would have benefitted William's Dutch advisers. Issuing the biblically inspired warning that 'should this Bill pass, it will bring as great Afflictions on this Nation, as ever fell upon the *Egyptians*', Knights asserted that already 'one of their Plagues we have at this time very sever upon us; I mean that of their Land bringing forth *Frogs* in abundance, even in the Chambers of the King: For there is no entring the Courts of St. *James* and *Whitehall*, the Pallaces of our Hereditary Kings, for the greatest Noise and Croking of the *Frog-Landers*'. In response to this perceived Dutch threat to English freedoms, customs, and land ownership, Knights concluded his speech with the motion 'that the *Serjeant* be commanded to open the Doors, and let us first Kick the Bill out of the HOUSE, and then Foreigners out of the KINGDOM'.[15] John Tutchin's *The Foreigners* (1700), the poem that triggered the publication of *The True-Born Englishman*, exploited these anti-Dutch sentiments in the aftermath of the Standing Army Controversy. While ostensibly excluding the king from his bigoted assault on the Dutch, Tutchin nevertheless characterizes Holland and its people in dehumanizing terms:

> Its Natives void of Honesty and Grace,
> A Boorish, rude, and an inhumane Race;
> From Nature's Excrement their Life is drawn,
> Are born in Bogs, and nourish'd up from Spawn.

Moreover, the king's subhuman Dutch advisers had only one goal, asserted Tutchin, namely impoverishing England:

---

[12] For a discussion of the Standing Army Controversy, see Lois G. Schwoerer, '*No Standing Armies!*' *The Antiarmy Ideology in Seventeenth-Century England* (Baltimore, MD: Johns Hopkins University Press, 1974), 155–87.

[13] Claydon, *Europe*, 136.

[14] Gilbert Burnet, *History of His Own Time*, cited in Craig Rose, *England in the 1690s* (Oxford: Blackwell, 1999), 54.

[15] *The following Speech being spoke off hand upon the Debates in the House of Commons* (1694), 7, 8.

> Like Beasts of Prey they ravage all the Land,
> Acquire Preferments, and usurp Command:
> The Foreign Inmates the Housekeepers spoil,
> And drain the Moisture of our fruitful Soil.[16]

The echoes of the anti-Dutch propaganda of the 1670s, which had painted Netherlanders as dangerously ambitious, immoral, ungodly, and inhumane, while stressing England's greater civilization, were visible during the 1690s.[17] However, the inherent sinfulness of William's countrymen was considered to be most clearly visible in their attitude towards benefactors: ingratitude was, in the English imagination, 'the clearest indictment' of a Dutch lack of civilization; moreover, this 'charge of ingratitude was linked with anti-Orangeism'.[18]

Williamite Defoe responded to anti-army arguments and the wave of hostility towards the king and his Dutch entourage by asserting that by denying England's monarch a meaningful army, that is, the metonymical 'sword' that enabled William to fulfil his royal duty of defending the nation, Parliament would effectively dismantle his kingship: 'A Military Power must be made use of with a Regal Power; and as it may follow *no King, no Army*, so it may as well follow, *no Army no King*'.[19] In other words, it was the English Parliament that was, in fact, upsetting the balanced constitution of the nation by denying the monarch adequate military funding. However, ultimately Defoe was most indignant about the general disrespect he felt Parliament was exhibiting towards the man whom a majority of English MPs had celebrated as their Protestant saviour only a decade earlier.[20] *The True-Born Englishman*, Defoe's imaginative response to the Standing Army Controversy and its immediate aftermath, turned the table on seventeenth-century anti-Dutch and more recent anti-Williamite rhetoric: the recent controversy and Parliament's actions should serve as a reminder that it was the English who had a habit of showing the greatest ingratitude towards their benefactors: 'Ingratitude, a Devil of *Black Renown*, / Possess'd her very early for his own' (lines 159–60). Moreover, if Netherlanders were products of 'Nature's excrement' and 'born in Bogs', the English, due to a long history of European invasions of and migrations to the island, had equally unsavoury origins: 'We

---

[16] John Tutchin, *The Foreigners* (1700), 5–6.

[17] For the 1670s context, see Claydon, *Europe*, 141–50.

[18] Claydon, *Europe*, 141, 143–4. Douglas Coombs notes that during the late seventeenth and early eighteenth centuries the relationship between the English and the Dutch was 'a story of the complex interplay of engrained hostility and growing consciousness of common interest'. *The Conduct of the Dutch: British Opinion and the Dutch Alliance During the War of the Spanish Succession* (The Hague: Martinus Nijhoff, 1958), 1.

[19] Defoe, *Some Reflections on a Pamphlet lately Publish'd, entituled, An Argument Shewing that a Standing Army is Inconsistent with a Free Government* (1697), *PEW*, i. 44.

[20] Defoe's initial reaction to the success of the anti-army campaign came in the ballad *An Encomium upon Parliament* (1699), a sarcastic attack on William's fourth parliament. The ballad echoed sentiments Defoe had expressed in his pro-army pamphlets, such as the ineffectiveness of the militia, the country's ingratitude towards William and his troops, and the excessive limitations he believed Parliament had placed on the king's prerogative.

have been *Europe's* sink, *the Jakes* where she / Voids all her Offal Outcast Progeny' (lines 249–50; *SFS*, i. 92). Moreover, England's flagrant ingratitude towards her Dutch saviour showed that the nation had been guilty of a thoroughgoing moral failure:

> *Ingratitude*, the worst of Human Guilt,
> The basest Action Mankind can commit;
> Which like the Sin against the Holy Ghost,
> Has least of Honour, and of Guilt the most. (lines 1108–11)

There was thus no plausible reason why Englishmen should show hostility and disrespect to their European neighbour and Protestant ally: their (misconceived) Englishness did not confer superiority. Personal merit, not ancestry or nationality, earned an individual status and respect, and by this criterion William was unassailable.

Alongside his inversion of older anti-Dutch rhetoric, Defoe harnessed more recent anti-French English attitudes in his support of the king. Even if one accepted that an army could be employed as an instrument of oppression, there were different types of oppression, asserted Defoe: 'a Slavery under a Protestant Army would differ very much from a Slavery under a Popish and French Army'.[21] In the British imagination, Catholic Louis XIV was Europe's perfidious arch-persecutor of Protestants, whose bloody thirst for power and territorial dominance threatened to overthrow the all-important European 'balance of power' that was considered the continent's and Britain's only protection from French absolutism.[22] Defoe projected the bloody bigotry with which the French king had become widely associated, not least because of his ruthless treatment of the Protestant Huguenots, directly onto the French army's brutal tendencies. Defoe challenged his readers to 'ask the Protestants of *Languedoc* if the *French Dragoons* were not worse than the *Spanish Inquisition*'.[23] Given that the Spanish Inquisition was associated with arbitrary Catholic cruelty, Defoe was implying that it was the soldiers' French-ness, shaped as it was by Louis's personality and policies, that exacerbated the ingrained Romanist tendency towards persecution and brutality.

THE WAR OF THE SPANISH SUCCESSION: ALLIES AND ENEMIES

Louis's influence on his subjects and the very character of France remained a dominant theme in the *Review*. Renewed conflict in the War of the Spanish Succession led Defoe

---

[21] Defoe, *Some Reflections*, *PEW*, i. 48.

[22] On the concept of the 'balance of power', see Stella Ghervas, 'Balance of Power vs. Perpetual Peace: Paradigms of European Order from Utrecht to Vienna, 1713–1815', *International History Review*, 39:3 (2017), 404–25.

[23] Defoe, *Some Reflections*, *PEW*, i. 48.

to assess Britain's Catholic rival: 'Our Ancient *English* Histories have always spoken of the *French* with a great deal of Contempt, and the *English* Nation have been apt enough to have very mean Thoughts of them from Tradition, as an Effeminate Nation'. This traditional English 'mean Opinion' of the French, concluded Defoe, 'must be acknowledg'd to be very just', due to the historical fact of repeated English victories over French armies, in particular between the late thirteenth and early fifteenth centuries. However, Defoe is quick to point out that, after having been ruled by Louis XIV for several decades, 'the Case is altered with them, and we find them to our loss, a Bold, Adventurous, Wise, Politick and Martial People'.[24] The personal qualities of the head of state thus influenced the character of the nation as a whole. National character is shown to be flexible and adaptable: a strong and aggressive monarch such as Louis will cause the nation to adopt the same traits, while a weak and indecisive ruler will enfeeble the nation. France no longer suffered from its medieval effeminacy and military weakness, since Louis's aggressive expansionism and ruthlessly persecutory inclinations had altered the character of the French people.[25] This 'new' masculine France represented a grave threat to Europe, Defoe explained, and Britain's war effort had to be adjusted accordingly.

Louis's military force readily reflected this changed national character. While the battle at Blenheim was generally considered to have been won by Marlborough's vision and decisiveness, with around a third of the French forces killed or wounded, Defoe's depiction of French soldiers is respectful and commendatory:

> So much they scorn'd the general Rules of War,
> Such Strangers to, so unconcern'd in Fear,
>   They'd calmly stand the fiercest Shock,
>   Delay the sure returning Stroke;
> Throw by the useless Engines of the War,
> The Sword's their Bullet, and their Name the Fire:
> The Pistol and the Carabin disdain'd,
> And carry'd all before 'em Sword in hand. (lines 648–55; SFS, i. 313)

Defoe's positive comments were undoubtedly designed further to aggrandize the British victory, but his depiction of the French army at Blenheim also reflected the notion of a Louis-emboldened France. What had allowed England to defeat the French in Germany was the determination of Queen Anne's representative on the battlefield, the Duke of Marlborough. Just as Louis had instilled a new martial spirit in French soldiers, so the transformation of the English, begun in the 1690s by the warrior-king William III, found its completion in the decisive military strategy of England's military leader in 1704 (a strategy that, quite remarkably, the duke had not disclosed to the Dutch allies). Through the queen's political support and Marlborough's strategic boldness, English soldiers had

---

[24] *Review*, i. 10 (19 February 1704).

[25] Defoe also credits Cardinal Richelieu (1585–1642) with the strengthening of the French nation. *Review*, i. 15 (26 February 1704). Richelieu centralized power in the monarch.

been allowed to show their fearless, eager, and powerful character, that is, to become an overwhelming force that even a foe as formidable as France could no longer defeat.[26]

Similar national character shifts to those that Defoe had recognized in France and England could be discerned in other European nations, albeit with an inverted trajectory. The Swedish warrior-king Gustavus Adolphus (1594–1632) was one of Defoe's Protestant heroes, and he frequently viewed Sweden through the lens of this monarch's military triumphs over Catholic nations in the Thirty Years' War (1618–48). The 'Great *Gustavus Adolphus*', as Defoe frequently labelled this monarch, had been the saviour of Protestantism in northern Europe: 'In that War against *Ferdinand* II. in which the Liberties of *Germany*, and the Protestant Religion were resumed from the Tyranny of the House of *Austria*; ... [Gustavus Adolphus] help'd to deliver *Europe* from Universal Slavery, then as much fear'd from the *Austrian*, as now from the *Bourbonne* Race'.[27] But while Catholic France had risen to military pre-eminence on account of Louis XIV, Sweden's role as a defender of Protestantism had been relinquished by the country's present king, Charles XII (1682–1718), towards whom Defoe developed 'a well-worked-out, balanced but predominantly critical attitude'.[28] Preoccupied with fighting the Great Northern War (1700–21) against Russia, Charles, while undoubtedly a capable military leader, had abandoned the cause of international Protestantism: 'The King of *Sweden* is the Principle Article against the present Confederacy [against France]; what tho' he is not in the League with *France*, if he is not, he does the drudgery of the *French* [and] he pursues their real Interest while he follows his own imaginary Glory'. The failure of *Protestant* monarchs such as Charles XII to defend international Protestantism had ultimately enabled French power, lamented Defoe, before casting his verdict on Charles XII: 'I shall undertake to charge the K... of S ... , in the Process of this History, with Ambition, Injustice, Ingratitude, and above all, an Impolitick and Immoderate Fury, by which he Flies in the Face of the Protestant Interest, injures *those that sav'd him from Ruin*; and opening a large Breach in the Confederacy, makes way for the *French* Power to over-run, or at least to endanger all *Europe*'.[29] Ruled by a misguided monarch, Protestant Sweden was no longer a friend of the reformed people of Europe. Gustavus Adolphus's impressive legacy and Sweden's important pro-Protestant role in European geopolitics had been squandered.

Sweden's decline from glory reached a low point in 1717–18, in Defoe's estimation. Charles's intriguing with the Jacobites to undermine the Hanoverian succession showed beyond doubt that even a Protestant nation could pose a direct threat to the safety of

---

[26] However, in his own celebratory poem *A Hymn to Victory* (1704), Defoe deviated from the widespread glorification of Marlborough by only briefly praising the duke as a brave and calm leader in the midst of battle, and instead emphasizing the bravery and determination of English soldiers as central to the victory. See further Andreas K. E. Mueller, 'Politics, Politeness, and Panegyrics: Defoe, Addison, and Philips on Blenheim', *PQ*, 94:1–2 (2015), 121–47.

[27] *Review*, i. 260 (25 July 1704).

[28] P. N. Furbank and W. R. Owens, 'What If Defoe Did Not Write the *History of the Wars of Charles XII*?', *PBSA*, 80:3 (1986), 333–7 (337).

[29] *Review*, i. 234–5 (11 July 1704).

Britain. The threat of a Swedish invasion was considered real enough in 1717 for Defoe to produce a pamphlet on the matter, one in which he firmly takes Charles to task: 'So scandalous a Quarrel as this, against the King and Nation of *Great-Britain*' will cause the Swedish king's 'entire Overthrow and Destruction', asserted Defoe indignantly, and he exhorted his countrymen to forget Charles's former military heroism and instead 'look on him as an enrag'd Enemy'.[30] This additional decline from not-friend to enemy was caused by Sweden's failure as a reformed nation. Furbank and Owens have rightly explained that 'In Defoe's eyes, Charles was a "Gothic Hero" who could have done immense things for the Protestant cause, had not vainglory led him astray'.[31]

Defoe's angry comments on Sweden in 1717 illustrate a fundamental principle of Defoe's career as a commentator on continental affairs. European geopolitics and the wars they occasioned were, Defoe had claimed in 1701, essentially religious in nature. This was because religion—or rather confession—was closely aligned with political principles: Protestantism promoted an inclination towards limited monarchy, toleration, and the rule of law, while Catholicism encouraged ruthless persecution and absolutism. Thus, all debates about liberty and property were '*Circles drawn about the Great Center* Religion'.[32] By extension, the maintenance of the European balance of power, designed as it was to prevent Popish France from enslaving the rest of the continent, especially Protestant nations, was inevitably a religious mission: 'I see no War can be Rais'd in *Europe*, but what will of Course run into a War of Religion' (76). When threatened by a Catholic power, European Protestants, even if they held 'ill-natur'd Animosities' towards one another, needed to overcome these and show unity: 'Here is no Foreigners, no Refugees, no *Dutch* Men; 'Tis a *Protestant*' (72). However, experiences such as those with the wayward Swedes meant that a caveat had to be added to Defoe's confession-driven vision of European relations, one that saw religious affinities muted. Swedish support for a Jacobite invasion of Britain demonstrated that Protestantism alone did not make for a reliable ally: 'It is not enough that a Nation be Protestant, and the People our Friends; if they will joyn with our Enemies, they are Papists, Turks and Heathens, as to us'.[33] While he readily embraced William III's continental policy of defending the Protestant interest through strategic alliances, the 'policy of balance above affiliation' that had characterized the king's international politics did not straightforwardly find a place in Defoe's thinking, mainly because he saw European wars as essentially religious conflicts which demanded fundamental confessional loyalties.[34]

A further case in point that illustrates Defoe's overarching stance concerning the predominance of confessional affiliation, albeit in a somewhat different manner from the one above, occurred in 1711–12 when he strongly criticized Britain's Dutch allies. British

---

[30] Defoe, *And What if the Swedes should come?* (1717), 5.
[31] Furbank and Owens, 'What If', 338.
[32] Defoe, *The Danger of the Protestant Religion, PEW*, v. 59.
[33] *Review*, i. 337 (2 September 1704).
[34] Lawrence Poston III, 'Defoe and the Peace Campaign, 1710–1713: A Reconsideration', *HLQ*, 27:1 (1963), 1–20 (5).

dissatisfaction with the Netherlands reached a crescendo during the peace campaign of 1710–13, not least as a result of Jonathan Swift's popular *The Conduct of the Allies* (1711). Against the backdrop of the Tory ministry's secret, unilateral peace negotiations with France, Swift castigated the combination of Dutch bellicosity and self-interest as well as Whig warmongering as the main reason for the unnecessary prolongation of the expensive military conflict. While Defoe's attacks on the Dutch 'never approached the intensity of Swift's',[35] he too criticized Britain's long-time Protestant ally in strong terms. Dutch haughtiness, in particular the States General's pretence to being the deciding 'Voice in the Field', with control over British troops, meant that Britain had been manoeuvred 'into a State of Pupilage to the States'.[36] Asserting Britain's sovereignty and right to agree a peace advantageous to herself, Defoe asserted that British interests must not be subjected to '*Dutch* Avarice', reminding his readers of the 'many false Cards' the Dutch played at the Treaty of Nijmegen (1678–9).[37] With the British national interest at risk of being compromised, even England's closest Protestant allies could come into Defoe's line of fire.

However, while any Dutch attempts to take advantage of Britain were unacceptable and needed to be resisted, military conflict with the Netherlands, Defoe warned his readers, would ultimately be disastrous for all of Protestant Europe: 'If we fight with the *Dutch*, we certainly fight against the Protestant Religion in Defence of Popery'.[38] Indeed, while the Protestant German, Swedish, and Danish rulers on the continent were not altogether inconsiderable, these 'Northern Provinces', Defoe impressed on his readers, were not formidable enough to defend themselves against the combined popish powers of France, Spain, and Catholic Germany. Rather, he asserted, 'the Center of Protestant Strength lies in the joint Forces, Power and Wealth of the Two Maritime Potentates, *Great Britain* and *Holland*, their Forces by Land have alone been able to match the Popish Powers of *Europe*'. A 'bloody war' between these two 'brethren' nations would therefore inflict 'a mortal Wound' to international Protestantism. Equally invested in keeping popish power at bay, Britain and Holland were, in the final analysis, 'but one body'.[39] In other words, this Protestant ally deserved to be reprimanded and resisted, but by fighting the Dutch the English would inflict harm on themselves. Defoe's sense of a basic confessional affinity between Britain and the Netherlands remained intact even when competing demands caused a significant strain on the relationship between the two nations. What helped to maintain this bond was that, in contrast to Sweden in 1717, the Netherlands were not working to undermine British Protestantism.

Defoe's endorsement of the Williamite approach of strategic, balance-focused alliances to defend international Protestantism meant that Catholic nations occasionally had to become British allies, if not unproblematically so. While its authority had

---

[35] Poston, 'Defoe and the Peace Campaign', 6–7.
[36] Defoe, *Reasons Against Fighting* (1712), 7–8.
[37] Defoe, *Reasons Against Fighting*, 20–1.
[38] Defoe, *An Enquiry into the Danger and Consequences of a War with the Dutch* (1712), 13.
[39] Defoe, *An Enquiry*, 16, 18, 21.

been significantly weakened by the Thirty Years' War, the Habsburg empire remained another Catholic geopolitical entity that could significantly influence the European balance of power. Joining William III's England and the Dutch Republic, Leopold I (1640–1705), the longest-ruling Habsburg emperor, joined Austria in the Grand Alliance against France during the Nine Years' War (1689–97) and, with the integrity of the Habsburg empire under threat from the second Partition Treaty that was to determine the Spanish succession, Leopold once again joined the Dutch and the British in declaring war against France in May 1702 (Louis had allies in Spain, Savoy, Bavaria, and Cologne). The Habsburgs' status as a British ally against France did not, however, prevent Defoe from offering 'a fully developed anti-Austrian line in the *Review* and later pamphlets'.[40] Commenting on the tensions between Austria and Hungary in 1704, Defoe described the Habsburgs in terms that echoed those he habitually used to discuss the French: Leopold was guilty of behaving as 'a Bloody, a Barbarous, a Perfidious Wretch' towards the Protestant Hungarians, and 'the Oppressions and Tyrannies of the House of *Austria*' would justify Hungary's taking up arms against the Austrians. However, defending the 'Protestant Religion and Liberties of *Europe*', which could only be secured by a combined British-Austrian military campaign against France, outweighed the local grievances of the Hungarians. Consequently, no Protestant Englishman should hope for Hungarian success against Britain's confederate, the tyrannical Leopold.[41] The overarching importance of the European balance of power and the stability of international Protestantism justified the joining of forces, at least temporarily, with a Catholic ruler who was brutalizing Protestants elsewhere.

Defoe's strong antipathy towards the Habsburgs was not specifically tied to the person of Leopold. Upon Leopold's death in 1705, his eldest son Joseph I (b. 1678) became the new emperor. Joseph then died unexpectedly in 1711 and was succeeded by his younger brother, Charles VI (1685–1740). All three Habsburg rulers shared dishonourable character traits that made them questionable allies throughout the War of the Spanish Succession: these Austrian rulers had a habit of reneging on firm commitments and shamelessly tried to improve their empire's position by continuing a war that came largely at the expense of England. 'I could not but reflect, and that with Regret', lamented Defoe in late 1711, 'how many Years ago this War had been finish'd in a happy, safe and honourable Peace, had the former Emperors but exerted themselves as by their own Interest, and their firm Engagements to the Allies, they were bound to do'.[42] Given the family habit of making false promises, Charles's latest pledge to commit more Austrian troops to the war against France should not be trusted, Defoe asserted two months later: '*Now we ought to be Encouraged to the War*, because, *tho' the former Emperors had*

---

[40] Poston, 'Defoe and the Peace Campaign', 6.

[41] *Review*, i. 337 (2 September 1704). See *Review*, i. 302 (15 August 1704), in which Defoe places the containment of France above religious affiliation: 'He that will help *French* Power against us is an Enemy to *England*, and the Publick Interest of *Europe*, by what Name or Title soever *his Religion, if he has any*, is Dignified or Distinguish'd'.

[42] *Review*, viii. 525 (18 December 1711).

abus'd us, this [one] *would be Honest, and perform his Conditions*; to which, I think, we should do well to Answer; *Let the Court at* Vienna *refund the Expence of what they have been deficient in first*, and then we may believe their New Promises, otherwise, they have Cheated us once, and it was their Faults—And let those that would have us Trust them again, tell us, *Whose Fault will the second Cheat be?*'.[43]

Defoe's indignation concerning the brazenness of Britain's Habsburg ally reached a boiling point in the pamphlet *Imperial Gratitude* (1712), whose subtitle promised a 'farther View of the Deficiencies of our Confederates' (*PEW*, v. 179). Given that the Grand Alliance had supported his claim to the Spanish throne, Charles's refusal to send representatives to the Utrecht peace conference demonstrated the new emperor's profound ingratitude towards his supposed allies, especially Britain, and revealed a new, apparently status-induced haughtiness. In the past, with no other assistance available to him, this Austrian prince had been dependent 'on Her Majesty in all his Distresses, his being frequently relieved and supported, and indeed constantly, whenever he was in any Exigence, by Her Majesties Assistance' (198). Now that French power had been curtailed and a realistic prospect of peace existed, one may plausibly expect 'his *Catholick* Majesty' to express his 'due Acknowledgement of the great Things done for him' by Britain as well as 'to see Her *Britannick* Majesty receive suitable Amends and Satisfaction for all these Mighty Things done, and Assistance lent him' (205). However, Charles was instead obstructing the path to European peace by denying the queen's 'trifling Request' for his ambassadors to be sent to Utrecht for preliminary talks (214). This refusal, asserted Defoe, 'could but signifie some Diffidence, Distrust and Uneasiness in the Refuser of and at the Proposer' (215). Given the years of loyal support England had lent to the Habsburgs, this was 'very disrespectful' conduct, but, Defoe added with a bitter irony, perhaps this was the way in which 'those *Northern* Nations ... exprest their Gratitude for infinite Obligations' (215). Several years later, in *Memoirs of a Cavalier* (1720), Defoe was still reminding his readers of 'the tyranny' and the '*Cruelty and Fury of the Emperor* Ferdinand'[44] (Ferdinand II was Leopold's grandfather), depicting the Austrian emperor as a hot-headed warmonger bent on the destruction of European Protestantism. Defoe has his English protagonist, the Cavalier, join Ferdinand's army as a volunteer, and during his service he witnesses the 'dreadful piece of Butchery' that was the Sack of Magdeburg (1631): 'The Slaughter was dreadful, we could see the poor People in Crowds driven down the Streets, flying from the Fury of the Soldiers who followed butchering them as fast as they could, and refused Mercy to any Body' (45). 'This was a sad Welcome into the Army for me', concludes the Cavalier, 'and gave me a Horror and Aversion to the Emperor's People, as well as his Cause' (47). Cooperation with the Austrians may at times be required to oppose an even greater enemy, but, as far as Defoe was concerned, the successive moral and political failures of the Habsburg emperors had turned all of Austria into an abominable nation.

---

[43] *Review*, viii. 627 (12 February 1712).
[44] Defoe, *Memoirs of a Cavalier*, ed. J. T. Boulton (Oxford: Oxford University Press, 1978), 35, 39.

The kingdom at the centre of the early eighteenth-century European succession war, Spain, represented something of a contradiction. Commanding a formidable empire that included the Spanish Netherlands as well as Mediterranean and American territories, the ailing and childless Charles II, an 'unhappy product of excessive Habsburg inbreeding',[45] had no mind to let his dominions be dismembered by the second Partition Treaty agreed by William III and Louis XIV and, shortly before he died in November 1700, he produced a will that made Louis's grandson, Philip of Anjou, the heir of an undivided Spanish empire. Breaking the recent Treaty, Louis accepted Charles II's will and, yet more problematically, in British eyes, decreed that if Philip's older brother died without a heir the new Spanish king would relinquish the Spanish succession to the throne of France, which made a new Bourbon superpower of a united France and Spain a distinct possibility. Fearing the destruction of the balance of power, and with the Spanish crown apparently under French control, the Grand Alliance commenced war against the Bourbons of France and Spain.

The outcome of the War of the Spanish Succession, settled by the Peace of Utrecht in 1713, shifted the European power balance in significant ways, leaving Spain's influence much diminished. While Britain had become a leading European power, albeit with a tarnished reputation after she sidelined her allies in the peace negotiations, France lost some fortresses in Flanders and all lands east of the Rhine. Spain ceded her Mediterranean holdings of Gibraltar and Minorca as well as the coveted Asiento to Britain. The Spanish Netherlands became Austrian. French territorial ambitions had been checked and 'Spain was made to pay the bill for all the rest'.[46] Defoe's commentary on Spain frequently centred on the nation's relative decline. The second Partition Treaty's vision of a carved-up Spanish empire and an ailing Charles II had given Defoe the impression of a country whose glory days were behind it: Spain had become 'a Slothful and Impoverisht Nation' and 'the Antient Military Glory of the *Spanish* Infantry' could now only be revived with the assistance of France, Defoe wrote in the 4 March 1704 issue of the *Review*. But even a French-supported revival could not be easily achieved due to the haughty and bad-tempered Spanish demeanour: 'In the approaching War, tho' the *Spaniards* are able to Contribute little to themselves, we find the *French*, more put to it to consider what sort of Troops will please the *Spaniards*, than where to find Men to supply them with, to bring this Surly Nation to be Content with them'.

Indeed, Defoe's characterization of Spain and its people was overwhelmingly negative throughout the war. His commentary on European geopolitics and military activity contains frequent asides in which Spain was associated with both military inefficacy and thoroughgoing cruelty and barbarity. While their new Bourbon king was willing to act the warrior-king, his Spanish subjects failed to rise to the challenge: 'We see *Philip* the Vth. appears in the Field with 20 Battalions of *French*, *Irish*, and *Walloons*; as for the *Spaniards*, he makes little use of them, because indeed, he sees they are fit for little'.[47]

---

[45] Julian Hoppit, *A Land of Liberty? England 1689–1727* (Oxford: Oxford University Press, 2000), 107.
[46] *The Chronicles of an Old Campaigner M. De La Colonie 1692–1717*, trans. Walter C. Horsley (London: John Murray, 1904), 377.
[47] *Review*, i. 204 (24 June 1704).

However, there was no doubt in Defoe's mind that, faced with the unarmed, injured, and weak, the Spanish would readily indulge their inherent cruelty: during the siege of Barcelona (1705), had the French, who were forced to leave behind '1500 distress'd People, sick or wounded in the Camp', not appealed to the British for assistance, the Spanish 'would in cold Blood and with true *Spanish* Mercy have cut all their Throats'. Thus, even the ambitious French, who were themselves capable of considerable ruthlessness, showed themselves to be a virtuous and 'generous Enemy' by choosing 'rather to court the Generosity of the *English*, than trust the Cruelty of the *Spaniard*'.[48]

However, while Spanish cruelty was stereotypically presented by Defoe as an integral aspect of the nation's character, their present military weakness was not. 'The *Spaniards* are a brave Nation as any in the World, and tho' by the Errors of their Government, their Men are brought to be now of no Value in the Field', claimed Defoe in 1707. It was 'Poverty and neglect of Discipline' that had caused this severe decline, he continued, not a profound change in the Spanish character: 'The Men are the same, their Bloods as warm, their Hearts as Great'. Unpaid, untrained, and underequipped, a previously formidable Spanish army had been reduced 'from the best to the worst Troops in the World'. Defoe's suggestion that Spain's weakness was potentially only temporary was designed to advocate for a swift end to the war: if the allies allowed France to finance and discipline Spanish soldiers, 'as in the *French* Army is practised—I cannot but say, the only Advice is to push the War vigorously before these things can be done, for if the *Spaniards* recover themselves, all *Europe* will not be able to beat them'.[49] In addition to the propagandistic value of depicting Spain as a sleeping giant, one might point out that, in light of Defoe's usual formula that strong leadership will result in a strong nation, his commentary also represented a reflection on Philip V. Seven years after the Bourbon prince had become the king of Spain and three years after Defoe had shown him as a warrior-king, Philip had still not succeeded in reversing the nation's military fortunes. Almost two years after the above warning Defoe was still speaking of 'the weak ill-mannag'd *Spaniards*'.[50] The settlement provided by the Peace of Utrecht cemented this subordinated geopolitical position: Spain posed no real threat to the European balance of power after 1713.

Friends and Villains: National Character and the Individual

While Defoe's propaganda occasionally relies on supposedly ingrained national characteristics, he argued that the conduct of each European nation was largely determined by its government, especially the head of state, and that the manner in

---

[48] *Review*, iii. 400–1 (29 June 1706).
[49] *Review*, iv. 380 (5 August 1707).
[50] *Review*, v. 737 (29 March 1709).

which a given nation behaved was therefore variable over time. However, the rise and fall of Europe's nations and their international and military conduct were not necessarily reflected in the behaviour of individuals. As he asserted in *The True-Born Englishman*, it was not nationality or hereditary entitlement that made the individual great, but personal merit. Kathryn Rummell has argued that Defoe, in *A New Voyage Round the World* (1724), frequently drew on the 'Black Legend' in his depictions of Spain but ultimately showed a very different type of Spaniard: 'Defoe's presentation of the Spaniard turns the stereotype on its ear—the Spanish Planter is neither cruel nor greedy'.[51] This is true of Spanish characters in Defoe's other fictions: for example, Robinson Crusoe, even though his brother was killed by Spanish forces, and in spite of his musings about the 'Spaniards in all their barbarities practised in America ... for which the name of a *Spaniard* is reckon'd to be frightful and terrible to all People of Humanity', rescues a Spaniard from the cannibals and immediately equips the man with a pistol (145). He finds the Spaniard to be loyal, compliant, and prudent, and later refers to 'our friends, the *Spaniards*' (218). Due to scruples concerning his violent intervention in indigenous practices, Crusoe had initially decided not to attack the cannibals, until he notices that their next victim was a white '*European*, and had Clothes on' (196). The man's shared European origins evidently mean more to Crusoe than any moral doubt he might have about slaughtering indigenous people.

Defoe's reconfiguration of different European national characters is continued in *The Farther Adventures of Robinson Crusoe* (1719). When Crusoe helps to rescue a distressed group of French merchants and travellers who had to abandon their ship, he assigns their 'Excess of Joy' at their last-minute rescue to their national temper, which 'is allow'd to be more volatile, more passionate, and more sprightly, and their Spirits more fluid than other Nations', even though he cannot 'determine the Cause' for it.[52] In fact, as if to undermine the stereotype he immediately suggests that Friday behaved in a similar manner when he was reunited with his father years earlier. Moreover, the French were not guilty of the cardinal sin that Defoe had assigned to the English in *The True-Born Englishman*, namely ingratitude: 'Nothing of good Manners or civil Acknowledgments for the Kindness shewn them was wanting; the *French*, 'tis known, are naturally apt enough to exceed that way' (24). Crusoe's own affectionate reunion with the old Spaniard leads him to comment on his friend's kind exclamations towards him, 'as a well bred *Spaniard* always knows how' (41). Crusoe's summary of the Spaniard's experience with the three Englishmen, 'the most impudent, harden'd, ungovern'd, disagreeable Villains' (46), after his rescue from the island further inverts Defoe's earlier polemical demonization of the Spanish: the Spaniards (Crusoe's old friend had rescued several countrymen

---

[51] Kathryn Rummell, 'Defoe and the Black Legend: The Spanish Stereotype in *A New Voyage round the World*', *Rocky Mountain Review of Language and Literature*, 52:2 (1998), 13–28 (18). Rummell argues that Defoe modifies the Spanish stereotype away from cruelty and towards one that characterizes Spanish colonialism as inferior to that of the English, because the Spaniards fail fully to exploit the resources of their colonies.

[52] Defoe, *The Farther Adventures of Robinson Crusoe* (1719), 24, 21.

from the savages) are compassionate, well mannered, and industrious. In contrast, the three English rogues are lazy, quarrelsome, and destructive. If *A New Voyage* depicts the Spanish as bad colonialists, as Rummell has claimed, *Farther Adventures* sees the Spaniards approaching Defoe's colonial ideal.

A notable exception to Defoe's depiction of the inhabitants of the Iberian peninsula is the Portuguese. Notionally allied to France at the beginning of the War of the Spanish Succession, Portugal joined the Grand Alliance in 1703, which gave the allies a strategically important port in Lisbon and land access to Spain. In spite of the benefits that the Portuguese alliance offered, Defoe's view of the people of Portugal was frequently negative. In *The True-Born Englishman* he declares that 'Rage rules the *Portuguese*' while, in comparison, the Spanish were merely proud (line 143; *SFS*, i. 89). In 1704, in contrast to the earlier image of a rageful people, Defoe mocks Portuguese military weakness: 'An Army of *Portuguese*, An Army of Old Alms Women! we should say'.[53] In *Captain Singleton* (1720), Bob Singleton's reflections on the Portuguese offer the most damning national character that Defoe produced during his long career. The Portuguese taught Bob 'to be an arrant thief and a bad sailor'; from them he 'learn[ed] every thing that is wicked among the *Portuguese*, a Nation the most perfidious and the most debauch'd, the most insolent and cruel, of any that pretend to call themselves Christians, in the World'. Even in his own state of 'original wickedness', continues Singleton,

> I entertained such a settled Abhorrence of the abandon'd Vileness of the *Portuguese*, that I could not but hate them most heartily from the Beginning, and all my Life afterwards. They were so brutishly wicked, so base and perfidious, not only to Strangers [foreigners], but to one another; so meanly submissive when subjected; so insolent, or barbarous and tyrannical when superior, that I thought there was something in them that shock'd my very Nature. Add to this, that 'tis natural to an *Englishman* to hate a Coward, it all joined together to make the Devil and a *Portuguese* equally my Aversion.[54]

Defoe's condemnation of the Portuguese, through the experience of his fictional character, appears complete: reflecting on many years of contact with the Portuguese, Singleton cannot think of a single redeeming characteristic. Yet, what holds true in one context does not necessarily suit another: in *Robinson Crusoe*, published a year before *Captain Singleton*, Defoe's protagonist finds a saviour and loyal benefactor in a Portuguese captain.[55]

Defoe's interest in European national characters is equally visible in *Roxana* (1724). The novel's eponymous protagonist is a French child immigrant, more precisely a

---

[53] *Review*, i. 204 (24 June 1704).
[54] Defoe, *Captain Singleton*, ed. Shiv K. Kumar (Oxford: Oxford University Press, 1969), 6–7.
[55] For a discussion of the Portuguese captain's 'extraordinary charity' towards Crusoe, see Geoffrey Sill, 'Robinson Crusoe, "Sudden Joy," and the Portuguese Captain', Digital Defoe, 10:1 (2018), http://digitaldefoe.org/2018/11/01/robinson-crusoe-sudden-joy-and-the-portuguese-captain/. (Accessed 22 April 2020).

Huguenot who escaped the persecution of Protestants in France. Illustrating the relative superficiality of national character traits, Roxana explains that she 'retain'd nothing of the *French*, but the Speech' and became thoroughly anglicized.[56] Her scandalous international life sees her marry a good-for-nothing English brewer who bankrupts the family business and abandons her and their five children; she is pressured into an affair with her (presumably English) landlord, who exploits her inability to pay him rent; and she becomes the mistress of a German prince who lavishes expensive gifts on her. The most trustworthy and genuine of all Roxana's partners is, tellingly, a Dutchman, who helps her to escape imprisonment in France and truly wishes to marry her. The Dutch merchant is an honest man, who 'acted as honest Men always do: with an upright and disinterested Principle; and with a Sincerity not often to be found in the World' (122). Unlike the other men, the Dutchman is not only a role model for courteous and honest behaviour, but highly accomplished in matters of finance and trade. That Defoe would choose a Dutchman as Roxana's final and best-suited husband is hardly surprising, for, as Coombs has pointed out, the English 'widely believed that the Dutch had discovered the infallible technique of commercial success' and that their commercial methods ought to be imitated.[57] At the very least, the Dutch husband is a match for Roxana's own financial acumen and ambition.

Roy Porter claims that, in the eighteenth century, 'the English saw the Continent through eyes prejudiced by caricatures: they saw poverty, superstition and tyranny'.[58] Caricature has in common with stereotypes that it focuses on perceived prominent features that are presented in an exaggerated fashion. In his polemical responses to European geopolitics, Defoe undoubtedly utilized national stereotypes to give weight to his argument: the Austrians were haughty and untrustworthy, the French had strong tyrannical inclinations, the Spanish were cruel and the Portuguese even worse, and the Swedes had all but lost their moral compass. Even Britain's closest ally, the Dutch, could occasionally be said to be selfishly demanding. The English, on the other hand, were fair and honourable. But these depictions had a flipside: Englishmen were guilty of ingratitude and disrespect towards their most recent national saviour, William III, and could behave in more barbaric ways than the Spaniards, who, in turn, were shown to be compassionate and well-mannered elsewhere. Similarly, unlike the English, the French knew when to be appropriately thankful towards their saviour. Especially in his fictions Defoe played with and inverted national stereotypes, some of which he had employed himself, and, ultimately, he recognized that neither the character of a nation nor of an individual was categorically fixed. Predicated as it was on the personality of the ruler, a national character was to a significant degree fluid and changeable, and an individual could lose traits associated with their native country. Above all, Defoe embraced the

---

[56] Defoe, *Roxana*, ed. John Mullan (Oxford: World's Classics, 1996), 6. For Defoe's favourable view of immigration based on economic principles, see Daniel Statt, 'Daniel Defoe and Immigration', *ECS*, 24:3 (1991), 293–313.

[57] Coombs, *Conduct of the Dutch*, 8.

[58] Roy Porter, *English Society in the Eighteenth Century* (London: Pelican, 1982), 22.

notion of an interconnected Europe, in particular with regards to the all-important balance of power, and the need for Protestant unity in continental geopolitics. Outside of Europe's geographical bounds, he also recognized a basic affinity between Europeans. If frequent wars complicated the relationship between Europe's nations and did on occasion divide countries along confessional lines, at the personal level it was possible for an Englishman to trust a Spaniard, or even a Portuguese captain, and make common cause with him, especially if under attack from non-Europeans. Rising above the enmity between Catholics and Protestants, the French, Spanish, and English could be friends. The Dutch could produce the best of men, the Austrians perhaps less so.

Further Reading

Jeremy Black, 'The Theory of the Balance of Power in the First Half of the Eighteenth Century: A Note on Sources', *Review of International Studies*, 9:1 (1983), 55–61.

Tony Claydon, *Europe and the Making of England, 1660–1760* (Cambridge: Cambridge University Press, 2007).

Douglas Coombs, *The Conduct of the Dutch: British Opinion and the Dutch Alliance During the War of the Spanish Succession* (The Hague: Martinus Nijhoff, 1958).

Stephen Conway, *Britain, Ireland, and Continental Europe in the Eighteenth Century: Similarities, Connections, Identities* (Oxford: Oxford University Press, 2011).

Julian Hoppit, *A Land of Liberty? England 1689–1727* (Oxford: Oxford University Press, 2000).

Lawrence Poston III, 'Defoe and the Peace Campaign, 1710–1713: A Reconsideration', *HLQ*, 27:1 (1963), 1–20.

William Roosen, *Daniel Defoe and Diplomacy* (Selingsgrove, PA: Susquehanna University Press, 1986).

Kathryn Rummell, 'Defoe and the Black Legend: The Spanish Stereotype in *A New Voyage Round the World*', *Rocky Mountain Review of Language and Literature*, 52:2 (1998), 13–28.

Daniel Statt, 'Daniel Defoe and Immigration', *ECS*, 24:3 (1991), 293–313.

CHAPTER 29

DEFOE AND COLONIALISM

MARKMAN ELLIS

DANIEL DEFOE defended colonial endeavour throughout his writing career, from before the *Review* (1704–13) to his final publications. In *A Plan of the English Commerce* (1728), one of Defoe's last major works, he declares that '*The Commerce of the World … is an unbounded Ocean of Business*'. The most elevated manifestation of the commercial principle, he suggests, is '*New planting Colonies, and farther improving those already settled*'. The book was motivated, Defoe says, by the problem of how to increase English trade in the face of increasing competition—his term is 'imitation'—from European traders, especially in woollens. Colonies are his solution:

> *The World is wide: There are new Countries, and new Nations, who may be so planted, so improv'd, and the People so manag'd, as to create a new Commerce; and Millions of People shall call for our Manufacture, who never call'd for it before.*
>
> Nothing is to me more evident, than that the civilizing the Nations where we and other *Europeans* are already settled; bringing the naked Savages to Clothe, and instructing barbarous Nations how to live, has had a visible Effect already, in this very Article. (*PEW*, vii. 119, 120)

Colonial endeavour serves a commercial purpose and yields profits for promoters and their countries, but it also organizes the world into hierarchies of civilization and barbarism [SEE CHAPTER 24]. The defence and promotion of colonial projects preoccupied Defoe in his non-fiction writing, in tracts and essays [SEE CHAPTER 6]. Furthermore, his prose fictions and novels provide significant thought experiments in colonial foundation, plantation management, settlement practice, and colonial labour management, including slavery. As we will see below, in this '*Ocean of Commerce*' Defoe was a mercantilist and a gold bug, an apologist of trade, a philosopher of colonialism, and an imagineer of imperialism.

This chapter begins with a discussion of Defoe's idea of the colony as understood and practised in his non-fictional writing on political economy in the period 1704–15, when he developed a business plan for an English colony in the south of the Pacific seaboard of the Spanish-governed territory of Chile in South America. This proposal was repeated and elaborated in the *Review* and in his writings on the South Sea Company in 1711–12, and it had a later iteration in his *A General History of Discoveries and Improvements* (1725–6). The second section explores ideas of the colony and plantation as it is imagined in *Robinson Crusoe* (1719) and the *Farther Adventures* (1719). Defoe's fictions imagine how to build a colony from scratch, but also undertake important thinking about a colony's ideological status and legitimation. The third section returns to Defoe's proposal for an English colony in Chile, as it is explored in his last novel, *A New Voyage Round the World* (1724). There, issues of colonial settlement are embedded in broader discussions of global commerce and colonial practice, especially ideas of English commerce with indigenous peoples. As Maximillian Novak suggests, Defoe at various times was a mercantilist committed to state protectionism, and at other times a promoter of free trade, but he consistently wrote 'economic propaganda for the planting of new English colonies', both in his non-fiction works in journalism and political economy, and in his fictions.[1] The fictional plays an important role as an imaginative space for thinking through the ramifications of the colonial project.

Daniel Defoe, Colonial Projector

Defoe's long history as a colonial apologist began at least as early as 1704, when an essay on the 'Condition of our Colonies and Plantations' appeared in the *Review*.[2] His essay surveyed the politics of international trade at that juncture, promoting the importance of the trade in sugar and slaves with the colonies in the Caribbean, and of trade in and between the English colonies in North America. The main force of this essay is its warning that this lucrative trade was endangered by a suspected expansion of French naval power. It is not an especially important essay about colonialism, but it does establish how Defoe employs certain key terms conventional to the period. A colony was a settlement planted in a new country, composed of a body of people who form a political community that remains subject to the metropolitan state. As Defoe later reflected, colony and metropole are bound together in close concert: 'The Prosperity of our Colonies is our own Prosperity; That all the Wealth of our *Plantations* is our Wealth; their Strength our Strength.'[3] In Defoe's estimation, the term 'plantation' was a synonym for a colonial settlement: the action of establishing a colony was called 'planting'. A plantation was both a landed estate focused on agricultural production (such as a sugar plantation, dedicated to the production of sugar and its derivatives like rum and molasses), and a colonial settlement: when Defoe speaks in this essay of 'our plantations

---

[1] Maximillian E. Novak, *Economics and the Fiction of Daniel Defoe* (Berkeley, CA: University of California Press, 1962), 140.

[2] *Review*, i. 190–3 (17 June 1704).

[3] *Review*, viii. 607 (31 January 1712).

in *America*', he means the Atlantic colonies in North America, not just the agricultural properties located there. Defoe's usage of these terms was broadly in accordance with how they had been used a century earlier by Francis Bacon (1561–1626) in his essay 'Of Plantations', in which the plantation was a synecdoche for both the colony and its people: 'I like a Plantation in a pure soil; that is, where people are not displanted, to the end to plant in others; for else it is rather an extirpation than a plantation'. The metaphor (or discourse) of agriculture is not coincidental but integral to the polity of the plantation. Bacon continues: 'The people wherewith you plant ought to be Gardeners, Ploughmen, Labourers, Smiths, Carpenters, Joiners, Fishermen, Fowlers, with some few Apothecaries, Surgeons, Cooks, and Bakers'.[4] In his *Review* essay in 1704, Defoe reasserts the importance of commerce for Britain's colonial possessions in North America and the Caribbean, and the importance of naval superiority over the French for the maintenance of that commerce. Defoe argues that the ministry needs to be reminded that planting a colony must be reinforced by 'Mastership of the Sea' or naval superiority.

In July 1711 Defoe sent Harley a secret letter, under his code name Claude Guilot, containing 'A Proposall for Seizing, Posessing, and forming an English Collony on The kingdome of Chili in ye South Part of America' (*Correspondence*, 632). The proposal has an important political context, discussed below, and, although in Defoe's handwriting only five half-folio pages in length, it was also remarkable for the detail and comprehensiveness of the plan it outlined. The plan was not a philosophical defence of colonial endeavour, but, rather, offered a practical proposal or blueprint for action. Defoe defended the climate and fertility of the situation he had identified in the southern reaches of Chile: 'The Country Fruitfull, The Natives Courteous and Tractable, and The Wealth of ye Place in Gold Incredible' (*Correspondence*, 633). As an imaginary landscape for intercontinental trade and colonial exploitation, it was ideal, albeit somewhat idealized.[5]

The location he identified was known to him as 'the Port of Baldavia' (more usually Valdivia, now in Chile), a Spanish colonial settlement founded in the late sixteenth century in the southern reaches of the Viceroyalty of Peru. It was the site of extensive military fortifications, built by the Spanish—following raids by English and Dutch privateers in the seventeenth century—as the southernmost defensive complex of the lucrative colony of Peru.[6] This location, Defoe fantasized, could be seized and defended by a small British seaborne force: it was remote from Spanish land forces, and, with continuing British mastery of the sea, would be almost impregnable. His proposed colony was to be an interloper: an unauthorized trader who trespasses on the rights and privileges of the Spanish trade monopoly in South America. Defoe suggested that the area had never been fully settled by the Spanish, and that a commerce could be developed with

---

[4] Francis Bacon, 'Of Plantations', *Essays or Counsels, Civil & Moral* (1625), in *The Major Works*, ed. Brian Vickers (Oxford: Oxford University Press, 2002), 407–9 (408).

[5] Robert Markley suggests this 'climatological fantasy' was underpinned by geosymmetrical arguments. 'Defoe and the Imagined Ecologies of Patagonia', *PQ*, 93:3 (2014), 295–313 (304–7).

[6] 'The Defensive Complex of Valdivia', in *Tentative List of World Heritage Sites, UNESCO* (1998), https://whc.unesco.org/en/tentativelists/1202/. (Accessed 20 February 2020).

'the Natives', the Andean people known as Mapuche ('Araucan' in that period). Defoe claimed that the Mapuche 'Indians' have need of English woollen manufactures: 'These Natives are a foundačon of Commerče, because They Go Cloathed, and would Generally Cloth Themselves, if They Could Obtain Manufactures' (*Correspondence*, 633). His settlement, he suggested, might even use the Mapuche as intermediaries for a trade with Spanish merchants in Peru and the Argentine; furthermore, in a final hyperbolic flourish, he claimed the Mapuche would trade English manufactures for gold, for 'The Plenty of Gold in Chili Exceeds That on ye Coast of Guinea in Affrick' (*Correspondence*, 633). In short, Defoe's blueprint for a colonial settlement imagined a fortified 'factory' from which British merchants might trade to and from the indigenous peoples of South America and the Spanish colonists, facilitated by mastery of the sea. As this suggests, Defoe envisions a seaborne empire of scattered plantations and factories, imagined on a truly global scale, united by, and in the service of, commerce.

Defoe's plan for the Baldivia colony was embedded within the debate on the South Sea Company, a joint-stock company founded in London in the spring of 1711 by Defoe's patron, the Lord Treasurer, Robert Harley, Earl of Oxford. On its foundation, as an incentive to investors, Harley gave the company a monopoly on trade with Spain's colonies in South America, in return for taking on responsibility for the short-term war debt. As Harley knew, British trade with these colonies was prohibited by Spain, who vigorously defended against any interlopers. But Harley sensed an opportunity afforded by the War of the Spanish Succession (1701–14), which matched Britain and her allies against Spain and France. In June 1711 Defoe was encouraged to write a series of articles about colonies and plantations in the *Review*, arguing that as the Spanish had neglected their colonies in southern South America, this offered a great opportunity for English commerce. Defoe claimed that 'there is Room enough on the Western Coast of *America*, call'd the *South Seas*, for us to Fix, Plant, Settle, and Establish a Flourishing Trade, without Injuring, Encroaching on, or perhaps in the least Invading the Property or Commerce of the *Spaniards*', though this view was more than a little tendentious.[7] He was exercised by the success of the French trade with Spanish America, as permitted under the terms of their alliance. Defoe recognized that while Spain would not grant English merchants access or territory by negotiation, Britain might demand it at the war's end, when 'we shall carry on a free Trade with the *Spaniards* of America, throughout the rest of their Plantations, that is, with *Peru*, *Mexico* &c as the *French* do now'.[8] However, at the conclusion of the war in 1713, the Treaty of Utrecht did not reward Britain with a monopoly of trade to Spanish South America, but rather a thirty-year contract for the *Asiento dos Negros*, the exclusive right to sell 4,800 slaves each year to Spanish American colonies, transported from Africa. This was to become both enormously profitable for the company and a tragic disaster for those Africans kidnapped into slavery.[9] In the next decade,

---

[7] *Review*, viii. 243 (17 July 1711).
[8] Defoe, *Review*, viii. 233 (12 July 1711).
[9] Abigail L. Swingen, *Competing Visions of Empire: Labor, Slavery, and the Origins of the British Atlantic Empire* (New Haven, CT: Yale University Press, 2015), 184–90.

however, the promise of the profits from the *Asiento* induced the South Sea Company into offering a series of ambitious and innovative financial instruments derived from the national debt, the trade which led to the financial crisis known as the South Sea Bubble in 1720.

Defoe's plans for the Baldivia colony reflected wider currents of intellectual debate in London in 1711 and 1712 on the commercial potential of intercontinental trade and colony formation. A scheme very similar to Defoe's was proposed to Harley in September 1711 by the merchant and travel-writer Thomas Bowrey (d. 1713), a correspondent of Defoe.[10] Harley was also encouraged by the map-maker Herman Moll, who published a prose account of Baldivia in his geography *A View of the Coasts, Countries and Islands within the Limits of the South-Sea-Company* in 1711, which included an influential map of the region, including a large inset 'A Map of ye Port of Baldivia'.[11] Moll's cartography of the area was assisted by the observations of the buccaneer adventurers William Dampier and Woodes Rogers (who had rescued Alexander Selkirk from Juan Fernández). As Shinsuke Satsuma has discussed, the South Sea Company took the discussion far enough in 1712 for Harley to consider a developed plan for a military expedition to secure by force a commercial trading base in the South Seas arena of southern South America. Advised by the privateer Woodes Rogers, the plans made by the company were ambitious, but because they did not find sufficient support in the government, were abandoned as impractical before the end of 1712.[12]

Defoe's interest in a fortified South American colony was revisited the following year in *An Essay on the South-Sea Trade* (1712), a further contribution to the ministerial effort to energize the South Sea Company. Here Defoe took a more theoretical position, arguing that the South Seas trade would ideally allow an 'Open, Free Commerce' between Britain and the Spanish Colonies in South America, which might in part be facilitated by British merchants 'Settling in some Part' of Spanish America (*PEW*, vii. 50). There they might establish a factory or settlement to carry on their trade, either by force of conquest or by negotiated agreement.[13] As in his memorandum of the previous year, Defoe argued that the geographical circumstances of Chile would work in favour of the colony.

---

[10] Thomas Bowrey to [Robert Harley?], 'Proposal for taking Baldivia in ye So. Seas', 10 September 1771, BL Add. MS. 28140, ff. 31r–v (and copy at BL Add. MS. 70163, ff. 196r–197v). Margaret Hunt, 'Bowrey, Thomas (d. 1713)', *ODNB*. For a discussion of Bowrey's plan, see Shinsuke Satsuma, *Britain and Colonial Maritime War in the Early Eighteenth Century: Silver, Seapower and the Atlantic* (Woodbridge: Boydell and Brewer, 2013), 61–2.

[11] Herman Moll, *A View of the Coasts, Countries and Islands within the Limits of the South-Sea-Company* (1711), 49–59. On Defoe's reading in travel accounts, see J. A. Downie, 'Defoe, Imperialism, and the Travel Books Reconsidered', *Yearbook of English Studies*, 13 (1983), 66–83 (80–1).

[12] Shinsuke Satsuma, 'The South Sea Company and its Plan for a Naval Expedition in 1712', *Historical Research*, 85:229 (2012), 410–29 (423–8).

[13] John McVeagh, 'Introduction', *PEW*, vii. 6–7.

> By a Trade to the *South-Seas*, we are to understand our Seizing some such Port or Place in *America*, whether already possess'd, or not possess'd, as we shall think proper, and taking it as our own, by Virtue or the Treaty above noted, to settle, plant and inhabit the same as a Colony, erecting there such Trade with the Adjacent Countries, whether *Spaniards* or others, and improving the Native Fruitfulness of the Place as much as possible, taking at the same Time all Opportunities to open a Trade with the *Spaniards* as much as Circumstances will admit, and which there is no Question will be considerable.—And this is the Way a Trade may be carried on.—This I am of the Opinion is the Way of Trade the Government proposes, and what they mean by a Trade to the *South-Seas*. (*PEW*, vii, 50–1)

To Defoe at least, the South Seas trade was not simply a deal for the *Asiento*, but also a colonial project, in which the British, 'under the Protection, in the Name, and by the Power of Her Majesty', should

> *Seize, Take,* and *Possess,* such Port or Place, or Places, *Land,* Territory, Country or Dominion, *call it what you please,* as we see fit in America, and *keep it for our own*; keeping it implies Planting, Settling, Inhabiting, Spreading, and all that is usual in such Cases.

Having acquired this colony by force, Defoe proposes that to make it worth keeping it must be profitable, so 'we are to Trade *to* it, and *from* it' (*PEW*, vii. 52). As with the scheme presented to Harley on 23 July 1711, Defoe describes the foundation of the colony within the format or genre of a proposal, a practical scheme to be acted upon. To his mind, this explanation of the intention behind the South Seas Company was more credible than those who imagined they might plunder or exploit 'Golden Mountains', as the Spanish had in Peru in previous centuries. Although mechanistic and practical, Defoe's contribution to the South Sea debate, and the idea of a Chilean colony, was still a kind of thought experiment, a fiction about how a global commerce might be conducted had the world been ordered differently.

Defoe continued to be curious about this idea as late as 1726, when he wrote a chapter on it in his history of empires and global commerce, *A General History of Discoveries and Improvements*. Here he offers a '*Proposal for a new Settlement in America*' located in Patagonia, on the Atlantic coast of South America. He envisages an agricultural settlement, founded on ranching 'large black Cattle' on the extensive grasslands in the area's temperate climate. Recognizing that as an interloper the colony would be challenged, Defoe specifies the need for a 'Sufficient Force to preserve and protect the Settlement against any assault of the *Spanish*' (*TDH*, iv. 211–12). But the world offers almost unlimited potential, Defoe argues, for colonies and improvement:

> There are no doubt new Countries and Lands yet to be discover'd, new Colonies to be planted, which were never discover'd, or planted before; and which is still worth our Consideration, those already planted are capable of new Improvements, and farther Planting, which I think I may call improving. (*TDH*, iv. 223)

He further considers how a colony based on coffee production could be advantageously promoted somewhere at a latitude equivalent to that of Mocha in Arabia Felix, such as the Caribbean and Africa. Defoe notes how the Dutch have successfully transcultured coffee plants from Arabia to Java in the Dutch East Indies (now Indonesia). As Defoe suggests, the botanical geopolitics of colonial settlement have the capacity to reshape global landscapes and the environment.[14] In *A Plan of the English Commerce*, Defoe reasons:

> Let the same Climates be examin'd in other Parts of the World, and the Soil in those Climates be compared ... [and] as no visible Difference is found in them, why should they not produce the same Harvest, the same Plants, Fruits, Druggs; or, whatever grows and is produced in one, why should it not be planted, grow, and produce the same in another? (*PEW*, vii. 299–300)

Defoe revisits his proposal for a coffee colony, outlined in *A Plan of the English Commerce*, numerous times in the following years, such as in his pamphlets *The Advantages of Peace and Commerce* (1729) and *An Humble Proposal to the People of England, for the Encrease of their Trade* (1729).[15] Repetition of the idea in these pamphlets and tracts suggests something of how Defoe understands colonial discourse—debate on and promotion of colonial projects—as a kind of public propaganda or media campaign, in which an idea, with careful propagation, might take root in the political imagination.

Crusoe's Colony

In *The Life and Strange Surprizing Adventures of Robinson Crusoe*, Defoe offers a different kind of colonial thought experiment. It details what happens when an ordinary but resourceful Englishman is cast away on an uninhabited island off the Atlantic seaboard of South America. At the end of the novel, Crusoe has not only survived twenty-eight years on the island, but has, at least to his own satisfaction, established on the island something that he calls, variously, a plantation, settlement, and, eventually, a colony. How he achieved that is one of the questions the novel answers. Although early on in his sojourn Crusoe makes a joke about the island being his kingdom, by the end he does seem to claim for himself a form of sovereignty, or proprietorship over the colony. Having returned to England, Crusoe is tempted to renew his travels and revisit his island settlement. 'In this Voyage I visited my new Collony in the Island': there, he catches up with the news of his English and Spanish settlers, their 'Battles with the *Caribbeans*',

---

[14] Alfred W. Crosby, *Ecological Imperialism: The Biological Expansion of Europe, 900–1900* (Cambridge: Cambridge University Press, 1986).

[15] Defoe, *The Advantages of Peace and Commerce* (1729), 18–19; *An Humble Proposal to the People of England, for the Encrease of their Trade, and Encouragement of their Manufactures* (1729), 45–6.

and 'the Improvement they made upon the Island itself'. Crusoe brought from England, to reinforce his colony, 'Supplies of all necessary things' and some useful workmen, '*viz.* a Carpenter and a Smith', and promised to send some women from England. He also reinforced his legitimate authority over his island colony by enacting a reformation of property: 'I shar'd the Island into Parts with 'em [the colonists], reserved to myself the Property of the whole, but gave them such Parts respectively as they agreed on'.[16] Defoe's solution is for Crusoe to hold a 'property' in the whole, sharing the use of the land with his settlers by granting tenancies under his feudal sovereignty. Although no longer resident, the absentee Crusoe reforms landholding on the island, and by so doing, demonstrates that he is its legitimate ruler. In this way, *Robinson Crusoe* is not only a novel describing how to found a colony; it also promulgates a myth about colonial legitimacy: that settlers in new lands can establish and hold title to the property they have acquired.

Crusoe had long entertained thoughts about how to achieve legitimate rule of his island. Soon after the shipwreck, when he is first establishing himself on the island, he is struck with the thought that he is ruler of the land he occupies, if only because he is alone. Exploring the valleys around where he has been shipwrecked, he is pleased to find that 'the Country appear'd so fresh, so green, so flourishing, everything being in a constant Verdure, or Flourish of *Spring*, that it looked like a planted Garden'. Reflecting on 'that delicious Vale', Crusoe finds himself

> surveying it with a secret Kind of Pleasure, (tho' mixt with my other afflicting Thoughts) to think that this was all my own, that I was King and Lord of all this Country indefeasibly, and had a Right of Possession; and if I could convey it, I might have it in Inheritance, as completely as any Lord of a Mannor in *England*. (99–100)

Crusoe fantasizes that he is sovereign of the island, with a right of possession, that might be conveyed in inheritance or sale, prefiguring his achievements at the end of the novel, twenty-seven years later. Crusoe tries on several titles here: king and lord, but also lord of the manor, a feudal legal entity which recognized the sovereign but accorded the lord of the manor a freehold ownership of the land, which could then be leased to others under a system called copyhold. But these reflections are ironic, for as Crusoe recognizes he must defend his lordship from competing claims from other people, should there be any, and until then everything is moot, a joke. But if he could convey his claim, that is, prove his real property to others, his claim to a kind of feudal rule would be proved.

By the fourth year on the island, Crusoe still entertains these fantasies. The world, he admits, is a 'remote thing' that does not recognize, or even remember, him, or his claims.

---

[16] Defoe, *Robinson Crusoe*, ed. J. Donald Crowley (Oxford: Oxford University Press, 1972), 305. This section foreshadows events described in *The Farther Adventures of Robinson* (1719).

> I was Lord of the whole Mannor; or, if I pleas'd, I might call myself King, or Emperor over the whole Country which I had Possession of. There were no Rivals. I had no Competitor, none to dispute Sovereignty or Command with me. (128)

Crusoe can arrogate to himself the title of king or even emperor, but without connection to the world, his claims of sovereignty are useless. Alone on the island, there is no one who might dispute his absolute sovereignty, but without someone to rule, his claim is without force. He applies the same logic to the agricultural surplus that he might generate by his farming activities. 'I might have rais'd Ship Loadings of Corn; but I had no use for it' (128). As the solitary consumer of his surplus production, there is no market and no commerce. The irony of Crusoe's status as a Lord of Nothing is dramatized some considerable time later (probably around his fifteenth year on the island) when he reconceptualizes the scene of him dining with his domesticated animals as a feudal court:

> It would have made a Stoic smile to have seen, me and my little Family sit down to Dinner; there was my Majesty the Prince and Lord of the whole Island; I had the Lives of all my Subjects at my absolute Command. I could hang, draw, give Liberty, and take it away, and no Rebels among all my Subjects. (148)

Robinson Crusoe is king or lord of his island, he fantasizes, with absolute power over his subjects, but only because his reign is uncontested, and his subjects are animals who have no rights. As Frank Donoghue remarks, 'Crusoe's possessiveness of the island, is an expression of his fantasy of isolation and an attempt to suppress his more plausible suspicions that someone else owns it'.[17] In solitude on his island, Crusoe has a problem with others.

A few years later, however, others find Crusoe, and he finds he must defend his colony from their competition. His first encounter is with the local Caribbean indigenes, from whom he rescues Friday, and later Friday's father and a Spanish man. Crusoe establishes that Friday's people are Carib, noting that having asked Friday for 'the Names of the several Nations of his Sort of People' he 'could get no other name than Carib' (215).[18] With the Caribs and the Spaniard, Crusoe establishes his priority, impressing upon each that as he has saved them from certain death, they are his subjects. In the case of Friday, his place as Crusoe's slave is commemorated in an important ritual, in which Friday places his head under Crusoe's foot, while making 'all the Signs to me of Subjection, Servitude,

---

[17] Frank Donoghue, 'Inevitable Politics: Rulership and Identity in *Robinson Crusoe*', *Studies in the Novel*, 27:1 (1995), 1–11 (3).

[18] In *The Farther Adventures*, Crusoe comments this was a mistake: Friday's people are not Caribs, but Islanders (*Novels*, ii. 26). Defoe points to the distinction, still maintained by anthropologists, between Mainland Caribs (Kalinga) and Island Caribs (Kalinago). See Samuel M. Wilson (ed.), *The Indigenous People of the Caribbean* (Gainesville, FL: University Press of Florida, 1997). For discussion of Friday's religion, see Timothy C. Blackburn, 'Friday's Religion: Its Nature and Importance in *Robinson Crusoe*', *ECS*, 18:3 (1985), 360–82.

and Submission imaginable' (206). Friday's father, and the Spaniard, in his 'Debt for his Deliverance', further signal their acceptance of his legitimate sovereignty (235, 237–8). Their recognition of his status as lord of the island is fragile, however. Although he has been a long time alone on the island, Crusoe has to recognize that the indigenes, from whom he rescued Friday, have a prior claim, and are its real rulers if they can prove or enforce their claim. In Crusoe's thinking, only their status as cannibals downgrades their claim. In any case, Crusoe reasons,

> My Island was now peopled, and I thought myself very rich in Subjects; and it was a merry Reflection, which I frequently made, How like a King I look'd. First of all, the whole Country was my own meer Property, so that I had an undoubted Right of Dominion. 2dly, My People were perfectly subjected: I was absolutely Lord and Lawgiver; they all owed their Lives to me, and were ready to lay down their Lives, *if there had been occasion for it*, for me. (241)

Crusoe's summary of the political settlement on his island establishes that he is an absolute ruler, and all his subjects are slaves.

In *Robinson Crusoe*, Defoe argues that Crusoe's labour on the island contributes to his claim to his colony. Defoe's account of Crusoe's experience as a colonial landholder on his island is profitably examined by a comparison with arguments advanced by John Locke in his *Essay Concerning the True Original, Extent, and End of Government*, the second of his *Two Treatises on Government* (1690). Locke was materially engaged in colonial questions, including investment, constitutional arrangements, and colonial trade policy, and his theoretical model of colonial property rights was influential in colonial ventures. Defoe may even have had it in mind in Crusoe's deliberations.[19] Locke begins by developing an account of the state of nature, the condition of people prior to government and society, in which all people are in an equality, with the same undifferentiated power and jurisdiction. Crusoe's situation on his island, which he describes as having been 'reduced to a meer State of Nature', is similar to Locke's description of the indigenous peoples of America, living 'according to reason, without a common superior on earth' in 'a state of peace, good will, mutual assistance and preservation'.[20] Locke considers how in a state of nature all people have an equal right to a share in the goods of nature, and asks, if this is the case, how did people come to own property (that which one person owns separately from others)? Locke's solution to the problem was to state that:

> Though the earth and all inferior creatures be common to all men, yet every man has a 'property' in his own 'person.' This nobody has any right to but himself. The 'labour' of his body and the 'work' of his hands, we may say, are properly his. Whatsoever, then, he removes out of the state that Nature hath provided and left it in, he hath

---

[19] On Locke and Defoe see Ian A. Bell, 'King Crusoe: Locke's Political Theory in *Robinson Crusoe*', *English Studies*, 69:1 (1988), 27–36.

[20] John Locke, *Two Treatises of Government*, ed. Peter Laslett (Cambridge: Cambridge University Press, 1988), 280.

mixed his labour with it, and joined to it something that is his own, and thereby makes it his property.[21]

The ramifications of Locke's argument are relevant to colonial settlement. In the state of nature, men exert themselves in their work of the land; their labour in working the land establishes for them ownership of the goods it produces, and a property in the land.

Locke's argument is theoretical, but it has real world applications. In exploring his argument, he uses some of the same kind of imaginative reasoning that characters do in Defoe's novels. It is labour, Locke suggests, that invests natural resources with the status of property, using the example of the man harvesting acorns or apples for his private nourishment:

> He that is nourished by the acorns he picked up under an oak, or the apples he gathered from the trees in the wood, has certainly appropriated them to himself. Nobody can deny but the nourishment is his. I ask, then, when did they begin to be his? when he digested? or when he ate? or when he boiled? or when he brought them home? or when he picked them up? And it is plain, if the first gathering made them not his, nothing else could. That labour put a distinction between them and common.

Locke extends this argument to beasts as well:

> This law of reason makes the deer [the property of] that Indian's who hath killed it; it is allowed to be his goods who hath bestowed his labour upon it, though, before, it was the common right of every one.[22]

Crusoe's encounters with the wild goats on his island gives an instance of this process. The island's goats are at first 'so shy, so subtile, and so swift of Foot, that it was the most difficultest thing in the World to come at them' (61). They are wild, and not his. But when he shoots one of the goats, the meat unquestionably belongs to him, as his labour is mixed with it. And later, having wounded a goat, he 'took such Care of it' that it recovers, and by that labour of care, becomes his:

> By my nursing it so long, it grew tame, and fed upon the little Green at my Door, and would not go away: This was the first Time that I entertain'd a Thought of breeding up some tame Creatures, that I might have Food when my Powder and Shot was all spent. (75)

Later, he builds an enclosure for the goats, who can now be described as his possessions ('my goats'):

---

[21] Locke, *Two Treatises*, 287–8.
[22] Locke, *Two Treatises*, 288–9.

> In about a Year and a half I had a Flock of about twelve Goats, Kids and all; and in two Years more I had three-and-forty, besides several that I took and kill'd for my Food. After that I enclosed five several Pieces of Ground to feed them in, with little Pens to drive them into, to take them as I wanted, and Gates out of one piece of Ground into another. (147)

By domesticating the goats, Crusoe makes them his own: what was wild and free becomes his private property through his labour. In the state of nature, Locke says, a man can establish a right of property by his labour upon the land: 'As much land as a man tills, plants, improves, cultivates, and can use the product of, so much is his property'.[23] This is a very significant argument for colonial projectors, especially in those parts of the world where, Locke argues or imagines, mankind continues in the state of nature.

Just before he discovers the footprint in the sand, after almost eighteen years on the island, Crusoe casts up his accounts, describing in detail what his labours have achieved on the island. He describes how he has established a place of residence and also a farm on the island, describing them both as his 'plantations', using the term that usefully conjoins a place of cultivation and a colonial settlement:

> You are to understand, that now I had, as I may call it, two Plantations in the Island; one my little Fortification or Tent, with the Wall about it under the Rock, with the Cave behind me ... Near this Dwelling of mine, but a little farther within the Land, and upon lower Ground, lay my two Pieces of Corn Ground, which I kept duly cultivated and sow'd, and which duly yielded me their Harvest in its Season; and whenever I had occasion for more Corn, I had more Land adjoining as fit as that.
>
> Besides this, I had my Country Seat, and I had now a tollerable Plantation there also; for first, I had my little Bower, as I call'd it, which I kept in Repair ... Adjoyning to this I had my Enclosures for my Cattle, that is to say my Goats: and as I had taken an inconceivable deal of pains to fence and enclose this ground, so I was so uneasy to see it kept entire, lest the Goats should break thro', that I never left off till with infinite Labour I had stuck the Out-side of the Hedge so full of small Stakes, and so near to one another, that it was rather a Pale than a Hedge. (151–2)

A little later he re-enumerates this as 'my three Plantations, *viz.* my Castle, my Country Seat, which I call'd my Bower, and my Enclosure in the Woods' (166). In any case, what he is careful to do here is to show not only how these places are defended, but also that he has taken great pains to build them: that is, he has mixed his labour with the soil. Crusoe repeatedly describes how his ingenious reproduction of the trappings of civilized life take 'infinite labour' or an 'inconceivable deal of pains'—phrases that are not simply exaggeration, but also make philosophical claims about his expropriation of the island.

What Defoe learns from Locke, and explores through Crusoe's narrative, is that British colonists, through their labour on the land they occupy, establish property rights in it—rights they can maintain in spite of the manifestly prior claims of indigenous

---

[23] Locke, *Two Treatises*, 290–1.

peoples. In the *Review* for 24 April 1711, Defoe had considered how English colonies could be secured from rival European interlopers, asking 'What Title, What Claim do we make to our Colonies Abroad, either in *Virginia*, the Islands, *Africa*, and the Gold Coast, or any where else?'[24] The turn to Locke, as James Tully concludes, provides a partial answer: colonists were 'entitled to the land they cultivated, without native consent'.[25] This conclusion underlies Crusoe's claim that 'that the whole Country was my own meer Property; so that I had an undoubted Right of Dominion' (241). The narrative shows how Crusoe is able to justify this claim, and have it acknowledged by Friday, Friday's people, and the Spanish. Tully goes on to argue that Locke's reasoning informed contemporary practice in the American colonies, where arguments like Locke's were deployed in the dispossession of Native Americans of their land.

In relation to Crusoe's island, Defoe follows Locke in valuing European agricultural practices above the customary land use of American indigenes. Defoe and Locke understood that in the customary hunting and collecting practices of indigenous peoples the land remained in an unimproved primitive condition consistent with the state of nature. Tully concludes that this suggests that 'Amerindian government does not qualify as a legitimate form of political society'.[26] As indigene government is not on a par with European government, it need not (necessarily) be treated with the same respect or in the same manner. So although the island Crusoe occupies is clearly an important location in the religious calendar of the indigenous Caribs, as a site for ritual sacrifice and cannibal feasting, Crusoe is successfully able, at least in his own account, to degrade the claim of property rights embedded in their cultural practices. Crusoe's horror at their cultural cannibalism serves the political agenda of his colonial land policy.

In *Robinson Crusoe*, Defoe presents two overlapping arguments to show how his protagonist can successfully claim legitimate sovereignty in his island colony. The first shows that his claim to being its lord, with right of dominion, is acknowledged by others, albeit in the somewhat exceptional circumstances that they all owe him their lives. The second shows how he could establish a right of 'meer Property' by mixing his labour with the land and domesticating the wild flora and fauna. Both claims are endorsed in the events described in the opening section of *The Farther Adventures of Robinson Crusoe*, which narrates Crusoe's return to 'my Kingdom, my Island' (*Novels*, ii. 9). His narrative confirms the success of Crusoe's ideological ambition to suppress indigenous titles, establish his sovereignty, and have that recognized by fellow Europeans. On his return to the island, Crusoe finds that his rule of the island is still recognized by his Spanish colonists, who have had to defend it from two forces: a group of three English 'Rogues', and the cannibal indigenes from the mainland. The English rogues

---

[24] *Review*, viii. 76 (24 April 1711).
[25] James Tully, 'Placing the *Two Treatises*', in *Political Discourse in Early Modern Britain*, ed. Nicholas Phillipson and Quentin Skinner (Cambridge: Cambridge University Press, 1993), 253–80 (267). James Tully, *An Approach to Political Philosophy: Locke in Contexts* (Cambridge: Cambridge University Press, 1993), 138.
[26] Tully, *Approach*, 139.

rebel against Crusoe's Spanish subordinates when they declare they are unwilling to accept their status as equals within the colony. Instead, the '*English* Brutes' assert that as Englishmen they have a natural priority over the Spanish colonists, saying to the others that 'the Island was theirs, that the Governor, meaning me [Crusoe], had given them Possession of it, and no Body else had any right to it, and damn 'em'. The rebellion of these 'unnatural Rogues' is eventually suppressed by their ostracism and reformation (*Novels*, ii. 33–4). Their leader, Will Atkins, becomes a 'very industrious necessary and sober Fellow', whom Crusoe finds living in a curious circular wickerwork house, like a beehive, fabricated by his Carib slaves (*Novels*, ii. 73).

The challenge to Crusoe's dominion posed by the Caribs in the *Farther Adventures* is more sustained and dangerous, as they make repeated incursions on the island, initially to celebrate victories with ritual cannibal feasts. They are repelled only by violent resistance from Crusoe's colonists. Building on Crusoe's defensive fortifications, the colonists manage to defeat the Carib invaders, despite overwhelming inferiority in numbers. In the military defeat of the indigenes, Defoe's narrative encodes two important colonial myths. The first is that indigenous assertions of customary sovereignty can be reimagined as an unprovoked attack on the colony, and therefore the ensuing retaliation can be vindicated using just-war theory. Second, as Christopher Loar has argued, such violence ritually encodes the almost magical superiority of firepower afforded to the colonists by European firearms and gunpowder.[27] While the mere sound of gunfire alone is sometimes enough to enforce submission, Crusoe is also willing to commit atrocities. In a later naval battle in Bahia, Brazil, in which Friday is unexpectedly killed, a flotilla of 126 canoes confronts a lone English ship. Provoked by the indigenes' resistance—especially 'the ill Manners of turning up their bare Backsides'—Crusoe responds with a broadside of small shot from the ship's cannon, 'justify'd before God and man'. 'I can neither, tell how many we kill'd, or how many we wounded at this Broad-side; but sure such a Fright and Hurry never was seen among such a Multitude' (*Novels*, ii. 121). The myth of European military superiority is confirmed.[28]

ADVANTAGEOUS COLONIES IN *A NEW VOYAGE ROUND THE WORLD*

Defoe returned to the theme of South Seas colonization in his last novel, *A New Voyage Round the World*, and, more specifically, to his historically enduring scheme for an

---

[27] Christopher F. Loar, *Political Magic: British Fictions of Savagery and Sovereignty, 1650–1750* (New York: Fordham University Press, 2014), 104–141.

[28] See the discussion of Crusoe's proposal of a collective European holy war against non-Christian nations in Nicholas Seager, 'Crusoe's Crusade: Defoe, Genocide, and Imperialism', *Etudes anglaises*, 70:2 (2019), 196–212.

English settlement in South America. On the last page of the novel, his protagonist declares:

> I take the Liberty to recommend that Part of *America*, as the best and most advantageous Part of the whole Globe for an *English* Colony, the Climate the Soil, and above all, the easy Communication with the Mountains of *Chili*, recommending it beyond any Place that I ever saw, or read of. (*Novels*, x. 258)

The plot of the novel prosecutes this recommendation over two volumes through two overlapping and mutually reinforcing arguments about English colony-building, the first concerning the ideological and practical dominance of English commerce in cross-cultural encounters, and the second demonstrating the advantages of an English colony in South America. Arguments are emplotted to engage with Defoe's wider mercantilist ideas of economic nationalism and individual improvement. The novel begins in 1713, when the narrator, an unnamed merchant-adventurer, sets out on 'a cruising and trading voyage to the East'. Defeated in their attempt to round Cape Horn by bad weather, the merchant's expedition decides to sail east 'by a Course never sailed before',[29] crossing from the Cape of Good Hope to Southeast Asia, and then running from the Philippines into the South Pacific, and across the ocean to South America.

Disavowing the fictional status of the novel, the narrator declares that he will keep his observations not in a tedious seamen's journal, full of sailing jargon and details of the ship's course and sea conditions, but in 'a manner of relating... perfectly new in its Form', as a set of plotted observations (*Novels*, x. 31). In belated recognition of the geopolitics of the South Sea Company, frustrated by the advantage enjoyed by the French vessels permitted to trade with Spanish South America, the expedition engages in a complex subterfuge to get around the proscription against British trade with Spanish America. The Captain narrator equips his ship with 'letters of marque' issued by the new Ostend East India Company (established in 1722), so it can pretend to be a French vessel, with a French captain and sufficient French-speaking crew to fake their way through hostile naval inspection by Spanish authorities. All the while, the Captain-narrator remains in secret command, with English seamen manning his ship, in which guise 'we were *English* Cruisers' who could switch to privateering, a state-legitimated form of piracy, in which a privately owned armed vessel is commissioned to attack enemy shipping. With this 'mysterious Equipment', the voyage can undertake both legitimate 'French' trading activity, and at the same time resort to privateering (*Novels*, x. 31–2).

In the first volume, Defoe explores the utility and profitability of trading voyages to the myriad small islands encountered in the Pacific. This trade would, he suggests, facilitate a new trade route across the Pacific to America and so around the world. The merchant's

---

[29] The East India Company had inserted a clause in the act establishing the South Sea Company that proscribed exactly this east-to-west crossing of the Pacific, as also any trade conducted by British merchants between China or India, and the Americas. The Ostend Company was in part a response to these restrictions.

east-to-west trans-Pacific trade route was counter to the established practice of the previous century or more, in which ships sailed west with the prevailing trade winds. The exception, and it was a notable one, was the annual return voyage of the Spanish Manila galleon between Mexico and the Philippines, inaugurated in 1565 (which did not, as Defoe's merchant imagines, complete the voyage to Europe around Cape Horn).[30] In the Pacific, Defoe's merchant and his ships encounter a series of fictional islands where they trade very profitably with the indigenous peoples, using cheap goods purchased for the purpose in Britain. After the Philippines, they sail east to the Ladrones (Mariana Islands), known to the Spanish since 1521, and then south to hitherto unknown islands. As they do so, the voyage enters a zone primarily constructed by Defoe's global imaginary, derived from travel accounts, but larded with numerous wonders, a place of plenty that almost beseeches exploitation. One of the locations they navigate suggests they have encountered the northern edge of a larger southern continent, so remote that the 'wild People' there 'understood nothing' and 'had never seen any Ship or Bark of any Nation... but their own' (*Novels*, x. 107). These fictional indigenes are very excited by the merchant's trade trinkets, amongst which are cheap iron hatchets, an instrument the use of which, somewhat incredibly, has to be demonstrated to them. Using sign language, the voyage trafficks for bargains among them, exchanging a hatchet for a 'Cargo of Gold' which 'weigh'd near five Ounces, for about the Value of two Shillings'.[31] Another uninhabited island, deep in the Southern Ocean, they call the Pearl Islands, after the prodigious number of large pearls they find in the oysters they catch there.[32]

In each place the expedition trades with considerable profit. English commerce, which is global, private, bourgeois, and entrepreneurial, is dedicated to maximizing return to individual metropolitan investors, but it is also extraordinarily profitable for every member of the expedition, from the supercargo to the lowest-ranked crew member. Defoe's imagination scopes out several characteristics of this sort of trade, which, while not based on settlement and sovereignty, reflects his colonial and imperial world view. The first is Defoe's law of unequal exchange. At first, this takes the form of a fantasy in which European wares, including English woollens, are adequate goods to trade for Chinese silks and Asian spices, pearls, and other luxury commodities [SEE CHAPTER 30]. In its pure form, repeated across the Pacific, the merchant's trade exploits moments of miscomprehension in the cross-cultural reading of value, in which

---

[30] Jane H. Jack, '*A New Voyage Round the World*: Defoe's "Roman à Thèse"', *HLQ*, 24:4 (1961), 323–36 (330–1).

[31] The location of the large island or continent is unclear, but it is approximately in the Tasman Sea between Australia and New Zealand, although British geographical knowledge at the time placed the location in largely uncharted territory. Defoe says the expedition has sailed as far south as the 'Southern Tropick', to the latitude 32°S (*Novels*, x. 106–7).

[32] The narrator says this island is 49 or 50°S, after which, being driven further south (as far as 67°S), they encounter snow and icebergs, being the 'farthest Southern Latitude that any European Ship ever saw in those Seas' (*Novels*, x. 139). The narrator later says that 'those Islands, where we so successfully fish'd for Oysters, or rather for Pearl, are the same as the ancient Geographers have call'd *Solomon's* Islands' (*Novels*, x. 146).

indigenous people do not know the value of their luxury commodities such as pearls or gold, because of their local superabundance, and, as a result, can be defrauded or exploited to exchange luxuries for 'worthless' or overvalued European trade goods, such as the specially manufactured 'toys' they have brought with them. In this traffick of 'Knives, Cissars, Beads, Looking-Glasses, Combs, ... Glass-Beads and Glass-Earings', the rhetoric of the equality of the market is maintained, but only in order to defraud the ignorant indigene (*Novels*, x. 107). The second law proposes that every place the voyage encounters has utility for English commerce. Even the most unpromising island is good at least for victualling and water. But more often, these imaginary places supply a significant luxury product—such as pearls or gold—that is locally abundant and undervalued. The third is the law of compound accumulation, so that one voyage might use multiple exchanges to accumulate advantage: Defoe's narrator is able to trade his English goods for China manufactures (silk, porcelain), and then sell them on for fabulous sums in South America, compounding his profit. Defoe's fourth law, the most general, is that trade is the dominant and universal script of human encounter around the world [SEE CHAPTER 14]. Even when there is no common language for trade, the merchant and his crew are able to bring off peaceable and profitable commerce, using a universal semiotic of exchange. In the *Review*, Defoe argued that trade was part of God's providence: 'there is a kind of Divinity in the Original of Trade'. He continues: 'God, in the Order of Nature, not only made Trade necessary to the making the Life of Man Easy, and towards accommodating one Part of the World with what they might want for their Conveniences, from another part; but also qualified, suited, and adapted the Vegetative and Sensitive World, to be subservient to the Uses, Methods, and Necessities which we find them now put to, by the ingenious Artists for the Convenience of Trade'.[33] The world, even and especially that beyond the bounds of civilized Europe, is entranced by British commerce.

In the second volume of *A New Voyage Round the World*, the expedition makes landfall in South America, and Defoe develops a second colonial argument, on the utility and advantage of colonial settlement. Two overlapping narratives in the novel recommend the salubriousness, accessibility, and profitability of Baldivia in Chile as a location for the establishment of the British colony in the southern tip of South America. This is a return to the argument he has been making since the turn of the century, but cast in new narrative clothes. Having made their profitable progress across the Pacific, the merchant's vessels cruise the South American coast with a plan to trade if possible, using their French subterfuge, and to privateer if not. Using the remote island of Juan Fernández as a base, they seize a Spanish vessel, and are tempted to take the route of the privateer, like Dampier before them. But instead, the merchant befriends a wealthy Spanish landowner on the captured vessel, and coopts him to his plan in return for fair treatment and mutual profit. The Spanish landowner provides him with the connections and cover to trade profitably, under his forged French papers, in the

---

[33] *Review*, ix. 211 (3 February 1713).

Chilean colony. The 'Spanish landlord', as he is called, further invites the merchant to visit his estates up in the country, a conceit which allows the merchant to range widely in the Spanish colony, and so describe its natural resources, economy, and political and military situation. He finds the colony to be an agriculturally rich and fertile region that is not only self-sufficient in food supply, but also has the potential to be a ready market for English goods. He determines that the indigenous Mapuche 'Chileans', or 'Indians' as he calls them, are tractable and obedient, and that the Spanish are present in very low numbers, without significant military reinforcement. In short, the region is open to conquest. Furthermore, the Spanish landlord shows him an overland route to the Argentine, making possible Defoe's eccentric but long-cherished idea that an English colony would have an overland trade route to the Spanish colonies, perhaps brokered by indigenous Mapuche merchants. The merchant's tour of the southern Andean mountains also reinforces the idea that in Chile, as in Peru in the previous centuries, gold was plentiful, so much so that in many places the expedition halts, gold can literally be picked up off the ground: 'Here they took up the Sand, or Gravel with their Hands, and every handful brought up such a Quantity of Gold, as was surprising' (*Novels*, x. 215). Altogether, the narrative nourishes the fantasy that colonial settlement projects are feasible and profitable.

In the final section of the novel, the merchant sponsors a daring secret expedition of a group of his men led by a loyal lieutenant to test his hypothesis that a cross-Andean trade might be possible. They leave from Baldivia, journey up into the mountains guided by the Spanish landlord, and then cross the continental divide, entering the almost uninhabited waste lands of Patagonia. The merchant's ship sails around the Cape Horn to pick them up at the mouth of the River Camarones, an imagined detail Defoe had noticed on Moll's map of the South Seas Company territory. After a series of outlandish adventures, battling the hostility of the weather and landscape, the transcontinental party emerges to testify to the almost unlimited quantities and easy accessibility of gold, which they could literally pick up from the ground. 'It seems', the narrator reports, 'there is a kind of Satisfaction in the Work of picking up Gold, besides the meer Gain' (*Novels*, x. 230–56). So although the South Sea colony scheme begins with a practical and circumstantial mode of formal realism about British mercantile commercially driven colonial endeavour, Defoe's project ends up in gold bug territory, prosecuting the colonial projector's romance and myth of superabundant gold, and in this way exchanges the modern commercial British colonial model for the earlier, increasingly outmoded, model of Spanish colonialism.

Conclusion

Defoe's ideas about the benefits of colonization are not unchanging through his writing and political career, though his commitment to the Baldivia scheme is remarkably tenacious. Nonetheless, certain assumptions or expectations are baked in. Defoe argues in his political writing that the settlement of a colony is a heroic enterprise, to be accorded high status, the appropriate focus of aristocratic support. Colonies, he argues, should be commercially orientated, organized as a large-scale investment opportunity, appropriate to joint-stock companies, or aristocratic great men, with extensive finance or credit. Colonies should be organized on mercantilist principles, so that profits should accrue to metropolitan backers, and further increase British trade. The colonies and plantations Defoe imagines are politically subservient to the British crown, with the concomitant obligation on the crown to protect the colony, especially through its projection of naval power [SEE CHAPTER 31]. He argues a colony should aim for self-sufficiency in food production through local agriculture, but admits it may need reinforcement supply in its early years. He argues that the colonial population should grow not only through natural reproduction, but also through metropolitan migration and indentured labour, ideas he explores more fully in *Moll Flanders* (1722) and *Colonel Jack* (1722).[34] He argues that migrants should include useful trades, and women, not just unskilled labour, criminals, and adventurers. Defoe is open to experimental forms of government in the colony, the political settlement of which is not tied exactly to that of the metropolis, allowing for religious toleration, a wide variety of government systems from absolutism to representative government, a wide variety of forms of land tenure, and, above all, free toleration of slavery and other forms of unfree labour.

Defoe's assumptions are further situated within, and around, others that organize the world and its peoples. Colonial projects are undertaken within the context of international rivalry with European powers (especially France, Holland, Spain, and Portugal). Defoe sees the commercial impetus of international trade as civilizing and beneficial, in which trade is the agent of mutual moral improvement for both parties. On the other hand, Defoe for the most part does not entertain many higher philosophical or religious motives to his colonial schemes, such as Christian mission. As Dennis Todd argues, for Defoe the colonial experience is transformative for his protagonists (such as Crusoe or Colonel Jack), but not for the colonized like Friday or Mouchat, who remain servants and slaves even after their conversion to Christianity.[35] Despite his curiosity about different forms of colonial government, Defoe sees the status of indigene 'natives' and African 'slaves' in an ordered hierarchy that places the English at the apex, above even their European rivals [SEE CHAPTER 28]. In Defoe's fictions, colonial projects have the capacity to marshal capital, labour, and natural resources to suit British purposes, reorganizing the world into racial hierarchies as they do so.

---

[34] Defoe's interest in indentured labour as a form of moral reform is explored in Dennis Todd, *Defoe's America* (Cambridge: Cambridge University Press, 2010), 88–9, 140–9.

[35] Todd, *Defoe's America*, 108–33.

FURTHER READING

Timothy C. Blackburn, 'Friday's Religion: Its Nature and Importance in *Robinson Crusoe*', *ECS*, 18:3 (1985), 360–82.

Alfred W. Crosby, *Ecological Imperialism: The Biological Expansion of Europe, 900–1900* (Cambridge: Cambridge University Press, 1986).

J. A. Downie, 'Defoe, Imperialism, and the Travel Books Reconsidered', *Yearbook of English Studies*, 13 (1983), 66–83.

Jane H. Jack, '*A New Voyage Round the World*: Defoe's "Roman à Thèse"', *HLQ*, 24:4 (1961), 323–36.

Christopher F. Loar, *Political Magic: British Fictions of Savagery and Sovereignty, 1650–1750* (New York: Fordham University Press, 2014).

Robert Markley, 'Defoe and the Imagined Ecologies of Patagonia', *PQ*, 93:3 (2014), 295–313.

Maximillian E. Novak, *Economics and the Fiction of Daniel Defoe* (Berkeley, CA: University of California Press, 1962).

Shinsuke Satsuma, *Britain and Colonial Maritime War in the Early Eighteenth Century: Silver, Seapower and the Atlantic* (Woodbridge: Boydell and Brewer, 2013).

Nicholas Seager, 'Crusoe's Crusade: Defoe, Genocide, and Imperialism', *Etudes anglaises*, 70:2 (2019), 196–212.

Abigail L. Swingen, *Competing Visions of Empire: Labor, Slavery, and the Origins of the British Atlantic Empire* (New Haven, CT: Yale University Press, 2015).

Dennis Todd, *Defoe's America* (Cambridge: Cambridge University Press, 2010).

CHAPTER 30

DEFOE AND THE PACIFIC

ROBERT MARKLEY

DEFOE was fascinated, throughout his literary career, by the Pacific Ocean. From his early journalistic works to his last novel, he imagined the Pacific region as the ultimate blank space on the world map, and projected onto it, like many of his contemporaries, a vision of 'infinite Advantage'—the endless profits to be made by exploiting opportunities for trade, piracy, and colonization from the western coasts of South America to the '*Southern* unknown Countries' supposedly lying south and southeast of the Indonesian archipelago.[1] Yet in the early eighteenth century, the Pacific was perceived as a mosaic of distinct regions and spheres of influence: the trade-rich coastal waters of China; the unapproachable empire of Japan; the South Seas along the coasts of Chile and Peru, patrolled by Spanish war ships and raided by the British and French; the Spanish colony in the Philippines; the Dutch commercial empire in the East Indies; the known and hypothesized islands dotting the surface of the vast ocean. No one attitude or consistent, global view of the Pacific's vast regions existed during Defoe's lifetime; instead, the open ocean and its bordering lands served as ideological screens for the dreams and fantasies, the values and assumptions, that animated an ideology of 'infinite Advantage'.

Depending on what islands, colonies, or countries one zeroed in and on and what accounts from travellers and projectors one read, the lands washed by Pacific waters fulfilled three crucial, if imaginary, roles. First, the islands east of the Indonesian archipelago and the imaginary continent of Terra Australis Incognita offered both the prospect of an insatiable market for European exports, notably for Defoe and his readers new untapped markets for English woollens, and endlessly profitable supplies of gold, spices, and exotic goods [SEE CHAPTER 14]. Second, the west coast of the Americas stoked dreams of breaking the Spanish monopoly on gold and silver mining, disrupting Spanish trade across the Pacific, and blocking French designs to control the slave trade in the Caribbean and Central America [SEE CHAPTER 29]. And third, the civilizations

---

[1] Defoe, *A New Voyage Round the World*, Novels (1724), x. 131. On 'infinite advantage' see Jeremy Wear, 'No Dishonour to be a Pirate: The Logic of Infinite Advantage in Defoe's *Captain Singleton*', *ECF*, 24:4 (2012), 569–96.

of China and Japan offered both the luxury goods (notably tea, porcelain, and silk) in demand across Europe and access to the complex trading networks crisscrossing East Asia that western merchants believed could multiply their profits severalfold.[2] These different regions, however, were often joined in grand visions of British expansion across thousands of miles of ocean. Writing in *The Review* in 1711, Defoe cautions against get-rich-quick schemes for colonizing the Pacific, yet nonetheless asserts that 'there is Room enough on the Western Coast of *America*, call'd the *South Seas*, for us to Fix, Plant, Settle, and Establish a Flourishing Trade, without Injuring, Encroaching on, or perhaps in the least Invading the Property or Commerce of the *Spaniards*'.[3] This vision of a South Seas of infinite resources and endlessly 'Flourishing Trade' derived, in part, from the extravagant claims by seventeenth-century British explorers, notably William Dampier, and helped to fuel the speculative frenzy for South Sea Company stock between 1712 and 1720.[4] Yet British enthusiasm for Pacific exploration persisted after the collapse of the South Sea Bubble in the autumn of 1720, and this stubborn optimism suggests the ways in which the Pacific marked a fundamental dialectic in the national imagination: the hopes—even convictions—that Pacific trade and colonization would cement Britain's status as a global power, and the fears that failure in the South Seas would undermine its naval power, economic ambitions, and political influence.[5] To a significant extent, eighteenth-century fiction set in the Pacific, particularly Defoe's novels, can be read as compensatory efforts to reconcile these hopes and fears: what British expeditions to the Pacific failed to accomplish in reality could be imagined in fiction by projecting onto the South Seas fantastic visions of a 'Flourishing Trade'.

In different ways, Defoe recasts a long tradition of voyage literature—characterized by real and imagined ethnographies, tales of adventure, and schemes to reap vast profits from discovery, trade, and piracy—in order to define the Pacific as a theatre for reimagining Britain's national identity.[6] No realistic narrative could comprehend what seemed to eighteenth-century writers and readers an unbounded ocean whose shorelines faded off the northern and southern edges of maps. Defoe's novels, in this context, present always incomplete and always provisional refractions of British ventures in the Pacific, his heroes negotiating always incomplete transitions from piracy and opportunism to sustained commercial success. Given its roots in voyage literature,

---

[2] See Robert Markley, *The Far East and the English Imagination, 1600-1740* (Cambridge: Cambridge University Press, 2006); Neil Rennie, *Far-Fetched Facts: The Literature of Travel and the Idea of the South Seas* (Oxford: Clarendon Press, 1995); and Avan Judd Stallard, *Antipodes: In Search of the Southern Continent* (Clayton, Victoria, Australia: Monash University Press, 2016).

[3] *Review*, viii. 243 (17 July 1711).

[4] On Dampier, see Diana and Michael Preston, *A Pirate of Exquisite Mind: The Life of William Dampier: Explorer, Naturalist and Buccaneer* (Sydney: Doubleday, 2004).

[5] See John Carswell, *The South Sea Bubble* (Stanford, CA: Stanford University Press, 1960); Larry Neal, The *Rise of Financial Capitalism: International Capital Markets in the Age of Reason* (Cambridge: Cambridge University Press, 1990); and Malcolm Balen, *The Secret History of the South Sea Bubble* (New York: Fourth Estate, 2003).

[6] See the still-classic study by J. A. Downie, 'Defoe, Imperialism, and the Travel Books Reconsidered', *Yearbook of English Studies*, 13 (1983), 66–83.

it is hardly surprising that fiction set in the Pacific often seems tangential to the development of the eighteenth-century novel, particularly in criticism devoted to domestic fiction, psychological realism, explorations of gender, and narrative experimentation. Nonetheless, in the century before Britain established colonies in the Far East, *Captain Singleton* (1720) and *A New Voyage Round the World* (1724) demonstrate the ways in which the Pacific helped to shape the nation's ability to imagine itself, culturally as well as economically, as a global power.

THE SOUTH SEAS IN VOYAGE LITERATURE

Early in 1720 when Defoe sent his pirate-hero, Bob Singleton, into the Pacific, he could draw on a rich tradition of voyage literature that described both the hardships, in-fighting, and unrealized dreams of South Sea ventures as well as the freebooting, profit-taking, and flag-planting that stirred British dreams of 'infinite Advantage' [SEE CHAPTER 8]. Before the advent of steamships, voyages to the Pacific around Cape Horn were expensive, dangerous, and time-consuming, beset by the omnipresent threats of storms, scurvy, supply shortages, shipwreck, mutiny, and attacks from Spanish ships off the coasts of Chile and Peru and Dutch ships in the East Indies. Beginning in the sixteenth century with Magellan's circumnavigation, accounts of harrowing voyages to the Pacific constituted a popular genre that interlaced tales of adventure, shipwreck, mutiny, and naval raids with commercial reconnaissance, nationalist propaganda, skewed cultural anthropology, and schemes for future commerce and colonization.[7] In the late seventeenth century, readers in Britain avidly consumed the eyewitness accounts of the buccaneers, including Dampier, Basil Ringrose, and Lionel Wafer, who raided the Spanish colonies in South and Central America in the 1680s, and later, in Dampier's case, parlayed his experience into the command of three voyages to locate and explore Terra Australis Incognita.[8] Significantly, both tales of buccaneer raids and accounts of sanctioned naval expeditions display what Glyndwr Williams calls 'a process of

---

[7] C. R. Boxer (ed. and trans.), *The Tragic History of the Sea*, rev. ed. with additional translation by Josiah Blackmore (Minneapolis, MN: University of Minnesota Press, 2001); Margarette Lincoln, 'Mutinous Behavior on Voyages to the South Seas and Its Impact on Eighteenth-Century Civil Society', *ECL*, 31:1 (2007), 62–80.

[8] For the exploits of the buccaneers, see A. O. Exquemelin, *Bucaniers of America ... Inlarged with two Additional Relations, viz. The one of Captain Cook, and the Other of Captain Sharp* (1684), and Basil Ringrose, *Bucaniers of America. The Second Volume Containing the Dangerous Voyage and Bold Attempts of Captain Bartholomew Sharp and Others; Performed upon the Coasts of the South Sea* (1685). See Derek Howse and Norman Thrower (eds.), *A Buccaneer's Atlas: Basil Ringrose's South Sea* (Berkeley, CA: University of California Press, 1992); Philip Edwards, *The Story of the Voyage: Sea-Narratives in Eighteenth-Century England* (Cambridge: Cambridge University Press, 1994); Glyndwr Williams, *The Great South Sea: English Voyages and Encounters 1570–1750* (New Haven, CT: Yale University Press, 1997); Jonathan Lamb, *Preserving the Self in the South Seas, 1680–1840* (Chicago, IL: University of Chicago Press, 2001).

enlargement and literary polishing'[9]—a self-conscious recasting by ghostwriters of oral accounts, ships' logs, and officers' journals into literary artifacts designed to appeal to a readership eager for tales of adventure and investment opportunities. In this regard, the fictionalizing of the Pacific preceded and helped to define the contours of the novels of the 1720s.

Tellingly, Defoe's final novel, *A New Voyage Round the World*, appropriates the title of Dampier's *A New Voyage Round the World* (1697) and its recycling by later writers and publishers eager to cash in on a popular genre: William Funnell (Dampier's disgruntled mate on his third circumnavigation), Woodes Rogers, George Shelvocke, William Betagh, and Richard Walter and Benjamin Robins, the authors of the official version of George Anson's circumnavigation in the 1740s, all promised their readers 'new voyages around the world'.[10] The buccaneering roots of these works reflect the hard realities of ventures into the Pacific: because the British launched no successful commercial ventures in the Pacific before 1800, all of these 'new voyages' turned to preying on Spanish ships, raiding Spanish colonies in Chile and Peru, as Sir Francis Drake had done in the 1570s, and then sailing across the Pacific and using their booty to trade for spices, silks, and porcelain in the Far East.[11] Although the South Sea Company was formed ostensibly as a trading venture that would assume much of Britain's national debt, sell stock to raise money for Pacific trade, and then use the profits from that trade to pay off its investors, its schemes were based on the assumption that occasional successes, like Woodes Rogers's capture of a small Spanish treasure ship en route from Acapulco to Manila, provided a blueprint for British adventurism in the Pacific.[12] Rogers's mission, though, had no successor for thirty years, and the South Sea Company never sent a ship into the Pacific, preferring bribes and financial manipulation to outfitting ships.

To market their narratives of actual voyages, authors, ghostwriters, and booksellers had to compress radically the day-to-day entries of logbooks and journals of three to

---

[9] Williams, *Great South Sea*, 113.

[10] William Funnell, *A Voyage Round the World* (1707); Woodes Rogers, *A Cruising Voyage Round the World* (1712); George Shelvocke, *A Voyage Round the World by Way of the Great South Sea* (1726); William Betagh, *A Voyage Round the World* (1728); and Richard Walter, *A Voyage Round the World, in the Years MDCCXL, I, II, III, IV. By George Anson* (1748). The authorship of this text is vexed; see Glyndwr Williams, *The Prize of All the Oceans: The Dramatic True Story of Commodore Anson's Voyage Round the World and How He Seized the Spanish Treasure Galleon* (New York: Viking, 1999), 237–41; Glyndwr Williams, 'Anson at Canton, 1743: "A Little Secret History"', in *The European Outthrust and Encounter. The First Phase c.1400 to c.1700*, ed. Cecil H. Clough and P. E. Hair (Liverpool: Liverpool University Press, 1994), 271–90; and Robert Markley, 'Anson at Canton, 1743: Obligation, Exchange, and Ritual in Edward Page's "Secret History"', in *The Culture of the Gift in Eighteenth-Century England*, ed. Linda Ziokowski and Cynthia Klekar (New York: Palgrave, 2009), 215–33.

[11] Glyndwr Williams, '"The Inexhaustible Fountain of Gold": English Projects and Ventures in the South Seas, 1670–1750', in *Perspectives of Empire: Essays Presented to Gerald S. Graham*, ed. John E. Flint and Glyndwr Williams (London: Longman, 1973), 27–53.

[12] On the French in the Pacific, see Williams, *Great South Sea*, 135–6, 143–59; James Pritchard, *In Search of Empire: The French in the Americas, 1670–1730* (Cambridge: Cambridge University Press, 2004), 320–2; and Catherine Manning, *Fortunes á Faire: The French in the Asian Trade, 1719–48* (Aldershot: Variorum, 1996).

four years at sea and censor potentially sensitive navigational information that might prove more useful for Dutch, French, and Spanish rivals than for British readers. With few glorious successes to trumpet, tales of circumnavigation remained episodic and, in some ways, unfulfilling; even as their authors gesture towards the vastness of the Pacific and its resources, they seem to recognize that their accounts fall hopelessly, even comically, short of describing its promise and its realities. With an eye towards marketing his new voyage, Defoe begins his final novel by having his narrator disparage previous accounts of circumnavigation for being 'fill'd up with Directions for Sailors coming that way, the Bearings of the Land, the Depth of the Channels, Entrances, and Barrs at the several Ports, Anchorage in the Bays and Creeks, and the like Things, useful indeed for Seaman going thither again, *and how few are they*? but not at all to the Purpose when we come expecting to find the History of the Voyage' (30). For Defoe, 'the History of the Voyage' must link the various regions of the Pacific—from Terra Australis Incognita to Peru—*imaginatively*, and in his own work he counters what he sees as the conceptual as well as narrative shortcomings of his predecessors by harnessing tales of Pacific adventure to larger generic and ideological ends. In contrast to the brutal conflicts that frequently erupted aboard ships in the Pacific, Defoe's novels offer compensatory fictions of heroes who master the crises on which so many voyages to the South Seas foundered. Particularly in *A New Voyage*, his nameless hero embodies the virtues of an idealized commander, equally adept at overcoming mutinies, storms, scurvy, and the threat of shipwreck; defeating enemies on the high seas; winning the trust of indigenes on newly discovered shores; driving hard bargains with merchants in the Far East; befriending the native peoples of South America suffering under the Spanish Yoke; and maximizing the expedition's profits.[13] In Swift's *Gullivers Travels* (1726), this faith in an ideology of endless exploitation turns the 'History of the Voyage' into a satiric tale of comic disorientation and eroding selfhood that plagues the usually hapless Gulliver in voyages that never reach their ostensible destinations. But Defoe's novels set in the Pacific offer distinct but complementary visions of the South Seas that assert and reassert a belief in 'infinite Advantage'.

If *Captain Singleton* reworks a tradition of pirate literature that Defoe himself had helped shape, *A New Voyage* reasserts the novelist's faith in the prospects of a 'Flourishing Trade' in the wake of the South Sea Bubble that exposed the company's on-again, off-again schemes for trade, privateering, and exploration in the South Seas as little more than a smokescreen for financial manipulation and corruption. Published in June 1720, two months before the collapse of the company's stock, *Singleton* outlines the novelistic opportunities that the Pacific offers. In *The Farther Adventures of Robinson Crusoe* (1719), Crusoe, now in his late sixties, becomes a merchant in Southeast Asia, and his quest for profits eventually takes him along the coast of China, to Beijing, and then across Siberia in a caravan; Singleton, in contrast, reaches the waters of the far southwestern Pacific

---

[13] See Alan Frost, 'Shaking off the Spanish Yoke: British Schemes to Revolutionise America, 1737–1807', in *Science and Exploration in the Pacific: European Voyages to the Southern Oceans in the Eighteenth Century*, ed. Margarette Lincoln (Woodbridge: Boydell Press, 1998), 19–38.

and begins his transition from pirate to semi-respectable and intermittently penitent merchant. As Hans Turley has argued, Singleton, like the Crusoe of *Farther Adventures*, is distinguished not by an interiorized psychology, but by his rebellion against the rigid hierarchies of command on board navy vessels, standards of civilized behaviour, legal strictures, and moral self-consciousness.[14] What distinguishes Singleton, though, is not, or not simply, his outlaw status as an 'enemy to all mankind' (the period's legal definition of piracy), but the ways in which he internalizes and displaces the dangers of eighteenth-century voyages to the South Seas onto a vision of profit and ultimately reform.[15]

Singleton's adventures in the second half of the novel highlight the stark differences that Defoe and his contemporaries perceived among potential trading partners in the far western Pacific; they also dramatize the qualities that the hero must cultivate in order to become as successful as a merchant as he had been as a pirate. Singleton's dealings with the Dutch and with the Chinese, in this sense, contrast the dangers of inter-European rivalry for spices and silks to the opportunities for expanding British commerce in un- and under-exploited markets. Even given his tendencies to self-recriminations about his career as a pirate, the hero is chameleon-like in his ability to adapt to changing circumstances.[16] In his conversations with Quaker William, he offers a range of strategies and solutions to problems that are more complex and challenging than those the hero faces during his trek across Africa in the first part of the novel.

Confronted by Dutch ships among 'the infinite Number of Islands which lye in [the] Seas' of Southeast Asia, Singleton fights when he has the advantage and shrewdly negotiates when he senses the opportunity: after running a captured ship aground and stealing its merchandise, he gives its sailors the option of joining his crew.[17] Preying on Japanese ships and trading clandestinely with natives in the Moluccas to circumvent the Dutch monopoly of the spice trade brings Singleton enough money to convince him that '*we were rich enough*' to leave 'Rummaging among the Spice Islands' (198), and he adjusts to temporary setbacks by setting a new mercantile course. Blown by contrary winds

---

[14] Hans Turley, *Rum, Sodomy, and the Lash: Piracy, Sexuality, and Masculine Identity* (New York: New York University Press, 1999).

[15] Erin Mackie, *Rakes, Highwaymen, and Pirates: The Making of the Modern Gentleman in the Eighteenth Century* (Baltimore, MD: Johns Hopkins University Press, 2009).

[16] The literature on Defoe's heroes and heroines is extensive. For representative views, see, John Richetti, *Defoe's Narratives: Situations and Structures* (Oxford: Clarendon, 1975); Paula R. Backscheider, *Daniel Defoe: Ambition and Innovation* (Lexington, KY: University Press of Kentucky, 1986); Rachel Carnell, *Partisan Politics, Narrative Realism, and the Rise of the British Novel* (New York: Palgrave Macmillan, 2006), 75–102; Ann Marie Fallon, *Global Crusoe: Comparative Literature, Postcolonial Theory and Transnational Aesthetics* (Farnham: Ashgate, 2011); Maximillian E. Novak, *Transformations, Ideology, and the Real in Defoe's Robinson Crusoe and Other Narratives: Finding 'The Thing Itself'* (Newark, DE: University of Delaware Press, 2015); and Elizabeth R. Napier, *Defoe's Major Fiction: Accounting for the Self* (Newark, DE: University of Delaware Press, 2016.

[17] Defoe, *The Life, Adventures, and Pyracies of the Famous Captain Singleton*, ed. Shiv Kumar, intro. Penelope Wilson (Oxford: Oxford University Press, 1990), 191. The following paragraphs expand an argument I originally made in 'The Eighteenth-Century Novel and the Pacific', in *The Cambridge History of the English Novel*, ed. Robert Caesario and Clement Hawes (Cambridge: Cambridge University Press, 2012), 196–212.

toward the Chinese coast, he first plunders a Chinese junk, then 'resolve[s] now that we should leave off being Pyrates, and turn Merchants; so we told them [the Chinese] what Goods we had on board, and that if they would bring their Super-Cargoes or Merchants on board, we would trade with them' (199). Understandably torn between a desire to turn a profit and their fear of Singleton and his crew, the merchants negotiate a mutual pledge of faith: Quaker William sails as factor for the pirate goods that the Chinese ships are transporting, while two Chinese merchants remain on board Singleton's ship as hostages. Unlike the mutual suspicion that characterizes Singleton's encounters with the Dutch, his negotiations with the Chinese merchants are marked by a civility that is essential as both the basis *for* and the product *of* a mutually beneficial commerce. This scene is not Defoe's 'realistic' depiction of Anglo-Chinese trading encounters in the eighteenth century, but a fictional rendering of the mutually reinforcing values of mutual self-interest, good faith bargaining, and profitable trade that he had advocated in his 1711 numbers of *The Review*.[18] In this respect, the turn to commercial civility provides the moral platform for his eventual renunciation of his life as a pirate, if not the fortune he has accumulated.

When William returns from his thirteen-day trading mission, he describes 'how civilly he had been used, how [the Chinese had] treated him with all imaginable Frankness and Openness, that they had not only given him the full Value of his Spices and other Goods which he carry'd, in Gold, by good Weight, but had loaded the Vessel again with such Goods as he knew we were willing to trade for' (200). In return, William pledges that Singleton and his crew 'should use no Violence with [the Chinese], nor detain any of their Vessels after we had done trading with them'—a pledge that the hero eagerly puts into action. Singleton boasts that 'we would strive to outdo them in Civility, and ... make good every Part of his Agreement' (200). The ensuing negotiations over prices leave both the reformed pirates and the Chinese 'exceedingly well satisfied' (201). This episode tells us less about a change in Singleton's moral psychology or a dawning recognition of his past crimes than it does about his strategic flexibility and his new-found zeal for trade. It gestures metonymically, in this respect, towards a metanarrative of imagined British prosperity, a buccaneering pilgrim's progress from raiding the Spanish Main to unlocking the lucrative trade of the Far East. Because the wealthy regions of the China Sea hold the promise of nutmegs, cloves, silks, teas, and (above all else) gold bullion, trade becomes—for Defoe as it does for Singleton—the logical extension and evolutionary end of piracy. As Singleton leaves the Moluccas and heads into 'the open Sea ... South East of the *Philippines*, being the great Pacifick, or South Sea' (196), his

---

[18] On China in eighteenth-century literature, see David Porter, *Ideographia: The Chinese Cipher in Early Modern Europe* (Stanford, CA: Stanford University Press, 2001; Chi-ming Yang, *Performing China: Virtue, Commerce, and Orientalism in Eighteenth-Century England, 1660–1760* (Baltimore, MD: Johns Hopkins University Press, 2011); Eugenia Zuroski Jenkins, *A Taste for China: English Subjectivity and the Prehistory of Orientalism* (Oxford: Oxford University Press, 2013); and Eun Kyung Min, *China and the Writing of English Literary Modernity, 1690–1770* (Cambridge: Cambridge University Press, 2018). For a critical overview of work before 2014, see Robert Markley, 'China and the English Enlightenment: Literature, Aesthetics, and Commerce', *Literature Compass*, 11 (2014), 517–27.

moral self-questioning—his 'Horrour ... upon the just Reflection' (195) of his life as a pirate—allows him to transform his pillaging of defenceless vessels into a strategic mode of capital formation. Piracy offers him the means to invest in a complex regional economy that produces 'Civility' as well as profit.

In this respect, Singleton makes the western Pacific a logical stage for the theatrics of his repentance precisely because the novel asks its readers to imagine the mutually constitutive discourses of trade and civility as a means for the hero to secure a stable, if secretive, identity. Faced by a guilty conscience, Singleton and Quaker William can persuade each other of the impracticability of making restitution for their piracies only after they have secured their fortunes through the civilizing effects of trade in the South Seas. Wealth produces reformation, even if their future in London rests on the disguised homoerotic bonds that isolate them from society. Yet the riches that Singleton and William accumulate from 'turn[ing] Merchants' are themselves a fantastic projection of what trade in the 'great *Pacifick*' offers, and Defoe yokes their wealth to two of the great dreams—or delusions—of eighteenth-century voyage literature: reopening trade to the closed nation of Japan and finding a sea-route to the Pacific across the arctic wastes of North America.

Immediately after concluding their dealings with the Chinese merchants, William tries to persuade Singleton to sail to Japan in order to rescue thirteen English sailors shipwrecked 'upon a great Rock in a stormy Night where they lost their Ship and the rest of their Men were drowned' (201–2). Japan had been closed to all Europeans except for a single Dutch trading outpost since 1638, the year that professing Christianity was made a capital offence and native converts massacred.[19] The source of William's tale is 'a kind of Religious, or *Japan* Priest, who spoke some Words of *English*' (201), having learned them from the sailors who had been pressured to denounce the Christian religion and worship what Defoe calls 'their God, an Idol' (202). Through the priest's intervention, the English sailors have been spared and allowed to 'live their own Way, as long as they were quiet and peaceable' (202), but remain stranded, with no hope of returning to Europe. When Singleton asks what the Englishmen were doing sailing north of Japan, William tells him that the priest had

> pull'd out a little Book, and in it a Piece of Paper, where it was written in an *English* Man's Hand, and in plain *English* Words, thus; and says *William*, I read it my self: *We came from Greenland, and from the North Pole*. This indeed was amazing to us all and more to those Seamen among us who knew any thing of the infinite Attempts which had been made from *Europe*, as well as by the *English* as the *Dutch*, to discover a Passage that way into those Parts of the World; and as *William* press'd us earnestly to go on to the North, to rescue those poor Men, so that the Ship's Company

---

[19] See Derek Massarella, *A World Elsewhere: Europe's Encounter with Japan in the Sixteenth and Seventeenth Centuries* (New Haven, CT: Yale University Press, 1990), and Jacques Proust, *Europe through the Prism of Japan: Sixteenth to Eighteenth Centuries*, trans. Elizabeth Bell (Norte Dame, IN: University of Notre Dame Press, 2002).

began to incline to it; and in a Word, we all came to this, that we would stand into the Shore of *Formosa*, to find this Priest again and have a further Account of it all from him. ... [B]ut when [we] came there, the Vessels were very unhappily sail'd, and thus put an End to our Enquiry after them, and perhaps may have disappointed Mankind of one of the most noble Discoveries that ever was made, or will again be made in the World, for the Good of Mankind in general. (202–3)

In this embedded tale, Defoe gives fictional form to the centuries-long dream of finding a sea route across the Canadian Arctic, the fabled Northwest Passage, that motivated expeditions from the sixteenth to the late eighteenth centuries.[20] William sees for himself only a scrawled, one-sentence narrative, '*We came from Greenland, and from the North Pole*', that marks the limits of geographical knowledge, even of the epistemology of exploration, at the border between plausible narrative and pure fantasy. It is significant that the 'rest of [the English] Men were drowned' on the rocky coast of Japan rather than perishing somewhere between Greenland the North Pole, because apparently most or all of the crew survived a voyage that had defeated the 'infinite Attempts' of their real-life counterparts.

In *Singleton*, Japan exists beyond the horizons of first-hand knowledge, trade, and English ambition, linked to the tale of an impossible voyage and the sacrifice of Englishmen who cannot be rescued. Cutting themselves off from the kind of trade that Singleton embraces in his encounter with the Chinese merchants, the Japanese remain beyond the collective suggested by 'Mankind'. Although the crew captures and loots a Japanese merchant ship in one of their raids, the empire lies outside of the 'Adventures and Pyracies' that the title of the novel promises. Japan becomes instead a kind of talisman for two centuries of British ambitions to exploit the Northwest Passage as a comparatively fast and inexpensive sea route to the great empires and trading emporia of the Pacific. The marooned sailors who vanish from the narrative with the mysterious Japanese priest are Defoe's ciphers for the thousands of lost seamen who never completed their circumnavigations of the earth, even as their ghosts haunt English dreams of the Pacific. It is only, Defoe emphasizes in his final novel, in fiction that these dreams can be realized.

Defoe's *New Voyage*

In *A New Voyage Round the World*, Defoe relocates the prospect of an infinitely profitable trade from the China Sea to the shores of the imaginary Terra Australis Incognita. The undiscovered or under-explored lands of the South Pacific offer endless reserves of gold and valuable commodities. They are populated by natives willing to trade their

---

[20] See Glyn Williams, *Voyages of Delusion: The Search for the Northwest Passage in the Age of Reason* (London: HarperCollins, 2002).

riches for trinkets and capable of being civilized into consumers craving British goods, particularly the woollens the East India Company had spent two centuries trying to unload on reluctant merchants from Bombay to Canton. Although Defoe's unnamed hero and his crew engage in the usual gamut of activities in their voyage across the Pacific—privateering, illegal trading in Spanish and Dutch ports, and hoodwinking indigenous peoples—their discoveries liberate them from the psychological dilemmas faced by the half-penitent piratical subject, allowing them to dispense with the moral self-questioning that intermittently occupies Singleton. But even as the hero's moral self-consciousness gives way to kind of a Machiavellian managerial expertise, he anchors his identity in a network of mutually reinforcing interests: nominal service to king and country, fidelity to the voyage's unnamed financial backer, dedication to the belief that a contented and motivated crew is good for business, and a conflation of the sailors' self-interest with the owner's insistence on a huge return from his investment. The infinite profits that *A New Voyage* envisions in the Pacific both produce and are produced by redefining moral consciousness and psychological interiority as a kind of strategic inventiveness—the ingenuity and indirection that Defoe elevates into an art in *The Complete English Tradesman* (1725–7). The ins and outs of the narrator's schemes may be complicated, even opaque, but they are always guided by his commitment to minimizing risks and maximizing profits.

In contrast to *Singleton*'s focus on 'Adventures and Pyracies', *A New Voyage* offers fantasies of mercantile opportunism that reinvigorate the arguments that Defoe had made in 1711 when he devoted twelve numbers of his *Review* to promoting the South Sea Company. Repeatedly in these numbers of *The Review*, Defoe argues that if England were to seize ports in New Spain and thereby drive the French from the region, the ensuing trade would prove 'Fruitful of infinite Advantages' for Britain.[21] Underlying this assertion is his belief that 'the Countries in [these tropical] Latitudes [are] infinitely beyond the Plantations of *New England, Virginia, &c.* in the Fruitfulness of the Soil, Kind of Production, and other Advantages'.[22] Years later in *A New Voyage*, Defoe offers a vision of these 'infinite Advantages' by inverting the route of actual circumnavigations: an English voyage reaps vast profits by sailing eastward around the Cape of Good Hope and across the Indian Ocean, and then discovers a new continent in the Pacific, new trading opportunities in Chile, and ideal conditions for new colonies in the verdant but unpopulated interior of South America. In this manner, he dramatizes what might lie 'infinitely beyond' the disappointments of North American colonization by turning seaborne adventures into a sprawling commercial prospectus. In the post-Bubble disenchantment of the mid 1720s, no cartel of investors awaits the hero at the end of *A New Voyage* to claim the lion's share of the voyage's profits or to parcel out small shares of this booty to the crew. Instead, the financing for this improbable voyage comes from a

---

[21] *Review*, viii. 248 (19 July 1711).
[22] *Review*, viii. 283 (7 August 1711).

single anonymous investor in London, who conveniently dies in the final sentences of the novel so that the narrator can keep much of the voyage's profits.

Defoe begins *A New Voyage* by distancing his narrative from the traditions of voyage literature on which he draws. Asserting that 'a very good Sailor may make but a very indifferent Author', he rejects as narrative models the 'long Journals [and] tedious Accounts' that 'have little or nothing of Story in them, for the use of such Readers who never intend to go to Sea' (29, 30). In contrast, his 'Story' describes both the narrative and managerial strategies necessary to realize England's longstanding dreams of Pacific riches. Emphasizing the originality of his final novel, Defoe has his hero declare that he will 'give an Account of my Voyage, differing from all that I had ever seen before, in the nature of the Observations, as well as in the manner of relating them: And as this is perfectly new in its Form, so I cannot doubt but it will be agreeable in the Particulars, seeing either no Voyage ever made before, had such Variety of Incidents happening in it, so useful and so diverting, or no Person that sail'd on those Voyages, has thought fit to publish them after this manner' (30–1). Defoe's claims that his novel 'is perfectly new' are aesthetic, even metafictional; it is the imagination of the author that will make particulars 'agreeable' and ensure a narrative and conceptual unity that will turn a 'Variety of Incidents' into a believable first-person narrative. Yet even as Defoe mocks previous tales of circumnavigation, he appropriates and reworks the assumptions and values that underlie their voyages. His claim that he is offering 'an Account ... perfectly new in its Form' rests on his transforming the 'long Journals [and] tedious Accounts' of his predecessors into his 'useful and diverting'—that is, aesthetically pleasing as well as instructive—narrative. It is a 'History of the Voyage' related by an individual who becomes a function of his and his crew's adventures. What voyage literature can only promise, Defoe asserts his novel will deliver.

The 'indifferent Author' Defoe has in mind is Dampier, whose accounts of his three contentious and unprofitable missions to map the coasts of Australia and discover new markets for British trade devolve into long stretches of 'Directions for [future] Sailors coming that way' (30). Yet Dampier's narratives testify to the widespread faith that 'infinite Advantages' are to be found among the islands north of Australia. Dampier presents himself as always on the verge of discovering 'some fruitful Lands, Continent, or Islands, or both, productive of any of the rich Fruits, Drugs, or Spices (perhaps Minerals also, &c.) that are in other Parts of the Torrid Zone, under equal Parallels of Latitude'.[23] The fact that these 'fruitful lands' remain undiscovered after three voyages—as fanciful, in their own way, as Swift's imaginary islands in *Gulliver's Travels*—both frustrates and provokes his and his readers' faith in the commercial potential of Terra Australis Incognita. In *A New Voyage*, Defoe recasts this unbridled faith in the profitability of the Pacific by envisioning what lies beyond Dampier's reach: a triumphal voyage of discovery and trade.

---

[23] William Dampier, *A Voyage to New Holland: The English Voyage of Discovery to the South Seas in 1699*, ed. James Spencer (London: Alan Sutton, 1981), 147.

What distinguishes Defoe's novel from Dampier's narratives, then, is less its 'Form' or 'Variety of Incidents' than its redefinition of the genre to exclude descriptions of scurvy, dissension, violence, and death that are staples of non-fictional accounts of circumnavigation. The narrative coherence of Defoe's account reflects the single-mindedness of his visions of wealth to be made in the Pacific. If *Roxana*, published within a year of *A New Voyage*, reads as a cautionary tale about the seductions of luxury and sin, Defoe's final novel offers an inverted image of his guilt-ridden heroine: a hero who, unlike Singleton, does not suffer from pangs of conscience or indict himself for his sins, who has nothing to repent for and no guilt to expiate or explain away. Moll Flanders and Bob Singleton reform after they have become rich, but the narrator of *A New Voyage* has no need to leave a life of rampant acquisitiveness because he already exists in a privileged state: the success of the voyage legitimizes his actions and identity by redefining 'character' in the mutually constitutive terms of morality and trade.[24] Preserving the self in the South Seas, to borrow Jonathan Lamb's phrase, means subordinating self-reflection to mercantile duty: maximizing profits and minimizing dissension.[25]

In this sense, although the novel occasionally reads like a brief for Defoe's projects in the South Seas, it also dramatizes new strategies of command aboard ship and a new literary 'Form' that recasts the failures and frustrations of previous circumnavigations into a dream vision of mercantile aggrandizement. Unlike his real-life counterparts, the hero of *A New Voyage* exercises his authority by persuading sailors to consent to his plans, not by terrifying or threatening them. In this respect, he moulds his crew (like Defoe tries to mould his readers) into collaborators willing to hazard all on the success of the voyage. Early in the novel, the narrator is forced to put down a mutiny by members of the crew sceptical of his plans to sail east across the Indian Ocean, bypassing the trading monopoly of the East India Company in Bombay, Madras, and Calcutta, in order to reach the Pacific. The narrator, who until this time has concealed his command of the voyage, restores order on board by guile and generosity, claiming that 'Men were always secured in their Duty by a generous Kindness, better than by absolute Dominion and Severity' (60). 'Generous Kindness', however, is not a mark of gentlemanly sensibility or good nature, but a means of control, a way to enhance and mask the nature of his power. Even after the narrator reveals himself as the true commander of the voyage, relegating the French Captain to a glorified boatswain, his strategies remain more important than any intrinsic qualities he possesses.

The hero, in this regard, is no Bob Singleton, although he shares the pirate's ability to command by consensus. Defoe's treatment of the abortive mutiny in *A New Voyage* rewrites the Madagascar episodes in *Captain Singleton* by emphasizing the superiority of cogently planned trading ventures over piracy or mere opportunism. The hero quickly pardons all but two of the mutineers, then sends one of them, the second mate and ringleader, to spy on a crew of pirates on Madagascar. After learning that the pirates

---

[24] See Deidre Shauna Lynch, *The Economy of Character: Novels, Market Culture, and the Business of Inner Meaning* (Chicago, IL: University of Chicago Press, 1998).

[25] Lamb, *Preserving the Self*.

are merely 'a Crew of unresolv'd divided Rogues ... [with] no Body to command, and therefore no Body to obey' (71), the now-reformed second mate convinces those tired of their immoral, and not very profitable, ways to join the expedition for the remainder of the voyage. The second mate is named captain of their stolen vessel, having mastered the strategies of command—guile, indirection, foresight, rhetorical persuasiveness, and a focus on profit—that stem from and underwrite the consensual obedience of the crew. Defoe thus imbues his hero with sociopolitical, rather than personal, virtues. The aesthetic unity he claims for his novel stems from his conviction that self-discipline and efficient organizational hierarchies are fundamental to the South Seas trade.

Yet to the extent that the hero's moral and psychological identity is defined by his strategies of command and control, his integrity as a character becomes as imaginary as his vision of the boundless wealth of the Pacific. The fiction of limitless profits, in this regard, enables the fiction of a coherent, if temporally dislocated, self. Defoe's heroes, as they sail the Pacific, rely on the prospect of 'infinite Advantage' as a way to justify the coherence of a *retrospectively* constructed self: that is, Singleton can reform and the narrator of *A New Voyage* can disclaim the need to reform because they have returned to England wealthy men. The success of their voyages grants them the narrative authority to recount how they repurposed their strategies of self-command into tales of moral reclamation (in the case of the second mate) and consensual authority. The hero of Defoe's final novel, then, is a different kind of character from Roxana or Moll Flanders because his self-justification lies in already having overcome the dangers and frustrations of trade in the Pacific.

If *A New Voyage* follows the contours of voyage literature, it also brings to the fore the fantastic elements that characterize Defoe's novel-writing, and that are often downplayed or subsumed within a critical discourse of moral and descriptive realism. Even in novels that seem to foreground moral realism—*Robinson Crusoe*, *Moll Flanders*—the characters' circumstances hinge on improbabilities that rely on the author's sleights-of-hand, like Crusoe's agricultural success on his island and the absence of rats that typically devasted crops and grain stores on island colonies.[26] In his final novel, however, Defoe's generic experimentation pushes the bounds of speculative realism into the service of something approaching science fiction—an alternative history of commercial triumph. Set on a voyage that took place from December 1711 to spring 1713, the novel anticipates the now-familiar science-fiction genre of an alternative history, a genre that asks 'what if?' as a way to defamiliarize the history that readers already know or already have experienced.[27] Disgruntled by the lack of British ambitions in the Pacific, Defoe's novel charts lost opportunities that would have provided an imaginative roadmap to a glorious and wealthy national future.

---

[26] See Lucinda Cole, *Imperfect Creatures: Vermin, Literature, and the Sciences of Life, 1600–1740* (Ann Arbor, MI: University of Michigan Press, 2016), 143–71.

[27] Classics of alternative history include Philip K. Dick's *The Man in the High Castle* (1961)—the Nazis won World War II—and Kim Stanley Robinson's *The Years of Rice and Salt* (2002): a history of the world since 1350 based on the premise that almost all Europeans were wiped out by the Black Death.

The lands that Defoe describes in the South Pacific are alien enough that they might be lapped by the waters of an ocean on Aldebaran. Yet the fantastic elements of *A New Voyage*, in an important sense, extend the novelist's insistence that verisimilitude must be governed by—or indeed must be a function of—a larger moral or, I would suggest, ideological vision. In his preface to the third volume of his Crusoe trilogy, the *Serious Reflections* (1720), Defoe castigates his critics who claim that his novels elevate make-believe over moral purpose. Speaking in the persona of Crusoe, he declares 'that the Story, though Allegorical, is also Historical; and that it is the beautiful Representation of a Life … sincerely adapted to, and intended for the common Good of Mankind', while reminding his readers that 'the Fable is always made for the Moral, not the Moral for the Fable'.[28] Although *A New Voyage* shares more with Crusoe's *Farther Adventures* than with the better-known first volume of the trilogy, it too privileges a 'Moral' over a 'Fable', although the moral is defined in terms of the 'common Good' of British commercialism. Rather than the puritanical self-fashioning of the narrator's inner life, Defoe's unnamed hero devotes his time and energy to entwined narrative strategies of navigational specificity and detailed tableaux of idealized economic trade with willing natives.

Once the ships sail into the uncharted waters of the southwestern Pacific, the narrative often reads like one of the logbooks that Defoe began his novel by mocking:

> We stood away full *South*, to see if we could find out the Continuance of the former Land: But as we found no Land, so great a Sea coming from the South, we concluded, we should find no Land that Way. And varying our Course Easterly, we ran, with a fair fresh Gale at *N.W.* and by *W.* for seven Days more; in which Time, we saw nothing but the open Sea, every Way; and, making an Observation, [we] found we had pass'd the *Southern Tropick*, and that we were in the Latitude of six and twenty Degrees and thirteen Minutes; after which, we continued our Course still *Southerly* for several Days more; 'till we found by another Observation, that we were in two and thirty Degrees, and twenty Minutes. (106–7)

The parodic intensity of this passage encourages readers to plot the ship's course as it sails into unchartered waters east of Australia. Unlike the sick, scared, and often mutinous crews that are staples of Pacific voyage literature in the seventeenth and eighteenth centuries, the crew in *A New Voyage* lack individual voices or any novelistic markers of subjective experience. The 'we' who 'stood away', 'concluded', and made observations are effects of the commercial imperatives that motivate the voyage.

This specificity of the narrator's sailing directions is matched by the minutely detailed description of economic exchanges on imaginary lands. Sailing south southeast from the Ladrones (the Marianas Islands), the ships encounter the contours of a coastline that may be either an island or a continent, and peoples who perform the roles that 'mild and inoffensive' indigenous peoples ideally do in the one-sided contact narratives of

---

[28] Defoe, *Serious Reflections during the Life and Surprising Adventures of Robinson Crusoe* (1720), A2v, A2r.

centuries of European voyage literature. On the coast of this unknown country, the sailors encounter people whose social structures and forms of address mirror their own expectations. After saluting the 'King' in an elaborate and dignified pantomime,

> our Officer stept up to the Queen, and ties about her Neck, a most delicate Necklace of Pearl; *That is to say*, of large handsome white Glass Beads, which might in *England*, cost about Four Pence Halfpenny, and to every one of her Ladies, he gave another of smaller Beads and differing Colours than those which he gave the Queen: Then he presented her Majesty with a long String of Glass-Beads, which being put over her Head, reached down to her Waste before, and joyn'd in a kind of a Tossel, with a little Knot of blew Ribband, which she was also extreamly pleased with; and very fine she was. (113)

The narrator easily identifies—or projects onto this group of indigenous people—a sociopolitcal hierarchy defined by royalty and court attendants, despite the fact that neither natives nor Englishmen can speak the other's language. The glass beads serve the same function as 'a most delicate Necklace of Pearl' because they define economic and intercultural transactions in terms of a cost-benefit analysis: in exchange for these trinkets, the sailors receive about £10 worth of gold, a substantial return on their investment of 'Four Pence Halfpenny'. Defoe rewrites, in effect, 300 years of Eurocentric contact narratives as an idealized tableau of unproblematic and mutually satisfying exchange.

But unlike the analogous scenes in *Captain Singleton*—trading trinkets for gold in Africa—this Pacific encounter quickly turns into a detailed description of the Queen's sexualized body:

> Saving that her Skin was of a Tawny Colour, she was a very pretty Woman; very Tall, a sweet Countenance, admirable Features, and in a Word, a completely Handsome Lady [whose] Breasts were plump and round, not flaggy and hanging down, as it is General with all the *Indian* Women, some of whose Breasts hang as low as their Bellies; but Sitting as Beautifully up, as if they had been lac'd with Stays round her Body. (114)

In one respect, this scene reads like a primer of masculinist, imperialist appropriation that identifies the European male gaze with the appropriative logics of the colonialist subjugation of complaisant, feminized natives.[29] In another, the physical description of the Queen anticipates the erotic charge that defines accounts of the Pacific Islands in later eighteenth-century voyage literature.[30] Yet if the Queen is rendered in the

---

[29] See Heidi Hutner, *Colonial Women: Race and Culture in Stuart Drama* (Oxford: Oxford University Press, 2001).

[30] See Edwards, *Story of the Voyage*; John Gascoigne, *Captain Cook: Voyager Between Worlds* (London: Hambledon, 2007); and Harriet Guest, *Empire, Barbarism, and Civilisation: Captain Cook, William Hodges, and the Return to the Pacific* (Cambridge: Cambridge University Press, 2007).

appropriative and eroticized depictions of dozens, if not hundreds, of Indian Queens in seventeenth- and eighteenth-century literature, Defoe's description of her is entangled with a longer, compulsively detailed assessment of the materials and value of the cloak she puts on. This description is worth quoting at length:

> [The Queen's cloak] was made of an infinite Number and Variety of Feathers, odly, and yet very curiously put together, and was Spangl'd, as we may call it, all over, with little Drops or Lumps of Gold; some no bigger than a Pins-Head, which had Holes made thro' them, and were strung Six or Seven together, and so Tyed on to the Feathers: Some as big as a Large Pea, hanging single, some as big as a Horse-Bean, and beaten Flat, and all hanging promiscuously among the Feathers, without any Order or Shape, which notwithstanding were very Beautiful in the Whole, and made the Thing look Rich and Handsome enough. ...
>
> When their Majesties had just put on their Robes, you may guess how Glorious they look'd, but especially the Queen, who being a most charming beautiful Creature as before, was much more so, when she glitter'd thus all with Gold; our Men look'd very narrowly to observe whether there were no Diamonds, and particularly whether any Pearl among their Finery, but they could not perceive any. (115–16)

This over-determined scene of colonialist desire could serve as an emblem of exchanges between gold-rich indigenes and Europeans hell-bent on profit. On one level, this description seems stitched together from narrative accounts and reworks analogous scenes in *Singleton*: hatchets for provisions, trinkets for gold, a gun shot off as a demonstration of techno-western superiority, and mild and 'inoffensive' natives inclined to profitable 'Traffick'. It is significant that the feathered, gold embroidered vest, rather than the Queen's 'charming beautiful' body, becomes the object of the sailors' gaze. Their obsession with the 'Rich and Handsome' robes restages on an undiscovered island or continent a refracted version of the logic of economic striptease we find in *Roxana*, when the heroine and her Dutch husband reveal their jewels, stocks, bonds, and deeds, and other instruments of wealth to each other. The sailors' efforts to discover half-expected diamonds and pearls stitched into the feathered cloak suggests how the projective fantasy logic of accumulation operates. Gold, diamonds, and pearls form an inferential chain that follows from the 'what ifs' of Defoe's belief in the riches of the South Pacific.

In an important sense, the description of the Queen's robe seems a compensatory fantasy for the failures, false starts, and disappointing results of earlier British mercantile and naval expeditions to the South Seas. Like the navigational headings, wind directions, and measurements of latitude in the novel, the Queen's robe dresses fantasy in the garb of 'realistic' description; it is as though Defoe is trying to convince himself as much as he is the reader that his alternative history in *A New Voyage* has an overarching 'Moral' that holds together conceptually and narratively his imaginative vision of the wealth awaiting intrepid merchants in the '*Southern* unknown Countries'. The analogical reasoning that allows the sailors to leap from gold, to pearls, to diamonds in gazing on the feathered object of their desire is characteristic of a novel that projects into the unknown of what Defoe thinks he already knows about tractable natives, trinkets for gold, and the returns on investment that the narrator and his crew realize.

The undiscovered lands of the Pacific, for Defoe, exist in the overlap of colonial allegory and alternative history. In a striking passage that blurs projective fantasy and investment prospectus, the narrator echoes the language that Defoe had used fifteen years earlier in *The Review*. Generalizing from his encounters, the narrator declares that

> the People in the *Southern* unknown Countries, being first of all very numerous, and living in a temperate Climate which requires clothing, and having no Manufactures or Materials for Manufactures of their own, wou'd consequently take off a very great Quantity of *English* Woollen-Manufactures, especially when Civiliz'd by our dwelling among them and taught the Manner of Clothing themselves for their Ease and Convenience; and in Return for these Manufactures, 'tis Evident, we shou'd have Gold in Specie, and perhaps Spices; the best Merchandise and Return in the world. ...
>
> Nor can it be objected here, that this Nook of the Country [where his crew has reaped huge profits] may not easily be found by any One but by us, that have been there before ... I lay it down as a Foundation; that whoever, Sailing over the *South-Seas*, keeps a stated Distance from the Tropick to the Latitude of fifty six, to sixty Degrees, and steers *Eastward* towards the *Straights of Magellan*, shall never fail to discover new Worlds, new Nations, and new inexhaustible Funds of Wealth and Commerce, such as never were yet known to the Merchants of *Europe*. (131)

The 'beautiful Representation' that Defoe has in mind in *A New Voyage* underwrites fables of 'infinite Advantage': willing consumers eager to part with their gold and spices for England's surplus 'Woollen-Manufactures' become the fantasy figures of exploratory voyages not undertaken. The uncharted regions these peoples supposedly inhabit are the imaginary—and essential—landscape of an ideology of capitalist expansion, the fictions of 'inexhaustible Funds of Wealth and Commerce' that justify outlays of men, ships, and money. The promise of these 'new Worlds', for Defoe, renders schemes of Pacific trade and exploration rational enterprises, blurring distinctions between fiction and fact, speculation and investment. These 'new Nations', with 'no Manufactures or materials for Manufactures', must remain imaginary because to 'civiliz[e]' them would bring them into economies of scarcity, self-interest, and commercial competition. If that were to happen, these lands would offer not 'the best Merchandise and Return in the World', but only refractions of the contentious histories and ongoing antagonism that Swift satirizes in the rivalry between Lilliput and Blefuscu. In its own way, then, *A New Voyage* is as much a fantasy as *Gulliver's Travels*; but if the rhetoric of 'new Worlds, new Nations, and new inexhaustible Funds of Wealth and Commerce' is any indication, it is one that Defoe and at least some his readers fervently wished to believe. His final novel tests the bounds of realism and anticipates the generic postulates of later innovations in science fiction and fantasy.

Further Reading

J. A. Downie, 'Defoe, Imperialism, and the Travel Books Reconsidered', *Yearbook of English Studies*, 13 (1983), 66–83.

Philip Edwards, *The Story of the Voyage: Sea-Narratives in Eighteenth-Century England* (Cambridge: Cambridge University Press, 1994).

Jonathan Lamb, *Preserving the Self in the South Seas, 1680–1840* (Chicago, IL: University of Chicago Press, 2001).

Robert Markley, 'The Eighteenth-Century Novel and the Pacific', in *The Cambridge History of the English Novel*, ed. Robert Caesario and Clement Hawes (Cambridge: Cambridge University Press, 2012), 196–212.

Robert Markley, *The Far East and the English Imagination, 1600–1740* (Cambridge: Cambridge University Press, 2006).

Neil Rennie, *Far-Fetched Facts: The Literature of Travel and the Idea of the South Seas* (Oxford: Clarendon Press, 1995).

Jeremy Wear, 'No Dishonour to be a Pirate: The Logic of Infinite Advantage in Defoe's *Captain Singleton*', *ECF*, 24:4 (2012), 569–96.

Glyndwr Williams, *The Great South Sea: English Voyages and Encounters 1570–1750* (New Haven, CT: Yale University Press, 1997).

Glyndwr Williams, '"The Inexhaustible Fountain of Gold": English Projects and Ventures in the South Seas, 1670–1750', in *Perspectives of Empire: Essays Presented to Gerald S. Graham*, ed. John E. Flint and Glyndwr Williams (London: Longman, 1973), 27–53.

CHAPTER 31

AFRICA AND THE LEVANT IN DEFOE'S WRITINGS

REBEKAH MITSEIN AND MANUSHAG N. POWELL

> I look upon the Northern and Western Parts of *Asia*, and of *Africa* also, and the Eastern Parts of *Europe* too, to be like Mines of Gold and Silver ... left off before they were *half wrought*.[1]

DANIEL Defoe was a consistent cheerleader for mercantile colonialist projects. But, to quote Srinivas Aravamudan, his 'imperial aspirations for Britain are not undifferentiated'.[2] Indeed, Defoe displays geographical meticulousness in his texts on trade and exploration, even when addressing regions—particularly the Levant (broadly speaking, the eastern Mediterranean) and the continent of Africa, northern as well as sub-Saharan—where European limitations make meticulousness a challenge. A persistent fear of Islam, coupled with ambivalence over the unknown African subcontinent, led his writing to depict Africa as regressive and forbidding. The Levant is similarly treated with ambivalence: a major source of trade whose importance can be felt even in English towns, the Levant presented a worrisome and inconsistent contrast to European Christian identity.

Yet Defoe also saw opportunity in Africa and the Levant that he does not see elsewhere. In *A General History of Discoveries and Improvements* (1725–6), Defoe argues for more commercial and intellectual investment in Africa and the Levant rather than 'run[ning] away now, to *India*, *China*, the remotest Parts of *Asia*, to *Chili*, *Brasil*, and the farthest Part of *America*, for the very Product and Wealth which the Countries known [by the ancients] are qualified fully to supply us with; and perhaps with half the Hazard, Trouble, and Experience as the other' (*TDH*, iv. 24). There is, of course, the little matter of the Ottoman Empire and broader Muslim world to contend with. These represented

---

[1] Defoe, *A General History of Discoveries and Improvements* (1725–6), *TDH*, iv. 26.
[2] Srinivas Aravamudan, 'Defoe, Commerce, and Empire', in *The Cambridge Companion to Daniel Defoe*, ed. John Richetti (Cambridge: Cambridge University Press, 2008), 45–63 (56).

a formidable religious and geopolitical challenge to Western ambitions, but it often suits Defoe to depict that threat as lesser than the many inconveniences he attaches to other potential colonial directions. This chapter considers why Defoe selects Africa and the Levant for some of his most extreme mercantilist fantasizing, and how he shapes discourse around what was for him a vast and heterogeneous part of the unknown-but-knowable world. We follow a path through these Old-World geographies sketched out by Defoe's imaginative writing in 1719–20.

We begin in northern Africa and the Levant, where Robinson Crusoe, working euphemistically as a 'Guinea trader', is captured 'by a *Turkish* rover of *Sallee*' and forced into Barbary captivity.[3] The language here, which underscores cultural and political continuities more than territorial locations, alerts us to how interconnected Guinea, North Africa, and the Levant were in Defoe's economic imagination: Salé, on the northwest coast of Morocco, is nowhere near Turkey, and rather than being under Ottoman thrall had recently been turned from an independent pirate state into part of Alaouite Morocco. Defoe knew this, of course; 'Turkey' in this English usage means 'Muslim'. Escaping with a fellow captive, the Morisco boy Xury, Crusoe coasts southwest along the African continent. In Crusoe's *Farther Adventures* (1719) and in *Captain Singleton* (1720), Defoe's protagonists return to Africa: Crusoe to Madagascar, Singleton from thence to the mainland. The chapter will conclude with Defoe's highly speculative engagement with the continent's interior, wherein he offers the African subcontinent as one of the rewards of pushing back against the global economic power of the Muslim world, even as he acknowledges the immense difficulties of doing so.

ISLAM, THE LEVANT, AND NORTH AFRICA

Levantine interaction was a ticklish problem for the trade-minded Defoe, who saw its advantages but hesitated over its multicultural influence, which was not identical to but certainly inseparable from the Islamic religion. In *A System of Magick* (1726), Defoe speculates that the Devil, in seeking to gain power throughout Asia and Africa, made use of Islam, which has 'strangely triumph'd over the Christian World, has spread itself over *Asia* and *Africa*, from the utmost Islands of *India* East, to the utmost Corner of *Africa* to the West; and it was, 'till within a few Years past, Master of a fourth Part of *Europe* besides' (*SFS*, vii. 252).[4] The anxiety expressed in this moment, characterized by the repetition of 'utmost', is less over the content of Islamic belief than over the global scope of its dominance. Encompassing the Mediterranean area to the east of Italy, including

---

[3] Defoe, *Robinson Crusoe*, ed. Evan R. Davis (Peterborough, ON: Broadview Press, 2010), 61.
[4] Robert James Merrett argues that Defoe 'faults Mohammedanism [sic]' but 'in a limited way or for cultural reasons that extend beyond Islam', in contrast to Catholicism, which is intolerable. *Daniel Defoe: Contrarian* (Toronto: University of Toronto Press, 2013), 160–1. Defoe's views on Islam were complicated by his sense of English and European missteps, both at home and abroad (160–71).

Asia Minor and northeastern Africa, the Levant is a space of interstices that includes an ancient as well as modern European presence. It was not an area in Defoe's day where Europeans had untrammelled authority, yet it was a space where they aspired to significant influence, particularly as diplomatic solutions began to lessen the threat of Barbary corsairs. The Levant is a sort of econo-cultural halfway point between the factories of the west African coast, and the Indian Ocean (where due to Dutch monopolies and the closed off Chinese and Japanese trading powers, the English were insignificant indeed). The Levant provoked in Europeans a mix of desire and anxiety that fuelled a widespread response that Aravamudan terms levantinizations, cross-cultural experiments of the orientalizing intellect.[5]

To some extent, Defoe diverges from other literary accounts of the Muslim world because Crusoe's Barbary captivity includes no hint of conversion panic. As dependent as the Ottoman and Barbary economies were on some forms of captivity and enslaving, there was nonetheless an Islamic injunction against enslaving fellow Muslims, and conversion was supposed to mean an absolute end to enslavement; converting and manumitting a Christian captive could be an important demonstration of faith. Captivity narratives by redeemed or escaped Europeans often emphasized the captives' resistance to attempts to convert them, but Crusoe's Moroccan master apparently never broaches the topic. Defoe is more interested in exploring the increasing global trade in chattel-enslaved African people than in tracking the ancient and still-active slave networks of the Mediterranean. In this, he is perhaps even a little ahead of his time. As Linda Colley argues, 'before 1730, men and women in Britain and Ireland were exposed to far more information about Barbary slavery than about any other variety', a ratio reflected in popular writing as well.[6] There was considerable eighteenth-century public interest in the interactions of Britain and Ireland with North African corsairs. Accounts of Barbary captivity appeared in newspapers, pamphlets, verse, broadsides, and on stage. Eighteenth-century treaties with Morocco and the Ottoman Empire decreased the actual incidences of captivities dramatically during the 1720s, but did not diminish the public appetite for captivity stories.

Not only is Crusoe never tempted by Islam; he is never even tempted by Arabic. Charles Gildon, an early reviewer of Defoe, complained about the silliness of having Xury speak nothing but English, when 'it had been more natural to have made *Robinson* speak broken *Arabick*, which Language he must be forc'd in some Measure to learn'.[7] In a perversion of the usual conditions of Barbary captivity, Crusoe sells Xury, who had been his faithful friend, to a Portuguese captain on the promise that the boy will be freed after ten years upon converting; the (Presbyterian) Defoe leaves open the question of Xury's future with the Catholic Portuguese. Another travelling Defoe protagonist, Roxana, is in

---

[5] Srinivas Aravamudan, *Tropicopolitans: Colonialism and Agency, 1688–1804* (Durham, N.C.: Duke University Press, 1999), 16–23.

[6] Linda Colley, *Captives: Britain, Empire, and the World, 1600–1850* (New York: Anchor Books, 2004), 63.

[7] Charles Gildon, *The Life and Strange Surprizing Adventures of Mr. D[aniel] de F[oe]* (1719), 13.

Naples with a royal lover when he purchases for her 'a little Female *Turkish* Slave, who, being Taken at Sea by a *Malthese* Man of War, was brought in there; and of her I learnt the *Turkish* Language; their Way of Dressing and Dancing, and some *Turkish*, or rather *Moorish* Songs, of which I made Use, to my Advantage, on an extraordinary Occasion, some Years after', meaning in the orientalized masquerade performances that will raise her fortunes but be her undoing.[8] The Maltese corsairs, the highly problematic Catholic answer to Maghrebi sea predators, are registered with less alarm than the '*Sallee*' rovers were in *Crusoe*, and Roxana's linguistic acquisition is done from a position of dominance unavailable to Crusoe. Even so, a larger point remains that while his heroes are never 'forc'd' to pick up a language associated with Islam, let alone subject to outside instead of internal religious pressures, Defoe's English characters are readily tempted to economic intercourse. The driving force that underpins religious strife is economics, not heresy.[9]

Indeed, Defoe provokes levantinizations because English engagement in Ottoman trade caused complex 'internal structural changes' in order to compete in the Levant: 'Ottoman demand for English cloth was forcing towns to specialize and transforming regional industries ... Burstall in Yorkshire was now specialized in dying broad cloths since the market for kersey and shalloon had been captured by large towns', which in turn were out of the running with 'Wiltshire, Gloucestershire, Somerset, and Devon in producing kersies and drugets for the Turkey trade'.[10] The extent to which Defoe saw the Levant as having set up shop in England's interior appears markedly in the peculiar ending of *Captain Singleton*, in which the pirate protagonists, living large off of ill-gotten gains, attempt to ensure their safety while enjoying a quiet English retirement through laundering money in Venice and Naples and residing in London with 'Mustachoes [and] Beards' and wearing 'long Vests, that we may pass for *Grecians* and Foreigners'.[11] The price Bob Singleton and William Walters pay for security seems a high one, particularly to William, as Bob demands that they give up speaking English even in public, apparently forever. And yet they do not repine, in part because they also bring with them 'such a Cargoe to *London*, as few *American* Merchants had done for some Years' (312). The illegalities and deceptions they have practised have allowed them to outstrip the Caribbean and American trade, just as the theory set forth in *A General History of Discoveries and Improvements* suggested—but what the reader ought to think of their bargain is left undetermined.

Defoe's ambivalence concerning the Levant and North Africa is not limited to their presence in the English homeland as in *Singleton* or *Roxana*. In *Discoveries and Improvements*, he argues that Africa was once a populous place of sophisticated culture and vibrant trade, and that it might be again. In fact, he suggests that America was

---

[8] Defoe, *Roxana*, ed. Melissa Mowry (Peterborough, ON: Broadview Press, 2009), 131.
[9] See Defoe's proposals for commercial expansion in Africa in *A Plan of the English Commerce* (1728), *PEW*, vii. 298–309.
[10] Merrett, *Daniel Defoe*, 164.
[11] Defoe, *Captain Singleton*, ed. Manushag N. Powell (Peterborough, ON: Broadview Press, 2019), 312.

'peopled by the help of Navigation from the West-side of *Africa*' during a time when 'the *Carthaginians* possest that Coast' (*TDH*, vii. 75). But

> those Nations, which being once the Center of Commerce, as well as of Arts and Sciences, are since lay'd Desolate and over run with a Barbarous People, who utterly neglecting those Improvements, have turn'd the most delicious Countries, formerly *flowing with Milk and Honey*, into a Desolate Howling Wilderness. (25)[12]

Importantly, these 'Barbarous People' are not Black Africans, but the 'the *Moors* and *Turks*' of the Ottoman Empire and—of course—the Barbary Coast: 'an indolent rapacious Crew of Vagrants and Thieves, who neither have Trade, or seek any; who cultivate no Lands, but for immediate Food; who have neither Numbers to consume the Product of a fruitful Soil; Merchants to export it to other Countries, or People to raise a product for the Consumption which might be demanded' (88). The Moors and Turks have 'blocked up' commerce with the rest of Africa, and Defoe dedicates many pages of *Discoveries and Improvements* and other works to imagining how they might be 'root[ed] out' by the 'Christian Nations of *Europe*' (112, 119).

Again signalling his relative disregard for conversion panic, Defoe's justification for this dispossession does not lie in the fact that the North Africans are Muslim per se. Contra his position in *A System of Magick*, 'it is not sufficient', he writes, 'to say they are *Mahometans*, and not *Christians*; for then we have a right to make War upon and destroy all the Heathen Nations of the World, which I do not take to be just' (119). If they were making proper, peaceful, good use of the land, Defoe suggests, 'we might trade with them, as well as we do with their fellow Infidels at *Constantinople*, *Smyrna*, *Aleppo*, and other places' (120). However, their territorial possession is not honest, dependent as it is on the captivity and forced labour of Christians and the prevention of vigorous trade with the rest of Africa. This is justification enough, Defoe argues, for them to be driven from Africa's coasts. Doing so would leave room for the European powers either to 'conquer the Black Kings' of sub-Saharan Africa and 'reduce them to Reason', or simply to spread out and share the territory (123). Though North Africa was sometimes separate from sub-Saharan Africa in the eighteenth-century European imagination, for Defoe the two were inextricably linked, the barbarity and cruelty of the one inhibiting European trade with or conquest of the other.

Defoe's account of Africa in *Robinson Crusoe* reflects this economic and geographical vision. The Moors are the main impediment to European trade with Guinea, but they are also easily subverted by European initiative. Crusoe's first trip to the west coast of Africa is very lucrative. Travelling as a companion to the ship's captain, Crusoe transforms £40 worth of goods into £300 worth of gold dust under the captain's mentorship, establishing the potential value of honest trade with Africa under the governance of 'an honest, plain-dealing Man'. Crusoe believes himself 'now set up for a *Guiney* Trader' (60); however,

---

[12] 'Howling wilderness' is a phrase Defoe uses elsewhere to describe Africa; it was a popular biblical referent at the time for frightening, unmapped lands. See Deuteronomy 32:10.

this path to wealth is stymied by Barbary corsairs in the very next voyage. Crusoe's Moroccan master is uncouth, hypocritical, financially unsuccessful, and entirely lacking in foresight. Thinking he is cleverly outfitting his fishing boat with supplies in case it is ever blown off course with him in it, Crusoe's master effectively hands Crusoe the means of his escape (63). The master's dominance is a reality Crusoe must contend with, and it takes time—two years—to overcome, but by exploiting flaws that Defoe suggests are inherent to the Moor's way of life, Crusoe ultimately accomplishes this fairly easily. Defoe's characterization of Crusoe's captors suggests that though the Islamic Moors hold a certain amount of geopolitical control in Africa, this might be defeated through the dedicated application of European wit and ingenuity.

The payoff for taking on Barbary appears in Defoe's subsequent depiction of sub-Saharan Africa. As Crusoe makes his escape, along with Xury, they sail down the coast toward Guinea, hoping to arrive at 'that part where the English traded' (avoiding the closer factories that lie along the way controlled by rival European powers) and catch a ship to Crusoe's home. Initially, it appears that Crusoe and Xury are travelling away from a bad situation into a worse one. They lie awake in their boat at night listening to the 'dreadful Noises of the Barking, Roaring, and Howling of wild Creatures', terrified to go on shore lest they 'should be devour'd by savage Beasts, or more merciless Savages of humane kind' (67). For Defoe such descriptions are a mark not of Africa's inherent fruitlessness, but of its current mismanagement. Defoe contended that 'this part of the World call'd *Africa*, which at present seems to be given up to Barreness and to wild Beasts, once was, and still might be rendred useful to the trading World, wou'd the Christian Nations apply themselves first to the Conquest of it; and then to the planting and cultivating it' (*TDH*, vii. 90). Once Crusoe and Xury finally encounter the inhabitants of sub-Saharan Africa, they turn out to be generous, peaceful, and eager for trade. Crusoe kills a ferocious leopard that comes among them, and in gratitude these 'friendly *Negroes*' 'furnish' Crusoe with 'Roots and Corn … and Water' (72). Given that Africa's wild howling animals are emblematic for Defoe of a terrible neglect of the land, Crusoe's killing of the leopard, and the way the sub-Saharan Africans respond, suggest that the dispossession of Africa's Moors would be met with gratitude and generosity by the continent's other inhabitants.

About the long history of Islam in sub-Saharan Africa, Defoe is curiously muted, saying nothing directly about the Muslims of the Senegambia or the Swahili Coast, although the presence of the latter may be why Captain Singleton and his band leave the coast for the continent's unknown interior. These groups of Muslims, unlike the Ottomans, did not correspond to sovereign nations as Defoe would have understood them; they were perhaps better understood as an aggregate of culturally and economically connected regions (in the west) and city-states (in the east)—and hence they may not have registered as the same sort of geopolitical rival as 'the Turks', whom Defoe certainly sees as the main threat. In his call for more extensive trade with Ethiopia, for instance, Defoe suggests that even if the Turks cannot be removed entirely from northeast Africa, they 'may not be able wholly to stop the Current of such a beneficial Commerce, as might be open'd on that side of the World if the Trading Nations would join together to undertake it' (*TDH*, vii. 27). Ethiopia, markedly, was not a Muslim but a Christian nation; not coincidentally Defoe praises its 'docible People [who] are able, and indeed qualified, to bring ten times more Wealth into *Europe* by Trade, than all the Empires of *New Spain* ... do bring to the unimproving *Spaniards*' (27). He also believed that the government should regulate this beneficial commerce in order to protect not just the Africa trade itself, but also Britain's African settlements, which he intimated could grow, under the right leadership, from trade posts into a colonial vanguard.

The Royal African Company and the 'Guinea Trade'

Defoe's writings provide a valuable illustration of the continuities between Europe's economic relationship with sub-Saharan Africa, which was conducted largely through negotiations with local potentates and brokers, and Europe's early colonial aspirations regarding Africa [SEE CHAPTER 14]. These two interests are united in *Captain Singleton*. Like *Robinson Crusoe*, *Captain Singleton* introduces Africa through an episode of Barbary captivity: Bob is taken prisoner by an Algerine Rover. Before the Algerine Rover can make it to shore, condemning Bob to slavery, the ship is attacked by 'two great *Portuguese* Men of War, and taken and carried into *Lisbon*' (54–5). Bob, still a child, is largely confused throughout this episode, 'not indeed understanding the Consequences' of what is happening (55), but Defoe's reader can see the geopolitics of this scene. The text illustrates Defoe's notion that, however much they might otherwise disagree, the 'the *European* Princes' might 'joyn in the clearing the Coasts of *Africa* from this bloody Race of Infidels which now possess it' (*TDH*, vii. 117) in order to 'restore the Peace and Commerce of *Africa*, so profitable to *Europe*' (112). As is briefly represented in *Robinson Crusoe*, the sub-Saharan portion of *Captain Singleton* proposes a warrant for this investment (Africa is an untapped treasure trove) and sketches out what that should look like (carefully regulated government settlements in Africa, not free and open trade).

As several critics have shown, *Captain Singleton* stages a fantasy in which riches are to be found in Africa's interior, free, or cheap, for the taking. After participating in a mutiny, the teenage Bob Singleton and his new Portuguese fellows are marooned on Madagascar, cross the Mozambique channel to the mainland, and embark on a journey across the interior towards Angola, ultimately veering north and ending up at the Dutch and British factories of the Gold Coast. Along the way, Singleton and his men collect Africa's three most lucrative resources: gold that can be scooped out of a stream with little effort; ivory as far as the eye can see; and natives who, enslaved without the help of African or European middlemen, are eager to serve. These profitable imaginings are the continent's leitmotifs, resonant with Defoe's theory that investment in Africa 'bids fair to out-do in Profit to us the Commerce of both the *Indies*' (*TDH*, vii. 220). At the same time, Defoe was cautious about believing free trade would result in a limitless supply of wealth.

Defoe mapped out some thoughts on this issue during the dissolution of the Royal African Company's monopoly in the first two decades of the eighteenth century. Parliament opened trade to independent ships in 1698, provided these separate traders pay a 10% tax to the RAC to help the Company maintain the costs of its forts and of its alliances with local African leaders.[13] At the height of Defoe's interest in the matter, even this statute was set to expire, and he dedicated many issues of the *Review* from 1709 to 1713 to defending the RAC against independent traders who were pushing for greater freedoms. Defoe argued that a company monopoly was the only way to guarantee the stability of trade, which he deemed absolutely necessary to the financial well-being of Britain and its colonies. The separate traders undermined this stability by

> Bribing the Company's Officers and Factors Abroad; confederating and corresponding with the Company's Enemies in *Africa*, whether Natives or *Europeans*; running down the Price of their Goods to the Negroes, teaching them the Craft and Knowledge of Trade, and how to Buy and Sell to their Advantage; raising the Rates of the Slaves they buy; and thus in every Article rendring the Company's Trade more difficult to manage, and less profitable than it was before.[14]

Defoe suggested that while the RAC poured labour and resources into maintaining forts and settlements and into building alliances with local African potentates, the separate traders both took advantage of this work and injured it. Individuals may get rich quick by 'appear[ing] on the Coast of *Africa* in Defiance of the Company's Forts, carrying on an open Trade without Regard to the Laws of the Land or the Lawful Privileges of the Company' (12), but such a scheme chips away at the structural integrity of the trade and hobbles territorial expansion that might one day lead to lucrative mining ventures and plantation settlements.[15]

The fact that Singleton and his crew closely resemble the separate traders that Defoe decried in earlier writings as utterly immoral and financially irresponsible 'Pyrates' tempers the depiction of quickly and easily accumulated wealth that *Captain Singleton* initially offers.[16] Indeed, there was considerable crossover between pirates and separate traders. European pirate voyages to the African coast and especially the profitable Red Sea depredations would have been impossible to undertake without trading posts and watering holes run by separate traders, many of whom were former pirates themselves, like the prosperous Dutchman John Pro, who ran a settlement based in Madagascar and

---

[13] See William Pettigrew, *Freedom's Debt: The Royal African Company and the Politics of the Atlantic Slave Trade, 1672–1752* (Chapel Hill, N.C.: University of North Carolina Press, 2013).

[14] Defoe, *An Essay upon the Trade to Africa* (1711), 12.

[15] Beginning in 1719, around the time of *Captain Singleton*'s publication, James Brydges, Duke of Chandos, was attempting to revive the RAC with this very message. Pettigrew, *Freedom's Debt*, 166.

[16] Defoe, *Essay upon the Trade to Africa*, 18.

worked with native populations to undersell the RAC to pirates looking for supplies and enslaved Africans. Elsewhere, as in the *Review* and *The King of Pirates* (1719), Defoe muses upon the possibility of repatriating the pirate settlers he believes are prospering in Madagascar.[17] But Singleton at first encounters no pirate but himself.

Let loose on the shore of Africa to do as he wills, Singleton muses:

> I was now to enter upon a Part of independent Life, a thing I was indeed very ill prepared to manage, for I was perfectly loose and dissolute in my Behaviour, bold and wicked while I was under Government, and now perfectly unfit to be trusted with Liberty, for I was as ripe for any Villainy as a young Fellow that had no solid Thought ever placed in his Mind could be supposed to be. (63)

One of Defoe's arguments against opening up the African trade was that the separate traders were similarly 'ill prepared to manage' their 'independence' and 'unfit to be trusted with liberty'. He wrote that 'an open Trade, in which every Man was at Liberty to Export or not Export[,] to Trade or not to Trade, as his own Affairs Directed' offers no security, while the RAC promised that their trade was 'a great Trust from the Nation' that they 'Preserve and Maintain … for the Good of the whole Body'.[18] Security did not simply mean trade would continue. It meant that the 'Forts and Settlements' would be maintained, that there would always be '*a sufficient Stock of Goods always lying ready in the several Forts*' for the purpose of '*Preserving, Securing and Encreasing the number of Contracts and Alliances with the Natives, and the several Neighbouring Petty Kings of the Country*', and that the multitude of buyers and sellers on the coast would not depreciate the value of European goods and thus place all the bargaining power in the hands of African merchants and leaders (36–7). Defoe returned every few months in the *Review* to his contention that the separate traders had offered no guarantee that an open trade to Africa would be secure, acknowledging at one point that 'this Question has been ask'd over and, even till it is Threadbare'—but posing it anyway.[19]

When the separate traders were asked by Parliament how they would ensure stability, they suggested that a portion of their profits could go to maintaining the forts and factories, which Defoe countered is grounded in the specious reasoning that the 'Gain of the Trade' will be constant and always in the Europeans' favour. If trade is no longer profitable, the separate traders will simply start trading somewhere else. Not only will England lose any land gains and 'Friendship' in Africa they managed to carve out through their forts and settlements, plantations in the Americas will also suffer. The separate traders, in their naïveté and with their eye focused only on their own profits, offered no concrete solution beyond a proposal full of 'Uncertainties and Weakness'.[20]

---

[17] *Review*, iv. 550–4 (18 October 1707). On the attribution of *The King of Pirates*, see Maximillian E. Novak, 'Did Defoe Write *The King of Pirates?*', *PQ*, 96:4 (2017), 475–88 (480–1).

[18] Defoe, *Essay upon the Trade to Africa*, 63.

[19] *Review*, viii. 760 (24 April 1712).

[20] Defoe, *Essay upon the Trade to Africa*, 40.

Like Singleton's, their 'thoughts' are not 'solid'. They are unable to imagine beyond the present or invest in the future.

Singleton's smash-and-grab approach to seizing Africa's resources is thus the opposite of what Defoe and the RAC advocated. The scene in which Singleton and the crew enslave a group of locals in Mozambique, for instance, may 'reveal the necessary violence of imperialist ideology', as Laura Brown argues, but it is not clear that the narrative, or Defoe himself, endorses their tactics.[21] Aware that they will not be able to survive an overland journey without guides, translators, and drovers who know how to manage indigenous beasts of burden, Singleton proposes that they 'quarrel with some of the Negro Natives', with whom they had up to this point traded peacefully, and 'take ten or twelve of them Prisoners, and binding them as Slaves, cause them to travel with us' (102). The Portuguese pirates demur at this rather awful plan, but conveniently for Singleton the locals start the quarrel themselves when they deem insufficient the trinkets the cutler offers in exchange for their cattle. One of the Africans throws a lance. One of the Europeans shoots him through the heart. The unfamiliar discharge of a gun and the sudden death of their countryman creates chaos among the Africans, who rally and attack. It takes only a few volleys of shots to subdue the Africans, after which Singleton and his band 'secure about 60 lusty young Fellows, and let them know they must go with us; which they seemed very willing to do' (105). In order to manage this crew, the Europeans, who are blessed with the kind of preternaturally gifted surgeon who appears only in colonialist fiction, heal one of their leaders of his gunshot wound, 'one tall, well-shap'd, handsom Fellow, to whom the rest seemed to pay great Respect, and who, as we understood afterwards, was the Son of one of their Kings' (108). This 'Black Prince' swears fealty to Singleton and the Portuguese sailors and becomes their mediator and guide. The alternating power of European guns and European medicine cow the Africans into believing the Europeans have command over life and death. Once the Black Prince is healed, he apparently becomes a grateful slave, serving Singleton and his crew cheerfully and diligently.[22]

This scene rehearses imperial tropes that would become common in the latter half of the eighteenth century, in which technological difference justified European dominion over the savage and ignorant other [SEE CHAPTER 24]. Yet, as Wheeler and Loar point out, even as Singleton and his fellows revel in the social control that their guns afford, the text does not wholeheartedly embrace martial violence as proper and

---

[21] Laura Brown, *Ends of Empire: Women and Ideology in Early Eighteenth-Century English Literature* (Ithaca, N.Y.: Cornell University Press, 1993), 166.

[22] For a discussion of the 'grateful slave' trope in Defoe's fiction, see George Boulukos, *The Grateful Slave: The Emergence of Race in Eighteenth-Century British and American Culture* (Cambridge: Cambridge University Press, 2008), 75–94. Laura Brown reads this as a colonial strategy whereby the Black Prince, and thus Africa, are 'brought into the circle of the civilized, the Christian, the comprehensible, and the familiar'. 'Defoe's "Black Prince": Elitism, Capitalism, and Cultural Difference', in *Defoe's Footprints: Essays in Honour of Maximillian E. Novak*, ed. Robert M. Maniquis and Carl Fisher (Toronto: University of Toronto Press, 2009), 153–69 (156).

civilized European behaviour.[23] In a contrasting scene, written just a few months earlier in *The Farther Adventures of Robinson Crusoe*, Crusoe and his fellow English land on Madagascar and trade quite peacefully with the 'Indians' of the island until one of his men openly and violently rapes a girl; the cascade of hostilities that follows leads to a genocidal 'massacre' perpetrated by the English that horrifies Crusoe, who compares it, curiously, to '*Oliver Cromwell* taking *Drogheda*, in *Ireland*, and killing man, woman, and child' (*Novels*, ii. 135). The entire thing is an unprofitable atrocity. Similarly, the way Singleton and his fellows acquire their baggage carriers is precisely the kind of behaviour that Defoe argued undid the labour the RAC put into the continent and turned locals aggressive. The African potentates from whom the RAC rented the land for their forts had strict rules governing who the company could enslave and who could be transported out of Africa. Violation of these rules invited retaliation either as an outright attack or through the rescinding of trade and land agreements. As such, Defoe was wary of those who would 'rob the Inhabitants, and sometimes have trepann'd the innocent Natives on Board, on Pretence of Trade, and carry'd them away into Slavery'.[24] The capturing and selling of local elites into slavery—like the Black Prince—was particularly foolhardy. Unscrupulous traders occasionally did this, and the RAC had to expend considerable efforts and funds to get them back.[25]

Defoe explored this matter in a dialogue he wrote between an RAC supporter and a separate trader for the *Review* in 1709. The RAC supporter tells the separate trader, 'what you really are all by Profession' is 'A Parcel of Kidnapers ... for you come upon the Coast, invite the poor *Blacks* on board to trade with you, and then like Pirates, hoist your Sails, and carry them all away into Captivity'.[26] Defoe's deeming the *modus operandi* of separate traders 'Kidnapping' is not grounded in abolitionist sentiment, which, indeed, he lacked. *Captain Singleton* features a Quaker slave-trader as one of its main, and most moral, characters, and Defoe frequently remarked that without the slave trade the Caribbean colonies would irreparably suffer, once writing, 'were the Supply of *Negroes* but to stop one Year—The Plantations would fall Sick like a Body, when a Supply of Food is with-held from the Stomach'.[27] But he was aware, perhaps through his friendship with Dalby Thomas, who was chief factor at Cape Coast Castle from 1703 to 1711, that when enslaved Africans are transported out of a territory without the local potentate's say-so,

---

[23] Roxann Wheeler calls this scene a 'glorification of European technology and a critique of European behavior in Africa'. *The Complexion of Race: Categories of Difference in Eighteenth-Century British Culture* (Philadelphia, PA: University of Pennsylvania Press, 2000), 107. Christopher F. Loar argues that *Captain Singleton* illustrates the 'raw violence enabled by gunpowder, no longer cloaked by a rhetoric of civility and cultural superiority'. *Political Magic: British Fictions of Savagery and Sovereignty, 1650–1750* (New York: Fordham University Press, 2014), 120.

[24] *Review*, v. 682–3 (5 March 1709). See Randy J. Sparks, 'Gold Coast Merchant Families, Pawning, and the Eighteenth-Century British Slave Trade', *William and Mary Quarterly*, 70:2 (2013), 317–40; Kwame Yeboa Daaku, *Trade and Politics on the Gold Coast, 1660 to 1720: A Study of the African Reaction to European Trade* (Oxford: Oxford University Press, 1970), 73–92.

[25] See Sparks, 'Gold Coast Merchant Families', 323.

[26] *Review*, v. 699–700 (12 March 1709).

[27] *Review*, v. 663 (22 February 1709).

'the Natives' will 'in Revenge murther the Company's Servants, and all the *English* they can find'.[28] They might also abandon trade with the English and make an alliance with the Dutch instead. For this reason, though factors often flaunted their martial power, they tried to avoid actual violence.

If faced with trouble from the locals, the RAC might pay or otherwise persuade another African nation to subdue them.[29] But, just as most Barbary captivities were resolved through diplomacy and ransom, most disputes in Guinea were settled by 'palaver', which was a formal negotiation process, and the giving of gifts, which is why for Defoe and others 'securing' the trade meant keeping the forts stocked with goods for the purpose of keeping peace with African leaders.[30] Defoe once wrote that that African trade 'is no way to be carried on but by Force; for a mere Correspondence with the Natives as Merchants, is as impracticable, as it would be if they were a Nation of Horses'.[31] However, he goes on to define 'force' as the establishment and maintenance of forts and settlements, not aggressive conquest, which are distinct in Defoe's thinking, however alike they were in historical practice. Though the RAC accusing the separate traders of 'kidnapping' reads to contemporary eyes as a gross hypocrisy, early eighteenth-century conversations around the Africa trade made a distinction between purchasing enslaved Africans from local brokers and seizing Africans directly. The company argued, however erroneously, that the former could be done justly and humanely, and that only a joint-stock company would ensure both that the Caribbean plantations continued to receive a steady supply of labourers and that their acquisition was above board.[32] The separate traders, on the other hand, would only follow the rules if it suited them because nothing and no one held them accountable for their actions.

SUB-SAHARAN AFRICA AND *CAPTAIN SINGLETON*

Given Defoe's understanding of these nuanced political relationships, critics have often puzzled over the fact that Defoe wilfully fictionalizes Africa in *Captain Singleton*, stripping its people of their complexity and agency and playing up European access to its resources, when the contemporary travel accounts and geographies that Defoe knew so

---

[28] *Review*, v. 700 (12 March 1709). Defoe dedicated *An Essay upon Projects* (1697) to Thomas, calling him both a '*Friend*' and the '*Commissioner, &c., under whom I have the Honour to serve his Majesty*' (*PEW*, viii. 29). For more on their relationship, see Novak, *Daniel Defoe*, 114–19.

[29] For examples of Europeans attempting this tactic, with varying levels of success, see Daaku, *Trade and Politics on the Gold Coast*, 73–92.

[30] Defoe, *Essay upon the Trade to Africa*, 36–7.

[31] *Review*, v. 653 (17 February 1709).

[32] Pettigrew, *Freedom's Debt*, 180–3.

well and venerated show quite a different picture.[33] Not only did African elites have their own rules about who could be enslaved and how, they kept Africa's interior goldmines and goldfields from Europe until well into the nineteenth century, which traders and travellers frequently grumbled about. *Atlas Maritimus & Commercialis* (1728) admits that Europeans 'have not a Mark of Gold in the whole Trade, but what we must get out of the Negroes by fair trading. ... It is brought down from the Inland Countries by the Negroes, nor can we tell particularly from what Part of the Inland Countries it comes'.[34] Yet Singleton and his fellows are pulling gold out of streams, and the Black Prince does not even know what it is. One explanation for this inverted characterization of Africa may be that Defoe was more interested in writing propaganda than in realistically representing trade in Africa.[35] However, it is also possible that Defoe is counting on his knowledgeable reader to be critical of the ease with which Singleton plumbs Africa's depths, particularly given that Singleton himself repeatedly indicates that he is not honest, that he operates only according to his own interests, and that he kept no journal of his travels.[36] The unguarded and seemingly endless supply of wealth in the continent's interior may be less reflective of Defoe's vision for Africa than a caricature of the separate traders' vision for Africa—at least if we assume a common readership for works like *Singleton* and *A General History of Discoveries and Improvements*.

An idea of trade with Africa that was ever abundant, in which the need to make and maintain 'friendships' with jealous landlords could be ignored, was, after all, the fallacy of which he accused the separate traders and their supporters. Defoe understood, and he expected readers of the *Review* and his *Essay upon the Trade to Africa* to understand, that there would be times when trade with Africa would not be lucrative and when relationships with locals would not be harmonious. However, the only security that the separate traders could offer against this was the conjecture that it would keep producing profits at a rate that was infinite and steady. Defoe, who knew from personal experience that '*all Trade is subject to Disaster*', found this line of reasoning ludicrous and misleading.[37] The supporters of open trade had managed to persuade the public through 'Sophism' and 'the gaudy Surface of Words' that were 'no more than a superficial Gilding over a poysonous Pill' that trade to Africa would progress as it had indefinitely. Defoe despaired of the fact that if 'half the World pursue[d] Interest, and Half pursue[d] their blinded Inclination', there would be no place in the Africa trade for 'honest wise Men'.[38]

---

[33] Wheeler, *Complexion*, 107–8; Boulukos, *Grateful Slave*, 53; Novak, *Daniel Defoe*, 584; Peter Knox-Shaw, *The Explorer in English Fiction* (New York: Palgrave, 1986), 56.

[34] *Atlas Maritimus & Commercialis* (1728), 240. For the most thorough consideration of Defoe's involvement in the *Atlas*, see Jess Edwards, 'Daniel Defoe and *Atlas Maritimus & Commercialis*', in *Topographies of the Imagination: New Approaches to Daniel Defoe*, ed. Katherine Ellison, Kit Kincade, and Holly Faith Nelson (New York: AMS Press, 2014), 141–66.

[35] See Wheeler, *Complexion*, 136.

[36] On Bob Singleton as a self-consciously unreliable geographer, see Rebekah Mitsein, 'Upon a Voyage and no Voyage: Mapping Africa's Waterways in Defoe's *Captain Singleton*', *Digital Defoe*, 10:1 (2018).

[37] *Review*, viii. 760 (24 April 1712).

[38] *Review*, vi. 648 (2 February 1710).

Defoe's inclusion of an RAC factor gone rogue in *Captain Singleton*, who uses precisely these promises of infinite gain in order to convince Singleton and his fellows to pursue 'Interest' and 'blinded Inclination' over wisdom, offers a possible explanation for Defoe's own 'gaudy' and 'gilded' Africa in the narrative. Finally having crossed the wildest part of the continent, the crew is 'astonished to see a white Man ... stark naked, very busy near the Door of his Hut' (166). This Englishman turns out to be well educated and friendly, formerly 'a Factor for the *English Guinea* Company at *Siera Leon*, or some other of their Settlements which had been taken by the *French*, where he had been plundered of all his own Effects, as well as those entrusted to him by the Company' (170). Singleton is deliberately vague about how it is the Englishman ended up out of the RAC's service, whether 'the Company did not do him Justice' (170) or whether the Englishman abandoned his post. Either way the Englishman 'was employed by those called Separate Traders, and being afterwards out of Employ there also, traded on his own Account; when, passing unwarily into one of the Company's Settlements, he was either betrayed into the Hands of some of the Natives, or, somehow or other, was surprised by them' and carried away (170). The Englishman managed to flee his captors, moving from nation to nation until he 'had taken up his Abode where we found him, where he was well received by the petty King of the Tribe he lived with; and he, in return, instructed them how to value the Product of their Labour, and on what Terms to trade with those negroes who came up to them for Teeth' (170). For some critics, the Englishman serves as a litmus test for Defoe's thoughts on human difference. Defoe aligns Englishness with civility in this episode to the extent that, although the Englishman has effectively gone native, gentlemanly qualities shine through even his deplorable state of nakedness. He is all hospitality and helpfulness. Even so, the details of the Englishman's story might have caused readers familiar with the Africa of Defoe's *Review* to consider him with some wariness.

The inspiration for this character is presumed to be one John Freeman, who was a factor for the Royal African Company under Dalby Thomas until he was dismissed in 1705 or 1706 for 'arbitrary conduct', and Paula Backscheider suggests Defoe's readers would have recognized him as such.[39] *Atlas Maritimus & Commercialis*, which tells the story of a white man living 300 miles into the interior of Africa and alludes to a 'larger Account of the Journey of Thirteen Portuguese before they met with this white Man', identifies him by this name (252–3).[40] The real John Freeman was undeniably a reprobate. As Peter Knox-Shaw, quoted by Furbank, writes: 'Quite apart from the complaints that he abandoned an island to the French', Freeman was 'accused of embezzling dietmoncy by keeping his men on short commons, of dealing—against prescription—with freelance traders or the Dutch, of underhand hoarding and downright theft' (*Novels*, v. 227). After the RAC released him from service, Freeman set up as a separate trader, tried to coerce company men to defect to his band, burned African villages after he failed

---

[39] Backscheider, *Daniel Defoe*, 475.
[40] The resonances between *Captain Singleton* and Freeman's story in *Atlas Maritimus & Commercialis* is one reason scholars have attributed the latter to Defoe. See P. N. Furbank, 'The Naked White Man', in *Novels*, v. 227–31; Knox-Shaw, *Explorer*, 64.

to trade with them, eventually lost all influence in the region with both the Europeans and the Africans, and died in pathetic circumstances in 1713. Given Freeman's ignominious trajectory, Furbank and Knox-Shaw both remark on how surprising it is that in his accounts in *Singleton* and the *Atlas*, Defoe 'gives no suggestion that Freeman was a scoundrel' (*Novels*, v. 231). Yet there are indications in *Singleton*, if not in the *Atlas*, that he is not entirely a gentleman, either. If nothing else, his eventual fate is a good deal less positive than that of the novel's semi-repentant pirate protagonist.

Not only is the Englishman a self-confessed separate trader, but by teaching the Africans the value of their ivory he is engaging in what Defoe considered to be one of their most damning tendencies: educating the locals on the strategies of trade until they become 'sharp and crafty as an Exchange-Alley Stock-Jobber', able to price the goods they are both buying and selling to their advantage, and putting the RAC, the Dutch, and the separate traders into bidding wars around what they have to offer.[41] The east coast Africans who traded cattle for a handful of the cutler's trinkets are already a distant fantasy. The Africans the Englishman resides with are 'a more fierce and politick People than those we had met with before; not so easily terrified with our Arms as those, and not so ignorant, as to give their Provisions and Corn for our little Toys' (168–9). The Englishman also slowly and subtly persuades Singleton and the Portuguese away from their path to the security of European forts on the Gold Coast. He promises to guide Singleton and his crew safely to the Gold Coast, but before they go he implores them to stay and gather some riches, 'for', says he, 'there is not a River but runs Gold—not a Desert but without Plowing bears a Crop of Ivory. What Mines of Gold, what immense Stores of Gold, those Mountains may contain, from whence these Rivers come, or the Shores which these Waters run by, we know not, but may imagine that they must be inconceivably rich' (172). However, the Englishman's persuasive rhetoric is no testimony to his virtues.

Singleton and the crew agree to stay a while longer, and the venture proves profitable, but when they are ready to be done with it, the Englishman encourages them to stay longer still:

> He told us, tho' he had as much Reason to be sick of the Country as any of us, yet if we thought to turn our March a little to the South-East, and pitch upon a Place proper for our Head Quarters, we might find Provisions plenty enough, and extend ourselves over the Country among the Rivers for two or three Year to the Right and Left, and we should soon find the Advantage of it. (176)

The sailors are not keen on this proposal, profitable though it sounds. They are 'more desirous to get Home than be rich, being tired of the excessive Fatigue of above a Year's continual Wandring among Deserts and wild Beasts' (176). Yet, Singleton says, 'the Tongue of our new Acquaintance had a kind of Charm in it, and used such Arguments, and had so much the Power of Persuasion, that there was no resisting him' (176). Starting to

---

[41] *Review*, viii. 640 (19 February 1712).

sound very much like the sophists Defoe decried in the *Review*, as well as the persuasive devils Defoe criticized in his *Political History of the Devil* (1726) and *A System of Magick*, the Englishman sways everyone 'by his good Words' to stay another six months (177). At the end of six months, the Englishman coaxes them to prolong their stay yet again using logic that Singleton tells us was 'so forcible, so well argued, that it appeared in all our Faces we were prevailed upon: so we told him we would all stay: For tho' it was true to we were all eager to be gone, yet the evident Prospect of so much Advantage could not well be resisted' (180). To stay and gather these riches seems a fine idea. But the lure of easy gain keeps turning the Englishman's attention, and Singleton's attention, away from the long-term goal, and what is alluring in theory turns out to be a dead end in practice.

The Englishman himself points out that gold acquired for its own sake serves no purpose. In fact, he never bothered to gather the gold before, since without the means to make it on his own back to the European forts, it was no more advantage to him than if he 'had a Ton of Gold Dust, and lay and wallowed in it' (173). Without any momentum moving them back to Europe or larger strategic vision guiding them, Singleton and the sailors risk ending up in the same position as the Englishman. The Englishman may have the right idea, but the unsustainability of his approach is confirmed by the fact that his story ends not with a triumphant and lucrative return to England, but in loss and desperation. Finally able to head toward the Gold Coast, Singleton, the Englishman, and the Portuguese sailors arrive at a Dutch fort where the Englishman sends 'a thousand pounds sterling over to England, by the way of Holland, for his refuge at his return to his friends'. However, this ship is taken by the French and the money stolen. The Englishman 'remained in the *Dutch* factory some time, and, as [Singleton] heard afterwards, died there of Grief' (182). The fact that the Englishman remains at the Dutch fort rather than travelling to Cape Coast Castle with Singleton and simply boarding a ship bound for England as Singleton does reminds us that despite the Englishman's gentlemanly appearance and compelling speech, by RAC standards he is a renegade. Without the protection of the English forts and settlements to facilitate his passage home, the wealth the Englishman amassed amounts to nothing to Britain's economy, but well serves the French.

Singleton fares only slightly better. He does make it back to England with his riches, but he does not know how to manage his wealth, so that 'all that great Sum, which [he] got with so much Pains and Hazard, was gone in little more than two Years Time' (182). He observes, 'so this Scene of my Life may be said to have begun in Theft, and ended in Luxury; a sad Setting out, and a worse Coming home' (182). Thus, although *Captain Singleton* may stage Defoe's fantasies about what economic and colonial investment in Africa could bring, it seems in the end not to endorse Singleton's approach as either prudent or sustainable, nor is its fabulous account of Africa's resources as naïvely propagandistic as it initially appears. Rather, the novel suggests that without a guiding vision, and without long-term investment in the continent's British holdings, wealth from the Africa trade will be lost just as quickly as it is amassed. Mistaking the ease with which wealth in Africa is acquired for the stability of long-term trade is one of Crusoe's errors as well. On his first voyage to Africa, the £40 worth of baubles he trades for £300 worth of gold dust 'fill'd me with those aspiring Thoughts which have since so completed my Ruin' (60). The second time he attempts this voyage, he is captured by Barbary pirates. The third time he attempts this voyage, very clearly acting as a separate trader, he is shipwrecked. Crusoe's attempts to make a quick buck off of the Africa trade by avoiding proper channels end in disaster. However, that first lawfully acquired gain (under the guidance of a good and honest captain) was invested by the captain's widow, she of the 'unspotted integrity', and continues to turn a profit the whole time Crusoe is on the island. Indeed, earnest investment seems to be what Defoe advocates for regarding Africa in general, whether investment in the forts and settlements of the Guinea Coast or investment in wresting territorial control from North Africa's 'Turks'.

Conclusion

The Levant, North Africa, and sub-Saharan Africa have distinct associations in Defoe's writing, and each requires unique strategies of engagement as geopolitical and narrative objects, but they are connected like links in a chain in Defoe's global vision. If Britain were to direct its economic energies towards these Old-World geographies, which have been overlooked, he suggests, in the scramble to gain ground in the New World and the East Indies, the gains might include not only material wealth, but also Christian expansion and Muslim suppression. This is a struggle, he hints, that might be more readily won in Africa and the Levant than in the Far East. Defoe's staging of this vision through his fiction, though ideological, is not simplistic or naïve. His writings on Africa and the Levant, which in part dramatize his protagonists' shifts from captives to enslavers, showcase his ambition and his ambivalence regarding what participation in a global economy and colonial enterprise should ideally look like, and signal what the stakes of such engagement are for Britain's sense of national identity and place on the world stage. 'There is a vast Ocean of Improvement in View upon the African Coast', Defoe claims in *A Plan of the English Commerce*, both the east and west sides of which contain 'populous Nations, nay Empires, where there are Millions of People yet to trade with, who were never traded with before' (*PEW*, vii. 306). But of course no populous empire gets off the ground without trade, and the attitude of the *Plan*'s narrator—we can but try—is undercut by the Defoe of the *Review* and *Singleton*, who knew the trials had been made, and fallen short of golden ideals. Reaching these millions will only be possible if those who would make a hack of such trade relationships—Barbary Muslims, misguided separate traders—are discouraged and suppressed.

Further Reading

Srinivas Aravamudan, 'Defoe, Commerce, and Empire', in *The Cambridge Companion to Daniel Defoe*, ed. John Richetti (Cambridge: Cambridge University Press, 2008), 45–63.

George Boulukos, *The Grateful Slave: The Emergence of Race in Eighteenth-Century British and American Culture* (Cambridge: Cambridge University Press, 2008), 75–94.

Laura Brown, *Ends of Empire: Women and Ideology in Early Eighteenth-Century English Literature* (Ithaca, N.Y.: Cornell University Press, 1993).

Peter Knox-Shaw, *The Explorer in English Fiction* (New York: Palgrave, 1986).

Christopher F. Loar, *Political Magic: British Fictions of Savagery and Sovereignty, 1650–1750* (New York: Fordham University Press, 2014).

Robert James Merrett, *Daniel Defoe: Contrarian* (Toronto: University of Toronto Press, 2013).

Rebekah Mitsein, *African Impressions: How African Worldviews Shaped the British Geographical Imagination across the Early Enlightenment* (Charlottesville, VA: University of Virginia Press, 2022).

Rebekah Mitsein, 'Upon a Voyage and no Voyage: Mapping Africa's Waterways in Defoe's *Captain Singleton*', *Digital Defoe*, 10:1 (2018). https://digitaldefoe.org/2018/11/01/upon-a-voyage-and-no-voyage-mapping-africas-waterways-in-defoes-captain-singleton/#:~:text=As%20Singleton%20puts%20it%2C%20%E2%80%9Cwe,doing%E2%80%9D%20(emphasis%20original).

William Pettigrew, *Freedom's Debt: The Royal African Company and the Politics of the Atlantic Slave Trade, 1672–1752* (Chapel Hill, N.C.: University of North Carolina Press, 2013).

Roxann Wheeler, *The Complexion of Race: Categories of Difference in Eighteenth-Century British Culture* (Philadelphia, PA: University of Pennsylvania Press, 2000).

PART IV
AFTERLIVES

CHAPTER 32

THE CELEBRATED DANIEL DE FOE

Publication History, 1731–1945

NICHOLAS SEAGER

IN 1722 Defoe published three major fictions which since then have frequently been reissued. Counting new impressions, recensions, abridgements, serializations, excerpts, translations, rewrites, and appearances in collected works, by 1900 *Colonel Jack* had appeared at least thirty-one times, *A Journal of the Plague Year* at least forty-seven, and *Moll Flanders* at least sixty. These are impressive numbers but fall short of a less celebrated production of the same year. *Religious Courtship* was published at least sixty-three times by 1867. And whereas the novels were often popular in radically abridged or bowdlerized versions, most editions of the 358-page conduct book were complete and accurate.

The frequent reprinting of *Religious Courtship* for its first 150 years attests to the endurance of didactic literature well into the mid-Victorian period, just as the subsequent scarcity of editions indicates the converse. It also indicates that the circulation of Defoe's works down to 1945 is not just the story of *Robinson Crusoe* (1719), fantastically popular as that novel was. Nor is it just the story of Defoe's fiction. His political works, histories, travel books, commercial essays, and religious writings were repeatedly republished in Britain and America. However, just as anonymous publication was common in Defoe's lifetime, it persisted in his posthumous publication history: few editions of either *Moll* or *Religious Courtship* identified their author. And Defoe's works often circulated in versions he would hardly have recognized, as they were commonly abridged, extended, or rewritten. This essay shows that Defoe's publication history is best considered in terms of adaptation and appropriation in response to shifting tastes and sociopolitical contexts. It first examines non-fiction genres before turning to the novels and then collected editions.

Politics and History

Many Defoe works are topical pieces not republished after their original moment, though some required multiple editions or impressions in their first months. The exceptions to immediate obsolescence show that Defoe's ideas on political subjects were repeatedly applied to later debates. Like several Defoe pamphlets, *An Essay upon Publick Credit* (1710) was reprinted, for its historical interest, in *Somers Tracts* (1748)[1] but attributed there to Robert Harley, the politician whose fiscal management it promoted, as it was again in a 1797 standalone edition. Defoe's attention to financial crisis evidently resonated during Pitt's suspension of the gold standard following a run on the banks after reports of a French invasion. The 1797 titlepage explains that the Marquess of Lansdowne recommended *An Essay* in a Lords debate after the Bank of England began to refuse specie payments; it was then reprinted, with annotations, as 'a Work of the utmost Importance ... in the present awful Situation of Public Affairs'.[2]

Although *An Essay upon Publick Credit* was reprinted in 1797 regardless of Defoe's authorship, which remained unknown, eighteenth-century editions of his other works emphasized their topical relevance with reference to him. In 1735, *The Corn-Cutter's Journal* contributed to 'the present Universal Topick of Discourse'—standing army debates—by serializing *An Argument Shewing, That a Standing Army, With Consent of Parliament, is not Inconsistent with a Free Government* (1697). Though unsure whether Defoe should be remembered as '*famous* or *infamous*', as his reputation as a political turncoat persisted, the editor insists that the work is written 'with great Strength of Argument, as well as Sprightliness of Stile'.[3] We shall see that such early plaudits were common.

The Original Power of the Collective Body of the People of England (1702) is an important example of the political potential of Defoe republication. Reacting to the House of Commons' imprisonment of five men from Kent who petitioned it, Defoe's tract argues that sovereignty derives from and may revert to the landowning classes, his rather restrictive definition of 'the People'. Extracts of *Original Power* were reprinted in *The Modern Addresses Vindicated* (1710) in a wilful misapplication of Defoe's ideas by Tories orchestrating a petitioning campaign to pressurize Queen Anne into dissolving parliament, a position against which Defoe was simultaneously arguing. In 1769 a 'second edition' of *Original Power*, published by R. Baldwin, included a prefatory letter from a liveryman to his peers defending petitions protesting the Commons' expulsion of John Wilkes. By annulling the Middlesex elections at which voters repeatedly returned Wilkes, the author insists, representatives have betrayed the trust of voters. This 'excellent Tract' by 'the celebrated *Daniel De Foe*' is 'an undeniable and irrefragable Answer' to

---

[1] *A Collection of Scarce and Valuable Tracts*, 4 vols (1748), ii. 1–9.
[2] *An Essay upon Public Credit ... By Robert Harley* (1797).
[3] Spiro Peterson, *Daniel Defoe: A Reference Guide* (Boston, MA: G. K. Hall, 1987), 4.

'the Friends of Arbitrary Power'.[4] An undated 'third edition' of Baldwin's *Original Power* contains a different prefatory letter addressed not to ordinary voters, but to London's elected dignitaries. It attacks '*the Extension of the* Excise Laws' and appears from this internal evidence, and newspaper advertisements, to date to 1763, thus predating the 'second edition'. It also capitalizes on Defoe's burgeoning reputation as a tireless friend to liberty. Defoe '*understood as well as any Man the civil Constitution of the Kingdom*', and '*the Design of reprinting this Piece is to keep alive* the Original Right of the People'.[5] Baldwin's editions also contained extracts from Defoe's *Six Distinguishing Characters of a Parliament-Man* (1701), a critique of William III's last parliament deemed applicable to the 1763 and 1769 crops. Another edition of *Original Power*, published by J. Williams in 1771, signals its topicality on its title page, and is pitched at a yet more exalted readership: 'Addressed to the KING, LORDS, and COMMONS. Necessary to be read at this alarming crisis'. The last words frankly could refer to any one (or the sum) of the populace's grievances in the wake of the instalment of North's ministry. *The Morning Post* also printed excerpts of *Original Power* in 1775 to support objections to the British government's treatment of the American colonists.[6] Defoe's reputation as a champion of liberty, which displaced the image of a mercenary turncoat as the century advanced, ensured that even topical works found new readers.

Of Defoe's poems only *The True-Born Englishman* (1700/1) had a substantial posthumous publication history. Already in 1705, Defoe claimed it had gone through nine authorized and twelve pirated editions.[7] Defoe refreshed its topicality in 1716, adding new lines and a preface transferring the defence of a foreign king from William to George.[8] 1733 saw a twenty-third edition, the first posthumous one; there were at least twenty-eight further editions or impressions from 1740 to 1795, a rate of one every two years, plus numerous editions in the nineteenth century. Some major poems by Dryden and Pope get nowhere near these numbers. The poem's satire on notions of English racial purity ensured its continued relevance. It had particular resonance in the case of the first American edition, published in Philadelphia in 1778, during or just after British occupation of the city. It was perhaps enjoyed by the colonists as a satire on the enemy, as, like several eighteenth-century editions, it omitted the preface that contextualizes Defoe's satire, making it seem straightforwardly anti-English.[9] As late as 1904, selections from the poem were published in London and Mumbai (Bombay), with commentary to criticize British colonial policy in India.[10]

The True-Born Englishman's longevity and international reach was exceptional among Defoe's poems. Even an admirer like the early nineteenth-century radical satirist

---

[4] *The Original Power of the Collective Body of the People of England*, 2nd ed. (1769), iii, iv.
[5] *Original Power*, 3rd ed. (undated), iii, iv; *London Evening Post*, 11–13 August 1763.
[6] *Morning Post*, 21 February, 29 August 1775.
[7] Defoe, *A Second Volume of the Writings of the Author of the True-Born Englishman* (1705), A3r.
[8] *The True-Born Englishman . . . Corrected and Enlarg'd by the Author* (1716).
[9] *The True-Born Englishman* (Philadelphia, 1778).
[10] Nasarvanji Maneckji Cooper (ed.), *John Bull's Failings: Being Selections from Daniel Defoe's The True-Born Englishman* (London: Simpkin, Marshall & Co.; Bombay: K. & J. Cooper,, 1904).

and bookseller William Hone judged *Jure Divino* (1706) 'unfit for republication entire' because it was 'defective in arrangement and versification' and was cluttered with dated historical references; but Hone's *The Right Divine of Kings to Govern Wrong!* (1821) selects from and rearranges Defoe's poem, turning its satire on Divine Right theory against the revival of what Hone called 'Priestcraft' and 'Kingcraft' after Peterloo and the accession of George IV.[11] A 1748 version of *Caledonia* (1706), meanwhile, is a rare example of an originally onymous work made anonymous. Defoe's authorship is effaced, and the poem is presented as original. The text is also altered: stanzas referring to the prospective Union and Defoe's dedicatees, Queensberry and Queen Anne, are deleted. This version is dedicated to the Duke of Argyll, formerly Earl of Islay, a man whom incidentally Defoe had disliked. It updates Defoe's descriptions of the Scottish nobility, and Defoe's account of Scottish military triumphs is augmented by new lines on 'their late great Feat at Berg-op-Zoom', which surpass Defoe's worst poetic faults by rhyming 'perform'd' and 'redound'.[12] Whereas *Jure Divino* could be excerpted to support a republican cause in the Age of Reform, *Caledonia* apparently offered some welcome boosterism after the Forty-Five, as well as a route to patronage for one patriotic plagiarist.

Defoe's contributions to Scottish affairs better endured in other works: his ambitious histories. The vastness of *The History of the Union of Great Britain* (1709) precluded its republication for a long time, but it became freshly topical in the late eighteenth century. In 1786 John Stockdale issued a lavish new edition. Stockdale's advertising campaign emphasizes the *History*'s heft—'One large Volume Quarto, containing One Thousand Pages'—and touts bonus features: '*an elegant Engraving of the Author*'; a 'copious Index' by the British Museum's cataloguer, Samuel Ayscough, also issued separately as a prospectus;[13] an introduction by the constitutional theorist Jean-Louis de Lolme; and 'a Life of the Celebrated Author' by George Chalmers, which claimed that the *History* would have ensured Defoe's immortality even had he not written *Robinson Crusoe*. It cost £1.10s., or £1.11s.6d. on royal paper.[14] This prestige edition appeared in the wake of the Constitution of 1782, which freed Ireland from British rule and raised the prospect of an Anglo-Irish union. De Lolme's extensive 'Essay' reflects on this possibility, echoing Defoe in emphasizing the benefits of the 1707 Anglo-Scottish Union. Significantly, Defoe is not wheeled out as elementary propaganda, but credited for a complex consideration of the challenges of political union. De Lolme infers from Defoe that 'an incorporate Union of Great Britain and Ireland may be pronounced a most desirable object to both Kingdoms; yet it is certainly not without its difficulties'.[15]

After the 1798 uprising of the French-backed United Irishmen, Defoe's account of how unity came out of hostility in 1707, ending centuries of conflict (and keeping out

---

[11] William Hone, *The Right Divine of Kings to Govern Wrong!* (1821), 10–11.
[12] *Caledonia: A Poem in Honour of Scotland* (1748), 42.
[13] *In a few days will be published ... The History of the Union* [1786].
[14] *Morning Herald*, 7 February 1786; *Whitehall Evening Post*, 31 May–2 June 1787.
[15] *The History of the Union between England and Scotland* (1786), 81, 91.

French interference!), seemed highly relevant. In 1799 two selections from his *History* were issued by John Exshaw in Dublin to promote union. One comprises just sixty-six pages and urges that an Anglo-Irish union can be achieved despite its opponents' misrepresentations. This edition is adapted to demonstrate that union will guard against populist revolution, such as by comparing the 1707 Jacobites to the 1799 Jacobins.[16] Exshaw's more substantial, 214-page abridgement likewise emphasizes its pertinence to current debates and calls Defoe's 'the best and most copious source of information' on its subject, written in a 'clear and impressive stile'.[17] In different ways, the Stockdale and Exshaw editions of the *History* show that Defoe's abilities as an author and political thinker were rated highly.

Memoirs of the Church of Scotland (1717) was republished in 1734—like the original, anonymously—and retitled *An Ecclesiastical History of Scotland*. This was another topical intervention. Defoe's account of the Kirk's steadfastness despite persecution was reissued after the First Secession (1733) of ministers who cited doctrinal laxity as their reason for separating from the Church of Scotland. A century later, now assigned to Defoe, *Memoirs* merited three editions in the 1840s. The Reverend William Wilson provided scholarly notes and an admiring preface outlining Defoe's qualities as a historian: 'De Foe is no cold-hearted chronicler ... He does not seek to disguise his passionate admiration of the Church of Scotland'. Like those who resurrected *Original Power*, and like his namesake Walter Wilson, whose 1830 biography applied Defoe's writings to the contemporary struggle for Dissenters' rights, Wilson represents Defoe as a fighter against tyranny, motivated to defend the Church of Scotland by his 'enlarged love of liberty'. Wilson conjectures that *Memoirs* has been neglected due to Defoe's double offence of being English and pro-Union, denying it is 'ill-digested and hastily-arranged'. These Scottish-published, early Victorian editions of *Memoirs* were, again, occasioned by schism in the Church: the so-called Disruption of 1843 resulted in the formation of the Free Church of Scotland, whose adherents objected to the state's encroachments on the spiritual independence of the Kirk. Wilson was part of the breakaway and conscripts Defoe's anti-Erastian *Memoirs* to the cause: the mainstream Church, Wilson laments, 'has entirely destroyed the foundations of De Foe's eulogy. She is no longer a free Church, and she is no longer a Presbyterian Church'.[18]

The examples offered so far demonstrate that Defoe remained in the cultural memory long after his death as an enduringly relevant commentator on politics and history. He was invoked in new printings to address issues of the day, not just in hastily produced interventions, but in lasting editions which praise, discuss, and apply his ideas, attesting to a far better reputation and reach than Defoe is usually credited with.

---

[16] *Extracts from De Foe's History of the Union* (Dublin, 1799), iii, iv, 1.
[17] *The History of the Union between England and Scotland* (Dublin, 1799), preface.
[18] *Memoirs of the Church of Scotland* (Perth, 1844), iv, v, vii.

Travel and Trade

The regular new editions of Defoe's (anonymous) *Tour thro' the Whole Island of Great Britain* (1724–6) during the eighteenth century are not responses to particular political events like previous examples, but they do signal its enduring relevance to a nation undergoing seismic socioeconomic changes. Early serializations under different titles brought the *Tour* to wider readerships by spreading the cost of purchase—there was an elegant 540-page quarto (1734) and a scrappy farthing-newspaper plagiarism (1740–2).[19] Nine official editions appeared in the eighteenth century; these promptly moved from the original octavo to the more portable duodecimo format suited to use while travelling. This is not all that changed. The *Tour* was incrementally altered and augmented to reflect local developments, showing an effort not just to churn the thing out, but to curate, refresh, and update it for later generations. Each new edition came 'With very great additions ... which bring it down to the Year 1738', '... 1742', and so on. It was expanded to the extent that it went from three to four volumes in the 1742 third edition (9s. to 12s. in price).[20] The 1742 preface states that 'many very material Omissions' required the additions: the tourist overlooked cherished antiquities and 'pass[ed] wholly by several of the best Towns'.[21] 1742 added more than any other, both in terms of new sections and piecemeal augmentations. Its fourth volume, covering Scotland, adding two new letters to Defoe's three, was separately published in 1746, catering to curiosity about Scotland after the Forty-Five.[22] The 1769 seventh edition first announced Defoe's authorship and Samuel Richardson's role in expanding the earlier editions, stating that the *Tour* was 'Originally begun by the celebrated Daniel De Foe, continued by the late Mr. Richardson'.[23] The attribution is repeated in subsequent editions, though nothing more is made of it: the publishers thus presented the *Tour* as an up-to-date national survey, attachable to two famous dead writers, but not merely a historical artefact.

The overall effect of the textual revisions may be traced in miniature in the evolution of the *Tour*'s account of Leicester. In the original Defoe focused on current commerce—the city's weaving industry and the livestock that sustained it—with civic, geographic, and historical facts too (*TDH*, ii. 206–8). This account was progressively interlarded, in edition after edition, with facts about Leicester's ancient and modern history (Romans, Richard III, and Royalists), archaeological discoveries, and descriptions of new

---

[19] Pat Rogers, 'George Parker, Defoe, and the Whitefriars Trade: A "Lost" Edition of *A Tour thro' Great Britain*', *The Library*, 8:1 (2007), 33–59; Nicholas Seager, 'Serialization of Defoe's *Tour* in *All Alive and Merry* (1740–42)', *N&Q*, 62:2 (2015), 295–7.

[20] *London Evening Post*, 24 October 1738; *Universal Spectator, and Weekly Journal*, 10 April 1742. The 1778 eighth edition cost 14s.

[21] *A Tour thro' the Whole Island of Great Britain*, 3rd ed., 4 vols (1742), i. iv.

[22] *A Tour thro' that Part of Great-Britain called Scotland* (Dublin, 1746).

[23] T. C. Duncan Eaves and Ben D. Kimpel, *Samuel Richardson: A Biography* (Oxford: Clarendon, 1971), 72–6.

country houses (Staunton Harold, The Hastings, Gumley Hall).[24] By 1778, therefore, the *Tour*'s description of Leicester had doubled in length. A more leisurely paced *Tour* had evolved, which was perhaps more serviceable as a guidebook as domestic tourism bloomed, and it reflects growing pride in the national heritage; but it is a more diluted analysis of commercial systems than the book Defoe wrote.[25] That was not restored until a 1927 edition.[26] A letter to *The Gentleman's Magazine* in 1783 remembered Defoe's original as 'an entertaining and useful book' but called the latest edition 'the strangest jumble and unconnected hodge-podge that ever was put together'.[27] The additions, this reader had noticed, were often taken from other printed sources without acknowledgement. The *Tour*'s publication history illustrates that eighteenth-century readers enjoyed Defoe without necessarily knowing they were reading him, and his account of Britain remained serviceable at its core, even as it was supplemented.

The 1769 edition of Defoe's *The Storm* (1704) shows a similar impetus to 'modernize' Defoe's writings. It was published—like the original, anonymously—as *An Historical Narrative of the Great and Tremendous Storm Which happened on Nov. 26th, 1703*, so is transformed from an experimental mode of journalism into a history. The correspondence giving eyewitness accounts of the Great Storm of 1703, which Defoe reproduced verbatim and interspersed with religious and scientific commentary on meteorology, tends in 1769 to be reported in indirect speech more befitting a 'historical narrative'. Defoe's text is pruned, rewritten, and rearranged, as well as augmented with biblical references in the margins, poetic epigraphs for chapters, and accounts of later storms. Like the editions of the *Tour*, it offers an up-to-date version of Defoe's material.

A similar process of editing and updating occurred with *The Complete English Tradesman* (1725–7). After Defoe's death, it was published in a string of editions by the Rivingtons, reaching a fifth in 1745; several were paired with *A Plan of the English Commerce* (1728), as 'By the late Ingenious Mr. DANIEL DE FOE'.[28] These editions are another indicator of Defoe's favourable reputation in the years after his death, contradicting reductive accounts of Defoe's early reception which claim he was seen mainly as a slapdash journalist.[29] Animadversions on his political writings remained common, but there were many complimentary accounts of his works long before his reputation as a novelist rose, nowhere more so than on commerce. The 1738 fourth edition of *Tradesman* transformed the work from 'Two large Volumes in *Octavo*' to 'two

---

[24] *Tour*, 2nd ed., 3 vols (1738), ii. 332–5; *Tour*, 3rd ed., 4 vols (1742), ii. 372–7; *Tour*, 6th ed., 4 vols (1761[–2]), ii. 424–9; *Tour*, 8th ed., 4 vols (1778), ii. 391–5.

[25] Katherine Turner argues that 'the gradual accretion of new information transforms the *Tour* and thus mirrors the transformation of the physical and social "face" of Great Britain'; this is 'a dynamic, natural and sociable process of growth wholly in keeping with Defoe's own enterprise'. 'Defoe's *Tour*: The Changing "Face of Things"', *BJECS*, 24 (2001), 189–206 (202, 190).

[26] *Tour*, 2 vols, ed. G. D. H. Cole (London: Dent, 1927).

[27] *The Gentleman's Magazine*, 53 (1783), 409.

[28] *A Plan of the English Commerce*, 2nd ed. (1737).

[29] Ashley Marshall, 'Fabricating Defoes: From Anonymous Hack to Master of Fictions', *ECL*, 36:2 (2012), 1–35.

smaller and more portable Volumes' in duodecimo (around 750 pages), reducing the cost from 11s. to 6s.[30] An extension to Defoe's original preface accounts for the 'very great Alterations and Improvements' announced on the titlepage; it attributes *Tradesman* for the first time to that 'ingenious Gentleman', 'the celebrated Mr. DANIEL DE FOE, whose extensive knowledge in all the branches of the *British* Trade and Commerce is sufficiently known'. The editor maintains this respectful tone yet points out shortcomings that justify the additions, deletions, and rearrangements: Defoe can be 'too verbose and circumlocutory'. However, stylistic and structural faults are imputed as much to Defoe's circumstances as to his abilities: the 1738 editor explains that Defoe was paid by the sheet, so his books can seem padded out; *Tradesman* was written under time pressure in three disjointed instalments, whereas he, in 1738, can see more clearly the plan of the whole.[31] He reorders the chapters, drops the epistolary format of volume I, integrates the 1726 *Supplement* into the run of chapters, and adds topics Defoe did not tackle. Like the *Tour*, *The Complete English Tradesman* was a 'living document', not something to be allowed to slide into obscurity, but deserving refreshment.

The 1738 editor speculates that Defoe would have approved of his changes. Bram Dijkstra by contrast argues that the 'egregiously adulterated' 1745 fifth edition (based on that of 1738) amounts to a 'moral retrenchment', whitewashing Defoe's explorations of the moral dubiety of commerce.[32] The 1738/45 edition is more of a practical manual for the aspiring merchant, stripped of Defoe's exploratory episodes and reflections on the clash between capitalist and Christian ethics. Defoe's insights into the tortuous morality of nascent capitalism, which continue to interest readers in the book, were subordinate in the 1730s and '40s to a more functional educative plan. For purists, the 1745 edition of *Tradesman* is more offensive than that of 1738. First, it removes those additional paragraphs in the preface which acknowledge Defoe's authorship and justify the changes; second, it removes the [crotchets] with which 1738 signalled additions to Defoe's text. Hence, the edits became silent, and the book was restored to anonymity. In this adulterated form the 1738/45 text endured: the first volume was republished in 1766 as *The Mercantile Library, or Complete English Tradesman*, and the 1840–1 *Works of Daniel De Foe* used the 1745 text, another reminder that the Georgians and Victorians often read Defoe in adulterated states.

Religious Writings

Several of Defoe's theological books were repeatedly republished during the eighteenth and nineteenth centuries, indicating that they served readers' continuing religious

---

[30] *Daily Journal*, 12 July 1728; *Daily Gazetteer*, 3 December 1737.
[31] *The Complete English Tradesman*, 4th ed., 2 vols (1738), i. x–xvi.
[32] Bram Dijkstra, *Defoe and Economics: The Fortunes of Roxana in the History of Interpretation* (Houndmills: Palgrave, 1987), 9.

needs. *The Family Instructor* (1715) and *Religious Courtship* were the didactic works most frequently published, and their texts were more stable than many Defoe works with such extensive publication histories, including the novels. The lessons apparently mattered more than the teacher, because virtually all editions were anonymous until well into the nineteenth century, though Defoe's authorship of these works was generally acknowledged in biographies and criticism.

The last lifetime edition of *The Family Instructor* was the 'tenth' (1725), though several of its supposed predecessors are untraced, if they ever existed.[33] Edition statements for *The Family Instructor*—as for many enduringly popular eighteenth-century books—are unreliable. Different 'seventeenth' editions appeared as far apart as 1772 and 1794. The first American edition was published in Philadelphia in 1792, and there were at least six more in America in the next twenty-five years. Volume II of *The Family Instructor* (1718) was less popular, but it reached an 'eighth' edition in 1766. Volume II was often published in conjunction with volume I. For instance, the 'fifteenth' edition of volume I and 'seventh' of volume II were simultaneously published as a pair by Charles Hitch in 1761. In 1800, *The Complete Family Instructor* combined them in one volume; there were several further complete editions. *A New Family Instructor* (1727), a less practical and more polemical book, was considerably less popular, but there were new editions in 1732, 1742, and 1750.

The Family Instructor is the first work I have treated so far with much of a history of illustrated editions. Some nineteenth-century editions of volume I have frontispiece illustrations depicting moments from the book's dialogues, but the most extensively illustrated edition is the only abridged version I have examined [*c.*1815], published by the Religious Tract Society and targeting poorer readers. Entitled *The Two Apprentices; or, The Importance of Family Religion*, it gives just the five dialogues concerning the apprentices William and Thomas and includes twenty-seven illustrations. The earliest edition to make much of Defoe's authorship came in 1816, which included a biography derived from Chalmers's.

The Family Instructor is sometimes mentioned as Defoe's second most popular book in the eighteenth century (after *Crusoe*), but *Religious Courtship* was published more often. Their popularity declined sharply and simultaneously in the mid-Victorian period. With *Religious Courtship*, again, anonymity was the norm; again, it was usually published in full. The handful of abridgements are interesting for their different approaches. The first (1734) is about a third of the length of Defoe's original and skilfully digests the first two parts, comprising seven dialogues; it excludes the 'Appendix' containing three further dialogues. A new preface, supplied by the Independent minister John Bassett of Kenilworth, justifies editing the book (the practice of abridgement still needed defending), noting the price-reduction (1*s.* versus typically 3–5*s.*). Social and psychological richness is lost in abridgement. For example, when Defoe introduces

---

[33] Irving N. Rothman, 'Defoe Census of *The Family Instructor* and *The Political History of the Devil*', *N&Q*, 23:11 (1976), 486–92.

a woman whose priority in marriage is 'a good Settlement', he does so in a circumlocutory manner that attenuates judgement by acknowledging that this mindset is the consequence of social expectations and curtailed educational opportunities among women of her class, whereas the abridgement bluntly imputes to her 'a love of money'.[34] An undated 'third edition' of this abridgement includes the three dialogues of the 'Appendix' too. Basset is gone, and the same preface as 1734 is now signed 'D. D.', potentially an earlier association of Defoe with *Religious Courtship* than is currently recorded.[35] A 1760 abridgement with the novelistic title *The Cautious Lady* is derived from the 1734 text. The ubiquity of *Religious Courtship* is suggested by the fact that Goldsmith's Olivia Primrose in *The Vicar of Wakefield* (1766) enjoys its dialogues as much as she does those of Thwackum and Square or Crusoe and Friday. *Religious Courtship* was still going strong a hundred years after *The Cautious Lady* and *The Vicar of Wakefield*, 'known familiarly to most serious servant-maids, and formerly a favourite companion of their mistresses', as one writer put it in 1851, and 'scarcely less esteemed by the British public than *Robinson Crusoe*', claimed an 1855 editor.[36]

Like these conduct books, *The Political History of the Devil* (1726) was regularly reprinted until the mid-nineteenth century. A sixth authorized edition appeared in 1770, but since 1726 there had also been an early piracy, two editions claiming to be the third (1728, 1734), two claiming to be the fourth (1739, 1745), two editions of a French translation (1729, 1730), and two German translations (1733, 1748), though its continental presence waned after it was placed on the Catholic Church's index of banned books.[37] A 1772 Birmingham edition was published serially in fifteen numbers accompanied by a short, unrewarding picaresque narrative, *Genuine Anecdotes of a Scoundrel; or, Memoirs of Devil Dick*. 1772 uses new illustrations, the first since the original frontispiece. Several nineteenth-century editions are also illustrated, those published by Thomas Kelly, engraved by T. Wallis, being the most attractive. This edition has the illustration of a woman accused of being a witch being ducked while the Devil in the person of a blacksmith looks on that terrifies Maggie (and prefigures the flood and her spiritual crisis) in *The Mill on the Floss* (Figure 32.1). Mr Tulliver says he bought the book inadvertently with some sermons based on its good binding, unaware of the content that makes it unsuitable matter for his daughter.

Maggie Tulliver reads a slightly abridged version of *Political History*. 1772 was the last for a while to keep Defoe's text intact, because a 1777 edition cut the end of chapter I and all of chapter II from part I; that section then remained absent from most 'long' versions of *Political History* until the 1840s. From 1777 to 1854, there were nineteen 'long' editions, published in places as different as Alnwick and Philadelphia, York and New York, Exeter

---

[34] RDW, iv. 151; *Religious Courtship Abridg'd* (1734), vii–viii, 124.
[35] *Religious Courtship Abridg'd*, 3rd ed. [1735?], viii; Furbank and Owens, *Critical Bibliography*, 203.
[36] 'Daniel De Foe', *Chambers's Papers for the People*, 7 (1851), 1–32 (30); *Religious Courtship* (Cincinatti, OH: Applegate, 1855), i–ii.
[37] Margaret Bald, *Banned Books: Literature Suppressed on Religious Grounds* (New York: Facts on File, 2014), 259–60.

THE CELEBRATED DANIEL DE FOE: PUBLICATION HISTORY, 1731–1945   593

FIGURE 32.1 Frontispiece, *Satan's Devices; or, the Political History of the Devil: Ancient and Modern* (1819). © British Library Board.

and Ayr, which reflects the rise of publishing in America and provincial Britain. I designate these 'long' because they are either complete or lack only the section just specified. The reasons for that cut are not obvious. Towards the end of chapter I the Devil's historian intimates that his intelligence is diabolical, which may have perturbed later Georgians. Certain statements in chapter II could be deemed blasphemous, such as when the historian says it is 'as certain that there is a *Devil*, as that there is *a God*', though these seem no more objectionable than other parts of the book (*RDW*, vi. 45, 50).

Regardless, the slightly abbreviated version was the source for the more considerably abridged chapbook editions of *Political History*. Chapbooks were small-format, short, inexpensive books often sold by pedlars and often illustrated with simple woodcut engravings. Defoe's novels were often adapted into chapbooks. There are two chapbook versions of *Political History*, both twenty-four-page duodecimos. *The History of the Devil Ancient and Modern* (1794) is a skilful epitome, but its most curious feature is a topical addition at the end when the narrator asks: 'In our own times have we not seen Thomas Paine a willing volunteer for the Devil in every wickedness?'. But Satan's wiles are always defeated, and Paine fortunately 'now rots in a jail' in France during the Terror.[38] *The Political History of the Devil upon Two Sticks* [c.1794] is not based on Defoe, though it appropriates the title (and LeSage's) to attack Jacobins including Danton and Robespierre.[39] The other chapbook, published in Ayr in 1817, mainly covers just the opening four chapters of *Political History*: this is the weaker school of Georgian abridgement, merely stopping when there is enough to fill the volume rather than condensing the whole. Both chapbooks make cuts and alterations designed to suit the work to a less 'learned' readership, such as omitting Defoe's engagement with *Paradise Lost*.

Another Defoe treatise on the occult, *An Essay on the History and Reality of Apparitions* (1727), had a less extensive publication history than *Political History*, but there were several posthumous editions down to 1770. The text is stable, though the title changed to *The Secrets of the Invisible World Disclos'd* in 1729, 1735, 1738, and 1740 editions; these were not anonymous like the original, but rather attributed to Andrew Moreton, the pseudonym under which Defoe published reformist works including *The Protestant Monastery* (1726) and *Parochial Tyranny* (1727). *A View of the Invisible World; or, General History of Apparitions* (1752) is not an edition of Defoe's book, as bibliographers have assumed, but rather a motley collection of ghost stories whose principal source is Defoe's *Apparitions*, though it discards Defoe's theological reflections. The final eighteenth-century edition was *The Secrets of the Invisible World Laid Open* (1770), an abridgement and rewrite that again prioritizes the spooky stories over the religious reflections.

---

[38] *The History of the Devil Ancient and Modern* (1794), 23–4. An undated Edinburgh version of this abridgement lacks the Paine addition.

[39] In a small textual change, an 1837 edition replaces Louis XIV with Napoleon Bonaparte as the final inheritor of Nimrod's Satanic ambition: Frank Curry, 'De Foe and Napoleon Bonaparte', *N&Q*, ser. 11, 7 (1913), 405–6.

The 1770 edition of *Apparitions* contains a version of the short ghost story Defoe published as *A True Relation of the Apparition of One Mrs Veal* (1706). *Mrs Veal* was frequently reissued in the eighteenth century, either by itself or within Charles Drelincourt's enduringly popular *The Christian's Defence Against the Fears of Death* (1651). There were at least eleven iterations of *Mrs Veal* in Defoe's lifetime, though the last of those (1728) identifies itself as the twelfth edition.[40] And there were at least twenty-four iterations of *Mrs Veal* from 1731 to 1799. It is yet another work that circulated in huge numbers though with no association with Defoe in the editions themselves.

There is some truth in John Richetti's remark, concerning the period to Chalmers's 1785 biography, that 'Defoe seems to have been little read or remembered in the years after his death'.[41] These first fifty years are indeed fallow compared to what followed, and readers were not seeking out 'books by Daniel Defoe' in large numbers. However, the number of editions of his non-fiction works demonstrates that, down to the 1780s, Defoe was extensively republished, albeit often anonymously or in modified form, for readers of various social levels. So Defoe was being *read* far more than we have allowed, and when he is *remembered* in these editions' paratexts it is with reverence: as a powerful polemicist, skilled stylist, insightful historian, authority on commerce, and defender of liberty. Some of his religious non-fiction—*The Family Instructor*, *Religious Courtship*, and *The Political History*—continued to be individually published well into the nineteenth century, as well as appearing in collected editions. But by the 1780s Defoe was recognized as an important novelist, and this essay now turns to editions of his fictions, where publication history and creative adaptation overlap yet further.

'Factual' Fictions

Defoe's last novel, *A New Voyage Round the World* (1724), was among those published by the bookseller and circulating library proprietor Francis Noble in the late eighteenth century, having been republished only twice before then, both early serializations.[42] Noble's editions of *Moll Flanders*, *Roxana*, *Memoirs of a Cavalier*, and *New Voyage* were the earliest to assign them to Defoe; in the case of *Cavalier* and *New Voyage*, they were the first to present them as fictions. As Furbank and Owens demonstrate, Noble's editions were crucial in the process by which Defoe came to be regarded as a novelist.[43] *Daniel De Foe's Voyage Round the World* (3 vols, 1787) is prefaced by a '*Life of the Author, by William Shiells*', actually derived from *Robert* Shiells's 1753 biography. The text was carefully edited, but there is an odd moment when the voyagers touch for the first time

---

[40] Charles Drelincourt, *The Christian's Defence Against the Fears of Death*, 12th ed. (1728).
[41] Richetti, *Life of Daniel Defoe*, vii.
[42] Both undated: one in forty numbers published by George Read; one in forty-four numbers as a supplement to *The Chester Weekly News*.
[43] P. N. Furbank and W. R. Owens, 'Defoe and Francis Noble', *ECF*, 4:4 (1992), 301–13.

on Valdivia in Chile, early in the narrative. Defoe's subheading stating that this is '*the Continent of* America, South *of the River* De la Plata' is deleted, and an added footnote states this is 'the place Captain James Cook named Botany Bay'.[44] Everything else is kept the same as in Defoe, so it is otherwise clear we are in South America, and that is unmistakable in the later part when the travellers return and cross the Andes. Botany Bay seems like the editor's local misapprehension, but it has caused commentators to label the edition 'garbled' or 'mangled'.[45] Actually, the editor does a faithful and skilful job of reproducing Defoe's text, with minor stylistic changes.

The text of *Memoirs of a Cavalier* remained stable in eighteenth-century editions, but the work was variously presented as fiction or history. Across eight editions, the title changed from *Memoirs of a Cavalier* (1720, 1754) to *A Military History of Germany, and England* (1759, 1766, 1778) to *The History of the Civil Wars in Germany … Also, Genuine Memoirs of the Wars of England* (1782) to *Memoirs, Travels, and Adventures, of a Cavalier* (1784) to *Memoirs of the Honourable Col. Andrew Newport* (1792). The 1754 second edition initiated the Newport attribution to affirm the book's factuality despite rumours that it is a 'Romance'.[46] 1759 altered the title to reinforce its historical status on the basis that 'Memoirs' makes it sound like a French romance and 'Cavalier' only applies to the second half.[47] The Noble edition (1784) positions Defoe as the editor of a *manuscrit trouvé*, putting the original preface that describes its discovery in his name; but Noble's subsequent advertisements identified Defoe as the author and 'taught the world to regard *Memoirs of a Cavalier* as a work of fiction'.[48] 1792 missed that lesson, as it ignored Defoe, foregrounded the Newport attribution, and presented the book as military history; paratextual features including an index and a frontispiece portrait of the Earl of Essex reinforce this presentation.[49] Though included in collected editions of Defoe's novels during the nineteenth century, debate about whether *Cavalier* was genuine memoir or fiction continued into the twentieth century, including in editions.[50]

Whereas *New Voyage* and *Cavalier* were read primarily as novels by the early nineteenth century, *A Journal of the Plague Year* continued to divide readers on its truth status. This debate played out in editions during the eighteenth and nineteenth centuries; after its connection with Defoe was universally acknowledged, the question was whether he was the editor of an actual memoir, compiler of historical documents, author of an

---

[44] *Novels*, x. 37; *Daniel De Foe's Voyage Round the World*, 3 vols (1787), i. 57.

[45] P. N. Furbank and W. R. Owens, 'Defoe and Francis Noble', 310–11; Ashley Marshall, 'Did Defoe Write *Moll Flanders* and *Roxana*?', *PQ*, 89:2/3 (2010), 209–43 (226).

[46] *Memoirs of a Cavalier* (Leeds, [1754]), iii–v. For the date—hitherto unestablished—see *Leedes Intelligencer*, 17 December 1754 (copy in Bodleian Library, Leeds).

[47] *A Military History of Germany, and England* (Edinburgh, 1759), iv.

[48] *Memoirs, Travels, and Adventures, of a Cavalier*, 3 vols (1784), i. viii; Furbank and Owens, 'Defoe and Francis Noble', 310–12.

[49] *Memoirs of the Honourable Col. Andrew Newport* (1792), 432–9. *Memoirs* was presented as a novel written by Defoe in the 1785–6 German translation.

[50] Nicholas Seager, '"A Romance the likest to Truth that I ever read": History, Fiction, and Politics in Defoe's *Memoirs of a Cavalier*', *ECF*, 20:4 (2008), 479–505, esp. 491–2.

historical novel, or some combination of these roles.[51] The first new edition in 1754 does not name Defoe (Shiells a year earlier gave the first known attribution) and rebrands it a *History*. As late as 1835, Edward Wedlake Brayley's frequently reissued edition asserted that 'De Foe's work is *not* a fiction, nor is it *based* upon fiction', its details all being derived from factual sources; but even he acknowledges that 'where [Defoe] has thus acquired information, he has given additional interest to the subject by entering into a detail of circumstances which, if not to the letter true, still arrests disbelief'.[52] By contrast, an 1832 edition states that Defoe's powers of invention were applied to factual materials and he 'embellished his melancholy narrative with imaginary facts', an oxymoron that indicates the generic instability inherent in the book's reception.[53] One undated Victorian edition was titled *The Plague: A Fiction Founded upon Fact*. Perhaps because of the interest in it as a historical source, *Plague Year* bucks the trend of Defoe novels in that full-length or 'long' abridgements were far more numerous (at least thirty) in the nineteenth than in the eighteenth century.[54] Its popularity continued into the twentieth century.

Editions of *Plague Year* between that of 1754 and the 1809–10 *Novels* were short abridgements derived from a version first published in the *Pennsylvania Town and Country-Man's Almanack* (1762). This was separately published in Germantown, Pennsylvania the following year as *The Dreadful Visitation* and at least thirteen further times, with different titles, in the next fifty years, mainly in America, where epidemics were a common occurrence. None of these abridgements refers to Defoe, maintaining that the protagonist was a real survivor of the plague. The chapbook is crafted as a third-person summary of a longer, factual memoir. This enhances its hortatory purposes: switching to third-person allows the modern narrator to extrapolate lessons from H. F.'s account, particularly concerning the need for confession, repentance, faith in providence, and charity. Some versions end with H. F.'s recital of Psalm 91; some follow that by urging the duty to care for Christians of different denominations; some append 'A Hymn on Death and Eternity', an unacknowledged recycling of an Isaac Watts hymn. The abridgement emphasizes the pro-toleration aspects of *Plague Year*, repurposing its praise for Nonconformist ministers who remained in London in 1665 into a message for social cohesion despite denominational differences in Revolution-era America.

The emotional power of *Plague Year* has helped to ensure its continuous popularity since the early nineteenth century: editors, along with other commentators, commonly evoked the vividness of its scenes and its affective intensity. This response extends to several illustrated editions. The novel thematizes gaps between verbalization and

---

[51] Robert Mayer, 'The Reception of *A Journal of the Plague Year* and the Nexus of Fiction and History in the Novel', *ELH*, 57:3 (1990), 529–55.

[52] Defoe, *A Journal of the Plague Year*, ed. Edward Wedlake Brayley (1835), viii, xiv.

[53] *A Journal of the Plague Year* (1832), v.

[54] The earliest 'long' abridgement, about two-thirds the length of the original, was *An Abridgement of the History of the Great Plague in London, in the Year 1665* (1824). This text was used in abridgements in 1830, 1837, 1846, and 1858. The last two were SPCK productions, but the SPCK's 1871 *Abridgement* is different and was reissued in 1878 and 1881. All are accompanied by an extract from Evelyn's diary on the Great Fire.

visualization, especially with what H. F. calls the 'speaking sight' of the Aldgate burial pit. The frontispiece to an 1819 edition (Figure 32.2), designed by Henry Corbauld and engraved by James Tuck, depicts the emptying of the burial cart, a popular scene among illustrators (the 1795 chapbook's and 1835 edition's illustrations thereof make for good comparisons). Corbauld was a student of Fuseli's, and his engraving is suitably gothic, with ominous overhanging trees and the full moon peeping over clouds like H. F.'s compulsive but illicit witnessing of the scene. H. F. memorably describes a bereaved father

FIGURE 32.2 Frontispiece, *The History of the Plague Year in London, in the Year 1665* (1819). Personal copy of Nicholas Seager.

whose 'manly grief' dissolves when he sees his loved ones' bodies 'shot into the pit promiscuously' rather than laid down decently. In the image, the limp, entangled bodies contrast with the rigid recoil of the sexton holding the torch in one hand, gripping his shovel in the other. The sexton's alarmed expression mirrors the stricken, upside-down face hanging from the cart. Another slumped corpse reaches to the grave in an uncanny embrace. In the novel, H. F. reflects on how the naked or barely covered bodies are 'huddled together', giving rise to reflections on the common lot of humanity, elicited also by this illustration.

CRIMINAL FICTIONS

Captain Singleton (1720) was republished twice as a newspaper serial. One ran in Exeter's *Post-Master* (1720–1), albeit with a substantial section cut and summarized.[55] A second one (hitherto unrecorded) ran in 1740, but only one issue survives of the farthing paper in which it appeared.[56] *Singleton* was republished in 1737, 1757, 1768, and 1800. 1768 was by a consortium including Francis Noble; though the edition maintains that Bob himself is the author, advertisements identified Defoe's authorship for the first time.[57] *The Voyages, Travels, and Surprizing Adventures, of Captain Robert Singleton* (1800) is an abridgement within the *English Nights Entertainment* series, available for 6 or 9*d*. It prioritizes the first half, the trek across Africa; the second, piratical half occupies only a quarter of the text. A frontispiece depicts Singleton fending off a crocodile. This version would have encouraged boys to aspire to explore Africa at the turn of the nineteenth century. *Singleton* mainly appeared in collected editions thereafter, until the late nineteenth century, when separate editions restarted.

The most interesting version of *Singleton* is that of 1757. It contains two prefatory letters from William Walters. In the first the piratical Quaker sets aside his sect's habitual pacifism to reproach the disgraced Admiral Byng for cowardice in the country's service during the Seven Years' War. William suggests that if Byng, then under court-martial for his failure to relieve besieged Minorca, lives to read *Singleton* he will 'blush to find such manly Actions related, that give Glory to the Performers, and Shame to thee'.[58] The second prefatory letter regrets that Byng was then executed. This edition substantially rewrites the story, largely effacing Singleton's immorality, giving him a more respectable background and greater nobility of purpose in the first half, and making him more

---

[55] Nicholas Seager, 'The Novel's Afterlife in the Newspaper, 1712–1750', in *The Afterlives of Eighteenth-Century Fiction*, ed. Daniel Cook and Nicholas Seager (Cambridge: Cambridge University Press, 2015), 111–32.

[56] *The Evening Post*, 29 August 1740.

[57] *London Chronicle*, 23–25 June 1767. In 1783 Noble advertised an edition of *Singleton* but none has been traced, suggesting copies of 1768 were being reissued. *London Chronicle*, 1–4 November 1783.

[58] *The Memoirs and Adventures of Captain Robert Singleton, Alias Edward M---gr---e, Esq*; (1757), A1v.

of a patriotic privateer than a stateless pirate in the second. At sea, he and William unofficially act in the British service, targeting enemy vessels, including rival European powers and India's Angrian pirates, before they settle in England, where Bob is reunited with both his long-lost lover and his real father. He is transformed from an aimless sea-rover into a landed gentleman, 'Edward M---gr---e, Esq', and leads a polite, sociable life with William, a Dutchman they have picked up, and a 'faithful' African called Mungo (the slave from the mutiny ship whose life William saves and whom they do not sell). All four men get married. This hybrid of adventure and sentimental modes illustrates how changing ideals for prose fiction coalesced with imperial-national agendas in mid-century Britain.[59]

Colonel Jack was Defoe's most popular novel barring *Crusoe* until the middle of the eighteenth century, there being nine issues of the full novel by 1747, as well as translations into German and Dutch. The novel's pickpocketing and highwayman sections were excerpted and circulated in collections of criminal biographies—at least six from 1734 to 1793, some illustrated—which ignored Defoe's authorship and the book's fictionality.[60] Early nineteenth-century versions modified *Colonel Jack* to make the hero reform more fully. An 1801 abridgement digests the whole novel and adds a new ending in which Jack's innate sense of gentility is confirmed by the discovery of his true parentage, his inheriting an estate, and his retirement in England surrounded by a family including wife, children, and his 'faithful Negro and friend *Mouchat*'—like in the 1757 *Singleton*, the 'grateful slave' motif extends into lifelong companionship and the rewrite indulges the romance of rediscovered noble parentage.[61] An 1810 abridgement for children focuses on Jack's youthful crimes but has him charitably adopted by the gentleman to whom he restores a pocket-book; Jack reforms, and there the book ends, like a curtailed *Oliver Twist*.[62] Not enough research has been done on how modified versions of *Singleton* and *Jack* in particular respond to later Georgian attitudes to social issues including crime and class, empire and slavery, the family, childhood, and manliness.

Like *Colonel Jack*, *Moll Flanders* was immediately popular, but the text escaped authorial control more rapidly: that is, it was chopped and changed from the start.[63] By Defoe's death there had been three full editions, two newspaper serializations, a twenty-page abridgement issued by Edward Midwinter called *The History of Moll Flanders* [c.1725], a 188-page one issued by Thomas Read called *The Life and Actions of Moll Flanders* (1723) that continued the story to tidy up her repentance, and a production called *Fortune's Fickle Distribution* (1730). The last condenses Moll's story to ninety-one pages, then adds separate histories of her governess ('Jane Hackabout') and final

---

[59] See Nicholas Seager, 'The Afterlife of Defoe's *Captain Singleton* in the Seven Years' War', *RES*, 74:314 (2023), 307–21.

[60] Defoe, *Colonel Jack*, ed. Gabriel Cervantes and Geoffrey Sill (Peterborough, ON: Broadview, 2016), 38–41.

[61] *The Life and Singular Adventures of the Three Jacks of Rosemary Lane* (1801), 72.

[62] *Colonel Jack: The History of a Boy that Never Went to School* (1810).

[63] David Goldthorpe, 'Textual Instability: The Fortunes and Misfortunes of *Moll Flanders*' (doctoral thesis, Open University, 1995).

husband ('James Mac-faul'). *Fortune's Fickle Distribution* was published three further times (1737, 1759, 1770), these involving further plot changes. *Moll* was also republished in full in 1741, 1753, 1761, and 1765. The Noble edition, *The History of Laetitia Atkins, vulgarly called Moll Flanders* (1776), is an extensive rewrite that attenuates Moll's criminal and sexual misconduct, indeed clarifying that the heroine, Laetitia, is not even the real Moll Flanders: the criminal career is curtailed, and our heroine's identification with the transported Moll is a quickly resolved case of mistaken identity. The Noble 'edition'—really an appropriation—again suits the novel to sentimental tastes of the 1770s.

By then, a plethora of *Moll* abridgements had started, perhaps as many as forty in the period 1760–1830. Most are undated. They range from eight pages to 144, with the twenty-four-page (single-sheet) chapbook format being most common. The abridgements predictably focus on the action, mainly Moll's criminal adventures, worrying less about her reflections, though they tend to tidy up ambiguities in her repentance.[64] Many are illustrated with simple woodcuts. In the Victorian period, *Moll* was published only in collected Defoe editions until a standalone 1896 one. Editions have been plentiful since then.

Whereas *Moll* was usually republished in shortened form, *The Fortunate Mistress* (1724)—or *Roxana*—was generally republished in *extended* form. Six distinct continuations were added to editions between 1740 and 1775.[65] *Roxana* ends with uncertainty about the heroine's daughter Susan's fate, so the extensions provide neater closure, either punishing Roxana's transgressions or having her repent.[66] The serialized 1740 edition fashions a lengthy extension out of texts including Eliza Haywood's amatory novel *The British Recluse* (1722) and William De Britaine's conduct book *Humane Prudence* (1680). It is a happy ending that brings *Roxana* into line with contemporary domestic ideals.[67] By contrast, *The Life and Adventures of Roxana* (1745) has a punitive continuation, in which Roxana is cast off by her husband when he discovers her past career as a courtesan, and she dies in poverty. This edition follows a 1742 (non-continued) edition in spotlighting the 'Roxana' alias in its title. Other, distinct continuations in 1750, 1755, and 1765 take their cue from 1745.[68] Indeed, 1765 was the version published in Victorian collections of Defoe's works, before it was finally established as 'spurious' in the early twentieth century. *Roxana* has been published many times since then.

The History of Mademoiselle de Beleau; Or, The New Roxana, The Fortunate Mistress (1775), published by Francis Noble and Thomas Lowndes, carried the first known

---

[64] Pat Rogers, *Literature and Popular Culture in Eighteenth-Century England* (Brighton: Harvester, 1985), 183–97.

[65] Spiro Peterson, 'Defoe's *Roxana* and its Eighteenth-Century Sequels: A Critical and Bibliographical Study' (doctoral thesis, Harvard University, 1953).

[66] Robert J. Griffin, 'The Text in Motion: Eighteenth-Century *Roxanas*', *ELH*, 72:2 (2005), 387–406.

[67] Nicholas Seager, 'The 1740 *Roxana*: Defoe, Haywood, Richardson, and Domestic Fiction', *PQ*, 88:1/2 (2009), 103–26; Nicholas Seager, 'Prudence and Plagiarism in the 1740 Continuation of Defoe's *Roxana*', *The Library*, 10:4 (2009), 357–71.

[68] P. N. Furbank and W. R. Owens, 'The "Lost" Continuation of Defoe's *Roxana*', *ECF*, 9:3 (1997), 299–308.

attribution via a fabricated preface signed Daniel Defoe, dated 1730, in which 'Defoe' confesses to having altered the story: 'I afflicted her ... for the sake of the moral only'.[69] The restored 'true' version is now published for the first time, in which Roxana lives happily with her Dutch husband until his death, and the novel ends, like the 1757 *Singleton*, with a spate of marriages—Roxana weds 'Mr. Worthy', but Amy, the Quaker, Susan, and another daughter are also married. Again, this revision transformed *Roxana* into a novel palatable for sentimental, genteel readers, but the nineteenth century preferred the punitive ending.

The illustration history of Defoe's novels except *Crusoe* remains neglected. Several eighteenth-century editions of *Roxana* came with engravings. Despite the censorious attitude that inclined publishers to append new endings, they not only resisted removing the heroine's most scandalous actions, but often illustrated arguably the defining one: her appearance in the Turkish dress. The 1724 edition (Figure 32.3) contained her first depiction, replicated in 1742, and a fold-out engraving in 1755 and a rather matronly depiction in 1775 followed. The 1895 collected *Romances and Narratives*, for which Jack Butler Yeats provided illustrations, revisits this scene (Figure 32.4). Here, Roxana's body shape is similar to 1724, apparently its model, but rather than posing alone with a mirror, she is dancing in company. Her dress is less ornate and 'exotic' in 1895 but more revealing, especially at the arms and ankles, and the image emphasizes her youthful looks despite her actual age. Rather than being alone in a lavish interior scene, she is the centre of collective male attention in an indistinct setting, though her flirtatious smile and eyeline—and the caption from the novel—indicate her interest in Charles II. The image thus makes more explicit a point on which the narrator is guarded: that Roxana is a royal mistress. Indeed, Yeats's behatted royal figure resembles a 1680s portrait of the merry monarch by Jacob Jacobsz de Wet II (now in Holyrood Palace).

ROBINSON CRUSOE

The publication history of the *Robinson Crusoe* trilogy—RC1: *The Life and Strange Surprizing Adventures* (1719); RC2: *Farther Adventures* (1719); RC3: *Serious Reflections* (1720)—is so extensive that here it can receive only an overview. There are so many editions, in such varied guises, that bibliographers have been defeated. The fullest list of English-language editions of RC1, compiled by Robert Lovett, identifies 1,198 between 1719 and 1979.[70] The real number is higher. David Blewett's list of 'the principal illustrated editions', 1719–1979, contains ninety-four that meet Lovett's criteria, of which fifteen are not in Lovett.[71] Jordan Howell lists ninety-three versions of the two

---

[69] *The History of Mademoiselle de Beleau* (1775), 2.
[70] Robert W. Lovett, *Robinson Crusoe: A Bibliographical Checklist of English Language Editions (1719–1979)* (Westport, CT: Greenwood Press, 1991).
[71] David Blewett, *The Illustration of Robinson Crusoe, 1719–1920* (Gerrard's Cross: Colin Smythe, 1995), 191–225.

FIGURE 32.3 Frontispiece, *The Fortunate Mistress* (1724). Boston Public Library, Defoe 27.26.

"Among them only one with his hat on".

FIGURE 32.4 Frontispiece, *Romances and Narratives by Daniel Defoe*, ed. G. A. Aitken, 16 vols (1895), vol. 13. Keele University Library.

predominant abridgements identified for 1719–1800 (eighty-four definitely exist, nine are unconfirmed), of which twenty-three definites and six unconfirmed are again not in Lovett.[72] *Crusoe* was published at a rate that vastly outstrips just about every other literary classic ever written.

Melissa Free uses Lovett's checklist to highlight the fact that, until the early twentieth century, the majority of editions of RC1 also included RC2. Indeed, in the eighteenth century many included RC3 as well. *Moll Flanders* is not even close to being Defoe's second most frequently published novel, as *Farther Adventures* was repeatedly included with its precursor. Free calculates that in the eighteenth century, nearly 50% of English-language editions included all three volumes, 47% included the first two but not the third, and less than 4% just RC1. In the nineteenth century, only 4% contained all three, nearly 79% contained the first two, and around 17% contained just RC1. Clearly, RC3 dropped off first: a big plummet in the 1820s and very few inclusions after 1860 (about the same time that didactic works like *Religious Courtship* and *The Family Instructor* nose-dived). RC2 endured for longer, with editions of RC1 by itself only overtaking joint editions in the 1910s, which Free links to a decline in English confidence following World War I, on the basis that RC2 is more ambivalent than RC1 about English national superiority.[73] Moreover, the joint RC1-RC2 editions often elide the division of the works, creating a continuous narrative. RC1 and RC2 were published and read as one for almost 200 years: the marginalization of RC2 is a recent phenomenon.

Although eighteenth-century readers commonly read RC2 and RC3 with RC1, they were, again, often not reading the whole thing. Through abridgement, *Crusoe* had an extensive cultural reach. The many children's retellings are *adaptations* rather than *editions*, but the stream of rewrites and remediations of *Crusoe*, alongside the plays, pantomimes, boardgames, paraphernalia, and eventually films and TV shows, never sapped the relish for the novel itself, in full or shortened editions.[74] Because it was pervasive in western culture, *Crusoe* influenced a wide range of reader groups. *Crusoe*'s reception is not just about the voices of professional readers and writers—later novelists from Scott to Woolf to Coetzee, or critics from Chalmers to Leslie Stephen to Ian Watt. Victorian and Edwardian children, early emigrés to Australia, British navvies during the Napoleonic wars, American frontiersmen during the westward expansion, and working-class readers involved in the Labour Movement all got hold of it.[75] Many readers, of many kinds, in Britain and worldwide, also read editions supplemented by illustrations. *Crusoe* has been translated into many languages, though scholarship on

---

[72] Jordan Howell, 'Eighteenth-Century Abridgements of *Robinson Crusoe*', *The Library*, 15:3 (2014), 292–342.

[73] Melissa Free, 'Un-Erasing Crusoe: *Farther Adventures* in the Nineteenth Century', *Book History*, 9 (2006), 89–130. Free mentions seven joint RC1-RC2 editions not in Lovett.

[74] Kevin Carpenter, *Desert Isles and Pirate Islands: The Island Theme in Nineteenth-Century Juvenile Fiction: A Survey and Bibliography* (Frankfurt-am-Main: Peter Lang, 1984), 24–25.

[75] For these types of readers' engagements with *Crusoe*, including the variety of editions they could have accessed, see Andrew O'Malley, *Children's Literature, Popular Culture, and Robinson Crusoe* (Basingstoke: Palgrave Macmillan, 2012); Karen Downing, *Restless Men: Masculinity and Robinson*

this matter is outdated.[76] The cultural influence of *Crusoe* has been extensive, thanks to its adaptative and global publication history.

Collected Editions

Ashley Marshall's argument that Defoe the novelist is a fabrication of the past sixty years overlooks the fact that for as long as people have regarded the novel as an art form, starting in the later eighteenth century, they have acknowledged Defoe's achievements.[77] An author with no reputation as an important novelist before Watt's *Rise of the Novel* (1957), which is Marshall's claim about Defoe, would not have had collections of their novels published in eight multivolume editions from 1809 to 1928, some of these reissued too. The first such collection, *The Novels of Daniel De Foe* (12 vols, 1809–10), contained all three *Crusoes*, *Singleton*, *Cavalier*, *Colonel Jack*, *Plague Year*, and *New Voyage*. It omits *Moll* and *Roxana*, which were still held in sanctimonious disregard. Overall, the edition promotes Defoe as a moral author of masculine adventure stories. This is reinforced by the publisher John Ballantyne's 'Biographical Memoir'. Sir Walter Scott assisted Ballantyne with the memoir (supplying a 'superstructure'), annotated the edition with 'critical remarks', and later extended Ballantyne's memoir, apparently for a never-realized volume of *Ballantyne's Novelist's Library* (1821–4) dedicated to Defoe.[78] Focused on the novels, the edition whetted rather than satisfied appetite. An 1822 bookseller's catalogue commented: 'It is really a reflection on our National Literature that a complete edition of the Works of so great and original a Genius should never have been published', a sentiment echoed by Defoe's biographer Walter Wilson in 1830.[79]

Two 1840s collections reflected the growth in Defoe's reputation (and canon). Thomas Tegg's twenty-volume *Novels and Miscellaneous Works of Daniel De Foe* (1840–1) is more lavish and inclusive than Ballantyne's edition. Though RC3 is gone, *Moll* and *Roxana* are in. This was the first printing of *Moll* in the shape Defoe wrote it since 1765. *Roxana*, however, still included the 1765 continuation. Tegg included several novels we no longer

---

Crusoe, 1788–1840 (Basingstoke: Palgrave Macmillan, 2014); Lucinda Cole, 'Crusoe's Animals, Annotated: Cats, Dogs, and Disease in the *Naval Chronicle* Edition of *Robinson Crusoe*, 1815', *ECF*, 32:1 (2019), 55–78; Shawn Thomson, *The Fortress of American Solitude: Robinson Crusoe and Antebellum Culture* (Madison, WI: Fairleigh Dickinson University Press, 2009); Jonathan Rose, *The Intellectual Life of the British Working Classes* (New Haven, CT: Yale University Press, 2001).

[76] Hermann Ullrich, *Robinson und Robinsonaden* (Weimar, 1898), 29–61; Werner Hendrik Staverman, *Robinson Crusoe in Nederland* (Groningen, 1907); William Edward Mann, *Robinson Crusoé en France* (Paris, 1916); Otto Deneke, *Robinson Crusoe in Deutschland: Die Frühdrucke, 1720–80* (Göttingen, 1934).

[77] Marshall, 'Fabricating Defoes'.

[78] Sir Walter Scott, *Miscellaneous Prose Works*, 6 vols (Edinburgh, 1827), iv. 258–321; *Letters*, 12 vols, ed. Sir Herbert Grierson (London: Constable, 1932–7), ix. 224–5.

[79] *A Catalogue of the Curious and Extensive Library of the Late James Perry* (1822), 50; Walter Wilson, *Memoirs of the Life and Times of Daniel De Foe*, 3 vols (1830), i. ix.

attribute to Defoe, but also a range of his religious and political works which, we have seen, had quite involved publication histories of their own—*The Family Instructor, Religious Courtship, The Political History of the Devil, History of Apparitions, Conjugal Lewdness* (1727), *The Complete English Tradesman, An Appeal to Honour and Justice* (1715), *The True-Born Englishman*, and more. A topical work such as *A Seasonable Warning and Caution against the Insinuations of Papists and Jacobites* (1712) is included not because of some claim to enduring literary value or modern resonance, but because Defoe wrote it—and Defoe was a major writer.

William Hazlitt the younger edited a more functional compilation with smaller, more tightly packed text in two columns, *The Works of Daniel Defoe* (3 vols, 1840–3). It included Hazlitt's substantial, admiring memoir, which extended his praise for Defoe's rectitude and literary qualities first aired in a review of Walter Wilson's *Memoirs*.[80] For Hazlitt, 'De Foe was a giant in literature: there is no English author who has written so variously, and few who have written so well'. Hazlitt calls his the 'first and only complete collection of the writings of Daniel De Foe', though the edition's own catalogue of Defoe's works signals its incompleteness. The *Works* are offered at a 'price which will render them accessible to the humblest classes, and in a form which will not disgrace the book-case of the highest'.[81] The two 1840s collections, along with Wilson's *Memoirs*, heralded the emergence of the modern, capacious image of Defoe as an author, taking in novels, moralistic works, poetry, and political pamphlets, making efforts to relate aspects of his oeuvre to one another, and appraising him as a major writer, of interest at once to the masses and the elite.[82]

The collected editions, continuing with the seven-volume 'Bohn's British Classics' *Novels and Miscellaneous Works* (1854–6), which was reprinted several times, usually foregrounded Defoe's fictions and other longer books such as conduct and supernatural treatises, but they never wholly excluded political writings. Smaller mid-to-late Victorian compilations focused more on this facet of Defoe. Though his attributional methods are now considered dubious, William Lee's collection of early Hanoverian periodical essays presented Defoe the journalist and press censor.[83] *The English Garner* published almost 200 pages of Defoe's polemical works, including bits of the *Review*, giving him precedence as a prose writer ahead of Swift, Addison, and Steele.[84] Henry Morley collected *Earlier Works*, including then rarely published items such as *A Hymn to the Pillory* (1704) and *The Consolidator* (1705).[85] More inaccessible writings by Defoe were published in the late nineteenth and early twentieth centuries, including unfinished late works, the bulk of his correspondence, the full *Review*, and his early manuscript

---

[80] *Edinburgh Review*, 1 (January 1830), 397–425.

[81] *The Works of Daniel De Foe*, 3 vols, ed. William Hazlitt (1840–3), i, dedication.

[82] For the intellectual background to Wilson's and Hazlitt's readings of Defoe, see P. N. Furbank and W. R. Owens, *The Canonisation of Daniel Defoe* (New Haven, CT: Yale University Press, 1988), 56–61.

[83] William Lee, *Daniel Defoe: His Life and Recently Discovered Writings*, 3 vols (1869). Cf. Furbank and Owens, *Canonisation*, 62–74.

[84] *English Garner*, ed. E. Arber, 8 vols (1877–90), vii. 459–656.

[85] Henry Morley, *The Earlier Life and Chief Earlier Works of Daniel Defoe* (1889).

poetry.[86] Defoe studies enjoyed a heyday in the forty years after 1950 because more and more of his writings were in print.

Smaller, single-volume collections of Defoe's writings abounded, from J. S. Keltie's often-reprinted *Works of Daniel Defoe* (1869) to H. K. Hawkins's *Selections from Daniel Defoe* (1922), but G. A. Aitken's sixteen-volume edition, *Romances and Narratives by Daniel Defoe* (1895), was the most important multivolume edition since the 1840s, unsurpassed until the twenty-first-century *Works* (forty-four volumes, with Furbank and Owens as general editors). Aitken's edition put the novels to the fore, but the final volume included shorter criminal narratives, such as *The King of Pirates* (1720), most reprinted for the first time; although none is universally accepted as Defoe's now, their inclusion shifted understanding of Defoe as a narrative craftsman, as did Aitken's prefaces, which were influential critical interventions during the rise of English as a university subject. Aitken relates the novels to their contexts but also discusses style and technique, including formal questions about Defoe's realism, as well as compositional ones about how he adapted sources. As mentioned, Yeats provided illustrations. Aitken's edition was republished in 1900 and 1902. Two American-published collections followed. *The Works of Daniel Defoe* (16 vols, 1903–4), edited by G. H. Maynadier, similarly devotes considerable critical attention to Defoe, panning *Colonel Jack* but giving *Roxana* greater praise than usual, an indicative change in those novels' respective fortunes. An eight-volume collected edition was published in Philadelphia in 1908. The fourteen-volume *Shakespeare Head Edition of the Novels and Selected Writings of Daniel Defoe* (1927–8) was a functional, no-frills edition, generally less preferred by scholars than Aitken's or the separate editions of most of the novels that came out regularly in the early twentieth century to serve popular and educational readerships, and which commonly included apparatus such as critical introductions and annotations. *Moll*, for example, was edited and introduced by major scholars like Ernest Baker, Carl Van Doren, Godfrey Davies, and Mark Schorer before Ian Watt wrote about it.

Conclusion

The first two centuries of Defoe's posthumous publication amounted to a great extent to adaptation and appropriation of varying sorts, a complex morphology of his writings rather than bare reproduction. At the textual level are abridgement, continuation, augmentation, interpolation, editorializing, rewriting, and translation; at the paratextual

---

[86] Defoe, *The Compleat English Gentleman*, ed. Karl D. Bülbring (1890); Defoe, *Of Royall Educacion*, ed. Karl D. Bülbring (1895); *The Manuscripts of his Grace the Duke of Portland, Preserved at Welbeck Abbey*, 10 vols (1891–1931); Defoe, *Review*, 9 vols in twenty-two books, ed. Arthur W. Secord (New York: Columbia University Press, 1938); *The Meditations of Daniel Defoe*, ed. G. H. Healey (Cummington, MA: Cummington Press, 1946). For a publication and reception history of Defoe's letters, see *Correspondence*, lxxxi–xc.

level we have prefatory biographies, introductions, and illustration (at which I have only glanced). Publication history intersects with Defoe's reputation and the developing attribution situation at every turn [SEE CHAPTERS 33 AND 34]. In paratexts, the editions both hosted and fed debates about Defoe's quality, the slipperiness of genre in his oeuvre, and his importance to literary, intellectual, and political history. This publication history is inevitably bound up with market demand, evolving literary tastes, attitudes to genres, and 'canon' (meaning both Defoe's expanding oeuvre and the broader standards of literary valuation that help determine which books get reprinted and in what guise). These factors may be seen by, for instance, the *Tour* and shifting standards for travel literature, sentimentalism and moralism as these shaped the eighteenth-century treatment of *Roxana*, the fiction/history dyad as played out in the publication of *Plague Year*, and the unlikely guaranteed-bestseller status of *Religious Courtship*. Whether and how Defoe was republished was governed by political circumstances: Irish affairs impacted *The History of the Union*; naval warfare and imperial conquest occasioned modifications to adventure novels like *Singleton*; Scottish religious schisms sent publishers back to *Memoirs of the Church of Scotland*; and contested views of Englishness kept *The True-Born Englishman* relevant. Finally, Defoe's publication history has been steered by his reputation: the esteem in which he was held as a commentator on commerce ensured a continuing audience for *The Complete English Tradesman*; his championing of English 'liberty' helped *Original Power* find new purposes in George III's reign; and the high regard for *Crusoe* provided a basis on which other works have been kept 'alive' or 'resurrected' because anything penned by the author of that book was sure to attract interest. The evidence of publication history presented in this chapter explodes orthodoxies about Defoe's reputation such as that he faded to oblivion before the 1780s, that the Victorians impugned his novels, and that even his best topical writing did not outlast its original occasion. Defoe never really went away and is unlikely to do so now.

FURTHER READING

David Blewett, *The Illustration of Robinson Crusoe, 1719–1920* (Gerrard's Cross: Colin Smythe, 1995).
P. N. Furbank and W. R. Owens, *The Canonisation of Daniel Defoe* (New Haven, CT: Yale University Press, 1988).
P. N. Furbank and W. R. Owens, *A Critical Bibliography of Daniel Defoe* (London: Pickering and Chatto, 1998).
Robert W. Lovett, *Robinson Crusoe: A Bibliographical Checklist of English Language Editions (1719–1979)* (Westport, CT: Greenwood Press, 1991).
Spiro Peterson, *Daniel Defoe: A Reference Guide* (Boston, MA: G. K. Hall, 1987).
Pat Rogers (ed.), *Daniel Defoe: The Critical Heritage* (London: Routledge and Kegan Paul, 1972).

CHAPTER 33

DEFOE'S CRITICAL RECEPTION, 1731–1945

KIT KINCADE

WHEN Daniel Defoe died in April 1731, obituaries referred to him as a 'universal Genius', a 'natural Genius', an 'ornament of our Society', and a 'great Author', 'eminent for his many Writings'.[1] When these descriptions were not being ironic, they were likely written by Defoe's family (or based on ones written by them) or even by Defoe himself.[2] While they reflect ideals Defoe considered he embodied, there is one description on which both supporters and detractors might agree: that his interest was in 'civil and religious liberty'.[3] His contemporaries saw him as a writer whose oeuvre was a commentary on contemporary topics such as social justice, politics, moral and religious instruction, and commerce and economics [SEE CHAPTERS 14 AND 20]. And although Charles Gildon revealed Defoe's authorship of *Robinson Crusoe* (1719) in *The Life and Strange Surprizing Adventures of D[aniel] De F[oe]* (1719), as Defoe maintained the fiction of Crusoe's authorship throughout the remaining two volumes of this work, it did not significantly contribute to Defoe's reputation by the time of his death or for many decades thereafter.

Anonymity and pseudonymity skewed Defoe's reputation from the beginning, thus bringing up the secondary problem of attribution [SEE CHAPTER 34]. Although no list was compiled around the time of his death, approximately eighty works were claimed on the publications themselves as being by Defoe. As George Harris Healey states: 'Of the hundreds of works that he wrote, his name appears on the title page of only ten. Two of his title pages show his initials. Twelve of his works have signed dedications or prefaces, three with his name, nine with his initials. Fifty odd pieces of his are identified as being "by the Author of the True Born Englishman" or the like. All his other works either

---

[1] Spiro Peterson, *Daniel Defoe: A Reference Guide 1731–1924* (Boston, MA: G. K. Hall & Co. 1987), 1.
[2] Novak, *Daniel Defoe*, 704–5.
[3] Peterson, *Reference Guide*, 1.

lack any indication of authorship or pretend to be the work of somebody else.'[4] Because of the lack of external evidence for much of his work, and titles being attributed variously through hearsay, private acknowledgement or discovery, or sometimes tenuous connections between works, there are many titles that have been attributed to Defoe that cannot be safely or completely accepted as his that may have been believed to be by him. While the status of the canon of his writings has always contributed directly to Defoe's reputation, it is not the objective of this chapter to evaluate individual attributions.

From his death through to roughly the middle of the twentieth century, Defoe's reputation was something of a rollercoaster ride. Defoe was acknowledged as a controversial figure in his lifetime but was plunged into obscurity for over half a century after his passing, then rediscovered by the Romantics, who praised him as a realist able to present fictional situations with a kernel of historical accuracy that produced deeply psychological responses in his readers and conveyed powerful moral lessons. His reputation plummeted once again in the Victorian era with the discovery of the Delafaye letters that revealed Defoe's time as a double-agent political writer, occasioning debate as to whether he was a master of realism or a liar. Because of this dual attitude to Defoe, he was judged to be a more complex figure than had previously been recognized, worthy of broader study in the early twentieth century. The re-rediscovery of him was based on both his breadth of subject matter and admiration of his artistry by critics and authors of the first half of the last century [SEE CHAPTER 3]. And what remains constant through all of these changes is the positive effect of *Robinson Crusoe* on his reputation.

1731–1790

Immediately after his death, and for more than fifty years following it, Defoe's reputation was practically non-existent, as he was considered primarily a topical writer. Pat Rogers indicates that the 'most famous allusion to Defoe continued to be that in *The Dunciad*' (1728, 1743) by Alexander Pope.[5] In Book II, in the section concerning 'profound, dark, *and* dirty Party-writers', Defoe is recalled through his disgraceful appearance in the pillory in 1703: 'Earless on high, stood unabashed De Foe'.[6] However, in private Pope remarked that 'Defoe wrote a vast many things, and none bad, though none excellent. There's something good in all he has writ'.[7] Rogers notes that Defoe's name is absent from

---

[4] George Harris Healey, 'Review of *A Checklist of the Writings of Daniel Defoe*, by John Robert Moore', *PQ*, 40:3 (1961), 383–4 (383).

[5] Pat Rogers (ed.), *Defoe: The Critical Heritage* (London: Routledge & Kegan Paul, 1972), 12.

[6] See John Butt (ed.), *The Poems of Alexander Pope* (New Haven, CT: Yale University Press, 1963), 736, 741.

[7] Joseph Spence, *Observations, Anecdotes and Characters of Books and Men*, ed. James Osborn, 2 vols (Oxford: Clarendon Press, 1966), i. 213.

critical discussion of literature in the following decades because he preceded 'the rise of the literary review' which gained in popularity in the late 1740s and 1750s.[8]

Some works identified as Defoe's were infrequently mentioned, while there were also occasions when his works were invoked without connection to his authorship. Both *Moll Flanders* (1722) and *A Tour thro' the Whole Island of Great Britain* (1724–6) remained popular for decades before their association with Defoe. Samuel Richardson's editorial revisions helped sustain an already popular interest in the *Tour* through the 1730s and '40s as a document of social and economic geography, while readers' interests in crime literature kept *Moll Flanders* consistently in print throughout the rest of the century.

Defoe's name appeared as author of several works in the five-volume *Catalogus Bibliothecae Harleianae* (1743–5), which was researched and assembled by William Oldys, Samuel Johnson, and Michael Maittaire for the bookseller Thomas Osborne to facilitate the sale of Robert and Edward Harley's library. The catalogue was the first to provide a list of both previously attributed works, such as *The Shortest-Way with the Dissenters* (1702) and *The History of the Union* (1709), with unattributed ones, such as *An Essay on the History and Reality of Apparitions* (1727).[9] The catalogue was an important early step in assembling a literary history by identifying works with authors and inviting further study. Up until this point, when Defoe was mentioned it was usually in commentary about a specific work or about a type of work associated with him.

Theophilus Cibber and Robert Shiels's ('Shiells' or 'Shields' is also seen) *Lives of the Poets of Great Britain and Ireland* (1753) provided the first posthumous biography/bibliography of Defoe. More a discussion of his works than of his life, it was also the first reference work to list Defoe's works, including pamphlets that he was famous for (such as *The Shortest-Way*), works he published under pseudonyms (like *History of Apparitions*), and works published as written by fictional characters, such as *Robinson Crusoe*, or shadowy amalgams of historical accounts and creative narration like *A Journal of the Plague Year* (1722). Cibber and Shiels spend less than a paragraph on his life, while discussing in depth his political pamphleteering. The chapter ends with Pope's treatment of Defoe and a few sentences about his death.

One way of ascertaining her or his reputation is by looking at the popularity of an author, but another way is examining how his body of works was understood. For example, *A Journal of the Plague Year* was in its day, and for much of the eighteenth century, considered as historical. However, it began to be associated with Defoe, starting with the Cibber-Shiels account, and 'by the 1770s Defoe's authorship of the *Journal* began to be clearly established', causing it to be considered a work of fiction that was praised by authors such as Hester Thrale in 1778, meaning it was recategorized as a 'Romance'.[10]

---

[8] Rogers (ed.), *Critical Heritage*, 13.

[9] Rodney M. Baine, 'Chalmers' First Bibliography of Defoe', *Texas Studies in Literature and Language*, 10:4 (1969), 547–68 (563).

[10] Robert Mayer, 'The Reception of *A Journal of the Plague Year* and the Nexus of Fiction and History in the Novel', *ELH*, 57:3 (1990), 529–55 (534–5).

This type of reassessment exemplifies the direction his overall reputation took in subsequent periods, vacillating between accusations of lying and praise for inventive realism.

While recognition and authoritative discussion of Defoe's works was at an ebb during this period, artistic commentary was on the rise. Tobias Smollett and Oliver Goldsmith in their histories, both entitled *History of England* (1757-8 and 1764, respectively), barely acknowledged, much less expanded on, Defoe's status: Smollett only acknowledged that Defoe was 'one of the most remarkable political writers of his day'.[11] However, as Jane Austen's narrator in *Northanger Abbey* (1818) exclaims, 'Alas! If the heroine of one novel be not patronized by the heroine of another, from whom can she expect protection and regard?'.[12] Inclusion of his works in fiction and the discussion of fiction began to appear. Smollett mentions both *Robinson Crusoe* and *Colonel Jack* (1722) in *The Adventures of Roderick Random* (1748); in *Tom Jones* (1749), Henry Fielding's narrator invokes 'The Apparition of Mrs. Veale' (1706) and *History of Apparitions*, and the character Benjamin the Barber recommends *Robinson Crusoe*; and Goldsmith refers to both *Robinson Crusoe* and *Religious Courtship* (1722) in *The Vicar of Wakefield* (1766).[13] Of particular note is Jean-Jacques Rousseau's inclusion of *Crusoe* in *Émile: or on Education* (1762), since it is one of the few books he allows his pupil to read, for its presentation of education in the natural world which consequently connected *Robinson Crusoe* to children's literature. None of these works, however, named the author of the titles invoked.

Even though Defoe had been identified as the author of *Robinson Crusoe* during his lifetime, few seemed to consider him as the creator of this popular fictional narrative, much less any other of his texts we now refer to as novels, until nearly the end of the eighteenth century. In 1785, a reviewer in *The Gentleman's Magazine* vaguely recollected, 'I think Robinson Crusoe is allowed to have been the work of Defoe, but I know no particulars of Defoe's life, nor what other books he wrote'.[14] The defining fact of Defoe's reception from the turn of the nineteenth century onwards, his authorship of *Crusoe*, was apparently still not common knowledge. Yet as early as 1738, *Colonel Jack* had been identified on the title page as being 'By the Author of *Robinson Crusoe*', and then later the same year another edition appeared that attributed the authorship to Defoe at the end of the Preface; hence Cibber's and Shiels's reference to it in their collection.[15] But then, it, too, slipped back into anonymity until 1775. Beginning in 1770, the bookseller Francis Noble began to attribute to Defoe novels that he had previously printed without identification of authorship. He published *Roxana* (1724) in 1775, *Moll Flanders* in 1776, and *Memoirs of a Cavalier* (1720) in 1784.[16] And while *A New Voyage Round the World* was first attributed to Defoe in 1786 by J. R. Forster in his *History of the Voyages and*

---

[11] Rogers (ed.), *Critical Heritage*, 13.
[12] Jane Austen, *Northanger Abbey*, ed. Barbara M. Benedict and Deidre Le Faye (Cambridge: Cambridge University Press, 2006), 30.
[13] Peterson, *Reference Guide*, 9-16.
[14] Rogers (ed.), *Critical Heritage*, 55.
[15] Furbank and Owens, *Critical Bibliography*, 206.
[16] P. N. Furbank and W. R. Owens, 'Defoe and Francis Noble', *ECF*, 4:4 (1992), 301-14.

Discoveries Made in the North, it was exploited by Noble in his reprint in 1787.[17] It is from this point, then, that we can trace literary history's shift in Defoe's reputation away from topical journalist and cultural commentator to one of the founding fathers of the novel.

The early 1780s also saw Defoe's name connected to his travel writing. Despite the seventh edition (1769) of *A Tour thro' the Whole Island of Great Britain* being 'described in the title as "Originally begun by the celebrated Daniel De Foe, continued by the late Mr. [Samuel] Richardson";[18] it was not until the eighth edition was reviewed in *The Gentleman's Magazine* in 1783 that it was attributed to Defoe for the reading public.[19] The *Tour*, once attributed to Defoe, was regarded as perhaps his most successful book, both in terms of popularity and earnings, in the eighteenth century, and while it may not have had much of an impact on his reputation for the first fifty years after his death, its reabsorption into his canon would have positively affected his reputation thereafter.

By the mid-1780s, other Scottish commentators enlarged on *Crusoe*'s reputation where Smollett left off by actively praising the novel. Both Hugh Blair and James Beattie in 1783 believed that it was more than merely a novel of entertainment. Blair believed the novel had 'that appearance of truth and simplicity, which takes a strong hold of the imagination of all Readers, it suggests, at the same time, very useful instruction; by showing how much the native powers of man may be exerted for surmounting the difficulties of any external situation'.[20] Similarly, James Beattie stated that 'Robinson Crusoe must be allowed by the most rigid moralist, to be one of those novels, which one may read, not only with pleasure, but also with profit'.[21] Tracing the development of recent literary history, Clara Reeve, in *The Progress of Romance* (1785), echoed Beattie's assessment that the novel was 'written to promote the cause of religion and virtue' and labelled it safe for young readers because of both its morality and realism, issues that gain traction both in the Romantic period, and as a work fit for children.[22]

By the end of this period, two developments buoyed Defoe's formerly sinking reputation: the biographies about Samuel Johnson and the biographical and bibliographical work on Defoe by George Chalmers (1742–1825). Johnson's most famous biographer recorded that he actively valued and recommended Defoe's works. Boswell reports that Johnson paid special attention to *Robinson Crusoe* as one of three noteworthy novels (*Don Quixote* and *The Pilgrim's Progress* being the other two) that he believed 'were wished longer by their readers' and gave a list of all of Defoe's 'works of imagination' to Elizabeth Montagu because he had written 'so variously and so well'.[23] The importance

---

[17] Furbank and Owens, *Critical Bibliography*, 212.
[18] Furbank and Owens, *Critical Bibliography*, 210.
[19] Rogers (ed.), *Critical Heritage*, 55.
[20] Hugh Blair, *Lectures on Rhetoric and Belle Letters*, 2 vols (1783), ii. 310.
[21] James Beattie, *Dissertations Moral and Critical* (1783), 566.
[22] Clara Reeve, *The Progress of Romance*, 2 vols (Colchester, 1785), i. 125. Cf. Paul Baines, *Daniel Defoe: Robinson Crusoe, Moll Flanders: A Reader's Guide to Essential Criticism* (Basingstoke: Palgrave MacMillan 2007), 14.
[23] James Boswell, *The Life of Samuel Johnson, LL.D.*, 6 vols, ed. George Birkbeck Hill (Oxford: Clarendon Press 1887), i. 71; ii. 268.

of Johnson's comments cannot be undervalued in terms of the development of early literary commentary and criticism; later he employed Robert Shiels as an amanuensis for the *Dictionary*, and eventually his private recommendations and semi-public opinions in Defoe's favour were published. His opinions, combined with those of commentators like Blair, Beattie, and Reeve, provided a foundation for Defoe's increasing reputation as a writer of imaginary fictions.

The culmination of this period, one that unites literary study of both author and texts with authorship attribution, arrived with the work of Scottish antiquarian Chalmers. In 1785, Chalmers published anonymously *The Life of Daniel Defoe* as an advertisement for John Stockdale's forthcoming edition of Defoe's *History of the Union* (1786) in which Chalmers's biography was reprinted. Chalmers then revised the biography and added a researched bibliography of Defoe's works for Stockdale's 1790 edition of *Robinson Crusoe*. Chalmers's achievement constitutes 'the first formal biography of Defoe which utilizes sounds techniques of research'.[24] Chalmers considers Defoe a 'literary' man worthy of not only being remembered, but of serious 'study' despite the difficulties he said were to be found in doing such work.[25] Peterson describes the style and methodology of the original version: 'Although rising to a Johnsonian eloquence, Chalmers more characteristically presents information gleaned from the writing of Defoe's enemies, records at Doctors Commons, prefaces or autobiographical pieces in his *True Collection* [1703], surviving anecdotes, and especially the *Appeal to Honour and Justice* [1715]. From only a handful of pamphlets in the Defoe canon, he writes with considerable respect for Defoe as the staunch advocate of English liberty and trade'.[26] Chalmers created his own criteria for authorship attribution, along with expanding his picture of Defoe the social commentator to a more multifaceted writer, insisting 'he must be considered distinctly as a poet, as a novelist, as a polemic, as a commercial writer, and as a grave historian'.[27] While Chalmers did create and express a concerted methodology for his work, in hindsight his methods have given modern Defoe scholars some pause. Furbank and Owens ask, 'what sort of confidence should we be inclined to place in his powers of judgment in literary attribution',[28] based on an assessment of what they determined as his personal gullibility. Meanwhile Rodney Baine determined that Chalmers's sources 'vary widely in reliability', ranging from Defoe's self-identifications and self-referential promotion to 'untrustworthy attributions made a half a century after his death by booksellers or, during his own lifetime, by his enemies. Though Chalmers rejected the latter group of attributions, it should be clear that Chalmers' assignment of any particular item to Defoe constitutes in itself no evidence that Defoe wrote it'.[29] Regardless of what modern Defoe scholars

---

[24] Peterson, *Reference Guide*, 31.
[25] George Chalmers, *The Life of Daniel Defoe* (1790), 371.
[26] Peterson, *Reference Guide*, 31.
[27] Chalmers, *Life*, 435.
[28] P. N. Furbank and W. R. Owens, *The Canonisation of Daniel Defoe* (New Haven, CT: Yale University Press, 1988), 52.
[29] Baines, 'Chalmers' First Bibliography', 567.

might consider about Chalmers's methodology, what cannot be stressed enough about his biography and bibliography is that it was the first to use specific research methods. Chalmers effectively helped to resurrect Defoe as a multifaceted literary figure worthy of study (covering novels, essays, and poetry) and pulling together sources previously uncollected with some new attributions, such as *The Storm* (1704) and *The Consolidator* (1705), and rescued his literary reputation from the obscurity assigned to most writers of contemporary cultural subject matter.[30]

In this period, Defoe was not merely rescued from obscurity primarily based on the popularity among readers and critics alike of *Robinson Crusoe*; he was legitimized as an author worthy of serious study. At a time when novels were considered a lower form of art that catered to the mere entertainment of the masses, critical evaluations such as Beattie's, Blair's, and Reeve's established Defoe as a moral educator in addition to a master realist. And Chalmers's biography enlarged his reputation as a writer of a variety of type of works and an important historical figure of the early part of the century.

1790–1837

What late eighteenth-century critics did generally for Defoe was to solidify his body of works as one worthy of serious literary study, as well as specifically single out *Robinson Crusoe* as not merely praiseworthy, but useful for moral instruction. His usefulness for instruction was noted by Nathan Drake in *Essays: Biographical, Critical and Historical* (1805), who considered Defoe's *Review* (1704–13) as 'far superior to anything which had hitherto appeared'.[31] Additionally, Defoe was now also being compared to Jonathan Swift, particularly in regards to both men's use of realism, regardless of authorial intent, in *Robinson Crusoe* and *Gulliver's Travels* (1726).[32] Anna Laetitia Barbauld in 1810 compared their uses of 'grave irony', and William Hazlitt in 1821 described both as representatives of their respective stylistic achievements, Swift's being clarity and Defoe's 'naturalness'.[33] Robert Mayer recounts the rising controversy over the truthfulness or fictionality of *A Journal of the Plague Year* that arose from reviews in *The Gentleman's Magazine* of Edward Wedlake Brayley's topographical *The Beauties of England and Wales* (1801–15), as Brayley initially thought that Defoe actually based the work on his own experience.[34] Both of these lines of commentary point in the direction of later critical discussion: Defoe's realism.

---

[30] For discussions of Chalmers and his bibliographical methods, see Furbank and Owens, *Canonisation*, 51–5.

[31] Nathan Drake, *Essays, Biographical, Critical, and Historical, Illustrative of the Tatler, Spectator, and Guardian*, 3 vols (London, 1805), i. 23.

[32] Rogers (ed.), *Critical Heritage*, 16.

[33] Peterson, *Reference Guide*, 55, 73.

[34] Mayer, 'Reception', 535–6.

It is easy to trace how *Robinson Crusoe* became associated with children's literature. As early as 1731, the term 'robinsonade' had been coined by Johann Gottfried Schnabel 'to describe an already burgeoning body of narratives' that created a sub-genre of shipwreck stories.[35] The combination of adventure story with moral tale made this novel an early tool for easily digestible lessons for a young audience. Blair, Beattie, and Reeve all expressed this notion in the previous period, and these commentaries and recommendations continued in this era. Maria Edgeworth's character Forester in *Moral Tales for Young People* (1801), for example, used *Crusoe* as a philosophical guidebook. But others viewed Crusoe as an imperfect role model for children that should be read only with parental guidance. As Andrew O'Malley explains: 'Negotiating the line between Crusoe's exemplary qualities and his alluring invitation to waywardness became a matter of some import to writers and publishers who recognized the merit and appeal of the narrative and found innovat[iv]e ways to revise and so harness it to pedagogical ends.'[36] This spawned a side industry as publishers commissioned 'revised' and 'improved editions for children', as well as 'Crusoe theatricals for children' that can be traced back to Richard Brinsley Sheridan's pantomime (1781) but which rose in popularity specifically for families and children in the early nineteenth century.[37]

In terms of adaptation of a stranger sort, William Godwin's play *Faulkener* (1807) is a tragedy loosely based on a combination of *Roxana* (the 1745 edition, with a changed ending) and Samuel Johnson's *Life of Richard Savage* (1744). While the play received mixed reviews, Charles Lamb's prologue 'was deemed interesting enough to be printed in *The Times* on 17 December, 1807' and 'is a thinly veiled attempt to draw a parallel between Defoe and Godwin' that drew on Defoe's reputation as author of *Robinson Crusoe* to establish both men as 'underappreciated polymaths'.[38]

The two most important and influential commentators on Defoe's legacy during this period were Sir Walter Scott and Samuel Taylor Coleridge. Both in their own ways did more to enlarge Defoe's reputation than anyone since Johnson and Chalmers. Scott was both an editor and a scholar of Defoe, in a line of Scottish literary critics who distinguished Defoe. In 1809–10, Scott edited the twelve-volume *The Novels of Daniel Defoe* for John Ballantyne & Co. This was the largest collection of his works in a single edition to date, including six novels, Ballantyne's biographical note (published earlier and minimally augmenting Chalmers's *Life*), and a 'List of De Foe's Writings, As Far As They Have Been Ascertained' [SEE CHAPTER 32]. Most importantly, 'the idea was Scott's—to publish, with biographies uniform editions of such novelists as Defoe, Richardson, Fielding, and Smollett'.[39] Scott's work continued Defoe's elevation to the

---

[35] Andrew O'Malley, *Children's Literature, Popular Culture, and Robinson Crusoe* (New York: Palgrave Macmillan 2012), 2.
[36] O'Malley, *Children's Literature*, 26.
[37] O'Malley, *Children's Literature*, 46.
[38] David O'Shaughnessy, *William Godwin and the Theatre* (London: Routledge, 2016), 138.
[39] Peterson, *Reference Guide*, 55.

status of a major author worthy of extensive study and one foremost in the early development of the novel. As Rogers argues:

> Scott reveals himself a perceptive, shrewd and observant critic. His comments on Defoe's use of coincidence, of the supernatural, and of deliberate plain language, are all strikingly original as well as forceful. Again, Scott was the first critic to consider the *nature* of Defoe's literary impersonations, as opposed to the mere identity assumed. He makes another departure in attending with such care to the plot of *Robinson Crusoe*; no one previously had noted such characteristic features of Defoe's narrative method as the summary dismissal of Xury from the book ... All in all, Scott may be seen as the first critic sufficiently literal-minded and sufficiently alive to technical matters as to be able to cope with Defoe.[40]

Scott was not all praise, however. Of Defoe's prose he says 'Neither can it [*The History of the Plague*] be the artful conducting of the story, by which we are so interested. De Foe seems to have written too rapidly to pay the least attention to this circumstance; the incidents are huddled together like paving-stones discharged from a cart, and have as little connexion between the one and the other'.[41]

While Scott may have been the most prolific commentator of Defoe's works in this period, Coleridge became the most famous. Simon Frost discusses how the Romantics sought to 'establish new truths about old texts': 'Whether or not he was aware, when Samuel Taylor Coleridge through his creative powers discovered new truths to grievously misunderstood texts, he was setting a critical standard for much twentieth and twenty-first century literary criticism; in the aspiration that a scholarly close reading should reveal for the first time the true value of a text'.[42] While a group of powerful writer/critics of the era (Charles Lamb, Walter Wilson, William Wordsworth, and Coleridge predominantly) created what Simon Frost describes as 'The Romanticization of *Crusoe*', the fame of Coleridge's commentary rests on his estimation that Defoe was 'Worthy of Shakespeare', granting him 'a further ticket to the English (romantic) canon by writing "Shakespeare! Milton! Fuller! Defoe! Hogarth! ... these are unique"'.[43] Coleridge began his evaluation of Defoe's works in a lecture delivered in 1818, but the quoted comments are from his marginalia to his copy of *Robinson Crusoe*.

Romantic authors and critics began to fashion Defoe as the precursor to their idea of naturalism. A new generation of authors paid homage to Defoe by referring to him in their works of fiction, such as Mary Shelley's narrator in *The Last Man* (1826) comparing his lot to Crusoe's, and John Gibson Lockhart's biographical note on Defoe prefacing Cadell & Davies's edition of *Robinson Crusoe* (1820), marking a half-way point in the development of biographical and bibliographical studies between Chalmers and Walter

---

[40] Rogers (ed.), *Critical Heritage*, 17.
[41] Quoted in Rogers (ed.), *Critical Heritage*, 72.
[42] Simon Frost, 'The Romanticization of Close Reading: Coleridge, *Crusoe* and the Case of the Missing Comma', *Bibliologia*, 8 (2013), 85–110 (85).
[43] Frost, 'Romanticization', 86. 101.

Wilson's, and deemed 'probably the best assessment since Chalmers', for revisiting original material and using new sources.[44] Both Hazlitt (in 1818) and Charles Lamb turned their attentions to what at the time were considered Defoe's secondary novels. Not only was Lamb 'the first critic to make a serious claim for books such as *Captain Singleton*, and indeed the first to appreciate the link between *Crusoe* and the other novels, as they treat of endurance and survival in a hostile environment', but he was also influential on Wilson's work, so much so that Wilson used letters from Lamb (written in 1822 and 1829) in his biography.[45]

Wilson's *Memoirs of the Life and Times of Daniel De Foe* (1830) was the first major biographical and bibliographical work published since Chalmers. Spanning three volumes, compared to Chalmers's 'uncharacteristically short' commentary,[46] Wilson's biography 'was primarily concerned with Defoe the man and Defoe the patriot ... But ... in no way furthered a critical estimate of Defoe as a writer'.[47] Its value was that it brought 'Defoe into the mainstream of intellectual discussion'.[48] While Wilson's biography provided more coverage of and detail on Defoe's life than any previous ones, it is also both more biased (tending towards being apologist) and more uneven in its coverage of his life. All critics of Wilson's *Memoirs* indicate, to varying degrees, that it is more focused on the politics and history of Defoe's lifetime than on evaluating his literary merit. Wilson's work has been described as being a victim of a 'particular historical moment', written before and during the repeal of the Test and Corporation Acts partially as a propagandist move in support of repeal, paralleling Defoe's place in political discourses of his day. Furbank and Owens describe Wilson's work as 'stately and prosy in its style', while 'his concentration on history and general issues as opposed to personal biography'[49] tended to make his work more about the historical moment than about Defoe's life story. Wilson laments the paucity of extant information on his subject that has not 'escaped the ravages of time',[50] and justifies his approach by explaining that 'if he has been led further into the discussion of politics than may seem properly to fall within the province of biography, it must be remembered that De Foe passed the prime and vigour of his life in active employment, sometimes in the service of the state, and always occupied upon subjects in which the public took a warm interest. Upon these accounts, the history of his life is very much interwoven with the events of the times'.[51] He also defends his particular slant by explaining: 'A biographer of De Foe would have but little sympathy for his subject, if he were not a cordial friend to civil and religious liberty; and the present

---

[44] Peterson, *Reference Guide*, 70.
[45] Rogers (ed.), *Critical Heritage*, 18, 86.
[46] Furbank and Owens, *Canonisation*, 56.
[47] Frankie Jo Kirk, 'A Century of Defoe Criticism, 1731–1831' (masters thesis, Rice University, 1952), 107–9.
[48] Rogers (ed.), *Critical Heritage*, 19.
[49] Furbank and Owens, *Canonisation*, 57.
[50] Walter Wilson, *Memoirs of the Life and Time of Daniel De Foe*, 3 vols (London, 1830), i. v.
[51] Wilson, *Memoirs*, i. ix.

writer avows himself so in the largest sense that is consistent with the safety of government and the peace of society'.[52]

Wilson's literary discussion comes primarily from his friend, Charles Lamb, whose letters he quotes in the *Memoirs*. Wilson, bucking the trend of casting Defoe as the obvious predecessor of the Romantics, attempts to refocus attention on Defoe as a political writer and polemicist. Tracing the proliferation of his reputation outside of England, Rogers indicates that 'The earliest sustained consideration of Defoe to be found in any foreign source is that of Philarete Chasles, in *Revue de Paris* 1833 … a two-part biographical study, mostly derived from Chalmers and Wilson; it portrays Defoe as a loyalist and a martyr'.[53]

1837–1900

Although there was little sustained scholarly attention on Defoe following Wilson until mid-century, his rising reputation and commercial appeal are indicated by the appearance of two competing editions of Defoe's works released beginning in 1840. The publisher Thomas Tegg reprinted Scott's edition, including Chalmers's biography with updated notes, in twenty volumes (1840–1), and William Hazlitt (the younger) published a three-volume set (1840–3) described by Peterson as 'more functional but less elegant' and as 'crammed with reprints of the rarest pamphlets and tracts and all the major novels'.[54] There were comparisons of Defoe's work to other writers by critics such as Thomas De Quincey (1841) and Edgar Allan Poe (1841, 1843, and 1844), and references in works of fiction by Charles Dickens (*A Christmas Carol* [1843] and *David Copperfield* [1849–50]) and James Fenimore Cooper (*The Crater; or, Vulcan's Peak* [1847]). Where there were literary tributes, they tended to be patronizing: 'Most of these writers conceived of Defoe as a nursery classic, and though they give *Crusoe* unstinted praise, there is to modern eyes some condescension in their approach'.[55]

While *Robinson Crusoe* had been a subject of literary and historical attention for some time, from early critical engagement with the form and techniques used to the influence of Alexander Selkirk's story on the narrative, commentators in the 1850s began to show scholarly interest more widely. *Robinson Crusoe* had been established as the mainstay of Defoe's reputation, the one work that helped revive him from the clichéd dustbin of history, and while interest in this novel never diminished, attention was now turned towards other works thanks in no small part to the establishment of *Notes and Queries* in 1849. During the years 1850 to 1860, there were no fewer than sixty articles published on Defoe, ranging in topic from attribution, to biographical questions, to interpretive

---

[52] Wilson, *Memoirs*, i. xvii–xviii.
[53] Rogers (ed.), *Critical Heritage*, 24.
[54] Peterson, *Reference Guide*, 107.
[55] Rogers (ed.), *Critical Heritage*, 20.

issues both large and small, and across his works from the novels (still focused primarily on *Crusoe*), to the longer non-fiction pieces (such as about whether Duncan Campbell was a real person or referencing points from the *Tour*), to the pamphlets and periodicals (from 'Inquiry into the State of the Union' to the *Mercator*). The amount and breadth of coverage, for this ten-year period alone, is more than the sum total appearing in all of the other decades combined. Defoe was now being acknowledged for his foresight and modernity, exemplified in works like *Augusta Triumphans* (1728), *Second Thoughts are Best* (1729), and *An Essay upon Projects* (1697). Crusoe continued to be held up as a religious and prudent role model, appearing in works such as John Ruskin's *Notes on the Construction of Sheepfolds* (a query about the 'offices of the clergy' in 1851), Nathaniel Hawthorne's *The Blithedale Romance* (1852), and Charles Dickens's *Bleak House* (1852–3).[56] Those interested in his historical moment began to take notice of Defoe's social and political writings. Edwin Owen Jones included him in his *Eminent Characters of the English Revolution* (1853), and Margaret Oliphant singled out Defoe as a vivid recreator of the times in 'Evelyn and Pepys' (*Blackwood's Edinburgh Magazine*, 1854).[57] Finally, in this decade, Defoe criticism achieved a level of sophistication with an essay in the *National Review* (1856), likely written by Walter Bagehot: 'The article remains as good a short study of the novelist as can be found. For the first time the mechanics of Defoe's art are fully explored; the distinctive feel and atmosphere of his books are evoked; and the characteristics of his imaginative world are presented with cogency and force. The *National Review* essay set a standard to which few nineteenth-century critics aspired'.[58] The decade closed with an odd biography that both was and was not about Defoe. *The Life and Times of Daniel Defoe* (1859) by William Chadwick was based primarily on Wilson's *Memoirs* and was more concerned with his 'Times' than his 'Life'. Most curious about this particular biography was Chadwick's thesis that Defoe was the original precursor to all things Victorian. Chadwick argues that Defoe 'is seen as a champion of free trade amongst other things, and annexed to every Victorian cause that occurs to the writer ... Its purpose is to congratulate Defoe on having anticipated Victorianism in so many directions'.[59]

One example of Defoe's utility and relevance is the evolution of the Crusoe story as adapted, especially for children, which had gained huge popularity. O'Malley explains that 'the form has, since the beginning of the nineteenth century lent itself to countless other variations, including stories in which children, adults, groups containing adults and children, and even stranded animals have survival adventures in remote, if not "exotic" places, although by this time it had become a form most commonly produced for children. At the peak of British Empire in the Victorian period, the robinsonade was

[56] Peterson, *Reference Guide*, 131.
[57] Peterson, *Reference Guide*, 139.
[58] Rogers (ed.), *Critical Heritage*, 21.
[59] Rogers (ed.), *Critical Heritage*, 20.

perhaps the dominant form of boys' adventure story'.[60] This rise coincides with the rise in critical attention paid to Defoe and his works at large.

After 1860, commentary on Defoe quickened apace. This decade brought notable studies from abroad by Hippolyte Taine (1863) and Karl Marx (1867), as well as from home by Leslie Stephen (1868). Taine's 'Les romanciers' considers several of his novels (and 'The Apparition of one Mrs. Veal') as being full of facts and states of *Crusoe* that it proves to be both 'moral and English'.[61] Marx analyses the political economy on Crusoe's island, compared to the economy of the Middle Ages, concluding that Crusoe is the model of the individual modern man. Stephen's 'De Foe's Novels', a study primarily of works other than *Crusoe*, was for a time the most famous critical work on Defoe, overshadowing even the *National Review* essay. Stephen's primary thesis was that the strength of Defoe's art was that he was a skilful (if tedious) liar but not necessarily an evocative artist: 'Nor is the mere fact that he tells a story with the strange appearance of veracity sufficient; for a story may be truth-like and deadly dull'.[62] Novelists in this decade continued to allude to Defoe's works in their own as tools to reveal aspects of character, such as Maggie Tulliver in George Eliot's *The Mill on the Floss* (1860) accidentally dropping a copy of *The Political History of the Devil* (1726) that she had been perusing for the illustrations, and Gabriel Betteridge in Wilkie Collins's *The Moonstone* (1868) using *Robinson Crusoe* as one would a Bible, periodically dipping into the text to find words of solace or encouragement.

Finally, if the rise of critical interest and general respect in this twenty-year period, 1850 to 1870, was initiated by the positive, if belated, review of Wilson's *Life* in the *Eclectic Review* (1851), then it culminates in the publication, and subsequent reviews, of the work of James Crossley and of William Lee's *Daniel Defoe: His Life, and Recently Discovered Writings* (1869), a biography, bibliography, and edition of journalism published from 1716 to 1729 that Lee newly attributed to Defoe. Both men were long-time students of Defoe's work, with Crossley frequently contributing to *Notes and Queries*. After the publication of the six Delafaye letters in 1864, Lee undertook his book-length study and published several articles on the letters.[63] He was interested not only in correcting 'what he thought were glaring errors, both bibliographical and ideological, of Walter Wilson', but also in defending Defoe's reputation against the critical backlash that the publication of the Delafaye letters caused.[64] Furbank and Owens state:

> By the early part of the century, Defoe had become very much the hero, if not the property of political radicals like William Hone, Hazlitt and Godwin. Lee evidently felt the need to rescue Defoe from such hands, and he asserted stoutly that, contrary

---

[60] O'Malley, *Children's Literature*, 50.
[61] Peterson, *Reference Guide*, 165.
[62] Leslie Stephen, *Hours in a Library*, 3 vols (New York, 1894), i. 18.
[63] Furbank and Owens, *Canonisation*, 65; Nicholas Seager, 'Introduction', in *Correspondence*, lxxxii–lxxxiv.
[64] Furbank and Owens, *Canonisation*, 62, 65.

to Wilson's slanders, Defoe was always 'a liberal Conservative in politics' and, although personally a Dissenter, yet a firm supporter of the Church of England.[65]

Lee's copiously researched biography received 'a warm press', and while the reviewers scrutinized the character of Defoe from widely differing stances, Lee was criticized for two glaring faults: 'first, that he was an out-and-out idolater of Defoe ... and second, that he was wildly over-confident in his attributions'.[66] Illustrating his admiration for his subject, Lee pointed out how Defoe stood above all of his fellow party polemicists for his refusals to 'descend from the discussion of important principles to the defence of his own character', claiming that 'no controversial writer of that age was more perfectly free from this great fault than Defoe; yet none was more vilified by his opponents', even obliquely referring to Defoe as 'his hero'.[67] As for the interrelations of attribution and reputation, Lee added numerous topical pieces to the Defoe canon, many from a random collection of occasional journalism, that supported his reassessment of Defoe's political and religious commitments outlined by Furbank and Owens, taking the emphasis off Dissent. Meanwhile Crossley, a professed supporter of Lee's research, provided him with aid with some questions but withheld it from others, apparently in order to bolster his own work. He then criticized Lee in print for these omissions. Crossley never published his own extended list of attributions. While this story is not meant to undermine either Lee's or Crossley's work, it is meant to show how this public airing of disagreement on not only interpreting Defoe, but also on attribution of his works, played out.[68]

For a variety of reasons, Defoe studies was on the decline for the remaining thirty years of the nineteenth century. Rogers thinks that the discovery of Defoe's work as a political double-agent 'led to a veritable crisis of conscience among the critics, tough and tender-minded alike', possibly leading to this decline.[69] However, it is likely a combination of factors: (1) the preference for *Robinson Crusoe* above the other novels (particularly because of the racy subject matter of those like *Roxana* and *Moll Flanders*, which were deemed scandalous by the Victorians); (2) the reductive attitude towards *Robinson Crusoe*, rendering it predominantly a text for the moral education of boys (*pace* Stephen); (3) the changing novelistic tastes in the latter half of the century, and the fashioning by critics and writers alike of Defoe as novelist specifically rather than as a writer in general (or even a political and cultural commentator). A combination of factors contributed to this deterioration: the discovery of the Delafaye letters, Lee's over-zealous hero-worshipping, and problems of attribution as they played out in the public forum.

---

[65] Furbank and Owens, *Canonisation*, 67.
[66] Furbank and Owens, *Canonisation*, 68.
[67] William Lee, *Daniel Defoe: His Life, and Recently Discovered Writings*, 3 vols (London, 1869), i. vi, xx, xxii.
[68] For a discussion of the events summarized here, see Furbank and Owens, *Canonisation*, 62–82.
[69] Rogers (ed.), *Critical Heritage*, 22.

Lest it be considered a critical wasteland, however, there were noteworthy moments in the development of Defoe studies and in conversations about his place in cultural reception in these decades. William Minto in 1879 and Thomas Wright in 1894 both published biographies of Defoe. Minto had to negotiate the idolization of Defoe by scholars such as Lee and Wilson: 'It is Defoe's misfortune that his biographers on the large scale have occupied themselves too much with subordinate details, and have been misled from a true appreciation of his main lines of thought and action by religious, political, and hero-worshipping bias'. In Minto's assessment, Defoe 'was a great, a truly great liar, perhaps the greatest liar that ever lived'.[70] The result was a healthy dose of scepticism needed for a more realistic portrait of Defoe. Wright's biography, while adding important new details specific to Defoe's life, also 'strains credibility by pushing certain restrictive theories' that seek to interpret actions in Defoe's life by his works or attempt to explain certain seeming inconsistencies.[71] George A. Aitken's sixteen-volume edition of his works, *Romances and Narratives by Daniel Defoe* (1895), was the most significant collection since Scott's. Aitken articulated his belief in Defoe's 'skill in imparting verisimilitude' rather than accusing him of being a 'consummate liar', as well as believing 'his statements about himself to be true, in the absence of evidence to the contrary'.[72] In 1890 Karl D. Bülbring published for the first time Defoe's *The Compleat English Gentleman* (c.1728–9), the only known surviving book-length manuscript in Defoe's hand. Rounding off this period is Hermann Ullrich's bibliography *Robinson und Robinsunaden* (1898). This work provided the most comprehensive evaluation of Defoe's reception abroad to date. It established that he was known for only *Crusoe* and the plethora of translations, adaptions, and editions of that work, and that Defoe was recognized as the founder of the novel by the turn of the century. Ullrich records from 1719 to 1895: '196 English editions (this includes abridgments); 110 translations; 115 revisions; and 227 imitations ... Ulrich [*sic*] lists 49 French versions, beginning in 1720; 21 German (1720 onwards); 5 Dutch (1720–2); as well as Italian, Swedish, Hebrew, Armenian, Danish, Turkish, Hungarian, Bengali, Polish, Arabic, Estonian, Maltese, Coptic, Welsh, Persian and other translations'.[73]

Overall, Defoe's Victorian reputation reached its zenith in the late 1860s before falling away to some extent due to newly discovered biographical information. However, popular interest in Defoe remained high because of *Robinson Crusoe*. The tension caused by the discovery that he was a paid political agent, one willing and able to write on both sides of an issue, coupled with the diametrical opposition of the positions of his biographers Wilson and Lee, claiming respectively Defoe's liberalism and conservativism, seemed to take Defoe's reputation right back to where it began at his death.

---

[70] William Minto, *Daniel Defoe* (New York: Harper and Brothers, 1900), v–vi, 165.
[71] Peterson, *Reference Guide*, 272.
[72] George A. Aitken (ed.), *Romances and Narratives by Daniel Defoe*, 16 vols (London, 1895), i. xiii, xxxii.
[73] Rogers (ed.), *Critical Heritage*, 23–4.

1900–45

Defoe's reputation rebounded yet again in the early twentieth century. The general opinion of him as a writer improved, the range of topics he covered was better appreciated, and the novels besides *Crusoe* were increasingly analysed for their artistic merits. Scholars early in the century, particularly Aitken and W. P. Trent, enhanced both biographical and bibliographical understanding of Defoe. By 1905 Trent was already working hard to revise Lee. Aitken had acquired a cache of Crossley's working papers, including his unpublished list of attributions, and loaned them to Trent.[74] Trent published a series of articles in the New York *Nation* in 1907 and an entry for Defoe in the *Cambridge History of English Literature* (1912). In 1916 he released both an edition of *Robinson Crusoe* and *Defoe: How to Know Him*, a fairly conventional biography with excerpts from various types of Defoe's works. There were only two other biographies, Wilfred Whitten's in 1900 and John Masefield's in 1909, before Paul Dottin's three-volume biography and critical study, *Daniel Defoe et ses romans* (1924), dubbed as 'probably the most important piece of French scholarship and criticism' on Defoe.[75]

In terms of analyses and interpretations, Defoe's reputation was solidified as a progenitor of the novel and inventor of archetypes. In 1905 he was referred to as 'The Father of English Fiction' by W. J. Dawson.[76] Although James Joyce's observations on Defoe were shared in his lecture at the Università Popolare, Trieste, in March 1912, and therefore not widely disseminated until later, his evaluation indicates the evolution of the political aspects of literary interpretation.

> The true symbol of the British conquest is Robinson Crusoe, who, cast away on a desert island, in his pocket a knife and a pipe, becomes an architect, a carpenter, a knife grinder, an astronomer, a backer, a shipwright, a potter, a saddler, a farmer, a tailor, an umbrella-maker, and a clergyman. He is the true prototype of the British colonist, as Friday (the trusty savage who arrives on an unlucky day) is the symbol of the subject races. The whole Anglo-Saxon spirit is in Crusoe.[77]

Joyce's comments develop Leslie Stephen's association of *Crusoe* and Englishness, anticipating postcolonial assessments of the novel. In 1919, Virginia Woolf celebrated the bicentenary of *Robinson Crusoe* in 'The Novels of Defoe', published in the *Times Literary Supplement* (reprinted in the first *Common Reader* in 1925). Woolf's was an early feminist reading of both *Roxana* and *Moll Flanders* rather than *Crusoe*, highlighting both heroines' complexity and modernity with early strokes of psychological realism. Conversely, Willa Cather, in her introduction to *Roxana* (1924), complained that it 'has

---

[74] Furbank and Owens, *Canonisation*, 79.
[75] Peterson, *Reference Guide*, 391.
[76] Peterson, *Reference Guide*, 316.
[77] Quoted in Dominic Manganiello, *Joyce's Politics* (London: Routledge & Kegan Paul, 1980), 109.

ready invention, but lacks imagination'.[78] Woolf followed her earlier piece with an article solely on *Crusoe* in the second series of the *Common Reader* in 1932 that focused on Defoe's prose style. And E. M. Forster in *Aspects of the Novel* (1927) wrote that Moll 'fills the book that bears her name, or rather stands alone in it' and avers that the novel 'then shall stand as our example of a novel in which a character is everything and is given freest play'.[79] The year before, he had recorded in his *Commonplace Book* (not published until 1978) some of the musings of his Bloomsbury friends expressing his belief that '*Robinson Crusoe* is an English book, and only the English could have accepted it as adult literature' and recording that Virginia Woolf believed that *Robinson Crusoe* has '3 cardinal points of perspective, God, man, Nature, and Crusoe snubs us on each and forces us to contemplate "a large earthenware pot"—i.e. Defoe has a "sense of reality" which she also calls "common sense". Passing on to the dreary Bloomsbury conclusion that the pot's perspective may be as satisfying as the universe if the writer believed in a pot with sufficient intensity'.[80] Here, Forster invokes Woolf's idea of the symbolism of the pot and its connection to man (as manufacturer), nature (as material), and God (as maker of all). The pot is a religious symbol worthy of contemplation.

Not only were public intellectuals revising earlier stances and forging ahead with new interpretations of Defoe's works; scholars were also opening new venues for discussion. Defoe was 'early taken up by the Marxists', but new attention was paid to his 'life and ideas'.[81] Dottin emphasized Defoe's use of the occult in his works, addressed his obfuscatory work for Harley, and re-examined and reprinted Charles Gildon's pamphlet attacking *Crusoe*.[82] Carl Van Doren wrote an introduction for the Borzoi Classics edition of *Moll Flanders* (1923) supporting a Marxist interpretation of the novel as one fixated on economic conflicts. Arthur Secord published *Studies in the Narrative Method of Defoe* (1924) addressing the art of Defoe's authorship. James Sutherland's 1937 biography focused more on Defoe's life than interpretations of his literary works.[83]

The conclusion of this period would not be complete without noting one particular scholar who in many ways, whether intentionally or not, changed how we currently view Defoe's canon—John Robert Moore, who added more to Defoe's bibliography than any other previous scholar. He published his first book, *Defoe in the Pillory and Other Studies*, in 1939, attributing *A General History of the Pyrates* (1724–8) to Defoe, using internal evidence. This study was followed by his *Defoe's Sources for Robert Drury's Journal* (1943), which was reviewed negatively by Secord in 1945. Moore's reaction to Secord became personal and triggered Secord to research the *Journal*, resulting in a study bolstering his review, published posthumously in 1961.[84] These two early monographs

---

[78] Peterson, *Reference Guide*, 391.
[79] E. M. Forster, *Aspects of the Novel* (San Diego, CA: Harcourt Brace & Co., 1985), 56, 61.
[80] E. M. Forster, *Commonplace Book*, ed. Philip Gardner (Stanford, CA: Stanford University Press, 1985), 9, 10.
[81] Rogers (ed.), *Critical Heritage*, 26–7.
[82] Paul Dottin (ed.), *Robinson Crusoe Examin'd and Criticis'd* (London: J. M. Dent & Sons, 1923).
[83] James Sutherland, *Defoe* (London: Methuen, 1937), vii.
[84] For a discussion of the events summarized here, see Furbank and Owens, *Canonisation*, 100–21.

helped establish Moore's reputation as the pre-eminent Defoe scholar of the end of this period and laid the groundwork for his biography and bibliographies of Defoe, published in 1958 and 1960/1971 respectively.[85]

Defoe's reputation in the early twentieth century took on the complexity with which the period and his critics began to reassess him. Ideas of British national identity and colonialism were invoked and investigated by Leslie Stephen, James Joyce, and Virginia Woolf in terms of *Robinson Crusoe*. And new critical attention was paid to his other novels, such as in terms of feminism and economics, his works of non-fiction, and his place in political and cultural history.

What can be gathered from this overview of roughly 200 years of opinion about Defoe is how drastically his public reception evolved. He was considered at his death as a political polemicist and cultural and economic commentator. He then almost immediately plunged into obscurity for nearly fifty years. The Romantics took him up as one of their own, praising his naturalism and morality as a novelist. The Victorians championed his realism, until they were faced with the messy reality of his career. And it was this messiness that transitioned him into a complex figure and a progenitor of the novel because of his perceived modernity in the early twentieth century. And this critical wild ride, essentially, can be traced back to a single work. Of the many works he authored or expressed pride in or association with throughout his lifetime, it is the single publication of *Robinson Crusoe* that dictated for Defoe the scrutiny of posterity. While some of his other works had been admired by a few historians and critics alike, the general population's attraction to and fascination with this one novel led to a re-examination of his other works. And this re-examination, interestingly enough, turned his public image from that of a writer of social, political, and economic analysis (a prototype for our idea of the modern political pundit or even spin doctor on occasion) to that of one of the fathers of the English novel. While this evolution was neither completely laudatory nor condemnatory at any given time, it was always thought-provoking and contentious. And that complexity aided critics in re-evaluating his other novels, as well as his works of non-fiction, pamphleteering, and journalism.

Further Reading

Paul Baines, *Daniel Defoe: Robinson Crusoe, Moll Flanders: A Reader's Guide to Essential Criticism* (Basingstoke: Palgrave MacMillan 2007).

P. N. Furbank and W. R. Owens, *The Canonisation of Daniel Defoe* (New Haven, CT: Yale University Press, 1988).

P. N. Furbank and W. R. Owens, *A Critical Bibliography of Daniel Defoe* (London: Pickering and Chatto, 1998).

---

[85] John Robert Moore, *Daniel Defoe: Citizen of the Modern World* (Chicago, IL: University of Chicago Press, 1958); John Robert Moore, *A Checklist of the Writings of Daniel Defoe* (1960), 2nd ed. (Hamden, CT: Archon, 1971).

Robert Mayer, 'The Reception of *A Journal of the Plague Year* and the Nexus of Fiction and History in the Novel', *ELH*, 57:3 (1990), 529–55.

Andrew O'Malley, *Children's Literature, Popular Culture, and Robinson Crusoe* (New York: Palgrave Macmillan 2012).

Spiro Peterson, *Daniel Defoe: A Reference Guide 1731–1924* (Boston, MA: G. K. Hall & Co. 1987).

Pat Rogers (ed.), *Defoe: The Critical Heritage* (London: Routledge & Kegan Paul, 1972).

CHAPTER 34

ATTRIBUTION AND THE DEFOE CANON

BENJAMIN F. PAULEY

Many readers will come to a volume like this one by way of novels like *Robinson Crusoe* (1719) or *Moll Flanders* (1722), with an interest in exploring Defoe's wider oeuvre. It does not take long to discover, however, that there is considerable confusion as to just what 'Defoe's oeuvre' entails. Estimates of Defoe's output as a writer have varied from the merely astonishing to the frankly confounding: while George Chalmers attributed more than 120 works to Defoe in 1790, John Robert Moore's 1971 *Checklist of the Writings of Daniel Defoe* extends well past 500. Even after years of critical scrutiny of earlier attributions and a more sceptical assessment of what constitutes satisfactory evidence for attribution, P. N. Furbank and W. R. Owens's 1998 *Critical Bibliography of Daniel Defoe* lists above 250 works as either certainly or probably by Defoe.[1] The question of just what Defoe did and did not write was a vexed one in his own day, and has been the subject of sometimes heated debate pretty much ever since. As Furbank and Owens note, discussions of an author's career inevitably entangle questions of biography with questions of bibliography [SEE CHAPTERS 1 AND 33]. Our sense of what kind of person an author was is shaped by our understanding of what he or she wrote; but then our understanding of what an author wrote can be influenced by our sense of what kind of person he or she was. In the case of Defoe, this hermeneutic circle can seem a vicious one: the difficulty of knowing what Defoe wrote stems in part from the many unanswered questions about his life, yet the difficulty of knowing what Defoe was like arises in no small part from our uncertainty about what he wrote. If an author's name, as Foucault suggests, generally serves to 'group together a certain number of texts, define

---

[1] George Chalmers, *The Life of Daniel De Foe* (1790); John Robert Moore, *A Checklist of the Writings of Daniel Defoe*, 2nd ed. (Hamden, CT: Archon Books, 1971); and Furbank and Owens, *Critical Bibliography*.

them, differentiate them from and contrast them to others', then 'Defoe' proves to be most elusive.[2]

Defoe and the Landscape of Eighteenth-Century Publishing

That there should be such confusion over the body of Defoe's work is perhaps not so surprising when we consider the circumstances of print in his day [SEE CHAPTER 12]. The English Short Title Catalogue has more than 1,500 records for works printed in London (or printed elsewhere for sale in London) in 1719, the year when the first two *Crusoe* books were published.[3] When records for multiple editions, issues, or states of the same title are accounted for, these 1,500 records represent approximately 1,200 distinct works. Fewer than 750 of those works announced their authorship openly (either through a title page statement or a signed preface), and at least twenty of those statements of authorship are now considered to be false, though it is not clear whether all contemporary readers would have recognized them as such. Nearly a hundred titles are plainly pseudonymous (either using a classical-sounding pen name or referring simply to a role, such as 'A Gentleman at Edinburgh'), and twenty indicate their authorship only by reference to another work ('by the Author of … '). As many as 350 titles appear to be what we might call 'purely' anonymous, giving no indication of their authorship whatsoever. This admittedly hasty survey of a single year's publications tends to bear out Robert Griffin's suggestion that 'Anonymity during [the eighteenth and nineteenth centuries] was at least as much a norm as signed authorship'.[4]

Defoe affirmed his authorship of only a small handful of works, relative to the hundreds that have been attributed to him. Between them, *A True Collection of the Writings of the Author of the True-Born Englishman* (1703) and *A Second Volume of the Writings of the Author of the True-Born Englishman* (1705) assemble forty previously published works. Of the uncollected works that Furbank and Owens consider certain attributions, only seven seem to have carried Defoe's signature or initials, and an additional fifteen were said to be 'by the Author of' another of his works. Only ten of these, however, were linked to a work that Defoe had openly acknowledged: it is not clear that all readers of, for instance, *An Essay upon Loans* (1710) would have been able to identify 'the Author of the *Essay upon Credit*' as Defoe. Indeed, Defoe took some pains to

---

[2] Michel Foucault, 'What Is an Author?', in *Aesthetics, Method, and Epistemology*, ed. James D. Faubion, trans. Robert Hurley (New York: The New Press, 1998), 205–22 (210).

[3] This discussion is based on a copy of ESTC bibliographic data that I received in 2010. Queries of the live database hosted by the British Library would likely return different results reflecting subsequent additions to the catalogue, but I do not believe the differences would materially alter the patterns I describe.

[4] Robert J. Griffin, 'Anonymity and Authorship', *New Literary History*, 30:4 (1999), 877–95 (882).

ensure that *An Essay upon Publick Credit* (also 1710) would *not* be attributed to him. In the *Essay*, he affects to speak slightingly of 'the Author of the Review' ('TRADE, as the Author of the *Review* has told us, and who I can better submit to learn of on that subject, than some others he talks more about ... '); in a subsequent number of the *Review*, he offers a similarly grudging reflection on the author of the *Essay upon Credit* (who, he says, 'however wide in other Things, was right in this ... ').[5] Defoe's name is still more scarce in title page ascriptions. Indeed, the only work of any length to which Defoe seems to have set his name on the title page during his lifetime is *An Appeal to Honour and Justice* (1715)—a work, fittingly enough, in which he claims to set the record straight on what he had and had not written, but one in which he is not entirely forthcoming.

It seems safe to say that Defoe really did write the somewhat more than sixty works whose authorship he affirmed—there is no indication that he ever claimed another author's work as his own. That, however, is perhaps all we can say without qualification. Defoe clearly did not set his name to all that he wrote, but neither did he write all that was attributed to him, even in his own day. In *An Appeal to Honour and Justice*, Defoe complains of his contemporaries' readiness to see his hand in all manner of anonymous works:

> Every Libel, every Pamphlet, be it ever so foolish, so malicious, so unmannerly, or so dangerous, [is] laid at my Door, and ... call'd publickly by my Name. ...
>
> My name has been hackney'd about the Street by the Hawkers, and about the Coffee-Houses by the Politicians, at such a rate, as no Patience could bear. One Man will swear to the Style; another to this or that Expression; another to the Way of Printing; and all so positive, that it is to no purpose to oppose it.[6]

Whatever his hopes, *An Appeal to Honour and Justice* did not stop Defoe's contemporaries from attributing works to him that he did not claim, himself. In *The Political State of Great Britain* for June 1717, for instance, Abel Boyer declared *Minutes of the Negotiations of Monsr. Mesnager* (1717) and thirteen other pamphlets discussing political intrigues surrounding the accession of George I all to be the product of Defoe's 'FORGE of *Politicks* and *Scandal*'. Boyer insists that Defoe's authorship would be obvious 'to any one who shall take the Pains to consider the *loose Stile*, and *long-winded, spinning Way of Writing*, which is the same in all the Productions of this celebrated Author'.[7]

---

[5] *PEW*, vi. 51; *Review*, vii. 529 (21 December 1710). Such obfuscation seems to have been effective, as the *Essay* was attributed by contemporaries, variously, to Charles Davenant, the Duke of Shrewsbury, and Robert Harley. J. A. Downie, *Robert Harley and the Press* (Cambridge, Cambridge University Press, 1979), 125, 167; *Correspondence*, 516.

[6] *Appeal*, 46.

[7] Abel Boyer, *The Political State of Great Britain*, 13 (1717), 633. Maximillian E. Novak suggests, however, that Boyer would have had inside information from the world of London publishing, not all of it necessarily correct. 'Review of *The Canonisation of Daniel Defoe* by P. N. Furbank and W. R. Owens', *ECS*, 22:4 (1989), 579–84 (584).

Defoe almost surely did write some of the works attributed to him by Boyer and others—but not all of them. Of the fourteen titles Boyer mentions, for example, Furbank and Owens accept three as certainly by Defoe and three as probably by him (they consider the periodical *Mercurius Politicus* as a publication in which he had some hand).[8] Furbank and Owens de-attributed five titles from Boyer's list in *Defoe De-Attributions*, but, in light of further evidence, returned one of them as a 'probable' attribution in their *Critical Bibliography*. (Furbank and Owens did not weigh in on three of the titles mentioned by Boyer, presumably because they were among the 'many ancient attributions ... still to be found in library catalogues'.[9]) As this sampling suggests, the marks of Defoe's authorship are not so plain as Boyer would have us believe.

The question remains, however, how and why so *many* works should have come to be attributed to Defoe, not just in his own day, but after his death as well. Whatever the accuracy of his individual ascriptions, Boyer's charge—that Defoe was a prolific and unscrupulous hack, and that his style was instantly recognizable—foreshadows much of what was to come. As Furbank and Owens note, the Defoe canon grew under the hands of a succession of scholars, each convinced of his insight into Defoe's character and style. The more these scholars examined the pamphlet and periodical literature of the early eighteenth century, the more of it seemed to them to have flowed from the prolific (and, it seemed, occasionally unscrupulous) pen of Daniel Defoe. Revelations like Defoe's letters to Charles Delafaye (which contradicted his protestations in *An Appeal to Honour and Justice* to have left off pamphleteering upon the Hanoverian succession, and which suggested that he had, in fact, been paid by a Whig ministry to infiltrate Tory journals) affected perceptions of Defoe's character (*Correspondence*, 831–53). He came to seem a dissembler, able to take on multiple personae, to write in multiple voices (whether as a means of sly propaganda or from a lack of any genuine conviction). Those perceptions, in turn, coloured perceptions of what he might have written. If Defoe's own denials of authorship could not be trusted, and, especially, if he were thought regularly to have written on more than one side of a question, then the field of material that he could be suspected of having written became drastically wider. As Furbank and Owens note in their remarks on the work of William Peterfield Trent, 'If Defoe is thought capable of writing more or less anything, the conviction is liable to grow that he wrote more or less everything'.[10]

---

[8] P. N. Furbank and W. R. Owens, 'On the Attribution of Periodicals and Newspapers to Daniel Defoe', *Publishing History*, 40 (1996), 83–98.

[9] Furbank and Owens, *Critical Bibliography*, xx.

[10] P. N. Furbank and W. F. Owens, *The Canonisation of Daniel Defoe* (New Haven, CT: Yale University Press, 1988), 87. On Defoe's letters to Delafaye, see Furbank and Owens, *Canonisation*, 65. Donald F. Wing facetiously advised anyone contemplating a continuation of his *Short Title Catalogue* past 1700 to save themselves a great deal of trouble by simply attributing all anonymous tracts to Defoe. 'The Making of the "Short-Title Catalogue, 1641–1700"', *PBSA*, 45:1 (1951), 59–69 (67).

Furbank and Owens: Interrogating the Defoe Canon

Furbank and Owens were by no means the first to raise questions about the state of the Defoe canon. Defoe's Victorian editor, William Hazlitt, dismissed (sometimes tartly) more than thirty of the fifty-two then-current attributions that he considered questionable. Maximillian Novak's treatment of Defoe's works in the *New Cambridge Bibliography of English Literature* signalled the doubtful nature of many ascriptions as best it could, given the essentially list-like character of that project; and in the wake of Moore's *Checklist* scholars like Pat Rogers, Rodney Baine, Henry Snyder, and J. A. Downie (among others) offered strong arguments against particular attributions in article-length pieces.[11] Furbank and Owens's critique of the Defoe canon, however, is so extensive and systematic as to require separate attention. Their project unfolded in three phases. After a series of essays questioning the attribution of particular works to Defoe, their 1988 *The Canonisation of Daniel Defoe* canvassed the history of Defoe attribution culminating in Moore's *Checklist*. The second phase of their project is represented by the 1994 *Defoe De-Attributions*, in which they scrutinized Moore's *Checklist* more narrowly. Where they deemed the evidence for an attribution lacking or faulty, they argued that the work should be de-attributed, since provisional ascription lent it unearned status, in spite of any markers of doubt an editor might provide (like 'possibly' or 'perhaps' by Defoe). In the final phase of their project, Furbank and Owens turned from the critique of prior attributions to the presentation of an alternative view of the Defoe canon on what they argued was a sounder basis in their 1998 *Critical Bibliography*. In this volume, they adduce the evidence for Defoe's authorship of each work listed, distinguishing between attributions that they consider certain, ones that they hold to be merely probable, and ones that they acknowledge as 'unsolved problems'.

Furbank and Owens's winnowing of the Defoe canon has not been universally accepted by Defoe scholars. Some have disputed their de-attributions, individually or in bulk; others have suggested that they did not carry their scepticism far enough.[12] At the

---

[11] Daniel Defoe, *The Works of Daniel Defoe, with a Memoir of his Life and Writings*, 3 vols, ed. William Hazlitt (1840–1), i. 13–17; Maximillian E. Novak, 'Daniel Defoe', in *The New Cambridge Bibliography of English Literature*, 5 vols, ed. George Watson (Cambridge: Cambridge University Press, 1971), ii. 880–917; and, among others, J. P. W. Rogers, 'Defoe and *The Immorality of the Priesthood* (1715): An Attribution Reviewed', *PBSA*, 67:3 (1973), 245–53; J. P. W. Rogers, 'A Bibliography of British History (1700–1715): Some Additions and Corrections', *PBSA*, 69:2 (1975), 226–37; Rodney M. Baine, 'Daniel Defoe and Robert Drury's *Journal*', *Texas Studies in Literature and Language*, 16:3 (1974), 479–91; Henry L. Snyder, 'Daniel Defoe, Arthur Maynwaring, Robert Walpole, and Abel Boyer: Some Considerations of Authorship', *HLQ*, 33:2 (1970), 133–54; and J. A. Downie, 'Defoe and *The Advantages of Scotland by an Incorporate Union with England*: An Attribution Reviewed', *PBSA*, 71:4 (1977), 489–93. Rodney Baine sketches the outlines of a more thorough critique of the Defoe canon in 'Chalmers' First Bibliography of Daniel Defoe', *Texas Studies in Literature and Language*, 10:4 (1969), 547–68.

[12] For a good overview of the response to Furbank and Owens's interventions, see Katheleen 'Kit' Kincade, 'The Twenty Years' War: The Defoe Bibliography Controversy', in *Textual Studies and*

centre of these debates lie questions of evidence: what *kind* of evidence can adequately warrant attribution of a work to an author? In the first and second phases of their programme, Furbank and Owens sought to reframe the terms on which the Defoe canon was discussed. 'De-attribution', as they handle it, does not necessarily imply an affirmative conclusion that Defoe did *not* write the work in question, but rather a judgement that no adequate grounds had been advanced for believing that he *did*. As such, they do not see the burden of argument as lying on them to *disprove* Defoe's authorship of any given work (still less to provide an alternative candidate). Instead, the challenge they present to Defoe bibliography is to call for better-supported arguments *for* a disputed work's inclusion in the Defoe canon, if any are to be had.

At the same time, Furbank and Owens sought to change perceptions of the kind of evidence that should be considered admissible for questions of attribution, or at least to change the weight given to different kinds of evidence. They accord a categorically higher value to external evidence of a work's authorship. External evidence can take different forms: from a title-page statement, to Defoe's avowal of his authorship either publicly or privately (they turn to his correspondence with Harley for affirmations of the authorship of many pamphlets), to the testimony of a contemporary or near contemporary. As they demonstrate in *The Canonisation of Daniel Defoe*, many works came to be attributed to Defoe largely on the basis of scholars' intuitions that they had detected his hand in the works they were reading, based on 'internal' evidence found in the text itself—stylistic tics; allusions to other works known (or thought) to be Defoe's; congruity with views Defoe expressed elsewhere; and so on. Furbank and Owens do not discount such evidence entirely, but they note that its detection can be highly subjective and impressionistic. Furthermore, as Rodney Baine had cautioned in questioning some of Moore's attributions, the larger the body of work that is considered Defoe's, the more likely it becomes that stylistic parallels or phrasal echoes could be found in *any* piece of writing from the period.[13] Furbank and Owens thus make a point in their *Critical Bibliography* not to admit any work as 'certainly' by Defoe on the basis of internal evidence alone, and to avoid relying on any work that is not a 'certain' attribution as a source of parallels for arguments based on internal evidence. Where there is at least the 'smallest scrap' of external evidence, they are willing to entertain further argument on the basis of internal evidence; but they are not prepared to accept any attribution as more than 'probable' without some piece of external evidence.

Furbank and Owens's emphasis on external evidence is the nub of much of the debate surrounding their work. On the one hand, Novak argues that insisting on external evidence—whose survival is, by its nature, unlikely—entails rejecting many works that critically astute readers have been persuaded are Defoe's.[14] On the other hand, Furbank

---

the Enlarged Eighteenth Century: Precision as Profusion, ed. Kevin L. Cope and Robert C. Leitz III (New York: AMS Press, 2012), 133–68.

[13] Baine, 'Daniel Defoe and Robert Drury's *Journal*', 484.

[14] See, for instance, Maximillian Novak, 'Defoe's Role in the *Weekly Journal*: Gesture and Rhetoric, Archive and Canon, and the Uses of Literary History in Attribution', *Studies in Philology*, 113:3 (2016), 694–711 (703).

and Owens have been faulted for not always holding to their own insistence on external evidence. In several entries in *Defoe De-Attributions*, for example, they are not content simply to point out the absence of external evidence *for* Defoe's authorship, but feel compelled to adduce the internal evidence of a work's badness (or, they would insist, the *variety* of its badness) as an argument *against* Defoe's authorship.[15] Their privileging of external evidence also opens up the troubling possibility of giving greater weight to problematic external evidence (simply because it is external) than to highly plausible internal evidence—a possibility they have sought to walk back in subsequent work.[16]

UNINTENDED CONSEQUENCES: REVISITING *MOLL FLANDERS* AND *ROXANA*

Paradoxically, Furbank and Owens's efforts at retrenching the canon to a smaller but more solidly established list of works 'known' to be Defoe's have in some cases created uncertainty where there had been little before. Perhaps the most consequential question raised by Furbank and Owens's scrutiny of the Defoe canon lies, ironically enough, with works whose attribution they did *not* dispute, but whose status is inevitably (if inadvertently) unsettled by the logic of their critique—namely, some of the 'major' novels, particularly *Moll Flanders* and *Roxana* (1724). As Novak noted in a brief review of *The Canonisation of Daniel Defoe*, privileging external evidence over internal (and, particularly, stylistic) evidence for questions of attribution raises problems for the ascription of *any* of the novels commonly thought to be Defoe's.[17] Given the brevity of the review form, Novak does not fully unpack that observation, but we can note that none of the novels appeared with Defoe's name on the title-page (understandably so, since they all purport to be genuine first-person narratives). While Charles Gildon named him as the author of *Robinson Crusoe* in a hostile pamphlet shortly after publication, Defoe never confirmed or denied his authorship.[18] A 1738 edition of *Colonel Jack* (1722) carried Defoe's name a few years after his death, and Robert Shiells included *A Journal of the Plague Year* (1722) in the list of Defoe's works given in his 1753 *Lives of the Poets*, but the other novels mostly were not published with Defoe's name until decades later, in editions published by Francis Noble.

---

[15] See, for example, P. N. Furbank and W. F. Owens, *Defoe De-Attributions: A Critique of J. R. Moore's 'Checklist'* (London: Hambledon, 1994), 4, 11–12, 15–16, 20, and 22, to name a few. For a discussion of the problem of relying on literary critical evaluation for questions of attribution, see Nicholas Seager, 'Literary Evaluation and Authorship Attribution, or Defoe's Politics at the Hanoverian Succession', *HLQ*, 80:1 (2017), 47–69.

[16] P. N. Furbank and W. R. Owens, 'On the Attribution of Novels to Daniel Defoe', *PQ*, 89:2–3 (2010), 243–53, discussed below.

[17] Maximillian E. Novak, 'Review of *The Canonisation of Daniel Defoe*', *ECF*, 1:2 (1989), 147–9 (148).

[18] Charles Gildon, *The Life and Strange Surprizing Adventures of Mr. D[aniel] de F[oe]* (1719).

Furbank and Owens address these publication circumstances in a response to Novak's review and in a longer subsequent article. It is ultimately due to the testimony of Noble, they acknowledge, that Defoe 'came to be popularly thought of as a novelist' at all.[19] Restating their premise that there must be at least 'some scrap of external evidence' for an attribution to be entertained as certain, Furbank and Owens argue that an attribution made 'within a few decades of his death' must be recognized as external evidence of the same sort as an attribution made during the author's lifetime, since 'it is always possible that it might reflect some living memory or first-hand tradition'. They explain that they consider all attributions made before the publication of Chalmers' 1790 list as valid (though not necessarily dispositive) external evidence and note that 'on this basis the ascriptions of Francis Noble, for all the shadiness of his character, would qualify'.[20] Furbank and Owens maintained this position in their subsequent *Critical Bibliography*, and most of the novels first published under Defoe's name by Noble—*Moll Flanders*, *Roxana*, and *A New Voyage Round the World* (1724)—stand in their list as certain attributions, though the entries for both *Moll Flanders* and *Roxana* carry the same uneasy remark: 'The attribution by Noble is evidently questionable, but given its date it must count as external evidence'.[21]

By making so explicit Noble's role in the attribution of the novels, however, Furbank and Owens managed to raise more questions than they settled. As they acknowledge in a 2010 essay, several reviewers of their *Critical Bibliography* took note of the means by which the novels were preserved as certain attributions. Tom Keymer noted that defining 'contemporary' as extending to sixty years after Defoe's death seemed to be 'a convenient means of evading the startling logic of their position—which is to question *Moll Flanders* and *Roxana*'.[22] G. A. Starr noted that Furbank and Owens never hang an attribution *entirely* on so tenuous an authority as Noble's, but suggested that there was something troubling about allowing such dubious testimony to fill the role of the external evidence required to push an attribution from 'probable' to 'certain'. In fact, Starr suggests, Furbank and Owens may not have been rigorous enough in policing the 'certain' category.[23] The most forceful interrogation of Furbank and Owens's treatment of the novels has been offered by Ashley Marshall, who urges a still more thorough scepticism than Furbank and Owens. Marshall takes pains to say that her aim is not to *de*-attribute *Moll Flanders* and *Roxana*, but rather to insist on a plainer accounting of their

---

[19] P. N. Furbank and W. R. Owens, 'Reply to Maximillian E. Novak's Review of *The Canonisation of Daniel Defoe*', ECF, 1:3 (1989), 239–40; and P. N. Furbank and W. R. Owens, 'Defoe and Francis Noble', ECF, 4:4 (1992), 301–13.

[20] Furbank and Owens, 'Defoe and Francis Noble', 313.

[21] Furbank and Owens, *Critical Bibliography*, 200, 207.

[22] Tom Keymer, 'Review of P. N. Furbank and W. R. Owens, *A Critical Bibliography of Daniel Defoe*', RES, 50:200 (1999), 533–6 (535).

[23] G. A. Starr, 'Review of P. N. Furbank and W. R. Owens, *A Critical Bibliography of Daniel Defoe*', ECF, 12:4 (2000), 587–8. For Furbank and Owens's responses, see 'On the Attribution of Novels to Daniel Defoe', 253 n. 7.

status. Like Starr, she finds Noble's testimony worryingly insufficient—surely not credible enough to label the novels as 'certainly' Defoe's.[24]

In a response to Marshall's essay, Furbank and Owens detail what they consider to be the internal evidence in support of Defoe's authorship of those novels—something they say they had not felt a pressing need to do for attributions considered 'certain' in their *Critical Bibliography*. While they had always maintained that internal evidence could become persuasive when there is at least some piece of external evidence to warrant its consideration, there is no small irony in Furbank and Owens, of all people, appealing to internal evidence for their vindication of the attribution of the novels. It seems somewhat strained to adduce Noble's testimony (whose credibility they make no pretence of defending) as the decisive scrap of external evidence that warrants giving a hearing to the potentially quite persuasive internal evidence they muster. In an essay in the same volume, Robert Griffin makes the case that Furbank and Owens do not—that Noble's claims to insider knowledge of Defoe's authorship are not so transparently implausible as Marshall suggests. As Griffin demonstrates, Noble's business relationships going back to the 1740s (when he was among the publishers of an edition of *Moll Flanders* without Defoe's name) put him in partnership with booksellers (like Brotherton and Stagg) who had been involved in the publication of early editions of the novels in Defoe's lifetime. Brotherton and Stagg had, themselves, been partners with the bookseller Thomas Warner (one of the original publishers of *Memoirs of a Cavalier* [1720] and *Captain Singleton* [1720], who had known Defoe well enough to help bail him from prison in 1713); and Warner had, in turn, partnered with William Taylor (the original publisher of the *Crusoe* novels).[25]

Novak, who has been sharply critical of Marshall's interrogation of the Defoe canon, has cited Furbank and Owens's and Griffin's responses as decisive refutations of what he sees as her sceptical provocation about *Moll Flanders* and *Roxana*.[26] If the question, however, is (as it is for Marshall) whether we *know* that Defoe wrote *Moll Flanders* and *Roxana*, we cannot answer in the affirmative in the same way that we can for, say, *The True-Born Englishman* (1700/1). Marshall's argument (given fuller scope in a subsequent essay, 'Beyond Furbank and Owens') is that we must face up to the qualitative differences in the states of our knowledge about different works and not proceed as if we know more than we really *know*.[27]

In an early response to Furbank and Owens, Novak suggested, 'Surely no one is so attached to certainty as to trade the great Defoe of modern literary history for the somewhat lively but clearly minor poet and journalist who identified himself as the author of *The True-Born Englishman*'.[28] Marshall argues—I think rightly—that our 'preferences'

---

[24] Ashley Marshall, 'Did Defoe Write *Moll Flanders* and *Roxana*?', *PQ*, 89:2–3 (2010), 209–41.

[25] Robert J. Griffin, 'Did Defoe Write *Roxana*? Does It Matter?', *PQ*, 89:2–3 (2010), 255–62.

[26] Novak, 'Defoe's Role in the *Weekly Journal*', 697–8.

[27] Ashley Marshall, 'Beyond Furbank and Owens: A New Consideration of the Evidence for the "Defoe" Canon', *Studies in Bibliography*, 59 (2015), 131–90.

[28] Maximillian E. Novak, '*A Vindication of the Press* and the Defoe Canon', *SEL*, 27:3 (1987), 399–411 (400).

for one Defoe over another ought not really enter into the matter (though I am not sure we need therefore lump 'the great Defoe of modern literary history' with exploded theories like phlogiston and Ptolemaic astronomy, as she colourfully suggests).[29] If Novak was concerned that Furbank and Owens's approach would leave a greatly diminished, if more certain, Defoe, Marshall cautions in 'Beyond Furbank and Owens' that the Defoe presented in their *Critical Bibliography* is actually far less certain than their rhetoric would suggest,[30]

Marshall concedes that we naturally make certain common-sense evaluations of probability (an ascription to Defoe made by Jacob Tonson seems more trustworthy than one made by Edmund Curll). She calls *Robinson Crusoe* 'a virtually certain ascription', for example, even if the grounds for it are (in her taxonomy) 'contemporary attribution' rather than 'claimed by D[efoe]' or the less-positive 'signed'; and she notes that she is inclined to think Defoe probably did write some of the works for which the evidence is neither especially clear nor strong—her example is *A Letter to Mr. Bisset* (1709).[31] But she warns that we cannot quantify our uncertainty: there is no calculus by which we could say, for instance, that twelve faint textual echoes equal one clear one. Still more than Furbank and Owens, she is leery of the intermediate gradations of 'probably', 'possibly', 'perhaps', and so forth. Her concern with nailing down what we know *for sure* can create the impression of a field divided between 'certain' and 'anything less than certain'.

I do not take Marshall to mean, however, that the only 'Defoe' to be taken seriously is the Defoe of the 'certain' attributions. Rather, she suggests that, beyond that relatively narrow circle, we must venture with caution, weighing the evidence for and against Defoe's authorship of questionable works individually, rather than assuming that any attribution that survived Furbank and Owens's scrutiny to find a place in the *Critical Bibliography* must be a comparatively safe bet. Defoe scholars have, in fact, carried out just this sort of work for particular titles. While there have been no grand archival coups revealing new documentary evidence to settle all doubts, scholars have arrived at new arguments for and against Defoe's authorship of various works, both by reading more deeply in works associated with Defoe's name and by reading more widely in the printed materials of Defoe's day.[32]

---

[29] Marshall, 'Did Defoe Write *Moll Flanders* and *Roxana*?', 233.

[30] Marshall, 'Beyond Furbank and Owens', 155–90.

[31] Marshall, 'Beyond Furbank and Owens', 141, 142. This attribution has since been confirmed: Nicholas Seager, 'Defoe, the Sacheverell Affair, and *A Letter to Mr Bisset* (1709)', *PBSA*, 115:1 (2021), 79–86.

[32] For an example of an argument for reattributing de-attributed works, see Seager, 'Literary Evaluation and Authorship Attribution'. For an argument for shifting an attribution from 'probable' to certain, see Sheldon Rogers, 'Evidence for the Attribution of *Mere Nature Delineated* to Daniel Defoe', *N&Q*, 59:257 (2012), 209. For new attributions of previously un-attributed works based on a combination of internal and external evidence, see James Kelly, 'The Worcester Affair', *RES*, 51:201 (2000), 1–23; G. A. Starr (ed.), *Christianity Not as Old as the Creation: The Last of Defoe's Performances* (London: Pickering and Chatto, 2012); Nicholas Seager, '*The Clause Proposed in the English Parliament to Prevent the French Goods being Imported thro' Scotland* (1707): A New Defoe Attribution', *N&Q*, 66:265 (2019), 83–6. On the other hand, Stephen Bernard decisively de-attributes *A Vindication of the Press* (1718) and attributes it,

Recognizing Defoe's Style

Scrutinizing individual works may yield new arguments, but it is undeniably an arduous process. It is perhaps natural to wish for some other approach that might yield broader insights at less expense of labour. A recurring theme in discussions of Defoe attribution, going back to Boyer's assertion of Defoe's authorship of the *Minutes of the Negotiations of Monsr. Mesnager*, is the possibility that Defoe might be reliably recognized by his style of writing. The history of Defoe attribution is littered with conflicting claims made on the basis of Defoe's style—a work in which one scholar hears Defoe's voice clearly may be rejected by another as plainly un-Defoean. If pronouncements on the basis of readerly judgement are necessarily subjective, however, there has been some speculation that an empirical, statistical examination of patterns of language use in disputed works might shed a different kind of light on questionable cases.

Though 'stylometry' has an uneven track record, the last fifteen years or so have seen what appear to be considerable advances in computer-assisted authorship attribution.[33] Computer scientists seem confident that certain classes of attribution problems are now largely manageable. Assigning the authorship of a disputed piece to one of a small, closed set of candidates, for instance (as is the task with the *Federalist Papers*, which has become a canonical test case for proposed new methods) is something that several researchers have managed to do with high degrees of accuracy using a range of methods. Indeed, problems of literary attribution are seen by some as comparatively pedestrian: attributing a 2,000-word poem to an author for whom we have a verified corpus of tens of thousands of words is not so difficult as determining the authorship of a brief email, Tweet, or text message (problems that are, moreover, far more pressing in forensic settings).[34]

---

instead, to Giles Jacob, by virtue of Jacob's own previously overlooked testimony. 'After Defoe, Before the Dunciad: Giles Jacob and *A Vindication of the Press*', *RES*, 59:241 (2008), 487–507. Maximillian Novak, who has argued against Furbank and Owens's premises concerning the primacy of external over internal evidence, has adduced internal evidence and thematic parallels to Defoe's other works to argue for the reattribution to Defoe of texts de-attributed by Furbank and Owens. '*A Narrative of the Proceedings in France*: Reattributing a De-Attributed Work by Defoe', *PBSA*, 97:1 (2003), 69–80; 'Daniel Defoe and *Applebee's Original Weekly Journal*: An Attempt at Re-Attribution', *ECS*, 45:4 (2012), 585–608. A similar approach arguing for *de-*attribution appears in G. A. Starr, 'Why Defoe Probably Did Not Write *The Apparition of Mrs. Veal*', *ECF*, 15:3–4 (2003), 421–50.

[33] For a survey of early statistical approaches to authorship attribution, see Harold Love, *Authorship Attribution: An Introduction* (Cambridge: Cambridge University Press, 2002), 132–42. For a withering critique of the QSUM method, in particular, see Stephen Karian, 'Authors of the Mind: Some Notes on the QSUM Attribution Theory', *Studies in Bibliography*, 57 (2005–6), 263–86. For an overview of extant computer-assisted approaches, see Patrick Juola, 'Authorship Attribution', *Foundations and Trends in Information Retrieval*, 3:1 (2006), 233–334; and, for a briefer discussion, Efstathios Stamatatos, 'A Survey of Modern Authorship Attribution Methods', *Journal of the American Society for Information Science and Technology*, 60:3 (2009), 538–56.

[34] See, for example, Kim Luyckx and Walter Daelememans, 'The Effect of Author Set Size and Data Size in Authorship Attribution', *Literary and Linguistic Computing*, 26:1 (2011), 35–55.

What is likely to be discomfiting to literary critics, however, is that these methods seem to achieve surprisingly high rates of success despite taking what may seem like rather crude approaches to the texts they study. John Burrows's 'Delta' procedure, to take one conspicuous example, compares the relative frequency of the most-used words in a particular text against their frequency in a larger comparison corpus in order to calculate the text's 'mean divergence' from the corpus as a whole. Works by the same author tend to score similarly, and thus cluster together when plotted on a graph.[35] Burrows's Delta takes what is known as a 'bag-of-words' approach: it treats texts as collections of words to be counted, and so is indifferent to questions of word choice, syntax, figuration, allusion, and so forth. What is more, in the study used to test the Delta procedure, Burrows used only the 150 most frequently used words, a list which consists almost entirely of so-called function words ('the', 'of', 'to', 'and', and so on). In short, Burrows's Delta does not attend to most of the things that most people who read or write would think of as constituting a writer's 'style'.

And yet, in tests on a group of 200 Restoration poems by twenty-five authors (well beyond the complexity of the *Federalist Papers* problem), Burrows's Delta identified the correct author as the most likely candidate 47% of the time, identified the correct author as either the most or the second most likely candidate 59% of the time, and placed the correct author within the top five candidates almost 79% of the time. These may not seem like especially impressive results at first, but, as Burrows notes, a random distribution of 200 poems among twenty-five authors would correctly assign any given poem to its actual author only 4% of the time. (It should also be noted that the Delta procedure proved more reliable with longer works, achieving 95% accuracy for works of more than 2,000 words.) Just as important, Delta was seldom badly wrong: the correct author was placed lower than twenty-first less than 2% of the time, where a random distribution would have placed the correct author in the bottom quintile of choices 20% of the time. Despite relying on a fairly simple measure like the relative frequency of function words, then, Burrows's Delta seems to get at some genuinely authorial trace. Burrows does not present Delta as anything like the final word in authorship attribution (indeed, it is not even his own last word on the matter).[36] The advance that Delta represents over earlier approaches, Burrows notes, lies in its ability to cope with larger groups of candidate authors: it can serve, at the very least, to identify a list of most likely candidates from a wider field for further, closer testing.

This, some might object, may all be very well in practice, but how does it work in theory? The answer is, apparently, somewhat murky. In examining Burrows's Delta

---

[35] For Burrows's initial description of his Delta method, see John Burrows, '"Delta": A Measure of Stylistic Difference and a Guide to Likely Authorship', *Literary and Linguistic Computing*, 17:3 (2002), 267–87. For a cautionary critique of the potential for misinterpretation of such results (applied to a successor method to Delta), see Pervez Rizvi, 'The Interpretation of Zeta Test Results', *Digital Scholarship in the Humanities*, 34:2 (2018), 401–18.

[36] See, for instance, John Burrows, 'All the Way Through: Testing for Authorship in Different Frequency Strata', *Literary and Linguistic Computing*, 22:1 (2007), 27–47.

closely, Shlomo Argamon detected a conceptual mismatch between Burrows's method for normalizing word frequencies, on the one hand, and the method he used for measuring distances between a given text and the reference corpus, on the other. Curiously, however, the revisions that Argamon proposed to address this theoretical problem actually produced *worse* results in the empirical tests performed by Stefan Evert and his collaborators than did Burrows's original Delta method.[37] Other scholars have proposed adjustments to Delta that do show improved robustness in these empirical tests, but, as Evert et al. note, 'There is almost no other algorithm in stylometry that has been used as much as Delta and still there is no theoretical framework to explain its success'.[38]

I have singled out Burrows's Delta because it has been conspicuous for empirically verifiable success in correctly assigning texts to their authors, but other scholars have pursued other leads with similar success. Some have attended to units larger than the word by examining the frequencies of word collocations or of certain syntactic patterns (an approach that seems, intuitively, as if it would be well suited to recognizing examples of Defoe's 'long-winded, spinning Way of Writing' if it is actually as distinctive as many have felt). Some have attended to units not defined by the word at all, as is the case with character *n*-grams (strings of, say, six characters, irrespective of word boundaries: the 6-grams of 'character n-grams', for example, would be 'charac', 'haract', 'aracte', and so on).[39] The idea that attending to strings of characters—a phenomenon seemingly below the threshold of word choice—could reveal a text's authorship is perhaps difficult to come to grips with, even if it seems, empirically, to work. As Harold Love notes, experimentally rigorous efforts in computer-assisted stylistic analysis really do seem to be measuring 'the *effects* of the workings of language', but they have not yet been convincingly tied to an account of the workings of language, themselves.[40]

Even in the absence of such an account, however, the appeal of such methods for the study of works of unknown or contested authorship is considerable. As Love suggests, given the paucity of external evidence for the authorship of many works, the results of stylometric analysis may well be 'by far the best evidence we have'.[41] Furbank and Owens express scepticism about the potential of computer-assisted stylometric analysis to resolve the questions that surround Defoe attribution, as does Marshall.[42] I am more inclined to think, with Love, that such analysis could well shed light on at least certain problems. Much recent work in attribution cautions that results are clearest when we compare texts from the same period and the same genre: features that reliably distinguish the authorship of poems might not carry over to prose; an author's style might

---

[37] Stefan Evert et al., 'Understanding and Explaining Delta Measures for Authorship Attribution', *Digital Scholarship in the Humanities*, 32:supplement 2 (2017), ii4–16 (ii6–8).
[38] Evert et al., 'Understanding and Explaining Delta Measures', ii8.
[39] Stamatatos, 'Survey of Authorship Attribution Methods', 6–9.
[40] Love, *Attributing Authorship*, 158, 160–1. Italics mine.
[41] Love, *Attributing Authorship*, 161, 162.
[42] Furbank and Owens, *Canonisation*, 176–83; *Defoe De-Attributions*, xxxiii–xxxiv; Marshall, 'Beyond Furbank and Owens', 147–9.

change enough over time to make detecting common authorship of texts from different ends of an author's career difficult. It may be that we can never arrive at a single, generalizable 'fingerprint' that would allow us to know Defoe wherever we might see him; but smaller-scale successes might be within reach. Determining the authorship of the welter of early eighteenth-century anonymous pamphlets is a daunting task, but stylometric analysis might give us some further insight into Boyer's charges, for instance. Similarly, the body of early eighteenth-century English prose fiction is perhaps small enough (McBurney's *Check List* shows eighty distinct titles published between 1715 and 1725), and with enough texts of known authorship (by Manley, Haywood, Aubin, and others), that we might have some hopes of making headway with *Moll Flanders* and *Roxana* (both published within five years of *Robinson Crusoe*).[43] The phrase 'computer-assisted' can conjure visions of light work and quick answers that it is important to dispel: though a computer can *process* text at great speed, considerable transcription and editing work is needed to prepare a suitable corpus for that processing.[44] It is also important to bear in mind the nature of the answers that such methods could yield, which are not necessarily so unequivocal as we might wish they could be.

In calling for a thorough re-examination of the Defoe canon, Rodney Baine entertained the possibility that a computer-assisted analysis might settle otherwise insoluble problems:

> If Defoe studies are to progress on any firm foundation, the whole canon must be carefully re-examined for authorship, and stricter tests must be demanded for the determination of those items which can be unhesitatingly ascribed to Defoe. Defoe scholars must then recognize the large area of uncertainty—the scores of items which may have been written by Defoe but for which there is quite inadequate evidence to constitute certitude—unless Professor Edward L. McAdam demonstrates that the I.B.M. computer can infallibly detect Defoe's style.[45]

There is perhaps a note of scepticism here, but Baine holds out a tempting prospect: a computer delivering certitude otherwise beyond the reach of human readers. Even a carefully done stylometric analysis, however, could not deliver absolute certitude: by its nature, stylometric evidence for or against Defoe's authorship of a work could only ever be probabilistic. If a measure based on certain linguistic features was found to correctly

---

[43] William H. McBurney, *A Check List of English Prose Fiction* (Cambridge, MA: Harvard University Press, 1960).

[44] For a cautionary discussion of the requisite textual work, see Joseph Rudman, 'Unediting, De-Editing, and Editing in Non-Traditional Authorship Attribution Studies: With an Emphasis on the Canon of Daniel Defoe', *PBSA*, 99:1 (2005), 5–36.

[45] Baine, 'Chalmers' First Bibliography of Defoe', 567–8. Baine cited a *New York Times* article describing work being done at New York University's Institute for Computer Research in the Humanities, which mentions that McAdam was investigating whether Defoe was the author of 'about 100 anonymous articles for British political journals at the turn of the 18th century'. Thomas O'Toole, 'Erudite I.B.M. 360 Helping Scholars', *New York Times*, 20 February 1966, 26. Whatever the results, McAdam does not appear ever to have published on this topic.

discriminate works known to be by Defoe from works in a training corpus known to be by other authors, say, 90% of the time or more, and if that rate were to hold when applied to other texts of verifiable authorship in a separate test corpus, then we would know with what confidence we might bring that measurement to bear in testing a work of genuinely unknown authorship. But the probabilistic character of such an attribution would always have to be borne in mind: there would always be about a 10% chance of being wrong—and that does not mean being 'about 10% wrong', but rather being 100% wrong about 10% of the time.

Such uncertainty might give us pause. It is certainly far from the picture of infallibility limned in Baine's closing formula. But it might be preferable to our current predicament, in which, as Marshall suggests, 'We can take the *nature* of the dubiety into account, but not the *degree*. ... We cannot afford *not* to distinguish among degrees of probability—but neither can we sanely pretend that the differences are measurable.'[46] Being able to articulate explicitly the degree of uncertainty would offer a relative measurement of the probability or improbability of different attributions. Even if it cannot yield perfect certitude, such information might well bolster—or qualify—our sense of the likelihood that Defoe wrote particular works, especially when laid alongside other kinds of evidence.

Conclusion

It is perhaps well, however, to ask why we care so much about establishing what Defoe did and did not write. For some, the question will seem preposterous, because the answer will seem self-evident: it is only by clarifying the authorship of the disputed works that we can come to a true estimation of 'Defoe's oeuvre' (the phrase with which I began). If what we are interested in is 'the great Defoe of modern literary history', then an incorrect attribution of a mediocre work unfairly dilutes Defoe's greatness, while an incorrect de-attribution of a great work unjustly denies him his due. Even if we are less invested in questions of literary greatness, we do tend to want to understand who was writing what in the periods we study. If our interest is in Defoe the political writer, for instance, then surely it matters which pamphlets and periodicals he wrote—it makes a difference not just to our sense of Defoe as an individual author, but also to our sense of the broader terrain of political argument whether Defoe was really salting the Tory press with weak arguments (as he claimed to Delafaye) or not.

We should recognize, however, the extent to which our desire to reconstruct a picture of the Defoe canon is at odds with the practices of eighteenth-century publishing, generally (in which anonymity and pseudonymity were widespread), and with Defoe's approach to publication specifically: we are, after all, seeking to detect his authorship

---

[46] Marshall, 'Beyond Furbank and Owens', 138–9.

where he sought to conceal it. We have our own reasons for wanting to do so, and I do not expect that we will give over the effort any time soon. But we would do well to bear in mind that they are our own reasons, and not ones necessarily shared by Defoe or his contemporaries. If we are to understand Defoe's oeuvre, it is not enough to single out for attention the works that we believe to be by Defoe, with varying degrees of certainty. Rather, we must read those texts alongside and in dialogue with the mass of texts of unknown and unknowable authorship—and this is true whether we wish to approach the question computationally (in which case we need a broad corpus against which to test hypotheses) or with traditional methods of historical and bibliographical scholarship. With Defoe, to an unusual degree, I would argue, we cannot neatly isolate figure from ground, but must, rather, read these works—acknowledged, attributed, repudiated, and simply anonymous—as part of a larger texture of eighteenth-century print.

Further Reading

P. N. Furbank and W. R. Owens, *The Canonisation of Daniel Defoe* (New Haven, CT: Yale University Press, 1988).

P. N. Furbank and W. R. Owens, *A Critical Bibliography of Daniel Defoe* (London: Pickering and Chatto, 1998).

P. N. Furbank and W. R. Owens, *Defoe De-Attributions: A Critique of J. R. Moore's 'Checklist'* (London: Hambledon, 1994).

P. N. Furbank and W. R. Owens, 'On the Attribution of Novels to Daniel Defoe', *PQ*, 89:2–3 (2010), 243–53.

P. N. Furbank and W. R. Owens, 'On the Attribution of Periodicals and Newspapers to Daniel Defoe', *Publishing History*, 40 (1996), 83–98.

Katheleen 'Kit' Kincade, 'The Twenty Years' War: The Defoe Bibliography Controversy', in *Textual Studies and the Enlarged Eighteenth Century: Precision as Profusion*, ed. Kevin L. Cope and Robert C. Leitz III (New York: AMS Press, 2012), 133–68.

Ashley Marshall, 'Beyond Furbank and Owens: A New Consideration of the Evidence for the "Defoe" Canon', *Studies in Bibliography*, 59 (2015), 131–90.

Ashley Marshall, 'Did Defoe Write *Moll Flanders* and *Roxana*?', *PQ*, 89:2–3 (2010), 209–41.

John Robert Moore, *A Checklist of the Writings of Daniel Defoe*, 2nd ed. (Hamden, CT: Archon Books, 1971).

Maximillian Novak, 'Defoe's Role in the *Weekly Journal*: Gesture and Rhetoric, Archive and Canon, and the Uses of Literary History in Attribution', *Studies in Philology*, 113:3 (2016), 694–711.

Nicholas Seager, 'Literary Evaluation and Authorship Attribution, or Defoe's Politics at the Hanoverian Succession', *HLQ*, 80:1 (2017), 47–69.

CHAPTER 35

HABITS OF GENDER AND GENRE IN THREE FEMALE ROBINSONADES, 1767–1985

RIVKA SWENSON

The eponymous hero of *Robinson Crusoe*[1] has often been touted as an Everyman. Samuel Taylor Coleridge, for instance, exalted Crusoe as 'the universal representative, the person, for whom every reader could substitute himself'; Coleridge saw in Crusoe the face of 'humanity in general', a human emblem 'who can make me forget my specific class, character, and circumstances, and ... raise me while I read him, into the universal man'.[2] In truth, the colonial manner in which Crusoe apprehends the world is predicated on his specific sociological identity as a white, English, Protestant, able-bodied, putatively straight man [SEE CHAPTER 29]. Pace Coleridge, it actually seems impossible that Crusoe could be anything other than what he is. Nevertheless, despite or because of the systemic limitations embodied by *Robinson Crusoe* itself, the Robinsonade microgenre has been continuously defined and refreshed by the adaptive appropriations of non-traditional Crusoe figures.

What kinds of characters can don the generic mantle of 'Crusoe'?[3] Whose stories can the Robinsonade give voice to, and how? Unca Eliza Winkfield's early 'female

---

[1] The edition I reference in this essay is Daniel Defoe, *Robinson Crusoe* (1719), ed. John Richetti (London: Penguin Books, 2001).

[2] Samuel Taylor Coleridge, 'Lecture XI', in *The Complete Works of Samuel Taylor Coleridge*, 7 vols, ed. James Marsh and W. G. T. Shedd (New York: Harper & Brothers Publishing, 1853), i. 309–19, 316, 311, 312.

[3] For recent and general critical approaches to the literary Robinsonade stimulated by the tercentenary of Defoe's novel, see Jakub Lipski (ed.), *Rewriting Crusoe: The Robinsonade Across Languages, Cultures, and Media* (Lewisburg, PA: Bucknell University Press, 2020); Emmanuelle Peraldo (ed.), *300 Years of Robinsonades* (Newcastle-upon-Tyne: Cambridge Scholars Press, 2020); Andreas K. E. Mueller and Glynis Ridley (eds), *Robinson Crusoe after 300 Years* (Lewisburg, PA: Bucknell University Press, 2021).

Robinsonade' *The Female American* (1767) inaugurates a prominent strand of novelistic Crusoean descendants that explores what happens if the Crusoe figure is a woman.[4] Among these, we see the coevolution of two conventions that have been fundamental to the microgenre since its inception. First, the metafictional convention: Crusoe is nothing if not a self-aware storyteller and writer who composes his life story (the story of the island, the story of tending the goats, the story of Englishness) *as* a 'story' (for example, 175, 218) that, in the process of being told to others (Friday, the European newcomers, us), is organized and transformed from a 'collection of wonders' into a 'chain of wonders' (203, 215).[5] Second, the expression of this metafictional convention by way of sartorial and architectural allegory,[6] such that the power of linguistic and generic command is concretized by the trappings of physical dress, broadly imagined, from immediate bodily habits (clothing, accessories) to the body-sheltering metonyms of habitation (a gigantic hollow idol, a human-shaped island traversable by tunnel, an island-like house). Amid the array of modern novelistic novels that follow *The Female American* in using sartorial allegory to illustrate the challenges to generic habits that are posed by alternative Crusoe figures, Muriel Spark's *Robinson* (1958)[7] and Jane Gardam's *Crusoe's Daughter* (1985)[8] stand out for their depiction of female Crusoes who press upon the microgenre's seams in order to alter and revivify the Robinsonade's sartorial and architectural habits from the inside out in a strong tradition of ongoing self-remediation.

---

[4] Unca Eliza Winkfield (pseud.), *The Female American* (1767), ed. Michelle Burnham (Peterborough, ON: Broadview Press, 2000). The term 'female Robinsonade' comes from Jeanine Blackwell, 'An Island of Her Own: Heroines of the German Robinsonades from 1720–1800', *The German Quarterly*, 58:1 (1985), 5–26. A few studies since then have considered the phenomenon of the female Robinsonade: C. M. Owen, *The Female Crusoe: Female Hybridity, Trade, and the Eighteenth-Century Individual* (Amsterdam: Rodopi, 2010); Michelle J. Smith, 'Nineteenth-Century Female Crusoes: Rewriting the Robinsonade for Girls', in *Victorian Settler Narratives: Emigrants, Cosmopolitans and Returnees in Nineteenth-Century Literature*, ed. Tamara S. Wagner (London: Pickering & Chatto, 2011), 165–76; Terri Doughty, 'Deflecting the Marriage Plot', in *Colonial Girlhood in Literature, Culture, and History, 1840–1950*, ed. K. Moruzi and M. J. Smith (Basingstoke: Palgrave Macmillan, 2014), 60–78; Thomas Farr, '19th-Century English Girls' Adventure Stories: Domestic Imperialism, Agency, and the Female Robinsonades', *Rocky Mountain Review*, 68:2 (2014), 142–58; Christopher Palmer, *Castaway Tales: From Robinson Crusoe to Life of Pi* (Middletown, CT: Wesleyan University Press, 2016); Rebecca Hightower-Weaver, *Empire Islands: Castaways, Cannibals, and Fantasies of Conquest* (Minneapolis, MN: University of Minnesota Press, 2007).

[5] See my '*Robinson Crusoe* and the Form of the New Novel', in *The Cambridge Companion to Robinson Crusoe*, ed. John Richetti (Cambridge: Cambridge University Press, 2018), 16–31.

[6] See Chloe Wigston Smith, *Women, Work, and Clothes in the Eighteenth-Century Novel* (Cambridge: Cambridge University Press, 2013), for the deployment of sartorial cum writerly metaphors within numerous other literary texts during the period.

[7] Muriel Spark, *Robinson* (New York: New Directions Publishing, 2003).

[8] Jane Gardam, *Crusoe's Daughter* (New York: Europa Editions, 2012).

'Dressed in My New Habit': Mantling Authority in Defoe's *Crusoe*

Neither the metafictional component of Robinsonades nor its manifestation as 'dress' are surprising, considering the microgenre's Crusoean roots. *Robinson Crusoe* itself is explicitly metafictional, displaying from start to finish its writerly protagonist's overt concerns with how-to-tell-his-story and how-to-use-his-story. At key moments, Crusoe's linguistic authority is instantiated by, and finds metaphor in, aspects of adornment. For example, when Crusoe dresses Friday in the trappings (sartorial and otherwise) of Protestant Englishness, or when Crusoe later approaches the island's European newcomers under the guise of 'Governour' (211), a role that is enabled by splendid 'new habit[s]' (216) that signal both his fictional authority as the island's faux-governor and his fiction-making authority as its genius loci while he leads his new subjects into the intricacies of both his story and his literal habitation.

Crusoe's process of bringing Friday into his purview easily marries together the co-constitutive metafictional elements of language and dress. Crusoe, after interpretively glossing the nude body of the sleeping man with an excess of sensuous description, immediately proceeds both to rename and clothe the islander when the latter awakes. 'I let him know his name should be *Friday*', reports Crusoe, introducing himself simply as '*Master*' (163). The mantling of Friday (the dismantling of his previous self, the enfolding of his story within Crusoe's own story), is accompanied by Crusoe literally clothing him: 'I let him know I would give him some clothes; at which he seemed very glad, for he was stark naked' (163). The trimmings of language, custom, and culture follow in kind, and, by and large, Friday is formed into a fresh fiction that bears Crusoe's imprint easily.

Having dressed Friday in the literal and figurative paraphernalia of Englishness, Crusoe is presented with a new storytelling challenge when Europeans alight on shore and need to be convinced that they are on 'an [e]nchanted island' (209). The frightened sailors, who fear they have entered a place ruled 'by devils or spirits', threaten mutiny against their captain (211). Sober-headed Englishman Will Atkins saves the day by telling them the island has an English governor—Crusoe. Crusoe admires the lie, for, 'although it was but a fiction, it had its desired effect' (215). Empowered now by the fabric of fiction to 'g[i]ve them every part of my own story' (218), Crusoe is furthered empowered by a gift from the captain: new clothes. Having already conjured the spirit of his own submerged Englishness from under layers of 'Mahometan' whiskers and animal skins while captivating Friday, Crusoe is now outfitted perfectly for his new role, with a powerful arsenal of 'six new clean shirts, six very good neckclothes, one pair of shoes, a hat, and one pair of stockings' (215–16). Crusoe thus is dually mantled by story and dress to speak as governor, as Atkins' lie becomes reality: 'I came thither dressed in my new habit; and now I was call'd Governour' (216). In his 'very good suit of clothes' (215), bearing the concomitant gift of a tale he has had ample time to develop and refine, Crusoe 'let[s] them in to the story' (218) just as he lets them into the 'winding passage' of his 'amazing' habitation (203), and thus makes them, in this way, into his subjects and heirs.

'Sacred Vestments': Entering the Idol in Winkfield's *The Female American*

Winkfield's *Female American*, published just two generations after *Robinson Crusoe*, expands on and deepens Defoe's sartorial metaphors to include other kinds of material spaces while tailoring the Robinsonade's generic fit for a female Crusoe; for heroine (and pseudonymous author) Unca Eliza Winkfield, the result is empowering, if untenable. Unca not only learns to appropriate the material history of the dead (as instantiated by the 'sacred vestments' of their golden clothing and jewellery, which she steals from tombs [79]), she also achieves a bounded authorial agency by entering the architectural fabric of a larger-than-life gold idol in order to assume the guise of the Oracle of the Sun; under cover of this enabling carapace, she preaches to the Indians about female equality.[9] If the very term 'female Robinsonade' would seem to be a contradiction in terms, Winkfield nevertheless imagines a heroine with the power to claim the means of linguistic reproduction and fruitfully transform the generic-sartorial relics she encounters.

The Female American's writerly protagonist tests the confines of the Robinsonade microgenre both overtly and covertly. Unca opens the first chapter by emphasizing that her narrative stretches generic limits because she is a woman: her story contains 'experience' that is rare for women, indeed her experience resembles that 'of men' (35). Except, of course, where it does not. Notably, for instance, the act of rebellion that lands her on the island is different from Crusoe's: Unca finds herself on the island because she refuses to wed the son of the ship's captain, her property is stolen, and she is cast away. No wonder her deepest fear, when she achieves the shore, is neither of beasts nor cannibals, but simply of 'fall[ing] into the hands of man' (56). Unca's story *is* unusual in obvious and less obvious ways. Thus she declares the story, with its quasi-anti-generic genesis, 'more wonderful, strange, and uncommon' than any of its kind (35).

At the same time, *The Female American* highlights the difficulties of transforming tradition from within. In *Robinson Crusoe*, the hero spends most of his time either reforming things substantially, or, more often, making them outright, from clay pots to chairs. Upon coming to the island, Unca, who has wandered into an extant genre,

---

[9] See relevant scholarship: Kristianne Kalata Vaccaro, '"Recollection … sets my busy imagination to work": Transatlantic Self-Narration, Performance, and Reception in *The Female American*', *ECF*, 20:2 (2007-8), 127–50; Mary Helen McMurran, 'Realism and the Unreal in *The Female American*', *The Eighteenth Century: Theory and Interpretation*, 52:3-4 (2011), 323–42; ;Mary Helen McMurran, 'Collecting and Collected: Native American Subjectivity and Transatlantic Transactions in *The Female American*', *Early American Literature*, 54:1 (2019), 37–68; Betty Joseph, 'Re(playing) Crusoe/Pocahontas: Circum-Atlantic Stagings in *The Female American*', *Criticism*, 42:3 (2000), 317–35.

initially finds that there is nothing for her to invent or build or do: in tangible terms, there is a furnished hut, built by the island's previous inhabitant (whom she dubs the Hermit). Inside the hut are useful items that further serve to emblematize Unca's passive status as an inheritor rather than a creator: a written manuscript; some pre-made food and drink. The manuscript is filled with hundreds of pages of the Hermit's instructions about how to manage island life, milk the goats, and so forth. Upon first entering the hut, Unca eats from an old 'heap of Indian roots', and she proceeds to drink from a shell that contains stale water and another that holds old fermented grape juice 'grown strong with standing' (58, 59). The hut's contents are ample, but not savoury or fresh. This is the stuff of established genre, it seems. What is a heroine, thus provided, to do for herself?[10] She need neither make nor remake (unlike Peter Longueville's talented pickle-making, taxidermist-hero Philip Quarll in the highly popular and widely printed Robinsonade *The Hermit* [1727]);[11] instead, she simply follows the wisdom of the manuscript in learning how to milk the goats, and so forth.

Before long, however, Unca is roused by necessity from passive deference to the authority of the absent but seminal spirit of the place. She grows mysteriously ill, and, plunging her fevered body into the river, she then proceeds to suckle directly from a she-goat: 'I made shift to creep softly to her, and sucked her dugs, which she happily permitted' (67). With this action, Unca bypasses the manuscript's generic inertia and is healed; enabled to violently purge the remnants of her sickness, she discovers that her 'fever was now quite gone' (67). With this shift, no more mention is made of the Hermit's ur-text, and Unca begins exploring the island.

Going forwards, Unca endeavours to reauthorize the extant features of the island by placing herself at the centre. First, upon finding tombs filled with mummies whose wrappings bear 'Indian characters' that describe the deceased as 'priests of the sun' (74), Unca avails herself of their 'sacred vestments ... formed of gold wire, or rather of narrow plated gold curiously folded, or twisted together like net work' (79). She recontextualizes herself, adorning herself with masses of gold wrappings, coronets, bracelets, rings, an action that is consonant with her efforts to remaster an island and a genre from within.

Powerfully costumed, Unca is poised not only to enter but to possess the larger-than-life gold idol of genre itself, to become the 'Oracle of the Sun' and achieve the linguistic command of a Crusoe. The architecture of the idol is 'wonderfully constructed', with excellent 'mechanics', an awesome raiment that gives its inhabitant a limited, if untenable authority. She reports of her literal ascent into the gold carapace,

---

[10] See Laura Stevens, 'Reading the Hermit's Manuscript: *The Female American* and Female Robinsonades', in *Approaches to Teaching Defoe's Robinson Crusoe*, ed. Carl Fisher and Maximillian E. Novak (New York: Modern Language Association, 2005), 140–51.

[11] Peter Longueville, *The Hermit: Or, the Unparalled Sufferings and Surprising Adventures of Mr. Philip Quarll, an Englishman* (1727). See my "'Mushrooms, Capers, and other sorts of Pickles": Remaking Genre in Peter Longueville's *The Hermit*', in Lipski (ed.), *Rewriting Crusoe*, 9–22.

another flight of stairs ... led me up into the image of the sun. At last I got quite into the body of it, and my head within the head of it. There were holes through the mouth, eyes, nose, and ears of it; so that I could distinctly see all over the island before me, of which the height I was at gave me a great command. (80)

Thus Unca, mantled as Oracle, locates within the form of the idol some potential for her own authority. Her body within its body, her head within its head, she asks herself, 'What credentials had I to support the *novel* [emphasis mine] doctrines that I was to introduce? How was I to combat old opinions, handed down from father to son ... ?' (110). Determined to use the idol as its own self-justifying credential and thereby prepare the natives for her own intended eventual leadership over them, Unca-as-Oracle insists to them that 'sometimes women' are sent by 'God' to 'instruct mankind' (111). The natives accept this radical story, and, until her suitor-cousin Mr Winkfield intrudes upon the scene, the authority of the novel female American heroine seems assured.

Alas, Unca's sovereignty does not last. Although she never professes any desire to leave the island, her gendered fate, in the form of a hero (Mr Winkfield), pursues her. As Unca's future fiancé approaches in his ship, the spell begins to fail; Unca becomes constrained by gendered restrictions both internal and external to genre. At first, the enraptured Europeans sound like the Europeans whom Crusoe enchants in his gubernatorial guise; the new arrivals to Unca's island exclaim on the wonders of the '[e]nchanted' place that is filled with 'sweet, but strange ... sounds' (129, 125). Unca strides forth confidently: 'drest in my priestly habits, and with my staff and crown ... I pleased myself much with the surprize they would be in, to see me in a dress of which they could form no expectation, nor conceive the meaning of' (124). But Unca overestimates her power in this dress, this genre, this place. Where Crusoe's European newcomers were soothed by the fiction of his gubernatorial authority, and laid aside their apprehensions of his island as 'an inchanted' stew of 'devils and spirits' (*Crusoe*, 209), Unca is a woman, a woman of colour at that, and, her 'priestly habits' notwithstanding, they see naught but a witch: 'the sailors heard ... the musick from the statue, as the wind blew directly off from the island; this, together with my tawny complexion and strange dress, so terrified them, that they stopped rowing, and would come no nearer' (129). Unable to simply claim authority like Crusoe would, she is seen by her audience as 'that she-devil there, wrapt in gold', indeed 'the devil's wife' (129); the men claim, with some hysteria, that she flies away and leaves 'a terrible stink of brimstone behind' (133). Unca may be a Sycorax (like many Robinsonades, *The Female American* has intertextual connections not only to Defoe's novel, but to William Shakespeare's *The Tempest*), but she is no Prospero, no Crusoe.

The novel's ending, which sees Unca reluctantly sealed in marriage to her English cousin, is a let-down.[12] When Mr Winkfield asks for 'Unca's hand for ever', she puts him off: '"we must land"', she demurs, '"the Indians are waiting for us"' (135). But Mr Winkfield's response to this mild rebuff leaves little doubt that the future will involve

---

[12] In her edition of the novel, Michelle Burnham notes the shift in narrative authority after Mr Winkfield arrives. See Burnham, 'Introduction', in *The Female American*, 9–28 (21).

curbing Unca's tongue, under threat of abuse: 'I saw he was chagrined at this unexpected answer ... when, rising up, I gave him my hand to conduct me on shore, which he squeezed, as if he meant to punish it for the mortification my tongue had given him' (135, 136). This bit of squeezing, this punishment, which foreshadows the marital gift of hand and body, does not bode well. Unca is a woman who has 'fallen into the hands of man' after all (56). Mr Winkfield declares ominously to the crowd that he shall 'spend my days with my dear Unca, whether she will or no' (137). The heroine reports starkly that 'through his constant importunity, I was at last obliged to give up my hand, about two months after his arrival' (140–1). The remainder of the book trails away, as the narrative turns almost entirely to Mr Winkfield's story: his voice literally takes over; meanwhile, Unca becomes 'Mrs Winkfield', and the idol is blown up to prevent additional 'idolatry' (153, 154). A kind of rejection of the genre, or an admission of its untenable tenancy for heroines vis-à-vis the old world's intrusions upon it.

Ultimately, the wrappings of (covert) female authority give way to the trappings of coverture. The subsequent sartorial metaphor that obtains in Mr Winkfield literally redressing the heroine neatly symbolizes the shift: Mr Winkfield, 'as if certain of finding me living, and the naked inhabitant of a desolate island, [had] brought over apparel to me. The linen was very acceptable to me' (140). However, despite this lacklustre denouement, wherein the change in dress signals the narrative turn towards the marriage plot, *The Female American*'s radical refiguring of Crusoean form is undeniable: *in situ*, Unca thrives as the Oracle, and her story, however practically or generically untenable, expands powerfully within the idol of genre to suggest the possibilities that inhere in the female Robinsonade.

'AMONGST THE SALVAGE': POSSESSING THE ISLAND IN SPARK'S *ROBINSON*

Like Winkfield's inaugural female Robinsonade, Spark's *Robinson*, published almost 200 years later, is in part a metafictional and metageneric exploration of the transformative possibilities that are enabled by the introduction of female protagonists. *Robinson*, however overlooked by scholars of the female Robinsonade,[13] is narrated by plane-crash survivor January Marlow, a heroine in the writerly mode of her Crusoean forebears. January's task is, one, to utilize available materials and become master of her own island experience (in this case, her experience of Robinson Island, named for its owner and chief resident, Miles Mary Robinson), and, two, to achieve some authority in relation to the men on the island (Robinson, and two male crash survivors) who implicitly compete with her, in different ways, for dominance over the island, *and*, three, to do all

---

[13] For a recent exception, see Patrick Gill, '"If I Had ... ": Counterfactuals, Imaginary Realities, and the Poetics of the Postmodern Robinsonade', in Lipski (ed.), *Rewriting Crusoe*, 23–36.

of this by way of assuming a certain generic command in fictionalizing her journal into the novel that is *Robinson*. The novel charts January's effort to command the space (real space and fictional space) as a woman; from the start, she describes the island, and implicitly the genre it represents, as bearing a gender-neutral 'human shape' (17): obliquely, then, the default gender of the Robinsonade itself is not masculine. In the process of asserting her mastery over Robinson Island, January both steals clothing from Robinson himself and avails herself of 'the salvage' (128, 166) that washes ashore (the clothes and accoutrements of deceased fellow passengers), before finally entering Robinson Island's tunnelled interior at the book's climax in order to place her journal—the seed of the novel—inside the dress of the island's own body and thus stake a germinal claim from within.

January is initially loathe to utilize the tools of the dead when they wash ashore after the crash: 'It is salvage', she protests, flinging a jacket on the ground 'as if it were teeming with maggots' (30). But when squeamishness about recycling proves counterproductive to establishing authority among the others, she becomes 'callous' and 'free' with it (128). Told sternly by Robinson that 'The salvage is not your property', she evenly replies, 'There was no one to guard the salvage and so I helped myself' (166). And so she does, using a salvaged bathing suit to swim in the lake and making a rosary (in defiance of Robinson's ban against rosaries) out of salvaged beads. January knows well that a 'change of dress' can actually enable a fundamental change of 'mind' (87), whether in the wearer or the observer. Accordingly, she learns to make use of whatever sartorial tools present themselves, salvaged or otherwise (Robinson's raincoat, his green shirt, Jimmie's spotted scarf), repurposes them as she wishes (turning a red cashmere tablecloth into a sari, for example), and takes hold of the space of Robinson Island and the metonym of *Robinson*-the-novel.

Notably, January's arguments with Robinson himself about matters of adornment are corollary to her larger and more unfocused disagreements with him about how to best dress the eponymous body of the island and the pages of *Robinson* itself. The novel is a revision, January says, of the island journal (from the start, she intended to 'later dress [it] up for a novel', in defiance of Robinson's command to 'Stick to facts' [18, 8]). January decorates the truth at will, and ruminates on the joys of fictionalizing, the joys of disguise: 'I greatly missed my make-up', she says, because 'I do not care to go about with nothing on my face so that everyone can see what is written on it' (71). Moreover, January not only delights in the metaphors of dress-up; she finds utility, freedom, power, like Unca before her, in the masquerade: indeed, she 'once attended the Derby disguised as a gipsy' merely to frighten her misogynistic brother-in-law Ian Brodie (94).

If Winkfield's chief metafictional emblem for the microgenre is the gold idol she ascends into, Spark's is the human-shaped island January descends into. Long before January plants her journal within those depths, she establishes the island as an aesthetic object whose ideal appearance she and Robinson (her chief competitor for the role of the novel's primary Crusoe figure) disagree over. January relays that Robinson's lazy approach to the island's management 'offended my aesthetic sense'; he places a mustard field against a blue lake for effect, but refuses to cultivate the island or create 'pattern'

(84). In response, she yearns to take this 'mess' and 'make an art of it' (84); reseeing the island as analogous to and reflective of her own female body, she resonates emotively with 'the mustard field staring at me with its yellow eye, the blue and green lake seeing in me a hard turquoise stone' (174). Where Robinson likes the coolness of meagre ornamentation, the absence of emotional or fleshly things (he is mostly an ascetic), and the spare hardness of 'stick[ing] to facts' (18), January re-dresses the human-shaped island within the bounds of her novel—metonym for that space—as magical, transformative, and brimming with possibility.

Indeed, like the gipsy costume and the salvaged goods, Robinson the island and *Robinson* the novel become a kind of dress that enables January not simply to be herself, but to be more than herself. Confronted throughout by men's opinions (Robinson's, Ian Brodie's, and more) about what women should and should not do, January claims both island and microgenre as spaces that allow her to simultaneously embrace and transcend her gender, much like the symbolic wonder of the impossible cactus that grows from the rock in such a way that it seems 'as if from the plant itself, a small stream' of water gushes forth (63). For Robinson, the island is a place for self-denial (specifically the denial of that which he perceives as female, such as the Marian aspects of Catholicism). For January, by contrast, it is a place to indulge forbidden desires: a 'sweet and dreadful urge towards the moon' that suggests to her how 'the pagan mind runs strong in women at any time, let alone on an island' (8, 9); or the guilty pleasure of not thinking at all about her young son Brian who is back in England; or the knowledge that she could become a murderer and even revel in 'bloody delight' (as she almost does, defending herself in the tunnel from Tom Wells when he stalks her to try to steal her journal) if she had to. January is excited by the island's screaming, sighing volcanic vents, and, undeterred by Robinson's description of the island's caves and tunnels as 'slimy holes in the mountain' (73), she plumbs the depths without his permission, defends herself from Tom Wells in the interior, and exits the cave empty-handed after secreting her journal in a 'hole in the rock' (156). She then returns to England and revises and disguises her memories into the fiction of *Robinson*, thus staking her claim on the island and the microgenre: in her rendering, the Robinsonade is 'a place of the mind' (174), 'both dangerous and lyrical', where 'all things are possible' (175).

'DIFFERENT, BEAUTIFUL CLOTHES': REFRESHING HABITS IN GARDAM'S *CRUSOE'S DAUGHTER*

As its title suggests, but oddly enough considering its absence from studies of the female Robinsonade,[14] *Crusoe's Daughter* is bluntly self-aware of its own unsubtle obsession with dilemmas of inheritance. These dilemmas are concretized by Gardam's novel

[14] A recent exception is Ann Marie Fallon, 'Anti-Crusoes, Alternative Crusoes: Revisions of the Island Story in the Twentieth Century', in *Cambridge Companion to Robinson Crusoe*, ed. Richetti, 207–20.

as the sprawling architectural dress of the 'yellow house by the sea' where heroine Polly Flint's seafaring father casts her away as a young girl to be raised by aunts, and where she remains for the rest of her life. Young Polly, who has read *Robinson Crusoe* a couple of dozen times by the time she is in her early teens, both idolizes Crusoe for what she sees as his competent self-sufficiency and bemoans that the outlines of his experience do not fit her own: simply put, 'things' are 'easier' for him because 'he [is] a man' (52). Consonant with the metageneric Robinsonade tradition, Polly filters her scrutiny of her gendered difference from her titular generic father through a sartorial medium: 'One of the very few mistakes' she sees in *Robinson Crusoe* is the hero's relative lack of concern about 'clothes' (103), about appearance and fit—he has a certain freedom and confidence of the body that eludes her, as 'a girl' (96). She herself is not at home in the world, although she literally and figuratively tries to dress the part. Failing, she maroons herself in the house's toxic confines until middle age, obsessively consuming both whisky and *Robinson Crusoe* (she spends her days single-mindedly transcribing, glossing, colour-coding, and studying the novel). Where Crusoe built a massive fence to protect himself from the world, Polly has *Crusoe*. She inhabits, imbibes, and transcribes until she is in her forties, trying to appropriate what she views as Crusoe's own powerful state in isolation—until her enabling servant/helpmate Alice (the novel's Friday figure) decides to save Polly by leaving her. Without her Friday, middle-aged Polly is empowered to reject her toxic habits and locate possibility in renovation; she rehabilitates the house's weather-beaten fabric by turning it into a boarding school for children and then opening its doors to two war-refugee girls whom she adopts as her own.

For young Polly, the problem of dress, of habit, of clothes—'I never, ever seem to be wearing the right ones' (103)—is always tacitly a problem of gender and genre. Trundling along the beach as a teenager with *Robinson Crusoe* in hand after getting her first menstrual period and staining a white sheepskin rug, she envies Crusoe: 'He didn't have blood pouring out of himself every four weeks until he was old. He would never feel disgusting' (51–2). Consonantly, she worries about her 'goodness' or virtue as akin to a set of 'new clothes' that must be guarded against 'signs of wear and tear' (25), as a 'raiment' that must be kept 'bright' (26). By contrast, she sees Crusoe as a man who commands his world confidently, without worrying at all about his goodness, his body, or his embodied presentation. For Polly, Crusoe's lack of concern is a painful reminder that the contours of his experience fit her poorly. 'One of the very few mistakes' in the novel, opines young Polly, is the lack of relatability that inheres, she feels, in the hero's lack of concern about dress: 'there were clothes brought off the ship. He had them by him. He did not use them. Or scarcely. Perhaps he had never really cared about his appearance. I would guess this was true. One can imagine him as a boy of say fourteen'—unconcerned, that is to say, and at home in his habits (103). Young Polly muses that 'Clothes on the desert island are what I should very much have missed. Different, beautiful clothes as time went by' (103), as if a feminized version of the genre might require some alteration of the Crusoean prototype.

Rich neighbour Lady Celia offers entry into just such another kind of narrative trajectory and aesthetic space, one that Polly is at pains to reject out of loyalty to the model of her hero. Lady Celia broaches the subject of Polly's sartorial and readerly habits first by admonishing her: 'you ought to wear different clothes' (101). Polly agrees, rifling through Lady Celia's clothes press in a state of delight: 'So many materials were stacked inside the press that it looked like a pirate's cave. A female-pirate's cave. Flimsy bits and silky bits and thick velvety bits and long, lacy bits all crammed in and layered tight, all the colours there are, all textures' (103). The microgenre stretches along similar colour lines as Spark's *Robinson*, as Polly drapes herself in all the bright colours we miss in Defoe's tropical novel—'greens', 'yellows', 'Kingfisher blue' (103). The charm begins to fail when Lady Celia compels Polly to read aloud from Tennyson's 'The Lady of Shalott', then offers her a necklace as a bribe to reject the Crusoean ethos and revere Tennyson instead: 'It was seed-pearls, with a little diamond clasp like a diamond daisy. It was small. Made for a girl' (105). While the necklace swings in the air, Lady Celia interrogates her: 'Do you love Tennyson ... Better than anybody?' (105). When Polly insists Tennyson is not 'quite as good as Daniel Defoe', Lady Celia puts the necklace away (105). And so Polly gives up the promise of being 'dressed as a princess' (104).

Instead, Polly tries to make some social headway at the Thwaites' fancy party in her own quasi-Crusoean garb, but she makes a poor go of it in her 'sailor-blouse' and straw hat (114). Feeling as out of place as if she has wandered in from the wrong genre, she flees to a secluded meadow and strips to her waist, exhibiting the kind of un-self-conscious confidence she attaches elsewhere to her hero. Alas, when Gardam's half-naked heroine lies down 'in the long grass' and 'listen[s] to the river running by', there is no safety in this freedom; Polly awakens to find a young man watching her, to her shame (116). She feels seen in the way that 'the pink hyacinth' is seen 'displaying its un-seeable underparts to all who passed by' (117). Returning to Thwaite Hall to change into fresh clothing, despondent in her awareness of her experiential limitations as a young woman, she steels herself to rejoin the party and wander about 'so nondescript and friendless, in all my clothes' (117). Polly's Crusoean sartorial aspirations render her fit for nothing, it seems.

Resonating with the travails of Polly's fictional foremother Unca Eliza, Polly's fraught sartorial status inspires a metafictional and metageneric question about the place of heroines within the scope of the early novelistic tradition more broadly, where marriage typically constitutes the appropriate happy ending for heroines (outside of the Gothic form, anyway). The voice in Polly's head tells her that, like Jane Austen's heroine in *Northanger Abbey*,

> It's not as if there's anything else for you. You've no excuse to be different. You can't write poetry or paint or play very well and you'll never write a book. You've never been to school or felt you were a hyacinth. (117–18)

In fact, the voice admonishes her, 'All you can do is speak German and talk about *Robinson Crusoe*' (118). Eyeing her 'torn stockings' and the 'vest hanging out of her pocket', she 'change[s] her dress' for more respectable garb; she knows that she must do this, must 'go down and join them', must 'join in', must leave behind her inappropriate

Crusoean proclivities and, in a word, find some man to marry her (117). And then, almost immediately, suitors crop up to woo her.

The problem is, Polly does not crave the feminized marital narrative arc. She wants to thrive within the microgenre's architecture, not be forced out of it into the dissolving narrative course of 'marriage' wherein 'A shutter comes down' (96). She does not want an arc in which 'someone will come and marry me and make things complete and take me away' (96). Surely 'marriage' is not 'the only completing, necessary thing', she asserts (96). And, so, she chooses another way, what she sees as Crusoe's way, although she is denied the choice of going to sea like Crusoe himself or like her own actual father.

Faced with, as she sees it, the duelling options of marrying an unmet suitor or 'becom[ing] knitted into a landscape' (96), Polly chooses the latter, there in the yellow house by the sea. 'What a desert isle you live on', as one ill-fated suitor (he dies tragically) teases her in her youth (157). He is not wrong: 'We're—rather cut off here', she concedes (146). The would-be suitor, Paul, ribs her for her Crusoean zeal: 'I'd forgotten. Defoe's the one isn't he? Is he still? People usually move on from *Robinson Crusoe* after childhood' (158). But Polly insists: 'I shall never move on' (158), not from *Crusoe* and not from the yellow house that is her own figural island space: 'I clung now quite desperately to my island' (186).

Indeed she does, despite the detriment to her being. In effect, she spends long decades being dissolved into the landscape of her fixations: liquor, and *Robinson Crusoe*. Polly's preoccupation with transcribing (and so forth) the novel, which she believes will bring her fully into Crusoean experience, is overtly excessive: Crusoe is 'Monumental, godlike' (201); Crusoe is 'her King Charles's head' (202); and Defoe's novel is nothing less than that 'paradigm, *Robinson Crusoe* itself, the novel elect' (223). Noting of her hero, 'I envied him ... for knowing exactly where he was' (208), Polly labours to parrot what she sees as 'Crusoe's mastery of circumstances' (202). 'Sitting in the yellow house with nothing in the world to do', she tries to reproduce her sense of his stoically 'magnificent simplicity' (202). So doing, she 'blots out' the rest of the world and its myriad narrative possibilities, letting instead the 'being and presence of Crusoe become her devotion and her joy' (202). Soon enough, she is able to proudly parrot her hero, proclaiming, 'Thus in two years time I had a thick grove; and in five or six years time I had a wood before my dwelling, growing so monstrous thick and strong, that it was indeed perfectly impassable' (206). And so she deems herself 'safe behind my own hand-built stockade. Oh, Robinson Crusoe' (228).

But, if *Robinson Crusoe* is 'so much more than a book' to her, and indeed 'lie[s] close to the bone', if it is a 'metaphysical landscape' where she feels 'most at home' (221), it is also a toxic fabric in which, like the house's metonym, she cannot thrive without some adaptation and alteration. She knows all her efforts of translation and the like comprise 'a totally pointless exercise' (187), but it is more than just pointless: it is a poisonous if sexless 'love affair' (234), a debilitating 'fever' that spans 'Oh such a great many years' (234), as Polly tries in vain to mimic her sense of Crusoe's empowered status in isolation. Years of it: 'I had been translating Crusoe for hours, colouring in the chapter headings, underlining with very exquisite care, letting the fire die, the lamp go down, my feet go cold' (196). There is not much to say, between the whisky and the Crusoean obsession, simply: 'I became very odd. Oh, really quite odd then' (202). The world sees her 'disappearing' into this island of her own device, 'All washed up and marooned and far away' (233). Meanwhile, a great many years go unremarked upon, since 'like Crusoe, "I cannot say that any extraordinary things happened to me; but I lived on in the same course, in the same posture and places, just as before' (191). But Polly is not like Crusoe. She 'looked to ... *Robinson Crusoe* ... and thought of that straightforward, strong and sexless man sitting alone in the sunshine. How easy and beautiful life had been for him' (69); she is so different from him in her stasis, as she knits herself into the landscape of a fatal enervation.

Considering Polly's earlier denunciation to Lady Celia of Tennyson after reading aloud from 'The Lady of Shalott', it is ironic that Polly comes to occupy the Lady of Shalott's own island story. Indeed, the Lady of Shalott's tale emerges as an unwitting and unwelcome ancestor in the history of the female Robinsonade. Her back turned on society, Polly transmutes the world not through the Lady of Shalott's mirror, but through 'the glass' of her whisky tumbler and the lens of Crusoe (208). Polly sits at her 'desk, day after day', embroidering (as it were) upon the text of *Robinson Crusoe* 'with the bottle and the glass in front of me and the shadows of people I had known just over my shoulder out of sight, in the corners of the room' (208). Polly wanted to parrot confident Crusoe, but instead she resembles the pitiful Lady of Shalott.

Finally, however, Polly's helpmate Alice, having perceived the life-or-death nature of the situation, leaves the house and thereby forces Polly into detoxifying. Ultimately transforming both herself and the yellow house by the sea, Polly is unmarooned, and the house is no longer an Island of Despair: like Crusoe, 'I saw my deliverance indeed visibly put into my hands, all things easy, and a large ship'—the house itself, refigured now as she prepares to enter it with her adoptive daughters—'ready to carry me any whither I pleased to go' (234). The yellow house and its contents are thus transformed by the arrival of the girls: 'Is that ours?' one of the girls asks of the house as they approach together, and Polly replies, 'Yes. Ours' (255). The 'funny old house' is no longer a static landscape, but is instead a structure on the move: 'The doors slammed and the sea crashed and the windows shook, and we were all safe home' (255). No one is trapped, no one is oppressively 'knitted into a landscape' (96). Instead, 'the light shone through' the trees on the landside 'like knitting-loops when you draw the needle out' (254)—an image of possibility.

As Gardam says in her preface, she wanted to write a 'great universal novel', in the mode of Defoe's own allegedly universal novel, but '[i]t became clear to me that I could only write of what I knew' (13). *Crusoe's Daughter* complicates the historical claim of universality. One of Polly's young suitors laughs incredulously at her veneration of *Robinson Crusoe* for this very reason: 'Crusoe and women? He never needed a—gave a thought to a woman all those years' (160). Accordingly, Polly, though she defends Defoe's novel to Lady Celia as an 'attempt at a universal truth' (105), struggles in vain to mine *Robinson Crusoe* for lessons about her own life: 'Perhaps if Robinson Crusoe had been a woman—' (149). But he was not. Polly muses, 'The trouble ... is perhaps that I am a girl' (96). She would go 'To sea if I could' (72), but no. Settled into her spinster decades, Polly 'envied' Crusoe, she tells us six times, for experiences that she has no access to: she envies him for 'put[ting] up a fight', for 'seamanship', for 'sensible sexlessness which he seemed so easily to have achieved' (208). Polly may believe it when she tells Lady Celia that Defoe's novel 'reads like reality' (106), but for her that reality is toxic in its native state. The book ends with a postscript that conjures up the figure of Robinson Crusoe himself asking Polly, 'when my wife died, there were children. There was a daughter. We do not hear about the daughter. What happened to her?' (265). Gardam's book, seeking an answer to that question, unmoors itself from the solid ground of the patriarch novel 'like the blob in the ocean, the seed' that 'hold[s] in itself some fibrous strength' with the power to 'carry the form', through acts of appropriation and adaptation, 'further' (223).

* * *

The Robinsonade would not seem to lend itself naturally to female protagonists. To be sure, there are essentially no women in Defoe's ur-novel. In the closing bits of *Robinson Crusoe*, in the space of a sentence, Crusoe marries an unnamed woman, 'not either to my disadvantage or dissatisfaction' (240), and she has three children. In the next sentence, she dies. Longueville's *The Hermit*, which appeared just a few years after *Robinson Crusoe*, is even more pointed than Defoe's novel about female absence; however much the hero Quarll hungers (unlike Crusoe) for female companionship, he also emphasizes that women have no appropriate place on the island or in the microgenre: 'this is a second garden of Eden, only here's no forbidden fruit, nor women to tempt a man' (26). Indeed, one of Quarll's ruling mottoes is, '*Waste not your vigour or substance on women, lest weakness or want be your reward*' (26). Of course, many Robinsonades since then have challenged the supposition that the castaway microgenre is no country for women, including the three novelistic Robinsonades that this essay has scrutinized for their careful attention to the metafictional, metageneric question of how sartorial and architectural habits can be revised to accommodate the conundrum of a female Crusoe.

Further Reading

Rebecca Hightower-Weaver, *Empire Islands: Castaways, Cannibals, and Fantasies of Conquest* (Minneapolis, MN: University of Minnesota Press, 2007).
Betty Joseph, 'Re(playing) Crusoe/Pocahontas: Circum-Atlantic Stagings in *The Female American*', *Criticism*, 42:3 (2000), 317–35.
Jakub Lipski (ed.), *Rewriting Crusoe: The Robinsonade Across Languages, Cultures, and Media* (Lewisburg, PA: Bucknell University Press, 2020).
Mary Helen McMurran, 'Collecting and Collected: Native American Subjectivity and Transatlantic Transactions in *The Female American*', *Early American Literature*, 54:1 (2019), 37–68.
Mary Helen McMurran, 'Realism and the Unreal in *The Female American*', *The Eighteenth Century: Theory and Interpretation*, 52:3–4 (2011), 323–42.

Andreas K. E. Mueller and Glynis Ridley (eds), *Robinson Crusoe after 300 Years* (Lewisburg, PA: Bucknell University Press, 2021).

C. M. Owen, *The Female Crusoe: Female Hybridity, Trade, and the Eighteenth-Century Individual* (Amsterdam: Rodopi, 2010).

Christopher Palmer, *Castaway Tales: From Robinson Crusoe to Life of Pi* (Middletown, CT: Wesleyan University Press, 2016).

Emmanuelle Peraldo (ed.), *300 Years of Robinsonades* (Newcastle-upon-Tyne: Cambridge Scholars Press, 2020).

Kristianne Kalata Vaccaro, ' "Recollection ... sets my busy imagination to work": Transatlantic Self-Narration, Performance, and Reception in *The Female American*', ECF, 20:2 (2007–8), 127–50.

CHAPTER 36

DEFOE ON SCREEN
Robinson Crusoe, The Red Turtle, *and Animal Rights*

ROBERT MAYER

RESIDENTS of or visitors to London in the 1980s regularly saw signs at or near Tube stops announcing the goals of Chickens' Lib, a movement aimed at protecting birds—ducks and turkeys as well as chickens—from the depredations associated with the factory farming of domestic fowl.[1] Chickens' Lib originated in 1971 with the actions of two British women—Clare Druce and her mother, Violet Spalding—and adopted its catchy label (after being known for a time as the Barnes Action Group) in 1973.[2] The group was in the forefront of the emerging international movement for animal rights; the most prominent animal rights organization in the United States, People for the Ethical Treatment of Animals, or PETA, was founded in 1980. And the impact of the movement on behalf of animals, if not entirely successful, has been notable and widespread. At Wal Mart in the United States, one can currently buy 'Happy' eggs that are advertised as 'Quite Possibly the Free♥Est of the Free Range' and certified 'American Humane' by the American Society for the Prevention of Cruelty to Animals.[3] Indeed, the attitudes engendered by Chickens' Lib and other, similar groups have become so prominent that they are the subject of satire, notably in an episode of *Portlandia*, 'Farm' (2011), that represents a couple concerned about the lived experience of the chicken they might order ('Colin') in a restaurant in Portland, Oregon.[4]

Another, more recent, and more pertinent, measure of the effect of the push for animal rights is the 2016 animated film *The Red Turtle*, made by the Dutch filmmaker Michaël

---

[1] See Clare Druce, *Chickens' Lib: The Story of a Campaign* (Hebden Bridge: Bluemoose Books, 2013); for a short film laying out the claims of the movement, see 'Chickens' Lib: Hidden Suffering, 1992': https://www.youtube.com/watch?v=Wwy7k9m67Vs. (Accessed 21 May 2019).

[2] Druce, *Chickens' Lib* ('the media loved our new name').

[3] Quotations are from the packaging of eggs marketed by the Happy Egg Co., a UK company; see https://thehappyegg.co.uk. (Accessed 21 May 2019).

[4] www.imdb.com (*Portlandia*, Episode List); for an excerpt, see https://www.ifc.com/shows/portlandia/video-extras/season-01/episode-01/colin-the-chicken. (Accessed 21 May 2019).

Dudok de Wit, with support from both Arte France and Studio Ghibli, the Japanese production company responsible for such celebrated animated films as *Grave of the Fireflies* (1988) and *Spirited Away* (2001). Thus, one of the latest screen appropriations of *Robinson Crusoe* (1719) continues the rich tradition of such works based upon or making use of texts by Defoe by incorporating into the castaway narrative ideas and concerns, images and tropes, current in contemporary culture and political discourse [SEE CHAPTER 33]. Defoe's texts, that is, have been and continue to be 'sites of collective significance' for a wide range of writers and artists.[5]

This essay demonstrates this aspect of the afterlife of Defoe's work, particularly for screen artists, by looking closely at one recent, notable motion picture and seeing it within the context of earlier screen works indebted to Defoe (in sometimes very complicated ways).[6] The essay will show that such works are marked by an extraordinary topicality, resulting from a tendency to use Defoe as a means of telling familiar stories that both refer to the past (among other things, eighteenth-century texts and contexts) and represent and comment upon contemporary reality. That topicality arises in important part from the fact that Defoe, perhaps more than any other British fiction writer, sought to use his narratives to comment more-or-less directly upon a wide range of developments and problems of great importance to the readers who lived in the England (and especially the London) of his day. One of Defoe's biographers, Paula Backscheider, has written that Defoe wrote 'to set his countrymen straight, to guide them, and to help them make distinctions'; Backscheider is referring to a particular set of texts ('practical divinity', 'pamphlets on relations with Spain and on crime', and 'books on the supernatural') written in the 1720s, but, as others have shown, her comment is more generally applicable.[7] Maximillian Novak argues that narratives like *Moll Flanders* and *Colonel Jack* were reactions to a 'sudden surge in crimes of all sorts' in England from 1715 to 1725.[8] David Roberts describes *A Journal of the Plague Year* (1722) as 'topical' because of 'its response to the Marseilles plague', which began in 1720, and the consequent threat of plague in London.[9] And Thomas Keymer, at least in part accounting for the great popularity of *Crusoe* ('its lowbrow appeal'), declares that the author's most famous book 'contrives a narrative of human domination over raw nature in tune with the Whig ideology of progress that Defoe expresses more directly elsewhere'.[10] Such topicality

---

[5] Robert Mayer, 'Defoe's Cultural Afterlife, Mainly on Screen', in *The Afterlives of Eighteenth-Century Fiction*, ed. Daniel Cook and Nicholas Seager (Cambridge: Cambridge University Press, 2015), 233–52 (248); the quotation is from Ann Rigney, *The Afterlives of Walter Scott: Memory on the Move* (Oxford: Oxford University Press, 2012), 11–12.

[6] *The Red Turtle*, dir. Michaël Dudok de Wit (Sony Pictures Classics, 2016). The film won a Special Jury Prize at Cannes and was nominated for an Academy Award for Best Animated Feature.

[7] Backscheider, *Daniel Defoe*, 516.

[8] Maximillian E. Novak, *Realism, Myth, and History in Defoe's Fiction* (Lincoln, NE: University of Nebraska Press, 1983), 123.

[9] Defoe, *A Journal of the Plague Year*, ed. Louis Landa, intro. David Roberts (Oxford: Oxford University Press, 1990), viii.

[10] Defoe, *Robinson Crusoe*, ed. Thomas Keymer (Oxford: Oxford University Press, 2007), x, xxv.

explains why screen works indebted to Defoe need to be seen as 'figures of memory', defined by Jan Assmann as 'fixed points ... of the past, whose memory is maintained through cultural formation', because they are part of what Klaus Poenicke describes as 'a project of permanent rewriting' that is 'very much oriented toward the future'.[11] *The Red Turtle* shows how *Robinson Crusoe* is such a 'figure of memory'. The film recapitulates *Crusoe* in important ways, and it also makes the castaway narrative part of contemporary discussions of the being of animals and their relationship with humankind as well as twenty-first-century environmentalism.

A History of Defoe on Screen

Before turning to *The Red Turtle*, some historical context is in order. Movies based upon *Robinson Crusoe* first appeared in the early years of the history of film, and in the second half of the twentieth century screen artists produced works indebted to an ever wider range of texts by Defoe. Georges Méliès, one of the great pioneers of cinema, produced a *Robinson Crusoe* in 1903, just one year after making his most celebrated film, *A Trip to the Moon*. There were at least five Crusoe silent films made between 1913 and 1922 in the United States and France, one of them a six-hour serial.[12] More recently, major filmmakers like Luis Buñuel, Caleb Deschanel, and Robert Zemeckis have produced versions of the Crusoe story, and hardly a year goes by without a new addition to the series, for television or the movie theatre in the United States or Europe.[13] Starting around 1950—Buñuel's picture appeared in 1954—the Crusoe films frequently interrogate, critique, and rewrite Defoe's narrative, taking issue with its representation of relations between the Occidental castaway and the ethnic Other he encounters on the island, the piety of Defoe's hero, and the novel's seeming endorsement of the British colonial project. Indeed, the Crusoe screen works taken together make it clear that Defoe's text, as Ian Watt argues, embodies a central myth of Western Civilization, but one that is so fraught that it must be disrupted as it is retold or otherwise reinstantiated.[14]

---

[11] Jan Assmann, 'Collective Memory and Cultural Identity', *New German Critique*, 65 (1995), 125–33 (129); Klaus Poenicke, 'Engendering Cultural Memory: "The Legend of Sleepy Hollow" as Text and Intertext', *Amerikastudien/American Studies*, 43:1 (1998), 19–32 (20).

[12] See www.imdb.com, especially the pages on Méliès and Defoe; Robert Mayer, '*Robinson Crusoe* in the Screen Age', in *The Cambridge Companion to Robinson Crusoe*, ed. John Richetti (Cambridge: Cambridge University Press, 2018), 221–33. The list of works at www.imdb.com, while useful, is far from complete.

[13] The films by Buñuel and Zemeckis, respectively, are *Adventures of Robinson Crusoe* (1954) and *Cast Away* (2000). Caleb Deschanel, nominated for an Academy Award six times as a cinematographer, has also directed for film and TV, most notably in *Crusoe* (1988).

[14] Ian Watt, *Myths of Modern Individualism: Faust, Don Quixote, Don Juan, Robinson Crusoe* (Cambridge: Cambridge University Press, 1996), 141–92; Robert Mayer, 'Three Cinematic Robinsonades', in *Eighteenth-Century Fiction on Screen*, ed. Mayer (Cambridge: Cambridge University Press, 2002), 35–51 (48).

The Crusoe films and television programmes are perhaps best understood as a twentieth-century (and after) contribution to the Robinsonade, the literary genre resulting from the seemingly endless imitations, adaptations, or transformations of Defoe's narrative, which began to develop almost the moment the book appeared, and which endures to this day [SEE CHAPTER 35]. As Carl Fisher has shown, 'the Robinsonade refers to its source ... but [also] strikes out anew with each iteration', and this seems particularly true of the screen additions to the genre.[15] I have shown elsewhere that even films—like Buñuel's *Robinson Crusoe*—that seem to hew closely to Defoe's narrative in fact frequently depart from it dramatically by making the castaway narrative do ideological work quite different from that associated with Defoe's book. Many screen works feature a far more attenuated link to Defoe's source material, including as they do such science-fiction entrants as *Robinson Crusoe on Mars* (1964), *Lost* (2004–10), and *The Martian* (2015); a popular example of reality television, *Survivor* (2000–19); and the extraordinary trio of Robinson films made by Patrick Keiller between 1994 and 2010, treating such contemporary issues as 'the *problem* of England' and 'the possibility of life's survival on the planet'.[16] But what is striking about this rich and varied set of cinematic Robinsonades is the way the works demonstrate how Defoe's narrative, his hero and the dilemmas he faces, have been an almost endless source of productive reinvention and reimagining for early modern, modern, and post-modern artists and writers addressing their particular realities.[17]

The appropriation of Defoe's writing by filmmakers consisted almost exclusively of works indebted to *Crusoe* until about 1960, but after that, for a variety of reasons, other texts came to screen artists' attention. *Moll Flanders*, for example, was given two feminist renderings in the 1990s, and that novel was also the vehicle for both celebrating and lamenting the values and behaviour of men and women living in Anglo-American capitalist society.[18] The short, animated film *The Periwig-Maker* (2000) draws heavily on

---

[15] Carl Fisher, 'Innovation and Imitation in the Eighteenth-Century Robinsonade', in *Cambridge Companion to Robinson Crusoe*, ed. Richetti, 99–111 (99). See also Jakub Lipski (ed.), *Rewriting Crusoe: The Robinsonade across Languages, Cultures, and Media* (Lewisburg, PA: Bucknell University Press, 2020).

[16] I treat *Robinson Crusoe on Mars* in 'Robinson Crusoe in the Screen Age', 223–9; and *Lost* and *Survivor* in 'Robinson Crusoe on Television', *Quarterly Review of Film and Video*, 28:1 (2011), 53–65. The Keiller films are *London* (1994), *Robinson in Space* (1997), and *Robinson in Ruins* (2010). The first quotation is from Keiller's second film. The project of the three films, which comes to be called 'Robinsonism', was also continued in an exhibition at the Tate Britain and the book that grew out of that exhibition: Patrick Keiller, *The Possibility of Life's Survival on the Planet* (London: Tate Publishing, 2012). I discuss the Keiller films, book, and exhibition in 'Defoe's Cultural Afterlife', 242–7.

[17] To be sure, some iterations of the Crusoe myth are more subtle than others. *Crusoe*, a recent television series, takes issue with Defoe's representation of Friday by having its hero object when a Western pirate refers to Friday as a 'savage', informing the miscreant that Friday speaks twelve languages and knows *Paradise Lost* by heart. 'Rum and Gunpowder', *Crusoe*, dir. Duane Clark (NBC, 2008).

[18] *Moll Flanders*, dir. Pen Densham (MGM, 1995); *The Fortunes and Misfortunes of Moll Flanders*, dir. David Attwood (Granada Television, 1996). For Moll as a capitalist, see my discussion of a work that was projected (around 1970) but never completed, by the film director Ken Russell and the publisher of *Penthouse*, Bob Guccione, and an online characterization of Defoe's heroine by Robin Bates in connection with a class she was teaching. Mayer, 'Defoe's Cultural Afterlife', 235–6. On the feminist film

A Journal of the Plague Year, and especially that text's interest in and engagement with what we might call early modern epidemiology. The film focuses on the fate of a young girl who lives in London during the 1665 outbreak of the plague that is represented in the book. Along the way, *The Periwig-Maker*, through the thoughts of the eponymous central character, examines various 'remedies' for the epidemic, considering, for example, the question of the efficacy of 'the shutting-up of houses' that is so important in Defoe's narrative.[19] Whether or not the group that produced *The Periwig-Maker* was specifically inspired by contemporary fears of a new medical emergency—such as the COVID-19 pandemic the world has lived through since 2020—the film can be seen as part of the more general use of Defoe's *Journal* for reporting and reflecting upon such medical threats as the AIDS crisis of the 1980s and the SARS epidemic in China in 2003.[20] And, finally, there is Keiller's trilogy, in which the travels in contemporary England of a man named Robinson are undertaken 'to better understand a perceived "problem" by looking at, and making images of, landscape'.[21] The journeys, we are told in the second film, *Robinson in Space*, were inspired by the central character's 'reading [of] Daniel Defoe's *Tour through the Whole Island of Great Britain*'.[22] The *Tour* (1724–6) combines much reportage of what the narrator sees as he supposedly moves around England, Scotland, and Wales, as well as 'Useful Observations', embodying, as much as Keiller's dark assessments of Thatcherite and post-Thatcherite Britain, a particular ideological point of view, although in Defoe's case the tone is mostly celebratory, even triumphalist (*TDH*, i. 45).[23] Keiller's films, thus, are indebted to both the *Tour* and to Defoe's most famous novel; they are not in any way adaptations, of course, but Keiller's Robinson feels himself to be stranded in contemporary Britain, and he both reminds us of Defoe's protagonist (exploring his island, which he experiences as an alien environment) and self-consciously draws upon Defoe's traveller.[24] And Keiller's traveller aims not just to

---

versions, see Catherine Parke, 'Adaptations of Defoe's *Moll Flanders*', in *Eighteenth-Century Fiction on Screen*, ed. Mayer, 52–69.

[19] *The Periwig-Maker*, dir. Steffen Schäffler (AtomFilm, 1999); *A Journal of the Plague Year*, ed. Roberts, xviii.

[20] See David Black, *The Plague Years: A Chronicle of AIDS, the Epidemic of Our Time* (New York: Simon and Schuster, 1986), which drew upon Black's reporting on AIDS for *Rolling Stone* in 1985; and the 2013 exhibition in Hong Kong, 'A Journal of the Plague Year: Fear, Ghosts, and Rebels. SARS and the Hong Kong Story'. I discuss both Black's reporting and the Hong Kong show in 'Defoe's Cultural Afterlife', 234, 239–41. As to the fear of a contemporary plague (before COVID-19), see Dana Kerecman Myers, 'The Pandemic Everyone Fears', in the online weekly newsletter, *Global Health Now*, published by the Bloomberg School of Public Health at Johns Hopkins University (30 January 2018), www.globalhealthnow.org/2018-01/pandemic-everyone-fears. (Accessed 27 May 2019).

[21] Keiller, *Possibility of Life's Survival*, 9.

[22] Patrick Keiller, *Robinson in Space (and a Conversation with Patrick Wright)* (London: Reaktion Books, 1999), 20; the book is a virtual transcription of the film, lavishly illustrated, with marginal comments and notes.

[23] See Geoffrey M. Sill, 'Defoe's *Tour*: Literary Art or Moral Imperative?', *ECS*, 11:1 (1977–8), 79–83.

[24] Robinson represents himself as 'shipwrecked' in both *London* and *Robinson in Ruins*. In *Robinson in Space*, the traveller observes: 'We had ascended the Pennines at Blackstone Edge, by the route of Daniel Defoe'. Keiller, *Robinson in Space*, 142.

report on, but also to seek a solution to 'the *problem* of England'; in the second film in the trilogy, Robinson feels himself to be approaching 'his utopia'.[25] In short, what we find in the Robinson trilogy and in many of the screen works indebted to Defoe (especially those made after 1950) are appropriations of that writer's texts that seek to come to terms with contemporary reality, producing twentieth- and twenty-first-century essays, if you will, in epidemiology, ethnic and racial politics, political economy, and second-wave feminism. Artists who draw upon Defoe, in short, frequently engage in 'rewriting ... oriented toward the future'.

Humans and Animals

That Defoe's most famous narratives function in this way is clearly demonstrated by *The Red Turtle*, one of the most important recent additions to the body of screen works referring to, and generally reworking, Defoe's texts. The film begins, as many screen versions of *Crusoe* do, *in medias res*, with the castaway already in the water.[26] At first *The Red Turtle* appears to be a relatively straightforward retelling of the Crusoe story, but after a fairly conventional first act, the film changes, featuring a series of surprising, even magical, events that make it clear why the title of the film focuses not on the human being stranded on 'an un-inhabited Island', but rather on the reptile that passes most of its life in the sea.[27] In the early scenes of *The Red Turtle*, the human protagonist seeks to establish his control over his environment and overcome his difficulties by escaping from confinement, and in the process the film depicts the castaway's relationship with the other creatures around him as fundamentally adversarial. But as *The Red Turtle* develops, we see the human being change into someone who lives in harmony with other creatures in and around the island, a man who is finally disinclined to leave his island home. All this unfolds in a film without dialogue, although there is a rich, if subtle, soundtrack, including natural sounds (wind, rain, wave action), music, and human vocalizations—coughing, breathing, shouting, sighing, and such-like—but always without any specific language. The director, Dudok de Wit, observes that originally there was 'some dialogue ... [but] it didn't feel right. Suddenly you know his [the hero's] nationality'. So the film's narrative 'is told with the body language, with the editing, with the music, with the sound effects, with film language in general'.[28] Several commentators have attributed the film's refinement, its 'simple and elemental' style, to the filmmaker's decision to do without dialogue.[29] More importantly, the fact that the film does without

---

[25] Keiller, *Robinson in Space*, 6, 187.
[26] Buñuel's 1954 film, and a BBC serial, *The Adventures of Robinson Crusoe*, dir. Jean Sacha (Franco London Films, 1964), both begin with Crusoe emerging from the sea on to the shore of his island.
[27] Defoe, *Robinson Crusoe*, 1.
[28] *The Red Turtle*, Special Features, 'Commentary with Michaël Dudok de Wit'.
[29] Chuck Bowen, 'Review: *The Red Turtle*', *Slant Magazine*, 15 January 2017, https://www.slantmagazine.com/film/the-red-turtle. (Accessed 13 June 2019); A. O. Scott, 'Review: *The Red Turtle*, Life Marooned

human language and thereby eliminates 'nationality' makes perfect sense, given that this screen Robinsonade strikingly reworks the Crusoe story so as to reimagine the castaway's relationship with the natural world.

Early in Dudok de Wit's film, the castaway contends with the elements, trying desperately to swim in a stormy sea and then clinging to a capsized boat. In the next scene, he is ashore. Awakened by a curious crab, he begins the process of discovering where he has landed, much like Defoe's original, who reports: 'I began to look round me to see what kind of Place I was in'. In the novel, this action quickly becomes a general assessment of his new home, as when Crusoe undertakes 'a more particular Survey of the Island'.[30] As the castaway in *The Red Turtle* explores, we see that there are four 'regions' in his small world: the sea and shore, the extensive beach, a bamboo forest, and, within the forest, a freshwater lagoon. In the novel, Crusoe's exploration is part of his establishing mastery over his environment. He finds things he can eat and learns how to cultivate or process them, discovering grapes, for example, and deciding to 'keep them as dry'd Grapes or Raisins are kept'. More violently, he realizes that there are goats on the island and quickly begins to domesticate them, reporting in his journal that he 'Kill'd a young Goat, and lam'd another ... and led it Home ... and splinter'd up its Leg which was broke ... and the Leg grew well, and as strong as ever; but by my nursing it so long it grew tame ... and would not go away'.[31] Crusoe also learns to do all manner of things—his doing so inspired Jean-Jacques Rousseau to describe the book as 'a complete treatise on natural education'—and at one point Defoe's castaway famously observes, reflecting upon his own experience: 'every Man may be in time Master of every mechanick Art'.[32] When he saves a 'Savage' from 'Slaughter', he reflects at first, 'now was my Time to get me a Servant', names him Friday, notes with satisfaction what he sees as Friday's natural servitude, and teaches 'him to say *Master*, and then let him know that was to be my Name'. And later, when his island is peopled with not only himself and Friday but also the latter's father and 'the *Spaniard*', he reports 'I thought my self very rich in Subjects; and it was a merry Reflection ... How like a King I look'd'.[33] The dominance Crusoe enjoys on the island is implicitly rooted in the Judeo-Christian faith that God has given man 'dominion over the fish of the sea, and over the fowl of the air, and over the cattle, and over all the earth'.[34] Ian Watt emphasizes that the narrative has appealed to readers since 1719 as an image of '*homo economicus*'—'a model of industry', embodying 'the regulated diligence combined with accurate planning and stocktaking which is so important in modern economic organization'—and the original Crusoe's material success

---

with an Ornery Reptile', *New York Times*, 19 January 2017, https://www.nytimes.com/2017/01/19/movies/the-red-turtle-review.html.(Accessed 19 April 2019).

[30] Defoe, *Robinson Crusoe*, 41, 84.

[31] Defoe, *Robinson Crusoe*, 85, 65.

[32] Jean-Jacques Rousseau, 'A Treatise of Natural Education', in Defoe, *Robinson Crusoe*, ed. Michael Shinagel, 2nd ed. (New York: W.W. Norton, 1994), 262–4 (262); Defoe, *Robinson Crusoe*, ed. Keymer, 59.

[33] Defoe, *Robinson Crusoe*, 170, 171, 176, 174, 203.

[34] Genesis, 1:26.

on the island is based upon, and originates in, his more fundamental mastery of nature.[35] In Jack Gold's *Man Friday* (1975), Friday finally rejects Crusoe as 'sickness itself' in important part because of his insistence on his God-given 'dominion' over the whole of nature, but Zemeckis's *Cast Away* gives us a Crusoe-like figure who progresses in the narrative by becoming more at home in his island world, at least physically, even though we mainly see this in the latter film when he is expertly spearing fish for food.[36]

The human protagonist of *The Red Turtle* at first seems like Defoe's Crusoe, but ultimately he is very different. Establishing the limits of his world, he is momentarily startled by the bark of a sea lion and the call of a bird in the forest, but he easily establishes the source of those sounds and, in short order, finds water to drink and fruit that he can eat. (He, too—like the protagonist in *Cast Away*—is later seen spear-fishing under water with real skill.) Nature is not represented as wholly benign; the castaway is seen as dwarfed not only by the sea, but also by the hill which he ascends during his exploration of the island. Trying to climb down from a high bluff, he falls into a chasm and finds himself in a pool surrounded by sheer cliffs, barely escaping from what seems to be a death trap by diving and finding a way out to the open sea. When he tries to leave the island, something in the sea repeatedly destroys his raft. In the second half of the film, finally, a devastating tsunami inundates the island, all but destroying the forest, killing wildlife, and threatening the lives of not only the castaway, but also the others who by then have joined him on the island (of whom, more later). The island, then, is no paradise; it harbours dangers and threats.

The initial solutions to the protagonist's plight are human structures and efforts. He dreams ecstatically of a jetty that leads to his flying over the landscape. And he builds three rafts that are to be the vehicles of his escape. This man does not rest or take comfort from the peace and plenty of the island; he is determined to use his human ingenuity to escape. But his efforts are frustrated by something in the sea; each time the castaway sets forth, his raft is destroyed by violent blows from beneath. Just before trying one last time, he has a Crusoe-like moment of despondency. At the beginning of his journal, Defoe's protagonist identifies himself as 'poor miserable *Robinson Crusoe* ... on this dismal unfortunate Island, which I call'd *the Island of Despair*', and the man in *The Red Turtle* can barely rouse himself to build a third raft, this one huge, seemingly to protect against his unknown attacker.[37] He also prepares to fight back, taking a bamboo trunk with him as a weapon. Nevertheless, the third raft is broken up too, and the enraged man falls into the water, although he quickly pulls himself into a protective crouch when he finally sees his seeming antagonist, the red turtle, swimming towards him. The sea creature, however, merely comes close, looks intently, and then swims away. Is this creature his adversary? The turtle seems determined that the man should not leave, but it apparently does not

---

[35] Watt, 'Robinson Crusoe as a Myth', in *Robinson Crusoe*, ed. Shinagel, 288–306 (288, 299).

[36] Mayer, 'Three Cinematic Robinsonades', 42–5; I treat *Cast Away* in '*Robinson Crusoe* in Hollywood', in Maximillian E. Novak and Carl Fisher (eds), *Approaches to Teaching Defoe's* Robinson Crusoe (New York: MLA, 2005), 169–74.

[37] Defoe, *Robinson Crusoe*, 60.

wish to harm him. The two creatures seem to have arrived at a standoff; the man cannot escape, and the turtle leaves him to his own devices.

Back on land, the human protagonist throws a rock into the sea, wanders into the bamboo forest and shakes a tree violently, and screams at the sea from a hilltop. Seeing that the turtle has also, laboriously, come ashore, the man commits what Chuck Bowen describes as 'a shocking act of aggression'.[38] He runs to the turtle, struggling on land, and breaks a large piece of bamboo on its head, and when that seemingly has no effect, he turns the turtle on its back. The scene is bathed in a violent red-orange light, and the man completes his assault by jumping on the turtle's underside (or plastron), emitting a triumphant cry. He then dives into the ocean, leaving the turtle to wave its flippers helplessly, possibly injured by the man's violent leap. The castaway's mastery of the turtle is seemingly complete, and he begins a new raft, but then the fate of the turtle becomes the occasion for the man's 'transformation'.[39] As he works, he is increasingly troubled by the apparently dying beast. He dreams of it floating away, chasing after it as it rises. Eventually, the man tries to turn the turtle upright, but he cannot (presumably because it is by then dead weight), and he then carries water to it, wetting it. When there is no response, he kneels by the turtle and bends his head to the sand, in what seems like a gesture of repentance. And then he sleeps. He is awakened by the breaking open of the plastron, and suddenly (after the man has looked away), the shell no longer contains a turtle's body, but that of a woman, with abundant red hair. The turtle has become the vehicle for the man's deliverance. The rest of the film depicts the castaway's life on the island—there are no further escape attempts on rafts—with the family bequeathed to him by the turtle.

The film depicts the slow coming together of the wondrous couple. She is clearly of the sea, he is a creature of the land. It is the woman who pushes the empty turtle shell into the ocean, and on a sand bar, while they are still getting to know one another, she cracks open a clam and eats and then offers him a raw clam, which, after some hesitation, he accepts. Later, when they have had a child, the young one discovers a bottle by the shore. Displaying it to his parents, the boy looks out to sea, conscious, suddenly, of a world beyond the island; the father, by way of explanation, draws a mound of land with two adults and a child on it and then, at some distance away, a second mound, with more people and some animal shapes. In between the two, however, the mother draws only a turtle. The little boy, like his father before him, falls from a bluff into the pool surrounded by rock walls, but on a signal from his mother the boy easily finds his way out to sea, in the process encountering a turtle and swimming with it comfortably, naturally. Much older, probably in his teens, the boy plays with his father on the shore, leaps into the water, and then swims with two turtles in a way that suggests their physical kinship; the boy's arms momentarily seem like flippers. After the tsunami, the son swims out to

---

[38] Bowen, 'Review: *The Red Turtle*'.
[39] Isabel Stevens, '*The Red Turtle*—first look', *Sight and Sound* (updated 28 January 2019), https://www.bfi.org.uk/news-opinion/sight-sound-magazine/reviews-recommendations/red-turtle-first-look. (Accessed 1 April 2019). Stevens sees the 'theme of transformation' as central to the film.

sea to save his father, who is clinging to a floating tree trunk; the father—close to going under—is saved by the boy and three turtles who have joined him. And in the end it is the son who escapes the island; a young man near the end of the film, he finds the bottle again, considers it, and then has a dream in which he is at the top of a great, unmoving wave, looking landwards at his parents far below and seawards to the horizon. He must go. And his father, seeing him on the beach, from within the recovering bamboo forest, clearly understands that this is the case. This might seem somewhat sentimental and trite, but it is not. The film has a lovely, somewhat ecstatic quality, rooted in the harmonious encounter in the second half of the film between two distinct forms of being. 'Pictures are the film's currency', Isabel Stevens observes, 'and they are, without exaggeration, sublime'.[40] In any case, when the young man leaves, he builds no raft; instead, he straps a small bundle over his shoulder and swims away, accompanied by three turtles.[41] The film concludes with scenes with the parents, melancholy but content, swimming together, dancing, ageing. There is no hint of their leaving the island. When the father dies, the mother first goes into the sea and then returns to lie down next to the body of her companion. She places her hand on his, seen together in close-up, and it becomes a flipper. Once again a red turtle, she slowly returns to the sea.

The link between the man who is cast away on the island and the red turtle is, plainly, the central relationship of this version of the Crusoe-myth. There is no human Friday in this narrative; there is only a reptile. It is a turtle that keeps the man on the island, and a turtle that metamorphoses into his mate. Later, turtles commune with the son in the sea, assist in his rescue of his father, and in the end facilitate the young man's departure from the island. At first, however, the relationship between man and reptile seems to be straightforwardly antagonistic. The man wants to escape; the turtle prevents him from doing so. The film never asks why that would be so, nor does it really suggest an answer to that question. It offers only the single, dramatic moment in which the two creatures face one another under water (Figure 36.1). The man clearly feels threatened; the turtle seems curious, attentive, but then swims away. Although the man does not seem to be aware of it, this scene represents a moment of 'intercourse' ('communication' or 'connection') between these two very different beings. Something happens between them, something that determines the rest of the castaway's life on the island. Interestingly, whereas Dudok de Wit describes the turtle's gaze in the crucial confrontation as 'threatening', Bowen sees the creature's face as 'etched with lines that convey poignant, matter-of-fact benevolence'.[42] The turtle's bearing, expression, and intention are enigmatic, subject to strikingly different interpretations. But it is clear that there has been meaningful interaction between the two, and that sense is borne out by the turtle's act of crawling on to the beach, exposing itself to the man's anger, and, in effect, sacrificing itself for the man, giving up its being and becoming, at least for a time, a human companion for

---

[40] Stevens, 'The Red Turtle—first look'.
[41] Interestingly, the son's departure recapitulates a crucial element in Defoe's original: Crusoe's leaving home. I am grateful to my editor, Nick Seager, for bringing this point to my attention.
[42] Dudok de Wit, 'Commentary', The Red Turtle; Bowen, 'Review: The Red Turtle'.

FIGURE 36.1 *The Red Turtle* (2016), dir. Michaël Dudok de Wit.

the castaway. To be sure, this 'mythical' or 'mystical' or 'fantastic' cast of *The Red Turtle* cannot be read as any kind of argument.[43] The film is not in the least bit programmatic; Kate Stables argues that it 'hints rather than hollers' about the link between man and animal and 'leaves many things intriguingly open'.[44] Nevertheless, in representing crucial interaction between the two creatures, the film clearly suggests something like intentionality or agency in the turtle. In doing so, I believe, Dudok de Wit's film offers us a retelling of the Crusoe story that takes us into the realm of animal rights discourse.

ANIMAL RIGHTS AND ETHICS

The question of whether animals *have*, or can have, rights, philosophically speaking, comes down—to put the matter very simply—to the question of whether or not one believes that animals have, or can have, 'moral status'. Traditionally, Western philosophers have denied moral status to animals 'due to a lack of consciousness, reason, or autonomy'.[45] Recently, however, some have challenged this view of animals. Without

---

[43] I quote here from the reviews by Bowen and Stevens, already cited; and from Kate Stables, 'Film of the Week: *The Red Turtle* is a Dream of a Desert Island Movie', *Sight and Sound*, June 2017, updated 3 August 2017, https://www.bfi.org.uk/news-opinion/sight-sound-magazine/reviews-recommendations/red-turtle-michael-dudok-de-wit-dream-desert-island-movie. (Accessed 3 June 2019).

[44] Stables, 'Film of the Week'.

[45] Scott D. Wilson, 'Animals and Ethics', in *Internet Encyclopedia of Philosophy*, ed. James Fieser and Bradley Dowden, https://www.iep.utm.edu/anim-eth. (Accessed 3 June 2019). Wilson points out that, among others, Thomas Aquinas, René Descartes, and Immanuel Kant have enunciated this view of animals.

trying to enter into the complexities of a philosophical debate, one can simply point out that Tom Regan has made an influential case for the moral status of animals, arguing, according to Scott Wilson, that 'animals have rights in just the same way that human beings do' because they 'have the same moral status as human beings'.[46] Regan argues in *The Case for Animal Rights*, first published in 1983, that creatures have rights if they can be said to be 'the subject-of-a-life' and that

> individuals are subjects-of-a-life if they have beliefs and desires; perceptions, memory, and a sense of the future, including their own future; an emotional life together with feelings of pleasure and pain; preference- and welfare-interests; the ability to initiate action in pursuit of their desires and goals; a psychophysical identity over time; and an individual welfare in the sense that their experiential life fares well or ill for them, logically independently free of their utility for others and logically independently of their being the object of anyone else's interests.[47]

Whether or not all of Regan's criteria for saying that a creature is 'the subject-of-a-life' are met by the red turtles in Dudok de Wit's film, we can say with little difficulty that many or most are.[48] The turtle(s) clearly has/have memory: it/they stay in touch with the humans on the island over the lifetime of the castaway. It/they have preference-interests and desires: they want the castaway to stay on the island, and they seem to want to foster the humans' welfare. They clearly have the ability to initiate action, destroying, as they do, three successive rafts and coming ashore for an encounter with the man. They also seem to have an identity over time: one metamorphoses into a human woman and then changes back into a turtle after the castaway's death. And, finally, the film suggests that the turtle that comes ashore has an 'individual welfare' that is not merely dependent upon or defined in relation to the human castaway. The man is troubled by its suffering; the film establishes a clear sense of the fitness of the creature's final transformation and return to the sea. There is, of course, no reason to believe that the filmmakers who created *The Red Turtle* were seeking to satisfy Regan's criteria in order to demonstrate that a turtle can be said to be 'a subject-of-a-life'.[49] Nevertheless, the film can be said to participate in a growing discussion of the 'consciousness' of animals. Sy Montgomery, in *The Soul of an Octopus*, cites the 'historic' Cambridge Declaration on Consciousness which declared that 'humans are not unique in possessing the neurological substrates

---

[46] Wilson, 'Animals and Ethics'.

[47] Tom Regan, *The Case for Animal Rights* (1983), rev. edn (Berkeley, CA: University of California Press, 2004), 243.

[48] Wilson shows that arguments about the moral status of human beings and animals make use of the 'Argument from Marginal Cases', which stipulates that not all human beings possess all of the capacities or qualities that supposedly convey moral status and therefore rights (rationality or the ability to speak, for example), but that it does not follow, therefore, that those humans lack moral status. 'Animals and Ethics'.

[49] In the extensive commentary on the DVD of *The Red Turtle*, Dudok de Wit has a great deal to say about how the film was made, but he is quite reticent when it comes to discussing the turtle and its transformations.

that generate consciousness'.[50] Orangutans are said to have culture; farm animals, we are told, 'lead rich and complex emotional lives'.[51] Such assertions make it clear that many observers of animals now believe it is no longer possible to argue that, as a group, they lack consciousness or autonomy, and, therefore, that one cannot with any surety deny to a wide range of animals moral status and, consequently, rights.

The Red Turtle, in short, offers not an argument about, but a suggestion of, being, consciousness, in the turtle that implicitly asserts its worth, and its rights. Bowen hints at this in declaring that the film opens us both to the creature's 'otherness' and to its 'majesty'. When at the end of the film the woman reacts to the man's death by going into the water, then back to her companion, and then lying down and placing her hand on his, all preparatory to her transformation and return to the sea, the film unmistakably suggests an intentionality that is shared by the human and the sea creature—an ontological integrity for both orders of being. Richard Nash has argued that whereas 'traditional humanism defined culture around the privileged category of the human, the era of the posthuman coincides with an intellectual reorientation to a world in which we are responsive agents within nature-culture networks'. In our day, that is, '[t]he paradigm of dominion, in which the world was a resource at the disposal of the human, is giving way to a paradigm of responsive interaction and mutual interdependencies'.[52] *The Red Turtle*'s considerable achievement is that it enacts the paradigm shift described by Nash: from the sense of 'dominion' in Defoe's original and in the Robinsonade that came in its wake to the emphasis on 'interaction' and 'interdependencies' in Dudok de Wit's film.

Kate Stables argues that the film 'establishes man and nature as deeply connected'; her assertion serves to remind us that the material in this film also takes the viewer into the realm of ecology, a science the 'central insight' of which is 'that everything is connected'.[53] Critics of the film have seen it as an argument for 'balance' or 'the emotional bond between man and nature', not surprisingly, given that this Crusoe begins at

---

[50] Sy Montgomery, *The Soul of an Octopus: A Surprising Exploration into the Wonder of Consciousness* (New York: ATRIA Paperback, 2015), 224. Lucinda Cole cites the United Nations Declaration of the Rights of the Great Apes as an act that participates in the 'personhood movement' and seeks to extend 'basic rights' to animals. 'Animal Studies and the Eighteenth Century: The Nature of the Beast', *Literature Compass*, 16:6 (2019), 1–12 (7); I am grateful to Cole for sharing with me her excellent introduction to animal studies scholarship on the long eighteenth century in advance of its publication.

[51] Bob Grant, 'Orangutans Have Culture', *The Scientist*, 25 October 2011, https://www.the-scientist.com/the-nutshell/orangutans-have-culture-41766. (Accessed 3 June 2019). *The Emotional World of Farm Animals*, dir. Stanley M. Minasian (Earthview Productions, 2004), https://www.youtube.com/watch?v=524JoqSlBWo. (Accessed 6 December 2019).

[52] Richard Nash, 'Animal Studies', in *The Routledge Companion to Literature and Science*, ed. Bruce Clarke and Manuela Rossini (New York: Routledge, 2011), 253–63 (255).

[53] Stables, 'Film of the Week'; Bill McKibben (ed.), *American Earth: Environmental Writing since Thoreau* (New York: Literary Classics of the United States, 2008), 265 ('insight'). Nash argues that the paradigm shift he identifies in animal studies is part of a larger turn to 'ecological criticism'. 'Animal Studies', 255.

odds with his island home, but ends up living in it contentedly.[54] Thus, the film is about 'a man's (and thus Man's) relationship with nature', in important part because it gives credence to the idea that not only Man but also other creatures have consciousness and autonomy.[55] One can find in *The Red Turtle*, then, a certain kinship with, or openness to, the argument of Aldo Leopold, the 'father of environmental ethics', in the section from *A Sand County Almanac* (1949) 'Thinking Like a Mountain', which Bill McKibben calls 'the key Damascus Road Story of American environmental conversion'. In this famous piece, Leopold turns against the killing of wolves because he comes to understand that 'mountains have a secret opinion about them'. Leopold shows that mountains need wolves to keep deer herds under control so that bushes, seedlings, and trees are not stripped off the mountainside, and even deer need wolves so that deer herds are not done in by their own over-foraging. Thus a farmer or forester who kills wolves (as Leopold did when he was young) does so because '[h]e has not learned to think like a mountain'.[56] Mountains do not think, of course, in any traditional sense, but the ecological perspective insists upon the integrity—the being—of an ecosystem like a mountain, or a desert island. *The Red Turtle*, too, sees the interconnectedness of things. The film represents the plight of a Crusoe-like figure seen from a perspective large enough to recognize that other than human creatures inhabit the world of the castaway and that those creatures matter too.[57] Michaël Dudok de Wit's film is in one sense a landmark in the history of the Robinsonade, filmic and otherwise, but in another sense it is nothing new. Just as earlier such works took account of perspectives provided by critiques of Western colonialism or racism to interrogate or rework Defoe's original, so *The Red Turtle* appropriates Defoe's endlessly fruitful source material and makes it new by making a sea creature a crucial element in Defoe's mythic narrative.

Further Reading

Lucinda Cole, 'Animal Studies and the Eighteenth Century: The Nature of the Beast', *Literature Compass*, 16:6 (2019), 1–12.

---

[54] Bowen, 'Review: *The Red Turtle*'; Stables, 'Film of the Week'. A. O. Scott finds 'eco-mysticism' in the movie. 'Review: *The Red Turtle*'. Stables argues that *The Red Turtle* is more than 'an eco-message movie', thereby implicitly acknowledging that it does partake of an ecological point of view.

[55] Stables, 'Film of the Week'.

[56] Aldo Leopold, from *A Sand County Almanac*, in *American Earth*, ed. McKibben, 265, 274–6.

[57] Lucinda Cole, in her study of vermin in literature and life sciences in the early modern period, cites approvingly the work of Michel Serres, who asserts that humans 'are not "separated but plunged, immersed in the Biogea, in cousin company"'. Cole shows that in his celebrated book, *Biogea*, 'Serres' goal is to "think like that company, in it, by it, for it"'. Cole's own goal, she tells us, is 'to treat insects, rodents, and ... [other] vermin as subjects of a shared world'. There is thus a clear kinship between such scholarship and theory and *The Red Turtle*. See Lucinda Cole, *Imperfect Creatures: Vermin, Literature, and the Sciences of Life, 1600–1740* (Ann Arbor, MI: University of Michigan Press, 2016), 172. *Biogea* was first published in French (*Biogeé*) in 2010.

Lucinda Cole, *Imperfect Creatures: Vermin, Literature, and the Sciences of Life, 1600–1740* (Ann Arbor, MI: University of Michigan Press, 2016).

Robert Mayer, 'Defoe's Cultural Afterlife, Mainly on Screen', in *The Afterlives of Eighteenth-Century Fiction*, ed. Daniel Cook and Nicholas Seager (Cambridge: Cambridge University Press, 2015), 233–52.

Robert Mayer, '*Robinson Crusoe* in the Screen Age', in *The Cambridge Companion to Robinson Crusoe*, ed. John Richetti (Cambridge: Cambridge University Press, 2018), 221–33.

Robert Mayer, 'Three Cinematic Robinsonades', in *Eighteenth-Century Fiction on Screen*, ed. Mayer (Cambridge: Cambridge University Press, 2002), 35–51.

Richard Nash, 'Animal Studies', in *The Routledge Companion to Literature and Science*, ed. Bruce Clarke and Manuela Rossini (New York: Routledge, 2011), 253–63.

Ian Watt, *Myths of Modern Individualism: Faust, Don Quixote, Don Juan, Robinson Crusoe* (Cambridge: Cambridge University Press, 1996).

A Selective Checklist of Defoe Screen Adaptations

ROBINSON CRUSOE

FILM

Robinson Crusoe, dir. Georges Méliès (1903). Protagonist played by: Georges Méliès.
Robinson Crusoe, dir. Otis Turner (1913). Robert Z. Leonard.
Little Robinson Crusoe, dir. Edward F. Cline (1924). Jackie Coogan.
Robinson Crusoe, dir. M. A. Wetherall (1927). M. A. Wetherall.
Mr. Robinson Crusoe, dir. A. Edward Sutherland (1932). Douglas Fairbanks.
Robinson Crusoe of Clipper Island, dir. Ray Taylor and Mack V. Wright (1936). Ray Mala.
Robinzon Kruzo, dir. Aleksandr Andriyevsky (1947). Pavel Kadochnikov.
Miss Robin Crusoe, dir. Eugene Frenke (1954). Amanda Blake.
Robinson Crusoe, dir. Luis Buñuel (1954). Dan O'Herlihy.
Robinson Crusoe on Mars, dir. Byron Haskin (1964). Paul Mantee.
Lt. Robin Crusoe, U.S.N., dir. Byron Paul (1966). Dick Van Dyke.
Robinson Crusoe and the Tiger, dir. René Cardona, Jr (1970). Hugo Stiglitz.
Zhizn i udivitelnye priklyucheniya Robinzona Kruzo, dir. Stanislav Govorukhin (1973). Leonid Kuravlyov.
Man Friday, dir. Jack Gold (1975). Peter O'Toole.
Il signor Robinson, mostruosa storia d'amore e d'avventure, dir. Sergio Corbucci (1976). Paolo Villaggio.
Dobrodružství Robinsona Crusoe, námořníka z Yorku, dir. Stanislav Látal (1982). Václav Postránecký.
Enemy Mine, dir. Wolfgang Petersen (1985). Dennis Quaid.
Castaway, dir. Nicolas Roeg (1986). Oliver Reed.
Crusoe, dir. Caleb Deschanel (1988). Aidan Quinn.
Shipwrecked, dir. Nils Gaup (1990). Stian Smestad.
Robinson Crusoe, dir. Rodney K. Hardy and George Miller (1997). Pierce Brosnan.
Cast Away, dir. Robert Zemeckis (2000). Tom Hanks.
Robinson Crusoë, dir. Thierry Chabert (2003). Pierre Richard.
Robinson & Crusoe, dir. Jan Sabol (2013). Vica Kerekes and Roman Luknár.

The Martian, dir. Ridley Scott (2015). Matt Damon.
The Wild Life, dir. Vincent Kesteloot, Ben Stassen, and Mimi Maynard (2016). Matthias Schweighöfer.
The Red Turtle, dir. Michaël Dudok de Wit (2016).

TV
Les Aventures de Robinson Crusoë, cr. Jean Sacha (1964). Robert Hoffmann.
Gilligan's Island, cr. Sherwood Schwartz (1964–7).
Expedition Robinson [*Survivor*], cr. Charlie Parsons (1997–).
Lost, cr. Jeffrey Lieber, J. J. Abrams, and Damon Lindelof (2004–10).
Crusoe, cr. Stephen Gallagher, Justin Bodle, and Richard Mewis (2008–9). Philip Winchester.

MOLL FLANDERS

FILM
The Amorous Adventures of Moll Flanders, dir. Terence Young (1965). Kim Novak.
Moll Flanders, dir. Pen Densham (1996). Robin Wright.

TV
Moll Flanders, dir. Donald McWhinnie (1975). Julia Foster.
The Fortunes and Misfortunes of Moll Flanders, dir. David Attwood (1996). Alex Kingston.

A Journal of the Plague Year

FILM
The Periwig-Maker, dir. Steffen Schäffler (1999). Kenneth Branagh.

Index

For the benefit of digital users, indexed terms that span two pages (e.g., 52–53) may, on occasion, appear on only one of those pages.

Acts and Bills of Parliament
   Calico Act (1700) 227–28, 258–59
   Copyright Act (1709) 7, 215–16, 222, 223, 226
   Corporation Act (1661) 369, 619–20
   Foreign Protestants Naturalization Act (1708) 491–92
   Licensing Act (1662) lapses (1695) 126, 215–16, 217–18
   Occasional Conformity Act (1711) 115–16, 117, 378–79
   Occasional Conformity bills (1702–4) 117, 129–30, 320–21, 323, 369–70, 371, 372
   Schism Act (1714) 97–98
   Settlement, Act of (1701) 114–15
   South Sea Company, Act incorporating the (1711) 538n.29
   Stamp Act (1712) 216
   Stamp Act (1725) 216
   Test Act (1673) 369, 619–20
   Toleration, Act of (1689) 115–16, 117–18, 311–12, 315, 320–21, 369–70
   Transportation Act (1718) 62
   Uniformity, Act of (1662) 312
   Workhouse Act (1723) 246–47
Adas, Michael 361
Addison, Joseph 22, 162–63, 218, 241–42, 607–8
   see also 'Addison, Joseph, and Richard Steele'
Addison, Joseph, and Richard Steele 127, 247
   Spectator, The 482, 484–85
   Tatler, The 198–99, 484–85
   see also 'Addison, Joseph' *and* 'Steele, Richard'
AIDS 663–65
Aitken, G. A. 608, 624, 625

Alaimo, Stacy 464–65
Alexander the Great 161, 291
Almanza, Battle of 409
Altman, Janet Gurkin 182, 184, 190–91
American Society for the Prevention of Cruelty to Animals 660
Ames, William 108–9
Anderson, Agnes Campbell 224, 229, 273
Anderson, Benedict 503
Anderson, Misty 290–91
Anglesey, Earl of 135, 220, 380
Anglo-Dutch Wars 400, 508
Anne, Queen
   accession of 126, 311–12
   Anglicanism of 114–15, 311–12, 369
   death of 110–11, 115, 134–35, 167, 379–80, 396–97
   party politics under 3, 43, 130–31, 132, 207–8, 584–85
   speeches to Parliament of 113, 207–8
   suspension of theatres by 72–73
   see also under 'Defoe, Daniel, views on'
Annesley, Samuel 4–5, 8–9, 94–95, 313
Anson, George 547
Applebee, Elizabeth 64–65
Applebee, John
   Original Weekly Journal 126–27, 137, 475, 638–39n.32
Aravamudan, Srinivas 439–40, 562, 563–64
Archer, John Michael 384, 386, 391
Argamon, Shlomo 640–41
Argyll, Duke of 224, 378–79
Ashcraft, Richard 316–17
Assmann, Jan 661–62
Aubin, Penelope 641–42
Auden, W. H. 37, 44

Austen, Jane
   Northanger Abbey 613, 655
   Pride and Prejudice 240–41, 290
Avery, Capt. John 60
Ayres, Philip 488–89
Ayscough, Samuel 586

Backscheider, Paula R. 7–9, 67, 75–77, 79, 92–93, 96, 162, 180–81, 187–88, 217–18, 221–22, 311–12, 319–20, 324–25, 384–85, 387–88, 390, 392–93, 394, 396–97, 400–1, 414, 421–22, 438–39, 575–76, 661–62
Bacon, Sir Francis 324–25, 347–50, 352, 391, 482, 483–84
   Advancement of Learning, The 341
   De Dignitate & Augmentis Scientiarum 384
   Historie of the Raigne of King Henry the Seventh, The 384
   New Atlantis, The 384
   'Of Plantations' 525–26
Bagehot, Walter 620–21
Baine, Rodney M. 386, 615–16, 633, 634, 642–43
Baines, Paul 55
Baker, Ernest 608
Baker, Henry 190–91
Baker, John 8, 209–10, 226–28
Baker, Sophia 190–91
Baldwin, Abigail 226–27
Baldwin, R. 584–85
Ballantyne, John 606–7, 617–18
Barbauld, Anna Lætitia 75–76, 79, 616
Barber, John 229
Barcelona, Siege of 340–41, 518–19
Bassett, John 591–92
Baxter, Richard 313, 319–20
   Certainty of the World of Spirits, The 325
   Poor Man's Family Book, The 95–96
Beattie, James 614–15, 616, 617
Beattie, J. M. 419–20
Beckett, J. V. 240
Behn, Aphra 49–50, 70–71
Belhaven, Lord 44–45, 373–74
   Scots answer to a British vision An 393–94
Bellamy, Edward 209–10
Bellamy, Liz 281
Berwick, Duke of 412
Betagh, William 547

Bethell, Slingsby 316–17
Betterton, Thomas 70–71
Bettesworth, Arthur 227, 228
Bickham, George
   High Church Champion and His Two Seconds, The 20–22
   Whig's Medly, The 20–22, 207
Black, Jeremy 386, 507–8
Blackmore, Richard 33
Blair, Hugh 614–15, 616, 617
Blake, William
   'Tyger, The' 47
Blenheim, Battle of 42, 121–22, 371–72, 406, 508, 512–13
Blewett, David 238–39, 297, 602–5
Bludworth, Sir Thomas 427–28
Bohun, Ralph 453–54, 455–56
Bolingbroke, Henry St John, first Viscount 216, 220
Bononcini, Giovanni 481
Book of Common Prayer, The 312
Booker, Kristina 276–77, 283–84, 285–86
Boreham, William 227–28
Bosman, William 459–60, 461, 463–64
Boswell, James 614–15
Boulton, Jeremy 244
Boulukos, George 442–43
Bowen, Chuck 668, 669–70, 672
Bowes, George 240–41
Bowrey, Thomas 528
Bowyer, William 228–29
Boyer, Abel 133, 631–32, 639, 641–42
   Political State of Great Britain, The 135–36, 631
Boyle, Robert 324–25, 345–46, 351–52
Boyne, Battle of the 193
Bracegirdle, Anne 70–71
Bradbury, Thomas 115
Bradley, Richard 464–65
Bragg, Benjamin 16–17, 223
Brant, Clare 177–78
Brayley, Edward Wedlake 596–97
   Beauties of England and Wales, The 616
Bromley, William 43
Brooks, Thomas
   Apples of Gold for Young Men and Women and a Crown of Glory for Old Men and Women 97

Brotherton, John 227, 228, 637
Brown, Laura 571
Brown, Thomas 389
Buckingham, Duke of 33
Bülbring, Karl D. 624
Bullard, Rebecca 52–53, 397–98
Buñuel, Luis 662–63
Bunyan, John 79, 82, 89–90, 150, 319–20
   Holy War, The 317
   Israel's Hope Encouraged 317
   Life and Death of Mr Badman, The 317
   Pilgrim's Progress, The 77, 146, 147–48, 317
Burnet, Thomas (pamphleteer) 219–20
Burnet, Thomas
   Sacred Theory of the Earth, The 260, 360
Burns, Robert
   'Man's a Man for a' that, A' 483–84
Burrows, John 640–41
Butler, Samuel 41
   Hudibras 30n.6
Byng, Admiral John 599–600

Camden, William
   Britannia 488–89
Campbell, Duncan 620–21
Carlos II, King of Spain 121, 366, 506–7, 518
Caroline, Queen 272–73
Catalogus Bibliothecae Harleianae 612
Cather, Willa 625–26
Cervantes, Migeul de
   Don Quixote 614–15
Chaber, Lois 305–6
Chadwick, William 620–21
Chalmers, George 586, 591, 595, 605–6, 614–16, 617–20, 629–30, 636
Chapman, Paul 136
Character of a Turn-coat A 1
Charles I, King of England 2–3, 20, 36, 57–58, 111, 170, 171–73, 175–76, 313, 453–54
Charles II, King of England 33, 35–36, 70–71, 111, 241–42, 264–65, 272, 313–15, 319–20, 384–86, 387–88, 602
Charles VI, Holy Roman Emperor 131, 516–17
Charles XII, King of Sweden 407–8, 513–14
Chartier, Roger 219
Chasles, Philarete 620
Chetwood, William Rufus 157, 227

Chickens' Lib 660
Chico, Tita 362–63
Child, Sir Josiah 234, 248
Church of England 2, 4–5, 31, 114–15, 207–8, 312–13, 321, 341, 500–1, 502–3, 622–23
Church of Scotland 175–76, 323–24, 375, 500–2, 587, 608–9
Cibber, Colley 70–71
Cibber, Theophilus
   Lives of the Poets of Great Britain and Ireland 612–14
Cicero 78, 208
Clarendon, Earl of
   History of the Rebellion, The 1–2, 57–58, 162–63, 173–74, 412–13
Clarendon Code 4–5, 312
Clayton, Sir Robert 155, 270–71, 421–22, 434
Clerk of Penicuik, Sir John 376
Coetzee, J. M. 605–6
   Foe 457–58
Coke of Holkham, Thomas 240–41
Colbert 188
Cole, Sir William 421–22
Coleridge, Samuel Taylor 617–18, 645
Colley, Linda 439–40, 564
Collier, Jeremy
   Short View of the Immorality of the English Stage 70–71, 72, 73–74
Collins, Anthony
   Discourse of Free-thinking 326
Collins, John 237–38, 317–18
Collins, Wilkie
   Moonstone, The 622
Collinson, Patrick 506nn.4–5
Columbus, Christopher 160, 345–46
Congreve, William 70–71
   Way of the World, The 76
Conway, Alison 278–79
Conway, Stephen 506–7
Cook, Sir Charles 234
Cook, Captain James 595–96
Cooke, J. 64–65
Cooper, James Fenimore
   Crater, The 620
Coppola, Al 347–48, 352
Corbauld, Henry 597–99
Corelli, Arcangelo 481

Corn-Cutter's Journal, The 584
Cornhill Magazine 49
Cornish, Henry 316–17
Cotton, Charles 30
Cowan, Brian 125–26, 131
Cowley, Abraham 40, 454–55
Cox, T. 228
Cromwell, Oliver 20, 150–51, 384–85, 571–72
Cromwell, Thomas 390–91
Croome, George 209–10
Crossley, James 622–23, 625
Cumming, Sir Alexander 378
Curll, Edmund 218, 220–21, 225–26, 227, 228, 638

Daily Courant, The 12
Daily Gazetteer, The 136
Daily Post, The 126–27, 228–29
Dampier, William 57, 150, 156–57, 160, 391–92, 458, 528, 540–41, 544–45, 554–55
 New Voyage Round the World A 60–61, 147–48, 546–47
Danton, Georges 594
Darby Jr, John 229
Darrell, William
 Gentleman Instructed in the Conduct of a Virtuous and Happy Life, The 95–96
Davenant, Charles 112–13, 114n.14, 411, 457–58
Davies, Godfrey 608
Davis, Leith 503
Davis, Moll 36
Dawson, W. J. 625
De Britaine, William
 Humane Prudence 601
Deering, Mary 272
Defoe, Benjamin 190–91
Defoe, Daniel, life of
 appearance of 237
 aspires to be a 'Gentleman' 235, 237–39, 247–48
 attribution issues 629–44
 birth and upbringing of 4–5, 313, 471–72, 482
 business career of 9, 10–11, 30, 67, 218–19, 230, 237–38, 250, 273, 317, 318–19, 341–42, 419–20, 471, 486
 childhood of 451–52
 contemporary reputation of, vii, 3, 4, 11

 death of 159
 debts and bankruptcies of 9–11, 15, 30, 162, 370–71
 Dissenter, vii, 3–5, 89–90, 94–95, 97–98, 111–12, 313, 314–15, 316–17, 341, 368, 482, 500–1
 education of 4–5, 71, 341, 347–48, 482
 hosier 9, 15–16, 250, 317
 intelligence agent 144–45, 162–63, 164, 166, 250, 372, 373–75, 382–83, 387–88, 390, 395–96, 398, 497–98, 623
 marriage of 237–38
 Monmouth rebel 1, 272–73, 315–16, 388
 pantile factory owner 10–11, 250, 471, 486
 payment from secret service funds 7–8, 218–19, 374, 380, 390
 posthumous reputation 417–18, 611–27
 in prison 6–7, 9, 10–11, 110–11, 144–45, 162, 186–87, 208, 218–19, 220, 370–71, 387–88, 417–18, 637
 prophet of modernity, vi
 prosecution for seditious libel (1703) 6–7, 10–11, 181, 199–200, 208, 217, 272–73, 323–24, 370, 387–88, 390, 417–18, 421–22
 prosecution for seditious libel (1713) 209–10, 219–20, 272–73
 radical Whig 3, 111–13, 125–26, 131, 243–44, 322, 364, 380–81
 reconciled to the Whigs 380, 396–97
 recruited by the government (1703) 6–7, 162, 323–24, 371, 417–18, 438
 relations with book trade 221–25, 226–30
 relations with Harley 6–8, 129–31, 135, 144–45, 162–63, 167, 182, 186–91, 218–19, 220, 234, 323–24, 341–42, 364, 370–72, 373–75, 377–79, 380–81, 387–97, 399, 486, 497–98, 506–7, 526–28
 relations with King William III 10, 144–45, 322, 365–66, 388
 in Scotland 109–10, 162, 164, 250, 323–24, 373–75, 376, 378, 393–95, 496–98, 499–501
 social conservatism of, vi, 243–44, 246, 247
 subscription ventures 222, 223, 224–25
 tours of England (1704–5) 162, 372, 390, 392–93

trained for the ministry, v, 71, 314, 317–18, 328, 341–42
in trouble after Hanoverian succession 219, 220, 323–24, 380
Defoe, Daniel, views on
Anne, Queen of England 39, 43, 183, 202, 204–6, 272–73, 502–3
Catholicism 104–5, 322, 380–81, 396–97, 514
colonialism 394, 436–39, 478, 524–42, 544–45, 559–60, 562–63, 567–68, 578
Dissenters 115–17, 118–19, 189–90, 320–21, 323–24, 364, 369–70, 380–81
English Civil Wars 1–3
immigration 242–43, 245–46, 255, 483–84, 489–90, 491–92, 521–22
Jacobitism 1–2, 115, 165–66, 167–68, 208–9, 380–81, 396–97, 506–7, 514
occult and supernatural 324–25, 326, 327–28, 342–44, 347–49, 352, 357
property 111–13, 243–44, 247, 322, 535–36
religion, vii, 4–5, 92, 94–95, 104–6, 317–20, 328, 335, 339–41
Revolution of 1688, 1–4, 12, 111–12, 113–14, 115–16, 320–21, 322, 328, 364, 371–72, 380–81
Royal African Company 569–73
science and technology 345–46, 347–48, 351–52, 356–63
slavery 438, 441–42, 443–49, 476, 511, 513, 524, 541–42, 564–65, 571–73, 578
trade 118–20, 121–22, 133–34, 249–65, 341–42, 493, 506–7, 574, 578
war 39, 400–15, 505–6
William III, King of England 1, 2–3, 12, 33–34, 37, 114–15, 201–2, 204–6, 320–21, 322, 364–66, 367, 380–81, 510–11
Defoe, Daniel, works of
Account of the Conduct of Robert Earl of Oxford, An 169n.27
Advantages of Peace and Commerce, The 259–60, 530
Advice to all Parties 12, 113
Anatomy of Exchange-Alley, The 120, 250–51, 476
Answer to a Question that No Body thinks of, viz. But What if the Queen Should Die?, An 115, 208–9

Appeal to Honour and Justice, An 7, 22, 23, 24–25, 114n.14, 133, 209, 322, 323–24, 365–66, 379–80, 395–96, 397, 606–7, 615–16, 630–31, 632
Argument ... Employing and Enobling Foreigners, An 491–92
Argument Shewing, That a Standing Army, With Consent of Parliament, is not Inconsistent with a Free Government, An 243–44, 499, 584
Atalantis Major 51n.10
Atlas Maritimus & Commercialis 154n.15, 224–25, 228–29, 459–60, 573–74, 575–76
Brief History of the Poor Palatine Refugees Lately Arrived in England A 491–92
Brief Reply to the History of Standing Armies in England A 401n.4
Caledonia 44–45, 224, 373–75, 498–99, 585–86
Captain Singleton
  Africa in 563, 565–66, 567–78
  critical reception of 618–19
  domesticity in 304–5
  ecology in 452–53, 459–64
  'fiction of entertainment' 60–62
  money in 106, 252, 266–67
  national identity in 440–47, 448
  Pacific in 546–47, 548–54, 555–56, 558, 559
  Portuguese in 521
  publication history of 599–600, 601–2, 606, 608–9, 637
  travel in 151–53, 156–57, 158, 493–94
  violence in 412–13
Case of Mr. Law, Truly Stated, The 120, 228
Challenge of Peace, Address'd to the Whole Nation A 113, 371
Character of the Late Dr. Samuel Annesley, The 8–9
Christianity Not as Old as the Creation 326–27
Colonel Jack
  colonial migration in 541–42
  crime in 275, 417–18, 419–20, 423–26, 427, 428–29, 431, 434, 661–62
  critical reception of 608, 613
  family and marriage in 279–80, 299, 301–2, 304–10
  'fiction of entertainment' 61–62, 63–67
  gentility in 238–39

Defoe, Daniel, works of (*cont.*)
   history in 176
   Jacobitism in 63–64, 238–39, 268–69, 279–80, 308–9
   London in 478–80
   money in 252, 267, 268–69
   price of 418
   publication history of 583, 600, 606, 613–14, 635
   race and slavery in 442–43, 444–45, 446, 447–49, 483–84
   Spanish America in 59, 154–55, 309
   travel in 154–56, 157
   war in 400–1, 412–15
   women in 284, 286
Commentator, The 8–9, 76–77, 126–27, 137–38, 262–63, 396–97
Compleat English Gentleman, The 79–81, 86–87, 93, 100, 159–60, 179–80, 229, 237–38, 241–42, 341, 607–8, 624
Complete English Tradesman, The
   commerce and manufacture in 120, 146–47, 252, 262–64, 391–92, 552–53
   dialogue in 79–81, 84–86, 93, 100
   epistolary form of 93, 177–78
   prose style and 179–80
   publication history of 589–90, 606–7, 608–9
   Rivington's publication of 227, 589–90
   status in 233–35, 236, 237–38, 243
   women in 273, 274–75, 276, 277–78, 279, 286, 287–88
Conjugal Lewdness 93–94, 280–81, 294, 296–97, 298–99, 300–3, 305–6, 307, 309–10, 606–7
Consolidator, The 23, 42–43, 349, 350–52, 391–93, 607–8, 615–16
Continuation of Letters written by a Turkish Spy A 179–80, 188, 190–93, 383, 397
Danger of the Protestant Religion Consider'd, The 121, 320–21, 506–7
Director, The 8–9, 126–27, 475
Discourse Upon an Union of the Two Kingdoms of England and Scotland A 499–500
Dissenters Answer to the High-Church Challenge, The 118

Double Welcome, The 37, 42
Due Preparations for the Plague 58–59, 79–82, 84, 100n.29, 464–65
Dyet of Poland, The 42–43, 392–93
Edinburgh Courant, The 126–27, 375
Elegy on the Author of the True-Born-English-Man, An 39, 41
Eleven Opinions about Mr. H—y, 114n.14
Encomium on a Parliament, An 32–33, 510n.20
Enquiry into the Danger and Consequences of a War with the Dutch, An 515
Enquiry into the Disposal of the Equivalent, An 499–500
Enquiry into Occasional Conformity, An 369–70
Enquiry into the Occasional Conformity of Dissenters, An 106n.36, 116–17, 369
Essay at Removing National Prejudices against a Union with Scotland, Parts I–VI, An 109–10, 113, 373–74, 499–500, 501, 503
Essay upon Literature, An 359–60
Essay on the History and Reality of Apparitions, An 56–57, 67, 178n.5, 326, 327–28, 334–35, 339–40, 342, 355–56, 594–95, 606–7, 612–, 613
Essay on the Late Storm, An 10–11, 113
Essay on the South-Sea Trade, An 528
Essay upon Loans, An 630–31
Essay on the Regulation of the Press, An 7, 220–21, 481–82
Essay on the Treaty of Commerce with France, An 118–19
Essay upon Projects, An, vii–viii, 71, 145, 146–47, 148–49, 250–51, 272, 341–42, 362, 389, 403–4, 405, 408, 490, 573n.28, 620–21
Essay upon Publick Credit, An 251, 584, 630–31
Essay upon the Trade to Africa, An 569, 570, 574
Essay on the Treaty of Commerce with France, An 118–19
Every-Body's Business, is No-Body's Business 284–86, 398–99
Evident Approach of a War, The 122

Experiment, The 500n.24
Family Instructor, The
  dialogue in 74, 75–76, 78, 84, 89, 95, 100, 101–5
  didacticism in, vii–viii, 11, 92–93
  family relations in 275–76, 278–79, 280–81, 294, 297–99, 301
  illustrations of 591
  political contexts of 96–98
  publication history of 590–92, 595, 605, 606–7
  religion in 96–99, 105, 323–24
Family Instructor, Volume II, The 11, 78–81, 92–93, 100, 104–5, 294, 299–300, 301–2, 591
Farther Adventures of Robinson Crusoe, The
  advertisement for *Atlas* in 224–25
  Africa in 563, 571–72
  China in 361
  colonialism in 524–25, 532n.18, 536–37, 548–49, 557
  family relationships in 299, 302–3, 309–10, 439n.12
  'fiction of adventure' 55–57
  national identity in 520–21
  publication history of 602–6
  religion in 333
  travel in 149–50, 159
  women in 278
Felonious Treaty, The 121
Flying-Post and Medley, The 135, 379–80
Fortunate Mistress, The
  attribution to Defoe of 4, 635–38, 641–42
  critical reception of 608, 623, 625–26
  dialogue in 99–100
  espionage in 383, 397–98
  'fiction of entertainment' 51–52, 64–67
  gender in, v, 272, 274, 286, 287–88, 480–81
  illustrations of 602
  marriage and domesticity in 279, 304–5
  money in 123, 252, 267, 268–71, 275, 555, 559
  national identity in 521–22
  publication history of 601–2
  psychology in 58–59, 309–10
  publication history of 595–96, 601–2, 606–7, 608–9, 613–14, 617

  religion in 106, 327
  slavery in 445, 564–65
  status in 237, 276–77, 284, 289–90, 291–92
  theatricality in 88
  travel in 146, 155–56, 157, 159, 286
Freeholder's Plea against Stock-Jobbing Elections of Parliament Men, The 367–68
Friendly Epistle by Way of Reproof … to Thomas Bradbury A 115
General History of Discoveries and Improvements A 159, 259–60, 276, 347, 356–59, 400–1, 524–25, 529–30, 562–63, 565–66, 573–74
General History of Trade A 249, 256, 260
Genuine Works of Mr. Daniel D'Foe, The 11, 422n.16
Giving Alms no Charity 245–47, 254, 282–83, 490
Great Law of Subordination Consider'd, The 123–24, 236–37, 241–42, 244, 247, 276–77, 283–85, 291–92
High-Church Legion, The 392–93
Historical Account of the Bitter Sufferings … of the Episcopal Church in Scotland, An 501–2
Historical Collections 161, 188, 273, 274, 291
History of the Kentish Petition, The 162n.6
History of the Union, The 162–67, 168, 169–70, 171, 172, 174, 175, 224, 374–75, 376, 393, 502–3, 586–87, 608–9, 612, 615–16
History of the Wars, of his Present Majesty Charles XII, The 407–8
Humble Proposal to the People of England, An 118–19, 437–40, 530
Hymn to the Mob A 45–46
Hymn to Peace A 42
Hymn to the Pillory A 39–41, 42, 48, 208, 218, 228, 323, 607–8
Hymn to Victory A 42, 403–4, 513n.26
Impartial Account of the Late Famous Siege of Gibraltar, The 407–8
Impartial History of the Czar of Muscovy, An 407–8
Imperial Gratitude 517
Journal of the Plague Year A 46–47
  adaptations of 663–65

Defoe, Daniel, works of (*cont.*)
  attribution to Defoe 635
  COVID-19 and, v
  critical reception of 612–13, 616, 618
  dialogue in 79–81, 82–84, 99–100
  ecology in 452–53, 464–68
  'fiction of purpose' 57–59
  historical fiction in 173–74, 175
  illustrations of 597–99
  London in 153–54, 288–89, 474–77
  publication history of 583, 596–99, 606, 608–9
  religion and science in 339–40, 353, 354
  topicality of 661–62
  women in 283
Jure Divino
  critical reception of 29n.1, 34
  history in 161, 204
  pirated editions of 16–17, 207, 223
  political theory in 2–3, 43–44, 131, 243–44, 322–23
  portraits of Defoe in 12–17, 207, 210
  publication history of 585–86
  satire in 195, 196, 203–7, 210
  status in 239
  subscription publication of 221–24
King of Pirates, The 569–70, 608
Lay-Man's Sermon upon the Late Storm, The 10–11, 113
Legion's Memorial 110, 184, 367
Letter to a Dissenter from his Friend at the Hague A 6, 124, 189–90
Letter to the Dissenters A 189–90, 323–24
Letter to Mr. Bisset A 638
Letter to Mr. How A 116–17
Lex Talionis 121, 490
Manufacturer, The 8–9, 126–27, 134, 251–52, 258, 263–64, 396–97
Master Mercury, The 42, 126–27, 133, 400–1, 406
Meditations 30, 237–38, 314–20, 327, 607–8
Memoirs of a Cavalier
  'fiction of purpose' 57–58, 59–60, 63–64
  history in 2, 163–64, 170, 171–74, 175–76, 517
  military affairs in 154–55, 400–1, 412–15

  publication history of 595–97, 606, 613–14, 637
  travel in 150–51
Memoirs of the Church of Scotland 172, 174n.31, 587, 608–9
Memoirs of the Conduct of Her Late Majesty and Her Last Ministry 52–53
Memoirs of Count Tariff 118–19
Mere Nature Delineated 46
Mercator 8–9, 126, 133–34, 251–52, 377–79, 620–21
Mercurius Politicus 126–27, 135–36, 137, 380, 396–97, 632
Minutes of the Negotiations of Monsr. Mesnager 23–24, 52–54, 163–64, 170–72, 175–76, 383, 397, 631, 639
Mock Mourners, The 37–38, 108, 195, 201–2
Moll Flanders
  American colonies in 541–42
  attribution to Defoe 4, 635–37, 641–42
  crime in 276–77, 289, 290, 417–18, 423–24, 426–34, 446, 493–94, 661–62
  critical reception of 612, 623, 625–26
  dialogue in 94
  'fiction of entertainment' 49–50, 51–52, 58–59, 61–66, 171–72
  London in 471–72, 476–77, 478, 479, 480
  marriage in 86, 275, 280–81, 292, 297, 302–3, 304–10
  money in 94, 252, 264–65, 267–69, 555
  moral message of 69, 94, 556
  price of 418
  publication history of 49–50, 583, 595–96, 600–1, 605, 606, 608, 613–14
  retrospective form of 180
  screen adaptations of 663–65
  social status in 123, 235–38, 286, 289–91, 304–5
  theatricality of 87–88
  travel in 146, 152–54, 155–56, 157
  women's status in 84–85, 272, 275–76, 282–83, 284, 285, 287–88, 480–81
Monitor, The 8–9, 126–27
More Reformation 37–38, 39–40, 122–23, 195, 196–97, 200, 206–7

New Family Instructor A 30, 46, 47–48, 56–57, 67, 76–77, 92–93, 104–6, 280–81, 294, 326–27, 334–35, 591
New Test of the Church of England's Honesty A 109–10
New Test of the Church of England's Loyalty A 109–10
New Voyage Round the World, A
    attribution to Defoe of 595–96, 613–14, 636
    colonialism in 159, 266, 524–25, 537–41
    'fiction of purpose' 59, 67
    Pacific region in 545–46, 547–49, 552–60
    publication history of 595–97, 606
    Spanish in 519–21
    travel in 147–48, 156–57
Observations on the Fifth Article of the Treaty of Union 499–500
Of Royal Education 100
Old Whig and Modern Whig Revived, The 113–14
Original Power of the Collective Body of the People of England, The 34, 111–13, 243–44, 367–68, 584–85, 587, 608–9
Pacificator, The 33, 38–39, 200
Peace without Union 117
Plan of the English Commerce, A, vii–viii, 93, 120, 247–48, 251–52, 254, 437, 491–92, 495–96, 524, 530, 578, 589–90
Political History of the Devil, The 47, 56–57, 326, 327, 334–35, 339–40, 342–44, 383, 398, 576–77, 592–94, 595, 606–7, 622
Poor Man's Plea, The 37–38, 122–23, 241–42, 420–21, 422–24, 427
Present State of the Parties in Great Britain, The 178n.5
Protestant Monastery, The 123–24, 594
Quarrel of the School-Boys at Athens, The 51n.10
Reasons against Fighting 514–15
Reasons against the Succession of the House of Hanover 208–9, 210
Reflections on the Prohibition Act 119n.24
Reformation of Manners 33, 37–39, 122–23, 195, 196–97, 202–3, 421–24, 425–26
Remarks on the Letter to the Author of the State-Memorial 392–93

Review
    advertisements of *Jure Divino* in 210, 221–22
    colonial arguments in 524–26, 527–28, 535–36, 544–45, 549–50, 553–54, 560
    commerce in 60–61, 119, 146, 240, 242–43, 249, 251–65, 341–42, 360, 484, 539–40, 569, 570, 572–73, 574, 576–77, 578, 630–31
    contemporary reactions, vii, 12, 237
    Defoe's self-presentation in 15–16, 110–11, 220, 223, 317–18
    financing of 7–9
    history in 2, 161, 191
    immigration covered in 483–84, 491–92
    journalistic significance of 109–10, 125–33, 137–38, 484–87, 616
    literary discussion in 198, 482
    plague reportage in 474
    politics in 2, 20, 126–33, 136–37, 138–42, 220–21, 340–41, 371–73, 374, 376–78, 390, 392–93, 395–96, 499–500, 506–7
    publication history of 607–8
    publishers of 227, 229–30
    Scandal Club section of 8–9, 94–95, 139, 383, 422–23
    status in 233, 235, 241–42, 244, 245, 246–47
    theatre in 69, 71–74
    War of the Spanish Succession in 121–22, 400–1, 402, 403, 404–5, 406–12, 414, 415, 511–12, 515–16, 518
Robinson Crusoe
    adaptations and appropriations of 605–6, 621–22, 645–58, 660–73
    Africa in 563–65, 566–67, 577–78
    autobiographical claim of 24–25
    colonialism in, v, 83, 359–60, 459–60, 524–25, 530–37, 627, 647–48
    dialogue in 83, 88, 94, 99–100
    environment in 452–53, 455–59, 556
    family in 297, 299, 302–5, 307
    'fiction of adventure' 53–55
    Gildon's attack on 23–24, 69, 564–65, 610, 626, 635
    illustration of 53–54, 602
    money in 59, 62, 252, 265–66

Defoe, Daniel, works of (*cont.*)
    national identity in 442, 505–6, 519–20, 521, 625–26
    poetry in 31
    popularity of 157, 591–92, 602–6, 611, 613, 614–20, 623, 626
    property in 322
    publication history of 602–6, 615–16, 625
    publishers of 8, 224–25, 228–29, 637
    religion in 51–52, 56–57, 320, 323–24, 327, 330–34, 353
    Selkirk as model for 156–57, 620–22
    slavery in 361, 444–45
    status in 235–36, 245–46
    technology in 348–49
    travel in 146–48, 158
    truth claim in, vi, 23–24
    women in 278, 289–90
Roxana, see '*Fortunate Mistress, The*'
Scots Nation and Union Vindicated, The 503
Seasonable Warning and Caution against the Insinuations of Papists and Jacobites A 606–7
Second Volume of the Writings of the Author of The True-Born Englishman A 11, 12, 31–32, 195, 224, 418, 585, 630–31
Secret History of the October Club, The 52–53, 113–14, 167–68
Secret History of One Year A 52–53
Secret History of the Secret History of the White-Staff, The 22, 111, 169–70, 171, 174
Secret History of the White-Staff, The 22, 111, 115, 163–64, 166–70, 171, 172, 379–80
Secret Memoirs of a Treasonable Conference at S—House 52–53
Serious Inquiry into this Grand Question A 117
Serious Reflections ... of Robinson Crusoe
    didacticism of 24, 56, 309–10, 342, 557
    poetry in 30–31, 46
    publication history of 56, 602–6
    religion in 56–57, 326–27, 334–40, 352–54, 386, 412–13
    travel in 150
Shortest Way to Peace and Union, The 110–11
Shortest Way with the Dissenters, The
    Defoe's comments on 140–41
    Defoe's prosecution and punishment for 6–7, 10–11, 12, 16–17, 39, 108, 181, 199–200, 217–19, 272–73, 278, 387–88, 390, 400, 417–18, 421–22, 471, 486
    irony in 114–15, 207–8, 209–10
    notoriety of, vii, 110–11, 612
    political and religious contexts of 114n.14, 117, 207–8, 210, 320–21, 323–24, 369–70
Sincerity of the Dissenters Vindicated, The 113n.13
Six Distinguishing Characters of a Parliament-Man, The, 366–67, 584–85
Some Reflections ... Standing Army is Inconsistent with a Free Government 401n.4, 510–11
Some Sensible Queries on the Third Head, viz. a General Naturalization 490
Some Thoughts upon the Subject of Commerce with France 118–19
Spanish Descent, The 39
Storm, The 10–11, 42, 145–46, 147–48, 153–54, 161, 349–52, 452–56, 467–68, 589, 615–16
Succession to the Crown of England, Consider'd, The 114–15
System of Magick A 56–57, 326, 327–28, 334–35, 339–40, 342, 347–48, 356–58, 563–64, 566, 576–77
Tour thro' the Whole Island of Great Britain, A
    Britain in, vi, 494–97, 498, 500
    economics in 120, 251–52, 255, 256
    guidebook style of 11
    history in 1–2, 427–28
    Keiller films reworkings of 620–21
    London in 472–74
    publication history of 588–90, 608–9, 612, 614
    reworked in *Atlas Maritimus* 224–25
    status in 234, 391–92
    travel in 148, 157–59
True-Born Englishman, The
    national identity in 437, 439–41, 442, 489–92, 503, 506–7, 508–11, 519–21
    poetic quality of 34–37, 48
    political significance of 11–12, 43, 161, 365–66, 437, 482–84, 489–90

popularity of 3–4, 11–12, 29–30, 39–40, 110, 637–38
price of 418
publication history of 37–38, 223–24, 228, 418, 585–86, 606–7, 608–9
satire in 195, 196, 197–98, 201–2, 203, 209, 239, 420–21, 423–24
True Collection of the Writings of the Author of The True Born Englishman A 11, 12–16, 108, 421–22, 489–90, 615–16, 630–31
Trumpet Blown in the North … Duke of Mar A 115
Two Great Questions Consider'd. I. What the French King will do, with Respect to the Spanish Monarchy. II. What Measures the English Ought to Take 121, 366–67, 506–7
Vision, The 44–45, 373–74, 393–94
Weakest Go to the Wall, The 97–98, 115–16
What if the Pretender should come?, And 208–9, 272–73
Defoe, Hannah 273
Defoe, Mary (née Tuffley) 9, 23, 30, 161, 272, 273, 278
de Fonvive, Jean 126
De Krey, Gary 316–17
Delafaye, Charles 135, 184, 219, 229–30, 611, 622–23, 632, 643
de Lolme, Jean-Louis 586
DeLuna, D. N. 323
De Quincey, Thomas 620
Dennis, John 198–99, 200
Dent, Arthur
  Plain Man's Path-way to Heaven, The 95–96
Deschanel, Caleb 662
de Wet II, Jacob Jacobsz 602
Dialogue Betwixt Whig and Tory A 382–83
di Carli, Denis 459–60
Dickens, Charles 252, 471–72
  Bleak House 620–21
  Christmas Carol A 620
  David Copperfield 620
  Oliver Twist 600
Dickey, Laurence 499
Dijkstra, Bram 590
Dissent/Dissenters
  academies of 4–5, 97–98, 341, 347–48, 482

antitheatricalism of 70–74, 89–90, 481
occasional conformity of 110, 115–17, 118, 129–30, 320–21, 323, 369–72, 378–79
persecution of 4–5, 97–98, 311–14, 328, 500–1
Puritanism and 4–5, 70–71, 89, 111, 313, 326, 481
Reformation of Manners movement and 122–23
toleration of 97–98, 115–17, 128, 138–39, 187, 189–90, 311–14, 364, 369–70
trade and 5, 118–19, 120, 255, 264
Whig party and 111–18, 189–90, 255, 323–24, 369–70, 378–79
Dodd, Anne 227
Dodderidge, Sir John 236–37, 238, 239
Donne, John
  Holy Sonnets 319–20
Dormer's News-Letter 396–97
Dorset, Earl of 33
Dottin, Paul 625, 626
Downie, J. A. 7–8, 57, 72–73, 129, 130–31, 222, 387, 388, 390, 394–96, 633
Downing, Karen 279
Drake, Sir Francis 160, 547
Drake, James
  Memorial of the Church of England, The 392–93
Drake, Nathan
  Essays: Biographical, Critical and Historical 616
Drelincourt, Charles
  Christian's Defence Against the Fears of Death, The 595
Druce, Clare 660
Drury, Joseph 348–49
Dryden, John 37, 38, 70–71, 200–1, 206–7, 221, 318–19, 324–25, 585
  Absalom and Achitophel 31–32, 33, 198–99, 317
  Discourse on the Original and Progress of Satire 198–99
  Essay of Dramatic Poesie, An 31, 37–38
Dudok de Wit, Michaël
  Red Turtle, The 661–62, 665–73
Duncombe, Sir Charles 37
Dunton, John 8–9, 167–68
  Athenian Mercury 94–95
  Voyage Round the World A 144–45

D'Urfey, Thomas 38, 70–71
Dyer, John
  Dyer's Newsletter 135, 372

Earle, Peter 282, 283–84, 286, 292, 300
East India Company 119, 538, 552–53, 555
Easton, Fraser 283–84
Eclectic Review, The 622
Edgeworth, Maria
  Moral Tales for Young People 617
Edward I, King of England 502–3
Edwin, Sir Humphrey 116–17
Eliot, George
  Mill on the Floss, The 592, 622
Elizabeth I, Queen of England 282–83, 313, 384
Ellis, Frank H. 37–38
England, Church of, *see* 'Church of England'
English Civil Wars 1–3, 35, 57, 58, 70–71, 150–51, 170, 173–74, 311–12, 316–17, 322, 407, 408, 413–15, 479–80
English Garner, The 607–8
English Men No Bastards 34
Ennius 31–32
Equiano, Olaudah 483–84
Essex, Earl of 596
Etherege, George 70–71
Eugene, Prince 42, 403–4
Evelyn, John 454–55, 620–21
Evert, Stefan 640–41
Exclusion Crisis 314–15, 316–17, 387–88
Exshaw, John 586–87

Faction Display'd 16–17
Falconer, John 384
Falconer, Richard 157
Faller, Lincoln B. 430–31
Farquhar, George 70–71
Favret, Mary 402
Fawcett, Benjamin 95–96
Federalist Papers, The 639
Ferdinand II, Holy Roman Emperor 57–58, 513, 517
Fielding, Henry 49, 617–18
  Tom Jones 613
Fiennes, Celia
  Journeys 152n.11, 494
Fifth Monarchy Men 313, 314–15

Filmer, Sir Robert
  Patriarcha 295, 301, 323
Fisher, Carl 663
Fletcher, Andrew
  State of the Controversy betwixt United and Separate Parliaments 109–10
Flint, Christopher 296–97, 305
Flying-Post, The, see under 'Ridpath, George'
Foe, James 4–5, 225–26, 314n.14, 316–17
Foe, Jane 272
E. M. Forster
  Aspects of the Novel 625–26
Forster, J. R.
  History of the Voyages and Discoveries Made in the North 613–14
Foxe, John
  Acts and Monuments 87, 317
Franklin, Benjamin 229
Fransham, John 15, 190–91
Fraser, Peter 384–85
Free, Melissa 605
Freeman, John 575–76
French, Henry 241
Frost, Simon 618
Fuller, Thomas 618
Funnell, William 547
Furbank, P. N. 294–99, 575–76
  see also 'Furbank, P. N. and W. R. Owens'
Furbank, P. N. and W. R. Owens 50–51, 93, 126–27, 130–31, 133, 135, 137, 183, 320, 387, 390, 396–97, 513–14, 595–96, 608, 615–16, 619–20, 622–23, 629–31, 632–38, 641–42
  see also 'Furbank, P. N.' *and* 'Owens, W. R.'
Furnese, Sir Henry 234
Fuseli, Henry 597–99

Gallagher, Noelle 175
Ganz, Melissa J. 305–6
Gardam, Jane
  Crusoe's Daughter 645–46, 653–58
Garth, Samuel 33
  Medal, The 198–99
Gay, John 247
Geminiani, Francesco 481
General History of the Pyrates A 417–18, 626–27
Gentleman's Magazine, The 588–89

Genuine Anecdotes of a Scoundrel; or, Memoirs of Devil Dick 592
George, Dorothy 232–33
George I, King of Great Britain 45–46, 110–11, 125–26, 135, 137, 167, 220, 311–12, 322, 379–80, 387, 474–75, 585, 631
George II, King of Great Britain 1
George III, King of Great Britain 608–9
George IV, King of Great Britain 585–86
Charles Gildon
    Life and Strange Surprizing Adventures of Mr. D---- de F--, of London, The 23–24, 69, 564–65, 610, 626, 635
Gikandi, Simon 438
Gloucester, Duke of 114–15
Godolphin, Sidney, Earl of 7–8, 43–44, 182, 184, 185–86, 366, 370–74, 375–77, 390, 392–93, 394–96, 411
Godwin, William 58, 622–23
    Faulkener 617
Gold, Jack
    Man Friday 666–67
Goldie, Mark 4–5
Goldsmith, Oliver
    History of England, The 613
    Vicar of Wakefield, The 591–92
Gollapudi, Aparna 428–29
Grave of the Fireflies 660–61
Graves, John 227
Great Fire of London 313, 427–28, 473, 489–90
Great Northern War 400–1, 407–8, 513
Gregg, Stephen 292
Grey of Groby, Lord 316–17
Grierson, George 226
Griffin, Robert J. 630, 637
Guillory, John 178–79
Gustavus Adolphus, King of Sweden 57–58, 60, 171–74, 175–76, 391, 403–4, 406, 407, 414, 513
Gwyn, Nell 36

Habermas, Jürgen 484–85
Haddington, Earl of 394
Halifax, Earl of 182, 183–84, 185–87, 188, 365
Halley, Edmond 159, 224–25, 351–52, 391–92
Hamblyn, Richard 349–50
Hammond, Brean 230

Handel, George Frideric 481
Hannibal 158, 407, 463
Harcourt, Simon 379–80
Harley, Edward 612
Harley, Robert
    political career of 6–7, 8, 11, 23–24, 52–53, 113–15, 129–30, 163–64, 174, 220, 226–27, 251, 364–68, 370–75, 377–79, 384–86, 389, 475, 526–28, 584
    relations with Defoe 6–8, 129–31, 135, 144–45, 162–63, 167, 182, 186–91, 218–19, 220, 234, 323–24, 341–42, 364, 370–72, 373–75, 377–79, 380–81, 387–97, 399, 486, 497–98, 506–7, 526–28
Harrington, James 243–44
Hawkins, H. K. 608
Hawthorne, Nathaniel
    Blithedale Romance, The 620–21
Hay, Douglas 241
Haywood, Eliza 49–50, 641–42
    British Recluse, The 601
    Mercenary Lover, The 280
    Present for a Servant-Maid A 285
Hazlitt, William 89, 616, 618–19, 622–23
Hazlitt the younger, William 607, 620, 633
Healey, G. H. 30, 317–18, 395–96, 610–11
Hepburn, Sir John 412–13
Herbert, George 319–20
Hill, Christopher, vi
Hills, Henry 16–17, 207, 228
Hindle, Maurice 307–8
History of George a Green, Pindar of the Town of Wakefield, The 479–80
Hitch, Charles 591
Hoadly, Benjamin 20–22
    Nature of the Kingdom, or Church of Christ, The 117–18
Hobbes, Thomas 185–86, 204, 274, 447, 452
    Leviathan 443–44
Hodges, Nathanial
    Loimologia 465–67
Hodges, William 109–10
Hogarth, William 480, 618
Holder, Charles Frederick 460–61
Holmes, Geoffrey 232–33
Homer 139

Hone, William 622–23
  Right Divine of Kings to Govern Wrong!,
    The 585–86
Hoppit, Julian 311–12
Horace 139
Horsley, John
  Britannia Romana 488–89
Howe, John 116–17
Howell, Jordan 602–5
Hume, David 325–26
Hume, Robert D. 484
Hume, Thomas 226
Hunter, J. Paul 29–30, 70–71, 89–90, 94, 95–96,
    97, 104
Hunter, Michael 325–26
Hunt, Margaret 284–85
Hurl-Eamon, Jennine 283
Hurt, William 220
Huygens, Christiaan 355–56
Hyde, John 226, 228

Iliffe, Rob 324–25
Islay, Earl of 585–86

Jackson, Clare 503
Jacob, Margaret 325–26
Jacobitism 1, 121–22, 135, 138–39, 192, 365–66,
    380–81, 506–7, 513–14
  Invasion threat (1708) 129–30, 185–86
  Scottish politics and 165–66, 169–70,
    375–76, 378–79, 502–3, 586–87
  Tory politicians and 52–53, 113–15, 129–30,
    167, 168, 207–11, 220, 322, 368, 377
  Uprising of 1715, 45–46, 64, 98–99, 216–17,
    222–23, 309, 311–12
  see also 'Defoe, Daniel, *Colonel Jack*'
Janeway, Richard 8, 209–10, 220
Jeffreys, George 315–16
Johns, Adrian 223, 484–85
Johnson, Samuel 9, 70–71, 247, 612, 614–15,
    617–18
  Dictionary of the English
    Language, A, vi
  Life of Richard Savage, The 617
Jones, Edwin Owen
  Eminent Characters of the English
    Revolution 620–21

Jonson, Ben
  Bartholomew Fair 477
Jordan, Thomas 30
Joseph I, Holy Roman Emperor 130–31, 516–17
Joyce, James 625–26, 627
Juvenal 31–32, 33
  Satires 12–15

Kant, Immanuel 325–26
Keats, John 29–30
Keeble, N. H. 313
Keiller, Patrick 663–65
Keimer, Samuel 229
Kelly, Thomas 592
Keltie, J. S. 608
Kenyon, J. P. 23–24
Keymer, Tom 636–37, 661–62
King, Gregory 232–33, 240, 242, 244, 245, 246–47
Knights, Sir John 509
Knox-Shaw, Peter 575–76

Lamb, Charles 61, 617, 618–20
Lamb, Jonathan 555
Landau, Norma 418–19
Lansdowne, Marquess of 584
Laslett, Peter 232–33, 295–96
Law, John 120
Le Clerc, Jean
  Life of the Famous Cardinal Duke de
    Richlieu, The 57–58, 389, 397
Lee, William 137, 607–8, 622–25
Leipzig, Battle of 406
Leopold, Aldo 672–73
Leopold I, Holy Roman Emperor 515–17
LeSage, Alain-René 594
Leslie, Charles 110–11, 141, 486
  Rehearsal, The 72, 126
L'Estrange, Roger 223
Levellers 313
Lindert, Peter H. 245–47
Lindner, Oliver 287, 290–91
Lintot, Bernard 221
Loar, Christopher F. 464–65, 467–68,
    537, 571–72
Locke, John 322, 443–44, 453–54, 456–57
  Two Treatises of Government 317, 323, 452,
    533–34, 535–36

Lockhart, George 374
Lockhart, John Gibson 618–19
London Company of Weavers 134
Longman, Thomas 228–29
Longueville, Peter
   Hermit, The 648–49, 658
Lost 663
Louis XIV, King of France 34, 37, 111, 121, 171, 190–91, 320–21, 365, 366–67, 506–7, 508, 511–13, 515–16, 518
Love, Harold 641
Lovell, Sir Salathiel 421–22
Lovett, Robert 602–5
Lowndes, Thomas 64–65, 601–2
Lowndes, William 234
Lowther, Sir James 240–41
Lucian 78
Ludlow, Edmund
   Memoirs 1–2, 173–74
Lutzen, Battle of 172–73
Lynch, Kathleen 319–20

MacCulloch, Diarmaid 313
Macfarlane, Alan 295–96
Mackworth, Sir Humphry 112–13
   Vindication of the Rights of the Commons of England 367
Macky, John
   Journey Through England in Familiar Letters 494
Magdeburg, Sack of 57–58, 414, 517
Magellan, Ferdinand 546–47
Maittaire, Michael 612
Malešević, Siniša 402–3
Manley, Delariviere 49–50, 226–27, 641–42
Mar, Earl of 115, 378–79
Matthews, John 222–23, 229–30
Marana, Giovanni Paolo
   L'Espion du Grand Seigneur 179, 191–92, 397
Maranhão, Tullio 92
Markley, Robert 303–4, 309–10, 350, 452
Marlborough, Duke of 37, 42, 121–22, 185–86, 216–17, 371–72, 395–96, 403–4, 406, 412, 508
Marshall, Alan 384
Marshall, Ashley 174, 195–96, 203, 606, 636–38, 641–42, 643

Marshall, David 70, 82, 83, 88
Martian, The 663
Martin, Henry
   British Merchant, The 134
Marvell, Andrew 31–32, 33, 37, 39, 200
Marx, Karl 266, 622
Mary II, Queen of England 32, 196–97, 288–89
Masefield, John 625
Mason, Shirlene 273
Massie, Joseph
   Calculations of Taxes for a Family of each Rank, Degree or Class: For One Year 235, 241, 244–45
May, James E. 229
Mayer, Robert 616
Maynadier, G. H. 608
Mazarin 188
McAdam, Edward L. 642
McBurney, William H. 641–42
McDowell, Paula 283, 359–60
McKenzie, Alan T. 180–81
McKeon, Michael 295
McKibben, Bill 672–73
McVeagh, John 8–9, 125–26, 127–28, 263, 404, 408–9
Mead, Dr Richard 81, 464–65
Meadows, William 227, 228
Mears, William 227
Mede, Joseph 324–25
Meere, Hugh 228–29
Meier, Thomas Keith 495
Méliès, Georges
   Robinson Crusoe 662
   Trip to the Moon A 662
Memorial of the Church of England, The 392–93
Merrett, Robert James 281, 296–98, 301–2, 305–6
Merrill, Elizabeth 78, 82
Mesnager, Nicolas 23–24, 52–54, 163–64, 170–72, 175–76, 383, 397, 631, 639
Midwinter, Edward 228, 600–1
Mildmay, Col. Henry 316–17
Milhous, Judith 484
Milton, John 38–39, 41, 44, 46–48, 305–6, 313, 618
   Areopagitica 218
   Paradise Lost 327, 342–43, 594

Minto, William 624
Mississippi Company 120
Mist, Nathaniel 221, 222–23
    Weekly Journal 126–27, 135, 136–37, 219, 229–30, 396–97
    Modern Addresses Vindicated, The 584–85
Moll, Herman 60–61
    View of the Coasts, Countries and Islands within the Limits of the South-Sea-Company A 528
Moncur, John 229
Monmouth, Duke of 198–99
Monmouth Rebellion 1, 53–54, 144–45, 315–16, 388, 400
Montagu, Elizabeth 614–15
Montgomery, Sy 671–72
Moore, John Robert, vi, 247, 388, 626–27, 629–30, 633, 634
More, Henry 324–25
Morland, Samuel
    'Brief Discourse Concerning the Nature and Reason of Intelligence, A' 384, 386, 391
Morley, Henry 607–8
Morning Post, The 584–85
Morphew, John 220, 226–27
Morris (Morice), Roger 384–85
Morton, Charles 4–5, 341, 347–48, 482
Mueller, Andreas K. E. 29–30, 98–99
Mullan, John 51–52, 342–43

Napoleonic Wars 415, 605–6
Narborough, Sir John 57
Nash, Richard 672
National Review, The 620–21, 622
Nelson, James 234–35
Newbury, Battle of 150–51
Newman, Ian 441–42
Newton, Sir Isaac 345–46, 347–49, 352
    Treatise on Revelation 324–25
Nine Years' War 121, 508–9, 515–16
Noble, Francis 4, 49–50, 64–65, 595–96, 599, 600–2, 613–14, 635–37
Norden, John
    Speculum Britanniae 488–89
North, Lord 584–85
Notes and Queries 620–21

Nottingham, Earl of 158–59, 182–84, 217, 370, 371–72, 377, 378–79, 380, 390, 400
Novak, Maximillian E. 7–8, 57, 67, 76, 93–94, 95, 97–98, 125–26, 137, 139, 305–6, 318–20, 323, 393–94, 396–97, 407–8, 475, 524–25, 633, 634–36, 637–38, 661–62
Nutt, Elizabeth 227
Nutt, John 227
Nyquist, Mary 443–44

Oberwittler, Dietrich 418–19
Occasional conformity, *see under* 'Dissent/Dissenters'
Ogilby, John 459–61
    Africa 60–61
Oldham, John 36, 37
Oldmixon, John 7–8, 167–68
    History of England 3–4
Oldys, William 612
Oliphant, Margaret
    'Evelyn and Pepys' 620–21
O'Malley, Andrew 617, 621–22
O'Neill, Lindsay 385–86
Ormond, Duke of 115, 240
Orr, Leah 51–53, 56–57
Osborn, John 228–29
Osborne, Thomas 612
Otway, Thomas 70–71
Owen, Christine 286, 289–90
Owen, Edward 190–91
Owen, James 113n.13
Owens, W. R. 33, 34, 45–46
    see also 'Furbank, P. N. and W. R. Owens'
Oxford, Earl of, *see* 'Harley, Robert'

Pagden, Anthony 325–26
Paine, Thomas 594
Parker, Henry 228–29
Parker, Thomas 135, 220, 380, 396–97
Parkes, Christopher 495
Parrinder, Patrick 304–5
Partition Treaty 121, 130–31, 506–7, 515–16, 518
Paterson, William 184–86
Pauley, Benjamin F. 288–89
Penn, William 370
Pennsylvania Town and Country-Man's Almanack 597

People for the Ethical Treatment of
    Animals 660
Pepys, Samuel 384–85, 427, 620–21
Periwig-Maker, The 663–65
Peterson, Spiro 615–16, 620
Philip V, King of Spain 121, 518–19
Phillips, Roderick 306
Pierce, John 373–74
Pitt the Younger, William 584
Pittis, William 208
    *True-Born Englishman: A Satire, Answered,
    The* 483–84
Plague of 1665, 57–59, 81, 283, 313, 339–40,
    464–68, 474–77, 489–90, 597,
    663–65
Plato 78
Poe, Edgar Allan 620
Poems on Affairs of State 196
Poenicke, Klaus 661–62
Pope, Alexander 3–4, 44–45, 229, 247, 352, 487,
    585, 611–12
    Dunciad, The 22, 207, 218
    Iliad, The 221
Popish Plot 314, 317
Porter, Roy 326, 522–23
Portlandia 660
Post Man, The 126
Post-Master, The 599
Pretender 64, 114–15, 121, 208–9, 375–76,
    380, 395–96
Prior, Matthew 226–27
Pritchard, Jonathan 484
Pro, John 569–70
Procopius
    *Secret History of the Court of the Emperor
    Justinian, The* 52–53

Queensberry, Duke of 224, 371, 373, 375–76,
    378, 393–94, 585–86
Quincy, John 465–66

Raleigh, Sir Walter 324–25
    History of the World, The 347
Ramillies, Battle of 121–22, 340–41, 372, 404
Rapin, René 174–75
Read, Thomas 600–1
    Read's Journal 137

Reeve, Clara 614, 616, 617
    Progress of Romance, The 614
Reformation 172, 191–92, 312
Reformation of Manners movement 5, 37–38,
    122–23, 196–97, 200, 421
Regan, Tom 670–72
Religious Tract Society 591
*Remarks on the Review, Numb. 74. Concerning
    the New Chappel in Russel-Court,
    Covent-Garden* 73
Republican Bullies, The 7–8
Restoration 1, 4–5, 6, 31–32, 33, 35, 36, 39, 70–
    71, 113–14, 118–19, 196–97, 238, 241–42,
    244, 312–13, 314–15, 384–85, 387–88, 482
*Review Review'd. In a Letter to the Prophet
    Daniel in Scotland, The*, vii, 237
Revolution of 1688, 1–5, 12, 34, 53–54, 111–12,
    113–14, 118–19, 130–31, 172, 193, 203,
    206, 232–33, 311–12, 313, 320–24, 328,
    364–68, 374, 377, 378–79, 380–81,
    482, 484–85
Revolution, English, *see* 'English Civil Wars'
Rhames, Aaron 226
Richard I, King of England 479–80
Richard III, King of England 588–89
Richardson, Samuel 49, 84, 180–81, 588, 612,
    614, 617–18
    Pamela 82
Richelieu, Cardinal 188, 191, 327, 389, 390–91,
    397–98
Richetti, John, vi, 89, 203, 297–98, 307–8,
    318–19, 320, 397, 471, 595
Ridpath, George
    Flying Post, The 126–27, 135, 219–21, 379–80
    Observator, The 126, 132, 140–41
Ringrose, Basil 546–47
Risk, George 226
Rivington, Charles 227, 589–90
Roberts, David 661–62
Roberts, James 226–27
Robespierre, Maximilien 594
Robins, Benjamin 547
Robinson Crusoe on Mars 663
Rochester, Earl of 38–39, 44, 200–1, 318–20
    'Satire upon Mankind' 319–20
    'Upon Nothing' 47
Rogers, Nicholas 241, 242

Rogers, Pat, vi, 1–2, 44–45, 302–3, 391–92, 473, 474, 611–12, 617–18, 620, 623, 633
Rogers, Woodes 156–57, 160, 458, 528, 547
  Cruising Voyage Round the World A 147–48
Rooke, Sir George 133
Rosenthal, Laura 289–90
Rousseau, Jean-Jacques 666–67
  Émile 613
Roxburgh, Natalie 264–65
Roy, William
  Military Antiquities of the Romans in Britain, The 488–89
Royal African Company 60, 119, 251, 258–59, 461, 568–76, 577
Royal Society 156–57, 178–79, 346, 349–52, 384, 454–55
Rummell, Kathryn 519–21
Ruskin, John
  Notes on the Construction of Sheepfolds 620–21
Russell, Lord William 366–67
Ryswick, Treaty of 121, 365

Sacheverell, Henry 3, 15, 20–22, 46, 110–11, 115, 128–29, 138–39, 210, 216–17, 376–77
  Perils of False Brethren, The 11–12, 117–18
SARS 663–65
Satsuma, Shinsuke 528
Schnabel, Johann Gottfried 617
Schochet, Gordon J. 315
Schonhorn, Manuel 187, 382–83, 391
Schorer, Mark 608
Scotland, Church of, *see* 'Church of Scotland'
Scots Post-Man, The 126–27
Scott, Jonathan 322
Scott, Sir Walter 58–59, 605–6, 617–18, 620, 624
Scrimgeour, Gary J. 459–60
Seager, Nicholas 1–2, 125–26, 174, 354, 395–96
Secord, Arthur W. 57–58, 173–74, 412–13, 626–27
Sedgemoor, Battle of, *see* 'Monmouth Rebellion'
Selkirk, Alexander 458, 528, 620–21
Severin, Tim 227
Shaftesbury, Earl of 115–16, 198–99, 387–88
Shakespeare, William 70–71, 618
  Tempest, The 650

Shapiro, Barbara 174–75
Sheehan, Jonathan 402, 410–11
Shelley, Mary
  Last Man, The 618–19
Shelley, Percy Bysshe
  Ozymandias 474
Shelvocke, George 547
Sheridan, Richard Brinsley 617
Shiells, Robert
  Lives of the Poets, The 3–4, 75–76, 595–96, 612–13, 635
Shinagel, Michael 86, 93, 235, 238–39, 243, 252
Sill, Geoffrey 389
Slavery 305–6, 442–49, 483–84, 524, 541–42, 564, 600
Smith, Erasmus 389
Smith, Geoffrey 384
Smith, Capt. John 359
Smollett, Tobias 49, 617–18
  Adventures of Roderick Random, The 613
  History of England, The 613, 614
Snyder, Henry L. 633
Somers, Lord 365, 366–67, 368, 377
  Jura Populi Anglicani 367
Somers Tracts 584
Sorensen, Janet 493–94
South Sea Company 119, 120, 216–17, 262, 273, 474–76, 527–29, 538, 541, 544–45, 547–49, 553–54
Spalding, Violet 660
Spark, Muriel
  Robinson 645–46, 651–53, 654–55
Speed, John
  Theatre of the Empire of Great Britain, The 488–89
Spirited Away 660–61
Sprat, Thomas
  History of the Royal Society, The 178–79
Stables, Kate 669–70, 672–73
Stagg, R. 637
Stanhope, James, Earl 182, 396–97
St. James's Post, The 126–27
Starr, G. A. 56–57, 94–95, 102, 278–79, 326–27, 334–35, 353, 495, 636–37
Steele, Sir Richard 127, 132, 139, 141–42, 198–99, 216, 247
  Englishman, The 132

Guardian, The 126, 132, 134
  see also 'Addison, Joseph, and Richard Steele'
Stephen, Leslie 54–55, 66–67, 605–6, 622, 623, 625–26, 627
  History of English Thought in the Eighteenth Century 49–50
Stevens, Isabel 668–69
Stockdale, John 586–87, 615–16
Stone, Lawrence 295, 296–97, 301–2
Storm of 1703, 10–11, 41–42, 113, 145–46, 349–50, 451–52, 453–55, 457–58, 467–68, 589
Stow, John 472
Straub, Kristina 285–86
Strype, John
  A Survey of the Cities of London and Westminster 472
Stuart, James Francis Edward, *see* 'Pretender'
Stukeley, William
  Itinerarium Curiosum 488–89
Sunderland, Earl of 7–8, 44n.23, 182–83, 184, 185–86, 188, 372, 375–77, 395–96
Survivor 663
Sutherland, James 186–87, 328, 626
Swedish Intelligencer, The 57–58, 173–74, 412–13
Sweetapple, Sir John 421–22
Swift, Jonathan 7–8, 22, 41, 121–22, 123, 141, 142, 162–63, 216, 220, 226–27, 229, 241–42, 247, 264, 346, 377–79, 482, 483–84, 486, 607–8
  Conduct of the Allies, The 514–15
  Examiner, The 126, 128, 132, 484–85
  Gulliver's Travels 37–38, 64, 157, 547–48, 554, 560, 616
  Tale of a Tub A 349, 351–52
Sydenham, Thomas 464–65
Sydney, Algernon 367–68

Tadmor, Naomi 295–96, 298–99
Taine, Hippolyte 622
Tavernier, Jeremiah 12
Taylor, Thomas 30
Taylor, William 8, 53–54, 55–56, 224–25, 227, 228–29, 637
Tegg, Thomas 606–7, 620
Tennyson, Alfred Lord
  'Lady of Shalott, The' 654–55, 657

Thatcher, Margaret 663–65
Thomas, Dalby 572–73, 575–76
Thompson, F. M. L. 240–41
Thomson, James
  Seasons, The 41, 44–45, 47–48
Three Champions, The 16–17
Thurloe, John 384–85
Tilly, Count 58, 406, 414
Tindal, Matthew
  Christianity as Old as the Creation 326–27
Todd, Dennis 542
Toland, John 1–2, 135–36, 243–44, 370–71
  Art of Governing by Partys, The 367–68
Tonson, Jacob 221, 638
Tookey, Robert 229
Townshend, Charles 115, 135, 380, 396–97
Treaty of Commerce 118–19, 133–34, 258, 377–78
Trenchard, John 243–44
Trent, W. P. 29–30, 625, 632
Trevelyan, George Macaulay, vi, 232–33
Trollope, Anthony 252
Tuck, James 597–99
Tuffley, Joan 9
Turin, Siege of 409–10
Turner, William 425–26, 427, 428
Tutchin, John 15–17, 200, 486, 491–92
  Foreigners, The 34, 365–66, 439–40, 489–90, 509–10
  Observator, The 126, 132, 223
Twain, Mark 41

Ullrich, Hermann 624
Underdown, David 384
Union of Britain and Ireland 226, 586–87
Union of Great Britain 44–46, 109–10, 113, 128–29, 162–66, 169–70, 183–84, 224, 250, 255, 323–24, 373–76, 378, 380–81, 387–88, 393–94, 437, 486, 497–504, 505–6, 585–87
Universal Spectator, The 126–27
Utrecht, Treaty of 64, 96, 118–19, 257, 378–79, 506–7, 517, 518, 519, 527–28

Vanbrugh, Sir John 70–71, 72–73
Van der Gucht, Michael 12–15
van Doren, Carl 608, 626

Van Sant, Ann 348–49
Vauban 408–9
Vickers, Ilse 347–48, 482
Virgil 139, 221, 474
Vox Populi, Vox Dei 222–23

Wafer, Lionel 546–47
Wahrman, Dror 402, 410
Wall, Cynthia 302–3, 472
Wallis, T. 592
Walmsley, Peter 348–49
Walpole, Robert 131, 216–17
Walsingham, Sir Francis 188, 387–88, 390–91
Walter, Richard 547
War of the Spanish Succession 111, 120–22, 128–29, 130–31, 170, 251–52, 400, 404–5, 506–7, 508, 511–19, 521, 527–28
War, Thirty Years' 170, 233–34, 513, 515–16
Warner, Thomas 219, 227–28, 637
Waters, Edward 226
Watson, James 229
Watt, Ian, vi, 4, 49–50, 252, 472, 605–6, 608, 662, 666–67
Watts, Isaac 597
Watts, John 229
Watts, Michael 314–15
Webster, Noah 451–52
Weitzman, Arthur J. 191–92
Wharton, Earl of 182
Wheeler, Roxann 361, 436, 442–43, 448–49, 571–72
Whiston, William 347–48
Whitefield, C. 64–65
Whitehead, Julian 384
White-hall Evening Post, The 126–27, 137, 396–97
Whitelock, Bulstrode 173–74
  Memorials of the English Affairs 412–13
Whitten, Wilfred 625
Whores Rhetorick, The 425–26
Whyman, Susan E. 182, 183
Wild, Robert 30–31
Wildman, John 385–86
Wilkes, John 584–85
Wilkins, John 391
  Mercury; or the Secret and Swift Messenger 384

William I, King of England 35, 204
William III, King of England
  anti-Dutch attitudes towards 34, 437, 483–84, 489–90, 514
  colonialism and 59
  Defoe's writings in support of 1–3, 12, 32–35, 37–38, 114–15, 121, 130–31, 183–84, 201–2, 204–5, 206, 320–21, 322–23, 364–67, 380–81, 401, 439–40, 491–92, 522–23, 585
  employment of Defoe (alleged) 144–45, 181, 388
  European strategy of 508–11, 514, 515–16, 518
  Intelligence under 384, 388
  military skills of 193, 403–4, 407, 512–13
  partition treaties of 121
  politicians and 200, 365–67, 370–72, 584–85
  religion and 311–12
  standing army of 401, 506–7, 508–9
  see also under 'Defoe, Daniel, views on'
Williams, Glyndwr 546–47
Williams, J. 584–85
Williams, Raymond 295
Williamson, Jeffrey G. 245–47
Williamson, Sir Joseph 384–85
Wilson, Scott D. 670–71
Wilson, Walter 75–76, 606, 618–21
  Memoirs of the Life and Times of Daniel de Foe 61, 587, 607, 622–23, 624
Wilson, Rev. William 587
Winkfield, Unca Eliza
  Female American, The 645–46, 648–53
Wither, George 30–31
Woolf, Daniel 175
Woolf, Virginia 54–55, 66–67, 605–6, 625–26, 627
Wordsworth, William 618
Wren, Sir Christopher 473
Wright, Thomas 624
Wrightson, Keith 295–97
Wycherley, William 70–71

Yeats, Jack Butler 602, 608
Yeats, W. B. 37

Zemeckis, Robert
  Cast Away 662, 666–67